Brill's
New Pauly

CLASSICAL TRADITION
VOLUME I

A-Del

Brill's New Pauly

Brill's

Encyclopaedia of the Ancient World

New Pauly

Edited by
Manfred Landfester in cooperation with
Hubert Cancik and *Helmuth Schneider*

English Edition
Managing Editor *Francis G. Gentry*

Assistant Editors *Michael Chase, Tina Chronopoulos,
Edda Gentry, Susanne Hakenbeck, Tina Jerke,
Craig Kallendorf, Ingrid Rosa Kitzberger,
Daniel C. Mack, Sebastiaan R. van der Mije,
Joseph M. Sullivan, Frank J. Tobin and James K. Walter*

CLASSICAL TRADITION
VOLUME I

A-DEL

BRILL
LEIDEN · BOSTON
2006

© Copyright 2006 by Koninklijke Brill NV,
Leiden, The Netherlands

Koninklijke Brill NV incorporates the imprints
Brill Academic Publishers, Martinus Nijhoff
Publishers and VSP.

Originally published in German as DER NEUE
PAULY. Enzyklopädie der Antike. In Verbindung
mit Hubert Cancik und Helmuth Schneider
herausgegeben von Manfred Landfester.
Copyright © J.B. Metzlersche Verlagsbuch-
handlung und Carl Ernst Poeschel Verlag
GmbH 1996ff./1999ff. Stuttgart/Weimar

Cover design: TopicA (Antoinette Hanekuyk)
Front: Delphi, temple area

Data structuring and typesetting:
pagina GmbH, Tübingen, Germany

ISBN (volume) 90 04 14221 5
ISBN (set) 90 04 12259 1

This book is printed on acid-free paper.

PRINTED IN THE NETHERLANDS

Table of Contents

Notes to the User

Arrangement of Entries

The entries are arranged alphabetically and, if applicable, placed in chronological order. In the case of alternative forms or sub-entries, cross-references will lead to the respective main entry. Composite entries can be found in more than one place (e.g. *a commentariis* refers to *commentariis, a*).

Identical entries are differentiated by numbering.

Spelling of Entries

Greek words and names are as a rule latinized, following the predominant practice of reference works in the English language, with the notable exception of technical terms. Institutions and places (cities, rivers, islands, countries etc.) often have their conventional English names (e.g. *Rome* not *Roma*). The latinized versions of Greek names and words are generally followed by the Greek and the literal transliteration in brackets, e.g. *Aeschylus* (Αἰσχύλος; *Aischýlos*).

Oriental proper names are usually spelled according to the 'Tübinger Atlas des Vorderen Orients' (TAVO), but again conventional names in English are also used. In the maps, the names of cities, rivers, islands, countries etc. follow ancient spelling and are transliterated fully to allow for differences in time, e.g. both Καππαδόκια and *Cappadocia* can be found. The transliteration of non-Latin scripts can be found in the 'List of Transliterations'.

Latin and transliterated Greek words are italicized in the article text. However, where Greek transliterations do not follow immediately upon a word written in Greek, they will generally appear in italics, but without accents or makra.

Abbreviations

All abbreviations can be found in the 'List of Abbreviations'. Collections of inscriptions, coins and papyri are listed under their *sigla*.

Bibliographies

Most entries have bibliographies, consisting of numbered and/or alphabetically organized references. References within the text to the numbered bibliographic items are in square brackets (e.g. [1.5 n.23] refers to the first title of the bibliography, page 5, note 23). The abbreviations within the bibliographies follow the rules of the 'List of Abbreviations'.

Cross-references

Articles are linked through a system of cross-references with an arrow → before the entry that is being referred to.

Cross-references to related entries are given at the end of an article, generally before the bibliographic notes. If reference is made to a homonymous entry, the respective number is also added.

Cross-references to entries within the *Classical Tradition* volumes are added in small capitals; cross-references to entries in the *Antiquity* volumes are added in regular type.

It can occur that in a cross-reference a name is spelled differently from the surrounding text: e.g., a cross-reference to Mark Antony has to be to Marcus → Antonius, as his name will be found in a list of other names containing the component 'Antonius'.

List of Transliterations

Transliteration of ancient Greek

α	a	alpha
αι	ai	
αυ	au	
β	b	beta
γ	g	gamma; γ before γ, κ, ξ, χ: n
δ	d	delta
ε	e	epsilon
ει	ei	
ευ	eu	
ζ	z	z(d)eta
η	ē	eta
ηυ	ēu	
θ	th	theta
ι	i	iota
κ	k	kappa
λ	l	la(m)bda
μ	m	mu
ν	n	nu
ξ	x	xi
ο	o	omicron
οι	oi	
ου	ou	
π	p	pi
ϱ	r	rho
σ, ς	s	sigma
τ	t	tau
υ	y	upsilon
φ	ph	phi
χ	ch	chi
ψ	ps	psi
ω	ō	omega
ʽ	h	spiritus asper
ᾳ	ai	iota subscriptum (similarly ῃ, ῳ)

In transliterated Greek the accents are retained (acute ´, grave `, and circumflex ^). Long vowels with the circumflex accent have no separate indication of vowel length (makron).

Transliteration and pronounciation of Modern Greek

Only those sounds and combinations of sounds are mentioned which are different from Ancient Greek.

Consonants

β	v	
γ	gh	before 'dark' vowels like Engl. 'go'
	j	before 'light' vowels
δ	dh	like Engl. 'the'
ζ	z	like Engl. 'zeal'
θ	th	like Engl. 'thing'

Combinations of consonants

γκ	ng	
	g	in initial position
μπ	mb	
	b	in initial position
ντ	nd	
	d	in initial position

Vowels

η	i
υ	i

Diphthongs

αι	e	
αυ	av	
	af	before hard consonants
ει	i	
ευ	ev	
	ef	before hard consonants
οι	i	
υι	ii	

Spiritus asper is not pronounced. The Ancient Greek accent normally retains its position, but the distinction between ´, ` and ^ has disappeared.

Transliteration of Hebrew

א	a	alef
ב	b	bet
ג	g	gimel
ד	d	dalet
ה	h	he
ו	w	vav
ז	z	zayin
ח	ḥ	khet
ט	ṭ	tet
י	y	yod
כ	k	kaf

ל	l	lamed
מ	m	mem
נ	n	nun
ס	s	samek
ע	ʿ	ayin
פ	p/f	pe
צ	ṣ	tsade
ק	q	qof
ר	r	resh
ש	ś	sin
ש	š	shin
ת	t	tav

Pronunciation of Turkish

Turkish uses Latin script since 1928. Pronunciation and spelling generally follow the same rules as European languages. Phonology according to G. Lewis, Turkish Grammar, 2000.

A	a	French a in *avoir*
B	b	b
C	c	j in *jam*
Ç	ç	ch in *church*
D	d	d
E	e	French ê in *être*
F	f	f
G	g	g in *gate* or in *angular*
Ğ	ğ	lengthens preceding vowel
H	h	h in *have*
I	ı	i in *cousin*
İ	i	French i in *si*
J	j	French j
K	k	c in *cat* or in *cure*
L	l	l in *list* or in *wool*
M	m	m
N	n	n
O	o	French o in *note*
Ö	ö	German ö
P	p	p
R	r	r
S	s	s in *sit*
Ş	ş	sh in *shape*
T	t	t
U	u	u in *put*
Ü	ü	German ü
V	v	v
Y	y	y in *yet*
Z	z	z

Transliteration of Arabic, Persian, and Ottoman Turkish

ا ,ء	ʾ, ā	ʾ	ʾ	hamza, alif
ب	b	b	b	bāʾ
پ	–	p	p	pe
ت	t	t	t	tāʾ
ث	ṯ	s̱	s̱	t̲āʾ
ج	ǧ	ǧ	ǧ	ǧīm
چ	–	č	č	čim
ح	ḥ	ḥ	ḥ	ḥāʾ
خ	ḫ	ḫ	ḫ	ḫāʾ
د	d	d	d	dāl
ذ	ḏ	ẕ	ẕ	d̲āl
ر	r	r	r	rāʾ
ز	z	z	z	zāy
ژ	–	ž	ž	že
س	s	s	s	sīn
ش	š	š	š	šīn
ص	ṣ	ṣ	ṣ	ṣād
ض	ḍ	ḍ	ḍ	ḍād
ط	ṭ	ṭ	ṭ	ṭāʾ
ظ	ẓ	ẓ	ẓ	ẓāʾ
ع	ʿ	ʿ	ʿ	ʿain
غ	ġ	ġ	ġ	ġain
ف	f	f	f	fāʾ
ق	q	q	q, k	qāf
ك	k	k	k, g, ñ	kāf
گ	–	g	g, ñ	gāf
ل	l	l	l	lām
م	m	m	m	mīm
ن	n	n	n	nūn
ه	h	h	h	hāʾ
و	w, ū	v	v	wāw
ى	y, ī	y	y	yāʾ

Transliteration of other languages

Akkadian (Assyrian-Babylonian), Hittite and Sumerian are transliterated according to the rules of RLA and TAVO. For Egyptian the rules of the Lexikon der Ägyptologie are used. The transliteration of Indo-European follows Rix, HGG. The transliteration of Old Indian is after M. Mayrhofer, Etymologisches Wörterbuch des Altindoarischen, 1992ff. Avestian is done according to K. Hoffmann, B. Forssman, Avestische Laut- und Flexionslehre, 1996. Old Persian follows R.G. Kent, Old Persian, ²1953 (additions from K. Hoffmann, Aufsätze zur Indoiranistik vol. 2, 1976, 622ff.); other Iranian languages are after R. Schmitt, Compendium linguarum Iranicarum, 1989, and after D.N. MacKenzie, A Concise Pahlavi Dictionary, ³1990. For Armenian the rules of R. Schmitt, Grammatik des Klassisch-Armenischen, 1981, and of the Revue des études arméniennes, apply. The languages of Asia Minor are transliterated according to HbdOr. For Mycenean, Cyprian see Heubeck and Masson; for Italic scripts and Etruscan see Vetter and ET.

List of Abbreviations

1. Special Characters

→	see (cross-reference)	i̯, u̯	consonantal i, u
<	originated from (ling.)	m̥, n̥	vocalized m, n
>	evolved into (ling.)	l̥, r̥	vocalized l, r
√	root	|	syllable end
*	born/reconstructed form (ling.)	#	word end
∞	married	⟨ ⟩	transliteration
ă	short vowel	/ /	phonemic representation
ā	long vowel	[ ]	apocryphal
†	deceased		

2. List of General Abbreviations

Common abbreviations (e.g., etc.) are not included in the list of general abbreviations.

abl.	ablative
acc.	accusative
Athens, AM	Athens, Acropolis Museum
Athens, BM	Athens, Benaki Museum
Athens, NM	Athens, National Museum
Athens, NUM	Athens, Numismatic Museum
b.	born
Baltimore, WAG	Baltimore, Walters Art Gallery
Basle, AM	Basle, Antikenmuseum
Berlin, PM	Berlin, Pergamonmuseum
Berlin, SM	Berlin, Staatliche Museen
bk(s).	book(s)
Bonn, RL	Bonn, Rheinisches Landesmuseum
Boston, MFA	Boston, Museum of Fine Arts
Bull.	Bulletin, Bullettino
c.	circa
Cambridge, FM	Cambridge, Fitzwilliam Museum
carm.	carmen, carmina
Cat.	Catalogue, Catalogo
cent.	century
ch.	chapter
Cod.	Codex, Codices, Codizes
col.	column
conc.	acta concilii
Cologne, RGM	Cologne, Römisch Germanisches Museum
comm.	commentary
Congr.	Congrss, Congrès, Congresso
contd.	continued
Copenhagen, NCG	Copenhagen, Ny Carlsberg Glyptothek
Copenhagen, NM	Copenhagen, National Museum
Copenhagen, TM	Copenhagen, Thorvaldsen Museum
d.	died
dat.	dative
decret.	decretum, decreta
diss.	dissertation
ed.	edidit, editio, editor, edited (by)
edd.	ediderunt
epist.	epistulae
f.l.	falsa lectio
fem.	feminine
fig(s).	figure(s)
Florence, MA	Florence, Museo Archeologico
Florence, UF	Florence, Uffizi
fr.	fragment
Frankfurt, LH	Frankfurt, Liebighaus
gen.	genitive
Geneva, MAH	Geneva, Musée d'Art et d'Histoire
Ger.	German
Gk.	Greek
Hamburg, MKG	Hamburg, Museum für Kunst und Gewerbe
Hanover, KM	Hanover, Kestner-Museum

inventory no.	inventory number
Istanbul, AM	Istanbul, Archaeological Museum
itin.	itineraria
Kassel, SK	Kassel, Staatliche Kunstsammlungen
l.	lex
l.	line
L.	Lucius
l.c.	loco citato
Lat.	Latin
leg.	leges
lib.	liber, libri
ling.	linguistic(ally)
loc.	locative
London, BM	London, British Museum
Madrid, PR	Madrid, Prado
Malibu, GM	Malibu, Getty Museum
masc.	masculinum, masculine
Moscow, PM	Moscow, Pushkin Museum
MS(S)	manuscript(s)
Munich, GL	Munich, Glyptothek
Munich, SA	Munich, Staatliche Antikensammlung
Munich, SM	Munich, Staatliche Münzsammlung
Mus.	Museum, Musée, Museo
n.d.	no date
Naples, MAN	Naples, Museo Archeologico Nazionale
neutr.	neutrum, neuter, neutral
New York, MMA	New York, Metropolitan Museum of Arts
no.	number
nom.	nominative
N.S.	Neue Serie, New Series, Nouvelle Série, Nuova Seria
NT	New Testament
Op.	Opus, Opera
opt.	optative
OT	Old Testament
Oxford, AM	Oxford, Ashmolean Museum
p.	page
P	Papyrus
Palermo, MAN	Palermo, Museo Archeologico Nazionale
Paris, BN	Paris, Bibliothèque Nationale
Paris, CM	Paris, Cabinet des Médailles
Paris, LV	Paris, Louvre
pl.	plate
plur.	plural
pr(aef).	praefatio
Ps.-	Pseudo
rev.	revised

Rome, MC	Rome, Museo Capitolino
Rome, MN	Rome, Museo Nazionale
Rome, MV	Rome, Museo Vaticano
Rome, VA	Rome, Villa Albani
Rome, VG	Rome, Villa Giulia
Ser.	Serie, Series, Série, Seria
s.v.	sub voce
sc.	scilicet
schol.	scholion, scholia
serm.	sermo
s(in)g.	singular
Soc.	Society, Societé, Società
St.	Saint
St. Petersburg, HR	St. Petersburg, Hermitage
Stud.	Studia, Studien, Studies, Studi
The Hague, MK	The Hague, Muntenkabinet
Thessaloniki, NM	Thessaloniki, National Museum
tit.	titulus
trans.	translation, translated (by)
t.t.	terminus technicus
Univ.	Universität, University, Université, Università
v	verso
Vienna, KM	Vienna, Kunsthistorisches Museum
vol(s).	volume(s)

3. Bibliographic Abbreviations

A&A
  Antike und Abendland
A&R
  Atene e Roma
AA
  Archäologischer Anzeiger
AAA
  Annals of Archaeology and Anthropology
AAAlg
  S. GSELL, Atlas archéologique de l'Algérie. Édition spéciale des cartes au 200.000 du Service Géographique de l' Armée, 1911, repr. 1973
AAHG
  Anzeiger für die Altertumswissenschaften, publication of the Österreichische Humanistische Gesellschaft
AArch
  Acta archeologica
AASO
  The Annual of the American Schools of Oriental Research
AATun 050
  E. BABELON, R. CAGNAT, S. REINACH (ed.), Atlas archéologique de la Tunisie (1 : 50.000), 1893
AATun 100
  R. CAGNAT, A. MERLIN (ed.), Atlas archéologique de la Tunisie (1: 100.000), 1914

AAWG
: Abhandlungen der Akademie der Wissenschaften in Göttingen. Philologisch-historische Klasse

AAWM
: Abhandlungen der Akademie der Wissenschaften und Literatur in Mainz. Geistes- und sozialwissenschaftliche Klasse

AAWW
: Anzeiger der Österreichischen Akademie der Wissenschaften in Wien. Philosophisch-historische Klasse

ABAW
: Abhandlungen der Bayerischen Akademie der Wissenschaften. Philosophisch-historische Klasse

Abel
: F.-M.Abel,GéographiedelaPalestine2vols.,1933–38

ABG,
: Archiv für Begriffsgeschichte: Bausteine zu einem historischen Wörterbuch der Philosophie

ABr
: P. Arndt, F. Bruckmann (ed.), Griechische und römische Porträts, 1891 – 1912; E. Lippold (ed.), Text vol., 1958

ABSA
: Annual of the British School at Athens

AC
: L'Antiquité Classique

Acta
: Acta conventus neo-latini Lovaniensis, 1973

AD
: Archaiologikon Deltion

ADAIK
: Abhandlungen des Deutschen Archäologischen Instituts Kairo

Adam
: J.P. Adam, La construction romaine. Matériaux et techniques, 1984

ADAW
: Abhandlungen der Deutschen Akademie der Wissenschaften zu Berlin. Klasse für Sprachen, Literatur und Kunst

ADB
: Allgemeine Deutsche Biographie

AdI
: Annali dell'Istituto di Corrispondenza Archeologica

AE
: L'Année épigraphique

AEA
: Archivo Espanol de Arqueología

AEM
: Archäologisch-epigraphische Mitteilungen aus Österreich

AfO
: Archiv für Orientforschung

AGD
: Antike Gemmen in deutschen Sammlungen 4 vols., 1968–75

AGM
: Archiv für Geschichte der Medizin

Agora
: The Athenian Agora. Results of the Excavations by the American School of Classical Studies of Athens, 1953 ff.

AGPh
: Archiv für Geschichte der Philosophie

AGR
: Akten der Gesellschaft für griechische und hellenistische Rechtsgeschichte

AHAW
: Abhandlungen der Heidelberger Akademie der Wissenschaften. Philosophisch-historische Klasse

AHES
: Archive for History of Exact Sciences

AIHS
: Archives internationales d'histoire des sciences

AION
: Annali del Seminario di Studi del Mondo Classico, Sezione di Archeologia e Storia antica

AJ
: The Archaeological Journal of the Royal Archaeological Institute of Great Britain and Ireland

AJA
: American Journal of Archaeology

AJAH
: American Journal of Ancient History

AJBA
: Australian Journal of Biblical Archaeology

AJN
: American Journal of Numismatics

AJPh
: American Journal of Philology

AK
: Antike Kunst

AKG
: Archiv für Kulturgeschichte

AKL
: G. Meissner (ed.), Allgemeines Künstlerlexikon: Die bildenden Künstler aller Zeiten und Völker, ²1991 ff.

AKM
: Abhandlungen für die Kunde des Morgenlandes

Albrecht
: M. v. Albrecht, Geschichte der römischen Literatur, ²1994

Alessio
: G. Alessio, Lexicon etymologicum. Supplemento ai Dizionari etimologici latini e romanzi, 1976

Alexander
: M.C. Alexander, Trials in the Late Roman Republic: 149 BC to 50 BC (Phoenix Suppl. Vol. 26), 1990

Alföldi
: A. Alföldi, Die monarchische Repräsentation im römischen Kaiserreiche, 1970, repr. ³1980

Alföldy, FH
: G. Alföldy, Fasti Hispanienses. Senatorische Reichsbeamte und Offiziere in den spanischen Provinzen des römischen Reiches von Augustus bis Diokletian, 1969

Alföldy, Konsulat
G. ALFÖLDY, Konsulat und Senatorenstand unter den Antoninen. Prosopographische Untersuchungen zur senatorischen Führungsschicht (Antiquitas 1, 27), 1977
Alföldy, RG
G. ALFÖLDY, Die römische Gesellschaft. Ausgewählte Beiträge, 1986
Alföldy, RH
G. ALFÖLDY, Römische Heeresgeschichte, 1987
Alföldy, RS
G. ALFÖLDY, Römische Sozialgeschichte, ³1984
ALLG
Archiv für lateinische Lexikographie und Grammatik
Altaner
B. ALTANER, Patrologie. Leben, Schriften und Lehre der Kirchenväter, ⁹1980
AMI
Archäologische Mitteilungen aus Iran
Amyx, Addenda
C.W. NEEFT, Addenda et Corrigenda to D.A. Amyx, Corinthian Vase-Painting, 1991
Amyx, CVP
D.A. AMYX, Corinthian Vase-Painting of the Archaic Period 3 vols., 1988
Anadolu
Anadolu (Anatolia)
Anatolica
Anatolica
AncSoc
Ancient Society
Anderson
J.G. ANDERSON, A Journey of Exploration in Pontus (Studia pontica 1), 1903
Anderson Cumont/Grégoire
J.G. ANDERSON, F. CUMONT, H. GRÉGOIRE, Recueil des inscriptions grecques et latines du Pont et de l'Arménie (Studia pontica 3), 1910
André, botan.
J. ANDRÉ, Lexique des termes de botanique en latin, 1956
André, oiseaux
J. ANDRÉ, Les noms d'oiseaux en latin, 1967
André, plantes
J. ANDRÉ, Les noms de plantes dans la Rome antique, 1985
Andrews
K. ANDREWS, The Castles of Morea, 1953
ANET
J.B. PRITCHARD, Ancient Near Eastern Texts Relating to the Old Testament, ³1969, repr. 1992
AnnSAAt
Annuario della Scuola Archeologica di Atene
ANRW
H. TEMPORINI, W. HAASE (ed.), Aufstieg und Niedergang der römischen Welt, 1972 ff.
ANSMusN
Museum Notes. American Numismatic Society

AntAfr
Antiquités africaines
AntChr
Antike und Christentum
AntPl
Antike Plastik
AO
Der Alte Orient
AOAT
Alter Orient und Altes Testament
APF
Archiv für Papyrusforschung und verwandte Gebiete
APh
L'Année philologique
Arangio-Ruiz
V. ARANGIO-RUIZ, Storia del diritto romano, ⁶1953
Arcadia
Arcadia. Zeitschrift für vergleichende Literaturwissenschaft
ArchCl
Archeologia Classica
ArchE
Archaiologike ephemeris
ArcheologijaSof
Archeologija. Organ na Archeologiceskija institut i muzej pri B'lgarskata akademija na naukite
ArchHom
Archaeologia Homerica, 1967ff.
ArtAntMod
Arte antica e moderna
ARW
Archiv für Religionswissenschaft
AS
Anatolian Studies
ASAA
Annuario della Scuola Archeologica di Atene e delle Missioni italiane in Oriente
ASL
Archiv für das Studium der neueren Sprachen und Literaturen
ASNP
Annali della Scuola Normale Superiore di Pisa, Classe di Lettere e Filosofia
ASpr
Die Alten Sprachen
ASR
B. ANDREAE (ed.), Die antiken Sarkophagreliefs, 1952 ff.
Athenaeum
Athenaeum
ATL
B.D. MERITT, H.T. WADE-GERY, M.F. McGRECOR, Athenian Tribute Lists 4 vols., 1939–53
AU
Der altsprachliche Unterricht
Aulock
H. v. AULOCK, Münzen und Städte Pisidiens (MDAI(Ist) Suppl. 8) 2 vols., 1977–79

Austin
C. Austin (ed.), Comicorum graecorum fragmenta in papyris reperta, 1973

BA
Bolletino d'Arte del Ministero della Publica Istruzione

BAB
Bulletin de l'Académie Royale de Belgique. Classe des Lettres

BABesch
Bulletin antieke beschaving. Annual Papers on Classical Archaeology

Badian, Clientelae
E. Badian, Foreign Clientelae, 1958

Badian, Imperialism
E. Badian, Roman Imperialism in the Late Republic, 1967

BaF
Baghdader Forschungen

Bagnall
R.S. Bagnall et al., Consuls of the Later Roman Empire (Philological Monographs of the American Philological Association 36), 1987

BalkE
Balkansko ezikoznanie

BalkSt
Balkan Studies

BaM
Baghdader Mitteilungen

Bardenhewer, GAL
O. Bardenhewer, Geschichte der altkirchlichen Literatur, Vols. 1–2, ²1913 f.; Vols. 3–5, 1912–32; repr. Vols. 1–5, 1962

Bardenhewer, Patr.
O. Bardenhewer, Patrologie, ³1910

Bardon
H. Bardon, La littérature latine inconnue 2 vols., 1952–56

Baron
W. Baron (ed.), Beiträge zur Methode der Wissenschaftsgeschichte, 1967

BASO
Bulletin of the American Schools of Oriental Research

Bauer/Aland
W. Bauer, K. Aland (ed.), Griechisch-deutsches Wörterbuch zu den Schriften des Neuen Testamentes und der frühchristlichen Literatur, ⁶1988

Baumann, LRRP
R.A. Bauman, Lawyers in Roman Republican Politics. A study of the Roman Jurists in their Political Setting, 316–82 BC (Münchener Beiträge zur Papyrusforschung und antiken Rechtsgeschichte), 1983

Baumann, LRTP
R.A. Bauman, Lawyers in Roman Transitional Politics. A Study of the Roman Jurists in their Political Setting in the Late Republic and Triumvirate (Münchener Beiträge zur Papyrusforschung und antiken Rechtsgeschichte), 1985

BB
Bezzenbergers Beiträge zur Kunde der indogermanischen Sprachen

BCAR
Bollettino della Commissione Archeologica Comunale di Roma

BCH
Bulletin de Correspondance Hellénique

BE
Bulletin épigraphique

Beazley, ABV
J.D. Beazley, Attic Black-figure Vase-Painters, 1956

Beazley, Addenda²
TH.H. Carpenter (ed.), Beazley Addenda, ²1989

Beazley, ARV²
J.D. Beazley, Attic Red-figure Vase-Painters, ²1963

Beazley, EVP
J.D. Beazley, Etruscan Vase Painting, 1947

Beazley, Paralipomena
J.D. Beazley, Paralipomena. Additions to Attic Black-figure Vase-Painters and to Attic Red-figure Vase-Painters, ²1971

Bechtel, Dial.¹
F. Bechtel, Die griechischen Dialekte 3 vols., 1921–24

Bechtel, Dial.²
F. Bechtel, Die griechischen Dialekte 3 vols., ⁴1963

Bechtel, HPN
F. Bechtel, Die historischen Personennamen des Griechischen bis zur Kaiserzeit, 1917

Belke
K. Belke, Galatien und Lykaonien (Denkschriften der Österreichischen Akademie der Wissenschaften, Philosophisch-Historische Klasse 172; TIB 4), 1984

Belke/Mersich
K. Belke, N. Mersich, Phrygien und Pisidien (Denkschriften der Österreichischen Akademie der Wissenschaften, Philosophisch-Historische Klasse 211; TIB 7), 1990

Bell
K.E. Bell, Place-Names in Classical Mythology, Greece, 1989

Beloch, Bevölkerung
K.J. Beloch, Die Bevölkerung der griechisch-römischen Welt, 1886

Beloch, GG
K.J. Beloch, Griechische Geschichte 4 vols., ²1912–27, repr. 1967

Beloch, RG
K.J. Beloch, Römische Geschichte bis zum Beginn der Punischen Kriege, 1926

Bengtson
H. Bengtson, Die Strategie in der hellenistischen Zeit. Ein Beitrag zum antiken Staatsrecht (Münchener Beiträge zur Papyrusforschung und antiken Rechtsgeschichte 26, 32, 36) 3 vols., 1937–52, ed. repr. 1964–67

Berger
  E.H. BERGER, Geschichte der wissenschaftlichen Erdkunde der Griechen, ²1903
Berve
  H. BERVE, Das Alexanderreich auf prosopographischer Grundlage, 1926
Beyen
  H. G. BEYEN, Die pompejanische Wanddekoration vom zweiten bis zum vierten Stil 2 vols., 1938–60
BFC
  Bolletino di filologia classica
BGU
  Ägyptische (Griechische) Urkunden aus den Kaiserlichen (from Vol. 6 on Staatlichen) Museen zu Berlin 13 vols., 1895–1976
BHM
  Bulletin of the History of Medicine
BIAO
  Bulletin de l'Institut français d'Archéologie Orientale
BiblH&R
  Bibliothèque d'Humanisme et Renaissance
BiblLing
  Bibliographie linguistique / Linguistic Bibliography
BIBR
  Bulletin de l'Institut Belge de Rome
Bickerman
  E. BICKERMANN, Chronologie (Einleitung in die Altertumswissenschaft III 5), 1933
BICS
  Bulletin of the Institute of Classical Studies of the University of London
BIES
  The Bulletin of the Israel Exploration Society
BiogJahr
  Biographisches Jahrbuch für Altertumskunde
Birley
  A.R. BIRLEY, The Fasti of Roman Britain, 1981
BJ
  Bonner Jahrbücher des Rheinischen Landesmuseums in Bonn und des Vereins von Altertumsfreunden im Rheinlande
BKT
  Berliner Klassikertexte 8 vols., 1904–39
BKV
  Bibliothek der Kirchenväter (Kempten ed.) 63 vols., ²1911–31
Blänsdorf
  J. BLÄNSDORF (ed.), Theater und Gesellschaft im Imperium Romanum, 1990
Blass
  F. BLASS, Die attische Beredsamkeit, 3 vols., ³1887–98, repr. 1979
Blass/Debrunner/Rehkopf
  F. BLASS, A. DEBRUNNER, F. REHKOPF, Grammatik des neutestamentlichen Griechisch, ¹⁵1979
Blümner, PrAlt.
  H. BLÜMNER, Die römischen Privataltertümer (HdbA IV 2, 2), ³1911

Blümner, Techn.
  H. BLÜMNER, Technologie und Terminologie der Gewerbe und Künste bei Griechen und Römern, Vol. 1, ²1912; Vols. 2–4, 1875–87, repr. 1969
BMC, Gr
  A Catalogue of the Greek Coins in the British Museum 29 vols., 1873–1965
BMCByz
  W. WROTH (ed.), Catalogue of the Imperial Byzantine Coins in the British Museum 2 vols., 1908, repr. 1966
BMCIR
  Bryn Mawr Classical Review
BMCRE
  H. MATTINGLY (ed.), Coins of the Roman Empire in the British Museum 6 vols., 1962–76
BMCRR
  H.A. GRUEBER (ed.), Coins of the Roman Republic in the British Museum 3 vols., 1970
BN
  Beiträge zur Namensforschung
Bolgar, Culture 1
  R. BOLGAR, Classical Influences on European Culture A.D. 500 – 1500, 1971
Bolgar, Culture 2
  R. BOLGAR, Classical Influences on European Culture A.D. 1500–1700, 1974
Bolgar, Thought
  R. BOLGAR, Classical Influences on Western Thought A.D. 1650–1870, 1977
Bon
  A. BON, La Morée franque 2 vols., 1969
Bonner
  S.F. BONNER, Education in Ancient Rome, 1977
Bopearachchi
  O. BOPEARACHCHI, Monnaies gréco-bactriennes et indo-grecques. Catalogue raisonné, 1991
Borinski
  K. BORINSKI, Die Antike in Poetik und Kunsttheorie vom Ausgang des klassischen Altertums bis auf Goethe und Wilhelm von Humboldt 2 vols., 1914–24, repr. 1965
Borza
  E.N. BORZA, In the shadow of Olympus. The emergence of Macedon, 1990
Bouché-Leclerq
  A. BOUCHÉ-LECLERQ, Histoire de la divination dans l'antiquité 3 vols., 1879–82, repr. 1978 in 4 vols.
BPhC
  Bibliotheca Philologica Classica
BrBr
  H. BRUNN, F. BRUCKMANN, Denkmäler griechischer und römischer Skulpturen, 1888–1947
BRGK
  Bericht der Römisch-Germanischen Kommission des Deutschen Archäologischen Instituts
Briggs/Calder
  W.W. BRIGGS, W.M. CALDER III, Classical Scholarship. A Biographical Encyclopedia, 1990

Bruchmann
  C.F.H. BRUCHMANN, Epitheta deorum quae apud poetas graecos leguntur, 1893
Brugmann/Delbrück
  K. BRUGMANN, B. DELBRÜCK, Grundriß der vergleichenden Grammatik der indogermanischen Sprachen, Vols. 1–2, 1897–1916; Vols. 3–5, 1893–1900
Brugmann /Thumb
  K. BRUGMANN, A. THUMB (ed.), Griechische Grammatik, ⁴1913
Brunhölzl
  F. BRUNHÖLZL, Geschichte der lateinischen Literatur des Mittelalters 2 vols., 1975–92
Brunt
  P.A. BRUNT, Italian Manpower 222 B. C. – A. D. 14, 1971
Bruun
  C. BRUUN, The Water Supply of Ancient Rome. A Study of Imperial Administration (Commentationes Humanarum Litterarum 93), 1991
Bryer/Winfield
  A. BRYER, D. WINFIELD, The Byzantine Monuments and Topography of Pontus (Dumbarton Oaks Studies 20) 2 vols., 1985
BSABR
  Bulletin de Liaison de la Société des Amis de la Bibliothèque Salomon Reinach
BSL
  Bulletin de la Société de Linguistique de Paris
BSO(A)S
  Bulletin of the School of Oriental (from Vol. 10 ff. and African) Studies
BTCGI
  G. NENCI (ed.), Bibliografia topografica della colonizzazione greca in Italia e nelle isole tirreniche, 1980 ff.
Buck
  A. BUCK (ed.), Die Rezeption der Antike, 1981
Burkert
  W. BURKERT, Griechische Religion der archaischen und klassischen Epoche, 1977
Busolt/Swoboda
  G. BUSOLT, H. SWOBODA, Griechische Staatskunde (HdbA IV 1, 1) 2 vols., ³1920–26, repr. 1972–79
BWG
  Berichte zur Wissenschaftsgeschichte
BWPr
  Winckelmanns-Programm der Archäologischen Gesellschaft zu Berlin
Byzantion
  Byzantion. Revue internationale des études byzantines
ByzF
  Byzantinische Forschungen. Internationale Zeitschrift für Byzantinistik
BYzZ
  Byzantinische Zeitschrift
Caballos
  A. CABALLOS, Los senadores hispanoromanos y la

romanización de Hispania (Siglos I al III p.C.), Vol. 1: Prosopografia (Monografias del Departamento de Historia Antigua de la Universidad de Sevilla 5), 1990
CAF
  T. KOCK (ed.), Comicorum Atticorum Fragmenta, 3 vols., 1880–88
CAG
  Commentaria in Aristotelem Graeca 18 vols., 1885–1909
CAH
  The Cambridge Ancient History 12 text- and 5 ill. vols., 1924–39 (Vol. 1 as 2nd ed.), vols. 1–2, ³1970–75; vols. 3,1 and 3,3 ff., ²1982 ff.; vol. 3,2, ¹1991
Carney
  T.F. CARNEY, Bureaucracy in Traditional Society. Romano-Byzantine Bureaucracies Viewed from Within, 1971
Cartledge/Millett/Todd
  P. CARTLEDGE, P. MILLETT, S. TODD (ed.), Nomos, Essays in Athenian Law, Politics and Society, 1990
Cary
  M. CARY, The Geographical Background of Greek and Roman History, 1949
Casson, Ships
  L. CASSON, Ships and Seamanship in the Ancient World, 1971
Casson, Trade
  L. CASSON, Ancient Trade and Society, 1984
CAT
  Catalogus Tragicorum et Tragoediarum (in TrGF Vol. 1)
CatLitPap
  H.J.M. MILNE (ed.), Catalogue of the Literary Papyri in the British Museum, 1927
CCAG
  F. CUMONT ET AL. (ed.), Catalogus Codicum Astrologorum Graecorum 12 vols. in 20 parts, 1898–1940
CCL
  Corpus Christianorum. Series Latina, 1954 ff.
CE
  Cronache Ercolanesi
CEG
  P.A. HANSEN (ed.), Carmina epigraphica Graeca (Texts and Commentary 12; 15), 1983 ff.
CeM
  Classica et Mediaevalia
CGF
  G. KAIBEL (ed.), Comicorum Graecorum Fragmenta, ²1958
CGL
  G. GÖTZ (ed.), Corpus glossariorum Latinorum, 7 vols., 1888–1923, repr. 1965
Chantraine
  P. CHANTRAINE, Dictionnaire étymologique de la langue grecque 4 vols., 1968–80

CHCL-G
E.J. KENNEY (ed.), The Cambridge History of Classical Literature. Greek Literature, 1985 ff.

CHCL-L
E.J. KENNEY (ed.), The Cambridge History of Classical Literature. Latin Literature, 1982 ff.

Chiron
Chiron. Mitteilungen der Kommission für alte Geschichte und Epigraphik des Deutschen Archäologischen Instituts

Christ
K. CHRIST, Geschichte der römischen Kaiserzeit von Augustus bis zu Konstantin, 1988

Christ, RGG
K. CHRIST, Römische Geschichte und deutsche Geschichtswissenschaft, 1982

Christ, RGW
K. CHRIST, Römische Geschichte und Wissenschaftsgeschichte 3 vols., 1982–83

Christ/Momigliano
K. CHRIST, A. MOMIGLIANO, Die Antike im 19. Jahrhundert in Italien und Deutschland, 1988

CIA
A. KIRCHHOFF ET AL. (ed.), Corpus Inscriptionum Atticarum, 1873; Suppl.: 1877–91

CIC
Corpus Iuris Canonici 2 vols., 1879–81, repr. 1959

CID
Corpus des inscriptions de Delphes 3 vols., 1977–92

CIE
C. PAULI (ed.), Corpus Inscriptionum Etruscarum, Vol. 1–2, 1893–1921; Vol. 3,1 ff., 1982 ff.

CIG
Corpus Inscriptionum Graecarum 4 vols., 1828–77

CIL
Corpus Inscriptionum Latinarum, 1863 ff.

CIL III Add.
M. SASEL-KOS, Inscriptiones latinae in Graecia repertae. Additamenta ad CIL III (Epigrafia e antichità 5), 1979

CIRB
Corpus Inscriptionum regni Bosporani, 1965

CIS
Corpus Inscriptionum Semiticarum 5 parts, 1881–1951

CJ
Classical Journal

CL
Cultura Neolatina

Clairmont
C.W. CLAIRMONT, Attic Classical Tombstones 7 vols., 1993

Clauss
M. CLAUSS, Der magister officiorum in der Spätantike (4.–6. Jahrhundert). Das Amt und sein Einfluß auf die kaiserliche Politik (Vestigia 32), 1981

CLE
F. BÜCHELER, E. LOMMATZSCH (ed.), Carmina Latina Epigraphica (Anthologia latina 2) 3 vols., 1895–1926

CM
Clio Medica. Acta Academiae historiae medicinae

CMA
Cahiers de l'Institut du Moyen Age grec et latin

CMB
W.M. CALDER III, D.J. KRAMER, An Introductory Bibliography to the History of Classical Scholarship, Chiefly in the XIXth and XXth Centuries, 1992

CMG
Corpus Medicorum Graecorum, 1908 ff.

CMIK
J. CHADWICK, Corpus of Mycenaean Inscriptions from Knossos (Incunabula Graeca 88), 1986 ff.

CML
Corpus Medicorum Latinorum, 1915 ff.

CMS
F. MATZ ET AL. (ed.), Corpus der minoischen und mykenischen Siegel, 1964 ff.

CodMan
Codices manuscripti. Zeitschrift für Handschriftenkunde

Coing
H. COING, Europäisches Privatrecht 2 vols., 1985–89

CollAlex
I.U. POWELL (ed.), Collectanea Alexandrina, 1925

CollRau
J. V. UNGERN-STERNBERG (ed.), Colloquia Raurica, 1988 ff.

Conway/Johnson /Whatmough
R.S. CONWAY, S.E. JOHNSON, J. WHATMOUGH, The Prae-Italic dialects of Italy 3 vols., 1933, repr. 1968

Conze
A. CONZE, Die attischen Grabreliefs 4 vols., 1893–1922

Courtney
E. COURTNEY, The Fragmentary Latin Poets, 1993

CPF
F. ADORNO (ed.), Corpus dei Papiri Filosofici greci e latini, 1989 ff.

CPG
M. GEERARD (Vols. 1–5), F. GLORIE, (Vol. 5), Clavis patrum graecorum 5 vols., 1974–87

CPh
Classical Philology

CPL
E. DEKKERS, A. GAAR, Clavis patrum latinorum (CCL), ³1995

CQ
Classical Quarterly

CR
Classical Review

CRAI
Comptes rendus des séances de l'Académie des inscriptions et belles-lettres

CRF
O. RIBBECK (ed.), Comicorum Romanorum Fragmenta, 1871, repr. 1962

CSCT
Columbia Studies in the Classical Tradition
CSE
Corpus Speculorum Etruscorum, 1990 ff.
CSEL
Corpus Scriptorum ecclesiasticorum Latinorum, 1866 ff.
SCIR
Corpus Signorum Imperii Romani, 1963 ff.
Cumont, Pont
F. CUMONT, E. CUMONT, Voyage d'exploration archéologique dans le Pont et la Petite Arménie (Studia pontica 2), 1906
Cumont, Religions
F. CUMONT, Les Religions orientales dans le paganisme romain, ³1929, repr. 1981
Curtius
E.R. CURTIUS, Europäische Literatur und lateinisches Mittelalter, ¹¹1993
CVA
Corpus Vasorum Antiquorum, 1923 ff.
CW
The Classical World
D'Arms
J.H. D'ARMS, Commerce and Social Standing in Ancient Rome, 1981
D'Arms/Kopff
J.H. D'ARMS, E.C. KOPFF (ed.), The Seaborne Commerce of Ancient Rome: Studies in Archaeology and History (Memoirs of the American Academy in Rome 36), 1980
Dacia
Dacia. Revue d'archéologie et d'histoire ancienne
Davies
J.K. DAVIES, Athenian Propertied Families 600–300 BC, 1971
DB
F. VIGOUROUX (ed.), Dictionnaire de la Bible, 1881 ff.
DCPP
E. LIPIŃSKI ET AL. (ed.), Dictionnaire de la Civilisation Phénicienne et Punique, 1992
Degrassi, FCap.
A. DEGRASSI, Fasti Capitolini (Corpus scriptorum Latinorum Paravianum), 1954
Degrassi, FCIR
A. DEGRASSI, I Fasti consolari dell'Impero Romano, 1952
Deichgräber
K. DEICHGRÄBER, Die griechische Empirikerschule, 1930
Delmaire
R. DELMAIRE, Les responsables des finances impériales au Bas-Empire romain (IVᵉ-VIᵉ s). Études prosopographiques (Collection Latomus 203), 1989
Demandt
A. DEMANDT, Der Fall Roms: die Auflösung des römischen Reiches im Urteil der Nachwelt, 1984

Demougin
S. DEMOUGIN, Prosopographie des Chevaliers romains Julio-Claudiens (43 av.J -C.–70 ap.J.-C.) (Collection de l'École Française de Rome 153), 1992
Deubner
L. DEUBNER, Attische Feste, 1932
Develin
R. DEVELIN, Athenian Officials 684–321 B.C. 1949
Devijver
H. DEVIJVER, Prosopographia militiarum equestrium quae fuerunt ab Augusto ad Gallienum (Symbolae Facultatis Litterarum et Philosophiae Lovaniensis Ser. A 3) 3 vols., 1976–80; 2 Suppl. Vols.: 1987–93
DHA
Dialogues d'histoire ancienne
DHGE
A. BAUDRILLART, R. AUBERT (ed.), Dictionnaire d'Histoire et de Géographie Ecclésiastiques 1912 ff.
DID
Didascaliae Tragicae/Ludorum Tragicorum (in TrGF Vol. 1)
Diels, DG
H. DIELS, Doxographi Graeci, 1879
Diels/Kranz
H. DIELS, W. KRANZ (ed.), Fragmente der Vorsokratiker 3 vols., ⁹1951 f., repr. Vol.1, 1992; Vol. 2, 1985; Vol. 3, 1993
Dierauer
U. DIERAUER, Tier und Mensch im Denken der Antike, 1977
Dietz
K. DIETZ, Senatus contra principem. Untersuchungen zur senatorischen Opposition gegen Kaiser Maximinus Thrax (Vestigia 29), 1980
Dihle
A. DIHLE, Die griechische und lateinische Literatur der Kaiserzeit: von Augustus bis Justinian, 1989
DiskAB
Diskussionen zur archäologischen Bauforschung, 1974 ff.
Dixon
S. DIXON, The Roman Family, 1992
DJD
Discoveries in the Judaean Desert, 1955 ff.
DLZ
Deutsche Literaturzeitung für Kritik der internationalen Wissenschaft
DMA
J.R. STRAYER ET AL. (ed.), Dictionary of the Middle Ages 13 vols., 1982–89
Dmic
F. AURA JORRO, Diccionario Micénico, 1985
Dörrie/Baltes
H. DÖRRIE, M. BALTES (ed.), Der Platonismus in der Antike, 1987 ff.
Domaszewski
A.V. DOMASZEWSKI, Aufsätze zur römischen Heeresgeschichte, 1972

Domaszewski /Dobson
A.V. DOMASZEWSKI, B. DOBSON, Die Rangordnung des römischen Heeres, ²1967

Domergue
C. DOMERGUE, Les mines de la péninsule Iberique dans l'Antiquité Romaine, 1990

Drumann /Groebe
W. DRUMANN, P. GROEBE (ed.), Geschichte Roms in seinem Übergange von der republikanischen zur monarchischen Verfassung 6 vols., 1899–1929, repr. 1964

DS
C. DAREMBERG, E. SAGLIO (ed.), Dictionnaire des antiquités grecques et romaines d'après les textes et les monuments 6 vols., 1877–1919, repr. 1969

Dulckeit /Schwarz /Waldstein
G. DULCKEIT, F. SCHWARZ, W. WALDSTEIN, Römische Rechtsgeschichte. Ein Studienbuch (Juristische Kurz Lehrbücher), 1995

Dumézil
G. DUMÉZIL, La religion romaine archaïque, suivi d'un appendice sur la religion des Etrusques, 1974

Duncan-Jones, Economy
R. DUNCAN-JONES, The Economy of the Roman Empire. Quantitative Studies, 1974

Duncan-Jones, Structure
R. DUNCAN-JONES, Structure and Scale in the Roman Economy, 1990

DVjS
Deutsche Vierteljahrsschrift für Literaturwissenschaft und Geistesgeschichte

EA
Epigraphica Anatolica. Zeitschrift für Epigraphik und historische Geographie Anatoliens

EAA
R. BIANCHI BANDINELLI (ed.), Enciclopedia dell'arte antica classica e orientale, 1958 ff.

EB
G. CAMPS, Encyclopédie Berbère 1984 ff.

Ebert
F. EBERT, Fachausdrücke des griechischen Bauhandwerks, Vol. 1: Der Tempel, 1910

EC
Essays in Criticism

Eck
W. ECK, Die Statthalter der germanischen Provinzen vom 1.–3. Jahrhundert (Epigraphische Studien 14), 1985

Eckstein
F.A. ECKSTEIN, Nomenclator philologorum, 1871

Edelstein, AM
L. EDELSTEIN, Ancient medicine, 1967

Edelstein, Asclepius
E.J. and L. EDELSTEIN, Asclepius. A Collection and Interpretation of the Testimonies, 1945

Eder, Demokratie
W. EDER (ed.), Die athenische Demokratie im 4. Jahrhundert v. Chr. Vollendung oder Verfall einer Verfassungsform? Akten eines Symposiums, 3. – 7. August 1992, 1995

Eder, Staat
W. EDER (ed.), Staat und Staatlichkeit in der frühen römischen Republik: Akten eines Symposiums, 12. – 15. Juli 1988, 1990

EDM
K. RANKE, W. BREDNICH (ed.), Enzyklopädie des Märchens. Handwörterbuch zur historischen und vergleichenden Erzählforschung, 1977 ff.

EDRL
A. BERGER, Encyclopedic Dictionary of Roman Law (TAPhA N.S. 43,2), 1953, repr. 1968

EEpigr
Ephemeris Epigraphica

EI
Encyclopaedia of Islam, 1960 ff.

Eissfeldt
O. EISSFELDT (ed.), Handbuch zum Alten Testament, ³1964 ff.

Emerita
Emerita. Revista de linguistica y filologia clasica

EncIr
E. YARSHATER (ed.), Encyclopaedia Iranica, 1985

Entretiens
Entretiens sur l'antiquité classique (Fondation Hardt)

EOS
Atti del Colloquio Internazionale AIEGL su Epigrafia e Ordine Senatorio: Roma, 14–20 maggio 1981, 2 vols., 1982

EpGF
M. DAVIES, Epicorum graecorum fragmenta, 1988

EpGr
G. KAIBEL (ed.), Epigrammata Graeca ex lapidibus conlecta, 1878

Epicurea
H. USENER (ed.), Epicurea, 1887, repr. 1963

EPRO
Études préliminaires aux religions orientales dans l'Empire Romain, 1961 ff.

Eranos
Eranos. Acta Philologica Suecana

Er-Jb
Eranos-Jahrbuch

Erasmus
Erasmus. Speculum Scientiarum. Internationales Literaturblatt der Geisteswissenschaften

Eretz Israel
Eretz-Israel, Archaeological, Historical and Geographical Studies

Ernout/Meillet
A. ERNOUT, A. MEILLET, Dictionnaire étymologique de la langue latine, ⁴1959

Errington
R.M. ERRINGTON, Geschichte Makedoniens. Von den Anfängen bis zum Untergang des Königreiches, 1986

ESAR
T. FRANK (ed.), An Economic Survey of Ancient Rome 6 vols., 1933–40

Espérandieu, Inscr.
E. Espérandieu, Inscriptions latines de Gaule 2 vols., 1929–36

Espérandieu, Rec.
E. Espérandieu, Recueil généneral des bas-reliefs, statues et bustes de la Gaule Romaine 16 vols., 1907–81

ET
H. Rix (ed.), Etruskische Texte (ScriptOralia 23, 24, Reihe A 6,7) 2 vols., 1991

ETAM
Ergänzungsbände zu den Tituli Asiae minoris, 1966 ff.

Euph.
Euphorion

EV
F. Della Corte et al. (ed.), Enciclopedia Virgiliana 5 vols. in 6 parts, 1984–91

Evans
D.E. Evans, Gaulish Personal names. A study of some continental Celtic formations, 1967

F&F
Forschungen und Fortschritte

Farnell, Cults
L.R. Farnell, The Cults of the Greek States 5 vols., 1896–1909

Farnell, GHC
L.R. Farnell, Greek Hero Cults and Ideas of Immortality, 1921

FCG
A. Meineke (ed.), Fragmenta Comicorum Graecorum 5 vols., 1839–57, repr. 1970

FCS
Fifteenth-Century Studies

FdD
Fouilles de Delphes, 1902 ff.

FGE
D.L. Page, Further Greek Epigrams, 1981

FGrH
F. Jacoby, Die Fragmente der griechischen Historiker, 3 parts in 14 vols., 1923–58, Part I: ²1957

FHG
C. Müller (ed.), Fragmenta Historicorum Graecorum 5 vols., 1841–1970

Fick/Bechtel
A. Fick, F. Bechtel, Die griechischen Personennamen, ²1894

FiE
Forschungen in Ephesos, 1906 ff.

Filologia
La Filologia Greca e Latina nel secolo XX, 1989

Finley, Ancient Economy
M.I. Finley, The Ancient Economy, ²1984

Finley, Ancient Slavery
M.I. Finley, Ancient Slavery and Modern Ideology, 1980

Finley, Economy
M.I. Finley, B.D. Shaw, R.P. Saller (ed.), Economy and Society in Ancient Greece, 1981

Finley, Property
M.I. Finley (ed.), Studies in Roman Property, 1976

FIRA
S. Riccobono, J. Baviera (ed.), Fontes iuris Romani anteiustiniani 3 vols., ²1968

FIRBruns
K.G. Bruns, TH. Mommsen, O. Gradenwitz (ed.), Fontes iuris Romani antiqui, 1909, repr. 1969

Fittschen/Zanker
K. Fittschen, P. Zanker, Katalog der römischen Porträts in den capitolinischen Museen und den anderen kommunalen Museen der Stadt Rom, 1983 ff.

Flach
D. Flach, Römische Agrargeschichte (HdbA III 9), 1990

Flashar
H. Flashar, Inszenierung der Antike. Das griechische Drama auf der Bühne der Neuzeit, 1991

Flashar, Medizin
H. Flashar (ed.), Antike Medizin, 1971

FMS
Frühmittelalterliche Studien, Jahrbuch des Instituts für Frühmittelalter-Forschung der Universität Münster

Fossey
J.M. Fossey, Topography and Population of Ancient Boiotia, Vol. 1, 1988

FOst
L. Vidmann, Fasti Ostienses, 1982

Fowler
W.W. Fowler, The Roman Festivals of the Period of the Republic. An Introduction to the Study of the Religion of the Romans, 1899

FPD
I. Piso, Fasti Provinciae Daciae, Vol. 1: Die senatorischen Amtsträger (Antiquitas 1,43), 1993

FPL
W. Morel, C. Büchner (ed.), Fragmenta Poetarum Latinorum epicorum et lyricorum, ²1982

FPR
A. Bährens (ed.), Fragmenta Poetarum Romanorum, 1886

Frazer
J.G. Frazer, The Golden Bough. A Study in Magic and Religion, 8 parts in 12 vols., Vols. 1–3, 5–9, ³1911–14; Vols. 4, 10–12, 1911–15

Frenzel
E. Frenzel, Stoffe der Weltliteratur, ⁸1992

Friedländer
L. Friedländer, G. Wissowa (ed.), Darstellungen aus der Sittengeschichte Roms 4 vols., ¹⁰1921–23

Frier, Landlords
B.W. Frier, Landlords and Tenants in Imperial Rome, 1980

Frier, PontMax
B.W. Frier, Libri annales pontificum maximorum. The origins of the Annalistic Tradition (Papers and Monographs of the American Academy in Rome 27), 1979

Frisk
    H. FRISK, Griechisches etymologisches Wörterbuch (Indogermanische Bibliothek: Reihe 2) 3 vols., 1960–72

FRLANT
    Forschungen zur Religion und Literatur des Alten und Neuen Testaments

Fuchs/Floren
    W. FUCHS, J. FLOREN, Die Griechische Plastik, Vol. 1: Die geometrische und archaische Plastik, 1987

Furtwängler
    A. FURTWÄNGLER, Die antiken Gemmen. Geschichte der Steinschneidekunst im klassischen Altertum 3 vols., 1900

Furtwängler/Reichhold
    A. FURTWÄNGLER, K. REICHHOLD, Griechische Vasenmalerie 3 vols., 1904–32

Fushöller
    D. FUSHÖLLER, Tunesien und Ostalgerien in der Römerzeit, 1979

G&R
    Greece and Rome

GA
    A.S.F. GOW, D.L. PAGE, The Greek Anthology, Vol. 1: Hellenistic Epigrams, 1965; Vol. 2: The Garland of Philip, 1968

Gardner
    P. GARDNER, A History of Ancient Coinage, 700–300 B.C., 1918

Gardthausen
    V. GARDTHAUSEN, Augustus und Seine Zeit, 2 parts in 6 vols., 1891–1904

Garnsey
    P. GARNSEY, Famine and Food Supply in the Graeco-Roman World. Responses to Risk and Crisis, 1988

Garnsey/Hopkins/Whittaker
    P. GARNSEY, K. HOPKINS, C.R. WHITTAKER (ed.), Trade in the Ancient Economy, 1983

Garnsey/Saller
    P. GARNSEY, R. SALLER, The Roman Empire, Economy, Society and Culture, 1987

GCS
    Die griechischen christlichen Schriftsteller der ersten Jahrhunderte, 1897 ff.

Gehrke
    H.-J. GEHRKE, Jenseits von Athen und Sparta. Das Dritte Griechenland und seine Staatenwelt, 1986

Gentili/Prato
    B. GENTILI, C. PRATO (ed.), Poetarum elegiacorum testimonia et fragmenta, Vol. 1, ²1988; Vol. 2, 1985

Georges
    K.E. GEORGES, Ausführliches lateinisch-deutsches Handwörterbuch 2 vols., ⁸1912–18, repr. 1992

Gérard-Rousseau
    M. GÉRARD-ROUSSEAU, Les mentions religieuses dans les tablettes mycéniennes, 1968

Germania
    Germania. Anzeiger der Römisch-Germanischen Kommission des Deutschen Archäologischen Instituts

Gernet
    L. GERNET, Droit et société dans la Grèce ancienne (Institut de droit romain, Publication 13), 1955, repr. 1964

Geus
    K. GEUS, Prosopographie der literarisch bezeugten Karthager (Studia Phoenicia 13 Orientalia Lovaniensia analecta 59), 1994

GGA
    Göttingische Gelehrte Anzeigen

GGM
    C. MÜLLER (ed.), Geographi Graeci Minores 2 vols., Tabulae, 1855–61

GGPh¹
    F. ÜBERWEG (ed.), Grundriß der Geschichte der Philosophie; K, PRÄCHTER, Teil 1: Die Philosophie des Altertums, ¹²1926, repr. 1953

GGPh²
    W. OTTO, U. HAUSMANN (ed.), Grundriß der Geschichte der Philosophie; H. FLASHAR (ed.), vol. 3: Die Philosophie der Antike, 1983, vol. 4: Die hellenistische Philosophie, 1994

GHW 1
    H. BENGTSON, V. MILOJCIC ET AL., Großer Historischer Weltatlas des Bayrischen Schulbuchverlages 1. Vorgeschichte und Altertum, ⁶1978

GHW 2
    J. ENGEL, W. MACER, A. BIRKEN ET AL., Großer Historischer Weltatlas des Bayrischen Schulbuchverlages 2. Mittelalter, ²1979

GIBM
    C.T. NEWTON ET AL. (ed.), The Collection of Ancient Greek Inscriptions in the British Museum 4 vols., 1874–1916

Gillispie
    C.C. GILLISPIE (ed.), Dictionary of scientific biography 14 vols. and index, 1970–80, repr. 1981; 2 Suppl. Vols., 1978–90

GL
    H. KEIL (ed.), Grammatici Latini 7 vols., 1855–80

GLM
    A. RIESE (ed.), Geographi Latini Minores, 1878

Glotta
    Glotta. Zeitschrift für griechische und lateinische Sprache

GMth
    F. ZAMINER (ed.), Geschichte der Musiktheorie, 1984 ff.

Gnomon
    Gnomon. Kritische Zeitschrift für die gesamte klassische Altertumswissenschaft

Göbl
    R. GÖBL, Antike Numismatik 2 vols., 1978

Goleniščev
    I.N. GOLENIŠČEV-KUTUZOV, Il Rinascimento italiano e le letterature slave dei secoli XV e XVI, 1973

Gordon
    A.E. GORDON, Album of Dated Latin Inscriptions 4 vols., 1958–65

Goulet
    R. GOULET (ed.), Dictionnaire des philosophes anti-
    ques, 1989 ff.
Graf
    F. GRAF, Nordionische Kulte. Religionsgeschichtli-
    che und epigraphische Untersuchungen zu den Kul-
    ten von Chios, Erythrai, Klazomenai und Phokaia,
    1985
GRBS
    Greek, Roman and Byzantine Studies
Grenier
    A. GRENIER, Manuel d'archéologie gallo-romaine 4
    vols., 1931–60; vols. 1 and 2, repr. 1985
GRF
    H. FUNAIOLI (ed.), Grammaticae Romanae Frag-
    menta, 1907
GRF(add)
    A. MAZZARINO, Grammaticae Romanae Fragmenta
    aetatis Caesareae (accedunt volumini Funaioliano
    addenda), 1955
GRLMA
    Grundriß der romanischen Literaturen des Mittelal-
    ters
Gruen, Last Gen.
    E.S. GRUEN, The Last Generation of the Roman Re-
    public, 1974
Gruen, Rome
    E.S. GRUEN, The Hellenistic World and the Coming
    of Rome, 1984, repr. 1986
Gruppe
    O. GRUPPE, Geschichte der klassischen Mythologie
    und Religionsgeschichte während des Mittelalters
    im Abendland und während der Neuzeit, 1921
Gundel
    W. and H-G. GUNDEL, Astrologumena. Die astro-
    logische Literatur in der Antike und ihre Geschichte,
    1966
Guthrie
    W.K.C. GUTHRIE, A History of Greek Philosophy 6
    vols., 1962–81
GVI
    W. PEEK (ed.), Griechische Vers-Inschriften, Vol. I,
    1955
Gymnasium
    Gymnasium. Zeitschrift für Kultur der Antike und
    humanistische Bildung
HABES
    Heidelberger althistorische Beiträge und epigraphi-
    sche Studien, 1986 ff.
Habicht
    C. HABICHT, Athen. Die Geschichte der Stadt in hel-
    lenistischer Zeit, 1995
Hakkert
    A.M. HAKKERT (ed.), Lexicon of Greek and Roman
    Cities and Place-Names in Antiquity c. 1500 B.C. –
    c. A.D. 500, 1990 ff.
Halfmann
    H. HALFMANN, Die Senatoren aus dem östlichen Teil
    des Imperium Romanum bis zum Ende des 2. Jahr-
    hunderts n. Chr. (Hypomnemata 58), 1979

Hamburger
    K. HAMBURGER, Von Sophokles zu Sartre. Griechi-
    sche Dramenfiguren antik und modern, 1962
Hannestad
    N. HANNESTAD, Roman Art and Imperial Policy,
    1986
Hansen, Democracy
    M.H. HANSEN, The Athenian Democracy in the Age
    of Demosthenes. Structure, Principles and Ideology,
    1991, repr. 1993
Harris
    W.V. HARRIS, War and Imperialism in Republican
    Rome 327–70 B.C., 1979
Hasebroek
    J. HASEBROEK, Griechische Wirtschafts- und Gesell-
    schaftsgeschichte bis zur Perserzeit, 1931
HbdOr
    B. SPULER (ed.), Handbuch der Orientalistik, 1952
    ff.
HbdrA
    J. MARQUARDT, TH. MOMMSEN, Handbuch der rö-
    mischen Alterthümer, vols. 1–3, ³1887 f.; vols. 4–7,
    ²1881–86
HBr
    P. HERRMANN, R. HERBIG, (ed.), Denkmäler der
    Malerei des Altertums 2 vols., 1904–50
HDA
    H. BÄCHTOLD-STÄUBLI ET AL. (ed.), Handwörter-
    buch des deutschen Aberglaubens 10 vols., 1927–42,
    repr. 1987
HdArch
    W. OTTO, U. HAUSMANN (ed.), Handbuch der Ar-
    chäologie. Im Rahmen des HdbA 7 vols., 1969–90
HdbA
    I. V. MÜLLER, H. BENGTSON (ed.), Handbuch der
    Altertumswissenschaft, 1977 ff.
Heckel
    W. HECKEL, Marshals of Alexander's Empire, 1978
Heinemann
    K. HEINEMANN, Die tragischen Gestalten der Grie-
    chen in der Weltliteratur, 1920
Helbig
    W. HELBIG, Führer durch die öffentlichen Sammlun-
    gen klassischer Altertümer in Rom 4 vols., ⁴1963–72
Hephaistos
    Hephaistos. Kritische Zeitschrift zu Theorie und
    Praxis der Archäologie, Kunstwissenschaft und an-
    grenzender Gebiete
Hermes
    Hermes. Zeitschrift für klassische Philologie
Herrscherbild
    Das römische Herrscherbild, 1939 ff.
Herzog, Staatsverfassung
    E. V. HERZOG, Geschichte und System der römi-
    schen Staatsverfassung 2 vols., 1884–91, repr. 1965
Hesperia
    Hesperia. Journal of the American School of Clas-
    sical Studies at Athens

Heubeck
A. HEUBECK, Schrift (Archaeologia Homerica Chapter X Vol. 3), 1979

Heumann/Seckel
H.G. HEUMANN, E. SECKEL (ed.), Handlexikon zu den Quellen des römischen Rechts, ¹¹1971

Highet
G. HIGHET, The Classical Tradition: Greek and Roman Influences on Western literature, ⁴1968, repr. 1985

Hild
F. HILD, Kilikien und Isaurien (Denkschriften der Österreichischen Akademie der Wissenschaften, Philosophisch-Historische Klasse 215; TIB 5) 2 vols., 1990

Hild/Restle
F. HILD, M. RESTLE, Kappadokien (Kappadokia, Charsianon, Sebasteia und Lykandos) (Denkschriften der Österreichischen Akademie der Wissenschaften: Philosophisch-Historische Klasse 149; TIB 2), 1981

Hirschfeld
O. HIRSCHFELD, Die kaiserlichen Verwaltungsbeamten bis auf Diocletian, ²1905

Historia
Historia. Zeitschrift für Alte Geschichte

HJb
Historisches Jahrbuch

HLav
Humanistica Lavanensia

HLL
R. HERZOG, P.L. SCHMIDT (ed.), Handbuch der lateinischen Literatur der Antike, 1989 ff.

HM
A History of Macedonia, Vol. 1: N.G.L. HAMMOND, Historical geography and prehistory, 1972; Vol. 2: N.G.L. HAMMOND, G.T. GRIFFITH, 550–336 BC, 1979; Vol. 3: N.G.L. HAMMOND, F.W. WALBANK, 336–167 BC, 1988

HmT
H.H. EGGEBRECHT, Handwörterbuch der musikalischen Terminologie, 1972 ff.

HN
B.V. HEAD, Historia numorum. A manual of Greek numismatics, ²1911

Hodge
T.A. HODGE, Roman Aqueducts and Water Supply, 1992

Hölbl
G. HÖLBL, Geschichte des Ptolemäerreiches. Politik, Ideologie und religiöse Kultur von Alexander den Großen bis zur römischen Eroberung, 1994

Hölkeskamp
K.-J. HÖLKESKAMP, Die Entstehung der Nobilität. Studien zur sozialen und politischen Geschichte der Römischen Republik im 4.Jh. v. Chr., 1987

Hoffmann
D. HOFMANN, Das spätrömische Bewegungsheer und die Notitia dignitatum (Epigraphische Studien 7) 2 vols., 1969 f. = (Diss.), 1958

Holder
A. HOLDER, Alt-celtischer Sprachschatz 3 vols., 1896-1913, repr. 1961 f.

Honsell
H. HONSELL, Römisches Recht (Springer-Lehrbuch), ³1994

Hopfner
T. HOPFNER, Griechisch-ägyptischer Offenbarungszauber 2 vols. in 3 parts, 1921–24, repr. 1974–90

Hopkins, Conquerors
K. HOPKINS, Conquerors and Slaves. Sociological Studies in Roman History, Vol. 1, 1978

Hopkins, Death
K. HOPKINS, Death and Renewal. Sociological Studies in Roman History, Vol. 2, 1983

HR
History of Religions

HRR
H. PETER (ed.), Historicorum Romanorum Reliquiae, Vol. 1, 1914; Vol. 2, 1906, repr. 1967

HrwG
H. CANCIK, B. GLADIGOW, M. LAUBSCHER (from Vol. 2: K.-H. KOHL) (ed.), Handbuch religionswissenschaftlicher Grundbegriffe, 1988 ff.

HS
Historische Sprachforschung

HSM
Histoire des sciences médicales

HSPh
Harvard Studies in Classical Philology

Hülser
K. HÜLSER, Die Fragmente zur Dialektik der Stoiker. Neue Sammlung der Texte mit deutscher Übersetzung und Kommentaren 4 vols., 1987 f.

Humphrey
J.H. HUMPHREY, Roman Circuses. Arenas for Chariot Racing, 1986

Hunger, Literatur
H. HUNGER, Die hochsprachlich profane Literatur der Byzantiner (HdbA 12, 5) 2 vols., 1978

Hunger, Mythologie
H. HUNGER (ed.), Lexikon der griechischen und römischen Mythologie, ⁶1969

Huss
W. HUSS, Geschichte der Karthager (HdbA III 8), 1985

HWdPh
J. RITTER, K. GRÜNDER (ed.), Historisches Wörterbuch der Philosophie, 1971 ff.

HWdR
G. UEDING (ed.), Historisches Wörterbuch der Rhetorik, 1992 ff.

HZ
Historische Zeitschrift

IA
Iranica Antiqua

IconRel
T.P. v. BAAREN (ed.), Iconography of Religions, 1970 ff.

ICUR
A. Ferrua, G.B. De Rossi, Inscriptiones christianae urbis Romae, 1922ff.

IDélos
Inscriptions de Délos, 1926 ff.

IDidyma
A. Rehm (ed.), Didyma, Vol. 2: Die Inschriften, 1958

IEG
M. L. West (ed.), Iambi et elegi Graeci ante Alexandrum cantati 2 vols., 1989–92

IEJ
Israel Exploration Journal

IER
Illustrierte Enzyklopädie der Renaissance

IEry
H. Engelmann (ed.), Die Inschriften von Erythrai und Klazomenai 2 vols., 1972 f.

IF
Indogermanische Forschungen

IG
Inscriptiones Graecae, 1873 ff.

IGA
H. Roehl (ed.), Inscriptiones Graecae antiquissimae praeter Atticas in Attica repertas, 1882, repr. 1977

IGBulg
G. Mihailov (ed.), Inscriptiones Graecae in Bulgaria repertae 5 vols., 1956–1996

IGLS
Inscriptions grecques et latines de la Syrie, 1929 ff.

IGR
R. Cagnat et al. (ed.), Inscriptiones Graecae ad res Romanas pertinentes 4 vols., 1906–27

IGUR
L. Moretti, Inscriptiones Graecae urbis Romae 4 vols., 1968–90

IJCT
International Journal of the Classical Tradition

IJsewijn
J. IJsewijn, Companion to Neo Latin Studies, ²1990 ff.

IK
Die Inschriften griechischer Städte aus Kleinasien, 1972 ff.

ILCV
E. Diehl (ed.), Inscriptiones Latinae Christianae Veteres orientis 3 vols., 1925–31, repr. 1961; J. Moreau, H.I. Marrou (ed.), Suppl., 1967

ILLRP
A. Degrassi (ed.), Inscriptiones Latinae liberae rei publicae 2 vols., 1957–63, repr. 1972

ILS
H. Dessau (ed.), Inscriptiones Latinae Selectae 3 vols. in 5 parts, 1892–1916, repr. ⁴1974

IMagn.
O. Kern (ed.), Die Inschriften von Magnesia am Mäander, 1900, repr. 1967

IMU
Italia medioevale e umanistica

Index
Index. Quaderni camerti di studi romanistici

InscrIt
A. Degrassi (ed.), Inscriptiones Italiae, 1931 ff.

IOSPE
V. Latyschew (ed.), Inscriptiones antiquae orae septentrionalis ponti Euxini Graecae et Latinae 3 vols., 1885–1901, repr. 1965

IPNB
M. Mayrhofer, R. Schmitt (ed.), Iranisches Personennamenbuch, 1979 ff.

IPQ
International Philosophical Quaterly

IPriene
F. Hiller von Gärtringen, Inschriften von Priene, 1906

Irmscher
J. Irmscher (ed.), Renaissance und Humanismus in Mittel- und Osteuropa, 1962

Isager/Skydsgaard
S. Isager, J.E. Skydsgaard, Ancient Greek Agriculture, An Introduction, 1992

Isis
Isis

IstForsch
Istanbuler Forschungen des Deutschen Archäologischen Instituts

Iura
IURA, Rivista internazionale di diritto romano e antico

IvOl
W. Dittenberger, K. Purgold, Inschriften von Olympia, 1896, repr. 1966

Jaffé
P. Jaffé, Regesta pontificum Romanorum ab condita ecclesia ad annum 1198 2 vols., ²1985–88

JBAA
The Journal of the British Archaeological Association

JbAC
Jahrbuch für Antike und Christentum

JCS
Journal of Cuneiform Studies

JDAI
Jahrbuch des Deutschen Archäologischen Instituts

JEA
The Journal of Egyptian Archaeology

Jenkyns, DaD
R. Jenkyns, Dignity and Decadence: Classicism and the Victorians, 1992

Jenkyns, Legacy
R. Jenkyns, The Legacy of Rome: A New Appraisal, 1992

JHAS
Journal for the History of Arabic Science

JHB
Journal of the History of Biology

JHM
Journal of the History of Medicine and Allied Sciences

JHPh
Journal of the History of Philosophy

JHS
Journal of Hellenic Studies

JLW
Jahrbuch für Liturgiewissenschaft

JMRS
Journal of Medieval and Renaissance Studies

JNES
Journal of Near Eastern Studies

JNG
Jahrbuch für Numismatik und Geldgeschichte

JÖAI
Jahreshefte des Österreichischen Archäologischen Instituts

Jones, Cities
A.H.M. Jones, The Cities of the Eastern Roman Provinces, ²1971

Jones, Economy
A.H.M. Jones, The Roman Economy. Studies in Ancient Economic and Administrative History, 1974

Jones, LRE
A.H.M. Jones, The Later Roman Empire 284–602. A Social, Economic and Administrative Survey, 1964

Jones, RGL
A.H.M. Jones, Studies in Roman Government and Law, 1968

Jost
M. Jost, Sanctuaires et cultes d'Arcadie, 1985

JPh
Journal of Philosophy

JRGZ
Jahrbuch des Römisch-Germanischen Zentralmuseums

JRS
Journal of Roman Studies

Justi
F. Justi, Iranisches Namenbuch, 1895

JWG
Jahrbuch für Wirtschaftsgeschichte

JWI
Journal of the Warburg and Courtauld Institutes

Kadmos
Kadmos. Zeitschrift für vor- und frühgriechische Epigraphik

KAI
H. Donner, W. Röllig, Kanaanaeische und aramaeische Inschriften 3 vols., ³1971–1976

Kajanto, Cognomina
I. Kajanto, The Latin Cognomina, 1965

Kajanto, Supernomina
I. Kajanto, Supernomina. A study in Latin epigraphy (Commentationes humanarum litterarum 40, 1), 1966

Kamptz
H. v. Kamptz, Homerische Personennamen. Sprachwissenschaftliche und historische Klassifikation, 1982 = H. v. Kamptz, Sprachwissenschaftliche und historische Klassifikation der homerischen Personennamen (Diss.), 1958

Karlowa
O. Karlowa, Römische Rechtsgeschichte 2 vols., 1885–1901

Kaser, AJ
M. Kaser, Das altrömische Jus. Studien zur Rechtsvorstellung und Rechtsgeschichte der Römer, 1949

Kaser, RPR
M. Kaser, Das römische Privatrecht (Rechtsgeschichte des Altertums Part 3, Vol. 3; HbdA 10, 3, 3) 2 vols., ³1971–75

Kaser, RZ
M. Kaser, Das römische Zivilprozessrecht (Rechtsgeschichte des Altertums Part 3, Vol. 4; HbdA 10, 3, 4), 1966

Kearns
E. Kearns, The Heroes of Attica, 1989 (BICS Suppl. 57)

Keller
O. Keller, Die antike Tierwelt 2 vols., 1909–20, repr. 1963

Kelnhofer
F. Kelnhofer, Die topographische Bezugsgrundlage der Tabula Imperii Byzantini (Denkschriften der Österreichischen Akademie der Wissenschaften: Philosophisch-Historische Klasse 125 Beih.; TIB 1, Beih.), 1976

Kienast
D. Kienast, Römische Kaisertabelle. Grundzüge einer römischen Kaiserchronologie, 1990

Kindler
W. Jens (ed.), Kindlers Neues Literatur Lexikon 20 vols., 1988–92

Kinkel
G. Kinkel, (ed.), Epicorum Graecorum Fragmenta, 1877

Kirsten /Kraiker
E. Kirsten, W. Kraiker, Griechenlandkunde. Ein Führer zu klassischen Stätten, ⁵1967

Kleberg
T. Kleberg, Hôtels, restaurants et cabarets dans l'antiquité Romaine. Études historiques et philologiques, 1957

Klio
Klio. Beiträge zur Alten Geschichte

KlP
K. Ziegler (ed.), Der Kleine Pauly. Lexikon der Antike 5 vols., 1964–75, repr. 1979

Knobloch
J. Knobloch et al. (ed.), Sprachwissenschaftliches Wörterbuch (Indogermanische Bibliothek 2), 1986 ff (1st installment 1961)

Koch/Sichtermann
G. Koch, H. Sichtermann, Römische Sarkophage, 1982

Koder
  J. KODER, Der Lebensraum der Byzantiner. Histo-
  risch-geographischer Abriß ihres mittelalterlichen
  Staates im östlichen Mittelmeerraum, 1984
Koder/Hild
  J. KODER, F. HILD, Hellas und Thessalia (Denk-
  schriften der Österreichischen Akademie der Wis-
  senschaften, Philosophisch-Historische Klasse 125;
  TIB 1), 1976
Kraft
  K. KRAFT, Gesammelte Aufsätze zur antiken Ge-
  schichte und Militärgeschichte, 1973
Kromayer/Veith
  J. KROMAYER, G. VEITH, Heerwesen und Kriegfüh-
  rung der Griechen und Römer, 1928, repr. 1963
Krumbacher
  K. KRUMBACHER, Geschichte der byzantinischen
  Litteratur von Justinian bis zum Ende des oström-
  ischen Reiches (527–1453) (HdbA 9, 1), ²1897, repr.
  1970
KSd
  J. FRIEDRICH (ed.), Kleinasiatische Sprachdenkmä-
  ler (Kleine Texte für Vorlesungen und Übungen
  163), 1932
KUB
  Keilschrifturkunden von Boghazköi
Kühner/Blass
  R. KÜHNER, F. BLASS, Ausführliche Grammatik der
  griechischen Sprache. Teil 1: Elementar- und For-
  menlehre 2 vols., ³1890–92
Kühner/Gerth
  R. KÜHNER, B. GERTH, Ausführliche Grammatik der
  griechischen Sprache. Teil 2: Satzlehre 2 vols.,
  ³1898–1904; W. M. CALDER III, Index locorum,
  1965
Kühner/Holzweißig
  R. KÜHNER, F. HOLZWEISSIG, Ausführliche Gram-
  matik der lateinischen Sprache. Teil I: Elementar-,
  Formen- und Wortlehre, ²1912
Kühner/Stegmann
  R. KÜHNER, C. STEGMANN, Ausführliche Gramma-
  tik der lateinischen Sprache. Teil 2: Satzlehre, 2 vols.,
  ⁴1962 (revised by A. THIERFELDER); G.S. SCHWARZ,
  R. L. WERTIS, Index locorum, 1980
Kullmann/Atlhoff
  W. KULLMANN, J. ALTHOFF (ed.), Vermittlung und
  Tradierung von Wissen in der griechischen Kultur,
  1993
Kunkel
  W. KUNKEL, Herkunft und soziale Stellung der rö-
  mischen Juristen, ²1967
KWdH
  H.H. SCHMITT (ed.), Kleines Wörterbuch des Hel-
  lenismus, ²1993
Lacey
  W.K. LACEY, The Family in Classical Greece, 1968
LÄ
  W. HELCK ET AL. (ed.), Lexikon der Ägyptologie 7
  vols., 1975–92 (1st installment 1972)

LAK
  H. BRUNNER, K. FLESSEL, F. HILLER ET AL. (ed.),
  Lexikon Alte Kulturen 3 vols., 1990–93
Lanciani
  R. LANCIANI, Forma urbis Romae, 1893–1901
Lange
  C.C.L. LANGE, Römische Altertümer, Vols. 1–2,
  ²1876–79; Vol. 3, 1876
Langosch
  K. LANGOSCH, Mittellatein und Europa, 1990
Latomus
  Latomus. Revue d'études latines
Latte
  K. LATTE, Römische Religionsgeschichte (HdbA 5,
  4), 1960, repr. 1992
Lauffer, BL
  S. LAUFFER, Die Bergwerkssklaven von Laureion,
  ²1979
Lauffer, Griechenland
  S. LAUFFER (ed.), Griechenland. Lexikon der histo-
  rischen Stätten von den Anfängen bis zur Gegen-
  wart, 1989
Lausberg
  H. LAUSBERG, Handbuch der literarischen Rhetorik.
  Eine Grundlegung der Literaturwissenschaft, ³1990
LAW
  C. ANDRESEN ET AL.(ed.), Lexikon der Alten Welt,
  1965, repr. 1990
LCI
  Lexikon der christlichen lkonographie
LdA
  J. IRMSCHER (ed.), Lexikon der Antike, ¹⁰1990
Le Bohec
  Y. LE BOHEC, L'armée romaine. Sous le Haut-Em-
  pire, 1989
Leitner
  H. LEITNER, Zoologische Terminologie beim Älte-
  ren Plinius (Diss.), 1972
Leo
  F. LEO, Geschichte der römischen Literatur. I. Die
  archaische Literatur, 1913, repr. 1958
Lesky
  A. LESKY, Geschichte der griechischen Literatur,
  ³1971, repr. 1993
Leumann
  M. LEUMANN, Lateinische Laut- und Formenlehre
  (HdbA II 2, 1), 1977
Leunissen
  P.M.M. LEUNISSEN, Konsuln und Konsulare in der
  Zeit von Commodus bis zu Alexander Severus
  (180–235 n. Chr.) (Dutch Monographs in Ancient
  History and Archaeology 6), 1989
Lewis/Short
  C.T. LEWIS, C. SHORT, A Latin Dictionary, ²1980
LFE
  B. SNELL (ed.), Lexikon des frühgriechischen Epos,
  1979 ff. (1st installment 1955)
LGPN
  P.M. FRASER ET AL. (ed.), A Lexicon of Greek Per-
  sonal Names, 1987 ff.

Liebenam
 W. LIEBENAM, Städteverwaltung im römischen Kai-
 serreich, 1900
Lietzmann
 H. LIETZMANN, Geschichte der Alten Kirche,
 ⁴ᐟ⁵1975
LIMC
 J. BOARDMAN ET AL. (ed.), Lexicon Iconographicum
 Mythologiae Classicae, 1981 ff.
Lippold
 G. LIPPOLD, Die griechische Plastik (HdArch III),
 1950
Lipsius
 J.H. LIPSIUS, Das attische Recht und Rechtsverfah-
 ren. Mit Benutzung des Attischen Processes 3 vols.,
 1905–15, repr. 1984
Lloyd-Jones
 H. LLOYD-JONES, Blood for the Ghosts – Classical
 Influences in the Nineteenth and Twentieth Centu-
 ries, 1982
LMA
 R.-H. BAUTIER, R. AUTY (ed.), Lexikon des Mittel-
 alters 7 vols., 1980–93 (1st installment 1977), 3rd
 vol. repr. 1995
Lobel/Page
 E. LOBEL, D. PAGE (ed.), Poetarum lesbiorum frag-
 menta, 1955, repr. 1968
Loewy
 E. LOEWY (ed.), Inschriften griechischer Bildhauer,
 1885, repr. 1965
LPh
 T. SCHNEIDER, Lexikon der Pharaonen. Die altägyp-
 tischen Könige von der Frühzeit bis zur Römerherr-
 schaft, 1994
LRKA
 Friedrich Lübkers Reallexikon des Klassischen Al-
 tertums, ⁸1914
LSAG
 L.H. JEFFERY, The Local Scripts of Archaic Greece.
 A Study of the Origin of the Greek Alphabet and its
 Development from the Eighth to the Fifth Centuries
 B.C., ²1990
LSAM
 F. SOKOLOWSKI, Lois sacrées de l'Asie mineure,
 1955
LSCG
 F. SOKOLOWSKI, Lois sacrées des cités grecques,
 1969
LSCG, Suppl
 F. SOKOLOWSKI, Lois sacrées des cités grecques,
 Supplément, 1962
LSJ
 H.G. LIDDELL, R. SCOTT, H.S. JONES ET AL. (ed.), A
 Greek-English Lexicon, ⁹1940; Suppl.: 1968, repr.
 1992
LThK²
 J. HÖFER, K. RAHNER (ed.), Lexikon für Theologie
 und Kirche 14 vols., ²1957–86

LThK¹
 W. KASPER ET AL. (ed.), Lexikon für Theologie und
 Kirche, ¹1993 ff.
LTUR
 E.M. STEINBY (ed.), Lexicon Topographicum Urbis
 Romae, 1993 ff.
LUA
 Lunds Universitets Arsskrift / Acta Universitatis
 Lundensis
Lugli, Fontes
 G. LUGLI (ed.), Fontes ad topographiam veteris urbis
 Romae pertinentes, 6 of 8 vols. partially appeared,
 1952–62
Lugli, Monumenti
 G. LUGLI, I Monumenti antichi di Roma e suburbio,
 3 vols., 1930–38; Suppl.: 1940
Lustrum
 Lustrum. Internationale Forschungsberichte aus
 dem Bereich des klassischen Altertums
M&H
 Mediaevalia et Humanistica. Studies in Medieval
 and Renaissance Society
MacDonald
 G. MACDONALD, Catalogue of Greek Coins in the
 Hunterian Collection, University of Glasgow 3 vols.,
 1899–1905
MacDowell
 D. M. MACDOWELL, The law in Classical Athens
 (Aspects of Greek and Roman life), 1978
MAev.
 Medium Aevum
Magie
 D. MAGIE, Roman Rule in Asia Minor to the End of
 the Third Century after Christ, 1950, repr. 1975
MAII
 Mosaici Antichi in Italia, 1967 ff
MAMA
 Monumenta Asiae minoris Antiqua, 1927ff.
Manitius
 M. MANITIUS, Geschichte der lateinischen Literatur
 des Mittelalters (HdbA 9, 2) 3 vols., 1911–31, repr.
 1973–76
MarbWPr
 Marburger-Winckelmann-Programm
Marganne
 M.H. MARGANNE, Inventaire analytique des papy-
 rus grecs de médecine, 1981
Marrou
 H.-I. MARROU, Geschichte der Erziehung im klassi-
 schen Altertum (translation of Histoire de l'éduca-
 tion dans l'antiquité), ²1977
Martinelli
 M. MARTINELLI (ed.), La ceramica degli Etruschi,
 1987
Martino, SCR
 F. DE MARTINO, Storia della costituzione romana 5
 vols., ²1972–75; Indici 1990
Martino, WG
 F. DE MARTINO, Wirtschaftsgeschichte des alten
 Rom, ²1991

Masson
O. MASSON, Les inscriptions chypriotes syllabiques. Recueil critique et commenté (Études chypriotes 1), ²1983

Matz/Duhn
F. MATZ, F. v. DUHN (ed.), Antike Bildwerke in Rom mit Ausschluß der größeren Sammlungen 3 vols., 1881 f.

MAVORS
M.P. SPEIDEL (ed.), Roman Army Researches 1984 ff.

MDAI(A)
Mitteilungen des Deutschen Archäologischen Instituts, Athenische Abteilung

MDAI(Dam)
Damaszener Mitteilungen des Deutschen Archäologischen Instituts

MDAI(Ist)
Istanbuler Mitteilungen des Deutschen Archäologischen Instituts

MDAI(K)
Mitteilungen des Deutschen Archäologischen Instituts (Abteilung Kairo)

MDAI(R)
Mitteilungen des Deutschen Archäologischen Instituts, Römische Abteilung

MDOG
Mitteilungen der Deutschen Orient-Gesellschaft zu Berlin

MededRom
Mededelingen van het Nederlands Historisch Instituut te Rome

Mediaevalia
Mediaevalia

Mediaevistik
Mediaevistik. Internationale Zeitschrift für interdisziplinäre Mittelalterforschung

MEFRA
Mélanges d'Archéologie et d'Histoire de l'École Française de Rome. Antiquité

Meiggs
R. MEIGGS, Trees and Timber in the Ancient Mediterranean World, 1982

Merkelbach/West
R. MERKELBACH, M.L. WEST (ed.), Fragmenta Hesiodea, 1967

Mette
H.J. METTE, Urkunden dramatischer Aufführungen in Griechenland, 1977

MG
Monuments Grecs

MGG¹
F. BLUME (ed.), Die Musik in Geschichte und Gegenwart. Allgemeine Enzyklopädie der Musik 17 vols., 1949–86, repr. 1989

MGG²
L. FINSCHER (ed.), Die Musik in Geschichte und Gegenwart 20 vols., ²1994 ff.

MGH
Monumenta Germaniae Historica inde ab anno Christi quingentesimo usque ad annum millesimum et quingentesimum, 1826 ff.

MGH AA
Monumenta Germaniae Historica: Auctores Antiquissimi

MGH DD
Monumenta Germaniae Historica: Diplomata

MGH Epp
Monumenta Germaniae Historica: Epistulae

MGH PL
Monumenta Germaniae Historica: Poetae Latini medii aevi

MGH SS
Monumenta Germaniae Historica: Scriptores

MGrecs
Monuments Grecs publiés par l'Association pour l'Encouragement des Etudes grecques en France 2 vols., 1872–97

MH
Museum Helveticum

MiB
Musikgeschichte in Bildern

Millar, Emperor
F.G.B. MILLAR, The Emperor in the Roman World, 1977

Millar, Near East
F.G.B. MILLAR, The Roman Near East, 1993

Miller
K. MILLER, Itineraria Romana. Römische Reisewege an der Hand der Tabula Peutingeriana, 1916, repr. 1988

Millett
P. MILLETT, Lending and Borrowing in Ancient Athens, 1991

Minos
Minos

MIO
Mitteilungen des Instituts für Orientforschung

MIR
Moneta Imperii Romani. Österreichische Akademie der Wissenschaften. Veröffentlichungen der Numismatischen Kommission

Mitchell
S. MITCHELL, Anatolia. Land, Men and Gods in Asia Minor 2 vols., 1993

Mitteis
L. MITTEIS, Reichsrecht und Volksrecht in den östlichen Provinzen des römischen Kaiserreichs. Mit Beiträgen zur Kenntnis des griechischen Rechts und der spätrömischen Rechtsentwicklung, 1891, repr. 1984

Mitteis/Wilcken
L. MITTEIS, U. WILCKEN, Grundzüge und Chrestomathie der Papyruskunde, 1912, repr. 1978

ML
R. MEIGGS, D. LEWIS (ed.), A Selection of Greek Historical Inscriptions to the End of the Fifth Century B.C., ²1988

MLatJb
  Mittellateinisches Jahrbuch. Internationale Zeit-
  schrift für Mediävistik
Mnemosyne
  Mnemosyne. Bibliotheca Classica Batava
MNVP
  Mitteilungen und Nachrichten des Deutschen Paläs-
  tinavereins
MNW
  H. MEIER ET AL. (ed.), Kulturwissenschaftliche Bi-
  bliographie zum Nachleben der Antike 2 vols.,
  1931–38
Mollard-Besques
  S. MOLLARD-BESQUES, Musée National du Louvre.
  Catalogue raisonné des figurines et reliefs en terre-
  cuite grecs, étrusques et romains 4 vols., 1954–86
Momigliano
  A. MOMIGLIANO, Contributi alla storia degli studi
  classici, 1955 ff.
Mommsen, Schriften
  TH. MOMMSEN, Gesammelte Schriften 8 vols.,
  1904–13, repr. 1965
Mommsen, Staatsrecht
  TH. MOMMSEN, Römisches Staatsrecht 3 vols., Vol.
  1, ³1887; Vol. 2 f., 1887 f.
Mommsen Strafrecht
  TH. MOMMSEN, Römisches Strafrecht, 1899, repr.
  1955
Mon.Ant.ined.
  Monumenti Antichi inediti
Moos
  P. v. MOOS, Geschichte als Topik, 1988
Moraux
  P. MORAUX, Der Aristotelismus bei den Griechen
  von Andronikos bis Alexander von Aphrodisias (Pe-
  ripatoi 5 und 6) 2 vols., 1973–84
Moreau
  J. MOREAU, Dictionnaire de géographie historique
  de la Gaule et de la France, 1972; Suppl.: 1983
Moretti
  L. MORETTI (ed.), Iscrizioni storiche ellenistiche 2
  vols., 1967–76
MP
  Modern Philology
MPalerne
  Mémoires du Centre Jean Palerne
MRR
  T.R.S. BROUGHTON, The Magistrates of the Roman
  Republic 2 vols., 1951–52; Suppl.: 1986
MSG
  C. JAN (ed.), Musici scriptores Graeci, 1895; Suppl.:
  1899, repr. 1962
Müller
  D. MÜLLER, Topographischer Bildkommentar zu
  den Historien Herodots: Griechenland im Umfang
  des heutigen griechischen Staatsgebiets, 1987
Müller-Wiener
  W. MÜLLER-WIENER, Bildlexikon zur Topographie
  Istanbuls, 1977

Münzer¹
  F. MÜNZER, Römische Adelsparteien und Adelsfa-
  milien, 1920
Münzer²
  F. MÜNZER, Römische Adelsparteien und Adelsfa-
  milien, ²1963
Murray/Price
  O. MURRAY, S. PRICE (ed.), The Greek City: From
  Homer to Alexander, 1990
Muséon
  Muséon Revue d'Études Orientales
MVAG
  Mitteilungen der Vorderasiatischen (Ägyptischen)
  Gesellschaft
MVPhW
  Mitteilungen des Vereins klassischer Philologen in
  Wien
MythGr
  Mythographi Graeci 3 vols., 1894–1902; Vol. 1,
  ²1926
Nash
  E. NASH, Bildlexikon zur Topographie des antiken
  Rom, 1961 f.
NC
  Numismatic Chronicle
NClio
  La Nouvelle Clio
NDB
  Neue Deutsche Biographie, 1953 ff.; Vols. 1–6, repr.
  1971
NEAEHL
  E. STERN (ed.), The New Encyclopedia of Archaeo-
  logical Excavations in the Holy Land 4 vols., 1993
Neoph.
  Neophilologus
Newald
  R. NEWALD, Nachleben des antiken Geistes im
  Abendland bis zum Beginn des Humanismus, 1960
NGrove
  The New Grove Dictionary of Music and Musicians,
  ⁶1980
NGroveInst
  The New Grove Dictionary of Musical Instruments,
  1994
NHCod
  Nag Hammadi Codex
NHS
  Nag Hammadi Studies
Nicolet
  C. NICOLET, L' Ordre équestre à l'époque républi-
  caine 312–43 av. J.-C. 2 vols., 1966–74
Nilsson, Feste
  M.P. NILSSON, Griechische Feste von religiöser Be-
  deutung mit Ausschluss der attischen, 1906
Nilsson, GGR,
  M.P. NILSSON, Geschichte der griechischen Religion
  (HdbA 5, 2), Vol. 1, ³1967, repr. 1992; Vol. 2, ⁴1988
Nilsson, MMR
  M.P. NILSSON, The Minoan-Mycenaean Religion
  and its Survival in Greek Religion, ²1950

Nissen
  H. Nissen, Italische Landeskunde 2 vols., 1883–
  1902
Nock
  A.D. Nock, Essays on Religion and the Ancient
  World, 1972
Noethlichs
  K.L. Noethlichs, Beamtentum und Dienstverge-
  hen. Zur Staatsverwaltung in der Spätantike, 1981
Norden, Kunstprosa
  E. Norden, Die antike Kunstprosa vom 6. Jh. v.
  Chr. bis in die Zeit der Renaissance, ⁶1961
Norden, Literatur
  E. Norden, Die römische Literatur, ⁶1961
NSA
  Notizie degli scavi di antichità
NTM
  Schriftenreihe für Geschichte der Naturwissenschaf-
  ten, Technik und Medizin
Nutton
  V. Nutton, From Democedes to Harvey. Studies in
  the History of Medicine (Collected Studies Series
  277), 1988
NZ
  Numismatische Zeitschrift
OA
  J.G. Baiter, H. Sauppe (ed.), Oratores Attici 3 vols.,
  1839–43
OBO
  Orbis Biblicus et Orientalis
OCD
  N.G. Hammond, H.H. Scullard (ed.), The Ox-
  ford Classical Dictionary, ²1970, ³1996
ODB
  A.P. Kazhdan et al. (ed.), The Oxford Dictionary
  of Byzantium, 1991 ff.
OF
  O. Kern (ed.), Orphicorum Fragmenta, ³1972
OGIS
  W. Dittenberger (ed.), Orientis Graeci Inscripti-
  ones Selectae 2 vols., 1903–05, repr. 1960
OLD
  P.G.W. Glare (ed.), Oxford Latin Dictionary, 1982
  (1st installment 1968)
OIF
  Olympische Forschungen, 1941 ff.
Oliver
  J.H. Oliver, Greek Constitutions of Early Roman
  Emperors from Inscriptions and Papyri, 1989
Olivieri
  D. Olivieri, Dizionario di toponomastica lombar-
  da. Nomi di comuni, frazioni, casali, monti, corsi
  d'acqua, ecc. della regione lombarda, studiati in rap-
  porto alle loro origine, ²1961
Olshausen/Biller/Wagner
  E. Olshausen, J. Biller, J. Wagner, Historisch-
  geographische Aspekte der Geschichte des Ponti-
  schen und Armenischen Reiches. Untersuchungen
  Zur historischen Geographie von Pontos unter den
  Mithradatiden (TAVO 29), Vol.1, 1984

OLZ
  Orientalistische Literaturzeitung
OpAth
  Opuscula Atheniensia, 1953 ff.
OpRom
  Opuscula Romana
ORF
  E. Malcovati, Oratorum Romanorum Fragmenta
  (Corpus scriptorum Latinorum Paravianum 56–58);
  vols., 1930
Orientalia
  Orientalia, Neue Folge
Osborne
  R. Osborne, Classical Landscape with Figures: The
  Ancient Greek City and its Countryside, 1987
Overbeck
  J. Overbeck, Die antiken Schriftquellen zur Ge-
  schichte der bildenden Künste bei den Griechen,
  1868, repr. 1959
PA
  J. Kirchner, Prosopographia Attica 2 vols., 1901–
  03, repr. 1966
Pack
  R.A. Pack (ed.), The Greek and Latin Literary Texts
  from Greco-Roman Egypt, ²1965
Panofsky
  E. Panofsky, Renaissance und Renaissancen in
  Western Art, 1960
Pape/Benseler
  W. Pape, G.E. Benseler, Wörterbuch der griechi-
  schen Eigennamen 2 vols., 1863–1870
PAPhS
  Proceedings of the American Philosophical Society
Parke
  H.W. Parke, Festivals of the Athenians, 1977
Parke/Wormell
  H.W. Parke, D.E.W. Wormell, The Delphic Ora-
  cle, 1956
PBSR
  Papers of the British School at Rome
PCA
  Proceedings of die Classical Association. London
PCG
  R. Kassel, C. Austin (ed.), Poetae comici graeci,
  1983 ff.
PCPhS
  Proceedings of the Cambridge Philological Society
PdP
  La Parola del Passato
PE
  R. Stillwell et al. (ed.), The Princeton Encyclo-
  pedia of Classical Sites, 1976
Peacock
  D.P.S. Peacock, Pottery in the Roman World: An
  Ethnoarchaeological Approach, 1982
PEG I
  A. Bernabé (ed.), Poetae epici graeci. Testimonia et
  fragmenta. Pars I, 1987

Pfeiffer, KPI
R. PFEIFFER, Geschichte der Klassischen Philologie. Von den Anfängen bis zum Ende des Hellenismus, 1978

Pfeiffer KPII
R. PFEIFFER, Die Klassische Philologie von Petrarca bis Mommsen, 1982

Pfiffig
A.J. PFIFFIG, Religio Etrusca, 1975

Pflaum
H.G.PFLAUM, Les carrières procuratoriennes équestres sous le Haut-Empire Romain 3 vols. and figs., 1960 f.; Suppl.: 1982

Pfuhl
E. PFUHL, Malerei und Zeichnung der Griechen, 1923

Pfuhl/Möbius
E. PFUHL, H. MÖBIUS, Die ostgriechischen Grabreliefs 2 vols., 1977–79

PG
J.P. MIGNE (ed.), Patrologiae cursus completus, series Graeca 161 vols., 1857–1866; Conspectus auctorum: 1882; Indices 2 vols.: 1912–32

PGM
K. PREISENDANZ, A. HENRICHS (ed.), Papyri Graecae Magicae. Die griechischen Zauberpapyri 2 vols., ²1973 f. (1928–31)

Philippson /Kirsten
A. PHILIPPSON, A. LEHMANN, E. KIRSTEN (ed.), Die griechischen Landschaften. Eine Landeskunde 4 vols., 1950–59

Philologus
Philologus. Zeitschrift für klassische Philologie

PhQ
Philological Quarterly

Phronesis
Phronesis

PhU
Philologische Untersuchungen

PhW
Berliner Philologische Wochenschrift

Picard
CH. PICARD, Manuel d'archéologie grecque. La sculpture, 1935 ff.

Pickard-Cambridge/Gould/Lewis
A.W. PICKARD-CAMBRIDGE, J. GOULD, D.M. LEWIS, The Dramatic Festivals of Athens, ²1988

Pickard-Cambridge/Webster
A.W. PICKARD-CAMBRIDGE, T.B.L. WEBSTER, Dithyramb, Tragedy and Comedy, ²1962

Pigler, I
A. PIGLER, Barockthermen. Eine Auswahl von Verzeichnissen zur lkonographie des 17. Und 1 8. Jahrhunderts. 2 vols., ²1974; Ill. Vol.: 1974

PIR
Prosopographia imperii Romani saeculi, Vol. I-III, ²1933 ff.

PL
J.P. MIGNI (ed.), Patrologiae cursus completus, se-

ries Latina 221 vols., 1844–65 partly repr. 5 Suppl. Vols., 1958–74; Index: 1965

PLM
AE. BAEHRENS (ed.), Poetae Latini Minores 5 vols., 1879–83

PLRE
A.H.M. JONES, J.R. MARTINDALE, J. MORRIS (ed.), The Prosopography of the Later Roman Empire 3 vols. in 4 parts, 1971–1992

PMG
D.L. PAGE, Poetae melici graeci, 1962

PMGF
M. DAVIES (ed.), Poetarum melicorum Graecorum fragmenta, 1991

PMGTr
H.D. BETZ (ed.), The Greek Magical Papyri in Translation, Including the Demotic Spells, ²1992

Poccetti
D. POCCETTI, Nuovi documenti italici a complemento del manuale di E. Vetter (Orientamenti linguistici 8), 1979

Pökel
W. PÖKEL, Philologisches Schriftstellerlexikon, 1882, repr. ²1974

Poetica
Poetica. Zeitschrift für Sprach- und Literaturwissenschaft

Pokorny
J. POKORNY, Indogermanisches etymologisches Wörterbuch 2 vols., ²1989

Poulsen
F. POULSEN, Catalogue of Ancient Sculpture in the Ny Carlsberg Glyptotek, 1951

PP
W. PEREMANS (ed.), Prosopographia Ptolemaica (Studia hellenistica) 9 vols., 1950–81, repr. Vol. 1–3, 1977

PPM
Pompei, Pitture e Mosaici, 1990 ff.

Praktika
Πρακτικά της εν Αθήναις αρχαιολογικάς εταιρείας

Préaux
C. PRÉAUX, L'économie royale des Lagides, 1939, repr. 1980

Preller/Robert
L. PRELLER, C. ROBERT, Griechische Mythologie, ⁵1964 ff.

Pritchett
K. PRITCHETT, Studies in Ancient Greek Topography (University of California Publications, Classical Studies) 8 vols., 1969–92

PropKg
K. BITTEL ET AL. (ed.), Propyläen Kunstgeschichte 22 vols., 1966–80, repr. 1985

Prosdocimi
A.L. PROSDOCIMI, M. CRISTOFANI, Lingue dialetti dell'Italia antica, 1978; A. MARINETTI, Aggiornamenti ed Indici, 1984

PrZ
Prähistorische Zeitschrift
PSI
G. Vitelli, M. Norsa, V. Bartoletti et al. (ed.),
Papiri greci e latini (Pubblicazione della Soc. Italiana
per la ricerca dei pap. greci e latini in Egitto), 1912 ff.
QSt
Quellen und Studien zur Geschichte und Kultur des
Altertums und des Mittelalters
Quasten
J. Quasten, Patrology 2 vols., 1950–53
RA
Revue Archéologique
RAC
T. Klauser, E. Dassmann (ed.), Reallexikon für
Antike und Christentum. Sachwörterbuch zur Aus-
einandersetzung des Christentums mit der antiken
Welt, 1950 ff. (1st installment 1941)
RACr
Rivista di Archeologia Cristiana
Radermacher
L. Radermacher, Artium Scriptores. Reste der vor-
aristotelischen Rhetorik, 1951
Radke
G. Radke, Die Götter Altitaliens, ²1979
Raepsaet-Charlier
M-T. Raepsaet-Charlier, Prosopographie des
femmes de l'ordre sénatorial (l. – II. siècles) (Fonds
René Draguet 4) 2 vols., 1987
RÄRG
H. Bonnet, Reallexikon der ägyptischen Religions-
geschichte, ²1971
RAL
Rendiconti della Classe di Scienze morali, storiche e
filologiche dell'Academia dei Lincei
Ramsay
W.M. Ramsay, The Cities and Bishoprics of Phrygia
2 vols., 1895–97
RAssyr
Revue d'assyriologie et d'archéologie orientale
Rawson, Culture
E. Rawson, Roman Culture and Society. Collected
Papers, 1991
Rawson, Family
B. Rawson (ed.), The Family in Ancient Rome. New
Perspectives, 1986
RB
P. Wirth (ed.), Reallexikon der Byzantinistik, 1968
ff.
RBA
Revue Belge d'archéologie et d'histoire de l'art
RBi
Revue biblique
RBK
K. Wessel, M. Restle (ed.), Reallexikon zur byzan-
tinischen Kunst, 1966 ff. (1st installment 1963)
RBN
Revue Belge de numismatique

RBPh
Revue Belge de philologie et d'histoire
RDAC
Report of the Department of Antiquities, Cyprus
RDK
O. Schmitt (ed.), Reallexikon zur deutschen Kunst-
geschichte, 1937ff.
RE
G. Wissowa et al., (ed.), Paulys Real-Encyclopädie
der classischen Altertumswissenschaft, Neue Be-
arbeitung, 1893–1980
REA
Revue des études anciennes
REByz
Revue des études byzantines
REG
Revue des études grecques
Rehm
W. Rehm, Griechentum und Goethezeit, ³1952,
⁴1968
Reinach, RP
S. Reinach, Répertoire de peintures greques er ro-
maines, 1922
Reinach, RR
S. Reinach, Répertoire de reliefs grecs et romains 3
vols., 1909–12
Reinach RSt
S. Reinach, Répertoire de la statuaire greque et ro-
maine 6 vols., 1897–1930, repr. 1965–69
REL
Revue des études latines
Rer.nat.scr.Gr.min
O. Keller (ed.), Rerum naturalium scriptores Gra-
eci minores, 1877
Reynolds
L.D. Reynolds (ed.), Texts and Transmission: A
Survey of the Latin Classics, 1983
Reynolds/Wilson
L.D. Reynolds, N.G. Wilson, Scribes and Schol-
ars. A Guide to the Transmission of Greek and Latin
Literature, ³1991
RFIC
Rivista di filologia e di istruzione classica
RG
W.H. Waddington, E. Babelon, Recueil général
des monnaies grecques d'Asie mineure (Subsidia epi-
graphica 5) 2 vols., 1908–1925, repr. 1976
RGA
H. Beck et al. (ed.), Reallexikon der germanischen
Altertumskunde, ²1973 ff. (1st installment 1968);
Suppl.: 1986 ff.
RGG
K. Galling (ed.), Die Religion in Geschichte und
Gegenwart. Handwörterbuch für Theologie und Re-
ligionswissenschaft 7 vols., ³1957–65, repr. 1980
RGRW
Religion in the Graeco-Roman World
RGVV
Religionsgeschichtliche Versuche und Vorarbeiten

RH
Revue historique
RHA
Revue hittite et asianique
RhM
Rheinisches Museum für Philologie
Rhodes
P.J. RHODES, A commentary on the Aristotelian Athenaion Politeia, ²1993
RHPhR
Revue d'histoire et de philosophie religieuses
RHR
Revue de l'histoire des religions
RHS
Revue historique des Sciences et leurs applications
RIA
Rivista dell'Istituto nazionale d'archeologia e storia dell'arte
RIC
H. MATTINGLY, E.A. SYDENHAM, The Roman Imperial Coinage 10 vols., 1923–94
Richardson
L. RICHARDSON (Jr.), A New Topographical Dictionary of Ancient Rome, 1992
Richter, Furniture
G.M.A. RICHTER, The Furniture of the Greeks, Etruscans and Romans, 1969
Richter, Korai
G.M.A. RICHTER, Korai, Archaic Greek Maidens, 1968
Richter, Kouroi
G.M.A. RICHTER, Kouroi, Archaic Greek Youths, ³1970
Richter, Portraits
G.M.A. RICHTER, The Portraits of the Greeks 3 vols. and suppl., 1965–72
RIDA
Revue internationale des droits de l'antiquité
RIG
P-M. DUVAL (ed.), Recueil des inscriptions gauloises, 1985 ff.
RIL
Rendiconti dell'Istituto Lombardo, classe di lettere, scienze morali e storiche
Rivet
A.L.F. RIVET, Gallia Narbonensis with a Chapter on Alpes Maritimae. Southern France in Roman Times, 1988
Rivet/Smith
A.L.F. RIVET, C. SMITH, The Place-Names of Roman Britain, 1979
RLA
E. EBELING ET AL. (ed.), Reallexikon der Assyriologie und vorderasiatischen Archäologie, 1928 ff.
RLV
M. EBERT (ed.), Reallexikon der Vorgeschichte 15 vols., 1924–32
RMD
M.M. ROXAN, Roman military diplomas (Occasion-

al Publications of the Institute of Archaeology of the University of London 2 and 9), Vol. 1, (1954–77), 1978; Vol. 2, (1978–84), 1985; Vol. 3, (1985–94), 1994
RN
Revue numismatique
Robert, OMS
L. ROBERT, Opera minora selecta 7 vols., 1969–90
Robert, Villes
L. ROBERT, Villes d'Asie Mineure. Etudes de géographie ancienne, ²1902
Robertson
A.S. ROBERTSON, Roman Imperial Coins in the Hunter Coin Cabinet, University of Glasgow 5 vols., 1962–82
Rohde
E. ROHDE, Psyche. Seelenkult und Unsterblichkeitsglaube der Griechen, ²1898, repr. 1991
Roscher
W.H. ROSCHER, Ausführliches Lexikon der griechischen und römischen Mythologie 6 vols., ³1884–1937, repr. 1992 f.; 4 Suppl. Vols.: 1893–1921
Rostovtzeff, Hellenistic World
M.I. ROSTOVTZEFF, The Social and Economic History of the Hellenistic World, ²1953
Rostovtzeff, Roman Empire
M.I. ROSTOVTZEFF, The Social and Economic History of the Roman Empire, ²1957
Rotondi
G. ROTONDI, Leges publicae populi Romani. Elenco cronologico con una introduzione sull' attività legislativa dei comizi romani, 1912, repr. 1990
RPAA
Rendiconti della Pontificia Accademia di Archeologia
RPC
A. BURNETT, M. AMANDRY, P.P. RIPOLLÈS (ed.), Roman Provincial Coinage, 1992 ff.
RPh
Revue de philologie
RQ
Renaissance Quarterly
RQA
Römische Quartalsschrift für christliche Altertumskunde und für Kirchengeschichte
RRC
M. CRAWFORD, Roman Republican Coinage, 1974, repr. 1991
RSC
Rivista di Studi Classici
Rubin
B. RUBIN, Das Zeitalter Iustinians, 1960
Ruggiero
E. DE RUGGIERO, Dizionario epigrafico di antichità romana, 1895 ff., Vols. 1–3: repr. 1961 f.
Saeculum
Saeculum. Jahrbuch für Universalgeschichte

Saller
R. SALLER, Personal Patronage Under the Early Empire, 1982
Salomies
O. SALOMIES, Die römischen Vornamen. Studien zur römischen Namengebung (Commentationes humanarum litterarum 82), 1987
Samuel
A.E. SAMUEL, Greek and Roman Chronology. Calendars and Years in Classical Antiquity (HdbA I 7), 1972
Sandys
J.E. SANDYS, A History of Classical Scholarship 3 vols., ²1906–21, repr. 1964
SAWW
Sitzungsberichte der Österreichischen Akademie der Wissenschaften in Wien
SB
Sammelbuch griechischer Urkunden aus Ägypten (Inschriften und Papyri), Vols. 1–2: F. PREISIGKE (ed.), 1913–22; Vols. 3–5: F. BILABEL (ed.), 1926–34
SBAW
Sitzungsberichte der Bayerischen Akademie der Wissenschaften
SCCGF
J. DEMIAŃCZUK (ed.), Supplementum comicum comoediae Graecae fragmenta, 1912
Schachter
A. SCHACHTER, The Cults of Boiotia 4 vols., 1981–94
Schäfer
A. SCHÄFER, Demosthenes und seine Zeit 3 vols., ²1885–87, repr. 1967
Schanz/Hosius
M. SCHANZ, C. HOSIUS, G. KRÜGER, Geschichte der römischen Literatur bis zum Gesetzgebungswerk des Kaisers Justinian (HdbA 8), Vol. 1, ⁴1927, repr. 1979; Vol. 2, ⁴1935, repr. 1980; Vol. 3, ³1922, repr. 1969; Vol. 4,1, ²1914, repr. 1970; Vol. 4,2, 1920, repr. 1971
Scheid, Collège
J. SCHEID, Le collège des frères arvales. Étude prosopographique du recrutement (69 –304) (Saggi di storia antica 1), 1990
Scheid, Recrutement
J. SCHEID, Les frères arvales. Recrutement et origine sociale sous les empereurs julio-claudiens (Bibliothèque de l'École des Hautes Études, Section des Sciences Religieuses 77), 1975
Schlesier
R. SCHLESIER, Kulte, Mythen und Gelehrte – Anthropologie der Antike seit 1800, 1994
Schmid/Stählin I
W. SCHMID, O. STÄHLIN, Geschichte der griechischen Literatur. Erster Theil: Die klassische Periode der griechische Literatur VII 1) 5 vols., 1929–48, repr. 1961–80
Schmid/Stählin II
W. CHRIST, W. SCHMID, O. STÄHLIN, Geschichte

der griechischen Litteratur bis auf die Zeit Justinians. Zweiter Theil: Die nachklassische Periode der griechischen Litteratur (HdbA VII 2) 2 vols., ⁶1920–24, repr. 1961–81
Schmidt
K.H. SCHMIDT, Die Komposition in gallischen Personennamen in: Zeitschrift für celtische Philologie 26, 1957, 33–301 = (Diss.), 1954
Schönfeld
M. SCHÖNFELD, Wörterbuch der altgermanischen Personen- und Völkernamen (Germanische Bibliothek Abt. 1, Reihe 4, 2), 1911, repr. ²1965)
Scholiall
H. ERBSE (ed.), Scholia Graeca in Homeri Iliadem (Scholia vetera) 7 vols., 1969–88
SChr
Sources Chrétiennes 300 vols., 1942 ff.
Schrötter
F. V. SCHRÖTTER (ed.), Wörterbuch der Münzkunde, ²1970
Schürer
E. SCHÜRER, G. VERMÈS, The history of the Jewish people in the age of Jesus Christ (175 B.C. – A.D. 135) 3 vols., 1973–87
Schulten, Landeskunde
A. SCHULTEN, Iberische Landeskunde. Geographie des antiken Spanien 2 vols., 1955–57 (translation of the Spanish edition of 1952)
Schulz
F. SCHULZ, Geschichte der römischen Rechtswissenschaft, 1961, repr. 1975
Schulze
W. SCHULZE, Zur Geschichte lateinischer Eigennamen, 1904
Schwyzer, Dial.
E. SCHWYZER (ed.), Dialectorum Graecarum exempla epigraphica potiora, ³1923
Schwyzer, Gramm.
E. SCHWYZER, Griechische Grammatik, Vol. 1: Allgemeiner Teil. Lautlehre Wortbildung, Flexion (HdbA II 1, 1), 1939
Schwyzer/Debrunner
E. SCHWYZER, A. DEBRUNNER, Griechische Grammatik, Vol. 2: Syntax und syntaktische Stilistik (HdbA II 1,2), 1950; D. J. GEORGACAS, Register zu beiden Bänden, 1953; F. RADT, S. RADT, Stellenregister, 1971
Scullard
H. H. SCULLARD, Festivals and Ceremonies of the Roman Republic, 1981
SDAW
Sitzungsberichte der Deutschen Akademie der Wissenschaften zu Berlin
SDHI
Studia et documenta historiae et iuris
SE
Studi Etruschi
Seeck
O. SEECK, Regesten der Kaiser und Päpste für die

Jahre 311 bis 470 n. Chr. Vorarbeiten zu einer Pro-
sopographie der christlichen Kaiserzeit, 1919, repr.
1964
SEG
Supplementum epigraphicum Graecum, 1923 ff.
Seltman
C. SELTMAN, Greek Coins. A History of Metallic
Currency and Coinage down to the Fall of the Hel-
lenistic Kingdoms, ²1905
Sezgin
F. SEZGIN, Geschichte des arabischen Schrifttums,
Vol.3: Medizin, Pharmazie, Zoologie, Tierheilkunde
bis ca. 430 H., 1970
SGAW
Sitzungsberichte der Göttinger Akademie der Wis-
senschaften
SGDI
H. COLLITZ ET AL. (ed.), Sammlung der griechischen
Dialekt-Inschriften 4 vols., 1884–1915
SGLG
K. ALPERS, H. ERBSE, A. KLEINLOGEL (ed.), Samm-
lung griechischer und lateinischer Grammatiker 7
vols., 1974–88
SH
H. LLOYD-JONES, P. PARSONS (ed.), Supplementum
Hellenisticum, 1983
SHAW
Sitzungsberichte der Heidelberger Akademie der
Wissenschaften
Sherk
R.K. SHERK, Roman Documents from the Greek
East: Senatus Consulta and Epistulae to the Age of
Augustus, 1969
SicA
Sicilia archeologica
SIFC
Studi italiani di filologia classica
SiH
Studies in the Humanities
Simon, GG
E. SIMON, Die Götter der Griechen, ⁴1992
Simon, GR
E. SIMON, 1 Die Götter der Römer, 1990
SLG
D. PAGE (ed.), Supplementum lyricis graecis, 1974
SM
Schweizer Münzblatter
SMEA
Studi Micenei ed Egeo-Anatolici
Smith
W.D. SMITH, The Hippocratic tradition (Cornell pu-
blications in the history of science), 1979
SMSR
Studi e materiali di storia delle religioni
SMV
Studi mediolatini e volgari
SNG
Sylloge Nummorum Graecorum

SNR
Schweizerische Numismatische Rundschau
Solin/Salomies
H. SOLIN, O. SALOMIES, Repertorium nominum
gentilium et cognominum Latinorum (Alpha –
Omega: Reihe A 80), ²1994
Sommer
F. SOMMER, Handbuch der lateinischen Laut- und
Formenlehre. Eine Einführung in das sprachwissen-
schaftliche Studium des Latein (Indogermanische
Bibliothek 1, 1, 3, 1), ³1914
Soustal, Nikopolis
P. SOUSTAL, Nikopolis und Kephallenia (Denk-
schriften der Akademie der Wissenschaften, Philo-
sophisch-Historische Klasse I 50; TIB 3), 1981
Soustal, Thrakien
P. SOUSTAL, Thrakien. Thrake, Rodope und Hai-
mimontos (Denkschriften der Österreichischen Aka-
demie der Wissenschaften, Philosophisch-Histori-
sche Klasse 221; TIB 6), 1991
Sovoronos
J.N. SOVORONOS, Das Athener Nationalmuseum 3
vols., 1908–37
Spec.
Speculum
Spengel
L. SPENGEL, (ed.), Rhetores Graeci 3 vols., 1853–56,
repr. 1966
SPrAW
Sitzungsberichte der Preußischen Akademie der
Wissenschaften
SSAC
Studi storici per l'antichità classica
SSR
G. GIANNANTONI (ed.), Socratis et Socraticorum Re-
liquiae 4 vols., 1990
Staden
H. V. STADEN, Herophilus, The Art of Medicine in
Early Alexandria, 1989
Stein, Präfekten
A. STEIN, Die Präfekten von Ägypten in der römi-
schen Kaiserzeit (Dissertationes Bernenses Series 1,
1), 1950
Stein, Spätröm.R.
E. STEIN, Geschichte des spätrömischen Reiches,
Vol. 1, 1928; French version, 1959; Vol. 2, French
only, 1949
Stewart
A. STEWART, Greek sculpture. An exploration 2
vols., 1990
StM
Studi Medievali
Strong/Brown
D. STRONG, D. BROWN (ed.), Roman Crafts, 1976
Stv
Die Staatsverträge des Altertums, Vol. 2: H. BENGT-
SON, R. WERNER (ed.), Die Verträge der griechisch-
römischen Welt von 700 bis 338, ²1975; Vol. 3: H.H.
SCHMITT (ed.), Die Verträge der griechisch-römi-
schen Welt 338 bis 200 v. Chr., 1969

SVF
    J. V. ARNIM (ed.), Stoicorum veterum fragmenta 3
    vols., 1903–05; Index: 1924, repr. 1964
Syll.²
    W. DITTENBERGER, Sylloge inscriptionum Graeca-
    rum 3 vols., ²1898–1909
Syll.³
    F. HILLER VON GAERTRINGEN ET AL. (ed.), Sylloge
    inscriptionum Graecarum 4 vols., ³1915–24, repr.
    1960
Syme, AA
    R. SYME, The Augustan Aristocracy, 1986
Syme, RP
    E. BADIAN (Vols. 1,2), A.R. BIRLEY (Vols. 3–7) (ed.)
    R. SYME, Roman Papers 7 vols., 1979–91
Syme, RR
    K. SYME, The Roman Revolution, 1939
Syme, Tacitus
    R. SYME, Tacitus 2 vols., 1958
Symposion
    Symposion, Akten der Gesellschaft für Griechische
    und Hellenistische Rechtsgeschichte
Syria
    Syria. Revue d'art oriental et d'archéologie
TAM
    Tituli Asiae minoris, 1901 ff.
TAPhA
    Transactions and Proceedings of the American
    Philological Association
Taubenschlag
    R. TAUBENSCHLAG, The law of Greco-Roman Egypt
    in the light of the Papyri: 332 B. C. – 640 A. D.,
    ²1955
TAVO
    H. BRUNNER, W. RÖLLIG (ed.), Tübinger Atlas des
    Vorderen Orients, Beihefte, Teil B: Geschichte, 1969
    ff.
TeherF
    Teheraner Forschungen
TGF
    A. NAUCK (ed.), Tragicorum Graecorum Fragmenta,
    ²1889, 2nd repr. 1983
ThGL
    H. STEPHANUS, C. B. HASE, W. UND L. DINDORF ET
    AL. (ed.), Thesaurus graecae linguae, 1831 ff., repr.
    1954
ThlL
    Thesaurus linguae Latinae, 1900 ff.
ThlL, Onom.
    Thesaurus linguae Latinae, Supplementum onoma-
    sticon. Nomina propria Latina, Vol. 2 (C – Cyzistra),
    1907–1913; Vol. 3 (D – Donusa), 1918–1923
ThLZ
    Theologische Literaturzeitung Monatsschrift für das
    gesamte Gebiet der Theologie und Religionswissen-
    schaft
Thomasson
    B.E. THOMASSON, Laterculi Praesidum 3 vols. in 5
    parts, 1972–1990

Thumb/Kieckers
    A. THUMB, E. KIECKERS, Handbuch der griechi-
    schen Dialekte (Indogermanische Bibliothek 1, 1, 1),
    ²1932
Thumb/Scherer
    A. THUMB, A. SCHERER, Handbuch der griechischen
    Dialekte (Indogermanische Bibliothek 1, 1, 2),
    ²1959
ThWAT
    G.J. BOTTERWECK, H.-J. FABRY (ed.), Theologisches
    Wörterbuch zum Alten Testament, 1973 ff.
ThWB
    G. KITTEL, G. FRIEDRICH (ed.), Theologisches Wör-
    terbuch zum Neuen Testament 11 vols., 1933–79,
    repr. 1990
TIB
    H. HUNGER (ed.). Tabula Imperii Byzantini 7 vols.,
    1976–1990
Timm
    S. TIMM, Das christlich-koptische Ägypten in ara-
    bischer Zeit. Eine Sammlung christlicher Stätten in
    Ägypten in arabischer Zeit, unter Ausschluß von
    Alexandria, Kairo, des Apa-Mena-Klosters (Der
    Abu Mina), des Sketis (Wadi n-Natrun) und der Si-
    nai-Region (TAVO 41) 6 parts, 1984–92
TIR
    Tabula Imperii Romani, 1934 ff.
TIR/IP
    Y. TSAFRIR, L. DI SEGNI, J. GREEN, Tabula Imperii
    Romani. Iudaea – Palaestina. Eretz Israel in the Hel-
    lenistic, Roman and Byzantine Periods, 1994
Tod
    M.N. TOD (ed.), A Selection of Greek Historical In-
    scriptions to the End of the Fifth Century BC, Vol. 1:
    ²1951, repr. 1985; Vol. 2: ²1950
Tovar
    A. TOVAR, Iberische Landeskunde 2: Die Völker und
    Städte des antiken Hispanien, Vol. 1 Baetica, 1974;
    Vol. 2: Lusitanien, 1976; Vol. 3: Tarraconensis, 1989
Toynbee, Hannibal
    A.J. TOYNBEE, Hannibal's legacy. The Hannibalic
    war's effects on Roman life 2 vols., 1965
Toynbee, Tierwelt
    J.M.C. TOYNBEE, Tierwelt der Antike, 1983
TPhS
    Transactions of the Philological Society Oxford
Traill, Attica
    J. S. TRAILL, The Political Organization of Attica,
    1975
Traill, PAA
    J. S. TRAILL, Persons of Ancient Athens, 1994 ff.
Travlos, Athen
    J. TRAVLOS, Bildlexikon zur Topographie des anti-
    ken Athen, 1971
Travlos, Attika
    J. TRAVLOS, Bildlexikon zur Topographie des anti-
    ken Attika, 1988
TRE
    G. KRAUSE, G. MÜLLER (ed.), Theologische Realen-
    zyklopädie, 1977 ff. (1st installment 1976)

Treggiari
S. TREGGIARI, Roman Marriage. Iusti Coniuges from the Time of Cicero to the Time of Ulpian, 1991
Treitinger
O. TREITINGER, Die Oströmische Kaiser- und Reichsidee nach ihrer Gestaltung im höfischen Zeremoniell, 1938, repr. 1969
Trendall, Lucania
A.D. TRENDALL, The Red-figured Vases of Lucania, Campania and Sicily, 1967
Trendall, Paestum
A.D. TRENDALL, The Red-figured Vases of Paestum, 1987
Trendall/Cambitoglou
A.D. TRENDALL, The Red-figured Vases of Apulia 2 vols., 1978–82
TRF
O. RIBBECK (ed.), Tragicorum Romanorum Fragmenta, ²1871, repr. 1962
TRG
Tijdschrift voor rechtsgeschiedenis
TrGF
B. SNELL, R. KANNICHT, S. RADT (ed.), Tragicorum graecorum fragmenta, Vol. 1, ²1986; Vols. 2–4, 1977–85
Trombley
F.R. TROMBLEY, Hellenic Religion and Christianization c. 370–529 (Religions in the Graeco-Roman World 115) 2 vols., 1993 f.
TU
Texte und Untersuchungen zur Geschichte der altchristlichen Literatur
TUAT
O. KAISER (ed.), Texte aus der Umwelt des Alten Testaments, 1985 ff. (1st installment 1982)
TürkAD
Türk arkeoloji dergisi
Ullmann
M. ULLMANN, Die Medizin im Islam, 1970
UPZ
U. WILCKEN (ed.), Urkunden der Ptolemäerzeit (Ältere Funde) 2 vols., 1927–57
v. Haehling
R. v. HAEHLING, Die Religionszugehörigkeit der hohen Amtsträger des Römischen Reiches seit Constantins I. Alleinherrschaft bis zum Ende der Theodosianischen Dynastie (324–450 bzw. 455 n. Chr.) (Antiquitas 3, 23), 1978
VDI
Vestnik Drevnej Istorii
Ventris/Chadwick
M. VENTRIS, J. CHADWICK, Documents in Mycenean Greek, ²1973
Vetter
E. VETTER, Handbuch der italischen Dialekte, 1953
VIR
Vocabularium iurisprudentiae Romanae 5 vols., 1903–39

VisRel
Visible Religion
Vittinghoff
F. VITTINGHOFF (ed.), Europäische Wirtschafts- und Sozialgeschichte in der römischen Kaiserzeit, 1990
VL
W. STAMMLER, K. LANGOSCH, K. RUH ET AL. (ed.), Die deutsche Literatur des Mittelalters. Verfasserslexikon, ²1978 ff.
Vogel-Weidemann
U. VOGEL-WEIDEMANN, Die Statthalter von Africa und Asia in den Jahren 14–68 n.Chr. Eine Untersuchung zum Verhältnis von Princeps und Senat (Antiquitas 1, 31), 1982
VT
Vetus Testamentum. Quarterly Published by the International Organization of Old Testament Scholars
Wacher
R. WACHER (ed.), The Roman World 2 vols., 1987
Walde/Hofmann
A. WALDE, J.B. HOFMANN, Lateinisches etymologisches Wörterbuch 3 vols., ³1938–56
Walde/Pokorny
A. WALDE, J. POKORNY (ed.), Vergleichendes Wörterbuch der indogermanischen Sprachen 3 vols., 1927–32, repr. 1973
Walz
C. WALZ (ed.), Rhetores Graeci 9 vols., 1832–36, repr. 1968
WbMyth
H.W. HAUSSIG (ed.), Wörterbuch der Mythologie, Teil 1: Die alten Kulturvölker, 1965 ff.
Weber
W. WEBER, Biographisches Lexikon zur Geschichtswissenschaft in Deutschland, Österreich und der Schweiz, ²1987
Wehrli, Erbe
F. WEHRLI (ed.), Das Erbe der Antike, 1963
Wehrli, Schule
F. WEHRLI (ed.), Die Schule des Aristoteles 10 vols., 1967–69; 2 Suppl. Vols.: 1974–78
Welles
C.B. WELLES, Royal Correspondence in the Hellenistic Period: A Study in Greek Epigraphy, 1934
Wenger
L. WENGER, Die Quellen des römischen Rechts (Denkschriften der Österreichischen Akademie der Wissenschaften. Philosophisch-Historische Klasse 2), 1953
Wernicke
I. WERNICKE, Die Kelten in Italien. Die Einwanderung und die frühen Handelsbeziehungen zu den Etruskern (Diss.), 1989 = (Palingenesia), 1991
Whatmough
J. WHATMOUGH, The dialects of Ancient Gaul. Prolegomena and records of the dialects 5 vols., 1949–51, repr. in 1 vol., 1970

White, Farming
  K.D. WHITE, Roman Farming, 1970
White, Technology
  K.D. WHITE, Greek and Roman Technology, 1983, repr. 1986
Whitehead
  D. WHITEHEAD, The demes of Attica, 1986
Whittaker
  C.R. WHITTAKER (ed.), Pastoral Economies in Classical Antiquity, 1988
Wide
  S. WIDE, Lakonische Kulte, 1893
Wieacker, PGN
  F. WIEACKER, Privatrechtsgeschichte der Neuzeit, ²1967
Wieacker, RRG
  F. WIEACKER, Römische Rechtsgeschichte, Vol. 1, 1988
Wilamowitz
  U. v. WILAMOWITZ-MOELLENDORFF, Der Glaube der Hellenen 2 vols., ²1955, repr. 1994
Will
  E. WILL, Histoire politique du monde hellénistique (323–30 av. J. C.) 2 vols., ²1979–82
Winter
  R. KEKULÉ (ed.), Die antiken Terrakotten, III 1, 2: F. WINTER, Die Typen der figürlichen Terrakotten, 1903
WJA
  Würzburger Jahrbücher für die Altertumswissenschaft
WMT
  L.I. CONRAD ET AL., The Western medical tradition. 800 BC to A.D. 1800, 1995
WO
  Die Welt des Orients. Wissenschaftliche Beiträge zur Kunde des Morgenlandes
Wolff
  H.J. WOLFF, Das Recht der griechischen Papyri Ägyptens in der Zeit der Ptolemaeer und des Prinzipats (Rechtsgeschichte des Altertums Part 5; HbdA 10, 5), 1978
WS
  Wiener Studien, Zeitschrift für klassische Philologie und Patristik
WUNT
  Wissenschaftliche Untersuchungen zum Neuen Testament
WVDOG
  Wissenschaftliche Veröffentlichungen der Deutschen Orient-Gesellschaft
WZKM
  Wiener Zeitschrift für die Kunde des Morgenlandes
YCIS
  Yale Classical Studies
ZA
  Zeitschrift für Assyriologie und Vorderasiatische Archäologie

ZÄS
  Zeitschrift für ägyptische Sprache und Altertumskunde
ZATW
  Zeitschrift für die Alttestamentliche Wissenschaft
Zazoff, AG
  P. ZAZOFF, Die antiken Gemmen, 1983
Zazoff, GuG
  P. ZAZOFF, H. ZAZOFF, Gemmensammler und Gemmenforscher. Von einer noblen Passion zur Wissenschaft, 1983
ZDMG
  Zeitschrift der Deutschen Morgenländischen Gesellschaft
ZDP
  Zeitschrift für deutsche Philologie
Zeller
  E. ZELLER, Die Philosophie der Griechen in ihrer geschichtlichen Entwicklung 4 vols., 1844–52, repr. 1963
Zeller/Mondolfo
  E. ZELLER, R. MONDOLFO, La filosofia dei Greci nel suo sviluppo storico, Vol. 3, 1961
ZfN
  Zeitschrift für Numismatik
Zgusta
  L. ZGUSTA, Kleinasiatische Ortsnamen, 1984
Zimmer
  G. ZIMMER, Römische Berufsdarstellungen, 1982
ZKG,
  Zeitschrift für Kirchengeschichte
ZNTW
  Zeitschrift für die Neutestamentfiche Wissenschaft und die Kunde der älteren Kirche
ZpalV
  Zeitschrift des Deutschen Palästina-Vereins
ZPE
  Zeitschrift für Papyrologie und Epigraphik
ZKG
  Zeitschrift der Savigny-Stiftung für Rechtsgeschichte. Romanistische Abteilung
ZRGG
  Zeitschrift für Religions- und Geistesgeschichte
ZVRW
  Zeitschrift für vergleichende Rechtswissenschaft
ZVS
  Zeitschrift für Vergleichende Sprachforschung

4. Ancient Authors and Titles of Works

Abd	Abdias
Acc.	Accius
Ach.Tat.	Achilles Tatius
Act. Arv.	Acta fratrum Arvalium
Act. lud. saec.	Acta ludorum saecularium

Acts	Acts of the Apostles	Mac.	Macedonica
Aet.	Aetius	Mith.	Mithridatius
Aeth.	Aetheriae peregrinatio	Num.	Numidica
Ael. Ep.	Aelianus, Epistulae	Reg.	Regia
NA	De natura animalium	Sam.	Samnitica
VH	Varia historia	Sic.	Sicula
Aen. Tact.	Aeneas Tacticus	Syr.	Syriaca
Aesch. Ag.	Aeschylus, Agamemnon	App. Verg.	Appendix Vergiliana
Cho.	Choephori	Apul. Apol.	Apuleius, Apologia
Eum.	Eumenides	Flor.	Florida
Pers.	Persae	Met.	Metamorphoses
PV	Prometheus	Arat.	Aratus
Sept.	Septem adversus Thebas	Archil.	Archilochus
Supp.	Supplices	Archim.	Archimedes
Aeschin. In Ctes.	Aeschines, In Ctesiphontem	Archyt.	Archytas
Leg.	De falsa legatione	Arist. Quint.	Aristides Quintilianus
In Tim.	In Timarchum	Aristaen.	Aristaenetus
Aesop.	Aesopus	Aristid.	Aelius Aristides
Alc.	Alcaeus	Aristob.	Aristoboulos
Alc. Avit.	Alcimus Ecdicius Avitus	Aristoph. Ach.	Aristophanes, Acharnenses
Alex. Aphr.	Alexander of Aphrodisias	Av.	Aves
Alci.	Alciphron	Eccl.	Ecclesiazusae
Alcm.	Alcman	Equ.	Equites
Alex. Polyh.	Alexander Polyhistor	Lys.	Lysistrata
Am	Amos	Nub.	Nubes
Ambr. Epist.	Ambrosius, Epistulae	Pax	Pax
Exc. Sat.	De excessu Fratris (Satyri)	Plut.	Plutus
Obit. Theod.	De obitu Theodosii	Ran.	Ranae
Obit. Valent.	De obitu Valentiniani (iunioris)	Thesm.	Thesmophoriazusae
Off.	De officiis ministrorum	Vesp.	Vespae
Paenit.	De paenitentia	Aristot. An.	Aristotle, De anima (Becker 1831–
Amm. Marc.	Ammianus Marcellinus		70)
Anac.	Anacreon	An. post.	Analytica posteriora
Anaxag.	Anaxagoras	An. pr.	Analytica priora
Anaximand.	Anaximander	Ath. Pol.	Athenaion Politeia
Anaximen.	Anaximenes	Aud.	De audibilibus
And.	Andocides	Cael.	De caelo
Anecd. Bekk.	Anecdota Graeca ed. I. Bekker	Cat.	Categoriae
Anecd. Par.	Anecdota Graeca ed. J.A. Kramer	Col.	De coloribus
Anon. De rebus	Anonymus de rebus bellicis (Ireland	Div.	De divinatione
bell.	1984)	Eth. Eud.	Ethica Eudemia
Anth. Gr.	Anthologia Graeca	Eth. Nic.	Ethica Nicomachea
Anth. Lat.	Anthologia Latina (Riese	Gen. an.	De generatione animalium
	²1894/1906)	Gen. corr.	De generatione et corruptione
Anth. Pal.	Anthologia Palatina	Hist. an.	Historia animalium
Anth. Plan.	Anthologia Planudea	Mag. mor.	Magna moralia
Antiph.	Antiphon	Metaph.	Metaphysica
Antisth.	Antisthenes	Mete.	Meteorologica
Apc	Apocalypse	Mir.	Mirabilia
Apoll. Rhod.	Apollonius Rhodius	Mot. an.	De motu animalium
Apollod.	Apollodorus, Library	Mund.	De mundo
App. B Civ.	Appianus, Bella civilia	Oec.	Oeconomica
Celt.	Celtica	Part. an.	De partibus animalium
Hann.	Hannibalica	Phgn.	Physiognomica
Hisp.	Iberica	Ph.	Physica
Ill.	Illyrica	Poet.	Poetica
It.	Italica	Pol.	Politica
Lib.	Libyca	Pr.	Problemata

Rh.   Rhetorica
Rh. Al.   Rhetorica ad Alexandrum
Sens.   De sensu
Somn.   De somno et vigilia
Soph. el.   Sophistici elenchi
Spir.   De spiritu
Top.   Topica
Aristox. Harm.   Aristoxenus, Harmonica
Arnob.   Arnobius, Adversus nationes
Arr. Anab.   Arrianus, Anabasis
    Cyn.   Cynegeticus
    Ind.   Indica
    Peripl. p. eux.   Periplus ponti Euxini
    Succ.   Historia successorum Alexandri
    Tact.   Tactica
Artem.   Artemidorus
Ascon.   Asconius (Stangl Vol. 2, 1912)
Athan. ad Const.   Athanasius, Apologia ad Constantium
    c. Ar.   Apologia contra Arianos
    Fuga   Apologia de fuga sua
    Hist. Ar.   Historia Arianorum ad monachos
Ath.   Athenaeus (Casaubon 1597) (List of books, pages, letters)
Aug. Civ.   Augustinus, De civitate dei
    Conf.   Confessiones
    Doctr. christ.   De doctrina christiana
    Epist.   Epistulae
    Retract.   Retractationes
    Serm.   Sermones
    Soliloq.   Soliloquia
    Trin.   De trinitate
Aur. Vict.   Aurelius Victor
Auson. Mos.   Ausonius, Mosella (Peiper 1976)
    Urb.   Ordo nobilium urbium
Avell.   Collectio Avellana
Avien.   Avienus
Babr.   Babrius
Bacchyl.   Bacchylides
Bar   Baruch
Bas.   Basilicorum libri LX (Heimbach)
Basil.   Basilius
Batr.   Batrachomyomachia
Bell. Afr.   Bellum Africum
Bell. Alex.   Bellum Alexandrinum
Bell. Hisp.   Bellum Hispaniense
Boeth.   Boethius
Caes. B Civ.   Caesar, De bello civili
    B Gall.   De bello Gallico
Callim. Epigr.   Callimachus, Epigrammata
    Fr.   Fragmentum (Pfeiffer)
    H.   Hymni
Calp. Ecl.   Calpurnius Siculus, Eclogae
Cass. Dio   Cassius Dio
Cassian.   Iohannes Cassianus
Cassiod. Inst.   Cassiodorus, Institutiones
    Var.   Variae

Cato Agr.   Cato, De agri cultura
    Orig.   Origines (HRR)
Catull.   Catullus, Carmina
Celsus, Med.   Cornelius Celsus, De medicina
Celsus, Dig.   Iuventius Celsus, Digesta
Censorinus, DN   Censorinus, De die natali
Chalcid.   Chalcidius
Charisius, Gramm.   Charisius, Ars grammatica (Barwick 1964)
1 Chr, 2 Chr   Chronicle
Chron. pasch.   Chronicon paschale
Chron. min.   Chronica minora
Cic. Acad. 1   Cicero, Academicorum posteriorum liber 1
    Acad. 2   Lucullus sive Academicorum priorum liber 2
    Ad Q. Fr.   Epistulae ad Quintum fratrem
    Arat.   Aratea (Soubiran 1972)
    Arch.   Pro Archia poeta
    Att.   Epistulae ad Atticum
    Balb.   Pro L. Balbo
    Brut.   Brutus
    Caecin.   Pro A. Caecina
    Cael.   Pro M. Caelio
    Cat.   In Catilinam
    Cato   Cato maior de senectute
    Clu.   Pro A. Cluentio
    De or.   De oratore
    Deiot.   Pro rege Deiotaro
    Div.   De divinatione
    Div. Caec.   Divinatio in Q. Caecilium
    Dom.   De domo sua
    Fam.   Epistulae ad familiares
    Fat.   De fato
    Fin.   De finibus bonorum et malorum
    Flac.   Pro L. Valerio Flacco
    Font.   Pro M. Fonteio
    Har. resp.   De haruspicum responso
    Inv.   De inventione
    Lael.   Laelius de amicitia
    Leg.   De legibus
    Leg. agr.   De lege agraria
    Lig.   Pro Q. Ligario
    Leg. Man.   Pro lege Manilia (de imperio Cn. Pompei)
    Marcell.   Pro M. Marcello
    Mil.   Pro T. Annio Milone
    Mur.   Pro L. Murena
    Nat. D.   De natura deorum
    Off.   De officiis
    Opt. Gen.   De optimo genere oratorum
    Orat.   Orator
    P. Red. Quir.   Oratio post reditum ad Quirites
    P. Red. Sen.   Oratio post reditum in senatu
    Parad.   Paradoxa
    Part. or.   Partitiones oratoriae
    Phil.   In M. Antonium orationes Philippicae

Philo.	Libri philosophici
Pis.	In L. Pisonem
Planc.	Pro Cn. Plancio
Prov. cons.	De provinciis consularibus
Q. Rosc.	Pro Q. Roscio comoedo
Quinct.	Pro P. Quinctio
Rab. perd.	Pro C. Rabirio perduellionis reo
Rab. Post.	Pro C. Rabirio Postumo
Rep.	De re publica
Rosc. Am.	Pro Sex. Roscio Amerino
Scaur.	Pro M. Aemilio Scauro
Sest.	Pro P. Sestio
Sull.	Pro P. Sulla
Tim.	Timaeus
Top.	Topica
Tull.	Pro M. Tullio
Tusc.	Tusculanae disputationes
Vatin.	In P. Vatinium testem interrogatio
Verr. 1, 2	In Verrem actio prima, secunda
Claud. Carm.	Claudius Claudianus, Carmina (Hall 1985)
Rapt. Pros.	De raptu Proserpinae
Clem. Al.	Clemens Alexandrinus
Cod. Greg.	Codex Gregorianus
Cod. Herm.	Codex Hermogenianus
Cod. Iust.	Corpus Iuris Civilis, Codex Iustinianus (Krueger 1900)
Cod. Theod.	Codex Theodosianus
Col	Letter to the Colossians
Coll.	Mosaicarum et Romanarum legum collatio
Colum.	Columella
Comm.	Commodianus
Cons.	Consultatio veteris cuiusdam iurisconsulti
Const.	Constitutio Sirmondiana
1 Cor, 2 Cor	Letters to the Corinthians
Coripp.	Corippus
Curt.	Curtius Rufus, Historiae Alexandri Magni
Cypr.	Cyprianus
Dan	Daniel
Din.	Dinarchus
Demad.	Demades
Democr.	Democritus
Dem. Or.	Demosthenes, Orationes
Dig.	Corpus Iuris Civilis, Digesta (Mommsen 1905, author presented where applicable)
Diod. Sic.	Diodorus Siculus
Diog. Laert.	Diogenes Laertius
Diom.	Diomedes, Ars grammatica
Dion. Chrys.	Dion Chrysostomus
Dion. Hal. Ant. Rom.	Dionysius Halicarnasseus, Antiquitates Romanae
Comp.	De compositione verborum
Rhet.	Ars rhetorica

Dionys. Per.	Dionysius Periegeta
Dion. Thrax	Dionysius Thrax
DK	Diels /Kranz (preceded by fragment number)
Donat.	Donatus grammaticus
Drac.	Dracontius
Dt	Deuteronomy = 5. Moses
Edict. praet. dig.	Edictum perpetuum in Dig.
Emp.	Empedocles
Enn. Ann.	Ennius, Annales (Skutsch 1985)
Sat.	Saturae (Vahlen ²1928)
Scaen.	Fragmenta scaenica (Vahlen ²1928)
Ennod.	Ennodius
Eph	Letter to the Ephesians
Ephor.	Ephorus of Cyme (FGrH 70)
Epicurus	Epicurus
Epict.	Epictetus
Eratosth.	Eratosthenes
Esr	Esra
Est	Esther
Et. Gen.	Etymologicum genuinum
Et. Gud.	Etymologicum Gudianum
EM	Etymologicum magnum
Euc.	Euclides, Elementa
Eunap. VS	Eunapius, Vitae sophistarum
Eur. Alc.	Euripides, Alcestis
Andr.	Andromache
Bacch.	Bacchae
Beller.	Bellerophon
Cyc.	Cyclops
El.	Electra
Hec.	Hecuba
Hel.	Helena
Heracl.	Heraclidae
HF	Hercules Furens
Hipp.	Hippolytus
Hyps.	Hypsipyle
Ion	Ion
IA	Iphigenia Aulidensis
IT	Iphigenia Taurica
Med.	Medea
Or.	Orestes
Phoen.	Phoenissae
Rhes.	Rhesus
Supp.	Supplices
Tro.	Troades
Euseb. Dem. evang.	Eusebios, Demonstratio Evangelica
Hist. eccl.	Historia Ecclesiastica
On.	Onomasticon (Klostermann 1904)
Praep. evang.	Praeparatio Evangelica
Eust.	Eustathius
Eutr.	Eutropius
Ev. Ver.	Evangelium Veritatis
Ex	Exodus = 2. Moses
Ez	Ezechiel

Fast.	Fasti	Hippoc.	Hippocrates
Fest.	Festus (Lindsay 1913)	H. Hom.	Hymni Homerici
Firm. Mat.	Firmicus Maternus	Hom. Il.	Homerus, Ilias
Flor. Epit.	Florus, Epitoma de Tito Livio	Od.	Odyssea
Florent.	Florentinus	Hor. Ars P.	Horatius, Ars poetica
Frontin. Aq.	Frontinus, De aquae ductu urbis	Carm.	Carmina
	Romae	Carm. saec.	Carmen saeculare
Str.	Strategemata	Epist.	Epistulae
Fulg.	Fulgentius Afer	Epod.	Epodi
Fulg. Rusp.	Fulgentius Ruspensis	Sat.	Satirae (sermones)
Gai. Inst.	Gaius, Institutiones	Hos	Hosea
Gal	Letter to the Galatians	Hyg. Astr.	Hyginus, Astronomica (Le Bœuffle
Gal.	Galenus		1983)
Gell. NA	Gellius, Noctes Atticae	Fab.	Fabulae
Geogr. Rav	Geographus Ravennas (Schnetz	Hyp.	Hypereides
	1940)	Iambl. Myst.	Iamblichus, De mysteriis
Gp.	Geoponica	Protr.	Protrepticus in philosophiam
Gn	Genesis = 1. Moses	VP	De vita Pythagorica
Gorg.	Gorgias	Iav.	Iavolenus Priscus
Greg. M. Dial.	Gregorius Magnus, Dialogi (de mi-	Inst. Iust.	Corpus Juris Civilis, Institutiones
	raculis patrum Italicorum)		(Krueger 1905)
Epist.	Epistulae	Ioh. Chrys. Epist.	Iohannes Chrysostomus, Epistulae
Past.	Regula pastoralis	Hom. ...	Homiliae in ...
Greg. Naz. Epist.	Gregorius Nazianzenus, Epistulae	Ioh. Mal.	Iohannes Malalas, Chronographia
Or.	Orationes	Iord. Get.	Iordanes, De origine actibusque Ge-
Greg. Nyss.	Gregorius Nyssenus		tarum
Greg. Tur. Franc.	Gregorius of Tours, Historia Fran-	Iren.	Irenaeus (Rousseau/Doutreleau
	corum		1965–82)
Mart.	De virtutibus Martini	Is	Isaiah
Vit. patr.	De vita patrum	Isid. Nat.	Isidorus, De natura rerum
Hab	Habakkuk	Orig.	Origines
Hagg	Haggai	Isoc. Or.	Isocrates, Orationes
Harpocr.	Harpocrates	It. Ant.	Itinerarium, Antonini
Hdt.	Herodotus	Aug.	Augusti
Hebr	Letter to the Hebrews	Burd.	Burdigalense vel Hierosolymita-
Hegesipp.	Hegesippus (= Flavius Josephus)		num
Hecat.	Hecataeus	Plac.	Placentini
Hell. Oxy.	Hellennica Oxyrhynchia	Iul. Vict. Rhet.	C. Iulius Victor, Ars rhetorica
Hen	Henoch	Iuvenc.	Iuvencus, Evangelia (Huemer
Heph.	Hephaestio grammaticus (Alexan-		1891)
	drinus)	Jac	Letter of James
Heracl.	Heraclitus	Jdg	Judges
Heraclid. Pont.	Heraclides Ponticus	Jdt	Judith
Herc. O.	Hercules Oetaeus	Jer	Jeremiah
Herm.	Hermes Trismegistus	Jer. Chron.	Jerome, Chronicon
Herm. Mand.	Hermas, Mandata	Comm. in Ez.	Commentaria in Ezechielem (PL
Sim.	Similitudines		25)
Vis.	Visiones	Ep.	Epistulae
Hermog.	Hermogenes	On.	Onomasticon (Klostermann
Hdn.	Herodianus		1904)
Hes. Cat.	Hesiodus, Catalogus feminarum	Vir. ill.	De viris illustribus
	(Merkelbach /West 1967)	1 – 3 Jo	1st – 3rd letters of John
Op.	Opera et dies	Jo	John
Sc.	Scutum (Merkelbach	Jon	Jona
	/West1967)	Jos. Ant. Iud.	Josephus, Antiquitates Iudaicae
Theog.	Theogonia	BI	Bellum Iudaicum
Hsch.	Hesychius	Ap.	Contra Apionem
Hil.	Hilarius	Vit.	De sua vita

Jos	Joshua	Salt.	De saltatione
Jud	Letter of Judas	Somn.	Somnium
Julian. Ep.	Julianus, Epistulae	Symp.	Symposium
In Gal.	In Galilaeos	Syr. D.	De Syria dea
Mis.	Misopogon	Trag.	Tragodopodagra
Or.	Orationes	Ver. hist.	Verae historiae, 1, 2
Symp.	Symposium	Vit. auct.	Vitarum auctio
Just. Epit.	Justinus, Epitoma historiarum Phi-	Lv	Leviticus = 3. Moses
	lippicarum	LXX	Septuaginta
Justin. Apol.	Justinus Martyr, Apologia	Lydus, Mag.	Lydus, De magistratibus
Dial.	Dialogus cum Tryphone	Mens.	De mensibus
Juv.	Juvenalis, Saturae	Lycoph.	Lycophron
1 Kg, 2 Kg	1, 2 Kings	Lycurg.	Lycurgus
KH	Khania (place where Linear B tables	Lys.	Lysias
	were discovered)	M. Aur.	Marcus Aurelius Antoninus Augus-
KN	Knossos (place where Linear B ta-		tus
	bles were discovered)	Macrob. Sat.	Macrobius, Saturnalia
Lactant. Div.	Lactantius, Divinae institutiones	In Somn.	Commentarii in Ciceronis som-
inst.			nium Scipionis
Ira	De ira dei	1 Macc, 2 Macc	Maccabees
De mort. pers.	De mortibus persecutorum	Mal	Malachi
Opif.	De opificio dei	Manil.	Manilius, Astronomica (Goold
Lam	Lamentations		1985)
Lex Irnit.	Lex Irnitana	Mar. Vict.	Marius Victorinus
Lex Malac.	Lex municipii Malacitani	Mart.	Martialis
Lex Rubr.	Lex Rubria de Gallia cisalpina	Mart. Cap.	Martianus Capella
Lex Salpens.	Lex municipii Salpensani	Max. Tyr.	Maximus Tyrius (Trapp 1994)
Lex Urson.	Lex coloniae Iuliae Genetivae Ur-	Mela	Pomponius Mela
	sonensis	Melanipp.	Melanippides
Lex Visig.	Leges Visigothorum	Men. Dys.	Menander, Dyskolos
Lex XII tab.	Lex duodecim tabularum	Epit.	Epitrepontes
Lib. Ep.	Libanius, Epistulae	Fr.	Fragmentum (Körte)
Or.	Orationes	Pk.	Perikeiromene
Liv.	Livius, Ab urbe condita	Sam.	Samia
Lc	Luke	Mi	Micha
Luc.	Lucanus, Bellum civile	Mimn.	Mimnermus
Lucil.	Lucilius, Saturae (Marx 1904)	Min. Fel.	Minucius Felix, Octavius (Kytzler
Lucr.	Lucretius, De rerum natura		1982,²1992)
Lucian. Alex.	Lucianus, Alexander	Mk	Mark
Anach.	Anacharsis	Mod.	Herennius Modestinus
Cal.	Calumniae non temere creden-	Mosch.	Moschus
	dum	Mt	Matthew
Catapl.	Cataplus	MY	Mycenae (place where Linear B ta-
Demon.	Demonax		bles were discovered)
Dial. D.	Dialogi deorum	Naev.	Naevius (carmina according to
Dial. meret.	Dialogi meretricium		FPL)
Dial. mort.	Dialogi mortuorum	Nah	Nahum
Her.	Herodotus	Neh	Nehemia
Hermot.	Hermotimus	Nemes.	Nemesianus
Hist. conscr.	Quomodo historia conscribenda	Nep. Att.	Cornelius Nepos, Atticus
	sit	Hann.	Hannibal
Ind.	Adversus indoctum	Nic. Alex.	Nicander, Alexipharmaca
Iupp. trag.	Iuppiter tragoedus	Ther.	Theriaca
Luct.	De luctu	Nicom.	Nicomachus
Macr.	Macrobii	Nm	Numbers = 4. Moses
Nigr.	Nigrinus	Non.	Nonius Marcellus (L. Mueller
Philops.	Philopseudes		1888)
Pseudol.	Pseudologista	Nonnus, Dion.	Nonnus, Dionysiaca

Not. Dign. Occ.	Notitia dignitatum occidentis	Pall. Agric.	Palladius, Opus agriculturae
Not. Dign. Or.	Notitia dignitatum orientis	Laus.	Historia Lausiaca
Not. Episc.	Notitia dignitatum et episcoporum	Pan. Lat.	Panegyrici Latini
Nov.	Corpus Iuris Civilis, Leges Novellae (Schoell/Kroll 1904)	Papin.	Aemilius Papinianus
		Paroemiogr.	Paroemiographi Graeci
Obseq.	Julius Obsequens, Prodigia (Rossbach 1910)	Pass. mart.	Passiones martyrum
		Paul Fest.	Paulus Diaconus, Epitoma Festi
Opp. Hal.	Oppianus, Halieutica	Paul Nol.	Paulinus Nolanus
Cyn.	Cynegetica	Paulus, Sent.	Julius Paulus, Sententiae
Or. Sib.	Oracula Sibyllina	Paus.	Pausanias
Orib.	Oribasius	Pelag.	Pelagius
Orig.	Origenes	Peripl. m. eux.	Periplus maris Euxini
OrMan	Prayer to Manasseh	Peripl. m.m.	Periplus maris magni
Oros.	Orosius	Peripl. m.r.	Periplus maris rubri
Orph. A.	Orpheus, Argonautica	Pers.	Persius, Saturae
Fr.	Fragmentum (Kern)	1 Petr, 2 Petr	Letters of Peter
H.	Hymni	Petron. Sat.	Petronius, Satyrica (Müller 1961)
Ov. Am.	Ovidius, Amores	Phaedr.	Phaedrus, Fabulae (Guaglianone 1969)
Ars am.	Ars amatoria		
Epist.	Epistulae (Heroides)	Phil	Letter to the Philippians
Fast.	Fasti	Phil.	Philo
Ib.	Ibis	Philarg. Verg. ecl.	Philargyrius grammaticus, Explanatio in eclogas Vergilii
Medic.	Medicamina faciei femineae		
Met.	Metamorphoses	Philod.	Philodemus
Pont.	Epistulae ex Ponto	Phlp.	Philoponus
Rem. am.	Remedia amoris	Philostr. VA	Philostratus, Vita Apollonii
Tr.	Tristia	Imag.	Imagines
P	Papyrus editions according to E.G. Turner, Greek Papyri. An Introduction, 159–178	VS	Vitae sophistarum
		Phm	Letter to Philemon
		Phot.	Photius (Bekker 1824)
P Abinn.	Papyrus editions according to H.I. Bell et al. (ed.), The Abinnaeus Archive papers of a Roman officer in the reign of Constantius II, 1962	Phryn.	Phrynichus
		Pind. Fr.	Pindar, Fragments (Snell/Maehler)
		Isthm.	Isthmian Odes
		Nem.	Nemean Odes
		Ol.	Olympian Odes
P Bodmer	Papyrus editions according to V. Martin, R. Kasser et al. (ed.), Papyrus Bodmer 1954ff.	Pae.	Paeanes
		Pyth.	Pythian Odes
		Pl. Alc. 1	Plato, Alcibiades 1 (Stephanus)
P CZ	Papyrus editions according to C.C. Edgar (ed.), Zenon Papyri (Catalogue général des Antiquités égyptiennes du Musée du Caire) 4 vols., 1925ff.	Alc. 2	Alcibiades 2
		Ap.	Apologia
		Ax.	Axiochus
		Chrm.	Charmides
		Clit.	Clitopho
P Hercul.	Papyrus editions according to Papyri aus Herculaneum	Crat.	Cratylus
		Crit.	Crito
P Lond.	Papyrus editions according to F.G. Kenyon et al. (ed.), Greek Papyri in the British Museum 7 vols., 1893–1974	Criti.	Critias
		Def.	Definitiones
		Demod.	Demodocus
		Epin.	Epinomis
P Mich	Papyrus editions according to C.C. Edgar, A.E.R. Boak, J.G. Winter et al. (ed.), Papyri in the University of Michigan Collection 13 vols., 1931–1977	Ep.	Epistulae
		Erast.	Erastae
		Eryx.	Eryxias
		Euthd.	Euthydemus
		Euthphr.	Euthyphro
P Oxy.	Papyrus editions according to B.P. Grenfell, A.S. Hunt et al. (ed.), The Oxyrhynchus Papyri, 1898 ff.	Grg.	Gorgias
		Hp. mai.	Hippias maior
		Hp. mi.	Hippias minor
		Hipparch.	Hipparchus

Ion	Ion
La.	Laches
Leg.	Leges
Ly.	Lysis
Men.	Menon
Min.	Minos
Menex.	Menexenus
Prm.	Parmenides
Phd.	Phaedo
Phdr.	Phaedrus
Phlb.	Philebus
Plt.	Politicus
Prt.	Protagoras
Resp.	Res publica
Sis.	Sisyphus
Soph.	Sophista
Symp.	Symposium
Thg.	Theages
Tht.	Theaetetus
Ti.	Timaeus
Plaut. Amph.	Plautus, Amphitruo (fr.according to Leo 1895 f.)
Asin.	Asinaria
Aul.	Aulularia
Bacch.	Bacchides
Capt.	Captivi
Cas.	Casina
Cist.	Cistellaria
Curc.	Curculio
Epid.	Epidicus
Men.	Menaechmi
Merc.	Mercator
Mil.	Miles gloriosus
Mostell.	Mostellaria
Poen.	Poenulus
Pseud.	Pseudolus
Rud.	Rudens
Stich.	Stichus
Trin.	Trinummus
Truc.	Truculentus
Vid.	Vidularia
Plin. HN	Plinius maior, Naturalis historia
Plin. Ep.	Plinius minor, Epistulae
Pan.	Panegyricus
Plot.	Plotinus
Plut.	Plutarchus, Vitae parallelae (with the respective name)
Amat.	Amatorius (chapter and page numbers)
De def. or.	De defectu oraculorum
De E	De E apud Delphos
De Pyth. or.	De Pythiae oraculis
De sera	De sera numinis vindicta
De Is. et Os.	De Iside et Osiride (with chapter and page numbers)
Mor.	Moralia (apart from the separately mentioned works; with p. numbers)

Quaest. Graec.	Quaestiones Graecae (with chapter numbers)
Quaest. Rom.	Quaestiones Romanae (with ch. numbers)
Symp.	Quaestiones convivales (book, chapter, page number)
Pol.	Polybius
Pol. Silv.	Polemius Silvius
Poll.	Pollux
Polyaenus, Strat.	Polyaenus, Strategemata
Polyc.	Polycarpus, Letter
Pompon.	Sextus Pomponius
Pomp. Trog.	Pompeius Trogus
Porph.	Porphyrius
Porph. Hor. comm.	Porphyrio, Commentum in Horatii carmina
Posidon.	Posidonius
Priap.	Priapea
Prisc.	Priscianus
Prob.	Pseudo-Probian writings
Procop. Aed.	Procopius, De aedificiis
Goth.	Bellum Gothicum
Pers.	Bellum Persicum
Vand.	Bellum Vandalicum
Arc.	Historia arcana
Procl.	Proclus
Prop.	Propertius, Elegiae
Prosp.	Prosper Tiro
Prov.	Proverbs
Prudent.	Prudentius
Ps (Pss)	Psalm(s)
Ps.-Acro	Ps.-Acro in Horatium
Ps.-Aristot. Lin. insec.	Pseudo-Aristotle, De lineis insecabilibus
Mech.	Mechanica
Ps.-Sall. In Tull.	Pseudo-Sallustius, In M.Tullium Ciceronem invectiva
Rep.	Epistulae ad Caesarem senem de re publica
Ptol. Alm.	Ptolemy, Almagest
Geog.	Geographia
Harm.	Harmonica
Tetr.	Tetrabiblos
PY	Pylos (place where Linear B tablets were discovered)
4 Q Flor	Florilegium, Cave 4
4 Q Patr	Patriarch's blessing, Cave 4
1 Q pHab	Habakuk-Midrash, Cave 1
4 Q pNah	Nahum-Midrash, Cave 4
4 Q test	Testimonia, Cave 4
1 QH	Songs of Praise, Cave 1
1 QM	War list, Cave 1
1 QS	Comunal rule, Cave 1
1 QSa	Community rule, Cave 1
1 QSb	Blessings, Cave 1
Quint. Smyrn.	Quintus Smyrnaeus
Quint. Decl.	Quintilianus, Declamationes minores (Shackleton Bailey 1989)

ANCIENT AUTHORS AND TITLES OF WORKS

Inst.	Institutio oratoria
R. Gest. div. Aug.	Res gestae divi Augusti
Rhet. Her.	Rhetorica ad C. Herennium
Rom	Letter to the Romans
Rt	Ruth
Rufin.	Tyrannius Rufinus
Rut. Namat.	Rutilius Claudius Namatianus, De reditu suo
S. Sol.	Song of Solomon
Sext. Emp.	Sextus Empiricus
Sach	Sacharia
Sall. Catil.	Sallustius, De coniuratione Catilinae
Hist.	Historiae
Iug.	De bello Iugurthino
Salv. Gub.	Salvianus, De gubernatione dei
1 Sam, 2 Sam	Samuel
Schol. (before an author's name)	Scholia to the author in question
Sedul.	Sedulius
Sen. Controv.	Seneca maior, Controversiae
Suas.	Suasoriae
Sen. Ag.	Seneca minor, Agamemno
Apocol.	Divi Claudii apocolocyntosis
Ben.	De beneficiis
Clem.	De clementia (Hosius ²1914)
Dial.	Dialogi
Ep.	Epistulae morales ad Lucilium
Herc. f.	Hercules furens
Med.	Medea
Q Nat.	Naturales quaestiones
Oed.	Oedipus
Phaedr.	Phaedra
Phoen.	Phoenissae
Thy.	Thyestes
Tranq.	De tranquillitate animi
Tro.	Troades
Serv. auct.	Servius auctus Danielis
Serv. Aen.	Servius, Commentarius in Vergilii Aeneida
Ecl.	Commentarius in Vergilii eclogas
Georg.	Commentarius in Vergilii georgica
Sext. Emp.	Sextus Empiricus
SHA Ael.	Scriptores Historiae Augustae, Aelius
Alb.	Clodius Albinus
Alex. Sev.	Alexander Severus
Aur.	M. Aurelius
Aurel.	Aurelianus
Avid. Cass.	Avidius Cassius
Car.	Carus et Carinus et Numerianus
Carac.	Antoninus Caracalla
Clod.	Claudius
Comm.	Commodus
Diad.	Diadumenus Antoninus
Did. Iul.	Didius Iulianus
Gall.	Gallieni duo
Gord.	Gordiani tres
Hadr.	Hadrianus
Heliogab.	Heliogabalus
Max. Balb.	Maximus et Balbus
Opil.	Opilius Macrinus
Pert.	Helvius Pertinax
Pesc. Nig.	Pescennius Niger
Pius	Antoninus Pius
Quadr. tyr.	Quadraginta tyranni
Sev.	Severus
Tac.	Tacitus
Tyr. Trig.	Triginta Tyranni
Valer.	Valeriani duo
Sid. Apoll. Carm.	Apollinaris Sidonius, Carmina
Epist.	Epistulae
Sil. Pun.	Silius Italicus, Punica
Simon.	Simonides
Simpl.	Simplicius
Sir	Jesus Sirach
Scyl.	Scylax, Periplus
Scymn.	Scymnus, Periegesis
Socr.	Socrates, Historia ecclesiastica
Sol.	Solon
Solin.	Solinus
Soph. Aj.	Sophocles, Ajax
Ant.	Antigone
El.	Electra
Ichn.	Ichneutae
OC	Oedipus Coloneus
OT	Oedipus Tyrannus
Phil.	Philoctetes
Trach.	Trachiniae
Sor. Gyn.	Soranus, Gynaecia
Sozom. Hist. eccl.	Sozomenus, Historia ecclesiastica
Stat. Achil.	Statius, Achilleis
Silv.	Silvae
Theb.	Thebais
Steph. Byz.	Stephanus Byzantius
Stesich.	Stesichorus
Stob.	Stobaeus
Str.	Strabo (books, chapters)
Suda	Suda = Suidas
Suet. Aug.	Suetonius, Divus Augustus (Ihm 1907)
Calig.	Caligula
Claud.	Divus Claudius
Dom.	Domitianus
Gram.	De grammaticis (Kaster 1995)
Iul.	Divus Iulius
Tib.	Divus Tiberius
Tit.	Divus Titus
Vesp.	Divus Vespasianus
Vit.	Vitellius
Sulp. Sev.	Sulpicius Severus
Symmachus, Ep.	Symmachus, Epistulae
Or.	Orationes

Relat.	Relationes
Synes. epist.	Synesius, Epistulae
Sync.	Syncellus
Tab. Peut.	Tabula Peutingeriana
Tac. Agr.	Tacitus, Agricola
Ann.	Annales
Dial.	Dialogus de oratoribus
Germ.	Germania
Hist.	Historiae
Ter. Maur.	Terentianus Maurus
Ter. Ad.	Terentius, Adelphoe
An.	Andria
Eun.	Eunuchus
Haut.	H(e)autontimorumenos
Hec.	Hecyra
Phorm.	Phormio
Tert. Apol.	Tertullianus, Apologeticum
Ad nat.	Ad nationes (Borleffs 1954)
TH	Thebes (place where Linear B tables were discovered)
Them. Or.	Themistius, Orationes
Theoc.	Theocritus
Theod. Epist.	Theodoretus, Epistulae
Gr. aff. Cur.	Graecarum affectionum curatio
Hist. eccl.	Historia ecclesiastica
Theopomp.	Theopompus
Theophr. Caus. pl.	Theophrastus, De causis plantarum
Char.	Characteres
Hist. pl.	Historia plantarum
1 Thess, 2 Thess	Letters to the Thessalonians
Thgn.	Theognis
Thuc.	Thucydides
TI	Tiryns (place where Linear B tablets were discovered)
Tib.	Tibullus, Elegiae
1 Tim, 2 Tim	Letters to Timothy
Tit	Letter to Titus
Tob	Tobit
Tzetz. Anteh.	Tzetzes, Antehomerica
Chil.	Chiliades
Posth.	Posthomerica
Ulp.	Ulpianus (Ulpiani regulae)

Val. Fl.	Valerius Flaccus, Argonautica
Val. Max.	Valerius Maximus, Facta et dicta memorabilia
Varro, Ling.	Varro, De lingua Latina
Rust.	Res rusticae
Sat. Men.	Saturae Menippeae (Astbury 1985)
Vat.	Fragmenta Vaticana
Veg. Mil.	Vegetius, Epitoma rei militaris
Vell. Pat.	Velleius Paterculus, Historiae Romanae
Ven. Fort.	Venantius Fortunatus
Verg. Aen.	Vergilius, Aeneis
Catal.	Catalepton
Ecl.	Eclogae
G.	Georgica
Vir. ill.	De viris illustribus
Vitr. De arch.	Vitruvius, De architectura
Vulg.	Vulgate
Wisd	Wisdom
Xen. Ages.	Xenophon, Agesilaus
An.	Anabasis
Ap.	Apologia
Ath. pol.	Athenaion politeia
Cyn.	Cynegeticus
Cyr.	Cyropaedia
Eq.	De equitandi ratione
Eq. mag.	De equitum magistro
Hell.	Hellenica
Hier.	Hiero
Lac.	Respublica Lacedaemoniorum
Mem.	Memorabilia
Oec.	Oeconomicus
Symp.	Symposium
Vect.	De vectigalibus
Xenoph.	Xenophanes
Zen.	Zeno
Zenob.	Zenobius
Zenod.	Zenodotus
Zeph	Zephania
Zon.	Zonaras
Zos.	Zosimus

List of Authors

Altekamp, Stefan
Apel, Hans Jürgen
Arbeiter, Achim
Bachmaier, Helmut
Bäbler, Balbina
Behrwald, Ralf
Berger, Albrecht
Berges, Dietrich
Bergfeld, Christoph
Bichler, Reinhold
Borgmeier, Raimund
Böschenstein, Renate
Boschung, Dietrich
Bouzek, Jan
Bredow, Iris von
Brunet, Michèle Moretti, Jean-Charles
Brunner, Karl
Busch, Werner
Christof, Eva
Crüsemann, Nicola
Csapodi, Csaba
Dally, Ortwin
Dierse, Ulrich
Döhl, Hartmut G.
Dölemeyer, Barbara
Döring, Klaus
Dolezalek, Gero
Dominik, William J.
Drost-Abgarjan, Armenuhi
Dyson, Stephen L.
Effenberger, Arne
Eickhoff, Birgit
El-Abbadi, Mostafa
Eleuteri, Paolo
Febel, Gisela
Feistner, Edith
Fischer, Klaus
Fischer, Wolfdietrich
Fornaro, Sotera
Forssman, Bernhard
Forssman, Berthold
Frahm, Eckart
Freyberger, Klaus Stefan
Frielinghaus, Heide
Frobenius, Wolf, Barth, Andreas
Gauß, Walter
Gechter, Marianne
Geerlings, Wilhelm
Geus, Klaus
Gnilka, Christian
Graf, Fritz

Greiner, Bernhard
Groppe, Carola
Grosse, Max
Günther, Hubertus
Günther, Linda-Marie
Guthmüller, Bodo
Hartmann, Elke
Hartmann, Jana
Hauser, Stefan R.
Helas, Philine
Hellwig, Karin Wenzel, Carola
Hetzer, Armin
Hinz, Berthold
Hošek, Radislav
Höcker, Christoph
Hölter, Achim
Hünemörder, Christian
Irmscher (†), Johannes
Jakobi-Mirwald, Christine
Kader, Ingeborg
Kern, Manfred
Kilian, Barbara
Koerrenz, Ralf
Kopka, Alex
Krasser, Helmut
Kreikenbom, Detlev
Kuhlmann, Peter
Kuhn-Chen, Barbara
Kümmerling-Meibauer, Bettina
Kytzler, Bernhard
Landfester, Manfred
Lošek, Fritz
Lohr, Charles H.
Lück, Heiner
Luig, Klaus
Eickhoff, Birgit
Makris, Georgios
Mašek, Miro
Marshall, Peter K.
Martínková, Dana
Matthäus, Hartmut
Meier, Hans-Rudolf
Meier, Mischa
Mergenthaler, Volker
Michel, Raphael
Mohnhaupt, Heinz
Moser, Christian
Müller-Richter, Klaus
Näf, Beat
Niemeyer, Hans Georg
Nutton, Vivian

Peña, P. Bádenas De La
Pfarr, Ulrich
Pingel, Volker
Raeburn, David Antony
Ranieri, Filippo
Ratkowitsch, Christine
Rebenich, Stefan
Reinsch, Diether Roderich
Renger, Johannes
Repgen, Tilman
Reudenbach, Bruno
Rheidt, Klaus
Ricken, Friedo
Rollinger, Robert
Rommel, Bettina
Rudolph, Kurt
Rudolph, Wolf
Rüpke, Jörg
Saleh, Mohamed
Schalles, Hans-Joachim
Scharf, Friedhelm
Schevtschenko, Galina Ivanovna
Schiering, Wolfgang
Schlesier, Renate
Schmidt-Dengler, Wendelin
Schmitz, Thomas A.
Schneider, Helmuth
Schneider, Jakob Hans Josef
Schulze, Christian
Schulze, Janine
Schupp, Volker
Schütte, Sven
Schwandner, Ernst-Ludwig
Schweizer, Beat
Schweizer, Stefan

Sguaitamatti, Lorenzo
Stärk, Ekkehard
Stehlíková, Eva
Stenzel, Hartmut
Stillers, Rainer
Strohmaier, Gotthard
Stroszeck, Jutta
Strothmann, Jürgen
Stückelberger, Alfred
Stumpf, Gerd
Suntrup, Rudolf
Suter, Claudia E.
Svatoš, Martin
Talbert, Richard
Tinnefeld, Franz
Toral-Niehoff, Isabel
Tsakmakis, Antonis
Ungefähr-Kortus, Claudia
Usener, Sylvia
Vidmanová, Anežka
Wachter, Rudolf
Walther, Gerrit
Waquet, Françoise
Warland, Rainer
Werdehausen, Anna Elisabeth
Westbrook, Raymond
Wiater, Werner
Wiegels, Rainer
Wildung, Dietrich
Willers, Dietrich
Wyss, Beat
Zaminer, Frieder
Zeman, Herbert
Zervoudaki, Eos
Ziegler, Sabine

Classical Tradition translators

Annette Bridges
Simon Buck
Rolf Bueskens
Michael Chase
Annette Corkhill
Maarten Doude van Troostwijk
Dorothy Duncan
Karoline Krauss
David Levinson
Brian Murdoch
Michael P. Osmann
Michael Ovington
Charlotte Pattenden
David Richardson
Maria Schoenhammer
Barbara Schmidt-Runkel
Duncan A. Smart
Barbara Souter
Suzanne Walters

List of Entries

A

Academy
I. General II. Musical

I. General
A. Definition B. Humanism D. 19th Century E. 20th Century

A. Definition
The word 'academy' is not used in a uniform manner. In addition to scholarly academies dedicated to research, the term denotes various scholarly, pedagogical and social establishments. There are medical academies; music, dance and art academies; as well as church-related ones (→ A. II. musical). Scholarly (i.e. research) academies, on the other hand, are associations of scholars with the purpose of furthering research and academic communication. Their names have been changed many times over the centuries: they have been known as *societas* (society), *sodalitas* (sodality), association, institute, and by others terms. Since the 15th cent., the word academy has encompassed the widest variety of social and intellectual associations and organisations. It no longer exclusively refers to the ancient academy, more specifically, Plato's school, but also to scholarly associations and pure teaching institutions. In view of the loss of importance of universities, the prestigious term *academy* was assumed by other institutions of higher learning – specifically German ones – to promote themselves as places of scholarship and teaching. Following the French example, scholarly institutions in Germany were first called academies in the course of the 18th cent.

B. Humanism
The Platonic Academy, closed in 529 by Justinian, was rediscovered in Italian humanistic circles around the turn of the 15th cent. [9; 39; 55]. It is debatable to what extent the circle that existed at the court of Charlemagne under the Anglo-Saxon Alcuin can be called an academy. The link was consciously made to the Academy in Athens, both in content and in name, in order that its secular scholarship would be perfected by Christian teaching (cf. Alcuin, epist. 170, ed. Dümmler). But this link to ancient tradition was an isolated episode. The reason for this was also the negative connotation of the word in the Latin Middle Ages, which, following from Augustine's *Contra Academicos* (or *De Academicis*; cf. the commentary to bk. 2 and 3 by Th. Fuhrer, 1997) considered the sceptical tradition of the academy as an absolute or rejected it ([3]; L. Boehm in: [19. 65–111]). It was not until the professors, clerics, notables and merchants who set themselves up in private groups in Florence around 1400 in the monastery of Santo Spirito and in the Paradiso degli Alberti in order to debate literary, philosophical and political themes based on ancient texts that the idea of the Platonic Academy was taken up in a systematic manner. To be sure, these social discussion groups were not organized in a formal way (S. Neumeister in: [19. 171–189]). In 1427, inspired by Cicero's Tusc. 3,3,6f., Poggio Bracciolini planned to set up an Academy on his Tuscan estate to read the classics in the original, with an educated circle of friends. Then in 1454 in the house of the Florentine notable Alamanno Rinucci, young humanists came together in a *Nova Academia* or *Chorus Academiae Florentinae*, there to devote themselves, observing definite rules, above all to the writings of Plato and Aristotle. The study of ancient philosophers received a strong impetus through the works of the Byzantine scholar Johannes Argyropulos. The important influence of Greek philosophy on the humanistically aware Florentines was also reflected in the group collected together by Marsilio Ficino in 1462 that was commonly (albeit falsely, cf. [26]) dubbed *Accademia Platonica* and was the first occidental academy of modern times [15; 39. 101ff.; 40]. It also lacked a firm organisational framework and precise statutes. Its biggest achievement was the rediscovery of Platonic writings for the Latin West, through precise translations of which Ficino saw the opportunity to reform Christianity [57]. The express aim was the resurrection of the ancient academy 'antiquam Academiam resurgentem': M. Ficino, Opera omnia, ²1576, Repr. 1959, I 909), to which one demonstrated commitment through *exercitatio literarum*, i.e. educated debate, oratorical exercises and philosophical interpretations of Platonic teachings. The head of the academy, Ficino, dubbed the *pater Platonicae familiae*, managed the renewal of the ancient model in a villa in Careggi, which was given to him by Cosimo de Medici. *Symposia* were held following the Platonic example; November 7, Plato's supposed birthday and death day was kept as a holiday; the walls were decorated with aphorisms; and a bust of Plato, allegedly from the ancient Academy, was set up. At the same time, the Academy, which had close ties to the Medici, was to develop its influence – in a humanistic context – as a place of universal education and of the culture of urbane conversation. Although only a few selected individuals from the Florentine political and intellectual elite took part in individual meetings (such as Cristoforo Landino, Giovanni Pico della Mirandola, Angelo Poliziano), Ficino's conception proved exceptionally effective and influenced other humanistic circles outside Florence, such as the *Accademia Pontaniana* in Naples. The *Accademia Pontaniana* was founded in 1458 as the discussion group of Alfons I. It continued in 1471 under the guidance of Giovanni Pontano, the most important Neapolitian humanist; which also contributed to the fame of the court of Aragon. Together they studied ancient authors, specifically Virgil. In 1464 Pomponio Leto founded the *Accademia Romana* (after its founder also called the *Accademia Pomponiana*) on the Quirinal in

Rome. The most important Italian humanists belonged to it. It was temporarily banned for anticlerical statements by Pope Paul II. In Venice in 1484, Aldo Manuzio organised his *Neoacademia* in his publishing house. It not only pressed ahead with editions of Greek authors, but also developed rules of order, written in Greek, and discussions were carried on in Greek.

In the 15th cent. the idea of the academy found many disciples north of the Alps, specifically through the mediation of Conrad Celtis. 'Sodalities', literary/historically oriented, and informally organised, which in many ways picked up their inspiration from Italy, were founded in Buda, Krakow, Basel, Vienna, Ingolstadt, Heidelberg, Nuremberg, Augsburg, Erfurt, Straßburg and in many other towns [19. 951ff., 1069ff.; 56. 128ff.; 62]. The circles, which were formed by means of academic friendships and exchange of letters of their members, reflect a new formation of intellectual associations, founded through private initiative, but taken seriously by the Early Modern courts; they spread the classical legacy through editions, translations and relevant publications as well as historical/geographical studies of individual regions.

The level of popularity that the concept of the academy had in humanistic Italy can be seen in the fact that from the middle of the 15th to the end of the 16th cent., around 400 academies were founded (granted some existed only for a short time). In these, educated burghers came together to debate scholarly questions and the cultivation of the arts [19. 190–270; 44]. They continued the traditions of the first humanistic academies, in most cases not surviving the death of their founders. The number of academies, which had clear statutes and membership rules, procedural rules for meetings, apportioning of offices, fields of activity etc., grew from the first half of the 16th cent. on. In the period of early Absolutism the princes gradually assumed direction of the academies. In the context of the late humanist search for universal knowledge (Universalwissenschaft), the principal focus was on literary texts; scientifically based academies constituted only a small proportion.

The academies developed a new field of expertise in the course of the 16th cent.: the investigation and standardisation of literature in the national languages. Already at the beginning of the 1540s, the *Accademia Fiorentina* occupied itself with Dante, Petrarch and the contemporary language of Tuscany. The *Accademia della Crusca* was founded in 1583 – likewise in Florence – and formed its program to illustrate its name. Its task was, based on established authors of the 14th cent., to sort in the Italian language the worthless bran (*crusca*) from the flour. The first edition of the Italian dictionary of the *Accademia della Crusca* appeared in 1612. The German societies, however, initially held fast to Latin; Sprachgesellschaften in Germany as in other European countries, were formed on the Italian model only later. The *Fruchtbringende Gesellschaft* [19. 230ff.] was founded in Weimar in 1617, and Cardinal Richelieu set up the *Académie Française* [19. 348ff.] in 1635. Their declared aim was to derive standards and concepts for literature written in their national languages from ancient rhetoric and poetry. This deliberate turning towards the vernacular put the language societies of the 17th cent. in opposition to the universities, which still held tightly onto their tradition of Latin language and education.

C. 17TH AND 18TH CENTS.

Between 1660 and 1793, 70 official academies were founded in Europe and America. In addition there were numerous scholarly associations of a private and semi-private nature (such as the classical philological societies in German university towns [65]). In contrast to the academies, they were not, as a rule, licensed by the state, though they were recognised (Overview [45. 261ff., 281ff.]). The academies differed, sometimes considerably, in their orientation, organisation and social composition (L. Hammermayer in [2. 1ff.; 19; 29; 64; 66]). The Platonic model, that was modified already in the 16th cent., was no longer relevant for the content of their studies and organisational structure. The academies concerned themselves with scholarship and arts of the most different types, and in their variety reflected the enormous differentiation in the fields of knowledge. Most notably they accounted for the beginning rise of the natural sciences since the late 16th cent. The integration of scientific research and formulation of research problems in the work of the academies led to a deep division. There was far less discussion of the contribution of language and literature to establishing identity and culture than in the humanistic societies. Research in the service of scientific advancement was now the basic premise of the academy movement. It is against this background that, beginning in the second half of the 17th cent., the turn of the academies towards an experimental-inductive methodology in the sciences and the development of historical and philological source criticism is to be viewed. What the academies had in common was that they contributed to supraregional research communication and their members were only rarely obliged to teach in the universities. Before the Enlightenment, the universities, which were bound to the scholastic tradition, lost both esteem and significance to the academies, which offered themselves as central research institutions. By the end of the 18th cent. the academies were the standard organizational form of scholarly collaboration. Acting as the central academic institutes of their respective countries, they gathered together well-known academics and dedicated themselves more frequently to large scholarly projects that an individual scholar would not be able to tackle. Aside from custom prevailing in the Sprachgesellschaften, Latin first served as the international scholarly language, but was soon joined by French. From the middle of the 18th cent., national languages were used in the academies.

The informal scholarly associations soon came under the influence of the state and the ruler: absolutist princes assumed the roles of patrons, who supported existing organisations and founded new academies. In Europe, academies were a prominent tool of royal support for academia. The private circles of scholars, interested in literary and scientific studies, became state controlled organisations of an elitist cultural policy. Significantly, this absolutist academy movement played no role in the constitutionally republican Netherlands and Switzerland (Academy foundations did not occur there until 1808 and 1815 respectively). In Paris the *Académie des Sciences* and the *Académie des Inscriptions et Belles Lettres* had already been founded in 1666 and 1667 respectively to take their places alongside the *Académie Française* [19. 348ff.]. In London in 1662, the *Royal Society* was founded, which was oriented towards the natural sciences, and in 1683 the *Philosophical Society* in Dublin [19. 669ff.]. In Berlin, the Elector Frederick III, according to the concept of Gottfried Wilhelm Leibniz, founded the *Kurfürstliche Brandenburgische Societet der Scientien* in 1700 [7; 20; 21; 27; 28]. Vienna and Dresden tried to imitate the Berlin model, but in vain (it was not until 1847 that the opening of the *Kaiserliche Akademie* was officially announced in Vienna) [33; 46]. It was only in St Petersburg under Peter the Great in 1724/25 that the plan for an academy following the Prussian model could become reality [19. 966ff.]. In other European centres too, academies arose as institutions supported and funded by the state: in Edinburgh in 1731, in Madrid in 1714 (*Real Academia Española*) and in 1738 (*Real Academia de la Historia*), in Lisbon 1717 (*Academia Portuguesa da Historia*) and in 1779 (*Academia das Sciências*), in Stockholm 1739, in Copenhagen 1742 and in Brussels 1772.

In the 18th cent., an academy was to be found in every larger town in Italy some of which carried out important archaeological, as well as local and regional historical research such as that at Cortona on the Etruscans. In France there were not just academies in Paris, but also provincial academies were set up in many towns – often through private initiatives – all of which had a different focus; by 1789 there were 32 of them. The academy movement also gained a foothold in East and Southeast Europe [2; 11; 19. 1031ff.]. There was an extensive wave of formations in the German Reich in the second half of the 18th cent. To begin with the Olmütz Society was founded in 1746, though it was dissolved in 1751. Of great importance was the reorganisation of the Berlin Academy under Frederick II in the 1740s, which from now on was called the *Königlich Preußische Akademie der Wissenschaften*. Over the next four decades, countless academies and scholarly societies were founded in the country's various regional capitals, especially in central and southern Germany: The *Königliche Sozietät der Wissenschaften* in Göttingen (1751) [2. 97ff.; 29. 97ff.], the *Akademie nützlicher Wissenschaften* in Erfurt (1754) [1], the *Bayerische*

Akademie der Wissenschaften in Munich (1759) [24; 25], the Pfälzische *Akademie der Wissenschaften* in Mannheim (1763), the *Fürstlich Jablonowskische Gesellschaft der Wissenschaften* in Leipzig (1774) [42], the *Gesellschaft der Altertümer* in Kassel (1777) und the *Königlich Böhmische Gesellschaft der Wissenschaften* in Prague (1785). In North America too the academy movement met with response. The *Philosophical Society* was initially set up in Philadelphia in 1743/44 and the *American Academy of Arts and Sciences* with its headquarters in Boston in 1779. In the 18th cent. the concept of the academy reached Central and South America as well as Asia via the Portuguese and the Spanish.

The science-oriented academies grew in importance: After the brief flowering of the *Academia Secretorum Naturae* in Naples between 1560 and 1568, the *Accademia dei Lincei* was founded in Rome in 1603, in 1652 the *Academia Naturae Curiosorum* in Schweinfurt (which later became the *Leopoldina* in Halle), the *Royal Society* in London in 1660 and in 1666 the *Académie des Sciences* in Paris. The expansion of research in mathematics and the natural sciences found different institutional solutions and led to continuous controversies about the division of the scholarly fields within the academies. Basically it came down to the followingl alternatives: Either academies for sciences – such as in Schweinfurt, London and Paris – could be set up as independent organisations (partly in addition to academies for languages, literature and history), or science and humanities were merged into a single academy which would then be divided into different classes or departments. The idea of the unity of scholarship was advocated by Gottfried Wilhelm Leibniz and successfully put into practise in the Berlin Academy. Here, history, languages and natural sciences were all dealt with under the same roof. Many French and (after the second half of the 18th cent.) Italian provincial academies were modelled on the Berlin *Sozietät* [44; 54].

The frequently stressed connections of the academies with each other in a supranational and interfaith *république des sciences* or *république des lettres* have, up to now, only been verified in a few cases (e.g. for Berlin and St Petersburg). Munich's connections with academies elsewhere, however, were insignificant in the 18th cent. (cf. summary of previous research [66. 28f.]). Respected foreign scholars were frequently invited to become members of an academy. These choices were based not only upon position, but also their scholarly achievements. However, there are definitive studies on the members' social denominational and geographical origins only for the French and some German academies. It seems likely that already before the middle of the 18th cent. the majority of academy members came from the upper middle classes. Non-noble scholars entered the exclusive academic meritocracy on an equal footing with noble members and used their activities in the academy as a means of social mobility.

The Catholic Church also established comparable institutions. One may note the Maurist Congregation, which since the middle of the 17th cent. in Saint-Germain-des-Prés had been publishing exemplary editions of Church history and which also became renowned for its significant studies of ancillary historical material and for works on French history.

Despite the diversification in scholarship and the intensive focus of research on the natural sciences, the study of the ancient world retained a prominent position in the work of academies. It profited from the systematic collection and editions of historical sources which were now being started. Naturally the study of ancient history (just as that of universal history) was not on the agenda of every academy (cf. the German academies in general [38]; Paris: [5. 171ff.; 63. 230ff.]; Mannheim: [12; 18]; Munich: [37]). The transcriptions of monumental and epigraphic texts were large-scale classical research projects: Archaeological campaigns were carried out in Tuscany and the towns at the foot of Vesuvius, → POMPEII and → HERCULANEUM [14], but also in Gallia Romana and in the Palatinate [13]. Local academies, too, made important research contributions to regional ancient history; in Italy, for example, they made important contributions to intensive research in Etruscan history [4]. Prize contests sponsored by the academies frequently treated classical themes. The *Académie des Inscriptions et Belles Lettres*, for example, alternated questions from Classical Antiquity and the Middle Ages and even admitted non-French participants. In 1775 Herder addressed the theme: *Quels furent les noms et les attributs de Vénus chez les diverses nations de la Grèce et de l'Italie* [64. 65].

The academy movement, however, suffered a crisis in the 18th cent. The vast and extensive variety of academy foundings, which reflected the advances in scholarly specialisation, made intraregional coordination and cooperation ever more difficult. The unavoidable institutionalisation led to ossification and inflexibility. Various reform projects were discussed, including the suggestion for a Europe-wide *République des Lettres*, which in 1795 led to the establishment of the *Institut de France*. At the same time the middle class turned, under the influence of the Enlightenment, to organisations that were largely independent of the courts, so that the academies lost their principal socio-politial and scientific organisatorial function.

D. 19TH CENT.

This stagnation crisis was overcome by the reform movement at the beginning of the 19th cent. The Parisian model of a central academy, which had originated after the liquidation of the old academy structure during the French Revolution, had an effect on various European states, such as the *Kaiserlich Russische Akademie* reorganised in 1803 and the newly established *Königlich Bayerische Akademie der Wissenschaften* in 1807. In Prussia, Wilhelm von Humboldt started a thorough and wide-ranging reform in the division and

structure of scholarly fields that led to the founding of the University of Berlin (1810) and the reorganisation of the Academy (1812). In the 19th cent. the *Königlich Preußische Akademie der Wissenschaften* became a model example of a modern and efficient scholarly academy, whose central function lay in the overall organisation, representation and coordination of scholarly work. At the same time Humboldt's conception, the unity of research and teaching, prevented the universities from taking second place to the academies, as was the case in France, for instance. The members of the German Academy were frequently university professors. The Berlin Academy enlarged its distance, already stressed since the 17th cent., to theology and jurisprudence, the normative practical orientation of which was not considered reconcilable with an enlightened concept of science and innovation. Exponents of these subjects, such as the theologian Adolf Harnack, could only be taken on as historians. The neo-humanistic epistemology constructed a model of the academy which combined an idealised concept of an almost timeless Platonic academy with a positivist understanding of scholarship and a highly efficient scholarly organisation.

Before this background, Classical Studies in the 19th cent. experienced a boom without parallel [51; 52]. Led by Theodor Mommsen, since 1858 a full member and from 1874 to 1895 secretary of the Berlin Academy, the great classical undertakings were started: the fundamental research on source criticism, which established the international reputation of German classical scholarship. The entire historical source material of the ancient world was to be collected, indexed and published in large corpora. According to the methodological credo, advancement in scholarship could only be made via comprehensive editions of sources. In his reply to Harnack's inaugural speech, Mommsen in 1890 had redefined the task of the Academy in the age of positivism: *Auch die Wissenschaft hat ihr sociales Problem: wie der Großstaat und die Großindustrie, so ist die Großwissenschaft, die nicht von Einem geleistet, aber von Einem geleitet wird, ein nothwendiges Element unserer Kulturentwicklung, und deren rechte Träger sind die Akademien oder sollten es sein* ('Scholarship, too, has its social problem: just as the national state and corporate industry so also large-scale scholarship, which is not accomplished by [just] one individual but rather is led by one, is an essential element of our cultural development; and the responsible institutions for that are the academies or should be', Minutes, Berlin 1890, 792; TH. MOMMSEN, Reden und Aufsätze, 1905, 209). Hermann Diels, Mommsen's successor as secretary of the philolosophical-historical section, shared his views. He expressed his thoughts on *Die Organisation der Wissenschaften* in 1906 (in: [32]). Harnack, who inherited Mommsen's leading role in Academy politics after 1895, penned his programmatic essay in 1911 *Vom Großbetrieb der Wissenschaften* (now in: [49. 1009–1019]).

In 1815 on the initiative of August Böckh the *Corpus Inscriptionum Graecarum* was founded (4 vols., 1825–1859; 1877 index) and in 1817 Immanuel Bekker started the Aristotle edition (4 vols., 1827–1836; index 1870), which since 1874 was supplemented with the *Commentaria in Aristotelem Graeca* and the *Supplementum Aristotelicum*. After years of argument, the Berlin Academy approved Mommsen's plan in 1854 for a *Corpus Inscriptionum Latinarum*. Individual fascicles have been appearing since 1863; up to now 17 volumes with around 180,000 inscriptions as well as numerous supplements. From work on the indices of Latin inscriptions emerged the *Prosopographia Imperii Romani saec. I.II.III.*, edited by Hermann Dessau, Elimar Klebs and Paul von Rohden 1897/98. At Mommsen's suggestion Friedrich Imhoof-Blumer started to collect the ancient coins of northern Greece in 1888. Since 1898 individual volumes of the *Griechische Münzwerk* have been appearing at irregular intervals. In 1891 the corpus of Greek Christian writers of the first to third cents., commonly called the Church Fathers' Edition or 'Kirchenväterausgabe', was founded on the initiative of Mommsen and Harnack. The interdisciplinary project, on which ancient historians, classical philologists and theologians worked together, is a good example of the epoch-making cooperation of 'classical studies' and church history at the end of the 19th cent. After 1945 the series was broadened to include texts from later centuries (up to the 8th cent.). The Commission in charge of the Church Fathers' Edition became, at the end of 1901, also responsible for the *Prosopographia Imperii Romani saec. IV. V. VI*; the large-scale undertaking was intended to be a basic biographical tool for both secular and ecclesiastic historians, as well as for theologians and philologists; but in the end it failed because of its unrealistic goal, for which its initiator Mommsen had to take the blame. After many setbacks, the work was halted in 1933. In 1897, work was started on the dictionary of Ancient Egyptian under the leadership of Adolf Erman. By 1947 it contained around 1.75 million definitions of ancient Egyptian words (13 vols., 1926–1963). In 1901 Hermann Diels together with Ludvig Heiberg started the *Corpus Medicorum Graecorum*. Under the aegis of Ulrich von Wilamowitz-Moellendorff 1903 saw a new plan for the *Inscriptiones Graecae*, the sister project for the *Corpus Inscriptionum Graecarum*; cooperation with other academies, especially the Wiener Akademie, was strongly pushed and resulted in a geographical division of labour. From now on, Berlin focused its attention on the Greek mainland and the Aegean islands. To date 45 volumes (with almost 50,000 inscriptions) have appeared. In addition, Theodor Mommsen inaugurated the *Vocabularium iurisprudentiae Romanae*, a complete word index to the Digests and the pre-Justinian legal sources (5 vols., 1903–1987), an edition of Fronto, which was, however, not completed, as well as an index *rei militaris imperii Romani*. Plans for a comprehensive survey of ancient art and for a *Corpus Papy-*

rorum never came to fruition. The Prussian Academy had a personnel and administrative influence on several local, non-academic ventures and institutions in Berlin, and others like the Monumenta Germaniae Historica, the DAI (*Deutsches Archäologisches Institut*) with its branches in Rome, Athens, Cairo and Constantinople, the Reichslimeskommission headquartered in Heidelberg and the Römisch-Germanische Kommission in Frankfurt [52].

Also the newly established academies in the German-speaking countries (1846 the *Königlich-Sächsische Akademie der Wissenschaften* in Leipzig [42], 1847 the *Kaiserliche Akademie der Wissenschaften* in Vienna [33; 46], 1906 the Akademie in Straßburg and 1909 the Heidelberger Akademie [67]) carried out classical research and took part in joint ventures. In Vienna in 1864, the Commission to edit the works of the Latin Church Fathers was set up (CSEL); the Asia Minor Commission, which among other things was responsible for excavations at Ephesus, followed in 1890 [16. 9ff.], and in 1897 the Commission for research on the Roman Limes. Straßburg and Heidelberg increased their research on papyri. After 1918, the Heidelberg Academy took over a part of the work of its Straßburg sister organisation, specifically the *Acta Conciliorum Oecumenicorum* which had been advanced by Eduard Schwartz since 1909 [53. 41ff.].

Likewise, in many European and overseas nations, in order to manifest newly-won or aspired-to national sovereignty, in the 19th cent. academies were founded: in Poland (Krakow 1816), in Mexico (1824), in Hungary (1825), in Finland (1838), in Belgium (1841/42), in Norway (1857), in Croatia (1866), in Romania (1866), in Serbia (1866), in Bulgaria (1869) und in Japan (1879). These newly founded academies concerned themselves to a greater or lesser extent with classical research and were to some degree shaped by the Prussian Academy and its organisation (compare the individual articles on these countries). Academies played a lesser role in the USA, a result of the decentralisation of scholarly organisation and the prominent importance of private institutes; it was not until 1919 that the most important humanities organisations joined together as the *American Council of Learned Societies*. The Berlin Academy had a decisive influence on the works of other already existing academies – such as the one in St Petersburg [61]. In addition they were strengthened by the numerous personal relationships of members of individual academies, via elaborate correspondence (a nice example: the series of letters between Wilamowitz and M.I. Rostovzev [10]) and by inviting foreign scholars into the circle of members. (for the classical studies of the Berlin Academy: [35]).

In the face of the ever more costly projects that went beyond the organisatorial and financial possibilities of any one academy, and the need to avoid overlaps in the pursuit of research projects, at the end of the 19th cent. the possibility of a 'cartel' of scholarly academies was discussed. In 1893 the academies of Göttingen (in whose reorganisation Wilamowitz had a decisive share), Leipzig, Munich and Vienna formed the *Verband der wissenschaftlichen Körperschaften*. Berlin, which up to now had only worked in individual joint ventures, and Heidelberg joined in 1906 and 1911 respectively. On the initiative of the cartel, the International Association of Academies (IAA) came into being in 1899. Active until 1914 it brought together 24 European and American academies [23; 31]. The cartel oversaw over 30 projects, including the *Thesaurus linguae Latinae*, which was tackled by the academies in Berlin, Göttingen, Leipzig, Munich and Vienna, and on which today more than 20 academies on three continents are working [41]. There was also the edition of the Septuagint started by Rudolf Smend and Alfred Rahlfs in 1907 which now has its home in Göttingen[58]. Other projects were realised by arrangements between individual academies; the publication of the *Corpus Inscriptionum Etruscarum* since 1893 with the support of the Prussian and Saxon academies. Work on the *Corpus Medicorum Graecorum* was supported by the Berlin and Leipzig academies as well as the Royal Society in Copenhagen.

The 'industry-style management of research', funded by state support and private foundations, changed the character of the academy at the end of the 19th cent. This can be seen clearly at the Berlin Academy [52]. It was no longer a place of learned discourse, but rather an institution which had to accommodate itself to the requirements of large-scale, 'industrialised' research. Classical Studies initiated and exemplified an organisatorial modernisation, international cooperation, flexible methods of financing research and methodological diversity. Its innovative potential had its effect on other areas and even the physical and natural science section followed this model. Undertakings in Classical Studies strengthened at the same time a tendency towards subject specialistion. Using other areas of study as models, the study of Antiquity was divided into different sections and the unity of Classical Studies was destroyed forever.

E. 20TH CENT.

The most recent history of the academy reflects the changes and ruptures of the 20th cent. Chauvinism and military aggression, which culminated in two World Wars, robbed the scholarly community of vital material, personnel and ideational resources, and broke down the internationality of the scientific *republic*. The National Socialist regime had tried since 1933 – with varying degrees of success – to influence the personnel structure, the scholarly orientation and the organisation of the German, and after 1938 the Vienna and Prague Academies too (preliminary observations: [17; 43; 52a]). The academy system in Germany was reorganised along federal lines immediately after the end of World War II; in 1946 the individual academies joined together as the network, *Konferenz der deutschen Akademien der Wissenschaften*. [60]. The Russian Acad-

emy had been steered onto communist lines by Stalin in 1929 and reshaped into the Academy of Science of the USSR; since 1934 it had been meeting in Moscow; between 1961 and 1963 a basic reorganisation of the academy made allowance for the for the increasing differentation of the sciences and the quantative expansion of positions and institutes[34]. The division of Europe during the Cold War carried with it the transformation of a formerly pluralistic scholarly community in Eastern Europe into ideologically organised research academies, set up with well-staffed institutes, which had a central role in the scholarly organisation of their countries. The former *Preußische Akademie der Wissenschaften* in Berlin was also affected by this process; reopened in 1946 as the *Deutsche Akademie der Wissenschaften*, it underwent a far reaching reorganisation in 1969 ([48]; first results of the history of the institutes of Classical Studies [68]). The political changes that shook up former Warsaw Pact countries from the mid-1980s onwards and the ensuing disintegration of the Soviet Union and its satellites had a wide-ranging impact even on scholarly organisations. Many academies in Eastern Europe were newly-established or refounded: national sovereignty demonstrated itself in scholarly independence. The process of restructuring and reestablishing academic traditions was in no way a smooth process, nor indeed is it over. After the destruction of these older organisational structures, research is threatened in many places by an uncertain future and lack of resources (cf. on Russia [47]). In the Federal Republic of Germany after reunification the *Sächsische Akademie der Wissenschaften* was continued, the *Akademie gemeinnütziger Wissenschaften* in Erfurt was reconstituted and after the various institutes of the *Akademie der Wissenschaften* of the former German Democratic Republic had been dissolved, the *Berlin-Brandenburgische Akademie der Wissenschaften* was newly constituted (for an informative historical snapshot of the year 1989: [59]).

Specialisation within Classical Studies continued in the 20th cent. Numerous new enterprises were added to the projects pursued up to that point, achieved in part by individual academies, in part in national or international cooperation (cf. the publications of the individual academies in their *Jahrbücher* and *Sitzungsberichte*, and in the Internet). Many academies are represented by archaeological institutes in centres of Mediterranean culture (Madrid, Rome, Athens, Istanbul, Damascus, Jerusalem and Cairo, etc.). The *Internationale Assoziation*, set up in 1901 on the initiative of the London-based *Royal Society*, was joined by 18 academies and was replaced in 1919 by the *Union Académique International* (headquartered in Brussels). Within this international association, various academies have been working on *Catalogue des Manuscrits alchimiques grecs et latins*, on the *Corpus vasorum antiquorum*, on the *Tabula Imperii Romani* and the *Corpus des timbres amphoriques*. The German-speaking academies are jointly publishing the *Mittellateinische Wörterbuch* (together with the *Novum Glossarium*); there are comparable projects on medieval lexicography in many other European academies. Other large-scale joint projects include the *Corpus Signorum Imperii Romani*, the *Sylloge Nummorum Graecorum*), the *Lexicon Iconographicum Mythologiae Classicae*, a *Corpus fontium historiae Byzantinae* and the *Année Philologique*. The British Academy founded in 1901 (cf. Proceedings of the British Academy 1. VII–IX) supported textual criticism research on the Greek New Testament, the *Corpus Platonicum medii aevi*, the *Prosopography of the Later Roman Empire* and the *Patristic Greek Lexicon*; today among other things, a *Prosopography of the Byzantine Empire*, the *Corpus Inscriptionum Iranicarum*, the *Oxyrhynchus Papyri* and the *Roman-British Writing Tablets* are being published; furthermore, the *British Academy* is linked with the *British Schools and Institutes* and their various areas of research. The *Académie des Inscriptions et Belles Lettres* in Paris has also been concerned and occupied itself with numerous philological, epigraphic and archaeological projects; it is worth mentioning the *Corpus Inscriptionum Semiticarum* (since 1867) and the *Répertoire d'épigraphie sémitique*, the French complete edition of the works of Bartolomeo Borghesi, the *Inscriptiones Graecae ad res Romanas pertinentes*, the *Inscriptions latines de la Gaule et de l'Afrique*, the *Inscriptions grecques et latines de la Syrie*, the *Inscriptions grecques chrétiennes d'Asie mineure*, the inscriptions of Delos, the *Carte archéologique de la Gaule*, the *Recueil général des mosaïques de la Gaule* and, together with Yale University, the excavations in Dura-Europos; in its remit are the administration of the *Écoles françaises d'Athènes et de Rome* and the *École biblique et archéologique française de Jérusalem*. The Italian academies and the *Unione Accademia Nazionale* are overseeing, among others, numerous archaeological projects, the editing of Greek and Latin authors, the *Inscriptiones Italicae* (with the *Supplementa Italica* and the *Iscrizioni greche d'Italia*), the *Corpus dei Manoscritti Copti Letterari* and the *Corpus delle antichità fenicie e puniche*. The south and eastern European academies, as well as those from Scandinavian and the Benelux countries, have distinguished themselves by the deciphering and analysis of archaeological and epigraphic evidence, the publishing of academic journals and publications, the translation of classical authors in respective national languages, and collaborative work with international joint projects (cf. also the entires on individual countries).

In addition the commissions set up for international projects, the Austrian Academy in Vienna supports further working groups on Byzantine studies, the Corpus of ancient mosaics of Asia Minor, Mycenean research, Iranian studies and the history of ancient law. Together with the *Nordrhein-Westfälische Akademie der Wissenschaften* it publishes the *Inschriften griechischer Städte in Kleinasien*. After World War II, the Berlin Academy started work on a *Polybios-Lexikon* and a *Prosopographie der mittelbyzantinischen Zeit*. The

academy in Göttingen devotes itself to Byzantine legal sources, the *Septuaginta-Edition*, a *Lexikon des frühgriechischen Epos*, the *Reallexikon der germanischen Altertumskunde* and research on early Christian monasticism. The Bavarian Academy worked with the Vienna Academy on the *Corpus griechischer Urkunden des Mittelalters und der neueren Zeit* and, set up in several study groups, is currently engaged in examining cuneiform texts and Near Eastern archaeology; research on urban life in Late Antiquity and late Roman Raetia; the publication of a second series of *Acta Conciliorum Oecumenicorum*; onomastics; and an index to the Novellae of Justinian. In Heidelberg there are research positions on archaeometry, an epigraphic database, the *Lexicon Iconographicum Mythologiae Classicae*, the *Année Philologique*, publications from its papyri collection, the collection and study of Balkan pre-history. In the *Akademie der Wissenschaften und der Literatur* in Mainz, founded in 1949, commissions have been working and publishing on ancient slavery, coins of the Roman period found in Germany, Greek papyrus documents from Egypt, an Augustinus-Lexikon, the Corpus of Minoan and Mycenean seals, indices to Latin literature of the Renaissance, Coptic textiles, translations and commentaries on the works of Plato, a demotic book of names, and cuneiform texts from Bogazköy. The *Nordrhein-Westfälische Akademie der Wissenschaften*, founded in 1950 and headquartered in Düsseldorf, financed a critical edition of Athanasius and the *Bibliographia patristica*, is taking part in the publication of the *Reallexikon für Antike und Christentum* and the *Jahrbuch für Antike und Christentum*; it supports the edition of the works of Gregory of Nyssa as well as publications on papyri. The academies of Berlin, Düsseldorf, Göttingen, Heidelberg, Mainz und Munich together maintain the Patristic Commission.

The significance of the academies in terms of research policy and organisation for modern Classical Studies lies on the one hand in their mission to function as places of interdisciplinary discourse and international cooperation; on the other hand, in their responsibility for the dissemination of scholarly results through publications (protocols, yearbooks, monographs, special series, etc.), and, finally, in their function in carrying out long-term projects, which frequently conduct basic research in critical source analysis. Contrary to the natural sciences, Classical Studies have to a much smaller degree set up their own research institutions outside the academy and the university (in Germany, for instance, they have never been represented in the Kaiser-Wilhelm-/Max-Planck-Gesellschaft). The traditional leading role in Classical Studies in numerous academies in the 19th cent., above all in the Preußische Akademie der Wissenschaften has now been lost. For the most part, classical research projects are only a small part of the whole programme of the academy and often suffer consideral pressure for legitimisation as the result of tighter financial resources in the academic arena.

→ Academy; → Justinian; → Plato
→ BAROQUE IV. ART AND PAINTING

1 H. R. ABE, J. KIEFER, in: Mitteilungen der Akademie. der gemeinnützigen Wissenschaften zu Erfurt 1, 1990, 17–32 2 E. AMBURGER et al. (eds.), Wissenschaftspolitik in Mittel- und Osteuropa, 1976 3 M. BALTES, s.v. Academia, in: Augustinus-Lexikon 1, 1986/94, 39–45 4 P. BAROCCHI, D. GALLO (eds.), L'Accademia etrusca (exhibition catalogue), 1985 5 B. BARRET-KRIEGEL, Les historiens et la monarchie III: Les Académies et l'histoire, 1988 6 M. BIRCHER, F. VAN INGEN (eds.), Sprachgesellschaften, Sozietäten, Dichtergruppen, 1978 7 H.-ST. BRATHER, Leibniz und seine Akademie. Ausgewählte Quellen zur Geschichte der Berliner Sozietät der Wissenschaften, 1993 8 R. J. BRUNNER, J. HAHN (eds.), Johann Andreas Schmeller und die Bayerische Akademie der Wissenschaften, 1997 9 A. BUCK, Die humanistische Akademie in Italien, in: 29. 27–46 (= Studia humanitatis, 1981, 216–224) 10 W. M. CALDER III(ed.), Further Letters of Ulrich von Wilamowitz-Moellendorff, 1994, 191–205 (together with A. K. GAVRILOV) 11 A. CAMARIANO-CIORAN, Les académies princières de Bucarest et de Jassy et leurs professeurs, 1974 12 H. CHANTRAINE, Das Bild der römischen Kaiserzeit in den Acta der Mannheimer Akademie, in: K. CHRIST, E. GABBA (eds.), L'Impero Romano fra storia generale e storia locale, 1991, 225–240 13 Id., Archäologisches in den Acta der Mannheimer Akademie, in: R. STUPPERICH (ed.), Lebendige Ant., 1995, 107–112 14 E. W. COCHRANE, Tradition and Enlightenment in Tuscan Academies 1690–1800, 1961 15 A. DELLA TORRE, Storia dell'Accademia Platonica di Firenze, 1902 16 G. DOBESCH, G. REHRENBÖCK (eds.), Die epigraphische und altertumskundliche Erforschungen Kleinasiens. Hundert Jahre Kleinasiatische Kommission der Österreichischen Akademie der Wissenschaften, 1993 17 Leopoldina-Symposion. Die Elite der Nation im Dritten Reich. Das Verhältnis von Akademie und ihrem wissenschaftlichen Umfeld zum Nationalsozialismus, Acta Historica Leopoldina 22, 1995 18 P. FUCHS, Palatinus illustratus. Die historischen Forschungen an der Kurpfälzischen Akademie der Wissenschaften, 1963 19 K. GARBER, H. WISMANN (eds.), Europäische Sozietätsbewegung und demokratische Tradition. Die europäischen Akademien der Frühen Neuzeit zwischen Frührenaissance und Spätaufklärung, 2 vols., 1995 20 C. GRAU et al., Die Berliner Akademie der Wissenschaften in der Zeit des Imperialismus, 3 vols., 1975/1979 21 Id., Die Preußische Akademie der Wissenschaften zu Berlin, 1993 22 Id., Berühmte Wissenschaftsakademien., 1988 23 Id., Die Wissenschaftsakademien in der deutschen Geschichte: Das Kartell von 1893 bis 1940, in: 17, 31–56 24 L. HAMMERMAYER, Geschichte der Bayerischen Akademie der Wissenschaften 1759–1807, 2 vols., 1983 (vol. 2 ²1983) 25 Id., Freie Gelehrtenassoziation oder Staatsanstalt? Zur Geschichte der Bayerischen Akademie der Wissenschaften in der Zeit der Spätaufklärung und der Reform (1787–1807), in: Zschr. für Bayerische Landesgesch. 54, 1991, 159–202 26 J. HANKINS, The Myth of the Platonic Academy of Florence, in: Ren. Quarterly 44, 1991, 429–475 27 A. HARNACK, Geschichte der Königlich Preußischen Akademie der Wissenschaften, 3 vols. in 4 parts, 1900 28 W. HARTKOPF, G. WANGERMANN, Dokumente zur Geschichte der Berliner Akademie der Wissenschaften von 1700 bis 1990, 1991 29 F. HARTMANN, R. VIERHAUS (eds.), Der Akademiegedanke im 17. und 18. Jahrhundert,

1977 30 K. TH.V. HEIGEL, Über den Bedeutungswandel der Worte Akademie und Akademisch, 1911 31 W. HIS, Zur Vorgeschichte des deutschen Kartells und der internationalen Association der Akademien, 1902 32 P. HINNEBERG (ed.), Die Kultur der Gegenwart, Part 1, Section 1, 1906, 591–650 33 O. HITTMAIR, H. HUNGER (eds.), Akademie der Wissenschaften. Entwicklung einer österreichischen Forschungsinstitution, 1997 34 W. KASACK, Die Akademie der Wissenschaften der UdSSR, ³1978 35 CHR. KIRSTEN (ed.), Die Altertumswissenschaften an der Berliner Akademie. Wahlvorschläge, 1985 36 P.-E. KNABE, Die Wortgeschichte von Akademie, in: Archiv für das Studium der neueren Sprachen und Literatur 214, 1977, 245–261 37 A. KRAUS, Die historische Forschung an der churbayerischen Akademie der Wissenschaften. 1759–1806, 1959 38 Id., Vernunft und Geschichte. Die Bedeutung der deutschen Akademien für die Entwicklung der Geschichtswissenschaft im späten 18. Jahrhundert, 1963 39 P. O. KRISTELLER, Humanismus und Renaissance, 2 vols., 1974/76 40 Id., The Platonic Academy of Florence, in: Ren. News 14, 1961, 147–159 41 D. KRÖMER (ed.), 'Wie die Blätter am Baum, so wechseln die Wörter'. 100 Jahre Thesaurus linguae Latinae, 1995 42 E. LEA, G. WIEMERS, Planung und Entstehung der Sächsischen Akademie zu Leipzig 1704–1846. Zur Genesis einer gelehrten Gesellschaft, 1996 43 H. MATIS, Zwischen Anpassung und Widerstand. Die Akademie der Wissenschaften in den Jahren 1938–1945, 1997 44 M. MAYLENDER, Storia delle Accademie d'Italia, 5 vols., 1926–30 45 J. E. MCCLELLAN, Science Reorganized. Scientific Societies in the 18th Century, 1985 46 R. MEISTER, Geschichte der Akademie der Wissenschaften in Wien 1847–1947, 1947 47 E. Z. MIRSKAYA, Russian Academic Science Today: Its Societal Standing and the Situation within the Scientific Community, in: Social Stud. of Science 25, 1995, 705–725 48 P. Nötzoldt, Wolfgang Steinitz und die Deutsche Akademie der Wissenschaften zu Berlin. Zur politischen Geschichte der Institution (1945–1968), Diss. Humboldt-Universität Berlin 1998 49 K. NOWAK (ed.), Adolf von Harnack als Zeitgenosse, 2 vols., 1996 50 K. F. OTTO, Die Sprachgesellschaften des 17. Jh., 1972 51 ST. REBENICH, Theodor Mommsen und Adolf Harnack. Wissenschaft und Politik im Berlin des ausgehenden 19. Jahrhunderts, 1997 52 Id., Die Altertumswissenschaft und die Kirchenväterkommission an der Akademie, in: J. KOCKA et al. (eds.), Die Königlich Preußische Akademie der Wissenschaften zu Berlin im Kaiserreich, 1999, 169–203 52 a) Id., Zwischen Anpassung und Widerstand? Die Berliner Akademie der Wissenschaften von 1933–1945, in: B. NÄF (ed.), Antike und Altertumswissenschaft in der Zeit von Faschismus und Nationalsozialismus, 203–4 53 A. REHM, Eduard Schwartz' wissenschaftliches Lebenswerk, 1942 54 D. ROCHE, Le siècle des lumières en province. Académies et académiciens provinciaux 1680–1789, 2 vols., 1978 55 W. RÜEGG, s.v. Akademie, in: Lexikon des Mittelalters, 1, 248f. 56 Id., Humanistische Elitenbildung in der Eidgenossenschaft zur Zeit der Renaissance, in: G. KAUFFMANN (ed.), Die Renaissance im Blick der Nationen Europas, 1991, 95–133 57 W. SCHEUERMANN, Marsilio Ficino oder die Lehrjahre eines Platonikers, in: G. HARTUNG, W. P. KLEIN (eds.), Zwischen Narretei und Weisheit, 1997, 158–178 58 R. SMEND, Der geistige Vater des Septuaginta-Unternehmens, in: AAWG 190, 1990, 332–344 59 I. STARK, Der Runde Tisch der Akademie und die Reform der Akademie der Wissenschaften der DDR nach der Herbstrevolution 1989, in: Gesch. und Ges. 23, 1997,

423–445   60 M. Stoermer, Zur Geschichte der Konferenz der Akademie der Wissenschaften in der Bundesrepublik Deutschland, in: Akad.-Journ. 1, 1997, 11–13
61 K. Svoboda, Die klassische Altertumswissenschaft im
vorrevolutionären Rußland, in: Klio 37, 1959, 241–267
62 Chr. Treml, Humanistische Gemeinschaftsbildung.
Soziokulturelle Untersuchung zur Entstehung eines neuen
Gelehrtenstandes in der frühen Neuzeit, 1989 63 J. Voss,
Das Mittelalter im historischen Denken Frankreichs,
1972   64 Id., Die Akademie als Organisationsträger der
Wissenschaften im 18. Jahrhundert, in: HZ 44, 1980,
43–74 65 Id., Akademie, gelehrte Gesellschaft. und wissenschaftliche Vereine in Deutschland (1750–1850), in: E.
François (ed.), Sociabilité et société bourgeoise en
France, Allemagne et en Suisse (Geselligkeit, Vereinswe-
sen und bürgerliche Gesellschaft in Frankreich, Deutschland und der Schweiz), 1750–1850, 1986, 149–167
66 Id., Akademie und Gelehrte Gesellschaft, in: H. Reinal-
ter (ed.), Aufklärungsgesellschaften, 1993, 19–38   67 U.
Wennemuth, Wissenschaftsorganisation und Wissen-
schaftsförderung in Baden. Die Heidelberger Akademie
der Wissenschaften 1909–1949, 1994   68 M. Willing,
Althistorische Forschung in der DDR. Eine wissenschafts-
geschichtliche Studie zur Entwicklung der Disziplin Alte
Geschichte vom Ende des II. Weltkrieges bis zur Gegenwart, 1991

Additional Bibliography: D. Chambers (ed.), Italian Academies of the Sixteenth Century, 1995; W.
Fischer et al. (eds.), Die Preußische Akademie der Wissenschaften zu Berlin 1914 – 1945, 2000; M. Gierl,
Geschichte und Organisation. Institutionalisierung und
Kommunikationsprozess am Beispiel der Wissenschaftsakademien um 1900, 2004; D.-O. Hurel (ed.), Académies et sociétés savantes en Europe (1650 – 1800), 2000;
J. Kocka et al. (eds.), Die Berliner Akademien der Wissenschaften im geteilten Deutschland 1945 – 1990, 2002; R.
Mayntz et al. (eds.), East European Academies in Tran-
sition, 1998; F. A. Yates, The French Academies of the
Sixteenth Century, 1947 (repr. 1988).

II. Musical

In the history of music, many institutions (schools,
societies) and their events became significant under the
designation academy. Many academies, in the sense of
societies, discovered or imitated ancient music (Alterati
Florenz, late 16th cent.; Académie de Poésie et Musique
Paris, 1570), furthered or carried on musical theatre
(Intronati Siena, 1531; Invaghiti Mantua, 1607; Académie Royale de Musique, Paris after 1669; Royal
Academy of Music, London 1719–28; Arcadia Rom,
1690) and staged concerts or performed music, especially ancient music (Academy of Vocal Music London,
1726–31; Academy of Ancient Music London,
1710?/31–92; Sing-Akademie Berlin, after 1791; Sing-
Akademie Breslau, after 1825). Whereas some private
academies employed professional musicians to teach its
members (and in doing so became not infrequently the
basis for a conservatory), other academies were from
the beginning conceived as schools of music (Filarmonica Verona, after 1543; Floridi, later Filarmonica,
Bologna, after 1614/15; Royal Academy of Music London, after 1832; Santa Cecilia Rome, 1839; Dublin

1848; Zurich 1891; Vienna 1908; Glasgow 1929; Hel-
sinki 1939; Basel 1948). Just like the sessions or meetings of societies that designate themselves as 'academies', also their concerts may be called 'academies'
metonymically, so that in this context, one did not need
an academy to stage the event. A report about the musical life in Vienna in 1800 differentiates – apparently
depending on the type of locale – between 'public' und
'private academies' and in both categories between
'fixed' und 'ad-hoc' (the 'ad-hoc' private academies
evolved in the course of decades into what is called salon music). In a further metonymic sense, academy can
even mean works composed for a function at the academy (cantatas) (Pellegrini Amor tiranno 1616, Pasquini
1687).

W. Frobenius, N. Schwindt-Gross, Th. Sick (eds.),
Akademie und Musik, 1993 (with a detailed bibliography
317ff.).   WOLF BARTH, ANDREAS FROBENIUS

Acculturation

A. History of the Concept
B. Acculturation in the Historical
Disciplines

A. History of the Concept

The concept of *acculturation* originally derives from
the conceptual apparatus of American-style → Cultural anthropology, and is based on the concept of
culture essentially developed by S. Tylor, which, in the
course of the 20th cent., gradually replaced the norma-
tive-judgmental concept of culture that had been dominant until then. As an alternative to the latter, which
classified human societies on a scale between primitive
peoples and complex civilizations, 'Cultural Anthropology' near the end of the 19th cent. developed the
model of a non-judgmental comparison of individual
cultures. The underlying concept of culture embraces
all areas of human endeavor (thus including politics,
economics and religion) [4]. The study of 'acculturation' takes into consideration the modes and results of
cultural change that are the consequence of cultural
contact. In 1936, the following definition, still largely
valid today, was developed by R. Redfield, R. Lindon
and M. Herskvits: 'Acculturation comprehends those
phenomena which result when groups of individuals
having different cultures come into continuous first-
hand contact, with subsequent changes in the original
patterns of either or both groups' [14. 149]. In this context, the mechanisms and contexts of areas of contact
were at the center of these authors' considerations, for
instance the circumstances of encounter and criteria of
selection in cases of exchange. The concept was fine-
tuned in a workshop in 1953, by considering social
structures more intensely and classifying the possible
reactions to cultural contact [16]. Since acculturation
also offered a welcome explanatory model for cultural
change, the concept was soon utilized in many other
disciplines like sociology [11], archaeology [15] and the
historical disciplines.

B. Acculturation in the Historical Disciplines

The transferal of the anthropological acculturation model, initially conceived for cultural encounters within a colonial context, to historical societies (in particular ancient cultures), nevertheless revealed a series of problems. In particular, the concept lost some of its rigor, since the nature of the sources seldom permitted the exact observation of 'first-hand contact' and gradual change. In addition, the idea of homogeneity of the cultural entities involved turns out to be highly problematic, for it neglects the complexity of historical cultures, and it does not take historical development into consideration [7].

These problems have led to various modifications of the acculturation model: for instance, U. Bitterli's typology of cultural contacts [1] (primarily with regard to the contact of Europe with non-European cultures); building upon the latter, the more flexible concept of 'cultural borders' by J. Osterhammel [13] and the research on 'cultural transfer', established by M. Espagne and M. Werner [3] (particularly tailored to inter-European cultural exchange); finally, the flexibilized acculturation model specially developed for research on Classical Antiquity by U. Gotter. Gotter understands cultural entities as identity groups, and he limits the possibility of making relevant statements about acculturation to cases in which (1) groups can be determined and delimited, (2) the degree of foreignness between the groups can be determined (particularly with reference to perception), (3) the dynamics of reception can be described, and (4) the transformation of 'original patterns' can be observed. Since this is often impossible for ancient cultures, many of which can be grasped only on the basis of artifacts (this is true especially for the ancient 'marginal cultures' such as the Germanic, Celtic, and Iberian), according to Gotter the acculturation model should not be used in such cases [7]. As an example, Gotter has demonstrated his concept in a work on the process of Hellenization of the city of priests, Olba in Cilicia [6]. Important and well-attested processes of acculturation in Antiquity are Hellenization (for instance of Egypt [8], Southern Italy [10], Phoenicia [17], and Asia Minor [12]), the Orientalization of Greece in the Archaic Period [2], and Romanisation [9]. A particularly complex case are the processes of acculturation between Greece and Rome [5; 18]. The reception of the cultural and institutional achievements of the subjugated Hellenized population by Islam can also be interpreted as a process of acculturation.

→ Hellenization; → Olba; → Romanisation

1 U. Bitterli, Alte Welt – Neue Welt. Formen des europäischen-überseeischen Kulturkontakts vom 15.–18. Jahrhundert, 1986   2 W. Burkert, The Orientalizing Revolution, 1995   3 M. Espagne, M. Werner, Deutschfranzösischer Kulturtransfer im 18. und 19. Jahrhundert. Zu einem interdisziplinären Forschungsprogramm des CNRS, in: Francia 13, 1985, 502–510   4 J. Fisch, s. v. Zivilisation; Kultur, in: O. Brunner et al. (eds.), Geschichtliche Grundbegriffe, Vol. 7, 1992, 679–774   5 U. Gotter, Griechenland in Rom? Zur politischen Bedeutung von Akkulturation in der klassischen und spätrömischen Republik. Unpublished dissertation, Freiburg i.Br. 2002   6 Id., Tempel und Großmacht: Olba/Diokaisareia, in: E. Jean (ed.), La Cilicie: espaces et pouvoirs locaux, 2002, 286–366   7 Id., Akkulturation als Methodenproblem der historischen Wissenschaften, in: W. Essbach, wir/ihr/sie. Identität und Alterität in Theorie und Methode, 2001, 373–406   8 S. Grallert, Akkulturation im ägyptischen Sepulkralwesen. Der Fall eines Griechen in der 26. Dynastie, in: U. Höckmann, D. Kreikenbom (eds.) Naukratis. Die Beziehungen zu Ostgriechenland, Ägypten und Zypern in archaïscher Zeit. Akten der Table Ronde in Mainz, 25.–27. November 1999, 2001, 183–196   9 A. Haffner (ed.), Internationales Kolloquium zum Schwerpunktprogramm Romanisierung 1998, 2000   10 K. Lomas, Rome and the Western Greeks, 350 BC – AD 200, Conquest and Acculturation in Southern Italy, 1993   11 E. Long, Engaging Sociology and Cultural Studies: Disciplinary and Social Change, in: Id. (ed.), From Sociology to Cultural Studies. New Perspectives, 1997, 1–32   12 St. Mitchell, Ethnicity, Acculturation and Empire in Roman and Late Roman Asia Minor, in: Id. (ed.), Ethnicity and Culture in Asia Minor, 2000, 117–150   13 J. Osterhammel, Kulturelle Grenzen in der Expansion Europas, in: Saeculum 46, 1995, 101–138   14 R. Redfield et al., Memorandum for the Study of Acculturation, in: American Anthropologist 38, 1936, 149–152   15 J. Slofstra, An Anthropological Approach to the Study of Romanization Processes, in: R. Brandt, J. Slofstra (eds.), Romans and Natives in the Low Countries. Spheres of Interaction, 1983, 71–104   16 The Social Science Research Council Summer Seminar on Acculturation on 1953, in: American Anthropologist 56, 1954, 973–1002   17 R. A. Stucky, Acculturation et retour aux sources: Sidon aux époques perse et hellénistique, in: R. Frei-Steba (ed.), Recherches récentes sur le monde hellénistique, 2001, 247–258   18 G. Vogt-Spira, Auseinandersetzung Roms und Griechenlands als europäisches Paradigma, 1998.   Isabel Toral-Niehoff

Acoustics see → Natural sciences

Adagium see→ Aphorism;

Adaptation

A. Definition   B. Epics Based on Classical Models   C. Compilation   E. Verse and Prose Paraphrases   G. Translation   H. Periphrastic Translation   I. Travesty   J. Emblematic Adaptation   K. Other Forms

A. Definition

In the narrower sense, adaptation is understood by literary scholarship to mean the arranging of a literary work according to the rules of another genre or medium. Looking at the reception of classical texts in the literature of the Middle Ages and the modern age, adaptation is, to be sure, in a broader sense an adjustment to the conditions present in another, i.e. vernacular literature. The boundaries of this expanded concept of adaptation are translation on one hand and → *imi-*

tatio on the other. Whereas the latter, as imitation of mostly formal and poetological characteristics, will remain on the sidelines, translation must be seen as a form of adaptation. Because different periods view translations in different terms, to modern eyes those of the Middle Ages and the Early Modern period appear, to a greater or lesser extent, as free adaptations. In this general sense, adaptation mainly implies the following three aspects: 1. Insofar as the adaptation intends an adjustment to the ideology, view of the world, people or society and ethics of the adapting epoch, the changing methods of adaptation throw a significant light on the dominant self-awareness of the era, specifically on its relationship to antiquity. 2. With regard to literary-aesthetic matters, the potential of creativity in genre, language and style is a significant feature of adaptation.

The significance of adaptation reveals, to what extent classical literature and which aspects are perceived as important for their own time. Adaptation contributes to the development of emerging genres (for example in the epics of the courtly Middle Ages based on those of Classical Antiquity), reinforces the validity of developed genres (for example in the adaptation of the *Aeneid* or *Metamorphoses* in the → RENAISSANCE which interact with modern epic forms); or adaptation implicitly postulates a change in the concept of a genre (for example in the mock heroic epic of the 17th and 18th cents.). 3. The co-existence of different expectations, for example of an academic and popular nature, which can lead to completely opposing forms and functions of adaptation in the same era, demonstrates the close connection between adaptation and public taste. The following sections should be seen as an account of the historical forms of adaptation of Classical literature. The period covered is limited to the Middle Ages and the Early Modern period, as it is then when the most important forms manifest themselves. A second concentration can be found in French and Italian literature, as it is here where the reception of antiquity in general, and the various types of adaptation appear first. In the literature of other countries (Spain, Germany, Britain), they were mostly received after a certain interval. The methods of adaptation will be shown principally through the reception of the Classical epic, since no other genre shows a comparable variety of possibilities.

B. ROMANCES SET IN ANTIQUITY

The romance set in Antiquity (*Antikenroman*) is the most characteristic form of adaptation to show the relationship of the Middle Ages to Classical Antiquity. This genre emerged in Anglo-Norman French literature of the 12th cent. and was then taken up in other countries, notably Germany and Italy. The three most important texts are the anonymous *Roman de Thèbes* (c. 1150), the likewise anonymous *Roman d'Eneas* (c. 1160) and the *Roman de Troie* by Benoît de Sainte-Maure (c. 1165). The main sources for these works are Virgil (*Aeneid*), Statius (*Thebaid*) and the pseudo-his-

torical writings of Dares Phrygius (*De excidio Troiae*) and Dictys Cretensis (*Ephemeris belli Troiani*). In addition to clerics, the educated upper classes of society were the audience for these romances. These texts flourished only for a brief time. The reading public soon turned to the Arthurian legend. All the same, this type of adaptation is, from the viewpoint of the history of the genre, of wide-ranging importance since it prepared the ground for the characteristic features of the courtly epic. In that way the *Roman d'Eneas* most likely had an exemplary influence on the work of Chrétien de Troyes.

These romances set in Antiquity took great liberties in dealing with their sources and also in how they combined them. In spite of that, the public at the time perceived them as adequate and historically balanced treatments. The formal characteristics, specifically their structuring into moderate-size, relatively homogeneous, discrete narrative units, point to a predominantly oral transmission of the epics. When compared to the ancient versions, the story lines are often severely altered in terms of chronology and rhythm. In places they are compressed or abbreviated, and in others they are expanded either by amplification or by the introduction of new elements. The method of presentation can be generally viewed as a 'modernisation' of Classical Antiquity. Mythological elements are greatly reduced; motivation, which in the classical texts emerges from the meddling of the gods, is transferred into an inter- or intrapersonal sphere. Conventions and customs, perceptions of morals, institutions and social structures are made to approximate those of the High Middle Ages in order to acquaint the readers with the foreign world through the familiar. Classical personages become kings, knights, dukes, bishops, burghers and so on. Further, typical of the age is the social mindset, continually shaped by *cortoisie* (courtly attitude). In this way, the romance set in Antiquity anticipates an element that will have a fundamental ideological function in the courtly epic. A similar point holds for the concept of love, which again mirrors the courtly ideal. A characteristic feature is the change of emphasis in the *Roman d'Eneas*: drawing on elements from Ovid, the heroic plot becomes a love story. Two concepts of love are introduced and they are contrasted by a significant expansion of the original plot. In the end, the passionate love between Dido and Aeneas is contrasted with the courtly ideal, the love between Aeneas and Lavinia, with whose marriage the *Roman d'Eneas* ends. This ideological rounding off was so convincing to posterity that as late as 1428 the humanist M. Vegio composed, in Latin, a 13th book of the *Aeneid*, telling of Aeneas' marriage, rule and, in the end, apotheosis. This supplementary book appeared in most editions and translations of the *Aeneid* in early modern times (e.g. in G. Douglas 1513 and Th. Murner 1515).

Characteristic of the medieval relationship to the Classical world is also the reception of French romances of this type in other countries, notably in German and Italy where, via edited translations, secondary adaptations were generated. Heinrich von Veldeke's *Eneit* (*c.* 1170–90) almost certainly did not have recourse to the ancient texts, rather it adhered closely to the subject matter of the *Roman d'Eneas*. Nonetheless the romance was adapted to the linguistic and ideological norms of its author's surroundings. In this way he weakened the compilatory traits of its model, strengthened the structural coherence, gave the text a strongly rhetorical revision and highlighted the courtly idealisation of people, society and love. As in France, the German adaptation of the *Roman d'Eneas* comes particularly close to a contemporary understanding of courtly epic. Because Ovid's stories did not correspond to the taste dominated by the romance set in Antiquity, the German version of the *Metamorphoses* by Albrecht von Halberstadt from 1217 found no resonance, although it was the very first one done in the Middle Ages,

C. COMPILATION

That the romances set in Antiquity were appreciated less as literary texts than as works transmitting historical knowledge, is seen by the fact that they were often included in historical compilations. As manuscripts they were often combined in collections, in which the order could vary. In this way a kind of world history was constituted, which started with Trojan origins and flowed into the history of Britain, more specifically, the Arthurian era. Like the *Roman d'Eneas*, the *Roman de Troie* was utilized for a *Histoire ancienne jusqu'à César*, which at the same time assembled and adapted other ancient sources, e.g. the *Excidium Troiae* of Dares or a number of Ovid's *Heroides*. This type of compilation was repeated in other countries, for instance in Italy in the 14th cent. The *Fiorita* by Armannino da Bologna (1325), a mixture of poetry and prose passages, represents a history of mankind up to the age of Caesar; it also used the subject matter of the *Aeneid*. Similarly, Guido da Pisa in his *Fiore d'Italia* (start of the 14th cent.) used classical and medieval sources for a history of the Hebrew, Greek and Roman world. His second book, titled *I fatti di Enea* traces the story line of Virgil's epic in simple prose.

D. *Cantare*

The *Cantari* are a popular variation of the medieval courtly epic, intended mainly for public oral presentation. They use material from Old French heroic epics and courtly epics as well as Classical epics (Virgil, Ovid, Statius). In terms of adaptation, the *Cantari* with Classical subject matter share certain similarities with the romances set in Antiquity. Here too heroes and mythological figures are transposed to the world of the Middle Ages; the heroes show chivalric characteristics, and the action is structured in imitation of the courtly epic. Nonetheless, the *Cantari* should be understood as a form of adaptation in their own right. They took their material from medieval paraphrases, or *volgarizzamenti* (see below), and at times from the Old French verse adaptations of Classical epics. They were not

aimed at a highly-educated courtly audience, rather at the more simple, unequally educated levels of the Italian communes, where the *cantari* were enjoyed as a literary form of entertainment. This is borne out by the formal characteristics of the genre: a lot of action, fast narrative pace, relatively simple syntax and a striking arrangement of plot. The earliest *cantari* with Classical themes go back to the 14th cent. (for example the *Cantare di Piramo e Tisbe*); numerous others from the 15th and 16th cents. rework the subject matter of the *Aeneid* or episodes from the *Metamorphoses*. Then they were gradually replaced by adaptations, which followed the form of the *cantare*, now enhanced into an artistic genre called the *romanzo* (Boiardo, Ariosto).

E. VERSE AND PROSE PARAPHRASES

Characteristic of medieval paraphrases is the combination with commentary. It was not until the beginning of the Renaissance that textual adaptation and commentary diverged. By far the best example for the paraphrasing adaptation is the anonymous Old French *Ovide moralisé* (1316–28), a comprehensive didactic epic of 72,000 verses that supplies the themes of the *Metamorphoses* with a moralising explanation. The actual transmission of the Ovidian text is a simplified retelling of the plots, which are often structured after the style of late medieval romances or are connected with each other. The huge expansion results from three components: from the insertion of adaptations of other Ovidian texts (*Heroides*), from the integration of mythological stories from other sources (for example the *Aeneid*) and from the addition of allegorical interpretations, which for the most part go back to Latin commentaries on the *Metamorphoses*. The aim of the *Ovide moralisé* is to provide as complete a mythography as possible, aimed at an educated audience that, however, does not know Latin. At the same time the *Ovide moralisé* is this era's adaptation of the *Metamorphoses* with the greatest impact. Its reception reaches into the 16th cent. A prose version of the work appeared in 1466/67, and it is on this version that W. Caxton (1480) based the first English prose version of the *Metamorphoses*. Like this version the *Bible des Poètes*, published in 1484, also takes over the allegories of the *Ovide moralisé* and augments them with further allegories taken from the *Ovidius moralizatus* of a Latin commentatary by P. Bersuire (1347). It was not until the 16th cent. that the interest in themes from classical stories as fiction began to outweigh their interest as allegorical exegesis. In 1532 a modernised version of the *Bible* under the title *Le Grand Olympe* appeared, which turned its back on allegories and in the introduction explicitly stated its interest in the style and aesthetic qualities of the Classical epic – a decisive step away from the medieval paraphrase towards a literary interest in the original text.

F. *Volgarizzamento*

By *volgarizzamenti* we mean the transmission and translation of Latin texts into Italian (*volgare*), which flourished in Italy between the 14th and 16th cents. more strongly and more varied than in other countries, possibly via the intermediate stage of French adaptations. *Volgarizzamenti* do not constitute a unique form of adaptation, since in principle they can include every contemporary genre. Functionally, however, they must be differentiated from other adaptations: they developed mainly in the specific social context of the Italian city-states for a non-educated, but culturally-interested bourgeois audience. The most important texts of the 14th cent. were the *Metamorphoses*, the *Heroides*, the *Aeneid* as well as the tragedies of Seneca. The *volgarizzamenti* act similarly as mediators between the paraphrase and the original text as those examples cited in the previous section. The differences in level of the *volgarizzamenti* are characteristic of a broadly-diverse audience with a variety of interests. Working from the Latin prose adaptation of G. del Virgilio, G. dei Bonsignori (1375/77) translated the *Metamorphoses* into a simple language merely summarising the contents of the stories. In contrast, A. Simintendi (before 1333) earlier translated the same work, also into prose, but did so from the original text, on which he based his Italian. Another characteristic of *volgarizzamenti* is their multiple function. Although, like the paraphrases, they are often accompanied by allegorical or moral comments, new kinds of intentions are apparent in the transmission of knowledge, in rhetorical enrichment and with that the increasing appreciation of the vernacular, as much as in the transmission of the poetic themes of ancient texts. These intentions were motivated by the strong presence of Latin authors in contemporary vernacular literature, which was not comprehensible to a readership ignorant of Latin and without the knowledge of Classical texts, themes and forms. It was not least the especially early appearance of → HUMANISM in Italy that was responsible for the phenomenon of the *volgarizzamenti*. Under the influence of the Italian *volgarizzamenti* and together with beginning Humanism in Spain around 100 years later, similar transmissions appeared there in the 15th cent., often not based on Latin, but rather on Italian texts.

G. TRANSLATION

Due to their broad understanding of translation the medieval paraphrases and the *volgarizzamenti* of the early Italian Renaissance view themselves as translations of their Classical sources. Prose translations which make relatively free with the original are already encountered in the late 15th and in the 16th cents. – a French rendering of the *Aeneid* (1483), one of Homer, also in French (1519–1530) and the first Spanish version of the *Metamorphoses* (J. de Bustamante, 1546). Another of the first translations of the *Metamorphoses* dating from the 16th cent. into Italian follows a medieval pattern by not going back to Ovid's original, but to the paraphrase of Bonsignori. The first German version of Homer, translated by S. Schaidenreisser (1537), likewise goes back to a Latin version. At the same time,

however, the first accurate translations appeared, in which the effects of the Humanistic philological confrontation with Antiquity are visible. These translations are based on the original classical texts, follow them word for word as much as possible and aim for a textually faithful account, formally, rhetorically and semantically. This is true – at least in its intention – of the first French translation of the *Aeneid* by Octovien de Saint-Gelais (1500), more so of Cl. Marot's French translation of the *Metamorphoses* (Book I/II, 1534/43), B. Aneau (Book III, 1556) and F. Habert (complete, 1549–57). The first translations of Classical epics also appeared in other languages. In 1515 Th. Murner penned the first German *Aeneid* (which also has certain elements of a paraphrase), G. Douglas translated the same epic for the first time into English, and Chapman, between 1598 and 1611, the Homeric epics.

H. PERIPHRASTIC TRANSLATION

In the wake of translations of Classical literature, which were based on the original text and shaped by Humanistic-philological standards, the awareness of the complementary possibility emerged more clearly: namely of a translation that orientated itself on the taste or the expectation of the reader and allowed the features of the adapted text to recede in favour of the aesthetic principles of contemporary literature. This form of adaptation, resulting in a periphrastic rendering, represents an extraordinarily widely disseminated form in all European literatures. Characteristic examples are encountered especially in Italy from the beginning of the 16th cent. with A. Cerretanis' (1566) and A. Caros' (1570) versions of the *Aeneid* or L. Dolces' (1553) and G.A. dell'Anguillaras' (1561) versions of the *Metamorphoses*. In a sense Th. Murner's translation of the *Aeneid* (1515) and the conspicuously large number of adaptations in Restoration England, such as J. Dryden's renderings of Virgil and Ovid (1693, 1697) or A. Pope's Homer, should be included as well. On the surface the periphrastic translation has similarities with the romance set in Antiquity. In both cases, characteristics of contemporary genres are devolved onto the Classical text. The periphrastic rendering, however, was not meant to impart either historical or substantive knowledge. Its novelty lies in its aesthetic quality, which was viewed as an adequate equivalent of the Classical form. The Classical text was adapted with the conviction that the Classical author, had he lived in the modern age, would have shaped it the same way. In that respect, the periphrastic rendering really follows the broadly understood principle of *imitatio*. The intention of this type of adaptation is the improvement of the original with the means of one's own language and poetics so that the adaptation achieves the level of an independent and effective literary work.

An illuminating example is Murner's version of the *Aeneid* mentioned above, which may be placed between a translation and a paraphrase. This adaptation aims to turn the Classical work into a lively form and make it accessible to the German public. For that purpose Murner takes up the nearest contemporary epic form, the minstrel epic, and transposes the Classical world into the mores and customs of his time. However, the Italian Renaissance adaptations of Virgil and Ovid that try to link the *imitatio* of Classical Antiquity with contemporary literature become decisive for these adaptations. Most adaptors of epic texts chose the octave, common in vernacular epic; in stylistic and rhetorical terms, as well as in the composition of characters, plot development, scenery and décor they orientated themselves on the most successful genre of the epoch, the chivalric tale (romanzo), as it was first elevated to an artistic form by M.M. Boiardo (*Orlando innamorato*), and then by L. Ariosto (*Orlando furioso*). The plots of the Classical originals were rearranged, embellished or expanded according to the structural principles of these models. Above all, the predilection for long accounts of emotions and expanded descriptive passages were taken over. Generally, just as in the romanzo the represented reality was made to match the culture and ideology of the Renaissance. Classical heroes appear as princes; in their attitudes people follow courtly habits and manners. The marriage of the Classical with the contemporary model is eased by the fact that Renaissance literature in the vernacular picks up on the imitated Classical texts. Thus Ovid's epic is already in many places the model for Ariosto's *Orlando furioso*, which in turn affected the *Metamorphoses* adaptations in the Renaissance.

I. Travesty

Travesty is the adaptation of a Classical subject into a style which is not appropriate for it, specifically the adaptation of an elevated and heroic plot into a witty, funny or burlesque style. From a literary-historical point of view, it presupposes the linguistically and stylistically free adaptation of Classical works as practised in the periphrastic translations. Apart from that, it implies that Classical texts still have an exemplary character for contemporary poetics, but that at the same time a certain distance regarding the concept of a strict *imitatio* has occurred. That explains why the first parody of Virgil's *Aeneid*, G.B. Lalli's 1633, turns up in Italian literature, which already had a rich tradition of parodistic writing. Simultaneously with the emergence of the first chivalric tales, raised to the level of an art form, comic variations of the genre appeared. The immediate predecessors of the epic travesties are epic parodies, or mock-heroic epic, the best known example of which is A. Tassoni's *Secchia rapita* (1624). In it, the typical motifs, plot elements, character and mythological set up of the classical epic are caricatured within a trite plot that takes place in the contemporary world. Travesty differs from this comic variation of the *imitatio*, primarily in that it does not take up individual formal elements or plot features, but transforms a given epic subject as a whole, which it adheres to like a translation. Choosing a low or vulgar style, Lalli and his followers

were aiming not to mock the Classical work, but to create a new one, an amusing and witty variation of a known text, which in its transformation would find favour with the audience. The implied criticism is aimed rather at the implausibility of the models for a contemporary audience, and in the case of the Ovid travesty also at the tradition of allegorical elevation in mythological stories. This distancing highlighted the contrast between the original gravity of plot and characters and the everyday world in which they were placed. Heroes and gods are situated in a profane, trivial and bourgeois setting. A typical device that is used here – e.g. in P. Scarron's *Virgile travesty* (1648–52) or in L. Richer's *Ovide bouffon ou travesty* (1649) – is the mixture of high and colloquial language, of archaic, scholarly, Latinising elements with an informal to vulgar parlance. Through this the presentation of characters is often radically transformed: For example, in Scarron's version, Aeneas remains courageous and righteous, but at the same time feeble, vain and pompous. Scarron tries to find the burlesque equivalent for every grand situation of the original text. The travesty therefore presumes the reader's complete familiarity with the original. Without this knowledge, the comedy of contrast cannot be appreciated. The fact that travesty enjoyed a strong but brief fashion confirms that the genre indicates a shifting appreciation of the exemplary nature of Classical Literature. In France, most of the travesties were written around the middle of the 17th cent., in Britain between 1660 and 1680 (e.g. Ch. Cotton's *Scarronides: Or, Virgile Travestie*, 1664). Marivaux's Homer travesty (1716) or A. Blumauer's *Abenteuer des frommen Helden Äneas* (1784–1788) are rather the exceptions.

J. Emblematic Adaptation

The adaptation of Ovid's *Metamorphoses* enjoyed a certain popularity in the 16th and 17th cents. in the form of the emblem book (→ Emblems). In 1557 P. Bernard, for example, designed a *Metamorphose d'Ovide figurée*, in which the pictorial representation (*pictura*) of the most important tales and scenes of the epic are combined with a description (*subscriptio*) of that scene in an epigrammatic eight-line poem (probably from the Ovid translator B. Aneau). What differentiates this work from emblem books in the proper sense is that here, the interpretation of the mythological scene is not yet given in the *subscriptio*, whereas in later examples the tendency increases to interpret the Ovid episode allegorically as a moral exemplum (e.g. in G. Symeoni, 1559). In doing so, authors could follow either the route of humanistic tradition of interpretation, guided by moral philosophy (J. Posthius, 1563), or the Christian one (J. Spreng, Latin 1563, German 1564). The best known example of this genre is I. de Benserade's *Métamorphoses d'Ovide en rondeaux* (1676). The lyric form of the *rondeau* that Benserade chose for the *subscriptio* allows him to handle the moralising only occasionally seriously, but much more often playfully, jokingly or even ironically. Contributory to this is the fact that Benserade did not just transpose the *Metamorphoses* into emblematic form, but adapted them at the same time with the poetic means of a different popular, contemporary genre, the → FABLE, as it appears in exemplary form in the collections of J. de La Fontaine.

K. OTHER FORMS

Since the 'naturalisation' of a Classical theme in a form familiar to the public is an essential feature of every adaptation, basically no genre can be excluded as a potential target form. Thus a certain P. Galleni adapted Book 2 of the *Aeneid* into the form of a sonnet cycle. At the start of the same century, A. Metzger tailored episodes from the *Metamorphoses* into song forms of late *Meistergesang*. A Tuscan adaptor in the 18th cent. converted Ovid's epic into a cycle of novellas. However, the numerous lyrical, partial adaptations of Ovidian scenes in the Early Modern period as well as the dramatic compositions of classical themes belong in the large border area between adaptation and *imitatio*. New dramatic works using material of Classical tragedy and comedy since the Renaissance have not, as a rule, been perceived as adaptations (like the epic version of the *Aeneid* or *Metamorphoses*), but rather as original creations. On the other hand, it is clear that the earliest dramas (e.g. Angelo Poliziano's *Favola di Orfeo*, 1480) and the early libretto (e.g. *Dafne* by Ottavio Rinuccini, 1598) are basically partial adaptations of individual episodes from Ovid. Aside from the *Metamorphoses*, in the 16th and 17th cents., the dramatic adaptation of the Dido and Aeneas episode from Virgil's epic became especially popular as source material for the theatre (G.B. Giraldi 1541, L. Dolce 1547, E. Jodelle 1558, Ch. Marlowe 1580, A. Hardy 1627, G. de Scudéry 1637, Fr. de Boisrobert 1643). While Ovidian themes were chosen because of the fact that they were well-known and allowed a number of interpretations, the fourth book of the *Aeneid* provided an opportunity for developing a contemporary, hotly debated ethical-political topic: the conflict between the duty of the ruler and his passion. But here too, in addition to the question of a functionalisation of the material in the light of the perceived values of the epoch concerned, it is at the same time a matter of conforming to contemporary aesthetic principles, to the imitation of Greek or Roman tragedy in the Italian Renaissance or to the generic norms in the period of French classicism which were based on those. → COMMENTARY; → EPIC; → HUMANISM; → IMITATIO

1 G. AMIELLE, Recherches sur des traductions françaises des Métamorphoses d'Ovide, 1989   2 E. BERNSTEIN, Die erste deutsche Äneis, 1974   3 CH. BIET, Énéide triomphante, Énéide travestie, in: Europe 765/66, 1993, 130–144   4 U. BROICH, Studien zum komischen Epos, 1968 (trans. D. H. WILSON, The Eighteenth-Century Mock-Heroic Poem, 1990)   5 TH. BRÜCKNER, Die erste französische Aeneis, 1987   6 A. BUCK, M. PFISTER, Studien zu den 'volgarizzamenti' römischer Autoren in der italienischen Literatur des 13. und 14. Jahrhunderts, 1978   7 P. DEMATS, Fabula, 1973   8 F. GÖRSCHEN, Die Vergiltravestien in Frankreich, 1937   9 B. GUTHMÜLLER, Ovidio Metamorphoseos Vulgare, 1981   10 Id., Studien zur antiken Mythologie in der italienischen Renaissance, 1986   11 R. HOWELLS, Rewriting Homer in the 'Querelle des Anciens et des Modernes', in: Romance Studies 90, 1990, 35–51   12 M. HUBY, L'adaptation des Romans courtois en Allemagne au XII e et au XIII e siècle, 1968   13 A. HULUBEI, Virgile en France au XVI e siècle, in: Revue du seizième siècle 18, 1931, 1–77   14 H. LOVE, The Art of Adaptation, in: A. COLEMAN, A. HAMMOND (eds.), Poetry and Drama 1570–1700, 1981, 136–155   15 C. LUCAS, Didon. Trois réécritures tragiques du livre IV de l'Énéide dans le théâtre italien du XVI e siècle, in: G. MAZZACURATI (ed.), Scritture di scritture, 1987, 557–604   16 J. MONFRIN, Les translations vernaculaires de Virgile au Moyen Âge, in: Lectures médiévales de Virgile, 1985, 189–249   17 M. MOOG-GRÜNEWALD, Metamorphosen der *Metamorphosen*, 1979   18 F. MORA-LEBRUN, L'Énéide' médiévale et la naissance du roman, 1994   19 E. G. PARODI, I rifacimenti e le traduzioni italiane dell'Eneide di Virgilio prima del Rinascimento, in: Stud. di filologia romanza 2, 1887, 97–368   20 R. SCHEVILL, Ovid and the Renaissance in Spain, 1971   21 U. SCHÖNING, Thebenroman, Eneasroman, Trojaroman: Studien zur Rezeption der Antike in der französischen Literatur des 12. Jahrhunderts, 1991   22 J. VON STACKELBERG, Vergil, Lalli, Scarron, in: arcadia 17, 1982, 225–244

ADDITIONAL BIBLIOGRAPHY: B. J. BONO, Literary Transvaluation: From Vergilian Epic to Shakespearean Tragicomedy, 1984; R. J. CORMIER, One Heart, One Mind: The Rebirth of Virgil's Hero in Modern French Romance, 1973; C. KALLENDORF, The Aeneid Unfinished: Praise and Blame in the Speeches of Maffeo Vegio's Book XIII, in: Id., In Praise of Aeneas: Virgil and Epideictic Rhetoric in the Early Italian Renaissance, 1989, 100–128; L. PROUDFOOT, Dryden's Aeneid and Its Seventeenth-Century Predecessors, 1970; S. SHANKMAN, Pope's Iliad: Homer in the Age of Passion, 1983.

RAINER STILLERS

Advertizing

I. DEFINITION AND SYSTEMATICS II. HISTORY

I. DEFINITION AND SYSTEMATICS

Economically, advertizing denotes an instrument of a company's marketing policy; from the viewpoint of communications theory, it is a specific practice of the communicative use of signs. It has an ulterior goal, viz. to strengthen the advertized product's position in the market. In more recent times, this exclusively or predominantly heteronomous determination of advertizing has been qualified with a view to its artistic character and the aesthetic means it increasingly brings to bear (depending in each case on the underlying conception of art).

These means include the utilization of a 'very diverse' array of 'cultural elements', taken *inter alia* from Antiquity [9.88], drawn on in order to credit a given advertized product and to form a distinctive image. This adaptation may be laid out openly, but it may also be done less obviously, 'since reaching the goal of such

Fig. 1: Advertisement of the car manufacturer Citroën (from: *Der Spiegel* 15, 1960, 58)

communication', that is, successful sales, is not 'linked to the cognitive decipherment of a motif' [11.24]. What is decisive is not 'whether all who view the advertizement perceive' or 'recognize the ancient sources adapted in each case as such', since advertizing is directed 'not just to connoisseurs and experts, that is, to an audience trained in philology or art history', but to 'potential purchasers of every social origin and group affiliation' [13. 134–135]. For advertizing to be successful, it is much more critical that the 'cultural elements' [9 88] can be identified as borrowed from the world of Antiquity, and hence as 'classical'. A peculiar characteristic of the use of ancient elements in advertizing consequently consists in transforming [4] the 'classical' as a characteristic of a period, derived from a concept of style and valuation and subsequently (a-historically) attributed to the whole of Antiquity, into the 'classical' as a characteristic of quality, and attributing it [10 41] to the advertized products, 'preferably (...) luxury consumer goods and services' [11 27]. Like the ancient prop, the advertized merchandise or service is also considered to be 'classical', now in the sense of 'first class, exemplary (...), consummate, timeless' [2. 2132]. In this process, preferential use is made of mythological personages, ancient works of art and architecture, and the ideologems that come with them (for instance, norms of beauty or bodies). Thus, for instance, Myron's discuss-thrower (with the head in an altered position) vouches for an automobile and attributes 'classical harmony of mind and body, form and performance' to it; in this

way, 'the Citroen' becomes a 'car of classical beauty' (Fig. 1).

However, Antiquity becomes the object of appropriation through advertizing not only in such a substantial or material sense, as an arsenal of single parts potentially effective for advertizing, vaguely perceived and used in a historically undifferentiated way. On the contrary, in order to achieve its goal and move its recipient to buy merchandise or make use of a service, advertizing uses a theoretically well-grounded and systematically elaborated concept from Antiquity: that of → RHETORIC [12. 157, 165]. The systematic mapping of persuasive techniques by rhetoric is of special interest for the advertizing industry [3]. To be sure, 'tropes and figures are for the most part applied (...) unconsciously' [3. 73]; 'advertizing teams are by no means associations for the promotion of ancient rhetoric' [3. 73], yet in their choice of linguistic means (in the broadest sense of the term) they inevitably fall back on proven concepts that have been used in rhetorical practice since Antiquity and systematized in ancient theory. Ancient heritage finds its place in advertizing insofar as the latter is rhetorical. Since advertizing is closely connected to trade and is based on the experience of competition, it belongs, like trade, 'to the most archaic impulses of the human race' [1. vol. I.11]. But as an anthropological phenomenon, it is subject to historical modification. Looked at from a historical perspective, the extent to which it draws on an arsenal of ancient texts, images, and ideologems is subject to strong fluctuations. Decisive factors in this connection are, on the one hand, the knowledge about and status of Antiquity (for instance, as an aesthetic paradigm in the → CLASSICISM around 1800), on the other hand, the popularity of receptive processes (for instance, in the craze for allusions in Postmodernism).

→ Advertizing

1 H. BUCHLI, 6000 Jahre Werbung. Geschichte der Wirtschafts-Werbung und der Propaganda, 1962–1966   2 Duden. Das große Wörterbuch der deutschen Sprache, ³1999   3 U. FÖRSTER, Moderne Werbung und antike Rhetorik, in: Sprache im technischen Zeitalter 81 (1982), 59–73   4 M. FUHRMANN, Klassik in der Antike, in: H.-J. SIMM (ed.), Literarische Klassik, 1988, 101–119   5 H. KIMPEL, Von der Ware zum Kunstwerk. Das imaginäre Museum der Werbung, in: U. GEESE, H. KIMPEL (eds.), Kunst im Rahmen der Werbung, 1982, 43–57   6 R. KLOEPFER, H. LANDBECK, Ästhetik der Werbung, Der Fernsehspot in Europa als Symptom neuer Macht, 1991   7 M. SCHIRNER, Werbung und Geschichte, in: K. FÜSSMANN et al. (eds.), Historische Faszination. Geschichtskultur heute, 1994, 267–281   8 C. SCHMIEDKE-RINDT, Eine verhängnisvolle Affäre, Körpersprachliche Strategien im Reich der Wünsche, in: H. A. HARTMANN, R. HAUBL (eds.), Bilderflut und Sprachmagie, Fallstudien zur Kultur der Werbung 1992, 174–189   9 S. J. SCHMIDT, B. SPIESS, Die Geburt der schönen Bilder, Fernseh-Werbung aus der Sicht der Kreativen, 1994   10 U. SCHNEIDER-ABEL, Von der Klassik zum 'Klassischen. Herrenhemd', Antike in der Werbung, in: Journal für Geschichte 1 (1979), Heft 3, 41–46   11 M. SEIDENSTICKER, Werbung mit Geschichte,

Ästhetik und Rhetorik des Historischen, 1995　12 G.
UEDING, B. STEINBRINK, Grundriß der Rhetorik,
Geschichte, Technik, Methode, ²1986　13 J. ZÄNKER,
Amor & Psyche, Werbung, Mythos und Kunst, in: H. A.
HARTMANN, R. HAUBL (eds.), Bilderflut und Sprachma-
gie, Fallstudien zur Kultur der Werbung, 1992, 122–139.
VOLKER MERGENTHALER

II. History
A. Introduction B. From the End of the 19th to the First Half of the 20th Cent. C. Contemporary Advertizing D. Summary

A. Introduction

Advertizing is omnipresent: in posters, newspapers, journals, radio, television commercials, movies, internet, illuminated signs, display windows, packing material for consumer goods, marketing for events, advertizing vehicles and models, etc. For German-speaking regions, despite the increasing importance of electronic media, poster and newspaper advertizing are considered the best yardsticks of advertizing activity because of their large number of recipients.

Advertizing is a medium of information whose main task is the attractive display and sale of products. It must attract the attention of consumers and at the same time awaken in them needs which the product being offered promises to satisfy. Successful advertizing does the work of psychological persuasion and influences behaviour [49]. In light of its varied content (advertizing for products, for services, for firms, financial advertizing, non-commercial advertizing, etc.), and the inexhaustible possibilities of the world of advertizing, advertizing which makes use of Antiquity appears relatively seldom. Nevertheless, the direct or indirect use of archaeological objects and other Latin or Greek quotations indicates that Antiquity offers society as a whole a current and universal field of reference even outside of learned discourse.

Advertizing existed in Antiquity as well. Entrepreneurs announced their goods and services on shop signs [38; 46]. Drinking cups of terra sigillata from the Imperial Period were provided with their manufacturer's stamp in a clearly visible spot on the vessel [52], and were thereby designated as 'brand-name wares'.

B. From the End of the 19th to the First Half of the 20th Cent.

The medium of advertizing arose in the 19th cent. [37; 40] as a result of the interplay of social transformations (the collapse of the guilds, the introduction of free trade, the separation of producers and consumers, and rise of big-city culture) and technical achievements (use of machines, mass production of consumer goods, industrialization). Whereas in the first half of the 19th cent., advertizing was limited to ads in books, pictorial advertizements and posters came to the fore in German-speaking areas in the 2nd half of the 19th cent. In printing and reproduction technology, the foundations

which made possible the production of large numbers of color posters at an affordable price were laid by Alois Senefelder's *Lehrbuch der Steindruckerei* (Textbook of Lithography), published in 1818, and G. Engelmann's application for a patent on chromolithography in 1837. In 1855 in Berlin, Ernst Litfass introduced the columns which were named after him as bearers of advertizing, at the same time ensuring for himself a monopolistic concession on city billposting [54].

Commercial artists and lithographers worked alongside plastic artists in this new trade. Early advertising, both that designed for artistic interests and that designed for commercial purposes, was characterized by a harmonic-aesthetic tenor. Allegories and ideal figures, which the educated bourgeois deciphered on the basis of his knowledge, were highly popular as means of artistic expression. For instance, many companies advertised by personifying their hometown, represented as a woman with a mural crown after the manner of Roman personifications of cities: in 1883, 'Vienna' advertised for a play; from 1885 the Cologne-based company 4711 introduced a 'Colonia', and in 1893 a 'Stuttgart' appeared as the main figure in a poster for the municipal tourist organization [5; 9; 40] (Fig. 1). Contemporary content was clothed in ancient mythology. In taking over the characteristic tokens of the ancient gods, however, pictorial language corresponded completely to contemporary forms of expression. The gods were represented in restful, majestic posture. Athena was quite popular. [6. 144–145, catalogue no. 213, color pl. 20; 40]. On a poster by Ludwig von Hofmann from 1893, Ganymede, the incarnation of beauty, feeds Zeus' eagle [3. Fig. 202; 5. 140–141, catalogue no. 209, color pl. 17], in a metaphor for the relationship between art and the state. In an ad for Odol mouthwash from 1906 [13], the onlooker's gaze is directed to some ruins of a make-believe amphitheater, in the arena of which the company's name is indelibly inscribed in large stone blocks. For a beauty-product advertisement from 1919 [11], an independent domestic scene was invented, borrowing from the pictorial language of Attic vase-painting. The beauty products, which are not depicted, are described by a great deal of explanatory text. The vase-painting scheme serves to create an ideal world. In an ad for 'Triumph' beer from around 1904 [4], a triumphant Emperor is depicted on his quadriga, a concept probably most closely connected with relief sculpture on Imperial monumental arches like the Arch of Titus at Rome, the Arch of Trajan at Beneventum, or the Arch of Septimius Severus at Leptis Magna. Ads for Audi from 1909/1912 show the company founder August Horch in front of his car with his hand cupped at his ear in the gesture of 'listening or hearing', for the Latin word *audi* [8. Fig. 92].

From 1905 on, the object poster, with its representation of the product, began to be commonplace. Object posters were often enriched by citations from Antiquity, whose task was to illustrate the ideal conception of the product. Thus, in an automobile ad from 1928, a miniature car, with a driver and with two ladies in flounced dresses has been added to Myron's Discus-thrower at thigh-height [8. Abb. 109]. By the position of his head and hand, the Discus-thrower appears to support the car, which, to judge by the speed-lines accompanying it, is racing by. In place of the discus is the laurel-crowned Fiat label. In an ad for Opel from 1932, an illustration of the car is complemented by a drawing of the → BELVEDERE APOLLO [3]. Original photos of famous statues were never used as models in early advertising

In its quest for objectivity the Bauhaus devoted considerable attention to graphics and text. An advertising flyer by Herbert Bayer (1900–1985) for Dessau has a graphic representation of a columns express the city's ancient character and that of a glistening machine part its new [2]. The reception of Antiquity in the advertizing of the 1930s was characterized by the graphical abstraction and distancing of ancient architecture, ancient models, and forms [10; 14; 12; 51].

C. CONTEMPORARY ADVERTIZING

20th cent. marketing [49] works essentially with three methods: 1) an appeal to the emotions (success, freedom, friendship, love, sex, security, happiness, interest, independence, safety, anxiety, etc.) and offering a 'total' lifestyle or artwork concept; 2) intellectual mechanisms (surprise, novelty, intellectual conflict and contradiction). Difficult presentations must first be decoded by the recipient and thereby convey to him the experience of 'I have grasped what was to be said to me and only me' [57. 211]; 3) physical and optical attractions (color, variegation, size, contrast). According to the branch of communication science which concerns itself with 'imagery' [47], images are easier to memorize the more concrete, the more characteristic, and the larger they are. Representations of people and images that trigger personal feelings and associations are also effective. Positive concepts meet with greater success. Images are the quickest transmitters. The time an ad in a magazine is looked at is generally less than two seconds, which is enough for reception and processing. In advertizing in general, pictures, and hence representations of antiquities, are not an end in themselves, but are displayed by means of modifications and citations as well as being controlled by linguistic means, to achieve their goal.

In an ad for the financial advising company Ptech [2] the computer model of a skyscraper bearing an integrated, coloured structural diagram which displays the essential points of corporate strategy is set against a retouched detail of the decaying → PARTHENON; thus, classical Antiquity is set up as a world of contrast to the present. The old has been rendered distant and obsolete, but nevertheless represents a foundation. The same principle underlies the contrast between a cave-painting and an automobile in an ad for Audi [23], and a Xerox ad with a painted clay pot and scrolls [17], which strongly emphasizes the contrast of the old with the new

technologies offered by the company. Le Corbusier, in his essay *Des yeux qui ne voient pas: les automobiles* (1920) had already contrasted automobiles with a temple from Paestum and the Parthenon [50] in order to show the aesthetic kinship between the world of machines and Classical Greek architecture (→ PAESTUM, FIG. 6).

By inserting traffic lights, a collection of antiquities is represented as an environment in which people drive around in Lexus automobiles [26]. A seminar on business technology in Israel with the title 'Mosaic' [15] makes an argument for the advantages of a site rich in tradition. Syria, Lebanon, and Israel are well known by many for their Imperial-era mosaic finds which can therefore embody the cultural tradition of those countries. To bridge the gap to the present, a computer mouse looking as if it were made of mosaic pebbles in the style of an ancient mosaic was added to the picture. In an ad for Condor airlines [29], three runners are placed as black silhouettes against a yellow background. Unusually, they communicate by means of balloons, as in → COMICS. The figures themselves were copied from a black-figured vase-painting from an Attic prize amphora [36]: they evoke the association of speed and culture. The speed with which design in advertizing can be quickly rededicated to new ends is illustrated by a poster of the city of Frankfurt for an Aids benefit run from 2000 (Fig. 2). This time, the same three runners are depicted as blue silhouettes on a red background. Moreover, for reasons of gender equality, the central male figure has, through the hint of a breast and the addition of a hair braid, been transformed into a woman. An unusual example of the transformation of an ancient image is offered by an ad for British Airways [28]: a seated man designated by an inscription on his sedan chair as 'Chairman' is contrasted with a sleeping 'Wise man' sprawled under a canopy. In Antiquity, rest positions and sedan chairs are indeed signs of comfort, but this iconography is always found in a sepulchral context [45].

With its illustration from the equestrian statue of Marcus Aurelius from the Capitol at Rome (→ EQUESTRIAN STATUES) [31], the international credit institution Morgan Stanley Dean Witter & Co. seeks to transfer the Roman emperor's strength along with his philosophical insight and his leading position to the corporation. The newspaper *Frankfurter Allgemeine Zeitung* surprises its readers with a picture running over two pages of the monumental pillars of the Temple of Apollo at → DELPHI [19]. Here, the shrine's significance as an oracle and site of wisdom is transferred to the newspaper. The architectural designers M. Thun and Th. Schriefers, according to their own statement, intentionally chose classical architecture for their advertizing collages in the 1990s, for instance the Athenian acropolis, in order to position their 'product as an exclusive', top-quality product and to achieve the association of 'classical, exemplary, solid and high-quality' [7]. The Hellenistic statue of the → VENUS OF MILO,

Fig. 2: R. Nachbauer, Stuttgart (Germany), Tourist Office, before 1893. Chromeolithography, 86×62 cm. Early poster advertisements from the 2nd half of the 19th cent. featured allegories of ancient gods represented in contemporary forms.

discovered in 1820 and found today in the Louvre, which already inspired Prosper Mérimée (1803–1870) for his novella *The Venus of Ille* (1837) [41], and was reified, modified and ironized by Salvador Dali by the addition of drawers in 1934 [35], stands in advertizing for 'Greece, vacations, independence' (Fig. 3), for 'tradition and culture', and for 'erotic women' [27; 30; 34].

In an advertizing campaign launched several times since the late 1990s by Radio Ö1–Club of the ORF [16], the head of Lysippus' Apoxyomenos becomes the ideal listener (Fig. 4). The typical seams that arise in the process of plaster molding are clearly visible. The use of plaster and trivial copies in the ad is explained by its easy availability. Many large antiquities museums (Munich, Berlin, Basel, etc.) have set up workshops specializing in the exact reproduction of works of art, which are sold, and not only to specialized institutions, as → cast collections. Plaster casts of ancient works are also used in 20th cent. art [44; 56; 42. 238–239]. Advertizing and art tend towards use of classical and classicistic models of time-tested and aesthetically appealing objects, first and foremost statues. Art is much sooner open to experimentation like multiplication, alignment

in rows, insertion within spatial relations, addition of foreign materials, colouring, disguise, negation, and dissociation. Whereas in the art of the 20th cent. the goal is the dissolution of all original content and all historical significance, Antiquity functions in advertizing in a precisely converse way: as a classical ideal, incorporating timeless values.

Brand names have been and still are an essential component of advertizing. They provide key information and indicate quality. Since the beginnings of the advertizing business, unusual names have been preferred, often taken from Greek or Latin sources [48]: 1. Names of ancient gods and persons: Artemis (publishing), Diogenes (publishing), Clio (an automobile), Penaten (a cream), Nike (sporting apparel), Merkur (insurance, supermarket). 2. Speaking names: Audi ('Listen!', 1st half of the 20th cent.), Volvo ('I roll', 1927). 3. Word formations from meaningful Latin and Greek words or elements, including phantasy constructions: a hair-loss remedy in H. Balzac's *Histoire de la grandeur et de la décadence de César Birotteau* (1838) is called Kephalol; Alete, Kaloderma (as early as 1857), Nivea (the beauty ideal of 'snow-white'), Xerox (from xerography, ξερος/

xéros, dry, and γράφειν/ *gráphein*, to write, plus -ox as an exotic and symmetrical final syllable. 4. General prestige words denoting superiority, value and classicism. Their abstract character makes them, in part, applicable to very different products: 'Triumph' (beer, clothing), 'Olympia' (typewriters), 'Omega' (watches).

On a linguistic level, short and succinct slogans, easy to remember in daily life are effective. In accordance with this principle, Greek and Latin citations are also limited to → DICTA. The Horatian saying *Carpe diem* (Horace, Odes 1, 11) is used by an airline [18] and the eco-friendly cardboard packaging of a collection of scarves and cloths [1]. The words 'I came, I saw, I conquered', which according to Plutarch (Caes. 50,3), Caesar uttered to characterize his lightning-like victory in the battle of Zela, is used among others by the credit-card company Visa ('veni vidi visa') [21. 22]. An ad in the newspaper Gewinn *Win* for the winners of a competition chose as its title 'the die is cast' [20]. This expression, also known as *alea iacta est*, was, according to Plutarch, again uttered by Caesar when he quoted the Greek proverb κύβος ἀνερρίφθω/ *kýbos anerríphthō* ('let the die be cast'), alluding to the risk of an uncertain outcome. *Alea iacta est* also appears as the motto of the strategic approach of the German software company Veritas [29]. The Raiffeisen Bank, which always has a solution ready for its clients' problems, advertizes by using the 'Gordian knot', here simply a very tightly knotted rope before a neutral green background [33].

D. SUMMARY

The following points in approaches to Antiquity can be noted: 1. The advertizing of both the 19th and 20th cents. uses, among other things, very well-known monuments which already have a lengthy history of reception. 2. Complete sculptures with their own aesthetic value are preferred. 3. Brand names are formed from Greek or Roman components. 4. The use of the Greek and Latin language, as well as of antiquarian or historical themes, is restricted to proverb-style quotations. 5. For the most part, highly valued, rather expensive goods and services like automobiles, airlines and air-travel vacations, banks, software, and computers are advertized: less often is it products of daily need. 6. In the 19th cent., advertized products are represented by allegory. 7. Ancient objects are valued for their age, their dignity, their character as ruins, and their value as art. The aura of the remote and the exotic is attributed to them, and so they function either as the foundation for modern times or else as a contrast to the present. A classicism is cultivated in advertizing, which sees ethical and aesthetic standards, an ideal, grandeur, wisdom, culture, quality, and high social prestige embodied in Antiquity. 8. Content-value is attributed to sculptures: the Venus of Milo stands for a woman's beauty and sexuality, the Belvedere Apollo for the ideal male, Myron's Disk-thrower for concentrated strength. In all these cases, the ancient object is positioned as possessing prototype status and spiritual supremacy. 9. With

no basis in reality, products are upgraded and deliberately mystified by association with Antiquity. The feeling of 'uniqueness' is transmitted by means of a dictionary-style treatment of 'rara avis' [24] and the appeal to a Latin technical term. 10. Ancient works are retouched by use of omission or addition, reproduced as details, as drawings or graphics, and combined with modern elements.

SOURCES: 1 W. K. ALBRECHT-SCHOECK, Verpackung, Design, Umwelt, 1993, 85–88 2 U. BRÜNING (ed.), Das A und O des Bauhauses, 1995, 218–219 3 Deutsche Historisches Museum (ed.), Kunst Kommerz Visionen, 1992, 192 4 G. DIETRICH (ed.), Litfass Bier, 1998, Abb. (Fig.) 176 5 E. KOLL, Article on catalogue no. 49, in: B. DENSCHER (ed.), Tagebuch der Straße. Wiener Plakate (Exhibition catalogue), Vienna 1981 6 C. KORTE, Das wechselvolle Bild der Antike in der Berliner Malerei und Graphik von Adolph Menzel bis zur Gegenwart, in: W. ARENHÖVEL (ed.), Berlin und die Antike (Exhibition catalogue I), Berlin 1979, 132–150 7 E. KÜTHE, M. THUN, Marketing mit Bildern, 1995, 87, 147, 170 8 H. RIMMLER, Die Imagebildung des Automobils im Plakat 1900–1930, 1991, Ill. 92, 109 9 W. SCHÄFKE (ed.), Oh! De Cologne. Die Geschichte des Kölnisch Wasser, 1985, 70–71 10 P. SPARKE, Italienisches Design. Von 1870 bis heute, 1988, 73 11 U. THOMS, Dünn und dick, schön und häßlich. Schönheitsideal und Körpersilhouette in der Werbung, 1850–1950, in: P. BORSCHEID, C. WISCHERMANN (eds.), Bilderwelt des Alltags, 1995, 245–247, Ill. 2 12 A. WEILL, Plakatkunst International, 1985, Ill. 408, 414 13 M. WEISSER, Deutsche Reklame. 100 Jahre Werbung. 1870–1970, 1985, 165, 173 14 H. WICHMANN, Design contra Art Déco (1927–1930), 1993, 158, 162

EXAMPLES OF ADVERTIZING FROM MAGAZINES: 15 CT Magazin für Computertechnik 18, 2000, 75 16 Das Österreich1 Magazin 18, Juni 1997 (title page) 17 Der Spiegel 20, 1999, 321 18 Der Spiegel 36, 1999, 51 19 Der Spiegel 41, 2000, 44–45 20 Gewinn 2, 1995, 32 21 Gewinn 2, 1995, 167 22 Gewinn 10, 1998, 181 23 Gewinn 2, 1999, 25 24 Harvard Business Review. 3–4, 1999, 169 25 Harvard Business Review. 1–2, 2000, 78 26 Harvard Business Review. 1–2, 2000, 102 27 PSK Sportmagazin Sonderheft 9a, Okt. 1998, 9 28 Profil 31, 2000, 175 29 Stern 53, 22.12.1998, 10 30 The Economist, March 11–17, 2000, 4 31 The Economist, July 8–14, 2000, 79 32 The Economist Sept. 2–8, 2000, 71 33 Trend 7–8, 1999, 51 34 Wirtschaftswoche 37, 1999, 38

LITERATURE: 35 A. BAMMER, Antike- Moderne – Postmoderne, in: JÖAI 59, 1989, 101–109, Ill. 3 36 M. BENTZ, Panathenäische Preisamphoren. Eine athenische Vasengattung und ihre Funktion vom 6.–4. Jh. v. Chr., (= Antike Kunst 18. Beiheft), 1998, Nr. 5.184, Fig. 82 37 S. BRUNE-BERNS, Im Lichte der Großstadt – Werbung als Signum einer urbanen Welt, in: P. BORSCHEID, C. WISCHERMANN (eds.), Bilderwelt des Alltags, 1995, 90–115 38 M. DONDERER, Weder Votiv- noch Grabrelief, sondern Werbeschild eines Steinmetzmeisters, in: Epigraphica 56, 1994, 41–52; 39 B. DOERING, Die Avantgarde und das Plakat. Künstlerplakate vom Historismus zum Bauhaus, 1998 40 C. FRIESE, Plakatkunst 1880–1935, 1994 41 G. GRIMM, Prosper Mérimées tödliche Frauen oder 'Die Venus von Ille' und ihr Vorbild aus Melos, in: Antike Welt 6, 1999, 577–586 42 N. HIMMELMANN,

Minima Archaeologica, 1996   43 I. JENSEN, Archäologie und Computer- Werbung, in: R. STUPPERICH (ed.), Lebendige Antike, Rezeptionen der Antike in Politik, Kunst und Wissenschaft der Neuzeit, Kolloquium für Werbung, Schiering, 1995, 213–220   44 B. JUSSEN (ed.), Archäologie zwischen Imagination und Wissenschaft: Anne und Patrick Poirier, 1999   45 D. E. E KLEINER, Roman Sculpture, 1992, Ill. 61, Ill. 88–89   46 P. KRUSCHWITZ, Römische Werbeinschriften, in: Gymnasium 106, 1999, 231–253   47 W. KROEBER-RIEL, Bildkommunikation. Imagerystrategien für die Werbung, 1996   48 A. LÖTSCHER, Von Ajax bis Xerox, Ein Lexikon der Produktenamen, ²1992   49 G. MEYER-HENTSCHEL, Alles was Sie schon immer über Werbung wissen wollten, 1996   50 S. v. MOOS, Industrieästhetik, in: Ars Helvetica 11, 1992, 198–199, ill. 199   51 Nützliche Moderne. Graphik und Produkt-Design in Deutschland 1935–1955, ed. by J. KRAUSE (Exhibition catalogue), Münster 2000, 38–72   52 H. OTTOMEYER, Garantiert Qualität, in: S. BÄUMLER (ed.), Die Kunst zu werben, 1996, 16–18   53 J. PICKRUN, U. SCHÄDLER, Antike Motive in der Frankfurter Werbung gestern und heute, in: M. HERFORT-KOCH, U. MANDEL, U. SCHÄDLER (eds.), Begegnungen. Frankfurt und die Antike, 1994, 483–491, 569–570   54 D. REINHARDT, Vom Intelligenzblatt zum Satellitenfernsehen. Stufen der Werbung als Stufen der Geschichte, in: P. BORSCHEID, C. WISCHERMANN (eds.), Bilderwelt des Alltags, 1995, 44–63   55 Schweizerisches Landesmuseum (ed.), Recycling der Vergangenheit. Die Antike und das heutige Marketing (Exhibition catalogue), Lausanne-Vidy 1997   56 M. UNTERDÖRFER, Die Rezeption der Antike in der Postmoderne: der Gipsabguß in der italienischen Kunst der siebziger und achtziger Jahrhundert, 1998   57 D. URBAN, Kauf mich! Visuelle Rhetorik in der Werbung, 1995.

EVA CHRISTOF

Aegina

A. SANCTUARY OF APOLLO   B. SANCTUARY OF APHAEA   C. OROS AND OTHER ARCHAEOLOGICAL SITES   D. MUSEUMS   E. HISTORY OF RECEPTION

A. SANCTUARY OF APOLLO

(Fig.1,1) Since the end of the 17th cent. travel accounts have mentioned temple remains on the island of Aegina (A.). The first investigations in Colonna took place in 1811 after the excavations at the site of the Sanctuary of Aphaea. These were discontinued after three days by C.R. Cockerell since the hoped-for sculptural finds failed to appear. In 1829 the temple foundations were, for the most part, removed for the construction of the port. This state of affairs was shown by the survey of the Expédition de Morée [55. 12–17]. A. Furtwängler and G. Loeschcke conducted small excavations in 1878, and V. Stais in 1894 [6. 41; 29; 36]. In 1904, A.D. Keramopoullos exposed parts of the nearby Mycenean necropolis on the Hill of Windmills where the A. Treasure, subsequently bought by the British Museum, was found in 1891. With the exception of W. Kraiker's outline of geometric and archaic pottery and several preliminary reports [20; 40–48; 50], the extensive excavations of the sanctuary by A. Furtwängler (1903–1907), P. Wolters and G. Welter (1924–1941) remain unpublished. Furtwängler's hopes to make simi-

larly rich finds as at the Sanctuary of Aphaea, were not fulfilled. The settlement in late antiquity as well as the scavenging of stone in both ancient and later times is mainly responsible for this. [50. 2; 54; 55. 78]. The only significant sculpture found is the statue of a sphinx from the early 5th cent. BC, a bronze replica of which adorns Furtwängler's grave in Athens [39. 80 Nr. 52; 50. 2]. Furtwängler focused on topographical questions involving interpretations of Pausanias which set the tone for the subsequent excavations of Wolters and Welter in 1924. These led to the renaming of the sanctuary, then known as the Sanctuary of Aphrodite, as the Sanctuary of Apollo, a name that still stands today. Moreover preliminary excavations were also carried out on the long-inhabited prehistoric settlement and fortifications which, after the resumption of excavations in 1966 by H. Walter, were almost completely uncovered [38]. In the course of these a shaft grave dating to the middle Bronze Age was discovered [18]. Since 1974 the structural survey of the late archaic Temple of Apollo [55] has been published and a gradual reconsideration of the older finds has taken place[13–14; 18; 38; 51; 54–56]. Since 1993 excavations in the sanctuary have been continued by F. Felten and S. Hiller [5].

B. SANCTUARY OF APHAEA

(Fig. 1,2) The temple is first mentioned in 1675 by J. Spon and G. Wheler. The first investigation of the site, which had been plundered by metal treasure hunters, was undertaken in 1765 by the → SOCIETY OF DILETTANTI. Further excavations followed in 1804 (M. Leake) and 1805 (E. Dodwell). In 1811 Cockerell, C. Haller v. Hallerstein, J. Linckh and J. Foster discovered the famous pedimental statues. In the wake of this, many scholarly treatises were published about the temple, most of which identified the site with Zeus Panhellenios or Athena. [7. 10–21; 35. 163–165; 52. 47–62]. In 1894 Stais excavated around the east terrace wall and found several fragments of sculpture. The unsatisfactory inventory and restoration as well as the hope of finding further sculpture fragments led Furtwängler to start up excavations again in 1901. In the process, the temenos and the late archaic structure, south and west of the sanctuary, were exposed, and the designation of Aphaea as the patroness of the cultic site was confirmed [7. I–IX, 1–9; 49]. The site's cultic uses must have started in the late Bronze Age [32]. The temple ruins, which were threatening to collapse, were extensively restored in the 1950s by the Greek Ministry for Monuments. Since 1962 there have been further investigations aiming at a definitive clarification of the pedimental arrangement, and since 1967 there have been further excavations by D. Ohly, the most important result of which has been the new arrangment of the pediment sculptures [26–27]. More specific dating and mythological interpretations of the *Ägineten* are still subjects of discussion [23. 244–248; 27; 35]. New excavation results have been continuously published since 1965 [1; 8; 25; 28; 34] and have replaced the old publications [7].

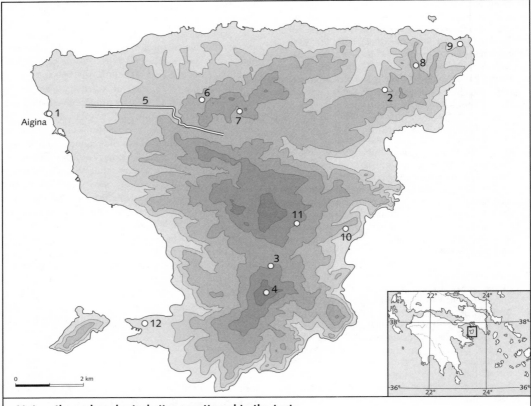

Aigina: the archaeological sites mentioned in the text

1 Sanctuary of Apollo (Cape Kolonna) and the town of Aigina. Settled since the Neolithic, fortified settlement from the early Bronze Age; sanctuary from the Protogeometric period; also: main town in antiquity, with commercial and naval ports, as well as ship sheds, theatre, stadium, city fortifications and graves from Mycenaean to Hellenistic times; synagogue and early Christian churches.

2 Aphaea Sanctuary. Sanctuary in the Late Mycenaean and again from Geometric period.

3 Sanctuary of Zeus Hellanios at the foot of the Oros, from Archaic period.

4 Oros: Bronze Age peak settlement and sanctuary in Late Mycenaean and again from Geometric period.

5 Water pipe

6 Dragunera: 'minor sanctuary' (Geometric?)

7 Palaeochora: the ancient Oie (?), main town of Aigina in Byzantine and medieval times.

8 Tripiti: small sanctuary and settlement of the Classical and Hellenistic periods

9 Pyrgazi: Archaic (?) and Classical (?) settlements

10 Kilindra: Mycenaean graves

11 Lazarides: Mycenaean settlement and graves

12 Perdika: Mycenaean graves

Altitute (in metres)

0   50   100   200   300   400

C. Oros and Other Archaeological Sites

(Fig.1, 3–4) The highest mountain on A. is often mentioned in travel writings of the 19th cent. The first survey of remains was carried out by the Expédition de Morée in 1829, followed by the first excavations of Stais in 1894. The brief excavations by Furtwängler (1905, 1907) and Welters (1933) have never been fully published [45. 91–92; 46. 8–14]. They confirm, however, the localisation of the Sanctuary of Zeus Hellanios at Oros [33] contrary to the commonly held view, which sited the Sanctuary of Aphaea here on the terraced area at the foot of Oros. Furtwängler's and Welter's dating and reconstruction have been confirmed since 1995 by surveys [15] and since 1996 by secondary excavations carried out by H.R. Goette. The excavations of Furtwängler and Welter on the summit (Illustration 1,4) likewise remain almost completely unpublished. A middle Bronze Age settlement and a Mycenean sanctuary are likely [7. 473–474; 31; 33; 41. 187; 45. 26; 46. 14–16]. Since geometric times, the Summit Sanctuary of Zeus-Hellanios-in addition to an altar [33; 46. 14–16]-was provided with a roofed cultic structure possibly fromaround 500 BC [15]. Apart from the two large excavation sites of Aphaea and Colonna and the mountain of Oros, a topographical survey and preliminary digs have been carried out at many sites on the island (Illustration 1): the town of A. with its harbour, synagogue and early Christian churches (1) [19], the aqueduct (5), the so-called small sanctuary in Dragunera (6), Palaeochora (7), Tripiti (8), Pyrgazi (9), Kilindra (10). The results of these were to appear in volumes of the series started by Furtwängler (Vol. 1: Aphaea [7]), but they were never published. Additional sites from Antiquity are marked on the map by H. Thiersch [7]. New unmarked finds include A. Town (1) [30], Lazarides (11) [4] and Perdika (12) [10. 26].

D. Museums

The institution of a national museum was part of the self image of the newly founded Greek state. Between 1829 and 1832 it was in A., the first Greek capital [16. 11–40]. During this period, finds from all over Greece were brought to A. Some, such as funerary steles from Greater Delos, remain in the Museum of A. Others, such as the Stele from Salamis [3. 396–398 Nr. 1550], possibly from A. originally, were transferred to Athens after 1832. In 1927, the Museum of A. was moved to the old school building by Welter [43]. The collection suffered losses in World War II, notably sculpture fragments from the Sanctuary of Aphaea [27. XII]. The new museum of A. Colonna was opened in 1981 and finds that were in the older museum have, for the most part, been transferred there. Finds from Colonna, sculpture fragments and the famous inscription from Aphaea as well as finds from other sites on the island have been displayed since the museum was re-opened in 1997. The Aphaea Museum, which includes a partial reconstruction of the older Poros Temple, was built in 1968.

E. History of Reception

The first attempts at interpretation came with the rediscovery of the Temple of Aphaea in the 19th cent. The ruins were generally identified either with the Temple of Zeus Panhellenios or Athena and together with the sculptures, linked with the Persian War. This corresponds with its interpretation as a Victory or National monument [24. 678; 35. 132, 162–165]. The pedimental statues from the temple (*Ägineten*) were bought in 1823 by the crown prince of Bavaria, later King Ludwig I, and first displayed in the workshop of M. Wagner in Rome. Between 1816 and 1818 they were restored and completed in a modern fashion by B. Thorvaldsen and staff under Wagner's supervision, something which earned praise and admiration as well as criticism. [9; 21; 27. XII; 52. 23–72]. Through the restoration, Thorvaldsen was stimulated (for his own work), e.g. the *Hoffnung* later acquired by C.v. Humboldt [2. 155; 11. 64–74; 21. 40; 27. XV]. In 1828, following Cockerell's recommendations, the *Ägineten* were grouped together in the room called the Äginetensaal in the Glyptothek, itself designed by L.v.Klenze to be a classical work of art. Although desired by Ludwig I, the exhibition was disowned by Wagner and Thorvaldsen, [52. 68–70; 53. 37–41, 98–100]. It was with the discovery of the *Ägineten*, which were up until then the first original pre-classical sculpture known, that research into archaic sculpture began. At the same time, in accordance with the *zeitgeist*, significance was attached to the *Ägineten* in terms of cultural development, Winckelmann's writings, and the already-known Elgin Marbles, although their aesthetic value was received with reserve [21. 40; 23. 10–11]. Thus Goethe's judgement inclined towards the negative (Sophienausgabe IV. 29, Nr. 8024) [9. 314; 37. 108], while K. O. Müller and – in his later works – Cockerell, too, made more positive comments about the *Ägineten* [21; 24.

677–679]. After much intense discussion, Thorvaldsen's restorative additions were removed for the new display in 1966 [9; 21; 22; 26].

→ Aegina; → Aphaea; → Apollo; → Architectural sculpture; → Dictynna; → Oros; → Water pipes; → Zeus

1 H. Bankel, Der spätarchaische Tempel der Aphaia auf Aegina, 1993   2 K. Bott, Wechselbeziehungen zwischen Thorvaldsen und seinen deutschen Auftraggebern, in: Analecta Romana Instituti Danici, Suppl. 18, 1991, 149–167   3 C. W. Clairmont, Classical Attic Tombstones. vol. I, 1993   4 K. Efstratiou, Lazarides, in: Archaiologikon Deltion 34 Chron, 1979, 70–71   5 F. Felten, S. Hiller, Ausgrabungen in der vorgeschichtlichen Innenstadt von Ägina-Kolonna (Alt-Ägina), in: Österreichische Jahreshefte 65, 1996 Beiblatt, 29–112   6 A. Furtwängler, G. Loeschcke, Mykenische Vasen, Berlin 1886, 41   7 A. Furtwängler, Aegina. Das Heiligtum der Aphaia, 1906   8 G. Gruben, Die Sphinx-Säule von Aegina, in: MDAI(A) 80, 1965, 170–208   9 C. Grundwald, Zu den Ägineten-Ergänzungen Bertel Thorvaldsens, in: Bertel Thorvaldsen. Untersuchungen zu seinem Werk, 1977, 305–341   10 J. P. Harland, Prehistoric Aegina., 1925   11 J. B. Hartmann, Antike Motive bei Thorvaldsen, 1979.   12 R. Higgins, The Aegina Treasure, 1979   13 K. Hoffelner, Ein Scheibenakroter aus dem Apollon-Heiligtum von Ägina, in: MDAI(A) 105, 1990, 153–162   14 Id., Die Dachterrakotten des Artemistempels vom Apollon-Heiligtum in Ägina, in: Hesperia Suppl. 27, 1994, 99–112   15 Jahresbericht des DAI 1995 s.v. Ägina, in: AA 1996, 582–583   16 P. Kavvadias, Glypta tou Ethnikou Mouseiou, 1890–92   17 A. D. Keramopoullos, Mykenaikoi taphoi en Aigine kai en Thebais, in: Archaiologike Ephemeris 1910, 177–208   18 I. Kilian-Dirlmeier, Alt-Ägina IV. 3, 1997   19 P. Knoblauch, Die Hafenanlagen der Stadt Ägina, in: Archaiologikon Deltion 27 Mel, 1972, 50–85   20 W. Kraiker, Aigina Die Vasen des 10.–7. Jahrhunderts, 1951.   21 L. O. Larsson, Thorvaldsens Restaurierung der Ägineten-Skulpturen, in: Konsthistorik Tidskrift 38, 1969, 23–46   22 M. Maass, Nachträgliche Überlegungen zur Restaurierung der Ägineten, in: MDAI(A) 99, 1984, 165–176   23 W. Martini, Die archaische. Plastik der Griechen, 1990   24 K. O. Müller, Kleine deutsche Schriften, vol. 2, Breslau 1848   25 Aegina, Aphaia-Tempel Iff., in: AA 1970ff.   26 D. Ohly, Die Neuaufstellung der Ägineten, in: AA 1966, 515–528   27 id., Die Aegineten, 1976   28 id., Tempel und Heiligtum der Aphaia auf Ägina, ⁴1985   29 L. Pallat, Ein Vasenfund aus Aegina, in: MDAI(A) 22, 1897, 265–333   30 E. Papastavrou, Synolo omadikon taphon sten A., in: Archaiologike Ephemeris 1986, 49–59   31 K. Pilafidis-Williams, The Sanctuary of Aphaia on Aigina in the Bronze Age, 1998   32 Id., A Mycenaean Terracotta Figurine from Mount Oros on Aegina, in: BICS Suppl. 63, 1995, 229–234   33 J. Schmidt, s.v. Oros, RE 18, 1175–1177   34 E. L. Schwandner, Der ältere Poros-Tempel der Aphaia auf Aegina, 1985   35 U. Sinn, Aphaia und die 'Aegineten'. Zur Rolle des Aphaiaheiligtums im religiösen und gesellschaftlichen Leben der Insel Aigina, in: MDAI(A) 102, 1987, 131–167   36 V. Stais, Proistorikoi synoikismoi en Attike kai Aigine, in: Archaiologike Ephemeris 1895, 235–264   37 H.v. Einem, Goethe-Studien, 1972   38 H. Walter, F. Felten, Alt-Ägina III. 1, 1981   39 E. Walter-Karydi, Alt-Ägina II. 1, 1987   40 G. Welter, Archaische Funde aus den Jahren 1923/24, Griechenland, in: AA 40, 1925, 317–321   41 Id., Ausgrabungen in

Ägina, in: Gnomon 5, 1929, 185–186, 415   42 Id., in: G.
KARO, Archaische Funde vom Sommer 1931 bis Mai
1932. Griechenland und Dodekanes, AA 1932, 162–165
43 Id., Ek tou Mouseiou Aigines, 1937   44 Id., Aigineti-
sche Keramik, in: AA 1937, 19–26   45 Id., Aigina, 1938
46 Id., Aeginetica I–XXIV, in: AA 1938, 13–24, 480–540
47 Id., Aeginetica XXV–XXXVI, in: AA 69, 1954, 28–48
48 Id., Aigina, 1962   49 D. WILLIAMS, Aegina, Aphaia-
Tempel IV, in: AA 1982, 55–68   50 P. WOLTERS, Forschungen auf Aigina, in: AA 40, 1925, 1–12   51 R. WÜN-
SCHE, Studien zur äginetischen Keramik der frühen und
mittleren Bronzezeit, 1977   52 Id., Ludwigs Skulpturen-
erwerbungen für die Glyptothek, in: Glyptothek München 1830–1980, 1980, 23–83   53 Id., 'Göttliche, paßli-
che, wünschenswerte und erforderliche Antiken'. Leo von
Klenze und die Antikenerwerbungen Ludwigs I., in: Ein
griechischer Traum. Leo von Klenze, 1986, 9–115
54 W. W. WURSTER, F. FELTEN, Alt-Ägina I.2, 1975
55 W. W. WURSTER, Alt-Ägina I.1, 1974   56 Reihe Alt-
Ägina I.1ff., 1974ff.
URL: http://www.dainst.org/index_536_en.html

WALTER GAUSS

Aequitas
A. THE CONCEPT   B. ANCIENT ROOTS
C. RECEPTION IN THE MIDDLE AGES   D. FURTHER
DEVELOPMENTS IN THE MODERN ERA

A. THE CONCEPT
Since the late Middle Ages, the legal concept of
aequitas has been translated by equity, although a differentiation was made between the two terms, particularly in the 19th cent.

Equity can best be described as a source of law,
which claims validity in addition to the positive legal
system and helps to decide individual cases. Martinus
Gosia (*around 1100), for instance, designated equity
as *fons et origo iustitiae* ('source and origin of justice').
As a particular manifestation of → justice, equity is
both a means of interpreting positive laws and a complementary legal norm for correcting legal resolutions
that appear to be unjust in individual cases, as well as
for filling lacunas. Since the beginning of European jurisprudence in the Middle Ages, it has taken its place
among the central institutions of law. It was mainly
developed in civil law and in canon law, and later was
also used in criminal and public law.

B. ANCIENT ROOTS
The doctrine of *equity* in post-Antiquity is a continuing development of three ancient elements: Aristotelian
epieíkeia ('propriety'), Roman legal *equity* and their
elaboration by the Church Fathers.

The concept of *epieíkeia* as developed by Aristotle
(Eth. Nic. 5,14, 1137a–1138a; Rhet. 1,13, 1373b–
1374b) means a justice higher than that of positive
laws. In Aristotle, *aequitas* means that one must not
stick to the letter of the text in the interpretation of the
law, but rather pay attention to its meaning. Owing to
unforeseen circumstances, abstract laws can be unjust
in an individual case. *Epieíkeia* then enables a mitiga-

tion or even a deviation from the law, in favor of single
case justice. Thus, what is at stake here is the adaptation
of general norms to the particular, factual circumstances of the case, according to the spirit of the legislator.

In ancient Roman law, *aequitas* denoted the ethical
requirements for the law, for instance in the definition
of law as *ars aequi et boni* (Celsus, Dig. 1,1,1 pr.). First
and foremost, *aequitas* meant equality of service and
service in return, in other words, the exchange of justice. In the post-Classical era, equity was a criterion for
the action of legislators and judges. Under the influence
of Latin Patristics the concept of *equity* was broadened
quite generally to that of overarching justice. The concepts of *caritas, humanitas, misericordia, benignitas*
and *clementia* were brought into connection with
aequitas. *Aequitas* received a religious foundation in
the equality of mankind before God and in the command to love one's neighbor.

C. RECEPTION IN THE MIDDLE AGES
Medieval jurisprudence was dominated by the idea
of *ratio scripta*. The *Corpus iuris civilis* enjoyed unconditional authority, from which to deviate no judge possessed any justification whatsoever. The special obligatory force of Justinian law was the direct result of the
fact that the law in question was written down. For that
reason it is one of the signal achievements of the
→ GLOSSATORS to have integrated the idea of *equity*
within the legal system as it was understood, so that, for
instance, one reads in the *Exceptiones Petri* (around
1160): *Si quid inutile, ruptum aequitative contrarium in
legibus reperitur, nostris pedibus subcalcamus* ('If
something useless, damaging, or contrary to equity is
found in the laws, we shall crush it beneath our feet').
[9]. The Glossators solved the apparent contradiction
between Cod. Iust. 1,14,1 (fair [in the sense of *aequitas*]
interpretation is permitted only to the Emperor) and
Cod. Iust. 3,1,8 (the judge shall give preference to justice and equity above the law in the strict sense) by going back to Cicero (Top. 2,9 and 5,28), with his distinction between *aequitas scripta* and *non scripta*. Cod.
Iust. 3,1,8 was seen as an expression of *aequitas scripta*:
within the context of the letter of the text, the judge was
to accentuate the *aequitas* that is contained within the
law itself. A genuine deviation from the law on grounds
of *aequitas non scripta* should be reserved for the legislator (Cod. Iust. 1,14,1).

Cino da Pistoia (1270–1336/7) established the following rule for the relation between positive law and
aequitas: 1. If neither *ius* nor *aequitas* is written down,
then *aequitas* has precedence. 2. If one of the two is
written down, it has precedence. 3. If both are written
down, the more specific norm outweighs the more general one; if both are equally specific or general, then
aequitas again gets precedence [7] All the elements of
ancient *aequitas* are attested in legalistic and canonistic
jurisprudential literature. The latter brought *aequitas*
above all into connection with → NATURAL law (cf.

Decretum Gratiani I, ch. 7), which justified the non-applicability or correction in individual cases of possibly unjust laws. Legal studies and studies of Canon law have in common that *aequitas* is always sought rather in interpretation than in the correction of a law. Equity was thus granted a supervisory function with regard to positive law. Among the important mediators of Aristotelian *epieíkeia* for posterity was Thomas Aquinas [1].

Germanic law of the Middle Ages also was aware of considerations of equity, which resembled ancient *equity* in their function, although no direct dependence upon ancient concepts can be proved in this area. Following canon law, Thomas More defined the most important cases in which to apply *equity* as 'to help in conscience fraud, accident and things of confidence'. As with ancient *aequitas*, equity in English law was originally concerned with the balancing of a deficit in justice arising as a result of the strict application of norms. Over the course of time, *equity* developed into its own normative system, alongside *common law*.

D. FURTHER DEVELOPMENTS IN THE MODERN ERA

Aequitas has maintained its function as a regulatory criterion until today. Norms must be interpreted in such a way that they do not give rise to unjust results in individual cases. In this context, particular attention must be paid to the meaning of rules. Similar to *epieíkeia* is the definition of equity in a treatise by Johannes Oldendorp (*c.* 1488–1567): *Billigkeit ist ein Urteil der natürlichen Vernunft, wodurch weltliche Gesetze gemildert und auf ein rechtes Leben ausgerichtet werden* ('equity is a judgment of natural reason, whereby secular laws are mitigated and directed towards an upright life') [6]. Moreover, the circumstances of the individual case should be of critical importance. Spanish Late Scholastic thought consolidated the medieval doctrine of *aequitas* in a way that long remained authoritative. In agreement with ancient tradition, Francisco Suárez (1541–1617) defined the most important cases where equity must be applied: to mitigate oppressive and unjust obligations, as well as to realize the true meaning of the law [11]. The Early Modern era produced a plethora of essays on *aequitas* [5]. In *usus modernus*, a mitigation of the law in individual cases by the judge was fully recognized. In these cases, frequent reference was made to ancient roots [10]. Unlike the jurists of previous times, theorists of natural law even used the argument of equity to establish rules that were positively standardised in Roman law [8. lib. cap. 15, § 9]. Grotius, building on Thomas Aquinas, took over the Aristotelian doctrine of *epieíkeia* [3]. Deviation from the law because of the circumstances of an individual case was also just for Pufendorf [8. lib. 2, § 10]. As in Aristotle, *aequitas* was to be taken into account, above all in the interpretation of law.

In Early Modern literature, there are repeated warnings against *aequitas cerebrina*, or equity judgments that have their origin not in objective grounds, but only in the judge's 'head'. Because of the danger of arbitrariness, Christian Thomasius (1655–1728) in particular sought drastically to limit the field of applicability of *aequitas* [12]. Yet equity continued to assert itself, even in the face of the 18th-cent. idea of codification, which saw the legislator alone as bound to equity, whereas the judge was not to evaluate the justice of the laws. Only the *Codex Maximilianeus Bavaricus Civilis* (1756) sought to implement this ideal completely (I 1 § 11). Later codifications increasingly moved away from this goal, and finally returned to the traditional conception (cf. Prussian Civil Code, Introd. §§ 20, 49; § 7 General German Civil Code; Art. 565, 1135 Code civil; §§ 242, 315, 660, 745, 829 BGB; Swiss Book of Civil Law, Art. 4): interpretation according to the meaning of the law, and filling in lacunae from the viewpoint of equity.

The 19th cent. saw the appearance, alongside traditional doctrines [2], of those which understood equity as a concept of morality and not of law, since the law in a liberal constitutional state must have assessible norms, but equity is non-assessible [13]. Nevertheless, equity in the sense of *epieíkeia* maintained its role in jurisprudence. As Windscheid wrote in his textbook on Pandects: *Billig ist das den thatsächlichen Verhältnissen angemessene Recht* ('the law that is appropriate to factual circumstances is valid') [4].

Equity maintained its position in the 20th cent. In the era of the constitutional state, of course, the contents of a fair judgement are strongly affected by constitutional principles. This is especially true of public law, which developed the principle of proportionality, as an expression of equity, into a central institution of law. Art. 20 III of the Basic Law of Germany binds all state action to law and justice. This prescription arose from the very experience that laws do not always yield just results, and it can therefore be understood as an expression of equity. The European Court of Justice has also taken up the Aristotelian idea of equity in the sense of a rule of equality and correction of laws that appear as unjust in individual cases (European Court of Justice, judgment of 20.5.1981, RS 152/80, in: Slg. 1981, 129ff.). The question still remains open as to who has actually benefited from the equity-argument throughout the various periods of legal history; in other words, [what is/was] its judicial-political function.

→ Aequitas

SOURCES: 1 THOMAS OF AQUINAS, Summa Theologica IIa IIae, q. 120   2 CH. F. GLÜCK, Pandecten, Erlangen ²1797, 1. Book, 1. Tit., § 26, 194–198   3 H. GROTIUS, De Aequitate, Amsterdam 1735   4 B. WINDSCHEID, Lehrbuch des Pandektenrechts, Vol. 1, Frankfurt/M. ⁶1887, § 28, S. 73   5 M. LIPENIUS, Bibliotheca Realis Iuridica, Leipzig from 1757, 36f.   6 J. OLDENDORP, Wat byllick unn recht ys. Eyne korte erklaring, allen stenden denstlick, Rostock 1529 (Reprint in Modern German in: E. WOLF, Quellenbuch zur Geschichte der Deutschen Rechtswissenschaft, 1950, 51–68, here 55f.)   7 CINO DA PISTOIA, In Codicem commentaria, C. 1,14,1, n. 12, tom. 1, Frankfurt/M. 1578, fol. 25, 25'   8 S. PUFENDORF, De officio hominis, Lund 1673 (German by K. LUIG, 1994) [Cf. The whole duty of man according to the law of nature, translated by Andrew Tooke, 1691; edited and with an Introduction by Ian Hunter and David Saunders. Two discourses and a commentary / by Jean Barbeyrac; translated by David Saunders, Indianapolis, IN., 2003 (Natural law and enlightenment classics) 9 Prologus zu den Exceptiones petri, in: F. C. VON SAVIGNY, Geschichte des römischen Rechts im MA, Vol. 2, Heidelberg ²1834, 321 10 G. A. STRUVE, Syntagma Jurisprudentiae, Frankfurt-Leipzig ³1738, nr. 44 on Dig. 1,4 11 F. SUÁREZ, De legibus 2,16, 1973, 77–98, 12 CH. THOMASIUS, Dissertationes Academicae, Vol. III, Diss. LXXIII: De Aequitate Cerebrina, 1777, 43–78; Vol. IV, Diss. CXVI: De Aequitate Cerebrina et exiguo usu, 1780, 230–259 13 C. WELCKER, s.v. B., in: ROTTECK, Staatslexikon, Altona 1846, Vol. 2, 526–533

LITERATURE: 14 P. G. CARON, 'Aequitas' romana, 'misericordia' patristica ed 'epicheia' aristotelica nella dottrina dell' 'aequitas canonica', 1971 15 N. HORN, Aequitas in den Lehren des Baldus, 1968 16 H. LANGE, Ius aequum und ius strictum bei den Glossatoren, in: ZRG 71, 1954, 319–347 17 M. RÜMELIN, Die Billigkeit im Recht, 1921 18 C. SCHOTT, Aequitas cerebrina, in: B. DIESTELKAMP et al. (eds.), Rechtshistorische Studien. Hans Thieme zum 70. Geburtstag, 1977, 132–160 19 H. SCHOTTE, Die Aequitas bei Hugo Grotius, 1963 20 G. WESENER, Aequitas naturalis, 'natürliche Billigkeit' in der privatrechtlichen Dogmen- und Kodifikationsgeschichte, in: M. BECK-MANNAGETTA et al. (eds.), Der Gerechtigkeitsanspruch des Rechts, 1996, 81–105 21 E. WOHLHAUPTER, Aequitas canonica. Eine Studie aus dem kanonischen Recht, 1931

ADDITIONAL BIBLIOGRAPHY: P. LANDAU, Aequitas in the corpus iuris canonici, in: Syracuse Journal of International Law and Commerce, 1994; (URL: http://faculty.cua.edu/pennington/Law111/LandauAequitas.htm).

TILMAN REPGEN

Aerial Archaeological Imaging
A. DEFINITION AND INTRODUCTION B. DEVELOPMENT C. PREMISES

A. DEFINITION AND INTRODUCTION
Aerial archaeological imaging (AAI) usually designates methods of remote sensing, which from high altitude make archaeological monuments visible or more easily viewed. Photographic procedures are normally employed for documentation of the information obtainable from a high altitude. The technical possibilities and scope of AAI have depended primarily on the development of air and space travel, and secondarily on that of photography. With the development of AAI, archaeology's grasp of humanity's history has been extended by a fundamental, distancing and abstracting perspective. With adequate surface conditions, AAI contributes greatly to the identification of fixed archaeological monuments covering large areas, offers vital data on the nature and extent of human activity in extended areas, and when satellite remote sensing is used, even over entire landscapes, AAI is an important means for the early identification and, therefore, the prophylactic protection of cultural resources.

B. DEVELOPMENT
[3. 33–44; 5. 1–84; 8] In a narrower sense AAI is based on the awareness that observation from high altitude allows one to perceive previously unknown archaeological monuments or some of their attributes, a procedure that one already had at one's disposal in a number of different, isolated places by the end of the 19th and the beginning of the 20th cent. In the field of classical archaeology the cooperation of some Italian archaeologists (Giacomo Boni among others) with specialists in military aerial photography and reconnaissance proved to be pioneering work to which we owe, among other things, the discovery of the remains of monumental inscriptions in the Augustan pavement of the Forum Romanum or the identification of the historical course of the Tiber's mouth at Ostia [2. 22–25, 29–31]. During the Italo-Turkish war of 1911–1912 pilots of the same military unit identified the remains of the ancient port installations of Sabratha in Tripolitania, which were covered by the sea. AAI developed significantly during both World Wars, a fact that illuminates the decades-long dependence of the practice of aerial archaeology on the development of aerial warfare and military aerial reconnaissance. The first attempts at a systematic use of AAI were made during World War I by, among others, the German-Turkish unit for the protection of monuments led by Theodor Wiegand in the Near East or by Carl Schuchhardt in Dobruja (Romania). These attempts proved above all useful in the documentation of settlements and military lines. At the same time Marc Bloch, an intelligence officer and later a co-founder of the journal Annales d'histoire économique et sociale, stimulated modern economic and social history by advocating the use of aerial prospection in the field of agrarian history [10. 101–107, 109f., 124f.] The methodological and practical breakthrough of systematic AAI took place in the 1920s in Great Britain through the efforts of Osbert Crawford [7]. Crawford created the necessary institutional support for AAI in his homeland, began a continued personal involvement which survived long after World War II, defined the relevant parameters for detection of archaeological monuments from the air and handled the publication of and publicity for the achievements of AAI. From 1925 to 1932 Antoine Poidebrad flew systematically over the former Roman border area in contemporary Syria and documented extended sectors of the limes constructions [9]. From 1934 to 1936, combining AAI and underwater research, he developed a layout of the remains of the docks of Tyre, the Phoenician port city, which were covered by the sea. From 1935 to 1937, Erich F. Schmidt, on behalf of the University of Chicago Oriental Institute, conducted flights in Iran, which served current excavations, the preparation of documentation for scheduled excavation sites and the systematic prospection of other territories in order to iden-

tify unknown archaeological monuments [11]. Parallel to the general production of maps with the aid of aerial images, especially of vertical exposures, AAI and archaeological cartography converged after World War I. In both fields, which were also intertwined in terms of personalities (e.g. through Osbert Crawford or Giuseppe Lugli), international meetings were organized which contributed to shared knowledge and to the general circulation of the results. The increased use of the respective air forces in World War II led to the emergence of aerial image archives of unprecedented dimensions, which afterwards were also able to be used for archaeological purposes. From these AAI received a further decisive impetus. Jean Baradez analyzed the topography of the border of Roman North Africa using aerial images, covering wide areas and taken from high altitude [4]. The series of aerial images taken by the Royal Air Force began a new phase in the study of the ancient cultural landscape of Italy, substantially initiated by the British School of Rome. The 1970s movement in Europe to protect monuments established AAI, in principle, as a standard tool of regional archaeology. However, adequate stability of infrastructure was not achieved in most of the relevant fields of activity. The profound political changes in Central and Eastern Europe have created conditions for a new beginning for AAI in these regions because many archived images, previously classified as military secrets, have become available for archaeological interpretation, and at the same time have made new AAI activities possible. When aerial prospection is practiced especially for archaeology the conditions of observation and documentation can be accurately established in accordance with scientific needs. The results of this exclusively archaeological aerial inspection are therefore considerably greater than the archaeological post processing of aerial images made for other purposes. Automatic data processing facilitates the subsequent elimination of deformations from oblique exposures and makes it possible to combine aerial archaeological images with other data, among others cartographic data, in geographic information systems (GIS), and thus to create integrated archaeological archives, which allow queries combining spatial- and object-related information. With the use of satellites offering images with increasingly better resolution, AAI is once again closely connected with the current development of military and civil remote sensing, as it was at the time of its nascency. AAI offers archaeological science an instrument which is able to quantify and describe, with increased precision, the potential of a given territory. At the same time it makes available for the first time specific individual sources as well as entire categories of information. Also in the field of Ancient archaeology AAI has provided the identification of entire settlements (e.g. Spina) and of isolated monuments, especially in areas with no modern construction. To the latter group belong border or fortification buildings and temporary military camps as well as farms or rural residences (villae). Fruitful research about ancient surveying is almost exclusively due to AAI.

C. PREMISES

Even those archaeological monuments which are not recognizable from the ground have to leave some markings or traces on the surface in order to be identified by remote sensing. Among them are slight differences in height which cast shadows and the differences in soil color, or the height of the vegetation which has grown over the archaeologically relevant remains and traces in ground. Results from AAI are influenced by the time of the day (incidence of the light), by the season (the density and height of the vegetation, snow covering), by the altitude of the flight, by the angle of vision or the camera angle. The full potential of AAI will only become evident in the long run through the successive joining of different sets of premises (for example, by the inclusion of the concomitant phenomenon of extreme drought). Fundamentally, the outlook for success with AAI depends on the extent of the subsequent modifications of the soil. Among these the utilization of the land is very important: agriculture, especially deep plowing, urban sprawl or soil sealing destroy archaeological remains or make them inaccessible to aerial inspection. Already by the beginning of the 20th cent. the parameters for the use of AAI were very different from region to region. Thus the remarkable success of AAI in countries such as Great Britain is due also to the local particularities of land-use history (with animal husbandry prevalent). The use of increasingly systematic aerial prospection over long periods of time also allows AAI to offer first-class documentation of the progressive loss of fixed archaeological sources.

→ ARCHAEOLOGICAL METHODS AND THEORIES;
→ UNDERWATER ARCHAEOLOGY

1 Aerial Archaeology Research Group News, Periodikum 1, 1990 sqq. 2 GIOVANNA ALVISI, La fotografia aerea nell'indagine archeologica, 1989 3 HELMUT BECKER (ed.), Archäologische Prospektion. Luftbildarchäologie und Geophysik, 1996 4 JEAN BARADEZ, Fossatum Africae. Recherches aériennes sur l'organisation des confins sahariens à l'époque romaine, 1949 5 JOHN BRADFORD, Ancient landscapes. Studies in Field Archaeology, 1974 6 RAYMOND CHEVALIER, Bibliographie des applications archéologiques de la photographie aérienne, 1957 7 OSBERT CRAWFORD, ALEXANDER KEILLER, Wessex from the Air, 1928 8 LEO DEUEL, Flights into Yesterday. The Story of Aerial Archaeology, 1973 9 ANTOINE POIDEBARD, La trace de Rome dans le désert de Syrie. Le limes de Trajan à la conquête arabe, 1934 10 ULRICH RAULFF, Ein Historiker im 20. Jahrhundert: Marc Bloch, 1995 11 ERICH F. SCHMIDT, Flights over Ancient Cities of Iran, 1940. STEFAN ALTEKAMP

Aesthetics see → BEAUTY, → BODY, ATTITUDES TOWARDS, → PROPORTIONS, THEORY OF

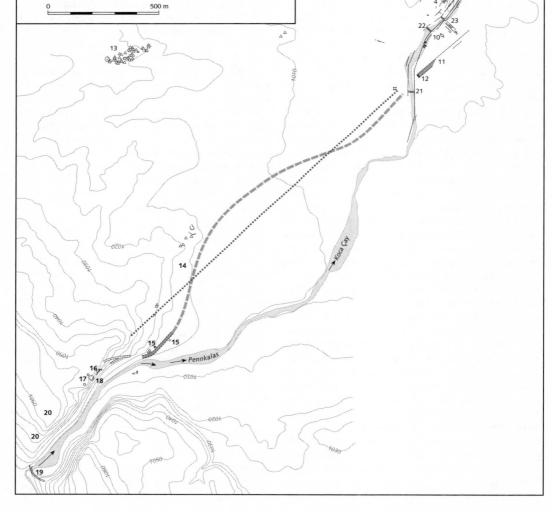

Aezani: topographical map

‿	Ancient water pipe
::	Ancient ruins
△	Grave/Sarcophagus
‒ ‒ ‒	Route of procession to the cave of Meter Steunene (conjectural)
••••••	Visual axis: colonnaded street-gate building-cave of Meter Steunene

1 Temple of Zeus (2nd quarter of 2nd cent. AD)
2 Agora
3 Heroon
4 Courtyard with Doric columns
5 Baths
6 Circular construction (tomb?)
7 Stadium (2nd half 2nd cent. AD)
8 Theatre
9 Baths (3rd cent. AD)
10 Round building (Macellum?) with Diocletianic Price Edict (AD 303) and late antique colonnaded street
11 Colonnaded street
12 Gate building
13 West Necropolis
14 South-west Necropolis
15 Funerary buildings
16 Grotto
17 Round pits (Bothroi)
18 Cave of Meter Steunene
19 Dam
20 Traces of quarry
21-24 Roman bridges

Survey of ancient buildings by the German Archaeological Institute's Aezani excavation
Map based on Turkish land survey
Surveyor: C. Hermann 1990/91
Edited by: K. Rheidt 1992
As of September 1991

N

0   500 m

Aezani

A. Location   B. History and Significance
C. The History of Discovery   D. Excavation
and Monuments

A. Location

Aezani (A.) is situated in a rural area near the town of Çavdarhisar, *c.* 50 kilometres southwest of the provincial capitol Kütahya in modern Turkey. A. occupied a central location on the Aizanitis, a plateau *c.* 1000 metres above sea level in western Phrygia, and belonged to Phrygia Epiktetos (Str. 12,8,12). The village houses of the older parts of Çavdarhisar stand in part on ancient foundation walls and contain numerous elements of ancient building. After destruction by an earthquake in 1970 a new town center was established about 2 kilometres to the southeast. Since then the houses of the old village have been gradually abandoned and allowed to deteriorate.

B. History and Significance

In its founding legend A. referred to its Arcadian descent in the early Imperial Period. Pausanias (8,4,3; 10,32,3) mentions the hero Azan, born of a liaison with the nymph Erato, as the mythical ancestor of the Phrygians who lived in the area around the Steunos cave and the Pencalas river. The oldest finds show that the city area was settled from the Early Bronze period at the latest (1st half of the 3rd cent.). In the Hellenistic period the area around Aizanoi was the object of contention between the kingdoms of Bithynia and Pergamon and came under Roman control in 133 BC. The first mintings are known from the 2nd/1st cent. BC, which bear the city name Ezeanitōn from the last third of the 1st cent. BC onwards. Since the time of Augustus the coins almost always say Aizanitōn or Aizaneitōn. An imperial inscription mentions donations of land by the kings of Pergamon and Bithynia to the temple and the city, which speaks for a certain significance for A. in the Hellenistic period [6; 22].

Citizens of A. held high offices beginning in the Augustan period and helped to bring the city to a position of importance through their connections to the Roman imperial house and through material donations. A. experienced a time of growth under Hadrian, whose arbitration made possible the collection of rents from the lands donated for the sanctuary of Zeus and with these the building of the temple of Zeus. Members of rich land-owning families were by then Roman citizens. Some of them played leading roles in the province as Asiarchs and even became consuls. A. was especially proud of its membership in the Panhellenion and of the honour of being counted among the most important cities of the realm with Greek tradition and culture [6; 10; 22; 26; 33]. In the Byzantine period A. was the seat of a bishop and had several churches, of which the largest was built over the temple of Zeus. In the 11th and 12th cents. this church was part of a settlement on the temple plateau. The fortified walls of this settlement were made of ancient structural elements and in the 13th cent. they served as a base for the tribe of the Çavdar Tartars and gave the modern site its name Çavdarhisar (Çavdar-Fortress) [6; 9; 22].

C. The History of Discovery

In 1824 Saint-Asaph, the later Earl of Ashburnham, was the first European to visit the well-preserved ruins. A.D. Mordtmann, G.Th. Keppel and W.J. Hamilton followed him a few years later. In 1838 L. de Laborde, in 1839 Ch. Texier and in 1847 Ph. Le Bas and E. Landron published the first extensive pictures of the buildings. A new phase in the history of its discovery began when A. Körte worked on dating the temple of Zeus in 1890 and 1895. The Steunos cave, in which the Anatolian mother goddess was worshipped as Meter Steunene (Fig.1: 16, 17, 18), was discovered by J.G.C. Anderson in 1898 and examined closely by Th. Wiegand in 1908 [16; 22; 31]. The first excavations of the → Deutsches Archäologisches Institut under the leadership of M. Schede and D. Krencker were carried out in 1926 and 1928. They were resumed by R. Naumann in 1970 and continue until today [22].

D. Excavation and Monuments

The temple of Zeus was the center of the excavations in the 1920s (Fig.1: 1). The Ionic Pseudodipteros from the 2nd quarter of the 2nd cent. AD, with its 8 x 15 columns, stands on a podium with an open staircase. Stairs, leading from the Opisthodom into a cellar with vaulted ceiling and to the roof of the temple [22] (Fig.2), point to the performance of ritual acts both in the cellar and on the roof. But the excavators' hypothesis that the temple was a double sanctuary in which the cult of Cybele was observed in the cellar has not been confirmed [26]. The temple has a pronounced ancient appearance because of its overall design and the development of some details such as the Ionic arrangement of the ringed hall (Fig.3). The retrospective architectural

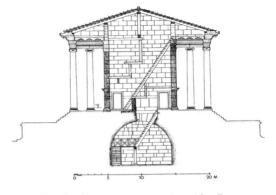

Fig. 2: Temple of Zeus; transverse section with cellar and reconstruction of stairs.
With Permission of the Aizanoi-excavation of the Deutsches Archäologisches Insitut

Fig. 3: Temple of Zeus; view from the northwest after completion of the measures to secure the timberwork 1996. *With Permission of the Aizanoi-excavation of the Deutsches Archäologisches Institut*

has the Diocletian price edict from the year AD 301 on its wall [21]. Regular excavations have taken place since 1978, concentrating on the thermal gymnasium from the 2nd half of the 2nd cent. AD (Fig.1: 5) [11, 12, 13]. From 1982 to 1984 Naumann, making individual investigations near the reservoir (Fig. 1: 19) and the Doric hall of columns (Fig.1: 4), uncovered a building made of large limestone blocks (Fig.1: 9), in which a second thermal bath with rich mosaics was added in the 3rd cent. AD From the 4th or 5th cent. onwards structural alterations were made to the main halls and given Christian furnishings [13; 14]. A. Hoffmann excavated from 1982 to 1990 in order to clarify the structural history of the theater-stadium complex (Fig.1: 7, 8), concluding that the stadium was constructed in several phases beginning in the 2nd half of the 2nd cent. AD, but was abandoned around the middle of the 4th cent. and used as a stone quarry [3; 4].

Since 1990 the members of the A. excavation team, under the leadership of K. Rheidt, have been investigating the entire city. By examining the urban relationships between monumental structures [23; 26], pottery [1], building ornaments, gravestones [5; 29] and inscriptions [6; 32; 33; 34] they are trying to work out a picture of A.'s topography and history in its various phases of development from its beginnings until the ruins were included in the houses and gardens of the village of Çavdarhisar, as well as placing it in a larger historical context. This new phase of the A. excavation, which was supplemented by emergency excavations of the Kütahya Museum [28; 35], yielded the fact that the city, in spite of its efforts to imitate Roman models with temples, thermal baths and theater-stadium, did not give up its Anatolian roots until well into the late Imperial period. The 2nd cent. AD system of urban planning could not be integrated with the new monumental structures. In contrast, the broad, columned street (Fig.1: 11) with an ornamental gate (Fig. 1. 12) [12],

language of the building and the reversion to Hellenistic models can be related to the desire for antiquity and for a Greek legacy, which reflected the city's membership in the Panhellenion [26; 30; 34]. The building of the temple of Zeus was the start of the representative expansion of the city center and was followed shortly afterwards by the so-called Agora (Fig.1: 2) with a small podium temple that has been interpreted as a Heroon (Fig.1: 3) [17; 22] by and the halls around the temple. Only the court with Doric columns (Fig.1: 4) [13; 22] was built before the temple of Zeus (Fig.4).

The excavations and research of the 1920s were not published until 1979 by R. Naumann, since Krenkker and Schede did not survive World War II. Naumann pleaded for the resumption of the excavation in A. in the aftermath of the earthquake of 1970 and began by examining several smaller structures, among them the Heroon on the Agora [17] and the circular building (Fig.1: 10) on the eastern bank of the Pencalas, which

Fig. 4: Town centre in the Imperial period; perspective reconstruction by D. Krencker, drawing by O. Heck. *With Permission of the Aizanoi-excavation of the Deutsches Archäologisches Institut*

Fig. 5: The late antique colonnade after anastylosis.
With Permission of the Aizanoi-excavation of the
Deutsches Archäologisches Institut

Fig. 6: Artemisium; this reconstruction of the temple
front incorporates elements that were built into the hall
architecture of the late antique colonnade.
With Permission of the Aizanoi-excavation of the
Deutsches Archäologisches Institut

which was the backbone of this system of streets, was
aligned with the sanctuary of Meter Steunene (Fig.1:
16, 17, 18) and was adorned with the tombs of the
richest families of A. around the middle of the 2nd cent.
AD [23; 26].

Between 1992 and 1995 a columned street from Late
Antiquity was uncovered, built around AD 400 out of
parts of older buildings (Fig.1: 10; Fig.5), into which
inscription bases and statues were integrated [7].
Among them were building parts from the temple of
Artemis from the middle of the 1st cent. AD (Fig.6).
There was a regularly arranged city precinct on the eastern bank of the Pencalas river by the 1st half of the 1st
cent. AD, which replaced late Hellenistic workshops
and potteries [1; 24; 26]. Since 1996 excavation in A.
has concentrated again on the temple of Zeus (Fig.1: 1)
[25]. Excavations are being carried out south of the
temple and at the southern corner of the temple plateau,
which have been identified as the remains of a settlement mound.

1 N. Atık, Die Keramik aus Aezani, in: AA 1995, 729–739
2 W. Günther, Ein Ehrendekret *post mortem* aus Aezani,
in: MDAI(Ist) 25, 1975, 351–356   3 A. Hoffmann,
Aezani. Erster Vorbericht über die Arbeiten im Stadion
1982–1984, in: AA 1986, 683–698   4 Id., Aezani Zweiter
Vorbericht über die Arbeiten im Stadion 1987. 1988 und
1990, in: AA 1993, 437–473   5 K. Jes, 'Gebaute' Tür-
grabsteine in Aezani, in: MDAI(Ist) 47, 1997, 231–250
6 B. Levick, S. Mitchell, J. Potter, M. Waelkens
(eds.), Monuments from the Aizanitis recorded by
C.W.M. Cox, A. Cameron, and J.Cullen, MAMA IX,
1988   7 H. C. v. Mosch, Eine neue Replik des Satyrs mit
der Querflöte und ihre Aufstellung in spät antikem Kontext, in: AA 1995, 741–753   8 Id., Ein neuer Portraitfund
aus Aezani, in: AA 1993, 509–515   9 C. Naumann, Die
mittelalterliche Festung von Aezani -Çavdarhisar, in:
MDAI(Ist) 35, 1985, 275–294   10 F. Naumann, Ulpii von
Aezani, in: MDAI(Ist) 35, 1985, 217–226   11 R. Naumann, F. Naumann, Aezani. Bericht über die Ausgrabungen und Untersuchungen 1978, in: AA 1980, 123–136
12 R. Naumann, Aezani. Bericht über die Ausgrabungen
und Untersuchungen 1979 und 1980, in: AA 1982, 345–
382 13 R. Naumann, F. Naumann, Aezani. Bericht über
die Ausgrabungen und Untrsuchungen 1981 und 1982, in:
AA 1984, 453–530 14 Id., Aezani. Bericht über die Ausgrabungen und Untersuchungen 1983 und 1984, in: AA
1987, 301–358 15 R. Naumann, Die Bedeutung der Türsteine bei den Kaianlagen an der Agora in Aezani, in:
MDAI(Ist) 25, 1975, 343–350 16 Id., Das Heiligtum der
Meter Steunene bei Aezani, in: MDAI(Ist) 17, 1967, 218–
247 17 Id., Das Heroon auf der Agora in Aezani, in:
MDAI(Ist) 23/24, 1973/74, 185–197 18 Id., Römische
Friese und Schrankenplatten aus Kleinasien, in: MDAI(R)
86, 1979, 331–337 19 Id., Ein römischer Brunnen in
ezani, in: Boreas 6, 1983, 162–167 20 Id., Römischer
Grabbau westlich des Zeus-Tempelareals in Aezani, in:
MDAI(Ist) 44, 1994, 303–306 21 R. Naumann, F. Nau-
mann, Der Rundbau in Aezani, 10. Beih. MDAI(Ist),
1973 22 R. Naumann, Der Zeustempel zu Aezani, in:
Denkmäler Ant. Architektur 12, 1979 23 K. Rheidt,
Aezani. Vorbericht über die Forschung zur historischen
Topographie, in: AA 1993, 475–507 24 Id., Aezani.
Bericht über die Ausgrabungen und Untersuchungen 1992
und 1993, in: AA 1995, 693–718 25 Id., Aezani. Bericht
über die Ausgrabungen, Restaurierungen und Sicherungs-
arbeiten 1994, 1995 und 1996, in: AA 1997, 431–473
26 Id., Römischer Luxus – Anatolisches Erbe. Aezani in
Phrygien – Entdeckung, Ausgrabung und neue For-
schungsergebnisse, in: Ant. Welt 28, 1997, 479–499 27 L.
Robert, Documents d'Asie Mineure XVIII. Fleuves et
Cultes d'A., in: BCH 105, 1981, 331–360 28 M. Türk-
tüzün, Zwei Säulensarkophage aus der Südwestnekro-
pole in Aezani, in: AA 1993, 517–526 29 M. Waelkens,
Die kleinasiatischen Türsteine, 1986 30 H. Weber, Der
Zeustempel von Aezani – Ein panhellenisches Heiligtum
der Kaiserzeit, in: MDAI(A) 84, 1969, 182–201 31 Th.
Wiegand, ΜΗΤΗΡ ΣΤΕΥΝΗΝΗ, in: MDAI(A) 36, 1911,
302–307 32 M. Wörrle, Inschriftenfunde von der Hal-
lenstrassengrabung in Aezani 1992, in: AA 1995, 719–727
33 Id., Neue Inschriftenfunde aus Aezani I, in: Chiron 22,
1992, 337–376 34 Id., Neue Inschriftenfunde aus Aezani
II: Das Problem der Ära von Aezani, in: Chiron 25, 1995,
63–81 35 U. Wulf, Zwei Grabbauten in der Südwest-
nekropole von Aezani, in: AA 1993, 527–541

KLAUS RHEIDT

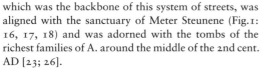

Affects, Theory of (Musical) Although affects were themes in Classical philosophy and rhetoric, incidentally also in the ethical doctrine of music (→ Music), there was no specific theory of musical affects. That melodies and rhythms affected different souls in different manners had been demonstrated by Boethius inst. mus. 1,1) as a transmitter of the idea (Pythagoras, Plato rep. 3,398–401). After the 11th cent., the attempt was made to link the → Musical theory of keys in Gregorian chant with the ethical doctrine of music. Connected with the reception of Aristotle (pol. 8; eth. Nic.), commentaries which discussed the question of ethics and affects in musical keys used in church first appeared around 1300 (Petrus de Alvernia and Guido von Saint-Denis [13], Walter Burley [12]). In the Renaissance, though the idea originated with words set to music in the late Middle Ages, the combination of music and words changed into a 'speaking art', which absorbed elements of both classical rhetoric and rhythm. Just as art's most noble challenge was to imitate nature, so too music's was to represent human affects. The theory of musical affects arising in the 16th cent. came out of the study of living speech and was joined to Classical rhetoric with its requirement that it entertain and move (*delectare, movere*, Quint. inst. or. 12,10,59). Added to this came the Greek teachings of the four humours (Galen; → Humoral Theory). Ramos de Pareja [7. 56f.] associated the four basic keys to the four humours (temperaments): *tonus protus* associated with the *phlegmatic temperament, tonus deuterus* with the *colic, tonus tritus* with the *sanguine* and *tonus tetrardus* with the *melancholic*. Renaissance theoreticians stressed that the ethical and affective content of a text should be expressed in a musical key [1]. In another development, Gioseffo Zarlino [8. 3, 10. Kap.], constructed a new system: intervals 'without half tones' (whole tones, major third, major sixth) express joyful affects; those 'with half tones' (minor third, minor sixth), sad affects. In Germany the musical or rhetorical theory of figures absorbed the theory of affects. The theory of musical affects acquired its greatest importance, with a precursor in the Italian madrigals, in the rise of monody at the end of the 16th cent. On the advice of philologist Girolamo Mei, the Florentine Camerata around Giovanni Bardi rejected polyphony and announced that the song of passionate expression was the new ideal (*cantare con affetto*) [2]). In Claudio Monteverdi's madrigals (1567–1643) the three affects were *ira, temperanza* and *humilta*, which corresponded to his *stile concitato, stile temperato* and *stile molle* [6]. After the first experiences with the new genre called → Opera particularly those of Monteverdi, Giovanni Battista Doni [3] differentiated three styles of new singing: simple recitative (*stile recitativo*), a style in which song clarified the affective content of the words (*stile espressivo*) and impassioned and dramatic singing (*stile rappresentativo*). Marin Mersenne [5] offered an elaborate system of musical affects that embraced both polyphony and instruments. Affects in music and the theory of musical affects played

an important role in the teaching of music in the following era (e.g. Rameau, Mattheson, Marpurg, Kuhnau, Heinichen), but here at this point one can hardly still speak of a Classical reception.

→ Aristotelianism; → Music

SOURCES: 1 N. BURTIUS, Musices opusculum, Bologna 1487 (repr.1969)   2 G. CACCINI, Nuove musiche, Preface, Florence 1602,   3 G. B. DONI, *Annotazioni sopra il Compendio* (...) Rome 1640   4 H. FINCK, Practica musica, Wittenberg 1556   5 M. MERSENNE, Harmonie universelle, Paris 1636   6 C. MONTEVERDI, Preface to Vol. 8 of Madrigals, Venice 1638   7 R. de Pareja, Musica practica (1482), (ed.) J. WOLF, 1901   8 G. ZARLINO, Istitutioni harmoniche, Venice 1558

LITERATURE: 9 H. ABERT, Die Musikanschauung des Mittelalters und ihre Grundlagen, 1905 (repr.1964)   10 W. BRAUN, Affektenlehre, MGG 2.1, 31–41   11 R. DAMMANN, Der Musikbegriff im deutschen Barock, ²1984, 215–396   12 M. HAAS, Musik und Affekt im 14. Jahrhundert: Zum Politik-Kommentar Walter Burleys, in: Schweizer Jahrbuch für Musikwissenschaft., Neue Serie 1, 1981, 9–22   13 S. VAN DE KLUNDERT, Guido von Saint Denis Tractatus de tonis, Dissertation Utrecht, 1996   14 W. SERAUKY, Affektenlehre, MGG 1.1, 113–121. Zaminer, Frieder   FRIEDER ZAMINER

Africa

A. AFRICAN LITERATURE IN THE LATIN LANGUAGE (16TH–18TH CENTS.)   B. AFRICAN POETRY AND PROSE (19TH–20TH CENTS.)   C. AFRICAN DRAMA (20TH CENT.)   D. CLASSICAL LANGUAGES AND CLASSICAL STUDIES IN AFRICAN SCHOOLS, UNIVERSITIES AND MUSEUMS (18TH–20TH CENTS.)

A. AFRICAN LITERATURE IN THE LATIN LANGUAGE (16TH–18TH CENTS.)

The earliest and probably best known African poet from this period was Juan Latino (1516–c. 1594), who was born in West-A. and who came to Spain around 1528. He translated Horace and wrote poetry in Latin. Five published works are extant, for the most part panegyric poems with numerous mythological allusions: The *Epigrammatum liber* (Granada 1573), which is set mostly in elegic metre following the example of Ovid, celebrates the birth of Prince Ferdinand in the year 1571; an elegy (Granada 1573) to Pius V.; the *Austriad* (Granada 1573), which is set in hexametres and which begins with an appeal to Apollo, compares the battle of Lepanto between the Turkish and Spanish fleets with a battle between Greeks and Trojans and narrates the victory of Don Juan of Austria with an occasional recourse to formulations from classical poetry; *De Translatione* (Granada 1574), in which Philipp II. is praised for his filial devotion; and a short poem (1585), which is dedicated to the Duke of Sesa. Among the African poets who wrote in Latin, Anton Wilhelm Amo (1703–after 1753) and Jacobus Eliza Johannes Capitein (1717–47) are also known to some extent. Amo wrote on legal and philosophical topics: *De jure Maurorum in Europa*

(Halle 1729), *De humanae mentis* ἀπάθεια *seu sensionis ac facultatis sentiendi in mente humana absentia* (Halle 1734) and the *Tractatus de arte sobrie et accurate philosophandi* (Leiden 1738). Capitein published some of his sermons and a speech entitled *Dissertatio politico-theologica de servitute libertati Christianae non contraria* (Wittenberg 1742).

B. AFRICAN POETRY AND PROSE (19TH–20TH CENTS.)

Numerous works by African poets show influences of the Classics. Among a series of Cape Verdean poets, the work of José Lopes (1872–1962) is most strongly influenced by Classical Antiquity. This can be seen most readily in the titles of his works: *Jardim das Hespérides* (1916), *Hesperitanas* (1929) and *Alma Arsinária* (1952); he also wrote poems in Latin. Lopes was especially influenced by the Classics in his bond with the epic world view and its mythical apparatus, in the assumption of the 'universality' of his poetry and the concept of the poet as the interpreter of the 'collective soul' of his people. Several other Cape Verdean poets, who show an inclination to Antiquity in the titles of their books of poems and individual poems, in quotations from the literature of antiquity, in lyrical elements, heroic odes, erotic themes, ancient deities, bucolic framework (→ BUCOLIC/IDYLL), mythological inferences and stories, are Januário Leite (1865–1930), Mário Pinto (1887–1958), Pedro Monteiro Cardoso (*c.* 1890–1942), Eugénio Tavares (1867–1930), Jorge Barbosa (1902–71), Manuel Lopes (1907–2005) and António Nunes (1917–1951). The interest of poets from the African mainland in Antiquity shows itself most obviously in the titles of numerous poems, for example *Creation of a Caryatid* by Wole Soyinka (b. 1934). While the Senegalese poet Birago Diop (1906–1989) used a classical metre in some of his poems, the poems in the works of his countryman Léopold Sédar Senghor (1906–2001) from *Chants d'ombre* (1945) to *Elégies majeures* (1979) are saturated with the influence of Greco-Roman poetry and Greek philosophy (pre-Socratic, Platonic as well as the post-Socratic). The poems of Christopher Okigbo (1932–1967) are reminiscent of the voice of the choir in classical Greek poetry. Musaemura Bonas Zimunya (b. 1949) from Zimbabwe uses allusions to Antiquity in his poetry. In some of his formulations and in his metric variety he resembles Latin poets, especially Catullus, while the style of the Cameroonian poet Louis-Marie Pouka M'Bague (b. 1910) has echoes of Horace and Virgil.

Other African poets and a few prose writers have also adopted protagonists, motives and themes from classical authors. Wole Soyinka uses the archetype Odysseus in his anthology of poems entitled *A Shuttle in the Crypt* (1972), while the god Ogun takes a journey into the deep in his book *Idanre and Other Poems* (1967), which appears elsewhere as a descent to Hades; the hunter Akara-Ogun in the fictional work *Ogboju ode ninu igbo irunmale* (1938) by Daniel Olorunfemi

Fagunwa (1903–1963) is an Odysseus figure. Nigerian 'books of ballads' are written in a spirit related to that of Ovid *Ars amatoria* in order to introduce the reader to the art of love. The novelist Ibrahim Issa (b. 1922) from Niger uses Homeric images in his work *Les Grandes eaux noires* (1959) in order to explore the historical possibility of Roman soldiers destroying the kingdom of a local ruler on the Niger River after the 2nd Punic War in the year 182 BC. In general the influence of Classical Antiquity on African writers is obvious not only in the frequent use of references to ancient literature and Latin expressions, but also in the balanced sentences and well-rounded paragraphs reminiscent of the style of Cicero. This goes back to the Greek and Latin studies, especially the latter, in the secondary schools and universities in the 19th and 20th cents. and the use of Latin in the Roman Catholic Church until 1965.

C. AFRICAN DRAMA (20TH CENT.)

A series of African dramatists, especially those of the Yoruba tribe in West-A., have adapted motifs and elements from Antiquity in their pieces and occasionally even kept the characteristics of individual Greek dramas. The Yoruba dramatist Wole Soyinka, recipient of the Nobel prize for literature for the year 1986, readapted Euripides' *Bacchants* in his piece *The Bacchae of Euripides: A Communion Rite* (1973), but was fairly faithful to the main scenes. In his portrayal of Dionysus Soyinka allows Apollan, Dionysian and Promethean characteristics to blend and refers to the Greek idea that a scapegoat must be offered to the gods, especially to Dionysus, in order to assure the fruitfulness of the grain. The influence of Greek tragedy can be seen in his other pieces as well, e.g. *Kongi's Harvest* (1967), in which strategies which correspond to the *deus ex machina*, the *prologos* and the *exodos* of the Greeks are used to give structure. Ola Rotimi (1938–2000), a countryman of Soyinka, transfers a Greek tragedy model and the Oedipus myth over to a Yoruba setting in *The Gods Are Not to Blame* (1971). The plot of Rotimi's piece is more or less identical to Sophocles' *Oedipus Rex*, and the chorus of the people from the city has a socio-philosophical text that can be compared to the role of the choir in Greek tragedy. Duro Ladipo (1931–1978), another Yoruba dramatist, composed a piece entitled *Oba Koso* (1973), which has some characteristics reminiscent of *Oedipus Rex*. John Pepper Clark (b. 1935), of Ijo-Yoruba background, went back to the proto-theatrical sources of Greek drama (origin in 'fertility cults') when he wrote *Song of a Goat* (1962), a piece about sterility and fertility. The title of the drama, in its literal translation of the Greek elements of the word 'tragedy', as they are commonly understood, is clear enough. After the sacrifice of a ram and the laments of a half-possessed aunt, a Cassandra figure who foresees everything and who prophesies evil in parabolic language but who is not believed and not respected because she is mad, the three main figures die, one of them in the Greek style behind the scenes. *The*

Song of a Goat is the first part of a trilogy of pieces which show that course of a family curse, a Nigerian version of *Oresteia* by Aeschylus. In The *Masquerade* (1964), the second piece of the cycle, choirs of neighbours and priests comment on the plot and report acts of violence that took place behind the scenes and are relevant to the plot just like in Greek tragedies. Femi Osofisan (b. 1946), a countryman of the abovementioned dramatists wrote an unpublished version of Sophocles' *Antigone* with the title *Tegonni: An African Antigone*. The Ghanaean Efua Theodora Sutherland (1924–1996) published *Edufa* (1967), a new interpretation of *Alcestis* by Euripides and included a choir since it is indispensable for Greek drama. Just like in Euripides' piece the wife in *Edufa* promises to die for her husband and keeps her promise under similar circumstances, which are marked by tender love. *The Beautiful Ones Are Not Yet Born* (1968), the work of another Ghanaean, Ayi Kwei Armah (b. 1939), echoes Juvenal's satire and Platonic teachings including the simile of the cave.

D. CLASSICAL LANGUAGES AND CLASSICAL STUDIES IN AFRICAN SCHOOLS, UNIVERSITIES AND MUSEUMS (18TH–20TH CENTS.)

Classical languages and studies have a marked tradition in African schools and universities. Latin and Greek were first taught in school in the 18th cent. This practice was able to continue in places with strong missionary and colonial influence. Latin is still taught in some public and private (mostly mission) schools, Greek much less, mostly in countries where these subjects are taught on a university level. One of the most famous schools is the Kamuzu Academy (Malawi), where pupils are required to study Latin, Greek and Classical history. Most Classics Departments in universities were established about the middle of the 20th cent. or later. In West-A. Classical philology and Classical studies are taught at the Universities of Sierra Leone, Cheikh Anta Diop (Senegal), Ibadan (Nigeria), Ghana and Cape Coast (Ghana). In 1966 the Classics Department in Cape Coast opened a Classical Museum, which was later taken over by the *Museums and Monuments Board* of Ghana. In central and southern A. Classical Philology and Classical Studies are taught at the Universities of Kikwit (Democratic Republic of Congo), Malawi and Zimbabwe. The University of Zimbabwe owns the world famous *Courtauld Collection of Greek and Roman Coins* and has published two catalogs of the collection.

→ Africa; → Myth; → Tragedy
→ SCHOOLS; → SOUTH-AFRICA; → UNIVERSITY

1 N. ARAUJO, A Study of Cape Verdean Literature, 1966 2 F. L. BARTELS, Jacobus Eliza Johannes Capitein 1717–1747, in: Transactions of the Historical Society of Ghana 4, 1959, 3–13 3 U. BEIER, Public Opinion on Lovers, in: Black Orpheus 14, February 1964, 4–16 4 B. BRENTJES, Anton Wilhelm Amo: Der schwarze Philosoph in Halle, 1976 5 M. L. CASTELLO, Greek Drama and the African World: A Study of Three African Dramas in the Light of Greek Antecedents (Diss. University of Southern California), 1981 6 W. J. DOMINIK, Classics Making Gains in Sub-Saharan Africa, in: The American Classical League Newsletter, Fall 1993, 4–7 7 Id., Classics in West and Central Africa, in: Prospects, Spring 1996, 3–4 8 A. EEKHOF, De negerpredikant Jacobus Elisa Joannes Capitein, 1717–1747, 1917 9 A. BAMGBOSE, The Novels of D.O. Fagunwa, Benin City 1974 10 P. J. CONRADIE, 'The Gods Are Not to Blame': Ola Rotimi's Version of the Oedipus Myth, in: Akroterion 39, 1994, 27–36 11 J. JAHN, Geschichte der neoafrikanischen Literatur, 1966, 31–35 12 M. KANE, 'Les Contes d'Amadou Coumba': Du conte traditionnel au conte moderne d'expression française, Dakar 1968 13 Id., Birago Diop: L'Homme et l'œuvre, 1971 14 A. LUVAI, For Whom Does the African Poet Write? An Examination of (Form/Content in) the Poetry of Okigbo and Soyinka, in: Busara 8.2, 1976, 38–52 15 G. MARIANO, Convergência lirica portuguesa num poeta cabo-verdiano na língua crioula do séc. XIX, in: II. Congresso da communidades de cultura portuguesa, Moçambique 1967, Bd. 2, 497–510 16 J. A. MARITZ, Some Thoughts on the Classical Allusions in the Work of M.B. Zimunya, in: Akroterion 41, 1996, 151–160 17 A. M. OCETE, El negro Juan Latino, 1925 18 J. W. SCHULTE Nordholt, Het Volk dat in duisternis wandelt, 1950, 17 19 O. SANKHARE, Enfers greco-romains et bibliques dans la poésie de Léopold Sédar Senghor, in: Afri-cult 4.3, Dakar, April 1992 20 Id., Senghor et la philosophie grecque, in: Scholia 8, 1999 21 M. SCHAETTEL, Léopold Sédar Senghor: Poétique et Poésie, 1997 22 V. B. SPRATLIN, Juan Latino: Slave and Humanist, 1938 23 H. DE VILHENA, O poeta caboverdiano José Lopes e o seu livro 'Hesperitanas', in: Novos escritos, 1939

ADDITIONAL BIBLIOGRAPHY: N. BISHOP, A Nigerian Version of a Greek Classics: Soyinka's Transformation of the Bacchae, in: J. GIBBS AND B. LINDFORS (eds.), Research on Wole Soyinka, Trenton 1993, 115–26; P. J. CONRADIE, Syncretism in Wole Soyinka's Play *The Bacchae of Euripides*, South African Theatre Journal 4.1, May 1990, 61–74; O. R. DATHORNE, African Literature in Latin, in: The Black Mind: A History of African Literature, 1974, 67–75; W. J. DOMINIK, The Classical Tradition in Africa, in: C. Kallendorf (ed.), A Companion to the Classical Tradition, 2007 (forthcoming); K. J. WETMORE JR., The Athenian Sun in an African Sky, 2002; F. BUDELMANN, Greek Tragedies in West African Adaptations, in: Proceedings of the Cambridge Philological Society 50, 2004, 1–25; M. McDONALD, Black Dionysus: Greek Tragedy from Africa, http://www2.open.ac.uk/ClassicalStudies/GreekPlays/Conf99/mcDon.htm.   WILLIAM J. DOMINIK

Agriculture

A. INTRODUCTION   B. EFFECTS OF LANDSCAPE CHANGE   C. TRANSMISSION OF AGRARIAN KNOWLEDGE   D. ANCIENT LEGISLATION   E. SPECIALIST LITERATURE

A. INTRODUCTION

Although questions of continuity within the tradition of intellectual history are apparent, hardly any other area of Classical civilisation has had such a lasting effect on European history as agriculture. Various levels may be distinguished: 1) the effect of measures used during Antiquity itself which changed the landscape; 2) the transmission of agricultural knowledge to successor cultures; 3) the consequences and exemplary nature of Classical legislation and social structures; 4) the indirect effects through specialist agrarian literature and calendars.

That agriculture's impact in the Mediterranean differs from that in the provinces or in areas of possible absorption outside the former empire is clear. In many cases it is a question of continuity of special developments that came about in Late Antiquity, which were in no way typical of the classical Mediterranean world. The main focus of the following survey is on the Latin West; long-term continuity in the Graeco-Byzantine world and the enormous achievements in transmission by Islamic cultures can only be sketched. Adaptations in the agrarian sector at the time of the Crusades were comparatively minor; the Graeco-Latin contact zones in southern Italy and in the Balkans had more of a regional effect. An important aspect that is not to be underestimated is the social prestige that aptitude in agriculture granted the *cives Romanus*, something that is also apparent in literary works (e.g. Virgil, Horace). Romanticised as early as the Augustan period, the republican farmer-warrior was viewed as an ethical model, with which an individual member of the upper classes, for whom the specialist literature was intended, could identify. This attitude was, it is true, not immediately understood within a Western warrior culture, but did have an effect where Latin written works became particularly well-known: in Medieval monasteries for whom the Roman example of large farms could be of use, in the Renaissance and, last but not least, in the reconstitution of the Baroque manor system.

B. Effects of Landscape Change

Certain characteristics of ancient agriculture have left a stamp on the European landscape: small scale, intensive crops are found e.g. in the lower Rhone valley and in former Raetia. Whether artificial irrigation in South Tyrol today through 'Waale' (from *aquale*) harks back to ancient roots is probable, but not attestable. Specialisation in specific crops in Antiquity (areas were used when suitable primarily for olives, wine, cereal crops or animal husbandry) had a lasting effect on large areas of land later on. The exploitation of forests for ship-building and for military uses laid waste entire regions, allowing them to erode and turn to karst; animal husbandry (especially of goats) was also responsible. In some regions (e.g. Salzburg, Bavaria) the Roman 'quadra' field system is still recognisable today.

C. Transmission of Agrarian Knowledge
1. Continuity and Breaks 2. Individual Crops 3. Agricultural Implements

1. Continuity and Breaks

Direct continuity in the Byzantine empire and in the Islamic world cannot be followed here in greater detail.

Artificial irrigation and intensive cultivation right up to market garden level were of course also seen in the European Mediterranean world, but they lost their markets with the decline of the Empire.

In spite of political fragmentation, the need for exchange of agricultural products over large distances might have contributed to a residual Italian identity because of the continuation of certain specialised products: until late in the 5th cent. (*Vita Severini*) even the region north of the Alps was accustomed to imports of olive oil.

2. Individual Crops

The most prominent example of Roman continuity is Alpine agriculture. There are numerous examples of Latin loan words from this activity in the German language (*alpes > Alm, butyrus > Butter, caseus > Käse, senior > Senn* and so on). Evidence of continuity is also found in place names. Alpine agriculture was of a special kind, typical for the mixed Celtic/Roman culture of the Alps. Demographic exchange in these areas was limited.

On the other hand animal husbandry was to a great extent culturally dependent. Cattle especially belonged to the prestigious Roman, Celtic and Germanic upper classes. This may also have had the consequence that there was no continuation of Roman breeding: the size of early medieval cattle breeds are noticeably smaller. The herding of sheep is older than Roman civilisation and therefore not really influenced by it; the continuation of shepherding culture is difficult to assess because of the lack of written sources. Sheep were replaced with pigs in parts of Europe as a generic animal raised for meat. Horse rearing had little to do with agriculture; horses were not used as agricultural draft animals until the late Middle Ages.

Similar to other crops, viticulture north of the Alps probably followed adaptations made necessary by climate, even during Roman times. For this reason, it is difficult to differentiate, from the written tradition, the share of continuity from that of reacquisition. Hardly any branch of fruit growing is conceivable without the influence from Antiquity. In this area one must differentiate between the improvement of local fruit (apples, less so pears) and the introduction of new varieties (pears, cherries, chestnuts etc.), whose prestige was higher the harder they were to grow. Continuity in herbs and vegetables can be presumed on a case-by-case basis, but because of a lack of sources, is difficult to prove. Individual varieties (peas, beans, herbs) come from the Mediterranean; but caution is needed as the European garden was strongly shaped by the Latin world of the monastery. Because of their erudition, monks from the early Middle Ages were able to draw on tradition as much as they drew on books. Strains of herbs, known from books, were either given up ('garum') or substituted (lavender for nard). Pepper and cloves were imported to Europe throughout the Middle Ages.

In the cultivation of cereals there is little to show for concerning continuity from the Roman period. In a few regions with particularly strong Roman continuity, Roman ploughing techniques must have predominated until the early Middle Ages: the crosswise ploughing of the ground with a digger plough rather led to square fields, while the post-Roman swivel plough is most applicable to long fields. Continuity is possible in wheat (cereals), and in millet, which, however, almost vanished from the sources, though it is difficult to assess whether that is because of low value or decreasing use. For other cereal types it is best to think in terms of independent development.

3. AGRICULTURAL IMPLEMENTS

Without going into the details which belong to the field of archaeology, two basic lines of development may be compared here: individual pieces of equipment reached such an optimal state in Antiquity so as to have required no further innovation to this day. An example that can be cited is the knives used to cut vines or fruit trees, practically a status symbol for the manorial lord.

Other implements required change due to shifts in the social structure, primarily because of the abolition of slavery. An effective example is the plough: the wide ploughshare required more oxen as draft animals, and the whole span had to be driven by several people. From the 5th cent. on, ploughshares became smaller and set at a slant. These required less pulling power and turned over the soil.

Until late in the Middle Ages, cereal crops were cut with a sickle. Because there was no need for a large supply of hay in the Mediterranean, large sickles were certainly sufficient for cutting grass. The innovation from Late Antiquity was to introduce a bend between the sickle blade and the handle, so that a person could cut parallel to the ground while standing–leading to the development of the scythe.

D. ANCIENT LEGISLATION

Of specific relevance for European agriculture were provisions of Antiquity which had been originally developed to secure areas on the edges of desert and mountainous regions which were difficult to cultivate. A *Lex Hadriana de rudibus agris* and a *Lex Manciana*, both of which have survived as inscriptions (e.g. CIL VIII 25902, 25943, 26416), assured specific rights for colonists in such regions. The so-called *Tablettes Albertini* from North Africa illustrate the relationships within an estate where tenant farmers could manage and trade almost entirely freely. Even an Italian papyrus (P. Ital. 3) attests to the classical roots of the 'two part agriculture', which was to become characteristic of the Middle Ages: the overlord or later the feudal lord cultivated only a part of his land centrally, passed a larger part on to more or less dependent people, who to a large extent worked independently on their holding in return for commensurate payments.

E. SPECIALIST LITERATURE
1. SOURCES 2. TRANSMISSION 3. IMPACT

1. SOURCES

The work of the Carthaginian Mago, translated into Latin after the fall of Carthage in 146 BC, has been lost, but was cited with great respect by Roman agronomists. Brief synopses survived (Diophanes) in Greek. The *Geoponika*, preserved only in fragments, was compiled in the 6th cent. AD and newly edited around 950 under Constantine VII Porphyrogenitus. The oldest Roman agricultural work is M. Porcius Cato's (234–149 BC) *De agri cultura*. The work, probably intended for private use, originated from his notes and did not appear in his lifetime, but influenced later authors. From its conception, M. Terentius Varro's (116–27 BC) work *De re rustica*, was a consciously systematic instruction manual. The *Georgics* by P. Vergilius Maro (70–19 BC) were by far more influential, although, or indeed because, they were written as a work of literature. The author himself had little practical knowledge even though Isidore of Seville categorised him as a specialist writer (Orig. 17,1,1). The 17th and 18th books of Pliny the Elder's (23–79 AD) *Historia naturalis* are a compilation of agricultural knowledge and commentaries on the calendar. In terms of content the work of L. Iunius Moderatus Columella, *De re rustica* from the 1st cent. AD is remarkable even today. The work of an unknown author, *De arboribus*, was combined with Columella's work already in Late Antiquity.

The most important intermediary of agricultural knowledge is Rutilius Taurus Aemilianus Palladius with his work *Opus Agriculturae*, probably written in the first half of the 5th cent. His work organises agrarian work for the first time almost entirely by the calendar, and for this reason enjoyed enormous popularity.

As in many other areas, Isidore of Seville had a decisive role in handing down ancient knowledge about agriculture; the relevant chapter 17 begins by mentioning the most important authors on the subject and thus ensures, while continually citing Virgil, acquaintance with the most important concepts.

2. TRANSMISSION

Transmission of the works of Virgil and Pliny was for the most part independent of their agrarian content; numerous manuscripts of both authors are in existence. All modern editions of Cato and Varro are based on a lost Florence manuscript (Marcianus). The younger authors on the subject have generally been transmitted in codices, and experienced their 'renaissance' in the Carolingian period and at the end of the Middle Ages. Palladius is also transmitted in individual manuscripts. To these must be added numerous excerpts and partial collections.

The calendars presented a special case for the transmission of agrarian knowledge. Roman holidays were closely connected to the farming year. The *Menologia rustica* should be understood in their connection with the Julian calendar reforms and list the agricultural activities assigned to particular months. The topics of illustrations in manuscripts of calendars, which for the most part show a typical activity for the season, remain noticeably constant, except for the reinterpretation of pagan elements e.g. a priest in front of a sacrificial altar becomes an old man warming himself over a fire. Little by little, the poems which accompanied the months, dealing with the names of the months, astronomical details and agrarian activities were expanded. One of the most extensive is that of Wandalbert of Prüm (813 – c. 870), who perhaps still directly drew on a calendar in the tradition of Filocalus (4th cent.).

3. IMPACT

Thus, the agrarian expertise of Antiquity remained available on farms and monasteries and was regularly drawn upon in the years of incisive agricultural reforms, most recently by experts in biological [organic] agriculture. From the outset, the size of the Roman empire made it necessary, depending on the region, to consider time conversions and climatic adjustments. Every era drew different lessons from its models. What one could and still can learn, affects not just the use of individual techniques and methods, but more basically – similar to jurisprudence – the development of a systematic scientific approach to agriculture: the concept *experimentum* which was derived from astronomy and there initially meant the systematic observation of celestial events, was adopted by Columella for agriculture and expanded through the element of repeated experiments. It was then possible to acquire a market-oriented, income-related mindset, which then came about above all in modern times.

Writers in the Middle Ages made use of specialist Classical literature for their agronomical works: Palladius and Varro were important sources for Petrus de Crescentiis, whose *Opus ruralium commodorum* was one of the most influential of medieval works in the field. Most medieval agronomical works also include books on veterinary science, though the transmission of these parts is smaller in volume. This may be in part because veterinary science was considered a subject in its own right (horse breeding was left mostly to the military); perhaps magical practises had become obsolete; but it is more likely that the post-Roman peoples had developed their own methods of animal husbandry and appropriate medical treatment.

1 W. ABEL, Geschichte der deutschen Landwirtschaft vom frühen Mittelalter bis zum 19. Jahrhundert, ²1967 2 C. BAUFELD, Antikenrezeption im deutschsprachigen Raum durch eine Landwirtschaftslehre. Columellas Werk 'De re rustica' in Heinrich Österreicher's translation, in: C. TUCZKAY et al. (eds.), Ir sult sprechen willekomen, 1998, 521–538 3 W. BERGMANN, Der römische Kalender: Zur sozialen Konstruktion der Zeitrechnung, in: Saeculum 35, 1984, 10–12 4 S. BÖKÖNYI, The Development of Stockbreeding and Herding in Medieval Europe, in: D. SWEENEY (ed.), Agriculture in the Middle Ages, 1995, 41–61 5 P. BRIMBLECOMBE, Climate Conditions and Population Developments in the Middle Ages, in: Saeculum 39, 1988, 141–148 6 K. BRUNNER, Continuity and Discontinuity of Roman Agricultural Knowledge in the Early Middle Ages, in: D. SWEENEY (ed.), Agriculture in the Middle Ages, 1995, 21–40 7 O. BRUNNER, Adeliges Landleben und europäischer Geist. Leben und Werk W. Helmhards von Hohberg, 1979 8 K. W. BUTZER, The Classical Tradition of Agronomic Science, in: K. W. BUTZER, D. LOHMANN (eds.), Science in Western and Eastern Civilisation in Carolingian Times 1993, 540–596 9 C. COUTOIS (ed.), Tablettes Albertini, actes privées de l'epoque vandale, 1952 10 D. HERLIHY, Three Patterns of Social Mobility in Medieval Society, in: Journal of Interdisciplinary History 3, 1973, 623–647, (Repr. in: Collected Studies, 1978) 11 J. KODER, Gemüse in Byzanz. Die Versorgung Konstantinopels mit Frischgemüse im Lichte der Geoponika, 1993 12 U. MEYER, Soziales Handeln im Zeichen des 'Hauses': Zur Ökonomik in der Spätantike und im frühen Mittelalter, 1998 13 A. RIEGL, Die mittelalterliche Kalenderillustration, in: Mitteilungen des Instituts für österreichische Geschichtsforschung. 10, 1889, 1–74 14 F. STAAB, Agrarwissenschaft und Grundherrschaft. Zum Weinbau der Klöster im Frühmittelalter, in: A. GERLICHEL (ed.), Weinbau, Weinhandel und Weinkultur 1993, 1–47 15 J. O. TJÄDER, Die nichtliterarischen Lateinischen Papyri Italiens aus der Zeit 445–700, 1955, 184–189 16 A. M. WATSON, Arab and European Agriculture in the Middle Ages: A Case of Restricted Diffusion, in: D. SWEENEY (ed.), Agriculture in the Middle Ages, 1995, 62–75 17 L. WHITE (ed.), The Transformation of the Roman World, 1966 18 V. WINIWARTER, Zur Rezeption antiker Agrarliteratur im frühen Mittelalter, 1991 19 Id., Landwirtschaftliche Kalender im frühen Mittelalter, in: Medium Aevum Quotidianum 27, 1992, 33–55 20 Id., Böden in Agrargesellschaften. Wahrnehmung, Behandlung und Theorie von Cato bis Palladius, in: R. P. SIEFERLE, H. BREUNINGER (eds.), Natur-Bilder, 1999, 181–221

ADDITIONAL BIBLIOGRAPHY: M. ADAS, Agricultural and Pastoral Societies in Ancient and Classical History, 2001; M. BARCELÓ; F. SIGAUT (eds.), The Making of Feudal Agricultures?, 2004; A. BURFORD, Land and Labor in the Greek World, 1993; S. ISAGER; J.-E. SKYDSGAARD, Ancient Greek Agriculture: An Introduction, 1992.   KARL BRUNNER

Albania
A. RENAISSANCE AND HUMANISM B. EFFECTS OF ANTIQUITY C. ARCHAEOLOGY

A. RENAISSANCE AND HUMANISM

In the Middle Ages, A. was only a geographical concept, and a loosely defined one at that. In the north, even what is now the Montenegrin coast was defined as Venetian A., while in the south, the name Epirus applied also to modern day A. In the 15th cent., the country was caught in a protracted defence against the Turkish conquest, so that there were no favourable requisites for the development of → HUMANISM. Nonetheless, as a result of the various waves of refugees fleeing to the West, native Albanians did take part in the → RENAISSANCE of the arts and sciences, primarily in the city states of Ragusa (Dubrovnik) und Venice. Individuals of note include [7. 28]: Johannes Gasulius (Ginus Gaxulus, Gjon Gàzulli, 1400–1465), Michele Marullo (Mikel Maruli,

1453–1500), Leonicus Thomeus (Leonik Tomeu, 1456–1531), Marinus Becichemus Scodrensis (Marin Beçikemi, born 1468). The most important, without question, was Marinus Barletius (Marin Barleti, c. 1440–1512). His works in Latin about the siege of Scùtari (Shkodra) and General Gjergj Kastrioti, known as Skanderbeg (Skënderbeu, 1405–1468) were disseminated throughout Europe and were translated into many languages (Italian, French, German and Polish, just to name a few). In these, the author described contemporary events in an educated style of Classical authors. In his first book of [1], he described Shkodra as a city in 'Madeconia' and mentioned that in antiquity, the Macedonians conquered the East, as far as India. Thus, Albanians sometimes confuse Alexander the Great (Leka i Madh) and Skanderbeg, since the Arabic/ Turkish form of Alexander's name, Iskender, sounds the same. Also the allegedly Illyrian twin-horned helmet of Skanderbeg feeds this contamination, because it is reminiscent of Ẕu'l Qarnayn in the Koran (18th Sura, 83–98), who is traditionally interpreted to be Alexander.

Another native Albanian, known internationally under his Russian name, is Maksim Grek (Mihal Artioti, 1475–1556). The master builder, painter and sculptor Andrea Nikollë Aleksi from Durrës (Andrija Alešija, 1425–1505) worked predominantly in Dalmatia. The fresco painter Onuphrios from Elbasan (Onufri, 16th cent.), belongs to the Greek renaissance and was active in Berat and Kastoria. A good late example of Humanism is the inclusion of the 10 classical sibyls with the prophets in the bi-lingual Italian-Albanian work of Catholic theological literature *The Host of Prophets*. The author Petrus Bogdanus (Pjetër Bogdani, c. 1625–1689) was named archbishop of Skopje (Macedonia) in 1677 and died in Pristina (Kosovo).

B. Effects of Antiquity

In ethnography, elements of national dress (e.g. the 'bell' dresses of women or men's 'fustanella') and individual themes and motifs of folk poetry have been discussed in terms of relics from Classical times. Albanian customary law (*Kanun*) is said to have retained elements from Indo-European prehistoric times. No consensus has been reached in all of these cases and any evaluation must be made with caution. Classical tradition played no serious role in the education system, and in the 20th cent., the interest of Albanians was limited to the issue of their ancestry. Within the purview of the Catholic Church, Latin was taught in North A. (1859–1944), and there are isolated examples of translations from Latin, but because of prevailing illiteracy in pre-War A. they did not reach a wide public. In the 18th cent., the influence of Greek neo-Aristotelianism reached briefly into southern A. Under the leadership of Theōdoros Kaballiōtēs, the Academy of Voskopoja (Moschopolis), which had been founded in 1744, had an exchange with the Μαρούτσειος σχολή in Ἰωάννινα (Epirus); in this way Eugenios Bulgarēs' ideas came to

southern A. In scholarly writings of the 17th and 18th cents., the Croats are described as Illyrians and the Albanians as Epirotes or Macedonians. P. Bogdanus (1685) described himself as 'Macedo' and the Italo-Albanian Nicola Chetta (1742–1802) described his people as 'Macedoni' [7. 24]. The self-designation *Albanoi > Arbër/Arbën* can hardly have become customary in medieval A. without foreign influence since the change *l>r* is not otherwise attested in the language development. The serious attempt at a scholarly explanation for the origin of the Albanians started with Thunmann [36], who grouped the Albanians with the classical Illyrians and the Rumanians (=Walachians) with the Thracians. Still the leading opinion today, it was, nonetheless, questioned from various sides at the start of the 19th cent. Adelung saw in the Albanians relics of non-Slavicised Proto-Bulgarians and linked them with the Iranian Ἀλανοί, or Caucasian A. [5. 793]. The alternative is therefore immigration versus autochthonic development, and since Xylander (1835), in the field of linguistics, the theory has prevailed of Albanian as a continuation of a paleo-Balkan language [15. 199–201]. A dead end in terms of the history of ideas which had serious consequences was Hahn's thesis of the Pelasgian character of Albanian. He suggested that the ancestors of the Albanians settled the Balkan peninsula before the Greeks [14. 211–254; 301–309]. This assertion that the *Pelasgians* (Πελασγοί) 'were the first European bearers of culture' [14. 245] has fired Albanian national consciousness until today, although linguists have never seriously pursued Hahn's theory. He determined: 'Epirotes, Macedonians and Illyrians originate from the same tribe. (...) Illyrian = Pelasgian in the broader sense' [14. 215]. Hahn equated the Albanian tribal name, the *Toski* with the classical *Tusci* and deduced: 'We consider ourselves justified in taking not only the Epirotes but also the Macedonians as Tyrrhenian Pelasgians, and seeing in them the nucleus of a large ethnos which was spread over the entire northern extent of the peninsula, a nucleus which connects the Tyrrhenian Pelasgians in Thrace and in Italy' [14. 233]. Camarda (1864) adopted this theory and spoke of a 'Thracian-Pelasgian or Greek-Latin stem' ('ceppo traco-pelasgico, o greco-latino') [8. 5], to which Albanian must be reckoned, in which Albanian was closer to Greek than Latin. We also find here the untenable theory anonymously expounded, in which Albanian is 'nothing less than a rather deformed dialect of basic Greek' ('poco meno che un dialetto, comunque assai disforme, del linguaggio fondamentale greco') [8. 7]. This theory – but with anti-Greek overtones – took a turn into politics through the writings of Pashko Vasa (1879) and Sami Frashëri (1899). For the Albanians, the majority of whom had converted to Islam since the 18th cent. the theory of the Pelasgian = Indo-European descent was an ideological justification for their ambitions first of all for self-administration and eventually for independence from the Ottoman Empire. 'The Pelasgians, who derive from a certain Pelasgus I.(Πελασγός), were without question the first, and compared to those who came later, had the character of autochthonic people' [37. 5f.]. P. Vasa explained the most important names in the Greek pantheon from Albanian etymology [37. 16–19]. S. Frashëri continued such exaggerations and as a practical conclusion derived from this a demand for the cultivation of the Albanian language. 'We are the oldest nation in Europe, the most noble and heroic; we speak the oldest and best language of the Aryan race'. The Pelasgian theory vanished from research after World War II; but the Illyrian descent from now on became a vehicle of political justification, in that it served to rebuff the territorial claims of its neighbours. In Kosovo particularly, one seized on the designation of the Illyrian Dardanians and postulated a continuity of settlement since Classical times. Following a methodology practised by Hahn and Camarda, the name *Dardania* was etymologically explained from the Albanian word *dardhë-a* ('pear'). A late literary resumption of the Pelasgian theory was ventured by the internationally known author Ismail Kadare, in which he declared that the Albanian folk epic came from pre-Homeric times. With this he went against the predominant scholarly view of a recent adoption from the Serbo-Bosnian epic-cycle.

C. Archaeology

During Turkish rule (until 1912), the archaeological sites in Albania and Kosovo were not systematically investigated, at first. They were only mentioned in travel reports with Greek and Roman antiquities attracting the most interest. There were only occasional excavations, e.g. 1899–1900 by P. Traeger in Koman. An early expedition report, based on fieldwork is that of C. Patsch [26]. On the Albanian side, archaeology lay in the hands of educated laymen and amateurs like Sh. Gjeçov [23. 61–73]. During occupation in World War I, excavations were carried out in the north of the country by B. Árpád, C. Praschniker and A. Schober [28. 6–9, 17]. After World War I, C. Praschniker and L. Ugolini carried out excavations in Apollonia (Ἀπολλωνία) and Butrint (Βουθρωτόν). It was not until the founding of the Archaeological-Ethnographic Museum in Tirana (1948) that archaeology in A. received an institutional framework [12. 37]. The museum with the greatest number of exhibits is that in Durrës. In 1976 the Centre for Archaeological Studies was founded as part of the Albanian Academy of Sciences. Between 1971–1990, the journal *Iliria* appeared, which published the results of academic research on Antiquity, while the journal *Monumentet*) was dedicated to medieval studies and the preservation of historical monuments. Excavations range from pre- and early history to Classical antiquity and the medieval period.

1. Pre- and early history   2. Illyrians
3. Colonial Towns   4. Middle Ages
5. Kosovo

1. Pre- and early history

Research focused on the Korça basin (Maliq, Dunavec, Tren) in the south east of the country and on the Mat valley in the middle of A. Neolithic, Bronze Age pile villages and cave dwellings were discovered and burial mounds were excavated. Early Iron Age depictions of hunting scenes were reported from the site of Spileja (Tren) [33. 26–29; 11. 28]. From prehistoric, Bronze and Iron Age finds, Albanian archaeology infers a continuity of settlement up to modern times. 'The most important conclusion to come from the rich Bronze Age finds (...), is that the various levels of culture with their content from the early, middle and late Bronze Age, confirm an unbroken cultural continuity during this period and, with that, an autochthonic development. The broad ethnic community which emerged at the end of the 2nd millennium BC with the common economic, cultural, religious and linguistic characteristics is described as Ur-Illyrian' (M. Korkuti in: [11. 22]).

2. Illyrians

Because there is no written transmission of the Illyrian culture, archaeology must carry the whole burden for the historical line of argument. Scodra (Shkodra), Pelion (Πήλιον in Dassaretien, Selca) [11. 56f.], Amantia (Plloça), Antigoneia [11. 59–61] and Byllis (Βυλλίς, Hekal near Ballsh) [11. 72–79] are known to have been important Illyrian fortified settlements. The city of Albanopolis (Ἀλβανόπολις), mentioned by Ptolemy is believed to be Zgërdhesh near Kruja in central A. Koch, on the other hand, [21. 136, 151] maintains that Persqop south of Tirana is Albanopolis and that Zgërdhesh is a settlement not known by name from antiquity. Aside from Dyrrhachion and Apollonia, the larger Illyrian towns (either tribal conglomerations or kingdoms) minted their own (bronze) coins with Greek inscriptions. The existence of some Illyrian towns is only substantiated by coin finds with corresponding marks. Silver and gold coins that have been found in the country usually came from Athens, Epirus (Pyrrhos) or Macedonia [11. 260–276].

3. Colonial Towns

Durrës (Dyrrhachion/Epidamnos), Apollonia and Butrint are the most important Greek colonial towns on the Albanian coast, which are nowadays the most visible with the most accessible ruins. The old town of Durrës is partly built on the remains of the ancient amphitheatre, meaning that up to now it has only been partly excavated. Butrint has an ancient lion gate, a theatre, the remains of early Christian sacred buildings as well as Venetian fortifications from the Middle Ages. The nearby ancient town of Phoinike (Finiq) was the main city of the Epirote Chaones. With reference to Stephanos of Byzantion, Albanian archaeology assumes that the Greek colonies were generally founded on already existing Illyrian settlements and had a mixed population (N. Ceka [11.39f.]). Consequently, the town constitution would represent the real Greek factor and not the ethnic composition of the population. Grave inscriptions right up to Roman times have been interpreted to that effect when the proper names contained Illyrian elements [9].

4. MIDDLE AGES

The Archaeology of medieval sites began with the excavation of burial grounds, but is now opening up above all the fortified settlements and castles which were destroyed during the Turkish conquest and thereafter abandoned, e.g. Pogradec, Berat, Kanina (near Vlora) and Butrint. The process works hand in hand with the conservation of monuments, which aims for the preservation and reconstruction of medieval and modern structures up to urban groupings (e.g. the 'museum towns' of Berat and Gjirokastra). At the entrance to the castle of Kruja, a museum in the shape of a medieval castle was set up in 1982 [28. 732f.; 11. 157] according to the design of the architects Pr. Hoxha and P. Vaso- one of the most dubious achievements of Albanian conservation.

5. KOSOVO

Old Dardania features numerous prehistoric and Classical sites, which were systematically opened up only after 1954 [24. 267]. The remains of the town Ulpiana (Ουλπιανόν, Iustiniana Secunda, Lipljan near Gračanica) were partly excavated in 1954–56. Among the most important discovery sites is one called 'The Spinning Mill' (*predionica – tjerrtorja*), a prehistoric site near Prishtina. In 1971 work started in the prehistoric burial ground of Romaja, northwest of Prishtina. Already in antiquity the country must have had several ore mines; Novo Brdo was explored in 1955 as a medieval mining town. In 1975–76, the medieval conditions were studied intensively in connection with the work on the *Historischer Atlas des Mittelalters*.

→ Alexander [4] the Great; → Epirus; → Pelasgian

SOURCES: 1 M. BARLETIUS, De obsidione Scodrensi, Venedig 1504, Albanian translation by H. LACAJ, Rrethimi i Shkodrës, Tirana ³1982. 2 Id., Historia de vita et gestis Scanderbegi Epirotarum principis, Rom c. 1508, Albanian translation by ST. I. PRIFTI: Historia e jetës dhe e vepravet të Skënderbeut, Tirana ²1967 3 P. BOGDANUS, Cvnevs prophetarvm de Christo salvatore mvndi, et eius evangelica veritate, italice e epirotice contexta, Padua 1685 (Reprint. 1977) 4 C. H. TH. REINHOLD, Noctes Pelasgicae vel symbolae ad cognoscendas dialectos Graeciae Pelasgicae, Athens 1855

LITERATURE: 5 J. CH. ADELUNG, Mithridates oder allgemeine Sprachenkunde mit dem Vater Unser als Sprachprobe in beynahe fünfhundert Sprachen und Mundarten, Part 2, Berlin 1809 6 B. ÁRPÁD, Régészeti kutatás Albániában, Kolozsvár (Klausenburg) 1918 7 M. CAMAJ, Der Beitrag der Albaner zur europäischen Kultur, in: Balkan-Archiv, N.S., 9, 1984, 23–30 8 D. CAMARDA, Saggio di grammatologia comparata sulla lingua Albanese, Livorno 1864 9 N. CEKA, Mbishkrimet byline, in: Iliria 1987/2, 49–115 10 F. DRINI, Bibliographie de l'archéologie et de l'histoire ancienne d'Albanie. 1972–1983, Tirana 1985

11 A. EGGEBRECHT (ed.), Albanien. Schätze aus dem Land der Skipetaren, Exhibition catalogue, 1988 12 Fjalor enciklopedik shqiptar, Tirana 1985 13 R. GALOVIĆ, Predionica, Neolitsko naselje kod Prištine. Priština 1959 14 J. G. v. HAHN, Albanesische Studien, Jena 1854 (Reprint. Athens 1981) 15 A. HETZER, Zur Geschichte der deutschsprachigen Albanologie, in: Balkan-Archiv. N.S., 10, 1985, 181–217 16 Id., Gesellschaftliche Modernisierung und Sprachreform, in: Balkan-Archiv, N.S., 17/18, 1992/93, 255–416 17 Iliri i albanci, Belgrade 1988 18 B. JUBANI, Bibliographie de l'archéologie et de l'histoire antique de l'Albanie, 1945–1971, Tirana 1972 19 I. KADARE, Autobiographie des Volkes in seinen Versen, Tirana 1988 (Albanian original Tirana 1980) 20 Id., Dosja H, Tirana 1990 21 G. KOCH, Albanien. Kunst und Kultur im Lande der Skipetaren, 1989 22 I. MARTINIANOS, Hē Moschopolis 1330–1930, Thessalonikē 1957 23 R. MATA, Shtjefën Gjeçovi. Jeta dhe vepra, Tirana 1982 24 Z. MIRDITA, see Arkeologjia, Kosova, in: KSA, Enciklopedia e Jugosllavisë, Vol. 1, Zagreb 1984 25 Id., Studime dardane, Prishtina 1979 26 C. PATSCH, Das Sandschak Berat in Albanien, 1904 27 C. PRASCHNIKER, A. SCHOBER, Archäologische Forschungen in Albanien und Montenegro, 1919 28 FR. PRENDI, Kërkimet arkeologjike në fushën e kulturës pre dhe protohistorike ilire në Shqipëri, in: Iliria 1988/1, 5–33 29 M. PRENUSHI, Kontribut shqiptar në Rilindjen evropiane, Tirana 1981 30 E. RIZA, Qyteti-muze i Gjirokastrës, Tirana 1981 31 I. RUGOVA, Vepra e Bogdanit 1675–1685, Cuneus Prophetarum, Prishtina 1982 32 SAMI BEY FRASHËRI (ŞEMSETTIN SAMI), Was war Albanien, was ist es, was wird es werden? Gedanken und Betrachtungen über die unser geheiligtes Vaterland A. bedrohenden Gefahren und deren Abwendung, 1913 (Albanian original Bucharest 1899, Reprint. Prishtina 1978 = Werke, Vepra, Vol. 2) 33 Shqipëria arkeologjike, Tirana 1971 34 Studime ilire, Prishtina, 2 Vols., 1978 35 P. THOMO, Banesa fshatare e Shqipërisë Veriore, Tirana 1981 36 J. THUNMANN, Untersuchungen über die Geschichte der östlichen europäischen Völker, Part I, Leipzig 1774 (Part reprint of pages 169–366: Über die Geschichte und Sprache der Albaner und Wlachen, 1976) 37 WASSA EFFENDI (PASHKO VASA), Albanien und die Albanesen. Eine historisch-kritische Studie, Berlin 1879 38 J. v. XYLANDER, Die Sprache der Albanesen oder Schkipetaren, Frankfurt/M. 1835.

ARMIN HETZER

Alchemy see → NATURAL SCIENCES

Alesia see→ BATTLEFIELDS

Alexandria

I. HISTORY II. HISTORY OF THE EXCAVATIONS AND FINDS

I. HISTORY

A. LATE ANTIQUITY B. ARAB RULE (642–1172) C. UP TO THE OTTOMAN CONQUEST D. MODERN ALEXANDRIA

A. LATE ANTIQUITY

In Alexandria (A.), as in other cities of the Roman Empire, the transition from the pagan Graeco-Roman times to Christian Late Antiquity was accompanied by violence. A decisive event was the destruction in AD 391 of the Serapeum and the library annexed to it. A church was built on its ruins and the 'Great Church' was founded on the site of the Caesareum. Christian A. soon acquired significance owing to its leading role in the Church and thanks to the catechistic school under the leadership of distinguished scholars such as Clement and Origen and the Patriarchs Petrus I and Athanasius. Nevertheless the pagan Hellenistic cultural tradition continued to exist and could boast of the 'Wisdom of Hypatia' (Synes. epist. 136). Furthermore, in the 6th cent AD, after Justinian had ordered the shutting down of the Academy in 529 AD, the Neo-Platonist Damascius fled from Athens and may have settled in A. (Agathias 2,30).

Economically, A. remained an important centre for trade, with the production of glass, textiles, papyrus, and wine, though of poorer quality than before. It also served, as before, as a place of transfer for trade between the Indian Ocean and the Mediterranean. After the *Annona* from AD 330 on were no longer delivered to Rome, but to Constantinople, the sea route from A to the Bosporus became the most important trade route. As late as the 5th cent. AD Jerome wrote that Rome was enriched by A. and its treasures (epist. 91).

B. ARAB RULE (642–1172)

In 642 the Arab general ʿAmr b. al-ʿAs occupied A., but only three years later the Byzantines reconquered the city, so that ʿAmr had to take it by storm in 645. These events resulted in destruction on a large scale. The loss of a great part of the Greek Byzantine population and leading citizens and the Arabs' establishment of Fustat as a new capital had a negative effect on the further development of A. (John of Nikiou 117,2–3; Al-Baladhuri 214; ʿAbd-al-Hakam 72). In spite of this A. retained a certain economic significance, since the Lighthouse and the harbour installations were in as good a condition as ever. As a result A. continued to be the most important port in Egypt. Even if trade relations with Europe and Constantinople continued only to a restricted extent, they were maintained with other parts of the Islamic world and with India. Shipbuilding and textile production remained concentrated in A., but the manufacture of glass and papyrus, owing to the altered circumstances, gradually decreased.

Around 800 the rise of Venice as a leading trading power in the Mediterranean was a sign of the intensifying of trade relations with Europe, as Venetian ships traded between Italy, Constantinople, Egypt, and Syria. As a result of this revival of Mediterranean trade the autonomous Sultan Ibn Tulun had the city fortifications and the Lighthouse restored in the second half of the 9th cent., after the uppermost storey had collapsed in an earlier earthquake in 796. To a large extent these improvements enabled A. to reconfirm its role as a port of reshipment for trade between the Indian Ocean and the Mediterranean (Al-Masʿudi, al-Tanbih 19). During the

following two centuries under the Fatimid Dynasty (969–1172) A. became not only a base for its strong navy, but also a central port for merchant ships sailing throughout the Mediterranean to Andalusia, northern Africa, Amalfi, Genoa, Venice and Syria. Associations of foreigners with their own trade settlements and offices (*funduqs*) were widespread in A.

Throughout the period of Arab rule (642–1172) the population and culture gradually changed. At first the Greek character of A. could be preserved, since the Arab garrison kept itself primarily to its own quarter and Greek remained, as before, the official language of administration of the country for almost a century. Being able to speak Greek was still of importance: it has been reported from the 8th cent. that an Omajjad prince 'commanded a group of philosophers in Egypt to translate medical books from Greek and Coptic into Arabic' (Ibn al-Nadim 338–339). There is also evidence that in the 9th cent. Hunain b. Ishaq, the famous Abbasid translator, 'went to A. to learn Greek' (Ibn Abi Usaibiʿa 1,189).

With increasing Arabisation more Arabs settled in the city, particularly soldiers and merchants. This also had an effect on the topographic face of A., with mosques and trade settlements (known as caravanserais or *funduqs*) being most significant, but there were also luxurious houses and theological schools (Ibn Ǧubair 39; Al-Maqqari 3,60–61). It should be emphasised that two Sunnite schools experienced their prime in A. under the Shiʿite Fatimid dynasty.

C. UP TO THE OTTOMAN CONQUEST

After the fall of the Fatimids, Saladin founded in Cairo a new Sunnite dynasty, the Ajjubids (1172–1250). Because of his personal war experience he decided to fortify A. and strengthen the navy. During a visit to the city he arranged for the establishment of a new school at which secular as well as theological subjects were to be taught. The school provided accommodation for those students who came from far away, and had baths and a hospital (Ibn Ǧubair 42; Abu Shama, Akhbar al-Dawlatain 1,269). Despite constant disputes with the Crusaders in Palestine, Saladin maintained the same friendly trade relations as his predecessors with the Italian city republics and other Europeans, a policy which operated for the greater good of A. The Spanish traveller Benjamin de Tudela (1166–1173) saw in the city associations and representatives from almost every European land as well as from Muslim and other eastern peoples as far away as India, and every nation had its own *funduq* (De Herreros, Quatre Voyageurs 29,3; Ibn Ǧubair 39–40).

At this time, after five years silence, a story of the fate of the Library of A. was spreading among Arab authors. According to this (as told at the beginning of the 13th cent. by Ibn al-Qifti, p. 354) the Arab general ʿAmr b. al-ʿAs destroyed the library, by having the books used as fuel for the baths in A. The truth of this story has been doubted in modern times since the 17th cent. The currently accepted interpretation stems from the assumption that the story is a 12th cent. fabrication to justify Saladin's selling the great Fatimid Library of Cairo and that of ʿAmid on the upper Tigris when he urgently needed money to finance the furthering of his campaign against the Crusaders (Al-Maqrizi, Khitat 2,255; Abu Shama 1,200). To justify Saladin's action Ibn al-Qifti, one of his most faithful followers, evidently considered it appropriate to include in his work the fantastic story of ʿAmr's desecration of the books. Today the prevailing opinion is that the ancient Royal Library was unintentionally burnt in Caesar's Alexandrian War in 48 BC, whereas the sister library of the Serapeum, mentioned above, was destroyed in 391 AD. Thus the library had long ceased to exist when ʿAmr occupied A.

During the subsequent rule of the Mamelukes (1250–1517) A. was able to maintain a relatively high standard of living. Economic growth in various parts of Europe had led to an increased demand for eastern goods. Correspondingly, more capital was also invested in international east-west trade, in which Egypt played a central role, as a pivot between the Red Sea and the Mediterranean. Merchandise flowed in abundance to A., and from there to practically every Mediterranean port. Recent archaeological finds show that A. was part of a broad branching international trade network, which stretched over the whole of the Mediterranean and reached as far as the Far East, India and China.

In 1303 an earthquake destroyed the ancient Lighthouse, or what was left of it. Attempts to reconstruct it were unsuccessful and so a new Lighthouse was built over on the end of Cape Lochia (now Silsila) (Ibn Battuta 10). On the old site Sultan Qait Bey had a fort built using parts of the old Lighthouse (1480), to defend the entrance into the eastern harbour. Only a short time later the discovery of the Cape of Good Hope in 1497 provided sea trade to India with the route round Africa. This substitute represented a decisive turning-point in the significance of A. as a trade metropolis. Even the Ottoman conquest of Egypt in 1517 could not offset the problems that had arisen or stop the decline of the city. Many inhabitants withdrew to Rosetta, particularly after the fresh water channel which connected A. with the Nile became choked with mud. When the members of the French expedition came to the largely deserted city in 1798, they estimated the population still to be 8000, but when they left again the number of inhabitants had decreased to 7000 (G. Le Père, Description de l'Égypte, 18).

D. Modern Alexandria

The departure of the French gave rise to a power vacuum, which soon led to dispute between British, Ottoman and Mameluke forces. An Egyptian popular uprising certainly brought about that the conflict ended favouring Mohammad ʿAli, an officer of Albanian descent in the Ottoman army. In 1805 the Sultan designated him Viceroy of Egypt. In 1807 British troops occupied A., but were defeated at Rosetta and forced to evacuate A. on 20 September 1807. The following day Mohammad ʿAli entered the city. He set in motion measures to restore A. to its old greatness. First he connected A. with the rest of Egypt by having a new fresh water channel dug (the Mahmudiya Canal), which reaches to the western branch of the Nile. Then he repaired the western harbour, extended it, and provided it with a new lighthouse. Europeans soon settled in large numbers in A.: British, French, Greeks, Italians, Swiss, but also Syrians and Egyptians from all parts of the land, as well as Jews of various nationalities. The population of the city multiplied from 7000 to 60,000 in 1840, and by 1874 the number had risen to 270,000.

After a revolt in 1882 under Ahmed ʿOrabi Pasha, violent unrest again broke out after the First World War in 1919 against the British Protectorate, this time under the leadership of Zaghlul Pasha. In the end, the British agreed to full independence in 1922. In 1923 a constitution for Egypt was concluded, and Sultan Fuad was invested with the title of king. At this time A. had the status of a second capital, as the Cabinet occasionally met there in the summer. Trade also increasingly intensified in A., and the Stock Exchange acquired an international significance.

During the Second World War A. was one of the most important British naval bases and so was the target of German air raids. In 1942 a modern university was founded in A., considerably stimulating cultural life. Shortly after the end of the War in 1952 a military coup forced King Faruq to abdicate in A. on 26 July. Egypt became a republic with General Nagib as its first president, succeeded in 1954 by Gamal ʿAbd al-Nasser. It was in A. that Nasser announced the nationalisation of the Suez Canal in 1956. The failure of attempts by the United Kingdom, France and Israel to regain the Canal caused many Europeans in A. and the rest of Egypt to leave the country. The widely applied nationalisation and requisition measures of 1961/1962 drove a great proportion of the Europeans out of A. Because of the more strongly centralised administration in Cairo the government no longer met in A. in summer. In 1990 the population exceeded three million, but A. had lost its economic significance, since business activities had increasingly also concentrated themselves in Cairo and several western agencies had transferred from A. to Cairo.

→ Alexandria; → Library

1 M. El-Abbadi, Life and Fate of the Ancient Library of Alexandria, ²1992 2 A. J. Butler, The Arab Conquest of Egypt, 1902 3 C. Décobert, J.-Y. Empereur (eds.), Alexandrie Médiévale, 1998 4 C. Haas, Alexandria in Late Antiquity, 1997 5 W. Heyd, Histoire du Commerce du Levant au Moyen Âge, 1983 6 A. A. Ramadan, Modern Alexandria, in: G. I. Stehen (ed.), Alexandria Site and History, 1992, 109–126 7 A. A. Salem, Tarikh al-Iskandariyah wa-hadaratuha fi al-ʿasr al-Islami hattā fath al-ʿUthmani, 1961 (History of Alexandria and its Civilization in Islamic Times) 8 P. J. Vatikiotis, Modern History of Egypt, 1969 9 L. C. West, Phases of Commercial Life in Roman Egypt, in: JRS 7, 1917, 45–58

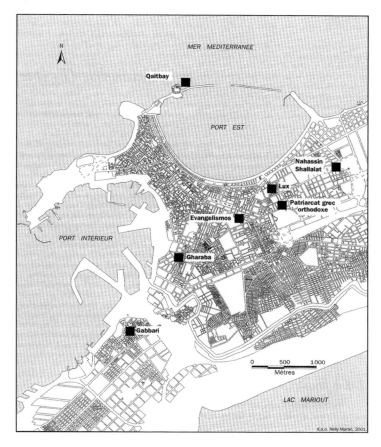

Fig. 1: Plan of Alexandria showing the locations of sites excavated by the Centre d'Études (2000)

ADDITIONAL BIBLIOGRAPHY: A. HIRST, M. SILK (eds.), Alexandria, Real and Imagined, 2004; A. WOLFF, How Many Miles To Babylon? Travels and Adventure to Egypt and Beyond. 1300–1649, 2003.   MOSTAFA EL-ABBADI

II. HISTORY OF THE EXCAVATIONS AND FINDS
A. INTRODUCTION B. FATE OF THE MONUMENTS UP TO THE BEGINNING OF THE 19TH CENTURY C. EXCAVATIONS AND FINDS D. THE NAME ALEXANDRIA IN MODERN TIMES

A. INTRODUCTION
Despite the great economic and cultural significance of the city of A., which was founded by the Macedonian King Alexander on the Egyptian Mediterranean coast in 331 BC, the preservation of the ancient remains and the state of scholarship are poor. Most of the ancient public buildings are still attested to only in literary sources (Strab. 17,791ff.).

B. FATE OF THE MONUMENTS UP TO THE BEGINNING OF THE 19TH CENTURY
Until the Arab conquest of Egypt in 640 most of the public buildings presumably remained intact. After the decision of Caliph Omar to expand the city of Fustat at Gizah into a new finance and trade centre, A. quickly

became depopulated. Sedimentation and natural changes in the water level led to the city being gradually filled in. There is certain evidence that the lighthouse, the ancient landmark of A., fell victim to an earthquake in 1303. The ancient buildings subsequently served as a quarry [33].

C. EXCAVATIONS AND FINDS
In the 17th and 18th cents., European travellers visited A. repeatedly, though only sporadically mentioning the ancient relics of the city. The first plan was drawn up by the Frenchman Dominique Vivant Denon (1747–1825) and his collaborators, who also documented the ancient remains of the city. They were members of the Commission des Sciences et des Arts of General Napoleon Bonaparte's Eastern Army, founded in 1798 [8]. The beginning of the systematic study of A. is connected with the name of Mahmud-Bey el-Falaki, who began excavations between 1863 and 1865 by order of the Egyptian Viceroy Ismail Pasha for the *Histoire de Jules César* of the French Emperor Napoleon III. If the exact extent and appearance of the city is unclear even today, el-Falaki's basic perception that the city possessed a system of orthogonally crossing streets retains validity [12]. The opportunity to pursue extensive excavations in A. was lost in the course of the 19th

Fig. 2: Architectural fragments
in the Archaeological Museum of
Alexandria (1923)

cent.: as a result of the decision of Mohammed 'Ali, the Ottoman Governor of Egypt (1769–1849), to expand A. into a great port, the modern city came to cover the ancient settlement area completely, making archeological investigation difficult to this day [14]. It also explains why many questions regarding the topography of ancient A. still remain unanswered despite numerous research activities, particularly during the 20th century. This concerns a complete plan of the city [19; 32] as well as the location and furnishings of many graves [34], the waterway network [5], the picture of the royal palaces with the tomb of Alexander the Great [4] and the nearby world-famous library [22]. After el-Falaki, the Greek physician T.D. Neroutsos contributed greatly to the exploration of the city with his archaeological and topographical investigations, esp. from 1874 to 1885 [24]. The endangering of the ancient structures by the rapid growth of A. led on 17 October 1892 to the foundation of the Archaeological Museum, which is active to this day as a research institute and conserves part of the antiquities found in the excavations (Fig. 2: architectural fragments in the Archaeological Museum) [15]. The first director, Giuseppe Botti (1892–1903), principally carried out emergency digs, which had become necessary owing to the extension of the eastern harbour and the demolition of the Arab fortification walls. Between 1892 and 1902 he worked in the rich necropolis of Kôm el-Chougafa alongside renowned German archaeologists, whose work was financed by the Stuttgart industrialist Ernst von Sieglin [9]. Botti also established the first catalogue of the Museum and was one of the driving forces in the founding of the Society Archéologique Royale d'Alexandrie, publisher since 1898 of the Bulletin d'Archéologie d'Alexandrie [7]. Botti's successor, Evaristo Breccia (1904–1932), continued the work of his predecessor, primarily presenting evidence that he had found in his excavations in the necropoleis of the ancient city. The third director of

the Museum, Achille Adriani (1932–1939 and 1947–1953), is a man of outstanding merit not only for conducting numerous excavations, but also for initiating a still unfinished compendium Repertorio d'Arte dell'Egitto Greco-Romano of the sculptures [2], paintings, architecture [3] and artefacts of Greek and Roman Egypt, with special emphasis on those found in A. Alan Rowe, who administered the Museum between 1941 and 1947, uncovered the foundations of the Serapeum, one of the few monuments in the interior of the city of whose history and reconstruction an approximate idea is possible [28]. Since 1954 the Museum has been headed by Egyptian archaeologists. Substantial insights into the city in Late Antiquity have resulted from the activities of the Mission Archéologique Polonaise (since 1960), which has been active in the region of Kôm el-Dikka. The Polish team were the first to document an insula in the centre of the ancient city, and they were able to reconstruct the development of the area from the second century AD into the early modern period [20; 27]. Work on a smaller scale was carried out by the Cairo Section of the Deutsches Archäologisches Institut from 1975 to 1977 (Gabbari necropolis) [29]. New impulses for archaeological field work in the city have come from the Centre d'Études Alexandrines and its director Jean-Yves Empereur (Fig. 1: Plan of Alexandria showing the locations of sites excavated by the Centre d'Études (2000). [This plan may need to go to GeoMüller – to give it the Pauly look, and I think for legal reasons as well.]) [11]. The Centre has committed itself to intensifying its excavation work to support conclusions about the appearance of the ancient metropolis. Their investigations are now spread across the entire city [10]. Underwater excavations east of the Mameluke fort at Quaitby (at the eastern end of the lighthouse island) led to the discovery of colossal architectural and statue fragments, which can be attributed to the pharaonic and Ptolemaic eras. Their exact origin and significance however are still not entirely explained [16]. It remains unclear, for example, whether a colossal torso from the excavations (Fig. 3: Torso of a Ptolemaic pharao) in fact can be identified as portraying Ptolemy II (283–246 BC). The patchy knowledge of A. arises not only from the many inadequately documented or published excavations, but also from the impossibility of reconstructing the exact location of objects from many rapidly executed emergency digs. Most of the finds are now in museums in Europe and overseas. It has been possible to achieve an approximately satisfactory state of research only in some areas (e.g. Ptolemaic architectural fragments) [25]. Many questions about chronology and production of sculpture [31], ceramics [23], terracotta, toreutics, glyptics, and glass are still open [1; 30].

Because of its rich literary and epigraphical tradition A. has been a particularly interesting subject for ancient historical research [6]; two areas of special study are emerging: A. under the Ptolemies [13] and A. in Late Antiquity, a period during which the city's population was made up not only of pagans, but also comprised a significant Jewish community and a growing number of Christians [17]. Detailed attention has been paid to the life and art [35] as well as the elaborately adorned processions and festivals at the court of the Ptolemies [18; 26]; since the early 1970s many archaeological studies and those focussing on the history of religion have examined the Greek and Greco-Egyptian cults of A., esp. the Serapis cult and the iconography of its images [21].

D. The Name Alexandria in Modern Times
The name Alexandria plays no great role in modern times. Only in connexion with the last Ptolemaic Queen Cleopatra, after Jacques Amyot's 1559 translation into French of Plutarch's Lives, did it become, since the 17th cent., a favourite topic of European literature, fine arts and – in the 20th cent. – the film industry. The name Alexandria stands for proverbial ostentation and riches at the court of the Ptolemaic queen [36]

→ Alexandria; → Plutarch

Sources: 1 G. Grimm, Alexandria. Die erste Königsstadt der hellenistischen Welt. Sonderheft Antike Welt, 1998

Literature: 2 A. Adriani, Repertorio d'arte dell'Egitto greco-romano. Serie A: Scultura I–II, 1963 3 Id., Repertorio d'arte dell'Egitto greco-romano. Serie C: Architettura e topografia I–II, 1963 4 Id., La tomba di Alessandro. Realtà, ipotesi e fantasie, 2000 5 G. Brands, Die Wasserversorgung Alexandrias und der Kanal von Kanopos, in: W. Hoepfner, E.-L. Schwandner, Haus und Stadt im klassischen Griechenland, 21994, 247–256 6 M. Clauss, Aexandria. Schicksale einer antiken Weltstadt, 22003 7 E. Combe, Le Cinquentenaire de la Société Royale d'Archéologie 1893–1943, in: Bulletin de la société archéologique d'Alexandrie 36, 1943–1944, 104–113 8 D. V. Denon, Voyage dans la Basse et la Haute Égypte pendant les Campagnes du Général Bonaparte en 1798 et 1799, Paris 1802 9 Expedition Ernst von Sieglin: Ausgrabungen in Alexandria, vols. 1–3, 1908–1927 10 J.-Y. Empereur, Alexandrie 2000, in: BCH 125, 2001, 679–700 11 Id., Alexandria rediscovered, 1998 12 M. B. el-Falaki, Mémoire sur l'antique Alexandrie, ses faubourgs et environs decouvertes par les fouilles, sondages, nivellements et autres recherches, faits d'après les ordres de son Altesse, Ismail Pacha, Vice Roi d'Égypte, Copenhagen 1872 13 P. M. Fraser, Ptolemaic Alexandria, vols. 1–3, 1972 14 Id., Alexandria from Mohamed Ali to Gamal Abdal Nasser, in: N. Hinske (ed.), Alexandrien. Kulturbegegnungen dreier Jartausende im Schmelztiegel einer mediterranen Großstadt, 1981, 63–74 15 Y. el-Gheriani, The Graeco-Roman Museum. Foundation, Addition and Renovation from 1892 to 1992, in: Alessandria e il mondo ellenistico-romano. Atti del II congresso internazionale italo-egiziano (1992), 1995, 49–53 16 F. Goddio et al., Alexandrie. Les quartiers royaux submergés, 1998 17 C. Haas, Alexandria in Late Antiquity. Topography and Social Conflict, 1997 18 H. von Hesberg, Temporäre Bilder oder die Grenzen der Kunst. Zur Legitimation frühhellenistischer Königsherrschaft im Fest, in: JDAI 104, 1989, 62–66, 76, 78–79 19 W. Hoepfner, Geschichte des Wohnens, vol 1: 5000 v. Chr.- 500 n. Chr. Vorge-

schichte – Frühgeschichte – Antike, 1999, 455–471 20 Z. Kiss, G. Majcherek, H. Meyza, H. Rysiewski, B. Tkaczow, Alexandrie VII. Fouilles polonaises à Kôm-el-Dikka (1986–1987), Warsaw 2000, 131–143 21 LÄ, s.v. Serapis, vol. V, 1984, 870–874 22 R. MacLeod, The Library of Alexandria. Centre of Learning in the Ancient World, 2002 23 M.-D. Nenna, M. Seif el-Din, La vaisselle en faïence d'époque gréco-romaine. Catalogue du Musée gréco-romain d'Alexandrie, Cairo 2000 24 T. D. Neroutsos, L'ancienne Alexandrie. Étude archéologique et topographique, Paris 1888 25 P. Pensabene, Repertorio d'arte dell'egitto greco-romano. Serie C III: Elementi architettonici di Alessandria e di altri siti egiziani, 1993 26 E. E. Rice, The Grand Procession of Ptolemy Philadelphus, 1983 27 M. Rodziewicz, Record of the Excavations at Kôm-El-Dokka in Alexandria from 1960 to 1980, in: Bulletin de la société archéologique d'Alexandrie 44, 1991, 1–118 28 A. Rowe, Discovery of the Famous Temple and Enclosure of Serapis at Alexandria, in: Annales du service des antiquités de l'Égypte, suppl. 2, 1946 29 M. Sobottka, Ausgrabungen in der West-Nekropole Alexandria (Gabbari), in: Das römisch-byzantinische Ägypten, Symposium Trier 1978, 1983, 195–203 30 St. Schmidt, Katalog der ptolemäischen und kaiserzeitlichen Objekte aus Ägypten im akademischen Kunstmuseum Bonn, 1997 31 Id., Grabreliefs im griechisch-römischen Museum von Alexandria (= ADAIK 17), 2003 32 B. Tkaczow, Topography of Ancient Alexandria. An Archaeological Map, Warsaw 1993 33 A. L. Udovitch, Medieval Alexandria. Some Evidence from the Cairo Gizeh Documents, in: Alexandria and Alexandrinism, Symposium Malibu 1993, 1996, 273–284 34 M. S. Venit, Monumental Tombs of Ancient Alexandria, 2002 35 G. Weber, Dichtung und höfische Gesellschaft. Die Rezeption der Zeitgeschichte am Hof der ersten drei Ptolemäer, 1993 36 C. Ziegler, L'Écho de Cléopâtre, in: La gloire d'Alexandrie. Exhibition catalogue Paris 1998, 295–303.   ORTWIN DALLY

Alexandrinism
A. Philosophy B. Theory of Art and Culture C. Alexandrinisme as a Literary Mark of Style

A. Philosophy
1. Ancient Basis of the Term 2. Reception in the Middle Ages 3. Alexandrinism in the Renaissance

1. Ancient Basis of the Term
As a term in the history of philosophy Alexandrinism describes a direction of → Aristotelianism informed by the writings of the most significant ancient Aristotelian commentator, Alexander of Aphrodisias. By removing inconsistencies in the works of Aristotle, Alexander endeavoured (around AD 200) to present a naturalistic base position. His doctrine of the threefold *nous* had particularly far-reaching influence: he distinguishes 1. the *physikós nous*, which primarily describes the *nóesis* in its potentiality, 2. the *epíktetos nous*, which contains the capacity of the *noeín* for application, and 3. the *nous poiētikós*, which effects the devel-

opment from 1 to 2, invades humans from outside and is identified with the divine. The human soul dies with the body; no divine providence exists as far as the particular individual is concerned [13; 18. 564f.; 21].

2. RECEPTION IN THE MIDDLE AGES

Alexander of Aphrodisias's works were known to the Scholastic philosophers mainly through the Latin translations of Wilhelm von Moerbeke (c. 1215–1286), but also through Latin versions of Arabic translations [19. 348f., 368]. It was Alexander's theses and particularly his teaching on the threefold *nous* that occupied Thomas Aquinas, Albertus Magnus, Dietrich von Freiberg, and others [19. 410, 434, 558].

Alexander's writings were known in the East no later than about AD 850–900 [19. 301], and Averroes (= Ibn Rushd, 1126–1198) in his comprehensive commentary on Aristotle's writings also expounded on the works of Alexander. Like Alexander so also Averroes rejected the idea of an individual immortal soul. He was, however, of the opinion– in the sense of monopsychism–that there was a continuation of the soul as a part of a common intellect (i.e., the 'divine soul') for the whole of humanity [19. 313–322].

Whereas the Jewish philosopher Moses Maimonides (1135–1204) apportioned great significance to the Commentaries of Alexander and Averroes for the understanding of the writings of Aristotle [19. 340], the Catholic Church repeatedly pronounced prohibitions against the 'false doctrines' of Alexandrianism and Averroism, as they denied both the immortality of individual souls and divine providence in regard to individual humans [7. 452].

3. ALEXANDRINISM IN THE RENAISSANCE

Renaissance Aristotelianism was also accompanied by an intensive occupation with the Aristotelian commentators of Antiquity and the Middle Ages and it led to a clear polarisation between champions of Alexandrinism and of Averroism. In the Introduction to his translation of Plotinus, the Platonist Marsilio Ficino (1433–1499) characterised contemporary Aristotelianism in these terms: *Totus fere terrarum orbis a Peripateticis occupatus in duas plurimum sectas divisus est, Alexandrinam et Averroicam* ('Almost the whole world is occupied by Peripatetics and divided for the most part into two schools, the Alexandrian and the Averroic').

Pietro Pomponazzi (1462–1524) is considered the chief advocate of Alexandrinism in the Renaissance period. He taught in Bologna, Ferrara, and Padua and caused deep controversy, especially through his *De immortalitate animae* (1516) [10. 63–78; 20. 22f., 26–30], with the defenders of Averroism, but particularly also with the Catholic Church. In it Pomponazzi stated that the doctrine of the absolute immortality of the soul was indeed true on account of its firm basis in Holy Scripture, but at the same time called into doubt whether it could be proved rationally, and independently of the convictions of faith (P. Pomponazzi, De immortalitate animae, ch. 8). Already by 1512 a prohibition from the Church against Alexandrinism and Averroism

had occurred, and Pope Leo X commissioned the Aristotelean commentator Augustinus Niphus (1473–1546) to write a refutation of *De immortalitate animae*. Other advocates of Alexandrinism in the Renaissance include the Neapolitan philosopher Simon Porta (d.1555) and the Spaniard Sepulveda (d. 1572), a pupil of Pietro Pomponazzi [20. 30f.].

B. THEORY OF ART AND CULTURE

1. ANCIENT BASIS OF THE TERM 2. USE OF THE ADJECTIVE 'ALEXANDRIAN' IN THE WORKS OF FRIEDRICH NIETZSCHE 2.1 THEORY OF ART AND CRITICISM OF CULTURE 2.2 THEORY OF EDUCATION 3. 20TH CENT. DISCUSSION OF EDUCATION

1. ANCIENT BASIS OF THE TERM

The use of the adjective 'Alexandrian' in the sense of 'cultured', 'educated' can be traced back to ancient Alexandria, which had been a significant cultural centre in the Mediterranean since about 300 BC and distinguished itself by the flourishing of literary, natural and spiritual learning, the rise of new branches of knowledge such as philology in particular and also by the institution of the Museum with its comprehensive Library. The literati of Alexandria were often scholars and poets in one person and concentrated on their activities as philologists. In their own poetry they mostly preferred small literary forms, strove for particularly painstaking elaborations of the texts, frequently chose unusual themes, in accordance with the ideal of the *Poeta Doctus*, and included learned allusions and excursuses [8. 88–99, 193–194; 16].

2. USE OF THE ADJECTIVE 'ALEXANDRIAN' IN THE WORKS OF FRIEDRICH NIETZSCHE

2.1 THEORY OF ART AND CRITICISM OF CULTURE

In his *Die Geburt der Tragödie aus dem Geist der Musik* ('The Birth of Tragedy out of the Spirit of Music') Friedrich Nietzsche traces the decline of ancient tragedy both to an increasing dominance in rational thought and theoretical contemplation of the world and to optimism about knowledge, citing Socrates as its creator. The rebirth of tragedy and, with it, of Hellenism can only result by establishing the limits of knowledge. He uses the adjective 'Alexandrian' as a synonym for 'theoretical', 'Socratic', and 'learned' [4. 610] in the sense of a quixotic accumulation of knowledge and an exaggerated confidence in the possibilities of human cognition. Alexandrian humans, 'who are basically librarians and proofreaders sacrificing their sight to book dust and printing errors' (Geburt der Trag. ch. 18, Werke III.1, 116), oppose art, myth and everything Dionysian; they are at best epigones, but are never themselves productive. Nietzsche therefore singles out the educational aspect of ancient Alexandrian culture and uses 'Alexandrian' in a purely pejorative way to characterise Roman Antiquity, the Renaissance and particularly his own time, which is wholly 'caught in the net of Alexandrian culture' and the highest ideal it knows is 'the theoretical man, equipped with the highest powers of understanding and working in the service of science' (Geburt der Trag., ch. 18, Werke III.1, 112). Nietzsche's interpretation of art is dealt with in detail in [12].

2.2 THEORY OF EDUCATION

Friedrich Nietzsche accuses the philologists of his time of unproductive erudition (Fragment 5,47, Werke IV.1, 129) and criticises: *Aufklärung und alexandrinische Bildung ist es – besten Falls!–, was Philologen wollen. Nicht Hellenenthum* ('Elucidation and Alexandrian education are – at best! – what philologists want. Not Hellenism.' Fragment 5,136, Werke IV.1, 151). An adequate understanding of Antiquity can not be arrived at in this manner. Nietzsche repeated his rebukes in *David Strauß*, characterising the eponymous hero as a 'cultural Philistine' (David Strauß, ch. 2, Werke III.1, 161) and remarking: *Vieles Wissen und Gelernthaben ist ... weder ein nothwendiges Mittel der Kultur, noch ein Zeichen derselben und verträgt sich nöthigenfalls auf das beste mit dem Gegensatze der Kultur, der Barbarei* ('Much of what is known and learnt is ... neither a necessary instrument of culture nor a sign of the same, and of necessity it at best complies with the antithesis of culture, barbarity'. David Strauß, ch. 1, Werke III.1, 159).

3. 20TH CENT. DISCUSSION OF EDUCATION

The central points of the criticism of scholarship and education expressed by Nietzsche were often taken up and discussed with great controversy at the end of the 19th cent. and the beginning of the 20th [15. 8off.]. By the end of the 20th cent., the question of the demarcation of true education from pure accumulation of factual details had gained in topicality in the face of an abundance of new interpretive possibilities. In 1998 Wolfgang Frühwald titled his article on education in the information age 'Athen aus Alexandrien zurückerobern' ('Reconquering Athens from Alexandria'). He was referring to a quotation from E.R. Curtius, which probably originated in a remark by the historian of art and culture Aby Warburg [2. 230; 9. 5], and asserted: *In der technizistischen Debatte um die Effizienz der Hochschulen geht oft der Blick dafür verloren, daß bloße »Belehrtheit« nicht das Ziel der Bildung sein kann* ('In the technicist debate on the efficiency of the universities one often loses sight of the fact that simple learnedness cannot be the goal of education') [2. 228].

C. ALEXANDRINISME AS A LITERARY MARK OF STYLE

Proceeding from the characteristics of ancient Alexandrian literature presented in B.1, French employs the noun *alexandrinisme* as a description of a subtle, somewhat dark style with a predilection for strong embellishments, allegories, and learned allusions. In contrast to Nietzsche's usage, there is no exclusively pejorative connotation [17. 491f.], although this is contained in the English term Alexandrianism or Alexandrinism.

→ Aristotelianism; → EDUCATION/CULTURE; → PHILO-

SOPHY; → RENAISSANCE
→ Alexander [26] of Aphrodisias; → Alexandria;
→ Aristotle, commentators on; → Aristotelianism;
→ Hellenism; → Museum; → Peripatos

SOURCES: 1 M. FICINO, Opera omnia, Basel 1561, (repr. 4 vols, 1959–1961) 2 W. FRÜHWALD, Athen aus Alexandrien zurückerobern. Bildung im Informationszeitalter, in: Forschung & Lehre 5, 1998, 228–232 3 F. NIETZSCHE, Werke. Kritische Gesamtausgabe, (eds.) G. COLLI, M. MONTINARI, 1967ff. 4 Id., Die Geburt der Tragödie. Schriften zu Literatur. und Philosophie. der Griechen, (ed. and comm.) M. LANDFESTER, 1994 5 PETRUS POMPONATIUS, Tractatus de immortalitate animae. Testo e Traduzione a cura di G. MORRA, 1954 6 PIETRO POMPONAZZI, Abhandlung über die Unsterblichkeit der Seele. Latin-German ed. B. MOJSISCH, 1990

LITERATURE: 7 H. FLASHAR, Aristoteles, in: id. (ed.), Die Philosophie der Antike 3: Ältere Akademie. Aristoteles-Peripatos, 1983, 175–458 8 H.-J. GEHRKE, Geschichte des Hellenismus., ²1995 9 P. GODMAN, T.S. Eliot and E.R. Curtius. Eine europäische Freundschaft, in: Liber. Europ. Kultur-Zschr. 1, 1989 10 P. O. KRISTELLER, Acht Philosophen der italienischen Renaissance, 1986 (= Eight Philosophers of the Italian Renaissance, 1964) 11 Id., Aristotelismo e sincretismo nel pensiero di Pietro Pomponazzi, 1983 12 T. MEYER, Nietzsche und die Kunst, 1993 13 P. MORAUX, Der Aristotelismus bei den Griechen von Andronikos bis Alexander von Aphrodisias, 3 vols, 1973ff. 14 B. NARDI, Studi su Pietro Pomponazzi, 1965 15 U. PREUSSE, Humanismus und Geschichte: zur Geschichte des altsprachlichen Unterrichts in Deutschland von 1890 bis 1933, 1988 16 E. R. SCHWINGE, Künstlichkeit von Kunst. Zur Geschichtlichkeit der alexandrinischen Poesie (= Zetemata 84), 1986 17 Trésor de la langue française. Dictionnaire de la langue du XIXᵉ et du XXᵉ siècle (1789–1960), publié sous la direction de P. IMBS, vol. 2, 1973 18 F. UEBERWEG, Grundriß der Geschichte der Philosophie 1: Die Philosophie des Altertums, (ed.) K. PRAECHTER, ¹²1926 (repr. 1961) 19 Id., Grundriß der Geschichte der Philosophie 2: Die patristische und scholastische Philosophie, (ed.) B. GEYER, ¹¹1927 (repr. 1961) 20 Id., Grundriß der Geschichte der Philosophie 3: Die Philosophie der Neuzeit bis zum Ende des XVIII. Jahrhundert, completely revised by M. FRISCHEISEN-KÖHLER, W. MOOG, ¹³1953 21 J. WONDE, Subjekt und Unsterblichkeit bei Pietro Pomponazzi (= Beitr. zur Altertumskunde 48), 1994. JANA HARTMANN

Allegorism

I. LINGUISTICS AND LITERARY STUDIES II. HISTORY OF RELIGIONS AND MYTHOLOGY

I. LINGUISTICS AND LITERARY STUDIES

A. INTRODUCTION: THE CONCEPT B. HOMERIC ALLEGORISM C. BIBLICAL ALLEGORISM D. VIRGILIAN ALLEGORISM E. OVIDIAN ALLEGORISM AND ALLEGORICAL-INTEGUMENTAL MIXED FORMS

A. INTRODUCTION: THE CONCEPT

In recent linguistic and literary-historical studies, as in theology, allegorism designates the methodically reflective development of a multiple meaning that goes beyond the literal meaning of religious, poetical, and other normative texts. As a hermeneutic-interpretative procedure, allegorism is to be distinguished from the grammatical, rhetorical, and productive-poetic forms (cf. below, *ad finem*) of → ALLEGORY. Like the latter, it proceeds according to the fundamental law of transference. Allegorism begins with a situation of creative reception in which a canonical text needs to be explained under altered cultural circumstances that lead to the assumption that its wording no longer constitutes its unique or proper meaning, but rather that the genuine (theological, philosophical or ethical) spiritual meaning (*nous*), or that which is 'concealed beneath (*hypó*) the literal meaning', still remains to be discovered. In the oldest texts, as in the Homeric allegorism of Theagenes of Rhegium and the end of the 6th cent. BC, allegorism is therefore designated as *hypónoia*. This concept is gradually replaced, near the dawn of our era at the latest, by *allegoria*, a word found in works of literary hermeneutics since the 1st cent. AD(Ps.-Heraclitus, Sextus Empiricus, Philo of Alexandria) and is current in patristic literature since Origen.

B. Homeric Allegorism

The beginnings of Western textual allegory are found in the criticism of Homeric poetry and myth by the grammarian Theagenes of Rhegium of the 6th cent. BC, who interpreted Homeric texts in the direction of cosmogony or philosophy of nature. It was practiced systematically in the 5th/4th cent. by Ionic natural philosophers from among the Pre-Socratics. The first 'ethical' allegorism was that of Anaxagoras of Clazomenae and his student Metrodorus of Lampsacus. Homeric allegorism was handed down in scholia from the 2nd cent. BC on down into the Byzantine period. Homeric allegorism found wide acceptance in the 1st cent. AD in the school of Pergamum (L. Annaeus Cornutus, *Theologiae Graecae Compendium*; Ps.-Heraclitus, *Allegoriae Homericae*), which was much influenced by Stoicism. Choeroboscus (6th or 7th cent.), with his allegorism of Homer to explain nature, is characteristic of the further development of the theory of allegorism in the Greek world. Homeric allegorism was still known in the 12th cent. to the Byzantine scholar Eustathius (archbishop of Thessalonica), who continued it in his own commentary on the *Iliad*.

C. Biblical Allegorism

Allegorical exegesis of the Bible, whose pre-Christian roots lie in Hellenistic Judaism, constitutes the core of allegorism. Philo of Alexandria furnished large parts of the Mosaic books with an ethical-moral allegorism. This had an important influence on Clement of Alexandria. The Antiocheans Diodorus of Tarsus and Theodore of Mopsuestia rejected allegorism. The NT is familiar with a rudimentary form of allegorism, and developed, especially through Paul and the Letter to the Hebrews, the related thought form of → TYPOLOGY.

Throughout the Middle Ages allegorism remained the authoritative form of reception of the Bible in a wide variety of commentaries, particularly on *Genesis*, the *Psalms*, the *Song of Songs* and the *Apocalypse*. In the High and Late Middle Ages allegorism was extended to the entire Bible. From there, it spread to such neighboring fields as sermons, liturgy, visionary literature, the interpretation of history and philosophy of nature. Common to the various concepts of allegorical interpretation of scripture evolving over time is the claim that it is founded on the facts of sacred history and is therefore true. On the other hand, poetic allegorism was evaluated as *figmentum, mendacium* (John of Salisbury, *Policraticus* 3,6 and 9), or as an 'enveloping' transformation of reality (*integumentum, involucrum*, Isidore of Seville, *Etymologiae* 8,7,10; William of Conches, Bernardus Silvestris). Origen was decisive for the beginnings of Christian allegorism of scripture with his model of meaning on three levels, transferred from the order of creation to scripture (*Peri archon* 4,2,4).Following him, the Middle Ages down to the 13th cent. developed various outlines of systems. Gregory the Great conceived of a threefold explication of the Bible in the literal, allegorical-typological and tropological-moral sense (*Moralia in Iob* = CCL 143,4). More influential was the doctrine, already defended by Cassian (*Conlationes* 14,8,4 = CSEL 13,405) around 420 and further propagated in the 12th and 13th cents., of the fourfold meaning of scripture: *historia/sensus litteralis – allegoria* including typology, *tropologia/sensus moralis and anagogia*. Essential for the expansion of allegorism was the theory of signs originating in Augustine (*De doctrina christiana* 2,10,15 = CCL 32,41), which then in the 12th and 13th cents. further developed into a theory of meaning not only of words, but also of things. This, according to Hugh and Richard of St. Victor, enabled one to differentiate spiritual literature from worldly literature. The way was thus prepared for an all-embracing allegorism of everything found in the Bible, in creation and in all utterances of human culture and history (cf. PL 175,20–24; PL 177,205B). Substantial transformations in allegorism were brought about by the rise of → SCHOLASTICISM and can be identified in → HUMANISM (Trithemius; Erasmus of Rotterdam, *Enchiridion*), in the literature of the Reformation, and in Protestant schoolbooks of the early modern period.

D. Virgilian Allegorism

The beginnings of the allegorical interpretation of the *Aeneid* lie in the 4th and 5th cents.in the *Vita* of Aelius Donatus, in Servius, and especially in Claudius Giordanus Fulgentius' (*Expositio Vergilianae continentiae secundum philosophos moralis*), whose richly transmitted work influenced the integumental interpretation of the *Aeneid* that was in evidence since the 12th cent. (Bernardus Silvestris, *Commentum super sex libros Eneidos Virgilii*). Medieval sermons were also familiar with Christian interpretations of Virgil (Alanus ab Insulis, Absalon von Springiersbach; see Gottschalk

Hollen [11. 259] for further material on integumental Virgil commentaries), and with lives of Virgil. Virgilian allegorism was still practiced by Ph. N. Frischlin (*P. Virgilii Maronis Bucolica & Georgica, paraphrasi exposita*, 1580; a modification of earlier interpretations by J.L. Vives and a plagiarizer).

E. Ovidian Allegorism and Allegorical-Integumental Mixed Forms

Knowledge of Ovid already appears in the early Middle Ages. Since its beginnings, in addition to the reception of extracts of Ovidian material, motifs and formal patterns, 'the possibility of the allegorical interpretation of mythology' constituted a central aspect of Ovid reception [4. 252]. Conceptual and actual transitions to *integumentum*, that is, to 'the interpretative allegorism of poets and philosophers' became manifest with particular clarity in the forms of medieval Ovid allegorism, as did 'expressive-creative poetic allegory, formed with this as its model' [6. 9]. Authoritative models of the latter were given, for instance, by Prudentius, *Psychomachia*; Martianus Capella, *De nuptiis Mercurii et Philologiae*; Boethius, *De consolatione philosophiae*; and Alanus ab Insulis, *De planctu naturae* and *Anticlaudianus*). Whereas authors like Bernardus Silvestris and John of Salisbury sought to separate *allegoria* and *integumentum*, this separation was not maintained in the systematic commentaries on Ovid that began in the 12th cent. (Arnolphe of Orléans, *Allegoriae super Ovidii Metamorphosin*; John of Garlandia, *Integumenta Ovidii*); for many other examples of allegorizing interpretations of Ovid: [2. 286–288]. The *Ovidius moralizatus* (c. 1340) of Petrus Berchorius (Pierre Bersuire), which stood methodologically close to biblical allegorism, may be considered the high point of allegorism of the *Metamorphoses*; the Old French *Ovide moralisé* arose independently from it (c. 1350).

→ Adaptation

→ Philo of Alexandria

1 W. Freytag, Allegorie, Allegorismus, in: Historisches Wörterbuch der Rhetorik 1, 1992, 330–392 (with extensive bibliography)   2 H.-J. Horn, U. Krewitt, Allegorismus. Außerchristliche Texte, I. Alte Kirche, II. Mittelalter, in: TRE 2 1978, 276–290   3 J. C. Joosen, J. H. Waszink, Allegorismus, in: Reallexikon für Antike und Christentum 1, 1950, 283–293   4 H. Kugler, Ovidius Naso, P., in: Die deutsche Literatur des Mittelalters: Verfasserlexikon (Second completely revised edition) 7, 1989, cols. 247–273 (medieval reception)   5 H. Meyer, Schriftsinn, mehrfacher, in: Historisches Wörterbuch der Philosophie 8, 1992, 1431–1439   6 Ch. Meier, Überlegungen zum gegenwärtigen Stand der Allegorie-Forschung, in: Frühmittelalterische Studien 10, 1976, 1–69   7 H. de Lubac, Exégèse médiévale. Les quatre sens de l'écriture, 1–4, 1959–1964   8 F. Ohly, Schriften zur mittelalterliche Bedeutungsforschung, ²1983   9 H. Graf Reventlow, Epochen der Bibelauslegung, vol. 1, 1990; vol. 2, 1994; vol. 3, 1997; vol. 4, 2001   10 H.-J. Spitz, Allegoresis/Allegorie/Typologie, in: Fischer Lexikon der Literatur 1, 1996, 1–31   11 F. J. Worstbrock, Vergil (P. Vergilius Maro), in: Die deutsche Literatur des Mittelalters: Verfasserlexikon (Second completely revised edition) 10, 1999, cols. 247–284 (medieval reception)

ADDITIONAL BIBLIOGRAPHY: D. C. Allen, Mysteriously Meant: The Rediscovery of Pagan Symbolism and Allegorical Interpretation in the Renaissance, 1970; C. Baswell, Virgil in Medieval England: Figuring the Aeneid from the Twelfth Century to Chaucer, 1995; H.-J. Horn, Die Allegorese des antiken Mythos in der Literatur, Wissenschaft und Kunst Europas, 1997.   RUDOLF SUNTRUP

II. History of Religions and Mythology
A. Introduction B. Origin C. The Jewish-Christian Tradition of Antiquity D. Middle Ages E. Early Modern Period

A. Introduction

Allegorism, from the Greek *allēgoreín*, 'to interpret figuratively', is the understanding of a traditional text in a figurative sense; the term was coined in Hellenistic discussions and replaced the expression *hypónoia*, 'deeper (literally, lying underneath) meaning', which was generally used in Plato's time. As a method, it is to be distinguished from the historical interpretation of myths, or euhemerism, as well as from purely etymological interpretation, even though allegorism often makes use of them, and also from Christian typology, which by means of non-literal interpretation of the Old Testament, transforms it into the forerunner and announcer of the salvific events described in the New Testament. Here, of course, the terminology in Christian discussion since Galatians 4,24 is often easy to misunderstand (cf. Origen, *Peri archōn* 4,2,6). Allegorism as an exegetical method is also to be distinguished from → ALLEGORY, which is a literary creation that is, under the influence of a poetics that goes back to allegorism, deliberately unintelligible on a literal level. Allegory was particularly vital in the Middle Ages and beyond through the examples of Prudentius, Martianus Capella and Boethius. A comprehensive historical presentation of allegorism is lacking. Precisely for this reason, the best synthesis will be a systematic approach ([1], cf. also [2; 3; 4]).

B. Origin

Allegorism arose in Greek Antiquity as a means of interpreting Homer. As a consequence of pre-Socratic criticism of mythical tales in Homer, carried out in particular by Xenophanes of Colophon and Heraclitus of Ephesus, there was an apologetic concern. This was at least as important as the claim of Late Archaic exegetes of Homer that they were reading the poet in an original way [5; 6]. Already in Antiquity, the Homeric interpreters Theagenes of Rhegium and Stesimbrotus of Thasus (FGrH 107), from the end of the 6th cent. BC were considered its inventors. Its most important early defender was thought to be the Anaxagorean Metrodorus of Lampsacus (late 5th cent. BC). He was held to have interpreted Homer in line with the physical sciences, as can be seen in detail in his commentary on a cosmogonic poem by Orpheus from a grave at Derveni (*c.* 320 BC) [7], whereas his teacher Anaxagoras himself was regarded as the founder of the ethical allegorism of Homer (Diogenes Laertius 2,3,11). However, ethical allegorism of mythic tales must have already arisen in the circle of southern Italian Pythagoreans, as Plato suggests (Gorgias 493 ab). In the following period, physical allegorism, taken up and expanded particularly by the Stoa, was to dominate [8]. The model of *theologia tripertita* or 'threefold speech about the gods' found in M. Terentius Varro probably goes back to the Hellenistic Stoa. In addition to the literal sense (*theologia poetice*), it added an underlying physical sense (*theologia physice*) and a text's application to political life (*theologia civilis*) [9]. Important authors writing in Greek include Cornutus and Heraclitus, the latter of whom wrote Homeric allegorism in the imperial period. Physical allegorism predominates in both these authors [10]. In his *De natura deorum*, Cicero has the Epicurean Velleius and the Sceptic Academic Cotta strongly criticize the allegorism of the Stoic Balbus. Nevertheless, it was at least handed down as a method for posterity by one of the chief Latin authors. Despite the indifference of Plato and the hesitant attitude of Plutarch (*Isis et Osiris* 374 E; [11]), allegorism became important for the Neoplatonists (with the exception of Plotinus), as is shown, for instance, in Porphyry's work on the cave of the nymphs in Homer, or Julian's discourse on the Great Mother [12; 13]. Particularly important for posterity was the commentary on Cicero's *Somnium Scipionis* by Macrobius [14].

C. The Jewish-Christian Tradition of Antiquity
1. Jewish   2. Christian

1. Jewish
Apologetic allegorism of the Old Testament began in Alexandrian Judaism. Fragmentarily preserved are the interpretations of the Jewish Peripatetic Aristobulus (2nd cent. BC) in his Commentary on the Pentateuch (Eusebius, *Preparatio Evangelica* 8,10; 12,12), and the allegorical exegesis of the dietary laws in the *Letter of Aristeas* (143–50); however, the fact that the *Song of Songs* was taken up into the canon also presupposes its allegorical interpretation. It was Philo's allegorism, however, that became central, particularly his moral allegorizing, although he is also familiar with physical allegorism. He sought to grasp the true reality of the biblical text, whose literal meaning was merely a shadowy image of the truth. By means of this Platonizing construct, he succeeded, despite privileging the allegorical meaning, in maintaining the literal sense so indispensable for religious practice (cf. in particular, Philo, *Legum allegoriae* 2,71–73; *De Abrahami migratione* 89f.; De *providentia* 2,72; *De mutatione nominum* 8–10) [15].

2. Christian
Imperial Christians used allegorism both for the rejection of pagan myths and for the interpretation of their own scriptural tradition. In this process, Varro's *theologia tripertita* became one of the foundations of allegorism and is referred to both by apologists and Church Fathers [16; 17].

The consequences of physical allegorism for pagan religion are easily seen. It eliminates the reality of the gods (Aristides, *Apologia* 13,7). At the same time, however, it provides myths with an acceptable validity, to which apologists and Church Fathers objected. Not only allegorism, but also pagan myths as such were to be rejected (for a detailed account, see, for instance, Athenagoras leg. 22 or Arnob. 4,33; 5,32–41). This attitude survives in the sermons of Augustine (see the detailed account in a sermon for the calends [18]).

In addition, a tradition of allegorizing the Old Testament existed since the New Testament times, whereas the gospels, as historical truth, were not subject to allegorism. Paul already read Genesis 16,1–15 (Sara and Agar) *per allegoriam* (Galatians 4,24), that is, typologically. This legitimized allegorism of the Old Testament for the whole of Christian exegesis. Following Alexandrian tradition, Origen formulated a system of allegorism and distinguished between the literal (somatic) meaning, accessible to all; the more advanced moral (psychic) sense; and the mystical (pneumatic) sense, open only to a few (*Peri archōn* 4,2,4). He often rejected the literal sense, in contrast to his successors; yet through his system he influenced the three scriptural meanings of later times. In the Latin West, Ambrose in particular, following Philo, pursued allegorism, both moral and mystical. As with Philo, however (and Ambrose's predecessor Hilary of Poitiers), the literal meaning remained indisputably steadfast; moreover, the *sensus historialis* and the *sensus mysticus* (moral allegorism) took their place within the taxonomy. Augustine subscribed to this view in a nuanced way, insofar as he ascribed greater psychagogical effect to allegorical interpretation (*Epistolae* 55,21), and correspondingly used it in his sermons, whereas he preferred the historical sense in his Bible commentaries [19]. Both interpretative levels consequently coexist. This became valid for all those who followed, especially once Gregory the Great clearly stood up for this twofold path (*In evangelio Johannis* 40,1). From its roots in scriptural interpretation, allegorism became clearly discernible in Fulgentius' commentary on Statius' *Thebaid* and, thus secularized, was transferred to the interpretation of pagan literary works as well. Despite the objections of the late Augustine (*De doctrina christiana* 3,8,12), this linked the allegorizing literary interpretation of imperial grammar with Christian allegorism. On the other hand, a Christian allegorical literature arose from creative contact with exegetical procedure. Its most important exponents in the Latin West were Prudentius and Boethius [20; 21].

D. Middle Ages
1. Scriptural Exegesis and Allegorical Poetry 2. The Allegorism of Ancient Myths

1. Scriptural Exegesis and Allegorical Poetry

Following the Church Fathers, particularly Augustine, the Middle Ages continued the allegorical exegesis of scripture, as well as the secularized exegesis of pagan poetry. In the School of Chartres (see below), this led to elaborate theoretical schemes, like that of *indumentum*, or the literal surface of the 'textual skin', which was to be penetrated. Under the influence of Prudentius and Boethius, the Latin Middle Ages provided itself in addition with a highly vital allegorical poetry. Understanding it, whether in an ethical or edifying sense, historically or politically, did not take place via the exegetical procedure of allegorism, but was already pre-planned within the literal sense. We cannot elaborate on this here.

2. The Allegorism of Ancient Myths

Rhetorical tradition classified the mythical tale (*fabula*) as fiction (Cicero, *De inventione* 1,27 and *Rhetorica ad Herennium* 1,12 down to Isidore, *Etymologiae* 1,44,5). Although they understood this fiction as an 'image of truth' (Theon, *Progymnasmata* 3; Aphthonius, *Progymnasmata* 1; Sopater, *Rhetores Graeci* 10, p. 59 Walz), they derived the necessity of allegorism from this fact [22]. It was ultimately on this foundation, but above all on Porphyry's theoretical comprehension in his confrontation with Colotes on the subject of Platonic myth (Porphory, Fragment 182 Smith) that Macrobius, in his commentary on Cicero's *Somnium Scipionis* (1,2,7–12), constructed a complex classification of fictional texts (*fabulae*). According to it, fictional texts fall into two categories: the purely entertaining (and hence rejected) textual genre of comedy and novel, and the useful (animal fables, myths of the gods, philosophical myths). This classification, absorbed by Isidore (*Etymologiae* 1,40), became fundamental for the Western Middle Ages and in the School of Chartres, with its concept of the narrative surface (*indumentum, integumentum*) of fictional texts, particularly influenced the exegesis of literary fiction in general [23]. It also became the starting-point for an independent philosophical treatment of myth [24]. Above all, however, allegorism, both physical and moral, was the means that permitted the Middle Ages contact with ancient mythology. In addition to Cicero's *De natura deorum*, the central texts were the *Mythologiae* of Fulgentius [25], and often Servius' commentaries on Virgil as well. Boccaccio's *De genealogiis deorum* still embraced these basic approaches in the form of a genuine encyclopedic compendium. The Middle Ages sought the same approach to pagan authors, above all to Virgil and Ovid. Virgil had already been the subject of allegorical interpretation by Macrobius, and in Carolingian times Theodolphus of Orleans had formulated the general opinion that in the works of both poets 'there lies hidden a great deal of truth under a false surface' (*plurima sub falso tegmine vera latent* [26]). This was the origin of, among other things, the moralistic allegorism of the Ovidian *Metamorphoses*, with its high point in the *Integumenta Ovidii* of John of Garland and the *Ovid moralisé* of the 13th cent. [27; 28].

E. Early Modern Period

On one level, the Renaissance and Baroque periods continued this tradition uninterruptedly [29]. Needless to say, new access to Greek texts as well opened up a broad spectrum of interpretative possibilities. In addition to physical and moral allegorism, political allegorism appeared in an ever-increasing degree. Following the lead of Augustus' utilization of the myth of Aeneas, this allegorism used ancient myths for the legitimation of political rule. Florentine → Neo-Platonism in particular employed theological-philosophical allegorism. Its role for understanding iconography has still not been given adequate treatment [30; 31].

Allegorism underwent a fundamental transformation beginning in the late 16th cent. through the gradual appearance of a scientific mythology in connection with the discoveries and elaboration of ethnography [32; 33]. Knowledge of non-European myths, with their often striking resemblances to ancient mythology, led to a historicization of the → myth phenomenon, and a conceptual disengagement from other fictional genres, particularly animal fables (La Fontaine). Myth was understood for the first time, but with lasting consequences, by Bernard de Fontenelle [34] as a story that belongs to the dawn of humanity, and whose narrative peculiarities are not deliberate surfaces placed over a deeper truth, but involuntary distortions of physical and historical facts. From an exegetical procedure that sought the narrator's actual intentions, allegorism was thus transformed into the decoding of early human psychic reactions and excluded all moralistic exegesis. Central in this process was the systematization by Christian Gottlob Heyne. Instead of the current technical term *fabula*, he coined the term *mythus*, whereby he declared the independence of myth from literary genres and codified the division of myth into a *genus physicum* and a *genus historicum*. Although these contents relied completely on the categories of traditional allegorism, he turned expressly against the understanding of myth as allegory, designating it as a symbol [35]. He thereby laid the foundations for the Romantic interpretation of myth and the consequent debate on the differentiation between allegory and symbol.

→ Allegoresis, → allegory.

1 A. Fletcher, Allegory. The Theory of a Symbolic Mode, ²1970 2 W. Haug (ed.), Formen und Funktionen der Allegorie, 1979 3 J. C. Joosen, J. H. Waszink, Allegorism, in: Reallexikon für Antike und Christentum 1, 1950, 283–293 4 J. Gruber et al., Allegorie, Allegorism, in: Lexikon des Mittelalters 1, 420–427 5 J. Tate, The Beginnings of Greek Allegory, in: CR 41, 1927, 214–215 6 Id., On the History of Allegorism, in: CQ 28, 1934, 105–114 7 A. Laks, G. W. Most (eds.), Studies on the

Derveni Papyrus, 1996   8 P. Steinmetz, Allegorische Deutung und allegorische Dichtung in der alten Stoa, in: Rheinisches Museum für Philologie 129, 1986, 18–30   9 G. Lieberg, Die theologia tripertita in Forschung und Bezeugung, ANRW I 4, 63–115   10 G. W. Most, Cornutus and Stoic Allegoresis. A Preliminary Report, ANRW II 36.3, 2014–2065   11 P. Hardie, Plutarch and the Interpretation of Myth, in: ANRW II 33.6, 4743–4787   12 R. Lamberton, Homer the Theologian, 1986   13 Y. Vernière, L'empereur Julien et lexégèse des mythes, in: J. Hani (ed.), Problèmes du mythe et de son interprétation, 1978, 105–118   14 A. Hüttig, Macrobius im Mittelalter. Ein Beitrag zur Rezeptionsgeschichte der Commentarii in Somnium Scipionis, 1990   15 D. Dawson, Allegorical Readers and Cultural Revision in Ancient Alexandria, 1992   16 H. Chadwick, Antike Schriftauslegung. Pagane und christliche Allegorese. Activa und Passiva im antiken Umgang mit der Bibel, 1998   17 J.-C. Fredouille, La théologie tripartite, modèle apologétique (Athénagore, Théophile, Tertullien), in: D. Porte, J.-P. Néraudau (eds.), Res Sacrae. Hommages à Henri Le Bonniec, 1988, 189–219   18 F. Dolbeau, Nouveaux sermons de saint Augustin pour la conversion des païens et des donatistes (IV), in: Recherches Augustiniennes 26, 1992, 69–141   19 M. Marin, Allegoria in Agostino, in: La terminologia esegetica nell'antichità, 1987, 135–161   20 R. Herzog, Die allegorische Dichtkunst des Prudentius, 1966   21 Id., Exegese – Erbauung – Delectatio. Beiträge zu einer christlichen Poetik der Spät-Antike, in: W. Haug (ed.), Formen und Funktionen der Allegorie, 1979, 52–69   22 J. Pépin, La tradition d'allégorie. De Philon d'Alexandrie à Dante, 1987   23 E. de Bryne, Etudes d'esthétique médiévale, 1946   24 P. Dronke, Fabula. Explorations into the Use of Myth in Medieval Platonism, 1974   25 H. Liebeschütz, Fulgentius metaphoralis. Ein Beitrag zur Geschichte der antiken Mythologie im Mittelalter, 1926   26 De libris quos legere solebam20, in: Poetae Latini Aevi Carolini 1, (Berlin 1881, 543   27 F. Ghisalberti (ed.), Ovid moralisé, 1933   28 Curtius, 211f.   29 G. M. Anselmi, Mito classico e allegoresi mitologica tra Beroaldo e Codro, in: Id., Le frontiere degli Umanisti, 1988, 13–51   30 E. Panofsky, Studies in Iconology. Humanistic Themes in the Art of the Renaissance, 1939   31 E. Wind, Pagan Mysteries in the Renaissance, 1958   32 F. E. Manuel, The Eighteenth Century Confronts the Gods, 1959   33 M. T. Hodgen, Early Anthropology in the Sixteenth and Seventeenth Centuries, 1964   34 B. de Fontenelle, De l'origine des fables, A. Niderst (ed.),(= Œuvres complètes, Vol. 3), 1989, 187–202   35 F. Graf, Die Entstehung des Mythosbegriffs bei Christian Gottlob Heyne, in: Id.(ed.), Mythos in mythenloser Gesellschaft. Das Paradigma Roms, 1993, 284–294.   FRITZ GRAF

Allegory
I. Literary history   II. Art history

I. Literary history

Since Antiquity, the term has had a productive and a receptive aspect. In rhetoric it denotes the generation of texts based on the linking of metaphors (cf. Quint. Inst. 8,6,44) and the use of personifications. With regard to hermeneutics, it refers to the interpretation of mythical texts (Euhemeros) or biblical texts (cf. Aug. Doctr. christ.) which is, in a spiritual sense, clearly different from the literary sense. Nowadays we prefer to subsume this under the term allegorism. Already in the *Psychomachia* of Prudentius (AD 405), the first larger allegorical work of literature, expressive and interpretative allegory work together since an allegorical text always identifies itself as such and presents interpretative aids to the readers e.g. through the proem or the speeches of the personifications. According to Christian understanding, not only texts but also their references can be interpreted allegorically (*allegoria in factis*) [8]; thus, in Prudentius Abraham's battles in the Old Testament prefigure the battle between virtues and vices within the Christian soul. The allegory presupposes a dualistic world view, the separation between a sphere of the sensual regarded as inferior and, by contrast, a distinguished intelligible world; consequently, allegory has an affinity to → Platonism and Christianity. As 'poetry of the invisible' [4. 28] allegorical literature makes the intelligible evident. Therefore, allegorical personifications are popular in the visual arts (manuscripts of allegorical texts are often illuminated in the Middle Ages), in the art of memory as *imagines agentes*, in the religious plays of the late Middle Ages and the Baroque, in the European → festive processions from the *entrées royales* of the Middle Ages to the triumphal processions of the Italian Renaissance and the political celebration of the 'Highest Being' in the French Revolution.

Besides Prudentius, Boethius (*De consolatione philosophiae*) and Martianus Capella determined the further development of the allegory, especially the neo-Platonic literature of the 12th cent. replete with allusions to and quotations from classical authors. Partly in prosimetric and partly in epic hexameter, Alanus ab Insulis (*De planctu Naturae, Anticlaudianus*), Bernardus Silvestris (*Cosmographia*) and Johannes de Hauvilla (*Architrenius*) describe the cosmological order and the position of humans in it. The often Christological allegories of animals from the *Physiologus* were adapted in all vernacular languages of the Middle Ages, in the most original fashion by Richard de Fournival, whose *Bestiaire d'Amours* (mid-13th cent.) refers not to salvation history but to the amorous history of the author. A similar tendency towards secularization and psychologization of the allegory can also be found in the very influential *Roman de la Rose* by Guillaume de Lorris and Jean de Meun (*c.* 1240–1280), in which a love allegory is narrated in the first person as a dream vision; there the mistress is split into personifications such as *Fair Welcome* or *Danger*. Probably the most complex allegory in European literary history is Dante's *Divina Commedia* (*c.* 1310–1314); besides the subjective allegory of the vision, it fully integrates both the Latin poetical and allegorical tradition as well a the tradition of the theological interpretation of the Bible. Dante was the first vernacular author to call for a reading of his text according to the fourfold method of interpretation (cf. Epist. 13); this, once again, demonstrates the complementarity of the productive and the receptive allegory. In direct addresses (e.g. Inf. 9,61–63 und Purg. 8,19–21) the reader is assigned to interpret the *Commedia* allegorically, but the *dottrina* is not revealed. Francesco Colonna's *Hypnerotomachia Poliphili* (1499) influenced by Dante, a love allegory in stilted Latinizing prose, reveals a strong antiquarian interest in the archaic heritage of Antiquity; therefore, images and descriptions of monuments gain importance as opposed to the narrative. It is From this combination of picture and allegorical text that the field of → EMBLEMS arose in the 16th cent. The Spanish baroque allegory of the Counter Reformation, however, dissolves the earthly world into mere illusion. In the works of Pedro Calderón de la Barca this is expressed in the allegorical equation of life and dream (*La vida es sueño*) (1635) and that of world and theatre *El gran teatro del mundo* (1655). The very diverse plots (*argumentos*) of the Corpus Christi plays always refer to the same, the only substantial topic (*asunto*), i.e. the Eucharist. Empiricism and secularization, therefore, necessarily lead to a depreciation of the allegory [1]; Goethe gave priority to the primacy of the appearance in the symbol over the primacy of the concept of all allegory (*Maximen und Reflexionen*, no. 1112). The rehabilitation of the allegory in Baudelaire [3. 686–700] and W. Benjamin [2] is not a restauration of pre-modern world views, but it is linked to the insight into the split nature of the subject and the external determination by psychological forces such as melancholy.

→ ALLEGORISM; → EMBLEMS

→ Allegoresis; → Allegorical poetry; → Allegory

1 P.-A. ALT, Begriffsbilder. Studien zur literarischen Allegorie zwischen Opitz und Schiller, 1995 2 W. BENJAMIN, Ursprung des deutschen Trauerspiels, GS I.1, 203–430, 1974 3 W. HAUG (ed.), Formen und Funktionen der Allegorie, 1979 4 H. R. JAUSS, Alterität und Modernität der mittelalterlichen Literatur, 1977. 5 CHR. MEIER, Überlegungen zum gegenwärtigen Stand der Allegorie-Forschung, in: FMS 10, 1976, 1–69 6 J. PÉPIN, Dante et la tradition de l'allégorie, 1971 7 M. QUILLIGAN, The Language of Allegory. Defining the Genre, 1979 8 A. STRUBEL, *Allegoria in factis* et *Allegoria in verbis*, in: Poétique 23, 1975, 342–357 9 J. WHITMAN, Allegory. The Dynamics of an Ancient and Medieval Technique, 1987

A. FLETCHER, Allegory. The Theory of a Symbolic Mode, 1964   MAX GROSSE

II. ART HISTORY
see → PERSONIFICATION

Amsterdam, Allard Pierson Museum

A. THE INSTITUTION B. HISTORY OF THE COLLECTION C. ACTIVITIES OF THE MUSEUM

A. THE INSTITUTION

The Allard Pierson Museum (APM) is located at Oude Turfmarkt 127, 1012 GC Amsterdam, the Netherlands. It is funded by the University of Amsterdam. The museum receives active support and is anchored in the public domain through the *Vereniging van Vrienden Allard Pierson*, with its own journal [12]. (Website: www.uba.uva.nl/apm; e-mail: APM @UBA.UVA.nl)

B. HISTORY OF THE COLLECTION

The APM, with around 14,000 objects, is the second most important collection of antiquities in the Netherlands after the National Museum in Leiden. It was founded relatively recently, on November 12, 1934, when the Allard Pierson Stichting (Foundation) was transferred to the University of Amsterdam. The collection of C.W. Lunsingh-Scheurleer from 's-Gravenhage (The Hague), which was housed in his private museum, Carnegielaand, forms its core [1]. As such, the APM serves, like other museums in this country, as an example of a civic museum. It originated in the context of a bourgeoisie broadly interested in art, antiquities and learning. Its collection was assembled between 1900–1932 through purchases on the international art market.

Important names of the 20th cent. history of European collections are represented in the APM. The collection Lunsingh-Scheurleer in turn, for instance, absorbed the large sets of Greek, Roman and Coptic artefacts of the collection of Freiherr Friedrich W. von Bissing. This represented, apart from the Sieglin Collection (Stuttgart/Tübingen), one of the most important European collections of art and craft of Greco-Roman Egypt. The Egyptian objects of the von Bissing collection came into the possession of the APM only after 1934 when von Bissing saw an opportunity to keep large parts of his collection together there [2]. In addition, there are important items from the collections of Paul Arndt, Munich and of Hans Schrader, Frankfurt/M, that had been acquired primarily in Athens.

In the post-war period the APM continued the systematic study of items in its collection, a process started under difficult circumstances during the war [3; 4]. In addition, the APM devoted itself actively to the education of young archaeologists while at the same time cultivating and enlarging its stock [5; 6]. Thus, in 1976, on the occasion of the move to the Oude Turfmarkt, some 1400 objects were donated, a sign of the broad support and recognition of the work done [7]. The APM received further donations in more recent times, too. Worth mentioning in this respect are the collection of black-figured Attic vases of Dr. J.L. Theodor (1995) [12] in the classical field as well as the collection van Leer in the Egyptian department [13; 14]. The remaining stock of the former collection Lunsingh-Scheurleer was finally transferred from The Hague to the APM in the summer of 1998 which means that the museum has a considerable collection of classical vases from all parts of the Greek world at its disposal.

C. ACTIVITIES OF THE MUSEUM

The strength of the institution lies in its collections in the areas of Greece, Italy, and Greek-Roman Egypt. The predominance of minor arts lends the institution its special character, something that becomes apparent in the permanent exhibition which is set out in modern display cases according to geographical and historical viewpoints. Detailed (multilingual) labels guide the visitor and familiarise him with the distinctive features and strengths of the APM collections.

The ceramics collection contains more than 4000 vessels and fragments and includes a broad repertoire of ancient forms of pottery from the Greek Bronze age through the Etruscans to Roman Terrasigillata [6]. Undecorated consumer ceramics stand next to vessels decorated with figures or black varnish. Attic black-figured goods are particularly richly represented in the Greek section, in part by some outstanding examples. Figured terracotta is another main subject representing all important centres of production of the ancient world from the 6th cent. BC until the [Roman] Empire. These provide a good insight of the cultural and religious history of Antiquity and are rich in mythological depictions, bridging the time span between Antiquity and the present.

Ancient sculpture is represented by burial and other reliefs; this department is particularly proud of a few busts, among them the basalt bust of a man from the 2nd or 3rd cent. BC [15]. Metalwork is represented both by bronze vessels and gold and silver jewellery [16]. Of particular interest are the moulds for metal casts, as a model for a helmet from Greek Egypt shows. Faience and glass are also abundantly represented. The extensive collection of W.N.G. van der Sleen belongs, as a special subject, to the latter category comprising a compendium of glass beads from Antiquity to modern times [10]. Besides, finds from Roman times point at Holland's own ancient past.

While the APM as the sole archaeological Museum of Amsterdam – the largest Dutch city – has to perform important public tasks, it has developed at the same time into an important research centre as part of its academic duties [11; 13]. This way, museum work and basic research are developed further through the combination of academic and public duties. The APM has above all made a name for itself through publications on Greek ceramics of the archaic period. Worth mentioning are, among other things, studies on Laconian ceramics which for the first time systematically opened up this important local class of ceramics [17]. The continuing study of Greek-Roman antiquities from Egypt is also one of the initiatives resulting from the work of the museum.

1 C. W. Lunsingh-Scheurleer, Catalogus eener Verzameling Egyptische, Grieksche, Romeinsch en andere Oudheden, 1909 (re.: the private collection before the museum's founding) 2 G. A. S. Snijder (ed.), Allard Pierson Museum, Algemeene gids, 1937, Repr. 1956 (general handbook for the period after the museum's founding) 3 H. G. van Gulik, Catalogue of the Bronzes in the Allard Pierson Museum. 1940 4 C. S. Ponger, Katalog der griechischen und römischen Skulptur, der steinernen Gegenstände und der Stuckplastik im Allard Pierson Museum, 1942 5 God and Men in het APM, 1972 (Exhibition

catalogue) 6 H. A. G. Brijder (ed.), Griekse, Etruskische en Romeinse kunst, Allard Pierson Museum, ²1984 7 Gifts to Mark the Re-Opening, 1976 (catalogue) 8 R. Lunsingh-Scheurleer(ed.), Eender en anders (Exhibition catalogue), Allard Pierson Museum, 1984 9 Id., Grieken in het klein. 100 antieke terracottas, 1986 10 G. Jurriaans-Helle, Kralen Verhalen, 1994 11 Allard Pierson Series, 1980ff.; Allard Pierson Series, Scripta Minora, Stud. in Ancient Civilizations, 1989ff. 12 P. Heesen, The J.L. Theodor Collection of Attic Black-Figure Vases, AP Series Vol. 10, 1996 13 (Journal) MVAPM = Mededelingenblad Vereniging van Vrienden Allard Pierson MVAPM 65, 1996, 1 14 J. M. A. Janssen, Egyptische Oudheden verzameld door W.A. van Leer, Mededelingen en verhandelingen van het genootschap, in: Ex Oriente Lux 12, 1957 15 R. Lunsingh-Scheurleer, Egypte Geschenk van de Nijl, 1992 16 Id., Antieke Sier, Goud en zilver van Grieken und Romeinen, 1987 17 C. Stibbe, Laconian Mixing Bowls. A History of the krater Lakonikos, Laconian Drinking Vessels and Other Open Shapes, Laconian Black-glazed pottery pt. 1 & 2, AP Series, Scripta Minora, Vols. 2 and 4, 1989 and 1994.   WOLF RUDOLPH

Anacreontic poetry, Anacreontica

A. The Figure of Anacreon as a Literary Subject and as Eudaimonistic Model B. The Adaptation of Anacreontic Motifs, Translation and Stylistic Creation in Western Poetry C. The Neo-Latin and Vernacular Anacreontic Poetry of Europe under the Banner of the Renaissance and Humanism D. The German Anacreontic Movement E. European Anacreontic Poetry in the 18th–19th Cents.

A. The Figure of Anacreon as a Literary Subject and as Eudaimonistic Model

The lasting influence of Anacreon and the *Anacreontea* can best be expressed by the title of a book by L. A. Michelangeli: *Anacreonte e la sua fortuna nei secoli* ('Anacreon and his posthumous fame throughout the centuries'). In order to form a picture of the poet's personality, it is not necessary to rely on the historical or ahistorical testimony of later poets (Aulus Gellius, Horace), on his own works or on those of the *Anacreontea*, for Anacreon himself had already been canonized in the Hellenistic period as one of the great ancient lyric poets. After the discovery, publication (1554) and interpretation of the *Anacreontea* by the French Humanist Henricus Stephanus (1528–1598) and later literarily ambitious interpreters, Anacreon, identified as the lyric alter ego of the poems considered authentic, finally became one of the leading figures of European Eudaimonism with Enlightenment tendencies, or the so-called 'Anacreontic' period of the 18th cent. The image of Anacreon, literarily reconstructed to be sure, corresponded to the concept of the Socratic Sage. Goethe maintained this image in the epigram *Anakreons Grab* ('Anacreon's Tomb', 1784).

B. The Adaptation of Anacreontic Motifs, Translation and Stylistic Creation in Western Poetry

Connected with this image, Anacreontic poetry immediately spread throughout Europe. In addition to poetic translations and adaptations (→ ADAPTATION), the Anacreontic style of writing became prevalent first in Neo-Latin, then later also in vernacular tongues (unrhymed catalectic iambic or catalectic ionic dimeter in meter; witty and graceful, often also tenderly flirtatious or casually narrative in style; in subject-matter: erotic playfulness, often in allegorical guise; poems of friendship and marriage; meditations).

C. The Neo-Latin and Vernacular Anacreontic Poetry of Europe under the Banner of the Renaissance and Humanism

The Neo-Latins were to some extent already composing anacreonizing verse in the various national literatures before the *editio princeps* of Anacreon in 1554: for example, the Italian Angelo Poliziano (1454–1494), the Englishman Thomas More (1478–1535,) and the Dutchman Johannes Secundus (1511–1536); somewhat later, the Germans Johannes Aurpach (1531–1582) and Caspar Barth (1587–1658). The poetry of the recent national literatures followed the *editio princeps* of 1554: in France, beginning with Pierre Ronsard (1524–1585) and Remy Belleau (1528–1577); in Italy, with Torquato Tasso (1544–1595) and Gabriello Chiabrera (1552–1638); in Spain, beginning with Manuel de Villegas (1589–1669); in Holland with Daniel Heinsius (1580–1655) and Petrus Scriverius (1576–1666); in Britain with Robert Herrick (1591–1674) and Abraham Cowley (1618–1667); in Poland with Jan Kochanowski (1530–1584); in Germany with Georg Rudolph Weckherlin (1584–1653) and Philipp von Zesen (1619–1689). The anacreontic style, which could also take on sentimental features, was particularly appropriate for occasional poetry from the 16th to the 18th cent. Neo-Latin and vernacular anacreontic wedding-poems were a common artistic exercise. Finally, in the poetry of the Catholic orders the style and meter were transferred to Christian themes: By the Jesuits, for instance – the German-Czech Jacobus Pontanus (1542–1626), from France Gilbertus Ioninus (1596–1638), from Belgium Nicolaus Susius (d. 1619), from Holland Petrus Stratenus and finally from Italy Carlo d'Aquino in 1726. There was also an *Anacreon christianus* in the Protestant camp – for instance with Wilhem Alardus (1572–1645) and Caspar Barth. This kind of *parodia christiana* reminds one of the Christian 'Anacreontea', as they had been constituted since the 7th cent. by Sophronius of Damascus, Bishop of Jerusalem, and his successors Helias and Michael Syncellus (8th and 9th cents.), and had later become characteristic of Byzantine culture through the poems of the Patriarch Photius, Emperor Leo, Leo Magister, Gregory of Nazianzen and others.

D. The German Anacreontic Movement

German Anacreontic poetry reached a high-water mark in the 18th cent. A number of Anacreon editions and translations had sustained interest in this lyric poetry until this point. The inexhaustible gracious poetry of the French – the historically last poets of a long line: Chaulieu (1639–1720), La Farre (1644–1712), de la Motte (1672–1731), and Gresset (1709–1777) come to mind – provided with numerous *odes anacréontiques* the very cadence and motifs which were decisive for German anacreontic poetry, the center of the so-called Anacreontic in the 18th cent. The literary-historical concept of Anacreontic thus focusses on that buoyant lyric poetry of the German Enlightenment (→ ENLIGHTENMENT), which, in view of a new understanding of a secularized and optimistic existence supported by the bourgeoisie, took the Anacreontic as its model with regard to content, meter, and style. The figure of Anacreon became the ideal for the attitude toward life of a poetic youth movement. The poetic translation, *Die Oden Anakreons in reimlosen Versen* (The odes of Anacreon in unrhymed verses), published in 1746 by Johann Nikolaus Götz (1721–1781) and Johann Peter Uz (1720–1786) had its effect: in 1760 it appeared once again, revised by Götz. The young Enlightenment thinkers, often 'anacreontically' confederated in friendship-leagues, had their own German Anacreon, translated in the new style of pleasantries and gracefulness. Johann Wilhelm Ludwig Gleim (1719–1803), known as the 'German Anacreon', propagated the style of unrhymed anacreontic short verses developed by his friends Uz and Götz through his own attempt at humorous songs devoted to friendship, love, and (moderate) wine-drinking (1744/45). Gleim attracted other Anacreontics into his circle of friends: Karl Wilhelm Ramler (1725–1798), Johann Georg Jacobi (1740–1814) and others. The anacreontic style, extended onto numerous topics, found from then on supporters in Goethe (1749–1832) and his friend Karl Ludwig von Knebel (1744–1834), August Graf von Platen (1796–1835), Wilhem Müller (1794–1827), Eduard Mörike (1804–1875) down to Otto Julius Bierbaum (1865–1910) and Hugo von Hofmannsthal (1874–1929).

E. European Anacreontic Poetry in the 18th–19th Cents.

The reception of Anacreon in other European nations took a similar course as in Germany: the Italians developed an enthusiastic taste for anacreonizing in: Paolo Rolli (1687–1765), Pietro Metastasio (1698–1782) and Lorenzo da Ponte (1749–1838); from Sweden, based on German models, anacreontic verses by Carl Michael Bellmann (1740–1795) rang forth; likewise from Holland by Jacobus Bellamy (1757–1786). In England, the adaptation of the *Anacreontea* by Thomas Moore (1779–1852) called forth an unheard-of enthusiasm for Anacreon. There was no end to the anacreonizing, when at the end of the 18th cent., under the influence of the Europe-wide classicistic enthusiasm for Antiquity, and influenced by German literature, Russian lyricists also gave their contribution: after Antioch Dmitrijevich Kantemir (1709–1744), who provided the first Russian translation of the *Anacreontea*, M.V. Lomonossov (1711–1765) and A.P. Sumarokov (1717–1777) tried their hand at it, the latter taking Gleim as his model. Finally, Michail Matvejevich Cheraskov (1733–1807), together with the poets close to him, brought life to a Russian Anacreontic, which was influential long into the 19th cent., and was promoted by the complete translation of the *Anacreontea* by J.J. Martynov (1771–1833).

→ Anacreon

1 M. BAUMANN, Die Anakreonteen in englischer Übersetzung, 1974 2 W. KÜHLMANN, 'Amor liberalis'. Ästhetischer Lebensentwurf und Christianisierung der neu-lateinischen Anakreontik in der Ära des europäischen Späthumanismus, in A. BUCK, T. KLANICZAY (eds.), Das Ende der Renaissance – Europäische Kultur um 1600, 1987, 165–186 3 L. A. MICHELANGELI, Anacreonte e la sua fortuna nei secoli con una rassegna critica su gl'imitatori e i traduttori italiani delle 'Anacreontee', 1922 4 J. O'BRIEN, Anacreon Redivivus: A Study of Anacreontic Translation in Mid-Sixteenth-Century France. 1995 5 P. ROSENMEYER. The Poetics of Imitation: Anacreon and the Anacreontic Tradition. 1992 6 A. RUBIO' Y LLUCH, Estudio critico-bibliográfico sobre Anacreonte y la Coleccion Anacréontea, y su influencia en la literatura antiqua y moderna, 1879 7 D. SCHENK, Studien zur anakreontischen Ode in der russischen Literatur des Klassizismus und der Empfindsamkeit, 1972 8 H. ZEMAN, s.v. Anakreontische Dichtung, Anakreontik, Literarisches Rokoko, in: Fischer Lexikon der Literatur, 1996 9 Id., Die Entfaltung der deutschen Anakreontische Dichtung des 17. Jahrhunderts an den Universitäten und ihre Wirkung im städtischen Lebensbereich, in: Stadt-Schule-Universität, Buchwesen und die deutsche Literatur im 17. Jahrhundert, 1976, 396–409. 10 Id., Goethes anakreontische Lyrik der Weimarer Zeit, in: Zeitschrift für deutsche Philologie, 94, 1975, 203–235. 11 Id., Die deutsche anakreontische Dichtung, 1972.   HERBERT ZEMAN

Ancient History (Greece, Rome, Late Antiquity) see → HISTORIOGRAPHY

Ancient Languages, Teaching of
I. GERMANY II. GREAT BRITAIN III. ITALY
IV. FRANCE V. USA

I. GERMANY
A. DEFINITION B. HISTORY C. THE CURRENT SITUATION

A. DEFINITION
Methodical instruction in the classical languages Latin and Greek (in earlier times also Hebrew) as well as guided reading and interpretation of Latin and Greek texts is designated as instruction in the classics.

B. HISTORY
Classical languages have been taught since ancient times, when Greek was studied in Rome. In medieval preparatory schools/Latin schools, Latin was the focus of instruction. Grammar, rhetoric and dialectics were taught and practised using Classical texts. This instruction was intended to prepare students for reading philosophical and scholarly works. In the → RENAISSANCE, renewed interest in the ancient world led to the establishment of instruction in the Classics. Cicero's works were now regarded as an expression of Classical Latin style; *latine legere, scribere, loqui* was the goal of the new kind of Latin teaching, and Greek began to be taught as well. Latin instruction in particular had not only academic, but also practical purposes, since proficiency in *eloquentia* ('eloquence') was useful as long as Latin remained the language of the Church, diplomacy, scholarship and jurisprudence. After 1700, as the German language was increasingly placed on an equal footing with Latin and also gained more acceptance at the → UNIVERSITY, the importance of teaching Latin declined.

Against this backdrop, the 18th cent. Classical scholars J. M. Gesner and C. G. Heyne developed a new concept of the ancient world and stressed the value of cultural tradition in → EDUCATION/CULTURE. *In der Kritik an dem rhetorischen Bildungsideal (→ RHETORIC) des ersten Humanisten mit seiner Latinitätsdressur verleg(t)en sie den Schwerpunkt von der Imitation auf die Interpretation der antiken Schriften, deren idealem Gehalt sie schon vor dem Einfluß Winckelmanns und Herders eine humanisierende Wirkung zuschr(ie)ben* ('In their critique of the rhetorical ideal of education (Rhetoric) put forth by the first humanists, which was characterized by an emphasis on Latinate rote learning, they shifted the emphasis from imitation to the interpretation of Classical writings, ascribing a humanizing effect to the ideals contained in such works, even before the influence of Winckelmann and Herder was felt' [10. 5]). This new appreciation for the Classical tradition encouraged a view of education in which the Greek language as well as Greek art and philosophy offered a historical model of the highest levels of human perfection, and thus the ancient world served as the focus of education. After 1780, Heyne's pupil F. A. Wolf developed the academic field of Classical languages into that of Classical philology, making it an independent discipline. At the same time, J. G. Herder was including similar ideas in his *lectures*. He emphasized that the ideal formation of a human being is based on the harmonious development of his talents, and that this goal can be furthered by learning Classical languages and studying exemplary works from the ancient world. Around the year 1800, W. von Humboldt built upon this foundation to establish the new humanist theory of education. Like F. A. Wolf, he was convinced that the Greeks had achieved a particularly pure concept of humanity in their culture and the works they produced. Accordingly, education should focus on the study of

Greek antiquity, particularly Greek language, literature and art, since only such studies were capable of stimulating thinking and one's aesthetic and moral sense in the desired way.

Humboldt presumed that every human being possesses 'capabilities' suited for perceiving and learning about the world. These capabilities must be developed in a harmonious and well-rounded manner. To that end, stimuli are required from a variety of situations and encounters, as well as from various kinds of subjects; education requires using one's powers to deal with subjects and situations with which one comes into contact. The primary means of stimulation is language, since it is the unique mode of expression that distinguishes human beings from other creatures. Languages such as ancient Greek and Latin, which have ceased to change and are no longer spoken, and which convey great cultural accomplishments, are, in their clarity, particularly suitable for practicing one's capabilities. Together with the study of the mother tongue and mathematics, they offer fundamental stimuli to shape a personality that is capable of thinking independently, assessing situations, and acting in accordance with the dictates of morality.

During the Prussian educational reform that began in 1809, these ideas played a significant role in the concept of the humanistic *Gymnasium*. Instruction in the Classics represented the core of the *Gymnasium*'s curriculum. It was Latin, not Greek, however, that became the fundamental language in the schools, while instruction in Greek was added two years later. But this *Gymnasium* curriculum, which was developed by J. W. Süvern, reflected the fact that it was no longer Humboldt's position to require pupils in the *Gymnasium* to study both Latin and Greek over a period of many years. Pupils working toward the final qualifying examination (*Abitur*) were now required to study both Classical languages up to their final school year, to express themselves in Latin both in writing and orally, and later to translate from Greek into Latin. It soon became clear that an important function of instruction in the Classics was not so much to educate young people through the study of Classical languages, but to carry out social selection. After 1832, the study of Latin was also introduced for the first time in the secondary schools for the bourgeoisie; no heed was paid to the need to teach the emerging natural sciences, and only later were the sciences integrated into the curriculum to a limited degree. For a long time, the influence of the Classical philologists made it impossible to receive an education at the *Gymnasium* by studying other subjects. Thus instruction in the Classics remained the core subject and the most imposing obstacle to passing an *Abitur* examination. It was not until the last third of the 18th century that the number of hours devoted to the Classics declined somewhat; for instance, the Latin essay was eliminated from the *Abitur*. Finally, the school conference of 1900 abolished the monopoly of the → HUMANIST GYMNASIUM as the only pathway by which one could gain general qualification for university entrance. Concurrently, there were discussions and testing of ways to reform the *Gymnasium* by shortening the duration of instruction in the Classics.

In this situation, proponents of instruction in the Classics saw a way to underscore its importance by seeking to interpret Classical texts in the prevalent spirit of German nationalism [1]. This stabilized the situation for a brief period, but the Classics' position in education again became precarious after 1918. The old charges – that it was outmoded, elitist, excessively demanding, not appropriate for children, socially selective, reactionary – were again raised during the Weimar Republic. The decline of instruction in the Classics was unstoppable. Nor was the → THIRD HUMANISM movement founded by W. Jaeger, whose proponents idealistically emphasized the educational effects of Classical studies, able to gain widespread acceptance. Furthermore, advocates of instruction in the Classics neglected to adapt to the need for political education that encouraged a republican way of thinking. *Das liebevoll weiter ausgemalte Bild des frühen Rom als einer verklärten Welt, die von fides, auctoritas, labor, pietas und magnitudo animi erfüllt war, konnte nicht nur historische Nachprüfung nicht standhalten, sondern stellte auch kein geeignetes Leitbild für die Jugend eines demokratischen Staates dar* ('The lovingly painted portrait of ancient Rome as an idealized world filled with fides, auctoritas, labor, pietas and magnitudo animi not only failed the test of historical accuracy, but also offered no suitable model for young people in a democratic state' [9. 37]). A further devaluation of instruction in the Classics occurred under the National Socialists [1] (→ NATIONAL SOCIALISM). They demanded that the study of Latin and Greek be used to promote a spirit of nationalism. There is some dispute as to the practical effects of these demands on the schools. In most cases, it meant ideologization; however, sometimes the Classics were also used as a means of distancing oneself from Nazi ideology. Two strands of development can be reconstructed for the period between 1945 and 1990, one West German, the other East. In West Germany attempts were successful, despite strong American objections to the humanistic *Gymnasium*, to reestablish instruction in the Classics as it was traditionally understood. Indeed, it experienced a brief flowering in the 1950s, before steadily losing ground in the 1960s. There are a number of reasons for the dramatic decline: 1. the familiar, above-mentioned objections to the humanistic *Gymnasium*, 2. the establishment of new subject concentrations in the *Gymnasium*, which proved more attractive to many parents, 3. the expansion of the study of the natural sciences, 4. discussion of an impending disaster in education and attempts to attract pupils, 5. the opening of the *Gymnasium* to a wider segment of the population, 6. the reform of the *Gymnasium*'s upper level with the introduction of elective subjects, which often led students to drop courses such as Latin that had occupied a privileged position in the curriculum, and 7. discussion about modernizing the curriculum, introducing clearly defined instructional and learning goals. Within the curriculum discussion, it was apparently no longer possible to identify appropriate goals, content and methods for instruction in the Classics. In 1970, it seemed that it would be 'only a matter of time' until such instruction was done away with altogether [10. 7].

However, the threatened demise of instruction in the Classics mobilized efforts to legitimize and reestablish it within the framework of the modern curriculum discussion. The Classical philologists sought to draw up 'concrete descriptions of the content and functions of Classical instruction' [11. 1], in place of the familiar emotional appeals that underscored the value of Classical studies in shaping the human mind. A new pedagogy was developed in which clear goals for instruction in the Classics were formulated, as well as appropriate content and methods. The theory that Classical works were useful in themselves was abandoned in favour of arguments that language instruction was valuable for developing existing capabilities by focusing on socially relevant topics. This more objective approach was reflected in the following learning goals, formulated in terms of behaviour: instruction in the Classics encourages the development of scholarly procedure. By teaching translation, it helps the student to practise choosing the appropriate word in a given situation and to understand the context of written materials. It introduces the student to interpretive techniques and provides insight into unfamiliar grammar and means of expression. As such goals were formulated, appropriate texts for reading were chosen and methods of instruction were selected. On this basis, Classical philologists were able to participate in constructing new curricula in the 1970s. The curricular approach – goals, content, methods, evaluating the achievement of learning goals – was also practised in the case of the Classics curricula. Learning goals were formulated with a view to general educational goals, and content was determined with those goals in mind. Subsequently, procedures were identified for achieving and assessing the goals that had been set. In this context it was decided that learning goals should reflect social needs. Thus the teaching of Latin might concentrate on specific questions relating to Rome as a world power, such as its policies toward conquered nations, its legal system and so on, which in effect uses the past to encourage thinking about central issues of the present. The language itself and the texts composed in that language were no longer regarded as indispensable pillars of a good education; they had to be justified through logical learning goals as appropriate subjects to be taught. Accordingly, the instructional aims became clearer, and they were reflected in concrete subject matter. Thus the pedagogy of Classical language teaching gained intellectual status in the curricular discussion; instruction in the Classics was accepted as a part of education in the schools. It was now a subject that needed to compete with the other school subjects and

prove convincing in terms of its goals. In the case of Latin, especially, these efforts were sufficiently successful to appeal to parents of *Gymnasium* students, and interest in studying Latin has remained steady ever since the 1980s.

In East Germany (beginning in 1949, the German Democratic Republic) the secondary schools continued to offer so-called C branches with Classes in Latin and Greek until the mid–1960s (→ GDR). Even in the secondary schools that focused on modern languages or the natural sciences, Latin was a required subject up to the 'Kleines Latinum' [6. 313]. After 1964, when the educational system shifted to a socialist model featuring a polytechnical secondary school (which went up to the 10th form, *Polytechnische Oberschule, POS*) and an expanded secondary school (11th/12th form, *Erweiterte Oberschule, EOS*), the Classes that had focused on Classical languages were eliminated. In all of the GDR, there were now nine schools in which instruction in the Classics was compulsory. In addition, Latin was offered as a mandatory elective course in the 11th and 12th years of the expanded secondary school, for three hours, twice a week. In the 1980s fewer pupils were able to study the Classical languages because of a worsening shortage of teachers qualified to teach Latin or Greek. At the same time, 'the demand for courses in Classical languages at the universities by far exceeded the resources of the foreign language departments' [6. 313]. This gap between supply and demand drew renewed attention to the importance of instruction in the Classics in a well-rounded education and as a basis for university training. An initial step toward remedying the shortage was the decision in 1985 that the University of Halle would again train Latin teachers; subjects were combined: German plus Latin or Russian plus Latin, with the option of earning certification to teach Greek as well. However, by 1990, there had been no success in expanding instruction in the Classics in order to bring 'secondary school education in the GDR up to a level comparable to the rest of Europe' [6. 316].

C. THE CURRENT SITUATION

More recent curricula include the Classical languages on an equal footing with the modern languages and other subjects. The characteristic structure of the *Gymnasium*, as a multi-functional school that offers a variety of choices, puts instruction in the Classics in competition with other subjects, particularly the modern languages. The struggle to attract students begins in the first year, and continues every two years thereafter. Students and parents may choose between Latin–later Greek– and, each time, a modern foreign language. Accordingly, proponents of the Classics today must seek to attract students through open competition with other subjects. This has led to numerous efforts to provide a rationale for learning Latin, while Greek has been promoted to a lesser degree. Statistics for the period from 1980 to 1992 from the Conference of Ministers of Education and the Arts (*Kultusministerkonferenz,*

KMK) show that the share of students who took Latin at the first and second secondary school levels has fallen steadily, but appears likely to remain stable at the new levels. The percentage dropped from 40.7% (1980) to 27.3% (1992), but the absolute number of pupils studying Latin has recently increased somewhat. There are, however, differences among the German states in how often pupils choose to study Latin. By far the largest percentage of pupils to take Latin is found in Bavaria (41.9%). By comparison, there appears to be almost no interest in taking Greek: during this period, the percentage of all pupils studying Greek at the first and second secondary school levels declined from 1.4% to 0.7%, according to the *KMK*. While 559,134 pupils were taking Latin in 1992, only 13,656 chose to study Greek.

In discussing the reasons for studying various subjects, arguments for the importance of Latin teaching in particular were brought up very early on. The new humanists (→ NEO-HUMANISM) underscored its role in conveying formal principles. In 1900, Willmann stressed the 'inherent logic' of the Latin language and described instruction in the Classics as a 'regime of intellectual exercise' [13. 364], while also pointing out the importance of the cultural content of Latin works for a proper education. Similar arguments are now couched in modern terms. F. Maier lists the five most important: 1) 'Latin is the keep-fit path of the mind': courses in Latin provide a training ground for logical thinking that requires methodical, thorough and concentrated work on clear text passages. Text analysis encourages intellectual discipline and forces the student to follow certain rules in order to work through unfamiliar sentence structure. Translating constantly requires comparison of the Latin content with the German. This enriches one's language. 2) Latin is the 'basic language of Europe'. It is the foundation for numerous languages and forms a bridge to the Romance languages. 3) Latin is the 'fundamental language of scholarship'. Having learned Latin, one can decipher many common scholarly concepts. 4) Latin is a 'key language in European culture'. It is the language in which the basic texts of European thought were written up to the modern age. 5) Latin is the 'core subject of a humanistic education' [8]. The Latin tradition includes texts about political, ethical and philosophical issues that are comparable to the basic issues confronting us today. These texts can be used as models in 'intensive study of the foundations of human existence' [8. 400]. They offer impetus for developing a humanistic perspective with regard to historical and social situations. These are the central arguments. Sometimes the additional argument is made that Latin is an appropriate first foreign language, since it does not involve difficulties in pronunciation or writing.

The introduction of the multi-functional *Gymnasium* meant that Latin was taught in four different segments, beginning in the fifth year with Latin I, in the seventh with Latin II, in the ninth with Latin III, and in the tenth or eleventh with Latin IV. This means differ-

ent numbers of hours of instruction, and requires finding a balance between the teaching of language and of reading. 'The shorter the language-teaching phase, the more demands are placed on reading instruction, in order to consolidate, reinforce and expand the pupils' knowledge of the language' [7. 109]. Accordingly, the various types of Latin teaching must reflect age-specific abilities and interests. In any case, it is problematic to teach reading adequately to convey the ancient way of life, given a limited amount of language instruction. The new pedagogy has developed models for both content and methods to address this issue.

In order to encourage the study of Greek, particular emphasis has been placed on the importance of ancient Greek civilization and its literary works. Even more than Latin, the study of Greek requires a willingness to deal with a foreign tradition with precision, concentration and persistence; accordingly, a stronger focus has been placed on learning to read Greek and examining basic texts that deal with issues of politics, ethics and knowledge.

Two thousand years after Cicero, then, we can conclude that, despite undiminished opposition, instruction in the Classics has withstood the crisis of the 1970s. Indeed, it has emerged from this period even stronger, and with new approaches to both content and methodology. At present, efforts are focused on seeking to consolidate the competitive position of instruction in the Classics relative to the other subjects in the curriculum by linking the issues it raises to the present day; this seems to have been more successful in the case of Latin, since it is a more accessible language and more people appear to be convinced of its importance. Greek, on the other hand, while favoured by the new humanists, continues its long-term fight for survival.

→ CLASSICISM AFTER CLASSICAL ANTIQUITY;
→ COURSE OF INSTRUCTION; → GERMANY; → SCHOOLS

1 H. J. APEL, S. BITTNER, Humanistische Schulbildung 1890–1945, 1994   2 G. BAHLS, W. KIRSCH, Fünfjähriges Diplomlehrerstudium auch in der Ausbildung von Altsprachenlehrern, in: Fremdsprachenunterricht 7/8, 1988, 390–395   3 H.-J. GLÜCKLICH, Lateinunterricht, 1993   4 J. GRUBER, F. MAIER (eds.), Alte Sprachen, 2 vols. 1979   5 W. v. HUMBOLDT, Der königsberger und der litauische Schulplan, Werke 13, 1920   6 W. KIRSCH, Gegenwart und Zukunft des Altsprachenunterrichts, in: Fremdsprachenunterricht 7, 1990, 313–320   7 F. MAIER, Lateinunterricht zwischen Tradition und Fortschritt, vol. 1, 1984   8 Id., Latein liegt im Trend der Zeit, in: Forschung und Lehre 9, 1994, 398–400   9 K. MATTHIESSEN, Altsprachlicher Unterricht in Deutschland, in: J. GRUBER, F. MAIER (eds.), Alte Sprachen, vol. 1, 1979, 11–42   10 C. MENZE, s.v. Altsprachlicher Unterricht, in: Neues Pädagogisches Lexikon, 1971, 4–7   11 R. NICKEL, Altsprachlicher Unterricht, 1973   12 K. WESTPHALEN, Neue Perspektiven für den Latein- und Griechischunterricht, in: Gymnasium 100, 1993, 144–158   13 O. WILLMANN, Didaktik als Bildungslehre, 1909.   HANS JÜRGEN APEL

II. Great Britain
A. From the Renaissance to the 20th Cent.
B. 20th Cent.   C. Current Situation

A. From the Renaissance to the 20th Cent.

From the Renaissance until the early 20th cent., the teaching of Latin and (to a lesser degree) Greek occupied the most prominent place in the school curriculum for the British educated classes. Long after Latin had lost its function as Europe's lingua franca, the Classical languages and Classical literature formed the foundation of schooling for children of the ruling aristocracy and academic families. This situation was not appreciably changed by the industrial revolution in the 19th cent.: the established schools were hesitant to introduce instruction in the natural sciences, and the new industrial leadership class wanted its own sons to enjoy an education similar to that provided for the landed gentry. When state-run *secondary schools* were established in 1902, their curriculum was intended to approximate the model of the traditional *grammar schools* and the so-called *public schools* as closely as possible. The Classical subjects continued to be defended with the argument that they offered a comprehensive general education (→ Education/Culture) that schooled the intellect and offered the optimum preparation for public government service, whether in → Great Britain or in other parts of the British empire.

One of the main methodological features of instruction in the Classics, beginning in the early 19th cent. and continuing up to the 1960s, was the great importance attached to translation (→ Adaptation) from English into Latin and Greek. Stylistic exercises in both prose and verse were developed into a high art that was regarded as a central element in linguistic education, along with the stylistic integration of Greek and Latin authors.

B. 20th Cent.

In the course of the 20th cent., the Classical subjects lost their preeminence in the curriculum, while other subjects such as the natural sciences and modern languages have steadily increased in importance. First Greek, then Latin, lost its position as a subject required for admission to the universities at Oxford and Cambridge. A further factor was the development in the state-run educational sector of non-selective *comprehensive schools*, which, in many places, were replacing the state-run *grammar schools* that had offered Latin. Theoretically, the Classical languages could still be taught in the comprehensive schools, since individual schools maintained control over their curricula, and indeed, some head teachers offered Latin and – albeit only rarely – Greek as an elective for their more talented pupils. After 1988, however, when a uniform curriculum (the so-called *National Curriculum*) was introduced in all state-run schools, only few pupils were able to take Latin, and Greek disappeared almost entirely from the schools. In the so-called public schools, which offered a more academically oriented programme, Latin continued to be taught, but was only rarely compulsory. A few schools also offered Greek, but this frequently depended on the willingness of individual teachers to take on additional unpaid work.

During the second half of the 20th cent., these developments caused teachers to rethink the real goals of teaching the Classical languages and the rationale for them as part of the curriculum (→ Course of Instruction). Owing to the limited amount of time allotted in the curriculum, it seemed necessary to attach more importance to teaching translation so that pupils might read the ancient Latin and Greek texts. It was no longer possible to maintain the traditional emphasis on stylistic exercises in the Classical languages. Classical language instruction was generally justified in terms of cultural considerations rather than as a way of sharpening one's intellect, which was presumed to be a benefit of their study as well. The new language courses for beginners included historical and other kinds of background material, which captured and held pupils' interest. Advanced classes attached less importance to knowledge of grammar than to the development of a critical literary sense. All the same, the argument continued to be made that the real reason for learning Latin was to develop the ability to apply learning methods to other subjects, particularly as utilitarian considerations gained the upper hand in the materialistic climate of the 1980s. A new movement arose in 1977 with the development of modern learning materials for introducing Latin in the state-run *primary schools*, which may well be useful in helping to teach English grammar.

Constant worry about the survival of the subject also led to a change in methodology. In the first half of the 20th cent., a campaign was initiated by the *Association for the Reform of Latin Teaching*, urging the use of the so-called 'direct approach', which is normally associated with teaching modern languages. While this method produced some enthusiastic teachers, it failed to gain general acceptance, since oral communication is not among the main goals of learning Greek and Latin. However, enhancing knowledge of the original → Pronounciation did indeed lead to improvements in the ability to recite Classical poetry and prose. The *Classical Association* continues to support regional competitions for pupils in which Classical texts are read aloud and quoted from memory.

C. Current Situation

The most significant influence on instruction in the Classics during the second half of the 20th cent. came from the *Joint Association of Classical Teachers* (JACT), founded in 1962. In its publications and conferences, this association proposed a number of innovations and provided help to teachers in adjusting to changed circumstances. One of its achievements was the development of a textbook for teaching Greek that is still widely used in schools and universities, both in Great Britain and abroad. In addition, the JACT founded *summer schools* for older pupils studying Latin and Greek. This again enabled more pupils to learn the Classical languages, and many young people were encouraged to continue their study at the → UNIVERSITY level.

Currently, most university departments of Classical philology offer courses for students who want to begin studying the Classical languages, whether in order to read Classical texts in the original or as a foundation for studies in other areas. Moreover, there is considerable interest in such courses in the field of adult education. The wide dissemination of texts in translation as well as many other sources of information, including television and travel, has led to increasing public interest in Classical literature and ancient civilizations. Such factors – and not so much the established position of the Classical languages in the English school system – will undoubtedly keep instruction in the Classics alive in Great Britain in the 21st cent. and beyond.

→ SCHOOLS

1 T. W. BAMFORD, The Rise of the Public Schools, 1967, 86–115 2 J. E. SHARWOOD SMITH, On Teaching Classics, 1977, 23–36 3 C. A. STRAY, Classics Transformed: Schools, Universities and Society in England, 1830–1960, 1998 4 M. J. WIENER, English Culture and the Decline of the Industrial Spirit, 1981, 16–24

ADDITIONAL BIBLIOGRAPHY: M. L. CLARKE, Classical Education in Britain 1500–1900, 1959; C. A. STRAY, The Living Word: W. H. D. Rouse and the Crisis of Classics in Edwardian England, 1992.   DAVID ANTONY RAEBURN

III. ITALY
A. HISTORY TO THE END OF THE 19TH CENT.
B. 20TH CENT.

A. HISTORY TO THE END OF THE 19TH CENT.

As it was in the Roman Empire's school system, which continued in place in Italy up to the time of the Lombards, the teaching of Latin grammar and rhetoric were characteristic of the Italian system. These subjects aided in occupational training that was based primarily on the study of law. Following directly in the tradition of the legal academies of the Roman Empire, beginning in the 4th cent. the Church established cathedral schools (→ CATHEDRAL SCHOOLS) for educating priests as well as parish schools that were open to all, in which the basics of Latin were taught; these can be considered the forerunners of today's primary schools. The goal of mediaeval schooling was the pupils' religious education; accordingly, the 'non-Christian' writers Virgil and Ovid as well as Classical culture in general were largely ignored and viewed as dangerous. The 'secular' answer to the Church's system of instruction came during the period of the city-republics with the establishment of state-run schools in which arithmetic and writing were taught rather than elementary Latin; at a higher level, there were the → UNIVERSITIES, which had their roots in the culture of the city. At the same time the humanistic schools emerged, a mid-level model that was common

in the most prominent Italian cities. The main proponents of this model were educational theorists like Guarino Guarini and Vittorino da Feltre, whose aim was to educate young people to become good citizens, taking care to respect their dignity, by reviving the Classical ideal of *humanitas* (→ HUMANISM). The schools taught rhetoric as well as the philological and historical interpretation of Classical texts.

The *studia humanistica* did not last long; their 'humanistic and religious' ideals were taken up during the Counter-Reformation by the Jesuit colleges, which dissociated themselves from the free universities and developed into public schools par excellence, in Italy as well as in other countries (cf. [2]; → JESUIT SCHOOLS). The Jesuit *ratio studiorum* (1599) provided for instruction in Latin grammar during the first four years of study. The teaching method was based on mnemonics, and the goal was to practise the rhetorical use of Latin. In addition, these schools taught the fundamentals of Greek (cf. [2. 911; 6; 11]). The Jesuits required Greek in order to understand Biblical texts and documents of church history, as well as to keep pace with the Protestants, who had excellent training in Greek. By and large, Greek, which was considered an 'oriental' language, was taught relatively infrequently from the end of the 16th until the 19th century, even at the university level, a fact lamented by the Classical scholar Scipione Maffei (*Parere sul migliore ordinamento della R. Università di Torino*, 1718), among others. Latin, in contrast, was always a main subject in the schools, for example in the Savoyan Piedmont, where the schools were reorganized by Vittorio Amedeo II through the *Costituzioni* that were passed in 1729, as well as during the Napoleonic occupation; Vittorio Amedeo II had taken charge of organizing the school system and teacher training even before the Jesuits were banned (1773).

The *legge Casati* (1859) introduced the first school system in a united Italy and took as its models not only reforms that had already been made in the Savoy kingdom (such as the *legge Boncompagni* of 1848), but also, in particular, the Prussian system. This resulted in the humanist *liceo classico*, which was divided into the five-year *ginnasio* and the three-year *liceo* (a distinction that is echoed today in the anachronistic terms 'fourth and fifth forms' of the *ginnasio* used for the first two years of the *liceo classico*). According to the *legge Casati*- which, to be sure, witnessed regular curriculum amendments up to the year 1923 – Greek was taught beginning with the third form of the *ginnasio*. Latin lessons, which were allotted more than three times as many hours as Greek, accounted for about one fourth of all class time in the *ginnasio*, but this amount was drastically reduced in the *liceo*, where the natural sciences were given preference. Overall, between 1860 and 1923, Latin and Greek were assigned about 50 hours per week in the *ginnasio*, and in the *liceo* about 25, out of a total of 179 hours each week (precise figures: [1. 95]). Rhetorical use of Latin continued to be important; a great deal of time was devoted to practising writing essays in Latin. It was not until 1867 that uniform curricula were established by law. The curricula regarded the study of Latin and Greek as preparation for reading texts considered exemplary for a sense 'of the aesthetic and art'. The authors read in the *ginnasio* included Cornelius Nepos, Phaedrus, Caesar (*De bello Gallico*), Ovid (*Fasti*), Cicero (*Briefe*), Virgil (several books of the *Aeneid*), Livy (excerpts) and Sallust (*De coniuratione Catilinae* or *De bello Iugurthino*). In the *liceo*, pupils read Tacitus's *Historiae*, Cicero's rhetorical and philosophical works, Horace, Virgil's *Georgica* and portions of Quintilian's *Institutio oratoria*. Readings in Greek classes included not only Xenophon, the author par excellence for the *ginnasio*, but also Homer and the orators. The German model was followed also in selecting textbooks. The standard textbook for Greek was Georg Curtius's grammar, namely, Giuseppe Müller's translation that was published by Hermann Loescher, the first Italian publisher specializing in Latin and Greek textbooks. This translation was preferred especially by those who advocated a 'logical', 'algebraic' and 'linguistic' approach to Greek. Sometimes, however, Raphael Kühner's 'empirically' based grammar was used as well (both of these served as a foundation for Karl Schenkl's widely-used grammar as well as his exercise book, translated in 1868). Kühner's grammar was used in teaching Latin. The Greek and Latin authors were regarded as the foundation of knowledge, while the Classical languages, owing to the 'memory training' required in order to learn them, were seen as the 'key' to every other subject, including the natural sciences. This view was the subject of later criticism of instruction in the Classics, and particularly of Latin instruction (the study of which, according to the Italian anthropologist Cesare Lombroso, 1893, supposedly weakened the nervous system).

The discussion of the Italian school system following the unification of Italy was, then, oriented toward Germany and France. The time had passed when school instruction was solely in the hands of the Church. All the same, the influence of the clergy remained crucial among the people and in the political arena, and any attempt at reform was subject to criticism and tension emanating from Church circles. Opinion polls were taken in preparation for planning school reform. The poll initiated by Minister of Education Antonio Scialoia (1872) [10] provides a good picture of the polemics of that time with respect to the teaching of Latin and Greek. Latin was rejected not only in favour of more practically oriented subjects, but also because the content of the Latin texts was regarded as 'immoral' and as practically inciting attempts to overthrow the government. Greek was naturally met with resistance by the utilitarians, but also by the 'humanists', who rejected philological Classical studies that were focused on the languages. Even among the clergy there were no teachers trained to teach Greek. Accordingly, many at the end of the 19th cent. advocated doing away with the teaching of Greek in the *liceo* [12. 430ff.]; in 1904, a

legislative decree permitted a choice between Greek and mathematics in the second year of the *liceo*.

The 'philologists', in particular the Turin group in the *Rivista di filologia e d'istruzione classica*, founded in 1872, launched a campaign to save Greek, causing them to be accused of Germanophilia (for more on the other side of this attitude: [12]). The voice of the *Società italiana per la diffusione e l'insegnamento degli studi classici* was the magazine *Atene e Roma* (today the periodical of the *Associazione italiana di cultura classica*), which was founded in 1898 and published in Florence. On the opposing side were those who rejected philological studies in favour of the rhetorical and artistic use of the Classical texts, such as the school periodical *Il Baretti*. The *Civiltà cattolica* was untiring in its advocacy of Latin studies that were neither historical nor linguistic, but rhetorical in nature, which represented one of the strengths of the parochial schools. On the other side, the extreme position of the philologists led to viewpoints that were utterly opposed to the idea of disseminating scientific advances in the schools: adopting the German model for the organization of Classical studies encouraged scientific research, but it also led to a stark division between academic and university work, on the one hand, and the teaching of Latin and Greek in the secondary schools, on the other.

B. 20TH CENT.

The task of the *liceo classico* in a united Italy was to educate the ruling classes (and in many respects that remains true today). The difficult and 'unnecessary' study of the Classical languages and philosophy served as a means of social discrimination. Latin and Greek teachers, for example, received a higher salary. The reform project initiated by Gaetano Salveminis (1908; with the help of Alfredo Galletti) supported elite schools, particularly for the Classical subjects. Giovanni Gentile's reform (1923) also saw the *liceo classico* as having central importance as the aristocratic school that offered access to all university departments, which held true until 1970. Although numerous changes have been made in some areas, this reform continues to be a heavy burden on the Italian school system, because the structure of the *liceo classico* remains unchanged: the natural sciences and modern foreign languages are substantially underrepresented; during the first two years all of Greek and Latin morphology and syntax are covered (about 10 hours per week), and all 'humanistic' subjects are taught by the same teacher. The last three years, in which extensive excerpts from the Classics are read, are devoted to the whole of literary history. With the reform of 1923, the *liceo scientifico* was introduced, which had a natural science orientation and served to train qualified technicians; Greek was not part of the curriculum. Another new school type was the *istituto magistrale* (previously: *scuola normale*) for training primary-school teachers, which included Latin in its curricula for all four years; it replaced more practically-oriented subjects such as agronomy, needlework and handwriting. Finally, a state examination which included tests in translating from Latin and Greek was introduced as part of the final qualifying examination taken upon completion of the *liceo*. In line with the ideological exaggeration of the importance of Latin by the fascist regime, the Minister of Education Giuseppe Bottai made Latin the basic subject in his reform of the 'unified' middle school (*scuola media 'unica'*). Until 1962, when the three-year obligatory *scuola media unica* was introduced, this *scuola media* provided access to higher education. While Latin was optional in the last year of the *scuola media* until 1977, it was eliminated altogether at that time, following numerous fierce debates. As in the 19th cent., → COURSES OF INSTRUCTION were not drawn up until long after structural reforms had been agreed upon; it was not until 1944 that curricula for the secondary schools were in place. In 1967 they were examined (the Latin curricula used today in the *liceo scientifico* and the *istituto magistrale* are from that year) and in 1978 they were revised for the *ginnasio* and in 1980 for the *liceo classico*, after Latin and Greek had begun simultaneously in the first year of the *liceo*. A comprehensive reform to standardize the curricula is underway. During the last few years, there has been growing interest in the didactics of the Classical languages, also at the university level, while the final examinations to gain certification to teach at the *ginnasio* (1993) still require, anachronistically, translation from Greek into Latin.

→ ITALY; → SCHOOLS

1 G. BONETTA, G. FIORAVANTI, L'istruzione classica (1860–1910), 1995 2 G. P. BRIZZI, Strategie educative e istituzioni scolastiche nella Controriforma, in: A. ASOR ROSA (ed.), Letteratura Italiana, Vol. I: Il letterato e le istituzioni, 1982, 899–920 (with bibliography) 3 M. L. CHIRICO, La fondazione della rivista 'Atene e Roma' e la filologia classica italiana, in: M. CAPASSO et al. (eds.), Momenti della storia degli studi classici fra Ottocento e Novecento, 1987, 87–104 4 V. CITTI (ed.), Discipline classiche e nuova secondaria. Vol. I: Aspetti generali, 1986 5 A. CURIONE, Sullo studio del greco in Italia nei secoli XVII e XVIII, 1941 6 A. LA PENNA, Università ed istruzione pubblica, in: Storia d'Italia, V.2, 1973, 670–765 7 D. LASSANDRO, Sull'insegnamento del latino, in: E. BOSNA, G. GENOVESI (eds.), L'istruzione secondaria superiore in Italia da Casati ai giorni nostri. Atti del IV Convegno Nazionale, 1988, 289–298 8 M. RAICICH, Il professore nella scuola italiana, in: Belfagor 15, 1960, 614–622 9 Id., Gli studi classici nell' Ottocento, in: Belfagor 19, 1964, 229–234 10 Id., Le polemiche sugli studi classici e l'inchiesta Scialoia, in: Belfagor 18, 1963, 257–268 und 534–551 (Repr.: Scuola cultura e politica da De Sanctis a Gentile, 1981) 11 G. RICUPERATI, Università e scuola in Italia, in: A. ASOR ROSA (ed.), Letteratura italiana, I: Il letterato e le istituzioni, 1982, 983–1007 (with bibliography) 12 S. TIMPANARO, Il primo cinquantennio della Rivista di filologia e d'istruzione classica, in: RFIC 100, 1972, 387–441.   SOTERA FORNARO

IV. FRANCE
see → FRANCE

V. USA
see → UNITED STATES OF AMERICA

Ancient Near Eastern Philology and History (Assyriology)

A. NAME AND DEFINITION B. ORIGINS AND BEGINNINGS C. END OF THE 19TH CENT. D. THE 1920S AND 1930S E. SINCE THE END OF WORLD WAR II F. STRUCTURES AND INSTITUTIONS OF THE DISCIPLINE G. ANCIENT NEAR EASTERN PHILOLOGY AND HISTORY IN THE CONTEXT OF ITS CULTURAL AND POLITICAL ENVIRONMENT H. PERSPECTIVES FOR THE FUTURE

A. NAME AND DEFINITION

Ancient Near Eastern Philology and History (ANEPH) is part of Ancient Near Eastern Studies, which includes the archaeology of the ancient Near East as well as philology and history. The term 'ancient Near Eastern', in the context of Western European and American scholarship, refers to the geographical area of the Near East and its pre-Christian or pre-Islamic civilizations in the territory of present-day Turkey, Syria, Lebanon, Israel, Jordan, Iraq, the Arabian peninsula and Iran. As understood by Eastern European scholars, the term ancient Near Eastern includes all ancient advanced civilizations between the Mediterranean and the China Sea. Originally, and to some degree even today, the discipline has borne the traditional name Assyriology, since it was inscriptions from ancient Assyria that marked the beginning of research on the culture of ancient Mesopotamia. In comparison with that term the designation Ancient Near Eastern Studies proved to be increasingly appropriate the more ancient Near Eastern civilizations became known. The enormous increase in inscriptions and archaeological material over the years led to the development of two sub-disciplines: Ancient Near Eastern Philology and → NEAR EASTERN ARCHAEOLOGY, which, however, remain linked by a shared goal – which is to reconstruct an ancient advanced civilization on the basis of written and material evidence. In that regard, ANEPH, as a historical and cultural discipline, is very closely associated with Near Eastern Archaeology and unthinkable without the contributions of that discipline. The work of the latter, in turn, can only be successful by taking into consideration the findings of philology, when dealing with epochs that can be studied through written sources.

ANEPH concerns itself with the languages, history and civilizations of the Ancient Near East. Their written relics can be understood primarily through the medium of Akkadian (Assyrian-Babylonian) and Sumerian cuneiform script; through Hittite and other ancient Anatolian languages passed down in cuneiform writings (Hattic, Luwian, Palaic); and through (hieroglyphic) Luwian, familiar from numerous hieroglyphic texts.

ANEPH cultivates close ties to the historical and Near Eastern disciplines that address the languages and civilizations of the ancient Near East whose written expressions are extant in non-cuneiform alphabetic writings. These include → SEMITIC Studies, insofar as they deal with Ugaritic, Phoenician, Aramaic and other Western Semitic languages, Old South Arabian and aspects of comparative linguistics; furthermore → IRANIAN Studies and Ancient History insofar as they focus on the reign of the Achaemenids, Arsacids (Parthians) and Sasanids. There are close links between Anatolian Studies, which deals with the oldest known Indo-European languages, and Indo-Germanic Studies, which focuses, among other things, on the ancient Anatolian languages of the 1st millenium (for example Lydian, Lycian, Phrygian).

B. ORIGINS AND BEGINNINGS

Soon after the→ DECIPHERMENT of Old Persian, Elamite and Akkadian cuneiform script during the 1st half of the 19th cent. some of this work occurring at the same time as extensive English and French excavations were being carried out in the palaces of the Assyrian capitals of Kalu (Nimrud), Dūr-Šarru-ukīn and Nineveh, inscriptions found there on orthostats were published, as were texts from the library of the Assyrian king Ashurbanipal that was discovered in Nineveh (E. Botta, *Monument de Ninive* (= Dūr-Šarru-ukīn), 1849; A.H. Layard, *Inscriptions in the Cuneiform Character from Assyrian Monuments*, 1851; H.C. Rawlinson, E. Norris, Th. Pinches, *The Cuneiform Inscriptions of Western Asia*, 5 volumes 1861–1880). Having become accessible, these texts made it possible to undertake a comprehensive study of ancient Mesopotamia that went beyond merely deciphering the language.

Public interest in the artistic and written relics of ancient Mesopotamia arose from a variety of motives: for one, attempts by European powers to gain political and economic influence in the Ottoman Empire had the side effect of leading to an occupation – initially pursued by amateurs – with the relics of the civilization of ancient Mesopotamia. Second, a certain competitiveness arose among the major countries of that time in seeking to acquire important works of art for their museums. A related factor, at the end of the 19th cent., was the decision by the political and intellectual elite of Germany, and in particular Prussia, to conduct excavations of their own in Mesopotamia, and likewise to display ancient Near Eastern antiquities in the museums of Berlin, as such materials were displayed in the → LOUVRE and the British Museum. The public exhibitions there of reliefs from the palaces of the Assyrian rulers now introduced to an educated public another pre-classical advanced civilization, in addition to ancient Egypt, with works of art of an impressive appeal. Third, the development of the discipline must be viewed against the backdrop of a general contemporary interest in foreign civilizations that encompassed the ethnography of the non-European world as well as the history

of antiquity. In this context, the Near East assumed a significant position in a universally-oriented historiography, when it involved the investigation of the beginnings of history. Finally, the theological discussion in Europe-and the United States [7; 11] concerning the Old Testament as a historical source and its accuracy, played a significant role insofar as certain inscriptions from Assyrian rulers shed light on Old Testament reports of contacts and conflicts involving the nations of Judah and Israel. Thus, it was a sensation in 1874 when George Smith, curator at the British Museum in London, published an extensive fragment of the Epic of Gilgamesh, which was discovered among the clay tablets in the library of Ashurbanipal, and which contained the story of a 'flood' that shows astonishing parallels to the story of the Flood in the Old Testament (Gen. 6–8).

C. END OF THE 19TH CENT.

Especially those scholars engaged in historical and critical investigation of the Old Testament provided crucial impetus for establishing Assyriology as an independent academic discipline. The articles by the Old Testament scholar Eberhard Schrader were of landmark importance: *Die Basis der Entzifferung der babylonisch-assyrischen Keilinschriften geprüft* (ZDMG 23, 1869, 337–374) and *Die assyrisch-babylonischen Keilschriften. Kritische Untersuchungen der Grundlagen ihrer Entzifferung* (ZDMG 26, 1872,1–392) as well as his monograph *Die Keilinschriften und das Alte Testament* (1872, ³1903). Not least because of these works, Schrader was appointed in 1875 to the first professorial chair for Assyriology, which was created for him in Berlin at the initiative of the Royal Prussian Academy of Sciences.

For a long time, the new discipline was met with considerable scepticism. Objections were raised, for example, to what were regarded as careless philological methods; this was warranted given that the discipline was still in its beginning stages. Not justified in its absoluteness was the criticism of numerous errors in the reading of place names and personal names due to the multiple meanings of the cuneiform script. Above all, it is thanks to Friedrich Delitzsch that a change occurred in this regard. His roots were in Indo-Germanic Studies, a discipline noted for its methodological stringency; he wrote his Habilitation thesis in 1874 in Leipzig, the first to do so in the field of Assyriology, and immediately thereafter received a position at that university as an associate professor (*außerordentlich*). In a methodically convincing manner, Delitzsch laid the groundwork for the discipline in terms of grammar (*Assyrische Grammatik*, 1889) and lexicon (*Assyrisches Handwörterbuch*, 1896) and thus established Assyriology as a recognized academic discipline in the canon of the other Near Eastern subjects. His reputation as an outstanding scholar drew students from many countries, who subsequently established an Assyriological tradition in their own countries. Assyriology was shaped by

Delitzsch's many students in the United States in particular. Paul Haupt founded Ancient Near Eastern studies in Baltimore; his student W. Muss-Arnoldt compiled the first English-language dictionary of Akkadian, which far exceeded Delitzsch's in its scope.

In the 1880s it was above all the French excavations (L. Heuzy, E. de Sarzec, *Découvertes en Chaldée*, 1884–1912) in southern Iraq that revealed numerous monumental inscriptions from rulers of the city-state of Lagash dating from the 25th to the 22nd cents. BC as well as thousands of administrative documents. They were written in Sumerian, a language whose study had only just begun at that time. This meant that ANEPH, whose horizon had initially been limited to the Assyrian and Babylonian history of the 1st millennium, was expanded to a substantial degree chronologically, geographically and linguistically, since the newly discovered texts came from the second half of the 3rd millennium. Previous research on the Sumerian language, which had at first been regarded by many researchers not as an independent language, but as a cryptographic rendition of Assyrian-Babylonian, was based in large part on bilingual Sumerian-Akkadian texts from the 1st millennium. Of fundamental importance were the works of the French scholars F. de Lenormant and J. Oppert, as well as of A.H. Sayce in England, who recognized the essential grammatical principle of Sumerian – an agglutinative language that up to today no one has been able to assign to one of the known language families [13]. Building on this, in 1907 the French scholar of Ancient Near Eastern Studies F. Thureau-Dangin published his masterly translation of the Gudea of Lagash (22nd cent. BC), which – apart from certain details – has not been surpassed even today. When Delitzsch subsequently published his *Grundzüge der Sumerischen Grammatik* (1914) and his *Sumerisches Glossar* (1914), the first stage of research on the Sumerian language had come to an end.

As the 19th cent. gave way to the 20th, ANEPH received enormous impetus from numerous excavations in Iraq; of these, particular mention should be made of the American excavations in Nippur conducted by H.V. Hilprecht and those carried out by the → DEUTSCHE ORIENT-GESELLSCHAFT in → BABYLON and in Ashur by R. Koldewey and W. Andrae, among others. An important role was played at that time by the British Museum, where Assyriological research was carried out with great foresight in its organization. One example is the *Catalogue of the Kujundjik Collection of the British Museum* (1889–1896) published by Carl Bezold, which still today remains indispensable. It deciphers the scholarly records of ancient Mesopotamia (largely in Akkadian as well as in bilingual Sumerian-Akkadian texts) collected in the library of Ashurbanipal. In particular, it enabled scholars to fit together texts that had been unearthed as fragments – which was generally the case for the text records from Mesopotamia – and to identify duplicates. It is often necessary to have several dozen partially overlapping duplicates in order to reconstruct

a text completely. The major museums in London, Paris and Berlin began to publish their extensive holdings of clay tablets (*Cuneiform Texts from Babylonian Tablets in the British Museum*, 1869ff.; *Textes cunéiformes du Louvre*, 1910ff.; *Vorderasiatische Schriftdenkmäler der Königlichen Museen zu Berlin*, 1907–1917). The same was true of the important American collections, which had acquired thousands of cuneiform texts in the antiquities market: for example *Yale Oriental Series, Babylonian texts* (1915ff.); University of Pennsylvania Museum: *Publications of the Babylonian Section* (1911–1930); *Babylonian Expedition of the University of Pennsylvania* (1893–1914). Thus researchers had an extensive body of material available for most of the periods of Mesopotamian history and linguistic development. As excavations, text publications and the editing and translation of important texts significantly increased knowledge of the history and culture of Babylonia and Assyria, the relationship of Assyriology/ANEPH to Old Testament studies was also affected. Triggered by lectures given by Delitzsch, this led in Germany to the so-called Babel-Bible controversy (→ BABYLON, E, 4).

Of particular significance was the discovery of the Hammurabi Stele, found in the course of the French excavations at Susa (1902) – containing the text of what remains today the most comprehensive code of laws from preclassical Antiquity – by the French scholar V. Scheil, who also made a great contribution by publishing an impressive number of texts. The Stele text – written in the Old Babylonian dialect Akkadian – opened up new dimensions in the study of Akkadian grammar. Moreover, this find led to the development of an independent branch of ANEPH, Ancient Near Eastern Legal History. This discipline was shaped by the prominent legal historians Josef Kohler, Paul Koschaker, Mariano San Nicolò and Sir John Miles. For a long time, Ancient Near Eastern Legal History could claim to be on an equal methodological footing with its parent discipline, Roman Legal History. Otherwise, this holds true only for the research on Babylonian → MATHEMATICS and mathematical astronomy conducted by Otto Neugebauer. Studies of the literature and religion of ancient Mesopotamia have gradually been linked with the respective parent disciplines, as the appropriate methodological approaches are being adopted.

D. THE 1920S AND 1930S

With his *Grundzüge der sumerischen Grammatik* (1923) and the morphological analysis formulated in it, which remains essentially valid today, Arno Poebel laid the foundation for further research into the Sumerian language. A. Deimel, who worked at the Pontificio Istituto Biblico in Rome, made a landmark contribution when he published administrative documents from the 24th cent. BC in their original archival context, and on that basis, for the first time, depicted systematically the administrative and economic structures of an early

Mesopotamian city-state (beginning in 1920). His *Sumerisches Lexikon* (1928–1933), organized by cuneiform signs, remains an indispensable lexical aid for Sumerology, despite the obvious shortcomings in it that have since become evident. The English scholar Stephen Langdon contributed in a variety of ways to our knowledge of Sumerian through the publication of numerous texts and studies.

A new branch of ANEPH began to emerge in 1915, when the Czech orientalist Bedrich Hrozny recognized as Indo-European the language on the clay tablets that had been discovered by August Winckler in 1907 at the Anatolian site of Boghazkoy, and thus laid the foundation for the new cuneiform discipline of → Hittite Studies. In the United States, the Egyptologist James Henry Breasted, Director of the Oriental Institute in Chicago, launched the *Chicago Assyrian Dictionary* project in 1922. Following the model of the Egyptian dictionary that had been started under the leadership of A. Erman and under the patronage of the Royal Prussian Academy of Sciences in Berlin, Breasted planned to compile a thesaurus of the Assyrian-Babylonian language. Scholars from all over the world were recruited to go through and translate entire groups of texts, some of them as yet unpublished, as a basis for cataloging the language's vocabulary. The goal of Bruno Meissner, Professor of Assyriology in Berlin, was a more modest one; with the support of the Prussian Academy of Sciences, after extensive preliminary work, he sought in 1930 to compile a concise dictionary of Assyrian-Babylonian. It was not until after World War II that both dictionary projects were successfully continued. C. Bezold had sought to meet the need for a dictionary. His *Babylonian-Assyrian Glossary* (without references) was published posthumously in 1926 by his student A. Götze.

In the 1920s, the young scholar Benno Landsberger (1890–1968), who was teaching in Leipzig, provided, with his fundamental grammatical and heuristic insights, a valuable impetus for ANEPH that continues today. Particularly groundbreaking was his work entitled *Die Eigenbegrifflichkeit der babylonischen Welt*. (1926, repr. 1965). In it, Landsberger put an end to so-called Pan-Babylonianism, while at the same time calling into question the sometimes rash application of Old Testament concepts to the religious phenomena of Mesopotamia. He showed how to gain insight in a methodologically rigorous manner into the ways of thinking and the values that were specific to Mesopotamian culture. In this way, he anticipated the later discussion of group-specific and scientific concepts that was to become well known under the terms 'emic' and 'etic' in the fields of linguistics and social anthropology. His findings in the sphere of grammar were further developed by his students in later years, and became a fundamental part of the discipline.

Hitler's dictatorship led to the exodus of numerous scholars from Germany and Austria – among them scholars in the field of Ancient Near Eastern Studies such as Benno Landsberger, Julius and Hildegard Lewy, Otto Neugebauer, Hans-Gustav Güterbock, Fritz Rudolf Kraus, Leo Oppenheim, Ernst Herzfeld and Albrecht Goetze. As modern universities were being established under the leadership of Kemal Ataturk, Landsberger, Güterbock and Kraus founded the field of ANEPH in Turkey. Oppenheim, Goetze, the Lewys, Neugebauer and Herzfeld found a new home in the United States and had a profound effect on APG in that country.

E. Since the End of World War II

After the war, Landsberger, Güterbock and Oppenheim were called to the Oriental Institute of the University of Chicago and, together with I. J. Gelb and T. Jacobsen, they guided the decisive phase of the *Chicago Assyrian Dictionary* (CAD) project. The original plan to compile a thesaurus had been abandoned, since the publication of the myriad unpublished texts in museums and private collections, as well as the new texts that were constantly being added from of the numerous excavations in Iraq and Syria, would only have been possible to achieve with the help of generations of researchers. Therefore, it was decided that work should proceed on the basis of the text material that was already accessible. In 1956 the first volume appeared and in July 2005 a conference was held at the Oriental Institute to celebrate the completion of the CAD project. According to its long-term publisher, Leo Oppenheim, the CAD is not intended to be just a dictionary, but a compendium that depicts the culture of Mesopotamia through the concepts that are inherent in its language. This is accomplished, for example, by citing the entire context of a given word, which permits the user a direct critique of its interpretation. The CAD continued the tradition of international cooperation, even after the actual writing process had begun: many young as well as older scholars from all over the world were recruited to work on this project. In contrast, Wolfram von Soden's three-volume *Akkadisches Handwörterbuch*, which was compiled – based on Meissner's preliminary work – between 1954 and 1981, was largely one man's accomplishment. Conceived as a concise dictionary, it attaches particular importance to the etymological equivalents of the other Semitic languages and to the grammatical (morphological and syntactical) characteristics of individual words, which makes it a valuable supplement to the CAD. Thus the study of Akkadian has at its disposal modern lexicographic aids that are comparable to those used in studying the classical languages. In addition to the dictionary, von Soden contributed to ANEPH an *Akkadian Syllabary* (1948), the basis for a well-founded interpretation of the various meanings of the signs of cuneiform script, and above all the descriptive *Grundriss der Akkadischen Grammatik* (1952), which remains the standard today. Modern linguistic theory forms the foundation of the grammatical presentations of Erica Reiner (*A Linguistic Analysis of Akkadian*, 1966), I. J. Gelb (*A Sequential Reconstruc-*

tion of Akkadian, 1969) and G. Buccellati (*A Structural Grammar of Akkadian*, 1996).

Research on the Sumerian language after 1945 was shaped by the work of Adam Falkenstein (1906–1966), Thorkild Jacobsen (1904–1993) and Samuel Noah Kramer (1897–1990). Falkenstein's *Grammatik der Sprache des Gudea von Lagasch* (1949/50), important aspects of which are based on Poebel (see above), introduced a new era of research into Sumerian grammar. Since then, a sometimes controversial discussion of the grammatical structure of Sumerian has followed, which has led, among other things, to important new discoveries regarding the Sumerian verb system. While previously the grammar had been based for the most part on bilingual Sumerian-Akkadian texts (known to scholars from copies dating from the 1st millennium) and bilingual grammatical lists, Falkenstein based his analysis on a monolingual Sumerian text corpus of high literary quality. The advantage of using this text corpus was that its formation could be limited to a time span of some 20 years, and that it had not been subsequently 'modernized' as it was handed down. Kramer's lasting contribution lies in the publication of Sumerian myths, epics and cultic songs in autographic and philological editions. Together with the help of numerous dissertations instigated by him, the most important components of the Sumerian literary tradition were made accessible. Lexicographic research on Sumerian is based to a substantial degree on the series edited by B. Landsberger and M. Civil entitled *Materials for the Sumerian Lexicon* (17 volumes since 1938), which contains bilingual Sumerian-Akkadian vocabularies and lists of objects organized by subject groups. The compilation of a Sumerian dictionary based on the CAD model has been under way since 1984 at the University of Pennsylvania (PSD) under the leadership of Å. Sjöberg and continued by Steve Tinney. In recent years, the project's focus has shifted more toward a digital existence. PSD has issued a web-release of its second Beta of the ePSD in 2005 and expects to have a Web, CD and print-release of a first full version of the PSD in 2006.

F. Structures and Institutions of the Discipline

Since the 1950s, ANEPH has been established as a new discipline in many countries beyond the group of North American and Western European countries that were prominent in the past (for example, in China, Iraq, Israel, Japan, Spain, Syria) or has launched a new beginning, as in the former Soviet Union (in that country, the entire field of Near Eastern Studies in Leningrad fell victim to the Stalinist 'purges' following Kirov's murder in 1934), Poland, Hungary and the former Czechoslovakia. In Iraq, Israel, Syria and Turkey, an important motivation for addressing the cultures of the Ancient Near East arose from interest in those countries' own history and the search for a national identity.

Since the beginning of the 20th cent., ANEPH has been repeatedly enriched by surprising text discoveries.

These discoveries have not only deepened our understanding of Babylonian civilization, but above all they have substantially increased our knowledge of the culture and history of northern Mesopotamia and Syria (among others, Alalaḫ, Ebla, Emar, Kaneš, Mari, Nuzi, Ugarit). Research has turned to the Syrian region because of the favorable working conditions found there, but also because of the political situation in Iraq. The enormous expansion in the amount of source material, not only in terms of regional, but also in its linguistic variety, chronological dimension (3200 – approx. 100 BC) and content (e.g., literary and religious texts, administrative and legal documents, letters), has led to increased specialization within the field of ANEPH: in the sub-disciplines of Sumerology, Akkadian studies and Hittite Studies, interest is emerging to varying degrees in certain language and historical periods and in certain content areas (among others, economic and social history, literary traditions, medical, mathematical and astronomical texts). While the situation varies from country to country, as a result of these developments there are now two professorships in the field of ANEPH at many universities. Unlike the United States, France and Italy, where ancient Near Eastern history is taught on a large scale within the general history curriculum, in Germany it has not proved possible so far, despite a great deal of effort, to integrate the non-European history of Asia and Africa into the academic training offered to historians, although it is an integral part of the secondary-school curriculum. In Western Europe and North America, many new professorships in ANEPH were established as the universities were expanded in the 1970s; however, since the mid–1990s these positions again find themselves in jeopardy as a wave of 'consolidation' is taking place in the tertiary educational sphere.

In some countries, ANEPH has been a subject of study not only at the universities, but also at research institutions outside of the universities or affiliated with them: for example at the Carsten Niebuhr Institute in Denmark, the Oriental Institute in Chicago, the Netherlands' Historisch-Archaeologisch Instituut in het Nabije Oosten, Centre National de la Recherche Scientifique (CNRS) in France, Consiglio Nazionale delle Ricerche (CNR) in Italy, Consejo Superior de Investigaciones Científicas (CSIC) in Spain, at the major museums in Philadelphia, Paris, London and Berlin, and the Academies of Sciences in the former Soviet Union or Russia, the former Czechoslovakia or the Czech Republic, and the former East Germany. In countries with no national research centers, research projects at the universities are financially supported by the relevant national organizations for promoting research (among others, the National Endowment for the Humanities in the United States, the Netherlands' Organization for Pure Research, the Deutsche Forschungsgemeinschaft).

An important part in the extensive scholarly cooperation that occurs within the sphere of ANEPH is contributed by the annual Rencontre Assyriologique

Internationale, which was established by French and Belgian Assyriologists in 1948. Since scholars in Ancient Near Eastern Studies in the socialist countries were long subject to travel restrictions, they began in 1974 to hold conferences at irregular intervals under the name 'Šulmu' (peace), with active participation by researchers from Western Europe and the United States.

G. Ancient Near Eastern Philology and History in the Context of its Cultural and Political Environment

In addition to discussing heuristic and methodological problems, in keeping with a general trend in the study of history, the discipline of ANEPH itself has become the subject of investigation and critical reflection [12; 16]. Central themes in this regard include the concentration on certain research subjects favored by the trends of the time, the use of specific methods, as well as issues of the discipline's place and significance in the university's canon and in university education. Looking back, it also becomes clear to what degree the circumstances of a given era have affected the discipline's development and choice of themes. This holds true not only for the 19th cent. In later years as well, the discipline has become entangled in the ideological currents of the time. In the Soviet Union, V.V. Struve participated in the 1930s in formulating the so-called Stalinist formation theory (the development from a primitive society to communism via a slaveholder society, feudalism and capitalism). To counter Struve's one-sided ideological positions, I.M. Diakonoff was able to put forth, successfully, a well-founded critique, strictly focused on the message of the texts, (1967). In so doing, Diakonoff helped to shape ancient Near Eastern research in the former Soviet Union, East Germany and Czechoslovakia, as well as in Poland and in Hungary. In the winter semester of 1933/34, as part of the political education of students at the University of Berlin, Bruno Meissner lectured on a topic entitled Introduction to the 'Ethnogeny of the Ancient Near East' [14. 191]. T. Jacobsen's *Primitive Democracy* (JNES 2, 1943, 149–72) can be viewed as a young scholar's declaration of allegiance to the political system of his adopted country, while his work *The Assumed Conflict between Sumerians and Semites in Early Mesopotamian History* in the Journal of the American Oriental Society (JAOS) 59, 1939, 485–95) is a response to the view – by no means limited to Germany – that historical developments can be explained by national characteristics or racial differences [4].

H. Perspectives for the Future

In view of the fact that new texts are continually being discovered, and with more than 150,000 unpublished texts now found in museums (in particular in the British Museum in London, the Archaeological Museum in Istanbul and the Iraq Museum in Baghdad), ANEPH finds itself in a dilemma: first, the urgent task remains to make unpublished material in the form of autographies accessible; in addition, there is a pressing need to edit the content of known material and to develop syntheses. In the near term, then, it is important not only to continue the editing of the large quantities of unpublished texts, but also to come up with newly-edited publications of texts that have long been available. In the last few decades, exemplary editorial standards have been developed for this purpose. This included making hand-drawn copies of and collating the texts. In view of the many duplicates of literary texts, the reader not only had to be informed of variants, but the actual degree of preservation of each text passage had to be laid out as well, in the form of a 'Partitur' (i.e. 'textual matrix' format). In this context, increasing attention has been paid to issues of paleography and the scribal culture. A large quantity of texts in the rich scholarly tradition of ancient Mesopotamia (in particular myths, epics, texts of divination and incantation, medical, mathematical and astronomical texts) has been made accessible not only editorially, but also with respect to content. There is an emerging tendency to approach the intellectual concepts of Mesopotamian civilization and its values and world view in such a way that intuition, methodological stringency and understanding of what is specific to that civilization are rooted in strict philological discipline [10].

Since the 1960s, problems of social and economic history in the ancient Near East have drawn increasing attention (I. J.Gelb, *Approaches to the Study of Ancient Societies*, JAOS 87, 1967, 1–8). The groundwork for such inquiries was laid by Koschaker, Miles and San Nicolo (see above) and their students, who conducted numerous investigations in legal history. Research dealing with this region's social and economic history currently has at its disposal a unique and far richer body of source material than is available for other ancient civilizations, with a present total of around 100,000 published letters and legal and administrative documents. However, since they are dispersed among a large number of museums and collections – coming, in many cases, from illicit excavations – they first have to be put back into their original context. In the case of document holdings of significance for economic and social history research, this is achieved primarily by the use of prosopographic methods. With the help of archives or dossiers reconstructed in this manner, it is then possible to depict the structures and processes of a society and its economy. While the texts do not enable us to draw statistical conclusions that meet the standards of social science, the extant individual texts are of great temporal and localdensity; for example, frequently 10,000–20,000 texts are spread over a span of only a few decades. As sources have been made accessible, an intensive and sometimes controversial theoretical debate has ensued, primarily regarding the question of whether modern, neoclassical economic theories are suitable for analyzing pre-modern economies. Those who answer in the negative base their view on the work of the economic historian Karl Polanyi and the ancient historian Moses Finley, among others [15].

Increasingly, ANEPH is launching interdisciplinary research projects dealing with such issues as cultural, social, religious, economic and scientific history, or participating in related colloquia or research groups. In so doing, it is expanding the spectrum of knowledge that, in the past, has often been limited by Western ways of thinking. ANEPH enables us to examine and understand an independent and significant ancient advanced civilization, in the light of its own circumstances and concepts. Moreover, it is clear that the knowledge and achievements of this civilization have remained influential up to the present day, through the mediation of the Old Testament and the classical Mediterranean world. For its part, ANEPH has also gained new perspectives for considering its own sources by working together with other disciplines (such as sociology, social anthropology, economic, legal, cultural, medical, mathematical, astronomical and religious history, and comparative literature) and by gaining experience with the methods of those disciplines.

→ Achamenids; → Akkadian; → Ancient Southern Arabian; → Aramaic; → Assurbanipal; → Atraḫasīs; → Cuneiform script; → Gilgamesh, Gilgamesh Epic; → Hammurapi; → Hattic; → Ḫattusa; → Hieroglyphs; → Hittite; → Judah and Israel; → Luwian; → Nineveh; → Palaic; → Parthia; → Phoenicians, Poeni; → Sassanids; → Sumerian; → Ugaritic

→ Iraq Museum Baghdad; → Berlin II. Vorderasiatisches Museum; → Egyptology; → London, British Museum

1 R. Borger, Altorientalische Lexikographie – Geschichte und Probleme, in: Nachrichten der Akad. der Wiss. Göttingen, Philos.-Histor. Kl. 2/1984, 71–114 2 J. S. Cooper, Posing the Sumerian Question: Race and Scholarship in the Early History of Assyriology, in: Aula Orientalis 9, 1991, 47–66 3 Id., From Mosul to Manila: Early Approaches to Funding Ancient Near Eastern Stud. Research in the US, in: Culture and History 11, 1992, 133–164 4 Id., Sumerian and Aryan Racial Theory, Academic Politics and Parisian Assyriology, in: RHR 210, 1993, 169–205 5 Id., G. M. Schwartz (ed.), The Study of the Ancient Near East in the Twenty-First Century, 1996 6 I. J. Gelb, Introduction, in: Chicago Assyrian Dictionary Vol. A/1, 1964, VII–XXIII 7 B. Kuklick, Puritans in Babylon – The Ancient Near East and American Intellectual Life 1880–1930, 1996 8 M. T. Larsen, Orientalism and Near Eastern Archaeology, in: Domination and Resistance, ed. D. Miller et al., 1986, 229–239 9 Id., The Conquest of Assyria, 1996 10 S. M. Maul, Wiedererstehende Welten, in: MDOG 130, 1998, 266–274 11 C. W. Meade, Road to Babylon, Development of US Assyriology, 1974 12 A. L. Oppenheim, Assyriology – Why and How, in: Id., Ancient Mesopotamia, ²1977, 7 31 13 S. A. Pallis, The Antiquity of Iraq, 1956 14 J. Renger, Die Geschichte der Altorientalistik und der Vorderasiatischen Archive in Berlin 1875–1945, in: W. Arenhövel (ed.), Berlin und die Antike, 1979, 151–192 15 Id., On Economic Structures in Ancient Mesopotamia, in: Orientalia 63, 1994, 157208 16 M. W. Stolper, On Why and How, in: Culture and History 11, 1992, 13–22 17 Bibliography of current publications can be found in the journals: Archiv für Orientforschung and Orientalia.
                                                    JOHANNES RENGER

Andalucia see→ Arabic-Islamic cultural sphere

Animal Epic
A. Concept, Origin, Classical Models
B. History

A. Concept, Origin, Classical Models

The animal epic (AE) is an epic work of varying length (from several hundred to more than 10, 000 lines) with animals as the protagonists, who plan, act, reflect and speak like human beings. Animals appear as well-spoken participants in the myths, stories and other literature of a wide range of peoples and cultures, in oral tradition as well as in literary works that have come down to us in written form. The inclination to reflect human activity in narrative form in the world of the animals may be seen as an anthropological universal, and it manifests itself in literary genres as varied as the → epic, the → fable, didactic writing, Christian redemption-allegory in the tradition of the *Physiologus*, as well as in the → fairy-tale. These genres have been grouped together in modern literary criticism since the 19th cent. under the heading of 'animal poetry', although in classical and medieval poetics fictional texts with animals as protagonists are not classified under an individual category, and even the sub-classification of AE is unknown.

The anthropomorphic treatment of animals always has an alienating effect, whether the emphasis is upon the similarity between animal and human behaviour in the didactic parable, or whether it is on the deliberate discrepancy for parodistic purposes between an elevated style and actions carried out by lower orders. In the AE the reduction of the epic hero, who stands out above his fellow-humans through his special abilities, to an animal fulfils a parodistic or satirical function. Since the animal is never fully humanised, and in certain situations retains its natural instincts to seize its prey or to run away, it is precisely this oscillation on the part of the protagonist between its animal and its human nature that gives the AE its particular charm [1]. Both in form and content (verse-form, use of epic formulas and epithets, narrative, use of dialogue, battle-descriptions and to an extent cyclic structures, in post-classical times also love-themes) the AE, as is so often the case with comic genres, feeds upon 'serious' or 'high-level' models in the relevant literature. This is already apparent in the single surviving animal-epic from the classical period, the late Hellenistic pseudo-Homeric *Batrachomyomachia*, which describes in only around 300 lines of verse the battle between the frogs and the mice, using the *Iliad* as a model. Although the *Batrachomyomachia* was unknown in the West during the Middle Ages and had no influence on the development of post-classical Latin and vernacular AEs, it was used as a school text in → Byzantium, and provided a model for a satirical book-drama by Johannes Prodromos, the *Katomyomachia* ('War of the Cats and the Mice', 1st. half of the 12th cent.). Not until 1472 was the pseudo-Homeric epic parody translated into Latin by the Italian humanist C. Marsuppini, and it became known in Western European literature from the 16th century on. In spite of the assumption made by J. Grimm, it is impossible to determine a straightforward genealogy which would lead from the oral tradition of the 'animal legend' (which is practically impossible to reconstruct) directly to the medieval AE [5. 12–23]. An important classical precedent for the development of the AE in the Middle Ages in Western Europe, however, is the fable; numerous narrative themes, such as that of the unfairly divided booty by the lion, were taken over into the AE and given epic treatment. The AE is a heterogeneous genre, for which it is impossible to point to a single source or claim a single tradition line of development; multiple origins of the genre has to be assumed, given that the humanisation of animals is a familiar feature of all agrarian societies. Folklore, Christian tradition (*Physiologus*, Balaam's ass in Numbers 22, 28, as the only speaking animal in the Bible) and the Latin school tradition (especially collections of fables, *Avianus*) all have a combined effect [10. 1–46].

B. History

The history of the AE is a discontinuous one; its most important points of development are the formation in the High Middle Ages (12th cent.) of large-scale epic cycles with named individual protagonists, and the productive use of the classical genre *Batrachomyomachia* as a model, which begins only in the → Renaissance (16th cent.).

Shorter animal-poems in various metres have survived from the early Middle Ages which, like Alcuin's *The Cock and the Wolf* take up themes from fables, but no generic tradition of AE developed [10.129]. The first more extensive AE of the Latin Middle Ages is the anonymous *Ecbasis cuiusdam captivi* in 1229 leonine hexameters (*c.* 1043–1046); the author interpolates into an autobiographical framework on the distractions of his youth the tale of the flight of a calf, which would have been devoured by a wolf had the latter not been outwitted by the fox. The artistry of the story, with the interweaving of various episodes and narrative levels, as well as borrowings from Horace, is, however, not really an epic, but presumably a monastic Easter entertainment designed to be performedt with different voices for different roles. The first genuine Latin AE is the *Ysengrimus* of Nivardus of Ghent (mid–12th cent.) in elegiac distichs. The otherwise unknown author integrates the individual comic episodes with different adventures of the wolf by way of flashbacks, to make it an epic whole, which ends with the protagonist torn apart by a herd of swine. Nivardus individualises the animals for the first time by providing names. The wolf, a deceiver deceived, falls prey, as a caricature of a monastic bishop, to Fortuna [7]; the cunning of the fox is developed in carefully worked-out rhetorical dialogues and inner monologues, which show the contradiction of thought and word.

Around 1170 there emerged the first episodes (Fr. *branches*) of the Old French *Roman de Renart* in rhymed octosyllabic couplets, the metre of the courtly romance. The Old French AE shares with the romance the description of a feudal world under the rule of King Noble. Even the parodistic reversal of courtly love in a crude rape-scene (Renart the fox woos the she-wolf Hersent, only to force himself on her) is to be read against the background of the courtly world. The action is motivated by the antagonism between the cunning fox and the constantly outwitted wolf, and in generic terms is characterised as the opposite of heroic poetry [5. 219–239]; the entire Renart-cycle of over 30, 000 lines also shows us, like other ramified large-scale epics, the childhood and the death of the hero. Renart constantly shows himself to be a master of verbal equivocation, mockery and deceit [8]. Thus the trickster-figure of the cunning fox can, in French allegories of the 13th cent. (e.g. Jacquemart Gielee, *Renart le Nouvel*), be stylised into the embodiment of evil as such. The Renartmaterial was welcomed into other medieval literatures, as for example in the *Reinhart Fuchs* (late 12th cent.) of Heinrich der Glîchezære from the Alsace, who warns against disloyalty, in the anonymous Middle English version *The Vox and the Wolf* (second half of the 13th cent., see [4. 181–197]), the Flemish *Van den Vos Reinaerde* (first half of the 13th cent.) or the Low German AE *Reynke de Vos* of 1498, which was to serve in 1793 as Goethe's model when he was working on his own AE *Reineke Fuchs*.

During the Renaissance the Homeric epics, and also the pseudo-Homeric *Batrochomyomachia* became once again the focus of literary attention. As early as 1521 Teofilo Folengo published his burlesque AE *Moschaea* in three books of elegiac distichs, dealing with the victorious struggle of the ants against the flies. The parodistic mismatch between epic style and trivial subject, which is a constitutive feature of the burlesque genre, is here augmented in two respects: first through the reduction of the heroes to insects, and secondly through the 'macaronic' mixture of the scholarly language, Latin, and the dialect of Padua. In 1595 in his *Froschmeuseler* the German humanist Georg Rollhagen inflated the classical model into a gigantic didactic epic with moral, economic and scientific excursuses. Against that, Lope de Vega's *Gatomaquia* is more comic and wittier, written in 1635 in *silvas*, the favoured strophic form of his arch-rival Góngora, who had been branded as 'dark.' The battle of the juvenile cats is set off by their rivalry for the beautiful but flighty lady cat, Zapaquila. The introduction of the jealousy-motif is an indication that beside the classical epic, the genre of the Italian romanzo, which grew out of a mixture of medieval *romance*, medieval heroic epic and classical epic, most notably Ariosto's *Orlando Furioso*, is also being parodied. The parodistic AE serves as a foil, therefore, to whatever epic genres are available or popular at any given time. Against this, the gradual loss of interest in the epic and the eventual dominance of the ironic

→ NOVEL towards the end of the 18th and the beginning of the 19th cent. also lead to the disappearance of the AE, although it bids farewell from the heights of European literature and in fine style with Goethe's *Reineke Fuchs*, published in 1794, and Giacomo Leopardi's incomplete *Batracomiomachia*, begun in 1831. Where Goethe cast his medieval material into hexameters in order to castigate human foibles in general and as a personal diversion from the genuine epic activities on the 'world stage', the French → REVOLUTION, Leopardi was concerned in his work, full of allusions and composed in *ottava rima*, the metre of the *romance*, precisely with a satirical treatment of the political struggles between Italian patriots and adherents of the restoration in Naples in the years 1820–1831. George Orwell's anti-Stalinist satire *Animal Farm* (1945), in terms of genre, is no longer determined by the epic, but by the fable and the novel. Beyond that, in the 20th cent. talking animals have withdrawn into → COMICS and children's books, where their improbability is most likely to be accepted. Alan Alexander Milne's children's classic *Winnie-the-Pooh* was even translated into Latin in 1958, so that Bear, Piglet and Rabbit appear one last time in classical dress.

→ Batrachomyomachia;→ Epic, animal
→ FABLE

1 G. BIANCIOTTO, Renart et son cheval, in: FS Félix Lecoy, 1973, 27–42 2 R. DITHMAR, Die Fabel, ⁷1988 3 J. FLINN, Le Roman de Renart dans la littérature française et dans les littératures étrangères au moyen âge, 1963 4 TH. HONEGGER, From Phoenix to Chauntecleer. Medieval English Animal Poetry, 1996 5 H. R. JAUSS, Untersuchungen zur mittelalterlichen Tierdichtung, 1959 6 F. P. KNAPP, Das lateinische Tierepos: Untersuchungen zur mittelalterlichen Tierepik, 1979 7 J. MANN (ed.), Ysengrimus, 1987 8 J. R. SCHEIDEGGER, Le Roman de Renart ou le texte de la dérision, 1989 9 A. STRUBEL, La Rose, Renart et le Graal, 1989 10 J. M. ZIOLKOWSKI, Talking Animals. Medieval Latin Beast Poetry, 750–1150, 1993.
MAX GROSSE

Animal studies see → ZOOLOGY

Anthologia Graeca see→ LYRIC POETRY

Anthologia Latina see→ LYRIC POETRY

Antiquarianism (Humanism until 1800)
A. CONCEPT, CONTENT AND FORM   B. HISTORY AND GENRES   C. ANTIQUARIANISM AND MODERN ANCIENT STUDIES

A. CONCEPT, CONTENT AND FORM
During the period covered here, *antiquities antiquitates, antiquités*, 'Antiquitäten', 'Alterthümer' were understood as the totality of written documentation or material remains (such as coins, monuments, objects of art and everyday items) that might provide information about the daily conditions, customs, practices, cults, institutions, in short the culture, of an ancient people.

An *antiquarius* was an authority, a collector and archivist of such documents and fragments. After Jacob Spon (1685 [76]) both terms were often used synonymously with 'archaeology' and 'archaeologist'. This arbitrariness in terminology shows that antiquarianism was not regarded as a self-contained *ars* or academic discipline but rather as an arsenal of facts, the ordering and erudite description of which did not follow any firm set of rules but rather the interest and competence of the individual antiquarian. In a period that required every academic field to draw on ancient models, this openness can be readily explained by the multiplicity of possible models. Even if Varro's *Antiquitatum rerum humanarum et divinarum libri XLI*, that masterpiece of Antiquity praised by Cicero, had been lost and were known to us only through Augustine's scant list of its contents (Civ. 6,4), there were various other authors to turn to, such as Aulus Gellius (*Noctes Atticae*), Athenaeus of Naucratis (*The Learned Banquet*), Strabo, Pausanias, Stephanus of Byzantium or other late Roman-Hellenistic lexicographers. This plethora of varied models gave antiquarians significantly greater freedom of manoeuvre in the presentation and literate structure of their material than was available to historians, for example [112].

Like the latter, however, pre-modern antiquarianism pursued a fundamentally philological goal: it was expected to help reach a better understanding of the works of classical authors. Information derived from those authors helped, in turn, to identify ancient objects. Antiquarianism and history were thus expected to extend and validate each other, with the latter concentrating on the dynamic factor and the former, the static, systematic or structural factor: While ancient authors mostly depicted events and changes and often left the political and cultural constants simply to be guessed at, it fell to antiquarianism to portray just those 'circumstances and attitudes' [89. 54–55]. In the early modern period of Classical studies, it therefore encompassed constitutional, legal, economic and cultural history. Antiquarianism usually took the form of a reference work: *Bibliotheca* or *Thesaurus*, which bundled together excerpts or entire works on specific themes (e.g. [39–42; 82]), *Lexica*, which condensed such texts into short items of information (e.g. [62]), or *Catalogi*, which described and classified the pieces in a collection (e.g. [7–8; 26; 34; 71; 87]). From the late 16th cent. on, illustrations in woodcuts or copperplate engravings increasingly accompanied the textual description. In the 18th cent. the leading antiquarian publications were often expensive works with illustrated plates (e.g. [49]). Even if the external appearance of the publications was modified in this way, their structure nevertheless remained relatively unchanged. In 1459, in imitation of Varro, who had divided his *Antiquitates* into religious and temporal antiquities, Flavius Blondus developed the modern model, by breaking up his *Roma triumphans* (in: [10]) into *antiquitates publicae, privatae, sacrae* and *militares*. In 1583, Johannes Rosinus adopted a sharper differentiation in his *Romanarum Antiquitatum libri X* [67], which, in its revision by the Scottish Etruscologist Thomas Dempster (Utrecht, 1710) remained a standard work until well into the 19th cent.: the books covered Rome's topography and populations (I), the sacred items of Antiquity (II–IV), customs, games and festivals (V), *comitia* assemblies and magistrates (VI–VII), the legal (IX) and martial items of Antiquity (X). Items of Antiquity were always classified according to subject matter. In the middle of the 18th cent. categorisation changed to using periods and phases of artistic development. That heralded the end of traditional antiquarianism and its merging with history into modern *Altertumswissenschaft* (study of Antiquity).

B. History and genres
1. ROME AS THE CENTRE OF HUMANISTIC ANTIQUARIANISM   2. ANTIQUARIANISM AND ARISTOCRATIC REPRESENTATION   3. FORMS OF ANTIQUITATES PUBLICAE   4. GREEK AND BIBLICAL ANTIQUARIANISM   5. NATIONAL ANTIQUARIANISM   6. CRISIS AND TRIUMPH OF ANTIQUARIANISM AFTER 1700

1. ROME AS THE CENTRE OF HUMANISTIC ANTIQUARIANISM
Interest in material remains from Antiquity never faded during the Middle Ages [109, ch. 1; 124, ch. 1]. Ancient buildings were incorporated into churches, residential or defensive complexes, while inscriptions, sculptures und fragments were used as booty, and jewels and coins were fashioned into decorative items and cult objects. Saintly cults and local legends developed out of grave finds. Ancient monuments were used as evidence of the longevity of one's own city, family or period of rule – signifying a valuable political legitimisation in an era when legal and property claims and pretensions to power had to have a basis in tradition. This pragmatic, direct relationship with Antiquity was to change fundamentally at the beginning of the Renaissance. It gave way to the consciousness of a deep historical gap, separating the (depressed) present from (the brilliance of) Antiquity [105]. That is why Humanists no longer looked at ancient remains with a naive pleasure in the old and unusual, but with admiration and a spirit of enquiry. The beauty and artistic perfection of ancient objects confirmed for them that Antiquity had been an exemplary era in every respect, and they served as exemplars for the humanistic project of systematically orienting all fields of existence towards ancient models. Thus, scholars began to explore all these things specifically to gain from them a vivid, historical impression of the politico-cultural reality of life for people in Antiquity [129].

Like → HUMANISM in general, antiquarianism also came to life in Italy. The city of Rome remained its centre until the 18th cent. [99; 100; 111]. In the service of the Popes, who deliberately linked with Rome's im-

perial tradition on their return from Avignon (1377), distinguished Humanists like Poggio Bracciolini propagated a *renovatio* of Augustan Rome under curial direction (J. Hankins in: [99. 47–85]). Families who supplied cardinals, like the Orsini, Colonna or Barberini, on the other hand, promoted instead study that recalled the republican-senatorial tradition of ancient Rome. This political-ideological antagonism also dominated the relationship between Rome's antiquarian attitudes and those of other Italian states (e.g. Venice or Florence) and, from the time of the Reformation, between Catholic and Protestant antiquarianism. The fascination for antiquarianism in early modern Europe is to be explained not least by its importance as a cultural medium for political power struggles [127].

Roman antiquarianism began as a search for the topography of ancient Rome. In 1429, in *De varietate fortunae urbis Romae et de ruina eiusdem*, Poggio Bracciolini wistfully described the Roman ruins that he – following Petrarch's advice to read the classicists on ancient ruins – attempted to identify from literary sources (in: [63]). In 1432/34, for his treatise *De re aedificatoria* (1452, printed 1485), the architect Leon Battista Alberti measured and sketched several Roman buildings [1]. The first topographic manual of ancient Rome, however, was produced by Papal secretary Flavius Blondus in his *Roma instaurata* (1444–47, printed 1471), the sequel to which, *Roma triumphans* (1457–59, printed 1472), also encompassed Christian antiquities (in: [10]). In 1462 Pope Pius II (Enea Silvio Piccolomini) renewed an edict issued in 1363 for the protections of Roman antiquities. In 1515 Julius II appointed the painter Raffael Santi inspector of Roman monuments and antiquities and commissioned him to see to their systematic documentation. The results – the *Antiquitates urbis* of Andrea Fulvio and a map of ancient Rome by Fabio Calvo – appeared in 1527, shortly before the destruction of many ancient monuments in the 'Sacco di Roma' (Sack of Rome). In 1553, Calvo's map was superseded by the one that Pirro Ligorio drew in his *Libro delle antichità di Roma* [46] and then surpassed in 1561 with his monumental woodcut-depiction of a bird's-eye view of ancient Rome (*Antiquae urbis imago accuratissime ex vetustis monumentis formata*) [97]. Similar attempts were made by Leonardo Bufalini (1551), Antonio Tempesta (1593) and many others after them (Grafton in: [99. 87–123]).

Rome's importance as a travel destination for pilgrims, members of the nobility and artists ensured that such maps and pictures of ancient buildings, statues and works of art quickly spread throughout the whole of Europe and shaped the contemporary image of Antiquity with local colouring [103]. Especially influential were the *compendia* of Ulisse Aldrovandi [2; 3] of Bologna, the *Vestigi delle Antichità di Roma* of the copperplate engraver of the Prague court, Aegidius Sadeler [68], the plates depicting Roman statues and bas-reliefs by François Perrier [57–58], and in the 18th cent. the *vedute* of the Venetian Giovanni Battista Piranesi [61].

Until 1657 the Roman antiquarian Cassiano dal Pozzo had distinguished artists like Nicolas Poussin encyclopaedically document all extant monuments of Antiquity and the Early Middle Ages in an enormous archive of illustrations. By the time of his death there were some 7000 drawings and etchings in 23 folio volumes (Museo Cartaceo) [17].

2. ANTIQUARIANISM AND ARISTOCRATIC REPRESENTATION

Until the discovery of → POMPEII, Rome remained the central stage for significant finds of classical works of art (→ LAOCOON GROUP in 1506, the Farnese bull in 1545, the Farnese Hercules in 1546, Ara pacis in 1568, the Aldobrandi wedding in 1582, Niobe in 1583) [102]. In 1471 Pope Sixtus IV opened the first Antiquity museum in the Conservatory palace. From 1503, Julius II created at Belvedere the Antiquity gallery that became a model throughout the world. Soon, not only Roman cardinals (Borghese, Farnese, Ludovisi, Barberini, Colonna, Chigi), but prestige-minded cities and princes in Europe began collecting works of art or at least establishing for themselves a *studiolo*, a study fashioned in antique style. Famous Italian collections were those of the Gonzaga in Mantua and the Este in Ferrara. In just Venice alone in the 17th cent. there were about 70 fairly small exhibition rooms of antiquities. Among the French aristocracy, antiquities-collecting was popular under Francois I (1515–1547) [102. 1–6]. Emperors in the Holy Roman Empire from Maximilian I (1493–1519) onward maintained antiquarian collections at their courts in Vienna, Innsbruck and Prague. As early as 1570 the dukes of Bavaria established in their residence at Munich the *Antiquarium*, the only Antiquity museum outside Italy [92. 133–192], in competition with the collection of the Palatine Electors in Heidelberg [7], while the courts of Saxony and Brandenburg did not develop their significant → ANTIQUITIES COLLECTIONS until the 17th cent. [8. 103]. In England, in addition to the collection of King Charles I (1625–1649), that of the diplomat Thomas Howard, 2nd Earl of Arundel, was world-famous [104]. Its catalogue, completed by John Selden in 1629 [71], set new scholarly standards.

Supervised by reputable antiquarians, such collections and (private) museums reflected the status, wealth, good taste, education and extensive contacts of their owners. They thus served scholarly and social purposes at the same time. As attractions for distinguished travellers, they became a meeting-place for nobles, artists, scholars and other members of the new upper class that often transcended social levels [127]. Under the influence of antiquarianism, aristocratic-elite circles, which constituted a Europe-wide network of communications and correspondence, formed themselves into → ACADEMIES. One of the earliest and most influential was the Roman one of Pomponius Laetus (1428–1497), who held lectures on old chronology, linguistic and legal items of Antiquity and together with his pupils collected inscriptions [99]. In the 16th cent. all larger Italian cities

had similar academies, which pursued, proposed and financed antiquarian research. In → NAPLES, they united in 1738 to form the *Accademia degli Ercolanesi*, which had been recording the finds from → HERCULANEUM, and those from Pompeii after 1760. In Augsburg, Laetus' pupil Conrad Peutinger established around 1495 the first German collection of antiquities (which contained *inter alia* the *Tabula Peutingeriana*) and an academy that had links with the humanist sodalities promoted by Emperor Maximilian I [92]. In England 1572 a *Society of Antiquaries* was formed in 1572 but was banned by King James I in 1604 as a bastion of political resistance. In 1732 wealthy private individuals established the → SOCIETY OF DILETTANTI, which financed several antiquarian research expeditions in the eastern Mediterranean. The most important French academy for antiquarian studies was the royal *Académie des Inscriptions et belles-lettres* (founded 1663), which after its re-establishment in 1716/17 published *Mémoires* annually. A *Collegium Antiquarium* was established in Uppsala in 1666 [122; 126. 47–49].

3. FORMS OF ANTIQUITATES PUBLICAE

The most widespread form of reputable antiquarianism was work with gems and coins. These fascinated contemporaries as symbols of princely power, as a starting-point for politico-moralistic reflection and for the attempts, characteristic of the period, to produce genealogical lines of descent from the Caesars to the collection's owner. For that reason, ancient numismatics flourished above all at the imperial court. Here, the court historiographer Wolfgang Lazius dreamed as early as 1558 of a complete corpus of all ancient coins [45], before Adolf III Occo outlined in 1579 a method for their chronological recording [52] – two goals that were, however, not reached until Joseph Hilarius Eckhel as Director of the Vienna Court Coin Cabinet, completed its massive catalogue in 1779 and in 1792 founded modern → NUMISMATICS with his *Doctrina nummorum veterum* [26–27]. In the 17th cent., the leading numismatists were working in France, where, in 1514, using antiquarian techniques, Guillaume Budaeus had developed a comparative metrology and monetary theory [16]: Jean Foy Vaillant (1632–1706), who in the course of his adventurous life wrote a great number of treatises, particularly on Roman provincial and Hellenistic coins, and was the first to concentrate consistently on original items can be mentioned, but also Charles Patin [56] and the Palatine-Brandenburg diplomat Ezechiel Spanheim [75].

The first comprehensive compendia of gem and coin portraits were created by the Spanish court painter Hubert Goltzius [33] and distinguished collectors like Fulvius Ursinus [83–84] and Abraham Gorlaeus, a resident of Antwerp ([36; 37] cf. Zazoff in: [90. 363–378]). The spectacular plan for a publication on all ancient jewels, however, on which Peter Paul Rubens and Nicolas Fabri de Peiresc, the most famous antiquarian of his time, had been working between 1621 and 1637, did not come to fruition, because of the latter's death [117.

21]. The pioneering work of modern glyptography was created in 1724 by Philipp von Stosch [79], whose much admired collection was catalogued by Johann Joachim Winckelmann in 1760 [88. 130].

Aesthetic-moralistic and political interests interfered not only in the debate over coins but also in consideration of the classical forms of *antiquitates publicae* and of inscriptions and legal antiquities. In both cases, contemporaries admired not least the art of pithy, well-constructed mottoes. Most of all, though, they hoped to obtain information on the organisation and leadership structure of a model polity. Poggio published the first Roman inscriptions in 1429 in *De varietate fortunae* ([in: 63]). The first German collection was produced in 1505 by Conrad Peutinger 1505 in his *Romanae vetustatis fragmenta in Augusta Vindelicorum* [60]. Some 30 years later, his fellow citizen, the banker Raymund Fugger financed an edition [4] that remained the leading work on Roman provincial inscriptions until Janus Gruter, librarian of the Heidelberg Palatine Inscriptions, together with Joseph Justus Scaliger, published in 1602/03 the *Inscriptiones antiquae totius orbis Romani*, the authoritative edition until Mommsen [43].

In 1550 the Augustinian monk Onuphrius Panvinius [54] from Verona and Carolus Sigonius from Modena [74] undertook the first attempts to reconstruct the ruins of the Roman *fasti*, discovered a little earlier on the forum. From such beginnings there developed, on the one hand, chronological antiquarianism, which culminated in Joseph Justus Scaliger's efforts in 1583 und 1606, using antiquarian, philological and mathematical methods, to combine Biblical and ancient time-systems into one objective world chronology [69; 70; 98]. On the other hand, Panvinius [55] und Sigonius [72] became the founders of antiquarian legal history, which was later developed in particular by Protestant scholars. Thus, Franciscus Balduinus [6] in 1550 and Jacobus Gothofredus [38] of Geneva in 1616 completed pioneering reconstructions of the Law of the Twelve Tables. Via Holland, this branch of antiquarianism reached Germany in the 17th cent., where, in 1719, Johann Gottlieb Heineccius compiled the collection of Roman legal antiquities that was be canonical for the whole of Europe for many decades [44].

4. GREEK AND BIBLICAL ANTIQUARIANISM

The first steps in non-Roman, especially Greek antiquarianism [94; 106. 16–24] were taken in Italy as well. At the beginning of the 15th cent., the Florentine priest Cristoforo de' Buondelmonti, financed by Cardinal Girolamo Orsini, researched both Christian churches and ancient temples in the Aegean. Between 1423 and 1455 the long-distance trader Cyriacus of Ancona conducted even more intensive investigations into the ancient sites of this region. Of his *Antiquarum rerum commentaria*, however, there remain only copies of individual pages. After the fall of Constantinople in 1453, such journeys became rarer – that of the French doctor Petrus Belonius [9] being an exception to the rule. The most important pioneers of Greek antiquarianism –

Johannes Meursius [48], Ubbo Emmius [29], Samuel Petitus [59], Jacob Gronovius [42], Lambert Bos [12] and Johann Albert Fabricius [30] – never saw Greece. A new chapter of Greek travel began only in 1675/76 with Jacob Spon, a physician from Lyons, [78; 95]. From 1751 the → SOCIETY OF DILETTANTI financed several English research expeditions to → GREECE and Asia Minor: these included those of the architects James Stuart and Nicholas Revett, who for several years systematically recorded the *Antiquities of Athens* [80], and of Richard Chandler, who had catalogued the *Marmora Oxoniensia* [20], before he researched the *Ionian Antiquities* in Asia Minor [19]. In 1799, Thomas Bruce, 7th Earl of Elgin, began his efforts, successful in 1804, to transport the Parthenon friezes (the so-called Elgin Marbles) to London.

Biblical antiquarianism, i.e. for the most part Hebrew-Ancient Near Eastern, was at least as intensively pursued as classical antiquarianism throughout the whole period under discussion. In 1583 Sigonius wrote, in turn, the first authoritative study [73]. In 1593 there followed Jewish-Rabbinical antiquities of the Spanish publisher of the polyglot Bible, Benito Arias Montanus [5]. The Utrecht orientalist, Hadrian Reeland [64–65], produced a collection of sacred Hebrew antiquities (1708) and a pioneering antiquarian topography of Palestine (which he had never seen). From 1744 the Venetian Blasius Ugolinus combined these and many other works on Hebrew antiquities into one thesaurus of 34 folio volumes [82]. Some 100 years earlier, Antonio Bosio had produced the foundational work of Christian antiquarianism with his topography of Roman catacombs [13].

A pre-Champollion Egyptian antiquarianism was inspired by the re-erection of Roman obelisks under Sixtus V (1585–1590). Imbued by the desire to portray the Egyptians to his contemporaries as a model people whose political and private lives moved in perfect, contented harmony with the precepts of almighty priest-kings, the polyglot Jesuit Athanasius Kircher studied their sacred antiquities and the meaning of the hieroglyphs (Grafton in: [99. 87–123]). Nicolas Fabri de Peiresc in Aix-en-Provence was especially interested in Egyptian antiquarianism. A universal scholar, he published nothing, but was, on the basis of his letters alone, regarded as the most significant antiquarian of his time [121].

5. NATIONAL ANTIQUARIANISM

Parallel with the intensive study of Classical antiquarianism, research into individual national antiquities began in all European countries. Princes and authorities promoted efforts, intensified by the growing spirit of nationalism, to (re-)construct with critical methods as glorious an early history as possible from the monuments, ruins and finds in one's own country. In competition with the Papal-imperial *renovatio* of Rome, Italian cities started to discover their pre-Roman and – in Sicily and southern Italy – Greek origins [112. 104–106; 113]. → ETRUSCOLOGY flourished in Tuscany ([23; 34; 35; 36] cf. [112. 91–92]). Following Blondus' example, authorities such as Scipione Maffei [47] or Lodovico Antonio Muratori [50–51] established, as late as the 18th cent., impressive collections of urban and regional antiquities.

Even in France, where Joachim du Bellay's sonnet cycle *Les Antiquitéz de Rome* (1558) co-founded national literature, cities like Nîmes (1559), Bordeaux (1565), Paris (1576), Arles (1625), Vienne (1658) and Lyons (1678) undertook research into their monuments and antiquities ([77. 85–86]; further evidence in: [119; 95]). It was no accident but an indication of a political alliance that André Duchesne followed up his *Antiquités et Recherches de la grandeur et majesté des Rois de France* with a collection in 1610 of antiquities of French cities and fortresses [24–25]. In 1643, in his *Ulysse françois*, Louis Coulon wrote a guidebook to Gallo-Roman antiquities. Finds like those of the 'Venus of Arles' (1651), the 'Childeric grave' in Tournai (1653) and the Gallic 'grave of Cocherel' (1685) inspired the search for the Gallic past that in the 18th cent. was conducted on an academic basis and produced a great number of works on regional antiquarianism [119. 31–57].

In the Holy Roman Empire as well, urban scholars in particular (especially in Alsace, Franconia and Swabia) were engaged in demonstrating the greatness of the Germanic past through their antiquarian research and thus providing a historical-ideological accompaniment to the Emperors' efforts of political unification. Even before Beatus Rhenanus of Schlettstadt in his *Rerum Germanicarum libri III* (1531) put antiquities on an equal footing with textual sources [66], Sigismund Meisterlin had accorded them a great deal of attention in his *Augsburger Chronik* (Augsburg Chronicle) (1485/88). But even a royal historian of the court like Johann Turmair, also known as Aventin, thoroughly investigated his lord's property around 1520 in systematic search for Roman and pre-Roman remains [81]. Even before the Catholic project of *Germania Sacra* was translated into reality, the Jesuit Christoph Brouwer produced a model piece of modern religious-monastic antiquarianism with his antiquarian works on the history of the Fulda and Trier bishoprics [14–15].

After the Reformation, the attention given to national antiquities was strengthened by the anxiety that learned scholars felt at seeing the destruction of age-old monasteries, churches and monuments. In England, John Leland, who had been King's Antiquary since 1533, undertook extensive journeys following the closure of monasteries to save MSS, record place names and study local antiquities such Hadrian's Wall [109]. His jottings remained unpublished – like John Aubrey's notes on the *Monumenta Britannica* from the 1660s. William Camden, however, used them in 1586 for his influential *Britannia*, a collection, using Blondus as a model, of name-studies, urban histories, coins and inscriptions [118. 33–53]. *The Roman Antiquities*, in which Thomas Godwin drew parallels in 1614 between Roman and English institutions [31] were an antiquar-

ian expression of such inspiration of national feeling [96]. There was now a universal effort to use excavations to enlarge antiquities [118]. In Sweden, Johan Bure (1568–1652) and Olof Rudbeck (1630–1702) were commissioned by the king to research rune stones and grave-mounds. In Denmark, Ole Worm (1588–1654) displayed his finds in his much-visited 'room of wonders'. In Hamburg, Andreas Albert Rhode's *Cimbrisch-Hollsteinische Antiquitaeten-Remarques* appeared in 1719/20 as the first antiquarian publication [124]. In Holland, Ubbo Emmius researched the antiquities of his native Frisia [28]. In Russia, where the Scythians had been discovered as national ancestors, the Czars, starting with Peter the Great, promoted research into Scythian graves and antiquities [123]. The combination of antiquarianism, topography and ethnography ensured that national antiquarianism – even more than the rather literature-fixated classical antiquarianism – became a laboratory for modern archaeological methods.

6. Crisis and Triumph of Antiquarianism after 1700

In the 17th cent. the universities in the Netherlands became centres of antiquarianism and places of refuge for leading antiquarians from all over Europe. Here, at the cutting-edge of advanced philology, mathematical inspiration and modern science, worked Philipp Cluverius of Danzig, who updated the topography not just of Germany but also of Old Italy [21–22], Johann Georg Graevius [39–41] of Naumburg and Jacob Gronovius [42] of Hamburg. Their life's work consisted of massive collections of texts, in which they brought together the work of earlier antiquarians, often with modern commentary, into mighty storehouses of knowledge and thus provided representative overviews of the status of individual branches of antiquarianism. The articles in the *Lexicon antiquitatum Romanarum* of Samuel Pitiscus [62] summarized the more extensive information contained in those publications. Such large-scale projects were also a reaction to a growing crisis in the meaning of antiquarianism, i.e. to the fact that consensus as to what 'Antiquity' was and should be, was clearly disappearing in the flood of finds and publications. In the process, the pedagogical-moral aim of antiquarianism moved so far away from its focus that it could appear as a frivolous end unto itself. Moreover, intensive philolological-antiquarian research had exposed so many mistakes in transmission that sceptics (so-called Pyrrhonists) disputed that antiquarianism could yield any reliable knowledge of value [112]. Defenders of antiquarianism had therefore to first of all identify what was credible in the accumulated wisdom on Antiquity and what of that was worth knowing at all. In the process, however, antiquarianism acquired a revolutionary new significance. To be sure, Cyriacus of Ancona had already prized antiquities as *sigilla* of historical accuracy, as Patin had praised coins as 'les marques les plus assures' of history, and Spon monuments as better books, fashioned out of stone and metal. Now, however, the relationship between history and anti-quarianism was being completely reversed: whereas classical texts had previously accorded antiquities their status and authority, the latter had now become judges of textual credibility [120].

Antiquarianism's new claim, to be able to determine, better than history could, the substance and meaning of Antiquity was embodied in 1719 by *L'Antiquité expli-quée et représentée en figures* of the Benedictine Bernard de Montfaucon [49]. The work, composed in French (with Latin translations at the foot of each page) was the most lavish and most expensive that antiquarianism had produced up to that time. In some 40,000 copperplate illustrations it documented ancient remains – divided into sacred, private, martial and funerary items of Antiquity – from pictures of deities to everyday objects from the whole Mediterranean (non-Jewish) world. Montfaucon saw pictures not as illustrations of textual information but as its sensory essence. He therefore defined Antiquity as precisely that *qui peut tomber sous les yeux, et ce qui se peut représenter dans des images*: and he regarded *la belle antiquité* as having declined in the 3rd cent., with the Theodosius Column as its last monument. On the other hand, he only touched peripherally on state, legal and constitutional antiquities, hitherto the central concerns of antiquarianism, or on chronology and topography.

This tendency to explain Antiquity as a sensory-aesthetic phenomenon and antiquities as autonomous, aesthetic objects was given a boost in 1752 by the *Recueil d'antiquités egyptiennes, etrusques, grecques et romaines* of the French diplomat, Asia Minor traveller and patron of the arts Anne Claude Philippe de Thubires, Comte de Caylus [18]. He discussed only items from his own collection and insofar adopted a distinctly anti-academic approach, although he attached great importance to exactness in measurements and physical descriptions and although he preferred fragments to intact items, sherds to statues. He constantly searched for the specific way in which each people in each period created its works so as to determine artistic progress or variations (*ses progrès ou ses alterations*) from the differences. In 1761, well ahead of Winckelmann, Caylus described an evolution from Egypt through Etruria to Greece *ou le savoir joint la plus noble élégance*, so that art reached its highest 'perfection' here, and by comparison that of the Romans represented something of a decline.

This transition to a genetic structure of antiquarianism, driven by the aristocratic principle of inherent aesthetic intuition, was completed in 1764 by Johann Joachim Winckelmann's *Geschichte der Kunst des Alterthums* (*History of the Art of Antiquity*) [88]. Art was no longer divided according to objects or artists but into a theoretical-typological section, which described artistic development according to its character, and an evolutionary history, which studied the same process in connection with the external conditions of the period. In so doing, he stipulated a parallelism between aesthet-

ic and political development, taking art, in the emancipatory spirit of the Enlightenment, as the product and measure of political freedom [107; 108; 122]. That he, like Caylus, celebrated Greek culture as the apogee of Antiquity, and disparaged Roman culture, by contrast, as a phenomenon of decadence, shifted antiquarianism's traditionally most important field of study out of the limelight.

C. ANTIQUARIANISM AND MODERN ANCIENT STUDIES

Winckelmann thus gave antiquarianism its own immanent criteria – those of style and organic development – for independent classification of its material. This historizing completely freed antiquarianism from its bondage to ancient texts and did away with the old distinction between antiquarianism and history. At the beginning of the 19th cent. both disciplines – together with philology – merged into one new discipline: that of historically oriented 'Altertumswissenschaft' (ancient studies), which Christian Gottlob Heyne had been practicing since 1763 at the University of Göttingen,– with its powerful international reach – as the universal study of culture [93] and the programmatic representation of which was subsequently developed by his pupil Friedrich August Wolf in 1807 [89]. From being an aspect of aristocratic representative culture, an elitist hobby for wealthy collectors, or a demanding secondary activity for professors of poetry and jurisprudence, antiquarianism had become a professional academic subject. Without changing its name, it became the systematic discipline of archaeology, which in modern humanistic studies had the role of making material sources available. August Böckh's *Staatshaushaltung der Athener*, the first document of the new modern antiquarianism, appeared in 1817 in that context. [11]. Whoever then, by contrast, pursued antiquarianism in the old way, immediately ran the risk of acquiring the reputation of being an unsystematic, unhistorical eclectic, or even of being *merely* an antiquarian.

→ ARCHAEOLOGICAL METHODS AND THEORIES; → CHRISTIAN ARCHAEOLOGY; → CLASSICAL ARCHAEOLOGY; → HISTORIOGRAPHY; → PRINTS, BOOKS CONTAINING; → QUERELLE DES ANCIENS ET DES MODERNES; → ROMAN LAW

SOURCES: 1 L. B. ALBERTI, De re aedificatoria. L'architettura, G. ORLANDI, P. PORTOGHESI (eds.), 2 vols., 1966 2 U. ALDROVANDI, Antiquarum statuarum urbis Romae icones, Rome 1584 3 Id., Delle Statue Antiche, che per tutta Roma, in diversi luoghi, & case se veggono, in: L. MAURO, Le Antichità della Città di Roma, Venice 1558 4 P. APIAN, B. AMANTIUS, Inscriptiones sacrosanctae vetustatis non illae quidem Romanae, sed totius fere orbis summo studio maximis impensis terra marique conquisitae, Ingolstadt 1534 5 B. ARIAS MONTANUS, Antiquitatum Judaicum libri IX, Leiden 1593 6 F. BALDUINUS, Libri duo ad Leges Romuli Regis Romani Legum XII Tabularum, Leiden 1550 7 L. BEGER, Thesaurus ex Thesauro Palatino Selectus, sive gemmarum et Numismatum quae in Electorali Cimeliarchio continentur. Elegantiorum aere expressa, et convenienti commentario illustrata

Dispositio, Heidelberg 1685 8 Id., Thesaurus Brandenburgicus ..., 3 vols (with different titles), Neuköln 1696–1701 9 P. Belonius, Les Observations de plusieurs singularitéz & choses mémorables trouvées en Grèce, Asie, Iudée, Egypte, Arabie & autres pays estranges, Paris 1553 10 F. Blondus, Opera omnia, Basle 1559 11 A. Böckh, Die Staatshaushaltung der Athener, 2 vols, Berlin 1817 12 L. Bos, Descriptio Antiquitatum Graecarum praecipue Atticarum descriptio brevis, Franecker 1714 13 A. Bosio, Roma sotteranea, Rome 1632 14 Ch. Brouwer, Fuldensium Antiquitatum libri IV, Antwerp 1612 15 Id., Antiquitatum et annalium Trevirensium libri XXV, J. Masenius (ed.), 2 vols, Lüttich 1670 16 G. Budaeus, De asse, Paris 1514 17 C. dal Pozzo, The Paper Museum. A Catalogue Raisonnée, F. Haskell, J. Montagu (eds.), 1996ff. 18 A. C. Ph. de Thubires, Comte de Caylus, Recueil d'antiquités egyptiennes, etrusques, grecques et romaines, 7 vols (from vol. 3 on with addition 'et gaulois" in the title), Paris 1752–1767 19 R. Chandler, N. Revett, Ionian Antiquities. Ruins of Magnificent and Famous Buildings in Ionia, published at the expense of the Society of Dilettanti in 1769 20 R. Chandler, Marmora Oxoniensia, Oxford 1763 21 Ph. Cluverius, Germaniae antiquae Libri III. Adiectae sunt Videlicia et Noricum, Leiden 1616 22 Id., Italia antiqua, Leiden 1624 23 Th. Dempster, De Etruria regali libri VII, Th. Coke (ed.), 2 vols, Florence 1723 and 1726 24 A. Duchesne, Les Antiquités et Recherches de la grandeur et majesté des Rois de France, Paris 1609 25 Id., Les Antiquités et Recherches des Villes, châteaux et places remarquables de toute la France, suivant l'ordre des huit parlements, Paris 1610 26 J. H. Eckhel, Catalogus Musei Caesarei Vindobonensis numerorum veterum distributus in partes II ..., 2 vols., Vienna 1779 27 Id., Doctrina nummorum veterum, 8 vols, Vienna 1792–1798 28 U. Emmius, De origine atque antiquitate Frisiorum, Groningen 1603 29 Id., Vetus Graecia illustrata, 3 vols, Leiden 1626–1632 30 J. A. Fabricius, Bibliotheca Graeca, sive notitia scriptorum veterum Graecorum, quorumcumque monumenta integra aut fragmenta edita existant: tum plerorumque e Mss. ac deperditis, 14 vols, Hamburg 1705–1728 31 Th. Godwin, Romanae Historiae Anthologia. An English Exposition of the Roman Antiquities, wherein many Roman and English Offices are paralleled, and diverse obscure Phrases explained, Oxford 1614 32 H. Goltzius, Icones Imperatorum Romanorum e priscis numismatibus ad vivum delineatae, Bruges 1558 33 Id., Romanae et Graecae antiquitatis monumenta e priscis numismatibus eruta, Antwerp 1645 34 A. F. Gori, Mus. Florentinum, 6 vols, Florence 1731–1743 35 Id., Mus. Etruscum, 3 vols, Florence 1737–1743 36 A. Gorlaeus, Dactyliotheca, seu annulorum sigillorumque promptuarium, Nuremberg 1601 37 Id., Thesaurus Numismatum familiarum Romanarum, Leiden 1608 38 J. Gothofredus, Fragmenta Duodecim Tabularum, suis nunc primum tabulis restituta, probationibus, notis et indice munita, Heidelberg 1616 39 J. G. Graevius, Thesaurus Antiquitatum et Historiarum Italiae, 27 vols, Leiden 1704–1723 40 Id., Thesaurus Antiquitatum et Historiarum Siciliae, 5 vols, Leiden 1723 41 Id., Thesaurus Antiquitatum Romanorum, 12 vols, Utrecht 1694–99 42 J. Gronovius, Thesaurus Graecarum Antiquitatum, 13 vols, Leiden, 1694–1703 43 J. Gruter, Inscriptiones antiquae totius orbis Romani in corpus absolutissimum redactae ingenio ac cura Jani Gruteri: auspiciis Josephi Scaligeri ac Marci Velseri, 2 vols, n.p. 1602 and 1603 44 J. G. Heineccius, Antiquitatum

Romanarum Jurisprudentiam illustrantium Syntagma secundum ordinem institutionum Iustiniani digestum, in quo multa iuris Romani atque auctorum veterum loca explicantur atque illustrantur, Halle 1719 45 W. Lazius, Specimen Commentarii veterum numismatum maximi scilicet operis et quattuor sectionibus multarum rerum publicarum historiam etc. comprehendentis, Vienna 1558 46 P. Ligorio, Delle antichitá di Roma, (ed.) D. Negri, 1989 47 S. Maffei, Verona Illustrata, Verona 1731 and 1732 48 J. Meursius, Opera omnia, J. Lamius (ed.), 12 vols, Florence 1741–1763 49 B. de Montfaucon, L'Antiquité expliquée et représentée en figures, 15 vols, Paris 1719–1724 50 L. A. Muratori, Antiquitates Italicae medii aevi, sive dissertationes de moribus italici populi, ab inclinatione Romani imperii usque ad annum 1500, 6 vols, Milan 1738–1742 51 Id., Novus Thesaurus veterum Inscriptionum, in praecipuis earundem collectionibus hactenus praetermissarum, 6 vols, Milan 1739–1742 52 Adolf III. Occo, Imperatorum Romanorum numismata a Pompeio Magno ad Heraclium, Antwerp 1579 53 O. Panvinius, Fasti et triumphi Romani, Venice 1557 54 Id., Fastorum libri V, eiusdem in Fastorum libros commentarii, Venice 1558 55 Id., Reipublicae Romanae commentatorium libri III, Venice 1558 56 Ch. Patin, Introduction à l'histoire par la connaissance des Médailles, Paris 1665 57 F. Perrier, Icones et segmenta illustrium e marmore tabularumque Romae quaedhuc exstant, Rome and Paris 1645 58 Id., Segmenta nobilium signorum et statuarum quae temporis dentem invidiamque evaserunt, Rome and Paris 1638 59 S. Petitus, Leges Atticae, Paris 1635 60 C. Peutinger, Romanae vetustatis fragmenta in Augusta Vindelicorum, Augsburg 1505 61 G. B. Piranesi, Antichitá Romane, Roma 1756 62 S. Pitiscus, Lexicon antiquitatum Romanarum in quo ritus et antiquitates cum Graecis ac Romanis communes, tum Romanis peculares, sacrae et profanae, publicae et privatae, civiles et militares exponuntur, 2 vols, Leeuwarden 1713 63 G. F. Poggio Bracciolini, Opera omnia, Basle 1538 64 H. Reeland, Antiquitates sacrae veterum Hebraeorum, Utrecht 1708 65 Id., Palestina ex monumentis veteribus illustrata, Utrecht 1714 66 B. Rhenanus, Rerum Germanicarum libri III, Basle 1531 67 J. Rosinus, Romanarum antiquitatum libri X, ex variis scriptoribus summa fide singularique diligentia collecti, Basle 1583 68 A. Sadeler, Vestigi delle antichitá di Roma, Tivoli, Pozzuoli et altre luochi, Prague 1606 69 J. J. Scaliger, Opus novum de emendatione temporum, Paris 1583 70 Id., Thesaurus temporum, Leiden 1606 71 J. Selden, Marmora Arundelliana, n.p. 1629 72 C. Sigonius, De antiquo iure civium Romanorum libri II; De antiquo iure Italiae libri III, Venice 1560 73 Id., De republica Hebraeorum libri VII, Bologna 1582 74 Id., Regum, consulum, dictatorum ac censorum Romanorum Fasti, Modena 1550 75 E. Spanheim, Dissertationes de usu et praestantia numismatum antiquorum, Rome 1664 76 J. Spon, Miscellanea eruditae antiquitatis, in quibus marmora, statuae, musiva, toreumata, gemmae, numismata, Grutero, Ursino, Boissardo, Reinesio, aliisque antiquorum monumentorum collectoribus ignota, et hucusque inedita referuntur ac illustrantur, Lyons 1685 77 Id., Recherche des antiquités et curiositás de la ville de Lyon, Ancienne Colonie des Romains et Capitale de la Gaule Celtique. Avec un Mémoire des Principaux Antiquaires et Curieux de l'Europe, Lyons 1673 78 Id., Voyage d'Italie, de Dalmatie, de Grece, et du Levant, fait aux années 1675 et 1676 par Iacob Spon, Docteur Medecin Aggregée à Lyon, et George

Wheler, Gentilhomme Anglois, 3 vols, Lyons 1678
79 PH. BARON von Stosch, Gemmae Antiquae Caelatae,
Sculptorum Nominibus insignatae, Amsterdam 1724
80 J. STUART, N. REVETT, The Antiquities of Athens, 4
vols, London 1762–1816   81 J. TURMAIR named Aventinus, Baierische Chronik (ed. M. LEXER), in: Id., Sämmtliche Werke, vols 4–5, 1881–1908   82 B. UGOLINUS, Thesaurus antiquitatum sacrarum complectens selectissima
clarissimorum virorum opuscula, in quibus veterum
Hebraeorum mores, leges, instituta, ritus sacri et civiles
illustrantur, 34 vols, Venice 1744–1769   83 F. URSINUS,
Familiae Romanae in antiquis numismatibus ab urbe condita ad tempora Divi Augusti ex bibliotheca Fulvii Ursini,
Rome 1577   84 Id., Imagines et elogia virorum illustrium
et eruditorum ex antiquis lapidibus et numismatibus
expressae cum annotationibus bibliotheca, Rome 1570
85 E. VINET, L'Antiquité de Bordeaux, de Bourg sur mer,
d'Angoulème et autres lieux, Bordeaux 1565   86 Id.,
L'Antiquité de Saintes et de Barbezieux, Bordeaux 1571
87 J. J. WINCKELMANN, Description des Pierres gravés du
feu Baron de Stosch, Florence 1760   88 Id., Gesch. der
Kunst des Alt., Dresden 1764 with Ann. 1767 (ed. L.
GOLDSCHEIDER, 1934, repr.1982)   89 F. A. WOLF, Darstellung der Alterthums-Wissenschaft, in: Mus. der Alterthums-Wissenschaft, vol. 1, Berlin 1807, 1–145
(repr.1986)

LITERATURE: 90 H. BECK, P. C. BOL, W. PRINZ, H.V.
STEUBEN (eds.), Antikensammlungen im 18. Jahrhundert,
1981 91 P. BERGHAUS (ed.), Der Archäologe. Graphische
Bildnisse aus dem Porträtarchiv Diepenbroick. Herausgegeben in Verbindung mit K. KNECKTYS, A. SCHOLL-
MEIER (Katalog Westfälisches Landesmuseum für Kunst
und Kulturgeschichte), 1983   92 R. VON BUSCH, Studien
zu deutschen Antikensammlungen des 16. Jahrhunderts,
(Diss. Tübingen) 1973   93 Der Vormann der Georgia Augusta. Christian Gottlob Heyne zum 250. Geburtstag.
Sechs akademische Reden, 1980   94 R. AND F. ÉTIENNE,
Le Grèce antique. Archéologie d'une découverte, 1990
95 R. ÉTIENNE, J.-C. MOSSIÈRE (eds.), Jacob Spon, 1993
96 A. B. FERGUSON, Utter Antiquity. Perceptions of Prehistory in Renaissance England, 1993   97 R. GASTON
(ed.), Pirro Ligorio, Artist and Antiquarian, 1988
98 A. T. GRAFTON, Joseph Scaliger, 2 vols., 1983/92
99 Id. (ed.), Rome Reborn. The Vatican Library and Renaissance Culture, 1993   100 H. GÜNTHER, Die Renaissance der Antike, 1997   101 F. HASKELL, Die Geschichte
und ihre Bilder. Die Kunst und die Deutung der Vergangenheit, 1995   102 Id., N. PENNY, Taste and the Antique.
The Lure of Classical Sculpture 1500–1900, ⁴1994
103 G. HERES, Archäologie im 17. Jahrhundert, in: M.
KUNZE (ed.), Archäologie zur Zeit Winckelmanns. Eine
Aufsatzsammlung, 1975, 9–39   104 D. HOWARTH, Lord
Arundel and his Circle, 1985   105 P. JOACHIMSEN,
Geschichtsauffassung und Geschichtschreibung in
Deutschland unter dem Einfluß des Humanismus, 1910
(repr. 1968)   106 W. JUDEICH, Topographie von Athen,
1931 107 C. JUSTI, Winckelmann und seine Zeitgenos-
sen, 1943   108 M. KÄFER, Winckelmanns Hermeneutische Prinzipien, 1986 109 J. M. LEVINE, Humanism and
History, 1987 110 W. MCCUAIG, Carlo Sigonio, 1989
111 C. MOATTI, A la recherche de la Rome antique, 1989
112 MOMIGLIANO, 1955, 67–106 113 Id., 1984, 115–132
114 Id., 1984, 133–153 115 Id., The Rise of Antiquarian
Research, in: Id., The Classical Foundations of Modern
Historiography, 1990, 54–79   116 S. PIGGOTT, Ancient

Britons and the Antiquarian Imagination, 1989   117 Id.,
Antiquity Depicted. Aspects of Archeological Illustration,
1978 118 Id., Ruins in a Landscape. Essays in Antiquarianism, 1976   119 P. PINON, La Gaule retrouvée, ²1997
120 M. RASKOLNIKOFF, Histoire romaine et critique historique dans l'Europe des lumières, 1992 121 A. REINBOLD
(ed.), Peiresc ou la passion de connaître. Colloque de
Carpentras, novembre 1987, 1990   122 W. SCHIERING,
Zur Geschichte der Archäologie, in: U. HAUSMANN (ed.),
Allgemeine Grundlagen der Archäologie, 1969, 11–161
123 V. SCHILTZ, Histoire de Kourganes. La redécouverte
de l'or des Scythes, 1991 124 A. SCHNAPP, La Conquête
du passé. Aux origins de l'archéologie, 1993 (engl. 1996)
125 J. B. TRAPP, Virgil and the Monuments, in: Id., Essays
on the Renaissance and the Classical Tradition, 1990 (VI)
126 B. G. TRIGGER, A History of Archaeological Thought,
1988. 127 G. WALTHER, Adel und Antike. Zur politischen
Bedeutung gelehrter Kultur für die Führungselite der
frühen Neuzeit, in: HZ 266, 1998, 359–385 128 M. WEG-
NER, Altertumskunde, 1951 129 R. WEISS, The Renaissance. Discovery of Classical Antiquity, 1969
130 ZAZOFF, GuG

ADDITIONAL BIBLIOGRAPHY: M. DALY DAVIS,
Archäologie der Antike, in: exhibition catalogue of the
Herzog August Bibliothek, vol. 71, 1994; S. FORERO-
MENDOZA, Le temps des ruines. L'éveil de la conscience
historique à la renaissance, 2002; PH. JACKS, The Antiquarian and the Myth of Antiquity. The Origins of Rome
in Renaissance Thought, 1993; P. N. MILLER, Peiresc's
Europe. Learning and Virtue in the Seventeenth Century,
1995; G. PARRY, The Trophies of Time. English Antiquar-
ianism of the Seventeenth Century, 1995; TH. WEISS (ed.),
Von der Schönheit weißen Marmors. Zum 200. Todestag
Bartolomeo Cavaceppis, in: Wissenschaftliche Bestands-
kataloge der Kulturstiftung Dessau-Wörlitz, vol. 2), 1999;
M. WINNER, B. ANDREAE & C. PIERANGELI (eds.), Il Cortile delle Statue. Der Statuenhof des Belvedere im Vatikan.
Akten des internationalen Kongresses zu Ehren von
Richard Krautheimer, Rom, 21–23 October 1992, 1998.

GERRIT WALTHER

Antiqui et moderni see→ QUERELLE DES ANCIENS ET
DES MODERNES

Antiquities, Collections of
A. INTRODUCTION   B. PERIODS IN THE HISTORY
OF COLLECTIONS   C. CATEGORIES OF
COLLECTIONS

A. INTRODUCTION
The history of collections was the object of intensive
investigation around 1900, in Germany above all by
Adolf Michaelis [1–3] and Christian Hülsen [4]. In
recent decades, it has once again, for various reasons,
come to occupy the center of interest. Cultural history
discovered collections and their classification systems
as sources for research on mentality. Great museums
occupied themselves increasingly with their own histories. Added to this was an increased attention to processes of reception. On the archaeological side, the new
interest for the context of finds led to the investigation
of the provenance of 'old finds'. It thus became possible

to trace the history of the Berlin (Praying boy) back through many collections to its discovery at Rhodes [5], or to clarify the provenance of the *Duncombe Discobolus* in a convincing way [6]. Because of these heterogeneous scientific interests and various methodological starting-points, the history of collections presents itself until today primarily as a mosaic of individual studies. Because of the one-sided state of research, the following presentation is largely limited to collections of sculptures.

B. PERIODS IN THE HISTORY OF COLLECTIONS
1. ANTIQUITY AND BYZANTIUM 2. THE MIDDLE AGES 3. THE RENAISSANCE UNTIL THE COUNCIL OF TRENT 4. THE BAROQUE 5. THE AGE OF ENLIGHTENMENT 6. FUTURE PROSPECTS

1. ANTIQUITY AND BYZANTIUM
Because of their religious and political significance, ancient statues were initially created only for exhibition in shrines and grave precincts, later on in public squares as well. Only when aesthetic appreciation asserted itself and consideration from art-historical viewpoints established itself did museum-style exhibitions become possible. Since Late Hellenistic theories of art attributed an exemplary role to works of the 5th and 4th cents. BC, the latter were particularly treasured and sought after by connoisseurs. Greek originals reached Rome in large numbers as spoils of war, and served as adornments of public buildings, but also of private villas and gardens [7; 8]. In addition, the development of the copyists' trade made older masterworks available for new exhibition contexts – at least in three-dimensional reproductions [9].

In Christian Late Antiquity a fundamental conflict was articulated, which was to remain decisive for the reception of statues down to modern times. To be sure, wealthy villas could still be fitted out with older statues, which often had to be repaired for their new exhibition. Here again, a primarily aesthetic appreciation of the sculptures came to the foreground [10]. On the other hand, the religious significance of the statues resulted in an aggressive rejection by the Christians, which often expressed itself in the destruction of ancient figures of the gods (for instance, the destruction of the cult-statue of Serapis in Alexandria [11]). Several collections of statues are attested at Byzantium [12–14; 15], of which that of Lausos is said to have contained some of the most famous Greek cult statues [16].

2. THE MIDDLE AGES
Owing to their interpretation as 'heathen' idols, ancient statues were also problematic in the Middle Ages [17; 18]. The smashing of 'idols' was even celebrated as a pious deed of saints. Showing the debris of ancient statues in public was considered proof of the victory of Christianity over the pagan deities [17; 45–47]. Occasionally, conflicts determined by content could be resolved through a Christian reinterpretation. Where no religious implications were perceived, particularly with

primarily decorative pieces, ancient sculptures could be reused in a variety of ways: urns as reliquaries or stoups [19]; sarcophagi for the burial of important personages, or even saints [20]; reliefs as decorations for façades or choir screens, etc.

Publicly shown collections of antiquities, which served as legitimation of power and demonstration of political success, are attested in many places. In Rome, publicly exhibited ancient statues (the Lateran she-wolf, the Capitoline group of fighting animals) marked the site of a massacre [21]. The figures displayed on the papal Lateran Palace testified to continuity since the time of the Roman emperors (equestrian statue of Constantine), and at the same time to the triumph of Christianity over the pagan divinities (colossal head of Sol) [17. 46; 22]. The sculptures brought to Aachen by Charlemagne underlined his claim to continue the Roman Empire in a new form [23; 24]. In Venice, the bronze horses and porphyry reliefs taken from Constantinople and exhibited in St. Mark's Square proclaimed the city's successes, although the contexts were soon forgotten [25; 26]. Many cities exhibited ancient inscriptions and figures as proof of their long and glorious history [25. 115–167]. The presentation of spolia in many churches was a visible expression of the overcoming and simultaneous monopolization of Antiquity [27; 28].

3. THE RENAISSANCE UNTIL THE COUNCIL OF TRENT
The intense concern of the → RENAISSANCE with the literature of Antiquity also led to a modified concept of the meaning of ancient sculptures. Artists and scholars made them the object of systematic study [29; 30], and not infrequently possessed antiquities themselves, as for example Lorenzo Ghiberti [31]. In addition to their traditional evaluation as historical and antiquarian testimonies (see above), the aesthetic appreciation of ancient works of art came more and more to the fore [32], as they became the unquestioned models for architects, painters and sculptors. Complete series of portraits, preferably of Roman emperors, became very popular: they could be regarded as parallels to historical texts, such as the Lives of the Caesars by Suetonius. Knowledge of ancient coins enabled a methodologically well-grounded procedure for the identification even of figures in the round [22. 48–50], which of course did not exclude continuing capricious identifications. Added to this was the effort to tie in preserved statues with literary accounts about famous monuments and artists.

In Rome, Venice, Florence and other cities of Northern Italy, cardinals and princes acquired their own collections of antiquities. In Rome in 1471, Pope Sixtus IV had some of the city's most famous antiquities (the she-wolf; the colossal head of the bronze statue of an emperor and its bronze hand; the Spinario; Camillus) transferred from the Lateran Palace to the Capitol [22]. Gradually, the Piazza del Campidoglio was adorned with sculptures alluding to Rome's historic grandeur [32; 33] (Fig. 1). Under Julius II (1503–1513) the Bel-

Fig. 1: Rome, Capitol Square with ancient statues. View from 1618, anonymous engraving

Fig. 2: Rome, collection of antiquities in the Casa Santacroce. Drawing by Marten van Heemskerck

Fig. 3: Rome, Courtyard of the Palazzo Valle-Capranica with antiques. Engraving by Hieronymus Cock

Fig. 4: Leiden, statue collection of the university. Drawing by Jacob van Werven, *c.* 1745

vedere Court at the Vatican received its decoration of statues, which, with the Apollo (→ BELVEDERE APOLLO), the Antinoos, the Belvedere Torso and the → LAOCOON GROUP, included some of the most valued and frequently-copied figures [2; 34].

Cardinals and noble families filled the gardens and courts of their palaces with fragments of statues, busts, and reliefs [30. 471–480; 35]; one of the first to do so may well have been the Cardinal Prospero Colonna (d. 1463) [35; 90]. Inventories give some idea of the numerous and often very extensive collections of antiquities in Rome, as do the sketchbooks of artists like Maerten van Heemskerck (Fig. 2), but also the description written in 1550 by Ulisse Aldroandi, entitled *Le statue di Roma*. Among the antiquities collections described were those of the Cardinals Andrea Della Valle (d. 1534) [35. 117ff.; 36], Paolo Emilio (d. 1537) as well as Federico (d. 1564) Cesi [4. 1–42; 36; 87–91] and Rodolfo da Carpi (d. 1564) [4. 43–84] and that of Stefano Del Bufalo [37]. Antiquities thus often remained incomplete and were frequently arranged according to decorative considerations, but also often according to theme or content [36]. A pioneering innovation for the exhibition of antiquities was illustrated by their integration within architecture, as it was undertaken around 1525 in the Palazzo Valle Capranica [4. VI.; 36] (Fig.3). Outside of Italy, King François I of France proceeded to set up his own collection of antiquities [38].

4. THE BAROQUE

The increasingly strict moral ideas of the Counter-Reformation brought about a drastic reduction of the

papal antiquities collections in Rome under Pius V (1566–1572) and Sixtus V (1585–1590), and even the hiding of the Belvedere Court antiquities in wooden crates [2. 42–48; 36. 114–115]. The same period, however, also witnessed the rapid expansion of the antiquities collections of Cardinal Alessandro Farnese (d. 1589) [39] and Ferdinando de Medici (d. 1609) [40]. Only slightly later followed the collections of Marchese Vincenzo Giustiniani [41; 42], of the Cardinals Scipio Borghese (d. 1633) [43] and Lodovico Ludovisi (d. 1632) [44–46] as well as that of Pope Urban VIII (1623–1644) in the Palazzo Barberini. All of them were integrated within magnificent palaces or villas.

The 17th cent. saw the rapid spread of antiquities collections north of the Alps as well, where they soon became an integral part of royal representations. For instance, antiquities collections were acquired by Albrecht V, Elector of Bavaria [47]; Charles I of England [48; 49], Christina of Sweden [50–52]; Louis XIV of France [53; 54] and Philip IV of Spain [55]. In France and England, powerful court figures were also active as collectors (for example, Richelieu [56], Mazarin [57; 58] (Fig. 4), J.-B. Colbert [59], N. Foucquet [60] in France; the Earl of Arundel [61], and the Duke of Bukkingham [62] in England). They were able to make use of diplomatic channels in Constantinople, Rome, and Venice to build up their antiquities collections rapidly and on a large scale. They also employed their own agents, who searched for statues in Greece and Asia Minor. In addition to Rome, Venice also played an important role in the procurement of ancient sculptures destined for Germany, England, and the Netherlands [63]. The representative function of sculptures then caused them to be almost completely restored. Here the gallery emerged as a new form of exhibition, enabling the presentation of a large number of sculptures in a unified manner. [64].

Also the Republic of Venice exhibited the sculptures bequeathed by Domenico and Giovanni Grimani publicly in a gallery (*statuario pubblico*) that was connected to the Biblioteca Marciana [65]. In the Netherlands, a number of antiquities collections of the haute bourgeoisie came into existence [66]; most of these, however, were short-lived. Despite the striking increase in antiquities collections, ancient statues once again became problematic for religious and political reasons (Reformation, Counter-reformation, Puritanism). In England this led, around the middle of the 17th cent., to the dissolution of all significant antiquities collections, and in France to the partial destruction of Mazarin's collection.

5. THE AGE OF ENLIGHTENMENT

The antiquities collections of the 18th cent. stood completely under the sign of the English 'milords' (milordi) [1; 67–69]. Whereas English collections of the 17th cent. had been connected with the royal courts, it was now the aristocrats, concerned to maintain their distance from the crown, who set up antiquities collections on their country estates. Their emergence usually followed a well-established course: in the context of their 'grand tour', the young Lords visited Rome, where alongside the famous galleries they were also shown the offerings of art dealers. English art agents in Rome (G. Hamilton, Th. Jenkins [70]) obtained ancient sculptures from excavations or from old Roman collections, had them restored, and organized their export. Numerous antiquities collections thus appeared in England in quick succession. English collectors were often in close contact with each other. Many were members of the → SOCIETY OF DILETTANTI, which also backed archaeological explorations in Greece and Asia Minor.

The picture at Rome itself changed in the course of the 18th cent. [71]: a few well-known collections were dissolved (Mattei, Montalto Negroni), whereby many pieces came to England; other collections left as a whole (1728 A. Chigi to Dresden; 1780–88 A. Medici to Florence; 1787 A. Farnese to Naples; later, in 1808, A. Borghese to Paris). At the same time, at the initiative of the Popes, the Capitoline Museum (1734) (→ ROME, Capitoline Museum), and the Museo Pio-Clementino at the Vatican (since 1769; → ROME, Vatican Museums) came into being. The Cardinal Alessandro Albani's (→ ROME, Villa Albani) elaborately staged antiquities collection gained wide renown, and was given additional radiance by the activity of J. J. Winckelmann [72].

The model of English art collections was most of all imitated in Northern Europe: near the end of the 18th cent., similarly conceived antiquities collections arose in Germany (for example Wörlitz [73]), Poland (for example, Arkadia/Nieborow [74; 75]) and Russia.

6. FUTURE PROSPECTS

The establishment of the → LOUVRE as a National museum has, since 1792, created a new model of antiquities collections. In the following years, similarly ambitious national museums came into being in many countries; moreover, in many places were municipal collections, which included large antiquities sections. In contrast to these large politically-driven projects, carried out energetically and with substantial means, the significance of private antiquities collections declined rapidly and irrevocably. Nevertheless, significant antiquities collections continued to be started from time to time, even until most recent times. Thanks to the philanthropic attitude of their founders, many of them were transferred in one way or another to public museums.

C. CATEGORIES OF COLLECTIONS

Despite the individual character of many antiquities collections, categories may be formed on the basis of the various intentions underlying the collections [76]. Publicly displayed antiquities have been known since the Middle Ages (see above). In such cases collections came into being more or less accidentally, usually as the result of accumulations of fragments of statues. The earliest examples of deliberately compiled antiquities collections were closely connected with attempts to legitimatize authority through reference to Antiquity. The antiquities collection on the Capitol received a new quality through the donation of Sixtus IV in the year 1471 (see above), which became the seedbed of the Capitoline Museums. Through foundations and the conversion of private antiquities collections, public museums came into existence, soon eagerly visited by travelers, in Venice (*statuario pubblico*), Florence (→ UFFIZI GALLERY) and Verona (Museo Maffeiano).

Until the late 18th cent., aristocratic and royal collections represented the most important, frequent, and sumptuous group of antiquities collections. Here, ancient sculptures often formed only a part of the collections, which might also include paintings, gems, coins, etc. They were frequently combined with modern antiquities: copies of bronze, tin, stone or plaster, which reproduced the famous masterpieces in Florence or Rome [77]. Decorative statues were regarded as a representation form of the rulers, so that they were mainly used on facades, and in areas for formal representation and reception. Their integration into ostentatious architecture led to the fact that aristocratic antiquities collections, once established, could be maintained over generations. Scholars' collections included inscriptions, coins, gems, and minor arts, yet scarcely any sculptures. On the other hand, many universities acquired great antiquities collections in the course of the 18th cent. (Turin 1723; Leiden 1743, see Fig. 5; Oxford 1755).

Antiquities collections belonging to artists, who were often active as restorers and art dealers, are attested since the Renaissance. Whereas P. P. Rubens – although only for a short time – purchased an extensive antiquities collection, his colleagues contented themselves with smaller collections. Their possessions included mainly fragments of sculptures, which they were able to use as three-dimensional models for their work. This same function was often assumed by plaster casts. Copies of ancient statues, the study of which served for the training of artists, had been gathered since the 17th cent. in art academies.

Collections of members of the bourgeoisie are scarcely to be found before the 19th cent. The usually short-lived collections of Dutch merchants had a distinctive imprint. They presented antiquities lined up warehouse-style in intimate domestic settings.

→ Cast Collections

1 A. Michaelis, Ancient Marbles in Great Britain, Cambridge 1882, 1–205 2 Id., Geschichte des Statuenhofes im vaticanischen Belvedere, in: JDAI 5, 1890, 5–72 3 Id., Storia della Collezione Capitolina di antichita fino all'inaugurazione del Museo (1734), in: MDAI(R) 6, 1891, 3–66 4 Ch. Hülsen, Römische Antikengärten des XVI. Jahrhunderts, in: Abhandlungen der Heidelberger Akademie der Wissenschaften, Philosophisch-historische Klasse 4, 1917 5 G. Zimmer, N. Hackländer, Der betende Knabe, 1997, 25–34 6 P. C. Bol, Der antretende Diskobol, 1996, 19–27 7 M. Pape, Griechische Kunstwerke aus Kriegsbeute und ihre öffentliche Aufstellung in Rom, 1975 8 G. Waurick, Kunstraub der Römer. Untersuchungen zu seinen Anfängen anhand der Inschriften, in: Jahrbuch des römisch-germanischen Zentralmuseum Mainz 22, 1975, 1–46 9 R. Neudecker, Die Skulpturenausstattung römischer Villen in Italien, 1988 10 E. M. Koppel, Die Skulpturenausstattung römischer Villen auf der iberischen Halbinsel, in: W. Trillmich et al. (eds.), Hispania antiqua. Denkmäler der Römerzeit, 1993, 202 11 W. Hornbostel, Sarapis, 1973, 398–400 12 J. B. Clarac, Musée de sculpture antique et moderne III (1850), CXVII–CLXVIII 13 C. Mango, Antique Statuary and the Byzantine Beholder, in: Dumbarton Oaks Papers 17, 1963, 55–75 14 R. Stupperich, Das Statuenprogramm in den Zeuxippos-Thermen, in: MDAI(Ist) 32, 1982, 210–235 15 S. Guberti Bassett, Historiae custos: Sculpture and Tradition in the Baths of Zeuxippos, in: AJA 100, 1996, 491–506 16 C. Mango, M. Vickers, E. D. Francis, The Palace of Lausus at Constantinople and its Collection of Ancient Statues, in: Journal of the History of Collections 4, 1992, 89–98 17 N. Gramaccini, Mirabilia. Das Nachleben antiker Statuen vor der Renaissance, 1996 18 N. Himmelmann, Antike Götter in der Spät-Antike, in: Trierer Winckelmannsprogramme 7, 1985, 3–22 19 D. Manacorda, Amalfi. Urne romane e commerci medioevali, in: Aparchai, FS PAOLO ELEUTERI Arias, vol. II, 1982, 713–752 20 B. Andreae, S. Settis (eds.), Colloquio sul reimpiego dei sarcofagi romani nel medioevo, Pisa 1982 (= Marburger Winckelmann-Programm, 1983), 1984 21 A. Erler, Lupa, Lex und Reiterstandbild im mittelalterlichen Rom, in: SB der wissenschaftlichen Gesellschaft an der Johann Wolfgang Goethe-Univ. Frankfurt a.M. 10, Nr. 4, 1972, 123–142 22 T. Buddensieg, Die Statuenstiftung Sixtus IV. im Jahr 1471, in: Römisches Jahrbuch für Kunstgeschichte 20, 1983, 35–73 23 L. Falkenstein, Der 'Lateran' der karolingischen Pfalz zu Aachen, 1966 24 B. Brenk, Spolia from Constantine to Charlemagne: Aesthetics versus Ideology, in: Dumbarton Oaks Papers 41, 1987, 103–109 25 M. Greenhalgh, Ipsa ruina docet: L'uso dell'antico nel Medioevo, in: S. Settis, Memoria dell'antico nell'arte italiana I, 1984, 149–151 26 Die Pferde von San Marco (exhibition catalogue, Berlin 1982), esp. 17–33; 55–72 27 H. Saradi, The Use of Ancient Spolia in Byzantine Monuments. The Archaeological and Literary Evidence, In: IJCT 3, 1997, 395–423 28 L. de Lachenal, I Normanni e l'antico. Per una ridefinizione dell'abbaziale incompiuta di Venosa in terra lucana, in: BA 81, Ser. VI 96–97, 1996, 1–80 29 H. Ladendorf, Antikenstudium und Antikenkopie, in: Abhandlungen der sächsischen Akademie der Wissenschaft zu Leipzig, philosophisch-historische Klasse 46/2 1953 30 Ph. P. Bober, R. Rubinstein, Renaissance Artists and Antique Sculpture. A Handbook of Sources, 1986 31 L. Medri, La collezione di Lorenzo Ghiberti, in: Lorenzo Ghiberti. Materiali e ragionamenti (exhibition catalogue, Florence 1978), 559–567 32 T. Buddensieg, Zum Statuenprogramm im Kapitolsplan Pauls III., in: Zeitschrift für Kunstgeschichte 32, 1969, 180–182 33 L. Spezzaferro, M. E. Tittoni (eds.), Il Campidoglio e Sisto V, 1991, 85–115 34 M. Wimmer, B. Andreae, C. Pietrangeli (eds.), Il Cortile delle statue. Der Statuenhof des Belvedere im Vatikan, 1998 35 P. G. Hübner, Le statue di Roma, 1912 36 H. Wrede, Römische Statuenprogramme des 16. Jahrhunderts in: [33] 91–94 37 Id., Der Antikengarten der del Bufalo bei der Fontana Trevi, in: Trierer Winckelmannsprogramme 4, 1982, 3–28 38 S. Favier, Les collections de marbres antiques sous François Ier, in: Revue du Louvre 24, 1974, 153–156 39 Ch. Riebesell, Die Sammlungen des Kardinal Alessandro Farnese, 1989 40 C. Gasparri, La collection d'antiques du cardinal Ferdinand, in: A. Chastel (ed.), La Villa Medici II, 1991, 443–485 41 Id., Materiali per servire allo studio del Museo Torlonia di scultura antica, in: Atti dell'Accademia Nazionale dei Lincei. Memorie Ser. VIII 24/2, 1980, 53–61; 71–124 42 L. Guerrini, 'Indicazioni' giustiniane, in: Xenia 12, 1986, 65–96 43 K. Kalveram, Die Antikesammlung des Kardinals Scipione Borghese, 1995 44 B. Palma, I Marmi Ludovisi: Storia della Collezione, 1983 45 Id., L. de Lachenal, I Marmi Ludovisi nel Museo Nazionale Romano, 1983 46 Id., L. de Lachenal, M. E. Micheli, I Marmi Ludovisi dispersi, 1986 47 E. Weski, H. Frosien-Leinz, Das Antiquarium der Münchner Residenz. Katalog der Skulpturen, 1987, esp. 32–64 48 A. H. Scott-Elliot, The Statues from Mantua in the Collection of King Charles I, in: Burlington Magazine 101, 1959, 218–227 49 O. Millar, The Inventories and Valuations of the King's Goods, in: Walpole Society 43, 1970–72 50 H. H. Brummer, Till belysning av drottning Christinas antiksamling i Stockholm, in: Konsthistorisk Tidskrift 32, 1963, 16–33 51 W. A. Bulst, Die Antikesammlungen der Königin Christina von Schweden, in: Ruperto-Carola 41, 1967, 121–135 52 C. van Tuyll van Serooskerken, Königin Christina als Sammlerin und Mäzenatin in: Christina Königin von Schweden (exhibition catalogue, Osnabrück 1997/98), 211–225 53 A. Bertoletti, P. Nicard, Objets d'art transportés de Rome en France, in: Nouvelles archives de l'art français II 2, 1880/81, 72–74 54 S. Hoog, Les sculptures du Grand Appartement du Roi, in: Revue du Louvre 26, 1976, 147ff. 55 P. Leon, Die Sammlung Klassische Skulptur im Prado, in: S. F. Schröder, Katalog der antiken Skulpturen des Museo del Prado in Madrid, 1993, 10–15 56 J. Schloder, M. Montembauld, L'album Canini du Louvre et la collection d'antiques de Richelieu, 1988 57 A. Le Pas de Secheval, Aux origines de la collection Mazarin, in: Journal of the History of Collections 5, 1993, 13–21

58 P. MICHEL, Rome et la formation des collections du cardinal Mazarin, Histore de l'art 21/22, 1993, 5–16 59 F. DE CATHEU, Le château et le parc de Sceaux, in: Gazette des Beaux-Arts 21, 1939, 86–102; 287–304 60 E. BONNAFFÉ, Les amateurs de l'ancienne France. Le surintendant Foucquet, Paris 1882 61 D. E. L. HAYNES, The Arundel Marbles, 1975 62 M. VAN DER MEULEN, Rubens Copies after the Antique, 1994, I, 220–231 63 I. FAVARETTO, Arte antica e cultura antiquaria nelle collezioni venete al tempo della Serenissima, 1990, esp. 82–83; 143–157 64 W. PRINZ, Galerien und Antikegalerien, in: [68] 343–356 65 I. FAVARETTO, G. L. RAVAGAN (ed.), Lo Statuario Pubblico della Serenissima (exhibition catalogue, Venice 19 ? 66 J.G. van Gelder, I. JOST, Jan de Bisshop and his Icones and Paradigmata, 1985, 35–50 67 H. OEHLER, Foto + Skulptur. Römische Antiken in englischen Schlössern (exhibition catalogue, Cologne 1980) 68 H. BECK et al. (eds.), Antikesammlungen im 18. Jahrhundert, 1981 69 D. BOSCHUNG, H. VON HESBERG (eds.), Antikensammlungen des europäischen Adels im 18. Jahrhundert als Ausdruck einer europäischen Identität, 2000 70 G. VAUGHAN, Thomas Jenkins and his international Clientele, in: [69] 71 P. LIVERANI, La situazione delle collezioni di antichità a Roma nel XVIII secolo, in: [69] 72 H. BECK, P. C. BOL (eds.), Forschungen zur Villa Albani, 1982 73 F.-A. BECHTOLDT, TH. WEISS (eds.), Weltbild Wörlitz, 1996 74 T. MIKOCKI, Collection de la Princesse Radziwill, 1995 75 Id., Antiken-Sammlungen in Polen, in: [69] 76 D. BOSCHUNG Eine Typologie der Skulpturen- Sammlungen des 18. Jahrhundert: Kategorien, Eigenarten, Intentionen, in: [69] 77 F. HASKELL, N. PENNY, Taste and the Antique. The Lure of Classical Sculpture, 1500–1900, 1981 78 L. SALERNO, Collezioni archeologiche, in: EAA Suppl., 1973, 242–259 79 C. GASPARRI, Collezioni archeologiche, in: EAA 2. Suppl. II, 1994 192–225 80 A. GROTE (ed.), Macrocosmos in Microcosmo. Die Welt in der Stube: Zur Geschichte des Sammelns 1450–1800, 1994 81 K. POMIAN, Der Ursprung des Museums: Vom Sammeln, 1993 82 D. VON BOTHMER, Greek Vase-Painting: Two Hundred Years of Connoisseurship, in: Papers on the Amasis Painter and his World, 1987, 184–204 83 J. CHAMAY, S. H. AUFRERE, Peiresc (1580–1637). Un précurseur de l'étude des vases grecs, in: AK 39, 1996, 38–51 84 P. ZAZOFF, GuG.

DIETRICH BOSCHUNG

Antiquity

A. HISTORY OF THE CONCEPT B. DIVISION OF HISTORY INTO ANTIQUITY, MIDDLE AGES AND MODERN TIMES

A. HISTORY OF THE CONCEPT

The term *antiquity* originated as a borrowing from the French adjective *antique*. It came to designate, after a fairly lengthy semantic development, a historical period (→ EPOCHS, CONCEPT OF) that, since the 18th cent. is synonymous with the German substantive 'Altertum' (ancient times) that had been used for centuries to denote Greco-Roman Antiquity. The adjective *antique* (from the Latin *antiquus*) was introduced into French in the 16th cent. by the Humanists and at first meant 'old' and then, since Rabelais, also antique, i.e., referring to the ancient world. Already in the Latin of the Early

Middle Ages *antiquus* or *antiquitas* could denote the period of Greco-Roman Antiquity (e.g. Beda, temp. rat. 37,2; Notker Balbulus Gest. 1,28: *antiquitas*). In Italy Dante used the adjective *antico* in his *Convivio* (2,5,1), written in 1303–1308, to refer to pre-Christian ancient history: *per difetto d'ammaestramento li antichi la veritade non videro de le creature spirituali* ('for lack of instruction, ancient people did not yet see the truth of spiritual creatures'). The noun *antichità* as a term for Antiquity as a historical period first appears around 1350 in Boccaccio. The French *antique* as a feminine noun has since 1530 referred specifically, unlike in Italian, to an ancient work of art [6; 12], and as a masculine noun has, in archaeology, signified since the 18th cent. the art of Antiquity in general. By way of contrast, the noun *antiquité* (since Montaigne, 1580 [5]) has been used to refer to the culture and historical period of the ancient world. In German archaeological technical literature, *Antique* accordingly refers to an individual work of art from the 16th–17th cents. (Hagedorn 1743) [1] and then, as a delimiting term, to ancient works of sculpture (Winckelmann 1755) [10]. In the 18th cent. its usage began to broaden and served as a generic concept for the style of ancient works of art considered worthy of imitation, but it also referred to the totality of those works of art (since Heyne 1777) [3]. In 1798/99 Novalis spoke of the 'godliness of antiquity' that is created in the eyes of those who contemplate ancient works of art [7]. The adjective *antique* or *antik* was already used, even before the noun, in connection with works of art from Egypt, Greece and Italy (Hagedorn 1727) [4]; otherwise, 'old' took on the function of 'antique'. The German noun 'die Antike' was considered to relate to the adjective *antik* as 'breadth' relates to *broad* [13]. A.W. and F. Schlegel were the first, beginning in 1796, to expand the usage of 'antique' as a contrast to 'modern' [13. 31] to mean the culture of antiquity in general and literature in particular [13. 30f.]. The corresponding epoch itself was called by F. Schlegel, starting in 1797, 'the classical ancient world' (*klassiches Altertum*) [13. 33] in the sense of a normative aesthetics. This conceptual pair (*klassisches Altertum*) was generally disseminated and translated into other languages (English: *Classical Antiquity*, French: *antiquité classique*). Only Greeks and Romans were included in this epoch. At the same time, however, in W. v. Humboldt the concept 'antiquity' expresses 'a special characteristic of human existence' and is thus not necessarily tied to a specific epoch ([9. Vol. VI, 487], 1819). Yet Humboldt, Eichendorff and others contrasted the inner posture of pagan Antiquity –as that of a lost paradise–, with Christian culture and German folk traditions ([9, IV. 83f.] 1813; [2]). The transformation in meaning of *antiquity* from a term referring to a stylistic and generic term in art history to one referring more generally to a historical period took place gradually in the 19th cent., first among art historians (e.g. Lübke and Springer since 1860 and 1862 [8]). In literary history, *antiquity* is first used to refer to a period of time in W. Scherer's

Geschichte der deutschen Literatur ('History of German Literature', 1883). The concept *antiquity*, not as an example of a culture expressing a normative function, but rather a historical period designating, in a historicist sense, the ancient world as a whole was first introduced by Th. Zieliński's book *Die Antike und Wir. Vorlesungen* ('Antiquity and Ourselves' [11]) at the beginning of the 20th cent. and thereafter began to replace the concept *ancient world* ('Altertum'; Stemplinger, Crusius, Immisch). This means that, at the very moment when the term 'antiquity' subsumed the existing concept *(classical) ancient world* ('klassisches Altertum'), the normative effect of that concept was being lost [13].
→ Period, Era; → Pompeius,*III. Schrifsteller und Redner* [III 3] P. Trogus

SOURCES: 1 T. BADEN (ed.), Briefe über die Kunst von und an Christian Ludwig von Hagedorn, Leipzig 1797, 2 und 11 2 J. VON EICHENDORFF, Das Marmorbild, 1819 3 Chr. G. Heyne an Chr. G. von Murr, in: Journal zur Kunstgeschichte und zur allgemeinen Litteratur, IV, Nürnberg 1777, 39 4 G. DE LAIRESSE, Grundlegung zur Zeichen-Kunst, (trans.) CHR. L. VON HAGEDORN, Nürnberg 1727, 52 5 Essais de MICHEL, SEIGNEUR DE MONTAIGNE, III, (Didot) Paris 1802, 120 6 J. PALSGRAVE, L'esclarcissement de la langue françoise, London 1531, 487 7 R. SAMUEL (ed.), Novalis Schriften, I–V, 1960–1988: III, 469; IV, 274 8 A. SPRINGER, Das Nachleben der Antike im Mittelalter, in: Die Grenzboten 1 (1862) 489–499, 25 9 A. VON SYDOW (ed.), Wilhelm und Caroline von Humboldt in ihren Briefen, I–VII, 1906–1916 10 J. J. WINCKELMANN, Gedanken über die Nachahmung der Griechischen Werke in der Malerey und Bildhauerkunst, Dresden,²1756, 13, 16, 32 11 TH. ZIELIŃSKI, Die Antike und Wir. Vorlesungen, (trans.) E. SCHOELER, ²1909

LITERATURE: 12 P. IMBS (ed.), Trésor de la langue française. Dictionnaire de la langue du XIXᵉ et du XXᵉ siècle (1789–1960), III, 'antique,' 1974, 171 13 W. MÜRI, Die Antike. Untersuchungen über Ursprung und Entwicklung der Bezeichnung einer geschichtlichen Epoche, in: A&A 7, 1958, 14 W. RÜEGG, Antike als Epochenbegriff, in: MH 16, 1959, 309–318 15 P. B. STADLER, Wilhelm von Humboldts Bild der Antike, 1959, 191.

B. DIVISION OF HISTORY INTO ANTIQUITY, MIDDLE AGES AND MODERN TIMES

During Antiquity itself, in addition to the mythological theory of the ages of the world, which described a decline from the Golden Age through the Silver and Bronze Ages to the Iron Age, there was a precursor of a historically oriented classification of eras; namely, the so-called 'theory of world empires' based on the ideas of Pompeius Trogus. According to this theory, world history was divided into the four great empires, one succeeding the other: Assyria, Persia, Macedonia, and Rome. The theory of world empires continued to be used to some extent until modern times. The fall of the Roman Empire and the founding of new states in its place did not at first lead to a new conceptual division of eras because the newly formed states, especially the Germanic ones, sought to preserve the continuity by adopting the Christian-Roman culture and Latin as their written language. Christian authors, however, did distinguish themselves as *moderni* from the pagan *antique*. Cassiodorus in the 6th cent. was the first to do so, and then, in like manner, Charlemagne regarding his empire;(→ QUERELLE DES ANCIENS ET DES MODERNES). Only with the rise of → HUMANISM in Italy beginning in about the 14th cent. did an awareness develop of an ancient period (*antiquitas*) and a present epoch separated by a *medium aevum* or *tempus* (first in Petrarch 1373 [8. 245]). Whereas the present (*nova aetas*) was considered, in accordance with a cyclical conception of history, to be a resurrection of pagan Greco-Roman *antiquitas*, the period in between was seen as a transitional period of decay (*media barbaria* in Poliziano and others). The fact that there was nevertheless no perception of a sharp break between 'Antiquity' and the 'Middle Ages' can be seen in the description of this epoch as *media antiquitas* in Humanists from Poliziano (1484), Beatus Rhenanus (1531) and Vadian (1547) through the beginning of the 19th cent. (Grotius 1611; Blondel 1654 [8. 245–265]; Humboldt 1813 [3, IV. 83]). The exact points in time dividing the three epochs from one another were for a long time not precisely defined. Within the Holy Roman Empire and among Catholic historians, the emphasis was rather on the continuity between 'Antiquity' and the time thereafter for political and religous reasons (→ SACRUM IMPERIUM). The three categories of the historical periods in the contemporary sense did not find general acceptance until the threshold of the 18th cent. with Cellarius [1] [8. 165–175]. According to this division, the transition from Antiquity to the Middle Ages occurred during the period of time between Constantine the Great and the end of the Roman Empire in the West in the 5th cent., and the modern era began in the 15th–16th cents. Since the Enlightenment, the victory of Christianity with Constantine's conversion is considered to mark specifically the end of Antiquity. This can be seen in Hölderlin's model of history [9]. L. v. Ranke defined 'ancient times' as the 'Greco-Roman world', i.e., the Mediterranean as 'it had been assembled through conquest' and 'united through culture'. The rise of non-Roman states through the great migrations and the Arab invasion, the uniting of the Roman-Germanic world, the end of Rome as the centre of things and the victory of Christianity mark the end of Antiquity. The 'modern age' begins when the lack of religious liberty of the Middle Ages was overcome and the New World was discovered [2]. Determining the exact border between Antiquity and the Middle Ages remains both difficult and controversial because it depends on the criteria used and whether they derive from political or cultural considerations, or are based on literary history [7]. Thus the culture of feudalism, for example, has been identified with the Middle Ages, while the modern era has been defined as beginning when an economy based on payment in kind was replaced by early capitalism. The division of history into three eras is problematic because of its geographical restriction to Western European cultural areas as the continuation of Latin Antiquity.

SOURCES: 1 CH. CELLARIUS, Historia universalis, Jena 1704–8 2 L. VON RANKE, Geschichte des Mittelalters, Vorlesungen 1840/41, in: Id., Aus Werk und Nachlaß, Vol. 4, 1975, 140–143 3 A. VON SYDOW (ed.), Wilhelm und Caroline von Humboldt in ihren Briefen, I–VII, 1906–1916

LITERATURE: 4 W. FREUND, Modernus und andere Zeitbegriffe des Mittelalters, 1957 5 H. GÜNTHER, Neuzeit, Mittelalter, Altertum, in: Historisches Wörterbuch der Philosophie 6, 782–798 6 P. E. HÜBINGER (ed.), Zur Frage der Periodengrenze zwischen Altertum und Mittelalter, 1969 7 H.-D. KAHL, Was bedeutet 'Mittelalter'?, in: Saeculum 40, 1989, 15–38 8 U. NEDDERMEYER, Das Mittelalter in der deutschen Historiographie vom 15. bis zum 18. Jahrhundert, 1988 9 P. SZONDI, Hölderlins Brief an Böhlendorff vom 4. Dez. 1801, in: Euphorion 58, 1964, 260–275

ADDITIONAL BIBLIOGRAPHY: Alejandro Coroleu, On the Awareness of the Renaissance, in: Il latino nell'età dell'Umanesimo (ed.) G. B. PERINI, 2004, 3–15; W. GOEZ, Translatio imperii. Ein Beitrag zur Geschichte des Geschichtsdenkens und der politischen Theorien im Mittelalter und der frühen Neuzeit, 1958; T. E. MOMMSEN, Petrarch's Conception of the 'Dark Ages', in: Speculum 17, 1942, 226–242; T. E. MOMMSEN, St. Augustine and the Christian Idea of Progress, in: Journal of the History of Ideas 12, 1951, 346–374.   PETER KUHLMANN

Antiquity, Romance set in see → EPIC, → ADAPTATION

Anti-Semitism see→ Judaism

Aphorism The short, pithy form of the aphorism holds, in its core, the potential to go beyond the bounds of any system. Consequently, in recent scholarship less emphasis has been placed on the pointed wording [1] as the main characteristic of the aphorism, than on the inherent conflict between the singular and the general, between the sensual and the intellect [9. 829ff.]. The aphorism is defined by a 'thinking in fractures'. It is 'nonconformist' [6. 7f.], which also gives it its its special licence. In the modern age, the aphorism can be conceived of as a 'form of playing' or a 'playing with concepts' [2. 22ff.; 3. 99f.], i.e. as an instrument to explore the scope between thinking and the self in society. Thus, it often employs rhetorical figures of contradiction, such as paradox, antithesis, paronomasia, antinomia and contrafacture, but it is also close to the joke and to irony [12. 188ff.; 2. 114ff.; 3. 99ff.; 8. 305ff.]. As a witty idea, and in contrast to the proverb, it seeks to distance itself from common usage [12. 248f.; 4. 140ff.]. The aphorism is marked by its 'contextual isolation' [4. 10]. It exists on its own, which makes it capable of being quoted. Whoever cites it, partakes of the social prestige of the invention and of the enigmatic nimbus of the aphorism as an 'oracle' (La Bruyère) [11.

1116f.]. The aphorism, like F. Schlegel's 'fragment', is complete unto itself 'like a hedgehog' (F. Schlegel, 'Fragmente', *Athenäum. Eine Zeitschrift von August Wilhelm Schlegel und Friedrich Schlegel*. Vol. I/2, 1798, 230), but it often appears in 'swarms of aphorisms' [9. 829], in collections or in diary-like notebooks such as G.Ch. Lichtenberg's *Sudelbücher*.

The aphorism adopted from Hippocrates and Tacitus (on the history of the term, cf. [1; 8. 215]) experiences its Golden Age in Spain and France in the 17th cent. and in England and Germany in the 18th cent. [4]. An independent literary genre and a specific aphoristic style evolves in combination with the aphoristic style derived from Seneca and the Horacian dictum *aut prodesse aut delectare*. Up until quite recently, two tendencies prevailed: on the one hand, an ethical/moral subject matter; on the other, an attitude critical of metaphysics and knowledge. Under the influence of the Spanish reception of Tacitus, in B. Gracián's *Oráculo manual*, the dramatization of the intelligent, quick-witted self, as it is also demanded by B. Castiglione in *Il Cortegiano* ('The Courtier'), becomes a yardstick for measuring social status [8. 413ff.]. In his *Maximes et réflexions*, the French moralist La Rochefoucauld develops the aphorism from the conversations of the drawing-room culture, on whose ethical foundations he reflects ironically at the same time. La Bruyère, Chamfort, Montesquieu and Vauvenargues continue in the moralistic vein [5. 33ff.]. Goethe's maxims, Lichtenberg's satirical aphorisms and Schopenhauer's *Aphorismen zur Lebensweisheit* ('The Wisdom of Life' [¹¹1911] and 'Counsels and Maxims' [²1891], trans. by T. Bailey Saunders)can be counted among them, as well as the sharp-tongued, socio-critical aphorisms of K. Kraus in the 20th cent. In the Anglo-Saxon world, O. Wilde, M. Twain and G.B. Shaw can be named as representatives of the ethical tradition [7. 311, 319ff.]. Humanist and existentialist variants can be found in the 20th cent. in E.M. Cioran and A. Camus.

Based on Erasmus and F. Bacon, the aphorism that is critical of knowledge and has the power to explode the system is brought forward, for instance, in B. Pascal's *Pensées* as an open form of theodicy, in Lichtenberg's rationalism as a rupture in positivistic thinking, but also in in the contemplation of aesthetic principles in the relation between poetics and philosophy by F. Schlegel and Novalis. In the 20th cent., R.M. Rilke and Paul Valéry [5. 160ff., 257ff.] continue the aesthetic self-reflection within the genre of aphorism. As 'fractured knowledge' [8. 27], the aphorism is also the appropriate form of expression for F. Nietzsche's critique of metaphysics [6. 76ff.]. In the 20th cent., the aphorism shows an affinity towards being absorbed by the aphoristic style that is related to the essay, as in R. Musil [10. 69ff.]. At the same time, a return of gnomic forms is noticeable in surrealism and in 'image aphorism', e.g. in R. Char [5. 103ff.]. The boundaries to experimental literature and to the joke now become doubtful, whereas already in Lichtenberg's *Hofbandit* (*Court Bandit*) –

the conflict so essential to the aphoristic form is reduced to compounds [3. 48f.]. Ultimately, the modern age questions the very consistency of the literary genre: P. Válery proposes the phantasy term 'rhumb' [2. 47] as a new name for the 'family resemblances' of the aphorism [3. 189]. The apophthegm, an often historically founded saying that is ascribed to a public figure and related to the anecdote, and the gnome as a maxim couched in verse form or rhythmic prose, also belong to this family. In contrast to the original idea and the exceptional nature of the aphorism, the *sententia* is allocated to the realm of rhetoric and considered to be generally valid and of an authoritative character. As a rule of life it emphasizes the ethical aspect, much like the rather individual maxim that is often used as a synonym for aphorism in French. Designations such as *pensée*, 'splinters of thought' and 'reflection' accentuate the theoretical aspect of the aphorism. A vulgarized form of the quotation-like aphorism is the proverb. Joke and riddle ultimately resolve the tension inherent in aphorism, whereas the fragment and the essay continue its openness in narrative form.

→ Chreia; → Gnome

→ Dicta

1 H. A. Gärtner, s.v. Aphorismos, DNP 1, 834f.   2 G. Febel, Aphoristik in Deutschland und Frankreich, 1985   3 S. Felder, Der Aphorismus, 1990   4 H. Fricke, Aphorismus, 1984   5 W. Helmich, Der moderne französische Aphorismus, 1991   6 H. Krüger, Über den Aphorismus als philosophische Form, 1988   7 L. R. Lind, The Aphorism, in: Classical and Modern Literature 14/4, 1994, 311–322   8 G. Neumann (ed.), Der Aphorismus, 1976   9 Id., Ideenparadiese, 1976   10 P. C. Pfeiffer, Aphorismus und Romanstruktur, 1990   11 H. Schlaffer, Aphorismus und Konversation, in: Merkur 573, 1996, 1114–1121   12 K.v. Welser, Die Sprache des Aphorismus, 1986

Additional Bibliography: P. Sinclair, Tacitus the Sententious Historian: A Sociology of Rhetoric in Annales 1–6, 1995; J. Geary, The World in a Phrase: A Brief History of the Aphorism, 2005.   Gisela Febel

Apollonian/Dionysian The polarity between Apollo and Dionysus and the phenomena linked with these gods was introduced into modern aesthetic discussion by Friederich Nietzsche. Nietzsche understood the 'duplicity of Apollo and Dionysus' as a fundamental opposition of Greek aesthetics: *An ihre (sc. der Griechen) beiden Kunstgottheiten, Apollo und Dionysus, knüpft sich unsere Erkenntnis, daß in der griech. Welt ein ungeheurer Gegensatz, nach Ursprung und Zielen, zw. der Kunst des Bildners, der apollinischen, und der unbildlichen Kunst der Musik, als der des Dionysus, besteht* ('it is by those two art-sponsoring deities, Apollo and Dionysus, that we are made to recognize the tremendous split, as regards both origins and objectives, between the plastic, Apollonian arts and the nonvisual art of music inspired by Dionysus', The Birth of Tragedy, Chap. 1). In the process, Nietzsche adds further pairs of opposites to this polarity: night and day, dream and intoxication, visual and emotional. In this polarity, Nietzsche links the opposition between the plastic arts and the musical, which had been important since Romantic aesthetics and which Schopenhauer, for instance, had set up as the principle of dividing the arts as such, with the names of the two Greek gods.

Their relation was by no means unambiguous in ancient theological speculation, especially during the period of the Empire; yet they were occasionally brought into relation with one another. Thus, as two forms of the sun-god, they could be regarded as ultimately identical (Macrobius, *Sat.*, 1, 18, 1, with reference to Ps.-Aristotle *Theologoumena*) while at the same time Apollo could be distinguished as the daytime sun, and Dionysius as the nighttime sun of the Underworld (*ibid*. 1, 18, 8). The opposition alluded to in this differentiation takes on central importance in Delphic theology, which places Apollo and Dionysus in opposition to one another (Plut. *De E* 9). Neoplatonic speculation adopted the opposition as that between creative division (Dionysus) and creative, harmonic unification (Apollo), to which the allegorical interpretation of the Orphic myth of Dionysus also contributed (Proclus, In Platonis Timaeum 35 b, vol. 2, p. 197 Diehl). Unlike other Neoplatonic concepts, this one was not really taken up in the Renaissance, yet Friedrich Creuzer, in particular, returned to the Neoplatonic exegesis of Orpheus and spoke of the 'opposition of the religion of Apollo and Bacchus', which includes an opposition between solar and darkly ecstatic conceptions of religion, reconciled in another 'School of Orphics'. F. Chr. Baur and J. J. Bachofen followed Creuzer. On the one hand, Bachofen went back beyond Creuzer to take up the opposition between the nocturnal solar god Dionysus and the day god Apollo of Late Antiquity, and set up Dionysus–as feminine-substantial and chthonic against a masculine-spiritual, celestial Apollo–in his evolutionary scheme ('Das Mutterrecht – [An English Translation of Bachofen's Mutterrecht (Mother right) (1861): A Study of the Religious and Juridical Aspects of Gynecocracy in the Ancient World', abridged and translated by David Partenheimer, 2003]). Nonetheless, he held fast to the coexistence of both as world-rulers, basing his view on the Neoplatonic interpretation of Orpheus (*Die Unsterblichkeitslehre der orphischen Theologie*, repr. 1967). Baur, on the other hand, understood both (based ultimately on Plato's doctrine of *mania* in the *Phaedrus*), as being linked to two kinds of ecstasy: pure spiritual contemplation (Apollo) and the sensual 'drunken ecstasy'. When he likewise linked two kinds of music and poetry with both [gods] – the harmony of poetry versus the rapture of the dithyramb – he prepared the way for the musical-poetic categorization set forth by Nietzsche's academic teacher Friedrich Ritschl, according to which Apollo was connected with Greco-Dorian stringed-instrument music, and Dionysus with un-Greek, Phrygian flute music. This opposition, which Nietzsche presupposed, became a commonplace in classical studies. However, no influence between Nietzsche and Bachofen should probably be assumed.

In the following period, the pair of contraries coined by Nietzsche played a much larger role outside philological research than it did within. In particular, German literature, beginning with the turn of the century, took it up in ever-new metamorphoses. However, even classical philology could not completely escape Nietzsche's coinage, insofar, for instance, as Apollo was understood as 'the most Hellenic of all the gods', or, in a fruitful transcendence of earlier opinions, the Dionysian was seen 'as a mighty, ultimate source of that which is Greek' (W.F. Otto).

→ Apollo; → Dionysus

→ ANCIENT LANGUAGES, TEACHING OF

1 S. BARBERA, Das Apollinische und Dionysiche. Einige nicht-antike Quellen bei Nietzsche, in: D. W. CONWAY, R. RHEN (eds.), Nietzsche und die antike Philosophie, 1992 2 H. CANCIK, Der Einfluß Friedrich Nietzsches auf Klassische Philologen in Deutschland bis 1945, in: H. FLASHAR (ed.), Altertumswissenschaft in den 20er Jahren. Neue Fragen und Impulse, 1995, 381–402 3 A. HENRICHS, Loss of Self, Suffering, Violence. The Modern View of Dionysos from Nietzsche to Girard, in: HSPh 86, 1982, 206–240 4 M. LANDFESTER, (ed.), in: F. NIETZSCHE, Die Geburt der Tragödie, 1994, 486–492 and 521–530.

FRITZ GRAF

Apologos see→ FABLE

Apophtegm see→ APHORISM

Apotheosis Although apotheosis as such contradicts the principle of monotheism and therefore cannot occur in Christianity, Christian society from the time of Constantine found ways to maintain the elevation of the ruler above the mortal plane and into the sphere of divinity. In addition, individual forms of apotheosis can be observed again and again, intended either to correspond precisely to this need or to exemplify Christ's ascension. A type of the latter, which shows Christ being wafted away in a mandorla, flanked by two angels (reliquary, Jerusalem, 7th/8th cent., Vatican, Museo Sacro; ivory, Metz, c. 1000, Paris, Lv Inv. no. OA 6000: Reichenauer Evangelary, 11th cent., Kupferstichkabinett der Staatlichen Museum Preussischer Kulturbesitz Cod. 78A2; cover page of the Evangelary of Abbess Theophanu, Stift Essen, Treasury; Spiez, apse of the romanesque castle church; Barnaba da Modena, Ascension, 14th cent., Rome, KM) goes back to the representation of the divinized Roman emperor in a medallion, flanked by two winged figures (ivory from 306, Constantine, Paris, LV) continued in Byzantine imperial diptychs of the 6th cent. (Basel, Historisches Museum; Paris, LV; Milan, Castell Sforzesco [19 nr. 48–50]), and ultimately to the kind of representation of the apotheosis of Antoninus Pius and Faustina, without a medallion, but in the same arrangement between two flying eagles (base of the column of Antoninus Pius from 161, Rome, VM). This type was transferred to the Assumption of Mary (cf. Florence, S. Maria del Fiore, Porta

della Mandorla, 1414–1421) and later served for the representation of the resurrection or ascension of ordinary mortals, for instance, c. 1100, on the sarcophagus of Doña Sancha in Jaca [6]. More frequent in the Western cultural sphere was the representation of the hand of God, raising Christ skywards [15.270f.].

The emperor Constantine, who sought to maintain his status through recourse to Christianity, like his divine predecessors, drives in the representations of his consecration coins a quadriga towards heaven, but is simultaneously seized by a divine hand. The obligatory eagle-flight was abandoned, and finally Constantine's mortal remains, uncremated, were buried, according to Christian custom [12. 518–523]. Constantine found his tomb 'amid the Apostles', probably as the 13th Apostle [13]. Eusebius knew how to replace the peculiar status of the Roman emperor as *divus* with that of a *Vicarius Dei divus* of the one God, who shares in the heavenly Kingdom (De laudibus Constantini 3,4–5; 5,1).

Henceforth, Christian rulers legitimized themselves as *vicarii Christi* or *Vicarii Dei* (in particular Charlemagne), as *alter Christus* and *Christus Domini*. Their status with regard to the people remained peculiar: around 1100, the Norman Anonymous, like Eusebius, conceived of the king as *Deus per gratiam*; that is, by the grace of God like unto God [10.69f.]. Landulfus Sagax remarked with regard to Augustus, that he was not undeservedly considered to be particularly like God (7, 21). Following Exodus 7: 1, Innocent III designated the Pope as *vicarius Iesu Christi, successor Petri, Christus domini, Deus Pharaonis*, and saw himself as standing between God and mankind, and could only be judged by God alone (4,294f. = PL 217, 657C–658A). Emperor Frederick II compared himself with Christ, and was designated by his chancellor as an 'imperial Christ' [4.433]. Pope Boniface VIII, who understood himself as *Christ* on earth and God of gods [4.433], was accused of black magic and of leading people into idolatry, among other reasons because of his statues [16.73].

One current of transmission, from Suetonius via Isidore of Seville down to Petrus Diaconus – another runs from Suetonius through Orosius, Historiarum adversus paganos 6,22,4, to Otto von Freising, Chronica 3,4 – knew of Augustus's refusal of apotheosis, although it was not reported that he meant this to apply only to his lifetime. According to the Mirabilia Urbis Romae, Augustus acknowledged Christ's lordship after Mary appeared to him with her child, and he therefore declined his apotheosis [18].

Louis XIV of France was designated as the living image of God [5.21, 55, 63], which can probably already to be assigned to the domain of allegory. Whereas the occasional designation of the medieval ruler as *divus* (→ RULER) utilized ancient imperial titles, and with that an element of Emperor-apotheosis (Dante to Henry VII; [4. 324]; Carmen de gestis Frederici I. in Lombardia, v. 71, for Frederick Barbarossa), identifications with ancient gods during the Middle Ages (for instance Jupiter and Apollo in [2]), and especially in the

Baroque must be considered as allegories. Thus, Louis XIV was represented as the Sun, Apollo, Jupiter, Hercules, and Neptune [5. 39, 46, 137] and also as hurling thunderbolts in a Roman war-chariot, accompanied by Minerva, Hercules, Gloria and Victoria [5. 112].

Not only were pagan elements of the exaltation of mortals maintained along with the victorious march of Christianity, but also a general need for 'divine men' was met. A. Angenendt speaks persuasively of a 'structural kinship' and 'analogy' between Greek heroes and Christian saints [3. 22]. Whereas the reasons for the exaltation of gentle martyrs must have been alien to pagan thought, the holy rulers, lawgivers (Stephen the Holy of Hungary) and warriors who were soon to follow them thoroughly resembled ancient divine men and divinized humans in their function for the dynasty. They were not merely elevated above the mass of mortals, but differed from them essentially, through the immortality they achieved. If [2. 50, v. 1605, 233] Frederick II was designated as living eternally, so were prominent ancestors considered as saints, long before formal papal canonizations, e.g. in Serbia [9], Norway (Olaf, who fell in battle in 1030, died, similarly to Knut of Denmark, of a spear wound like Christ, and was known as *rex perpetuus*, [8. 281ff.]) and Bohemia (Wenzel was considered an eternal prince of the land, [7. 340]). Through their living on after death, they thereby ensured for their descendants the necessary sacral aggrandizement and continuity. A proper procedure of canonization was in use among the Holy Emperors of the medieval Roman Empire, so for Henry II by Pope Eugene III (1146), and for Charlemagne at the instigation of Emperor Frederick Barbarossa (1165). To a certain extent, burial in proximity to saints replaced, as it had already done for Constantine, the eagles' flight of the Roman emperors' apotheosis. In the process, a particular sanctifying force is ascribed to the tomb of the holy first ancestor, as it was to Alexander the Great for the Diadochs. Last not least, a more modern relative of a ruler's apotheosis can be found in the neo-classical fresco on the rotunda of the US Capitol, *The Apotheosis of George Washington*, painted in 1856 by Constantino Brumidi.

→ Consecratio; → Ruler; → Ruler cult

SOURCES: 1 LANDULFUS SAGAX, Historia Romana, A. CRIVELLUCCI (ed.), 2 vols. 1912f. 2 PETRUS DE EBULO, Liber ad honorem Augusti sive de rebus Siculis, TH. KÖLZER, M. STÄHLI (eds.), 1994

LITERATURE: 3 A. ANGENENDT, Heilige und Reliquien, 1994 4 K. BURDACH, Briefwechsel des Cola di Rienzo 1, 1913–28 5 P. BURKE, Ludwig XIV., ²1996 6 J. ENGEMANN, s.v. Apotheosis, in: Lexikon des Mittelalters 1, 801f. 7 A. GIEYSZTOR, Politische Heilige im hochmittelalterlichen Polen und Böhmen, in: [14. 325–341] 8 E. HOFFMANN, Politische Heilige in Skandinavien und die Entwicklung der drei nordischen Reiche und Völker, in: [14. 277–324] 9 F. KÄMPFER, Herrscher, Stifter, Heiliger: Politische Heiligenkulte bei den orthodoxen Südslaven, in: [14. 423–445] 10 E. H. KANTOROWICZ, Die zwei Körper des Königs, (1957) 1990 (Eng. The King's Two Bodies: A Study in Mediaeval Political Theology, [1957] 1990) 11 L. KOEP (A. HERMANN), s.v. Consecratio II, Reallexikon für Antike und Christentum 3, 284–294 12 L. KOEP, Die Konsekrationsmünzen Kaiser Konstantins und ihre religionspolitischen Bedingungen, in: A. WLOSOK (ed.), Römische Kaiserkult 1978, 509–527, first published in: JbAC 1, 94–104 13 R. KRAUTHEIMER, Zu Konstantins Apostelkirche in Konstantinopel, in: id., Ausgewählte Aufsätze, 1988, 81–90 (orig. in: A. STUIBER und A. HERMANN, Mullus. Festschrift Theodor Klauser, 1964) 14 J. PETERSOHN (ed.), Politik und Heiligenverehrung im Hochmittelalter, 1994 15 A. A. SCHMID, s.v. Himmelfahrt Christi, in: Lexikon der christlichen Ikonographie 2, 268–276 16 T. SCHMIDT, Der Bonifaz-Prozeß, 1989 17 A. F. SEGAL, Heavenly Ascent in Hellenistic Judaism, Early Christianity and their Environment, in: ANRW II 23.2, 1333–1394 18 J. STROTHMANN, Kaiser und Senat, 1998 19 W. F. VOLBACH, Elfenbeinarbeiten der Spätantike und des frühen Mittelaters, 1976.   ME.SCH.

Arabic Medicine

A. ORIGINS B. TRANSLATIONS BEFORE AD 700
C. THE AGE OF HUNAIN D. THE TRANSLATIONS
E. ARABIC GALENISM F. CRITICISM G. YUNANI MEDICINE

A. ORIGINS

By AD 500, Greek medicine had become largely Galenic → GALENISM. Alternative medical theories no longer flourished, and even pragmatists like Alexander of Tralles did not reject Galenic ideas entirely. In Alexandria, and elsewhere in the Byzantine world that followed Alexandrian traditions, e.g. Ravenna, there was a teaching syllabus of Galen, the so-called 16 books – *Summaria Alexandrinorum*, and of Hippocrates that was commented upon by lecturers who expected of their audience also a grasp of Aristotelian philosophy. A division thus grew up between formal medicine, expressed in terms of books studied, and other types of healing. Those who had studied formal medicine were increasingly reluctant to call those who had not 'doctors'.

B. TRANSLATIONS BEFORE AD 700

The first translations of medical texts from Greek into a vernacular language of the Middle East were done by the priest-doctor Sergius of Resaena (d. 536), who translated at least 37 works of Galen into Syriac, five of them twice, as well as other non-Galenic medical tracts. Other Greek medical writings may also have been translated into Pahlavi at about the same time, while David Anhacht (c. 500), who had studied in → ALEXANDRIA, conveyed Galenic medical ideas in his Armenian philosophical writings. [1] Authors, writing in Syriac, also further developed Galen's medicine either in specific tracts, e.g. that by Sergius on dropsy, or in large compendia of general medicine, like the Pandects of Ahrun or those of Theodokos (7th cent.). This medicine was far more sophisticated and wide-ranging that that practised by the Muslim Arab conquerors themselves in the 7th cent., and it is not surprising that Christian physicians and a Christianised Galenic medicine continued to hold sway for several centuries.

C. THE AGE OF HUNAIN

Information is scanty, however, before the 9th cent. Then, with the strong encouragement of caliphs like al-Ma'mūn (d. 833) and wealthy courtiers, like Djibril ibn Bakhtishu' (d. 827), himself a doctor and a (poor) translator, a massive wave of translations occurred, usually first into Syriac, and then into Arabic. The leading spirit in this was Hunain ibn Ishaq (d. 873), assisted by his son Ishaq (d. 910), and his nephew Hubaish (d. c. 900), working in Baghdad, but there were others like Theophilos of Edessa (d. 785) and Job of Edessa (Ayyub al-Ruhawi, d. after 832), who were active elsewhere, especially in the largely Christian frontier region of Northern Syria. By 900, over 129 treatises of Galen were available in Arabic, some of them in several different versions, including works on logic and philosophy as well as on medicine. [2] A smaller proportion of the Hippocratic Corpus was translated into Syriac or Arabic, sometimes only indirectly via the lemmata to Galen's commentaries, but the Arabs possessed more works by Rufus of Ephesus than survive today, as well as the encyclopedists of Late Antiquity, Oreibasius, Aetius, and Paulus, and a variety of productions by late Alexandrian writers like Palladius. [3,4,5] Dioscorides and those authors writing on physiognomy and agriculture were also available in Arabic. The *Summaria Alexandrinorum* were also translated into Syriac and into Arabic (and, much later, into Hebrew, by Shimson ben Shlomo in 1322). From Arabic, in turn, translations were made into Armenian (9th/10th cents.), Pahlavi, and Hebrew (e.g. by Samuel ibn Tibbon, fl. 1200), and, from the late 11th cent. onwards, into Latin. There is even a report that some of Galen was translated, or at least transcribed, from Arabic into Chinese.[6]

D. THE TRANSLATIONS

The quality of the translations by Hunain and his school in the 9th cent. is remarkably high. Hunain himself in his *Risala* detailed his own careful methods of collation and translation, preferring to keep the sense of a passage rather than the exact word order, and at times confessing his inability to translate a word because of its rarity and its lack of context. Wherever possible, Hunain followed closely the Greek, only making occasional modifications to avoid offending religious sensibilities or to omit some of Galen's etymological comments that would be meaningless in Arabic. How far his methods were followed elsewhere is unclear, since many of the translations of others have been lost, but one should not necessarily believe Hunain's dismissive descriptions of his competitors' abilities. Modern historians of ancient medicine depend on these versions in a variety of ways.[7] (→ MEDICINE) Some ancient writings survive only in Arabic or Hebrew, e.g. Galen's treatise *De examinando medico* or his commentary on

the Hippocratic treatise 'On the Environment'. Others, no longer extant in full, are cited in part by Arabic or Jewish authors, e.g. Rufus of Ephesus' writing on melancholy in the adaptation of Ishaq ibn Imran (d. 907), or Galen's work on the avoidance of grief as found in the version by ibn Aknin (fl. 1300). other works, like Galen's treatises on the eye, formed the basis for subsequent development in Arabic authors, although what is development and what represents the Greek original is not clear. Even when the Greek survives, the Arabic often permits a view of the text, thanks to the remarkable accuracy of Hunain and his school, at an earlier and often less corrupt stage in the process of → TRANSMISSION.

E. ARABIC GALENISM

Most significant is the overall Galenic nature of formal Arabic medicine. Galen's perspective dominated all others, and its monotheistic ideas on causation and purpose made it attractive to Jews, Christians, and Muslims alike, even if they rejected some of Galen's own doubts about the nature of God or creation. Learned doctors studied Galen with their masters, following the Alexandrian syllabus, and it is no coincidence that many of the great names in Arabic and Jewish medicine, like Ibn Sina (Avicenna, 980?–1037) and Moses ben Maimon (Maimonides, 1138–1204) were, like Galen, famous as philosophers as much as doctors. But the sheer size of the Galenic Corpus, even in translation, was daunting. Ibn Ridwan (d. c. 1068) was already unusual in his day for the breadth of his knowledge of Galen, and few followed him in his insistence that an acquaintance with Galen's own writings was far more beneficial to the practitioner than any reading in subsequent handbooks. His opponent in a celebrated controversy, Ibn Butlan (d. c. 1068) took a more pragmatic line, relying on contemporary writings in the Galenic tradition. [8] Both sides had a point. Summaries and handbooks were effective in presenting the main outlines of Galen's theories, but the process of abridgment inevitably left out Galen's hesitations and much of his empirical evidence. Authors like al-Majusi (Haly Abbas, d. c. 999) and Ibn Sina, above all in his *Canon*, provided logically constructed syntheses that took Galen's ideas, e.g. on the three *spirits* (→ Pneuma), far beyond what he had written. Writers on → PHARMACOLOGY and → DIETETICS, like Ibn Butlan in his 'Tables of Health', applied Galen's incomplete theory of different degrees of efficacy of Arabic pharmacology systematically to a wide range of substances. But, while impressive in their organisation and clarity, these handbooks lost some of the energy and immediacy of Galen's original. The best Arabic medicine often begins with a Galenic or Hippocratic model, but goes far beyond it. Ibn Ridwan's treatise, 'On thePrevention of Bodily Ills in Egypt' (eds. A. S GAMAL, M W. DODS, 1984), develops ideas from the Hippocratic writing on the environment; al-Razi 's (Rhazes, 865–925) treatise on smallpox and measles refines Galen's nosology, while his experiments on animals recall those of Galen. The surgeon al-Zahrawi (Albucasis, *c.* 936–1013) constantly proclaims his debt to Galen, while describing many new operations and techniques.

F. Criticism

Arabic authors saw themselves as building upon solid foundations. While Galen's theology and philosophy came in for vigorous attack, criticism of the Greeks in medical matters took the form of adding new information rather than abandoning the old.[9] Abd-al Latif al-Baghdadi's (d. 1231) discovery from examining skulls that Galen had wrongly described the human jaw did not lead to widespread criticism of Galenic anatomy – and dissection of humans was almost impossible. [10] Ibn al-Nafis (d. 1288) discovered the passage of blood from one side of the heart to the other via the lungs by a mixture of observation (presumably of an animal heart) and meditation on the words of Galen in a thought-experiment. Although his discovery, expressed in his commentary on Ibn Sina, was often reported in later texts, it was merely placed without further comment alongside Galen's alternative theory, and ibn an-Nafis himself did not draw further conclusions from it.

G. Yunani Medicine

Greek humoralism in Arab dress, Yunani medicine, came under attack from religious fundamentalists from the 10th cent. on who sought to impose on Muslims the so-called Medicine of the Prophet, but it was never entirely replaced as the primary medicine of the educated doctor until the 19th and 20th cents. Western→ RENAISSANCE discoveries in anatomy, physiology and Paracelsian medical chemistry were assimilated where necessary [11]. Only with the advent of colonialism and the imposition of modern Western medicine did Yunani medicine come to be seen, at least by the ruling classes, as inferior and ineffective.[12] Nonetheless, as mediated through Ibn Sina's 'Canon of Medicine', it still remains today an important medical tradition in Pakistan and elsewhere in the Muslim world (including in Western Europe), and scholars trained in that tradition are ready to use the latest of modern Western technology or pharmacochemistry to prove the validity of recipes and diagnoses that go back to Galen, if not to Hippocrates.

Anatomy; → Galen; → Hippocrates; → Pharmacology; → Training (medical)

→ → Arabic-Islamic Cultural Sphere

1 M. Ullmann, Die Medizin im Islam, 1970, 17, 19 2 G. Strohmaier, Der syrische und arabische Galen,in: ANRW 37.2, 1987–2017 3 U. Weisser, Das Corpus Hippocraticum in der arabischen Medizin, in: G. Baader, R. Winau (eds.), Die hippokratischen Epidemien, 1989, 377–408 4 M. Ullmann, Die arabische Überlieferung der Schriften des Rufus von Ephesos, in: ANRW 37.2, 1293–1349 5 Id., Die Schrift des Rufus De infantium curatione und das Problem der Autorenlemmata in den Collectiones medicae des Oreibasios, in: Medical History 10, 1975, 165–190 6 M. Davies, A Selection from the Writings of Joseph Needham, 1990, 138–139 7 G. Strohmaier, Galen in Arabic: Problems and Prospects, in: V. Nutton (ed.), Galen: Problems and Prospects, 1981, 187–196 8 J. Schacht, M. Meyerhof, The Medico-Philosophical Controversy between Ibn Butlan of Baghdad and Ibn Ridwan of Cairo, 1937 9 J. C. Bürgel, Averroes contra Galenum, 1967, 263–340 10 E. Savage-Smith, Attitudes towards Dissection in Medieval Islam, in: JHM 50, 1995, 67–110 11 Id., Europe and Islam, in: I. Loudon (ed.), Western Medicine, 1997, 40–53 12 N. E. Gallagher, Medicine and Power in Tunisia, 1780–1890, 1983 13 L. I. Conrad, Arab-Islamic Medicine, in: W. F. Bynum, R. Porter (eds.), Companion Encyclopedia of the History of Medicine, 1993, 676–727 14 D. Gutas, Greek Thought, Arab Culture, 1998 15 D. Jacquart, F. Micheaud, La Médecine arabe et l'Occident médiéval, 1990 16 J. Moulirac (ed.), À l'ombre d'Avicenne: La Médecine au Temps des Califes, 1997 17 F. Sezgin, Geschichte des arabischen Schrifttums, vol. 3, Medizin -Zoologie-Tierheilkunde, 1970 18 G. Strohmaier, Denker im Reich der Kalifen, 1979 19 M. Ullmann, Islamic Medicine, 1978. VIVIAN NUTTON

Arabic Studies
A. Definition B. The Beginnings of Arabic Studies in Europe C. Changes in the Image of the Orient in the 18th Cent. D. Development in the 19th Cent. until the First World War E. Between the Two World Wars F. Post-1945

A. Definition
'Arabic studies' (AS) designates the philological investigation of the Arabic language and of the works composed in that language. As a linguistic discipline it is a part of → Semitic studies; as a cultural discipline, it is the central focus for Islamic studies.

B. The Beginnings of Arabic Studies in Europe
Although a number of works of AS as well as religious writings were translated into Latin by the school of translators founded by Alfonso X the Wise (1252–84), this did not lead to the creation of institutions where Arabic was taught. Many translators came from the parts of Spain that had been or still were under Arab domination. Where others, like Gerard of Cremona (d. 1187) or Robertus Ketenensis (the first translator of the Koran, d. *c.* 1160) had obtained their knowledge of Arabic is unknown. Knowledge of the Arabic language could only have been obtained from native speakers who had been driven to Europe, or in lands of the Orient itself. The founders of AS at the universities belonged to the latter category: Guillaume Postel (1510–1581, Paris), Jacob Golius (1596–1667, Leiden) and Eduard Pocock (1604–1691, Oxford).

In the 17th cent. collections of Arabic manuscripts were made at Heidelberg, Leiden, and Rome, later at the Escorial and elsewhere. The leading Arabists taught at Leiden: Johann Jacob Erpenius (1584–1624) wrote the first methodical presentation of the Classical Arabic language; Jacob Golius created the first usable lexicon. It was there that Johann Jacob Reiske (1716–1774), the most significant Arabist of the 18th cent., found the manuscripts for his editions of texts and translations; he did not, however, get the recognition he deserved during his lifetime.

C. CHANGES IN THE IMAGE OF THE ORIENT IN THE 18TH CENT.

As a result of the growth of the economic and military interests of European powers, the Orient entered public awareness ever more strongly near the end of the 18th cent. Under the influence of the → ENLIGHTENMENT, Europe's image of the Orient was transformed from that of a world of infidels needing evangelization to that of a world with its own cultural achievements. Antoine Galand's (1646–1709) translation of *The Thousand and One Nights* (1704–1717) had great influence on the creation of a romantic image for the Orient. J.G. Herder (1744–1803) understood Europe's contact with Spanish-Arabic culture to be one of the sources of the European Enlightenment.

D. DEVELOPMENT IN THE 19TH CENT. UNTIL THE FIRST WORLD WAR

With the new image of the Orient, conditions were ripe for the blossoming of AS. An initial summary of what had been accomplished up to his own time was provided by Christian Friedrich Schnurrer's *Bibliotheca Arabica* (1811). The first learned Orientalist Societies arose: the *Société Asiatique* in Paris in 1821, the *Royal Asiatic Society* in London in 1823, and the *Deutsche Morgenländische Gesellschaft* in Leipzig in 1845. Other countries soon followed their example. At the beginning of this development stood Antoine Isaac Silvestre de Sacy (1758–1838) in Paris and Josef von Hammer-Purgstall (1774–1856) in Vienna.

Trained as a so-called 'language-student' in Vienna, Hammer-Purgstall knew the Orient first-hand. In order to make the literature of the Orient known, he founded the first specialized journal, *Fundgruben des Orients* in 1809. His achievements were largely in the field of Persian literature, whereas as an Arabist he was subjected to fierce criticism. His student Friedrich Rückert (1788–1866) far surpassed his teacher as a philologist. His translations, like that of Ḥarīrī 's *Maqāmen*, skillfully imitated the originals and became part of German literature. His translation of the Koran (ed. A. MÜLLER 1888, H. BOBZIN 1995) transmits not only the meaning, but also the rhetorical form of the text.

De Sacy molded AS into a strictly philological discipline. Many orientalists of the first half of the 19th cent. were his students. Whereas subsequent French Arabists mainly placed themselves in the service of colonial interests as translators, or pursued historical interests as scholars, philological foundations were developed by, among others, De Sacy's student Heinrich L. Fleischer (1801–1888, Leipzig) and his students. They developed lively editorial activity, adopting the text-critical

methods developed in classical philology. Arabists from Germany like Georg Wilhelm Freytag (1788–1861), Gustav Flügel (1802–1870), Ferdinand Wüstenfeld (1808–1899), but also Dutch, English and French scholars – for instance Reinhart P. Dozy (1820–1883), William Wright (1830–1889) and M. Jan de Goeje (1836–1909) – participated in this process. At the same time, an ever more exact knowledge of the texts was achieved, as more and more knowledge was gained concerning the use of works of the Islamic scholarly tradition. Theodor Nöldeke (1836–1930) wrote his epoch-making *Geschichte des Korans* (History of the Koran 1860, frequently new and revised editions 1909–2000). Scholars like Wilhelm Ahlward (1828–1909), Th. Nöldeke and Charles J. Lyall (1845–1920) made the difficult texts of Old Arabic poetry accessible. The edition, undertaken in common by European Arabists, of the great historical work by Ṭabarī provided sources that enabled more profound presentations of history, exemplified by the works of Julius Wellhausen (1844–1918). R. Dozy devoted himself to the history of Spain under Arab domination. The reception of ancient scholarship in Islam found its first editors in Fr. Dieterici (1821–1903) and Moritz Steinschneider (1816–1909). The latter also presented the contribution of Jewish authors to Arabic literature (*Die arabische Literatur der Juden*, 1902–the Arabic literature of the Jews). Those who resided for longer periods in Arab lands often devoted themselves to the study of local dialects. French Arabists founded Arabic dialectology on a linguistic level; their work concerned primarily the vernaculars of North Africa and Syria.

Many works of this period are still valuable tools today, for instance Wright's *Grammar of the Arabic Language* (1874) or C. Brockelmann's (1868–1956) *Geschichte der arabischen Literatur* (history of Arabic literature 1898–1902; 3 Supplemental volumes 1937–1942), where Arab authors that had become known up until that time were listed together with their works. The problem of a dictionary compiled from texts remained unsolved. Ed. William Lane (1801–1876) was not able to complete his Arabic-English lexicon, which he began in Cairo in 1842, and which still relied on works of Arabic lexicography. A dictionary planned by August Fischer (1865–1949), in which the *Academy of the Arabic Language* in Cairo later also participated, was not completed because the flood of newly-edited texts pulled the rug out from under the project. After World War II, this project was pursued once again by Jörg Kraemer (1917–1961) and Helmut Gätje (1927–1986); in it they took up where Lane had left off (*Wörterbuch der klassischen Arabischen Sprache*, 1957ff.-Dictionary of the classical Arabic languages). Driven by personal experience of the Orient, there arose a tendency to make the investigation of the history of Islamic culture its special task. These foundations were laid by Alfred von Kremer (1828–1889, Vienna) with his *Kulturgeschichte des Orients unter den Chalifen* (history of Oriental culture und the Caliphs, (1875–1877), and the

Hungarian-born Ignaz Goldziher (1850–1921), who introduced the methods of → HISTORICISM into AS. In his *Muhammedanische Studien* (1889–1890 [Eng.: Muslim Studies, 1966]), he showed the effect of the power struggles in early Islamic times on the genesis of the traditions of the Prophet (*ḥadīt*), which earned him bitter criticism from Islamic scholars. Henri Lammens (1862–1937), who taught at the Université St.-Joseph in Beirut, went a step farther in the direction of source-criticism; he put forth the thesis, which is still defended today, that the biography of Mohammed was fabricated out of the Koran and is largely legendary. Carl Heinrich Becker (1876–1933, Prussian Minister of Culture from 1925–1930) gave Islamic studies in Germany the prestige they already had in other nations, and which found expression in the jointly-edited (by German, English and French scholars) *Encycloapedia of Islam* (1908ff., 2nd English and French edition 1954ff.).

E. BETWEEN THE TWO WORLD WARS

The close connections that had existed among Europe's Arabists were broken off by the First World War. In most European countries, Islamic studies now predominated, represented by a few eminent personalities, like the versatile D.S. Margoliouth (1858–1940, Oxford), or in France by Louis Massignon (1883–1962), who became prominent with studies on Islamic mysticism. The *School of Oriental and African Studies* was founded in 1917 in London, and the first to represent AS there was Theodor W. Arnold (1864–1930). The philological school was continued by C.A. Nallino (1872–1938, Naples), and in Germany by August Fischer (Leipzig). His student, Gotthelf Bergsträßer (1886–1933, Munich), made important contributions to the linguistic history of Arabic. Joseph Horovitz (1874–1931, Frankfurt) had a decisive influence on AS at the Hebrew University of Jerusalem, founded in 1925. Helmut Ritter (1892–1971), a student of Carl Heinrich Becker, made the manuscript treasures of Istanbul accessible. Because of the limited possibilities for contact with other scholars available to German Arabists, an important position was the holding of the Guest Professorship for Semitic scholars at the University of Cairo; it was administered by G. Bergsträßer, A. Schaade (1883–1952) and E. Littmann (1875–1958). Some of the most able Arabists were forced to leave Germany during Hitler's years in power, including Richard Walzer (1900–1975) and Joseph Schacht (1902–1969), who found new avenues for their activity in England, and Gustav E. von Grunebaum (= Grünebaum, 1909–1972) and Franz Rosenthal, who built up important centers of Islamic studies at Los Angeles and Yale.

F. POST-1945

German AS gained international attention with two outstanding works: Johann Fück's (1894–1974) *Arabiya, Untersuchungen zur arabischen Sprach- und Stilgeschichte* (»Arabiya: Studies on the History of Arabic

Language and Style«, 1954), which gave rise to a lively discussion about the history of the rise of Classical Arabic, and the *Arabisches Wörterbuch für die Schriftsprache der Gegenwart*, compiled from the sources (known internationally in its English version *Dictionary of Modern Written Arabic*, ed. J. MILTON COWAN, ⁴1994).

Whereas AS had previously been a phenomenon of European scholarly activity, after 1960 it spread as far as Japan. Arabists who had studied in Europe, and later also in the USA, and had assimilated the methods of modern scholarship, taught, to an increasing degree, at Arab universities. Since that time text editions have been prepared predominantly by Arabists from Arab countries. New centers of AS have also arisen in Europe and the USA. Larger-scale projects could thus be undertaken, such as the cataloguing of oriental manuscripts in Germany, initiated by Wolfgang Vogt (1911–1982), or the continuation of Brockelmann's work by Fuat Sezgin (*Geschichte des arabischen Schrifttums*, 1970ff.). At the same time, research horizons were broadened by the inclusion of contemporary themes, such as modern Arabic literature, as well as questions of political science and sociology. Sojourns in Arab countries, necessary for such studies, were supported by research support-centers like the Orient Institute of the *Deutsche Morgenländische Gesellschaft* in Beirut and similar institutions in other lands. The result of these developments has been a stronger specialization in research.

→ LINGUISTICS; → SEMITIC STUDIES

1 J. FÜCK, Die arabischen Studien in Europa bis in den Anfang des 20. Jahrhunderts, 1955   2 Id. Grundriß der arabischen Philologie, vol. 1: Sprachwissenschaft, 1982, vol. 2: Literaturwissenschaft, 1987, vol. 3: Supplement, 1992   3 R. PARET, Arabistik und Islamkunde an deutschen Universitäten, 1966; U. HEYD, Studies in Islamic History and Civilization, 1961

ADDITIONAL BIBLIOGRAPHY: M. M. BAKALLA, Arabic Culture through its Language and Literature, 1984; The Encyclopaedia of Islam (Brill Academic Publishers), 2002– Online ed., and CD-ROM (updated irregularly); B. LEWIS, Islam and the West, Oxford 1993; E. W. SAID, Orientalism, New York 1979.   WOLFDIETRICH FISCHER

Arabic-Islamic Cultural Sphere, the
I. THE NEAR EAST   II. AL-ANDALUS

I. THE NEAR EAST
A. ORIGIN AND DEVELOPMENT OF THE ARABIC-ISLAMIC CULTURAL SPHERE   B. THE SURVIVAL OF ANTIQUITY AMONG THE SYRIANS   C. ARAB RECEPTION   D. MIGRATIONS OF NARRATIVE MATERIALS   E. THE GRECO-ARABIC FIELD OF RESEARCH AND ITS IMPLICATIONS

A. ORIGIN AND DEVELOPMENT OF THE ARABIC-ISLAMIC CULTURAL SPHERE

In a power vacuum between Byzantium and Persia, the prophet Mohammed founded a new theocratic and militant state on the Arabian peninsula in 622. Within less than a century, it extended from the Atlantic Ocean to the Indus. These conquests were facilitated by mild taxation laws and tolerant religious policies: Jews and Christians, who for the most part belonged to national churches hostile towards the Imperial church, were incorporated into the new society with minimal discrimination; their culture was left untouched. This turned out to be a decisive factor in the survival of ancient knowledge. In the west, the Islamic empire encompassed Spain, North Africa, Sicily, some Greek islands, Egypt and the Syro-Mesopotamian region, which had all been shaped by Greco-Roman culture, and in the east, with Persia and Bactria, areas which had once been included in the conquests of Alexander the Great. Here the Muslims broadened their dominion as far as Khorezm, a river oasis situated where the Oxus (modern Amu Darya) flowed into the Aral Sea, and towards Transoxania with the cities of Bukhara and Samarqand. While incursions towards France and Constantinople met with failure, expansion was carried further towards India from the end of the 10th cent. on. North of the Mediterranean, Islamic conquests created a precondition for a European self-consciousness that would not dawn until the → RENAISSANCE and the → ENLIGHTENMENT – a consciousness no longer oriented towards the Roman Empire and its reestablishment, but to the liberation of the Greeks from Islamic domination and towards an exclusive spiritual kinship with them. The result of this expansion was the creation of a relatively homogeneous cultural area, to which many peoples brought their cultural assets. Among these, the Syrians contributed their cultivation of Greek → MEDICINE and science. The remarkable mobility of scholars and a book trade that flourished thanks to the adoption of Chinese paper led to a lively exchange between regions. Moorish Spain [117. 376–381] retained its own peculiar characteristics. Pre-Islamic Arabs had enjoyed a remarkable linguistic culture, poetic literature with complicated metres, and an essentially non-religious view of man and the world, which continued to be highly regarded (cf., for instance, the role of Homer in Byzantium). A tendency towards purism restricted the introduction of foreign words, even in translated literature.

Some of the terms adopted from the Greek by the older language included: *failasūf* (philosopher, also used in popular speech for 'infidel charlatan',), *hayūlā* < ὕλη ('matter'), *usṭuqus* < στοιχεῖον ('element'), *sūfisā ī* ('Sophist', in a pejorative sense) [117. 146–150]; from Latin: *barīd* ('post') < *veredus* ('post-horse'), *isṭabl* ('stable') < *stabulum*, *ṣirāṭ* < *strata*, as in the first Sura for the 'straight path' which the faithful must follow. The Jewish heritage included the Koran's strict monotheism and the prohibition on depicting living beings [117. 130–137], which limited the survival of ancient elements in the visual arts, at least in public. Inoffensive geometrical and vegetal decorative forms like the so-called arabesque, already found at → POMPEII, lived on in Islamic art. The wall mosaics of the Umayyad Mosque at Damascus (c. 715) depict trees and architectural scenery in the tradition of ancient fantasy landscapes. In the private realm, representations of living beings remained permissible, and specifically Greek material found entrance, for instance, in the constellations and the allegorical figures in the frescoes of the Umayyad desert castles [12; 36. 30–35].

B. THE SURVIVAL OF ANTIQUITY AMONG THE SYRIANS

The transmission of ancient scholarship to the Muslims did not occur through the Latin-speaking Christians of North Africa, who gave up their religion and language after the 11th cent. [79], and only to a very negligible degree by way of the Copts and the Spanish Christians. A favorable factor was the relocation of the centre of power into the cultural area marked by Syrian and Greek Orthodox Christianity, first to Damascus, and then in 750, after the bloody overthrow of the Umayyad dynasty by the Abbasids, to Iraq, where al-Mansur founded his capital Baghdad in 762. The Syrians, who were active as merchants, did not lag behind the Byzantine Greeks in their zeal to accummulate knowledge. Divided along religious and political lines between the Persian empire and Byzantium, they now found themselves united under the rule of Islam. The Syrian language had taken on many foreign elements, Hellenisms, and had thus become a useful means of expression for the various disciplines. Under Islam, cultured Syrians gradually abandoned their ancient Greco-Syrian bilingualism in favor of a Syro-Arabic one; hence the need for translations arose. The belles lettres of Antiquity, together with the whole of Latin literature, were excluded from the Syrian syllabus. Of their compatriot Lucian, Christian Syrians only translated his essay: *Ne facile credenda calumnia*. Syrian reception provided a filter upon which the Arab reception depended. The ancient Academy in → ALEXANDRIA, with its emphasis on Galenic medicine and Aristotelian philosophy in Neo-Platonist interpretation [124], still existed at the time of the Arab conquest of 641. Arab reports point to a solidly-structured educational organization [65]. The school was tightly linked to the Greek settlement, and received no backing from the Copts after the Arab conquest. Accounts claiming that the academy then, stage by stage, relocated to Baghdad, where its survival depended on the succession of individual teachers, are fictional [78; 117. 313–322]. Rather, the Academy had held a strong pre-conquest influence over the Syrian clergy and its schools in Edessa and Nisibis. The eminent translator Sergius of Rēšʿainā (Theodosiopolis) (d. 536) had studied in Alexandria under John Philoponus [10. 167–173; 64. 121–143; 113. 92f.]. Medical instruction was attached to the hospital in Persian Gundishapur. It gained particular importance, since the most competent Syrian doctors were called to the court in Baghdad because of their geographical proximity. The image of the ancient pre-Christian world was partially dependent on Christian chronicles of a popular nature [62]. One often encounters an astonishing knowledge of details. For instance, the Christian translator Qusṭā ibn Lūqā (d. *c.* 912) knew the story of the compilation of Homeric verses under Peisistratus, and used it to raise doubts about the authenticity of the Koranic suras in his correspondence with his Muslim patron [104. 640–643]. In addition to the Christian Syrians, a role was played by the Sabians of Ḥarrān (ancient Carrhae), who were known in Baghdad as proponents of Greek science and ancient paganism. Their Old Babylonian star-cult was amalgamated with Neoplatonic theology and Hermetism: they worshipped Hermes, Agathodaimon and Pythagoras, among others, as their prophets. At a temple in Ḥarrān, the writer al-Masʿ. 956) was shown a door-knocker with the inscription of a saying by Plato: 'He who knows himself becomes divine' [50. 166f.]. Their cult, which survived into the 11th cent., also influenced the Muslim conceptions of ancient pre-Christian religion; the encyclopedic scholar al-Bīrūnī (973–1048) believed that Socrates was condemned because he refused to call the planets gods [112. 155].

C. ARAB RECEPTION
1. SOCIAL CONDITIONS   2. TRANSLATION METHODS   3. BRANCHES OF LEARNING   3.1 MEDICINE AND PHARMACOLOGY   3.2 PHILOSOPHY   3.3 MATHEMATICS   3.4 ASTRONOMY AND ASTROLOGY   3.5 GEOGRAPHY AND GEODESY   3.6 OPTICS   3.7 MECHANICS AND STATICS   3.8 ZOOLOGY AND BOTANY   3.9 MAGIC AND ALCHEMY   3.10 THE INTERPRETATION OF DREAMS   3.11 ECONOMICS

1. SOCIAL CONDITIONS
In the 9th and 10th cents., a vibrant intellectual life developed in Baghdad as money flowed in from the provinces. The institution of the *maǧlis* ('session') included lectures given in private homes on theology, medicine or philosophy, as well as debating clubs in which Christian Aristotelians met Arabs and Persians to argue, for instance, about whether or not the earth is cone-shaped [112. 132f.]. This too aroused a desire for Arabic translations. Some Caliphs promoted learning: Al-Maʾmūn (reigned 813–833) maintained a so-called

'House of Wisdom', a kind of academy-cum-library, which devoted itself primarily to astronomy and mathematics [9]. He fitted out an expedition to measure degrees of latitude by Eratosthenes' method [112. 84f.], and tried in vain to hire the Byzantine mathematician Leon [51. 74f.]. Attitudes were still highly receptive in the 9th cent.: significant in this regard is an aphorism by the Syrian court physician Yūḥannā ibn Māsawaih: 'If Galen and Aristotle agree on a subject, then that is the way things are. When they are of different opinions, it is very difficult for the intellect to determine the right one' [67. 116]. On the other hand, this faith in authority fostered the problem of pseudepigraphy, which continued from Greek Antiquity into the Syrian and Muslim Orient. There was an academic proletariat that lived on transcription, and the temptation was great to augment one's income by producing rarities. Critical judgements on authenticity were scarce. In subsequent times, the Greek heritage was cultivated by court secretaries, doctors, and astrologers whose positions and offices had been increased in the course of political decentralization. Much depended on the whims of the sovereign, or the pressure put on him by orthodox preachers and the popular masses they incited [46]. Later on, however, theologians active in the *madrasas* ('schools') made considerable contributions in religiously inoffensive disciplines. An awareness of the the indigenous nature of the ancient tradition allowed people to speak without bias of the 'books of the ancients'. Only their opponents preferred the label 'Greek' in order to denigrate them as foreign. A broader, somewhat simplistic reception of the Neoplatonism of Late Antiquity existed among heretical movements such as the Ismailis and the 'Pure Brethren' of Basra [8]. In their efforts to fuse religion and philosophy through an allegorical exegesis of the Koran, they provoked the resistance of their orthodox opponents. The decisive blow against Neoplatonic philosophers was dealt by al-Ġazālī (d. 1111) in reaction to their denial of the world's beginning within time and the resurrection of the dead. He saw no conflict, however, with rational Galenic medicine [115. 140f.] and Aristotelian logic, which still in the 19th cent. was experiencing scholastic hypertrophy in individual *madrasas* [117. 358–362]. Symptomatic of an intellectual stagnation was, among other things, the continued study and copying of translated Greek literature– even down to most recent times– instead of note being taken of European innovations.

2. TRANSLATION METHODS
We possess instructive reports about the master translator Ḥunain ibn Isḥāq (808–873) [3], a Nestorian Arab who probably acquired his perfect knowledge of Greek during a lengthy period of study in Constantinople. He could even recite Homer, without, of course, daring to attempt a translation [113. 95f.]. In a *Risala* (letter) on the various *translations of Galen*, he gave an account of his predecessors and colleagues, and of his own philological methods [11]. He bought the majuscule manuscripts that he collated and then translated

into Syrian and Arabic in the course of his travels throughout the entire Near East [113. 91, 97]. As a rule, they were several centuries older than the ones that have come down to us. The importation of Byzantine books played a minor role. His translations reveal an insightful understanding; they were not, however, done word for word and are easy to read. Unfortunately, secondary stylistic editing by scribes can often be determined. Half the recorded Arabic translations of Galen were prepared by a student following Ḥunain's previous Syrian translation [113. 100]. Also noteworthy are accumulations of synonyms, that is, the replacement of one expression in the source by two in the target language [118]. Perhaps in this case, allowance was being made for the client's literary taste despite the translator's desire for precision [11. 25]. Names of peoples and countries appear modernized; thus, for instance, the Scythians as Turks [117. 272–277]. Another peculiarity is the monotheistic distortion of all specifically pagan statements, already observable in earlier Syrian translations [117. 219f., 227–262]. The corruption of foreign proper names except for those that had taken on an Arab look, e.g. Arisṭū, Baṭlamiyūs, Buqrāṭ or Ǧālīnūs, must be attributed to scribes.

3. Branches of Learning

3.1 Medicine and Pharmacology

The pronounced historical interest on the part of Muslims found rich nourishment in translated medical literature, e.g. in the myth of Asclepius [97. II, III], the pseudo-Hippocratic correspondence or the scattered autobiographical reminiscences in Galen [115. 136–138]. Hippocrates stood entirely in the shadow of his commentator Galen; although Ḥunain had also translated the Hippocratic works separately, the surviving Arabic Hippocratic texts were put together from the lemmas of the commentaries [117. 71–73, 219]. In the market official's manuals one finds the regulation that doctors, upon opening their practice, must take the → Hippocratic Oath; for the first time, then, this document of ancient guild-ethics was taken up by a state institution for the protection of patients [117. 216]. Dioscorides *Materia medica* received a full Arabic edition, complete with illustrations and the frontispiece portrait of the author [36.; 107. III. 58–60; 119; 122. 257–264]. Owing to the pre-eminence of the Alexandrian School, Byzantine and Islamic doctors formed a single Galenic sect (→ Galenism). Writings by adherents of other medical schools are preserved only in a few Arabic fragments [107. III. 51–68; 120; 122. 69–79]. Thanks to Ḥunain and his students, the Galenic corpus was almost completely translated; hence some material lost in Greek has been preserved in Arabic [113. 102–105]. Post-Galenic authors like Oribasius, Nemesius of Emesa, Palladius and Paulus of Aegina were highly esteemed and translated because they were followers and compilers of Galen [107. III. 152–170; 122. 83–87]. With his conception of homogeneous ('homoiomeric') bodily parts formed from the four elements earth, water, air and fire, and his rejection of → Atomism,

Galen was in agreement with Aristotle. However, Arab Peripatetics opposed him because he had gone beyond Aristotle in his anatomical investigations, for instance with regard to the functions of the heart and the brain [15; 130]. His copious writings demanded a pedagogical summary that practitioners could handle, and one such project was begun with the Alexandrian canon of 16 Galenic works and their shortened adaptation, extant only in Arabic: the *Summaria Alexandrinorum* [65]. Systematization reached its peak in Avicenna's (d. 1037) *Qanun fil tibb* ('Canon of Medicine'). Galenic humoral pathology, with its four bodily humors of blood, phlegm, yellow and black bile seems to indigenous practitioners today to be something genuinely Islamic and, in contrast to mechanized Western medicine, to be the 'medicine of the future' [71. 89].

3.2 Philosophy

Pre-Socratic material is preserved only in quotations [20; 113. 28–42], in the doxography of Aetius [19] and in collections of sayings and anecdotes, the so-called gnomologies. Of the latter, several collections are extant, some of them illustrated [36.; 73. I. 289]. Their content is identical only in part with that of the Greek transmission. However, the all-pervasive confusion of names should warn us to view the historicity of either version with skepticism [53; 55; 99; 113. 43–49]. Tendentiously falsified doxographies are found among the heretical writers, who constructed a tradition of age-old wisdom from them [101]. The atomism of early Islamic theology, in which even time is atomized and the atoms are mere points in space, was probably inspired more by Indian than by Greek sources [7]. Another atomism, more oriented towards Greek thought, was proposed by Rhazes (d. 925 or 932), who was significant as a physician and rationalistic alchemist. It is not clear to what extent the Platonic dialogues were translated [96. II; 125]; they were available in Galen's *summaries*, in which their dialogic character was abandoned. In a quotation from the summary of *The Republic* or the *Phaedo* [45] there is an interesting remark about Christians, who believe in myths but live a philosophical life – this obviously being a contemporary analogy to the education of the guardian caste. Thanks to his description in the Platonic dialogues, Socrates, who as a result of some confusion in the gnomologies was assigned Diogenes' tub as his dwelling-place, became a cult-figure for Muslim intellectuals. Rhazes, who depicted the prophets of revealed religions as frauds, chose him as his imam. Even Khomeini could appreciate him as an ascetic and preacher of monotheism, though al-Ǧazālī had classed him among the heretics [1; 69. 78–89; 113. 50–58]. Apocryphal sayings of Socrates are found in inscriptions on a mausoleum of the Timurid family in Samarqand [113. 59–61]. In the Alexandrian tradition, the greatest authority was enjoyed by Aristotle: the 'example' which, in the words of Averroes (1126–1198) 'nature devised in order to exhibit the ultimate human perfection within matter' [5; 24; 126]. Except for the *Politics* [13], the Aristotelian corpus was available in a complete translation; additional material exists in the shape of a letter to Alexander the Great, the authenticity of which is still a matter of debate [91]. In contrast to the Greek tradition, the *Organon* included the *Rhetoric* and the *Poetics*; the form of the latter, owing to the translator's lack of familiarity with the field, is not entirely masterful. Because of Aristotle's authority, a particularly large number of forgeries came to be associated with his name [29. 53f.; 84. 55–75]. In the course of Neoplatonic interpretation, endless room for discussion was provided by the allusions in *De anima* 3,5 (430 a 14–25) to the role of an 'active intellect', coming from outside, in the awakening of human thought [68]. Avicenna finally defined it as a stage of emanation connected with the Ptolemaic sphere of the moon: from the inspiring union with it, a blessed immortality was granted to the individual soul [47. 123–183]. He was thus contemplating ideas approaching the essence of prophethood. This led to a renewed flourishing of Neoplatonic philosophy in Shi'ite Persia of the 16th and 17th cents., which continues to reverberate to this day in the ideology of the Ayatollahs [18. 725–757; 63].

The work of Theophrastus is preserved in fragments; among them the *Meteorology*, lost in Greek [23; 26; 54]. The principal philosophical work 'On demonstration' (Περὶ ἀποδείξεως) of Galen, who was also valued outside medical circles as a proponent of practical causal thought, is preserved in Arabic citations which go beyond the remnants of the Greek text; they are especially numerous in Rhazes' *Doubts about Galen* [111]. Galen most likely communicated some doctrines of the Stoa as well, of which nothing else was translated. His opponents among the Peripatetic philosophers invoked the commentator Alexander of Aphrodisias, who was considered to be authoritative, and who was said to have personally argued with Galen at Rome; Galen's writings would seem to confirm this [25. 294; 39; 40; 49]. Alexander's work *On the Principles of the Universe*, preserved only in Arabic, contains in rudimentary form the hierarchy of the planetary souls in the Ptolemaic heavenly spheres, which reached full development with al-Fārābī (d. 950) and Avicenna. Plotinus was highly influential, without being known by name, through a forgery that probably first appeared in the 9th cent.: the *Enneads* 4–6, slightly adapted, had been published as the 'Theology of Aristotle' [4; 29. 53; 60]. Here, the doctrine of the eternity of the world was already linked to the notion of creation; nevertheless, it remained a constant annoyance to the orthodox factions. A paraphrase of Aristotle's *Metaphysics* and a letter to the Emperor Julian the Apostate by the philosopher and rhetor Themistius are extant only in an Arabic version [6. 100ff., 166–180; 109]. Proclus, an extract from whose commentary on the *Timaeus* is preserved in Arabic [85], was known as a defender of the eternity of the world [6. 60–73, 119f.; 127]. Also known was the polemic directed against him by the Christian professor John Philoponus. The latter was valued by many because of his theory of creation, which agreed with that

of Islam, as well as for his kinematics, which went beyond Aristotle, and with which he came close to the modern theory of gravitation [117. 168f.]. Another tendency of Late Antiquity that influenced certain groups in Islam was Hermetism. The Sabians must be considered as its intermediaries, together with the circle around al-Kindī (d. after 870), tutor to the young prince and 'first philosopher of the Arabs' [43].

3.3 MATHEMATICS

Greek → MATHEMATICS was united in a fruitful way with a comparatively strong Indian tradition; however, positional notation with a zero was accepted more readily among merchants than among the learned who, following the Greek model, stayed with an alphabetical notation for a long time. Euclid's *Elements of Geometry* was translated several times and amply commented upon; his *Data* was also available. Other translated authors, some of whose texts only survive in Arabic, included Apollonius of Perga, Menelaus, Pappus, Archimedes, Heron of Alexandria and Theo of Alexandria and Diophantes, whose arithmetical algebraic approach paved the way for Indian methods. A mystically-tinged Neopythagorean conception of numbers was imparted by the *Introduction to Arithmetic* (Ἀριθμητικὴ εἰσαγωγή) of Nicomachus of Gerasa [102; 107. V. 81–186; 110].

3.4 ASTRONOMY AND ASTROLOGY

Here there was an initial competition with an Indian tradition that for its part had taken up elements of pre-Ptolemaic Greek astronomy. Of the early Greek astronomers the following were available in translation in the 9th cent.: Aristarchus with 'On the Sizes and Distances of the Sun and Moon' (Περὶ μεγεθῶν καὶ ἀποστημάτων ἡλίου καὶ σελήνης), while his heliocentric concept remained unknown [83. 37–45]; others were Autolycus, Hypsicles, Theodosius and Menelaus [107. VI. 73–81]. The standard work, Ptolemy's *Almagest*, was translated into Arabic several times in the 9th cent. [76. 17–34]; Copernicus still used the Latin version by Gerard of Cremona that was based on it. The *Planetary Hypotheses* and the *Phaseis* are fully preserved only in Arabic. The latter work catalogues the heliacal risings of stars, which also played a part in popular Arab star-lore. The *Handy Tables* were also translated [88; 107. VI. 83–96]. The program formulated by Ptolemy of reducing the complicated movements of the heavenly bodies to the simplest possible kinematic models with epicycles, eccentrics, *punctum aequans* and so forth, were continued by several generations of Muslim astronomers. The goal pursued in the *Planetary Hypothesis* of representing mathematical constructs as physical realities was also further developed by some scholars. The return to Eudoxus model of homocentric spheres, picked up by Aristotle and chiefly posited by Spanish philosophers, could not compete [87]. In order to improve the accuracy of observations it became necessary to increase the size of the instruments, some of which were of Greek origin. The astrolabe, a precision mechanical instrument, served more for private use; in its common planispheric variant, the fixed stars of the celestial dome had to be projected onto a plane [57]. The Romans had no practical application for it, but by the year 1000 it had been introduced into Western Europe by way of Northern Spain. With the reproduction of the celestial spheres, the Greek constellations were also taken over [105]; to facilitate their understanding, Aratus *Phainomena* were translated [107. VI. 75–77]. The sequence of images drawn on paper by Abd ar-Raḥmān aṣ-Ṣūfī (d. 986) was also used in the West to illustrate the list of fixed stars of the *Almagest*, since it was more precise than the miniatures of the Latin Aratus tradition [116]. Astrology, scorned by orthodox religious thinkers and by most philosophers but highly valued at the courts, relied on a combination of Persian and Greek traditions. Among the better-known names were Teucrus of Babylon, Dorotheus of Sidon, Vettius Valens and Ptolemy with his *Tetrabiblos* [107. VII. 30–73; 123. 278–286].

3.5 Geography and Geodesy

The requisite orientation of mosques towards Mecca was a motive for the reception and further development of spherical trigonometry. Ptolemy's geography and system of climates, with its division of peoples into 'northern' and 'southern', was adopted all the more readily, as the Muslim territory extended primarily over the central fourth climate. Interest was also stimulated by Hippocrates' treatise 'On Airs, Waters, Places' (Περὶ ἀέρων ὑδάτων τόπων), on which a commentary by Galen, lost in Greek, is preserved [113. 113–117]. Greek methods of determining longitude and latitude were adapted for solving cartographical tasks [70]; the astronomers surrounding al-Ma'mūn introduced improvements to Ptolemy's world map, which found their way through Byzantine intermediaries into maps of the Renaissance, where they were ascribed to Ptolemy [107. X–XI; 108].

3.6 Optics

The conflict between Euclid's extramission theory of sight that has the ray of light emanating from the eye, and the correct theory of intromission inspired by Aristotle, was decided experimentally by Ibn al-Haytam (d. 1039). In addition to Euclid's 'Optics', texts by Pseudo-Euclid, Heron, Ptolemy, Theo of Alexandria and Anthemius of Tralles were also available [93. 643–729; 103].

3.7 Mechanics and Statics

Following Philo of Byzantium and Hero, the art of engineering also turned its attention to the construction of music boxes and Tantalus' cups, as well as to the investigation of the laws of leverage and the construction of scales, including hydrostatic ones following the model of Archimedes [61; 92. 65–75, 132–140; 100].

3.8 Zoology and botany

Aristotles books on animals were included in his translated corpus. His and Theophrastus' lost botanical writings were worked up into a book by Nicolaus of Damascus that is extant in Arabic [27]. In addition, there was a rich literature of a more agricultural, medical and magical character [107. IV. 310–312; 123. 8–18].

3.9 Magic and Alchemy

Late ancient magic lived on in the popular, non-literary tradition, accompanied by a primitive literature of largely pseudonymous character. A *Book of Stones* supposedly by Aristotle had already been recognized as a false attribution by al-Bīrūnī [123. 96–114]. The existence of a similar non-literary tradition must be assumed for alchemy, which was largely rejected by mainstream philosophy. The attendant literature indulges in vague allusions and aliases; pseudepigraphy included names like Hermes, Pythagoras, Democritus, Socrates, Plato, Aristotle, and Apollonius of Tyana [2; 90; 107. IV. 31–104; 123. 151–163; 129]. Zosimus was known as a genuine author of alchemical treatises; it is in his work that the concept of an elixir (*al-iksīr* < ξηρίον, 'dry powder') [121] is first attested, which by merely being scattered was supposed to transform various base metals into gold or silver. This miracle transformation was performed in a cleverly staged fraud by the emperor Constantine V Copronymus in the presence of an ambassador of the Caliph al-Manṣūr [113. 147f.].

3.10 The Interpretation of Dreams

In view of the belief in revelation through dreams, widespread in the Orient, it is not surprising that the standard work by Artemidorus was also translated. Here the translator was often overwhelmed by the details of daily life in Antiquity [106].

3.11 Economics

In addition to Aristotle's thoughts on the subject, one made use of a treatise, attributed to the Neopythagorean Bryson and now preserved only in Arabic, on the subject of money, slaveholding, marriage and the raising of children [89].

D. Migrations of Narrative Materials

Sura 18, 60–98 contains vague reminiscences of the Alexander Romance. In Persian → EPIC poetry, Alexander the Great appears as the illegitimate descendant of the Persian royal house [16; 35]; this falsification of history was censured by al-Bīrūnī [112. 117]. Elements of the Latin tradition in turn permeated Andalusian versions of the Alexander legend [42. LX-LXVI]. Material from novels, whose circulation in the Syrian region is attested by mosaics, found its way into Arabic and Persian literature [56; 117. 174–181], and Hellenistic or pan-Mediterranean narrative matter is a component of the stories from the *Thousand and One Nights* [51. 376–405]. Animal fables resurface in the corpus attributed to Aesop [98], for which one may assume both an oral and a literary transmission. The same holds true for jokes, where there is a blurred transition to the pithy anecdotes of the gnomologies [81; 99].

E. The Greco-Arabic Field of Research and its Implications

After Western European scholasticism had profited from the Greek scholarship preserved in Arabic, the Renaissance painted this path of transmission in a negative light; doctors who swore by Galen were particularly eager to engage in polemics [72]. Out of an interest in the history of science, the demand for the reconstitution of a text lost in Greek was addressed by Frederick the Great to J.J. Reiske, the founder of German Arabic studies. The work in question was Heron's *Baroulcus* [117. 516f.]. Since the end of the 19th cent., so-called Graeco-Arabic studies have functioned as an ancillary discipline to classical philology and philosophy, as well as the histories of medicine and science. The goal has been a text-critical evaluation, or else, where the original version is lost, to produce an Arabic edition with facing translation into a European language. This, for instance, is the program of the *Supplementum Orientale* to the Berlin *Corpus Medicorum Graecorum*. The creation of a lexical aid particularly for works in translation has now been undertaken by a team organized around D. Gutas and G. Endreß in Bochum [33]. An ideologically explosive issue is the fate of the Greek heritage in Islam and why, after such a promising beginning, it did not lead to the same results and breakthroughs as it did in Western Europe, but finally atrophied, so that → UNIVERSITIES in Muslim lands, unable to connect to an indigenous tradition in the relevant disciplines, are condemned to perpetually catch up with European and American research. Among Muslim intellectuals and lesser-informed European commentators, this has led to resentment-filled distortions, insofar as those innovations which are unquestionably present are exaggerated, and a kindling effect for subsequent Western European developments is ascribed to them. This claim, however, disregards the fact that Christian→ SCHOLASTICISM, because of its initially limited incorporative capability, relied on basic handbook knowledge which was, generally speaking, of Greek origin. On the basis of this latter phenomenon, philologists of a Eurocentric mindset pronounce judgement on Arabic-Islamic culture as a whole, which is equally mistaken. After racist explanations [37; 94. IIIf.] and those stemming from a deterministic view of the rise and fall of civilizations [74] can be considered outdated, reasons as to why the potential present in the Greek legacy did not undergo a development in Islamic regions analogous to that in Europe are being sought by more recent Oriental Studies in a particular intellectual development within Islamic society [14; 66. 231; 82]. Muslim intellectuals regret that Averroes' option of a rationalist Aristotelianism, seized upon in Western Europe, missed its calling in Islam [75]. Vis-à-vis these explanations oriented towards the history of ideas, the deterioration of social and economic conditions must also be taken into consideration [114]. Parallels may be drawn with the Byzantine pattern of development.

→ Aristotelianism; → Geography; → Occultism; → Natural sciences; → Platonism; → Pythagoras [2]
→ Alexander Romance

1 I. Alon, Socrates in Mediaeval Arabic Literature, 1991 2 G. C. Anawati, Arabic Alchemy, in: [93. 853–885] 3 Id., A. Z. Iskandar, s.v. Ḥunayn ibn Isḥāq al-ʿIbādī, Abū Zayd, in: Dictionary of Scientific Biography 15, 1978, 230–249 4 M. Aouad, s.v. La Théologie d'Aristote, in: [48. I. 541–590] 5 Id. et al., s.v. Aristote de Stagire, in: [48. I. 413–534] 6 ʿA. Badawi, La transmission de la philosophie grecque au monde arabe, 1968 7 C. Baffioni, Atomismo e antiatomismo nel pensiero islamico, 1982 8 Id., Frammenti e testimonianze di autori antichi nelle epistole degli Iḫwān aṣ-Ṣafāʾ, 1994 9 M.-G. Balty-Guesdon, Le Bayt al-ḥikma de Baghdad, in: Arabica 39, 1992, 131–150 10 A. Baumstark, Geschichte der syrischen Literatur, 1922 11 G. Bergsträsser (ed.), Ḥunain ibn Isḥāq über die syrische und arabische Galenübersetzungen, 1925 (AKM 17,2) 12 J. M. Blázquez, Las pinturas helenísticas de Qusayr ʾAmra (Jordania) y sus fuentes, in: AEA 54, 1981, 157–202; 56, 1983, 169–212 13 R. Brague, Note sur la traduction arabe de la Politique d'Aristote, derechef, qu'elle n'existe pas, in: P. Aubenque (ed.), Aristote politique, 1993, 423–433 14 Ch. Bürgel, Allmacht und Mächtigkeit, 1991 15 Id., Averroes 'contra Galenum' (= Nachrichten der Akademie der Wissenschaften in Göttingen, 1. Philologisch-historische Klasse, Nr. 9), 1967 16 Cl. A. Ciancaglini, Alessandro e l'incendio di Persepoli nelle tradizioni greca e iranica, in: A. Valvo (ed.), La diffusione dell'eredità classica nell'età tardoantica e medievale. Forme e modi di trasmissione, 1997, 59–81 17 Ch.-F. Collatz et al. (eds.), Dissertatiunculae criticae. Festschrift für G.Ch. Hansen, 1998 18 M. Cruz Hernández, Historia del pensamiento en el mundo islámico, 3 vols., 1996 19 H. Daiber (ed.), Aetius Arabus. Die Vorsokratiker in arabischer Überlieferung, 1980 20 Id., Democritus in Arabic and Syriac Tradition, in: Proceedings of the 1st International Congress on Democritus, 1984, 252–265 21 Id., Doxographie und Geschichtsschreibung über griechische Philosophen in islamischer Zeit, in: Medioevo 16, 1990, 1–21 22 Id., Hellenistischkaiserzeitliche Doxographie und philosophischer Synkretismus in islamischer Zeit, in: Aufstieg und Niedergang der Römischen Welt II 36.7, 4974–92 23 Id., The Meteorology of Theophrastus in Syriac and Arabic Translation, in: W. W. Fortenbaugh, D. Gutas (eds.), Theophrastus. His Psychological, Doxographical, and Scientific Writings, 1992, 166–293 24 Id., Salient Trends of the Arabic Aristotle, in: [34. 29–76] 25 Id., Semitische Sprachen als Kulturvermittler zwischen Antike und Mittelalter. Stand und Aufgaben der Forschung, in: Zeitschrift der Deutschen Morgenländischen Gesellschaft 136, 1986, 292–313 26 Id., A Survey of Theophrastean Texts and Ideas in Arabic, in: [41. 103–114] 27 H. J. Drossaart Lulofs, s.v. Nīḳūlāʾūs, in: EI 8, 36f. 28 G. Endress, Die arabisch-islamische Philosophie. Ein Forschungsbericht, in: Zeitschrift für Geschichte der Arabisch-Islamischen Wissenschaften 5, 1989, 1–47 29 Id., The Circle of al-Kindī. Early Arabic Translations from the Greek and the Rise of Islamic Philosophy, in: [34. 43–76] 30 Id., The Defense of Reason: The Plea for Philosophy in the Religious Community, in: Zeitschrift für Geschichte der Arabisch-Islamischen Wissenschaften 6, 1990, 1–49 31 Id. (ed.), Symposium Graeco-Arabicum II, 1989 32 Id., Die wissenschaftliche Literatur, in: H. Gätje (ed.), Grundriß der

Arabischen Philologie II, 1987, 400–506; III, 1992, 3–152
33 Id., D. GUTAS (eds.), A Greek and Arabic Lexicon,
1992ff.   34 Id., R. KRUK (eds.), The Ancient Tradition in
Christian and Islamic Hellenism, 1997   35 J. VAN ESS, s.v.
Alexander der Große X. Islamische Literatur, in: Lexikon
des Mittelalters I, 1980, 365   36 R. ETTINGHAUSEN, Islamic Painting, 1977   37 H. FÄHNDRICH, Invariable Factors
Underlying the Historical Perspective in Theodor Nöldeke's Orientalische Skizzen, in: A. DIETRICH (ed.), Akten
des VII. Kongresses für Arabistik und Islamwissenschaft
(= Abhandlungen der Akademie der Wissenschaften in
Göttingen, Philologisch-historische Klasse, 3. Folge, Nr.
98), 1976, 146–154   38 M. FAKHRY, Philosophy, Dogma
and the Impact of Greek Thought in Islam, 1994   39 S.
FAZZO, L'Alexandre arabe et la génération à partir du
néant, in: [58. 277–287]   40 S. FOLLET, s.v. Alexandros de
Damas, in: [48. I. 140–142]   41 W. W. FORTENBAUGH
(ed.), Theophrastus of Eresus. On his Life and Works,
1985   42 E. GARCÍA GÓMEZ (ed.), Un texto árabe occidental de la leyenda de Alejandro, 1929   43 CH. GENE-
QUAND, Platonism and Hermetism in al-Kindī's Fī al-nafs,
in: Zeitschrift für Geschichte der Arabisch-Islamischen
Wissenschaften 4, 1987/88, 1–18   44 Id., Vers une nouvelle édition de la Maqāla fī mabādiʾ al-kull d'Alexandre
d'Aphrodise, in: [58. 271–276]   45 ST. GERO, Galen on
the Christians. A Reappraisal of the Arabic Evidence, in:
Orientalia Christiana Periodica 56, 1990, 371–411   46 I.
GOLDZIHER, Stellung der alten islamischen Orthodoxie
zu den antiken Wissenschaften (= Abhandlungen der
Königlich Preußischen Akademie der Wissenschaften,
philosophisch-historische Klasse, Nr. 8), 1915; (Engl. The
Attitude of Orthodox Islam toward the Ancient Sciences,
in M. L. SWARTZ (ed.), Studies on Islam, 1981, 185–215)
47 L. E. GOODMAN, Avicenna, 1992   48 R. GOULET (ed.),
Dictionnaire des philosophes antiques, 1989ff. 49 Id., M.
AOUAD, s.v. Alexandros d'Aphrodisias, in: [48. I. 125–
139]   50 T. M. GREEN, The City of the Moon God. Religious Traditions of Harran, 1992   51 G. E. VON GRUNE-
BAUM, Medieval Islam: A Study in Cultural Orientation,
1946; ²1953, ⁷1969   52 D. GUTAS, Avicenna and the Aristotelian Tradition, 1988   53 Id., Greek Wisdom Literature in Arabic Translation. A Study of the Graeco-Arabic
Gnomologia, 1975   54 Id., The Life, Works, and Sayings
of Theophrastus in the Arabic Tradition, in: [41. 63–102]
55 Id., Sayings by Diogenes Preserved in Arabic, in: M.-O.
GOULET-CAZÉ (ed.), Le cynisme ancien et ses prolongements. Actes du Colloque International du CNRS, 1993,
475–518   56 T. HÄGG, The Oriental Reception of Greek
Novels, in: Symbolae Osloenses 61, 1986, 99–131; Id. and
B. UTAS, The Virgin and her Lover: Fragments of an Ancient Greek Novel and a Persian Epic Poem, 2003   57 H.
HARTNER, s.v. asṭurlāb, EI 1, 722–728   58 A. HASNAWI et
al. (eds.), Perspectives arabes et médiévales sur la tradition
scientifique et philosophique grecque, 1997   59 CH. HEIN,
Definition und Einteilung der Philosophie. Von der spät-
antiken Einleitungsliteratur zur arabischen Enzyklopädie,
1985   60 P. HENRY, H.-R. SCHWYZER (eds.), Plotini Opera
II, 1959   61 D. R. HILL, s.v. Engineering, in: [93. 751–
795]   62 H. HORST, Über die Römer, in: U. HAARMANN, P.
BACHMANN (eds.), Die islamische Welt zwischen Mittelalter und Neuzeit. Festschrift für H.R. Roemer, 1979, 315–
337   63 M. HORTEN, Das philosophische System von Schi-
rázi, 1913   64 H. HUGONNARD-ROCHE, Note sur Sergius
de Rešʿainā, traducteur du grec en syriaque et commen-
tateur d'Aristote, in: [34. 121–143]   65 A. Z. ISKANDAR,
An Attempted Reconstruction of the Late Alexandrian

Medical Curriculum, in: Medical History 20, 1976, 235–
258   66 D. JACQUART, F. MICHEAU, La médecine arabe et
l'occident médiéval, 1990   67 D. JACQUART, G. TROU-
PEAU (eds.), Yūḥannā ibn Māsawayh, Le livre des axiomes
médicaux (Aphorismi), 1980   68 J. JOLIVET, Étapes dans
l'histoire de l'intellect agent, in: [58. 569–582]   69 Id.,
Philosophie médiévale arabe et latine, 1995   70 E. S. KEN-
NEDY, s.v. Mathematical Geography, in [93. 185–201]
71 M. S. KHAN, Islamic Medicine, 1986   72 F. KLEIN-
FRANKE, Die klassische Antike in der Tradition des Islam,
1980   73 J. KRÄMER, Arabische Homerverse, in: Zeitschrift der Deutschen Morgenländischen Gesellschaft
106, 1956, 259–316; 107, 1957, 511–518   74 Id., Das
Problem der arabischen Kulturgeschichte, 1959   75 A.
VON KÜGELGEN, Averroes und die arabische Moderne.
Ansätze zu einer Neubegründung des Rationalismus im
Islam, 1994   76 P. KUNITZSCH, Der Almagest. Die Syntaxis Mathematica des Claudius Ptolemäus in arabisch-
lateinischer Überlieferung, 1974   77 Id. (ed.), Claudius
Ptolemäus, Der Sternkatalog des Almagest, 3 vols., 1986–
1991   78 J. LAMEER, From Alexandria to Baghdad:
Reflections on the Genesis of a Problematical Tradition,
in: [34. 181–191]   79 T. LEWICKI, Une langue romane
oubliée de l'Afrique du Nord: observations d'un arabi-
sant, in: Rocznik Orientalistyczny 17, 1951–52, 415–480
80 M. MARÓTH, Ibn Sīnā und die peripatetische Aussa-
genlogik, 1989   81 U. MARZOLPH, Philogelos arabikos.
Zum Nachleben der antiken Witzesammlung in der mittelalterlichen arabischen Literatur, in: Der Islam 64, 1987,
185–230   82 T. NAGEL, Die Festung des Glaubens. Triumph und Scheitern des islamischen Rationalismus im 11.
Jahrhundert, 1988   83 B. NOACK, Aristarch von Samos,
1992   84 F. E. PETERS, Aristoteles Arabus. The Oriental
Translations and Commentaries of the Aristotelian Corpus, 1968   85 F. PFAFF (trans.), Kommentar des Proklos
zu Platons Timaios C.43 (89 E – 90 C), in: Corpus Medicorum Graecorum Suppl. III, 1941, XLIf., 53–60   86 SH.
PINES, Studies in Arabic Versions of Greek Texts and in
Mediaeval Science, 1986   87 D. PINGREE, s.v. ʿilm al-
hayʾa, EI 3, 1135–1138   88 M. PLESSNER, s.v. Baṭlamiyūs,
EI 1, 1100–1102   89 Id. (ed.), Der OIKONOMIKOS des
Neupythagoreers 'Bryson' und sein Einfluß auf die islamische Wissenschaft, 1928   90 Id., Vorsokratische Philosophie und griechische Alchemie in arabisch-lateinischer
Überlieferung. Studien zu Text und Inhalt der Turba Phi-
losophorum, 1975   91 M. PLEZIA, Der arabische Aristo-
telesbrief nach 25 Jahren, in: [17. 53–59]   92 D. K. RAÏOS,
Archimède, Ménélaos d'Alexandrie et le 'Carmen de pon-
deribus et mensuris', 1989   93 R. RASHED (ed.), Encyclopedia of the History of Arabic Science, 3 vols., 1996   94 E.
RENAN, Averroès et l'averroïsme, ³1866, repr. 1986   95 F.
ROSENTHAL, The Classical Heritage in Islam, 1994   96 Id.,
Greek Philosophy in the Arab World, 1990   97 Id., Science
and Medicine in Islam, 1990   98 Id., A Small Collection of
Aesopic Fables in Arabic Translation, in: M. MACUCH et
al. (ed.), Studia Semitica necnon Iranica, 1989, 233–256
99 Id., Witty Retorts of Philosophers and Sages from the
Kitāb al-Ajwibah al-muskitah of Ibn abī ʿAwn, in: Grae-
co-Arabica 4, 1991, 179–221   100 M. ROZHANSKAYA, s.v.
Statics, in: [93. 614–642]   101 U. RUDOLPH (ed.), Die
Doxographie des Pseudo-Ammonios. Ein Beitrag zur neu-
platonischen Überlieferung im Islam, 1989 (AKM 49,1)
102 A. I. SABRA, s.v. ʿilm al-ḥisāb, EI 3, 1138–1141
103 Id., s.v. manāẓir, EI 6, 376f.   104 KH. SAMIR, P.
NWYIA (eds.), Une correspondance islamo-chrétienne
entre Ibn al-Munaǧǧim, Ḥunayn ibn Isḥāq et Qusṭā ibn

Lūqā, 1981   105 E. SAVAGE-SMITH, Islamicate Celestial Globes: Their History, Construction, and Uses, 1985 106 E. SCHMITT, Lexikalische Untersuchungen zur arabischen Übersetzung von Artemidors Traumbuch, 1970 107 Sezgin   108 F. SEZGIN, The Contribution of the Arabic-Islamic Geographers to the Formation of the World Map, 1987   109 I. SHAHID (ed.), Epistula de re publica gerenda, in: H. SCHENKL (ed.), Themistii orationes quae supersunt III, 1974, 73–119   110 M. SOUISSI, s.v. ʿilm al-handasa, EI Suppl. 1982, 411–414   111 G. STROH-MAIER, Bekannte und unbekannte Zitate in den Zweifeln an Galen des Rhazes, in: K.-D. FISCHER et al. (eds.), Text and Transmission. Festschrift for Jutta Kollesch, 1998, 263–287   112 Id. (trans.), Al-Bīrūnī, In den Gärten der Wissenschaft. Ausgewählte Texte, ²2003   113 Id., Hellas im Islam. Interdisziplinäre Studien zur Ikonographie, Wissenschaft und Religionsgeschichte, 2003   114 Id., Medieval Science in Islamabad and in Europe: Interrelations of Two Social Phenomena, in: Beiruter Blätter 10–11, 2002–2003, 119–127   115 Id., Réception et tradition: la médecine dans le monde byzantin et arabe, in: M. D. GRMEK (ed.), Histoire de la penseé médicale en Occident I, 1995, 123–149   116 Id., Die Sterne des Abd ar-Rahman as-Sufi, 1984   117 Id., Von Demokrit bis Dante. Die Bewahrung antiken Erbes in der arabischen Kultur, 1996   118 P. THILLET, Réflexions sur les 'traductions doubles', in: [58. 249–263]   119 A. TOUWAIDE, La traduction arabe du Traité de matière médicale de Dioscoride: état de recherche bibliographique, in: Ethnopharmacologia 18, 1996, 16–41 120 M. ULLMANN, Die arabische Überlieferung der Schriften des Rufus von Ephesos, in: Aufstieg und Niedergang der Römischen Welt II 37.2, 1293–1349   121 Id., s.v. al-iksīr, EI 3, 1087f.   122 Id., Die Medizin im Islam, 1970 (= Handbuch der Orientalistik, 1. Abteilung, Ergänzungs-band, VI, 1. Abschnitt)   123 Id., Die Natur- und Geheim-wissenschaften im Islam, 1972 (= Handbuch der Orientalistik, 1. Abteilung, Ergänzungs-Band VI, 2. Abschnitt) 124 M. VINZENT, 'Oxbridge' in der ausgehenden Spätantike oder: Ein Vergleich der Schulen von Athen und Alexandrien, in: Zeitschrift für antikes Christentum 4 (2000), 49–82   125 R. WALZER, s.v. Aflāṭūn, EI 1, 234–236   126 Id., s.v. Arisṭūṭālīs or Arisṭū, EI 1, 630–633 127 Id., s.v. Buruḳlus, EI 1, 1339f.   128 Id., Greek into Arabic. Essays on Islamic Philosophy, 1962 129 U. WEISSER, Das 'Buch über das Geheimnis der Schöpfung' von Pseudo-Apollonios von Tyana, 1980   130 F. W. ZIMMERMANN, Al-Fārābī und die philosophische Kritik an Galen von Alexander zu Averroes, in: A. DIETRICH (ed.), Akten des VII. Kongresses für Arabistik und Islamwissenschaft (= Abhandlungen der Akademie der Wissenschaften in Göttingen, Philologisch-historische Klasse, 3. Folge, Nr. 98), 1976, 401–414.   GOTTHARD STROHMAIER

II. AL-ANDALUS

A. THE NAME   B. HISTORICAL OUTLINE   C. THE RECEPTION OF HELLENISTIC CULTURE IN AL-ANDALUS   D. THE RECEPTION OF GREEK ANTIQUITY VIA THE EAST   E. THE TRANSLATION MOVEMENT IN MEDIEVAL SPAIN

A. THE NAME

The Arabs always called that part of the Iberian peninsula that was under Islamic domination by the name Al-Andalus, thus its borders fluctuated considerably between 711 and 1492. The modern place-name Andalucía is derived from this usage, and designates a particular Spanish region with strictly defined geographical borders. In etymological terms, Al-Andalus has traditionally been associated with the presence of the Vandals in Spain, but a Gothic origin has recently been proposed [1]. The name appeared fairly quickly after the Arab conquest on bilingual (Latin-Arabic) coins as a synonym for Hispania [2], and from then on denoted the Islamic part of the Iberian Peninsula.

B. HISTORICAL OUTLINE

The conquest of what had until then been Visigothic Spain was accomplished between 711 and 712 by contingents of Berber and Arab troops. It was part of the large-scale Islamic expansion towards Egypt and North Africa, which had the consequence of integrating North Africa into the Islamic world. The conquerors encountered surprisingly little resistance among the indigenous population, which had apparently suffered from oppressive taxation and political and economic instability under the last Visigothic kings. The conquest was followed by the rule of approximately 23 Arab governors who had to deal with numerous instances of tribal unrest among the Arab and Berber troops. Because of this unstable situation, a number of Visigothic noblemen were able to maintain some amount of regional independence (e.g. Tudmīr in Murcia). A period of relative peace only began with the arrival of Abd-ar-Raḥmān (756), an Umayyad prince who had escaped the Abbasid massacre of his family. With the help of his Syrian troops, he transformed the remote province of Al-Andalus into an Emirate, now with the capital at Cordoba, that was *de facto* independent from the Abbasids and which was modeled on the former Syrian Umayyad Caliphate. A specifically Spanish-Arabic culture arose, whose urban character resembled that of the Muslim Orient, and whose centers – the valleys of the Ebro and the Guadalquivir – coincided with those of Roman Spain. Because of the dynastic-political opposition to the Abbasid Caliphate in Baghdad, the period of the Umayyad Emirs (756–929), a phase of relative political calm, was characterized at first by a stronger cultural continuity with the Late Roman-Visigothic heritage. From around 830 a slow opening towards Eastern learning set in, and with it came a gradual reception of Hellenic culture that had already taken place in the East. The cultural and political zenith was reached in the time of the Umayyad Caliphate (929–1030), which began with Abd-ar-Raḥmān III's self-proclamation as Caliph. He organized his government and army on Oriental models, and centralized the Emirate, which was threatened by separatist tendencies when he assumed power. His reliance upon Berber mercenary troops would in time have fatal consequences for the state. Above all under such rulers as his bibliophile son al-Ḥakam II (961–976), who as a patron of the arts and sciences, made important contributions to the reception of Greek knowledge, Al-Andalus, now repacified, achieved a cultural flourishing that has scarcely been equaled since. Beginning in 1002, the Caliphate fell into a period of disorder similar to a state of civil war, in which Berbers, slaves, new Moslems and Arabs fought against each other in shifting alliances. Finally, in 1030 the era of the Taifa kings began, small regional princes who were organized after the model of the former Caliphate. Seeking to reproduce the bygone glory of Caliphate Cordoba at their courts, they promoted the arts and sciences. However, the consequence of this decentralization of political power was that in the course of the Reconquista (recapture of previously Visigothic territories) the Christian kingdoms in the north were successful for the first time in winning back extensive territories, and some Islamic kingdoms were forced to pay them tribute.

The recapture of Toledo (1085) finally forced the Taifa kings to call for help from the Berber Almoravids, who had established themselves as a force in North Africa. After defeating the Christians at Sagrajas (1086), the Almoravids assumed power in Al-Andalus. Being members of a fiercely rigorist sect, they were responsible for a phase of cultural stagnation and showed themselves to be highly intolerant toward liberal ideas as well as toward Christians and Jews. The same holds true for the Almohads, who succeeded them around 1150. Many leading intellectuals left Al-Andalus and resettled in the east of the country, while many Jews and Christians emigrated to the Christian north, where they played an important part in the Western reception of Oriental culture. The Almohad dynasty, which collapsed as a result of successful Castilian and Aragonese expansion in the 13th cent., was followed by the kingdom of the Nasrids in Granada, which was considerably reduced in territory and included the southeast portion of what is now Andalucía. It continued to pay tribute to the Christians and survived only because of a lack of unity among the Christian kingdoms, until it was finally conquered by the Catholic monarchs in 1492.

C. The Reception of Hellenistic Culture in Al-Andalus
1. Social Conditions 2. The Late Roman-Visigothic Substratum

1. Social Conditions
The specific composition of the population of Al-Andalus formed one of the most important determining factors for the transfer of knowledge: the indigenous population was comprised of a) Christians, who spoke a Romance dialect and used Latin as their cultural language, which from the 9th cent. on, was increasingly replaced by Arabic (= Mozarabs < musta'ribūn, i.e. 'Arabized' Christians); b) Jews, a large community of whom had already been living under the Visigoths, and whose numbers increased still further through immigration, owing to the relatively favorable Muslim legislation; c) a steadily growing contingent of new Muslims

(Spanish muladíes < Muwalladūn); d) initially, an unknown number of pagan non-Christians, who probably quickly converted to Islam.

The ruling class consisted mainly of a) Arab tribes, which were partly of Yemenite, partly of Syrian origin; b) Berber tribes; and c) an ever-increasing number of slaves of European origin. It is worth noting that the first two groups established themselves in extended family networks and therefore scarcely mixed, at least at first, with the indigenous population [3]. Embeddedness in Arabic culture and the use of written Arabic as the language of prestige soon were a common feature of at least the educated strata of these population groups: either the Romance dialect or else popular Arabic served as the vernacular. These linguistic conditions rendered communication possible across cultural and/or religious bounaries, creating a climate favorable to the processes of acculturation.

2. The Late Roman-Visigothic Substratum
Our insights into the cultural circumstances at the time of the first governors are limited by the dearth of available sources. Abd-ar-Raḥmān I was the first to attempt an orientalization of the region by introducing the fine arts as well as theological and judicial learning [4]; yet dynastic opposition to the Abbasids in Baghdad led to considerable isolation inside the Islamic world. Thus one was dependent on the knowledge of the indigenous population, which, however, was primarily acquainted with the encyclopedic knowledge of Isidore of Seville, so that one only enjoyed a reduced access to ancient learning. The issue of the translation and reception of Latin works in Al-Andalus is highly contentious, and closely linked to the question as to which ancient works were still known at all in Visigothic Spain. Our knowledge of Latin literature under the Visigoths [5] points to a strong predominance of ecclesiastical literature (hagiography, Latin Patristics) over profane literature. As a rule, ancient authors were known only through anthologies and drastically abridged summaries that were drawn from a very slim canon of mainly poetic authors. The monumental work of Isidore, who had probably not read ancient works in the original [6], became henceforth the foundation and filter through which knowledge of Antiquity reached the Spanish Christians.

Since the linguistic Arabization of indigenous Christians was already far advanced in the 9th cent. [7], it is not surprising that many works, such as the Gospels [8] and Eusebius' Chronicle [9. 38], were translated into Arabic. More significant was the reception of these translations by Muslim scholars. Thus, the Arabic translation of Orosius' Historia adversos paganos [10], of which fragments are preserved together with other works of Church history, also left traces in Islamic works. From Ibn Ǧulǧul's history of scholars, written in the time of the Caliphate [9. 37–43], we learn that up until the beginning of the 9th cent., the most important physicians in Al-Andalus were Christians, whose knowledge was based on a book entitled Aphorismoi

(Isidore's *Etymologiae*?), which was later translated into Arabic. Native traditions also seem to have lived on in astrology. In contrast, the reception of Latin works on agriculture, e.g. those of the Roman agronomist Columella, who is allegedly cited as Yūnīyūs in Andalusian geoponic writings [12], remains deeply controversial. Since we have scarcely any written sources available for this period, and the knowledge later imported from the East almost completely superseded this line of reception, we are more or less reduced to speculation. As far as engineering is concerned, Roman models apparently prevailed in the field of water management [13]. In the arts, not only were elements of Visigothic art taken over via the use of → SPOLIA, but there were also more creative adaptations: the horseshoe arch as a formative stylistic element is part of the Visigothic/ancient Spanish architectural heritage.

ISABEL TORAL-NIEHOFF

D. The Reception of Greek Antiquity via the East

Quite isolated until about 830, Al-Andalus began to open to Eastern influences in the 9th cent., adopting the Graeco-Hellenistic knowledge that had already been absorbed in the East. It must nevertheless be borne in mind that the consequence of Al-Andalus' peripheral situation with regard to the rest of the Islamic world was that, compared to the developments of the more central Islamic lands, it appeared as a) backward and provincial; b) because of its isolation, often surprisingly original; c) sometimes, as a dead end within the Islamic world. This situation was eventually reflected in the works that were translated into Latin and came to influence Medieval European thought. Three vehicles of this acculturation have been determined: 1) Official patronage of the respective sovereigns, who for the most part supported cultural transfer. 2) The initiative of private scholars, who by way of pilgrimage or business travel established contacts with Eastern colleagues and disseminated their new knowledge in Al-Andalus. 3) Eastern scholars and artists who, for a wide variety of reasons, had ended up in Al-Andalus.
1. MEDICINE AND PHARMACOLOGY 2. ASTRONOMY, ASTROLOGY AND MATHEMATICS 3. AGRICULTURE AND BOTANY 4. PHILOSOPHY

1. Medicine and Pharmacology
According to the historian of science Ibn Ǧulǧul (10th cent.), Hellenistically-oriented → MEDICINE had already been introduced into Al-Andalus at the beginning of the 9th cent. As in the East, the Galenic tradition in its late ancient abridged form and the Byzantine doctors like Paulus of Aegina and Oribasius were predominant, while Hippocrates was, to be sure, known, but far less popular [14]. The decisive impulse for medical science in Al-Andalus emanated from a new adaptation of Dioscorides' *Materia Medica*: thanks to a copiously illustrated manuscript given to the Caliph in Cordoba in 948 by his ally the Byzantine emperor, a more precise translation could be undertaken. This research left its mark on Andalusian pharmacology, giving it a botanical orientation. It occupied a large number of scholars who figure among the scientific mentors of Al-Andalus, including Sulaiman Ibn Ǧulǧul (mentioned above), author of the first Arab history of medicine, as well as the famous surgeon Abū al-Qāsim az-Zahrāwī (Lat. Abulcasis, d. 1002) of Cordoba. Of Arab physicians, especially ar-Rāzī (Lat. Rhazes, d. 950) enjoyed great popularity in Al-Andalus during his lifetime; later the medical writings of Ibn Sīnā (Lat. Avicenna, d.1037) were also held in high regard.

2. Astronomy, Astrology and Mathematics
An important factor in the development of Andalusian astronomy [15], and a symptom of the backwardness of Al-Andalus in this field of knowledge, was the preponderance of an Indo-Persian tradition that reflected a pre-Ptolemaic stage of astronomy (following the 'Sindhind' method), as it is embodied in the Tables of al-Ḫwārezmī. Before the arrival of Greek-oriented astronomy, the Indo-Persian tradition became known in Al-Andalus in the 9th cent., and in the 10th cent. Maslama al-Maǧrīṭī revised the *Ḫwārezmian* Tables, converting them to the meridian of Cordoba. It was this version that was then translated by Adelard of Bath and had a great influence in medieval Europe. A more detailed version of the Sindhind came to Al-Andalus in the 11th cent. through the commentary of Aḥmad ibn al-Muṯannā, and formed the basis of the Toledan Tables, which were compiled later that same century with contributions from the historian of science Ṣāʿid of Toledo and az-Zarqālī (Lat. Azarquel). The Alphonsine Tables were in turn derived from these.

Greek astronomy was available in the shape of Ptolemy's *Almagest*. However, Arab astronomers in the Greek tradition, like al-Battānī, Ibn Yūnus and Ibn al-Haytam, enjoyed no widespread recognition. In the field of mathematics, one noteworthy development was the beginning of positional notation.

3. Agriculture and Botany
In Al-Andalus, this area of science reached a peak that was never achieved in the East [16]. It was based on 1) Greek sources such as Vindanius Anatolius of Beirut (known to the Arabs in direct translation under the name Anaṭūlīyus, and through a Syriac translation under the transmogrified name Yūnīyus, who was falsely identified with Junius M. Columella), Cassianus Bassus Scholasticus and finally Bolus Democritus of Mendes; 2) possibly Latin sources, although this is disputed, since the Latin geoponic writers were scarcely known in the Visigothic period; 3) Arabic sources like the so-called 'Nabataean Agriculture'. It should be noted, however, that this textual genre – because it also absorbed many popular traditions – reflects a pre-Islamic substrate. Particularly representative of this tendency is the 10th cent. peasant calendar from Cordoba [17].

4. PHILOSOPHY

Here Al-Andalus did not catch up with developments in the Orient until comparatively late. This delay can be attributed to the repressive attitude of the predominantly Mālikite legal scholars, always highly suspicious of speculative thought. It is apparent in the following: a) the relatively quick and successful absorption of Neoplatonic thought (→ NEO-PLATONISM) via the Mu'tazila and the epistles of the Iḫwān as-Safā (Brethren of Purity). The most important representative of this philosophical strand was Ibn-Masarra (883–923), who constructed a synthesis of Mu'tazilite doctrines and the mystical theories of Ḏū-l-Nūn al-Miṣrī. His school had considerable influence on the development of Andalusian mystics like Ibn 'Arabī. b) a fairly late reception of the *Arabic Aristotle* and the so-called *falāsifa*, that is, Arab adherents of Hellenistic philosophy like al-Kindī, al-Fārābī and Ibn Sīna.

Initially, all that was known of Aristotle were his works on natural history and fragments of his *Organon*. In the course of the 11th cent., this knowledge was deepened, while the works on logic, together with Porphyry's *Isagoge*, were finally adopted and eagerly applied. However, the *Metaphysics* and the *Physics* remained excluded; first knowledge of them is attested in the 12th cent. The period of the great Andalusian philosophers began in the 12th cent., its first exponent being Ibn Baǧǧa (1070–1138, Lat. Avempace), who was responsible for the fruitful reception of the Eastern *falāsifa*, particularly Ibn al-Fārābī. His ideas had a considerable impact on, among others, Ibn Ṭufayl (born *c.* 1110), the author of the *Philosophus autodidactus* and successor of Ibn Sīna. The most important thinker of Al-Andalus, representing the summit of medieval → ARISTOTELIANISM, was Ibn Rušd (1094–1168, Lat. Averroes). He was a universal scholar who was also successful as a physician. His philosophy signifies a radical break with the Neoplatonic Aristotelian synthesis of Ibn Sīna and the establishment of philosophy as an independent discipline. In the Latin Middle Ages, he was understood first and foremost as a commentator on Aristotle; His enormous influence on Thomas Aquinas and the development of medieval Aristotelianism is a well-known fact. In the Islamic East, by contrast, his views found no successors.

The great historian and philosopher of history Ibn Ḫaldūn (1332–1406) deserves to be mentioned as the last significant thinker: though he lived in North Africa and Egypt, he was of Andalusian descent. He did not become known in the West until the 19th cent., at which time he was enthusiastically celebrated as a sociologist and theoretician of history; nevertheless, he exercised no influence on the development of European thought.

E. THE TRANSLATION MOVEMENT IN MEDIEVAL SPAIN

In conjunction with the fruitful reception of Hellenistic ideas, the peculiar makeup of the Andalusian population (see above) provided the most important

precondition for the move towards acculturation. Those Christians who were strongly Arabized, both linguistically and culturally, could thus act as middlemen between the two cultural regions, while the Jews could exercise their classic function as those who move between two worlds. Only a very cursory survey of the extent and effects of this momentous translation movement can be given here [19]. The first epicenter was the former Spanish March in northeastern Spain, where the immigration of Mozarabic Christians occurred in an environment that also allowed close contact with Gaul. A most important piece of evidence for this contact is a 10th cent. astrological treatise from the convent of Santa María de Ripoll [20].

In the 12th cent., through the patronage of the archbishop Raimund of Toledo, the focal point for these activities shifted to the former Visigothic capital. We are indebted to the translators of this generation for making ancient natural sciences known in the West, long before recourse to Greek originals was available. Mozarabs and Jews often prepared intermediary translations into Castilian, which then served as the basis for Latin versions. Important representatives were Plato of Tivoli (*c.* 1140), Juan de Sevilla (fl.1135–1153), Hermann the Dalmatian (fl. 1138–1143) and Adelard of Bath (*c.*1070–*c.* 1142). However, the most significant personality of the 12th cent. was Gerard of Cremona (1114–1187), whose translations covered all fields. By the time of his death, therefore, the great majority of ancient works transmitted by way of the East were available in Latin.

In the field of philosophy, it was the works of Aristotle, above all, that came to the West in this way, along with some pseudepigraphica, such as the so-called *Liber de causis*, which was based on Proclus' *Elements of Theology*. Of Arab philosophers, works by al-Kindī, Ibn Sīna and al-Ġazzālī (Lat. Algazel) were translated. In mathematics, the translation of Euclid's *Elements* by Adelard of Bath stands out, as does that of a book by al-Ḥwārezmī entitled *Liber Algebras et almucabola*, which brought Europe into contact with a heretofore unknown field of knowledge and a fully developed terminology to go with it. In astronomy, in addition to the relevant books of Aristotle, works by Euclid, Theodosius, Autolycus, Archimedes, Aristarchus, and Menelaus were translated, and finally Ptolemy's *Syntaxis mathematica*, under the title *Almagest*. In astrology, Ptolemy's *Tetrabiblos* was translated by Plato of Tivoli. Medical works include some treatises by Galen and works by many Arab doctors, particularly ar-Rāzī (Rhazes) and the *Qānūn* ('Canon') of Ibn-Sīna (Avicenna).

The 13th cent. in Spain was marked by the patronage of King Alfonso X of Castille, his role as a supporter of translations from Arabic into Spanish was frequently praised. Many Jews who were fluent in Arabic were in his service, as were converted Arabs or Mozarabs. Important Eastern works of belles-lettres were introduced into Europe through this channel (e.g. *Kalila wa-Dimna*), but also scientific treatises, chiefly on astronomy, from which the Alphonsine Tables were developed (see above). The most important translations from Arabic into Hebrew also fell into this period (especially those of the Ibn Tibbón family in southern France); some of these were then immediately translated into Latin.

In philosophy, more Aristotelian works were translated (*De anima* and the *Metaphysics* by Michael Scotus), along with pseudo-Aristotelian ones (*Liber de pomo*) and a revised version of Plato's *Phaedrus*. Doxographical collections like the book entitled *Bocados de oro* (Lat. *Bonium*), translated under Alfonso X, found their way into Europe. Proposed by Peter the Venerable, a corpus of Islamic theological writings as well as of the Koran were produced, which played an important role for later Christian, anti-Islamic polemics. There were also a large number of medical translations, although the names of the translators are for the most part unknown. From the the 14th cent. on, this translation activity rapidly declined, until finally in the Renaissance the original Greek sources became available, and the Arabs were unjustly condemned as flawed translators and transmitters of works of the ancients.
→ Hispania, Iberia; → Isidorus [9]

1 H. Halm, Al-Andalus und Gothica Sors, in: Der Islam 66, 2, 1989, 252–263   2 G. Miles, The Coinage of the Umayyads of Spain, 1950   3 P. Guichard, Structures sociales 'orientales' et 'occidentales' dans L'Espagne Musulmane, 1977   4 M. Makki, Ensayo sobre las aportaciones orientales en la España Musulmana, in: Revista del Instituto de Estudios Islámicos XI–XII,1 1963–64, 7–140   5 L. A. García Moreno, Historia de la España Visigoda, 1989, 365–378   6 M. C. Díaz y Díaz, Isidoro en la Edad Media Hispana, in: Id., De Isidoro al siglo XI, 1976, 141–202   7 D. Millet-Gerard, Chrétiens, mozarabes et culture islamique dans l'Espagne des VIIIe et IXe siècles, 1984   8 H. Goussen, Die christlich-arabische Literatur der Mozaraber, 1909   9 J. Samsó, Las ciencias de los antiguos en Al-Andalus, 1992   10 G. Levi Della Vida, La traduzione araba delle storie di Orosio, in: Al-Andalus 19, 1954, 257–293   12 L. Bolens, Les agronomes andalous du moyen âge, 1981   13 Th. F. Glick, Hydraulic Technology in Al-Andalus, in: [22. 974–986]   14 J. Vernet, Natural and Technical Sciences in Al-Andalus, in: [22. 937–951]   15 J. Samsó, The Early Development of Astrology in Al-Andalus, in: Journal of the History of Arabic Science 3, 1979, 509–22   16 E. García Sánchez, Agriculture in Muslim Spain, in: [22. 988–999]   17 Calendrier de Cordoue de l'année 961 (ed.) R. P. Dozy, (trans. C. Pellat), 1961   18 M. Cruz Hernández, Filosofía hispano-musulmana, 2 vols., 1957   19 J. S. Gil, La escuela de traductores de Toledo y los colaboradores judíos, 1984   20 J. M. Millás Vallicrosa, Assaig d'historia des idees físiques i matemátiques a la Catalunya medieval, 1931   21 Th. F. Glick, Islamic and Christian Spain in the Early Middle Ages, 1979   22 S. Kh. Jayyusi (ed.), The Legacy of Muslim Spain, 1994   23 E. Lévi-Provençal, L'Espagne Musulmane du Xe siècle, 1932   24 J. Vernet, La cultura hispanoárabe en Oriente y Occidente, 1978.   ISABEL TORAL-NIEHOFF

Arcadianism

A. THE ANCIENT MODEL   B. ARCADIANISM IN ANTIQUITY   C. THE REBIRTH OF ARCADIANISM   D. ARCADIANISM IN PAINTING   E. THE INSTITUTIONALIZATION OF ARCADIANISM   F. ARCADIANISM IN MODERN TIMES

A. THE ANCIENT MODEL

Arcadia, the mountainous landscape in the center of the Peloponnesus, played only an insignificant role in Antiquity. The foundation of Megalopolis in 368–67 BC underlined its civic independence, which until then had been only limited. Beginning with the second half of the 3rd cent. BC, the Arcadian poleis joined the Achaean League, whose fate was sealed by the Roman victory at Pydna in 168.

B. ARCADIANISM IN ANTIQUITY

Since very early times, Arcadia signified more than a mere geographical entity: it was an 'intellectual landscape' [2. 257] that embodied a cultural idea, upon which various ideals were based in the course of time. However, this development was linked not so much with Arcadia as with Sicily, where in the Hellenistic period the→ BUCOLIC emerged in the form of charming, unrealistic pastoral poetry. The fact that Bucolic poetry and Arcadianism came to be seen as almost equivalent, can be traced back not to a Greek poet, but to the Roman national poet Virgil (70–19 BC). Virgil knew the historical work of Polybius, with its affectionate description of his Arcadian homeland, which the Roman used as the backdrop for his *Bucolica* (Eclogues), set far from worldly events and therefore unobjectionable to the government in power.

C. THE REBIRTH OF ARCADIANISM

The theme of Arcadia awoke to full vigor at the time of the Renaissance. A precursor in this process was Francesco Petrarca (1304–1374) with his posthumously published *Bucolicum carmen*, which showed Virgil's influence, but which failed to achieve a broad impact because of its meager poetic value. The true founder of modern Arcadianism therefore did not appear until the following century in the person of the Neapolitan Jacopo Sannazaro (1456–1530) with his *Arcadia*, published around 1480. This pastoral novel borrowed abundantly from ancient classical authors, especially Virgil. It distanced itself from the daily routine of a shepherd's life even more than its predecessors, insofar as it gave form to the Arcadian idea as a vision of the 'Golden Age', which left no room for the Christian concept of Paradise. On the contrary, Sannazaro's Arcadianism included an anti-Christian, ancient concept of free love. *Arcadia* made an impressive effect both on its own time and in subsequent centuries, and far beyond Italy. A few striking examples of this phenomenon may be cited.

In 1590, Giovanni Battista Guarino (1538–1612), a nobleman from Ferrara, professor of literature and diplomat, composed with flawless poetic technique his tragi-comic pastoral novel *Il Pastor fido*, which became the model of its genre; this is even attested by a version in Vulgar Greek. Guarino's Arcadianism was based on a strict moral code, and, as he set out in his Prologue, on a moderate degree of freedom; the Golden Age is not introduced until near the end of the work. Characteristic for Spain in this context were Garcilaso de la Vega (1501–1536) with his Eclogues, Lope de Vega Carpio (1562–1635) with his pastoral novel *Arcadia*, and, last but not least, the great Miguel de Cervantes Saavedra (1547–1616), with his pastoral novel *La prima parte de la Galatea*, which met with little success at the time. In 1565 in France, Rémy Belleau, a younger member of the poetic circle known as the *Pléiade française*, published his poems under the title *Bergeries*; here, high-ranking personages in shepherds' garb debated public events in allegorical phrases. Similarly, the Dutchman Johan van Heemskerck (1597–1656) in his *Batavische Arcadia*, offered chatty conversations dealing with history and bygone customs. The Englishman Sir Philip Sidney (1554–1586) went even further, following established forms by setting forth Renaissance views on politics, society, morality, religion, and the fine arts in his *Arcadia*, posthumously published in 1590. A poetically gifted author, Sidney inserted sonnets and songs into his prose text. A German translation appeared in 1629, which was revised by the language reformer Martin Opitz (1597–1639) and published posthumously in 1642. Furthermore, drawing on ancient and humanistic sources, German literature of the 17th cent. developed an Arcadianism of a distinctive character. The desire for harmony and balance, peace and quiet were reflected in the pastoral novels and poetry of the turbulent period of the Thirty Years' Wars and its effects, as was the increasingly strong reaction to the unnatural character of courtly life. In his *Trutz Nachtigal*, only published after his death in 1639, the Jesuit Friedrich Spee (von Langenfeld; 1591–1635) combined spiritual themes with a bucolic setting. In the Pegnitz Order (named after the rivulet Pegnitz), founded by Georg Philipp Harsdörffer (1607–1658), Nuremberg patricians embraced the pastoral allegory-on the model of Harsdörffer's *Arcadia*-which made use of affected speech comparable to that of Italian Marinism. The emblem of the Pegnesians was the panpipe; in their activity, they sought to distance themselves from the bourgeois guild poetry of the Meistersinger.

D. Arcadianism in Painting

In addition to this varied literary Arcadianism, whose fundamental characteristic, despite all distance from reality, obviously contained elements of the ancient affirmation of worldly existence, there stood, largely independent from it, an Arcadianism of the visual arts and of no less importance; but it was, in contrast with the former, almost exclusively connected with the city of → ROME. It grew out of the newly-awakened sense of nature in the Renaissance, which

was reflected, on the one hand, in an inclination towards the heroic, and, on the other, in an idyllic tendency, in which gods and nymphs disported themselves, and shepherds watched over their flocks and otherwise gave themselves over to song and dalliances. The way for this trend was prepared by the Venetian Giovanni Bellini (c. 1430 to 1516), who was of course primarily concerned with Biblical subjects, but provided detailed depictions of flora and fauna; and by Bellini's student Giorgio Giorgione (c. 1477–1510) with his famous *Tempestà* (in the Accademia in Venice). The blossoming of artistic Arcadianism is linked with the Frenchman Nicolas Poussin (1594–1665), who lived almost continuously in Rome from 1624 on. Two of his paintings bear the epitaph 'Et in Arcadia ego' as a symbol of the fact that death is constantly present, even in utopian Arcadia; his *Les bergers d'Arcadie* hangs in the Louvre. Claude Lorrain (1600–1682) painted Greek temples, palaces and magnificent trees, and became a model for Classicism and other components of 18th cent. art, although he could not base his vision on a first-hand knowledge of what he was representing. Authentic representations of Arcadia first occur in travel literature in the early 19th cent.

IRMSCHER (†), JOHANNES

E. The Institutionalization of Arcadianism

Beyond literature and art, Arcadianism strove towards institutionalization. The most important of these foundations was the *Accademia degli Arcadi* in Rome. The former Queen Christine of Sweden (1626–1689), who resided primarily in Rome after her abdication in 1654, made her Palazzo available for meetings of literati and scholars. The aforementioned → ACADEMY, which was constituted in due form in 1690, arose from this; its spokesman was the canonicus Giovanni Mario Crescimbeni (1663–1728). This institution saw its main goal as restoring Italian poetry, which in the view of the Academy members had become barbarized. Here the charge was directed against the above-mentioned Marinism, the bombastic, baroque form of poetry named after Giambattista Marini (1569–1625), which, moreover, by no means disdained to make use of bucolic themes. The Academy countered with a call for stylistic simplicity and naturalness of content. Crescimbeni himself composed a novel *Arcadia*, as well as an impressive *Istoria della volgar poesia*. The members of the Academy adopted Arcadian names and gathered in the Bosco Parrasio. They came from the upper classes of society; remarkably, women were also accepted into their circle. *Mala carmina et famosa, obscoena, superstitiosa, impia* were excluded from readings. In 1711, under Pope Clement XI, the Academy counted 1195 members, and in 1725 King John V of Portugal erected a building for them on the Gianicolo. The Academy exercised its influence by promoting a formal Classicism; in 1807 it chose Goethe as a member, who prefaced the second part of his Italian travel journal with the motto 'I too am in Arcadia!'. The Academy survived periods of decline, and still has influence today as the *Accademia letteraria italiana dell'Arcadia*. There was also a short-lived Arcadian society in Germany, under the title of Phylandria. It was founded by the young Hessian nobleman Ernst Karl Ludwig Ysenburg von Buri (1747–1806), later an officer and dramatist. The Phylandria was initially a small group devoted to the performance of pastoral plays; it temporarily achieved a certain influence in its surroundings, and was later absorbed into the Freemasons. In 1764 Goethe, who was then still in Frankfurt, requested membership in the Phylandria, but is said to have been rejected for lack of virtue.

F. Arcadianism in Modern Times

The revolutions of the 19th cent. and the radical social, economic, and technological transformations in their aftermath caused the decline of Arcadianism. Not until recent decades has a return to the Arcadian idea of an organic union between nature, art, and human society manifested itself in Greece, supported by local associations as well as the Arcadian Academy at Athens, which devotes itself to regional concerns and the protection of the environment.
→ Vergilius

1 B. SNELL, Arkadien, Die Entdeckung einer geistigen Landschaft, in: Antike und Abendland 1, 1945, 26ff. 2 Id., Die Entdeckung des Geistes, ⁴1975 3 Id., The Discovery of the Mind in Greek Philosophy and Literature, New York: Dover, 1982. Repr. (Orig., 1960) 4 J. IRM-SCHER, Arkadismus und Revolutionarismus, in: Rivista Storica dell' Antichità   22/23, 1992/93, 267–274 4 Πραχτιχ Α' Συνεδρίου γιὰ τὴν ἀναβίωση τοῦ Ἀρκαδικοῦ ἰδεώδους, 1984. 5 R. POGGIOLI, The Oaten Flute: Essays on Pastoral Poetry and the Pastoral Ideal, 1975 6 A. SOARE (ed.), Et in Arcadia Ego, 1997

JOHANNES IRMSCHER (†)

Archaeological Institute of America
A. History B. Activities C. Publications and Research

A. History

The Archaeological Institute of America (AIA) was founded in 1879 in Boston, with the aim of encouraging archaeological research and American publications. The driving force behind the foundation and its first president, from 1879 to 1889, was Charles Eliot Norton (1827–1928), professor of Fine Arts at Harvard University. The organisation soon expanded outside Boston and became a national association. A network of local associations emerged in several cities, which were linked in a loose nationwide organization. The first local associations were founded in New York (1885), Baltimore (1885) and Philadelphia (1889). Gradually local associations gradually emerged in the whole country. An association was founded in Los Angeles in 1904, the first Canadian local association was founded in 1908. In the same year Francis W. Kel-

sey, of the University of Michigan, was the first president of the AIA who did not come from the Eastern States of the USA. In December 1998 there was a total of 101 local associations. From the beginning, the membership in the local associations united professional and part-time archaeologists. In 1906 the AIA was recognized as a corporate body by a law of the US Congress.

B. Activities

One of the first projects of the AIA was to encourage field research in the Old and the New World. Norton was of the opinion that Americans had to contribute creatively to archaeological field research. The first great project in the Mediterranean region were the excavations from 1881 to 1883 in Assos, conducted by John Thacher Clarke (1856–1921) and Francis H. Bacon (1856–1940). In the New World Adolph Bandalier studied in the 1880s Amerindian sites from the US Southwest and Mexico. The AIA financially supported from 1884 to 1885 the field research of William H. Ward in Mesopotamia. In the years up to World War I, AIA subsidized some small projects. In 1882, under the leadership of Charles Eliot Norton, AIA had a decisive role in the founding of the *American School of Classical Studies* in Athens. Thus the American students were able to use a study center in Greece. AIA was also involved in the founding of the institutes in Rome (1895), Jerusalem (1900) and Santa Fe, New Mexico (1907). These institutes soon developed their activities independently from the AIA and gradually took over its research activity. The expansion of the archaeological research of North American scholars made it imperative for the AIA to provide a journal for its publication.

C. Publications and Research

The first issue of the *American Journal of Archaeology* (AJA) was published in 1885, with Arthur L. Frothingham Jr. (1859–1923) as chief editor and Norton as advisory editor. In the beginning the journal was published by Frothingham and his colleague Allan Marquand. In 1897 the AJA was reorganized. The official publisher was now the AIA and John Henry Wright from Harvard was the editor. Whereas at the beginning, the AJA published a lot of non-classical materials, its contents, up to the years after Word War I, was limited mainly to materials from the Near East, Greece and Rome. In order to unify an organization made of local associations scattered over a large continent, the AIA instituted a national program with lectures and annual meetings. Within the framework of the national lecture program, organized in 1896, scholars were sent to the local associations, to present the most recent archaeological discoveries. The program was reinforced by the endowment of the Charles Eliot Norton Lectureship, instituted in the memory of the AIA founder by the archaeological philanthropist James Loeb. During its first years this lectureship served mainly to invite famous Europeans to the United States. D.G. Hogarth, Christian Huelsen, Franz Cumont and Eugenie Strong were only some of the first Norton Lecturers. Now AIA offers each local association three lecturers every year. The first Annual Meeting of the AIA took place in 1899, in New Haven, Connecticut, with lectures on the archaeology of the Old and of the New World. The aim of this meeting was to offer the members of a still fragmented American archaeological community the opportunity for a yearly exchange of information. The annual meeting quickly became the main communications center for professional activities and for the presentation of the most recent research results. Since 1905 it has been held together with the *American Philological Association*.

The AIA was always conscious of the necessity to speak both to professional and to amateur organizations. In 1914 the AIA inaugurated the publication of *Art and Archaeology*, a journal for the general public. It published articles on all archaeological and art historical fields, wishing to appeal to a readership of educated laymen. *Art and Archaeology* appeared until 1934, when lack of funds, caused by the Great Depression, and quarreling over marketing policy inside the AIA led to the demise of the journal. AIA certainly needed a publication for its non-professional members. In 1948 the journal *Archaeology*, which until then was very successful, took the place of *Art and Archaeology*. In the years between the World Wars the AIA faced several internal and external problems, which seriously weakened the organization. It became more and more difficult to set up research projects. The American archaeological research in the Mediterranean region was now run mainly by universities and overseas institutes. The last great American excavation financed by AIA was the Cyrene expedition from 1911. It ended with the assassination of Fletcher deCou, one of the members of the excavation crew, and the Italian invasion of Cyrenaica. Archaeologists who worked outside the Mediterranean area and the classical period increasingly looked for their identity outside the AIA. This led in 1912 to the founding of the *College Art Association*, and in 1936 of the *Society of American Archaeology*. The narrowing of the focus of the AIA was reflected in the research reports at the annual meetings and in the articles published in *American Journal of Archaeology*. The AIA was split between ideological and political standpoints. A group, led by Ralph Magoffin (1874–1942) from New York University, advocated the view that the AIA should strengthen its social backing by supporting such projects as *Art and Archaeology*. The other group, led by William Dinsmoor (1886–1973) from Columbia University, who was its president from 1937 to 1945, argued that such efforts would weaken its humanistic mission, which ought to concentrate mainly on the publication of articles in *American Journal of Archaeology*. The Great Depression severely weakened the organization and forced it to stop the publication of *Art and Archaeology*, to limit the conference program and to reduce the circulation of AJA.

After World War II, Sterling Dow (1903–1993) from Harvard brought the AIA to a new flourishing, during his presidency from 1946 to 1948. The journal *Archaeology* provided for a general respect, the financial situation improved and the lecture series was relaunched. The intensive work of the American archaeologists in the Mediterranean area after the war offered rich material for the A.J.A. and for the program of the annual meetings. Since the beginning of the 1960s the AIA has been offering modest financial support for student research. In 1983 the AIA moved is head office and the A.J.A. its offices at the Boston University.

Currently the number of the members is over 10,000, mostly laymen. AIA still supports national lectures and continues to publish the already mentioned two journals. Beside scholarships for graduates it offers a series of educational services.

→ UNITED STATES OF AMERICA

1 A. DONAHUE, One Hundred Years of the AJA, in: AJA 89, 1985, 3–30 2 A. V. DORT, The A.I.A. – Early Days, in: Archaeology 7/4, 1954, 195–201 3 ST. L. DYSON, Ancient Marbles to American Shores, 1998 4 PH. SHEFTEL, The A.I.A. 1879–1979. A Centennial Review, in: AJA 83, 1979, 3–17 5 S. H ALLEN (ed.), Excavating Our Past: Perspectives on the History of the Archaeological Institute of America, 2002.
URL: http://www.archaeological.org/   STEPHEN L. DYSON

Archaeological Methods and Theories
A. CONCEPT AND CONTENTS B. THE DEVELOPMENT OF ARCHAEOLOGICAL METHODS C. CONTEMPORARY ARCHAEOLOGICAL METHODS

A. CONCEPT AND CONTENTS
Archaeology is concerned with all aspects of human life in the past. Primarily it makes use of material remains which, for most of human history, from the Paleolithic to modern times, represent the only evidence. If at the beginning of archaeological research, focus was placed on individual objects, particularly ancient works of art, the framework was then broadened on the one hand by the inclusion of all kinds of material evidence from settlement systems to microanalyses of the contents of dwellings, and on the other by the expansion of the research question to include explanation of social change. The multiplicity of research topics led to the development of various archaeological disciplines, most of which were defined by space and time. Determined by their own research history, various issues were identified and developed and, connected with the latter, theories and archaeological methods based on them. In each instance, these questions reflect contemporary modern interests in and theories about past societies and as well as their proximity to the present. For want of other sources, most archaeological methods and theories were developed with a focus on the remains of non-literate societies. Their application to literate societies, particularly those of Classical Antiquity, took place only hesitantly due to their concen-

tration above all on individual objects and art-historical and chronological issues. The ever-increasing importance which is attributed to the explanatory power of material remains, both as a corrective and as a supplement to written sources, and the increasing utilization of both kinds of evidence – on an equal footing – yield particularly rich results, help to subject both kinds of evidence to the necessary criticism and also to evaluate the validity of many archaeological methods. The variety of archaeological traces and monuments corresponds to a variety of archaeological methods used for their interpretation. Many methods, for instance settlement-geographical and scientific investigations (archaeometry), were borrowed from other disciplines or based on their concepts, and then applied to archaeological matters. They are therefore methods within archaeology rather than archaeological methods. Conservation methods, museum studies and the conservation of monuments also belong to these.

B. THE DEVELOPMENT OF ARCHAEOLOGICAL METHODS

The history of archaeological methods developed with the question of the possibility of interpreting material culture, which ranges alongside memory, narration and textual sources as tangible evidence of the past. The history of archaeology and its methods has been marked by different notions of the proximity to Antiquity and, following from this, the possibility of insight into ancient thought and actions.

1. 15TH–18TH CENTURY: COLLECTING
2. MID–18TH TO MID–19TH CENT.: THE COMPARATIVE GAZE 3. FROM THE MID–19TH CENT.: COLLECTING AND ORDERING 4. THE EARLY 20TH CENT.: THE WILL BEHIND THE MATERIAL 5. THE MID–20TH CENT.: HUMANS IN THE ENVIRONMENT 6. THE 1960S: SOCIAL HISTORY 7. THE END OF THE 20TH CENT.: UNDERSTANDING THE ANCIENT LIFEWORLD

1. 15TH–18TH CENT.: COLLECTING

Archaeology requires an historical awareness, which presumes, on the one hand, a distance from the past and its otherness, as well as its contemporary significance. Archaeology therefore developed, both in the train of the early Enlightenment and its renewed interest in the literature, architecture and art of Greco-Roman Antiquity, and with growing patriotism in northern Europe [21, 45–52]. As early as the 15th cent., excavations were undertaken, especially in Rome, aimed at statues whose aesthetics were admired. In the Baroque period, scholarly interpretation of details superseded a more intuitive enthusiasm [3. 29]. Antiquarians put together catalogues of thousands of antiquities, without further classification or interpretation.

In northern Europe, too, interest in Classical and indigenous antiquities rose sharply in the 16th–18th cents. [21. 45–67]. In Britain, Sweden and Denmark, by around 1600, national antiquities such as runic stones

were systematically catalogued and grave finds even drawn on site. Already in 1697 O. Rundbecks not only began to draw sections, but also to speculate that barrows had developed through succeeding soil deposits [17. 200–3]. This was the beginning of the archaeological method of stratigraphy, which can be defined as reverse discovery and systematic description of stratification, that is, the accumulation of layers. Antiquities were granted a place in curiosity cabinets, along with geological and zoological oddities.

2. MID–18TH TO MID–19TH CENT.: THE COMPARATIVE GAZE

The establishment of archaeology occurred with the introduction of the 'comparative gaze' as an archaeological method. For Classical archaeology, this was linked to the application by J.J. Winckelmann (1764) of the concept of 'style' used in literature. 'Style' described those formal qualities that are common to works of art of a specific nation, era, workshop or artist [3. 32]. Winckelmann classified ancient art geographically and chronologically according to style and he hypothesised a succession of growth, acme and decline. For Winckelmann, art and political and social conditions were directly related. The zenith of art lay in a time of political freedom, the time of the Attic democracy, and ought to be a timelessly valid norm and model for the present time. Thus in its beginnings,→ CLASSICAL ARCHAEOLOGY was art history and normative aesthetics. However, this sense of an aesthetic norm disappeared in the 19th cent. in favour of the descriptive function of the concept of style. Based on C. Heyne and J. W. Goethe, a procedure developed early on that combined intensive description, classification according to such aspects as technique and material, as well as inspection of originals against imitations and the use of other sources for interpretation. Whereas Winckelmann's use of literary sources had opened up new possibilities in the interpretation of representations (iconography) as Greek myths, this was increasingly reversed, by the sculptures obtaining their meaning as illustrations of the texts.

A breakthrough in the field of archaeological dating methods was achieved by C. Thomsen in 1819, during his classification of the Danish collection of antiquities. He concentrated his efforts on find complexes, particularly of 'closed finds', i.e. finds from graves that had been deposited together. He first separated artefacts by material into stone, bronze and iron. Within each group of artefacts, for instance knives or pins, he then compared the objects according to form and decoration and separated them into types. The differences between them he interpreted in terms of chronology. He compared his typologies using closed finds and thereby identified parallel development of types. Based on this he came up with a chronological sequence for find complexes, in which all finds were classified according to material, form, decoration and context (types of graves). Thus he introduced seriation as an archaeological method. The 'Three-Age system' of the Stone, Bronze and Iron Ages, which he developed as a consequence, has since been successfully applied throughout the world. With stylistic analysis, typology and stratigraphy the basic archaeological dating methods had now been developed.

In 1859 C. Darwin opened up new perspectives in the search for early humans with his Theory of Evolution which was based on the survival of the best-adapted beings. However, by finding human bones and the bones of long-extinct animals in the same geological layers J. Boucher de Perthes had proven as early as 1841 that the age of humankind had to reach back beyond the time-span calculated using the Bible. By the mid–19th cent., therefore, the foundations for the investigation of archaeological cultures beyond Classical Antiquity had been laid by Thomsen, Boucher des Perthes and Darwin.

3. FROM THE MID–19TH CENT.: COLLECTING AND ORDERING

The second half of the 19th cent. was characterized by the development of a universal archaeology, which embraced all time periods, and defined societies by their artefacts. The above-mentioned archaeological methods were refined. This was especially true of excavation techniques. The focus was no longer on art objects, but on contexts. Introduced by E. Curtius at → OLYMPIA and A. Conze at Samothrace from 1873 onwards, all kinds of objects were increasingly surveyed three-dimensionally and on site, and stratigraphic relationships were documented. Excavations became scientific experiments, featuring experimental setups and exact observations. With a growing material assemblage from excavations and catalogues, artefacts were classified spatially and temporally, as in a periodic table. Works of art were ordered according to style and other artefacts according to typology. While Thomsen's typology had still been fairly crude, O. Montelius now compiled more detailed artefact typologies based on form, material, production technique and decoration. His typological method presupposed, on the one hand, that the products of a specific time and region were similar, and, on the other, that transformations were necessarily gradual and that these could help to identify developments. By seriating closed finds he established more exact spatial and temporal distributions of types and developed regional (relative) chronologies for the whole of Europe. He interpreted similarities between the artefacts from various regions as adaptations from more highly developed civilizations (of the Orient). He obtained absolute dates for non-literate cultures, for instance, from finds of Mycenaean pottery in Egypt in contexts that were precisely datable with the names of kings.

Antiquity and its investigation became more and more complex. Stylistic analysis, typology, iconography, the study of portraits and stratigraphy were used for the classification and attribution of objects. The historising approach diminished the ideational proximity of Classical Antiquity. Positivistic → HISTORICISM, which dominated cultural studies above all in Germany and, influenced by the emigrant F. Boas, also in the United States, increasingly emphasized the peculiarities and differences between individual societies.

4. THE EARLY 20TH CENT.: THE WILL BEHIND THE MATERIAL

Once artefacts could be dated and located by archaeological methods, the question of the meaning behind them moved into the foreground. A. Riegl turned against mere classification, connection with literary sources and the approach of G. Semper, who in the context of materialistic access to the world ('form is determined by materials'), sought to objectify and limit stylistic and formal investigations. Riegl understood the creation of objects as the result of a definite, deliberate will towards art, which asserted itself in its struggle with functionalism, raw material and technique. The development of art was therefore autonomous, albeit part of the transformation of successive world views. The content of art had to be discovered in the internal context of development and in a process of historical interpretation and every phenomenon had to be evaluated according to its own criteria. For H. Wölfflin, too, style reflected the atmosphere of the time and its attitude to life. The goal therefore had to be the pursuit of worldviews specific to a society and its development. According to E. Panofsky, however, these were not the cause of style, but rather phenomena of it; they did not provide an explanation, but required one. In the 1930s Panofsky therefore developed a threefold interpretative system, which was initially mainly taken in in the USA. The first, pre-iconographic stage was when formal and stylistic description was undertaken. In the second stage, the iconographic analysis, that which was represented was identified with the help of other sources and integrated into a typological history of the theme, and in the third, iconological stage, it was related to its philosophical, aesthetic, religious and political background.

Whereas iconology takes content as its starting point, in order to grasp the meaning behind art, structural studies, beginning in the 1920s, turned its attention to form. The nature and preconditions of a work of art were identified through its structure, that is, the internal organization of its form, its conception of space and shape, which was the expression of a supra-individual will to form and the bearer of the idiosyncrasy of its creation. This nucleus of art – supra-temporal constants of form and basic symbolic forms, which were assumed to be linked to regions and populations or races – was supposed to be objectively perceptible, even in modern times.

Beyond classical archaeology, archaeological cultures, defined as specific types of archaeological material constantly recurring together [21. 161–7], were now linked to ethnic groups. By mapping cultures defined in this way, G. Kossinna (1911) thought he could identify the settlement areas of specific ethnic groups. With his so-called settlement-historical method, he aimed to prove migrations of ethnic groups with typologically comparable finds. Kossinna's often absurd arguments were utilized particularly in Nazi Germany, in order to justify claims to land in eastern Europe. However, a positive contribution was that he drew the spatial dimension, i.e. the distribution of artefact types, into the discussion, and above all that he focused attention away from the pure development of artefacts towards the underlying historical processes. With his so-called historical approach, G. Childe further developed archaeological methods to represent archaeological cultures on distribution maps and in comparative chronological tables. Thus, human beings and the culture-historical development of various ways of life, rather than artefacts, became the subjects of archaeology. Childe turned away from the ethnic explanations of cultural differences and toward seeing the reasons for cultural change in the transformations of artefact technology and methods of production. His hypothesis of two revolutions which originated in the Near East and were of similar importance to the industrial revolution was of particular importance: 1. the transition from hunting and gathering to controlled agriculture and animal husbandry, the 'Neolithic revolution', and 2. the step from village-based subsistence farming to complex urban societies, the 'urban revolution'.

5. THE MID-20TH CENT.: HUMANS IN THE ENVIRONMENT

In the 1930s to 1950s, in a search for the conditions for the emergence of specific artefacts, L. White and J. Steward in the USA and G. Clark in Great Britain began to study the processes by which a society adapts itself to its natural and social environment. Their interest shifted from the investigation of individual cultures towards the relationships between types of evolutionary changes in the form and the function of material culture. From this they inferred a general cultural history of humanity, which White saw as linear, but Steward envisaged as multilinear. In archaeological methods, the focus was on describing central cultural attributes such as technology, subsistence and the organization of property, since economic organization was most closely connected with the variance of the environment. Artefacts were therefore interpreted functionally, regarding their adaptation to the environment. Foreign civilisations were no longer necessary for bringing about change, and internal transformation was possible through adaptation. Stewart saw settlement systems as an essential sign of a society's adjustment to its environment. He therefore initiated archaeological survey as an archaeological method, where all settlements traces in a region are recorded. Individual sites are dated by surface finds, and their size at different times is determined as closely as possible. With the reconstruction of settlement systems according to the sizes of sites, which point to their differential importance, ancient landscapes and the transformations in the intensity of their settlement become visible. This method was first applied by G. Willey in Peru from 1948 on and by R. McAdams in Iraq from 1955. Based on the increasing complexity

and centralization of settlement systems, they were able to observe the growth of political and social hierarchization. The settlement history of entire regions thus became accessible.

6. THE 1960S: SOCIAL HISTORY

In the 1960s, the further development of these ideas by the so-called 'New Archaeology' also brought about progress in the development of archaeological methods. Its proponents, now usually called processualists, turned against the traditional fixation with chronology, the assumption of change through diffusion or migration, the denial of internal differences of societies and of historical particularism. Archaeology was able to and had to explain, not describe similarities and differences between societies. Supra-cultural developmental processes (later also: laws of human behaviour), not historical events, ought to be of central interest [2. 2; 4. 12]. On the basis of systems theory societies were described as systems where alterations in one subsystem caused alterations in another, so for example in technology, which had an effect on the division of labour and thereby also on social relations. This made it possible to explain changes as internal to a system or brought about by external impetus, as multicausal rather than monocausal and as chronologically different from their causes. Long-term consequences of earlier decisions could then be discovered through simulations, that is, through experimental changes to models, intended to explain the origins of archaeological finds [1. 124–9]. However, the complexity of real life was greatly reduced by definitions of subsystems and essential variables and results were sometimes pre-determined.

The explanation of the processes, that is, of the dynamic relationships between the components of a system or of a system and its environment, which led to a social, political and economic evolution, was intended to take place by means of explicit archaeological methods and theories. This was the goal of the 'hypothetic-deductive' approach [1. 49–64], where hypotheses were first formulated on the basis of theories, then archaeological implications were deduced, and finally these were tested against the archaeological material, e.g. by excavation, whereas, traditionally, the excavation results and finds had been the starting points for further reflections (the inductive method). Methodological progress resulted in particular from the search for the archaeological correlations to social or economic developments, which helped to understand contexts that were not directly observable. For instance, if uniformity between the pottery production of different modern societies was linked to the tempering of clay, the forms and firing processes, then, with all due caution, it would be possible to deduce the manufacture, distribution and underlying methods of production from ancient pottery. As in this example, hypotheses and explanations were derived from analogies with modern populations based on so-called ethnoarchaeological investigations. Particular emphasis was placed on a society's internal differences. Tombs or architecture were no longer important for dating and questions of religion, but instead as indicators of social structure and organization, by focusing on the differences in the effort required for building them and the differences in their grave goods and their spatial organization. Great value was placed on the exclusion of random variation, e.g. in typologies, spatial distributions or in the agreement of analogies. In accordance with the claim of being scientifically rigorous, statistics and the probability theory were included in the argumentations. The approach of New Archaeology was generally positivistic: the answers lay in the material, and all one had to do was to ask the right questions. The point was not to try to adopt the internal ('emic') perspective of ancient societies, but to take up a neutral external ('etic') perspective, which also enabled cross-cultural comparisons.

A further essential development, which took place at the same time, was the question about the development of an archaeological context, a kind of archaeological source criticism. The explanation of formation processes, i.e. of the mechanisms by which an archaeological feature developed from a living system through human activity (discarding, redistribution of debris, abandonment, etc.) or natural conditions (erosion), has now become an independent branch of archaeology [16]. While it had been thought traditionally that finds came from contexts related to their use, it was now clear that most material that did not stem from tombs or conflagrations had already been discarded in Antiquity. This meant that the contexts of things during their period of use, that is, their actual historical context, had to be reconstructed. Correspondingly, ethnoarchaeological investigations were concerned with the frequency of the breaking and replacing of objects or with how societies discarded their refuse. Independently from the New Archaeology, interest in the organization of labour and trade also grew in Classical archaeology; construction crews were identified and quarries and mines were studied.

7. The End of the 20th Cent.: Understanding the Ancient Lifeworld

From the end of the 1970s, New Archaeology came under pressure from various sides. Marxist anthropologists emphasized its failure in considering the internal contradictions in social groups as transformative forces. Structuralist and contextual archaeologists criticized its lack of interest in the symbolic dimension of artefacts. However, whereas the former were seeking to find cross-culturally valid rules of the structure of cultural phenomena, contextual archaeologists emphasized the variety of culturally contingent meanings of material culture [9]. As a result of engagement with the Critical Theory of the Frankfurt School, and with Foucault and Derrida, the representation of the past as the logical preliminary stage for modernity was criticized as an ideology that had to be challenged. The 'etic' perspective was recognized as being subjectively constructed. The context-dependency of every interpretation, even the investigation of empirical data, was emphasized as being a physical practice in the present [19]. However, this criticism was also made possible by the progress of the New Archaeology, which enabled further research questions even in the case of non-literate societies through its archaeological methods, and thus contributed to a convergence of archaeological disciplines.

Critical archaeologists now unanimously agree that things do not simply have innate meaning, but that a contemporary interpretation is produced by re-contextualizing them with archaeological methods. This leads some to focus interpretations as a creative act less on explaining than on understanding or making 'sense of things', which results in a multiplicity of equally-justified interpretative possibilities. Although this approach is intended to be emancipatory, it can also excuse traditionally racist or nationalistic interpretations. In contrast, other approaches, particularly cognitive archaeology [14. 369–402], explicitly do not exclude explanations and promote progress on the path of the processualists by including symbolic dimensions. This coincides with widespread hermeneutic approaches, which aim to determine the original meanings of finds and features from the contexts in which they were created. However, often this is necessarily a process where the conditions for its creation are interpreted from the very material whose meaning they are intended to explain. Only when additional information is available, e.g. through analogies or literary sources, do the questions bear fruit. Thus in the case of representational art, questions are asked less about style or iconography than about iconology, about connotative meaning, implicit ideology and the effects that works of art had. This holds for statues as well as for burial contexts or temple inventories, which are no longer understood as the products of autonomous artists or founders, but as complex systems of signs, which were created within their general cultural and art-specific contexts, by producers and sponsors for specific purposes and effects. Artefacts thus become actors within the communicative process, as part of a visual sign language and at the same time they are part of an ideational system, with which society orients itself in the world and gives meaning to its actions. This focuses on the lifeworld-based context of the emergence of archaeological remains, where Husserl's concept of a *Lebenswelt* ('lifeworld') is to some extent used as a modern variation on the concept of culture.

C. Contemporary Archaeological Methods

The multiplicity of archaeological methods focuses on regional analyses and the discovery of archaeological sites, on their investigation, also through excavation, as well as on the analysis of excavation material and finds without context. On the level of finds, a distinction can be made between artefacts, i.e. things produced by human beings, such as statues or pottery, and ecofacts, i.e. organic and inorganic natural remains such as bones, plant remains and soil deposits. The former provide evidence for dates, origins, contacts, social structures and world-views. The latter also document diet, ecological conditions and human activities by means of their spatial distribution. Analogies, statistics [20] and the natural sciences [4; 15] assist in their interpretation.

1. REGIONAL SURVEYS   2. FINDING SITES
3. NON-INVASIVE METHODS   4. EXCAVATIONS
5. STRATIGRAPHY AND FORMATION PROCESSES
6. INTRA-SITE ANALYSES   7. TYPOLOGY   8. CHRONOLOGY   9. ANALOGIES AND ETHNO-
ARCHAEOLOGY   10. SOCIAL ORGANIZATION
11. TRADE AND EXCHANGE   12. MEANING
13. NATURAL SCIENCES

1. REGIONAL SURVEYS

Systematic archaeological surveys were introduced in the 1950s. In an archaeological survey, ideally the location and extent of all sites and artefact distributions of a region are documented with their surface finds. Instead of a complete record of all finds, which would be too time-consuming and expensive to create, a representative sample is taken [14. 70–5]. The results are plotted on maps to show the extent and intensity of settlement over time. The methods for the analysis of settlement systems came partially from economic geography. According to Christaller's theory of central places, specific sites assumed centralised political, economic and religious functions. Various hierarchic levels developed, depending on the complexity of the system. Places on the same level were, in theory, evenly distributed, although in practice this situation was modified by natural conditions such as mountains and rivers. The spheres of influence of central places have been described by Thiessen polygons [1. 153–80]. From the settlement areas determined in this way, population numbers could be estimated by analogies with modern or transmied numbers for the same region; however the population density could vary with the size and age of the settlements.

2. FINDING SITES

Whereas in the Mediterranean and in the Near East archaeological sites are predominantly recognizable as standing remains or rubbish deposits, other archaeological sites, north of the Alps almost as a rule, are covered by topsoil. Since settlement traces such as walls or ditches influence the moisture balance of the soil, they stand out on aerial photographs taken from specific angles, because of changes in vegetation or differential melting of snow on fields. In addition, stereoscopic and infrared photography, as well as satellite photography are nowadays available [11; 18]. An initial overview of the archaeological sites of a region can thus be obtained. The input of all known archaeological sites with their coordinates into GIS (Geographical Information System) [11], a database linking various thematic levels of data such as terrain, rivers, roads or finds with their spatial location, represents an important source for registering monuments or else can serve as preparation for a more detailed archaeological survey. GPS (Global Positioning System), which provides up-to-date coordinates via satellite, is increasingly used for orientation in the terrain or even, to some extent, for drawing up plans.

3. NON-INVASIVE METHODS

Work on a site always begins with the preparation of a topographical plan and a survey grid, in which the location of all finds and features can be recorded. Non-invasive surface studies have become increasingly important. They depend on (regional) conditions of preservation. Stone structures, e.g. Greek temples, are still to some extent so well-preserved that they can be directly subjected to a standing buildings survey. Plans, especially of single-phase settlements, can be obtained through techniques that measure anomalies caused by ancient walls or ditches in the electrical conductivity or the magnetic properties of the soil. In this process, electric resistance is measured based on the fact that damp soil is a better conductor than dry soil and that archaeological features can cause anomalies by being of a different composition to the surrounding soil. A magnetometry survey relies on the observation that structures, particularly those that have been burnt or fired, contain measurably greater concentrations of magnetic iron oxides [4. 543–53; 15. 319–52]. In the case of multi-phased settlement mounds, a more precise urban survey can help with the analysis of changes in population over time or with determining the functions of certain areas and places of production.

4. EXCAVATIONS

Excavations shape the image of archaeology and lend it an air of 'adventure', yet they make up only a small proportion of all archaeological activity. Since excavation always means that the original features are destroyed, it should only be undertaken in a clearly defined way and to answer concrete questions. On a practical level, most excavations worldwide are carried out as rescue or salvage excavations, now more commonly called contract archaeology or cultural resource management (CRM). They prevent the uncontrolled destruction of archaeological sites as a consequence of the building of roads, dams, etc. Since the documentation is all that remains and takes the place of the find, all archaeological units and finds have to be recorded, drawn and photographed with the greatest care. Historically, two excavation systems have primarily been used. An earlier system, the box grid, retained permanent sections across a site, which corresponded to the squares of the site grid. Baulks separating the squares were left standing so that a total stratigraphic record could be kept by drawing the sections. This meant, however, that a proportion of the site was permanently obscured by the baulks. This greatly impeded the efficient progress of the excavation and the interpretation of the site. With the more wide-spread use of single context recording systems, where each archaeological feature and deposit is recorded as a separate stratigraphic unit, and the introduction of the Harris matrix [7] in the 1970s, which provided an easy-to-understand and comprehensive record of the stratigraphy of a site, the box grid excavation was mostly supplanted by open area excavations. Here sections are more flexibly retained, recorded and removed where they are needed to facilitate an understanding of the stratigraphy of the site. This excavation system works particularly well in conjunction with the use of total stations for surveying the site as the excavation progresses.

5. STRATIGRAPHY AND FORMATION PROCESSES

Archaeological sites mostly developed as complex sequences of use, abandonment and re-use. This process is called stratification, that is, the deposition of various archaeological contexts. Primarily, contexts are all three-dimensional features such as soil or refuse deposits or walls. The retrospective description of the entire three-dimensional feature during its excavation and the analysis of its development over time is called stratigraphy. Conclusions are drawn from the relationships of contexts with each other about the sequence of their formation. The basic assumption is that a context that is above or cuts another context is more recent. Stratigraphy therefore is the transposition of the spatial dimension into a temporal one. Thus it makes sense also to consider cuts, e.g. of a pit, which take up no physical space but have a place in the chronological development of a site, as separate contexts [7].

The definition of contexts also created units useful for seriations. The context is the key to the reconstruction of past activity and for interpreting the meaning of the objects that were found. During excavation the contexts therefore have to be described exactly: their dimensions, their composition, their relationships with other contexts and their formation. A distinction is made between culturally determined formation processes caused by the activities of people (building houses, separating garbage) and non-cultural, natural formation processes, such as wind erosion, each of which leave behind specific traces [16]. Micromorphological analyses [6] of deposits provide further information about their formation or the use of space, particularly on the basis of organic residues. Special finds are measured in three dimensions, while other finds, e.g. pottery, are collected separately according to their context, to enable the reconstruction of past activities. Contexts are investigated horizontally to determine various past activities and vertically to gain an understanding of changes through time, and are combined into layers.

6. INTRA-SITE ANALYSES

The methods of → ARCHAEOLOGICAL STRUCTURAL RESEARCH are essential and integral components of archaeological methods. They include intra-site analyses, e.g. of the distribution of public and private buildings and of settlement plans, the interpretation of architecture, its elements and decoration and statistical analyses of the distributions of finds to study the different uses of individual buildings and sites.

7. TYPOLOGY

Artefacts from excavations or the art market can be classified typologically and stylistically. Typology as general classification is one of the oldest archaeological methods (see above). Although it was first only used to determine the spatial and temporal distribution of artefacts and the state of technology, its use today is highly diversified. In spite of the debate about the right methods for obtaining typologies and their exact value as evidence [1. 207–30], they are compiled based on the fact that specific attributes of objects, e.g. raw materials, colour, size and proportions, are important for answering specific questions. The concrete form of a typology thus depends on the research questions. This is best demonstrated in the case of pottery, since it is ubiquitous, can be shaped in an infinite variety of ways, is quickly produced and easily broken. Pottery therefore displays high rates of replacement and changes in shape and decoration. Ceramic typologies are based on wares, defined by clay type, temper, production technique and firing, or by shapes and possible decoration. Wares point to clay deposits and modes of production, shapes point to use, decoration to artists, messages and social contacts, and all three indicate dates and areas of origin [13]. There are, therefore, many meaningful possibilities for classification, although only in a few cases, for instance in that of Greek prize amphorae, is it certain that today's types correspond to ancient classifications.

8. CHRONOLOGY

Stratigraphy, typology, studies of style and seriation are archaeological methods for obtaining relative chronologies. Relative chronologies determine the chronological relationships of two or more archaeological contexts or objects. Absolute chronology, on the other hand, gives a precise date, by texts and coins, for example. The latter provide the contexts in which they were found with a date after which the contexts must have been created (*terminus post quem*). Most absolute dates rely on comparisons with securely dated objects. Through long archaeological practice a dense network of dates has thus been developed for almost all objects. Since the time of Thomsen, seriation (see above) has been one of the methods used in this. While at that time individual objects and generalised formal trends were compared, the method has become more precise with more finds from excavations. Since specific types developed, gained in popularity and fell out of fashion, no longer only their presence, but also their frequency is included in the seriation. With the Brainerd-Robinson matrix of 1951 [20], not only similar proportions of types in various units but also their differences were taken into account. Both were placed in relation to each other, and the percentage of similarity between any two units was thus compared. Since then, various coefficients of similarity and other statistical methods (cluster analysis) have been introduced to describe similarities between groups of artefacts.

Scientific methods provide absolute dates. Various methods are based on the measurement of the rates of decay of radioactive material. Of these, radiocarbon (14C) dating [4. 23–34] can also be used in historical periods. This method is based on the principle that living organisms absorb small quantities of radioactive 14C along with air. The difference between the quantity of 14C in dead organisms and that in living ones can be calculated in years by means of the known half-life of 14C. However, since the concentration of 14C has varied over the course of the earth's history, the dates have to be calibrated. This is done using dendrochronology [4. 35–46], which is based on growth rings of trees forming differently each year because of climatic variations. By comparing tree ring sequences, pieces of wood can be dated to a specific year, in central Europe as far back as *c.* 10,000 BC. Wood samples can, on the one hand, help with the calibration of 14C dates, while on the other hand, they can provide the date when the tree was felled, e.g. for the construction of a house. Thermoluminescence is a method for dating objects with mineral content, especially pottery. Here the radioactivity that has been absorbed since firing is released and measure by heating the sample to a high temperature [4. 46–62; 10. 398–418].

9. Analogies and Ethnoarchaeology

To be able to answer more specific questions of social and economic or functional history, archaeology makes intensive use of analogies, which are often obtained through ethnoarchaeology. From the beginnings of archaeology, artefacts were described using analogies, which were taken from ethnological observations, especially of one's own culture. This is as true of the identification of ceramic pottery vessels as jugs, as it is for that of sculptures as art. Ethnoarchaeology developed in the 1960s as a reflexive method out of dissatisfaction with the subjectivity and lack of consistency of analogies. Archaeologists themselves now studied behaviours in societies in specific ecological and social circumstances, in order to close the gap between archaeological finds and features and the past activities that had led to their creation. In the process, the demands that were made of analogies have grown constantly [1. 85–108]. The combination of various analogies aims to explain complex political and social relations, e.g. the behaviour of nomads between major polities.

10. Social Organization

The centrality of social organization as a topic in archaeology has been variously addressed above. The levels of social organization are inferred from settlement systems (see above) and communal building projects, e.g. temples and canals, and potential conflicts from fortifications. The intra-site comparison of the architecture and furnishings of private dwellings and the comparison of tombs and of their funerary furnishings enable more detailed analyses. The organization of labour may be inferred from the degree of specialization within settlements and in the manufacturing process, e.g. in its

standardization. Thus, it has been possible to distinguish the hands of different craftsmen on Greek temples or on the reliefs of Persepolis, and the organization of group labour has been clarified. The reconstruction of ancient technologies is a separate, quite diverse area, which ranges from the study of ancient mines and smelting to the analysis of tool traces and casting processes, or the production rate of pottery.

11. Trade and Exchange

An important aspect of social organization is how symbols and goods were exchanged [14. 335–68]. This includes limited exchange on a local or socially equal level (*peer polity interaction*) as well as super-regional trade. This is attested, e.g. by the discovery of imports and imitations of objects as well as of shipwrecks by underwater archaeology. Special cases are identifiable workshops of Greek vase-producers or stamped Roman amphorae, whose distribution as receptacles of the actual traded goods can be traced perfectly. Trade is represented on distribution maps. In the case of trade with Roman pottery the supply areas of specific workshops can be distinguished using distribution maps that incorporate quantified data. A multitude of scientific analyses of the compositions of the material [14. 343–50] can help to identify the provenance of metals, glass and pottery. The type of trade, i.e. direct, via middlemen or on a market, can be inferred from the distribution and manufacture of objects. The sum of these observations leads to the identification of general exchange mechanisms, which in economic history are separated into reciprocal exchange, redistribution and market exchange.

12. Meaning

As in the case of texts, the reception history of objects begins with their completion. Even their functional meaning can often be determined only by the contexts in which they were used. Function frequently varies with the contexts, e.g. as a cultic object or as an object of everyday use. However, new interpretative possibilities are opened up when, for instance, several statues in context receive a new meaning as a collective programme. Variation of meaning also holds for pictorial motifs, which are often considered to have represented explicit messages, but which may take on different meanings in the context of a grave or a household. Motifs may even have been chosen deliberately because of their ambiguity, or on the other hand by chance. A multitude of meanings certainly arises in past and, even more so, in modern interpretations, by incorporating different kinds of background knowledge. Antique pictorial motifs in Christian interpretation may serve as an example. Thus, interpretation is possible only within a broad concept of iconology. The symbolic, e.g. magical content of objects or meaning relevant to status, can, if at all, only be reconstructed through reflexive hermeneutic processes that make use of as many varied sources as possible (see above).

13. Natural Sciences

Zooarchaeology and archaeobotany are concerned with ecofacts, while physical anthropology and human osteology deal with human remains. Diet, domestication of animals and the development of agriculture can be inferred from the identification of animal bones and plant remains as well as from tooth wear. Bones of wild animals, mollusks and pollen analyses enable an extensive reconstruction of environmental conditions. Pollen cores attest to variations in climate. Slaughtering practices, identified by the age of slaughtered young animals, help to determine whether settlements were used seasonally. Vessels are increasingly studied for remains of their contents.

In addition to the scientific dating and prospection approaches, diverse methods of material analysis are available for identifying metal alloys or techniques. Specific combinations of minerals in ceramics facilitate the identification of the origin of clay. These combinations can be identified with thin section analysis or neutron activation analysis, where smallest quantities of ceramics are fired at with neutrons, which activate the trace elements [13. 140–50]. However, all too often scientific methods are not employed or remain unconnected alongside discourse in the humanities. A new example of the latter is the debate surrounding genetic analyses, which are used, e.g. for ascertaining kinship in burial grounds. But they are also used for determining ethnic relationships between ancient and modern peoples. In contrast, sociology and ethnology emphasize the socially constructed nature and changeability of ethnic definitions of foreignness and sameness, which have nothing to do with genes. This debate is part of a renewed discussion about whether humans are determined by biology or by culture which has accompanied the development of archaeological methods and theories since the 19th cent.

→ Antiquities collections; → Classical Archaeology; → Cultural anthropology; → Epochs, concept of; → Near Eastern archaeology; → Prints, books containing; → Style, Style analysis, Stylistic analysis; → Underwater archaeology;

1 R. Bernbeck, Theorien in der Archäologie, 1997   2 L. R. and S. R. Binford (eds.), New Perspectives in Archaeology, 1968   3 A. H. Borbein, Zur Entwicklung der archäologischen Forschung im 18. und 19. Jahrhundert, in: R. Kurzrock (ed.), Archäologie: Forschung und Information, 1977, 28–42   4 D. R. Brothwell and A. M. Pollard, Handbook of Archaeological Sciences, 2001   5 D. L. Clarke, Analytical Archaeology, 1968   6 M. A. Courty et al., Soils and Micromorphology in Archaeology, 1989   7 E. C. Harris, Principles of Archaeological Stratigraphy, ²1989   8 I. Hodder, The Archaeological Process, 1999   9 I. Hodder and S. Hudson, Reading the Past: Current Approaches to interpretation in Archaeology, ³2003   10 M. Johnson, Archaeological Theory, 1999   11 G. Lock, Using Computers in Archaeology, 2003   12 G. Lucas, Critical Approaches to Fieldwork, 2001   13 C. Orton et al., Pottery in Archaeology, 1993   14 C. Renfrew and P. Bahn, Archaeology: Theories, Methods and Practice, ⁴2004   15 R. Rottländer, Einführung in die naturwissenschaftlichen Methoden in der Archäologie 1983   16 M. B. Schiffer, Formation Processes of the Archaeological Record, 1987   17 A. Schnapp, La conquête du passé: aux origines de l'archéologie, 1993   18 I. Scollar et al., Archaeological Prospecting and Remote Sensing, 1990   19 M. Shanks and C. Tilley, Social Theory and Archaeology, 1987   20 S. Shennan, Quantifying Archaeology, ²1997   21 B. G. Trigger, A History of Archaeological Thought, 1991.   STEFAN R. HAUSER

Archaeological Park

A. Basic Concept B. Precursors C. Important Archaeological Parks D. Contemporary Uses

A. Basic Concept

The Archaeological Park (AP) concept is not well-defined, and how the AP differs from great excavation areas, with many restored, rebuilt or reconstructed buildings (such as → Athens, the agora with the stoa of Attalus; Ephesus, the library of Celsus; Pergamon, Traianeum) is not clear. The concept emerged for the first time in Germany at the beginning of the 1970s. Inspired by the methodological and theoretical discussions taking place at that time in the field of museum publicity, those in charge of managing archaeological cultural resources also started to reflect on their aims, subject matter and possible didactic initiatives. All this was further stimulated by the obvious growth of the interest of mass tourism in archaeological sites. The view developed that excavations should not be oriented only towards scientific goals and that, along with the necessary protection of building remains, the archaeological sites should meet the expectations of larger categories of visitors. A central role was assigned to the demand for visual realism. In many Mediterranean countries, because the remains of ancient buildings are better preserved, this is attainable by reusing original building parts in the reconstruction (*anastylosis*).

By contrast, more comprehensive forms of visitor-oriented treatment of the *in situ* remains are necessary in Central Europe. The AP concept pursues a particularly imaginative form of visualization. Exponents of traditional management of cultural resources, some of whom apply A. Riegl's categories of the monument value of the historical buildings also to AP, are critically opposed to this.

An AP does not just restrict itself to presenting the original foundations of buildings left visible in the field which it then usually protects with a little restoration masonry. Rather, it is characterized by an ensemble of wholly or partially reconstructed buildings on the historical site, i.e. superimposed on the original *in situ* finds which have usually only been minimally preserved (see *infra* on the concept of reconstruction). Both of these characteristics distinguish an AP from the usual open air museum, which mostly consists of a series of historical monuments, moved out of their original contexts, or freely adapted structures, i.e., those reconstructed on another site (Alphen a.d. Rijn/Holland, Archeon; Augst/Switzerland, the Roman House; Berg en Dal/Holland, the Bijbels Openluchtmuseum; Malibu/USA, the J.P. Getty Museum; Unteruhldingen/Germany, pile dwelling settlement). The reconstruction over the original finds is sometimes criticized as a violation of Art. 15 of the Venice Chart (1964), which only allows the use of *anastylosis* on archaeological sites. The surroundings of the buildings in an AP are usually created though landscape gardening; trees and hedges may partly serve as substitutes for previously existing architectural structures (Fig. 4). These attributes can be found already in the *castellum* from Saalburg im Taunus, which was partially rebuilt towards the end of the 19th cent. and can be seen as an early forerunner of the AP. Some older open air museums, organized especially on pre- and protohistorical settlement sites (such as those in Biskupin/Poland, Eketorp/Sweden, Gro(Raden/Germany) also show traits related to the AP. Finally, even before the 1970s, some archaeological sites, such as those in Magdalensberg/Austria, Schwarzenacker/Germany or sections from Hadrian's Wall/Great Britain, were shaped through comprehensive reconstruction, restoration and landscaping measures, and thus all have the characteristics of the present-day AP Isolated elements can be found also on archaeological sites of the Mediterranean area (Ampurias/Spain).

B. Precursors

Saalburg/Germany (reconstruction begun in 1898; full reconstruction of fortification wall, of the *principia*, of the *horreum*, and of two barracks; partial reconstruction of the *praetorium*); Magdalensberg/Austria (begun in 1949; full reconstruction of approximately 25 houses and trade shops), Römermuseum Schwarzenacker/Germany (begun in 1966; full and partial reconstruction of several houses.)

C. Important Archaeological Parks

The Xanten AP (begun in 1973; representation of the ancient road system in the environs; partial reconstruction of the amphitheater and of the port temple; full reconstruction of the guest house with protruding portico and baths, a section of the city wall with several towers and the northern city gate; protective building over the public baths, Fig. 3); the Cambodunum AP/Germany (begun in 1983; full or partial reconstruction of several sacred buildings and of the *portico* of the Gallo-Roman temple area); the Carnuntum AP/Austria (begun in 1988; full reconstruction of the Diana temple with protruding portico; partial reconstruction of the amphitheater planned).

The construction techniques and materials for the reconstructions of AP follow, as closely as possible, the ancient models. The compatibility of the modern additions with the construction materials used in the original finds is seen as an important criterion in the execution of the building. The dividing line between the original finds and the reconstructions is made recognizable mostly by the use of various visible means (protruding edges, a lead band, or rows of bricks). Besides the thorough analysis of the archaeological context, the preserved construction parts and other significant evidence, similar and better preserved buildings of the same type and, where appropriate, ancient written sources, such as M. Vitruvius Pollio are used as well in the reconstruction. The goal is to achieve the maximum of scientifically-founded realism and authenticity. Finally, an indirect goal of the reconstruction is a knowledge of ancient building techniques that can only be gained from practice. Nevertheless, no such replica can ever be an exact copy in every detail of its model: the knowledge gaps regarding many details admit alternative solutions. The necessity of deciding on one of several conceivable possibilities is inevitably a simplification that can only have the nature of an approximation. Thus the similarity of the replica to the ancient model varies. While the reconstruction of Mediterranean sacral architecture, because of its canonical use of forms, is possible even in great detail on the basis of a few significant building parts and can receive further authentication through comparison (Xanten, the port temple; Carnuntum, the Diana temple), the reconstruction of secular buildings, such as houses, trade shops, baths and the like, and also of indigenous sacred buildings is burdened with considerably greater uncertainty. That is why the reconstructions in AP are frequently better described as models at a 1:1 scale.

The model character of the reconstructions is especially obvious in those details carried out to achieve immediate didactic purposes: only partially plastered wall surfaces and wall segments (Xanten, amphitheater; Schwarzenacker, House 3; Kempten, the hall of the Gallo-Roman temple area), columns in various stages of completeness, and sections where polychromy is indicated (Xanten, the port temple), cut or half-finished walls (Xanten, city wall; Magdalensberg, houses from the south slope) are supposed to offer insights into ancient construction techniques and indications of the architectural characteristics of the original buildings. Finally, seared beam stumps and broken down walls are attempts to include in the reconstruction even the historical dimension, in this case, the destruction of the building (Schwarzenacker, house 16–17, Fig. 1).

Because of mostly fragmentary knowledge, the arrangement of the interior in full reconstructions is usually patterned on finds from better preserved sites and has, therefore, the character of an ideal type; also supplying the rooms with furniture, utensils, etc. is frequently accomplished by introducing copies of finds from other places or free imitations fashioned with the aid of pictorial representations. The wall paintings usually follow models from geographically neighbouring regions and from the same time period (Xanten, the guest house; Fig. 2), to which, in some cases, the similar function of the building is added (Xanten, the baths of the guest house). The reconstruction and organization

Fig. 1: Schwarzenacker, recreated wall of House 16–17.
With Permission of the author

Fig. 2: Xanten, Archeological park: guest rooms
at the park inn.
With Permission of the author

Fig. 3: Xanten,
Archaeological
park: amphitheatre,
inn, city wall,
towers and gates.
*With Permission of
the author*

Fig. 4: Kempten, Archaeological park: sacred buildings.
With Permission of the author

of space used for trade, such as *tabernae* or *thermopolia* is mostly based on well preserved counterparts from Ostia and from the towns near Vesuvius (Xanten, *thermopolium* in the guest house; Schwarzenacker, *taberna* house 1). These locations also offer the models for reconstructions of functional bath installations and windows true to the original (Xanten, the *thermae* from the guest house). A special case is the protective building over the public baths in Xanten which, although constructed of contemporary glass and steel, reproduces the overall appearance and size of the ancient building.

D. CONTEMPORARY USES

The reconstructed buildings are used in various ways. The most immediate connection between the ancient site and the reconstruction is realized when the contemporary building serves both to protect and to display the original remains (Xanten, the port temple: the podium extends freely over the foundation slab). But they may be also used as exhibition spaces (Magdalensberg; Saalburg), as halls for various kinds of performances (Xanten, Amphitheater) or for the housing of gastronomic facilities (Xanten, the Guest House; Schwarzenacker, House 1).

Publicity for the AP offers a wide range of information, geared to the needs of individual visitors, visitor groups, as well as special groups (short guides, display panels, visits guided by professionals, guided tours to the excavations, audio guides, special tours for the disabled, special events etc.). The possibility of actively engaging the visitor is greatly valued (Roman board- and skill games in the Xanten AP).

1 C. AHRENS, Wiederaufgebaute Vorzeit. Archäologische Freilichtmuseen in Europa, 1990   2 Architektur und Denkmalpflege. Bericht über ein Kolloquium, veranstaltet vom Architekturreferat des DAI in Berlin 6.–8.11.1975. Diskussionen zur archäologischen Bauforschung. 2, n.d.
3 W. EDER, Unsichtbares sichtbar machen – Überlegungen zum Nutzen und Schaden des Wiederaufbaus antiker Denkmäler, in: Denkmalpflege und Tourismus. Mißtrauische Distanz oder fruchtbare Partnerschaft. Vorträge und Diskussionsergebnisse. Internationales Symposion, 26.–29.11.1986 Trier, 1987, 38–57   4 R. G. K. F. GOLLMANN et. al., Archäologischer Park. Carnuntum 1, n.d.   5 W. JOBST (ed.), Symposion 'Antike Ruinen nördlich der Alpen und die Möglichkeiten ihrer Präsentation', 14.–17.7. 1988 Bad Deutsch Altenburg, Carnuntum Jahr-Buch, 1989, 1990 6 Landschaftsverband Rheinland (ed.), Colonia Ulpia Traiana. 1.–6. Arbeitsbericht zu den Grabungen und Rekonstruktionen. Veröffentlichungen zum Aufbau des A.P. Xanten, 1978–1984 7 A. MIRON, Denkmalpflege und Tourismus am Beispiel des Römermuseums Schwarzenacker und des Europäischen Kulturparks Bliesbrück-Reinheim, in: Denkmalpflege und Tourismus 2. Vorträge und Diskussionsergebnisse, 2. Internationales Symposion 9.–12.11.1988 Trier, 1989, 42–55   8 G. PICCOTTINI, H. VETTERS, Führer durch die Ausgrabungen auf dem Magdalensberg, ³1985   9 G. PRECHT, H.-J. SCHALLES, Archäologischer Park/Regionalmuseum Xanten – Entwicklungsmöglichkeiten und Zukunftsperspektiven, in: Id. (eds.), Spurenlese. Beiträge zur Geschichte. des Xantener Raumes, 1989, 297–305   10 A. RIECHE, Archäologische Rekonstruktionen: Ziele und Wirkung, in: Xantener Berichte 6, 1995, 449–473 11 H. SCHMIDT, Wiederaufbau. Denkmalpflege an archäologischen Stätten 2, 1993, 231–238 12 Id., Konservieren oder Rekonstruieren? Zur Präsentation archäologischer Grabungsplätze, Xantener Berichte. 5, 1994, 77–87 13 Verband der Landesarchäologen in der Bundesrepublik Deutschland (ed.), Sinn und Unsinn archäologischer Restaurierungen und Rekonstruktionen. Kolloquium Traunstein 17.–20.9. 1990, 1991 14 G. ULBERT, G. WEBER (eds.), Konservierte Geschichte? Antike Bauten und ihre Erhaltung, 1985 15 G. WEBER, APC. Archäologischer Park. Cambodunum. 1. Abschnitt. Der Gallo-römische. Tempelbezirk, 1989.
                    HANS-JOACHIM SCHALLES

Archaeological Structural Research
A. DEFINITION   B. HISTORY   C. FIELDS OF ACTIV-
ITY

A. DEFINITION
The concept of structural 'research' was coined by
Armin von Gerkan in 1924 to denote the field of activity of architects working exclusively or predominantly
on the history of monuments [2]. The historical period
to which the architect devoted his research was initially
irrelevant here. Thus, von Gerkan himself left behind a
scientific body of work stretching from Neolithic burial
structures to medieval churches, although the main
focus of his interest was Classical antiquity. Since the
career designation architectural 'researcher' is now
used officially by building physicists in modern civil engineering, the term 'archaeological structural researcher' has become customary to designate building historians who concern themselves with the science of
excavation. In contrast to a purely art-historical
approach to structures, for structural research the
building itself, with all its details, is the source of more
advanced historical knowledge. This means that the
graphic reconstruction of a building in its individual
developmental phases takes place by means of observation, measurement, and the drawing of all parts of the
building, the catalogued pattern and interpretation of
which is obtained by plotting both ground plan and
cross section [7] stone by stone, including deformations. Only when the global concept of a historical building has been obtained in this way does architectural
evaluation take place. The optimal precondition for
such a working procedure is architectural training,
since the architect, by means of his prior knowledge of
practical construction and his trained capacity for spatial representation, is best able to evaluate complex
structural ensembles, through their transposition into
two- and three-dimensional representations. Needless
to say, prior knowledge of measurement techniques and
statics is essential here [3].

B. HISTORY
Architectural structural research (ASR) appeals to
the confrontation, already attested many times in Antiquity, between architects and the architectural historical development prior to their time, as in the case of the
Roman architect Vitruvius in his 10 volumes *De architectura*. It is with the resumption of the paradigmatic
nature of ancient architecture in the → RENAISSANCE,
that we know of the earliest detailed technical drawings
by architects of ancient buildings and parts of buildings
[4] (Fig. 1). With the triumphant march of → CLASSI-
CISM in European architecture in the mid–18th cent.,
architects enthusiastic for Antiquity, primarily from
England and France, sallied forth more and more often
to Italy and the lands of the Eastern Mediterranean, still
under Ottoman rule, in order to study, measure, and
reconstruct the ruins of Classical Antiquity. Their
publications were eagerly received throughout Europe,

to serve as models of accomplished architectural art for
contemporary architecture [5] (Fig. 2). In the 19th and
20th cents., until the outbreak of the First World War,
knowledge of ancient architecture was the uncontested
goal of architectural training, even long after other historicist building forms had come into fashion. From the
outset, architects had assumed a leading role in the
great national excavations on classical soil, which were
not undertaken in Germany until after the foundation
of the Empire in 1871. In particular, students from the
Berlin *Bauakademie* refined their structural investigations, and also contributed in no small measure to the
development of excavating techniques. As the architect
Wilhelm Doerpfeld, having been trained since 1877 at
→ OLYMPIA, eventually took over as responsible leader
of various excavations in Greece and on the west coast
of Asia Minor, so, since 1898, the excavations of the
→ DEUTSCHE ORIENT-GESELLSCHAFT at → BABYLON
under Robert Koldewey, and subsequently at Assur
under Walter Andrae, were initially purely the domain
of architects. In Egypt as well, the architect Ludwig Bor-
chert led numerous digs since 1907, in particular the
state excavation of Tell Amarna.

After 1918, excavation activity on classical soil was
completely disrupted, and the unfortunate circumstance that ASR was not yet recognized as a fully-
fledged discipline of classical studies alongside the investigation of classical architecture led to difficult times
for many ASR professionals. This situation was criticized by Armin von Gerkan in his polemical essay [2],
which led in 1926 to many ASR professionals to form
the *Koldewey-Gesellschaft, Vereinigung fur baugeschichtliche Forschung,* in order to promote the recognition of their field and to support new talent.

Following some initially heated confrontations, the
association largely achieved this goal upon the resumption of the foreign excavations, especially since there
was not yet any lack of teachers and students in the
Departments of the history of architecture at the technical colleges, who were interested in ASR and were
ready to become engaged in it. This did not change immediately after 1945, although foreign excavations initially came to a standstill once again. Owing to the reconstruction of the destroyed cities, however, research
interests in German architectural training shifted drastically. Research on medieval architectural monuments,
preservation of historical monuments and theory of
architecture were then urgent concerns in the face of
dwindling historical interest[8] for which reasons ASR
was rolled back in most Institutes of architectural history. The → DEUTSCHES ARCHÄOLOGISCHES INSTITUT
(DAI) therefore established a Architecture Section at its
head office in Berlin in 1973, with permanent positions
for researchers, in order to take charge of the promotion of new talent, particularly in ASR, to meet the
needs of the excavation activities of its institutions,
alongside the Koldewey-Gesellschaft, now functioning
effectively, and several Chairs in architectural history
(Fig. 3). Only France, with the establishment of the

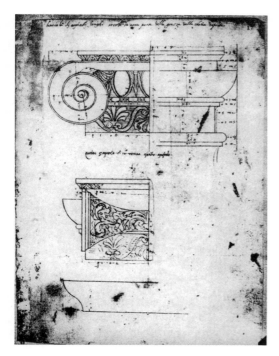

Fig. 1: Ionic capital in Rome,
Santi Apostoli. Anonymous scale
drawing, first half of the
16th cent.
*Reproduced with permission of
the Biblioteca Nazionale Centrale
di Firenze*

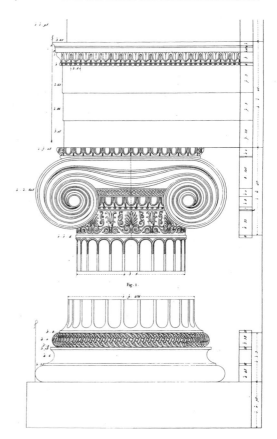

Fig. 2: Athens, Acropolis. Scale
drawing of the Erechtheum 1752

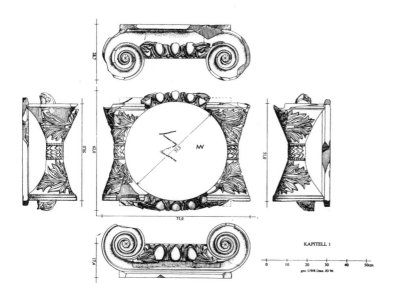

KAPITELL 1

Fig. 3: Ionic capital from Aezani,
first cent. AD. Drawing from the
Aezani excavation.
*Deutsches Archäologisches
Institut*

Institut de recherche sur l'architecture antique du CNRS, has gone beyond this attempt to render ASR more independent of the waning interest of the technical universities.

C. Fields of Activity

The widespread specialization and autonomization of many fields of Classical studies scarcely affected ASR, since the trained architectural researcher always approaches historical buildings from the most various eras and cultural circles with the same method. In addition, training in ASR additionally provides a basis for work in the conservation of monuments and in restoration projects. The breadth of the versatility of ASR is shown, for instance, by the DAI, under whose aegis work is being carried out by ASR specialists in the Egyptian, Mesopotamian, Hittite, Greco-Roman, Early Christian-Byzantine and Islamic cultural spheres. In recent times, they have been joined by ASR specialists who deal with the Pre-Hispanic architecture of America and the Eurasian cultural area. Essential to their profession is that they view themselves as researchers who work in cooperation with other branches of classical studies to illuminate the cultural history of ancient periods through the investigation of individual monuments, buildings, settlement layouts, and colonial structures, utilizing the most obvious heritage of ancient cultures, architecture. The coherence of ASR in German-speaking lands is promoted by the *Koldewey-Gesellschaft* with its biennial *Tagungen für Ausgrabungswissenschaft und Bauforschung* [6], and the Architecture Section of the DAI, with an informal series of colloquia on ASR [1].

→ Amarna; → Assur; → Babylon; → Olympia; → Vitruvius

1 Architektur-Referat des Deutschen Archäologischen Institut (ed.), Diskussionen zur archäologischen Bauforschung 1974; 2 A. von Gerkan, Die gegenwärtige Lage der archäologischen Bauforschung in Deutschland, 1924 (reprinted in: E. Boehringer (ed.), Von antiker Architektur und Topographie, 1959, 9–13).   3 Id., Grundlegendes zur Darstellungsmethode. Kursus für Bauforschung. 1930 (repr. in: E. Boehringer (ed.), Von antiker Architektur und Topographie, 1959, 99–106)   4 H. Günther, Das Studium der antiken Architektur in den Zeichnungen der Renaissance, 1988   5 W. Hoepfner, E.-L. Schwandner, Die Entdeckung der griechischen Bauten, in: Berlin und die Antike, Catalogue 1979, 291 ff   6 Koldewey-Gesellschaft (ed), Berichte über die Tagung für Ausgrabungswissenschaft und Bauforschung, 1926   7 G. Mader, Die Bauaufnahme, in: Petzet/Mader, Praktische Denkmalpflege, 1993, 156–167   8 W. Schirmer, Bauforschung an den Instituten für Baugeschichte der Technischen Hochschulen, in: J. Cramer (ed.) Bauforschung und Denkmalpflege, 1987, 25–29

Additional Bibliography: J. Bouquillard, La résurrection de Pompéi. Dessins d'archéologues des XVIIIe et XIXe siècles, 2000; N. T. De Grummond, An Encyclopedia of the History of Classical Archaeology, 1996; T. Doremus, Classical Styles in Modern Architecture: From the Colonnade to Disjunctured Space, 1994; F.

Salmon, Building on Ruins: The Rediscovery of Rome and English Architecture, 2000.

ERNST-LUDWIG SCHWANDNER

Archaic period see→ Epochs, concept of

Archaicism see→ Classicism

Architectural Copy/Citation
A. Introduction B. Middle Ages
C. 15th–17th Cent. D. 18th and 19th Cents.
E. Post-Modern period

A. Introduction

The terms 'copy' and 'citation' are not clearly defined or conceptually separated as far as their usage in the discipline of architectural history is concerned. While the literal adoption of a text or part of it is termed 'citation' in literature, the exact reproduction of a building or an architectural motif is referred to mainly as 'copy' in architecture. On the other hand, 'citation' tends to refer to the creatively modified adoption of individual elements and of forms taken out of a coherent whole, although the deliberate reference to the model must remain recognizable. The boundaries in relation to other methodologies of architectural reception and of the appropriation of forms from the architecture of previous periods cannot always be clearly defined.

B. Middle Ages

In spite of the continued use of individual Classical architectural elements such as columns, and apart from the special case of the Pantheon, it was the early Christian architecture of Late Antiquity that became particularly significant in the Middle Ages as a citable point of reference from the time of Antiquity. Reference to the architecture of early Christianity always aimed at the religious or political meanings attributed to these buildings, and thus was barely or only secondarily motivated by aesthetics. In general it can be said that the model was not replicated *in toto* but was recalled through the citation of a few architectural characteristics. Consequently, in the Middle Ages there were no copies in the sense of exact replicas of early Christian models from Late Antiquity; 'copying' occurred through citations, through the adoption of significant architectural features of the model [16]. This could be done by simply having the same number of columns as the model, a similar ground plan, a comparable sequence of space or through other such means.

The group of monuments that were taken as models was relatively limited. The buildings most frequently drawn upon were the early Christian basilicas of Rome, particularly St. Peter's, and the Church of the Holy Sepulchre in Jerusalem, both established by Constantine. The architectural features adopted from San Vitale in Ravenna (526–547) [2] (Figs. 1, 2), which left their mark on the architecture of the Palatine Chapel of Charlemagne in Aachen (786–800), still represent a

Fig. 1: Interior of the Palatine Chapel (now Cathedral) in Aachen

Fig. 2: Interior of San Vitale in Ravenna

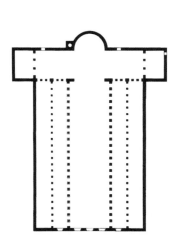

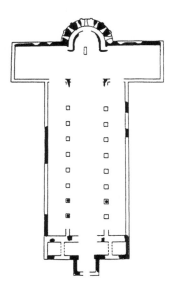

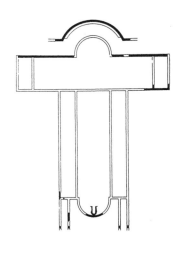

Fig. 3: Plan of Old St Peter's in Rome. *Reproduced with Permission of A. Arbeiter*

Fig. 4: Plan of the Carolingian abbey church of Saint Denis. *Copyright by Zeitschrift für Kunstgeschichte (Aachen/Basel)*

Fig. 5: Plan of the Abbey Church in Fulda. *Copyright by Zeitschrift für Kunstgeschichte (Aachen/Basel)*

unique case. The motivations for this choice of model, however, cannot be determined clearly, especially as other models besides the church of Ravenna were available to the Carolingians. Moreover, these architectural citations – octagonal central building with a two-storey gallery or the two-storey column arrangement with a triple arcade – were in this case expanded into a complex interlacing of references to the past through material borrowing in the form of *spolia* from Rome and Ravenna.

In the early Carolingian period the basilica in St. Denis (768–775) started the orientation towards the model of old St. Peter's, illustrated by the continuous transept of the Roman model and the imitation of the ring crypt of the tomb of Peter [14; 17] (Figs. 3, 4). The layout of a transept, especially a transept situated towards the west (e.g. Fulda *c*. 802–819, Fig. 5), and more generally the western orientation adopted from St. Peter's instead of the otherwise usual easterly direction, as well as an altar also situated in the west and dedicated to St. Peter, can since then be regarded as a reference to the Roman model. Even ifthe column or pillar arcades of Gothic cathedrals are, on the other hand, understood as allusions to early Christian basilicas [21. 22], then this is not so much in terms of a concrete building as a model; rather, this pillar motif more generally cites the model of the pillar basilica as a visualization of a concept of the early Christian and Roman Church. In spite of the respective time-specific differentiations, it is generally possible to relate the orientation towards Roman models and especially towards St. Peter's Basilica to the web of ideas of the universal primacy of Rome in political, religious or cultural life.

The same procedural methods of copying can be demonstrated for the Church of the Holy Sepulchre in Jerusalem [4; 10. 84–101]. The ground plan of a central building with an internal annular support structure, the number of columns, the expansion of the central building by means of three apsides – these architectural features alone or in combination can guarantee the reference to the model. In addition to these citations that identified a church as a replica of the Church of the Holy Sepulchre, the urban layout was able to portray the sacred topography of Jerusalem [19]. Such an architectonic visualization of the holy sites was suggested by the idea that the life Christ was reenacted in the liturgy during the Church year.

C. 15TH–17TH CENT.

→ HUMANISM and the studies of Antiquity conducted since the 15th cent. fundamentally changed the conditions for a recourse on the part of contemporary architecture to that of Antiquity. The architectural discovery of Classical buildings, their survey and recording that are already attested for Filippo Brunelleschi and Leon Battista Alberti and that reached their high point in Pope Leo X's plan for Raphael to make an inventory and reconstruct the entirety of ancient Rome,

had as a consequence a considerable increase in the knowledge of Classical architecture. The direct engagement with Classical edifices, the recording of ground plans, elevations or details of architectonic ornamentation are thus documented for just about every architect of the quattro- and cinquecento [12]. In the 17th cent. this architectural research became even more intensive [3].

The systematic scrutinization of traditional Classical architecture was ultimately motivated by the search for principles and standards of Classical architectural creation [6. 276f.]; Classical architecture was also reflected accordingly in the architectural theory of this period. The third book of Sebastiano Serlio's architectural treatise (*Il terzo libro ... nel quale si figurano e descrivono le Antichità di Roma*, Venice 1540) and the treatment of Classical buildings in the third and fourth book of Andrea Palladio's *I quattro libri dell'architettura* (Venice 1570) contributed significantly to the spreading of this practice. In this way the study of Antiquity had its place in the context of an art-theoretical discourse on the aesthetic conditions of architecture. In connection with this the model of Antiquity was primarily discussed in terms of the extent to which Classical architecture was able to set rules and standards which had to be emulated or even changed and surpassed [20].

Imitation of nature or Antiquity became a fundamental postulate of art and architectural theory that created – compared with the Middle Ages – completely new prerequisites for the adoption of Classical architectural styles whether through imitation or even through copying. This practice was no longer guided by occasional adoptions of meaning but developed into the normal case which was justified by aesthetics: architectural language that had been Classically trained made use of Classical vocabulary. First and foremost this included the system of Classical pillar arrangements as supports and the subdivision of walls, a system that with its elements – columns, wall pillars, cornices, architraves and triangular gables – had a determining influence on the outward appearance of architecture right through to the 19th cent. [11]. As the extant Classical pillar arrangements could not be made to conform to a standard pattern common to all of them and were not in keeping with the descriptions in Vitruvius, they became subjects that were constantly discussed anew in the debate surrounding the search for a rule and that were evaluated in varying ways with regard to form and proportions. So even when it repeatedly came to citations that were more or less faithful to the details, in terms of the application of this Classical system of form, [6] – Alberti already adopted the arrangement of wall pillars from the entrance to the Pantheon for the portal niche of Santa Maria Novella in Florence (1458/78) [22. 268; 25.41] (Fig. 6+7) – in the end it was more a matter of assimilation and 'improvement', of eclectic and innovative interpretations of Classical models [1; 5]. The same applies for the orientation towards Classical building types, ground plans and spatial solutions

Fig. 6: Portal of the Pantheon in Rome

Fig. 7: Portal of Santa Maria Novella in Florence

like those that are used in Raphael's Villa Madama (1518) project [7. 391ff.]. In contrast to what might perhaps be expected, exact copies of Classical buildings therefore play no part in Renaissance and Baroque architecture.

In view of the close correlation between 'citation', emendation and assimilation it is thus quite difficult to decide the extent to which recourse to a model was more generally aimed at the Classical architectural system or whether it referred to a concrete work instead [1. 556ff.]. The same is true for the extent to which the reference to a model therefore possibly also, at least occasionally as in the Middle Ages, had iconographic implications or was intended to be meaningful.

BRUNO REUDENBACH

D. 18TH AND 19TH CENTS.

It was not so much the search for rules as the fascination with the simple, pure form and the orientation towards this ideal (imbued with moral and pedagogical impulses) that determined the attitude of 18th- and 19th-cent. Classicism or Neo-Classicism towards Classical architecture [15]. Hand in hand with this went the discovery of Greece as 'true' Antiquity; knowledge of the Doric order (without a base) as the original order was for instance closely linked to the growing acquaintance with Greek temples in → PAESTUM from the middle of the 18 cent. [9; 23; 24]. Ruins and buildings from Greece itself were investigated at the same time and disseminated throughout Europe by means of the publication of engravings, primarily by Julien-David Le Roy's *Ruines des plus beaux monuments de la Grèce* (1758) and through *The Antiquities of Athens* (4 bks., 1762–1816) by James Stuart and Nicholas Revett, probably the most famous and influential work of its kind.

Fig. 8: The 'Tower of the Winds' in Shugborough

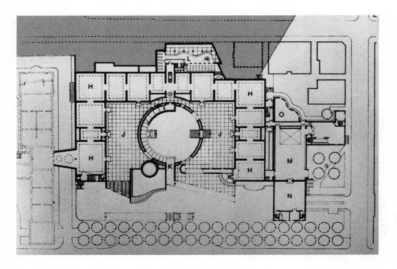

Fig. 9: Stuttgart, New State
Gallery, plan of a gallery floor
(J. Stirling)

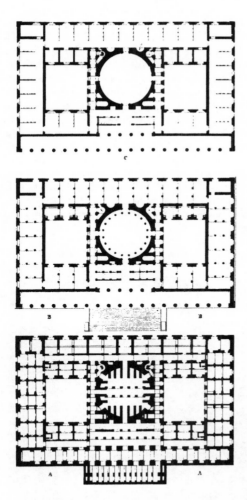

Fig. 10: Berlin, plan of the Altes Museum (R.F. Schinkel)

With regard to the question of architecture, the classicizing attitude towards Antiquity gave rise to a changed framework. Inasmuch as interest was directed at the authentic Classical form, archaeologically researched and disseminated in engravings, we probably owe to Classicism and the → GREEK REVIVAL the most faithful copies of Classical architecture. The influence that emanated from the publications of engravings can be demonstrated in many ways, both in terms of details of architectonic ornamentation and the replication of entire parts of buildings or complete edifices [24. 36–46]. The *Tower of the Winds* close to the Acropolis, for instance, depicted in the first volume of Stuart's and Revett's work (Fig. 11), was adopted by Stuart himself as a model for a garden building in Shugborough (1765) (Fig. 8), whilst James Wyatt identified the top part of the tower of the Radcliffe Observatory in Oxford (1773–1794) as a copy of the Athenian tower (Fig. 12).

However frequently such architectural citation was also adopted into the architecture of → CLASSICISM, the development of a 'Classical' architectural language that then spread throughout the whole of Europe and the USA was even more momentous. It was characterized less by the copying of concrete buildings than by the alignment with Classical stylistic imagery that showed itself particularly in the adoption of temple architecture, and here above all the temple façade as a portico with a triangular gable [15]. Although we can repeatedly see faithful adoptions of form in architectural terms, the reception of Antiquity as practiced by classicizing architecture and culminating in this omnipresent motif has to be understood as stylistic copy rather than as concrete architectural citation.

The garden buildings of the landscaped gardens, the *fabriques*, were of great importance for the popularization and implementation of the concept of different styles whose sequence determined the history of architecture and which lead to the phenomenon of → HISTORICISM [18]. These follies conveyed meaning and

Fig. 11: Athens, Tower of the Winds

Fig. 12: Oxford, Radcliffe Observatory

ambience in the various layouts of natural creations of gardens and depending on their style they were meant to induce different effects. Apart from exotic, Medieval or ruined buildings, use was also made of classicizing architectures, particularly that of Athens. Stuart, for instance, designed for Shugborough not only a replica of the Tower of the Winds but also additional copies of famous buildings in Athens, such as the Doric Temple which was modelled on the Theseion (c. 1760), Hadrian's Arch (1769) and the Monument of Lysicrates (1771) [8.56f.].

E. Post-Modern period

In the architecture of the so-called post-modern period, the playful or ironic adoption of classical architectural vocabulary and Classicist forms became a leitmotif, and this is already employed by a pioneer of this architecture, Charles Moore's Piazza d'Italia in New Orleans (1975–80). This architecture with its stance against the abstract, geometric planning grid of the International Style, reactivated semantic options for architectonic forms and to this extent delighted in working with copies and even more so with defamiliarized citations. The open internal rotunda in James Stirling's extension to the state gallery in Stuttgart (1977–83), for example, can be regarded as such (Fig. 9). It is inspired by the central rotunda in Karl Frierich Schinkel's Museum of Classical Antiquities (1823–30) in Berlin that for its part alludes to the Roman Pantheon (Fig. 10). The reproduction of the Villa dei Papiri in → Herculaneum which now houses a part of the Getty

collection (Malibu, end of the 1960s) owes more to the eccentricity of a billionaire than to an architectural concept in itself.

→ Basilica; → Forum/Square

1 H. H. Aurenhammer, Multa aedium exempla variarum imaginum atque operum. Das Problem der imitatio in der italienischen Architektur des frühen 16. Jahrhundert, in: Intertextualität in der Frühen Neuzeit (Frühneuzeit-Stud. 2) 1994, 533–605 2 G. Bandmann, Die Vorbilder der Aachener Pfalzkapelle, in: Karl der Große, Bd. 3, 1965, 424–462 3 A. Blunt, Baroque architecture and classical antiquity, in: Classical Influences on European Culture AD 1500–1700, 1976, 349–354 4 G. Bresc-Bautier, Les imitations du Saint-Sépulcre de Jérusalem (IXe-XVe siècles), in: Rev. d'histoire de la spiritualité 50, 1974, 319–342 5 T. Buddensieg, Criticism of ancient architecture in the 16th and 17th centuries, in: Classical Influences on European Culture AD 1500–1700, 1976, 335–348 6 H. Burns, Quattrocento architecture and the antique: some problems, in: Classical Influences on European Culture AD 500–1500, 1971, 269–287 7 Id., Raffaello e quell'antiqua architectura in: Raffaello architetto, 1984, 381–404 8 A.v. Buttlar, Der Landschaftsgarten, 1989 9 J. M. Crook, The Greek Revival, 1972 10 W. Erdmann, A. Zettler, Zur Archäologie des Konstanzer Münsterhügels, in: Schriften des Vereins f. Gesch. des Bodensees 95, 1977, 19–134 11 J. Guillaume (ed.), L'emploi des ordres dans l'architecture de la Ren. Actes du colloque tenu à Tours (1986), 1992 12 H. Günther, Das Studium der antiken Architektur in den Zeichnungen der Hoch-Ren. (= Röm. Forsch. der Bibliotheca Hertziana 24), 1988 13 W. Jacobsen, Gab es die karolingische 'Renaissance' in der Baukunst?, in: Zschr. für Kunstgesch. 51, 1988, 313–347 14 Id., Die Abteikirche von St.-Denis als

kunstgeschichtliches Problem, in: La Neustrie. Les pays au nord de la Loire de 650 à 850, Bd. 2, 1989, 151–185 15 W.v. KALNEIN, Architecture in the Age of Neo-Classicism, in: The Age of Neo-Classicism (The 14th Exhibition of the Council of Europe) 1972, liii–lxvi 16 R. KRAUTHEIMER, Introduction to an Iconography of Mediaeval Architecture, in: Journal of the Warburg and Courtauld Institutes 5, 1942, 1–33 17 Id., The Carolingian Revival of Early Christian Architecture, in: The Art Bull. 24, 1942, 1–38 18 M. MOSSER, Paradox in the Garden: a brief account of *fabriques*, in: Id., G. TEYSSOT (Eds.), The History of Garden Design: the western tradition from the Renaissance to the present day, 1999, 263–276. 19 R. G. OUSTERHOUT, The Church of Santo Stefano: A 'Jerusalem' in Bologna, in: Gesta 20, 1981, 311–321 20 G. POCHAT, Imitatio und Superatio – das Problem der Nachahmung aus humanistischer und kunsttheoretischer Sicht, in: Klassizismus. Epoche und Probleme. FS für Erik Forssman zum 70. Geburtstag, 1987, 317–335 21 W. SAUERLÄNDER, Das Jahrundert der großen Kathedralen, 1989 22 C. SYNDIKUS, Leon Battista Alberti. Das Bauornament, 1996 23 D. WATKIN, Greek Revival, in: The Dictionary of Art, Bd. 13, 1996, 607–614 24 D. WIEBENSON, Sources of Greek Revival Architecture (= Stud. in Architecture, 8), 1969 25 R. WITTKOWER, Architectural Principles in the Age of Humanism, ³1962   BRUNO REUDENBACH

Architectural theory/Vitruvianism
A. CHARACTERIZATION B. VITRUVIUS STUDIES, ITALY C. VITRUVIUS STUDIES, FRANCE

A. CHARACTERIZATION
Architectural Theory (AT) was an essential component of the architectonic culture of the 15th–18th cents. It was a result of the striving for greater scientific input and systematization that is generally characteristic of the → RENAISSANCE. Moreover it followed the ancient idea that lived on in the Middle Ages that the architect, much more than the artist, should also be well-versed in theory. In post-Medieval architecture, most of the architectonic decor and a considerable part of the layout can only be understood with reference to AT. In spite of this AT, as a whole usually had only a limited role in construction practice. It was directed first and foremost at patrons of the arts and an educated audience. Its actual purpose at precisely the period of its characteristic formation during the early Renaissance can only be partially established. From a pragmatic point of view, we can only concur with Francesco di Giorgio Martini when he criticized the epoch-making architectural treatise of L.B. Alberti (1452, published in 1485) because it was written in Latin and was not illustrated. For in this way, those for whom it was actually intended, the architects, could not understand it because of their lack of literary education while it remained closed to the literarily educated because of their lack of architectonic knowledge. Alberti, who was an exception in that he combined in one person the skills of a man of letters and those of an architect, did not take his own AT into account properly in the buildings which he himself designed.

In the course of the 16th cent., knowledge of AT spread. Humanistic treatises on architecture like that of Alberti long since ceased to originate in Italy. However, initially, similar works on AT, especially those of Philibert de l'Orme (1561/1567/1568) were again part of the reception of the Renaissance on the other side of the Alps; Albrecht Dürer's *Unterweisung der Messung* (1525) is worthy of mention here despite its more mathematical and scientific orientation. However this scholarly writing then also subsided on the other side of the Alps. Column books that could be used in an increasingly practical way dominated the field for a century (the most widespread being by Hans Blum, from 1550). From the late 17th cent. on, France again produced a wealth of scholarly writings on AT. The writings were now even further removed from practice than before; the authors were often laymen in matters of architecture. Again the areas of interest were, especially, general questions about basic architectonic principles, the value of artistic standards, the dependence of taste on the individual disposition of the observers or the relationship between feeling and reason in the evaluation of architecture.

AT was only partly oriented towards contemporary conditions and needs. In the Renaissance it even postulated a conscious break with the traditions that had evolved, and, instead, conjured up Antiquity, from where it took its guidelines, sometimes without much consideration of the extent to which they could really be implemented. Only very hesitantly did it venture to adapt, in a purposeful manner, the ancient set principles to modern conditions, to expand or even to adjust them. There was however an indirect form of adaptation of Antiquity: namely in the way in which one interpreted its ancient monuments. Mostly it was probably in a rather automatic manner that people visualized how conditions were during Antiquity, on the basis of the conditions to which they themselves were used and they therefore more or less consciously adapted Antiquity to their own circumstances. To be sure, this also was probably a significant prerequisite for their daring in carrying out the great experiment of the renaissance of Antiquity.

Ancient architecture was normally described in theory as exemplary. But what constituted ancient architecture, was determined in a different manner than it is today. Even Romanesque or Byzantine buildings were on many occasions considered to be ancient. In building practice, ancient architecture was usually imitated only in details (especially column arrangements) and in truth this by no means adhered perfectly to the principles of the Renaissance. Even the buildings that were considered to be the most beautiful monuments of Antiquity, the Pantheon and the Templum Pacis of Vespasian (nowadays the so-called Basilica of Constantine), showed striking defects according to the standards of the Renaissance. The discrepancy between such ancient works and the principles of the Renaissance come to light through the comparisons of the structures and drawings from the Renaissance that correct the defects as far as possible. The discrepancy was only rarely stated in the AT of the Renaissance. One of the few exceptions was Book III of the *L'Architettura* of Sebastiano Serlio (1540) that expressly aimed to teach people how to differentiate between good and bad architecture.

AT was primarily based on ancient writings. Its most important source was the treatise on architecture by Vitruvius that was already famous during Antiquity. Only copies are extant [1]. The best is a Carolingian codex (London, BM, Harleianus 2767). But the illustrations to which Vitruvius's text refers have, in many cases, been completely lost. Only one early Medieval manuscript (in Sélestat, Alsace) contains several illustrations but they do not appear to be ancient.

B. VITRUVIUS STUDIES, ITALY

Vitruvius's text continued to be well known throughout the entire Middle Ages. It was discussed at the court of Charlemagne by Alcuin and Einhard. Provost Goderamnus of St. Pantaleon studied it when his abbey church of St. Michael was built in Hildesheim (dedicated in 1022). Petrus Diakonus copied it at the end of the 11th cent. when he built the abbey of Montecassino. Vitruvius appears to have been highly regarded in northern Europe even more than in Italy. Albertus Magnus, Vincent of Beauvais and others refer to him. Many German, French or English → LIBRARIES owned copies of the treatise or copied it. The new interest in Antiquity that was awakened around 1350 in the Petrarch circle increasingly included Vitruvius as well. Petrarch and his friends, Boccaccio and G. Dondi, owned Vitruvius manuscripts.

In 1416 Poggio Bracciolini, the enthusiastic collector of ancient writings, discovered a Vitruvius manuscript in St. Gallen that in his time was probably considered to be ancient (unidentified, possibly Harleianus). In about 1485 G. Sulpicio in Rome edited and published Vitruvius for the first time. A re-emended text was printed in 1496 in Florence and in 1497 in Venice. After studying for decades, the Humanist, architect and engineer Fra Giocondo published a completely newly revised version of the text with 136 illustrations in Venice in 1511. This has been a basis for the emendation of Vitruvius [11] up to the present time.

One would assume that the early Vitruvius studies were centred in Florence. However, of these, only a few scattered attestations have come down to us: Vitruvius excerpts by Lorenzo Ghiberti and his grandson Buonaccorso [25. 30ff.] or Cronaca's illustration of Vitruvius's Doric portal [17]. At the court of Naples at the end of the 15th cent. a Vitruvius translation was prepared for F. di Giorgio. He copied it in his own hand and made excerpts from it as a basis for the second version of his treatise on architecture [14]. A manuscript by Pellegrino Prisciani, the librarian of d'Este who taught Isabella d'Este architecture as early as 1491 [21], bears testimony to early Vitruvius studies in Ferrara. The old ties between Alberti and the house of d'Este and then Isabella's link with Gian Cristoforo Romano must have reinforced this interest. In Milan the work on Vitruvius had already been documented in the Medieval cathedral stonemason's lodge. It was continued by Bramante, Gian Cristoforo Romano and others [17]. Studies of such kind gave rise to the splendidly produced translation of Vitruvius that Cesare Cesariano, who described himself as a student of Bramante, had printed in 1521 in Como. It comprises not just the translation but also numerous illustrations and a detailed commentary. At the beginning of the Renaissance the debate about Vitruvius at the Roman Curia (Alberti, Niccolò Perotti, G. Sulpicio and others) was particularly intensive. Around 1515/1520 Fabio Calvo translated Vitruvius at Raphael's house [13]. The high quality of this translation, occasional commentary and interpolations testify to the fact that extensive preliminary studies preceded this work. Notes written in Raphael's handwriting about the translation show that Humanists and artists discussed together the problems raised by Vitruvius. Around the same time as Raphael, Antonio da Sangallo also began studying Vitruvius [15; 17]. An enormous bundle of sketches and notes very vividly makes one aware how Antonio thought through difficult passages and looked for comparisons in ancient architecture. In 1531 and again in 1541 he planned to illustrate Vitruvius. But he did not get beyond a foreword. His brother Giovanni Battista realized the project on a more modest scale. In 1542 a group of Humanists formed in Rome with the aim of working on Vitruvius, re-emending his works, providing commentaries on them and illustrating them (*Accademia delle Virtù*). However only a carefully formulated programme was developed [26; 22]. None of these studies was published. Most influential in Italy were the Venetian studies of Vitruvius. The notes on architecture made by Albrecht Dürer during his stay in Italy, which are remarkably substantial for their time [12. Bk. II, 58–73], must be viewed against the background of the intensive studies of Vitruvius in Venice. The Venetian Humanist Silvano Morosini in particular is said to have completed a commentary on Vitruvius in 1495. The best Vitruvius commentary of the Renaissance was provided by the Venetian Humanist Daniele Barbaro in collaboration with the great architect Andrea Palladio, who did the illustrations (appeared from 1556 in many and varied editions in Venice). The voluminous and comprehensive, scholarly treatise on architecture published by Vincenzo Scamozzi in Venice in 1615 represents a certain end point in Vitruvius studies.

A new generation of French Vitruvius disciples profited from the flourishing antiquarian studies in Rome when they studied Antiquity there: Guillaume Philandrier (Vitruvius n., Lyon 1544) and de l'Orme. The Vitruvius editions that appeared on the other side of the Alps during the Renaissance were however not very independent. They were based to a large extent on Fra Giocondo and Cesariano (French Vitruvius translation by Jean Martin 1547, Philandrier's Vitruvius edition 1552, Walter Ryff's German Vitruvius translation in 1543 etc.).

After the misunderstandings of the early phase, expert knowledge of Vitruvius developed set forms in the early 16th cent. Fra Giocondo's edition, Calvo's translation and Antonio da Sangallo's studies are the most important evidence of it. Now for the first time differentiated knowledge of column arrangements was disseminated. They had been used for 100 years according to the model of mainly ancient buildings –mostly without being distinguished from one another – and they formed by far the most striking element of the reception of Antiquity. Only now did people gradually accept that an element as exotic as external porticos of columns represented a typical element of temples. Then people developed a diagrammatic concept of the Vitruvian house that has essentially been preserved right through to today although it is questionable whether it is actually in keeping with Vitruvius's concept.

Around the middle of the 16th cent. the studies of Vitruvius and of Antiquity again made significant progress overall. On the one hand with the publication of the great collected works, they became much more widespread. On the other hand, with Barbaro and Palladio, Venetian studies took prominence over the central Italian ones. With the increasing distance from Antiquity, the temptation for the architect to reflect his own tradition back on to it diminished.

Despite the transformation in style in the 17th cent. AT did not change significantly. The aesthetic guidelines were borrowed from Antiquity as before. With the growing progress in engineering and science and the increasing conviction that the ancient level had been regained, the social importance of the Vitruvius studies waned and the innovative spirit that had initially inspired them likewise subsided. Stereotypical paraphrases of the known results were highlighted while discussions withdrew to specialized corners of the field.

C. Vitruvius Studies, France

Colbert initiated a revival of Vitruvius studies and of AT. The revival was part of the broadly and systematically laid out framework of cultural and educational policy that was aimed at stylizing France as the leading cultural nation in the West (illustrated Vitruvius translation with a commentary by Claude Perrault, 1684). On the one hand, interest in the high civilization of Rome now declined in favour of a return to Greece as the root of Western art. Vitruvius himself makes it clear that he is based very much in the Greek tradition. On the other hand, through Colbert, people rediscovered the Gothic style as their national heritage. Even the Vitruvius edition of Perrault testifies to this. It was essential to combine these two components so as to develop an AT appropriate for France. The basic laws of statics formed the connecting link. They appeared to be realized as much in Gothic style as in the Greek temple. However the Italian Renaissance was criticized for not having taken these into consideration. Discussion about this brilliant combination lasted well into the 18th cent. It was linked with building projects of national significance: initially with the city façade of the Louvre and ultimately with the church of St. Geneviève, the patron saint of Paris

Colbert was already ensuring that Classical art works in Greece were recorded. However only in the course of the 18th cent. did large-scale expeditions to Greece begin. The French protagonist was Julien-David Le Roy who, on behalf of the French king, documented Greek buildings and published exact records of them for the first time (1758). Around the same time the temples of → Paestum were also rediscovered. Although these are well preserved and are situated in a prominent location, they were ignored throughout the whole of the Renaissance. The reason for the omission of the concrete manifestation of Greek architecture from the Western consciousness lay in the fact that – measured against what people knew, namely the Roman heritage – it appeared to them to be exotic and correspondingly repulsive. This can be seen in many reactions to the discovery of Greek architecture. One recognized that Vitruvius partly referred to this exotic architecture.

The disappointment about the true manifestation of Greek architecture (but also of the fine arts) intensified the dissolution of normative aesthetics that started to develop just before 1700. The distance from Vitruvius therefore grew. Increasingly he was transformed from a model to an archaic object.

Sources: 1 C. H. Krinsky, in: JWI 30, 1967, 36–70 2 L. Marcucci, in: 2000 Anni di Vitruvio. Studi e Documenti di Architettura VIII, 1978, 11–184 3 C. Fensterbusch, ⁵1991 4 F. Granger, Loeb Classical Library 251/280 5 H. Nohl, Leipzig 1876, Ndr. 1965 (index) 6 L. Cherubini, 1976 (index) 7 Vitruvius Pollio. Vitruvius: Ten Books on Architecture. Ingrid D. Rowland (trans.); commentary and illustrations by Thomas Noble Howe; with additional commentary by Ingrid D. Rowland and Michael J. Dewar, 1999

Literature: 7 J.v. Schlosser Magnino, La letteratura artistica, 1967 8 G. Germann, Einführung in die Geschichte der Architectur, 1980 9 H. W. Kruft, Geschichte der Architektur von der Antike bis zur Gegenwart, 1985 (bibliography) 10 L. A. Ciapponi, Il 'De architettura' di Vitruvio nel primo umanesimo, in: Stud. Medievale e Umanista III, 1960, 59–99 11 Id., Fra Giocondo da Verona and his edition of Vitruvius, in: JWI 47, 1984, 72–90 12 A. Dürer, Schriftlicher Nachlaß, H. Rupprich (ed.) 1956–69 13 V. Fontana, P. Morachiello, Vitruvio e Raffaello. Il 'de architettura' di Vitruvio nella traduzione inedita di Fabio Calvo Ravennate, 1975 14 F. di Giorgio Martini, Il 'Vitruvio Magliabechiano', G. Scaglia (ed.), 1985 15 G. Giovannoni, Antonio da Sangallo il Gio., 1959 16 J. Guillaume (ed.), Les Traités d'architecture de la Renaissance, 1988 17 H. Günther, Das Studium der antiken Architektur in den Zeichnungen der Hochrenaissance, 1988 18 Id. et al., Deutsche Architektur zwischen Gotik und Renaissance, 1988 19 Id., Alberti, gli umanisti contemporanei e Vitruvio, in: Leon Battista Alberti. Architettura e cultura, 1995 20 W. Herrmann, Laugier and 18th Century French Theory, 1962

21 F. Marotti, Lo spettacolo dall'umanesimo al manierismo, 1974 22 M. Maylender, Storia delle accademie d'Italia, 1926–30 23 P. N. Pagliara, Vitruvio da testo a canone, in: Memoria dell'Antico nell'Arte Italiana 1984–86, Bd. 3, 7–88 24 G. Scaglia, A Translation of Vitruvius and Copies of Late Antique Drawings in Buonaccorso Ghiberti's Zibaldone, in: Transactions of the American Philological Association 1979 25 J. von Schlosser, Lorenzo Ghibertis Denkwürdigkeiten, in: Kunstgesch. Jb. der K.K. Zentral-Kommission für Erforsch. und Erhaltung der Kunst- und Histor. Denkmale IV, 1910, 105–211 26 C. Tolomei, Delle lettere libri sette, 1547.

HUBERTUS GÜNTHER

Argumentation Theory
A. DEFINITION B. ANCIENT RHETORIC C. HISTORY OF INFLUENCE

A. DEFINITION
Argumentation theory analyzes and describes the structures and methods of argumentation, in particular, rhetorical argumentation. In Antiquity, persuasion was generally regarded to be the purpose of a speech, and argumentation, in turn, was seen as an instrument of persuasion (cf. Plato's definition of rhetoric as *peíthus demiurgós* – 'master of persuasion', Gorg. 453 a). Its primary tasks are to identify what is probable and to generate plausibility. The ethical implications of the fact that persuasive speech is not necessarily identical with truthful speech (Plat. apol. 17a) have been discussed in argumentation theory ever since sophistic rhetoric in the 5th cent. BC demonstrated the psychological power of the spoken word (*Gorgias*). Within the rhetorical system of the ancient world, which divided the composition of a speech into five stages of production (*officia oratoris*), argumentation theory is part of the first two phases: the discovery (*inventio*) and arrangement (*dispositio*) of the arguments, and thus precedes, in terms of the chronology of the system, linguistic expression (*elocutio*), memorization (*memoria*) and delivery (*pronuntiatio*). It forms the starting point for the speaker in terms of content. Argumentation is the framework for presenting the speaker's case; however, its full effectiveness depends on an appropriate linguistic formulation (Quint. inst. 5,12,6): *inventio/dispositio* (content) and *elocutio* (form) were regarded in the ancient world as integral and inseparable components of rhetoric; argumentation theory is firmly rooted in the system, both as a guideline for putting forth an argument (applied rhetoric) and for analyzing argumentation (theory of rhetoric).

B. ANCIENT RHETORIC
1. GREEK 2. ROMAN

1. GREEK
As far back as sophistic rhetoric, techniques of argumentation were developed that were often aimed solely at achieving a rhetorical victory, without regard for truth or morality 'turning the weaker into the stronger'.

This gave rise to heated discussions of the possibilities, purposes and responsibility of rhetoric (Plato; Isocrates). It was not until Aristotle's structural analysis that argumentation theory first became the subject of scholarly study. In his 'Rhetoric', Aristotle made what remains today the most significant contribution in the history of ancient argumentation theory. The oldest existing textbook, the 'Rhetoric' of Anaximenes of Lampsakos (*c.* 340 BC), provided specific practical aids for argumentation in diverse situations; there was at the time no systematic treatment of the material. Soon thereafter, Aristotle developed in the first volume of his 'Rhetoric' a detailed theory of argumentation, starting with a critique of his predecessors whose writings failed to examine the most important subject: the presentation of evidence (Greek *pisteis*), a term that may mean either 'evidence/evidentiary procedure' or 'means of persuasion') (rhet. 1,1,1354 a 11ff.). He immediately identified a structural analogy between rhetoric and dialectics, whose procedures are examined in 'Topics' and 'Analytics'). Both provide ways of finding arguments, and both, in principle, utilize the same system of inference (1,2,1356 a 34ff.). Those familiar with dialectical inferences are already familiar with rhetorical inferences as well. They need only be aware of specific differences. Rhetoric was regarded as a specialized discipline within dialectics, while argumentation theory was a core element within rhetoric. The primary task of rhetoric is to identify what is convincing and plausible. That, in turn, must be based on what is generally recognized to be true; its subject is the realm of the doubtful and disputed ('things that may be a certain way but also otherwise'. 1,2,1357 a 1ff.). Aristotle distinguishes between two types of proof: the 'inartificial' (*átechnoi*), such as witnesses' testimony, written documents and the like, and the 'artificial' (*éntechnoi*), arguments that still have to be found. This distinction has also been adopted by Roman rhetoric (Cic. orat. 2,27,116; Quint. inst. 5,1,1). Persuasion through speech can occur in three ways: through the plausible self-presentation of the speaker (*ethos*), by creating an emotional mood (*pathos*) and through rational evidentiary processes (*logos*). Although objective-logical and emotional argumentation work together, it is *logos* that occupies a primary position when Aristotle draws upon the instruments of logic to describe and define the processes of argumentation.

All evidentiary processes are based either on inductive or deductive inferences. An inductive inference in dialectics has its rhetorical equivalent in an inference drawn from an example (*paradeigma*), while the dialectical deduction (syllogism) corresponds to the rhetorical enthymeme (1,2,1356 b 2ff.), a three-step process consisting of argument, inference and conclusion [29. 73ff.]. Aristotle attributes the highest degree of evidentiary value to this enthymeme. Unlike the syllogism, however, the aim of the enthymeme (also referred to, particularly in its expanded form, as epicheirema) is not to arrive at strictly logical proof of truth but, by deducing from a generally recognized opinion, it seeks to determine what is probable (*eikós*); but not all of its steps must be carried out in their entirety. In addition to *paradeigma* and *eikos*, evidence is the third basis of inference. Using these distinctions, 'Aristotle carried out an analysis of the logical structure of argumentation that clearly remains valid today'[16. 919].

An important auxiliary discipline for rhetorical/dialectical inferences is the theory of topics or commonplaces. This is a link between logic and rhetoric which provides an inventory of argumentation patterns and plays a significant role in the further history of argumentation theory. Topoi (Latin *loci*, according to Quint. inst. 5,10,20, the *sedes argumentorum* – places where arguments are found) are based, according to Aristotle, on generally recognized values and patterns of thought that one may repeatedly refer to during the process of argumentation. With the help of normed categories, such as the topos from 'more or less', from an alternative action, from an analogy, or arguing from authority (rhet. 2,23,1397 b 14ff.), the theory of 'commonplaces constitutes' a store of conventionalized inferences that offers the speaker a labour-saving alternative to individual argumentation (Cic. orat. 2,130f.) [29. 87].

Because of the fragmentary nature of the rhetoric handed down from the Hellenistic and imperial periods, it is possible to construct only a rough sketch of the development of the theory of commonplaces and of argumentation theory after Aristotle's time. Theophrastus extended Aristotle's rhetorical teachings in the field of argumentation theory by compiling specific treatises on rhetorical inferences (enthymeme, epicheireme, *paradeigma*) (Diog. Laert. 5,2). Subsequently, questions of argumentation theory were taken up by a variety of disciplines: first, within the field of forensic rhetoric, Aristotle's rather general theory became more specialized, with increasing numbers of categories and a more finely tuned organization of the material. Here the influence of Hermagoras of Temnos (2nd cent. BC) was particularly felt, as his doctrine of *status* had a strong influence on Roman rhetoric.

This doctrine offered a kind of pattern [17. 103], consisting of questions (*status*, Greek *staseis*) one could pose in a juridical context to clarify the goal of the argumentation. They dealt with such issues as identification of the perpetrator; details of the incident, judgement regarding the deed and admissibility of the complaint or action. Moreover, argumentation theory maintained its close links to philosophical logic in the linguistic philosophy of the Stoa, who subdivided logic into rhetoric and dialectics, as disciplines with related aims, while excluding *pathos* as a means of rhetorical persuasion. The theory of syllogistic inference was further developed primarily by Chrysippus [30. 49ff.].

2. ROMAN

Although Roman rhetoric was based to a large degree on the Greek system and also retained much of the Greek terminology, there are nonetheless significant trends characteristic of Roman rhetoric. First, the specialization of legal rhetoric continued. The *status* doctrine became an integral part of rhetoric, and argumentation theory was adapted to meet legal needs. At the same time, the speaker's personality became a more central focus (Cicero), which led to a decline in the importance of logical argumentation.

A more practical orientation is apparent as early as Cicero's 'Rhetoric for Herennius' (c. 86–82 BC). Here argumentation theory is presented as a guide for argumentation in a forensic speech (2,2): 'which arguments, referred to by the Greeks as *epicheiremata*, should be selected and which should be avoided'. At the center is the *status* doctrine with the evidentiary commonplace (1,18–2,26), followed by a division of the argumentation into five sections: *propositio* (subject or putting forth the thesis), *ratio* (arguments based on logic and reason), *rationis confirmatio* (supporting arguments for the *ratio*), *exornatio* (additional embellishments) and *complexio* (summary) (2,27–46). Similarly, Cicero (inv. 1,57ff.) distinguishes propositio, *propositionis adprobatio* (proving the thesis), *adsumptio* (inference), *adsumptionis adprobatio* (proving the inference)and *complexio* as parts of the *ratiocinatio* or epicheirema). This, in turn, corresponds to a deductive argumentation, extending, in effect, the Aristotelian enthymeme by adding two supporting elements providing additional confirmation that are adapted to meet the needs of a forensic speech. Later, Quintilian reduced this number to three, or at least two elements (inst. 5,14,5f.). Unlike Aristotle, the theory of commonplaces in the *Rhetoric for Herennius* does not offer universal patterns of argumentation, but specializes in legal matters. Where Aristotle examined the logical structure of argumentation, the 'Rhetoric for Herennius' describes its linear progression and reveals a tendency toward segmentation and the development of new branches.

For Cicero, learned and systematic argumentation theory is of less importance than the persuasive power of the speaker's personality. (The ideal is the *orator perfectus*). The best arguments are not predetermined by a system of theories but are found through reasoning and experience (orat. 2,175). A great deal depends on powers of judgement. Referring to the Stoa, Cicero separates the *ratio iudicandi* (assessment of arguments), which corresponds to dialectics, from the heuristics of the theory of commonplaces (*ratio inveniendi*) (top. 2,6). Persuasion is a complex process whose elements *probare* (logical proofs), *conciliare* (arousing the audience's sympathy) and *movere* (moving the audience) reestablish the Aristotelian triad of persuasive means (orat. 2,115), albeit with a different emphasis. *Ethos* and *pathos*, for Cicero, are part of the profile of a persuasive speaker who seeks to win over the audience for his entire person. They serve to produce sympathy and/or to rouse the audience to action and form a second level of persuasion beyond argumentation in a narrower sense (part. 46; orat. 128). Accordingly, a significant share of rhetorical reflection (orat. 2,178ff.) is focused on the *captatio benevolentiae* (gaining good will) (inv. 2,22) and on controlling the emotions of the audience.

In the 1st cent. AD, Quintilian considers the question of argumentation theory in detail, although not always with terminological precision. He adopts the division into *probatio* (logical argumentation) and *adfectus* or *ethos/pathos* (inst. 6,2,4ff.). The *probatio* occurs through *signa, argumenta* or *exempla* (inst. 5,9,1; cf. the Aristotelian division into sign, *eikos* and *paradeigma* argumentation), and its logical structure is based on four basic patterns (inst. 5,8,7). For Quintilian, the concept *argumentum* corresponds to the Greek terms enthymeme, epicheireme and apodixis; its function is to clarify disputed questions by using undisputed facts (5,10,1ff.). Quintilian's analyses are also geared to practical goals; accordingly, his catalogue of topoi, with its fine distinctions, is concretely pragmatic (5,10,37ff.).

C. History of Influence
1. Late Antiquity and the Middle Ages 2. Renaissance and the Modern Age 3. Modern Times

1. Late Antiquity and the Middle Ages
The authors of Late Antiquity handed down the tenets of argumentation theory to the Middle Ages, sometimes as part of a complete system of rhetorical theories that was based mainly on the works of Cicero and Quintilian (Martianus Capella; Chirius Fortunatianus; Iulius Victor; Emporius). Sometimes, in the context of related disciplines such as dialectics or logic, it was above all Augustine and Boethius who were of far-reaching significance. Both were rooted in the tradition of ancient systematics and paved the way for further developments. Augustine influenced mainly the rhetoric of the Middle Ages, while Boethius, who studied argumentation theory in the field of dialectics, was the principal source for medieval logic.

Augustine (AD 354–430), who laid the groundwork for medieval sermon rhetoric (*ars praedicandi*) in the fourth book of *De doctrina christiana*, dealt in his early systematic works with argumentation theory (*Principia dialecticae; Principia rhetorices*), as the Stoa had before him, with the distinction between rhetoric (*scientia bene dicendi*) and dialectics (*scientia bene disputandi*), without subordinating the former to the latter. In Christian rhetoric, argumentation theory, in the narrow dialectical sense, became less important because the system in ancient times had developed a theory of proof and disproof (pro and con argumentation) that no longer seemed easily applicable to the goals of Christian homiletics.

Emotional influence, which Cicero had already placed on an equal footing with logical argument, was now considered to be of greater importance. Boethius (AD 480–525) also distinguishes between dialectics and rhetoric; however, he does not view them as equally

important but rather postulates the primacy of dialectics. In his *De topicis differentiis* (PL 64, 1174) he distinguishes between argument (content) and argumentation (formal structure) and, on the basis of the ancient definition of topos as a place in which arguments are found, he divides the theory of commonplaces into a dialectical (Books One and Two) and a rhetorical system (Book Four). Dialectical topoi are used for the purpose of discussing general questions (*théseis*), rhetorical topoi for examining specific cases (*hypothéseis*). This conception of the theory of commonplaces owes more to Roman than to Aristotelian thought. It follows, then, that dialectics is more universal than rhetoric, which applies dialectical methods only to concrete cases. However, this means that the structural analogy drawn by Aristotle continues to be valid.

The perpetuation of ancient argumentation theory in separate disciplines was preceded by the development of argumentation theory, first, in the narrow, logical sense, which leads to dialectics and ultimately to scholastic logic; and second, in a complex sense, encompassing *ethos* and *pathos*, leading to medieval sermon theory. The 'Aristotelian school' [27. 42] of argumentation theory became part of medieval philosophy, as in the works of John of Salisbury, through the mediation of Boethius, who devoted himself primarily to Aristotle's logic and systematic writings. The development of the medieval theory of disputation, as expressed, for example, in the works of Thomas Aquinas (*Summa theologica*, 1267–1273), is influenced in particular by the logic and systematical writings of Aristotle (top.; soph. el.), while the theories of argumentation logic contained in his 'Rhetoric' until William of Moerbeke's Latin translation (1270), survive only in the tradition of Arabic commentary. Thus, for example, Al-Farabi distinguishes in his commentary on Aristotelian rhetoric in the 9th cent. *logica demonstrativa, tentativa, sophistica, rhetorica* and *poetica* [27. 91f.]. In contrast, the Roman Ciceronian school becomes a model for the applied rhetoric of the Middle Ages.

In his treatise *Metalogicus* (1159) [3], which owes much to the rhetoric and dialectics of the ancient world, John of Salisbury addresses questions of argumentation theory but does not treat rhetoric as an independent discipline. He defines argumentation in the classical tradition as proof or disproof of a disputed issue (2,4) and distinguishes, following Boethius, between analytical logic (*logica demonstrativa*) and rhetorical, dialectical logic (*logica probabilis*). Logic as an overarching concept is defined as *loquendi vel disserendi ratio* (1,10); hence it fulfills the tasks which ancient theoreticians assigned either to rhetoric or dialectics. Grammar serves a propaedeutic function for logic. While here the task of achieving plausibility, which was part of ancient argumentation theory, is still present in a subcategory of logic, later medieval treatises on logic shift their focus to purely analytical logic, in which the communicative aspect of rhetorical argumentation is no longer significant.

With the emergence of new genera, the significance of argumentation theory and the theory of commonplaces, which became simply catalogues of commonplaces, both decline in medieval instruction in rhetoric; practically no further theoretical development occurs. Within the trivium, rhetoric is considered less important than grammar and dialectics; indeed, it is frequently not taught at all as an independent discipline. The ancient system of theories is broken down and assigned to different fields, and '... classical rhetoric as a theory of public argumentation did not exist in the Middle Ages' [16. 950].

2. RENAISSANCE AND THE MODERN AGE

Among the numerous Renaissance treatises on rhetoric (between 1400 and 1700 some 2,500 were published) there are, in addition to works in which argumentation theory is an integral part of the system, also those that consciously exclude argumentation theory, as well as others in which it is overshadowed by thematic specialization. Abundant production leads to a variety of types, dominated by three basic ones: first, argumentation rhetoric, represented by the 'humanistic-philological' type, which preserved the classical canon of Roman rhetoric; second, the rhetorical-dialectical type, *elocutio* rhetoric, which concerns itself exclusively with the linguistic-stylistic side of rhetoric; and third, specialized rhetoric, which concentrates on certain fields, such as sermons, letters, or poetry [16. 960f.; 14. 119ff.]. One model in particular, Cicero's ideal speaker, did not require a systematic argumentation theory. General rhetoric increasingly became stylistic rhetoric, and questions of argumentation theory are frequently excluded from rhetoric. Important in the history of argumentation theory is Rudolph Agricola's *De inventione dialectica* (1485 – 1515) [1], which develops a dialectics that refers back to the rhetorical argumentation theory of the ancient world and treats parts of a speech, *dispositio*, parts of the argument and the theory of emotion. The theory of commonplaces is also dealt with in detail. For Agricola argumentation belongs in the context of a situation requiring communication and seeks to achieve plausibility. The most important task is to inform the listener, and this is to be achieved by means of convincing and plausible argumentation. He classifies *inventio* and *dispositio*, as aspects of argumentation under dialectics, a consequence of the overlapping of the content of rhetoric and dialectics. Even in the ancient world this had caused classification problems for theoreticians.

Like Boethius, Philipp Melanchthon (1497–1560), in his writings on rhetoric and dialectics (*Elementa rhetorices; Erotemata dialectices*) [5; 6], distinguishes between the two disciplines based on specialization (rhetoric), on the one hand, and universality (dialectics), on the other, but regards *inventio* as part of both sciences. The rhetorical *inventio* refers to the four types of speeches: forensic, advisory, praise and didactic. Under dialectical *inventio* he treats general questions. It is primarily in dialectics that he discusses structural problems of argumentation theory, such as the relationship of enthymeme and example to syllogism and induction, while in his rhetorical treatise argumentation theory is given far less attention compared to the more comprehensive treatment of the components of a speech and the *elocutio*. For Melanchthon, the theory of commonplaces is, above all, an important instrument for biblical exegesis. As in Roman rhetoric, from which it derives, Melanchthon distinguishes between object topoi (*loci rerum*) and person topoi (*loci personarum*).

Finally, some Renaissance rhetoricians confine rhetoric to *elocutio* and *actio*, completely excluding argumentation theory, following the tradition of medieval logic. Others, with direct links to the ancient world, such as humanists venerating Cicero, seek to maintain the complete system of rhetorical theories, of which *inventio* and *dispositio* are integral parts.

A central role in this split was played by Peter Ramus (1515–1572), who in a polemic against Quintilian (*Rhetoricae distinctiones in Quintilianum*) sought to prove that argumentation theory should not be part of rhetoric. *Inventio* and *dispositio* are exclusively a subject of dialectics (*dialecticae partes propriae*) [7. 30]. Since every science has its own subject, argumentation theory cannot be part of both rhetoric and dialectics. Here Ramus clearly expresses his view on a problem of classification that has been present at some level throughout the history of argumentation theory. It is rooted above all in the dual function of argumentation theory, which is both to analyze the material and to provide practical guidelines. His *Dialectique* (1555) [8], equates dialectics (*disputer*) and logic (*raisoner*) and contains many elements of ancient argumentation theory, such as the treatment of unartifical evidence and rules for the use of means of rhetorical persuasion.

Ramus, Melanchthon and Agricola are part of the Aristotelian-scholastic tradition and thus find themselves confronted with a problem that is rooted in Aristotle's conception. His treatment of dialectics and rhetorical *inventio* as structurally equivalent led to the question whether argumentation theory is part of rhetoric at all. But Aristotle had built the structure of rhetoric on the foundation of argumentation theory, while argumentation theory had now become completely divorced from rhetoric.

Ramus and his successors, Audomarus Taleaus and Antoine Fouquelier, provided an impulse leading to the rise of many stylistic rhetorics that were limited to *elocutio*. The rhetoric taught in the schools, however, was still primarily the Classical rhetoric that handed down elements canonized by the ancient world. In Baroque theory, argumentation theory was again considered part of rhetoric. The definitive works of the period were the *Ars rhetorica* (1560) of Cyprian Soarez, which provided the foundation for Jesuit rhetorical teaching, and the *Rhetoric* of Gerhard Johannes Vossius (1605). Both relied on authorities in Antiquity, quoting from Aristotle, Cicero, and Quintilian. In seeking to establish a complete system, however, they tended to be strongly schematic. The ancient system found support from B. Gibert, who in his 1725 outline of ancient and modern rhetoric, *Jugemens des Savans sur les auteurs qui ont traité de la Rhétorique*, in contrast to Ramus, conceded to rhetoric its own *inventio* and *dispositio*, because it focused not only on persuading the intellect, as is dialectics, but also on steering the will (182f.). Accordingly, regarding *inventio* and *dispositio* as parts of dialectics does not rule out the possibility that rhetoric has such components as well.

The Enlightenment brought about a general devaluation of rhetoric, particularly of rhetorical argumentation theory. Influenced by Descartes' (1596–1670) theory of knowledge, the view gained prominence that rhetorical argumentation did not serve the search for truth but rather deception and manipulation. It was felt that inferences leading only to plausibility failed to deliver precise results and were incapable of yielding knowledge [29. 143]. This meant a clear shift in values from the beliefs of the ancient world. Procedures that were meant to produce plausibility in matters admitting of no ultimate certainty and thus to offer help in reaching a decision were now viewed as an instrument that deliberately obscured the truth. In his *Kritik der Urteilskraft* Kant sharply denounced rhetoric as the *Kunst, ... durch den schönen Schein zu hintergehen ... als Kunst sich der Schwächen der Menschen zu seinen Absichten zu bedienen, ... gar keiner Achtung würdig* ([the] 'art ... of deceiving by a beautiful illusion .... The art of the orator, as the art of making use of human weaknesses for one's own purposes... is worthy of no respect whatsoever') [53]. The type of logic that was developed at the Cistercian convent at Port-Royal continued the tradition in which argumentation theory was viewed as part of dialectics. Angélique Arnauld and Pierre Nicole, in their *La logique ou l'art de penser* (1662/1683) [2], criticized the theory of commonplaces as being of no use to logic. Their aim was to free argumentation theory from all rhetoric in the classical sense, since such rhetoric serves not logic, but other interests. Instead, they championed *véritable rhétorique* (true rhetoric), a purely analytical-logical process guided by the search for truth.

Bernard Lamy, who dealt in his work *De l'art de parler*,(1676) [4], first with *elocutio* (*l'art de parler*), then with argumentation theory (*l'art de persuader*), attempted to reconcile rhetoric and the rationality of the Enlightenment by giving special attention to *ethos* and *pathos*. In addition to rational argumentation, he considered it necessary to arouse emotion, thus enabling it to perform its cathartic function and liberate the spirit, encouraging it in its search for the truth. However, Lamy shared the view that the theory of commonplaces is useless for argumentation, since its procedures cannot replace real knowledge, and he argues in favour of profound familiarity with facts instead of a range of methods in argumentation (279ff.). The theory of commonplaces was then rehabilitated by Giambattista Vico (1668–1744), who argues that in human

intellectual development discovery precedes judgement. In his view the theory of commonplaces, or *ars orationis copiosae* ('the art of verbose speech'), should be distinguished from critique, or *ars verae orationis* ('the art of truthful speech') [9. 28f.]. The commonplace method corresponds to human nature; 'the theory of commonplaces is the discipline that makes the intellect creative, while criticism makes it precise' [10. 101]. However, despite this attempt and others to enhance the status of argumentation theory, or at least some portions thereof, it never regained the position it had occupied in the ancient system.

3. MODERN TIMES

Along with the general decline of rhetoric that began in the mid-eighteenth cent., construction of new theories largely ceased; argumentation theory now existed almost exclusively as a subject for logic and linguistic philosophy. It was not until the 'renaissance' of rhetoric in the 20th cent., starting in the 1930s in the United States with the *New Rhetoric* and after the war in Europe, that rhetorical argumentation theory was rediscovered as a scholarly discipline. It was of essential importance in this context that concepts such as consensus or 'universally accepted opinion' gain recognition as intellectually valid operational factors. This had been denied them by the scientism of the previous century in its focus on precise verifiability. Many modern theories assume that argumentation is necessary for consensus and decision-making ability as a basis for human society, which legitimizes argumentation theory as a intellectual discipline. Modern argumentation theory is the subject of various disciplines that are related to or touch on rhetoric, such as philosophy, sociology, communication science, political science, law, linguistics and literary scholarship. Many new concepts and perspectives are emerging, but they frequently contain elements of ancient argumentation theory, sometimes in the form of specific references, sometimes in analogies inherent to the material.

Of fundamental importance for legal, as well as general argumentation theory is Theodor Viehweg (*Topik und Jurisprudenz*, 1954), who, starting from criticism of traditional legal axioms, describes an inventive theory of commonplaces ('Téchné des Problemdenkens') as a methodological basis for jurisprudence. His theory draws on the theory of commonplaces of the ancient world (Aristotle; Cicero). The Viehweg school gave rise to topos catalogues in the realm of jurisprudence, but their meaning has been called into question [11; 34]. If Viehweg's approach is geared to practical use, then that of another basic work of modern argumentation theory, *Traité de l'argumentation* by Chaim Perelman und Lucie Olbrechts-Tyteca (1958), is structurally analytical. Contemporary argumentation theory, too, retains the ancient differentiation between guidelines and analysis. Perelman/Olbrechts-Tyteca attempt to construct a kind of argumentation logic from the procedures used in the Humanities and in jurisprudence to examine the structure of everyday argumentation, whose basic pattern, as with ancient enthymeme, is deductive. They develop a consensus theory, with consent of the universal audience being the gauge of the success of an argument, and they posit that a good argument leads inevitably to general consent. They also discuss the premises of argumentation, i.e.,the classification of *accords*, or generally conceded views, values and facts, as well as its techniques, such as linking and dissociating concepts as ways of drawing inferences.

Important in the realm of linguistic argumentation theory are the studies by Stephen Toulmin (*The Uses of Argument*, 1958), which, while not based on the rhetorical tradition, show considerable resemblance to ancient argumentation theory. Toulmin distinguishes between deductive *warrant-using arguments* and inductive *warrant-establishing arguments*, similar to M. Kienpointner's 'inferential-rule-using' and 'inferential-rule-establishing' argumentation patterns [23], which correspond to the Aristotelian enthymeme or *paradeigma* inference. The triad of argument, inference (in modern argumentation theory, inferential rule) and conclusion (according to Toulmin, *grounds, warrant, claim*) is supplemented by an element (*backing*) that provides additional reasons or support for the inference and thus serves a function comparable to that of *rationis confirmatio* or *adsumptionis adprobatio* (additional confirmation) of the ancient *epicheirema* (cf. Rhet. Her. 2,28ff; Cic. inv. 1,57ff.). New aspects in Toulmin's work are 'modality,' which allows for fine linguistic nuances (reinforcement or qualification) and *rebuttal*, in which any necessary limitations are formulated. In more recent years, a radicalization of linguistic argumentation theory can be observed, in which speaking and argumentation are considered the same (e.g. in the work of O. Ducrot). Certain concepts tempt one to draw certain inferences, and to this degree language is always argumentative. This approach 'implies that the vocabulary of a language is conceived as an area within the theory of commonplaces in which the topoi attached to each word are organized in their structural relationships' [16. 984].

Argumentation theory is viewed from an ethical standpoint in the communication theory of Jürgen Habermas. Habermas, too, sees the aim of argumentation in eliminating dispute or producing consensus and calls for 'rationally motivated agreement'. He lists four universal requirements for validity in argumentation: that it be understandable, sincere, true and correct. In this regard, any statement can be examined for its acceptability [19]. The language must be understandable, the speaker sincere, the statement accurate in substance and normatively correct, i.e., in keeping with the value system of the interlocutor. In ancient rhetoric, these requirements are divided among the areas of *elocutio, ethos, logos* and, insofar as value norms are at issue, the theory of commonplaces.

Examples of links to the Aristotelian theory of argumentative inferences are found in recent times in the work of G. Öhlschläger (*Linguistische Überlegungen zu einer Theorie des Argumentierens*, 1979) and M. Kienpointner (*Alltagslogik*, 1992). The latter sees the enthymeme as the prototype of every argumentation process. Kienpointner has also undertaken a classification of topoi that includes main and sub-classifications. Its content is based in large measure on the ancient theory of commonplaces. Ancient argumentation theory, like ancient rhetoric as a whole (particularly Aristotle, Cicero, Quintilian), is of definitive authority even today in introductory or descriptive works that seek to acquaint the reader with the substance and systematics of rhetoric in general [29]. Rhetorical argumentation theory in this context is usually presented in the form of ancient argumentation theory.

→ Argumentatio

→ CICERONIANISM; → FIGURES THEORY OF; → LOGIC; → RHETORIC IV.

SOURCES: 1 R. AGRICOLA, De inventione dialectica, L. MUNDT (ed.), 1992 (with a translation into German and commentary) 2 A. ARNAULD, P. NICOLE, La logique ou l'art de penser, ed. L. MARIN, 1970 (Eng.: The Art of Thinking, trans., with an introd. by J. DICKOFF and P. JAMES, 1964) 3 Johannes v. Salisbury, Metalogicon libri III, C. C. I. WEBB (ed.), 1919 (Eng.: trans. D. D. McGARRY, 1955) 4 B. LAMY, De l'art de parler, 1675 (Eng.: The Art of Speaking, 'written in French by Messieurs du Port Royal, in pursuance of a former treatise, intituled, The Art of Thinking; rendered into English', 1676) 5 PH. MELANCHTONS Rhetorik (ed.), J. KNAPE, 1993 (Eng.: M. J. LA FONTAIN, A Critical Translation of Philip Melanchthon's Elementorum rhetorices libri duo (Diss. University of Michigan), 1968) 6 Id., Erotemata dialectices (= Corpus reformatorum, Vol. 13) 7 P. RAMUS, Brutinae Quaestiones in Oratorem Ciceronis, Frankfurt 1593 (repr.: 1965) 8 Id., Dialectique, M. DASSONVILLE (ed.), 1964 9 G. VICO, De nostri temporis studiorum ratione (Latin-German edition),translation by W. F. OTTO, 1984 (Eng.: On the Study Methods of our Time, trans. E. GIANTURCO, 1965) 10 Id., Principi di una Scienza Nova, translated into German by E. AUERBACH, 1966 (Eng.: The New Science of Giambattista Vico, rev. trans. of the 3d ed. (1774) by T. G. BERGIN and M. H. FISCH, 1968)

LITERATURE: 11 R. ALEXY, Theorie der juristischen Argumentation, 1977 (Eng.: A Theory of Legal Argumentation: The Theory of Rational Discourse as Theory of Legal Justification, R. ADLER, N. MacCORMICK (trans.), 1989) 12 W. BARNER, Barockrhetorik – Untersuchungen zur ihren geschichtlichen Grundlagen, 1970 13 K. BARWICK, Augustins Schrift de rhetorica und Hermagoras, in: Philologus 105, 1961, 97–110 (see also 108, 1964, 80–101; 109, 1965, 186–218) 14 B. BAUER, Jesuitische ars rhetorica im Zeitalter der Glaubenskämpfe, 1986 15 R. BUBNER, Was ist ein Argument? in: G. UEDING, TH. VOGEL (eds.), Von der Kunst der Rede und Beredsamkeit, 1998, 115–131 16 E. EGGS, Argumentation, HWdR 1, 914–991 17 M. FUHRMANN, Die antike Rhetorik, 1984 18 K.-H. GÖTTERT, Argumentation. Grundzüge ihrer Theorie im Bereich theoretischen Wissens und praktischen Handelns, 1978 19 J. HABERMAS, Theorie des kommunikativen Handelns, 2 vols., 1981 (Eng.: The Theory of Communicative Action, T. McCARTHY (trans.), 1984–1987) 20 A. HELLWIG, Untersuchungen

zur Theorie der Rhetorik bei Platon und Aristoteles, 1973
21 W. S. HOWELL, Logic and Rhetoric in England 1500–
1700, 1956   22 G. A. KENNEDY, A New History of Classical Rhetoric, 1994   23 M. KIENPOINTNER, Alltagslogik,
1992   24 J. KLOWSKI, Zur Entstehung der logischen Argumentation, in: RhM 113, 1970, 111–141   25 J. KOP-
PERSCHMIDT, H. SCHANZE (eds.), Argumente – Argumentation. Interdiziplinäre Problemzugänge, 1985   26 E. A.
MOODY, Studies in Medieval Philosophy, Science and
Logic, 1975   27 J. J. MURPHY, Rhetoric in the Middle
Ages, 1974   28 Id. (ed.), Renaissance Eloquence, 1983
29 C. OTTMERS, Rhetorik, 1996, (with an extensive bibliography)   30 M. POHLENZ, Die Stoa. Geschichte einer
geistigen Bewegung, [7]1992, 49ff.   31 ST. E. PORTER(ed.),
Handbook of Classical Rhetorik in the Hellenistic Period,
1997   32 C. PRANTL, Geschichte der Logik im Abend-
lande, Vols. I–IV, Leipzig 1855–1870   33 W. RISSE, Die
Logik der Neuzeit, Vol. I, 1964, Vol. II, 1970   34 G.
STRUCK, Topische Jurisprudenz, 1971   35 G. UEDING, B.
STEINBRINK, Grundriß der Rhetorik – Geschichte, Technik, Methode, [3]1994

ADDITIONAL BIBLIOGRAPHY: H. GOTOFF, The Art of
Illusion. Harvard Studies in Classical Philology 95.
(1993): 289–313; G. A. KENNEDY, Focusing of Argu-
ments in Greek Deliberative Oratory. Transactions and
Proceedings of the American Philological Association 90.
(1959):131–138.; L. PERNOT, Rhetoric in Antiquity,
2005; J. J. MURPHY, A Short-Title Catalogue of Works on
Rhetorical Theory, 1981 (rev. ed. 2004 by J. J. MURPHY,
LAWRENCE GREEN); P. MACK, Valla and Agricola in the
Traditions of Rhetoric and Dialectic, 1993; W. J. ONG,
Ramus. Method, and the Decay of Dialogue, 1958.
                                                      SYLVIA USENER

Aristocracy see→ CONSTITUTION, TYPES OF

Aristotelianism
A. INTRODUCTION   B. GREEK ARISTOTELIANISM
C. ARABIC ARISTOTELIANISM   D. LATIN
ARISTOTELIANISM OF THE MIDDLE AGES   E. RE-
NAISSANCE ARISTOTELIANISMS   F. MODERN
ARISTOTLE RESEARCH   G. RECEPTION OF
ARISTOTLE IN THE 20TH CENT.

A. INTRODUCTION
The term 'Aristotelianism' refers to a particular form
of philosophy, named after Aristotle, that was already
developed during Antiquity and that has had adherents
up through the modern era. Aristotelianism emphasises
the theoretical sciences over the practical ones and the
synthetic representation of knowledge as a system derived from principles that are already known as opposed to the analytical search for principles of synthetic
representation. In this sense, Aristotelianism is a highly
developed form of the reception of Aristotle's philosophy that is much narrower in scope than the set of references – whether marginal or central – to aspects of
Aristotle's teachings and to his individual writings. In
the history of philosophy, Aristotelian theories have
been, and to some extent still are, employed and discussed in → LOGIC, → METAPHYSICS and → NATURAL

PHILOSOPHY as well as in → PRACTICAL PHILOSOPHY
and political philosophy; this does not, however, mean
that such discourses can be described as instances of
Aristotelianism. Aristotelian → RHETORIC and poetics
(→ TRAGEDY) have also had an inestimable influence on
those disciplines.

B. GREEK ARISTOTELIANISM
By focusing on empirical research in the sciences of
nature, ethics and politics, the older representatives of
Peripatos carried forward an approach to scientific inquiry that was grounded in the co-operative search for
concrete data. From around the beginning of the
Common Era, however, the encyclopaedic aspect of
Peripatetic philosophy became increasingly important
as a result of new scientific activity during late Antiquity. As a result of the Neoplatonic understanding of
Aristotle as an introduction to the higher wisdom of
Plato, the Aristotelian encyclopaedia of science was
transformed into a closed system. Proclus (c. 410–485),
in his *Elementatio theologica* and *Elementatio physica*,
presents his conclusions, with regard to the forms of
substance according to the geometric method proposed
by Aristotle and carried out by Euclid, in such a way
that they form the 'elements' of a continuous chain.
This 'synthetic' descent from principles to conclusions
assumes, according to Proclus, an 'analytic' ascent
behind all hypotheses to the sole principle of everything. However, by using the Platonic *Hen* as the first
principle, Proclus broke with the fundamental axiom of
Aristotelian science according to which all insight proceeds from previously existing knowledge.

At approximately the same time, Aristotle's logic
was expanded by Neoplatonic authors in such a way as
to include his *Rhetoric* and *Poetics* as well. In this way,
Simplicius (6th cent.), the last important representative
of the school of Athens, was able to regard poetic, rhetorical and dialectical argumentation as different stages
of participation in the ideal of absolute demonstration.
The Neoplatonic understanding of Aristotle gave rise to
a rich tradition of commentary in the Greek and Syrian
languages.

C. ARABIC ARISTOTELIANISM
Aristotle's works appeared in Islam as early as the
second half of the 8th cent. The Arabic reception of
Aristotle was based on an interest in Greek medicine.
Aristotle's categorisation of science presented a structure in which classical authors like Hippocrates and
Galen, Euclid and Ptolemy all had a place. With the
founding of the *bayt al-hikma* ('House of Wisdom') in
Bagdad in the year 830 by the Abbasid caliph al-
Ma'mûn (786–833), practically the entire corpus of Aristotelian works that had been preserved (except the
Eudemian Ethics, *Magna Moralia* and *Politics*) became
available, along with its Greek commentators. This
corpus laid a uniform foundation for Islamic Aristotelianism from Persia to Spain. In Baghdad there was, up
until the 10th cent., an established tradition of the study

of the logic and of the natural philosophical writings. Few commentaries on practical philosophy were written, since Aristotle's works were seen primarily as propaedeutics for the study of medicine [31].

The synthetic representation of an area of inquiry was, in accordance with Aristotle's and Euclid's methodology, used with great success in Arabic natural philosophical works, e.g. in the *Optics* by Alhazen (965–c. 1040) [2]. The shift in the Aristotelian theory of science in the direction of a first principle, which goes back to Proclus, was not followed in Islam. Even though the 'Book of Causes'(Lat. *Liber de causis*, c. 9th cent. [3]), which was erroneously attributed to Aristotle and which described the universe's structure according to the method of logical deduction from a first, highest principle, posited a creator god in place of the Platonic Hen, it had no effect in Islam.

From the beginning, Arabic philosophers understood Aristotle's books about natural philosophy and metaphysics as parts of a larger philosophical framework. Arabic Aristotelianism arose from the contact between this 'rational' science and the 'traditional' scholarship of the Arabs' (Koran, Arabic language and dialectical theology = *kalâm*). *Kalâm* had come into being in the 9th and 10th cents. as an answer to heresies that were arising in Islam. It was the theologians' task to provide believers with logical evidence for their faith. The first attempt to integrate the 'science of the Arabs' into the Aristotelian categorisation of knowledge was undertaken by Alfarabi (c. 870–950) in his *Catalogue of Sciences* [1]. While the philosophical theory of God was being incorporated into the speculative science of metaphysics, *Kalâm* as practical science served to defend the tenets of faith. A century later, Avicenna (980–1037) undertook a reform of theology according to the Aristotelian theory of demonstrative science. He tried to understand *Kalâm* not solely as apologetics but rather as Aristotelian metaphysics. He accordingly listed those types of premises that are permitted in the various forms of argumentation. If the theory of God is to be presented scientifically (that is demonstratively, not dialectically or rhetorically), then only axioms, sensory data and the unanimous agreement of Islamic tradition can serve as principles.

Aristotelianism in the strict sense of the word came into full flower with Averroes' (1126–1198) commentaries. In Averroes' opinion, Aristotle's demonstrative arguments lead to true and certain conclusions. The Aristotelian writings, Averroes stated, synthetically represented philosophical truth; just as Euclid completed geometry, so had Aristotle completed the speculative sciences. In cases in which the evidence leads to conclusions that clearly contradict Islamic theology, it was necessary to differentiate, according to Averroes, between a more exoteric meaning for the many and an esoteric meaning that is comprehensible only to a small elite. Philosophy was the profession of this intellectual elite, whose God-given task was to freely strive for truth. By the 14th cent., however, this elite as well as its scientific writings disappeared in Islam.

Aristotelian science was also used in medieval Judaism. In Spain and southern France, Hebrew translators made accessible the Islamic corpus of Aristotle's work as well as the associated commentaries by Averroes and the medical works that accompanied them. When conflicts arose between philosophy and the Jewish faith, some thinkers, among whom Moses Maimonides (1135–1204) is the most significant, argued that philosophical thought must proceed in accordance with the theory of demonstrative science without regard to theological teachings. In spite of this view there was in the 14th cent. within Judaism an increasingly critical evaluation of Aristotelian teachings in light of faith, and this in turn contributed to the development of a new scientific worldview.

D. LATIN ARISTOTELIANISM OF THE MIDDLE AGES

In the Latin West, Aristotle's works were made accessible and dealt with in three clearly differentiated phases. 1. The first phase began in the 6th cent. with the translation of the Aristotelian writings on logic by Boethius (c. 480–c. 524); in the monastic schools these were understood primarily as an introduction to the study of the Bible. 2. The 'scholastic' phase of Latin Aristotelianism began in the 12th cent. with gradual translation, first from the Arabic and later from the Greek, of practically the entire corpus of the science of Antiquity. In this phase the reception of Aristotle was greatly influenced by Averroes' synthetic understanding of science. 3. The last phase fell within the Renaissance era. It focused largely on addressing the irregularities that made the one-sided scholastic concept of science increasingly untenable [26].

In the scholastic Phase, Aristotle's works were received in connection with a comprehensive attempt to absorb the worldly knowledge of Greece, Judaism and Islam. The translations of the 12th and 13th cents. contributed significantly to the overall store of knowledge in the Middle Ages: Euclid, Ptolemy, Hippocrates and Galen, but above all Aristotle's books together with Averroes' commentaries. Already prior to translation of the Aristotelian corpus, the *magistri* of the new urban schools were led by Boethius in their search for a scientific conception that would include a systematic representation of philosophical and theological knowledge. Boethius understood science in the Aristotelian sense as a teaching that starts from first principles and proceeds by means of strict proofs to true and certain conclusions. Early scholastic authors were motivated by Boethius, and later by Euclid as well, to develop a general theory of scientific method from that model.

At the beginning of the 13th cent., Aristotle's natural philosophical books (including *Metaphysics* and *Liber de causis*) were available in the Latin West. But already in 1210 and 1215 the *libri naturales* were condemned in Paris. It seems as if these condemnations were not only directed at individual teachings of Aristotle's such as that of the eternity of the world, but also at the Proclian idea of a science based on first principles that had been transmitted by the Islamic *Liber de causis*. The *Regulae caelestis iuris* by Alain von Lille (d. *c.* 1203) resembles the axiomatic approach to inquiry. However, since that work – like 'De causis' – does not presuppose any axioms or postulates at the outset, Alain created the impression that his work was an attempt to prove articles of faith that were unprovable for Christians.

The fact that these condemnations between 1215 and 1255, when the Aristotelian corpus finally found acceptance in Paris, were for the most part observed, means that those 40 years were of decisive importance for the formulation of the scholastic method. Since Aristotle's logic was explicitly excluded from the condemnations, the *magistri artium* increasingly directed their attention to the theory of science of the *Second Analytics*. They worked on an axiomatic representation of the disciplines of the Quadrivium (especially on optics as a science subordinated to geometry), while the theologians for their part were seeking to justify their subject area not on the basis of *regulae* like those of Alain, but rather on the basis of articles of faith as axioms that were evident through revelation – unprovable, to be sure, yet certain nonetheless [24].

The foundation for the scientific progress of the 13th and 14th cents. was laid in the year 1255, when Aristotle's logic, natural philosophy and ethics were required for lectures at the Faculty of Arts in Paris. From that point on, Aristotle's works determined the structure of the philosophical teachings at the medieval → UNIVERSITIES. One of the first to pay attention to the entire corpus of Aristotelian knowledge was Albert the Great (*c.* 1200–1280). His paraphrases of all of Aristotle's basic works prepared the way for the extensive commentary literature by means of which the Middle Ages appropriated Aristotelian thought.

In the course of the next century extraordinary progress was made in natural philosophy. Aristotelian physics provided both the philosophical principles and the encyclopaedic structure for this development. The newly translated commentaries of Averroes, who understood Aristotle's works as a synthetic representation of philosophical truth, contributed to the solidification of Aristotle's rank as il maestro di color che sanno (Dante, Inferno 4,131). The progress extended to Aristotelian practical philosophy. New translations of *Nicomachean Ethics* and *Politics* from the Greek opened up a new way of perceiving human purpose and of conceiving of the state as secular [20].

The theologians, for their part, sought to justify a *concordia* between revealed teachings and the philosophical truth as represented by Aristotle and Averroes. Thomas of Aquinas (1225–1274) claimed, for apologetic purposes, that Aristotelian science on the one hand and the teaching of Christian revelation on the other were basically in agreement with one another. The acceptance of Christian doctrine was supposed to appear rational, since it agreed with basic philosophical suppositions like the existence of God and the immor-

tality of the human soul, both of which, for example, Aristotle was assumed to have proven.

In the year 1277, however, the bishop of Paris (Etienne Tempier) condemned 219 tenets, most of which represented Aristotelian positions [5]. For this reason, the condemnation had far-reaching effects on both theology and philosophy in the late Middle Ages. The fact that many of Aristotle's ideas contradicted Catholic teachings – his determinism, his theory of the eternity of the world as well as the uncertainty of his theory regarding the immortality of the soul – made it possible for philosophers to free the science of nature, to a certain degree, from its close adherence to Aristotle's authority in philosophical questions [17].

With that condemnation as a backdrop, Joannes Duns Scotus (1265–1308) defined the subject of Aristotelian metaphysics as a theory of being in such a way that it became a critique of the Aristotelian theory of speculative science. Whereas Aristotle was able to draw conclusions solely within the realm of physics, Scotus claimed that the first object of reason was not sensory reality but rather being as such. This determination makes possible the investigation of physical reality in a metaphysical manner, as finite being subject to change (*ens mobile*), in contrast to the consideration of the *corpus mobile* in physics as understood by Aristotle.

By means of these and similar modifications of Aristotle's theory of speculative science it became possible for the philosophers of the 14th cent. to go beyond Aristotle in the natural sciences. Thinkers like Johannes Buridan (*c.* 1295–*c.* 1358) were able, with the support of the Aristotelian idea that all science is autonomous within its own field, to develop theories in → PHYSICS, like the theory of the movement of a projectile, that were not dependent on Aristotle's views. Meanwhile, mathematicians like Nikolaus Oresme (*c.* 1320–1382) were able to turn their attention to areas that Aristotle had neglected and to develop, for example, new theories of proportions and infinite series [28].

E. Renaissance Aristotelianisms

The Aristotelianism of the clerical elite of the Middle Ages was based on a unified view of the wold that completely fell apart with the rise of new social groupings in the → RENAISSANCE, meaning that we must speak not of *one* Aristotelianism but rather of *various* Aristotelianisms for the period of 1450–1650 [12].

This third phase of Latin Aristotle reception began in 1438 with a treatise by the Byzantine philosopher Georgios Gemistos Pletho (*c.* 1360–1452) about Plato's precedence over Aristotle [6]. Pletho accused the Latinists of erroneously interpreting Aristotle as if his teachings agreed with Christian theology. Pletho stated that there was no idea of a provident creator god or of the immortality of the human soul to be found in Aristotle. He traced the Latinists' mistakes back to the Arab Averroes, who had claimed that Aristotle's works represented the completion of natural philosophy. In the Renaissance, Pletho's reproaches brought about a revolution in the Latin understanding of Aristotle. Facilitated by Byzantine thinkers who brought to Italy an Aristotle as yet unknown to the scholastics, Latin scholars from the middle of the 15th cent. onward produced new editions of the Greek text of Aristotle as well as new Latin and vernacular translations of his works. They furthermore created Greek editions and Latin translations of practically the entire corpus of ancient Greek commentaries. [26]. Finally, they wrote new commentaries on the Aristotelian corpus. It is noteworthy that the number of Latin Aristotle commentaries that were written during the century between Pietro Pomponazzi (1462–1525) and Galileo (1564–1642) is greater that that of those written during the entire millennium from Boethius to Pomponazzi.

In the 16th cent., new scientific interests led various scholars to consider individual works by Aristotle without taking into account his overall organisation of science. In Italy professional philosophers at the universities turned their attention to the natural philosophical and the zoological writings (→ ZOOLOGY). Humanistic scholars took up Aristotelian moral philosophy, while those who were interested in literature studied the 'Poetics'. Scholars concerned with constitutional reforms referred to Aristotelian logic in order to find new ways to interpret their legal doctrines. The Aristotelian *Politics* received new attention all over Europe, practically without any reference to other components of Aristotle's works [19].

1. CATHOLIC ARISTOTELIANISM 2. SECULAR ARISTOTELIANISM IN ITALY 3. BAROQUE SCHOLASTICISM 4. LUTHERAN ORTHODOXY 5. CALVINISTIC ARISTOTELIANISM

1. CATHOLIC ARISTOTELIANISM

With the end of the Council of Basel (1437), a new phase in the history of Catholic interpretation of Aristotelian science had already begun. The idea of a Christian Aristotelianism, as had been developed by the *via antiqua*, arose primarily at the northern European universities. Around the middle of the 15th cent. it was also brought to Italy. A fundamental transformation of Aristotelian science resulted from the meeting between Christian Aristotelianism and its secular counterpart in Italy.

Conflict arose in 1516 with the publication of Pietro Pomponazzi's *Tractatus de immortalitate animae* [7]. He claimed that according to Aristotle the theory of the soul was part of physics, albeit as a part of the theory of the animated body (*corpus animatum*). Since the soul was a material form, it was also transitory. The attempts to meet this challenge, which were undertaken primarily in the mendicant orders, were based on the search for metaphysical rather than physical proof of the soul's immortality. The Scotist definition of metaphysics as a science of uncreated and created being made it possible to regard the human soul and the world as metaphysical objects. This possibility, however, in turn implied the necessity of a systematic reinterpretation of Aristotelian philosophy in agreement with the principles that were considered to be its true principles – that is, those which led to conclusions that accorded with Catholic doctrine.

The first step in this direction was taken by Benito Perera (c. 1535–1610), a professor at the *Collegio Romano* of the newly founded Jesuit order. Perera claimed that the theory of the soul belonged to metaphysics. Since that science can only regard non-physical reality as a cause, however, he suggested subdividing traditional metaphysics into two special sciences: 'divine science', which addressed God, the intelligences and the soul, and 'primary philosophy', which reflected on 'being' as such.

The project of rewriting Aristotle was primarily undertaken at Iberian universities. The major systematic works of Spanish scholasticism attempted to represent metaphysics *per modum doctrinae*, that is, as an organic whole derived from the first principles of philosophy. The Jesuit Francisco Suárez (1548–1617), in his famous *Disputationes metaphysicae*, found the basis for his Christian reinterpretation of Aristotelian thinking in the relationship of finite reality with the infinite creative power of God. Finite being is being that can be constituted in its present being by means of God's absolute power because its essence does not contain any contradictory elements. The god that is recognised by means of natural reason is the principle of a system that descends through the various divisions of finite being [18].

2. SECULAR ARISTOTELIANISM IN ITALY

Because the faculties of arts at Italian universities were oriented toward medicine rather than toward theology, members were less concerned with metaphysics than with Aristotle's natural philosophical works. However, under pressure from the discoveries of Copernicus, Columbus and Galileo, from the various ancient philosophical schools- → PLATONISM, → STOICISM, → EPICUREANISM –, which had received increasing attention since the middle of the 15th cent., and from the enormous amount of scientific material that was uncovered during the Renaissance, Aristotelian authors sought to situate Aristotle's theory of science within a more all-inclusive context.

Whereas the Aristotelian tradition had since Proclus focused primarily on the compositive (synthetic) side of Aristotelian teachings about science, secular Aristotelianism in Italy rediscovered the – likewise Aristotelian – method of resolution (analysis) [13]. Understanding of these methods developed in the context of a theory of scientific *regressus*, which is made up of two moments. First one moves from a known effect to a confused recognition of the existence of the cause; then one apodictically proves the effect by means of a recognition of the essence of the cause, a recognition that has been acquired through a difficult *examen mentale*. By taking recourse in the *examen* to experimentation and mathematical deduction, Galileo Galilei (1564–1642) contributed to the formulation of modern science theory.

Toward the end of the 16th cent., the Paduan Aristotelian Jacopo Zabarella (1533–89) in his text De methodis (1578) [8], the sources of which are Aristotle's Analytica posteriora, Galen's Ars parva and Averroes' commentary on Aristotelian physics, related the theory of the *regressus* clearly to the Aristotelian differentiation between theoretical and practical science. The compositive method derives conclusions from first principles; the resolutive method takes as its point of departure the goal of an action and tries to discover the means and principles by which the goal can be attained. In Zabarella's opinion, however, it is necessary to differentiate 'methods' from 'orders' of representation. 'Methods' lead to the recognition of something that is unknown from something that is known; 'orders' pass on knowledge that has already been attained through human efforts. The two 'orders' correspond to the two 'methods': the compositive order represents the object of knowledge entirely as conclusions proceeding from first principles; the resolutive order sets up a system of *praecepta* and *regulae* for practice according to which a given goal can be attained [29].

3. Baroque Scholasticism

In the 17th cent. the ideas of both Christian and Italian secular Aristotelianism continued to be influential in the schools of Europe. The Christian Aristotelianism of the Catholic schools sought to defend a worldview in which acceptance of revelation seemed reasonable. From their teachings there arose a new literary form, the *cursus philosophicus* – e.g. the *Cursus conimbricensis* (1592–98) of the Jesuit order [14] and the summaries of scholastic philosophy by Eustachius a S. Paulo O.Cist. (d. 1640) and Johannes a S. Thoma O.P. (d. 1644). Suárez' division of reality into *ens infinitum, ens creatum immateriale* and *ens creatum materiale* provided a foundation for the *cursus*. It included the division of metaphysics into (what were later termed) the fields of *theologia naturalis, psychologia rationalis* and *cosmologia*. While the increasing need for independent treatment of the problem of God could thereby be addressed, it meant that the intensifying crisis of Aristotelian physics as a science of the *corpus mobile* became irrelevant for the Baroque scholastics.

4. Lutheran orthodoxy

Even though Aristotle and the scholastic mixture of theology and philosophy were rejected by Martin Luther, the Aristotelian conception of science became the primary one at Protestant universities in the 16th cent. [32]. In the areas that were oriented toward Luther in denominational terms, Aristotelian metaphysics was considered a suitable basis for the unity of doctrine needed by the Lutheran orthodoxy [25]. German philosophical textbooks, for example *Exercitationes metaphysicae* (1603–04) by Jakob Martini (1570–1649) and *Metaphysica commentatio* (1605) by Cornelius Martini (1568–1621) turned against disciples of Calvin and Melanchthon, but also against radi-

cal Lutherans who claimed that some aspects of the doctrine of faith, like that of the trinity, contradicted reason, and toward Suárez' idea of a possible, denominationally neutral world that could be accepted by anyone who accepted the idea of the creation. Even though there were Lutheran objections to the idea of natural knowledge of God, the theologians soon conceded, for apologetic purposes, the necessity of a natural theology. Already in 1621 a *Theologia naturalis* was published by Johannes Scharf (1595–1660). The Lutheran orthodoxy also tried to systematise the theology of revelation in agreement with the Aristotelian theory of practical science. Georg Calixt (1586–1656) applied Zabarella's idea of the analytical order to theology in his 1619 *Epitome theologiae*.

5. Calvinistic Aristotelianism

In the areas that leaned toward Calvinism, dogmatic theology was considered to be a speculative science that followed a synthetic method. Like Perera, reformed theologians differentiated between two metaphysical sciences. One considered God; the other was a general science of being that was definitive for the principles of the individual sciences. 'Ontology', according to Rudolphus Goclenius (1547–1628), who was the first to use the word, has the task of assigning to each of the various scientific disciplines its own place within a new encyclopaedia of knowledge. The idea of a systematic totality of knowledge was fundamental to Calvinistic thinking. In this vein, Bartholomäus Keckermann (1571/73–1609), Clemens Timpler (1567–1624) and Johann Heinrich Alsted (1588–1638) published, in the early 17th cent., systems of the various *artes*. In these systems the disciplines were understood not as sciences in the Aristotelian sense but rather as *artes liberales*, free arts, that are governed by *technologia* [33].

F. Modern Aristotle Research

The great number of Aristotelianisms in the Renaissance and the revolutionary understanding of science in the modern era put an end to Aristotelianism, in the strict sense of the word, around the middle of the 17th cent. Although individual works – *Logic*, the *Zoological Tracts, Politics, Poetics* – still attracted students, the scientific revolution of the 17th cent. evoked an entirely new way of thinking about the sciences. From the Enlightenment onward Aristotle was considered not so much the founder of a hierarchical system of science as one of those scholars who sought to understand reality by means of empirical research in individual disciplines. In the philosophy of the 19th cent., and particularly in 'German idealism', the break with the Aristotelianism that had until that time been dominant went hand in hand with intensified attention to the Platonic tradition (→ Platonism).

The publication of *Aristotelis opera* by the Berlin Academy between 1831 and 1870 and its edition of the *Commentaria in Aristotelem Graeca* between 1882 and 1909, as well as the edition of Aristoteles Latinus that was begun in 1939 by the *Union Académique Interna-*

tionale for the medieval Latin translation laid the foundation for modern research on Aristotle and the tradition of his philosophy.
→ Aristotle, commentators on; → Aristoteles
→ Arabic-Islamic Cultural Sphere, The

Sources: 1 Al-Farabi, Catálogo de las ciencias, A. González (ed. and trans., 1953   2 Opticae thesaurus. Alhazeni arabis libri VII, Basel 1572, (repr. with introduction by D. C. Lindberg), 1972   3 Die pseudo-aristotelische Schrift 'Ueber das reine Gute, bekannt unter dem Namen Liber de causis', O. Bardenhewer (ed.), 1882, (repr. 1958)   4 Le Liber de causis, A. Pattin (ed.), 1966 (Eng.: The Book of causes (Liber de causis), Dennis J Brand (trans.), rev., ²1984)   5 Aufklärung im MA? Die Verurteilung von 1277. Das Dokument des Bischofs von Paris, trans. and commentary by K. Flasch, 1989 6 G. G. Pletho, Περὶ ὧν Ἀριστοτέλης πρὸς Πλάτωνα διαφέρεται, Paris 1541, lat. Basel 1574 (= PL vol. 160, 773ff.)   7 P. Pomponazzi, Abhandlung über die Unsterblichkeit der Seele, lateinisch-deutsch, B. Mojsisch (ed.), 1990 8 Jacopo Zabarella: Über die Methoden (De methodis); Über den Rückgang (De regressu), R. Schicker (ed.), 1995

Literature: 9 E. Kessler et al. (eds.), Aristotelismus und Renaissance. In memoriam Charles B. Schmitt, 1988 10 Aristotelismo padovano e filosofia aristotelica: Atti del XII Congresso internazionale di filosofia, Venezia 1958, 1960, IX   11 L. Olivieri (ed.), Aristotelismo veneto e scienza moderna, 1983   12 Ch. B. Schmitt et al. (eds.), The Cambridge History of Renaissance Philosophy, 1988 13 E. Kessler et al. (eds.), Method and Order in Renaissance Philosophy of Nature: The Aristotle Commentary Tradition, 1998   14 L. Giard (ed.), Les jésuites à la Renaissance: Système éducatif et production du savoir, 1995 15 Platon et Aristote à la Ren. XVIᵉ Colloque International de Tours, Paris 1976   16 J. Kraye et al. (eds.), Pseudo-Aristotle in the Middle Ages, 1986   17 L. Bianchi, Il vescovo e i filosofi. La condanna Parigina del 1277 e l'evoluzione dell' aristotelismo scolastico, 1990   18 J.-F. Courtine, Suárez et le système de la métaphysique, 1990   19 H. Dreitzel, Protestantischer Aristotelismus und absoluter Staat, 1970   20 Ch. Flüeler, Rezeption und Interpretation der Aristotelischen Politica im späten Mittelalter, 2 vols., 1992   21 L. Giard, L'Aristotélisme au XVIe siècle, in: Les études philosophiques, 1986, Nr. 3, 281–405 22 P. O. Kristeller, La tradizione aristotelica nel Rinascimento, 1962   23 Id., Die Aristotelische Tradition, in: Humanismus und Renaissance, 1974, 30–49   24 A. Lang, Die theologische Prinzipienlehre der mittelalterlichen Scholastik, 1964   25 U. G. Leinsle, Das Ding und die Methode. Methodische Konstitutionen und Gegenstand der frühen protestantischen Metaphysik, 1985   26 Ch. H. Lohr, Latin Aristotle Commentaries: I. Medieval Latin Aristotle Commentaries, in: Traditio, 23–30, 1967,74; II. Renaissance Authors, 1988; III. Indices, 1995   27 Id., Latin Aristotle Commentaries V: Bibliography of the Secondary Literature, 2005   28 A. Maier, Studien zur Naturphilosophie der Spätscholastik, 5 vols., 1951–66   29 H. Mikkeli, An Aristotelian Response to Renaissance Humanism. Jacopo Zabarella on the Nature of Arts and Sciences, 1992   30 B. Nardi, Saggi sull'aristotelismo padovano dal secolo XIV al XVI, 1958   31 F. E. Peters, Aristoteles arabus, 1968   32 P. Petersen, Geschichte der Aristotelischen Philosophie im protestantischen Deutschland, 1921 (repr. 1964)   33 W. Schmidt-Biggemann, Topica universalis. Eine Modellgeschichte humanistischer und barocker Wissenschaft, 1983   34 Ch. B. Schmitt, Aristotle and the Renaissance, 1983 (Italian 1985, French 1992).
                                                        Charles H. Lohr

G. Reception of Aristotle in the 20th Cent.

1. Introduction 2. Anglo-Saxon Philosophy 3. The German-Speaking Region

1. Introduction

The reception of Aristotle in the 20th cent. can best be characterized in terms of its critical objective. The intent is to overcome, through Aristotle, the narrowing of modern philosophy since Descartes. Aristotle is not read as a systematist; rather, individual aspects of his philosophy are selected and further developed from the perspective of contemporary concerns. The following instances are especially noteworthy: a) the critique of rationalism and of idealistic speculations using Aristotle's method; b) the critique of empiricism using Aristotelian realistic ontology; c) the increased awareness that theoretical and practical reason cannot be traced back to one another and that simple formalism is insufficient for the justification of moral norms. The two main branches of reception will be sketched out here, and a) and b) will be considered more closely; c) will be addressed under → Practical philosophy.

2. Anglo-Saxon Philosophy

In opposition to Neo-Hegelian idealism, a renaissance of Aristotelian philosophy begins in Oxford with the work of the classical philologist and philosopher John Cook Wilson (1849–1915). Aristotle is viewed as a methodical example: Philosophy must be based on normal language and work out the multiple usage of words (which Aristotle demonstrates in exemplary fashion in Metaph. 5 using terms including that of 'being', 5, 7). Gilbert Ryle (1900–1976) differentiates, with the help of the theory of categories, meaningful from meaningless statements and thus solves philosophical dilemmas. With his method of 'linguistic phenomenology', John L. Austin (1911–1960), who like Wilson particularly values the 'Nicomachean Ethics', clarifies philosophical concepts – for example, via an investigation of the daily practice of making excuses, the concepts of action and freedom. Staying with the Aristotelian focus on the language of daily life, Peter Strawson, in *Individuals* (1959), differentiates between 'descriptive' and 'revisionary' metaphysics. Whereas revisionary metaphysics seeks to bring about a better structure, descriptive metaphysics is satisfied to describe the actual structure of our thinking about the world; in this way it shows that material individual objects, Aristotle's first substances, are fundamental to the ontology of our everyday language.

In Aristotle, Οὐσία (*ousía*) stands not only for substance but also for essence or form (*eídos*), which is indicated by sortal terms, e.g. 'person', 'leopard', 'water', 'gold'. For Aristotle, essence is a reality that is independent of our thinking and speaking. In contrast to the nominalism that harkens back to the Vienna Circle, denying the existence of such a real essence and recognising only conventions of speech, Saul A. Kripke, *Naming and Necessity* (1972), Hilary Putnam, *The Meaning of Meaning* (1975), David Wiggins, *Sameness and Substance* (1980) and others represent an Aristotelian realism. Sortal terms contain an indexical moment. They refer to reality; we can recognise their meaning only by investigating a natural specimen. The priority that Aristotle gives to the category of *ousía* is affirmed by the fact that the various aspects of our relationships with individual objects (counting, identifying, statements of existence) presuppose an ability on our part to understand the individual object as an instance of its kind, the second *ousía* of the Aristotelian writing on categories.

3. The German-Speaking Region

Repelled by the speculations of Fichte, Schelling and Hegel, Franz Brentano (1838–1917), under the influence of his teacher Adolf von Trendelenburg, devoted himself to the study of Aristotle. Important ideas for 20th cent. philosophy came from Brentano: He was Husserl's teacher and thus marks the beginning of phenomenology; he also decisively influenced contemporary ontology. Because of his method of linguistic-logical investigation he is close to analytical philosophy. Brentano is above all interested in analysis of psychological phenomena for which 'intentionality', that is the relationship to something, is essential, and in ontology. Both areas of inquiry are inspired by Aristotle. Brentano's dissertation investigates the four meanings of 'being' that Aristotle differentiates in Metaph. 5,7; his postdoctoral thesis deals with Aristotelian psychology; and the theology of Metaphysics XII [1] is at the heart of his later, comprehensive exposition of Aristotle.

Brentano's dissertation influenced Heidegger; his courses on Aristotle from the 1920s [2; 3] constitute the decisive impulse behind a new interest. According to Heidegger, philosophical historical interpretation has the task of destruction; it should lead to an original interpretation of tradition. Heidegger's relationship to Aristotle is ambivalent. For Heidegger, Aristotle determined the anthropology of the Greco-Christian understanding of life; therefore, Aristotle must be viewed critically with an eye to the kind of being that he saw in human life: 'The material realm that supplies the original meaning of being is that of objects that are fabricated and commonly used' [4. 253]. In Gadamer's judgment, Aristotle is for Heidegger more of a 'figure of tradition that had a masking function and prevented his own Western thinking from coming into its own' [5. 232]. But in the interpretation of the meaning of being that has been cited here, Aristotle represents for Heidegger simply the culmination of previous philosophy. In his physics, which is for Heidegger the centre of Aristotelian thinking, Aristotle is seen as achieving a new basic approach: the explication of Being in the How of its being moved 251].

Inspired by Heidegger's interpretations, other writers including Hans-Georg Gadamer, Hannah Arendt and Joachim Ritter fruitfully used ideas of Aristotle's for their own philosophy. The origins of Gadamer's *Wahrheit und Methode* (1960; Eng. 'Truth and Method', 1975) reach back to a seminar of Heidegger's in Freiburg about the sixth volume of the *Nicomachean Ethics* [5. 230f.], in which Aristotle differentiates among different forms of knowledge and truth. Practical knowledge is for Aristotle not reducible to the theoretical and the technical. It is not a knowledge that is object-based and that simply ascertains; rather, the knower is himself affected by this knowledge. It prescribes to him what he must do. Practical knowledge always has to do with the concrete situation; the culmination of practical knowledge, phronesis, is thus the ability to pass judgement, which can not be done according to a formula. Read as a renewal of Aristotelian phronesis, Gadamer's hermeneutics is a critique and demarcation of scientific-technical reason. Hannah Arendt, *The Human Condition* (1958), in a critical discussion of the impoverishment of social relationships in the modern world, wants to restore to the Aristotelian concept of action (*práxis*) its full meaning. From among the three forms of the Vita activa, labour, work and action, Arendt, along with Aristotle, grants the highest status to action, in which human beings develop themselves as life forms who are gifted in speech and destined for the polis, and which contains its goal within itself. Action takes place directly between people in the medium of language and without involvement of matter and things; it is life in the actual sense, for life means 'being among people'. It is an expression of human plurality and at the same time of the irreproducible uniqueness of the individual. In contrast to an abstract (Kantian) morality, Joachim Ritter, *Metaphysik und Politik. Studien zu Aristoteles und Hegel* (1969), refers to Hegel's morality to rehabilitate Aristotle's concept of the ethical, a category that includes custom, tradition and institution as well as virtue. In order to be effective, practical reason in his view must take on a concrete historical form, as it did for Aristotle in the polis.

→ Aristoteles

Sources: 1 F. Brentano, Von der mannigfachen Bedeutung des Seienden nach Aristoteles, 1862 (Eng.: On the Several Senses of Being in Aristotle, R. George (trans.), 1975); Die Psychologie des Aristoteles, insbesondere seine Lehre vom NOYΣ ΠOIHTIKOΣ, 1867 (The Psychology of Aristotle: In Particular his Doctrine of the Active Intellect: With an Appendix Concerning the Activity of Aristotle's God, R. George (trans.), 1977; Aristoteles und seine Weltanschauung, 1911 (Eng.: Aristotle and His World View, R. George & R. Chisholm (trans.), 1978) 2 M. Heidegger, Gesamtausgabe II. Abteilung: Vorlesungen 1919–1944, 17, 1994 (WS 1923/24), 6–41; 19, 1992 (WS 1924/25), 21–189; 21, 1976 (WS 1925/26), 127–196; 22, 1993 (SS 1926) 22–45; 33, ²1990 (SS 1931) 3 Id., Wegmarken, 1967, 309–372 (Eng.: Pathmarks, W. McNeill (trans.), 1998) 4 Id., Phänomenologische Interpretationen zu Aristoteles (Anzeige der hermeneuti-

schen Situation), in: H.-U. Lessing (ed.), Dilthey-Jahrbücher 6, 1989, 237–269 (Eng.: Phenomenological Interpretations of Aristotle: Initiation into Phenomenological
Research, R. Rojcewicz (trans.), 2001)

Literature: 5 H.-G. Gadamer, Heideggers theologische Jugendschrift, in: Dilthey-Jahrbücher 6, 1989, 228–
234 6 M.-Th. Liske, Aristoteles und der aristotelische
Essentialismus, 1985 7 Ch. Rapp, Identität, Persistenz
und Substantialität, 1995 8 F. Ricken, Die Oxford-Phi-
los., in: E. Coreth et al., Philosophie des 20. Jahrhunderts, ²1993, 158–176 9 F. Volpi, Heidegger e Aristotele,
1984 10 Id., Praktische Klugheit im Nihilismus der Technik: Hermeneutik, praktische Philosophie, Neo-Aristote-
limus, in: Internationale Zeitschrift für Philosophie 1,
1992, 5–23

Additional Bibliography: E. Booth, Aristotelian
Aporetic Ontology in Islamic and Christian Thinkers,
1983; R. Bosley, M. M. Tweedale, Aristotle and his Me-
dieval Interpreters, 1992; D. Des Chene, Physiologia:
Natural Philosophy in Late Aristotelian and Cartesian
Thought, 1996; H. S. Lang, Aristotle's Physics and its
Medieval Varieties, 1992; R. Pozzo (ed.), The Impact of
Aristotelianism on Modern Philosophy, in: Philosophy
and the History of Philosophy, vol. 39, 2004; C. B.
Schmitt, Aristotle and the Renaissance, 1983; R. Sor-
abji, Aristotle Transformed: The Ancient Commentators
and Their Influence, 1990; A. Tessitore, Aristotle and
Modern Politics: The Persistence of Political Philosophy,
2002. FRIEDO RICKEN

Arithmetic see→ Mathematics

Armenia
A. Introduction B. Middle Ages C. Modern Period

A. Introduction
Armenia (A.) is one of the cultural regions of the
Middle East shaped by Hellenism where the process of
reception had already occurred in ancient times. The
Temple of Garni, built in the 1st cent. AD and dedicated
to the sun god Mihr (Mithras), is, as the only preserved
pre-Christian temple in the area of A.- together with its
15–colour thermal bath mosaics with Greek inscriptions and mythical figures,– an impressive symbol of
this process.

A., which was divided between the great powers and
was struggling for its identity, had no intention of being
assimilated either by the Iranian – later the Arabian or
Russian – or the Greco-Roman/Byzantine – later the
Turkish/Mongolian culture groups. Thus, in its volatile
history, in addition to attempts at cultural synthesis,
clearly conflicting tendencies appear in the case of the
adoption of the prevailing cultural elements. A cultural
type was nurtured or rejected, depending on whether it
contributed to the protection of Armenian identity or
represented a danger to it. This criterion also applied to
Classical Antiquity and conditioned the history of its
influence in A.

The history of the reception of Greco-Roman Antiquity in A. has experienced three highpoints that will, in

the following, be paradigmatically characterized in the
reception of literature: 1. The period of the flourishing
of Hellenistic culture after the victory of Alexander the
Great (334 BC) when the kingdom of A. achieved its
independence from the Medes and Persians and the
emancipation of the Orontidic Dynasty added a new
Hellenistic dimension to the old Iranian component of
Armenian culture. At that time the Armenian state fell
within the circle of influence of ancient Greece, Hellenistic Syria and Cappadocia. The traces of these effects
can be observed throughout the entire Middle Ages and
beyond; 2. The period of the first Armenian cultural
renaissance (11th–13th cents.); 3. The period of the second renaissance (17th–19th cents.), which also represents a reaction to various risks to identity (in the first
case, through invasions from the east, in the second,
through loss of the governmental organisation). Models taken from national classicism (following Classical
Antiquity) were revived as bearers of the ideals of a
promising future with regard to hopes for national independence.

B. Middle Ages
As a result of the meeting of cultures in this region, a
highly developed, typically Armenian culture arose
which found its continuation in the early formation of
Armenian Christianity. This was closely followed in the
early Christian-Armenian period by translations of
Greek-language ancient and patristic works. In this
complex culture, the authority of the ancient world
played a large role. It was no coincidence that the final
spiritual formation of the key figure of this culture, St.
Grigor Lusaworič (Gregory the Illuminator), who determined the basic structures of Armenian Christian
culture in close correlation with the Cappadocian-East-
ern Roman culture, occurred in Cappadocian Caesaria
at the end of the 3rd cent. Also, the Armenian alphabet,
invented in the 5th cent. and conceived of as a prelude
to an extensive cultural programme, follows quite consciously the Greek alphabet's phonetic principles and
direction of writing. This alphabet became a symbol of
Armenian Christian literature and the basis for the
whole of medieval writing. The first Christian Armenian writers like Agat'hangełos and P'awstos of Byzantium (5th cent.) state that they wrote their works in
Greek, which, after Aramaic, was the second language
of administration and culture. In this way, even the
beginnings of Armenian written language and literature
relects a Graecophile tendency which will be seen in
later phases of the history of Armenian literature: in the
8th cent. (second Graecophile school, e.g. trans. of
Corpus areopagiticum), in the 12th cent. (cf. the works
of Grigor Magistros) or in the 18th–19th cents. (cf. the
poems, tragedies and epic poems utilizing Greek prosody or the historical, geographical and scientific works
of the Classicist school among the Mechithrists written
in Classical Armenian in imitation of Latin scientific
treatises). The Greek cultural centres of Athens, Caesaria, Edessa, Constantinople and Alexandria were also

centres of Armenian education and precursors of Armenian educational centres from the region of eastern A. to Cilicia and Jerusalem. But even in the later Armenian study centres, important works in the old tradition – in Armenian translation – remained the basis for education throughout the centuries, for instance the *Grammar* of Dionysios Thrax (2nd cent. BC) or the *Progymnasmata* of Aphthonios (4th/5th cent. AD).

The philosophical and theological works of the Greeks in the original and in translation (among others Aristotle, Plato, Proclos, Porphyrios, Iamblichus with their numerous interpretations, some of which were local – cf. Dawit' Anyałt', *David the Unconquerable* – as well as Aesop's *Fables*) were copied by several generations right through to the late 17th/18th cent. An example of this creative reception process is the work of Yovhannēs Sarkawag (1045/50–1129, also called 'Sophestos/Philosophos' and 'Poetikos') from the monastery of Hałpat who interpreted ancient and Christian authors in his writings and, among other things, also produced the Armenian variant of the Table of Pythagoras as well as the works of the above-mentioned Grigor Magistros, the translator of Euclid's *Elements* (Armenian: 'Principles') and admirer of ancient Greek mythology, poetry, philosophy, music theory and grammar. By working on these topics he attempted to revive interest in the art and culture of the ancient world. A further example is the creative work of Xačatur of Kečaris (1260–1331) who reconstructed the Armenian variant of the Alexander romance (Armenian: *Life of Alexander*) of Pseudo-Callisthenes, made 18 copies of it and illustrated them. The ancient tradition was adapted in a particularly lively fashion by the Armenian Chalcedonites, e.g. in the group centred around Simēon (1188–1255) from the monastery of Połnjahank', modern Achtala in the Lalwar Mountains, where the *Institutio theologica* of Proclos Diadochos, the writings of John of Damascus, the *Ladder of Divine Ascent* by John Klimakos and the Byzantine liturgical books were translated into Armenian (→ ADAPTATION).

C. MODERN PERIOD

It is in the modern period that the reflective, scholarly reception of Antiquity in the Armenian world has begun, especially through the work at the centres of Armenian science and culture in Constantinople (within the framework of the attempt by the learned Armenian Patriarch of Constantinople, Yakob Nalean, 1706–1764, to build a theological bridge in 18th cent. Istanbul between Orthodox churches of various traditions) and in Venice (later also in Vienna) among the Mechitharists, the colleagues and successors of the founder of the order, Mxit'ar of Sebaste (1676–1749). Particularly in their circle were laid the foundations for the Armenian cultivation of Ancient Studies and Classical philology, with the concept of Graeco-Roman Antiquity being so closely connected with the Classical period of Armenian culture that Armenians have continued to confuse the actual Graeco-Roman aspect of this field with that of Classical Armenological studies, right up until the present time.

In 1651 the *Institutio theologica* by Proclos Diadochos, translated in the 12th cent., was edited by Simēon of Juła, Bishop of Garni, and provided with a new commentary. The latter was later used as a school book. The fact that the Armenian scholar Step'annos of Lemberg translated the work *Liber de causis* in 1661 from Latin into Armenian under the title 'From the Book of Causes of Aristotle or as it is called by others, of Proclos', with reference to the parallel passages in Proclos, attests to the great interest in this work in the 17th and 18th cent among Armenians. It was published in 1750 in Constantinople. Xačatur of Ērzrum (1666–1740), a philosopher and scholar with encylopaedic knowledge and the spiritual father of Classicism in Armenian culture, wrote part of his philosophical, theological, rhetorical, geographical, geological, mathematical and scientific works in Latin (also in the polemics against Thomas Aquinas). In his two-volume work *A Short Outline of Philosophy* (Venice 1711) he portrays the image of man's sublimity, of the simplicity, harmony and symmetry of form and content, and links the progress of society with the educational role of art and culture. The concern for the cultivation of the Armenian language is mirrored in the publication of numerous grammar and language books for Old and Modern Armenian parallel to the compilation of Latin and Greek grammars, as well as multilingual dictionaries. Typical of the quality of philological work in this area is the two-volume Classical Armenian dictionary that is still highly significant today – *Nor bařgirk' haykazean lezui* (ed. by Gabriel Awetik'ean and Mkrtič Awgerean, Venice 1836/37, reprint Erevan 1979/1981) with Greek-Latin equivalents, etymological notes and references.

A further example of the appropriation of classical sources and European Classicist works and theories is *L'Art poétique* by Nicolas Boileau-Despréaux (1674), which was discussed by Xačatur of Ēzrum in his above-mentioned work. However other authors besides him wrote actively utilizing the genres and the metrics of ancient literature (cf. the three-volume edition of the Classicist poetic works of the Mechitharist Patres, 1852–1854) and were at the same time researchers of Classical Antiquity. They were often Constantinopolitans who either continued their career with the Mechitharists or worked in close academic collaboration with them there, e.g. Geworg Dpir of Palat (1737–1811) who rescued the Armenian version of Eusebius' *Chronicle* for later scholars and supplied the Mechitharists with many other, often unique copies of Classical works. From his pen came numerous translations from Greek and Latin that remain unedited among the Armenian manuscript collections in Jerusalem, Istanbul, Venice and Erevan (among others the first translation of Homer's *Iliad*).

Armenian Classicism, which began with Mxit'ar of Sebaste, Step'annos Agonc' (*Rhetoric*, Venice 1775),

Petrus of Łap'an (died in 1784) and was continued by the authors of the Classicist tragedies, Łukas Inčičean (*Historical Geography of Armenia*, Venice 1822), Manuel Jaxjaxean (trans. of Fénelon's *Continuation of the Fourth Book of Homer's Odyssey or the Adventures of Telemachus, Son of Odysseus*, Venice 1827) among others, reached its mature period in the work of famous admirers of Antiquity and creators of Classicist masterpieces like Arsen Bagratuni (epic poem *Hayk Diwc'azn* and the translation of Virgil's *Georgics*, Venice 1847, and of works by Sophocles, Aeschylus, Demosthenes and Cicero). This was the time of the editorial activities of Yovhannēs of Vanand (1772–1841) and Ełiay T'ovmačanean (translation and comparative studies of the *Homilies* of Johannes Chrysostomos in two volumes, Venice 1818, of the 'Parallel Biographies' by Plutarch in six volumes, Venice 1843–1848, as well as many metrical translations from the *Iliad* and *Odyssey* into Old Armenian). Eduard Hiwrmiwzean made the literary world of ideas of Antiquity accessible to the Armenian reader (*Poetics* and *Rhetoric*, Venice 1839, 'Mythology' as well as a description of the flora of A. modelled on Virgil's *Georgics* entitled *Burastan. The Fragrant Land*, Venice 1851). Mkrtič Awgerean alias J.B. Aucher translated from Latin into Old Armenian, e.g. Cicero's *De officiis* (Venice 1845), the *Dialogi* by Seneca (Venice 1849), as well as from Armenian into Latin, e.g. from the Armenian version of *Sermones* by Philo Judaeus lost in the Greek original or the *Chronicle* of Eusebius of Caesaria. Aside from the *Art of Rhetoric* (Venice 1832), Ep'rem Set'ean wrote works on Armenian law, discussing the body of thought in Graeco-Roman legal history.

A.'s long tradition of theatre, which goes back to Antiquity, was reconstructed in the works of Sargis Tigranean (1812–1875) and Petrus Minasean (1799–1867). From the pen of the former came the first complete investigation of the history and theory of Armenian theatre (in the light of Dawit' Anyałt's interpretations of tragedy and comedy) in which the first Armenian Classicist tragedy *The Blessed Virgin Hrip'sime*, (1668), which was supposed to serve to enlighten and educate the people, was also discussed. Hambarjum Limončean (1768–1839) and Minas Bžškean (1777–1851) dedicated their efforts to the investigation of Armenian medieval musical notation (*Chazen*) and its reproduction in the European notation system, with Limončean having Greek teachers for Greek Psaltarian theory and Byzantine neume study. Greek-Hellenistic elements are also found in Armenian book illumination.

Systematic research into the influence of Classical Antiquity on various fields of Armenian scholarship and culture is clearly required. Investigations in this regard are being carried out in the context of Armenological studies in the Republic of A. at the Academy of Sciences at the State University of Erevan and at the Institute of Ancient Manuscripts (Mesrop-Maštoc'-Matenadaran) as well as in the cultural centres of the Armenian diaspora. There is no special centre in A. for research into Graeco-Roman Antiquity (e.g. no chair in Classical philology at Erevan University). However the mosaics of the neo-Classical Mesrop-Maštoc'-Matenadaran on the hill above Erevan, produced in the 1960s and 1970s can be regarded as waves of an Armenian renaissance that continue to be observed into the present.

→ Armenia

1 A. ALPAGO-NOVELLO, Die armenische Architektur zwischen Ost und West, in: Die Armenier. Brücke zwischen Abendland und Orient, 1986, 131–224   2 S. P. COWE, Armenological Paradigms and Yovhannēs Sarkawag's 'Discours on Wisdom', in: Révue des études arméniennes 25, 1994–1995, 125–155   3 S. DER NERSESSIAN, Armenian Art, 1979   4 M. TADEVOSYAN, The Theory of Armenian Classicism, 1977 (Armenian)   5 N. TAHMIZYAN, Xačatur Ērzrumc'i as a Theoretician of Armenian Music, in: LHG (Periodical of the Academy of Sciences of the Republic of Armenia), 1966, Nr. 11 (Armenian)   6 R. W. THOMSON, Studies in Armenian Literature and Christianity, 1994   7 C. ZUCKERMAN, A Repertory of Published Armenian Translations of Classical Texts, 1995.
ARMENUHI DROST-ABGARJAN

Art Works, Acquisition of/Art Theft

A. DEFINITION   B. REASONS FOR THE ACQUISITION OF ART   C. ACQUISITION, GIFT-GIVING, DEDICATION   D. ACQUISTION BY FORCE (ART THEFT) IN HISTORICAL SUCCESSION   E. LEGAL ISSUES

A. DEFINITION

The acquisition of art/theft of art is necessarily linked to the idea of a specific object as a work of art. The prerequisite of an awareness of something as art is given only when an object is not primarily viewed for its material or political/religious value.

There is no word in Greek for 'work of art' or 'artist' in the contemporary sense. To the Greeks 'our' artist was a *bánausos*, a wage labourer in social terms, a *technítēs* in terms of his technical skills. Therefore, technites could be gods like Athena or Hephaestus when they produced something artistic, as well as cobblers, gold- and silversmiths, carpenters, weavers or doctors. Artistic works and valuable possessions are *keimélia*, cimelia (Hom. Il. 6,47; 9,330). Good workmanship was described by Homer as *kalos*, beautiful or as *daidálelos*, 'Daedalian'/skilfull, regardless of whether he refered to woven materials, buckles, brooches, necklaces, ear pendants, furniture for sitting, cauldrons or weapons (Hom. Il. 18,400–401). Homer described smiths from Sidon as *polydaídaloi*, as 'having many skills' (Hom. Il. 23,743).

The Greek term 'technítēs' is in contrast to the Latin 'artifex', the maker of artistic works; it is closer to the meaning of our word 'artist'.

B. Reasons for the Acquisition of Art

Motivations were primarily the perceived material or artistic value of an object, piety or demonstrations of power.

From early times, pious donations turned sanctuaries into museum-like compounds (in Greece, e.g. Delphi, Olympia; in Rome, e.g. the Capitol and the Temple of Fortuna).

Demonstrations of power became evident, when in a war specific statues from locally important deities or founding heroes were carried off (Paus. 8,46,1–4) or saved (Aeneas/Troy). Before a city was captured, the protective gods were invoked to leave the city (evocatio deorum: Plin. HN 28,18), and after capture the cult image was taken away (Paus. 8,46,1–4). That the Persians took the Athenian group of the tyrannicides (Paus. 1,8,5) was probably also a demonstration of power; otherwise it would be almost impossible to explain why several statesmen were appointed to secure their return to Athens: Antiochus (Paus. 1,8,5), Alexander (Plin. HN 34,70) and Seleucus (Val. Max. 2,10,ext.1).

Planned art collections only emerged in Hellenistic times, initially in connection with the libraries of the royal residences (Alexandria, Pergamon), but then also by private citizens (Cicero's Tusculum; Herculaneum, House of the Papyri; Lucian, Nigrinus 40).

In the the late Republic, demands were made that works of art ought to belong to the public (Agrippa: Plin. HN 34,9; Asinius Pollio: Plin. HN 36,33). Such demands were not again made with such consistency until the time of Napoleon.

Large numbers of works of art, similar to those of modern museums, were publicly exhibited in theatres (in Athens as early as the 4th cent. BC), public places, porticoes, gardens and baths.

C. Acquisition, Gift-giving, Dedication

Objects could be acquired directly from the manufacturer. This was how Thetis obtained the weapons she had commissioned from Hephaestus, the god of blacksmiths, for Achilles (Hom. Il. 18,368ff.). They could be given as private gifts or donated to sanctuaries (statues to Delphi as a tithe of war booty: Hdt. 8,27). They could awarded to to a person or be distributed as a prize (Hom. Il. 23). The same object could thereby serve completely different purposes: an ornate silver cauldron from Sidon originally was a gift given by a guest, then ransom for a prisoner and finally a prize in a competition (Hom. Il. 23,740–749).

In Roman times, fraud (and fraudulent borrowing) and public proscription increasingly featured alongside purchase, gift-giving and theft (also under torture: Polyb. 4,18) as a means for acquiring works of art. Not only the notorious Verres but also Augustus used proscription (Suet. Aug. 70).

D. Acquistion by Force (Art Theft) in Historical Succession

Looting and theft are already attested in early mythological times: At Troy Achilles conquered twelve towns by sea and eleven by land and in doing so looted numerous treasures (keimélia). The booty belonged to all Greeks in common and it was up to the army commander to distribute it. (Hom. Il. 9,328–337).

During the Persian wars, a Persian raid to plunder Delphi was unsuccessful only because of a miracle (Hdt. 8,35–39), other sites, including Athens, were plundered by the Persians/Greeks in 480 BC.

Although the Greeks often averred their respect for sanctuaries and temples, reports of looting appeared again and again: in 382 BC Dionysius I of Syracuse plundered a temple full of votive offerings in the Etruscan city of Argylla; the value of the booty was 1,000 talents, the profit from its sale was 500 talents (Diod. 15,14). In 381/80 BC, Titus Quinctius looted Praeneste and transported a statue of Jupiter to Rome where it was placed on the Capitol. An associated inscription however turns this statue into evidence for his personal triumph (Liv. 6,29,8–9). In 347 BC, the Phocian general Phayllus smashed up statues in Delphi to obtain money to pay mercenaries (minting?) while in the Temple of Apollo Phalaecus and other generals dug in the area near the hearth and tripod to find a legendary treasure; the excavation was only stopped because of an earthquake (Diod. 16,56). That same year the Athenians captured a ship with gold and ivory statues which Dionysius I had intended for the sanctuaries in Delphi and Olympia. When the ship's captain inquired as to the fate of the statues, the Athenians replied that it was not his business to ask what belonged to the gods, but rather what was important for the army (Diod. 16,57). When the Romans captured Capua in 211 BC, the priests' college in Rome was given the power to decide which of the looted bronze statues were deemed holy and which ones profane (Liv. 26,34,12).

The handling of captured works of arts varied. At the conquest of Volsinii in 264 BC, 2,000 Etruscan statues were taken (Plin. HN 34,34); when Dion and Dodona were plundered by the Aetolians in 221 BC, 2,000 statues were overturned and destroyed, with the exception of the images of gods (Polyb. 5,9). At the conquest of Syracuse in 212 BC, Marcus Marcellus robbed the town of its gods, while Fabius Maximus in 209 BC let Tarentum keep them (Liv. 27,16). After Scipio Africanus Minor captured Carthage in 146 BC, the soldiers who had taken part in the looting of the Temple of Apollo did not receive a share of the booty and Scipio also returned some of the booty previously taken by the Carthaginians to the Sicelian towns (App. Pun. 133).

When Marcus Marcellus captured Syracuse, paintings were also among the loot, as well as sculptures. Allegedly the value of (Greek) works of art was now recognised in Rome for the first time and from then on theft specifically for the sake of art was increasingly undertaken (Plut. Marc. 21; Liv. 25.40,1–3). More and more often paintings were also mentioned in connection with booty: 197 BC in Marcus Fulvius Nobilior (Polyb. 22,13), 197/194 BC in T. Quinctius Flaminius (Liv. 32,16,17).

With the triumphs of Lucius Scipio ('Asiaticus') over Antiochus and of Gnaeus Manlius Volso over the Asiatic Gauls, the first 'Asiatic luxury items' appeared in Rome in 189/187 BC: engraved silver vases, bronze beds, gold work from Pergamon, rugs, monopodia, costly gaming tables. 'With this triumph, luxury found its way to Rome' (Liv. 39,6,7; Plin. nat. 37,6,12).

Triumphs became more and more lavish, the looted art more and more costly. At Aemilius Paullus three-day triumph for defeating the Macedonian Perseus in 167 BC, statues and paintings on 250 wagons were displayed on the first day alone. This was booty from 77 destroyed towns (Plut. Aem.Paul. 32–33).

A new chapter opened in 146 BC with the destruction of Corinth by L. Mummius ('Achaicus'). Mummius had no understanding of art, yet filled Rome and the surrounding area with looted statues (Plin. HN 24,36; Vell. 1,13,4; Polyb. 40,7). Included in the loot were Corinthian bronzes, which from then on were sold in Rome at great cost (Plin. HN 34,6). Mummius placed a painting by Aristides, for which Attalus offered to pay 600,000 sesterces, in the Temple of Ceres; it was allegedly the first publicly displayed painting by a foreign artist in Rome. From then on, paintings by (Greek) artists were highly prized (Plin. HN 34,24).

Greece suffered terrible destruction at the hands of Sulla in 87/86 BC. He laid waste to the Acropolis and commandeered the temple treasures from Delphi, Olympia and Epidaurus (Sall. Catil. 11; Diod. 38,7,1; Plut. Sulla 12; Plin. HN 36,45). He was resented for displaying (commissioned?) paintings of many cities of Greece and Asia Minor in his triumph, but not a single one of a Roman city (Val. Max. 2,8,7).

The worst looter of art was C. V. Verres, who plundered Cilicia, the Greek islands, Asia Minor, Achaea and, above all, Sicily for his personal enrichment (73–71 BC; Cic. Verr. 2,1,49–51.81; 2,4,1; [1. 66–75]). Cicero acted for the prosecution in the case brought against him in Rome in 70 BC; the speeches for the prosecution make up the most extensive existing document about Classical misuse and theft of art.

In the meantime, professional art thieves had emerged, such as Tlepolemus who sculpted in wax, and the painter Hieron, who both worked for Verres (Cic. Verr. 2,4,30–31), and art dealers and agents like Atticus, Gallus, Damasippus, Junius, who worked for Cicero (Cic. Att.; Cic. fam. 7,23,1–3). In addition to declarations of value, the names of artists themselves became ever more important.

Scaurus, the stepson of Lucullus, spent great sums on building public spaces and art collections; 3,000 statues were displayed on the stage wall of a temporary theatre which he had erected (Plin. HN 34,36). He preferred paintings from Corinth; in Sicyon he requisitioned publicly owned pictures for Rome (Plin. HN 35,127). Murena and Varro had wall paintings removed from Sparta and sent them to Rome in wooden frames to decorate the Comitium (Plin. HN 35,173).

Scarus was the first person in Rome to build up a collection of gems, a dactyliotheca, Pompey donated a collection of gems from the booty of Mithradates to the Capitol, Caesar gave six dactyliothecae to the Temple of Venus Genetrix (Plin. HN 37,11; 37,6). Pearls and gems became treasured collectables in Rome following the Asiatic triumph of Pompey (Plin. HN 33, 151).

While Corinth was being rebuilt under Caesar/Augustus, painted earthenware vases, so-called Necrocorinthia (nekrós; Greek: corpse,) were found in graves. They became fashionable in Rome and this initiated systematic grave robbery (Strab. 8,6,23).

After defeating Mark Antony at Actium, Augustus took three obelisks and exotic works of Egyptian art back to Rome as well as other items. The Egyptian style was quickly integrated into local art. With Augustus the great interaction between art theft and study came to an end. Art continued to be stolen, but it did not have a transforming effect since one already knew and had everything.

Caligula had statues of gods of artistic or religious value taken from Greece, he intended the gold and ivory image of Zeus from Olympia to be transported to Rome and he had the heads of stolen (portrait) statues knocked off and replaced with his own image (Suet. Calig. 21. 57; Cass. Dio 59,28,4–5). Later this became common practice.

Nero ordered numerous Greek statues to be brought to decorate his Golden House (Plin. HN 34,84). When he visited Olympia, he had all (portrait) statues toppled and thrown into the latrines to expunge the memory of previous victors (Suet. Nero 24).

After the capture of Jerusalem, Vespasian and Titus politically demonstrated Rome's power in the display of the richest treasures at the triumph in AD 71. (Jos. BI 7,5,132ff.).

While Rome had long been the centre for stolen art, Byzantium/Constantinople came into focus at the end of the 2nd cent. AD and particularly when Constantine moved the imperial residence there in AD330. Under Constantine statues were brought from Athens, Rhodes, Cyprus, Syria, Egypt, Sicily and Greece for public buildings, especially the Baths of Zeuxippus and the Hippodrome; 60 of the statues at the Hippodrome came from Rome.

In Late Antiquity an awareness of the inherent value of art was lost more and more. In looting its material value was of primary concern and many works of art were deliberately smashed or destroyed because of religious sanctions against anything pagan.

When the Hagia Sophia was rebuilt in the 6th cent., during the increasing Christianisation of the empire under Justianian I, 427 predominantly Greek statues were removed from the church.

In 1204 Constantinople was sacked by the Crusaders and with that the last existing collection of Classical art was looted and destroyed.

Among the Crusaders, the Venetians more nearly seemed to have an understanding of art. Apart from gold and silver cimelia and reliquaries, they also brought Classical statues back to Venice. It was not until the Renaissance that the art collection became popular once more in Rome. Old style art theft only reappeared in the Thirty Years War, undertaken especially by the Swedes. Germany and Bohemia were particularly affected.

Large scale, systematically organised art theft was undertaken under Napoleon, who reached out as far as Italy, Spain and Egypt (1794–1814; Wescher [10]). In doing so he always also pursued scholarly goals; he planned a large public central museum, later the Musée Napoléon (today the Louvre), and had catalogues prepared for publication. Napoleon had an advisory staff of scholars and artists; the works that were to be taken were specified in lists before the robbery and comprehensive records were kept throughout the process. From Italy, in addition to works of art, he also took the famous archaeologist E. Q. Visconti back to Paris.

In opposition to Napoleon's motivation that art and science should be the accessible property of all, the motivation for the next systematic plundering of the art world, by the Nazis, was to a large extent characterised by primitive ideas and archaic brutality. Just as in Antiquity, private property in particular was completely expropriated either as war booty or proscription but without directed selection; much that was stolen never came into the possession of the state, but remained in the hands of individual members of the party elite.

E. LEGAL ISSUES

Legal questions in connection with art theft are contentious. More and more frequently countries in which certain works of art originated, demand that European museums should return them: The Pergamon Altar (Turkey), the Elgin/Parthenon Marbles (Greece), African and Latin American art, Schliemann's finds from Troy (Turkey and Germany). However, the question of repatriation can probably not be answered, as long as large central museums remove finds from regional sites (internal art theft) within the different countries.
→ Damnatio memoriae I. Historical

SOURCES 1 J. J. POLLITT, The Art of Rome c. 735 B. C.-337 A. D. (Sources & Documents in the History of Art Series), 1966
LITERATURE: 2 H. BECK, P. C. BOL, W. PRINZ, H.v. STEUBEN (ed.), Antikensammlungen im 18. Jahrhundert, 1981 3 C. PH. BRACKEN, Antikenjagd in Griechenland 1800–1830, 1977 4 FR. HASKELL, N. PENNY, Taste and the Antique, 1981 5 K. O. MÜLLER, Handbuch der Archäologie der Kunst. Mit Zusätzen von Fr.G. Welcker, Breslau ³1848 (Eng.: Ancient Art and its Remains, or, A Manual of the Archaeology of Art, 1852) 6 J. OVERBECK, Die antiken Schriftquellen zur Geschichte der bildenden Künste bei den Griechen, 1868 7 F. C. PETERSEN, Allge-

meine Einleitung in das Studium der Archäologie. Aus dem Dänischen von P. Friedrichsen, Leipzig 1829 8 W. TREUE, Der Kunstraub, 1960 9 L. VÖLKEL, Über die Wegführung der alten Kunstwerke aus den eroberten Ländern nach Rom, Leipzig 1798 10 P. WESCHER, Kunstraub unter Napoleon, 1976 11 W. WUNDERER, Manibiae Alexandrinae. Eine Studie zur Geschichte des römischen Kunstraubes, 1894.   HARTMUT G. DÖHL

Artemis of Ephesus see→ DIANA OF EPHESUS

Artes liberales

A. CONCEPT B. CAROLINGIAN EDUCATIONAL REFORM C. HUMANISM UNTIL THE 18TH CENTURY

A. CONCEPT

The Artes liberales (AL) describe a group of usually seven of study, 'worthy of a free man' (Seneca epist. 88; i.e.: grammar, logic/dialectics, rhetoric and arithmetic, music, geometry, and astronomy). They originate from the Greek educational programme of the *enkyklios paideia*, which were passed on to the Latin Middle Ages through the encyclopaedias of Martianus Capella, Cassiodorus, and Isidor of Seville. They are usually divided up into groups of three and four; since Boethius the group of four is (*De arithmetica* 1,1) called *quadruvium* or *quadrivium*; the group of three kept the name *trivium* which probably appeared for the first time in the marginal notes of Horace (*Scholia Vindobonensia ad Horatii artem poeticam* 307, ed. J. ZECHMEISTER, Vindobonae 1877, 36f.). The regular use of both expressions has only been documented from since the start of the 9th cent. [1. 183ff., 184 Note. 8; 3. 4–36]. The names *artes* or *scientiae sermocinales* (for the *trivium*) and *artes* or *scientiae reales* (for the *quadrivium*) became customary at the Faculty of Arts from the first half of the 13th cent. at the latest [4. 58ff.]. These names clarify the factual connection between the *artes*: the *trivium* deals with reality from the point of view of language. The *quadrivium* deals with reality from the point of view of the object in so far as it can be reduced to a mathematical structure on which it is based. This division of the *seven* AL in language- and object-based sciences goes back to the distinction Augustine made in *De doctrina christiana* 1,2 (= CCL 32, 1962, 7): 'omnis doctrina de rebus vel de signis'. The *artes* are classified correspondingly; for instance by Hugh of St. Victor (*Didascalicon. De studio legendi*, 2,20, ed. OFFERGELD, *Fontes christiani* 27, 1997, 192.): The *trivium* deals with words enunciated, the *quadrivium*, however, deals with thoughts or concepts grasped mentally [5]. The same distinction applies to what Bernard of Chartres (*The Glosae super Platonem of Bernard of Chartres*, ed. P. E. DUTTON, *Studies and Texts* 107, 1991, 143) calls the *studia humanitatis*: they differ (according to Calcidius) through the 'flourishing mind' (*animus florens*) for the *trivium* and the 'outstanding acumen' (*ingenium excellens*) for the *quadrivium*. As William of

Conches (*Glosae super Platonem/Accessus ad Timaeum*, ed. É. JEAUNEAU, 1965, 62 and 65) emphasizes with reference to Horace, this is a matter of an integrative knowledge with regard to everything that 'humans can possibly know'.

B. CAROLINGIAN EDUCATIONAL REFORM

The Carolingian educational reform [6. 800ff.] → CAROLINGIAN Renaissance, associated with the names of Alcuin and Hrabanus Maurus, entrusted the monastery schools and cathedral-schools → MONASTERY SCHOOLS with the task of providing adequate education for the understanding of the Scriptures. The free arts are the 'pillars' and 'steps' on which 'wisdom' (*sapientia*) rests – according to Alcuin in his Opuscula didascalica 1 (MPL 101, 853 C). Hugh of St. Victor (*Didascalicon* 3,3 ed. OFFERGELD, p. 228) describes the liberal arts as 'secondary school' and 'elementary school', as a road by which the active mind enters the secrets of wisdom: the 'foundation of all education (*omnis doctrinae*) lies in the seven free arts' (*Didascalicon* 3,4 ed. OFFERGELD, p. 235). His assertion: 'these are so interrelated and in their content so mutually dependent that, should only one of them be missing, all the others would not suffice to educate someone to be a philosopher', is no longer considered valid for the 13th and subsequent centuries. Even for the 12th cent. this view is questionable. It contributes more to making the educational system of the *arts* appear as an ideal than as a mirror of actual conditions. The knowledge of Aristotelian *Physics* and above all *Metaphysics*, and, further, of Arab sciences only adds to the dissolution of the uniform educational system.

The *trivium* [7. 279–302] describes the basic educational path in the Latin Middle Ages; the *quadrivium* follows it [8. 303–320; 9. 25ff., 120ff.]. In this respect, the educational system of the seven free arts is a unified whole, working in the background, from and in contrast to which, the individual sciences developed over the course of the 12th and 13th cents. [12. 151–184]. New sciences came up from outside, particularly natural philosophy, ethics and metaphysics. The seven free arts – according to Thomas Aquinas (*Expositio super Librum Boethii De trinitate* q. 5, a. 1 ad 3) -no longer suffice as divisions of theoretical philosophy. The history of AL is characterized by the dissolution of the uniform encyclopaedic educational system which in the beginning could be equated with a philosophical education: the individual *artes* became independent [13. 1–20]. The subjects of the *quadrivium* experienced a similar dissolution [14. 1736–1739]. The independence of the individual subjects of the *artes* was, in any case, decisive for their cohesion. Their common features consisted in the preparatory task. The faculty of arts as the indispensable preparation for higher study is a clear sign of the dissolution of the old *artes* structure. With the emergence of the university in the 13th cent., encyclopaedic general knowledge gives way to scientific specialist knowledge.

C. HUMANISM UNTIL THE 18TH CENT.

The revival of the *studia humanitatis* is the dominant viewpoint in humanism and in the Renaissance [15; 16; 17]. Language [18. 135ff.] becomes the object of human education. The *trivium* undergoes a revaluation: it is no longer simply propaedeutic, but to be understood as the goal of the moral education of man. The *studia humanitatis* and the *eruditio moralis* are very closely related; as in Philipp Melanchthon's work [19. 146ff.]. To the subjects of the *trivium* are added: poetics [20], history [21], and moral philosophy. [22.] Dante Alighieri (*Convivio* 2,13,8; [23. 174f.]) and also Francesco Petrarca have to be mentioned: the study of language and moral education go hand in hand. Grammar becomes historical philology – as for example with Gulielmus Budaeus. Logic and dialectics show a historical, humanistic trait [25]. The *Dialecticae disputationes* by Lorenzo Valla attempts to base them on language. Rudolf Agricola and particularly Petrus Ramus continue in this direction. Nonetheless, traditional logic is pursued further [26]. On the whole, rhetoric gains the upper hand. In contrast to the *quadrivium*, the *trivium* of the faculty of arts managed to hold its ground in the face of the new challenges [16. 372f., 377]. Whereas the *quadrivium* consisted of a juxtaposition of the four mathematical and physical disciplines and not of a uniform science of nature, the *trivium* possessed that integrated viewpoint in language, which now became effective. In addition to Latin, Greek and Hebrew became recognised university subjects as did rhetoric in addition to logic. Petrus Ramus deals in his *Scholae in liberales artes* (1569) with the classical subjects of the *trivium*; physics and metaphysics take the place of the subjects of the *quadrivium*. The inadequacy of the *quadrivium* was as apparent as the outstanding position of the *trivium*. This is also evident in Juan Luis Vives' *De causis corruptarum artium*. He retains the disciplines of the *trivium*; the *quadrivium* has disappeared. The 'historical-philological Ciceronianism' [17. 398ff.] refers more to the *artes* than to the *scientia*.

Thus, the *trivium* marked in the 16th and 17th cents. the educational path at the academic secondary schools in contrast to the philosophical faculties of the universities., i.e. the faculty of the arts. This is demonstrated by the curriculum adopted in 1586 and amended in 1599, the *Ratio atque Institutio Studiorum SJ*, which remained in force until 1773. The educational path at the Jesuit gymnasiums centred on the constitutions of Ignatius of Loyola [27]. The 'J'ai été nourri aux letters' (Descartes) represents education in the *studia humanitatis*, i.e. grammar, history (*historia*), poetics and rhetoric. [28. Vol.4, 100f., 112ff., 117f.]. Logic was often a subject on the upper level of the gymnasium and represents the entry into philosophy. One should understand logic here rather as dialectics – as Descartes noted critically [29. 116f.] and Michel de Montaigne (*Essais* 1,26; [30. 162, 280]) had already criticized – 'teaching us to talk about everything' (*disserere*) and thus 'distorting' rather than 'confirming' the *bon sens*, instead of logic, which 'provides proofs'. No longer is the *trivium* as a whole important but specialised knowledge. The original trinity of the *trivium* no longer exists. The Jesuit college in La Flèche, opposed by René Descartes in his *Discours de la méthode*, is an example of the organisation of knowledge along school lines. The *trivium* barely managed to survive as preparation for the secondary schools and as such does no longer belong at the university. It constitutes the entry level of philosophical education and is of propaedeutic character, as is normally the case these days at the so-called classical-humanist gymnasiums and the Grammar Schools. The *quadrivium* already stopped playing a role at the end of the Middle Ages. The AL became part of general education. General education and scholarship., gymnasium and university, split apart although the latter remains dependent on the former. Scholarship appears to be hardly possible without general education.

→ Artes liberales; → Education / Culture; → Enkyklios paideia

→ ANCIENT LANGUAGES, TEACHING OF; → EDUCATION/ CULTURE; → ENCYCLOPAEDIA; → JESUIT SCHOOLS; → PHILOSOPHY; → UNIVERSITY

1 H.-I. MARROU, Augustinus und das Ende der antiken Bildung, 1982 2 Id. Les arts libéraux au moyen âge, 1969, 5–27 3 P. RAJNA, Le denominazioni trivium e quadrivium, in: Studi medievali Nuova 1, 1928, 4–36 4 J. H. J. SCHNEIDER, Scientia sermocinalis/realis. Anmerkungen zum Wissenschaftsbegriff im Mittelalter und in der Neuzeit, in: Archiv für Begriffsgesch. 35, 1992, 54–92 5 Id., s.v. Trivium, Historisches Wörterbuch der Philosophie 10 6 G. SCHRIMPF, s.v. Philosophie. Institutionelle Formen. B. Mittelalter, Historisches Wörterbuch der Philosophie 7, 800–819 7 G. LEFF, Das trivium und die drei Philosophien., in: W. RÜEGG (ed.), Geschichte der Universität in Europa, 1: Mittelalter, 1993, 279–302 8 J. NORTH, Das quadrivium, in: W. RÜEGG (ed.), Geschichte der Universität in Europa, 1, 303–320 9 P. SCHULTHESS, R. IMBACH, Die Philosophie im lateinischen Mittelalter. Ein Handbuch mit einem bio-bibliographischen Repertorium, 1996 10 J. KOCH (ed.), Artes Liberales. Von der antiken Bildung zur Wissenschaft des Mittelalters, 1959 11 D. ILLMER, s.v.Artes Liberales, Theologische Realenzyklopädie 4, 156–171 12 R. McKEON, The Organization of Sciences and the Relations of Cultures in the Twelfth and Thirteenth Centuries, in: J. E. MURDOCH, D. SYLLA (eds), The Cultural Context of Medieval Learning. Proceedings of the First International Colloquium on Philosophy, Science, and Theology in the Middle Ages, September 1973, Boston Stud. in the Philosophy of Science 26, 1975, 151–184 13 D. E. LUSCOMBE, Dialectic and Rhetoric in the Ninth and Twelfth Centuries: Continuity and Change, in: J. FRIED (ed.), Dialektik und Rhetorik im frühen und hohen Mittelalter. Rezeption, Überlieferung und gesellschaftliche Wirkung antiker Gelehrsamkeit vornehmlich im 9. und 12. Jahrhundert. Schriften des Histor. Kollegs 27, 1997, 1–20 14 J. DOLCH, s.v. Quadrivium, Historisches Wörterbuch der Philosophie 7, 1736–1739 15 W. RÜEGG, Epilog. Das Aufkommen des Humanismus, in: Id. (ed.), Geschichte der Universität in Europa, 1: Mittelalter, 1993, 387–408 16 O. PEDERSEN, Tradition und Innovation, in: W. RÜEGG (ed.), Geschichte der Universität in Europa, 2: Von der Reformation bis zur französichen Revolution 1500–1800, 1996, 363–390 (Eng.: O. PEDERSEN, Tradition and Innovation, in, W. RÜEGG (ed.), A History of the University in Europe, Vol. 2, Universities in Early Modern Europe (1500–1800), (ed.) Hilde de Ridder-Symoens, 1996, 452–488) 17 W. SCHMIDT-BIGGEMANN, Die Modelle der Human- und Sozialwissenschaften in ihrer Entwicklung, in: W. RÜEGG (ed.), Geschichte der Universität in Europa, 2: Von der Reformation bis zur französischen. Revolution 1500–1800, 1996, 391–424 (Eng.: W. SCHMIDT-BIGGEMANN, New Structures of Knowledge, in No. 16, 489–530) 18 J. H. J. SCHNEIDER, Der Begriff der Sprache im Mittelalter, im Humanismus und in der Renaissance, in: Archiv für Begriffsgesch. 38, 1995, 66–149 19 PH. MELANCHTHON, De corrigendis adolescentiae studiis, in: Id., Glaube und Bildung. Texte zum christlichen Humanismus. Lateinisch./deutsch, (ed.) G.R. Schmidt, 1989 20 B. VICKERS, Rhetoric and Poetics, in: CH. B. SCHMITT, Q. SKINNER (eds.), The Cambridge History of Renaissance Philosophy, 1988, 1992, 715–745 21 D. R. KELLEY, The Theory of History, in: CH. B. SCHMITT, Q. SKINNER (eds.), The Cambridge History of Renaissance Philosophy, 1988, 1992, 746–761 22 J. KRAYE, Moral Philosophy, in: CH. B. SCHMITT, Q. SKINNER (eds.), The Cambridge History of Renaissance Philosophy, 1988, 1992, 301–386 23 D. ALIGHIERI, Opere, F. CHIAPELLI (ed.), 1963–1978 24 É. GILSON, Dante et la philosophie, 1986, 103ff. 25 L. JARDINE, Humanistic Logic, in: The Cambridge History of Renaissance Philosophy, 1992, 173–198 26 E. J. ASHWORTH, Traditional Logic, in: The Cambridge History of Renaissance Philosophy, 1992, 143–172 27 J. H. J. SCHNEIDER, s.v. Eruditio, Historisches Wörterbuch der Rhetorik 2, 1994, 1421–1425 28 R. DESCARTES, Discours de la méthode, É. GILSON (ed.), 1976 29 Id., Entretiens avec Burman. Manuscrit de Göttingen, CH. ADAM (ed.), 1975 30 M. DE MONTAIGNE, Œuvres complètes, A. THIBAUDET, M. RAT (eds.), 1962 (based on the edition of P. Coste, translated into German by J.D. Tietz, Leipzig 1753/54; Zürich 1992, Vol. 1 = I, 25th Chapter) (Eng.: The Complete Works: Essays, Travel-Journal, Letters, New York 2003) 31 U. LINDGREN, Die Artes Liberales in Antike und Mittelalter. Bildungs- und wissenschaftsgeschtliche Entwicklungslinien, 1992 32 F. DECHANT, Die theologische Rezeption der Artes Liberales und die Entwicklung des Philosophiebegriffs in theologischen Programmschriften des Mittelalters von Alkuin bis Bonaventura, 1993 33 B. ENGLISCH, Die Artes Liberales im frühen MA (5.–9. Jahrhundert). Das Quadrivium und der Komputus als Indikatoren für Kontinuität und Erneuerung der exakten Wissenschaften zwischen Antike und Mittelalter, 1994 34 O. WEIJERS, L. HOLTZ (eds.), L'enseignement des disciplines à la Faculté des arts (Paris et Oxford, XIIIᵉ -XVᵉ siècles). Actes du colloque international., 1997 35 M. L. W. LAISTNER, Thought and Letters in Western Europe AD 500–900, rev. ed., 1957 36 D. L. WAGNER, The 7 Liberal Arts in the Middle Ages, 1983 37 W. H. STAHL, R. JOHNSON, Martianus Capella and the 7 Liberal Arts, 1971 38 A. GRAFTON, L. JARDINE, From Humanism to the Humanities: Education and the Liberal Arts in 15th and 16th Century Europe, 1986.

JAKOB HANS JOSEF SCHNEIDER

Artists, Legends concerning
A. Subject Area   B. Written Information
about the Artist from Antiquity to the Mod-
ern Age   C. The Most Common Stereotypes
D. The Court Artist   E. The 'Unappreciated
Genius' of the modern period   F. The
Construct of the Artist

A. Subject Area
Anecdotes about artists have been passed down to us
in fragmentary form via Duris, the tyrant of Samos
(around 300 BC) and the student of Theophrastus
(FGrH II A Nr 76). C. Plinius Secundus the Elder took
up some of these in his notes about artists in the *Naturalis historia* (NH), that form the core of the legends
about artists. The anecdotes convey less about the
actual personality of the artist than about his role in
society. They generally characterize him as the embodiment of 'human wit' (see below). The legends about
artists show that there are certain stereotypes that are
constantly repeated in changed forms and that are attributed to individual artists. The tradition of legends
about artists moved through three historical high
points: in the Hellenistic and the Roman Imperial
periods, in Humanism of the 15th and early 16th cents.
as well as between Romanticism and the Classical Modern period (19th/20th cents.). Their relative importance
changes in each case when the social position of the
artist undergoes a change.

In Antiquity the clever artist proved through his wit
that his ability exceeded mere technical competence.
The artist in the Humanistic period, setting himself off
from the artist-craftsman of the guild, wished to prove
himself worthy of the court because he is a god-like
creator who is by nature gifted and talented. The modern artist has shaped the legend of the unappreciated
genius who – despite a philistine audience in a period of
capitalism and industrialization – works on his posthumous fame.

B. Written Information about the Artist
from Antiquity to the Modern Age
The ancient historians and philosophers took almost
no notice of the fine arts. Aristotle and Plato ranked
them below poetry and music. Painting and sculpture
were not assigned a Muse because they sprang from the
craft of artisans whose rank was low in a society of
slaveowners. In the Hellenistic period the attitude started to change. Pliny reported that it was thanks to the
influence of Pamphilos, the teacher of Apelles, that
painting became a subject taught to freemen (NH
35,77). It is certainly not true that slaves were forbidden
to practise it, but this assertion of Pliny is the basis of the
Humanist view of the supposedly high status of fine
artists in Antiquity. Anecdotes to the effect that artists
received no money for their work were meant to demonstrate their independence from the paid work of the
bánausoi, the artisans. Polygnotos painted the temple
of Delphi and the Poikile of Athens free of charge (NH
35,59). Zeuxis distributed his works with the remark
that they were priceless (35,62).

If information about artists backed up by written
evidence is lacking for the Middle Ages, this does not
mean that their work was held in low regard. Inscriptions from the 11th cent. on testify to pride in their
finished work. At the beginning of the 15th cent., however, it was not just the works but also the artists themselves who were again held in higher esteem. Competition between the courts developed as to who could keep
the most famous masters, and they were wooed with
privileges, stipends and aristocratic titles. As had already been the case in Antiquity, writers only gradually
attended the social rise of artists. The novellas of the
14th cent. by Giovanni Boccaccio and Franco Saccetti
tell of the amusing and droll nature of artists. Three
verses in Dante's *Divine Comedy* helped to lift the fine
arts to the high rank of poetry: 'Cimabue believed himself to be the master of the field of painting but now
Giotto is enjoying such popularity that the fame of the
other one is being obscured' (purg. 11,94–96). Commentaries about Dante regarding this tercet developed
in the 15th cent. into the first independent biographies
of artists. Giorgio Vasari's descriptions of the lives of
artists, first published in 1550, established the genre of
artists' biographies.

C. The Most Common Stereotypes
1. Conspicuous Behaviour   2. Wit and Clev-
erness   3. Friend of Princes   4. The 'Other
God'   5. Childhood and Discovery
6. Unworldliness   7. Melancholy

1. Conspicuous Behaviour
According to Pliny, Zeuxis is said to have worn his
name in gold letters on his clothing in Olympia (NH
35,62) and Parrhasios called himself 'habrodíaiton', a
foppish rake (35,7). Giovannantonio of Vercelli was
nicknamed 'Sodoma' because of his allegedly notorious
association with catamites; to this was added the extra
title of 'Mattaccio', arch-fool, because of his pranks
while painting in the monastery of Monte Oliveto
(Vasari 4,343ff.).

2. Wit and Cleverness
Artists proved their worth in rhetoric and art competitions with their counterparts and the audience. The
competition in drawing outlines between Apelles and
Protogenes in Rhodes (NH 35,81ff.) and the contest
between Zeuxis and Parrhasios involving painting illusions (NH 35,5) are famous. In the modern age the
competition idea continued in paragone literature with
respect to the claim for priority ranking among the
genres of painting and sculpture. There are countless
testimonials to the quick-wittedness of artists. Apelles
corrected a painted sandal whose representation was
found by a shoemaker to be faulty. When the latter now
claimed to have also noticed another mistake in a leg, he
received the response which is still a familiar phrase
today: 'Shoemaker, stick to your last!' (NH 35,85).

3. Friend of Princes

The Humanists traced equality of birth with the ruling classes back to a saying of Parrhasios, who is said to have called himself 'Prince of the arts' (NH 30,71). Apelles enjoyed the high regard of King Alexander who visited him in his workshop (NH 35,85ff.). Emperor Charles V felt that he was the 'Alexander' of Titian, his 'Apelles', and for whom, according to Carlo Ridolfi (*Meraviglie*, 1648), Charles picked up the fallen paintbrush. According to Carel van Mander (*Schilder-Boeck*, 1617), Emperor Maximilian I held the ladder for the artist Dürer while he worked.

4. The 'Other God'

Divine inspiration through the Muses was reserved for writers during Antiquity; not until Humanism was it also attributed to fine artists. Marsilio Ficino (*De vita triplici*, 1489) adopted Plato's concept of the *enthousiasmós* (in *Phaidros*) of divinely inspired madness, an idea which Giordano Bruno (*De eroici furori*, 1585) developed further in the sense of a modern concept of genius. The divine source of creativity was substantiated by the view that the artist himself was an '*alter deus*', 'another god' (according to H. Janitscheck, L. B. Alberti's minor writings on the theory of art, 1877, 90f.). Accordingly, great artists had no teacher to foster their talent: the painter Eupompus said that it was nature itself that had inspired him to imitate it (NH 34,61). This 'quality of talent' that that grew from nature itself is also emphasized by Vasari in the introduction to many of his biographies.

5. Childhood and Discovery

There are no ancient anecdotes about the childhood of artists. The topos developed together with the concept of the artist as the 'Other god'. The modern legends about artists therefore take over the ancient myths of gods and heroes like Zeus, Bacchus and Hercules, who, abandoned by their parents, are fed and raised by animal foster-mothers like goats, wolves and bears. Similarly the artist grows up in impoverished circumstances as a shepherd boy as in the case of Giotto, Domenico Beccafumi, Andrea Sansovino, Andrea del Castagno and Francisco de Goya. In his likeness to a god the boy-artist is similar to the young Christ, who was also born in a stable. Like the twelve-year old Jesus in the temple, the artist must assert this spiritual mission despite the lack of understanding from his natural parents. According to Ascanio Condivi (*The Life of Michelangelo Buonarotti*, 1553, trans. by R. Diel, 1939) the boy Michelangelo was beaten by his father out of hatred for the artistic career. But the one who is by nature gifted and talented asserts himself, practising untiringly, despite all his difficulties.

6. Unworldliness

The artist, by forgetting the everyday world through his work, comes to resemble the philosopher. The painter Protogenes who lived in Rhodes in his summerhouse outside the city wall is said not to have interrupted his painting during the storming of the city (NH 35,105). Paolo Ucello, unconcerned about profitable orders that could have alleviated his poverty, supposedly brooded about rules of perspective night after night while his wife called him to bed in vain (Vasari 2,81ff.). Aside from the 'unworldly creative rage' there is also the opposite-case scenario: Pontormo did not work for days on end; his living and working area on the first floor were accessible via a ladder that the artist pulled up after him so that he could protect himself from uninvited guests (Vasari 4,234ff.; 260).

7. Melancholy

Aristotle (problemata 30,1) concluded that everyone who was outstanding in philosophy, politics, writing and the fine arts was subject to melancholy. While the theologians of the Middle Ages castigated Melancholy as a disease, even as the vice of *acedia* ('lethargy'), the black bile temperament is again ennobled by Marsilio Ficino and others (*De vita triplici*, 1489). The melancholic was born under the star of Saturn. His character is like that of the dog: of a troubled brooder, a faithful sniffer seeking out truth. The concept of the intellectual and the artist as a melancholic developed into a platitude (R. Burton, *The Anatomy of Melancholy*, 1621).

D. The Court Artist

In the 17th cent. legends of artists became unfashionable. The profession adjusted to the etiquette of the court. Parallel to the tendency for art to be more academic was the move towards rationalism in philosophy, in which was the basis of René Descartes' *Discours de la méthode* (1637). Central to Baroque art literature were rules and style, not the whims of the artist. In his behaviour and clothing the artist demonstrated that he was an educated gentleman with good manners. Cavaliere d'Arpino (1568–1640), a founding member of the Roman Academy, appeared in public girded with a dagger and mounted high on a steed. A tendency towards parvenu-like behaviour continued via the Dandyism of the 19th cent. until today. The ideal of the courtier was perfected in Peter Paul Rubens: the artist, diplomat and multilingually educated man was happily married twice, good-looking and a man of the world in his interaction with kings and scholars – an *uomo universale*.

E. The 'Unappreciated Genius' of the Modern period

The translation of Vasari's biographies in the early 19th cent. coincided with the rebirth of the artist as an eccentric. Modern melancholy was transformed into the wanderlust of the German Romantics, the '*ennui*' ('boredom') of the Parisian poets in the Baudelaire circle and the affectation of the English dandies. The old topos of the unworldly brooding artist was reinvigorated under the conditions of the age of industrialization. Once again the legends about artists provided means of coping in an epoch of radical social change. The artist, released from the proscriptions, but also from the protection of the guild and the court had to prove his worth in the free market. The 'unappreciated genius' prevailed against the envy of his colleagues and the philistinism of his contemporaries. An ancient precursor motif is the anecdote of the slandering of Apelles at the court of King Ptolemy by his rival Antiphilus (D. Cast, *The Calumny of Apelles*, 1981). Rembrandt – as an artist whose talent was supposedly not valued in a fitting manner by his contemporaries and whose work only became more highly regarded as a result of his posthumous reputation – retrospectively became the prototype of the unappreciated genius. Suffering from the prevailing conditions in the world is a condition of creativity. Friedrich Nietzsche's *Ecce Homo* (1908) alludes to the scourged and mocked Christ of the Passion. William Blake, Paul Gauguin, Marc Chagall, James Ensor, Salvador Dali and Joseph Beuys present themselves as 'suffering Christs' who take up the cross for the sake of their revealed art. Certainly it is also possible here to trace a topos back to the late Middle Ages: in this way, for instance, Thomas a Kempis' (1380–1471) work *Imitatio Christi* influenced the religious motivation of the painters in the 15th cent., but in the modern period mystic self-abandonment became artistic role playing. The avant-garde artist was imbued with his messianic mission to gather humanity behind him in order to change the world. The modern artist as the suffering saviour also has as his models ancient titans and demigods: Prometheus, who brought fire to humans and for this was chained to the Caucasus by Zeus; Orpheus, who descended into the underworld to free his beloved Eurydice from Hades.

F. The Construct of the Artist

In the 1960s there was great discussion about the 'death of the author'. Post-structuralism replaced the artist with the observer who creates the image. Michel Foucault (*Qu'est-ce que c'est, un auteur?* 1969) sees in the author the interface of a function that, through the mask of a person, illustrates the existence, operation and circulation of discourses in society. The figure of the artist as a man passed down over the centuries contributes to the difficulty of populating legends of artists with females, since, according to tradition, the role of the Muse was intended for women. Art History has remained humanistic in its recording of artists' monographs. Any association between life and work involuntarily arranges the facts according to the pattern of the legends of artists; they provide the structural principle for that which we usually call 'the author', that figure in which we see the origin of ingenious ideas and of artistic skill.

→ Apelles

→ Ekphrasis; → Melancholy; → Mimesis, myths about

1 R. M. Comanducci, Buono artista della sua arte, Il concetto di artista e la pratica di lavoro nella bottega quattrocentesca, in: La grande storia dell'Artigianato, F. Franceschi, G. Fossi (eds.), 1999 2 H. Floerke, Die 75 italienischen Künstlernovellen der Renaissance, 1913 3 M. Foucault, Schriften zur Literatur, K. von Hofer, A. Botond (trans.), 1974 4 E. H. Gombrich, Art and Illusion, 1960 5 A. Jacobs, P. Whannel, Artist, Critic and Teacher, 1959 6 E. Kris, O. Kurz, Die Legende vom Künstler 7 E. Neumann, Künstler-Mythen, 1986 8 K. Jex-Blake (trans.), The Elder Pliny's Chapters on the History of Art, with Commentary and Historical Introduction by E. Sellers, 1968 9 O. Rank, Der Künstler, 1907 10 J. von Schlosser, Kunstliteratur, 1924 11 C. M. Soussloff, Absolute Artist, 1997 12 D. Spence, Narrative Truth and Historical Truth, 1982 13 R. Steiner, Prometheus, 1991 14 Topics of Discourse, 1978 15 G. Vasari, Le vite de piu eccellenti architetti, pittori, et scultori italiani: da Cimabue insino a' tempi nostri / descritte in lingua toscana, 1550; G. Vasari, Leben der ausgezeichnetsten Maler, Bildhauer und Baumeister (1568), E. Förster, L. Schorn (trans., 1832ff.), J. Kliemann (ed.), 1988f. 16 M. Warnke, Hofkünstler, 1985 17 M. and R. Wittkower, Born under Saturn, 1963 18 E. Zinsel, Die Entstehung des Geniebegriffs, 1926. WYSS, BEAT

Assyriology see → Ancient oriental philology and history; → Near Eastern archaeology

Astrology see → Natural sciences

Astronomy see → Natural sciences

Atheism see → Religion, critique of

Athens

I. History and interpretation II. Agora III. Acropolis IV. Kerameikos V. National Archaeological Museum VI. Other museums

I. History and interpretation

A. Introduction B. The Sources from the Classical Period – Firm Reference Points in Dealing with the History of Athens C. On the History of Athens and Interest in Athens and Its Ancient Legacy D. Characteristics and Tendencies in the History of Classical Studies E. Athens and the Creation of its Image

A. Introduction

Among the great places of antiquity that are of decisive importance for the culture and heritage of the western world, Athens (A.) plays a most important role. Nonetheless, it should be noted that the historical influence of → Rome is greater. Since time immemorial → Jerusalem, in particular, has been in competition with A. with respect to the question of which city was the foundation of history and culture and which should be regarded as such. → Sparta, on the other hand, was considered already in antiquity to be the politically more attractive counter-model and it did not completely lose this fascination even after the Second World War. Even the ancient states of the federation, particularly the Achaean Confederacy, are regularly assigned a role in the course of historically comprehensive discussions in the field of political thought. Undoubtedly → ATLANTIS (often connected with A.) then inspired utopian dreams particularly strongly.

The suggestive power of the symbol of A. to provide historical, political, social or cultural orientation always depended on what could be ascertained with certainty about A. based on the ancient sources and the information and images of A. provided by them. Likewise, the essential classifications of the symbols associated with A. are already to be found in the ancient sources.

B. THE SOURCES FROM THE CLASSICAL PERIOD – FIRM REFERENCE POINTS IN DEALING WITH THE HISTORY OF ATHENS

The core of what in all eras has been considered to be the history of A. essentially goes back to the numerous testimonials from the Classical age as well as to the ancient tradition of dealing with these testimonials [15; 23]. The history of A. is present in the mythological world of imagery (especially important: Athena, Theseus), in the texts of the philosophers (above all of Plato and Aristotle) and of the historians (Herodotus, Thucydides, Xenophon), in the works of the Atthidographers, authors of works on the myth, religion, history, culture, literature and topography of A. and Attica, in the works of the Attic orators (especially Isocrates and Demosthenes) above all in the eulogies to A., particularly to the fallen soldiers of the city, a tradition which was alive in the Roman Imperial period from Aelius Aristides to Himerius or Libanius and was drawn upon by Leonardo Bruni in 1428 to praise the fallen Florentine general Nanni Strozzi as well as Florence [2].

Yet more important perhaps are the Athenian structures of the Classical period (see [7; 8]) and the stories skillfully recorded by Plutarch and even more so his biographies of citizens of Athens with their enormous effect on future images of A. The tragedies and comedies that arose in A. kept the knowledge of the city, its institutions and peculiarities alive. Art works – in the form of vase painting, tomb reliefs and, especially, sculpture – played a more important role in the cultural heritage than the inscriptions.

Of course, a Pausanias in the 2nd cent. AD certainly knew to consult inscriptions. However it was not until the modern age that these were systematically re-evaluated and even in the 20th cent. important new discoveries were still recorded. The first article by Allen Brown West and Benjamin Dean Merritt in 1924, e.g. on the Attic tribute lists (edited by B.D. Merritt, H.T. Wade-Gery, M.F. Mac Gregor, 1939–1953) represented a breakthrough. Without the preliminary work of various scholars, the great systematic collections of inscriptions and the development of the casting technique – all present since from the beginning of the 19th cent. – this would not have been possible.

The *Athenaion Politeia* that is attributed to Aristotle and most certainly originated in his school was still known in the Imperial period, to be sure, but it was not until 1891 that its rediscovery was made known. In the same year Frederic George Kenyon produced the *editio princeps*. Since then [6] the text has been one of the most important points of reference in the study of Athenian democracy.

C. ON THE HISTORY OF ATHENS AND INTEREST IN ATHENS AND ITS ANCIENT LEGACY

[19; 21; 27; 29; 30] In the Roman Imperial and in the late Roman periods [14; 18] A. was a provincial city whose ancient remains were damaged especially by the Herulian's storming the city (AD 267). Nonetheless, as a cultural centre it was held in high regard, not least because the Neoplatonic Schools still exerted a considerable influence. The fact that – several decades before the closure of the Academy – Athenais (after her baptism: Eudocia), the poet daughter of the philosopher Leontius, became a Christian empress as the wife of Theodosius II testifies to the co-existence of Christian and pagan culture as well as to the significance of A.

The influential Irene (sole ruler from 797 to 802) and shortly afterwards her relative Theophano were further empresses from A., as Theophanes reports. The city was plundered by the Slavs in 582 but remained in Byzantine hands. Positive effects for the city were felt because Emperor Constantine II stayed there in 662/3 during his campaign against the Slavs [18. 117]. Certainly in the subsequent period people in Byzantium tended rather to regard A. in an unfavourable light because of its declining culture which was still pagan. In 1018 Basilius II celebrated his victory over the Bulgarians at St. Mary's Church in the Parthenon (John Skylitzes 364, 80–83 ed. THURN).

Of the bishops (since the beginning of the 9th cent. archbishops) of A., Michael Akominatos (Choniates) of Chonai in Phrygia showed the greatest amount of enthusiasm for the Classical past of A. and in his first sermon as the metropolitan in 1182 he reinterpreted it for his own purposes: whatever remained in the impoverished city of the former splendour and was obviously still known to the Athenians was to be surpassed in the present through the Christian way of thinking [1]. There are indeed numerous churches from the 11th/12th cents. – each one, however, with a small sanctuary. Moreover, in a similar manner to Michael Choniates, Pope Innocent III in Rome also respected the ancient greatness of A. [19. 227f.]: 'Antiquam Atheniensis gloriam civitatis innovatiogratiae non patitur antiquari'.

Nonetheless, as early as 1204 the Byzantine provincial dynast of Nauplia had devastated the lower part of the city of A. The 4th Crusade (1198–1204) led to the dismantling of the Byzantine Empire. A. was conquered and became a Frankish feudal duchy. Rule over the city, primarily by the Burgundian family de la Roche (1204–1311) and the Catalanian Compagnie (1311–85), was followed by the Florentine Acciaiuoli, during which the city in 1394 fell for a very short time into the hands of Venice. The links with Italy were significant for the rise

ATHENS 311 312

of the Renaissance. In 1446 the city again passed to Byzantium, but then fell in 1456 to the Turks with only the fortress holding out until 1458.

Apart from a series of isolated medieval references, we do not have coherent and more detailed descriptions of the ancient monuments until the end of the 14th cent., and from the 15th cent. from Cyriacus of Ancona, among others, who visited A. in 1436 and 1437 [13]. In medieval and early modern A. itself there was a certain interest in the ancient legacy, as the imaginative naming of ancient monuments attests. Sultan Mehmet II, the Ottoman conqueror of the city, treated A. generously, inspected the antiquities with interest and allowed A. to remain undamaged. The Athenian Laonicus Chalco-condylas (c. 1423–c. 1490) who grew up in Mistra reports in this regard in his history work but in view of the historical development he focuses on the rise of the Ottoman Empire. Regardless of this he belongs to the tradition of the great Athenian historians.

A revival of A. after 1456 was only of short duration. The city degenerated into just a provincial town. The time of Turkish rule was furthermore troubled because of the constant battles with Venice and this brought terrible destruction in the 17th cent., for instance to the Parthenon.

In the 17th cent. the French began to study the antiquities in A. The Jesuits and the Capuchins, who had been residing in A. since 1658 and who bought the Monument of Lysicrates, the so-called Lantern of Demosthenes from the Turks, and built their monastery there (Fig.1), had an important role in this. The expedition of the physician from Lyons Jacques Spon – together-er with George Wheler – led in 1678 to the publication of the first scientific topography of A. that continued to be of great significance for about a century.

After the French it was primarily the English who investigated A. The high point of their research was the work of the English architect James Stuart and of Nicholas Revett *The Antiquities of Athens* [4] that goes back to a mission – surpassing the rival French undertaking of Julien-David Le Roy – which the *Society of Dilettanti* that was founded in 1732 in London had inspired. The ambassador for the High Gate, Lord Elgin (Thomas Bruce), in 1816 suggested to the English government that it buy the sculptures from the Parthenon which he had shipped to London. The antiquities were to serve as models for his contemporaries and be 'beneficial to the progress of the Fine Arts in Great Britain' (Report from the Select Committee of the House of Commons on the Earl of Elgin's Collection of Sculptured Marbles, 1816, 2).

Philhellenism and Classicism, promoted by the hunt for art treasures, by travelers and scholars, museums and collections, images and books as well as a broad literary, artistic and intellectual movement, were not solely an aesthetic phenomenon. They went hand in hand with reforms in education and they had their social and political dimensions.

With the Greek War of Independence of 1821–1830, Greece and A. became central to interests in this regard. In 1833 A. which had been heavily destroyed became the capital city of the newly established Greek kingdom, which in view of the miserable condition of the city was by no means a matter of course. In this matter it needed the assistance of the Wittelsbach Ludwig I and his architect Leo von Klenze. Two until then unknown architects, students of Karl Friedrich Schinkel – the German Eduard Schaubert and the Greek Stamathios Cleanthes – drew up a city plan that emulated the Classical models (Fig.2). Bavarian, Prussian and Danish architects played an important part in the development of the city [25].

Directly after the wars, systematic investigations of the ancient monuments began: Greek legislation, the Central Archaeological Museum (already in the Theseion in 1833), later the Athenian National Museum that was completed in 1889, a Greek archaeological service – all of these contributed to conditions favourable as a framework to research. Worthy of mention here as well are individuals who were repeatedly important. In 1840 K.O. Müller (1797–1840) died in A. at the age of only 43; he was a scholar with great charisma who certainly also had a disastrous effect because of his descriptions of the nature of Ionians and Dorians. The Greek Archaeological Society (1837), the École Française d'Athènes (1846), a German Archäologisches Institut (1874), the American School of Classical Studies at Athens (1882), the British School at Athens (1886), in 1898 a centre of the Austrian Archäologisches Institut, in 1909 the Scuola Archeologica Italiana in Atene, in 1946 a Swedish institute and other institutions important for research have since then provided powerful momentum for investigations of ancient A. In addition to the excavations in A., the foreign schools also organized and financed scholarly activities in the Greek region – often on a grand scale.

D. CHARACTERISTICS AND TENDENCIES IN THE HISTORY OF CLASSICAL STUDIES

[16; 24] According to Walther Judeich [21. 16] modern Athenian local knowledge had grown slowly; this assessment was based not least on a seminal older work by L. Comte de Laborde (1854), in other words, works that are still used today did not appear until the 19th cent. Much faster progress was indeed made in the evaluation of the literary sources. An outstanding work was written in Italy in the 16th cent.: besides key books about Rome and Bologna, Carolus Sigonius (1523–1584) wrote a seminal as well as pioneering depiction of the Athenian state institutions [3], which went through many printings in subsequent cents. (*Gronovii Thesaurus Graecarum antiquitatum*, 13 Vols. Fol., Leiden 1697–1702, see Fig.3). French and Dutch philologists were also leaders in the field. The synoptic depiction of Greek state constitutions by the Frisian Ubbo Emmius (1547–1625) was of great influence. Eduardo Corsini (1702–1763), who came from a Florentine patrician family, published the *Fasti Attici* in 1744–56.

Fig. 1: The monument to Lysicrates with the Capuchin monastery. Engraving after a drawing of 1751

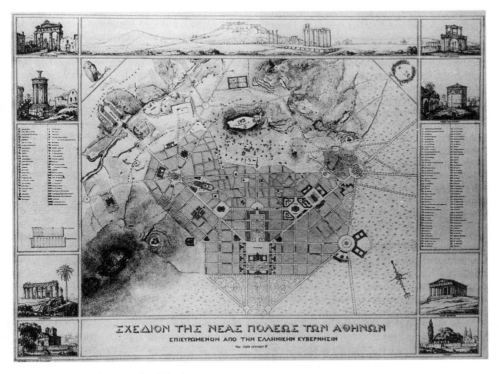

Fig. 2: Plan by St. Kleantes and E. Schaubert

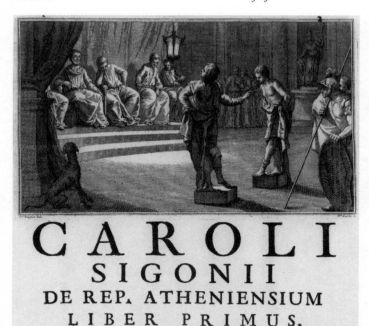

CAROLI
SIGONII
DE REP. ATHENIENSIUM
LIBER PRIMUS,
Qui de forma Reipublicæ infcribitur.

Fig. 3: C. Sigonius, *De republica Atheniensium*, 1564. Title page of the 1736 reprint

In the 17th cent. it became a prerequisite that the exact philological method used in the study of manuscripts be applied to inscriptions, coins and images. The groundbreaking life work of August Boeckh (1785–1867) whose *Staatshaushaltung der Athener* (State Finances of the Athenians, [5]) is not only a pioneering work but still of fundamental importance; it is based on his interest in historical interpretation and evaluation of all sources, including the inscriptions, in particular. A number of large scholarly projects in the research of Antiquity such as the *Realenzyclopädie* from 1837 onward goes back to the 19th cent., in which in the same way as in the numerous collections and museums worldwide A., of necessity, always assumes a central place. In addition there are text editions and commentaries, inscription editions as well as numerous other works about archaeology and numismatics as well as the grand historical syntheses.

Propelled and directed by A. Boeckh, the *Corpus Inscriptionum Graecarum* began to appear: The request of Boeckh to the Academy was made in 1815, and it was published from 1825 with the dating from 1828 to 1877. This was followed by the *Corpus Inscriptionum Atticarum* from 1873 and the *Inscriptiones Graecae* from 1903. *L'Année égraphique* (Academie des Inscriptions et Belles-Lettres, Paris) continues to publish classical, including Attic, inscriptions. An important evaluation of the sources and basis for further research was Johannes Kirchner's *Prosopographia Attica* (1901–1903). Alexander Christian Leopold Conze (4 Vols., 1893–1922) attended to a corpus of the Attic grave reliefs. Ernst Curtius (1814–1896) was a key figure in topography. Unsurpassed, as before, is the *Geschichte der Stadt Athen im Mittelalter* (History of the City of Athens in the Middle Ages, [19]) by Ferdinand Gregorovius (1821–1891), which he wrote primarily in Munich after his important work on Rome [19], at a time when Byzantine studies were receiving considerable attention. Great syntheses about the Attic festivals (e.g. L. Deuber, 1932) or Attic law (e.g. J.H. Lipsius, 1905) in the 20th cent. have their precursors in corresponding works from the 19th cent. In the 20th cent. John Davidson Beazley and John Boardman, in particular, promoted research on Attic vase painting centered on painters, schools of painting and images.

The excavations begun by the Greeks in 1882 in → ELEUSIS that were first Greek, then from 1913 German in the Ceramicus and the American excavation of the Agora (from 1931) are especially worthy of mention; the latter was impressive because of its immense organisational achievement and led to fundamental publications whose significance extends far beyond the Agora and A.

The depiction of the history of A. in the growing number of *Greek histories* since the 18th cent. but particularly since the 19th cent. always had a wide audience and regularly inspired discussions. One of the most influential authors was George Grote (1794–1871), even though the *Griechische Geschichte* by his later rival Karl Julius Beloch (1854–1929) is regarded more highly from an academic point of view. In Grote's *A History of Greece*, Athenian democracy is viewed as a form of government in which individuals were spurred on to the highest possible achievements, which consequently they were able to accomplish for the common good, thanks to the existing freedom.

Fig. 4: The Propyläen in Munich

The discussions about the advantages and disadvantages of Athenian democracy as well as the strengths and weaknesses of the state as an historic power took place however even in connection with the figures of Pericles, Socrates [22] and Demosthenes [28]. The comparisons between ancient and modern conditions have often unleashed great emotions. The moralizing impetus when using the ancient *exempla* was just as important here as the opportunity, with the aid of ancient A., to discuss the basic organization of the state.

In this point. scholars of Antiquity always had a wider audience in mind, for example the opponents of democracy Julius Schvarcz in the 19th and Hans Bogner in the 20th cent., who today are deemed to be interesting at most from the point of view of the history of the discipline, as well as great scholars of their discipline like Engelbert Drerup and even more importantly Ulrich von Wilamowitz-Moellendorff. Alfred Croiset crossed swords with the Action Française in 1909. In 1921 Arthur Rosenberg portrayed A. from a Marxist point of view. Moses I. Finley's plea for a democracy with broad participation (*Democracy Ancient and Modern*, 1973) is highly regarded. The German Jochen Bleicken, the French scholar Jacqueline de Romilly, the American Jennifer Talbert Roberts [26], the Finnish diplomat and expert in constitutional law, Tuttu Tarkiainen, and many others are worthy of mention. The Dane Mogens Herman Hansen dealt most comprehensively with the institutions of democracy, particularly in the 4th cent. BC, regularly drawing comparisons with modern democracy [9].

The excessive attention paid to Attic democracy and even more to a plaster cast version of A. reduced totally to Classicism has often been criticized (programmatic, for instance, is the title of a book by HANS-JOACHIM GEHRKE, *Jenseits Athen und Sparta. Das Dritte Griechenland und seine Staatenwelt*, 1986, [Beyond Athens and Sparta: The Third Greece and its States]; but also the earlier work by PAUL NERRLICH, *Das Dogma vom klassischen Altertum in seiner geschichtlichen Entwicklung*, 1894, [The Dogma of Classical Antiquity in its Historical Development]). There are however several prominent and impressive studies with a perspective not confined to Classicism. A perfect example of this is Christian Habicht's synthesis of Hellenistic history [10] or Hans Lohmann's study of the demos Atene based on the archaeology of settlements (1993).

E. ATHENS AND THE CREATION OF ITS IMAGE
[15; 20; 23; 24; 26] In Athenian self-depiction as well as in the ancient images of A., the city of A. was epitomized by its importance for education, science and culture, law and philanthropy, freedom, trade and prosperity, and for a brief period of considerable empire-building as well as for its religiosity [15; 23]. The dimensions of the symbol of A. are repeatedly being reformulated and become apparent in their diversity whenever A. is correlated with modern cities: the 'Spree-A.' Berlin, Dresden, Florence, the 'A. of America' La Paz, London, the 'Isar-A.' Munich (Fig.4), Paris or the 'Limmat-A.' Zurich (in the 18th cent.). Recurring allusions to science and philosophy take on shape with

the use of words like 'Academy', 'academic' or 'Athenaeum', and Pallas Athene still stands as a symbol of academic institutions.

A. as the first democracy has had a particular significance in connection with the processes of radical political change in the modern age, the English Glorious Revolution, the American and French Revolutions, as well as in modern thinking with regard to politics and the state. In a similar way as in Antiquity, reservations toward democratic institutions were very prevalent until the Second World War. Viewed from an historical perspective, those involved in 1993/94 in the 2500–year celebration of the introduction of democracy in A., Paris and Washington [11] have been supporting new positions. Moreover, the fact that Cleisthenian isonomy was so strongly foregrounded in the process of the development of democracy, was not previously the common perspective, although Cleisthenes, albeit in addition to Theseus and Solon, had already been mentioned regularly in the ancient tradition (Herodotus. 6,131).

The rediscovery of the *Politics* and *Ethics* of Aristotle in the 13th cent. greatly increased the number of references to A. but not the positive evaluation of democracy. Of primary importance remained the orientation towards the best possible constitution, as had already been outlined by Aristotle. This tendency was greatly reinforced by and ultimately culminated in the utopias, influenced by the Platonic Dialogues. The image of Athenian democracy as seen in the early modern period is, to an extent, a counterpoint to the lovely painting by Raphael 'School of A.', with Raphael reminding the viewer much more strongly of Roman thermal baths than of the Athenian environment, for here we are still far removed from the aesthetic turning point in the time of Winckelmann. The dynamic elements in Athenian democracy, above all the troubles which issued from the demos, repeatedly were viewed as negative factors. The fickle nature of the demos, its ingratitude in the rapid turning away from politicians and intellectuals or the unrest among the citizens – all of this was frequently criticized – likewise however also the change in the laws as well as a number of factors that were interpreted as evidence of moral and political decline, the most prominent of these being the defeat suffered in the war against the Macedonians.

Quite apart from this, Roman law and the history of Rome provided more detailed starting-points from an historical perspective, as can clearly be seen in Niccolò Machiavelli, for instance. Interest in the great texts from A. as the epitome of Greek education and science per se first grew gradually and probably not least because a return to the pre-Roman and pre-Christian periods opened up freedoms so that it was very possible at the same time to claim authority by an orientation towards tradition and that which was canonically valid.

Modern Republicanism liked to refer to the ancient examples and Thomas Hobbes already referred in a famous passage in his Leviathan (2,21) to this connec-

tion. He, like the American Founding Fathers or the revolutionaries in France, regularly commented on the shortcomings of Attic democracy, which meant that criticism of democracy certainly could be closely intertwined with an admiration for A. as the epitome of culture. It has been repeatedly stated that praise and high regard for the Classical model were ultimately used to substantiate one's own ideas. This is demonstrated in a number of academic studies in the history of the discipline on the treatment of Antiquity in the period of the American (M. Reinhold 1984; P. Rahe 1992; S.F. Wiltshire 1992; C.J. Richard, 1994) and French Revolutions (H. Parker 1937; J. Bouineau 1986; C. Mossé 1989 – as well as L. Guerci [20] and P. Vidal-Naquet, N. Loraux [31. 95ff.]).

Ancient texts are always used in this connedtion, and the most important are probably the philosophers Aristotle and Plato, the Attic dramas and the parallel biographies of Plutarch, then Herodotus and, since the 19th cent., Thucydides. Of course, great modern authors like Bodin, Hobbes and Montesquieu, and certainly not least the writers and thinkers of German Classicism became even more important, as did historical summaries – within the framework of great historical works, in lexica or as historical outlines in literature.

In political debates, speeches on festive occasions or in addresses to universities and grammar schools, A. is mentioned regularly. In the 19th cent. it became a set component of bourgeois education [31]. Always popular was the comparison with Sparta. When on March 22,1877 the great philologist Ulrich von Wilamowitz-Moellendorff spoke on the emperor's birthday of the 'splendour of the Attic Empire', he saw in the First Attic Delian League a successful federal state and a state in which the rule of law prevailed, whose common ground with Germany he believed to detect in the mind and thinking of the people.

A. always played a part when the humanities were called upon in the service of the nation during the World Wars as well as in discussions about the sociopolitical structuring in numerous countries [24]. In an atmosphere of such kind in 1926, the former French Prime Minister Georges Clemenceau had a *Démosthène* published (written by Robert Cohen). The *mater liberalium litterarum et philosophorum nutrix*, as it was called by Isidore of Seville (orig. 14,4,10) at the transition from Antiquity to the Middle Ages, remained even in the 20th cent. a central reference point for the history of culture and lack of culture.

→ Atlantis; → Rome; → Sparta

→ Bavaria; → Democracy; → Deutsches Archäologisches Institut; → École française d'Athènes; → Revolution

Sources 1 Sp. P. Lampros, Μιχαήλ κομινάτου τοῦ Χωνάτου τὰ Σωζόμενα, 2 vols., Athen 1879–80   2 S. Daub, Leonardo Brunis Rede auf Nanni Strozzi, Beiträge zur Altertumskunde 84, 1996   3 C. Sigonius, De republica Atheniensium, Bononiae 1564   4 J. Stuart, N. Revett, The Antiquities of Athens Measured and Delineated, 4 vols., London 1762–1816   5 A. Boeckh, Die

Staatshaushaltung der Athener, Berlin 1817 (M. FRÄNKEL (ed.), Berlin ³1886)   6 U. VON WILAMOWITZ-MOELLENDORFF, Aristoteles und Athen, 2 vols., 1893   7 J. TRAVLOS (I. TRAULOS), Bildlexikon zur Topographie des antiken Athen, 1971 (Eng.: Pictorial Dictionary of Ancient Athens, 1971)   8 Id., Bildlexikon zur Topographie des antiken Attika, 1988   9 M. H. HANSEN, Die athenische Demokratie im Zeitalter des Demosthenes, 1995 (Eng.: The Athenian Democracy in the Age of Demosthenes: Structure, Principles, and Ideology. Translated by J.A. Crook. Oxford, 1991)   10 CH. HABICHT, Athen. Die Geschichte der Stadt in hellenistischer Zeit, 1995   11 J. OBER, CH. HEDRICK (eds.), Demokratia. A Conversation on Democracies, Ancient and Modern, 1996   11a P. EUBEN, J. R. WALLACH, J. OBER (eds.), Athenian Political Thought and the Reconstruction of American Democracy, Ithaca, NY, 1994   11b J. A. KOUMOULIDES (ed.), The Good Idea: Democracy and Ancient Greece. Essays in Celebration of the 2500th Anniversary of its Birth in Athens, New Rochelle, NY., Athens, Moscow 1995   11c I. MORRIS, K. A. RAAFLAUB (eds.), Democracy 2500?, 1998

LITERATURE   12 Athènes. Ville capitale, sous la direction de Y. TSIOMIS, 1985   13 E. W. BODNAR, Cyriacus of Ancona and Athens, 1960   14 P. CASTRÈN (ed.), Post-Herulian Athens, 1994   15 D. LAU, s.v. Athen I (Sinnbild), Reallexikon für Antike und Christentum Suppl. 1, 639–668   16 R. AND F. ETIENNE, Griechenland. Die Wiederentdeckung der Antike, 1992 (French: La Grèce antique: archéologie d'une découverte 1990; Eng.: The search for Ancient Greece, 1992)   17 A. FRANTZ, s.v. Athen II (urban history), Reallexikon für Antike und Christentum Suppl. 1, 668–692   18 Id., Late Antiquity, AD 276–700. The Athenian Agora, 24, 1988   19 F. GREGOROVIUS, Geschichte der Stadt Athen im Mittelalter, Reprint of the ed. of 1889, ed. H. G. BECK, 1980   20 L. GUERCI, Libertà degli antichi e libertà dei moderni. Sparta, Atene e i philosophes nella Francia del Settecento, 1979   21 W. JUDEICH, Topographie von Athen, ²1931   22 M. MONTUORI, The Socratic Problem, 1992   23 B. NÄF, Die attische Demokratie in der römischen Kaiserzeit. Zu einem Aspekt des Athenbildes und seiner Rezeption, in: P. KNEISSL, V. LOSEMANN (eds.), Imperium Romanum. Festschrift für K. Christ, 1998, 552–570   24 Id., Von Perikles zu Hitler? Die athenische Demokratie und die deutsche Althistorie bis 1945, 1986   25 A. PAPAGEORGIOU-VENETAS, Hauptstadt Athen. Ein Stadtgedanke des Klassizismus, 1994   26 J. T. ROBERTS, Athens on Trial. The Antidemocratic Tradition in Western Thought, 1994   27 K. M. SETTON, Athens in the Middle Ages, 1975   28 U. SCHINDEL, Demosthenes im 18. Jahrhundert. Zehn Kapitel zum Nachleben des Demosthenes in Deutschland, Frankreich, England, 1963   29 E. K. STASINOPOULOS: Ἱστορία τῶν Ἀθηνῶν, 1973   30 J. TRAVLOS, (I. TRAULOS) Athènes au fil du temps. Atlas historique d'urbanisme et d'architecture, 1972 (Greek, 1960)   31 P. VIDAL-NAQUET, Die griechische Demokratie von außen gesehen, 2 vols., 1993–96 (French, La démocratie grecque vue d'ailleurs 1990)

ADDITIONAL BIBLIOGRAPHY: K. N. DEMETRIOU, George Grote and Athenian Democracy. A Study in Classical Reception, 1999 (Koinon, 2); M. FAKHRY, Philosophy, Dogma, and the Impact of Greek Thought in Islam, 1994; M. HALL (ed.), Raphael's School of Athens, 1997; M. H. HANSEN, The Tradition of Athenian Democracy AD 1750–1990, Greece and Rome 39, 1992, 14–30; H.

KASSIM, Aristotle and Aristotelianism in Medieval Muslim, Jewish, and Christian philosophy, 2000; M. NAFISSI, Ancient Athens and Modern Ideology. Value, Theory and Evidence in Historical Sciences. Max Weber, Karl Polanyi and Moses Finley, in: Bulletin of the Institute of Classical Studies, Supplement 80, 2005; E. PETERS, Aristotle and the Arabs: the Aristotelian Tradition in Islam, 1968; P. J. RHODES, Ancient Democray and Modern Ideology, 2003; N. URBINATI, Mill on Democracy. From the Athenian Polis to Representative Government, 2002.   BEAT NÄF

II. AGORA
A. INTRODUCTION   B. EXCAVATIONS TO 1930
C. EXCAVATIONS AFTER 1930

A. INTRODUCTION
The Athenian Agora, as a political, religious, social and economic centre of the city, is one of the most historic locations in Greece. To be sure, the remains of its buildings cannot directly relate its significance, since the only outstandingly well preserved building is the Hephaisteion from the Age of Pericles (second half of the 5th cent. BC) that was protected from destruction and dilapidation by a timely transformation into a Christian church (Fig.1). Because of its symbolic value, the Agora awakened archaeological interest at an early stage. As however fewer remains of buildings known through literature are recognizable today than formerly, the history of excavation has for a long time been marked by controversy. Only the excavations after the Second World War reduced the amount of leeway for speculation. The excavation of Agora was for a long time considered to be the special task and also the privilege of Greek researchers.

B. EXCAVATIONS TO 1930
Immediately after the Greek War of Independence (1821–1829), two outstanding architects, S. Cleanthes and E. Schaubert, were commissioned by the Greek government in 1832 to design a plan for the development of Athens as the capital city of the new kingdom. They recommended limiting the new site to the area north of the Acropolis so that the region of the ancient cities of Theseus and Hadrian would be available for later research. Initially financial difficulties prevented the systematic implementation of this plan but the Greek Archaeological Society took advantage of every opportunity that emerged in order to research individual buildings.

Their greatest contribution was the uncovering of the Stoa of Attalus (Attalus Hall) during a long series of excavation campaigns (1859–1862, 1874 and 1898–1902). Initially the archaeologists linked the remains with various names known from Antiquity (among others Stoa Poikile, Gymnasium of Ptolemy) that also found expression in the modern names of nearby streets. In 1861 however an inscription was discovered through which the building could be identified clearly as the Stoa of Attalus II of Pergamum (159–138 BC)

Area of the Agora from the Southwest: Mt. Lykabettos in the Background. Engraving by J. Thürmer, 1819.

Fig. 1: The Agora and surrounding area from the southwest, with the Lycabettus Hill in the background (after Joseph Thürmer, 1819)

Fig. 2: Model of the Agora from the northwest

that had previously only been known from Athenaios 5, 212f.

Also the now so-called Gymnasium of the Giants (1859, 1871 and 1912) and parts of the western Agora (1907–1908) were excavated by the Greek archaeologists. The huge marble figures in these remains of the building were still known in the 15th cent. (mentioned by the 'Viennese Anonymus', 1456–1458, in [6 vol. I.732] as statues of Zeus; a drawing of a statue as mermaid by Cyriacus of Ancona in 1436 or during the 1440s:), but they were then built over. Only after the destruction of these buildings in the Greek War of Independence did the large figures again become visible (now in the Agora Museum) and they gave occasion for much speculation. The German scholar Ludwig Ross, for instance, considered the group to be a reconstruction from Roman times of the eponymous heroes (heroes after whom the 10 phylae were named). After the excavations of the Archaeological Society, the row of statues proved to be part of a larger layout, whose purpose and time of origin however remained obscure. Only after the area had been completely uncovered in the 1930s was one able to determine that the Giants adorned the northern entry to a large Gymnasium from Late Antiquity.

In 1890–1891, for the construction of a railway section from Athens to Piraeus, a ditch with a width of *c.* 15 m was dug through the northern part of the Agora that brought to light extensive remains of ancient buildings and sculptures; these were measured and sketched by German archaeologists. The ditch, for the most part, ran through the square and therefore did little damage to the ancient buildings. Nevertheless remains at the north-western edge of the Agora fell victim to the construction of the railway. From 1891 to 1898 the *Deutsches Archäologisches Institut* began systematic excavations under the direction of Wilhelm Dörpfeld with the aim of investigating the exact site of the Agora. Between the Areopagus and the Pnyx (site of the people's assembly) the German archaeologists excavated a large area with private houses and small sanctuaries. These excavations allow a vivid insight into a residential area in ancient Athens.

In 1907–1908 the Greek Archaeological Society took over the area below the Temple of Hephaistos (Hephaisteion). In particular, they uncovered remains of the Temple of Apollo Patroos, remains of additional temples, of the Metroon (Sanctuary of μήτηρ θεῶν = Cybele; State Archive), of the Buleuterion (meeting chamber of the *búlē*, 'Council') and the four long stone seats on the eastern slope of the Colonus. The first identifications, primarily made by Dörpfeld, often proved to be wrong.

C. EXCAVATIONS AFTER 1930

The increase in population in Athens after the First World War and the influx of refugees from Asia Minor after 1922 forced the Greek government to decide between a continuation of the large scale excavations on the one hand and a loosening of the regulations and permission to build on the land on the other. Under the leadership of the Greek archaeologist Alexander Philadelpheus, a movement arose in support of the continuation of the diggings. After a corresponding draft bill put to the Greek parliament had initially failed, foreign archaeological institutions were asked for sponsorship. The American School of Classical Studies that received financial assistance from John D. Rockefeller and the Rockefeller Foundation, successfully supported the excavations. The Greek parliament in 1930 passed a bill by which the American School of Classical Studies, after compensating the property owners, was entitled to excavate the area and to publish the results; after the conclusion of the excavations the area was to be landscaped. All funds had to remain the property of the Greek government in Greece. At that time the land was almost completely developed. The area had over 300 houses in which about 5000 people lived. Although the position of the site had been established with great precision (two boundary stones that marked the exact extension of the site were found in 1938 and 1968), there was very little agreement about the precise locations of the individual buildings known from the ancient writings. Only the Stoa of Attalus had been clearly identified at this point.

The excavations began in 1931 and were continued until 1940 in annual digging campaigns lasting four to five months. The modern buildings for whose construction ancient materials had often been used first had to be demolished carefully and up to 12 m of silt and rubble had to be cleared away. By the outbreak of the Second World War, most of the area had been uncovered and the outline of the ancient site could be defined.

After the discovery of the Tholos (building for the Prytanes, 1934) which was clearly identifiable because of its round shape, the buildings situated to the north of it could also be identified with the aid of the list in Pausanias. (1,3,1ff.): the Bouleuterion, the Metroon, the Temple of Apollo Patroos (the discovery of a colossal statue of Apollo by the Greek Archaeological Society had already indicated in 1907 that there was a temple) and the Stoa of Zeus Eleutherios. The discovery too of the Altar of the Twelve Gods founded by Peisistratus the Younger in 521/20, whose central position in the ancient city's topography was known from literary sources, facilitated the identification and dating of its surroundings. In 1933 parts of the late ancient city wall that until then had been called the Valerian Wall were excavated south of the Stoa of Attalus. Through stratigraphic tests the wall could be dated to the period shortly after the Herulian destruction (AD 267). The fact that the entire wall had been constructed from recycled building materials explains the extremely derelict condition of the older buildings on the Agora. From 1935 more and more burial places were found that throw light on the early settlement of Athens and the burial rites: a family tomb mainly from the late 8th cent. BC south of the Tholos (1935), a Mycenaean chamber tomb on the northern slope of the Areopagus (1939, 1947), other Mycenaean burial places between the north-eastern and the north-western part of the ancient site (1949–1953), a cemetery from the early Geometric Period at the north-western foot of the Areopagus (1932, 1967) and an enclosed burial ground on the western slope of the Areopagus that was used from the 8th to the late 6th cents. BC (1939). In the mid–30s the major buildings on the southern side of the Agora were also excavated and identified: the Middle Stoa, the Odeum of Agrippa and a gymnasium from about AD 400 (Gymnasium of the Giants). After the north-eastern corner of the site had been cleared of late Roman and medieval rubble, a peristyle house from the late 4th cent. AD, a round well-house from the mid 2nd cent. AD and the 'Orators' Tribune built for the Roman generals' ('Bema', Ath. 5,212F) came to light, as well as a small columned hall that had for a long time been known as the North-eastern Stoa but in 1970 was identified as an extension to the large basilica that had been positioned past the site.

Further west, under the rubble, the Temple of Ares was discovered in 1937, whose proximity to the Odeum corresponded to Pausanias' description (Paus. 1,8,6; 14,1). The discrepancy between its superstructure which clearly comes from the mid 5th cent. BC and its foundation walls from the late 1st cent. BC can be explained by the practice in the 1st cent. of moving famous old temples from rural districts of Attica to the Agora. Once the actual Agora had, for the most part, been uncovered, archaeologists turned to the area between the southeastern corner of the square and the northwestern edge of the Acropolis. Here in three excavation campaigns between 1937 and 1939, the exact course of the Panathenaea road could be determined. The Eleusinium (Temple of Demeter), about whose position literary sources provide only imprecise information, was uncovered and identified.

The excavation of the northern slope of the Areopagus was begun in 1939. While researchers prior to the excavations mostly were of the opinion that many public buildings of the Agora must have stood on this slope, it now turned out that throughout Antiquity it was mainly covered with private houses with only sparse remains left. The Second World War interrupted the work but did not do any notable damage. After the war the work was resumed with the goal of uncovering the entire area up to the level it had had in Antiquity. This second series of excavation campaigns lasted from 1946 to 1960. At that time all the major buildings were explored according to the provisions of the original excavation permit and numerous probes were taken from deeper layers. A large part of the earliest layers remained untouched intentionally. It is true that, as a result, many early tombs, wells and minor monuments remained undiscovered but this method of proceeding made it possible to check through new diggings the conclusions of the first excavators.

The original excavation permit of 1930 allowed for investigations of the major part of the western Agora as well as the entire east and south sides. The north side of the ancient square had not yet been discovered. It had to lie north of the railway track to Piraeus that formed the northern boundary of the first excavation permit. The search for the north side began in 1969 in collaboration with the Greek government. The most recent excavations in this area led to the discovery of the Stoa Basilius at the farthest northwest corner of the square as well as a basilica at the northeast corner. The decorative addition of colonnades on the Panathenaea road, which are mentioned by ancient authors could now be understood with the aid of the finds. A series of modest houses, partly with shops from the Classical period, showed that the site was expanded on the east side only later. In the early Roman period these buildings were replaced by a stoa with a southerly orientation. The construction of a large and splendidly decorated basilica demonstrates both the reflourishing of Athens under Hadrian (Paus. 1,20,7) and the influence of Roman predilections in the architecture of public buildings on the old Greek city. New excavations along the north side of the Hadrian Road since 1980 have brought to light the Sanctuary of Aphrodite and the Stoa Poikile north of the square. Excavations in this area are still going on.

Just as the historical and architectonic development of the Agora in the Classical period of Athens became clear, so too did interest grow in the relationship between the ancient square and the large Roman buildings on its east side, the market of Caesar and Augustus and the library of Hadrian. Here too important excavations could be carried out from 1971 on. Originally, a museum was to be built between the Areopagus and the Hill of the Nymphs to house the finds from the excavations. This area however proved so rich in finds that a large new building seemed impossible. Instead of this it was decided in 1948 to reconstruct an ancient building as a museum. The Stoa of Attalus appeared to be the best suited because of its size and the possibility of exact reconstruction. From 1949 on the land around the Stoa on the east side of the square was therefore investigated first. In 1953 the work began on the reinforcing of the ancient foundation walls and on rebuilding the Stoa. The museum, opened in 1956, houses all the moveable objects found on the Agora since 1931 as well as several outstanding finds from earlier excavations, e.g. the statues of Apollo Patrous and the head of a Triton from the Gymnasium of the Giants. All the documentation from the most recent excavations is also stored here.

In the 1950s conservation of the excavations, as required by the law of 1930, as well as the laying out of a park began. Plantings are restricted to plants native to Greece and where possible they follow literary and archaeological notes with regard to ancient cultivation.
→ Athens
→ Deutsches Archäologisches Institut

1 The Athenian Agora: A Guide to the Excavation and Museum. American School of Classical Studies at Athens,

1990   2 J. M. Camp, The Athenian Agora. Excavations in the Heart of Classical Athens, 1986   3 H. R. Goette, s.v. Athenai II, Der Neue Pauly 2, 173   4 H. A. Thompson, R. E. Wycherley, The Agora of Athens. The History, Shape, and Uses of an Ancient City Center, 1972 (The Athenian Agora 14), 220–234   5 Travlos, Athen, 20–27   6 Travlos, Attika, 46   7 K. Wachsmuth, Die Stadt Athen im Alterthum, 2 vols., Leipzig 1874 (vol. 1) and 1890 (vol. 2.1).   BARBARA KUHN-CHEN

III. Acropolis
A. History of the Influence and Significance of the Acropolis – General Overview
B. Post-Antiquity: History of the Monuments to the Early 19th Cent. C. The History of Research, Excavation and Restoration in the 19th and 20th Cent. D. The Acropolis as Model and Epitome of Classicism

A. History of the Influence and Significance of the Acropolis – General Overview

As early as the turn of the 5th to the 4th cent. BC, the Acropolis took on a museum-like character in that its collection of monuments was of increasing symbolic significance due to its reference back to the 'great age' of Athens. Even though the Acropolis, in subsequent centuries, continued to remain the target of construction processes and monument dedications, the history of its reception nevertheless begins in Greek Antiquity. This is demonstrated by the few monuments that the autonomous polis of Athens had built on the Acropolis after the defeat at Aegospotamoi (for instance, dedications for the nauarchs Conon and Timotheus in 394 and 375 BC) and by the use of the Acropolis as a backdrop, for instance for the Theatre of Dionysos built in the mid 4th cent. BC on the southern slope in the massive stone technique of architecture.

Hellenistic and later Roman regents used the Acropolis intensively as a background for the staging of ostentatious productions, frequently insinuating an historical military reference to Athens' role in world politics in the 5th cent. BC Notable examples are Alexander's arms dedication from the Persian booty after the Battle of Granicus in 334 BC together with the bronze inscription on the epistyle of the Parthenon alluding to Athens' victories against the Persians in 480/79 BC (transmitted in Arr. Anab. 1,16,7); the incorporation of Roxane in the world of gods and heroes of Athens gathered in the Erechtheion; the Pergamene dedications (Eumenes' column in front of the Propylaeum in 178 BC as well as the 'small' Gallic anathema on the castle wall in front of the Parthenon that probably originated during the reign of Attalus II); the redesignation of the Eumenes' column to Agrippa in 27 BC; the building of the Monopteros for Roma and Augustus in front of the Parthenon; the honours for Nero (a statue with an accompanying inscription on the epistyle of

the Parthenon); the construction of an Odeum by the patron of the arts, Herodes Atticus, on the southern slope of the Acropolis (in the Hadrianic period) as well as the erection of two portrait statues, rich in allusions, of Julia Domna directly beside the Athena Parthenos in the Parthenon and the Athena-Polias-Xoanon in the Erechtheion (early 3rd cent. AD). A no less relevant part of the ancient history of the reception of the Acropolis is represented by the robberies and plunderings of the site, beginning with the desecration of the Erechtheion by Demetrius Poliorcetes (304 BC) and the tyranny of Lachares (297/96 BC), culminating in the subsequent capture of the city by the Herulians in AD 267; the dismantling of the immense sculptures of Athena Promachos and Athena Parthenos, presumably in the late 4th or 5th cent. AD (both sculptures were presumably taken to Constantinople and were lost there); and the willful, Christian-motivated destruction of numerous metopes of the Parthenon, probably in the 5th cent.

To the same extent that Athens was marginalized in the eastern Roman and later in the Byzantine Empire, the importance of the Acropolis declined. The Parthenon and Erechtheion were transformed into Christian churches although the Acropolis with St. Mary's Church in the Parthenon as a centre did not become an bishopric until the 9th cent.; in eloquent words, Archbishop Michael Choniates in 1145 lamented the decline of Athens. The military turmoil of the 12th–15th cents. (Frankish, Byzantine, Catalan, Florentine and Venetian conquests) as well as the progressive fixation of the world historical perspective on Byzantium and the Holy Land almost erased the city from memory so that in 1573 the Tübingen scholar, Martin Crusius (Kraus), even came to question the existence of the city; depictions of Athens, for instance in the Flemish Chronicle of Jean de Courcy (1473) or in Hartmann Schedel's World Chronicle (1493), are visual topoi of Gothic style without any specific details of the place and are not based on any close and rigorous examination. For an important inventory of buildings and depictions of the Acropolis immediately before the Turkish-Ottoman conquest (1457/58) we are indebted to the merchant Cyriacus di Piccicolle of Ancona, who visited Athens in 1436 and 1447, copied numerous inscriptions and among other things made sketches of the Parthenon.

In the almost 400 years of the Ottoman-Turkish occupation of Athens (1458–1827) the Acropolis was the centre of the local public administration; the ancient buildings were used in new contexts (the church in the Parthenon was transformed into a mosque and the Erechtheion into a harem) but it was by no means willfully destroyed. The area around the Acropolis itself experienced an increasingly dense settlement. Various views of the 17th–19th cents. (especially in Stuart-Revett and Dodwell) and reports like those of Jacques Spon (1678) describe uninhibited use of the Acropolis, the busy part of the city of Athens. The destruction of parts of the ancient monuments was to a large extent

Fig. 1: Sketch of the western side of the Parthenon. From the records of Cyriacus of Ancona, 1447

Fig. 2: Bombardment of the Acropolis and explosion of the Parthenon in 1687. Illustration from Francesco Fanelli, *Atene Attica*, Venice 1707 (after a contemporary drawing)

Fig. 3: Ascending to the fortified Acropolis: castellated defense walls, towers, and the walled-up intercolumnia of the Propylaea serve to secure access to the castle mount. Etching after a drawing by Joseph Türmer (1819/1825)

the product of acts of war (explosion of the gunpowder magazine in the Parthenon after the Venetian bombardment in 1687; the use of the Propylaeum and Nike Temple in entrenchments), as well as the consequences of targeted art theft. Since the 18th cent., in the course of the 'Rediscovery of Greece' (→ CLASSICISM; → GREECE), the Acropolis with its buildings and artifacts became synonymous with and a paradigm of idealized Classicism. The process of appropriation by the European cultural elites ranged from diagrammatic copying (among others LeRoy; Stuart-Revett) to seizure of property, via dismantling and robbing (among others the expeditions of Comte Choiseul-Gouffier 1787 and Lord Elgin in 1800–1803; → MUSEUM), to the extensive copying and refunctioning of [the ancient] buildings and art in Europe and America (see below) and the reconstruction on several occasions of the ancient ruins on site according to the respective standard of popular notions en vogue at that time (see below).

B. POST-ANTIQUITY: HISTORY OF THE MONUMENTS TO THE EARLY 19TH CENT.

(Figs. 1–4) An important turning-point in the history of the tradition of the Acropolis monuments is the dissolution of the pagan sanctuaries and the forced Christianization of Greece in the early 5th cent. The Parthenon and Erechtheion were transformed into churches, probably as early as the 5th or the early 6th cent. Especially at the Parthenon, the restructuring left clear traces

Fig. 4: The inhabited Acropolis, *c.* 1800. Aquatint plate in: Edward Dodwell, *Views in Greece from Drawings*, 1821

(moving of the entrance to the west side; finishing of the east side with an apse that was externally encased in a rectangular structure; installation of an altar; opening between the cella and opisthodomos – as well as side window openings?–; extension of the cella together with the galleries into a two-storey basilica with three naves; painting of the interior with Christian frescoes; destruction of various metope reliefs considered to be offensive because they were pagan). The reorientation and installation of an apse are also attested for the Erechtheion. In the Pinacoteca and the other annex buildings of the Propylaeum, formal rooms for church and secular dignitaries were provided (and they remained such, with interruptions, until the early 19th cent.). The actual Propylaeum complex continued to serve as a monumental gateway; because of its smallness as a building, the otherwise relatively unusable Temple of Nike, was utilized initially as a warehouse. The other buildings of the Acropolis became dilapidated. Their remnants were reused and the marble rubble was frequently burnt into lime. In the turmoil of the 13th and 14th cents. the Acropolis was extended into a fortress, the walls were raised with battlements and the Propylaeum was secured by the Franks with a solid fortified tower (which until its demolition in the 19th cent. was a landmark building in Athens). With the Ottoman-Turkish conquest, the Erechtheion was reorganized as a harem with the removal of all the Christian installations and building alterations (which left the external appearance of the building to a large extent untouched, although the interior with its many rooms was significantly changed); at the Parthenon the Christian frescoes were whitewashed, the altar was dismantled and the pulpit and prayer niche were installed, oriented in a strictly easterly direction towards Mecca, and a high minaret was added.

A second, highly significant turning-point occurred with the besieging, bombardment and conquest of the Acropolis by the Venetian troops of Francesco Morosini in 1687. As a defensive measure on the part of the garrison, the Nike Temple was completely demolished and used in the construction of fortification walls; at the same time the Intercolumnium of the Propylaeum was closed by being solidly walled up. The attempt by the Venetians to undermine the rock of the Acropolis and to completely blow it up failed. The key to the (short-lived) conquest of the Acropolis was a hit on the powder magazine in the Parthenon (26 September 1687); the explosion triggered by this devastated vast areas of the castle and cost the lives of over 300 soldiers who were defending it. The Parthenon which until then had largely been preserved as a building was blown apart and left lying in ruins in which after the retreat of the Venetians and after the return of the Turks a small, domed mosque was built. The drawings by Jacques Carrey of 1674 (now in the British Museum), which were carried out in the context of the Acropolis expedition of Marquis de Nointel, provide a priceless record of the building ornamentation of the intact Parthenon, although to this day

their details have been considered controversial and are the subject of debate among scholars.

Together with the Venetian conquest of the Acropolis began the modern history of its wanton plundering. Numerous fragments of sculptures were carried off as souvenirs (which later ended up in many different museums throughout the world). The attempt by the conqueror Morosini, to follow the tradition of the Byzantine conqueror Enrico Dandolo and dismantle the central group of the western gable of the Parthenon as a trophy of war came to nothing; the group of figures fell to the ground and was smashed to pieces (only a few fragments have to date been retrieved and properly assigned). The plundering reached its peak with the expedition of Lord Elgin – first started as an enterprise to obtain plaster casts – who, with a permit of the Sublime Porte, between 1800 and 1803 dismantled almost half of the frieze, 14 metope plates and 17 gable sculptures from the Parthenon, as well as a column and a Caryatid from the Erechtheion; gathered up frieze plates from the Nike Temple and other sculptures lying on the ground; and took them to London (where the Elgin Marbles later were to become an important nucleus of the British Museum; → LONDON, BRITISH MUSEUM).

Unlike the fate of the relatively well-documented history of the buildings, that of the free standing marble, bronze and gold ivory sculptures of the Acropolis is unknown. The Athena Parthenos and presumably also the colossal bronze Athena Promachos were shipped to Constantinople and destroyed there, at the latest in the inferno of sacking of 1204. The precious metal, bronze and ivory that were left on site went, as was generally the case, toward post-classical production; different from the archaic sculptures which were levelled and buried in the 'Persian rubble' after 479 BC and were thus inaccessible, marble sculptures are preserved only to a small extent; most of them were burnt into lime in the course of the century.

C. THE HISTORY OF RESEARCH, EXCAVATION AND RESTORATION IN THE 19TH AND 20TH CENTURY

(Figs.5–8) As early as 1834, i.e. only one year after the Acropolis was surrendered by the capitulating Turkish garrison to a Bavarian contingent of troops, the Acropolis was cleared by decree of all settlement, and after controversy and discussion on the future of the area that was now under the decisive influence of the Bavarian Leo von Klenze, it became the exclusive sphere of activity of archaeologists. Greeks and primarily Germans now worked on it together; within a few weeks, all existing, non-Greek ancient buildings were demolished. There is consensus among scholars today that the first excavation campaigns conducted until 1890/1891 are among the greatest disasters of modern field archaeology. The knowledge of excavation techniques that had been greatly refined in the 19th cent. were barely applied here; in the treasure hunting mentality of the 18th cent. people had, within a short

Fig. 5: Drawing of the western pediment of the Parthenon by Jacques Carrey, 1674

Fig. 7: Excavations on the Acropolis in the 1880s

Fig. 6: Rebuilding the Temple of Nike 1835/36, in: L. Ross, E. Schaubert, Ch. Hansen, *Die Akropolis von Athen nach den neuesten Ausgrabungen I: Der Tempel der Nike Apteros*, 1839, frontispiece

Fig. 8: Anastylosis work in the Parthenon 1988. *With Permission of the author*

time, dug right down to the rock and shifted the obstructive excavated material from place to place (and finally dumped it right off the Acropolis). There was practically no documentation of the findings at all. The consequences of these actions have been the subject of archaeological controversy down to the present, since key problems like the exact dating and the order of the layers of the 'Persian rubble' (with their effect on the entire chronology of Greek art) have to date remained just as unclarified, as the timing, the sequence and sometimes even, as in the case of the → PARTHENON, the precise number of building phases of individual architectures. The symbolic power and fame of the Acropolis of Athens still to this day contrast remarkably with the extremely scanty knowledge of its topography; even the meticulous analysis of photos and diary notes of the excavators conducted by J. Bundgaard in the 1970s could not contribute to the clarification of important facts in many instances. The collected finds from these campaigns have been housed to date in the Acropolis Museum that was constructed in 1874 on ground that had previously been probed only cursorily (a new building outside the plateau and demolition of the old museum are currently under discussion).

An additional problem of scholarly investigations of the Acropolis that has only recently been taken seriously – not only from a technical point of view – concerns the restorations of the Parthenon, Propylaeum, Nike Temple and Erechtheion, which at no time had followed objective historical criteria but were always the product of a desired ideal of the classical nature of the site. The goal not only of the excavations but also of the restoration efforts was the Acropolis of the 5th cent. BC; all other historical phases and constellations were not taken into account from the outset (and therefore their relics and traces were irretrievably wiped out to a large extent). What finally evolved through excavations and anastylosis measures was a skeleton construct of Classicism, a sight of the Acropolis that today seems self-evident but that did not exist in this form at any time before the 19th cent.

Immediately after the settlements on the acropolis hill were disbanded, one began to gather up scattered structural components and to reallocate them for the architectural structures. The greatest anastylosis measures of the 19th cent. were the complete reconstruction of the Nike Temple on the ancient bastion (1835/36 and 1843/44), utilizing the structural components salvaged from the entrenchment walls, and the restoration of the Caryatid porch of the Erechtheion (finished in 1844). More extensive restoration was carried out under N. Balanos: the Parthenon (1898–1902 and 1922–1933) was supplemented with vast parts of the peristasis shattered in 1687; on the Erechtheion (1902–1909) parts of the wall construction were restored; the Propylaea (1909–1917) were cleared of all non-Classical remnants; and the Nike Temple (1935–1939) was finally totally dismantled again and completely 'rebuilt'. It was not only the use of iron bars (which corroded in the

course of time, burst the marble and in this way caused further damage) that proved problematic but also the lack of uniformity in the methods of restoration as a whole. The aim was to 'beautify' a ruin, certainly to restore it but not to refine its completion properly; nonetheless new material was often used (and not only, for instance for reasons of authenticity, ancient material) and visually 'adapted' by purposely damaging the surface so that today it can barely be distinguished from the original building stone. The restoration project of the 1980s and 1990s, frequently discussed and controversial, was technically motivated because of the damage done in the Balanos restoration work, although it was fundamentally in the same Classicist tradition: Its reference point, with some exceptions, was to a large extent Classicism as an historical category; it also had as its goal the 'beautification' of the ruins, but not a completion of the main parts of the buildings, carried out in a methodically, theoretically and technically possible manner.

D. The Acropolis as Model and Epitome of Classicism

(Figs.9–12). Already in Antiquity, the Acropolis with its buildings and art works became a model, a universal ideal of Classical art and architecture, which was adapted and disseminated in the form of copies and reconstructions. A copy of Athena Parthenos decorated the library of Pergamum; copies were made of the Caryatids (Rome, Forum of Augustus; Tivoli, Villa Hadriana), of the ornamentation on the buildings (likewise on the Forum of Augustus) and of the Ionian column order of the Erechtheion (on the Monopteros for Roma and Augustus on the Acropolis itself) as well as extensive adaptations of building structures ('large' Propylaea in → ELEUSIS as a partial duplicate of the Mnesicles-Propylaea of the Acropolis). Of the Classical Greek sculptures preserved in Roman copies, quite a large number belong to the sculptures of the Acropolis.

In the course of the 'Rediscovery' of Greece, the Acropolis again became the paradigm of a Classical ideal. Detailed study of the ruins has become a basis for our own building activity. On numerous occasions, architectural motifs of the Acropolis, primarily the central part of the Propylaeum, the eight-pillar front of the Parthenon and the west wall of the Erechtheion have recently been adapted as ennobling citations with greater or lesser degrees of authenticity in Europe and North America (→ GREEK REVIVAL). Here the building records made on site (in addition to Stuart and Revett, the widely disseminated and frequently translated one-volume compendium by LeRoy, and later many and varied derivatives of these models) and occasionally also casts, guaranteed the imparting of shapes and proportions. Simultaneously, in the early 19th cent., the Acropolis in the context of → ROMANTICISM became a popular travel destination. Idyllic, bucolic visions that artistically interweave the landscapes and folkloric ambience with the silhouette of the Acropolis are to be

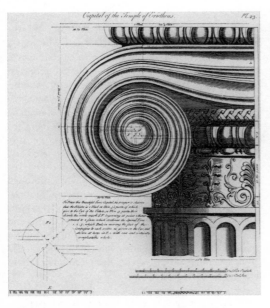

Fig. 10: The Parthenon as a decorative motif on the business card of the American architect J.H. Dawkin, 1833

Fig. 9: Drawing of the Ionic order of the Erechtheum, in: Julien David LeRoy, *Les ruines des plus beaux monuments de la Grèce, 1758*

Fig. 11: Erechtheum Korai adorning the 0176 of the boutique 'Hyper, Hyper' in London, Knightsbridge, 1988. *With Permission of the author*

Fig. 12: Copy of the Porch of the Maidens at St Pancras Church, London, by W. H. and W. Inwood, 1819–1822. *With Permission of the author*

found in great numbers as visual and textual topoi not only in printed graphics and the travel reports of the 19th cent., which were closely connected with these but also in poetry (e.g. Hölderlin's *Hyperion*), theatre and music (e.g. Beethoven's overture *Die Ruinen von Athen* composed to an opera fable of Kotzebue); dominant in all these manifestations is a mixture of authentic antiquity, freely invented ancient mythology and the timelessly transfigured world of the ancient Greeks. Visual adaptations of Acropolis motifs are still to be found in great numbers today and these are predominantly kitschy.

For the modern state of Greece the Acropolis and hence the Classical epoch of Pericles has since the foundation of the state assumed a significant role as a national symbol, often reproduced in whole or in part on coins, notes, stamps and other materials that bear sovereign images. However, with regard to the national identity of Greece, a virulent shift in emphasis has occurred to early Hellenism and the region of Macedonia -not least rooted in foreign policy-with the discovery of the royal tombs of Vergina in 1977.

SOURCES 1 R. BOHN, Die Propyläen der Akropolis von Athen, Berlin 1882 2 R. CHANDLER, Travels in Greece, London 1776 3 M. G. COMTE DE CHOISEUL-GOUFFIER, Voyage pittoresque de la Grèce, 4 vols. Paris 1782–1822 4 E. DODWELL, Views in Greece from Drawings, London 1821 5 P. KAVVADIAS, G. KAWERAU, Die Ausgrabungen der Akropolis im Jahre 1885 bis zum Jahre 1895, 1906/07 6 L. COMTE DE LABORDE, Athènes aux XVᵉ, XVIᵉ et XVIIᵉ siècles, Paris 1854 7 W. M. LEAKE, The Topography of Athens with Some Remarks on its Antiquity, London 1821 8 J. D. LEROY, Les ruines des plus beaux monuments de la Grèce, Paris 1758 (Eng.: Ruins of Athens: With Remains and other Valuable Antiquities in Greece. London 1759) 9 L. ROSS, E. SCHAUBERT, CH. HANSEN, Die Akropolis von Athen nach den neuesten Ausgrabungen 1: Der Tempel der Nike Apteros, Berlin 1839 10 J. SPON, Voyage d'Italie, de Dalmatie, de Grèce et du Levant, Lyon 1678 11 J. STUART, N. REVETT, The Antiquities of Athens, 4 vols. London 1762–1816

LITERATURE 12 N. BALANOS, Les monuments de l'Acropole. Relèvement et conservation, 1938 13 M. S. BROUSKARI, The Acropolis Museum, 1974 14 J. BUNDGAARD, The Excavations of the Athenian Acropolis 1882–1890. The Original Drawings, 1974 15 J. COLIN, Cyriaque d'Ancône. Le voyageur, le marchand, l'humaniste, (n.d._). 16 B. F. COOK, The Elgin Marbles, 1984 17 K. H. DITLEVSEN, Rejsen til Athen. Danske i Graekenland i 1800-tallet, 1978 18 F. GREGOROVIUS, Geschichte der Stadt Athen im Mittelalter, Stuttgart 1889 (repr. 1980) 19 H. HILLER, J. COBET, Die Akropolis von Athen. Verwandlungen eines klassischen Monuments, Ausstellungskatalog Xanten 1983 20 E. HARRIS, British Architectural Books and Writers 1556–1785, 1990 21 J. HAUGSTED, The Architect Christian Hansen. Drawings, Letters and Articles Referring to the Excavations on the Acropolis 1835–37, in: Analecta Romana Instituti Danici 10, 1982, 56–96 22 W. HAUTUMM (ed.), Hellas. Die Wiederentdeckung des klassischen Griechenland, 1988 23 W. D. HEILMEYER, H. SCHMIDT, Berliner Hausfassaden: Antike Motive an Mietshäusern der 2. Hälfte des 19. Jahrhunderts, Berliner Forum 4/81, 1981 24 CH. HÖCKER, L. SCHNEIDER, Pericle e la costruzione dell'Acropoli, in: S. SETTIS (ed.), I Greci 2/II, 1997, 1239–1274 25 CH. HÖKKER, Greek Revival America? Reflections on Uses and Functions of Antique Architectural Patterns in American Architecture between 1760 and 1860, in: Hephaistos 15, 1997, 197–240 26 H. KIENAST, Der Wiederaufbau des Erechtheion, in: Architectura 13, 1983, 89–104 27 R. A. MCNEAL, Archaeology and the Destruction of the Later Athenian Acropolis, in: Antiquity 65, 1991, 49–63 28 A. MICHAELIS, Der Parthenon, Leipzig 1871 29 M. PAVAN, L'avventura del Partenone, 1983 30 J. MORDAUNT CROOK, The Greek Revival. Neoclassical Attitudes in British Architecture, ²1995 31 L. SCHNEIDER, CH. HÖCKER, Die Akropolis von Athen, 1990 32 A. SCHOLL, Die Korenhalle des Erechtheion auf der Akropolis, 1998 33 K. M. SETTON, Athens in the Middle Ages, 1975 34 T. TANOULAS, The Propylaea of the Acropolis at Athens since the 17th Century, in: JDAI 102, 1987, 413–483 35 P. TOURNIKIOTIS (ed.), The Parthenon and its Impact in Modern Times, 1994 36 F.-M. TSIGAKOU, Das wiederentdeckte Griechenland, 1982 37 D. L. WIEBENSON, Sources of Greek Revival Architecture, 1969 38 Id., Stuart and Revett's Antiquities of Athens: The Influence of Archaeological Publications on the Neoclassical Concept of Hellenism, (Diss. Ann Arbor) 1983 39 The Acropolis at Athens: Conservation, Restauration and Research 1975–1983, Exhibition Catalogue Athens. 1985/86 40 Parthenon: Second International Meeting for the Restoration of the Acropolis Monuments, Congress Athens 1985 41 L. SCHNEIDER & C. HÖCKER, Die Akropolis von Athen, ²2001; 42 J.-D. LEROY, R. MIDDLETON (eds.), The Ruins of the Most Beautiful Monuments of Greece, 2004.   CHRISTOPH HÖCKER

IV. KERAMEIKOS

A. INTRODUCTION B. HISTORY OF THE EXCAVATION C. KERAMEIKOS MUSEUM AND RESTORATION MEASURES D. SIGNIFICANCE OF THE FINDS FOR THE HISTORY OF RESEARCH E. RECEPTION OF THE MONUMENTS

A. INTRODUCTION

The Kerameikos is an → ARCHAEOLOGICAL PARK situated between Piraeus and Hermes Roads in Athens (Fig. 1: plan of the excavations 1997). Its name is derived from the potters' quarter of the ancient city. In the lowlands of the Eridanus river now uncovered by the excavations, important roads ran to the Piraeus harbour, to Boeotia and to the Peleponnes. Graves had been plotted on the river banks since the Bronze Age, and from the Sub-Mycenaean Period until Late Antiquity the area was continuously used as a cemetery. After the building of the Themistoclean city wall (478 BC) the Classical cemetery of Athens occupied the grounds in front of the Sacred Gate and the Dipylon. Some of its monuments are still mentioned in Pausanias (Paus. 1,2,4; 1,3,1; 1,14,6). The archaeological site embraces a section of the city's defense system: the city walls with two gates and an outer wall and moat (proteichisma), also buildings within the city walls (Pompeium and private houses) as well as sanctuaries, public graves as well as private family graves, a bath and work-

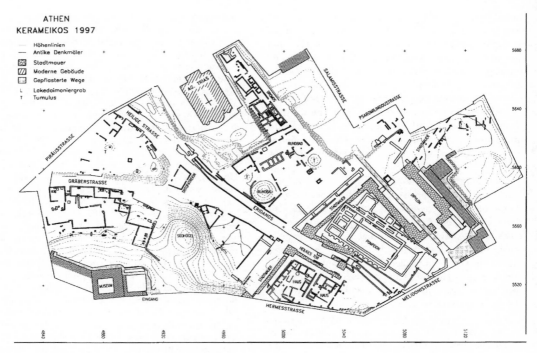

Fig. 1: Overview of the excavation site in the Kerameikos (1997).
Archive of the Deutsches Archäologisches Institut, Athens, Kerameikos excavation

shops outside the walls along the roads. Excavations brought to light monuments dating from the late 3rd millennium BC to the 7th cent. AD. In the 19th cent. a small church of the Hagia Trias stood on the grounds in front of the Porta Morea of the Turkish city wall [47]. In 1931 the church was torn down so that the excavations could be carried out. It was replaced in 1957 by a large new building which now dominates the archaeological site (Figs. 3: Church of the Haghias Trias and 4: The modern church 1995).

B. HISTORY OF THE EXCAVATION

The archaeological exploration of the Kerameikos was preceded by a collection of sources compiled by the scholar Joannes Meursius (1579–1639) and published in Utrecht in 1663 [20a]. The first excavations were undertaken at the beginning of the 19th cent. (for the excavations of the French ambassador, L.-F.-S. Fauvel, see [54. 13, 33], also [16. 415]). K.S. Pittakis (1798–1863) began documenting the finds from the Kerameikos and its neighbouring areas in 1838. Classical funerary reliefs were discovered during construction work for the new Piraeus Road (1860). In 1861 P. Pervanoglu (1833–1894) and St. A. Kumanudis (1818–1899) each led investigations in the vicinity of the Hagia Trias. K.S. Pittakis then conducted excavations in the area between the church and the new Piraeus Road, unearthing large quantities of human skeletons as well as a number of potters' workshops [50a; 36. 22]. The chance discovery in 1863 of the akroterion stele (Kerameikos, Inv. I 245;

IG II2 No. 8551) in the precinct of a family from Heraclea Pontica provided the impetus for a systematic study of the area. The stele still stood upright within the walls of the family precinct. These investigations along the Street of the Tombs were conducted by A.S. Rhusopulos (1823–1898) under the leadership of the Archaeological Society of Athens.

Several well-preserved family tombs were discovered, aligned side by side, and the find was understood as an opportunity to reconstruct on this site an Attic cemetery of the Classical period. Despite or rather precisely because of the political crisis in Greece at the time [11. 82, 264], the discoveries attracted particular public attention (cf. [36. 38]). The first comprehensive publication of the Street of the Tombs appeared as early as 1863 [55]. The Archaeological Society resumed the excavations in 1870 and with interruptions continued until 1913. The monuments on the Street of the Tombs were explored, as well as a large section of the city wall including the two city gates and parts of the Pompeium. Prominent politicians supported the research activities during this time: in 1889, the Minister of the Interior St. Dragoumis (1842–1923) made it a point to personally determine the routes for new roads along the excavation area, and in 1890 Prime Minister Charilaos Trikoupis (1832–1896) spoke out in favour of continued investigations along the Street of the Tombs.

In 1913 the Kerameikos excavation was handed over to the → DEUTSCHES ARCHÄOLOGISCHES INSTITUT, after years of fruitful collaboration between

Fig. 2: Sketch of the proposed Kerameikos
Museum by H. Johannes (1936)

Fig. 3: The Street of Tombs and the old Haghia Trias
Church, view from the west (late 1909).
Archive of the Deutsches Archäologisches Institut, KER 149

Fig. 4: City wall from the Kononian phase and the modern
Haghia Trias Church (1995).
Photo J. Stroszeck

German and Greek archaeologists ([9; 45; 14; 46]; A.
Brückner's *Der Friedhof am Eridanos* of 1909 is dedicated to Paniotis Kavvadias (1850–1928), the First Secretary of the Archaeological Society of Athens). A.
Brückner (1861–1936) and H. Knackfuß (1866–1948)
had last excavated at the Kerameikos on behalf of the
Preußische Akademie der Wissenschaften with the as-

sistance of the Archaeological Society [61]. Brückner
led the excavations from 1913 to 1916 and, after the
interruption of WWI, from 1926 to 1930. During this
period archaeologists began excavating the Classical
dromos [6; 59] between the Dipylon and the Academy
described by Paus. 1,29,1ff. Excavations also continued
along the Sacred Way, at the Dipylon and at the Pompeium. Among the most significant finds was the public
tomb of the Lacedaemonians (Xen. Hell. 2,4,33; [7])
who had fallen in battle in 403 BC. K. Kübler (1897–
1990) led the excavations from 1930 to 1943. He successfully explored the Sub-Mycenaean necropolis
under the Pompeium and the burial mound under the
Hagia Trias church. In a parallel campaign, K. Gebauer
investigated the grounds in front of the two gates and
the vicinity of the dromos. From 1926 to 1936 the excavation was financed by the German-American industrialist, G. Oberländer (1867–1936). The finds were published in the new series *Kerameikos: Ergebnisse der
Ausgrabungen* ('Kerameikos: Results of the Excavations') created by the Deutsches Archäologisches Institut,
the first volume of which appeared in 1939. After the
interruption on account of WWII (1943–1955) the
excavations were reopened in 1956 by the Deutsches
Archäologisches Institut. The first director was D. Ohly
(1911–1979), who resumed work on the necropolis and
the Themistocleian wall and dug a cross section
through the dromos next to the tomb of the Lacedaemonians [46a]. He was followed by F. Willemsen
(1910–1999), who oversaw the exploration of the area
in front of the central and northern segments of the
proteichisma from 1961 to 1974. Excavations were
also conducted on South Hill, the Dipylon and the
Sacred Way. Among the most important finds from
these years are several thousand ostraka from the Athenian ostracism [5a; 63a; 63b]. From 1974 to 1995 U.
Knigge (b. 1930) directed excavations on South Hill
and investigated a grave mound on the Sacred Way as
well as private houses behind the Sacred Gate. The investigation of the private houses is still ongoing [31a]. A
sensational new find was unearthed during a survey of
the Sacred Way outside the Sacred Gate in 2002 [45a].

Fig. 5: Stele of Lysanias in
the Kerameikos.
Photo J. Stroszeck

Fig. 6: Grave stele of the
archaeologist H.G. Lolling.
Athens, First Cemetery.
Photo J. Stroszeck

Fig. 7: Grave stele of the
archaeologist W. Reichel.
Athens, First Cemetery.
Photo J. Stroszeck

Fig. 8: Kerameikos, grave precinct of a family from the deme of Potamos.
Photo J. Stroszeck

Fig. 9: Grave column in the
First Cemetary of Athens.
Photo J. Stroszeck

C. KERAMEIKOS MUSEUM AND RESTORATION MEASURES

[32] A number of finds from the first, private explorations of the Kerameikos are now held by European museums [51; 62]. The finds from the excavations of the Archaeological Society remained on site or – through various intermediaries – made their way into the National Museum or the Epigraphical Museum of Athens (Museum at the Theseium: [24]; the small finds from the 1864 excavations were handed over to the ministry and on 23 July 1885 to the National Museum, while the finds from the excavations of 1890 were first exhibited at the Polytechneion before they went to the National Museum) [12; 22; 23; 31a]. After 1863 a guard was employed at the site and a cottage built for

him on South Hill that temporarily also functioned as a museum. A makeshift museum did exist from 1881, and in 1915 there was a museum room behind the Dipylon ([8; 25a]; still in use today as an excavation storeroom), to which another storage building was added in a pre–1931 extension. The construction of a new museum became possible in 1936 with a donation from G. Oberländer; it was planned by the German architect H. Johannes (1901–1945) and dedicated in October 1938 on the occasion of the 100th anniversary of the Archaeological Society of Athens (Figs. 2: Architect's sketch of the Kerameikos Museum 1936 and 10: Interior of the Archaeological Museum 1933 and 11: Interior of the Archaeological Museum 1968). The museum has seen several expansions since the post-war period.

Fig. 10: Interior of the
excavation museum (1933)
*Archive of the Deutsches
Archäologisches Institut*

Fig. 11: Interior of the
Oberländer Museum (1968).
*Archive of the Deutsches
Archäologisches Institut*

An overall extension and modernization of the exhibition concept was implemented in 2003/2004. The new display, which also features the sculptures found in 2002, was opened in time for the 2004 Olympic Games.

It appears that the German architect E. Ziller (1837–1923) carried out the first restoration work on the naskoi paintings in 1863. For the reconstruction of the Classical necropolis, many ancient sculptures were at first left in place or returned to their original location (e.g. the 1884 re-installation of the bull from the district of Dionysius of Collytus by the sculptor Lazaros Phytalis (1831–1909); cf. Praktika 1884, 23). In order to protect the monuments from the increasing environmental pollution, D. Ohly initiated a restoration programme which involves removing the ancient sculptures to museums and replacing them with casts. The programme continues to the present day.

D. SIGNIFICANCE OF THE FINDS FOR THE HISTORY OF RESEARCH

The Kerameikos excavations have been instrumental in clarifying crucial areas of the topography of ancient Athens [21; 59a; 60]: the course of the Eridanus before and after the installation of a sewage system under Themistocles, the development of the necropolises on its banks and on both sides of the arterial roads, furthermore the course and the various building stages of the city walls and fortifications [46] and the correct location of the two city gates (Sacred Gate and Dipylon) [2]. The Pompeium was identified and the history of its construction clarified [1; 19]. The closed grave-contexts of the Kerameikos cemetery have formed the basis for the study of Attic ceramics from the Sub-Mycenaean to the late Roman period. The first and largest Sub-Mycenaean (1100–1000 BC) cemetery known to date was excavated in the Kerameikos in 1927 and 1937/8 and the findings published by W. Kraiker and K. Kübler

[25. vols. I and IV]. Study of the Kerameikos material is still a prerequisite today for any further work on this period. The same is true of Attic Geometric pottery: the 'Dipylon style' was named after a group of Geometric vases found in 1873/74 at a nearby site on Piraeus Road, initially assumed to be the location of the Dipylon [5; 9; 52]. The funerary monuments of the Kerameikos ([10; 13; 15; 33; 53; 57]; re the Dipylon Head, Athens NM 3372: [18; 26; 40. 173ff.]) are of equal importance; they are milestones in the development of Archaic and Classical sculpture. Enquiries into ancient sociology are as unthinkable without the insights gained from the Kerameikos grave-contexts as is the study of Attic funerary customs [3; 4; 35; 43; 44; 63]. The finds from the rubble left after Sulla's destruction of Athens (86 BC; Paus. 1,20,4ff.; Plut. Sulla 14) provided a chronological reference point for the dating of the First Style of Roman wall painting [64]. And finally, the Kerameikos excavations have yielded material for the study of various artisan trades, esp. the pottery and foundry trades [3a; 31b; 42a; 66]. The epigraphical evidence from the Kerameikos (boundary markers, funerary inscriptions, ostraka, curse tablets) is important for the history of the city of Athens; it has helped shed light on the practice of Athenian ostracism as well as the prosopography of Athens [48]. Extensive new finds including columellae, trapezai and ostraka are still awaiting publication.

E. RECEPTION OF THE MONUMENTS

Reception of the Kerameikos and its monuments has been two-fold: both individual famous monuments, esp. the grave reliefs of Hegeso (Fig. 12: Funerary relief of Hegeso) and of Dexileus (Fig. 13: Funerary relief of Dexileus), as well as the district itself, in particular the Street of the Tombs with its interplay of sculpture and nature, have been a source of inspiration for modern artists. The planting of the area after the completion of the excavations played an important role.

The discovery of the Classical cemetery with its funerary sculptures along the Street of the Tombs had a direct impact on the design of late 19th cent. cemeteries and their monuments. The increased incidence of classicistic grave steles in cemeteries all over Europe at the time must be seen as a response to the excavations in the Kerameikos. The modern reception of individual monuments was brought about by the publications about the Kerameikos cemetery and the ready availability of copies: in 1875 the Italian sculptor Napoleone Martinelli began to offer plaster casts of Greek sculptures to customers world-wide, including casts of sculptures from the Kerameikos [38; 39]. Some classicistic grave monuments in the First Cemetery of Athens are reproductions of monuments from the Kerameikos. The palmette akroterion from the stele of Lysanias of Thoricus [42], for instance, was used for the graves of the archaeologists H.G. Lolling (1848–1894) and W. Reichel (1858–1900) and that of the botanist Th. von Heldreich (1822–1894) (Figs. 5: Stele of Lysanias and

Fig. 12: Tomb relief of Hegeso. Athens, National Museum Inv. 3624.
Archive of the Deutsches Archäologisches Institut, Athens, Kerameikos excavation KER 80

6: Stele of H.G. Lolling and 7: Stele of W. Reichel). Similarly, the grave column as a funerary monument can be traced, e.g., to the columns found in the precinct of a family from the deme of Potamos [31] (Figs. 8: Grave Precinct of the family from Potamos and 9: Stele in the First Cemetery).

The funerary relief of Dexileus (Fig. 13: Funerary relief of Dexileus) was the model for several modern works of art. It lent itself for re-application in war memorials, e.g. in a monument to the fallen of WWI in Coburg (Fig. 14: Coburg Monument). A large-format relief of 150 ceramic tiles laid out in six rows by Dimitris Mytaras (b. 1934) and the ceramicist Voula Gounela incorporates elements of the Dexileus relief in a montage symbolizing the link between the historical city of Athens and the modern capital. The artwork measuring 3 x 11 m has been on display in the Daphni metro station since 2000 (Fig. 15: Metro relief). Kerameikos monuments even found their way into the arts and crafts industry and into advertising. The bull from the precinct of Dionysius of Collytus (Fig. 16: Bull of Dionysius of Collytus) adorns the logo of the state-owned Greek ceramics factory 'Kerameikos' (Fig. 17: Kerameikos logo).

Fig. 13: Tomb relief of Dexileus (Kerameikos, Inv. P 1130). *Archive of the Deutsches Archäologisches Institut, Athens, Kerameikos excavation KER 5976*

Fig. 14: Coburg, Memorial for the Fallen of 1918. *Photo R. Kosellek*

Fig. 15: Ceramic relief by D. Mytaras and V. Gounellá (2000) in the Athenian underground station Daphni. *Photo J. Stroszeck*

Fig. 16: Kerameikos. Bull sculpture from the grave district of Dionysus of Collytus (Kerameikos, Inv. P 689). *Archive of the Deutsches Archäologisches Institut, Athens, Kerameikos excavation KER 6001.*

Fig. 17: Kerameikos bull. Logo of the Greek porcelain factory 'Kerameikos'. *Photo J. Stroszeck.*

The Street of the Tombs in its entirety, parts of it, or individual monuments of the Kerameikos provided motifs for painters and water colour artists, particularly in the decades between the end of the 19th cent. and World War II, when artists' impressions were sought after as souvenirs by tourists and Athenians alike. Representative examples are the water colours by Corcyra native Angelos Giallina (1857–1939) from 1891 [50], those by the Stuttgart art professor Otto Zaberer from 1912 [31. Fig. 162], or those by the Russian painter Alexander Barkoff from 1933–1934 [33a]. More recently, a new generation of painters has returned to the Kerameikos: in the 1990s Sarantis Karavousis (b. 1938) created a series of Kerameikos-themed oil paintings [41].

The period leading up to Word War II also saw notable photographers capturing views of the Kerameikos and its monuments, e.g. the brothers K. and A. Rhomaidis [14a; 20]. Walter Hege's (1893–1955) photographs were taken in the 1920 and 1930s; one series is held in the Kerameikos Archives of the *DAI* at Athens. Another photographer working with motifs from the Kerameikos at the time was Nelly, i.e. Elli Souyoultzoglou-Seraidari (1899–1998) [3b]. In 1991 the compound was chosen as a setting for the film adaptation of *Homo Faber* (US title: 'Voyager').

The monuments and excavations in the Kerameikos were primarily seized upon by modern Greek lyrical poets. As with the visual arts, the literary reception can be broken down into two distinct phases: the time before World War II and a more recent period beginning in the 1970s. In lyrical poetry, too, it was the grave reliefs of Hegeso and Dexileus – probably the two most famous grave reliefs of all – which elicited the strongest response. In 1892, the poet Kostis Palamas (1859–1943) dedicated famous verses to these two monuments; they also figure in poems, e.g., by Lili Iakovidi (1899) and Glafkos Alithersis (1897–1965). Other grave steles have received comparatively little attention and remain largely shrouded in anonymity [46b]. The excavations of Kurt Gebauer in the precinct of Theonichos form the framework for a 1943 short narrative by Ilias Venezis (1904–1973), *ΘΕΟΝΙΧΟΣ καί ΜΝΗΣΑΡΕΤΗ* ('Theonichos and Mnesarete', 1943). Occasionally, the Kerameikos or its monuments appear in the works of German poets, e.g. Pia Burger (b. 1897) and Durs Grünbein (b. 1962) [18a].

1 F. ADLER, Aus Kleinasien und Griechenland, in: Archäologische Zeitung 32, 1875, 161f. 2 G. VON ALTEN, Die Thoranlagen bei der Hagia Triada zu Athen, in: MDAI(A) 1878, 28–48 Taf. 3.4 3 J. BERGEMANN, Demos und Thanatos. Untersuchungen zum Wertsystem der Polis im Spiegel der attischen Grabreliefs des 4. Jahrhunderts vor Christus und zur Funktion der gleichzeitigen Grabbauten, 1997 3a B. BÖTTGER, Kaiserzeitliche Lampen vom Kerameikos (= Kerameikos XVI), 2002 3b I. BOUDOURI (ed.), Nelly's Sougioutzoglou-Seraidare. Archaiotetes: Hellada 1925–1939, 2003 4 A. BRÄUNING, Untersuchungen zur Darstellung und Ausstattung des Kriegers im Grabbrauch Griechenlands zwischen dem 10. und 8. Jahrhundert vor Christus, 1995 5 M. ΜΠΡΟΥΣΚΑΡΗ, Από τόν Ἀθηναϊκό Κεραμεικό του 8 ου π. Χ. αἰώρα, 1979 5a ST. BRENNE, Ostrakismos und Prominenz in Athen: attische Bürger des 5. Jh. v. Chr. Auf dem Ostraka, 2001 6 A. BRÜCKNER, Neue Kerameikos-Grabungen, in: AA 1914, 41ff. 91ff. 7 Id., Kerameikos, in: AA 45, 1930, 90, 102 Abb.5 8 Id., Berichte über die Kerameikos-Grabung 1914–1915, in: AA34, 1915, 109f. (Plan: 109) 9 Id., E. PERNICE, Ein attischer Friedhof, in: MDAI(A) 18, 1893, 73–191 Taf. 6–9 10 CH. W. CLAIRMONT, Classical Attic Tombstones, 1993, Suppl. Vol. 1995 11 R. CLOGG, Geschichte Griechenlands im 19. und 20. Jahrhundert. Ein Abriß, 1997 12 M. COLLIGNON, L. COUVE, Catalogue des vases peints du Museé National d'Athènes, 1902 13 A. CONZE, Die attischen Grabreliefs Vols. 1–4, Berlin 1893–1922 14 R. DELBRUECK, Über einige Grabhügel bei Agia Triada, in: MDAI(A) 25, 1900, 292ff. 14a J. DEMOS (ed.), Ελλάδα

1896–1906 Greece. Images from Stereoscopic Photographs, 2004, 54f. **15** H. DIEPOLDER, Die attischen Grabreliefs des 5. und 4. Jahrhunderts, 1931 **16** E. DODWELL, A Classical and Topographical Tour Through Greece During the Years 1801, 1805, and 1806, London 1819 **17** ΈΛΕΥΘΕΡΟΥΔΑΚΗΣ, Ἐγκυκλοπαιδικόν Λεξικόν, 1931 (Biographies of Greeks) **17a** G. EMRICH (ed.), Poetischer Athen-Führer. Athen – Attika – Klassische Stätten, 2000, 54–61, 140f., 160, 163, 170–175 **18** J. FLOREN, Die griechische Plastik, vol. I. Die geometrische und archaische Plastik, 1987, 251f. plate 23, 1 **18a** Hellenika. Jahrbuch für die Freunde Griechenlands, vol. 5, nos. 14–15, 1968, 65, 101 **19** W. HOEPFNER, Das Pompeion und seine Nachfolgebauten. Kerameikos. Ergebnisse der Ausgrabungen X, 1976 **20** G. HÜBNER, Bild als Botschaft. Das antike Erbe Athens in fotografischen Zeugnissen des 19. und 20. Jahrhunderts, in: Fotogeschichtliche Beiträge zur Geschichte und Ästhetik der Fotografie, 29, 1988, 15, Fig.17 (Photos by K. und A. Rhomaidis, Athen), 23, Note 23, 26, Fig.27 **20a** JOANNES MEURSIUS, Ceramicus Geminus, sive de Ceramici Atheniensium utriusque antiquitatibus, Trajectum ad Rhenum 1963 **21** W. JUDEICH, Topographie von Athen. ²1931 (Repr. 1994) **21a** N. KALTSAS, Sculpture in the National Archaeogical Museum, 2003 **22** S. KARUSU (S. KAROUZOU), Archäologisches Nationalmuseum. Antike Skulpturen, 1969, 81ff. **23** Π. ΚΑΣΤΡΙΩΤΗΣ, Γλυπτά τού Έθνικού Μουσειού, Άθήναι, 1908, Nr. 7, 38, 87, 2822, 3372 **24** R. KEKULÉ von Stradonitz, Die antiken Bildwerke im Theseion zu Athen, Leipzig 1869, 27ff. 385ff. et passim **25** Kerameikos. Ergebnisse der Ausgrabungen, Vols. I–XIV, 1939ff. **26** H. KNACKFUSS, Kerameikos, in: AA 1916, 157ff. **27** U. KNIGGE, Kerameikos. Tätigkeitsberichte 1975/76, in: AA 1978, 44ff. **28** Id., Tätigkeitsberichte. Kerameikos 1977, in: AA 1979, 178ff. **29** Id., Kerameikos. Tätigkeitsberichte 1978, in: AA 1980, 256ff. **30** Id., Kerameikos. Tätigkeitsberichte 1981, in: AA 1983, 209ff. **31** Id., Der Kerameikos von Athen, 1988 **31a** Id., Der Südhügel (= Kerameikos IX), 1976 **31b** A. KARIVIERI, The Athenian Lamp Industry in Late Antiquity, 1996 **32** A. KOKKOY, Ή μέριμνα γιά τίς ἀρχαιότητες στήν Έλλάδα καί τά πρῶτα μουσεῖα, 1977, 269–273 Abb.111, 112 **33** G. KOKULA, Marmorlutrophoren, 10. Beiheft MDAI(A), 1984 **34** ST. KUMANUDIS, Praktika 1876, 13ff.; 1880, 7f. **35** D. KURTZ, J. BOARDMAN, Greek Burial Customs, 1971 **36** F. LENORMANT, La voie sacrée, Paris 1864 **37** R. LULLIES, W. SCHIERING (eds.), Archäologenbildnisse, 1988, passim **38** N. F. MARTINELLI, Catalogo dei getti in gesso di diversi oggetti di scultura greca antica, Athen 1875, 28–30 Nr. 104–115 **39** Id., Catalogue of Casts in Gypsum, taken direct from the Masterpieces of Greek Culture existing in Athens and other Places in Greece ... 2, Athen 1881, 22ff. **40** W. MARTINI, Die archaische Plastik der Griechen, 1990 **41** D. MICHALOPOULOS, S. KARAVOUSIS, Perpetual Athens, 1996, 144–163 Figs. 23–32 **42** H. MÖBIUS, Die Ornamente der griechischen Grabstelen klassischer und nachklassischer Zeit, ²1968, plate 22 a **42a** M. CH. MONACO, Ergasteria. Impianti artigianali ceramici ad Atene ed in Attica dal Protogeometrico alle soglie dell'Ellenismo, 2000 **43** I. MORRIS, Burial and Ancient Society. The Rise of the Greek City-State, 1987 **44** Id., Death-Ritual and Social Structure in Classical Antiquity, 1992 **45** Κ. Δ. ΜΥΛΩΝΑΣ, Άι παρά του Δίπυλου αγασκαφαί, Praktika 1890, 19–25 **45a** W. D. NIEMEIER, Der Kuros vom Heiligen Tor. Überraschende Neufunde archaischer Skulptur im Kerameikos in Athen, 2003 **46** F. NOACK, Die Mauern Athens. Ausgrabungen und Untersuchungen., in: MDAI(A) 32, 1907, 123ff. **46a** D. OHLY, Kerameikos-Grabung. Tätigkeitsbericht 1956–1961, in: AA 1965, no. 2, 277–376 **46b** K. PALAMAS, Τα μάτια της ψυχής μου, 1892, reprinted, e.g., in B.P. Petrakos, Ο Μέντωρ 48, 1998, 168–171 **47** A. PAPANICOLAOU-CHRISTENSEN, Athens 1818–1853. Views of Athens by Danish Artists, 1985 **48** W. PEEK, Kerameikos. Ergebnisse der Ausgrabungen. Vol. 3: Inschriften, Ostraka, Fluchtafeln, 1941 **49** B. Χ. ΠΕΤΡΑΚΟΣ, Ἡ ἐν Ἀθήναις Ἀρχαιολογική Ἑτειρεία, (44, 46, 61, 85f., 111, 199, 344 und Fig.48), 1987 **50** A. TH. PHILADELPHEUS, Monuments of Athens, ¹¹1995, 147 **50a** K. E. PITTAKIS, in: Αρχαιολογική Εφημερίς 1860, 2102, no. 4150, note 1 **51** E. POTTIER, Vases antiques du Louvre, Paris 1897, 22–24 Nr. A 514–A 560 **52** F. POULSEN, Die Dipylongräber und die Dipylon-Vasen, 1905 **53** G. RICHTER, The Archaic Gravestones of Attica, 1961 **54** L. ROSS, Archäologische Aufsätze, vol. I, Leipzig 1855 **55** A. SALINAS, I monumenti sepolcrali scoperti nei mesi di maggio, giugno e luglio 1863 presso la chiesa della Santa Trinità in Atene, Turin 1863 **56** W. SCHIERING, s.v. Kerameikos, in: U. HAUSMANN (ed.), Allgemeine Grundlagen der Archäologie (Handbuch der Archäologie), 1969, 133 **57** B. SCHMALTZ, Griechische Grabreliefs, 1983 **58** F. STADEMANN, Panorama von Athen, München 1841, Plate. 8 **59** R. STUPPERICH, Staatsbegräbnis und Privatgrabmal, 1977 **59a** J. TRAVLOS, s.v. Kerameikos, in: Id., Bildlexikon zur Topographie des antiken Athen, 1971 (Engl. Pictorial Dictionary of Ancient Athens, 1971) **60** J. TRAVLOS, Attika **61** CHR. TSOUNTAS, Praktika 1907, 99 **62** H. B. WALTERS, Catalogue of the Greek and Etruscan Vases in the British Museum II, London 1893, 98 Nr. B 130 **63** S. WENZ, Studien zu attischen Kriegergräbern, 1913 **63a** F. WILLEMSEN, in: MDAI(A) 80, 1965, 100–126, suppl. 31–40 **63b** Id., ST. BRENNE, Verzeichnis der Kerameikos-Ostraka, in: MDAI(A) 106, 1991, 147–156 **64** F. WIRTH, Wanddekorationen ersten Stils in Athen, in: MDAI(A) 56, 1931, 33f. **65** H. YIAKOUMIS, La Grèce. Voyage photographique et littéraire au XIXᵉ siècle, ²1998, 117 **66** G. ZIMMER, Giessereieinrichtungen im Kerameikos, in: AA 1984, 63ff.

JUTTA STROSZECK

V. NATIONAL ARCHAEOLOGICAL MUSEUM

A. INTRODUCTION B. FOUNDATION AND OBJECTIVE C. THE BUILDING D. THE EXHIBITION CONCEPTS

A. INTRODUCTION

The National Archaeological Museum (NAM) is the largest archaeological museum in Greece and for Greek Antiquity the most important museum in the world. It houses an inestimable number of original works of every genre, a collection that for the most part comes from excavations in all regions of Greece from the period between the 5th millennium BC and the 5th cent. AD.

B. FOUNDATION AND OBJECTIVE

On the basis of the archaeological legislation of the newly established state of → GREECE, the museum was founded in 1834 as the 'Central Museum of Antiquities' at the time when the capital city was moved from Nau-

Fig. 1: The National Archaeological Museum (NAM). Drawing by L. Lange, 1860.
With Permission of the Ministry of Culture, Hellenic Republic

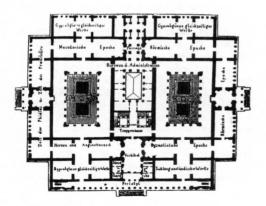

Fig. 2: NAM. Plan drawn by L. Lange, 1860.
With Permission of the Ministry of Culture, Hellenic Republic

plion to Athens. This had been preceded around 1829 by the foundation of the National Archaeological Museum on → AEGINA, the majority of the antiquities of which were now taken to Athens. The museum in Athens was not renamed the 'National Archaeological Museum' until 1888. Its designated aim was to collect 'the rarest antiquities ever discovered' that according to the above-mentioned law were considered to be 'works by the ancestors of the Greek people and the property of all Greeks'. The decision reflects the influence of → HUMANISM on the newly awakened national consciousness; an influence that in the last years of Turkish rule had already led intellectuals to seek effective protection of the plundered ancient sites. The scientific and didactic nature of the NAM was defined in 1893 when the setting up of the collections and their function were established by law: It was to serve the study and teaching of the field of archaeology, the dissemination of archaeological knowledge among the Greeks and the nurturing of interest in the fine arts. The consequence of the concentration of the antiquities discovered throughout the whole of Greece that was decreed by law and the postponement of the establishment of provincial museums, earmarked since 1834 but put off for many decades for reasons of cost, was that the NAM developed into a centre of outstanding importance for the study of the history of ancient art and life. After 1910 the collection of antiquities was mainly limited to finds from Attica, and after the Second World War collection activity came to a standstill with the development of the provincial museums. Enrichment of the NAM museum holdings now depended solely on gifts and purchases. The view that archaeological art works are not luxury articles, of interest only to a small group of experts, but are also interesting for broad circles of people became the ideological basis after the reopening of the NAM, which had been closed during World War II. The conviction that the museum as a social institution could also contribute to the education of young people in things national and in art also played a part in this [3; 6. 27–56, 201].

C. THE BUILDING

Internationally renowned architects who at that time were, in any event, occupied with the municipal planning of Athens and the construction of public buildings were commissioned to work on the planning and site allocation of the NAM. In 1836 Leo von Klenze

Fig. 3: NAM. Exterior design by E. Ziller, 1889.
With Permission of the Ministry of Culture, Hellenic Republic

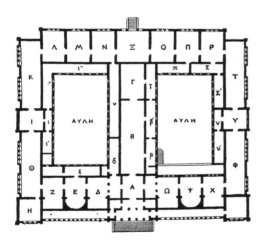

Fig. 4: NAM. Plan reflecting the changes made
by E. Ziller, 1889.
*With Permission of the Ministry of Culture,
Hellenic Republic*

presented the first plans in which he initially set aside a
site on the Acropolis for the NAM and, later, one on the
Ceramicus. In 1859 Theophil Hansen proposed that the
museum be built to the left of the university and then in
1887, rejecting the NAM that was now already being

built, the architects returned to plans for the south slope
of the Acropolis. In 1860, after the rejection by a committee of the Munich Academy of all 14 designs from an
architecture competition that had been announced in
1858, one of the members of this very committee,
Ludwig Lange, presented plans in which he suggested
that the site for the construction of the museum be the
Ceramicus (Figs. 1 and 2). Around 1866 the building of
the museum commenced according to the plans of
Lange, made possible by the transfer of the property of
Mrs. Eleni Tositsa on Patision Street and a donation
from Dimitrios Bernardakis (1856) – not without
objections on the part of some experts and the citizenry.
However, the architect Panagis Kalkos altered Lange's
designs for cost reasons; the planned row of columns
for the facade was cancelled. The design of the facade in
the neo-Classical form visible today goes back to Ernst
Ziller who in 1887/88 took over the completion of the
NAM with additional changes to the plan in the interi-
or, above all in the central wing (Figs. 3 and 4). The
interior of the building remained unadorned apart from
the mosaic floors and the mural decorations in the
rooms of the Mycenaean and Egyptian collections designed by G. Kawerau. The building fixtures and fit-
tings were completed through donations from the Archaeological Society and the government. The first extension was built in 1903–1906 with three adjacent

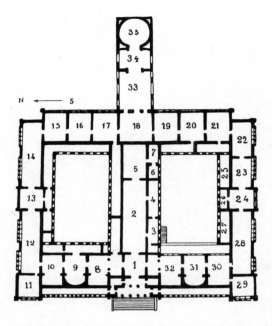

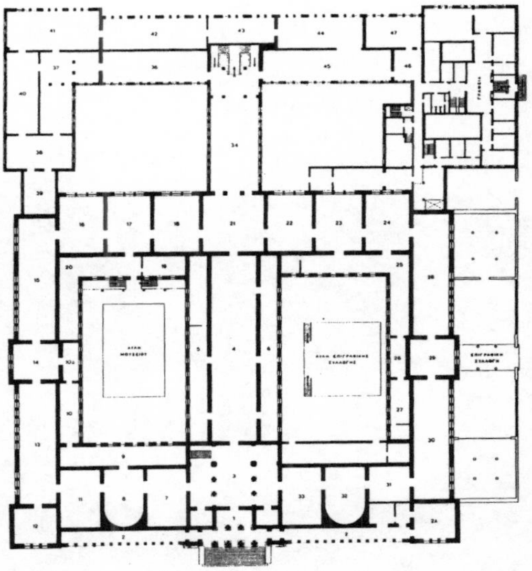

Fig. 6: NAM. Ground floor plan with the extensions
by G. Nomkos and P. Karadinos (NAM Archives).
With Permission of the Ministry of Culture, Hellenic Republic

Fig. 5: NAM. Plan of the building after addition of
the east wing. Drawing by A. Metaxas, 1903–1906.
*With Permission of the Ministry of Culture,
Hellenic Republic*

rooms in the centre of the east wing according to the
plans of Anastasios Metaxas (Fig.5). In 1932 it was decided to build a two-storey extension on the eastern side
by limiting the garden area, thereby tripling the exhibition space. The plans pertaining to this, in the neo-
Classicist style, are by Georgios Nomikos. After World
War II, the architect Patroklos Karadinos – parallel with
the repairs that had become necessary and in order to
set up the underground storerooms beneath the old
building – changed the vestibule of the entrance into its
present form. In addition he planned the extension of
the premises of the Epigraphical Museum in the south
wing (Fig.6). The NAM, in this form, is now recognized
as a monument worthy of preservation [3; 6. 201–246,
250–258].

D. THE EXHIBITION CONCEPTS

Antiquities have been housed in the courtyard of the
NAM from as early as the laying of the foundation
stone. The first exhibition was set up in the west wing
after it had been completed in 1874. However, it was
criticized by the press and experts [3; 6. 246–250]. In
his work *Die Museen Athens* (1881), A. Milchhöfer
describes antiquities still lying on the ground. In 1885
the Director General Panagiotis Kavvadias began to or-
ganize the antiquities that continued to be accumulated
in the building, which was only partly finished. In 1893
the NAM was completed and handed over to the public.
The works, installed according to art genres and following their chronological development, contained an
Egyptian collection and two rooms with Byzantine an-

tiquities. The latter two were later moved to a different
place. Set up in accord with the mentality and aesthetics
of its time, the exhibition attained the high regard of
scholars, although the arrangement of the objects on
the wall surfaces of the rooms made rather a decorative
impression in their layout [3; 4; 8]. In the course of
subsequent years, the continued expansion of the collections and the inclusion of every important ancient
object impaired the initial design of the exhibition and
tended to make the NAM appear like a storehouse
(Figs.7 and 8).

Preparations for new installations in 1939/40 were
interrupted by the outbreak of World War II that then
also necessitated the complete clearing of the NAM and
the hiding of all the antiquities. When in 1945 the building that had been used by various public authorities
during the German occupation was reassigned its original purpose, it required the work of many years to restore and modernize the building as well as to unpack
the crates and identify and restore the antiquities, which
had been buried under the floors. For educational
reasons, the responsible directors of the NAM, Semni
and Christos Karousos, as early as 1947, organized a
temporary exhibition in the rooms of the new east wing
with the most representative works from the collections
(Figs.9 and 10). This exhibition, in concept and appearance, was trend-setting with regard to the new museum
era that began all over Europe in the post-war period [3;
7]. The final refurbishing of the post-war NAM is associated with the work of a married couple by the name of
Karousos, and took an entire decade (1954–1964). The

Fig. 7: Tomb relief room. Design of the exhibition by P. Kavvadias, 1883 (NAM Archives).
With Permission of the Ministry of Culture, Hellenic Republic

Fig. 8: Archaic sculpture room. Design of the exhibition by P. Kavvadias, 1883 (NAM Archives).
With Permission of the Ministry of Culture, Hellenic Republic

Fig. 9: Temporary display, 1947.
With Permission of the Ministry of Culture, Hellenic Republic

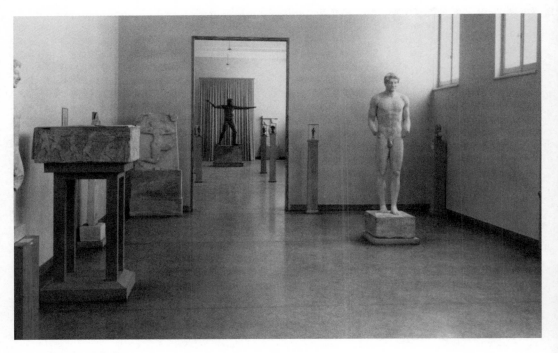

Fig. 10: Temporary display, 1947.
With Permission of the Ministry of Culture, Hellenic Republic

installation preserved the historic sequence according to art genres but attempted to link the didactic nature in the presentation of every artwork, i.e., the aesthetic display of the exhibits in the room. In principle, it was thought that at a time when the artifact itself was foregrounded at the expense its humanistic educational claim, emphasis on the artistic value of every work of art would promote the understanding and interpretation of the works [1; 2; 3; 5; 6]. The installation concept was directed at the circumspect and attentive visitor and not at the usual 'cultural consumers' who nowadays are often in a hurry. After 35 years the modern concept and the museum -based constraints led to the tackling of a new extension to the NAM and the reorganization of its exhibitions.

1 B. Andreae, Die Ausstellung der archaischen Sculpturen im Nationalmuseum Athens, Festschrift G. v. Osten (n.d), 257–266 2 XP. ΚΑΡΟΥΖΟΣ, Αρχαία Τέχνη, in: Ομιλίες-Μελέτες, 1972, 137–141 3 S. Karusu (S. Karouzou), Archäologisches Nationalmuseum. Antike Skulpturen. Beschreibender Katalog, 1969, I–XXVIII 4 Id., Η νέα Έκθεση των Ελληνικών Αγγείων στο Αυστριακό Μουσείο της Βιέννης, in: Νέ↑ Εστία 21 (242), 1937, 122–128 5 Id., Η νέα αίθουσα του Εηνικού Μθσειου, in: Νέα Εστία 59 (695), 1956, 849–855 6 A. Κοκκου, Η Μέριμνα για τις αρχαιότητες στην Ελλάδα πρώτα Μουσεία, 1977, 27–56; 61–67 7 E. Langlotz, The National Museum at Athens. Its New Arrangement, in: Archaelology 7 (3), 1954, 160–163 8 S. Reinach, Chronique d'Orient, in: RA 1893, 237.   EOS ZERVOUDAKI

VI. Other museums
see → Greece III Museums

Atlantis
I. The Platonic Myth II. Influence

I. The Platonic Myth
A. Name B. Introductory Scenario C. Scenario of Destruction D. Nature and Civilization of Atlantis E. Power and Decadence of Atlantis

A. Name
The island of Atlantis (A.) (Ἀ. νῆσος) is introduced in Plato's 'Timaeus' (Tim. 24e–25d) and described in the 'Critias' fragment (Critias 113b–121c). No tradition independent of this is attested [4]. Plato derived the name from Atlas' descendants (Critias 114a). This is etymologically correct. A. is derived from Atlas and τλῆναι = to bear or endure/to carry. Analogous terms are A. Μαίη (Hes. theog. 938), A. thálassa (Hdt. 1,202,4) and the Atlantes people (Hdt. 4,184,3–4). However, A. as 'the large/nameless island' can also be derived from the Egyptian [16; 8].

B. Introductory Scenario
The prologue to Timaeus by Plato begins with Socrates' desire to see a city that adheres to the ideal of the Platonic state by proving its worth in war (Tim. 17a–

20c). The statesman Critias recollects in this regard a tale, according to which 9,000 years before Solon a primeval Athens existed that embodied this ideal and repelled an invasion from A. (Tim. 20d ff.). This A. lay beyond the Pillars of Hercules and was bigger than Asia and Libya together (Tim. 24e). Critias' account claims not to be invented myth but true logos (Tim. 26e). Critias reports first a story of his grandfather by the same name (Tim. 21e–25d), who learned from Solon what priests at Sais read in 8,000 year old writings (Tim. 23e). Later, however, Critias refers to notes, allegedly a translation of the Egyptian report by Solon (Critias 113a-b). The Egyptian origin of the logos is probably a signal that it was fictional (cf. Phaidr. 275b), although it may at the same time indicate the use of Egyptian mythologems [8]. Egypt also becomes the paradigm of the Platonic state. For many institutions, which once the goddess Athene-Neith had taught the Ur-Athenians and then the Egyptians (Tim. 21e; 24a-d), are said to be located there. In the opinion of the Hellenistic exegete Crantor, Plato reacted here to those who mocked him with the reproach that his Politeia was merely an imitation of ancient Egyptian institutions (Proclus, In Timaeum 24 a-b p. 76 Diehl) [4]. This probably also relates to Isocrates' 'Busiris' [5. 183ff., 208ff.].

C. Scenario of Destruction
At a later time A. and the army of the Ur-Athenians are said to have sunk within one day (Tim. 25c-d) as victims of the third world-wide destruction before the Deucalionian Flood (Critias 112a). Such catastrophes occur periodically and annihilate all culture. Only in the protected Nile Valley could knowledge of prehistory be preserved (Tim. 22c–23c). Plato was fond of the idea of cyclical world catastrophes (polit. 269c–274d; leg. 3,677a ff.). He appears to allude concretely to the destruction of the city of Helice and its Temple of Poseidon in 373/2 BC [7]. The hypothesis that Plato as well as Pindar (fr. 38 Bowra) had used recollections of the Bronze Age Thera catastrophe remains mere speculation [15. 86ff.].

D. Nature and Civilization of Atlantis
A. is fascinating because of the juxtaposition of luxuriant nature and the highest civilization. There is an abundance of water, wood and precious metals, fruits and fragrances. Fauna is rich and exotic. There are even elephants (Critias 114d–115b). The cultivated land is divided into precise lots and supplied by a network of canals (Critias 118c-e). The image of the capital city is also characterized by strictly geometrical shapes. Concentric rings of land and water surround the acropolis. There a central sanctuary adorns the hill on which Poseidon and Cleito procreated and brought forth the royal house of A. (Critias 113d–114c; 116c). Next to it rises a colossal Temple of Poseidon. It is covered in gold, silver and unrefined ore and surrounded by golden votive statues. The cult image shows the god on a cart that is pulled by six winged horses and encircled by a hun-

dred Nereids riding on dolphins (Critias 116d-e). Four ring walls, covered in gold, unrefined ore, tin and copper enclose the central sanctuary, the acropolis and the inner and outer residential city (Critias 116a-c). The residential areas for the rulers, their guards, the warriors and the citizens are arranged running from the centre in the direction of the periphery. Roofed canal cuttings, bridges covered with coloured stone and houses, cold and hot basins and sporting facilities for people, horses and draught animals lend beauty to the metropolis (Critias 115d–116b; 117a-c). A large trading port, the outermost of three harbours, indicates lively foreign trade (Critias 117d-e).

E. POWER AND DECADENCE OF ATLANTIS

Power had been distributed by the god Poseidon among ten kings (Critias 114a-c). Atlas' descendants ruled the capital city. They commanded 10,000 war chariots, 60,000 light wagon teams, each had 120,000 Hoplites, archers and catapulters as well as a garrison of 240,000 men for 1,200 ships (Critias 119a-b). There were also the armies of the nine other kings (Critias 119b). A.'s power extended to many other islands in the huge ocean and parts of a mighty mainland that encircled it (Tim. 24e–25a). In the Mediterranean A.'s power extended to Tyrrhenia and Egypt (Tim. 25b; Critias 114c). Its further expansion failed because of the resistance of Ur-Athens (Tim. 25b-c). The debacle was meant to punish A.'s hubris (Tim. 24e; Critias 120e; 121 c). For a long time A.'s kings had known how to ensure that their rule was harmonious. An archaic bull sacrifice brought them together at a sanctuary of Poseidon in the middle of the island where they swore oaths to their fathers' statutes which were engraved on a stele of unrefined ore (Critias 119c–120d) [10]. With the disappearance of the divine portion of the inheritance in the house of the descendants of Atlas, they were corrupted. While they appeared outwardly handsome and happy, the hearts of the masters of A. were already full of desire for unlawful possessions and power (Critias 121a-c).

The Persian empire is reflected in this image of A. if one imagines it projected onto an imaginary West. Ur-Athens' merits are reminiscent of the deeds at Marathon and Salamis. In keeping with this is the legendary number of 1,200 enemy battle ships. The polychromatic ring walls of A. hark back to Herodotus' image of Ecbatana, an archetypical despotic city (Hdt. 1,98). In this way A. can be partly interpreted as an 'ideated Orient' [6. 214ff.]. In A.'s temples, harbours and wharves, its walls and its inordinately large war machine, however, characteristics can be found of what, according to Plato, became of Athens after the Persian Wars: a hybrid naval power whose external shine no longer corresponded to its internal strength. In this way, A. is also a memorial to the decline, experienced by the Athenians during the Peloponnesian War [19. 222ff.; 2].

II. INFLUENCE
A. ANTIQUITY B. EARLY MODERN PERIOD
C. 19TH AND 20TH CENTS.

A. ANTIQUITY

The reaction to the story of A. was initially purely literary. Theopompus parodied it in his tale of the land of Meropis on the true mainland on the other side of the (Atlantic) Ocean and of the military campaign of the ten million warriors of Machimos (FGrH 115 F 75c = Ael. VH 3,18). Euhemerus, on the other hand, gave his utopian island of Panchaea (Diod. Sic. 5,41–46; 6,1) characteristics reminiscent of Ur-Athens as well as A. [1. 191ff.]. However natural science posed the question whether A. should be regarded solely as a *plásma* and its decline only as a poetic device or whether it would not be worth assuming its actual existence (Posidonius in Str. 2,3,6). It is uncertain whether the history of such doubt goes back to Aristotle (deduced from the comparison of Str. 2,3,6 and 13,1,36). Pliny in any case shows that he still doubts the existence of A. (nat. 2,92,205). Plutarch leaves open the qualification logos or myth but takes as his starting point the Egyptian origin of the story (Plut. Solon 31). Later authors use A. without reservation as a geological or historical paradigm (Tert. Apol. 40,4; Amm. Marc. 17,7,13; Arnob. adv. gentes 1,5) [14. 194f.]. However, in the 6th cent. Cosmas Indikopleustes was still recording the fictional nature of the A. story (Topographia Christiana 12 p. 452c-p. 453b; p. 456c-d MIGNE). He thought it significant that Timaeus had based his report on the OT story of the Flood and had transferred the catastrophe to the west [18. 9].

B. EARLY MODERN PERIOD

The myth of A. had 'quietly survived' the Middle Ages [20. 72]. Its fascination as a → UTOPIA did not immediately appear with the Renaissance either. Thomas Morus declared his *Utopia* to be the rival of the *Civitas Platonica* [12], taking as a model a disciplined, exemplary state without, for instance, referring to A. [9]. The *Città del Sole* of Tommaso Campanella assumed to be on Taprobane (Ceylon) which with its seven concentric ring walls, the position of the buildings and the large temple is initially reminiscent of A. [9. 117ff.], is distinguished by strict regulations regarding even the most intimate spheres of life and so makes us think of Plato's *Nomoi* rather than the exuberant life on A. Only Francis Bacon, with his optimistic view of the ability of modernity even to surpass the admired model of the ancients with regard to civilization, made Nova A. into an explicitly utopian project: on the (fictitious) island of Bensalem in the South Seas, Christian Solomon-like wisdom directs a scholars' fraternity eager to experiment and thirsty for knowledge. Bacon took up – not without irony – the tradition of the old A. in which fairytale elements mingle with truth. Supposedly A. existed previously where America lies. A great flood had annihilated its arrogant power apart from the present day descendents of the few survivors [9. 188ff.].

Bacon, in pinpointing the location of A., paid tribute to fashion. From the 16th cent. onwards, a large number of variations with regard to geographical and geological speculation about A. had developed. The remains of the sunken continent were discovered, first following the Platonic text, in diverse islands in the Atlantic Ocean, then also in America, Africa and even in the South Seas [13. 361ff.]. This even provided justification for the claims behind Spanish Conquistador policy [20. 77ff.]. But soon there was more at stake. A. appeared to represent the origin of civilization as such. Its traces were now discovered as a cultural legacy at the most varied of places, nurtured national myths and stimulated the ambitions for great power. In this way, Olaus Rudbeck, toward the end of the 17th cent., elevated the Goths of Sweden to the rank of descendants of the Atlantians and linked A. with Upsala [18. 18ff.; 20. 81ff.]. On the other hand, as the cradle of culture, A. could also be projected into the far distance without severing the connection with the place of the observer. In the era of the French Revolution – through Jean-Sylvain Bailly – even Siberia was discovered as the country of origin of culture itself and associated with the tradition of A. [18. 28f.]. Such speculation lent a pseudo-historical normativeness to current cultural-ideological needs and contained a portentous tendency in its world view: the Jewish-Biblical tradition of Creation and history was to give way to a pseudo-ancient tradition [18; 20].

C. 19TH AND 20TH CENT.

With the advancement of historical-antiquarian research to a higher scholarly level, the paths of those academics who pinpointed the location of A. merely in a world of thought parted from those in the mainstream with their enthusiasm about A. The *Dissertation de l'Atlantide* by Thomas Henri Martin (1841) marks a milestone on this path and elevated the search for A. simultaneously to a topic for research. [13]. In recent times this search was enriched above all by aspects of reception research, ideological criticism and discussions about the phenomenon of the trivial popularization of the A. material. This meta-research on A. has a lot to do. The search for cultural traces of A. had in the late 19th cent., for instance, also taken hold of the Maya tradition and – through Le Plongeon – become mixed up with the fantastic story of the land of Mu and subsequently with speculation about a Lemuria sunk into the Pacific – a topic that became popular in occult circles [17. 34ff.; 3. 136ff.]. Claims that geological pseudo-knowledge about A. could be used beneficially also proved rich in tradition. Ignatius Donnelly who claimed to have discovered the legacy of A. in numerous ancient high cultures attained great popularity; of prime importance for him was the influence of Indo-European-Aryan peoples [17. 36ff.]. Speculation in National Socialist circles had an analogous racist basis. Alfred Rosenberg, for instance, in *Mythus des 20. Jahrhunderts* had the waves of 'Nordic blood' that he regarded

as a probable legacy of A., streaming so far that even Jesus became an Aryan in a Semitic environment. Such speculation was also purposefully instrumentalized by National Socialist institutions [20. 91f.; 3. 140ff.]. The discovery of A. near Helgoland popularized since the 1950s by Jürgen Spanuth is still rooted in 'Nordic enthusiasm' but emphasized above all the link between the catastrophe of A. and the migrations of sea peoples during the late Bronze Age [3. 157ff.; 20. 92]. This connecting line also dominates the tradition that – spurred on by the national-patriotic speculation of Spyridon Marinatos – transplants A.'s decline to the Aegean Bronze Age and associates it with the Thera catastrophe [20. 90f.; 17. 41ff.]. The linkage between A. and Homer's Troy, which Eberhard Zangger endeavoured to establish, also sought the model for Plato's tale in the history of the late Aegean Bronze Age [11]. The joy of discovery had led Adolf Schulten even further down the timeline when he postulated that the legendary city of Tartessus was a model for Plato's A. and sought to find it at the mouth of the Guadalquivir [3. 172ff.].

From this trend with its speculation that was becoming increasingly more scholarly, a movement can be delineated after the Second World War in which preoccupation with the catastrophe of A. appears to be a reaction to crises of modernity. In the 1950s, for instance, A. becomes for Otto Muck a monument to a cosmic-planetary catastrophe (supposedly June 5, 8498 BC) whose dreadful scenario evokes the image of atomic destruction and the catastrophic effect of poisonous gas. Fear of a threatening decline of values through alien cultural influences in the late period of the Economic Miracle and the era of the Cold War was likewise able to induce people to conjure up A. as an admonitory example, as in the 1980s the fear of the ecological self-destruction of humanity did [2]. On the other hand, the historical eclecticism of post-modernity is reflected in the project of Léon Krier to build a new A. on Teneriffa with the aim to rescue our planet through the humanitarian spirit. A. is still alive as a utopian project in the sense of Francis Bacon.

→ MYTH

1 R. BICHLER, Zur historischen Beurteilung der griechischen Staatsutopie, in: Grazer Beiträge 11, 1984, 179–206
2 Id., Die Position von Atlantis in der Geschichte der Utopie, in: G. POCHAT, B. WAGNER (eds.), Utopie. Gesellschaftsformen – Künstlerträume, 1996 (= Kunsthistor. Jb. Graz 26), 32–44   3 B. BRENTJES, Atlantis. Geschichte einer Utopie, 1993   4 A. CAMERON, Crantor and Posidonius on Atlantis, in: CQ 3, 1983, 81–91   5 CH. EUCKEN, Isokrates. Seine Position in der Auseinandersetzung mit den zeitgenössischen Philosophen, 1983   6 P. FRIEDLÄNDER, Platon I, ³1964   7 A. GIOVANNINI, Peut-on démythifier l'Atlantide?, in: MH 1985, 151–156   8 J. G. GRIFFITHS, Atlantis and Egypt, in: Historia 34, 1985, 3–28   9 K. J. HEINISCH (ed.), Der utopische Staat. Morus: Utopia. Campanella: Sonnenstaat. Bacon: Neu-Atlantis, 1960   10 H. HERTER, Das Königsritual der Atlantis, in: RhM 109, 1966, 236–259   11 M. KORFMANN, Troia und Atlantis, in: Ant. Welt H. 4, Jg. 1992, 299   12 B. KYTZLER, Zur neu-lateinischen Utopie, in: W. VOSSKAMP (ed.), Utopie-

forschung Interdisziplinäre Studien zur neuzeitlichen Utopie II, 1982, 197–209 13 Th. H. Martin, Dissertation sur l'Atlantide, in: Études sur le Timée de Platon, Bd. I, Paris 1841, 257–332 14 J. M. Ross, Is there any Truth in Atlantis?, in: The Durham Univ. Jour. 69/2, 1977, 189–199 15 F. Schachermeyr, Die mykenische Zeit und die Gesittung auf Thera (= Die ägäische Frühzeit II), 1976 16 W. Schenkel, Atlantis: die 'namenlose' Insel, in: Göttinger Miszellen 36, 1979, 57–60 17 W. H. Stiebing Jr., Ancient Astronauts, Cosmic Collisions and Other Popular Theories About Man's Past, 1984 18 P. Vidal-Naquet, Hérodote et l'Atlantide: entre les Grecs et les Juifs, in: Quaderni di Storia 16, 1982, 3–76 19 Id., Athen und Atlantis. Struktur und Bedeutung eines platonischen Mythos (French. 1964), in: Der Schwarze Jäger, 1989, 216–232 20 Id., Atlantis und die Nationen, in: Athen. Sparta. A., 1993, 61–94

ADDITIONAL BIBLIOGRAPHY: R. Ellis, Imagining Atlantis, 1998; P. Jordan, The Atlantis Syndrome, 2001; H-G. Nesselrath, Platon und die Erfindung von Atlantis, 2002.   REINHOLD BICHLER

Atomism

A. Introduction B. Middle Ages C. Rediscovery in the Renaissance D. Ideological Debate E. Reception in Physics and Chemistry

A. Introduction

Democritus' bold idea of a theory of atoms, which was taken up by Epicurus in a modified form and described in detail by Lucretius, was not accepted during Antiquity. Even through there are traces of a continuation of Atomism in the work of some Hellenistic physicians (Erasistratus, Asclepiades) and engineers (Philon of Byzantine, Heron) [7], the theory of atoms was to a great extent displaced by the overwhelming influence of Aristotle, of the Stoa and later of Christianity [8]. Criticism (such as Cic. Nat. D 2,93; Lactant. Div. inst. 3,17; Aug. contr. Acad. 3,23; Civ. 8,5) was directed less against an atom-based conception of matter than against the materialistic worldview connected with it, in which there was no room for *providentia* ('providence') and which therefore seemed close to atheism.

B. Middle Ages

Besides these critical judgements by widely-read authors, only two brief and more neutral outlines of the theory of atoms were accessible during the Middle Ages. They were found in two widely available collected works: *Etymologiae* by Isidor of Seville (13,2, around AD 600) and in the Byzantine lexicon *Suda* (s.v. ἄτομα, around AD 1000). Lucretius, who already during Antiquity was not widely disseminated, was lost. For that reason, the theory of atoms was, except for a few traces, for example in William of Conches (*c.* 1080–1154) [6], largely forgotten. The word 'atom' itself had lost any meaning in physics and referred to the smallest unit of time (C. Du Cange, Glossarium mediae et infi-

mae Latinitatis 1,462). In the Arabic realm, there was considerable interest in the theory of atoms, especially in the cosmology of the so-called Muʿtazilites of the 8th–10th. cents., but there as well it was later mostly pushed aside [2].

C. Rediscovery in the Renaissance

The history of the reception of Atomism begins with Poggio's discovery in 1417 [9] of a manuscript by Lucretius that caused quite a stir and of which multiple copies were made immediately. Lucretius, whose writings already appeared in print in 1473, was one of the first Latin authors to be accessible; with his work as well as the Latin translation of Diogenes Laertius that was edited in 1470, the most important source texts on Atomism had become available to a broader audience at the end of the 15th cent. One of the oldest instances of the renewed usage of the term 'atom' in the physical sense is then found in a tract by Leonardo da Vinci, written around 1500, that speaks of the *minutissimi e insensibili attimi* of the air (Cod. Leicester fol. 4r). The first more detailed reference to Antiquity's theory of atoms, in which the ancient corpuscular theory is used with reference to Democritus, Epicurus and Lucretius to explain material processes, can be found in the Italian physician Girolamo Fracastoro (de sympathia et antipathia rerum, Cap. 5, 1545).

D. Ideological Debate

After these first references to the atomistic conceptions of matter held during Antiquity, which tended to be rather selective, a more fundamental debate then came to the fore in which Atomism, along with its implications for a certain worldview, was contrasted with the Aristotelian view of the world that was for the most part supported by the Church. Giordano Bruno paid for his bold criticism of Aristotle and his references to Lucretius (such as de triplici minimo 1,9,1ff.) for the purpose of propagating the theory of atoms in 1600, when he was burned at the stake. Francis Bacon (1561–1626) [3] and Pierre Gassendi (1592–1655), who only accepted elements of Atomism but rejected its tendencies toward a certain worldview (materialism, randomness) were more careful.

E. Reception in Physics and Chemistry

Outside of natural philosophy the reception of Atomism plays an important role primarily in the area of → physics. Galileo had already taken a stand in favour of Atomism in his *Discorsi* (Leiden 1638) (1st Tag, 8,85f., Edizione nazionale). Credit for having paid careful attention to the theory of atoms and for having moved it, by means of his own observations, beyond that which was known by the ancients, goes to the German physician and chemist Daniel Sennert (1572–1637). In his text *De consensu ac dissensu chymicorum cum Galenicis et Peripateticis* (Wittenberg 1619) and in *Hypomnema physicum* (Wittenberg 1636) he disproved the Aristotelian theory of transmutation and pleaded for the theory of atoms, which seemed more suitable for explaining physical-chemical processes – such as dissipation and concentration of matter – (Hypomnema 3,1 de atomis). J. Jungius argued in a similar fashion in his *Praelectiones physicae* (around 1630). The discussion regarding Aristotle reached its high point in the programmatic text by Joh. Chrys. Magnien, *Democritus reviviscens* (Pavia 1646), in which a first calculation of the size of an atom was presented (Disputatio 2,3). With Newton, who stated his belief in an atombased understanding of matter in the 23rd Propositio of his *Philosophiae naturalis principia mathematica* (London 1687), and J. Dalton, who referred to that 23rd Propositio in his epoch-making lecture on January 27, 1810, the connection to modern atomic physics was established.

→ Atomism; → Democritus; → Lucretius
→ EPICUREANISM; → NATURAL SCIENCES

1 A. STÜCKELBERGER, Antike Atomphysik, (texts, translations, commentary), 1979 2 A. DHANANI, The Physical Theory of Kalām. Atoms, Space, and Void in Basrian Muʿtazilī Cosmology, 1994 3 B. GEMELLI, Aspetti dell'atomismo classico nella filosofia di Fr. Bacon e nel seicento, 1996 4 K. LASSWITZ, Geschichte der Atomistik vom Mittelalter bis Newton, Repr. 1963 5 A. G. M. VAN MELSEN, s.v. Atomtheorie, Historisches Wörterbuch der Philosophie 1, 1971, 606–611 6 B. PAPST, Atomtheorien des lateinischen Mittelalters, 1994 7 A. STÜCKELBERGER, Vestigia Democritea. Die Rezeption der Lehre von den Atomen in der antiken Naturwissenschaften und Medizin, 1984 8 Id., Die Atomistik in römischer Zeit, in: ANRW II 36.4, 2561–80 9 Id., Lucretius reviviscens, Von der antiken zur neuzeitlichen Atomphysik, in: Archiv für Kulturgesch. 54, 1972, 1–25

ADDITIONAL BIBLIOGRAPHY: A. G. M. VAN MELSEN, From atomos to Atom: The History of the Concept Atom, 1952; L. L. WHYTE, Essay on Atomism, from Democritus to 1960, 1961. ALFRED STÜCKELBERGER

Augustinism

I. DEFINITION   II. RECEPTION

I. DEFINITION

Augustinism is defined as the adoption and development of the basic teachings of the Church Father Augustine. As there was until the mid–13th cent. no serious theological alternative, it is possible to describe all theological thinkers up to this time as Augustinians. This is particularly apposite in regard to the doctrine of grace, theological epistemology, teachings on the nature of the Church and mysticism. Even after the 13th cent. Augustinism proved to be the most potent theological and philosophical current of the Middle Ages and modern times, asserting itself independently alongside Aristotelian and neo-Platonic thought. Augustinism in a narrower sense refers to a philosophy/theology concerned with three fundamental problems pervading the entire Augustinian canon: *beatitudo, ratio,* and *auctoritas.* In terms of content, the discussion of these three fundamental problems is formally determined by the hermeneutics of thing and sign (*res et signum*) developed in *De doctrina christiana.* Augustinism, being founded on these three problem areas and the hermeneutics associated with them, is, therefore, a highly distinctive phenomenon and manifests itself in characteristic ways in different thinkers. In a broad sense, the term *Augustinism* is used in the field of anthropology to refer to the teaching that grace takes precedence over nature and free will.

II. RECEPTION
A. FORMAL ASPECTS   B. ASPECTS OF CONTENT

A. FORMAL ASPECTS
Owing to its unsystematic character and to the enormous range of writings it engendered, Augustine's thought has never been subjected to investigation as a coherent whole. Soon after Augustine's death (430), around 450, Prosper Tiro of Aquitaine wrote a *Liber sententiarum ex operibus Sancti Augustini delibatarum* (CCL 68A, 221–252), which was an overview of Augustinian theology. He followed this with a *Liber epigrammatum ex sententiis Sancti Augustini* (PL 51, 497–532).

Before 550 Eugippius collated the comprehensive *Excerpta ex operibus Sancti Augustini* (CSEL 9), which was widely used during the Middle Ages. Alongside this, the most important mediaeval work was the *Aurelii Augustini milleloquium veritatis* (Brescia 1734) of Bishop Bartholomew of Urbino (d. 1350), which presented some 15,000 selected passages. This tradition of florilegial anthologies continues to this day, as F. Moriones' *Enchiridion theologicum Sancti Augustini* (1961) shows. The great complete editions of J. Amerbach (Basle 1506), Erasmus (Basle 1528/29) and the Maurines (Paris 1679–1700), as well as the reprint of the Maurines edition in PL 32–46 (1841/42), provided the basis for the widespread studies of Augustine in modern times.

B. ASPECTS OF CONTENT
1. Early Christianity. Four strands of Augustine's influence can be discerned in Early Christianity: 1. The not uncontroversial adoption of the Augustinian doctrine of grace. In the struggle against Pelagius and Julian of Eclanum, the Augustinian doctrine of grace prevailed and gained Church approval. At the Second Council of Orange in 529, it was ratified. In Lérins, a monastic settlement near Marseilles, and at Hadrumetum (North Africa), however, it met with resistance. What actually survived was an attenuated form of Augustinism (semi-Pelagianism). 2. Fulgentius of Ruspe, in his *De fide ad Petrum*, created the first systematic summary of Augustinism, which prefigured the scholastic *summa* tradition. He thus prepared the way for the development of the mediaeval system. 3. The acceptance by Western theology of Augustine's teachings on the sacraments and the nature of the Church was greatly aided by Leo the Great and Gregory the Great. Subsequent Western

ecclesiology has not developed in any essential way beyond the thought of Augustine. 4. In the development of the → ARTES LIBERALES tradition, Augustine is an important link to Boethius, Cassiodorus and Isidore of Seville,. In *De doctrina christiana* he prepared the ground for a Christian reception of the culture of Antiquity.

2. Middle Ages. Mediaeval Augustinism was primarily a matter of defining and developing Augustine's fundamental theses, but such development was often a question of reacting against various individual Augustinian teachings. Mediaeval Augustinism developed in two directions. 1. The philosophical Augustinism of the high Middle Ages was begun by Anselm of Canterbury who continued the Augustinian programme of *fides quaerens intellectum* and Augustinian epistemology. However, the Augustinism of the 13th cent. was a diverse movement which ranged from the Victorines to the School of Chartres and William of Auvergne and further to Bonaventure. It is possible to characterize this process as the formation of a Platonic-Christian anthropology. The more strongly theological Augustinism of the later Middle Ages, as represented by Thomas Bradwardine, Gregory of Rimini and Wyclif, paved the way for the alienation from the church as an institution, and thus for the Reformation. 2) Political Augustinism can only claim Augustine's *De civitate dei* as a source in a qualified sense since Augustine himself viewed history as a history of salvation but expressed no thoughts on specific forms of government. Aegidius of Rome is, along with Wyclif and Richard Fitzralph, the prime advocate for the concept of priestly and royal authority, which aimed, first and foremost, at securing more influence for the papacy.

3. Reformation. Luther's understanding of Augustine was shaped by the Augustinism of the Augustinian hermits [7]. He became acquainted with this form of Augustinism in the writings of Gregory of Rimini, Jacobus Perez and Johann von Staupitz. Luther's direct access to Augustine can be demonstrated by his work with the *Enarrationes in psalmos*, the commentary on the Epistle to the Galatians and his *De spiritu et littera* [4]. Although Luther found central concepts of his theology already present in Augustine, he read Augustine entirely in the light of his own understanding of Paul. The other conceptions of Augustine from the time of the Reformation (Karlstadt [10], Zwingli, Calvin [19]) are still largely unexamined.

4. Modern Era. In modern times Augustine has received most attention from Catholic circles. Various strands of his thinking, to some extent overlapping, can be shown to be present. 1. The Spanish Jesuits, specifically Luis de Molina, spoke out in opposition to strict Augustinism, which puts heavy emphasis on the doctrines of original sin and grace. What the Spanish Jesuits propounded was, in fact, a kind of semi-Pelagianism, emphasizing the power of the human agent in attaining salvation. 2. Their views were most strongly felt in the Netherlands and France, where, in opposition to them,

the book *Augustinus* by Cornelius Jansen, Bishop of Ypres (d. 1576) was published posthumously. It was the Augustinism of Jansen, not the historical Augustine, which shaped the modern conception of Augustine. One of the most prominent proponents of Augustinism was B. Pascal. 3. Modern research into Augustine was greatly facilitated by the great Augustine edition of the Maurines, published from 1679 to 1700. All modern editions are based upon it.

5. Contemporary Era. Through the 20th cent. the philosophy of Augustine was present in the work of thinkers such as Max Scheler, who drew on the Augustinian concept of love and its view of bliss in his moral philosophy [6]. A basic text for understanding the contemporary view of Augustine is H. Arendt's work on the Augustinian concept of love [2]. Probably the most significant appropriation of Augustine was that of M. Heidegger. His work *Sein und Zeit* ('Being and Time') (1927) could be described as a variation on the Augustinian concept of time and on the Augustinian categories of existence of 'Verfallenheit an die Welt.'[1].

With the diminishing importance of scholastic thinking in Catholic theology, Augustine has regained considerable influence. This influence is tangible, above all, in ecclesiology and sacramental theology. The 'existential' components of theology, clearly evident after *Vatican II*, with their emphasis on experience and mysticism, allowed Augustine once more full play. In contemporary Protestant theology, thanks to the legacy of the Reformation, Augustine is a constant presence. The conception of Augustine in the present is based substantially on the portrayal by A. von Harnack, who valued Augustine as a reformer of Christian piety and portrayed Augustinian thinking as the only system justified in Christianity [8]. Harnack's portrayal was corrected and expanded by Karl Holl [9]. These two authors heralded a period of intensive work on Augustine, during which the question of the Hellenization of the Christian faith and the problem of Augustine's personal conversion have been prime subjects of discussion.

→ Augustinus, Aurelius (Augustine)

1 C. ANDRESEN, Bibliographia Augustiniana, 1973   2 H. ARENDT, Der Liebesbegriff bei Augustin, 1929   3 H. X. ARQUILLIÈRE, L'Augustinisme politique, ²1955   4 D. DEMMER, Lutherus interpres, 1968   5 W. GEERLINGS, Augustin, Augustinism, in: LThK 31, 1240–1247   6 J. GROOTEN, L'Augustinisme de Max Scheler, Augustinus Magister II, 1111–1120   7 A. HAMEL, Der junge Luther und Augustinus, 2 vols., 1934/35   8 A. v. HARNACK, Lehrbuch der Dogmengeschichte, 1926   9 K. HOLL, Augustins innere Entwicklung, Gesammelte. Aufsätze zur Kirchengeschichte III, 1928, 54–116   10 E. KÄHLER, Karlstadt und Augustin, 1952   11 K. LEHMANN, Christliche Geschichtserfahrung und ontologische Frage beim jungen Heidegger, in: Philos. Jb. 74, 1966, 126–153   12 H. OBERMANN, Der Herbst der mittelalterlichen Theologie, 1965   13 J. ORCIBAL, Les Origines du Jansenisme, 1947   14 K. POLLMANN, Augustins de doctrina christiana, 1997   15 J. RATZINGER, Volk und Haus Gottes in Augustins Lehre von der Kirche, 1954   16 Revue des Etudes Augustiniennes 1ff., 1954ff. (running bibliography)   17 A. SCHINDLER

et al., Augustin, Augustinism, I–IV, TRE 4, 646–723
18 Ph. Sellier, Pascal et S. Augustin, 1970 19 L. Smits,
Saint Augustin dans l'oeuvre de Calvin, 1957/58 20 D.
Trapp, Augustinian Theology of the 14th Century, Augustiniana 6, 1965, 146–274
Additional Bibliography: P. Brown, Augustine of
Hippo: A Biography, 1968; A. Fitzgerald (ed.), Augustine through the Ages: An Encyclopedia, 1999; H. Marrou, Saint Augustine and His Influence through the Ages,
(Engl. translation by Patrick Hepburn Scott) 1957 (repr.
1993); G. Matthews (ed.), The Augustinian Tradition,
1999.   WILHELM GEERLINGS

Austria
I. Middle Ages to the 18th Cent.   II. 19th
Cent. and Outlook   III. 20th Cent.

I. Middle Ages to the 18th Cent.
A. The Name Austria   B. Severin and the
Non-End of the Roman Empire   C. Salzburg
as a Centre of Early Medieval Culture
D. The High Middle Ages   E. Late Middle
Ages   F. Reformation and Counter-Reforma-
tion   G. 17th and 18th Cents.

A. The Name Austria
The form *ostarrichi*, which underlies the modern
German name, is first found in a document of Otto III
addressed to the diocese of Freising and dated 1
November 996. It describes a small territory around
Neuhofen/Ybbs in western Lower Austria. In the following decades, Latin equivalents such as *terra* (*mar-
chia, plaga, regio*) *orientalis* are encountered. The form
Austria (A.), which underlies the modern term in English and the Romance languages, first occurs in a document drawn up by Conrad III for Klosterneuburg, dated
25 February 1147. With the rise of the Habsburgs as the
ruling dynasty, terms such as *domus Austriae, casa
d'Austria* ('the House of Austria') became established
[23. 43].

B. Severin and the Non-End of the Roman
Empire
1. The Northern Frontier of the Roman Empire   2. Contacts with the Interior of the
Empire

1. The Northern Frontier of the Roman
Empire
Against the backdrop of the end of Rome's supremacy and the harbingers of the Great Migrations, the
homo omnino latinus Severin (d. 482) appeared in the
three provinces of Raetia, Noricum and Pannonia, located in what is now modern A. Probably of noble
Roman descent, he maintained relations with the powerful of his age (Odoacer). In times of crisis, he cared for
the spiritual and physical well-being of the inhabitants
along the Danube frontier. He spent most of life at
Favianis, modern Mautern an der Donau in Lower A.
The *Commemoratorium vitae sancti Severini*, written

in 511 by Eugippius, a monk and student of Severin's, is
a source of exceptional quality for the study of Late
Antiquity in the region of the Danube and the eastern
Alps [21; 30.; 31].

2. Contacts with the Interior of the Em-
pire
Close military contacts not only existed between individual Roman forts along the Danubian frontier; the
economic dependence of the border areas necessitated
continuous communication with the interior as well.
Disruption or failure of communication resulted in disaster. Despite the evacuation of the Danubian provinces
by Odoacer in 488, part of the rural Roman population
remained in the country and passed on the cultural traditions of Antiquity and in some instances Christian
teachings to the immigrating and passing *gentes* of the
Great Migrations. Continuity into the 6th cent. of the
Christian era is evident in the Roman town of Teurnia
(modern St. Peter in Holz, Carinthia) in interior Noricum, which, as *metropolis Norici*, became an episcopal
see. The floor mosaic, donated by the *vir spectabilis
Ursus* and his wife *Ursina*, in the former cemetery
church combines motifs of ancient and pagan influences with Christian images based on the *Physiologus*.
The last dated Roman funerary inscription from the
entire Austrian region was found in the immediate vicinity of Teurnia: it is the headstone of the deacon Non-
nosus (d. 532) of Molzbichl [9; 21; 30; 31].

C. Salzburg as a Centre of Early Medieval
Culture
1. The Question of Roman Continuity
2. Abbots and Bishops   2.1 Carolingian
Reform   2.2 Elevation to the Status of Archbishopric   2.3 Education

1. The Question of Roman Continuity
During the chaos of the Great Migrations, the territory of modern A. was crossed and temporarily inhabited by a number of *gentes* (Huns, Avars, Lombards and
Rugians) [24]. The areas partially abandoned by the
Romans were not only settled by the remnants of these
peoples but in particular by the Baiuvari from the NE
and Slavs from the SE. The proximity of these peoples is
reflected in place names, though the romanization of
pre-Roman toponyms must also be considered. The
issue of continuity is clearly exemplified in the cases of
Iuvavum/Salzburg and, in a similar manner, of *Lauria-
cum*/Lorch (near Enns, Upper A.), which was a bishopric in the time of Severin but at the time of Rupert of
Salzburg (d. 715/16) appeared too exposed for the re-
establishment of the bishopric because of its location on
the river Enns (the boundary with the Avars) [6; 30].
The large number of *Romani tributales* in the Salzburg
sphere of influence on the rivers Salzach and Inn formed
a special group whose members, in spite of their economic dependence, were personally free and could improve their status [31. 295–297]. There was also
Roman continuity in the Carantanian territory (mod-

ern Carinthia and Styria), which was missionized by Salzburg, and the Danubian areas of modern Upper and Lower A., as numerous toponyms prove [29].

2. ABBOTS AND BISHOPS

Salzburg became a partner of the Agilolfingian dukes of Bavaria as well as a spiritual and intellectual centre under the first abbots and bishops of the monastery in St. Peter, which was founded around 700 by Rupert [19a].

2.1 CAROLINGIAN REFORM

Even before the reforms of Charlemagne, Salzburg developed into a local centre of medieval literature, both by creating texts of its own and preserving ancient and Christian Latin works. Rupert's most important successor was the Irishman Virgil (746/47–784), whose influence probably inspired the earliest hagiographic document of A., a *Vita Ruperti* of the mid–8th cent., preserved today in two versions (*Gesta Hrodberti*; *Conversio Bagoariorum et Carantanorum* cap. 1) [19]. Virgil also encouraged Arbeo of Freising to engage in literary activity. Perhaps the so-called *Aethicus Ister* is Virgil's own work, as suggested by the Irish colouring in its style [26]. The Irish insular influence is also evident in the Cuthbert Gospel of the late 8th cent., the most famous manuscript from the Austrian Middle Ages, along with the *Codex millenarius maior* of Kremsmünster (*c.* 800). Virgil also provided the impetus for building the first Salzburg cathedral. After the fire under archbishop Conrad III in the late 12th cent., one of the largest Romanesque cathedrals north of the Alps was erected in its place. Santino Solari ultimately modelled the present-day early Baroque cathedral on Il Gesù in Rome (1614–1628).

2.2 ELEVATION TO THE STATUS OF ARCHBISHOPRIC

Virgil's successor Arn, consecrated in 785, maintained close contacts with Charlemagne's court and with Charlemagne himself, a factor in Salzburg's elevation to the status of archbishopric in 798. The significance of Salzburg as promulgator of the Carolingian reforms is evident in Arn's correspondence with Alcuin. A lively exchange of students and manuscripts occurred between Salzburg, the court and Frankish monasteries (St. Amand, Tours). Under archbishop Arn the scriptorium of St. Peter grew by 150 volumes [3; 8]. Arn also gave his name to two estate surveys he initiated that demonstrate the monastery's economic significance. The edition and collection of the Latin poems now known as the *Carmina Salisburgensia* was written in the first half of the 9th cent. It constitutes an example of Carolingian utilitarian and occasional poetry [12. 32; 19a. 116–119]. Two poems of a cycle of the months based on models from Antiquity and Late Antiquity are deserving of note. They represent the literary accompaniment to an image cycle contained in a Salzburg Codex (now National Library, Vienna, cvp. 387). The last example of early medieval literary production in Salzburg is the probably genuine letter of Theotmar to the pope in which he and the Bavarian clergy complain about transgressions against Salzburg's sphere of missionary activity [19]. Theotmar died in or shortly after the battle of Preßburg against the Hungarians in 907. This defeat and the ensuing turmoil of the first half of the 10th cent. constituted a clear discontinuity in the cultural production of what is now modern A. [12. 36].

2.3 EDUCATION

Salzburg and other monasteries such as Mondsee (founded in 748) and Kremsmünster (founded in 777; the chalice donated by its founder Tassilo, the oldest communion chalice in the southern German region, is of considerable art-historical significance) were centres of missionary activity and thus the prime beneficiaries of measures undertaken to improve educational standards. These improvements became necessary because of the clergy's poor knowledge of Latin and the resulting problems (e.g., dispute between Virgil and Boniface over the validity of the baptismal formula *in nomine patria et filia*) [30. 255–257]. Up until the 8th cent., the only education available on Austrian soil had been on an elementary level. Rupert established a school at St. Peter, first the *schola interior* (*interna*) for training monks, later a *schola exterior* (*externa*) for youths of all classes but mainly of the nobility. Based on the pastoral instruction that every bishop must have a school in his city, Virgil transformed the Benedictine → MONASTERY SCHOOLS at St. Peter into a cathedral school (*schola ecclesiae cathedralis*). The school's large catchment area is indicated by the students' geographical origins, which were linked to Salzburg's mission in the southeast of the empire. Although nothing is preserved of the curriculum of the→ CATHEDRAL SCHOOL, it is likely to have included special training for the mission among the Slavs [7. vol. 1. 101–105]. Around 870, a conflict with far-reaching consequences arose between Salzburg and Methodius, who in the course of his educational activies had developed a Slavic script (Glagolica) with his brother Cyrillus. Their efforts were thought to infringe upon Salzburgian interests. The creation of the 'Freising Manuscripts' (the oldest source for the Slovene language, written in the 2nd half of the 10th cent.) has also been connected to Salzburg [12. 34].

D. THE HIGH MIDDLE AGES

1. THE OTTONIAN REFORM   2. THE AGE OF THE INVESTITURE CONTEST   3. FROM THE ELEVATION TO DUCHY TO THE BEGINNING OF HABSBURG RULE (1156–1278)

1. THE OTTONIAN REFORM

Despite the victory over the Hungarians on the Lechfeld in 955 and the enfeoffment of the Babenbergs in 976 with the Eastern March, the reform movement of the Ottonian period was virtually ineffective in the dioceses of Salzburg and Passau, which along with the archbishopric became increasingly active in the 9th cent. as the carriers of missionary activities especially in modern eastern A. [12. 49]. Again, it must be noted that after the 9th cent. it was primarily the clergy who retained the remaining basic principles of a late Roman education on this side of the Alps; their knowledge of Latin helped them form an intellectual elite. As in the Carolingian period, they were educated in cathedral schools, which were complemented by parochial schools at the end of the 12th and beginning of the 13th cent. [7. vol. 1. 110]. The curriculum can be reconstructed from the manuscript indices, however, some loss is to be expected. A vivid account of the teaching matter and method is contained in the first book of the metrical *Vita sancti Christophori* of Walther von Speyer (the so-called 'Scolasticus', 982/83), which is dedicated *ad collegas urbis Salinarum* Liutfrid, Benzo and Frederick. It is probably safe to assume that the canon of works and authors named in it (*Ilias Latina*, Martianus Capella, Horace, Persius, Juvenal, Boethius, Statius, Terence, Lucan, Virgil, Porphyrius, Plato, Cicero) was also used at Salzburg, provided the manuscripts in question were available [12. 36, 43].

2. The Age of the Investiture Contest

The internal Church reforms and the conflict between temporal and spiritual powers in the 11th and 12th cents. resulted in numerous monastic foundations in the territory of what is modern A. (Lambach 1040/1056, Gurk 1043/1123, Admont 1074, Reichersberg/Inn 1080/1084, Göttweig 1083/1094, Melk 1089, Millstatt 1080/1090, St. Paul im Lavanttal 1091, Klosterneuburg 1100/1133, Rein 1129, Heiligenkreuz 1133, Zwettl 1138, Seckau 1140, Wilhering 1146, Vienna/Schottenkloster 1150, Vorau 1163, Lilienfeld 1202). These foundations also became centres of cultural life and Latin literary production [12]: Reichersberg with the works of Gerhoh; Admont with sermons, exegesis and prose hagiography; Göttweig with a *Vita Altmanni* that was important for both the formation of a national identity and the knowledge of ancient mythology. The 11th cent. saw an early version of the Vita of the Irish pilgrim Coloman, who suffered martyrdom in modern Lower A. in 1012. The Babenberg margrave Henry I. had his body transferred to Melk, and Coloman went on to become A.'s first patron saint. After 1485 he was joined by the patron saint of Vienna, Lower and Upper A., Leopold III, who ultimately replaced him in 1663. The network of interdependency in Austrian annalism is widespread. Small works of verse poetry are traceable. The *Carmina Runensia* (named after the Cistercian monastery Rein in Styria, Ms. 20) holds a special position. It consists of six fragments of 93 verses making extensive use of ancient and late ancient models that may have been created at Rein. The treatment of these Classical literary models, as well as their content, places it in the proximity of goliardic literature [12. 89f.].

3. From the Elevation to Duchy to the Beginning of Habsburg Rule (1156–1278)

Otto of Freising, who was born in 1112 as the son of the Babenberg margrave Leopold III, reports this event in the history of his nephew, Emperor Frederick I Barbarossa (Gesta Friderici 2,54f.). He cites ancient (Cicero, Virgil, Lucan) and late ancient authors by name as he does in the historical and philosophical passages of his work *Chronica sive Historia de duabus civitatibus*, which was influenced by Augustine of Hippo. Otto became Bishop of Freising in 1138, after studying in Paris. Despite some criticisms, his writings belong in the corpus of Austrian ecclesiastical historiography [35. 104]. The collection of the *Carmina Burana* was came into being in the 1st half of the 13th cent. in the area of southern A. (Seckau in Styria, Carinthia), or in neighboring southern Tyrol [12. 407f.].

E. Late Middle Ages
1. The First Habsburgs

1. The First Habsburgs

In 1246 the male line of the Babenbergs became extinct with Frederick II. The territory of modern Lower and Upper A. as well as parts of Styria (which the Babenbergs had acquired in 1192, as a result of the the so-called Georgenberg Pact) initially came under the rule of the Bohemian king Ottokar II Premysl. In 1278, after the battle of Marchfeld, they fell to Rudolf of Habsburg, who in 1282 enfeoffed his sons Albrecht I and Rudolf II with the Austrian lands and founded the Habsburg rule, which only ended in 1918. With the acquisition of Carinthia (1335) and Tyrol (1363), the 'House of Habsburg' became the 'House of Austria' (*domus Austriae*).

1.1 The Privilegium maius

In reaction to not being included among the electors in the 'Golden Bull' of Charles IV, his father-in-law, in 1356, the Habsburg Rudolf IV had some documents forged in his chancellery in 1358/59 (collectively known since the mid–19th cent. as the *Privilegium maius*, as an extension of the *Privilegium minus*), with which he demanded certain privileges for his house. As historical proof of the ancient special status of A., he had two letters by Caesar and Nero inserted into a forged charter of Henry IV of 1058 [14]. Petrarch unmasked them as brazen forgeries in an appraisal commissioned by Charles IV [22]. Nevertheless, the provisions of the *Privilegium maius* were confirmed under the Habsburg Emperor Frederick III in the mid–15th cent. and resulted, for example, in the title of 'Archduke' being established for the Habsburgs, which Rudolf had invented as a contrast to the rank of elector [20. 138]. This seemingly odd invocation of Caesar, however, has a long tradition: for example, the place-name Melk/Medelicha was derived from the phrase *Mea dilecta*, which was attributed to Caesar. A similar folk etymology exists for the name Vienna, where Caesar supposedly stayed for a *biennium* [27. 144]. Caesar also led the series of real and fictional ancestors of the Habsburgs, as is evident, for example, in the figures on the tomb of Maximilian at Innsbruck [27. 309]. Likewise, in terms of regal virtues such as *clementia*, the Habsburgs considered themselves to be the heirs of the Julio-Claudian dynasty [27. 129].

1.2 THE FOUNDING OF UNIVERSITIES

The founding of the → UNIVERSITY of Prague by his father-in-law Charles IV in 1348 led Rudolf IV to found a university in Vienna. On the model of and with the help of scholars from the Parisian Sorbonne, the *Alma mater Rudolphina* was established in 1365. But the new university did not flourish or draw in new students until the theological faculty, originally rejected by the pope but established in 1384, caused an increased influx of professors from the Sorbonne in the late 14th cent. Teaching and learning methods conformed to the concerns of scholasticism [7. vol. 1. 203–215]. The clerically-oriented statutes were in force for almost 170 years. Only with the *Nova reformatio* of Emperor Ferdinand I of 1 January 1554 were they brought more closely in line with the objectives of the state [7. vol. 2. 349–373]. At Salzburg, a university had been proposed in the 15th cent., but it was Prince Archbishop Paris Lodron who finally opened the new institution in 1622. In 1585, Archduke Charles II of Inner A. founded the University of Graz and placed it under the supervision of the Jesuit order. The University of Innsbruck was founded in 1669 by Emperor Leopold I and remained under the influence of the Jesuits until 1773.

1.3 THE TRANSITION TO HUMANISM

The tension between the old principles of Scholasticism and the new ideas of Humanism still informs the rich and diverse literary oeuvre of Thomas Ebendorfer of Haselbach (1388–1464) [15]. After studying at the artistic and theological faculties, he became a teacher, dean and rector at the University of Vienna; in 1421 he was ordained as a parish priest and then participated in the Council of Basel as well as various imperial diets. Apart from theological writings, the main body of his work is concerned with historiography (*Cronica Austrie*, *Cronica regum Romanorum*) and reveals great dexterity in the use of Latin [15. 97–123]. Enea Silvio Piccolomini (1405–1464), a scion of Tuscan nobility, may well be considered a trailblazer of humanism in A. He arrived at the court of Emperor Frederick III in 1437 and was crowned *poeta laureatus* in 1442. In addition to speeches, letters and poems he, too, composed historical works, among which the *Historia Austrie (Australis) seu Friderici III* remains a major source of contemporary history. In 1455 he left the imperial court, became a cardinal a year later and in 1458 was elected pope as Pius II [20. 382–385]. In Tyrol the eminent early humanist Nicholas of Kues (Cusanus), while Bishop of Brixen, was a political opponent of Duke Sigmund the Rich. Maximilian I (emperor 1493–1519) brought many distinguished humanists into the country: Konrad Celtis (1st lecture on Tacitus' *Germania* in Vienna), Johannes Cuspinianus and Konrad Peutinger. The *Tabula Peutingeriana*, named after the latter, is a 6.82 m long and 34 cm wide copy of a road map of the Roman Empire last revised in the 5th cent. Purchased in 1720 by Prince Eugen and acquired after his death by the National Library in Vienna, it is a unique source of Austrian topography [28]. Maximilian himself was glorified in the account of his life 'Weiß Kunig', which was stylistically modelled on Caesar's *Commentarii*, and the *Austrias* of Riccardo Bartolini (c. 1475–1529), an epic based on classical precursors such as Virgil and Homer [10; 11].

F. REFORMATION AND COUNTER-REFORMATION
1. THE BROADENING OF PERSPECTIVE 2. THE NEW ORDERS

1. THE BROADENING OF PERSPECTIVE

The expansion of the Habsburg territories in the 16th cent., in conjunction with the Humanists' endeavours, fostered a growing interest in foreign cultures. In 1555, the Habsburgs' political adversaries at the Ottoman court, twice defeated outside Vienna (1529 and 1683), received an embassy from Ferdinand I. In Ankara, the Austrian diplomats led by the Fleming Ogier Ghiselin de Busbecq then discovered the *Monumentum Ancyranum*, a copy of the *Res Gestae* of Augustus [35. 240]. Johannes Kepler's (1571–1630) scientific work is closely associated with A. (Graz, Linz; the university there is named after him), and the study of alchemy was conducted in earnest at the Prague court of Rudolf II (1552–1612). Villach, Salzburg, Innsbruck, Vienna and Klagenfurt were stations in the life of the controversial physician and natural scientist Theophrastus Bombastus of Hohenheim, known as Paracelsus (d. 1541).

2. THE NEW ORDERS

In the 16th and 17th cents., the Austrian educational system was characterized by the religious disputes from which the Counter-Reformation emerged as the victor over Protestantism. When the Jesuits were founded in 1534, their significance on Austrian territory was first and foremost focused on the educational sector: schools established by Jesuits pursued the objective of an elitist education; they later developed into a highly organized form of grammar (secondary) school, the Gymnasium [7. vol. 2. 137]. Secondly, Jesuit theatre, which presented Latin plays by Classical and contemporary authors as part of the school curriculum, greatly influenced the development of stagecraft in A. One of their number, Nicholas Avancinus (1611–1686), who wrote sumptuous plays (*ludi Caesarei*) for the Imperial Court, also composed parodies of Classical authorities such as Horace [32. 1181–1189]. From the second half of the 17th cent., a large number of schools were operated by the Order of the Pious Schools (*Patres scholarum piarum*). Unlike the Jesuits, the Piarists, founded in 1597 by Joseph von Calasanz, put greater emphasis on an elementary education [7. vol. 3. 25–28, 34–38].

G. 17TH AND 18TH CENTS.

The → BAROQUE period saw the culmination of court culture under the Emperors Leopold I (1658–1705), Joseph I (1705–1711) and Charles VI (1711–1740), as evidenced in the buildings designed by Johann

Bernhard Fischer von Erlach, Lucas von Hildebrandt, Jacob Prandtauer and Josef Munggenast.

1. BAROQUE LITERATURE   2. THE REFORMS OF MARIA THERESIA

1. BAROQUE LITERATURE

The Latin literature of the Baroque retained its close affiliation with Antiquity; it was mostly written by members of the orders, and often served the ruling house. The Benedictine Simon Rettenbacher (1634–1706), who wrote about 6,000 Latin poems and plays (*Demetrius, Atys, Perseus, Ulysses*) may be considered a significant and prolific representative [7. vol. 3. 19]. The Augustinian Abraham a Santa Clara (Johann Ulrich Megerle, 1644–1709) enjoyed particular popularity on account of his mastery of language and witty wordplay.

2. THE REFORMS OF MARIA THERESIA

Under the rule of Maria Theresia (1740–1780) dramatic changes occurred in the education sector. In 1760 the Court Commission on Education (*Studienhofkommission*) was set up as the central regulating authority for universities and Gymnasien, and later for the entire educational system. Schools were to be removed from the influence of the Catholic Church and tied into the administration of the state. Johann Ignaz von Felbiger (1724–1788), who was called to Vienna in 1774, completely reorganized Austrian elementary schools with the General School Order (introduction of compulsory education in A.). The network of schools was expanded and more strongly adapted to regional requirements. At the ordinary and secondary schools Latin was only taught to those who wished to become surgeons or pharmacists, and those who wished to enter a Gymnasium [7. vol. 3. 102–118].

→ Odoacer

1 H. APPELT, Privilegium minus. Das staufische Kaisertum und die Babenberger in Österreich, 1976 2 R. & M. BAMBERGER, E. BRUCKMÜLLER, K. GUTKAS, Österreich-Lexikon, 2 vols., 1995 3 B. BISCHOFF, Die südostdeutschen Schreibschulen in der Karolingerzeit 2: Die vorwiegend österreichischen Diözesen, 1980 4 E. BRUCKMÜLLER, Sozialgeschichte Österreichs, 1985 5 K. BRUNNER, Herzogtümer und Marken. Österreichische Geschichte 907–1156, 1994 6 H. DOPSCH, H. SPATZENEGGER, Geschichte Salzburgs. Stadt und Land, 1983 7 H. ENGELBRECHT, Geschichte des österreichischen Bildungswesens, vols. 1–3, 1982–1984 8 K. FORSTNER, Die karolingischen Handschriften und Fragmente in den Salzburger Bibliotheken, Mitteilungen der Gesellschaft für Salzburger Landeskunde, Ergänzungsband 3, 1962 9 F. GLASER, Teurnia. Römerstadt und Bischofsstadt, 1992 10 E. KLECKER, Kaiser Maximilians Homer, in: Wiener Studien 108, 1995, 613–637 11 Id., Impius Aeneas – pius Maximilianus, in: Wiener Humanistische Blätter 37, 1995, 50–6512 12 F. P. KNAPP, Die Literatur des Früh- und Hochmittelalters. Geschichte der Literatur in Österreich, vol. 1, 1994 13 K. LECHNER, Die Babenberger. Markgrafen und Herzoge von Österreich 976–1246, 1985 14 A. LHOTSKY, Privilegium maius. Die Geschichte einer Urkunde, 1957 15 Id., Thomas Ebendorfer. Ein österreichischer Geschichtsschreiber, Theologe und Diplomat des 15. Jahrhunderts, Schriften der MGH 15, 1957 16 Id., Quellenkunde zur mittelalterlichen Geschichte Österreichs, Mitteilungen des Instituts für Österreichische Geschichtsforschung. Supplement 19, 1962 17 Id., Österreichische Historiographie, 1962 18 Id., Aufsätze und Vorträge 1, H. WAGNER, H. KOLLER (ed.), 1970 19 F. LOŠEK, Die Conversio Bagoariorum et Carantanorum und der Brief des Erzbischofs Theotmar von Salzburg, MGH Studien und Texte 15, 1997 19a Id., Die Auswirkungen karolingischer Politik und Reformen im Südosten des Reiches, in: Karl der Große, F.-R. ERKENS (ed.), 2001, 111–121 20 A. NIEDERSTÄTTER, Das Jahrhundert der Mitte. Österreichische Geschichte 1400–1522, 1996 21 R. NOLL (ed.), Eugippius, Das Leben des Heiligen Severin, 1981 22 P. PIUR (ed.), Petrarcas Briefwechsel mit deutschen Zeitgenossen, 1913 23 R. G. PLASCHKA, G. STOURZH, J. P. NIEDERKORN, Was heißt Österreich? Inhalt und Umfang des Österreichbegriffs seit dem 10. Jahrhundert bis heute, 1995 24 W. POHL, Die Awaren, 1988 25 G. SCHEIBELREITER, s.v. Österreich, in: LMA 6, 1993, 1520–1525 26 K. SMOLAK, Notizen zu Aethicus Ister, in: Filologia mediolatina 3, 1996, 135–152 27 K. VOCELKA, L. HELLER, Die Lebenswelt der Habsburger. Kultur- und Mentalitätsgeschichte einer Familie, 1997 28 E. WEBER, Tabula Peutingeriana. Codex Vindobonensis 324, 1976 29 P. WIESINGER, Antik-romanische Kontinuitäten im Donauraum von Ober- und Niederösterreich am Beispiel der Gewässer-, Berg- und Siedlungsnamen, in: Denkschriften der Österreichischen Akademie der Wissenschaften, philosophisch-historische Klasse 201, 1990, 261–328 30 H. WOLFRAM, Salzburg Bayern Österreich, Mitteilungen des Instituts für Österreichische Geschichtsforschung Ergänzungsband 31, 1995 31 Id, Grenzen und Räume. Österreichische Geschichte 378–907, 1995 32 H. ZEMAN, Die österreichische Literatur. Ihr Profil von den Anfängen bis ins 18. Jahrhundert, 1986 33 E. ZÖLLNER (ed.), Die Quellen der Geschichte Österreichs, 1982 34 Id., Der Österreichbegriff. Formen und Wandlungen in der Geschichte, 1988 35 Id., Geschichte Österreichs. Von den Anfängen bis zur Gegenwart, ⁸1994.   FRITZ LOŠEK

II. 19TH CENT. AND OUTLOOK

A. AUSTRIAN CLASSICISM   B. LITERARY JOSEPHINISM   C. THE HABSBURG MYTH   D. THE VIENNESE POPULAR THEATRE   E. OUTLOOK

A. AUSTRIAN CLASSICISM

A study and a drama on the Greek poetess Sappho were published almost simultaneously: in 1816 Friedrich Gottlieb Welcker wrote *Sappho von einem herrschenden Vorurtheil befreyt* [20], and Franz Grillparzer's blank verse tragedy *Sappho* premiered on 21 April 1818. The fair copy having been finished in August of 1817, it was first published in 1819 by J.B. Wallishausser in Vienna [9. 730ff.]. The writing of the tragedy was not preceded by a thorough study of the sources. At this point, Grillparzer (1791–1872) still obtained most of his knowledge of Greek life and thought from the works of Christoph Martin Wieland: *Geschichte des Agathon* (Agathon between the aging priestess Pythia and the young Psyche) and *Aristipp* (Lais at age 40 falls in love with a young Thessalian, who betrays her with Phryne). Only the poem to the goddess of love in Grillparzer's drama (I,6) is a free adaptation of a Sappho fragment [21. 4ff., No. VI]. Grillparzer's tragedy illustrates the embourgeoisement of the classical ideal of art, while suggesting in its formal composition an affinity with Goethe's *Iphigenie auf Tauris*. Sappho's mission as an artist, however, has been modified to accommodate Biedermeier notions of bliss: in Grillparzer's interpretation, the sole purpose of her art is to praise 'quiet domestic joys' (v. 96). Underneath the trappings of Antiquity we encounter (the values of) the early 19th cent. Viennese bourgeoisie. And yet, Sappho's death – her leap from the cliffs of Leucas – negates her dedication to ordinary life and restores the original artistic ideal, according to which the poet partakes of the divine.

Lord Byron praised the tragedy as a magnificent and sublime 'work of art': Grillparzer, he wrote, 'was great, ancient, not as simple as the ancients but very simple for a modern' [6. 46f.]. By contrast, the Viennese popular theatre immediately parodied the successful Burgtheater play, as e.g. in Franz Xaver Told's (von Toldenburg) 'comic melodrama' *Seppherl* [7. 46f.]. Friedrich Gottlob Welcker's study of Sappho's house as a school of the muses and boarding school for girls [20. 58ff.] influenced Ulrich von Wilamowitz-Moellendorff's *Sappho und Simonides. Untersuchungen über griechische Lyriker* (Berlin 1913). Welcker claims he felt compelled to respond to the *unsägliche Gemeinheit, welche sich oft, vordem und neuerlich, über die Sappho ausgesprochen hat* ('despicable meanness often expressed, in former times and recently, against Sappho', [20. 6]). He cites Plato, who called the poetess the tenth muse, and others who called her a female Homer. His prime concern was the rehabilitation of Sappho's *eros*, this he accomplished by lifting from it the air of scandal that had hung about her ever since she had been caricatured by the writers of Old Comedy. The cult of friendship and beauty surrounding Sappho is balanced by a love without desire on her side which, according to Grillparzer, is confirmed by her social reputation.

His elegy on ruins, *Campo vaccino* (1819), earned him a run-in with the censors: the poem had to be removed from all available copies of the pocketbook edition of *Aglaja*, after it was published in 1820. In court circles the conservative Grillparzer was now considered a 'Jacobin', because in his poem he had dared to play off the ancient sign system against Christian symbols.

Grillparzer's dramatic work is a focal point for the reception of Antiquity in 19th cent.-A. The dramatization of the legend of the Argonauts and that of the Hero and Leander myth illustrate his 'receptive' stance. His psychologizing approach is evident in the recurring opposition between processes of transgression and defiant postures of limitation. In his 1820/21 treatment of the legend of the Argonauts in the trilogy *Das Goldene Vlies: Der Gastfreund, Die Argonauten* and *Medea*, the material is reworked as a historical and philosophical tragedy involving society's Humanitarian ideals. The

characters' actions in history are being subjected to a judgment that must justify itself before the wisdom of the gods at Delphi: Delphi as the origin of the Humanitarian idea and Apollo as the divine symbol and protector of humanitas [16]. When Medea, after her deed, decides to take the fleece to Delphi and face the judgment of the priests there, she submits the totality of her actions to be judged by the Apollonian divinity, to be measured up against her commitment to the humanitarian ideal – in the full knowledge that the historical consequences of our actions may often stray far afield from this ideal. Grillparzer's epigram on the *Weg der neuern Bildung* (1848) rendered expression to his pessimism in the formula, *von Humanität durch Nationalität zur Bestialität* ('From humanity through nationality to bestiality', [9. 808]). The tragedy of *Medea* already traces this trajectory: first there is Delphi, followed by the contrast between Greeks and Colchians, finally the infanticide. Externally, the Fleeece creates a continuity between the parts of the trilogy, and functions as a leitmotif or a floating signifier. The Fleece trilogy also is a tragedy of words because their misinterpretation precipitates the catastrophe. Deviating from his previous practice with *Sappho*, Grillparzer conducted extensive preparatory studies for the trilogy. Once again, it was Wieland who provided the initial impulse (*Novelle ohne Titel* in *Hexameron von Rosenhain*). A.W. Schlegel's critique of Euripides' *Medea* in his lectures *Über dramatische Kunst und Literatur* stimulated Grillparzer's reading of the the Greek tragedy. His ancient sources were Seneca's treatment of the Medea myth, the Argonaut epics of Valerius Flaccus and Apollonius Rhodius, excerpts from Strabo and Hyginus, as well as Ovid's *Metamorphoses* (7th book) and the *Heroides* (e.g., Medea's letter to Jason). Grillparzer knew the *Medea* adaptations of Julius von Soden and Friedrich Wilhelm Gotter, played at the Burgtheater in 1815 and 1817, and the opera by Luigi Cherubini. He obtained a comprehensive understanding of the material from the *Gründliches mythologisches Lexikon* of Benjamin Hederich (1770 ed.), which he read in the summer of 1818.

Grillparzer's tragedy *Des Meeres und der Liebe Wellen* (1831) revolves around the individual identities of the two lovers Hero and Leander. Hero's evocation of the *Glück des stillen Selbstbesitzes* ('bliss of quiet self-possession', v. 392) states the central theme of the work: the ability to preserve one's sense of self. Hero flees from an oppressive family environment to discover her true self in the service of the goddess. Leander, through his love for Hero, is freed from an all-powerful maternal bond that had left him with his dead mother's memory as the sole purpose in his life. Ultimately, it is the prohibition of love imposed on priests, and the desire for love that that trigger the tragic conflict. Tragedy can only be avoided if 'Sammlung' (gathering), one of Grillparzer's primal words, becomes a maxim of everyday life. The diffuse expressions of human life are to be gathered, so as to form the basis of a more securely balanced and clearly focused, purposeful existence. Externally, Hero's tower dominates the stage as a symbol of all things solid and limited by their physical body, the male/phallic, while the sea represents that which is flowing, oceanic, feminine. In a poetics of space, the human figures are each linked to that section of the scenery which symbolizes the exact opposite of their personal nature: the tower is Hero's home, the sea becomes Leander's grave. Transgressions and violations of boundaries are an essential part of the action in this late Romantic tragedy of love. The plot is based on the Alexandrian fable of Hero and Leander, which shows parallels to the myth of Amor and Psyche. Grillparzer used as his sources Ovid's *Heroides* (letters 17 and 18), the epic of Musaeus *Hero and Leander*, Euripides' *Ion*, Schiller's ballad and Christopher Marlowe's fragmentary verse narrative of Hero and Leander, also the folk song *Es waren zwei Königskinder*.

B. LITERARY JOSEPHINISM

Authors such as Grillparzer liked to call themselves' Josephinians' – enlightened thinkers and dedicated to the policies of emperor Joseph II. The transition from Maria Theresia to her son Joseph II (1765–1790) marks the end of the Baroque period and the ascendancy of the literary Enlightenment in A. Wit, satire, travesty, criticism and a literature that could be both questioning and polemic were the trademarks of the age [5]. One representative example is Aloys Blumaur's (1755–1798) travesty of Virgil's *Aeneis* (1782/1788), which parodies the Roman epic by applying it to the founding of the Roman church and its opposition to the Emperor (*Abenteuer des frommen Helden Aeneas oder Virgils Aeneis travestiert*). Blumauer's Aeneas is the founder of both Rome and the Vatican. In his boat, he travels past fire-spewing mountains that disgorge hoods, rosaries, torture instruments and burnt human flesh. His descent into Hell leads to encounters with Luther, Hus and Rousseau and straight into the papal dens of iniquity. The entire travesty is an attack on the Catholic Church, the papacy and the Jesuit Order from the perspective of the Josephine Enlightenment. The hero Aeneas sheds all heroic traits along the way; at one point he gives one of Helen's petticoats to Dido as a gift. Blumauer's unfinished comic verse epic ties into Wieland's *Komische Erzählungen* (1765), which were in turn inspired by the spirit of Lucian [4; 15].

C. THE HABSBURG MYTH

The 'Austrian Plutarch' of Josef von Hormayr (1781–1848) played a significant role in the genesis of the Habsburg myth after the historical changes of 1806. Between 1807 and 1812 his *Österreichischer Plutarch oder Leben und Bilder aller Regenten und der berühmtesten Feldherren, Staatsmänner, Gelehrten und Künstler des österreichischen Kaiserstaats* was published in 20 parts. It recounts the history of A. as the gradual growing-together of the individual nations of the Danubian monarchy under the auspices of the House of Habsburg. Poetry, the author argues, is ideally suited to address these interdependencies and points of contact. In his work, therefore, he wishes to provide examples and inspirational material for this (new) kind of Austrian literature. His parallel biographies in the tradition of Plutarch, he says, are his contribution to the creation of a single Austrian identity and common culture. Hormayr was prompted to write his biographical work by Johannes von Müller, the Swiss historian who became custodian of the Viennese Court Library after 1800. Hormayr himself was made director of the House Court and State Archives in Vienna after 1808, and in 1816 Emperor Franz II appointed him Imperial Historiographer. Vol. 15 of the 'Austrian Plutarch' contains the history of the Bohemian king Przemisl Ottokar II; it became one of Grillparzer's primary sources for his Ottokar drama. Both Hormayr's and Grillparzer's work must also be read in the context of their Napoleonic experience [19].

The dramatist Heinrich Joseph von Collin (1771–1811), writer of 'Baroque national plays' ('barocker Staatsdramen', [9. 637]), celebrated successes as a classicistic orator-playwright. In his dramatic works, Collin gave voice to the Austrian imperial idea of nationhood in ancient dress: the continuity of the Austrian nation was to be built on the diversity of its peoples, guided by German education and Roman *virtus*. In a literary debate with Josef Schreyvogel, Collin expressed the opinion, entirely in line with Schiller and the Romantics, that the plot of tragedy illuminates the victory of freedom over necessity. The audience, representing mankind, benefits spiritually from the joyous triumph of their dignity. *Regulus* (1801) established Collin's reputation as the 'Austrian Corneille' among his contemporaries [17]. In 1802 his *Coriolanus* was performed at the Burgtheater. His source was the *Lives of Plutarch*, which Shakespeare had also used for his *Tragedy of Coriolanus*. Coriolanus stands accused of disregarding the will of the people. Enraged about his sentence, he severs all ties with home and country to enter the service of Rome's enemies. Torn between his oath of loyalty and a rekindled patriotism, Coriolanus seeks death as a stranger in the world. Beethoven's *Coriolanus Ouvertüre* (1807) was composed for Collin's tragedy. Collin's appreciation of and attitude towards Classical Antiquity is evident in his tragedy *Die Horatiansier und Curiatier*, which he composed for the emperor's name day [12].

D. THE VIENNESE POPULAR THEATRE

The theatre decree of 22 March 1776 marks Emperor Joseph's II attempt to reorganize the Viennese theatre. He appointed the Burgtheater as the court and national theatre and the Theater am Kärntnertor as the venue for travelling troupes and popular entertainment. This laid the groundwork for the separation of spoken and musical theatre. The cultural opposition between (metropolitan) Burgtheater and suburban popular theatre remained fairly significant: the Burgtheater per-

formed classical spoken pieces, which were then parodied on the suburban stage. The Viennese popular theatre thrived on this contrast and, aside from the Baroque
improvement play ('Besserungsstück') and farce, counted parody among its main genres [13; 14]. The Classical material was laced with contemporary allusions
and further customized through the liberal use of stage
machinery and typical Volkstheater allegory. Classical
reminiscences, allegories (often Lady Fortune), Greek
and Roman heroes relocated to Vienna, comic reworkings of ancient sources, these were all devices employed by authors ranging from Adolf Bäuerle, Joseph
Alois Gleich and Karl Meisl to Ferdinand Raimund and
Johann Nestroy – much to the pleasure of their largely
petty-bourgeois audiences [7]. Set in Vienna, the
'mythological caricatures' of Karl Meisl, and in particular his *Orpheus and Euridice* (1813), are just one representative example.

E. OUTLOOK

19th-cent.-Austrian authors drew on Classical
themes to gain, from the opposition between 'ancient'
and 'modern', an insight into their own sense of tradition, and to stimulate self-reflection. Psychologizing of
the myth is as much part of the Austrian reception of
Classical Antiqutiy as is parody. Within the context of
historical legitimization processes, both Greek and
Roman literature was utilized to support timeless
truths. However, the reference to the ancient world
could also signal a critical detachment from the present.
Some of these modes of reception are later found among
Austrian authors of the 20th cent., who continued the
practice and expanded upon it. A case in point are the
Greek plays of Hugo von Hofmannsthal [11] and Hermann Broch's novel *Der Tod des Virgil* [18; 10]. Egon
Friedell's *Kulturgeschichte des Altertums* (1936) is a
profound testament to the ironic subjectivity of a final,
comprehensive overview. Most recently, Christoph
Ransmayr has evoked an imaginative vision of antiquity in a contemporary setting in his Ovid novel *Die
letzte Welt* (1988) [8; 2; 3].

1 H. BACHMAIER (ed.), Franz Grillparzer, 1991 (with
select bibliography of secondary literature)   2 P. BACH-
MANN, Die Auferstehung des Mythos in der Postmoderne.
Philosophische Voraussetzungen zu Christoph Ransmayrs
Roman 'Die letzte Welt', in: Diskussion Deutsch, 21. Jahrgang, 1990, 639–651   3 K. BARTSCH, 'Und den Mythos
zerstört man nicht ohne Opfer'. Zu den Ovid-Romanen
An Imaginary Life von David Malouf und *Die letzte Welt*
von Christoph Ransmayr, in: Lesen und Schreiben (FS
MANFRED JURGENSEN), edited by V. WOLF, 1995, 15–22
4 B. BECKER-CANTARINO, Aloys Blumauer and the Litera-
ture of Austrian Enlightenment, 1973, 63–75   5 L. BODI,
Tauwetter in Wien. Zur Prosa der österreichischen Aufklärung 1781–1795, 1977   6 Briefe und Tagebücher des
Lord Byron, vol. 4, Braunschweig 1832   7 M. DIETRICH,
Jupiter in Wien oder Götter und Helden der Antike im
Altwiener Volkstheater, 1967   8 H. GOTTWALD, Mythos
und Mythisches in der Gegenwartsliteratur. Studien zu
Chr. Ransmayr, Peter Handke, Botho Strauß, George Steiner, Patrick Roth und Robert Schneider, 1996   9 F. GRILL-

PARZER, Werke in 6 Bänden, vol. 2, H. BACHMAIER (ed.),
1986   10 J. HEIZMANN, Antike und Moderne in Hermann
Brochs 'Tod des Vergil'. Über Dichtung und Wissenschaft,
Utopie und Ideologie, 1997   11 W. JENS, Hofmannsthal
und die Griechen, 1955   12 W. KIRK, Die Entwicklung des
Hochstildramas in Österreich von Metastasio bis Collin,
1978   13 V. KLOTZ, Bürgerliches Lachtheater, 1980
14 O. ROMMEL, Die Alt-Wiener Volkskomödie. Ihre
Geschichte vom barocken Welt-Theater bis zum Tode
Nestroys, 1952   15 E. ROSENSTRAUCH-KÖNIGSBERG,
Freimaurerei im josephinischen Wien. Aloys Blumauers
Weg vom Jesuiten zum Jakobiner, 1975, 116–155   16 W.
SCHADEWALDT, Der Gott von Delphi und die Humanitäts-
idee, 1975   17 P. SKRINE, Collin's *Regulus* Reconsidered,
in: BRIAN KEITH-SMITH (ed.): Bristol Austrian Studies,
1990, 49–72   18 O. TOST, Die Antike als Motiv und
Thema in Hermann Brochs Roman 'Der Tod des Vergil',
1996   19 L. CHR. TÜRKEL, Das publizistische Wirken des
Josef Freiherrn von Hormayr, 1980   20 FR. G. WELCKER,
Sappho von einem herrschenden Vorurtheil befreyt, Göttingen 1816   21 JOH. CHR. WOLF, Sapphus, poetriae Les-
biae fragmenta et elogia, Londini 1733.

HELMUT BACHMAIER

III. 20TH CENT.

A. EDUCATION   B. CLASSICAL STUDIES: TEACH-
ING AND RESEARCH   C. PSYCHOANALYSIS   D. LIT-
ERATURE

A. EDUCATION

After 1848, the efforts of the Austrian Empire in reforming universities and the Gymnasium were aimed at
eliminating the deficits that existed in the Austrian educational system compared to standards in Prussia and,
from 1871, in the German Empire. In essence, this
meant a modified adoption of the Humboldtian
reforms and a stronger differentiation within the scientific and technological secondary school system (10 to
17 or 18 years of age). This was accomplished, e.g., by
establishing the 'Technisches Gewerbemuseum' (now
Technologische Gewerbeschule = Technological Grammar School) in 1879. Another measure was to enforce
Latin and Greek instruction in the Gymnasium (eight to
six hours of Latin on average): the lower grades were
required to translate exclusively from German into Latin or Greek, but the same restriction still applied for the
Matura examination. Fierce debates in the last decade
of the 19th century about the value of the → TEACHING
OF ANCIENT LANGUAGES led to the removal of this requirement and a gradual reduction in the number of
hours. An indication of the nature of the debate is the
collection of statements published by Robert Scheu in
1898, *Was leistet die Mittelschule?* ('What are the benefits of the secondary school?') Aside from the assessments of eminent philologists, it also contained contributions from natural scientists, who argued vehemently
for a departure from the Humanist educational ideal.
Until WWI, only the humanist Gymnasium provided
unrestricted university access. After 1918, Otto Glök-
kel's (1874–1935) school reforms fundamentally
changed the education system; these meritorious

reforms emphasized the active participation of the pupils and pushed the formation of philological skills into the background. Latin and Greek continued to be taught in the humanist Gymnasium, but the *Realgymnasium* became the most popular school type between the world wars: Latin was compulsory from year three, and graduates could enter most branches of study, including *Jus* (= law) and medicine. This practice continued after 1945 in the so-called Second Republic. Before the school reform of 1965, the Humanist Gymnasia in Western Austria (Upper Austria, Salzburg, Styria, Carinthia, Tyrol, Vorarlberg) taught Latin from year one and Greek from year three, while in Eastern Austria Latin was taught from year three and Greek from year five in an eight-year curriculum; from the mid–1960s onwards, the Eastern Austrian solution became the norm for all of Austria. By the end of the millennium, a number of school reforms had caused further sharp reductions in the teaching of ancient languages, but even at the beginning of the 21st cent., the amount of ancient language teaching in Austria remains persistently above the European average.

B. Classical Studies: Teaching and Research

The rise of Classical studies in Austria in the second half of the 19th cent. was largely due to Hermann Bonitz (1814–1888) and Wilhelm von Hartel (1839–1907; 1900–1905 Minister of Education and Cultural Affairs), who were intent on reforming the teaching of Classical Studies at the university. There was a particular interest in Christian Latin literature, which led to the establishment of the series *Corpus Scriptorum Ecclesiasticorum Latinorum*. The Vienna Department of Classical Philology gained prominence first and foremost through the figure of Theodor Gomperz (1832–1912), who first made a name for himself as a papyrologist and was later known primarily for writing the standard work *Griechische Denker* ('Greek Thinkers'). The first edition was serialized from 1893 to 1909 and was recognized far beyond the confines of its immediate discipline. Gomperz' versatility is exemplified in his admiration for the social philosophy of John Stuart Mill, whose works he published in German (one volume, for instance, was translated by S. Freud, who counted *Griechische Denker* among his ten most important books). For his analysis of the Greek natural philosophers Gomperz sought to draw on the scientific thinking of his time (e.g. Helmholtz and Mach), displaying an anti-idealistic streak typical of Austrian intellectual traditions. The appointment of Ernst Mach to a chair in 'Geschichte und Theorie der induktiven Wissenschaften' ('History and Theory of the Inductive Sciences') was in no small way facilitated through the initiative of Gomperz and his son Heinrich. Gomperz, descendant of a wealthy Jewish family from Moravia, was a central figure in the social and intellectual life of his time. His son Heinrich Gomperz (1873–1942), subsequently Professor of Philosophy in Vienna, can be seen as one of the most stimulating influences on the members of the Vienna Circle gathering around Ernst Mach. Among his many pupils was Karl R. Popper, whose epoch-making work *Die offene Gesellschaft und ihre Feinde* ('The Open Society and its Enemies', 1945/1958) is indebted to Th. Gomperz' *Griechische Denker* not so much in terms of that book's vehement criticism but rather its interpretation of Plato; Popper also referred to it in his studies of Parmenides. The Austrian physicist and Nobel Prize laureate Erwin Schrödinger cited Gomperz in his publication *Die Natur und die Griechen* (The Greeks and Nature, 1956), arguing against Ernst Mach and for the importance and relevance of studying the writings of Pre-Socratic philosophers, even though they may no longer be valid from a scientific point of view.

The fact that in his youth Heinrich Gomperz wrote a *Grundlegung der Neusokratischen Lehre* (1897) is a significant illustration of the philosophical tendencies among the young intelligentsia in *Gründerzeit* Vienna: indeed, there was a *Klub der Neusokratiker* ('Neo-Socratic Society'). While its general attitude approached schoolboy humour, the club's first maxim was never to take anything seriously, since everything was the result of play, and God had created the world merely for the sake of play. Because he had been a stroller, like the Viennese, Socrates was made patron of the society. This was all thanks to a turn against Nietzsche, who had decried Socrates as a buffo and a caricature. Later on, Heinrich Gomperz advocated interpreting the Pre-Socratics according to psychoanalytical principles.

In the inter-war years, two eminent philologists were appointed from Germany: Ludwig Radermacher (1867–1952) and Hans von Arnim (1859–1931), one of whose areas of research was ancient tragedy. Another luminary in this particular field was Albin Lesky (1896–1980), whose *Griechische Literaturgeschichte* (*History of Greek Literature*, 1957) was translated into several languages, and who spoke out in favour of ancient language teaching at the Gymnasium during critical phases.

C. Psychoanalysis

The re-interpretation of ancient myths in the 20th cent. often bears a signature borrowed from the intellectual realm of psychoanalysis. And conversely, it is not absurd to ask what psychoanalysis owes to ancient thought and ancient literature. Above all, its founder Sigmund Freud (1856–1939) had enjoyed a solid classical education, which is reflected in his writings. The reference to the Oedipus model (affection of the son towards the mother and jealousy towards the father) first appears in a letter from 1897 addressed to W. Fließ and contains a self-analysis by Freud. This momentous theory was published with a detailed interpretation of Sophocles' drama in the *Traumdeutung* (*Interpretation of Dreams*, 1899; recte 1900). As has been expounded on numerous occasions, Oedipus was Freud's identification figure *par excellence*. Another such figure was the (Semitic) hero Hannibal, whose hatred of Rome he saw in analogy to his own aversion against the Catholic Church with its seat in Rome. In his essay *Zeitgemäßes über Krieg und Tod* (Thoughts for the Times on War and Death, 1915) Freud supported his rejection of the Christian view of an afterlife with Achilles' words from the *Odyssey*, according to which he would rather be a day labourer on earth than a Prince of Shadows. A passionate collector of archaeological objects, Freud admired Heinrich Schliemann and often compared his own work to that of an archaeologist, uncovering layer after layer in the speculative attempt to reconstruct that which has been destroyed. Appropriately, Freud's most extensive literary interpretation is dedicated to Wilhelm J. Jensen's novella Gradiva (1907), of which large parts are set in → POMPEII The close link between → PSY-CHOANALYSIS and Antiquity is further illustrated by the emergence of terms such as 'Electra complex' and 'narcissism'. And the fact that the concept of both a male and female disposition being present in every individual, proposed by Otto Weiniger (1880–1930) in his controversial yet phenomenally successful *Geschlecht und Charakter* (Sex and Character, 1903), specifically extracted by him from the narrative of Aristophanes in Plato's *Symposium*, is yet another example of the pervasiveness of ancient philosophy and literature in Vienna at the turn of the century.

D. LITERATURE

The enthusiastic exploration of ancient → MYTHOLOGY and literature was to a certain degree pre-conditioned by a familiarity with the material many authors had acquired in school: Sigmund Freud, Hugo von Hofmannsthal (1874–1929), Richard Beer-Hofmann (1866–1945), Arthur Schnitzler (1862–1931), Rudolf Kassner (1873–1959), Karl Kraus (1874–1936), Egon Friedell (1878–1938) as well as Stefan Zweig (1881–1942), all graduates of the Humanistic Gymnasium, were the last generation of literary authors committed to and shaped by this educational ideal. While many writers did take account of more recent insights in the study of Antiquity, perception of the subject-matter is often distorted through multiple refractions. Especially Nietzsche's concept of the Dionysian and Freud's psychoanalysis have left considerable marks. Even before Nietzsche's *Geburt der Tragödie aus dem Geiste der Musik* (*The Birth of Tragedy from the Spirit of Music*, 1872), Dionysus was one of those deities providing particular inspiration to poets. In Robert Hamerling's (1830–1889) epic poem *Ahasver in Rom* (1866), for instance, Nero appears as Dionysus. Under the rule of Dionysus as the god of ecstasy, moral norms are suspended – a notion also found in Arthur Schnitzler's one-act play *Das Bacchusfest* ('The Festival of Bacchus', 1915): the poet Felix Staufner invents an ancient festival, which allows unrestrained promiscuity to every man and woman for one night. Upon returning to everyday-life, the night's partners had to suppress their memories and were forbidden to continue their relationship. This fiction only served Schnitzler as a stylish

cloak for his own unfaithfulness and that of his wife. A dark festival dedicated to the goddess Astarte and characterized by an oppressive sexual licentiousness, is created by Richard Beer-Hofmann in the second chapter of his short novel *Der Tod Georgs* (1897/1900); in his descriptions, Beer-Hofmann drew on Lucian's treatise *De Dea Syriaca*, which had been brought to his attention by C.J. Burckhardt.

The most complex appropriation of ancient patterns is found in Hofmannsthal, who wrote an adaptation of Euripides' *Alcestis* (1893) while still attending the Gymnasium. In it, Admetus appears as a king in a fairy tale who promises his subjects a bright future through the death of his wife. He is thus freed from accusations often levelled against him on account of his wife's sacrifice. Egon Wellesz based his libretto for an opera (1923) on Hofmannsthal's version. His very free adaptation of Sophocles' *Electra* was a success on the Berlin stage in 1903. Set to music by Richard Strauss in 1909, it became a part of the standard operatic repertoire. In the stage directions, Hofmannsthal stipulates that *jene antikisierenden Banalitäten, welche mehr geeignet sind, zu ernüchtern als suggestiv zu wirken* ('those faux-antique banalities which are more likely to have a sobering rather than a suggestive effect') be avoided. Elements of the Archaic period, employed to avoid the merest hint of → CLASSICISM, gave a special quality the depiction of hysteria. The influence of Freud was already palpable for literary critics at the time. Ancient myths seemed perfectly suited to convey archetypal themes. Of the *verborgenen schuldigen Fluß-Gott des Blutes* ('hidden, sinful river-god of blood') we read in Rainer Maria Rilke's third *Duineser Elegie*; his *Sonette an Orpheus* and many of his poems speak of a profound immersion in Classical mythology. The striking alterations in Kafka's prose sketches *Prometheus* and *Das Schweigen der Sirenen* are succinct yet impressive manifestations of *Arbeit am Mythos* (Work on Myth, H. Blumenberg). The myth of Demeter forms the substrate of Herman Broch's (1886–1951) *Bergroman* (Mountain Novel). Begun in the 1930s and first published as *Der Versucher* (the Tempter) in 1954, it describes the goings-on in an alpine village at the eve of → NATIONAL SOCIALISM, and the struggle between good and evil chthonic powers. Broch's novel *Der Tod des Vergil* (*The Death of Virgil*, 1945), meanwhile, examines the relationship between the artist and authority: the Emperor Augustus demands from the poet, who senses his approaching death, the work that its creator sees *als erschreckend ungetan* ('as terrifyingly undone') and therefore wants to destroy. A similar motif underlies Christoph Ransmayer's (b. 1945) novel *Die letzte Welt* (1988): Ovid has destroyed his Metamorphoses before leaving Rome; in Tomi, Maximus Cotta does not find the poet, but the characters (e.g., Arachne, Ceys, etc.) from his work. Ransmayer's original intention, following a request from Hans Magnus Enzensberger, to re-tell Ovid's *Metamorphoses*, proved to be an impossibility. The novel, considered to be one of the most outstanding post-modern works in the German language, owes its peculiar tension to its portrayal of the exile's situation (the poet is banished by the authorities on nebulous grounds and, as a character in the novel, eludes all further investigation) and the principle of subjecting the narrative string of transformations itself to one more transformation. The novel's success may also be explained in light of the newly re-awakened interest in mythology in the 1980s. Written in direct opposition to Gustav Schwab, Michael Köhlmeier's (b. 1949) re-narrated mythological tales from Classical Antiquity (*Das große Sagenbuch des klassischen Altertums*, 1999) were a popular feature on Austrian radio. Köhlmeier is also engaged in an effort to fashion from the *Odyssey* a cycle of four novels, but the parts published so far would seem to indicate that the sheer volume of material is bound to exceed the proposed scope of the project. The first two novels, *Telemach* (1995) and *Kalypso* (1997), follow the respective portions of Homer's original, but by introducing pronounced anachronisms not unlike those used by Ransmayr, for instance, they distance themselves from a reconstruction of the archaic world of the myth. In his wholly unchallenged adaptations of Sappho, Archilochus, Catullus and Propertius published under the title *Die Erfindung der Poesie* (1997), Raoul Schrott has attempted to place ancient literature in a contemporary context. Of a different type are the translations by Peter Handke (b. 1942) from Aischylus (*Prometheus gefesselt*, 1986) and of Sophocles' *Oidipus auf Kolonos* (2003): they are rubbing and chafing against their originals. Handke's reflections continually take their departure from Classical literature, invoking Pindar, Lucretius, Homer and especially Virgil. The latter in particular is given canonical status with his *Georgica*, for an appropriation of nature that both preserves the essence of and applies a human measure to the natural world (cf. the novel *Die Wiederholung*, 1986). With his emphatic rejection of Kafka as the antithesis of Virgil, and his allegiance to Homer, Handke could also be provocative: *Kein Jesus soll mehr auftreten, aber immer wieder ein Homer* [4. 7].

1 K. G. Esselborn, Hofmannsthal und der antike Mythos, 1969 2 H. Gottwald, Mythos und Mythisches in der Gegenwartsliteratur. Studien zu Christoph Ransmayr, Peter Handke, Botho Strauß, George Steiner, Patrick Roth und Robert Schneider, 1996 3 R. Hank, Mortifikation und Beschwörung. Zur Veränderung ästhetischer Wahrnehmung in der Moderne am Beispiel des Frühwerkes Richard Beer-Hofmanns, 1984 4 P. Handke, Phantasien der Wiederholung, 1983 5 R. Hanslik, Das österreichische humanistische Gymnasium in seinem Werden und gegenwärtigen Sein, 1951 6 G. A. Höfler (ed.), M. Köhlmeier, 2001 7 W. Jens, Hofmannsthal und die Griechen, 1955 8 R. A. Kann (ed.), Thedor Gomperz. Ein Gelehrtenleben im Bürgertum der Franz-Josefs-Zeit, 1974 9 H. Politzer, Hatte Ödipus einen Ödipus-Komplex? Versuche zum Thema Psychoanalyse und Lit., 1974 10 K. R. Popper, Ausgangspunkte. Meine intellektuelle Entwicklung, 1979 11 M. Rohrwasser (ed.), Freuds pompejanische Muse: Beitr. zu Wilhelm Jensens Novelle 'Gradiva', 1996 12 W.

Schmidt-Dengler, Decadence and Antiquity: The Educational Preconditions of Jung Wien, in: E. Nielsen (ed.), Focus on Vienna 1900, 1982, 32–45 13 R. Scheu (ed.), Was leistet die Mittelschule?, Wien 1893 14 Ch. Zintzen, Von Pompeji nach Troja: Archäologie, Literatur und Öffentlichkeit im 19. Jahrhundert, 1998.

WENDELIN SCHMIDT-DENGLER

Autobiography
A. Introduction B. Middle Ages C. Humanism and Renaissance D. Representational Forms of Modern Autobiography

A. Introduction
Because autobiography is not considered to be a traditional literary genre, it does not follow a normative stylistic model. The *Confessiones* by Augustine are a product of Late Antiquity and therefore never achieved the status of a prescriptive model. The work was rarely imitated directly. Only individual elements (story of conversion, mystical ascent of the soul, meditation on memory) that Augustine himself had adopted from traditional early Christian contexts served as objects of imitation. [3]. The combination of different representational patterns in the *Confessiones* coupled with the lack of a normative model have contributed to the emergence of a multiplicity of autobiographical forms. Various forms such as the self-justification of a public person (Caesar), the biographical portrait (Suetonius, Plutarch), Stoic self-analysis (Seneca, Marcus Aurelius), and the philosophical *consolatio* (Boethius) all offer thematic as well as formal starting points for modern literary self-portrayals. Certain parts of research into autobiography favour a narrow definition of the genre which limits autobiography to the retrospective narration of one's own life [7. 14] but this view fails to do justice to the broad range of variation in representational patterns or to the complex history of their literary influence.

B. Middle Ages
Only a few autobiographies have survived from the period between the 7th and 11th cents. They do not follow Augustine's model but are oriented towards hagiography instead [8. 310–317]. Finally, during the → Renaissance of the 12th cent., an intensified study of the literary and philosophical heritage from Antiquity sparked a new interest in problems surrounding self-portrayal. The autobiographies of the High Middle Ages were written in a culture of increasing inwardness which manifests itself in more and more profound presentations of the sacrament of penance and in innovative, moral-philosophical approaches that place a higher value on freewill decisions than on actions [9]. The tendency to regard sin as subjective characterises the autobiography by the French abbot Guibert de Nogent, who was the first medieval author to consistently follow the model of the *Confessiones* in his *vita* (c. 1115) though he rejected Augustine's balance between

the confession of sins and praise of God in favour of the *confessio peccatorum*, thus moving self-portrayal closer to the act of private confession [17. 185]. Another path was chosen by the early scholastic theologian Peter Abaelard, who took up the ancient tradition of *epistolae consolatoriae* in his *Historia calamitatum mearum* (c. 1132). The consolation letter's form allows him to grant exemplary status to his tale of suffering and to combine it with an apology of his philosophical work. Although for the Middle Ages it presents an unusually complex picture of the personality, this picture is not presented for its own sake. The portrayal of individual life serves to confirm a given type, thus fulfilling a didactic and devotional function [2]. This is also the case with the numerous mystical stories of souls which appear in the 13th and 14th cents., outstanding among them being the autobiography of the Dominican monk Heinrich Seuse (1295–1366). The *vitae* of mystics offer *exempla* of a methodically trained discipline of the soul that aims for a divine, self-transcending experience.

C. HUMANISM AND RENAISSANCE

In the autobiographies of the Renaissance period, the individual becomes increasingly detached from religiously sanctioned models of interpretation. While Dante again raises the question whether it is morally appropriate to speak about oneself in the 1st treatise of the *Convivio*, thus once again subordinating self-portrayal to the purpose of edifying exhortation, the autobiographers of the 14th to the 16th cents. grant the individual its own worth [4; 16]. A sophisticated representation of personality becomes possible because the humanistic turn to the ancient culture of Antiquity-beyond the models of Augustine and Boethius quoted in Dante-opens up a diversity of representational patterns. Thus Petrarch uses the form of Cicero's → DIALOGUE in his *Secretum*. Enea Silvio Piccolomini follows ancient accounts of deeds in his *Commentarii*. Girolamo Cardano refers to Marcus Aurelius' example in his autobiography. Montaigne's essayist style orients itself towards the informal reflections in Seneca's letters and in the *Moralia* by Plutarch. The emancipation from religious methods of conveying meaning begins with Petrarch [13]: The *Secretum* (= *De secreto conflictu curarum mearum*, 1342) dramatises the process of self-analysis in the form of a dialogue between the autobiographer and the Church Father Augustine, who appears as the symbolic representation of Christian autobiography but fails to convince his dialogue partner to renounce all worldly goods. Conversion does not take place–the autobiographer deliberately remains caught in the inner conflict of his earthly existence. A secular perspective is even more apparent in the *Epistola ad posteritatem* (c. 1370) [6], where Petrarch offers a portrayal of an ideal humanist life, falling back on Suetonius' biographical structure. A similar tendency towards self-glorification aimed at securing future fame is prevalent in the *Vita* (1558–66) by the sculptor Benvenuto Cellini, although the latter does not center his life story around learning and erudition but on the artistic *ingenium* and on *virtù* as opposed to *fortuna*. Cellini's naïve self-glorification clearly stands in contrast to Petrarch's reflective attitude. It forms an even stronger contrast to the sceptical image of humanity that lies at the basis of Cardano's *De vita propria* (1575–76) and of Montaigne's *Essais* (published in 1580–95). The latter both take into account the finality of human existence by avoiding any form of idealisation. The narrative creation of a coherent image of life is abandoned; instead, these self-portrayals are organised according to topics, emphasising the idea that the self is incongruous [1. 113–126, 316–319].

D. REPRESENTATIONAL FORMS OF MODERN AUTOBIOGRAPHY

In the 17th and early 18th cents., secular self-portrayals lost status vis-à-vis religious autobiographies. The Puritan movement in England as well as German Pietism supported a culture of introspection, again referring to the example of the *Confessiones*. However, the followers of Augustine differ in their approaches: While the Spanish mystic Teresa de Jesus combines a retrospective narrative with meditative self-analysis in her *Libro de su Vida* (1562–65), the Protestant autobiographers (John Bunyan, George Fox, August Hermann Francke) emphasise the aspect of conversion, with the result that the narrative component becomes predominant in autobiography. Other factors that contribute to the success of retrospective autobiography toward the end of the 18th cent. are the secularisation of the Protestant story of the soul (Adam Bernd, Karl Philipp Moritz) [11. 62–75], the dominance of empiricist psychology in Enlightenment thinking which regards human memory as essential in personal identity, and the development of new representational forms in the genre of the novel [10]. In J.-J. Rousseau's *Les Confessions* (published in 1782–89), all of these threads are joined together. Rousseau, who in the title of his self-portrayal directly refers to the work of his ancient precursor, reverses Augustine's schema: His 'conversion experience' (the moment of inspiration at the gates of Vincennes described in the 8th book) does not reflect God's merciful intervention but instead the individual's disastrous entry into an alienated way of life within society; his childhood does not illustrate the weakness of the human being marked by original sin but is appreciated for the first time as an independent part of life that shapes his personality. In contraposition to the *Confessiones*, Rousseau's autobiography dramatises the liberation of the autonomous subject which adopts the divine attributes set forth by Augustine [5]. This new personality model is then enriched further by the dimension of external history in J.W.v.Goethe's autobiography *Dichtung und Wahrheit* (published in 1811–33): For Goethe, the purpose of autobiography lies in providing insights about how personality develops through the interaction between individual disposition and historical circumstances [15].

Rousseau and Goethe bestow a level of authority to this type of retrospectively narrated life story that remained uncontested all through the abundance of autobiographical literature of the 19th cent. (F.R. de Chateaubriand, Stendhal, J.S. Mill, J. Ruskin, Th. Fontane). While this style is still widely used in the 20th cent., it comes under increasing pressure from the more advanced representatives of literary modernism [12; 14]: The narrative recall of past life events is exposed as a mystification (A. Gide, J.-P. Sartre), resolution is replaced by fragmentary self-portraits that take up essayist traditions (M. Leiris); comprehensive memory is replaced by the decipherment of traces and documents (W. Benjamin); the ethos of sincerity gives way to a playful treatment of writing conventions (G. Stein, V. Nabokov) and to a deliberate blurring of the boundary between truth and fiction (A. Robbe-Grillet). A characteristic feature of 20th cent. autobiographical literature is a new diversity of representational forms.

→ Autobiography; → Biography; → Consolatio as a literary genre
→ BIOGRAPHY

1 M. BEAUJOUR, Miroirs d'encre. Rhétorique de l'autoportrait, 1980 2 E. BIRGE VITZ, Type et individu dans l'autobiographie médiévale, in: Poétique 6, 1975, 426–445 3 P. COURCELLE, Les Confessions de saint Augustin dans la tradition littéraire, 1963 4 M. GUGLIELMINETTI, Memoria e scrittura. L'autobiografia da Dante a Cellini, 1977 5 H. R. JAUSS, Gottesprädikate als Identitätsvorgaben in der Augustinischen Tradition der Autobiographie, in: O. MARQUARD, K. STIERLE (eds.), Identität, 1979, 708–717 6 E. KESSLER, Antike Tradition, historische Erfahrung und philosophische Reflexion in Petrarcas Brief an die Nachwelt, in: A. BUCK (ed.), Biographie und Autobiographie in der Renaissance, 1983, 21–34 7 PH. LEJEUNE, Le pacte autobiographique, 1975 8 G. MISCH, Geschichte der Autobiographie, II. ii, 1955 9 C. MORRIS, The Discovery of the Individual 1050–1200, 1972 10 K.-D. MÜLLER, Autobiographie und Roman. Studien zur literarischen Autobiographie der Goethezeit, 1976 11 G. NIGGL, Geschichte der deutschen Autobiographie im 18. Jahrhundert, 1977 12 H. R. PICARD, Autobiographie im zeitgenössischen Frankreich, 1978 13 T. C. PRICE ZIMMERMANN, Bekenntnis und Autobiographie in der frühen Renaissance, in: G. NIGGL (ed.), Die Autobiographie, 1989, 343–366 14 M. SCHNEIDER, Die erkaltete Herzensschrift. Der autobiographische Text im 20. Jahrhundert, 1986 15 E. SEITZ, Talent und Geschichte. Goethe in seiner Autobiographie, 1996 16 CH. WEIAND, 'Libri di famiglia' und Autobiographie in Italien zwischen Tre- und Cinquecento. Studien zur Entwicklung des Schreibens über sich selbst, 1993 17 M. ZINK, La subjectivité littéraire. Autour du siècle de saint Louis, 1985

ADDITIONAL BIBLIOGRAPHY: M. MOOG-GRÜNEWALD (ed.), Autobiographisches Schreiben und philosophische Selbstsorge, 2004; CHR. MOSER, Buchgestützte Subjektivität. Literarische Formen der Selbstsorge und der Selbsthermeneutik von Platon bis Montaigne, 2006.

CHRISTIAN MOSER

Automata see→ TECHNOLOGY, HISTORY OF

B

Baalbek

A. Introduction B. Research and
Excavation History C. The Significance of
the Excavations in Scientific and Political
Context D. Aspects of Conservation

A. Introduction

Baalbek, located in the fertile Beqaa plain northeast
of Beirut, has been the site of an indigenous Baal cult
since ancient times. The foundation of the Roman vet-
eran colony presumably began in AD 16 with the
construction of the sanctuary, whose monumental
construction lasted until the 3rd cent. AD. The old cult
remained alive among the population of the new colony. The sanctuary continued to be used even when
transformed by new cults in the Christian and Byzantine periods. In the 12th cent., the Ayyubids turned it
into a citadel. From this time on, the resident population has called the cult site Qalaa. The well-preserved
monumental buildings, of which the temple of Jupiter
Heliopolitanus is the largest known sacred building of
the Roman world, have made Baalbek a much visited
attraction and place of commemoration. To mark the
100th anniversary of the visit by the German imperial
couple, Wilhelm II and his wife Auguste Victoria, to
Baalbek on 10 November 1898, the newly built
museum in the passages of the lower floor of the altar
court and the south tower of the citadel was opened on
7 November 1998 [6].

B. Research and Excavation History

As early as in the post-Classical period the Roman
ruins of Baalbek received significant attention. The
earliest known written testimonies come from Arab historiographers and geographers of the 10th–14th cents.
Their writings lauded the beauty and monumentality of
the buildings and their decoration. Without considering
the historical context, the monuments were praised as
very ancient buildings. The historiographer Dimashki,
who was born in 1256 in Damascus, even believed that
the sanctuaries originated in the period of Abraham,
Moses and Solomon [1]. Starting in the early 16th cent.,
European travellers visited Baalbek with increasing frequency. One of the first Europeans known by name was
the knight Martin Baumgarten, who visited the site on
13 January 1508 [6]. In December 1647 Balthazar de
Monconys came to Baalbek and drew the first views of
the sacred buildings and the defences [9]. The first scientific documentation of the ruins of Baalbek came
from R. Wood, who together with his colleague J.
Dawkins produced detailed drawings of the buildings
in 1751 [16]. In the early 18th cent., L. de Laborde,
W.H. Bartlett and especially D. Roberts Veduten also
drew the buildings of Baalbek [11]. However, the scientific aspect was less important than the nostalgia
evoked by the ruins. Beginning in the mid–19th cent.,
the monuments became a focus of archaeological examinations, with attention concentrating on the architectural aspects. F. de Saulcy made significant discoveries during his stay in Baalbek in March 1851 [13]. He
was the first to recognize the large church building in
the sanctuary's altar court and was able to identify it
with the Theodosian basilica mentioned in the *Chro-
nikon paschale* (1,561). He assigned the monumental
podium wall of the Jupiter temple to the predecessor
building. He also examined the city wall and the north
slope of Sheik Abdallah, which was formerly the site of
a temple dedicated to Mercury. The visit of the German
emperor Wilhelm II in Baalbek on 10/11 November
1898 initiated a new phase of scientific study of the
town. The ruler was so impressed by the ruins that he
had an extensive and systematic excavation of the
buildings carried out. Sultan Abdul-Hamid II granted
permission for the project on 18 November. From 27
December 1898 to 16 January 1899 the architects R.
Koldewey and W. Andrae conducted preliminary investigations in Baalbek. As a precondition for excavating
the site, the land needed to be acquired first. The excavations began in September 1900 under the direction of
O. Puchstein with cooperation from B. Schulz and D.
Krencker. In four years, 150 workers using a field railway freed the buildings from the debris, which was several meters thick in some locations. Investigations were
initially limited to the Jupiter temple, but also the so-
called Bacchus temple, the 'Venus temple', as well as the
later Christian and Muslim architectural insertions and
conversions were recorded. The results were scientifically documented in maps, plans, sections, reconstructions and numerous photographs. Complementary surveys for the study of the site's Roman period were also
conducted. The buildings examined included the town
wall with its gates, the water supply system, the necropolises outside the town and the quarries. Twice during
the excavation campaigns in Baalbek, comparative
studies on temples in Syria and Lebanon were carried
out with the results being published in a separate monograph [8].

World War I interrupted the research until 1917
when work in Baalbek resumed under Th. Wiegand and
K. Wulzinger, who finally published the excavation
results [15]. From 1930 to 1935 French archaeologists
worked in the altar court of the Jupiter sanctuary. In
1933 P. Collart and P. Coupel completely removed the
ruins of the Theodosian basilica in order to uncover and
partially reconstruct the two altars [5]. In 1938 D.
Schlumberger discovered the monumental stairway
leading to the temple of Mercury on the north slope of
Sheik Abdallah, which presumably also functioned as a
procession route in Antiquity [14]. During the excavations of 1961/62, remains of a significantly older settlement mound were found in the area of the 'small altar'
in the court of the Jupiter sanctuary. In the Sueidiye

Fig. 1: Steps of the Jupiter Temple with foundations of the western apse of the Christian basilica

Fig. 2: Bustan al-Khan, building with a twelve-column portico, view from the north

Fig. 3: Citadel, south tower and remains of the dismantled wall on the southern side of the steps to the 'Temple of Bacchus'

quarter of the city Lebanese archaeologists excavated a Roman villa where polychrome floor mosaics were uncovered [2]. The most famous mosaic, a representation of the 'Seven Sages' found in the house of Patricius, is

now located in Beirut (National Museum). The Lebanese Antiquities Service conducted important excavations in an area south of Qalaa called Bustan al-Khan, which presumably was located outside the gates of Roman Baalbek [7].

This work, begun in 1967 and disrupted in 1975 by the civil war, resulted in the unearthing of monumental buildings. The assembly includes a building with a twelve-column portico, probably a profane representational building, a semi-circular stage-like facility (perhaps a council house or bouleuterion), the ruins of several residential buildings and a colonnaded street. The whole area remained in use until the Umayyad period. In the modern period the central court in front of the porticos was used as a khan (inn) for caravans, which is why the area is now called Bostan al-Khan, the Garden of the Khan.

C. The Significance of the Excavations in Scientific and Political Context

The German excavations provided a first scientific assessment of the Baalbek monuments from the Imperial to the medieval period. The objective of the work was a comprehensive documentation of the architectural state of the ruins. This publication remains the foundation of all architectural research on Baalbek. To be sure, the authors did not limit themselves to a systematic inventory of the buildings but also carried out a typological and stylistic examination of the structural and decoration types. Based on this method, a relative chronology of the buildings was established for the first time, according to which the temple of Jupiter was under construction in the 1st cent. AD, the altar court and the 'Bacchus temple' were completed in the 2nd cent. AD, the hexagonal court and the propylees in the 3rd cent. AD. The Christian basilica of the 4th cent. AD and the conversion of the sanctuary as a citadel in the Ayyubid period (12th cent.) constitute some of the later insertions. The research also contributed fundamental insights regarding the construction of a local sanctuary during the Roman period in the East. Elements, such as the temple with the inner sanctuary (*adyton*), the various precincts with their enclosures, the lustration pools and the altars are common cultic facilities that had specific functions in the performance of local rites. The later inserts of the Christian and Islamic periods attest to the continual use and functional transformation of the cult site. The studies also supplied important information on the ancient settlement and its environs. From the remains of the ancient and medieval town wall, the rhombic layout and 70 hectar area of Roman Baalbek were reconstructed. Study of the ancient water lines provided information on the town's water supply system. A survey conducted in the two ancient quarries located outside of Baalbek yielded new insights on quarrying technology as well as the transportation and setting of the stones during construction.

The German excavations in Baalbek became possible because of a change of German and Ottoman for-

Fig. 4: The 'Temple of Bacchus'

Fig. 5: Restored commemorative tablet in the cella
of the 'Temple of Bacchus'

eign policy and, therefore, are themselves an event in cultural politics. After his ascent to the throne the emperor Wilhelm II forcefully pursued contact with the Ottomans and engaged in friendly relationships especially with Sultan Abdul Hamid II. A memorial plaque that was set up on the occasion of the German imperial couple's visit to Baalbek on 10 November 1898 in the cella of the 'Bacchus temple' attests to this relationship. The text emphasizes the 'permanent mutual friendship' of the two rulers. Wilhelm II took a particular liking to the 'Bacchus temple', because it was completed under the rule of the emperor Antoninus Pius, whom Wilhelm II idealized as the Roman ruler to be a model for the German empire; and thus the decision was made to place the plaque into this sacred building. After World War I the English General Allenby ordered the plaque removed from the temple and the names and titles of the imperial couple erased. The plaque was nevertheless kept by the then owner of the Hotel Palmyra, M. Alouf, where it was found in the early 1970s by the German ambassador H.C. Lankes, who had the names restored and the plaque returned to its original site [12].

D. ASPECTS OF CONSERVATION

The German excavators carried out a series of measures to consolidate the monuments of Baalbek. They developed a concept for scrupulous conservation. Securing and supplementing work was only performed on buildings with a sufficient original construction substance. Supplementation should not imitate the original but should be marked as repairs. The original building substance was to be changed as little as possible so that the buildings' value as historical evidence was not diminished. One of the most important measures required was lifting the keystone of the door lintel above the portal of the 'Bacchus temple' into its original position because it threatened to collapse. During the French mandate in Lebanon, extensive restoration work was undertaken on the 'Bacchus temple' [10]. A tower from the Arabic period that stood on four columns over the temple's southeast corner was removed. Starting in 1934 all nine columns and the beams resting on them on the north side of the temple were returned to their original positions and consolidated. Using brackets and concrete, the subsequently reworked frieze and beam blocks were realigned. In 1935 the final clean-up work was performed in the temple's interior. Just before WW II the Ayyubid wall immediately in front of the temple was removed to permit an unencumbered view of the facade. A controversial decision that cannot be justified by the standards of modern conservation was the removal of the Christian basilica in the altar court, which was ordered by P. Collart and P. Coupel [5]. This measure was carried out to excavate and partially reconstruct the two altars [3; 4] but it would not have been necessary to demolish the west apse, with its two smaller apses, above the open staircase to the Jupiter temple, especially because it would not have impaired the work on the altars. This struc-

ture, which had been erected over the pagan sanctuary's central site of worship, was considered first rate historical evidence for the old site's continued use even though conversions and insertions for the new Christian cult resulted in an altered appearance. Since 1991 the Lebanese Antiquities Service has been concerned with an intensive consolidation of the buildings in Baalbek.
→ Baalbek

SOURCES: 1 G. LE STRANGE, Palestine Under the Moslems, London 1890 (Repr. 1965) (texts and translations)

LITERATURE: 2 M. CHEHAB, Mosaïques du Liban, in: Bull. du Mus. de Beyrouth 14, 1958, 29–52 3 P. COLLART, P. COUPEL, L'autel monumental de Baalbek, 1951 4 Id., Le petit autel de Baalbek, 1977 5 P. COUPEL, Travaux de restauration à Baalbek en 1933 et 1934, in: Syria 17, 1936, 321–334 6 M. VAN ESS (ed.), Heliopolis. Baalbek. 1898–1998. Forschen in Ruinen, 1998 7 H. KALAYAN, Les fouilles de Bostan – El Khan, in: Histoire et archéologie. Les dossiers 12, 1975, 31–35 8 D. KRENCKER, W. ZSCHIETZSCHMANN, Römische Tempel in Syrien, 1938 9 MONSIEUR DE MONCONYS, Journal des voyages de Monconys, conseiller du roi en ses conseils d'état, Paris 1665 10 F. RAGETTE, Baalbek, 1980 11 D. ROBERTS, The Holy Land II, London 1843 12 H. SADER, T. SCHEFFLER, A. NEUWIRTH, Baalbek: Image and Monument 1898–1998, 1998 13 F. C. DE SAULCY, Voyage autour de la Mer Morte II, Paris 1853 14 D. SCHLUMBERGER, Le temple de Mercure à B.-Héliopolis, in: Bull. du Mus. de Beyrouth 3, 1939, 25–36 15 TH. WIEGAND (ed.), Baalbek Ergebnisse der Ausgrabungen und Untersuchungen in den Jahren 1898–1905 I–III, 1921–1925 16 R. WOOD, The Ruins of Balbec, otherwise Heliopolis in Coelosyria, London 1757.

ADDITIONAL BIBLIOGRAPHY: N. JIDEJIAN, Baalbek: Heliopolis, City of the Sun, 1975

KLAUS STEFAN FREYBERGER

Babylon
A. PRELIMINARY NOTE B. INTRODUCTION C. GEOGRAPHY AND HISTORY OF RESEARCH D. MONUMENTS AS SYMBOL E. BABYLON AS ARGUMENT

A. PRELIMINARY NOTE
The name Babylon (B.) can refer to both the city and the country of the same name. Ancient Assyria can also be included under the latter. It is not always possible to distinguish between these meanings.

B. INTRODUCTION
In the first centuries AD, the ancient city of B. increasingly lost significance. Although the evidence of the Tabula Peutingeriana (3rd cent.) indicates it was still part of ancient travel routes (see map TAVO B S 1.2), Classical, Talmudic and Arabic sources record its decline [1. 136–145; 2. 44–60]. The available references to B. in the sources of subsequent centuries refer, on one hand, to the size of the city and country in the distant past, and on the other, consist of efforts to describe and locate the exact geographical position of the ruins of the present. Above all, two text categories form the funda-

mental points of reference for reception until the end of the 19th cent.: Biblical tales, of which the Tower of Babel and confusion of tongues (Gen. 11: 1–9), the visions of Daniel, and the Apocalypse of John are of particular importance, and descriptions of the city and Tower by ancient authors (Hdt. 1,178–187; Diod. Sic. 2,7–10; Str. 16,1,5–7; Curt. 5,1,24–35; Arr. Anab. 7,17). There are also numerous other links: Ninus, Nimrod, Semiramis, Nitocris, Belsazar, Nebuchadnezzar, Alexander, Susannah.

C. GEOGRAPHY AND HISTORY OF RESEARCH
Besides the ruins of B., Talmudic sources speak of 'Nebuchadnezzar's House' (remains of the palace?) and the 'bridge of B.' The location of the tower described by the rabbis as the 'House of Nimrod' in Borsippa and the equation of this location with B. already indicate a very early impression of a formerly enormous city. A small Jewish community also appears to have settled in the ruins [2. 59f., 103]. Early Arabic sources also mention a small village Bābil in addition to a district (ṭassūj). They record visits to the Den (ǧubb) of Daniel by Jewish and Christian pilgrims. The image of the ruins remains vague. The identification of the antiquities shows the influence of the Jewish Diaspora (Tower: Birs Nimrūd; Bridge: Jisr Bābil [2. 59 n. 41; 1. 23f., 83, 132ff.], see map TAVO B S 2). This is also still evident in the first Western European description by Rabbi Benjamin of Tudela (1178). The growing significance of the preserved ruins of ancient B. in occidental awareness is shown by notations in medieval maps of the world [33. 58, 126f.; 18. 56] as well as the mention of the Tower and city in fictitious or compiled travel reports by William of Boldensele (1336), Jean de Mandeville, and Hans Schiltberger (1475). At the end of the 16th cent., a new identification of the Tower with the ruins of ʿAqar Qūf, as opposed to Birs Nimrūd, was suggested (Leonhard Rauwulf), which found numerous adherents (Gasparo Balbi, John Eldred, Anthony Sherley, Thomas Herbert, Jean-Baptiste Tavernier, Jean Otter), but also opponents (Vincenzo Maria di Santa Caterina di Siena, Carsten Niebuhr, Domenico Sestini, Joseph de Beauchamp). However, the location of the city of B. by Pietro della Valle (beginning 17th cent.) at the site of the Arab village Bābil became generally accepted. Not much later, Johannes Kepler attempted to determine the precise geographical latitude of B. in the Tabulae Rudolphinae, using information from Ptolemy's Almagest [8. 504f.]. Claudius James Rich conducted the first systematic land survey, connected with an excavation and description of the ruin mounds in 1811. Further excavations were carried out in 1827 by Robert Mignan, and in 1850 by Austen Henry Layard. From 1852, a French expedition under Fulgence Fresnel worked in B. Meanwhile, the thesis equating Birs Nimrūd with the Tower of B. gained broad acceptance. Supported by the report of Herodotus, Julius Oppert developed in 1853 the idea of a 'Greater B.', which included Borsippa. Between 1899 and 1917, the territory of the ancient city was

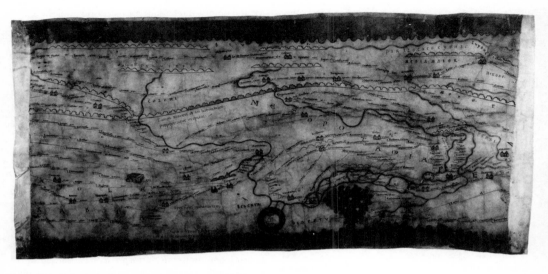

Fig. 1:Tabula Peutingeriana.
Austrian National Library, picture archives, Vienna: Cod. 324. Segm X

systematically excavated by Robert Koldewey [15; 28; 38; 43; 50. 182–184, 195–200].

D. Monuments as Symbol
1. The Tower of Babel 2. The Hanging Gardens and the Walls of Babylon

1. The Tower of Babel

In both the early Jewish-Hellenistic and the rabbinic traditions, the story of the building of the tower in Gen. 11:1–9 was broadly commented on and paraphrased. The theme of the building of the city, which dominates the original Biblical text, was suppressed in favour of numerous thematic enhancements. Among these are the destruction of the Tower and Nimrod as the first king, tyrant, and builder (Ios. Ant. Iud. 1,109–121), with Abraham set next to him as a contrasting figure of the 'just man' (Antiquitates Biblicae 6f.). The story of the Tower became interpreted and instrumentalized in a variety of ways. The Hellenized Diaspora connected it with the battles of the Titans in Greek myth as an outstanding event of early human history, and thus connected their own past to that of the ancient world (SamAn, OrSib 3). Philo interprets the event allegorically and documents the interest in the theme of the 'confusion of tongues' (*De confusione linguarum*). Early Christianity adopted the Jewish tradition and provided it with new patterns of interpretation. These allowed both a positive interpretation (tower as a symbol of the monolithic unity of the early Church, Shepherd of Hermas) and a negative (Church as an antitypical *turris corporis Christi*, Ephraim the Syrian *De nativitate* 1,44). Starting with the close of the 2nd cent., a moralizing point of view became more common. The building of the Tower and *superbia* were noticeably closely interwoven (Iren. Demonstratio 23; Tert. ad Prax. 16). At the same time, the story of the Tower was defended as historical with respect to the heathen world. From the 4th cent., the text was connected with the Pentecost miracle Acts 2, and the harmony of the Christian community was contrasted with the building of the tower, which was seen as wicked. This interpretation grew stronger through the equation by the Talmudic rabbis of the Tower with the ruins of a ziggurat. While the Septuagint and Old Latin Bible are silent about the location of the building of the Tower in B., it was authoritatively introduced by the Vulgate, through which the interpretation of B. as a godless realm given in Rev. 17 also was reinforced in connection with the Tower, and this ultimately became a *turris superbiae* (Jer. in Zech. 1,5,99.11). This point of view remained alive through the Middle Ages and into the 19th cent. (e.g. Isidore of Seville, Bede, Alcuin, Rabanus Maurus, Rupert of Deutz, Albertus Magnus, M. Luther, H. Zwingli, J. Calvin, K. Barth) [9 II/1. 446ff., 476ff., 488ff., 514ff.; II/2 647ff., 718, 807ff.; III/1 1062ff., 1081ff., 1113ff.; 10. 119–144; 50. 255–273]. Supported by the theses of Gerhard von Rad, modern exegesis sees the story of the building of the Tower as the highpoint of a Yahwist hamartiology, later expanded by the concept of human hubris [50. 273–290].

Not only the Christian, but also the Muslim tradition was strongly influenced by early Jewish ideas. The Koran takes up the story of the city, but does not name B. (Sura 16,28f.). The confusion of tongues and human hubris determine the point of view. Nimrod appears as a builder, the Tower itself as the first building after the Flood. A unique interpretation suggests the Tower as the 'palace of Nebuchadnezzar' [1. 138–141]. To a large extent, the Middle Ages and modern era fall back on ideas developed in Antiquity and shape them further. Thus, the Tower of Nimrod appears in the

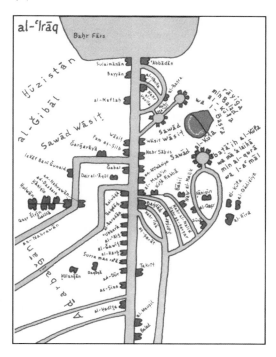

Fig. 2: Babylon as shown on the map of Ibn Haugal (late 10th cent.)
TAVO B S 2 Die Karten des Ibn Hauqual..., Gaube/Volle, 1982 © Dr. Ludwig Reichert Verlag Wiesbaden

'princes' mirrors' [9 II/2. 706ff.] as a negative type, which is also suitable for characterizing a papacy which both Petrarch [9 III/1. 959ff.] and Zwingli [9 III/1. 1081] considered despicable. On the other hand, the Counter-Reformation was able to brand heretical reformers with this image [9 III/2. 1266]. Rationalism and the Enlightenment emphasized the positive features of the king, who thus rose to be the first Grand Master of the Freemasons [9 III/2. 1404].

The pictorial representation of the Tower of B. has been extensively documented since the High Middle Ages. The wrath of God, overweening human pride, and the destruction of the Tower remained the predominant themes into the 15th cent. After that an 'archaeological-historical' point of view began to displace the 'moral-theological' one. The reports of ancient authors, above all Herodotus, became important foundations for reconstruction. In the 16th and 17th cents., the Tower was positively interpreted as an expression of human creativity and the beginning of architectural history. Stonemasons and bricklayers looked back on the Tower as the beginning and supreme achievement of their guild. Divine intervention was rationalized as the limit of human possibilities prescribed by natural law. At the same time, with the strengthening of national identity and the positive revaluation of national languages, the multitude of languages and, thus, the building of the Tower, were positively connoted [52]. For

example, Franciscus Irenicus (1518) says that the reason for the high status of the German language is that it goes back to Nimrod, whose grandson Trebeta brought it from B to Trier [45. 305]. Its representation reached a high point in Dutch art between 1550 and 1650 (J. and P. Brueghel the Elder, H. and M. van Cleve, L. van Valckenborch, T. Verhaecht). The interpretation of this phenomenon as an expression of Calvinist criticism of the Roman Catholic demands of the Spanish crown in the context of the Netherlands' struggle for freedom (1568–1648) [53; 18. 63–65] did not remain unchallenged [52]. Beginning in the 17th cent., the Tower entered the language of contemporary architecture as the epitome of human and divine wisdom (Trinity Church in Copenhagen by J. Scheffel 1637–1656; lanterns of Sant'Ivo alla Sapienza in Rome by F. Borromini 1642ff.). At the same time, there was a growing effort to represent both the Tower and other buildings in B. as components of a well-designed city layout which could be reconstructed in reality, with some contemporary colour added. A first high point in this development is found in the engravings of Coenrat Decker in the work *Turris Babel* by Athanasius Kircher (1679, Fig. 1), and a bit later in those of Johann Andreas Pfeffel in the work *Physika Sacra* by Johann Jakob Scheuchzer (1731). New accents were set by Johann Bernhard Fischer von Erlach's *Entwurf zu einer historischen Architektur* (1721–1723) (Design for an historical architecture). The Tower appears as part of a giant city, which appears to be a Versailles of early history [18. 60f., 67f.; 48. 503f.]. This development led to the first scientific, reconstruction attempts in the 19th cent., which represent a component of a lively discussion up into the present [43. 25–46; 6].

The Tower is present in the literature (A. Austin, *Tower of Babel*, 1874; P. Emmanuel, *Babel*, 1952), operas, and oratorios of the 19th and 20th cents. (C. Franck, *La Tour de Babel*, 1865; A. Rubinstein, *Der Turm zu Babel*, 1858/72; R. Barbier, *La tour de Babel*, 1932; I. Stravinsky, *Babel*, 1944/52). At the beginning of the 20th cent., the Tower became part of an ever more complex metaphorical symbolism, characterized by secularization and plurality. It was able to include both the fascinating possibilities of human creativity and the threat of an extravagant civilization. The Tower stood for human progress (A. Rodin's uncompleted design for a Monument du travail 1898), the fascinating possibilities of a new political order (V. Tatlin's design for a monument to the 3rd International 1919/20), as a pacifist signal for the reunification of a splintered humanity (S. Zweig's short text *Der Turm von Babel*, 1916), or as an image of biting social criticism, a symbol of discord, and sign of a political-ideological antagonism up until the most recent past [47. 49f., 126, 143, 144ff., 171ff.]. In the visual arts, it appears as part of a nuclear reactor by Pierre Brauchli (1979); as a structure in an urban metropolis by Jules C. van Paemel (1931), Hans Escher (1960), and Dominique Appia (1978); as a symbol for the history of humanity and its conflicts by Maurits Cornelis Escher (1928) and Cobi Reiser (1967). It serves as a stimulus and starting point for modern architectural fantasies and highrise architecture (L. Mies van der Rohe, H. Scharoun, O. Schubert, O. Kohtz, R. Tschammer, H. Ferris, Le Corbusier, H. Poelzig, A. Loos, F.A. Breuhaus de Groot), as a medium of political satire, as an artifact in the film industry (*Metropolis* by F. Lang, *The New Babylon* by G. Kosinzev and L. Trauberg, *The Bible* by J. Huston), or as a curiosity in contemporary amusement parks up to a lucrative brand-name product [33. 95f., 99f, 103, 254f., 259, 265, 269f., 273f., 275f.; 47; 49; 18. 70–89].

2. The Hanging Gardens and the Walls of Babylon

Since the earliest lists of the wonders of the world (→ Wonders of the world) in the Hellenistic era, the walls and the Hanging Gardens of B. have, for the most part, been part of those lists, only rarely being replaced by other *miracula*. To be sure, other structures in B. can also appear in addition to them, such as the obelisk of Semiramis (Diod. Sic. 2,11,5) or the bridge of B. (Curt. 5,1,24ff.). Ever since their description in Diod. Sic. 2,7,2ff., which goes back to Ctesias, the mighty walls of B. have been connected with Semiramis. The ancient lists were handed on through Late Antiquity to medieval authors (Nicetas of Heraclea, 11th cent.; Eustathius of Thessalonica, 12th cent.; the anonymus author of the Codex Ambrosianus gr. 886 fol. 180v, 13th cent.; Giorgio Sanguinato, about 1450). In this way the number of 'showpieces' were able to be extended to 30 (Codex Vaticanus gr. 989 fol. 144r, about 1300). The Renaissance led a return to the canonical number seven, and to an especial popularity of the ancient wonders of the world: Angelo Ambrogini vulgo Politianus (end of the 15th cent.), Hadrianus Iunius (about 1550). At the same time, they were also represented pictorially and interpreted contemporaneously: Maarten van Heemskerck (1572), Crispijn de Passe the Elder (1614). Only since this period have the Hanging Gardens also been connected with Semiramis [12. 9–20, 35–57, 92–117].

E. Babylon as Argument
1. General 2. Apocalyptic and Eschatological Concepts 3. World Empires and Ages of the World 4. Babel-Bible Controversy and Panbabylonism

1. General

For both the Islamic and the western worlds, the symbolic use of B. independent of theological interpretation is noticeable quite early on. Mandaean incantations repeatedly mention B. and a king of B. [13]. Tales of Sanherib ('King of Babylon'), Nebuchadnezzar, Daniel, and Belsazar found their way into Islamic legends of the prophets (*qiṣaṣ al-anbiyāʾ*) [25]. The only mention in the Koran (Sura 2,101f.) connects B. with the fallen angels Hārūt and Mārūt and depicts the location as an eerie, gloomy place, just as it is encountered

elsewhere in the early Islamic tradition [1. 187ff.]. A Shiite tradition has the ground of B. cursed [2. 59 n. 40]. At the same time, a positive connotation for B. can be perceived, which might go back to Persian sources. There, B. appeared as one of the seven great kingdoms of the world (*kišwar-iqlīm*), which exhibited both ideal climatic and cultural characteristics and whose borders were thought at times to extend to China. This idea was ultimately adopted by the Abbasids for their ruling ideology [1. 116–127].

Already in Late Antiquity, the capital of the Sassanids, Ctesiphon, was equated not only with ancient Susa (Lib. Or. 12,100; Ep. 331,2; Or. 18,243), but also with B. (Lib. Ep. 513, 2; 1452, 1; Or. 18,2,124; 1,136; 24,37); so also for the twin city Koch (Veh-Ardashir)-Ctesiphon (Lib. Or. 18,244). This tradition continued in the Middle Ages, where B. was used as a synonym for Baghdad (William of Boldensele, Hans Schiltberger [50. 195–197], Ludovico de Varthema [3.190]) or, in a fabulous context, even appears as a part of the Kingdom of Prester John ('Babilonem desertam iuxta turrim Babel' [4. 910:12]). The fantastic notion of a distant city of the Orient, mixed with realistic geographical knowledge (B. in Cairo), found its way into the *Spielmannsepik*, where Ymelot of Desert-Babylonia appears as the opponent of the western heroes in König Rother [11. 288–290]. In early modern magic, B. appears as an enticing place of enchantment, where three wells stand, from which flow poison, 'milk und red blood' [7]. Baroque theatre, musical drama, and oratorio put a Babylonian scenario on the stage with Calderón's *La cena del rey Baltasar* (1632), Metastasios' *Semiramide* (1729), and Händel's *Belshazzar* (1745). With the expansion of the geographic and historical horizon, as well as a generally emerging fascination with the Orient beginning in the early 18th cent., B. also becomes the projected image of Enlightenment social criticism. Voltaire's *Zadig* presents a contemporary Paris in B. (1747). In the tragedy *Sémiramis*, Ninus appears alongside the queen (1748), while Belus and Nimrod are characters in *La Princesse de Babylone* (1768). In addition, the young Goethe left behind a Belshazzar fragment (1767), and with Lord Byron, emotional Romanticism made use of the subject. In the *Hebrew Melodies* (1815), the Babylonian captivity of the Jews becomes a political allegory directed against exile and foreign domination (*On Jordan's Banks, To Belshazar, Vision of Belshazar*). Similar themes are found in Heinrich Heine's *Romanzero* (1851). The theme remains present throughout the whole of the 19th cent. It is taken up on the stage (J. Péladan's drama *Babylone*, 1895), in opera (plans by Mozart and Beethoven for a piece *Semiramis* and *Die Ruinen von Babylon* respectively; Verdi's *Nabucco*, 1842), and the visual arts (J. Martin, *Das Fest des Belsazar*, 1826, *Der Fall Babylon*, 1831; J.M.W. Turner, *Babylone*, 1834; Ed. Long, *The Marriage Market of Babylon*, 1875) [48. 358, 507f.; 30. 72–74, 77f.]. B. retains its complex network of semantic nuances into the present time. Franz Grillparzer polemized against [the use of] large projects as a symbol of German unity (poem *Kölner Dombau*, 1842), Roger Caillois used it as a means of linguistic criticism (*Babel*, 1948). Alfred Döblin's *Babylonische Wanderung* (1932) transported Marduk, cursed by the prophet Jeremiah, into the 20th cent. as Konrad. Jorge Luis Borges used the subject of B. in two stories in his *Ficciones* (1944): *La loteria en Babilonia* and *La Biblioteca de Babel*. Friedrich Dürrenmatt took up the theme in a political satire of power and divine mercy: *Ein Engel kommt nach Babylon* (three versions: 1953, 1957, 1980). The theme has been used simultaneously in modern criticism of the big city (J. Ponten, *Der babylonische Turm*, 1918; F.S. Fitzgerald's *Babylon Revisited*, 1931; F. Rosso's film *Babylon*, 1980) and in exactly the same way by its counterpart, the fascinating characterization of a pulsing metropolis (New York as 'New Babel'), which makes broader and more universal use of the metaphor [18. 77–88; 47. 214ff.]. Pop culture and esotericism have likewise resorted to B. Finally, B. has been given significant status in its role of identity creation in the politics of modern Iraq [14].

2. Apocalyptic and Eschatological Concepts

At the end of the 6th cent. BC, the term B. took on abstract characteristics in the prophecies of the Hebrew scriptures and became a symbol for powers hostile to Yahweh. In Isaiah 47, the female metaphor connected with Zion is transferred to B. ('Daughter of Babylon'). This image is strengthened in the Septuaginta Nahum 3: 4–5 (Niniveh as 'whore', *pórnē*) until one arrives at the concept, aimed at Rome, of B. as 'mother of whores' (*hē métēr tōn pórnōn*), as it is met in Rev. 17: 5 and which found wide circulation in Jewish-Christian circles [32; 40; 51]. Origen's and Augustine's interpretation of B. as a city of the devil had a great influence on patristic exegesis [17. 1131–1133; 34].

3. World Empires and Ages of the World

In addition, B. was judged in a more complex way in the Old Testament in connection with the idea of the four world empires (Dan. 3 and 7), of which B. figures as the first and Nebuchadnezzar becomes a believer in Yahweh (Dan. 4). This idea gained great effectiveness. Starting with Sulpicius Severus (about 400), the four world empires find their way into Christian salvation history, and can be traced through Orosius (417), Jordanes (about 550) to well into the Middle Ages: e.g. Frutolf of Michelsberg (1101), Hugh of Fleury (1110), Sigebert of Gembloux (1111), Honorius Augustodunensis (about 1135), and Otto of Freising (1157) [24; 26. 123–179; 35. 186] (→ Sacrum Imperium).

B. also played a vital role in various ideas about the division of world history into seven ages; since, in a tradition stemming from Augustine and which held great sway in the Middle Ages, the Babylonian Captivity represented the boundary between the fourth and fifth ages of the world [44; 46].

4. Babel-Bible Controversy and Panbabylonism

In 1902 and 1903, the Assyriologist Friedrich Delitzsch gave two lectures before an imperial audience with the programmatic title *Babel und Bibel* which led to a fierce dispute that drew in the greater public. Delitzsch based his arguments on the theological results of the discoveries brought about by the findings of the yet new field of cuneiform script, pointing out not only the Babylonian thought in Biblical literature, but also ultimately taking a position against the ecclesiastical concept of divine revelation. A public statement by Wilhelm II (*Hollmannbrief*) was perceived by the reading public as a reprimand from the emperor and the controversy was laid aside[23; 29].

Panbabylonism encompasses an attitude which is indirectly connected with the Babel-Bible controversy, which emerged around the turn of the century and was represented by noted Assyriologists with clearly different emphases. These included both scholars who strove to explain the mythology and world-view of all other peoples through diffusion from an astral-mythological system tracing back to B. (H. Winckler, H. Zimmern, E. Schrader, A. Jeremias), and those who attempted to interpret characters and narrative materials from the Old and New Testaments by means of literary influence originating in the Gilgamesh epic (P. Jensen) [23. 265–290; 29. 38–48].

Sources 1 C. Janssen, Babil, the City of Witchcraft and Wine, 1995 2 A. Oppenheimer, Babylonia Judaica in the Talmudic Period, 1983 3 Ludovico de Varthema, Reisen im Orient, 1996 4 F. Zarncke, Der Priester Johannes, Abhandlungen der Königlichen Sächsischen Gesellschaft der Wissenschaften, philosophisch-historische.-Klasse 7, 1879, 827–1030

Literature 5 I. Aghion et al., s.v. Semiramis, Flammarion Iconographic Guides. Gods and Heroes of Classical Antiquity, 1996, 268f. 6 W. Allinger-Csollich, Tieftempel-Hochtempel (Birs Nimrud II), in: Baghdader Mitteilungen 29, 1998, 95–330 7 Bächtold-Stäubli, s.v. Krebs, Handwörterbuch des deutschen Aberglaubens 5, 1933, 455–458 8 A. Becker, U. Becker, 'Altes' and 'Neues' Babylon?, in: Baghdader Mitteilungen 22, 1991, 501–511 9 A. Borst, Der Turmbau von Babel. Geschichte der Meinungen über Ursprung und Vielfalt der Sprachen und Völker, 4 Vols., 1959–63 10 H. Bost, Babel. Du texte au symbol, 1985 11 R. Bräuer (ed.), Dichtung des europäischen Mittelalters, 1991 12 K. Brodersen, Die sieben Weltwunder. Legendäre Kunst- und Bauwerke der Antike, 1996 13 E. S. Drower, The Book of Zodiac, 1949 14 Ch. Dyer, Der Golfkrieg und das neue Babylon, 1991 15 R. Fischer, Babylon. Entdeckungsreisen in die Vergangenheit, 1985 16 T. Ehlert, Deutschsprachige Alexanderdichtung des Mittelalters. Zum Verhältnis von Literatur und Geschichte, 1989 17 K. Galling, B. Altaner, see Babylon, Reallexikon für Antike und Christentum 1, 1118–1134 18 J. Ganzert (ed.), Der Turmbau zu Babel. Maßstab oder Anmaßung?, 1997 19 O. Holl, s.v. Baltassar, Lexikon der christlichen Ikonographie 1, 241f. 20 Id., s.v. Semiramis, Lexikon der christlichen Ikonographie 4, 149 21 Id., s.v. Weltalter, Lexikon der christlichen Ikonographie 4, 509f.   22 Id., s.v. Weltreiche, vier, Lexikon der christlichen Ikonographie 4, 523f.   23 K. JOHANNING, Der Bibel-Babel-Streit. Eine forschungsgeschichtliche Studie, 1988   24 K. KOCH, Europa, Rom und der Kaiser vor dem Hintergrund von zwei Jahrhunderten. Rezeption des Buches Daniel, 1997   25 R. G. KHOURY, Les légendes prophétiques dans l'Islam depuis le Ier jusqu'au IIIe siècle de l'Hégire, 1978   26 R. G. KRATZ, Translatio Imperii. Untersuchungen zu den aramäischen Danielerzählungen und ihrem theologiegeschichtlichen Umfeld, 1988   27 B. KUKLICK, Puritans in Babylon. The Ancient Near East and American Intellectual Life, 1880–1930, 1996   28 M. T. LARSEN, The Conquest of Assyria: Excavations in an Antique Land, 1840–1860, 1996   29 R. G. LEHMANN, Friedrich Delitzsch und der Babel-Bibel-Streit, 1994   30 J. M. LUNDQUIST, Babylon in European Thought, in: J. M. SASSON (ed.), Civilizations of the Ancient Near East, vol. I, 1995, 67–80   31 A. MANN, s.v. Babylonischer Turm, Lexikon der christlichen Ikonographie 1, 236–238   32 R. MARTIN-ACHARD, Esaïe 47 et la tradition prophétique sur Babylone, in: J. A. EMERTON (ed.), Prophecy. Essays presented to Georg Fohrer on his sixty-fifth Birthday, 1980   33 H. MINKOWSKI, Vermutungen über den Turm zu Babel, 1991   34 J. VAN OORT, Jerusalem and Babylon. A Study into Augustine's City of God and the Sources of his Doctrine of the Two Cities, 1991   35 N. H. OTT, Chronistik, Geschichtsepik, Historische Dichtung, in: V. MERTENS, U. MÜLLER (eds.), Epische Stoffe des Mittelalters, 182–204, 1984   36 B OTT, s.v. Jünglinge, Babylonische, Lexikon der christlichen Ikonographie 2, 464–466   37 S. A. PALLIS, The Antiquity of Iraq. A Handbook of Assyriology, 1956   38 A. PARROT, Ziggurat et tour de Babel, 1953   39 J. PAUL, W. BUSCH, s.v. Nabuchodonsor, Lexikon der christlichen Ikonographie 3, 303–307   40 M. RISSI, Die Hure Babylon und die Verführung der Heiligen. Eine Studie zur Apokalypse des Johannes, 1995   41 H. SCHLOSSER, s.v. Daniel, LCI 1, 469–473;   42 Id., s.v. Susanna, LCI 4, 228–231   43 H. SCHMID, Der Tempelturm Etemenanki in Babylon, 1995   44 R. SCHMIDT, Aetates mundi. Die Weltalter als Gliederungsprinzip der Geschichte, in: ZKG 67, 1955/6, 288–317   45 R. SCHNELL, Deutsche Literatur und deutsches Nationalbewußtsein in Spät-Mittelalter und früher Neuzeit, in: J. EHLERS (ed.), Ansätze und Diskontinuität deutscher Nationsbildung im Mittelalter, 247–319, 1989   46 K. H. SCHWARTE, Die Vorgeschichte der augustinischen Weltalterlehre, 1996   47 A. SENARCLENS DEGRACY, Der Turm von Babel als Thema der Kunst und Architektur des 20. Jahrhunderts (Diss. Graz), 1993   48 G. SIEVERNICH, H. BUDDE, Europa und der Orient, 800–1900, 1989   49 CH. W. THOMSEN, Architekturphantasien. Von Babylon bis zur virtuellen Architektur, 1994   50 CHR. UEHLINGER, Weltreich und eine Rede. Eine Deutung der Turmbauerzählung (Gn 11,1–9), 1990   51 S. UHLIG, Die typologische Bedeutung des Begriffs Babylon, in: Andrews University Seminary Studies 12, 1974, 112–125   52 U. B. WEGENER, Die Faszination des Maßlosen. Der Turmbau zu Babel von Pieter Bruegel bis Athanasius Kircher, 1995   53 S. E. WEINER, The Tower of Babel in Netherlandish Painting (Diss., Columbia University), 1985 (Microfiche New York 1986)   54 S. MAUL, Die Altorientalische Hauptstadt – Abbild und Nabel der Welt, in: Die orientalische Stadt – Kontinuität, Wandel, Bruch (= Colloquien der Deutschen Orient-Gesellschaft 1), 1997, 109–124. (Karten) TAVO B S 1.1: Karten des Klaudios Ptolemaios; B S 1.2: Tabula Peutingeriana; B S 2: Ibn Hauqal, c. 988

ADDITIONAL BIBLIOGRAPHY: *The Oxford Encyclopedia of Archaeology in the Near East*, prepared under the auspices of the American Schools of Oriental Research ERIC M. MEYERS (ed.) 1997.   ROBERT ROLLINGER

Bahgdad, Iraq Museum see → IRAQ BAGHDAD MUSEUM

Baltic languages

A. INTRODUCTION   B. LITHUANIAN   C. LATVIAN
D. OLD PRUSSIAN

A. INTRODUCTION

The term Baltic languages (BL) refers to an independent branch of the Indo-European family of languages, a branch that includes Lithuanian, Latvian and Old Prussian, the last of which died out c. 1700. Trade contacts between the Baltic peoples and the Romans (→ TRADE/TRADE ROUTES) had existed as early as Antiquity along the Amber Road, but evidence of linguistic contact at that early time does not exist. The Baltic peoples do not enter into the light of European history until the 13th cent. Church Latin at first had no direct influence on the vernacular languages, but Latin and Greek → LOAN WORDS were adopted by way of intermediary languages, that is, Lithuanian received words mostly from Polish and Belorussian, while Latvian and probably Old Prussian received them from German. The Reformation resulted in the increased influence of the Church, and beginning in the 19th cent., numerous → INTERNATIONALISMS from the areas of science, culture, technology or medicine entered into Lithuanian and Latvian, primarily through Russian.

B. LITHUANIAN

Among the loanwords that entered into Lithuanian by way of Polish and Belorussian beginning in the 13th/14th cent. were, for example, *adventas* 'advent' < Polish *adwent* from Latin *adventus*, *apaštala* 'apostle' < Polish *apostoł* from Greek ἀπόστολος, or *arnotas* 'ornate' < Polish *ornat* from Latin *ornatus*. Several borrowings that were mediated through German also fall into the same period, such as *mūras* 'Mauer' < Middle Low German *mūr* from Latin *murus* or *kalkės* 'Kalk' < German *kalk* from Lat. *calx*. In the course of the nationalist movement of the 19th cent., the vocabulary was expanded by internationalist terms that were adopted following Russian models, cf. the missing initial sound in *istorija* 'historia' < Russ. *istorija*. Furthermore, foreign words were usually adjusted to the specific linguistic circumstances of Lithuanian. In the areas of orthography and articulation, *ph* is changed to *f*, as in *filosofas* 'philosopher', *x* is replaced by *gz*, as in *egzaminas* 'exam', *qu* by *kv*, as in *kvadratas* 'quadrate', *y* by *i*, as in *gimnastika* 'gymnastics'. Stress is usually placed on the penultimate syllable as in *advokātas* 'advocate'. For the purpose of integration into the morphological system, masculine nouns usually receive the endings *-as* or *–(i)us* as in *docentas* 'docent' or *profesorius* 'professor', while

-a is the characteristic marker for feminine nouns, as in *problema* 'problem'. Common suffixes are *-ija* for feminine nouns as in *amnestija* 'amnestia' or *revoliucija* 'revolution' or *-izmas* for masculine nouns as in *komunizmas* 'communism'. Latin feminine nouns ending in *-as* are rendered with the masculine suffix *-etas, as in fakultetas* 'faculty', or *autoritetas* 'authority'. Adjectives usually end in *-us* (masc.) or *-i* (fem.), e.g. *konkretus/-i* 'concrete' or *momentanus/-i* 'momentary'. Adjectives are often formed with Lithuanian suffixes as well, for instance *-iškas/-a* as in *diplomatiškas/-a* 'diplomatic', or with *-inis/-ine* as in *kultūrinis/-e* 'cultural'. Verbs usually receive the infinitive ending *-uoti*, as in *emigruoti* 'to emigrate'.

C. LATVIAN

Latin or Greek words first entered Latvian via Middle Low German, for instance *alūns* 'alum' < Middle Low German *allûn* from Latin *alumen*, *ārsts* 'doctor' < Middle Low German *arste* (highly distorted) from Greek ἀρχίατρος or *pulveris* 'powder' < Middle Low German from Lat. *pulvis*. In the course of the movement of national awakening, the 'young Latvian movement' fought for the development of a literary language from the middle of the 19th cent. on, a movement which regarded the emergence of internationalist terms as unavoidable. Thus, beginning in 1863, foreign terms following Russian and German models were regularly introduced and explained in the newspaper 'Pēterburgas Avīzes'. In foreign words, the stress is always placed on the first syllable, as is common in Latvian, thus *pólitika* 'politics' or *'students'* student. Orthographically and phonetically, lexemes are adjusted as well, in that vowel lengths are marked by strokes, and *g* and *k* preceding high vowels are replaced by *ģ* or *ķ*, as in *kolēģis* 'colleague'. Double consonants are unknown, and *ph* is represented by *f*, *qu* by *kv*, *x* by *ks*, and *y* by *i*, as in *ksilofons* 'xylophone'. On the whole, the changes in the Latvian language are greater than those in Lithuanian. Foreign words are integrated into the linguistic system by adding *-s* or *-is* endings to masculine nouns and *-a* or *-e* to feminine nouns. One of the most common suffixes is *-ija* as in *koncentrācija* 'concentration'. Beginning in the 19th cent., this method was also used to form the names of countries, for instance *Francija* 'France' or the newly formed term *Latvija*. In this function, *-ija* was probably adopted from the Russian, where, in turn, it is of Latin origin, cf. Russian *Italija* 'Italy' Adjectives are often formed with the Latvian suffix *-isks/-a*, as in *fonētisks/-a*, while verbs usually end in *-ēt*, as in *integrēt* 'to integrate'.

D. OLD PRUSSIAN

The few preserved texts consist of glossaries and three translations of Luther's *Kleiner Katechismus* from the 16th cent. These texts hardly allow an understanding of the vernacular language, but a number of loanwords can be identified. The latter include church terms such as *altari* 'altar', *bīskops* 'bishop', *catechismus* 'cat-

echism', or *euangelion* 'gospel', as well as terms for cultural goods that might have been borrowed through German or Slavic, such as *kelks* 'chalice' from German Kelch < Latin *calix*, *kamenis* 'chimney' from Polish *komin* < Latin *camīnus*, or *knapios* 'hemp', probably from the older **kanapš* from Greek κάνναβις.

1 E. JAKAITIENĖ, Lietuvi̯ kalbos leksikologija, Vilnius 1980   2 S. JORDAN, Niederdeutsch im Lettischen, 1995   3 A. LAUA, Latviešu leksikologija, Riga ²1981   4 V. MAŽIULIS, Prūs̯ kalbos etimologijos žodynas, Vilnius 1988ff.   5 B. METUZĀLE-MUZIKANTE, The Morphological Structure of the Stem of International Words in Latvian, in: Lingua Posnaniensis XXII, 1979, 51–58   6 Z. ZINKEVIČIUS, Lietuvi̯ kalbos istorija I–VI, Vilnius 1984–1994.   BERTHOLD FORSSMAN

Baltimore Walters Art Gallery see → USA: MUSEUMS

Barberini Faun

A. OBJECT   B. DISCOVERY AND HISTORY OF THE SCULPTURE   C. RECEPTION

A. OBJECT

The so-called Barberini Faun is a 2.15 m high Greek sculpture from the 2nd half of the 3rd cent. BC. A youth is portrayed slumbering in a half-seated pose. The youthful, naked, muscular body of the BF reclines relaxed but not enfeebled on an animal skin spread over rocky ground, which combined with the ivy and corymbs in its hair suggests a Dionysian context. It reflects its inherent semi-animality less in its physicality than by → Aalen its openly displayed sensuality. Presumably the BF was originally set in a cultic context. The precise period of its transfer to Roma is unknown. Reuse of the statue during the Imperial Period is probably associated 'setting' with itssfdsto a secular on a fountain as decoration for a Roman villa [7].

B. DISCOVERY AND HISTORY OF THE SCULPTURE

It may be concluded from the inventory of Cardinal F. Barberini, completed between 1632 and 1640, that the BF was discovered in the course of structural works at Castel Sant' Angelo under the Barberini Pope Urban VIII between 1624 and 1628. The record of the transportation of a statue on May 5, 1627 to the Palazzo Barberini could relate to it. Its restoration by A. Gonelli is attested in 1628, the outcome being recorded in an engraving by H. Tetius [8. 181–184, 215] (fig.1). In a further restoration in 1679 G. Giorgetti and L. Ottoni developed legs and arm in stucco [3. 163–169; 227] and altered the pose to a half-seated one. The base was configured as an overgrown rock and the BF provided with a musical instrument. Engravings (by Maffei before 1704 [2. 87, XCIV], by B. Montfaucon in 1719 and by L. Deplaces after C. Natoire between 1720 and 1730) and copies document these additions. In spite of being the indisputable property of the Barberini family, in July 1799 the BF was sold to the sculptor V. Pacetti for 4000 scudi. Pacetti executed the missing limbs in mar-

Fig. 1: Barberini Faun, engraving
by H. Tetius (before 1642)

Fig. 2: Faun by Johan Tobias Sergel, 1774.
Photo: The National Museum of Fine Arts, Stockholm

Fig. 3: Bozzetto by Bernini
(in private ownership)

Fig. 4: Pencil drawing by Adolf von
Menzel, 1874.
*Staatliche Graphische Sammlung
München, Inv. Nr. 1975: 18 Z*

Fig. 5: Marble copy by Edme
Bouchardon. Between 1726 and 1730.
*With permission of Musée du Louvre,
Paris*

ble, not without altering the posture, especially by a
turning of the right leg toward the outside. This circumstance is shown in the 1874 pencil drawing by A.
Menzel (fig.4). In a dispute about the ownership of the
BF Pacetti had to return it to the Barberinis, who in
1814 sold it through the agent M. von Wagner to
Ludwig of Bavaria for 8000 scudi. After a delay in obtaining export approval it eventually reached Munich
in 1820, to take up the space reserved for it in the Glyptothek in 1827. In 1965 the additions, with the exception of the left leg with its original fragments, were removed, and in 1983 K. Vierneisel gave a new shape to
the right leg. A differing attempt at completion was carried out on the plaster cast in 1959/60 by H. Walter and
E. Luttner [9].

C. RECEPTION
It is difficult to disentangle the dynamic relationship
between reception and reconstruction of the BF Its initial installation as a horizontal reclining figure may be
explained by adoption of the concept of the sleeping
Endymion, or even of G.A. Montorsoli's 'Barberini
Pan', which in the 17th cent. was held to be antique.
This reconstruction of the BF was the model for Poussin's sleeping youth in his Bacchanal of 1635–36 [3].
The second restoration, which has come down to us
in a small bisque reproduction by G. Volpato and in E.
Bouchardon's copy of 1726 (today Paris, LV) (fig. 5),
was at first ascribed to G.L. Bernini, on account of an
entry in an inventory of 1738, as was the case with a
bozzetto, which may have been a preliminary model for
the reconstruction (fig. 3). Various attempts have been
made to establish relationships between works by Ber-

nini and the BF Müller [4. 56–60] sees an echo of the BF especially in the Ecstasy of St. Theresa in the sense of an iconic palimpsest. In 1774 J.T. Sergel produced a marble sculpture of a reclining faun, the initial terracotta model of which was more strongly oriented towards the BF than the completed figure, whose pose is concretely associated with insobriety by the presence of a wineskin and grapes (fig. 2). In the first years of the 19th cent. V. Agricola (Bauer) designed a decorative cameo in which he equipped the BF with various accoutrements, including a wineskin and a theatrical mask. The BF figures as decoration on the Nymphenburg Onyx Service of c. 1830 for the Residence in Munich. B. Thorvaldsen cites the pose of the BF in reverse on a Torlonia 'Cameo' designed in 1837 bearing the image of the sleeping Endymion. In 1861 a gilded copy of the BF was installed in the Grande Grotte at the Petershof as part of the sculptural decoration of the Grand Cascade. The BF has been the subject of highly different verdicts [1. 202–205]. When von Stosch judged the statue to be superior to the → BELVEDERE APOLLO, Winkelmann was provoked to damn the BF as a 'Wildman' [10].

Goethe has Paris (Faust II, 6453–6474) fall asleep upon his entrance on stage in living imitation of the pose of the BF He thus thematises the voyeuristic appeal implicit in the sensual quality of the marble youth, whose provocative unseemliness is accentuated to new heights of piquancy, particularly by the reaction of the female viewers.

To sum up, the artistic reception of the BF demonstrates a tendency to 'bestialize' the piece by means of laying superficial emphasis on its satyr-like, Dionysian character, probably in order to justify the portrayal of the naked male figure in such unwonted lascivious passivity.

→ Bacchus; → Dionysus

1 F. HASKELL, N. PENNY, Taste and the Antique. The Lure of Classical Sculpture, 1981   2 P. A. MAFFEI, Raccolta di Statue antiche e moderne, data in Luce da Domenico de Rossi, Roma 1704   3 J. MONTAGU, Roman Baroque Sculpture. The Industry of Art, 1989   4 A. MÜLLER, Die ikonische Differenz. Das Kunstwerk als Augenblick, 1997   5 D. NEBENDAHL, Die schönsten Antiken Roms. Studien zur Rezeption antiker Bildwerke im römischen Seicento, 1991   6 D. SPENGLER, Der Traum des Faun: Theorie und Praxis in der Kunst, 1993   7 Standorte – Kontext und Funktion anttiker Skulptur. (Ausstellung, Abguss-Sammlung Antiker Plastik FU Berlin, 1994/1995), ed. K. STEMMER, 1995, 212–213   8 G. TETI (H. TETIUS), Aedes barberinae ad Quirinalem ... descriptae, Roma 1642   9 H. WALTER, Der schlafende Satyr in der Glyptothek in München, in: Studien zur klassischen Archeologie. Friedrich Hiller zu seinem 60. Geburtstag, 1986, 91–122   10 J. WINKELMANN, Abhandlung von der Fähigkeit der Empfindung des Schönen in der Kunst, und dem Unterrichte in derselben. An den Freiherrn von Berg (KS und Briefe), 1960, 154.   PHILINE HELAS

Baron Thesis, the Fifty years ago Hans Baron (1900–1988), who had take refuge from Nazi Germany in the United States, put forth a comprehensive theory to explain the beginning of the Renaissance that anchored Florentine political events in the early 14th cent. into the Classical tradition of republican thought. During its first two generations, Baron argued, Italian humanism had maintained the medieval preference for monarchical government, which was traced back to Julius Caesar and Augustus. The same humanists had favored the contemplative over the active life, which allowed them to remain largely apolitical. By the summer of 1402, however, the thirteen-year-old war with Milan seemed about to overwhelm Florence, leading to a reappraisal of humanism and its role in civic life. Florence was a republic, which, it was felt, was the best form of government for fostering creativity and morality in the individual. Rome had also been a republic; indeed, her decline was due directly to the assault on republican freedoms by Julius Caesar and Augustus. To keep Florence from suffering the same fate at the hands of Milanese tyranny, the principles of classical republicanism must be revived and defended by Cicero's Florentine heirs. Milan was rebuffed, and the new republican ideology, which Baron called 'civic humanism,' received its first articulation a year afterwards in the *Laudatio Florentinae urbis* of Leonard Bruni. Twenty years after its original formulation, Baron's argument received an influential extension by J.G.A. Pocock, who argued that Classical republicanism had passed from Renaissance Florence to Oliver Cromwell's England, then to colonial America, where it formed the ideological foundation for the American revolution. In the 1980s civic humanism again united scholarship in the Classical tradition with active participation in political affairs in a movement called 'communitarianism,' whose sympathizers included William Clinton, Tony Blair, Jacques Delors, and Romano Prodi.

Critics of the Baron thesis have pointed out that the dates Baron has given to some of his key supporting documents are impossible to establish with certainty, that republican ideas can be found in some medieval thinkers, and that the commitment to Classical republican ideals is questionable on the part of both the Florentine state and its humanist defenders, especially Bruni. Other scholars like Paul Oskar Kristeller and Eugenio Garin have searched elsewhere for the origins of the Renaissance. Finally, Pocock's extension of the Baron thesis has led some scholars to argue that Classical republicanism does not constitute a distinct discourse in early modern society, that its various proponents are more different than alike, and that the system is hierarchical, elitist, and racist at its core. In the end, however, the first civic humanists succeeded in fusing scholarship and politics in a remarkable way that gave new life to the ideas of Cicero, Sallust, and Seneca in modern times.

CRAIG KALLENDORF

BARON, H. The Crisis of the Early Italian Renaissance: Civic Humanism and Republican Liberty in an Age of Classicism and Tyranny, 1955, ²1966 (Italian trans., 1970); HANKINS, J. The Baron Thesis after Forty Years and Some Recent Studies of Leonardo Bruni, in: Journal of the History of Ideas 56 (1995): 309–38; Id. (ed.). Renaissance Civic Humanism: Reappraisals and Reflections, 2000; POCOCK, J. G. A. The Macchiavellian Moment: Florentine Political Thought and the Atlantic Republican Tradition, 1975; WITT, R. AHR Forum: The Crisis after Forty Years, in: American Historical Review 101 (1996): 110–18.

Baroque

I. GERMANY II. GREAT BRITAIN III. ROMANCE COUNTRIES IV. ART AND PAINTING

I. GERMANY

A. THE CONCEPT AND ITS HISTORY C. LEARNING, EDUCATION AND KNOWLEDGE D. INSTITUTIONS OF CULTURAL SOCIETY

A. THE CONCEPT AND ITS HISTORY

The term, baroque, probably derived from the Portuguese word for an off-round, irregular pearl (barroco), appears from the 18th cent. on as a synonym for such terms as 'bizarre, bombastic, irregular.'

In its sense as a stylistic term or expression describing a cultural period, baroque did not come into use in the world of art-historical discourse until the second half of the 19th cent. – for the first time with J. Burckhardt [6], who saw Baroque as a continuing development ('reversion to the wild state' = Verwilderung) of stylistic elements of the Renaissance. Of course, the expression had been already extended to literature by Nietzsche (1879) and Borinski (1886); Nietzsche started out from the assumption of the commonality of all the arts and pointed to the close association of baroque style, understood by him as a timeless phenomenon, with rhetoric; Borinski spoke explicitly of a poetic baroque. But further work on the terminology initially remained the domain of Art History. Particular attention should be paid here to the studies of Wölfflin. With the intention of developing formal-analytical descriptive categories for art works, he demonstrated, by means of five contrastive pairs of terms, a fundamental difference between the artistic principles of Renaissance and Baroque, and thus postulated Baroque as an autonomous style. In the wake of Wölfflin, Walzel and Strich established the art-historical term Baroque for the study of literature, and undertook to extend Wölfflin's terminological apparatus to literature, seeing the Baroque as a Counter-Renaissance, and, especially in the case of Walzel, using the term to refer to a timeless type of style as well as a particular period (on the problems involved in the formation of the literary-historical terminology and its heuristic implications [2; 8; 11]).

Nevertheless it can be said that the concept Baroque has become established for German literature between → HUMANISM and the → ENLIGHTENMENT. In any case

the boundaries in each direction are fluid, and more recent scholarship, in contrast to older approaches, has emphasised the continuity between the learned culture of the Renaissance and that of the Baroque.

B. BAROQUE NATIONAL LANGUAGE AND LANGUAGE SOCIETIES

The significant feature of this period of literature is the propagation of a German literary language, a development that occurred distinctly late in Germany compared to the European norm. Martin Opitz first proclaimed the turn towards a national language in his Aristarchus sive de Contemptu Linguae Teutonicae (1617), and in 1624 in the first poetic primer in the German language, Buch von der deutschen Poeterey. For the content of his book Opitz built, for the most part, on the poetics of Scaliger and Ronsard.

The driving forces promoting the German language were the so-called language societies, which, modelled on the Italian Academy, were devoted to the advancement of the language. The first of these societies was the Fruchtbringende Gesellschaft, whose foundation in 1617 was brought about by Ludwig of Anhalt-Köthen. Other similar institutions were the Aufrichtige Tannengesellschaft (Straßburg 1633), the Deutschgesinnete Genossenschaft (Hamburg 1643), the Pegnesische Blumenorden (Nuremberg 1644) and the Elbschwanenorden (Hamburg 1653). The supporters of these societies were the educated nobility and the learned elite, who were in attendance at courts, in cities and universities. They gained increasingly in importance and, with few exceptions, dominated the language societies with their numbers.

Already during the Renaissance, this learned elite viewed itself as part of the European world of learning; its members were continually in contact by means of a highly intense degree of personal communication (letters, travel, study). Contemporary European literature was also eagerly received and translated.

C. LEARNING, EDUCATION AND KNOWLEDGE

Learning and education were the central elements of the literary elite's self-conception. The members of this group emerged from the educational institutions of the time (Protestant grammar schools, Jesuit secondary schools, → UNIVERSITY and educational institutions for the nobility like the → RITTERAKADEMIE), and were frequently attached to them professionally. An essential component of academic instruction was rhetoric, which was, without exception, based on ancient Classical theory and essentially taught in Latin. Therefore, bilingualism was the rule among writers and in literature, in spite of cultural partisanship on behalf of the German language. Mastery of the cultural canon and the rules of rhetoric, ostentatious display of knowledge and speech rich in allusion became the touchstones of learned competence, and thus an important component of social prestige. Such competence not only worked as an instrument of social advance: It also constituted a space within which it was possible to gloss over differences of status in the context of shared culture interest.

D. Institutions of Cultural Society

Apart from those rhetorical activities primarily connected with teaching (debate, declamation, Jesuit drama, school theatre), the institutions where scholarly education found practical application and could at the same time be demonstrated in the interests of personal prestige were the court and its ceremonial and festival culture, and above all the culture of conversation of the court and middle-class society.

Conversation therefore not only played a central role in 17th cent. life-style manuals (N. Faret, Baroque Gracián, E. Tesauro), but also motivated the reader's interest in polymathic/encyclopaedic literature, as for example the *Polyhistor Literarius, Philosophicus, et Practicus* of D.G. Morhof (1687). To this category also belong Ph. Harsdörffer's *Frauenzimmer-Gesprächspiele* (1641–1649) and his *Ars Apophthegmatica*, which appeared under the title *Kunstquellen Denckwürdiger Lehrsprüche und Ergötzlicher Hofreden* (1655). Writings of this kind were designed to provide the reader with an arsenal of learned material that could be reproduced in conversation, demonstrating him or her to be a versatile and profound conversationalist with a command of wit and *acutezza*.

Poetic literature too, as a component of learned culture, shares these essential features. *Doctrina*, the art of meaningful expression, stylistic variation and the mastery of literary and learned tradition were understood to be the prerequisites of the art of writing. This found expression inter alia in extensive commentaries on literary texts (e.g. in works by Opitz, Gryphius, Zesen and Lohenstein).

→ Germany

1 W. Adam(ed.), Geselligkeit und Gesellschaft im Barockzeitalter I/II, 1997 2 W. Barner, Barockrhetorik. Untersuchungen zu ihren geschichtlichen Grundlagen, 1970 3 K. Borinski, Geschichte der deutschen Literatur, vol. 2, Stuttgart 1893 4 G. Braungart, Hofberedsamkeit. Studien zur Praxis höfisch-politischer Rede im deutschen Territorialabsolutismus, 1988 5 Id., Ein Ferment der Geselligkeit: Zur Poetik des Apophthegmas, in: W. Adam (ed.), Geselligkeit und Gesellschaft im Barockzeitalter I/II, 1997, 463–472 6 J. Burckhardt, Cicerone, Basel 1855 7 G. E. Grimm, Literatur und Gelehrtentum in Deutschland. Untersuchungen zum Wandel ihres Verhältnisses vom Humanismus zur Frühaufklärung, 1983 8 H. Jaumann, Der Barockbegriff in der nicht-wissenschaftlichen Literatur und Kunstpublizistik um 1900, in: K. Garber (ed.), Europäische Barockrezeption, 1991, 619–633 9. W. Kühlmann, Gelehrtenrepublik und Fürstenstaat. Entwicklung und Kritik des deutschen Späthumanismus in der Literatur des Barockzeitalters, 1982 10 Id., Frühaufklärung und Barock. Traditionsbruch-Rückgriff-Kontinuität, in: K. Garber (ed.), Europäische Barockrezeption, 1991, 187–214 11 H.-H. Müller, Die Übertragung des Barockbegriffs von der Kunstwissenschaft auf die Literaturwissenschaft bei Fritz Strich und Oskar Walzel, in: K. Garber (ed.), Europäische Barockrezeption, 1991, 95–112 12 M. Schilling, Gesellschaft und Gesellschaft im

Pegnesischen Schäfergedicht und seiner Fortsetzung, in: W. Adam (ed.), Gesellschaft und Gesellschaft im Barockzeitalter I/II, 1997, 473–482 13 C. Schmölders (ed.), Die Kunst des Gesprächs. Texte zur Geschichte der europäischen Konversationstheorie, 1979 14 R. Zeller, Spiel und Konversation im Barock. Untersuchungen zu Harsdörffers Gesprächsspielen, 1974. HELMUT KRASSER

II. Great Britain
See → Classicism II. Literature (Great Britain)

III. Romance Countries
A. Conceptual Questions and General Remarks B. Adaptation and Aesthetic Exploitation of Ancient Texts in Romance Literatures between Renaissance and Baroque C. Tendencies towards a Deconstruction of Antiquity as a Model and the Beginnings of the Querelle des Anciens et des Modernes in the Baroque

A. Conceptual Questions and General Remarks

With regard both to general meaning and particular usage, the concept Baroque as applied to literature today denotes a period of development in literary history, or at least of its essential stylistic aspects, between roughly the second half of the 16th and the 17th cents., but, as controversy shows, can scarcely be defined within coherent chronological limits. Having entered, with varying emphasis, into the historiography of almost all European literatures, the concept Baroque in the most important Romance literatures has led to the definition of literary periods of different lengths. The period defined as preceding the Baroque, with various transitional periods depending on the different national literatures as Mannerism, especially in Italy, is the → Renaissance. It is followed by the more or less coherent (neo-)classicist tendencies (→ Classicism) of the second half of the 17th or (especially in Spain) of the 18th cent.

The retrospective reconstruction of styles or periods intended with the use of the term Baroque has been complicated by the its origins in art-historical debates of the 19th cent. The initial meaning it acquired then was expressive of a derogatory or at the least problematical view of the Baroque period. The term's previous history, stretching back into the 18th cent., demonstrates a range of meanings that includes negative connotations of the irregular, the diverging or the bizarre, taking it beyond the purview of an aesthetic perspective oriented toward rules (cf.: [10. 9f.; 21. 402–419; 25. 55ff.; 27. 69ff.]; also the Romance articles in [15; 20; 22]). Their effect is demonstrated in a famous quotation from Jakob Burkhardt's *Der Cicerone* (1855), where the term Baroque first enters art history: *Die Barock-Baukunst spricht dieselbe Sprache wie die Renaissance, aber einen verwilderten Dialekt davon* (Baroque architecture speaks the same language as the Renaissance, but in a corrupt dialect). Describing a period

Fig. 1: Emanuele Tesauro, frontispiece of
Il Cannocchiale aristotelico, 1670

Fig. 2: Emanuele Tesauro, title page of
Il Cannocchiale aristotelico, 1670

of dissolution of the artistic ideal attributed to Renaissance classicism, and (in spite of the artistic qualities of the Baroque, fully recognised since Heinrich Wölfflin, who in the wake of Burckhardt was the true originator of the term Baroque in art history) understanding it as a period of decline: that presents a basic problem in the qualifying use of the term, an obstacle which continues to affect its application to literary phenomena in spite of its increasing use since the 1920s in defining periods in connection with the national literatures of the Romance countries. Thus the important Italian philosopher and literary historian Benedetto Croce reacted to the first literary-historical applications of the concept with the verdict that 'art is never baroque, and what is baroque, is not art' (Foreword to [12. 37]), and as recently as 1980 the influential French literary historian M. Fumaroli warned against a term that was 'imported from Central Europe (and is) loaded with nationalistic prejudices and intellectual ambiguities' (Foreword to [24. 13f.]). The two verdicts have in common a classicist standpoint motivated by differing national literary concerns: from an Italian point of view the Baroque represents the decline of the Renaissance, which is seen as a golden age, while in France the acceptance of such a period threatens the superior status of 17th cent. Classicism.

These considerations already indicate that the use of the term Baroque is laden with value-judgments in which the qualification of the exemplary nature of ancient models, or the way these have been devalued by

literary developments, plays a significant role, at least implicitly. While the Baroque is conceived of as a period of rejection of the Renaissance, or of its dissolution – the latter being considered as a locus of harmonious artistic creativity – and in spite of the view developed since Wölfflin of the Baroque as an autonomous artistic constellation, critical assessment of it frequently continues to be determined by the idea of a norm attributed to the Renaissance, an exemplary model of rules, comprising aesthetic laws conceived of as harmonious, while the Baroque, with its lack of orientation and its incoherence, is seen as the dissolution of those rules. To be sure, such a conceptualisation of opposing epochs or styles based on art-historical premises had lost its normative historiographical claims a considerable time ago, esp. with regard to Spanish and Italian literature. This traditional viewpoint, however, is to some extent represented to this day in French scholarship, although here it is not the demarcation against the preceding Renaissance period that is the predominant concern, as it is especially in Italian literature, but a desire to devalue the Baroque in relation to the succeeding Classical period, which is seen as superseding it, the Baroque frequently being referred to in less recent scholarship as *préclassicisme*. That traditional view accentuates the fact that a qualification or devaluation of aesthetic and poetological positions, which are designed by taking recourse to models attributed to Antiquity, constitutes a fundamental problem of the period.

When for example Hugo Friedrich in a famous passage seeks to define the fundamental characteristic of Italian Baroque poetry as a *Überfunktion des Stils* (hyperfunction of style), as *Stilprunk* (stylistic ostentation) aiming at the *Großartigkeit des Scheins* (splendour of appearances) [13. 545ff., 562], then in pursuing such a perspective, which may also be found in many conceptualisations of the Baroque in Romance literatures, he is insisting upon turning away from the poetological ideal of → Mimesis, as it had been newly established during the Renaissance in the interpretation and adaptation of Aristotle's 'Poetics'. This way, however, in line with important trends in scholarship, the concept of the Baroque is given substance mainly through an accumulation of stylistic features deemed to be characteristic of it. Especially representative of this tendency is the work of H. Hatzfeld (cf. summary of research in [16] and more generally in relation to these questions [27. 76ff.; 10. 25ff., 71ff.]). Short of being able to consider such positions here more closely, especially with regard to the question of the relationship between the Baroque and Antiquity, it must be said that setting up a basis for the term Baroque on mainly phenomenological grounds (i.e. with regard to literary texts: stressing primarily those aspects that tend to intensify the *elocutio* and make it absolute), it is not possible to provide a systematising perspective on the contexts relevant to this question. In view of the lack of clear period boundaries, and of the plethora of Baroque texts in the Romance literatures, in some cases and in their stylistic peculiarities presenting an impression of chaos, it seems instead more desirable to provide a conceptualisation that is based less on epochal coherence or shared stylistic characteristics, but has as its goal the reconstruction of general tendencies in the dominant discourse that characterises the texts with widely varying degrees of intensity.

On the basis of a reconstruction of the concepts of Renaissance and Baroque suggested by J. Küpper (the following general reflections are in particular based on [19. 7–35, 230–304; 17]), it is first of all possible to grasp more precisely the much-cited 'discovery' of Antiquity by the Renaissance in terms of historical discourse, rather than to view it primarily as the disintegration of the totalitarianising theological system of discourse (esp. that of → Scholasticism), whose world view had used the ancient texts according to quite different principles – a disintegration that was due to the influence of nominalistic scepticism as well as to the availability of new ways of experiencing the world. This enables us to see the Renaissance as an epoch in which it becomes possible for ancient texts (both newly discovered and already known) to be productively received as locations for an increasingly open diversity of interpretation no longer directed by the hegemony of theological discourse. Humanist optimism has as its purpose the discovery of a multitude of ancient creative works that no longer have to be appropriated and interpreted under the terms of a primary imperative to correct a pagan falsification of revealed, scriptural truth. Although the ancient texts thus become important points of reference in the less than coherent discourse on the modelling of the universe in the Early Modern age, acquiring thereby a new legitimising function, in the context of the religious and political upheavals of the 16th cent. this process of re-evaluation becomes entangled in a crisis that, from the perspective of historical discourse, may be seen as the beginning of the age of the Baroque, namely as a new orientation of aesthetic reflection and literary discourse functions upon that crisis in widely varying ways. The outcome occurs in terms of a phase shift in the Romance countries, extending from the *Sacco di Roma* as the earliest historical focus of crystallisation of a crisis of the Renaissance via the French wars of religion to the beginning of the downfall of the Spanish Empire toward the end of the 16th cent. (cf. the historical panorama of events and mentality sketched by D. Souiller in [24. 20ff.]). As Humanist enthusiasm in drawing up new possibilities of thinking and writing by accessing and reinterpreting ancient tradition proves increasingly impotent in the face of ideological and social change (the philosophical and literary scepticism of a Montaigne or a Cervantes is paradigmatic here), at the same time the Council of Trent instigates efforts of ideological and aesthetic restoration, which also put undirected intercourse with ancient tradition solidly in question. The chaotic diversity of that tradition, which at the beginnings of → Humanism had even been given theological approval (e.g. in conceptions of *prisca theologia* ascribed to the ancients, or of parallel revelation), is henceforth seen as the uncontrollable tendency of a secularised system of thought. This applies not only to traditions such as Pyrrhonism or ancient materialism, which, starting in Italy, had inspired free-thinking philosophical tendencies influential in the Baroque, esp. in France; not only to Tacitus, who was regarded as the most important ancient source for the rationalisation of political theory, a tradition going back to Macchiavelli and widespread during the Baroque, but even to Aristotle, the ancient source of Scholasticism, from whose *Metaphysics* Italian Humanism had already developed arguments against the doctrine of the immortality of the soul.

Alongside such general aspects of ideological crisis, the validity of ancient tradition in the Baroque period was also qualified by the development of new strata of the population outside the circle of Humanist scholarship, in the realm of the social elites as well as at the princely courts. This occurred especially in the nation-states of Spain and France, which had become firmly established in spite of the crises of the age.

Although ancient traditions (with regard to both thought and myth) remained an influential cultural context for this new public far beyond the period of the Baroque, their significance waned markedly against the background of new worlds of thought and experience. The intensity of the ideological and political crisis of the period must not be allowed to hide the fact that not only in France, but primarily there, the Baroque was also a period of social and cultural modernisation. Indicative of the change involved is the fact that such pivotal representatives of Early Modern thought as Galileo and Descartes change from Latin to vernacular languages in their publications, with the strategic intention of reaching beyond the elite republic of scholars (whose language remained substantially Latin into the second half of the 17th cent.) to appeal to new strata of the population. All this was at least as definitive for the development of Baroque literature as the ideological and social crisis or the efforts toward a restoration of theological as well as political dominance over the chaotic diversity of discourse. A highly disparate development resulted in the various Romance literatures and even within individual national literatures from such contradictory premises, while at the same time in the adaptation and recasting of ancient models and texts showing a substantial, common characteristic.

B. Adaptation and Aesthetic Exploitation of Ancient Texts in Romance Literatures between Renaissance and Baroque

Literature oriented itself within the area of conflict, as outlined in a simplified way above, with an awareness of its own worth and special status learned and cultivated in the school of Renaissance Classicism. The resulting tendencies towards autonomy were advanced by qualifications introduced to the mimetic function of literary discourse, and the authority of the poet rendered more absolute. The most revealing measure of this process is the dynamism of poetological debate common to all Romance national literatures, developing from the 'rediscovery' of Aristotle's *Poetics c.* 1500 (first translation into Latin 1498). Upon closer examination it is most probably true that the explosive reception during the 16th cent. of the translation of this treatise, already known in the original Greek text, is itself a result of intensive reflection upon the distinctive status of literary discourse. Commentaries upon and adaptions of the *Poetics*, originating in Italy, as well as increasingly autonomous poetological treatises whose characteristic feature is the discussion and development of genre- and style-related rules capable of generalisation, flourished from the mid–16th cent. The most influential of these treatises across Europe into the 17th cent. is *Poetices libri septem* (1561) of Julius Scaliger, who claims Aristotle as his intellectual predecessor but already relativizes many of his judgements. In his work, Scaliger integrates the Latin poetological and rhetorical tradition and justifies the autonomy of the rules and thereby the poet's significance vis-vis the other *genera dicendi* on the basis of the particular nature of his voice, which enables him to transcend everyday reality and *velut alter Deus condere* [7.3]. Scaliger's tendency to elevate the function of the poet places him at the transition to those – for the most part not particularly systematic – Baroque treatises, in which reflections on the autonomous logic of poetic language increasingly take

the place of the hierarchically structured and mimetically oriented arguments characteristic of normative neo-Aristotelian poetics. This eclectic relativization of the authority of Aristotle shifts poetological argument into aspects of *elocutio* and *persuasio* (*persuasio* being seen primarily as a self-legitimising effect of ingenious stylistic expression, while a subordinate role is allotted to the *ratio dicendi* of tradition, which demands: *ut probemus vera esse, quae defendimus,* Cic. de orat. 2,27,115). The criteria for justifying the quality of literary discourse henceforth clearly move from the postulate of mimesis to the text structure created by the poet since they are more strongly oriented toward ancient tradition, from the *Rhetoric* of Aristotle himself down to Quintilian – sometimes even to Pseudo-Longinus and a Platonically inspired idea of the *furor poeticus* – than they were to that of the *Poetics*. In the perspective presented by Emanuele Tesauro in his *Cannocchiale aristotelico* (1655, Figs. 1, 2) the poet's power of imagination (*ingegno*) is a God-given ability, already approved by the ancients, to create imaginative speech, *argutie* or *argutezze* (with other theorists *acutezze*) in combination with the Latin etyma *acutus* (rhetorically: all forms of metonymic speech) and *argutus* as a characteristic of expressive language entail for Italian theorists of the Baroque the use of surprising, especially metaphorical images and figures (cf. [14. 628f.]); at the same time a privilege given by nature to individuals of genius ([8.83] cf. on this point and on the following [23.128ff.]). In his influential treatise, a kind of summing up of Italian Baroque poetics, Tesauro still ties in his conception of poetry, which fundamentally can be read as a genius-based poetics, with ancient tradition and also with a religious cosmology, using, among other things, the traditional argument for legitimising the importance of poetry: that *argutezze* are a means of revelatory annunciation or a representation of the divine among humans ([8. 1f., 59] et passim). But for him this poetry is no longer obliged to provide the illustration of a truth, but the use of surprising figures (*concetti*) aims at the creation of an effective illusion with great public appeal. Tesauro illustrates his modern intention of combining ancient rhetoric with a scientific world-view by using the bold metaphor embodied in his title and making of the *Rhetoric* of Aristotle a telescope (*cannocchiale*), with whose help poetry is enabled to view the sun (at the same time a traditional symbol of Apollo – cf. title-plate: Fig. 2 and [8. 2f.]), an intention also demonstrated by his extreme endeavours to make metaphorical language understandable and thus available. Such tendencies bring him close to other Baroque theorists, esp. Baltasar Gracián, one of the most important Spanish protagonists of a so-called dark poetic style (*conceptismo*), in his *Agudeza y arte de ingenio* (1648).

The claim of autonomy on behalf of literary discourse discernible in such tendencies of the Romance Baroque is in any case in itself entirely contradictory; the logic of the selective reading and re-interpretation of ancient texts on which it is based becomes understandable only when consideration is given to the background of ideological and political tension against which it arises, as described above. This may be demonstrated by reference to the category of the marvellous (*maraviglioso/meraviglia*), which is vital in this context and, not for the first time in Tesauro, plays a central role in the qualification or abnegation of the relationship of poetry to reality; this category of the marvellous may at the same time facilitate a clearer grasp of the tendencies leading to the Baroque's departure from the traditions of ancient poetics (especially those of Aristotle). Although elements of this conception may also be derived from Plato or from Aristotle's *Metaphysics*, in the *Poetics* it is accorded, at best, a functionally subordinate significance as against the dominant postulate of imitation (e.g. in the discussion of the Homeric Epic). At the transition between Renaissance and Baroque, in a critical departure from Aristotle, Italian commentaries on him, such as that of Castelvetro (1570) or Patrizi (1586), declared the marvellous to be the real aim of poetry, and precisely with regard to its effect: 'The aim of poetry [...] is pleasure; and it is particularly the marvellous that arouses pleasure' [2. 175]. But the departure from the postulate of mimesis expressed here derives not only from tendencies towards the autonomy of poetry, but also from efforts to restore theological dominance over literary discourse, insofar as the marvellous is capable of becoming a component of a religiously-based structuring of reality.

This is exemplified in the development of the epic, the genre that since the Renaissance (and deviating from the opinion of Aristotle), had been placed at the top of the genre hierarchy. At the same time Virgil gains acceptance as the great master of epic poetry, as opposed to Homer whose language since Scaliger is harshly criticised as uninspired and not sufficiently elaborate (cf. [7. 216ff.]); the critical comparison between the two epic poets, and between Greek and Latin poetry as a whole, which Scaliger made in Books V and VI of his work and where Latin is clearly preferred, remains typical of the reception of ancient literature in the Romance world down to the 18th cent. Whereas Pierre Ronsard, as late as the end of the Renaissance, in his fragmentary *Franciade* (1572) was still seeking to rewrite the *Aeneid* as a history of the foundation of France (supposedly the work of Francus, a putative son of Hector), there was, since Tasso and especially in Italian and French literature, a series of attempts extending across the entire period of the Baroque to remodel the national perspective of the genre in a religious direction. The cosmos of Virgil's text, which constructs a natural unity of divine and human action, is rewritten in Tasso's *Gerusalemme liberata* (1580/81) based in sacred history where the marvellous plays an extensive role, especially in the machinations of diabolic powers directed against the aims of the crusader army (the question of the extent to which Tasso can be regarded as a writer belonging to the Baroque, which has been the subject of intense academic debate, cannot be given

more detailed consideration here; in so far as the history of the genre is concerned, his epic is certainly a seminal text in the development of the Romance Baroque epic). It is certainly the case that the resulting plot strands (especially the enchantment of Rinaldo by Armida, modelled on the Dido episode) acquire their own logic that is difficult to reconcile with the domineering religious perspective (for which reason Tasso, under the influence of Counter-Reformation criticism, then rewrote his work as *Gerusalemme conquistata*). The marvellous, to which Tasso makes halfhearted attempts to give theoretical legitimacy by recourse to Platonism and Christianity (cf. [23. 79ff.]), acquired its own aesthetic dynamic, which, in spite of persistent efforts in all Baroque genres to endow it with a religious function and repeated attempts in the Baroque national religious epic to give it a religious foundation, subjected itself only to a limited degree to the powerful claims of a religious adaptation. Thus the French writer Desmarets de Saint Sorlin, who wrote an epic inspired by Virgil and Tasso on the baptism of the Frankish king Clovis as a scripturally-based foundation myth for the French monarchy, could still say: 'Everything that can be effected by the almighty power of God or by the power of demons is probable according to our religion' [6. 756]. Desmarets' explicit intention is to surpass the 'Aeneid', whose context of pagan foundation he claims is outshone by the light of Christian knowledge that pervades his work (cf. [6. 739f.]). It is, however, undeniable that this claim, present, if to a highly varying extent, in all Romance Baroque literatures, was only to be asserted at the cost of considerable qualification of the validity of poetological and literary texts from Antiquity.

This is shown most clearly in Spanish Baroque drama, which explicitly turns its back on ancient genre models, and, above all in its religiously didactic *autos sacramentales* but also in religiously inspired themes of the secular *comedia*, makes prominent use of elements of the marvellous. The best-known example of this is the first dramatisation of the Don Juan theme by Tirso de Molina (*El burlador de Sevilla o convidado de piedra*, 1630); similarly – in its complex Christian recodification and devaluation of ancient myth – Calderón's famous drama *La vida es sueño* (1636; cf. [18; 19]). Precisely because of the uninterrupted dominance of discourse in Spain by the Church, it is there that the dissolution of the Classical model is particularly pronounced. Even in Spain, however, this development is ambivalent, and must not be allowed to mask the modernising potential innate in Baroque deconstruction of Antiquity, which already contains elements of a → QUERELLE DES ANCIENS ET DES MODERNES. This is in any case present in its nascent state in Spanish debate. Thus a protagonist of the anti-Aristotelian *comedia nueva* founded by Lope de Vega goes so far as to set down reflections designed to legitimise the superseding of the ancients by this genre, postulating a development of thought in the scientific knowledge and the arts as the basis of a constant process of perfection of knowledge, which in Antiquity was still raw and incomplete. On the basis of this postulate, Antiquity can no longer serve as a model, for, as Aristotle himself is supposed to have said, 'ille melior artifex est, qui naturae propius accesserit'. From such assumptions it follows that it behooves a 'viro docto prudentique' ' ex his quae a maioribus inventa perfectaque sunt eximere multa, addere, mutare'. And, like Tesauro, in order to legitimise this relativizing of Antiquity and even extend it to the realm of ideas in general, he cites technical progress (*Appendix ad expostulationem Spongiae*, 1618, cited in [11. 564]).

C. Tendencies towards a Deconstruction of Antiquity as a Model and the Beginnings of the Querelle des Anciens et des Modernes in the Baroque

That the new meaning of the marvellous in Baroque literary discourse bears the seeds of its modernisation is shown with particular clarity at the beginning of the 17th cent. in the work of Giambatista Marino. As the central figure of the Baroque in Italy, in his lyric work Marino plays a complex deconstructive game with the ancient inventory of mythical images and characters (inter alia with the construct of Arcadia, present in all Romance literatures since the Renaissance; cf. [26]). Theoretically and practically, the marvellous as an aesthetic device is in various respects an essential element of his work. Thus, in a not only ironic sally against the author of a religious epic, he calls the worldly-oriented *maraviglia*, which are designed to astonish (*far stupir*), as the aim of the poet [4. 248]; but, in particular, in his *Adone* (1620/1623) he writes a sweeping epic that, in the last analysis, can be understood as a deconstruction not only of the Classical tradition of the genre but also of the religious use of the marvellous (not for nothing was it placed on the Index in 1627!). Building up a religious-cosmological framework that serves only as decor, and starting out from Ovid's greatly expanded text, this work, entirely episodic in structure, cites a broad inventory of mythic elements, which are deconstructed by combining them with fragments of modern world-experience and aesthetic play. To quote only one example: In the fifth book Venus and Adonis watch the story of Actaeon as a stage tragedy, and not only do they as spectators commit the very transgression (watching Diana bathing) whose punishment is the subject-matter of the myth, but in addition, in a transgression of the boundaries of the stage, the world of power represented by the myth is annulled as it invades that of the love of Venus and Adonis and the animals hunted by Actaeon flee into the arms of the loving couple. In an ironic turn against rule-based poetics, Marino calls his epic a 'hodgepodge confection', and explains elsewhere that it was written against the rules, but that the 'true rules' consist in 'breaking the rules at the right time and the right place in order to fit in with the prevailing customs and taste of the age' [5. 206, 397].

It is no accident that this modernising impetus based on the recasting and deconstruction of ancient tradition established the link from Italy to France, where the *Adone* appeared with a dedication to Louis XIII. And it is only a seeming paradox that Jean Chapelain, who later emerged as a theorist of French Classicism, expressly praised the style of this work for its innovations, because 'the light of Antiquity shines everywhere in them, and they wholly pervade the charm of modernity' [3. 82]. For it is the French debates of the first half of the 17th cent., together with the literary orientations of the period, to a large extent attributable to the Baroque, that consistently provide the clearest demonstration in the Romance region of that modernising potential of the literary Baroque, which manifested itself in a break with Humanism and a deconstruction of the Classical model. In the area of literary production, this upheaval is exemplified in the genre, discussed previously, by those very epic parodies which, originating in Italy, flourished in France (especially the *Virgile travesti* of Paul Scarron, appearing since 1648), or, again originating in Italy, by the series of burlesque journeys to Parnassus, to be found in all Romance literatures, and which spare neither Aristotle nor the chief of the Muses, Apollo, the stigma of ridicule (thus e.g. Cesare Caporale, *Viaggio in Parnaso*, 1582, Miguel de Cervantes, *Viage del Parnaso*, 1612, Traiano Boccalini, *De Ragguagli di Parnaso*, 1624; in France, as a later echo, Antoine Furetière, *Nouvelle allégorique ou Histoire des derniers troubles arrivés au Royaume d'Eloquence*, 1656).

But, precisely in French discourse, developments go far beyond a deconstructing dispute with the Antiquity.

Literature's claim to an autonomy no longer reliant on traditional models for legitimation leads c. 1630 to a dispute over modernism, and this may essentially be understood as the initial phase of the Querelle des Anciens et des Modernes. Positioned at the centre of this debate, Jean-Louis Guez de Balzac declares: 'I take the art of the ancients as they would have taken mine if I had been first in this world, but I am no slave to their spirit [...]. On the contrary, if I am not mistaken I am much cleverer in invention than I am in imitation; just as in our time new stars have been discovered that until now have remained hidden, so in eloquence I seek beauties unthought of until now' [1. 147]. Here Antiquity is accorded the status of a past whose material may still be available, but which, faced with the availability of the opportunities for knowledge and invention in the present, has lost its normative significance – and it is no accident that Balzac like Tesauro draws on the paradigm of astronomy for justification. In view of the progress of discovery during the Early Modern age, ancient tradition loses its function as the location for the normative accreditation of knowledge – and precisely thereby it is enabled to become a point of reference for aesthetic speculation and literary construction. In this development too, Baroque deconstruction of the Classical model plays its part. In France, for example, it constitutes an essential prerequisite for the Classicism of the 17th cent., in which a literary modernity founded on the speculative reconstruction of an idealised Antiquity is able to unfold, having developed only as a tendency within the heterogeneous field of discourse of Romance Baroque literature.

→ ARCADISM; → CLASSICISM AFTER CLASSICAL ANTIQUITY; → EPOCHS, CONCEPT OF; → POETICS; → RHETORIC

SOURCES: 1 H. BIBAS, K. BUTLER (eds.), Les premières Lettres de Guez de Balzac, Vol. 1, 1933 2 L. CASTELVETRO, Poetica d'Aristotele vulgarizzata e sposata, W. ROMANI (ed.), Vol. 2, 1979 3 J. CHAPELAIN, Opuscules critiques, A. C. HUNTER (ed.), 1936 4 G. GETTO (ed.), Opere scelte di Marino e di marinisti, vol. 1, ²1962 5 M. GUGLIELMINETTI (ed.), Marino, Lettere, 1966 6 D. DE SAINT SORLIN, Discours pour prouver que les sujets Chrestiens sont les seuls propres à la poësie Heroïque, 1673, in: R. FREUDMANN (ed.), Clovis ou la France Chrestienne, Poëme heroïque par J. Desmarets de Saint-Sorlin, texte de 1657, 1972 7 J. SCALIGER, Poetices libri septem, Lyon 1561, A. BUCK (ed.), repr.1987 8 E. TESAURO, Il Cannocchiale Aristotelico, Turin 1670, (repr.of 5th ed,1968)
LITERATURE: 9 W. BARNER (ed.), Der literarische Barockbegriff, 1975 10 A. BUCK, Forschungen zur romanischen Barockliteratur, 1980 11 Id., K. HEITMANN, W. METTMANN (eds.), Dichtungslehren der Romania aus der Zeit der Renaissance und des Barock, 1972 12 B. CROCE, Storia della età barocca in Italia, 1929 13 W. FLOECK, Die Literarästhetik des französischen Barock. Entstehung – Entwicklung – Auflösung, 1979 14 H. FRIEDRICH, Epochen der italienischen Lyrik, 1964 15 K. GARBER (ed.), Europäische Barockrezeption, 1991 16 H. HATZFELD, Der gegenwärtige Stand der romanistischen Barockforschung, 1961 17 J. KÜPPER, Die spanische Literatur des 17. Jahrhunderts und das Barockkonzept, in: K. GARBER (ed.), Europäische Barockrezeption, 1991, 919–941 18 Id., La vida es sueño: Aufhebung des Skeptizismus, Recusatio der Moderne, in: Id., F. WOLFZETTEL (eds.), (Re-) Dezentrierungen. Aspekte des Barock in der Romania, 1999 19 Id., Diskurs-Renovatio bei Lope de Vega und Calderón. Untersuchungen zum spanischen Barockdrama, 1990 20 Id., F. WOLFZETTEL (eds.), (Re-) Dezentrierungen. Aspekte des Barock in der Romania, 1999 21 B. MIGLIORINI, Etymologie und Geschichte des Terminus 'Barock', in: W. BARNER (ed.), Der literarische Barockbegriff, 1975 22 U. SCHULZ-BUSCHHAUS, Der Barockbegriff in der Romania. Notizen zu einem vorläufigen Resümee, in: Zschr. für Lit.-Wiss. und Linguistik 98, 1995, 6–24 23 G. SCHRÖDER, Logos und List. Zur Entwicklung der Ästhetik in der frühen Neuzeit, 1985 24 D. SOUILLER, La Littérature baroque en Europe, 1988 25 V. L. TAPIÉ, Baroque et classicisme, ²1980 26 W. WEHLE, Diaphorie. Über barocken Lustverlust in Arkadien, in: J. KÜPPER, F. WOLFZETTEL (eds.), (Re-) Dezentrierungen. Aspekte des Barock in der Romania, 1999 27 R. WELLEK, The Concept of Baroque in Literary Scholarship, in Id., Concepts of Criticism, 1963.
HARTMUT STENZEL

IV. ART AND PAINTING
A. INTRODUCTION B. ART THEORY AND ACADEMIES C. PAINTING AND SCULPTURE D. ARCHITECTURE

A. INTRODUCTION

As in the Renaissance, in the Baroque, too, art oriented itself on ancient models. During the 17th cent. ancient art for the first time underwent systematic examination, which contributed to an increased and more profound knowledge of it. Archaeological research brought many new ancient finds to light, and illustrated publications followed with images of the statues and structures concerned. Findings of ancient art enjoyed increasing popularity in circles of collectors. This was accompanied by a growing interest in ancient literature and history, encouraged, for the most part, by attractively illustrated new editions of ancient authors. The varied opportunities for theoretical as well as practical interaction with the ancient inheritance allowed reception in the Baroque to appear more multi-layered than was the case in the Renaissance. Ancient works of art were not used merely as objects of study and as sources, but, in addition, served as a corrective in the assessment of one's own artistic creation; at the same time, however, the models served to a greater extent than in the previous century as a stimulus for design. There was, however, hardly any consistent differentiation between Greek and Roman antiquities in their reception.

Not only in sculpture but also in the → PAINTING of the Baroque, mainly ancient sculptures were became of interest (statues, busts, tomb reliefs, coins, gems), since these had most frequently survived. The reception of ancient painting did not begin until the discovery of the cities of Vesuvius in the mid–18th cent. Preferences for particular artistic works shifted in the 17th cent. Whereas during the Renaissance the → BELVEDERE APOLLO was the most admired model, the artists of the Baroque oriented themselves more toward the → LAOCOON GROUP, the *Farnese Hercules* or the *Medici Venus*. Alongside studies of the originals, reception of the works occurred via copies and casts as well as via → PRINTS(BOOKS CONTAINING). Copies and casts in Curiosity Cabinets and → ANTIQUITIES COLLECTIONS made access to ancient art possible, also outside Italy. During the Baroque the reception of ancient works enabled the expression of new allegorical content.

During the course of the 16th cent. the ancient authors were translated into modern European languages and thus rendered accessible to artists, who for the most part had no knowledge of Latin or Greek. The number of received authors was, however, relatively small: Ovid, Herodotus, Tacitus, Livy, Flavius Josephus and Plutarch. Themes from Greek and Roman historiography were accorded scant attention by artists. It was Ovid's 'Metamorphoses' and his interpretations of ancient myths that were most often depicted from the 16th to the 18th cent.; at the same time, allegorical interpretations of the 'Metamorphoses' led to their use as

Fig. 1: Nicolas Poussin, *Et in Arcadia ego.*
With permission of Musée du Louvre, Paris

Fig. 1a: François Duquesnoy, *Santa Susanna.*
With permission of the Ministero Beni Culturali e Ambientali,
Instituto Centrale per il Catalogo e la Documentazione

sources of moral exemplars. Mythological themes were increasingly used in the iconographical programs of palaces and villas, entailing acceptance of the sometimes gross offence to Christian sensibilities caused by depiction of the ancient gods; clients wanted to show off their Humanist education by means of clever allusions, even if this often happened at the expense of morality and belief.

Unlike the late 18th cent., the 17th displayed no urge to comprehend Antiquity as a binding stylistic model and to view it in a doctrinaire fashion. As Baroque art did not possess a unified understanding of Antiquity, the approach, too, occurred in various ways: romantic, subjective, and also rational and scientific in manner. In all genres, two main tendencies may be detected: the emotive Baroque and the Classicistic, and these receive Antiquity in different ways. While artists of the Baroque tendency prized spectacular effects, the highest goal of the Classicists was the representation of ideal beauty, which was not to be found in never perfect nature, but was considered to have been achieved in the artworks of Antiquity. The most important representatives of the Classical tendency in the 17th cent. are, in painting, Carracci, Reni, Poussin, Lorrain and Sacchi, in sculpture Algardi and Duquesnoy; their spokesperson is the Italian writer on art and artists, Giovanni Pietro Bellori.

B. ART THEORY AND ACADEMIES

In traditional studios as in the academies founded during the course of the 17th cent., ancient art played a

Fig. 2: Peter Paul Rubens, *Descent from the Cross*.
Antwerp Cathedral.
With Permission of the Zentralinstitut für Kunstgeschichte München

Tempio antico nella Via Appia quale si vedevono non molti anni sono, una buona parte, ora è affatto consumato sino la superfice del terreno.

Fig. 3: Giovanni Battista Montano,
Tempio antico nella via Appia

vital role in the training of artists, and this in spite of the fact that writers of art treatises appearing in the wake of the Council of Trent (Paleotti etc.) demanded that ancient sculpture be consigned to the studies of the academics. The life-size casts of ancient statues enabled artists to carry out a thorough study of composition, stance, gesture and mimicry, and led them beyond faithful imitation to their own figurative inventions. In his writings Giovanni Pietro Bellori raises the demand for imitation of the ancients to the status of a doctrine. In a lecture on the 'Idea' at the Accademia di San Luca in Rome (1664) he advised artists to imitate not nature itself but the ancient artists, who in their works realised the idea of a perfect nature.

The normative conception of the perfection and beauty of ancient art was further developed in the eyes of Classicists at the Académie Royale de Peinture et de Sculpture founded in 1648. Antiquity had the status of an insurpassable exemplar, and was regarded as an absolute norm. Nature itself was subject to correction, in their opinion, insofar as it does not measure up to the Greek or Roman ideal of beauty. Jean-Baptiste Colbert in his capacity as Surintendant des Bâtiments and Vice-Protector of the Académie Royale initiated the creation of a → CAST COLLECTION of the most celebrated statues of Rome. Casts of sculptures such as the *Laocoon Group*, the *Antinous*, the → DIANA OF EPHESUS, the *Belvedere Apollo* and the *Medici Venus* served as objects of study, to be drawn by students before they

were allowed access to the live model class. The intention was that the proportions of the ancient statues should be transferred to the living models, as the former were regarded as perfect and undisputed exemplars for the representation of human beings. The central theme of the *conférences* held at the Académie Royale was ancient statues. Several *conférences* were devoted to the *Laocoon Group*, which was regarded as an exemplary representation of extreme suffering. During the second half of the 17th cent. a change came about in the assessment of Antiquity: if for Fréart de Chambray in his *Parallèle de l'architecture ancienne et moderne* (1650) it is still the standard by which all things are to be measured, the → QUERELLE DES ANCIENS ET DES MODERNES, pursued at the Académie Royale during the final three decades of the 17th cent., began to question the superiority and exemplary character of ancient art. This assault on the supposed perfection of Antiquity was a consequence of the development of French culture under Louis XIV, the advance of modern science and the promulgation of the modern philosophy of the Enlightenment. A protagonist of the *Modernes* was Charles Perrault, who in his seminal work *Parallèle des Anciens et des Modernes* (1693) represented the view that the present day was superior to Antiquity in almost all areas of art and knowledge. The most important out-

Fig. 4: Nicolas-François Blondel, Porte Saint-Denis, Paris. *With Permission of the Zentralinstitut für Kunstgeschichte München*

come of the 'Querelles' was the insight that ancient and modern art, being founded on historically different bases, were, thus, not capable of comparison. The questioning of the exemplary character and superiority of ancient art occasioned an historical view of that era, which eventually robbed it of its normative effect on contemporary art.

C. PAINTING AND SCULPTURE

The spirit of Antiquity may be detected most strongly in painting and sculpture in two motif areas: a) in the representation of gods and heroes of mythology and history and b) in the evocation of the ancient utopia of Arcadia. In numerous paintings, sculptural groups and murals the raw power of gods and heroes is celebrated in allegorical settings that endow it with a flavour of contemporaneity. At the same time, in the complex mythical/allegorical programs of the great ceiling frescoes absolutist rulers are presented in their palaces as heroes fit for divine worship. With Arcadia as a utopia pervaded by bliss and beauty, Antiquity became the definitive irretrievable era, the distant longed-for land, the quintessence of a happy clime to be 'sought with the soul'. Arcadia is set against the civilising constraints of the modern age as a symbol of the longing for Antiquity as a golden age, a imaginary state of harmony and freedom. The longing for original, paradisiacal states finds expression in harmonious landscapes populated with ancient or biblical figures in the paintings of Lorrain and Poussin (Fig. 1).

The fact that the painters oriented themselves closely on celebrated ancient models occasionally led to their figures appearing as unmoving as statues. While, with

regard to many of his paintings, Poussin emphasised this as a mark of quality, Rubens reacted to it critically, although at the time he was himself a prominent connoisseur of Antiquity and the owner of an antiquities collection. Rubens, who himself faithfully modelled many of his figures on marble statues (*Seneca, Descent from the Cross*; Fig. 2), in his critical study of 1630–1640 *De imitatione antiquarum statuarum* regards the study of antiquities by painters with a certain degree of reserve. Many artists followed his conception in imitating marble instead of flesh, using various colours in their depiction of it. Although close knowledge of the ancient models remained indispensable, at the same time painters had to endeavour to 'endow [those models] with flesh and blood, in such a manner that they in no way smack of stone'. The reception of Antiquity in Baroque sculpture is inseparable from the improving of antiquities. None of the celebrated Roman sculptors of the Seicento confined themselves to close conformity with the formal canon of ancient sculpture; instead, they improved and restored the antiquities in their own realisations, provoked to do this by the very fragmentary nature of the ancient models. In Bellori's estimation, Algardi and Duquesnoy were the only ones capable of reconstructing ancient statues *conforme la buona maniera antica*. A testament to the advanced state of knowledge of Antiquity in the early 17th cent. are the pseudo-ancient reliefs of the *Villa Ludovisi*, which passed for ancient works into our time. For Bernini the antiquities were *reliquie innamorte*, on which he relied so closely, especially in his early works, so that, for example, his *Goat Amalthea* was still at the beginning of the 20th cent. regarded as an ancient work.

D. ARCHITECTURE

While during the Renaissance theoretical involvement with ancient architecture was expressed in a multitude of treatises referring to Vitruvius' 'Ten Books on Architecture' and to knowledge gained from the writer's own studies of antiquities, such theoretical works by Italian architects of the 17th cent. are scarcely to be found. It should by no means be concluded from this that interest in ancient architecture had declined. It was merely expressed in other ways. Bernini's work for Pope Alexander VII in Rome is shaped by a study of Antiquity; in the oval form of the colonnaded St. Peter's Square, for example, he refers directly to the *Circus Neronianus*, which originally occupied the same space. Bernini's rival in Rome, Borromini, was also a recognised connoisseur of Antiquity; the ground-plan of *San Carlo alle Quattro Fontane*, for example, suggests a knowledge of the Roman-Hellenistic architecture of the *Villa Adriana*. In contrast to the reception of Antiquity during the High Renaissance, which – especially in Palladio – consisted in constructing entire buildings in the spirit of the canon that had come down from Vitruvius, the involvement of Baroque architecture with the ancient legacy is characterised by the adoption of individual forms as a basis for innovation. As had already been the case during the Renaissance, ancient forms such as the central-plan building on a circular plan (→ PANTHEON) were employed and re-interpreted in a Christian sense. While during the Renaissance exact drawings were prepared based on surviving buildings or elements of buildings, in the 17th cent. a new form of appropriation of Antiquity came into play: an outstanding example is Giovanni Battista Montano's *Raccolta de' tempij et sepolcri disegnati dall'antico* of 1624, which was frequently reissued; his designs are not reconstructions in the strict sense, but in part conceptions from his own imagination inspired by ancient models (Fig. 3). Borromini especially was inspired by such designs. Against the meticulous reconstruction of ancient forms during the Renaissance stands the imaginative revival of those forms during the Baroque. Even in the preference for particular orders, differences are evident. During the Renaissance the Dorian/Tuscan and Ionian orders were most frequently used, while now the much richer Corinthian is preferred (Bernini – design for the Louvre). Only the Palladian tradition of the 17th cent. esp. in Northern Europe, remains true to the Ionian order.

French Baroque architecture is inconceivable without its involvement with Antiquity, but this proceeded along essentially more academic lines than was the case in Italy. In 1671 Colbert founded the Académie Royale d'Architecture, placing it under the leadership of François Blondel. Its stated purpose was to work out a binding, systematic architectural doctrine and aesthetic, and to train young architects in it. Central to its teaching was Vitruvius, followed by the recognised Renaissance theorists. Claude Perrault was given the task of producing a new translation of Vitruvius. Travel grants were awarded in order to document ancient buildings in southern France and especially Italy. In his *Cours d'architecture* (1675–1683) Blondel cites the masters and buildings of Antiquity as models, but at the same time he regards it as the duty of architecture to supersede and perfect Antiquity. This culminates in the call for France to have its own national columnar order. French peculiarities are the setting of columns in pairs and the resulting absence of arcades of columns (Claude Perrault, colonnade of the Louvre). Under the aegis of French absolutism, the first → TRIUMPHAL ARCH of Baroque architecture rose 1670–1680 in Paris: an outstanding example is Blondel's *Porte Saint-Denis* in Paris (Fig. 4) – only a monumental form from Antiquity was appropriate for the greatness of the Sun King.

→ ARCADISM; → ARCHITECTURAL THEORY/VITRUVIANISM

1 H. BECK, S. SCHULZE (eds.), Antikenrezeption im Hochbarock, 1989   2 A. BLUNT, Baroque Architecture and Classical Antiquity, in: Classical Influences on European Culture, AD 1500–1700, 1976, 349–354   3 M. BULL, Poussin and the Antique, in: Gazette des Beaux-Arts 129, 1997, 116–130   4 E. FORSSMAN, Dorisch, jonisch, korinthisch. Studien über den Gebrauch der Säulenordnungen in der Architektur des 16.–18. Jahrhunderts, 1961   5 E. H. GOMBRICH, The Style all'antica, in: Stud. in Western Art 2, 1963, 31–41   6 Id., Norm and Form. Studies in

the Art of Renaissance 1, 1966   7 F. HASKELL, N. PENNY, Taste and the Antique. The Lure of Classical Sculpture 1500–1900, 8 M. JAFFÉ, Rubens and Italy, 1977   9 H. KELLER, Das Nachleben des antiken Bildnisses von der Karolingerzeit bis zur Gegenwart, 1970   10 H.-W. KRUFT, Die Quelle für die Ovalform von Berninis Petersplatz, in: Imagination und Imago, Festschrift Kurt Rossacher, 1983   11 H. LADENDORF, Antikenstudium und Antikenkopie, 1958   12 M. LYTTELTON, Baroque Architecture in Classical Antiquity, 1974   13 M. VAN DER MEULEN, Rubens' Copies after the Antique, 3 Vols., 1994 (= Corpus Rubenianum Ludwig Burchard 23)   14 J. MULLER, Rubens: The Artist as Collector, Princeton, 1989   15 D. NEBENDAHL, Die schönsten Antiken Roms. Studien zur Rezeption antiker Bildhauerwerke im römischen Seicento, 1990   16 W. OECHSLIN, Bildungsgut und Antike im frühen Settecento in Rom, 1972   17 E. PANOFSKY, Et in Arcadia ego. Poussin und die Tradition des Elegischen, in: Id., Sinn und Deutung in der bildenden Kunst, 1975, 351–377   18 Id., Idea, ein Beitrag zur Begriffsgeschichte der älteren Kunsttheorie, 1924   19 H. SEDLMAYR, Die Architektur Borrominis, 1986   20 W. STOPFEL, Triumphbogen in der Architektur des Barock in Frankreich und Deutschland, 1964   21 CH. TÜMPEL, Bild und Text: Zur Rezeption antiker Autoren in der europäischen Kunst der Neuzeit (Livius, Valerius Maximus), in: W. SCHLINK, M. SPERLICH (eds.), Forma et Subtilitas. Festschrift für Wolfgang Schöne zum 75. Geburtstag, 198–218   22 G. VALERIUS, Antike Statuen als Modelle für die Darstellung des Menschen. Die decorum-Lehre in Graphikwerken französischer Künstler des 17. Jahrhunderts, 1992   23 M. VIKERS, Greek and Roman Antiquities in the Seventeenth Century, in: O. IMPEY, A. MACGREGOR (eds.), The Origins of Museums. The Cabinet of Curiosities in Sixteenth and Seventeenth-century Europe, 1985, 223–231   24 M. WARNKE, P.P. Rubens. Leben und Werk, 1997.

KARIN WENZEL, CAROLA HELLWIG

Basilica

A. TERMINOLOGY AND DEFINITION   B. ARCHITECTURAL HISTORY OF THE CHRISTIAN BASILICA

A. TERMINOLOGY AND DEFINITION

1. PROFANE ARCHITECTURE   2. RELIGIOUS ARCHITECTURE

1. PROFANE ARCHITECTURE

In the Italian Renaissance (A. Palladio [11. lib. III, cap. 20]) the term *basilica* was applied to multifunctional communal palaces that contained commercial and meeting spaces (basilicas in Vicenza, Padua, Brescia) thus echoing the function of the ancient Roman basilica as market hall, administrative space, and courthouse.

2. RELIGIOUS ARCHITECTURE

The term *basilica* is first attested for church buildings in AD 303, and was regularly used in that sense since Constantine's time. At first the term was not confined to any particular architectural type: *basilica* could refer to both longitudinal and central-plan buildings, and in the early Christian Period even rotundas like S. Stefano Rotondo in Rome or S. Vitale in Ravenna went by the name of basilicas. In the early Middle Ages, the

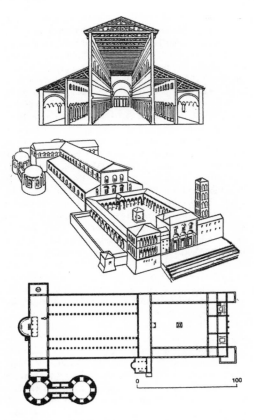

Fig. 1: Rome, Old Saint Peter's.
Late Constantinian. Section,
external view, plan (reconstruction)

term was used indiscriminately – e.g. by Widukind of
Corvey – for churches with both longitudinal and central building plans (*B. Caroli magni, in illa B., in
rotundum facta*), SS rer. germ. 43 1935, 65 [21. 910;
28. 213–215]). Its distinct conceptual specification did
not emerge until the 15th cent. Based on L. B. Alberti's
definition [1. VII, cc. 3, 14, 15] 'basilica' became an
established concept of architectural history and typology, and since then designates a longitudinal building,
divided by supports into three or more aisles ('pillared
basilica', 'columned basilica'); the side aisles are narrow
and lower, whereas the nave is wide and higher with
windows in the clerestory. If the nave is higher than the
side aisles but without its own clerestory, the building is
called a 'pseudo-basilica'. If a basilica consists of five or
more aisles, with interior side aisles that are higher than
the exterior ones, is called a 'stepped basilica'.

In canon law, the title basilica refers to the rank of a
church associated with certain privileges ('basilica
maior', 'basilica minor'), regardless of its architectural
type.

B. Architectural History of the Chris-
tian Basilica
1. Early Christian Period   2. Middle Ages
3. Modern Period

1. Early Christian Period
The era of Constantine created the conditions that
gave rise to Christian monumental architecture, with
the basilica as its most common representative. The
basic type of a Constantinian basilica features an axial
sequence of spaces with an outer court (atrium), a ves-

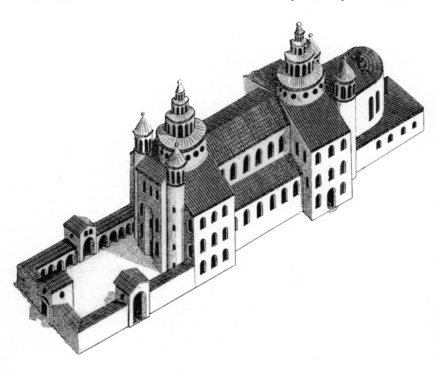

Fig. 2: General view of
Saint Riquier, Centula,
c. 790-799
(reconstruction)

tibule (narthex), an oblong space divided into three or five aisles with a flat wooden ceiling or open roof framework, and an apse sometimes preceded by a transept (Lateran Basilica, St Paul-outside-the-Walls, the Old St Peter, see Fig. 1, all in Rome). In addition, a specialised type developed in the 4th cent.: the three-aisled 'coemeterial basilica' with side aisles continuing as a rounded ambulatory around the choir area and apse (Santi Marcellino e Pietro, San Sebastiano, Santa Agnese, all in Rome). Constantinian basilicas are widely distributed (Palestine, Syria, North Africa), and are to be found in Byzantine art, where they are often conceived as 'galleried basilicas' (Demetrius Basilica/Thessaloniki 412, Johannes-Studios-Basilica, Constantinople 463). In Byzantium and the Christian East, the basilica concept was increasingly supplanted by cross-vaulted churches after the 6th cent. [26; 27. 1249–1259].

2. MIDDLE AGES

The basilica dominated church architecture in the West until the end of the Middle Ages. The Carolingian Period provided the foundation for the concept of the medieval basilica. In the service of the *Renovatio Imperii*, sacred architecture absorbed the model of Constantinian churches (monastery church, Fulda 791, monastery church, Hersfeld 831). Yet the early Christian basilica was modified to meet a succession of new needs (crypts, side chapels) resulting in new terminations for both east and west ends during the Carolingian-Ottonian Period. Among the preferred endings for the choir area were terminals like the square choir, inserted between transept and apse (Reichenau/Mittelzell 799), triapsal constructions (Agliate near Monza, 824), and staggered choirs (Cluny II, 981), as well as ambulatory choirs with radiating chapels (St-Philibert/Tournus 950). Innovations at the western end of the basilica included the development of substantial westwork (St-Riquier/Centula 790, Fig. 2), a two-towered façade (monastery church Hersfeld 831) or an apse at the western end of the church that could serve as a counter-choir in the liturgy (monastery church, Fulda 791, plan of St Gall 820). In addition, the west end could be granted its own transept with a crossing tower (St.Michael/Hildesheim c. 1000). With this clear emphasis on the west end, the basilica lost its directed spatial orientation in the Carolingian and Ottonian Period, and was therefore, in contrast to the early Christian basilica, conceived more strongly with a view towards a balance between east and west. With the reform movements of the 11th cent., the early Christian concept of the spatially oriented basilica prevailed once again in Romanesque church architecture (1000–1200): The flat-roofed episcopal churches, which soared to enormous heights (Strasbourg 1015, Speyer I, 1030, Pisa 1063), were based on the classic basilica scheme, as were the abbey churches of the reform orders (Cluniacs, Hirsau movement, Cistercians) whose construction activity in the 11th/12th cents. brought the basilica plan to wide parts of Europe. An innovation in Romanesque church architecture was the complete vaulting of the basilica ('vaulted basilica') that occurs in the late 11th cent. in Germany and France (Speyer II c. 1080, Cluny III 1089). With the exception of Italy, where the early Christian tradition of the flat roof was largely kept alive (Torcello 1008, Montecassino 1066), vaulting was accepted into the concept of a basilica. With their tower over the crossing, ambulatory choir, and galleries on the side aisles, buildings like Paray-le-Monial (1090), St-Madeleine/Vézelay (early 12th cent.) or Santiago de Compostela (completed 1128) exemplified the high Romanesque type of the completely vaulted basilica that culminated in French cathedral architecture. Characteristic of the basilica in its Gothic form (Notre-Dame/Paris 1163, Reims 1211) were the emphasis on the west-east orientation, the deliberate concentration of spatial units into one unified space, and the change in proportions of the central nave by increasing its height (from 1:2 at the cathedral in Pisa, through 1:2.5 at Chartres, to 1:3.5 at Beauvais). From France, the basilica spread to Belgian and Dutch regions (Brussels, early 13th cent., Utrecht 1321) as well as to England (Canterbury 1174) and Scandinavia (Uppsala 1270). In the 13th cent., basilicas increasingly appeared in Spain (Leon 1205, Burgos 1221), whereas in Germany its pure form was to be found only in a few large buildings (Cologne 1248, Strasbourg, nave 1250, Prague 1344). From the 13th cent. on, with its first peak in Germany around 1300, the hall church prevailed over the basilica, without ever completely replacing it. A few basilical constructions arose in Italy, in close association with German and French builder's guilds (Milan cathedral 1386, S. Petronio/ Bologna 1390), yet Northern European Gothic cathedrals remained fundamentally foreign to Italian stylistic sensibility. Significantly, important impulses for the post-medieval basilica came from this area [20; 22. 1356–1372].

3. MODERN PERIOD

Italy responded to the Gothic style with Renaissance architecture and its new formal canon, oriented towards Antiquity, which was accompanied by a revival of ancient building types, such as the basilica. All affinity to the central-plan building notwithstanding, the classical basilica was legitimized as a building concept for sacred architecture in the treatises (L. B. Alberti [1. lib. VII, capp. 3, 14]; Filarete [5. lib. X, 77r–78r]; F. di G. Martini [6. vol. II, lib. IV, esp. 372]; S. Serlio [16. lib. V, 215–218]), and its disposition and proportion were re-evaluated. After 1419, it was built in many variations: as a flat-roofed columned basilica with three aisles, a projecting transept and radiating side chapels (S. Lorenzo 1419, see Fig. 5, S. Spirito 1436, both in Florence), as a pillared basilica with three aisles and groin vaults with rows of chapels (S. Pietro/Modena 1476) or in the forward-looking shape of S. Andrea in Mantua (1472) where L. B. Alberti, inspired by the Roman Basilica of Maxentius, modified the side aisles to rows of chapels with cross-barrel vaults and replaced the flat ceiling of the central aisle with a huge coffered vault. Alberti's solution paved the way for the church

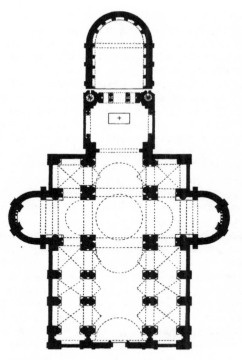

Fig. 3: Plan of San Giorgio Maggiore,
Venice (begun 1566)

Fig. 4: Interior of the 'Vor Frue Kirke',
Copenhagen (begun 1811)

Fig. 5: Interior of San Lorenzo, Florence (begun 1421)

architecture of the Counterreformation (P. Cataneo [3. lib. III pass.]). Modification of the basic scheme of the basilica in accordance with notions of ecclesiastical reform led to the emergence in 1560 of the 'Basilica della Riforma cattolica' [18], which appears in a basic oblong form, with a barrel-vaulted central nave and side aisles transformed into a series of chapels (Jesuit church Il Gesu/Rome), or as a spatial arrangement with several aisles built over a Latin cross (S. Giorgio Maggiore/Venice, Fig. 3). The pioneering longitudinal solution of St Peter/Rome (1607) ended several years of discussion over the conceptual shape of the church (Panvinius [12. 228ff.]; 24]) in favour of the Counterreformation and the basilica concept. These solutions encouraged the spread of the longitudinal basilica in the 17th and 18th cents. over wide areas of Europe (Theatine church/ Munich 1663, Jesuit church/Salamanca 1614, St Nicolas/Prague 1703, convent church Mafra 1717) as a successful alternative to the central-plan and hall buildings of the Baroque and Late Baroque Periods. French religious architecture of the 18th cent. also returned to the basilica scheme. From the middle of the century, the confrontation with ancient architecture and early Christian church construction, which theorists had demanded (J. Cordemoy [4. 193–222]; M. A. Laugier [10. 173–208]; Ch. Percier/P. Fontaine [13. pl. 92, 27]), found its implementation into barrel-vaulted columned basilicas of the classical type with three aisles (St-Symphorien/Versailles 1764, St-Louis/St-Germain-en-Laye 1765, St-Philippe-du-Roule/Paris 1768) [19. 123–136]. Their concept dominated Christian church architecture well beyond France and into the 19th cent. (Vor Frue Kirke (Church of Our Lady), Copenhagen 1811, see Fig. 4, Dionysios Church/Athens 1848). Building on early 19th cent. scholarly interest in the early Christian basilicas of Rome (for instance, building inventories etc. [7]) and the discussion it engendered, the basilica was pronounced appropriate for contemporary German-speaking lands as well ('The form of the basilica seems to speak most to the present time (...)', G. Moller to Goethe, 1818 [9. 6; 17. 154–223]). Treatises, pattern books and essays (L. v. Klenze [9]; Ch. Bunsen [2], G. Semper [15. 443–467]; H. Hübsch [8]) made the basilica practical for Protestant as well as Catholic church architecture. Theorists demanded a simple oblong floor plan, the basilica scheme, and a spacious central aisle covered either by a barrel-vault or a flat wooden ceiling, and these elements were largely constitutive of the church architecture of the 19th cent. (St Boniface/Munich 1828, Altlerchenfelder Church/Vienna 1848, Liebfrauenkirche/Zurich 1894) [22. 1372–1394]. The end of the 19th cent. saw the defeat of historicism in church architecture, and the rejection of classical spatial solutions like the basilica, which were replaced by new formal solutions. During the period of → NATIONAL SOCIALISM the basilica experienced – at least in theory – a *Renovatio* since it was regarded as 'the essence of Nordic spatial experience' (A. Rosenberg [14. 384]). In practice, however, the basilical type remained the exception as compared to the hall church, widespread in the 1930s (Hl. Kreuz/Würzburg 1934, Benedictine Abbey Münsterschwarzach 1935).

1 L. B. ALBERTI, De Re Aedificatoria, Florence 1485 (repr. 1975) 2 CH. V. BUNSEN, Die Basilika des christlichen Roms nach ihrem Zusammenhange mit Idee und Geschichte der Kirchenbaukunst, 2 vols., München 1842–44 3 P. CATANEO, I quattro primi libri di Architettura, Venice 1554 (repr. 1964) 4 J. CORDEMOY, Dissertation sur la manière dont les eglises doivent être bâties (...) in: Nouveau Traité de toute l'Architecture ou l'art de bastir (...), Paris 1714 (repr. 1966) 5 A. FILARETE, Trattato di Architettura, 2 vols., 1972 6 F. DI GIORGIO MARTINI, Trattati di Architettura, Ingegneria e Arte Militare, 2 vols., 1967 7 J. G. GUTENSOHN, J. M. KNAPP, Denkmale der christlichen Religion, oder Sammlung der ältesten christlichen Kirchen oder Basiliken Roms vom 4. bis zum 13. Jahrhundert, Tübingen/Stuttgart 1822–27 8 H. HÜBSCH, Die altchristliche Kirchen nach den Baudenkmalen und älteren Beschreibungen und der Einfluß des altchristlichen Baustyls auf den Kirchenbau aller späteren Perioden, Karlsruhe 1862 9 L. V. KLENZE, Anweisung zur Architectur des christlichen Cultus, München 1822 (repr. 1990) 10 M. A. LAUGIER, Essai sur l'architecture, Paris 1755 (repr. 1966) 11 A. PALLADIO, I Quattro Libri dell' Architettura, Venice 1570 (repr. 1968) 12 O. PANVINIUS, De Rebus antiquis memorabilibus (...), in: Spicilegium Romanum IX, Rome 1843, 194–382 13 CH. PERCIER, P. FONTAINE, Palais, Maisons et autres édifices modernes dessinés à Rome, Paris 1798 (repr. 1980) 14 A. ROSENBERG, Der Mythus des 20. Jahrhunderts, ³1932. 15 G. SEMPER, Über den Bau evangelischer Kirchen. in: KS, Berlin/Stuttgart 1884 (repr. 1979) 16 S. SERLIO, Tutte l'opere d'Architettura et Prospetiva, Venice 1619 (repr. 1964) 17 CH. L. STIEGLITZ, Encyklopädie der bürgerlichen Baukunst, 3 vols., Leipzig 1796, s.v. Kirche, 101–223 18 J. ACKERMAN, Il contributo dell'Alessi alla tipologia della chiesa longitudinale, in: Galeazzo Alessi e l'Architettura del Cinquecento. Atti del Convegno int. di Studi, 1975, 461–466 19 A. BRAHAM, The Architecture of the French Enlightenment, 1980 20 G. DEHIO, G. V. BEZOLD, Die kirchliche Baukunst des Abendlandes, 7 vols., 1892–1901 21 F. W. DEICHMANN, s.v. Basilika, Religion in Geschichte und Gegenwart 1, ³1957, 910–912 22 Id., G. BANDMANN, W. HAGER, H. HAMPE, s.v. Kirchenbau, Religion in Geschichte und Gegenwart 3, 1959, 1347–1406 23 J. HECHT, s.v. Basilika, Reallexikon zur deutschen Kunstgeschichte 1, 1480–1488 24 CH. JOBST, Die christliche Basilika, in: Aspekte der Gegenreformation, 698–749 (= Zeitsprünge 1, 1997, Sonderheft) 25 W. KOCH, Baustilkunde, europäische Baukunst von der Antike bis zur Gegenwart, 1982 26 R. KRAUTHEIMER, Early Christian and Byzantine Architecture, 1975. 27 E. LANGLOTZ, F. W. DEICHMANN, s.v. Basilika, Reallexikon für Antike und Christentum 1, 1225–1259 28 A. WECKWERTH, Die christliche Basilika – ein theologischer Begriff und eine theologische Gestalt, in: Westfälische Zeitung 112, 1962, 205–223. BARBARA KILIAN

Basle, Antikenmuseum and Sammlung Ludwig
A. INTRODUCTION B. SCULPTURE HALL C. THE
BUILDINGS HOUSING THE ANTIKENMUSEUM
D. COLLECTION E. ARRANGEMENT

A. INTRODUCTION
Although the Basle Antikenmuseum was founded
only a few decades ago, making it one of the youngest of
its kind in Europe, it houses an archaeological collection of great significance. Various genres of visual art
are represented by excellent examples both in terms of
their significance for cultural history as well as quality.
The museum was founded – and continues to be
supported – through a joint effort of municipal and private sponsorship. Therefore works on loan from private collectors supplement the museum's exhibits of its
own collections to a greater degree than is usually the
case in most other public collections in Europe. The
humanistic world view of the local bourgeoisie in the
19th cent. created the intellectual climate that led to the
foundation of the museum. Aside from private collections this is evidenced by the local tradition of subsequently integrating a → CAST COLLECTION into the
structure of the museum.

B. SCULPTURE HALL
Around 1830 a collection of casts of ancient sculptures was started in Basle. Initially, after 1849, the cast
collection was part of the University Museum until it
was moved into the Sculpture Hall at the Basle Kunst-
halle in 1887. Finally in 1963, after a varied history, it
found another home in a new, specially built sculpture
hall that allowed for a suitable display and included
studios as well. The Sculpture Hall had regular museum
hours and was administrated by the Antikenmuseum.
Unlike the cast collection of the 19th cent. its mission no
longer was to document a few chosen works but rather
to bring together the casts of ancient sculptures that are
scattered all over the world. With this objective in mind,
the collection of the Sculpture Hall grew multiple times
over the past decades; today it comprises several thousand objects and by quantity alone has a leading position internationally. For example, since the 1970s the
Sculpture Hall houses casts of almost all of the sculptural remains of the → PARTHENON in Athens. In 1982 they
provided the focus for a scholarly colloquium on the
Parthenon.

C. THE BUILDINGS HOUSING THE
ANTIKENMUSEUM
In 1966 the original collection was made available to
the public in a classicist townhouse (House A) and a
contemporary annex in the back. The increasing need
for more exhibition space was met in the 1980s by expanding into a neighbouring building that dates to the
first half of the 19th cent. as well (House B). Today the
museum complex provides a structured architectural
landscape, preserving a mostly traditional exterior
while in the interior new circulation patterns reflect

Fig. 1: Belly amphora, Amasis Painter. Antikenmuseum
Basel und Sammlung Ludwig. Inventory nr. Kä 420

Fig. 2: 'Basler Arztrelief' (relief depicting a physician).
Antikenmuseum Basel und Sammlung Ludwig.
Inventory nr. BS 236.

Fig. 3: 'Steinhäuserscher Kopf', replica of the Belvedere Apollo's head. Antikenmuseum Basel und Sammlung Ludwig. Inventory nr. BS 205.

Fig. 4: Portrait of a Republican. Antikenmuseum Basel und Sammlung Ludwig. Inventory nr. BS 209.

new usage priorities. Alterations to the structure of the buildings are limited; and in House B. the attempt was made to preserve the bourgeois interior style as much as possible. Around 1980 new construction was discussed, but in the end, renovation was preferred.

D. Collection

When the museum was established, its core was a small and scattered municipal collection; yet between 1960 and the opening of the museum it grew to twice its original size. Donations (especially the collections Käppeli and Züst) were equally represented. Half of the works shown in 1966 – there were c. 640 exhibits – came from private collections and were on loan as part of the permanent collection. Today, the collection is about four times as large, with a third coming from gifts. The largest donation, leading to an expansion of the museum, was given by Mr. and Mrs. Ludwig. The name *Sammlung Ludwig* was permanently added to that of the museum.

The collection focuses on sculptures, terracotta, vases and coins, but other genres, even weapons, are also well represented. From the outset, considerations of quality determined the acquisition of new objects. Thus the expansion of the holdings underwent a certain development; originally the focus was on Greek art between the 6th and 4th cents. whereas now works of art range from the 3rd millennium BC to the Byzantine period and sometimes include even marginal cultures. Attic vases of the 6th and 5th cents. BC are among the

most notable groups or individual works (e.g. an amphora of the Amasis Painter, Fig.1) as are an almost unique Ionic relief from the early 5th cent. with the portrait of a doctor (Fig. 2) and the replica of the head of the Vatican → Belvedere Apollo, considered its best ancient copy (Fig.3). The portraiture of the Roman Republic is also sufficiently represented (Fig.4).

E. Arrangement

Didactically the museum is guided by the principle to offer the visitor additional information in the exhibition halls without causing distraction from the works through an overabundance of specialised information. Individual sections or groups of works are explained on introductory panels. The complex architecture of the building prohibits a singular route through the collection that would lead from one department to the next. Therefore several tours are suggested, starting in the entrance hall of House A. The objects are organised mainly according to genres and within genres according to time periods. For example, Greek sculpture of the Archaic and Classical Periods is exhibited in the top floor of the modern extension with natural illumination from skylights, whereas Hellenistic and Roman sculptures are displayed in a room with artificial light a floor below; vases and objects of the minor arts, divided into groups, are placed on the various floors of Houses A and B. In assigning the vases to the various rooms, regional and chronological considerations were taken into account as well as the character of the particular rooms, e.g. Attic pottery of the late 6th and early 5th cents. BC- represented in masterworks – was placed into the most dignified rooms of House A. A separate building has been reserved for educational activities.

1 Antikenmuseum und Sammlung Ludwig. 120 ausge-wählte Werke (120 selected works), 1987   2 E. BERGER, Zur Eröffnung des erweiterten Antikenmuseum in Basel am 3. Mai 1988, in: AK 31, 1988, 29–44   3 Id., Hundert Jahre Skulpturhalle Basel (1887–1987), in: AK 31, 1988, 45–46   4 Id. (ed.), Antike Kunstwerke aus der Sammlung Ludwig 1–3, 1979–89   5 Id. (et al), Bauwerk und Plastik des Parthenon. – Zur Ausstellung Basel und die Akropolis in der Skulpturhalle, in: AK 23, 1980, 59–65   6 J. J. BER-NOULLI, Museum in Basel. Catalog für die antiquarische Abtheilung, Basel 1880   7 R. BURCKHARDT, Die Gipsab-güsse in der Skulpturhalle zu Basel, 1907   8 D. HUBER, M. SCHMIDT, Die Gebäude des Antikenmuseum, 1990   9 Kunstwerke der Antike aus der Sammlung Käppeli, 1963   10 K. SCHEFOLD, Klassische Kunst in Basel, 1955   11 Id., Führer durch das Antikenmuseum Basel, 1966.

DETLEV KREIKENBOM

Battlefields
A. HISTORY OF THE RECEPTION OF ANCIENT BAT-TLES   B. INDIVIDUAL BATTLES AND BATTLEFIELDS

A. HISTORY OF THE RECEPTION OF ANCIENT BATTLES
1. INTRODUCTION   2. MIDDLE AGES AND MOD-ERN TIMES   3. MILITARY SCIENCE AND HISTORY IN THE 19TH AND 20TH CENTS.

1. INTRODUCTION
The interest in → WAR in Antiquity encompasses a whole range of areas such as military technology, tactics and strategy, the great generals, as well as the impact of war on historical processes. Although military conflicts cannot be understood in terms of the military operations alone, the compressed events of bloody battle in time and space were seen as a key to the understanding of the history of war. For this reason a book genre came into being in the modern era which deals with European battles in the manner of a catalogue.

Already in 1600 in Venice, Giovanni Saraceni published a combat-historical index *Fatti d'arme famosi successi trà tutte le nationi del mondo* in such a catalogue. In London in 1676, James Health's *Chronicle of the war* [6. 1844f.] appeared. But the genre did not really become established until the 18th cent., when works such as Jean François Pétis de la Croix's *Dictionnaire des sièges et batailles mémnorables de l'histoire ancienne et moderne*, was published in Paris in 1770–71, or the *New Military Dictionary; or, the Field of War* came out in London in 1760.

From the 19th cent. onwards we find catalogues of classical battles as the first part of publications that also cover battles of the Middle Ages and the modern era; they also contain alphabetical and chronological compilations (dictionaries, lexica, encyclopedias, battles of world history, etc) or military-historical depictions.

Fig. 1: Alexandre Evariste Fraognard (1780–1850), *Léonidas*, undated. Paris, Musées de Sens

Older works start off chronologically with Greek history, while those from the 20th cent. begin with the hostilities of the old near eastern empires (Megiddo *c.* 1468 BC or Kadesh *c.* 1285 BC).

2. MIDDLE AGES AND MODERN TIMES
Already Charlemagne commissioned the Bendictine monk Herric to locate the battlefields of the Gallic Wars, specifically the site of Alesia. In 1477, in his edition of Caesar, Raimundus Marlianus appended an index of battlefields he had located. Classical reports of battles were often used as models in historiography. For example, in his portrayal of Frederick I's siege and capture of Milan in 1558 (*Gesta Frederici seu rectius Cronica*, III), Otto von Freising took over almost word for word passages from Flavius Josephus' *Peri tou Ioudai-kou polemou* ('Wars of the Jews') more specifically from the Latin translation of Pseudo-Hegesippus (4th or 5th cent. AD). In the same way, the reception of Vegetius accounted for the preoccupation with classical battles, as can be seen in the third book of *De regimine principum* by Aegidius Romanus in 1280, in *L'Arbre des batailles (1386/1390)* by Honoré de Bonet (Hono-rat Bovet) or the *Livre des faits d'armes et de chevalerie* (1410) by Christine de Pisan. In his instruction manual for the military *Le Jouvencel* (1462–1466/67), Jean de Bueil used classical examples like the Battle of Pharsalus (48 BC) and the war with Jugurtha. R. Valturio penned *De re militari libri XII* (Verona 1472), the first war manual to be printed [8. 358–362]. Apart from Vege-tius, the author also used Caesar and Ammianus Mar-cellinus as sources. In addition, he incorporated a pic-torial atlas that tried to represent the war machines de-scribed by the ancient authors (this atlas was adopted

Fig. 2: Jacques-Louis David (1748–1825), *Léonidas aux Thermophyles*, 1814. *With Permission of Musée du Louvre, Paris*

Fig. 3: Colossal statue of Vercingetorix by Aimé Millet (1865) in Alise-Sainte-Reine

Thereafter we come across increasingly numerous attempts to make the classical art of war relevant and useful for the present. The accessibility of texts through printing and the expansion of humanistic education, which also found its way into the military academies, could not by themselves have started this process. Among various historical factors, the renewed importance of heavy infantry formations in the 15th cent. is a case in point. Even Niccolo Machiavelli, in his work *Dell'Arte della guerra* (Florence 1521), developed his ideas of tactics and strategy based on classical patterns, inspired by such authors as Polybius, Caesar, Livy, Flavius Josephus, Frontinus or Vegetius. In doing so, he dipped regularly into the catalogue of the great classical battles.

The reform of the armed forces of the house of Orange, introduced by Johann der Mittlere von Nassau-Siegen after 1589, which drew on the classical tradition of war and was additionally inspired by the writings of Justus Lipsius, set new standards for army and battle formation [5; 9]. Further developed by Gustav Adolf, they contributed considerably to Sweden's great success in the 30 Years' War. In the German speaking countries it was Johann Wilhelm Neumair von Ramssla and Wilhelm Dilich who drew the parallels with ancient battles (from the Punic Wars and the time of Caesar) [8. 951–960]. Raimondo di Montecuccoli also repeatedly used examples from the battles of the Second Punic War and the Gallic Wars as evidence in his work.

The reception of Caesar and the preoccupation with battles fought by him was promoted by several European rulers, such as Charles V who annotated his copy of Caesar's writings with marginal notes [8. 448]. In 1575, Baldelli's translation of Caesar's *Commentarii* was enlarged by 41 drawings by Palladio depicting tactical formations or siege techniques. Henri Duc de Rohan created a leadership handbook based on the Gallic Wars, *Le parfait capitaine, l'abrégé des guerres*

by the first translation of Vegetius into German by Ludwig von Hohenwang in 1475). In 1487, the works of Aelian, Frontinus, Modestus and Vegetius were edited in a single redaction called *Veteres de re militari*. As early as 1421, L. Bruni in his work *De militia* tried to transfer classical tactics – for example from Polybius' descriptions of battles – to Florentine military affairs.

de la Gaule des Commentaires de César, which appeared in Paris in 1636. Following the publication in 1741 of Éclairissements géographiques sur l' Ancienne Gaule, the geographer Jean-Baptiste Bourguignon d' Anville brought out several works which centred on the locations of battles. In Art de la guerre, par principes et par règles (Paris 1748), after considering classical writers on war, J.F. de Chastenet Marquis de Puységur compared the the campaigns of Caesar and Turenne, and also analyzed the siege of Dyrrhachium (48 BC) and Caesar's oblique battle order at Pharsalus. When Jean Charles Chevalier de Folard, in the introduction to his Histoire de Polybe (Paris 1727), sparked off an agitated debate about the interpretation and actualisation of battle formations described in Polybius, Karl Gottlieb Guischardt's Mémoires militaires sur les Grecs et les Romains (2 vols, Den Haag 1758) countered Folard's theories with arguments which he had developed based on the description of battles in Polybius, Arrian and Caesar [8. 1478ff., 1824ff.]. In his Traité des Stratagèmes permis à la guerre ou Remarques sur Polyen et Frontin avec des observations sur les batailles de Pharsala et d' Arbelles (Metz 1765), Paul Gédéon Joly de Maizeroy analyzed the battle order at Arbela (331 BC) and Pharsalus. These debates about the relevance of classical accounts to military technology, above all Caesar but also Polybius, are representative of the central position which classical war and battle reports attained. Frederick the Great claimed to have learned only a few lessons from Caesar, but nonetheless encouraged a thorough study of classical warfare by his generals. His battle deployment of ordre oblique, with which he was able to beat much larger armies repeatedly, is reminiscent of the oblique battle order of Epaminondas at Leuctra (371 BC) or at Mantineia (362 BC). Napoleon I, an admirer of both Alexander and Hannibal, penned his Précis des guerres de Jules César on St. Helena, in which he analyzed Caesar's campaigns taking as his basis the works of Jean Baptiste d'Anville. Napoleon III appointed a topographical committee to do fieldwork headed by Eugène Stoffel (1861–1865), the results of which served as the foundation for the Histoire de Jules César (Paris 1866).

3. MILITARY SCIENCE AND HISTORY IN THE 19TH AND 20TH CENTS.

One cannot speak of military science as a subject in its own right until the 19th cent. Charles-Jean-Jacques-Joseph Ardant du Picq's book Études sur le Combat antique et Combat moderne (Paris 1868) analysed the battle of Cannae (216 BC) and Pharsalus as examples, with the accounts of Polybius and Caesar as his starting point, in order to bring out the features of the Classical art of war, such as surrounding and surprising the enemy, and to postulate their use in modern battle. Hans Delbrück's (1848–1929) idiosyncratic, four-volume Geschichte der Kriegskunst im Rahmen der politischen Geschichte (1900–1902) ascribes great importance to ancient battles for their understanding of tactics and strategy. Delbrück also recognized the connection with

the political, societal and economic structures. A further innovation and quirk on his part was his distrust of accounts of battles from the ancient world. These should undergo 'critical analysis': Delbrück identified the locations and tried to work out through analogies how certain events could have come to pass. In reaching his conclusions he took into account what was known on the basis of practical military exercises or from the reconstruction of ancient weapons. In particular, he repeatedly suggested that the, in his opinion, overly inflated numbers of soldiers given by Classical authors ought to be reduced. Johann Kromayer and the Austro-Hungarian colonel Georg Veith had at their disposal even more exact topographical knowledge of ancient battlefields. Their book Antike Schlachtfelder als Bausteine zur antiken Kriegsgeschichte (1903–1931) features the results of their reconstructions in maps with far-reaching influence.

Wilhelminian Germany was a fertile ground for war studies. The conviction that one could learn from history, coupled with the importance the elite placed on a humanistic education, led to a considerable regard for Antiquity in officer circles, even in the education of officers. The historically educated general – epitomized by Helmuth von Moltke – was absolutely the ideal. The vital role of the Classical history of war is apparent in Bernhard von Poten's overview of the education of officers in the German-speaking world Geschichte des Militär- Erziehungs- und Bildungswesens in den Landen deutscher Zunge, 5 vols, Berlin 1889–1897). Thus, the 'History of ancient armies' was taught alongside the 'history of war' and 'general history' at the War School in Berlin (military academy since 1859), at which Moltke and Alfred von Schlieffen had been pupils. The focusing of the course of events in the battle on the performance of the generals, already detectable in Classical reports of war, was adopted. Generals like Epaminondas, Alexander, Hannibal, Scipio or Caesar were given pre-eminent status. The high point of this military and theoretical development was the study of the battle of Cannae, published in 1909 by A. von Schlieffen, Chief of the German General Staff. The encirclement of the Roman army carried out by Hannibal at Cannae was at the centre of this work. It peaked with the thesis: 'the decisive battle can today be won according to the same plan that Hannibal had long ago devised'. Accordingly, Schlieffen analysed great battles of European history (from the time of Frederick the Great to the battles for unification) using Cannae as an example. For a future battle against France and Russia on two fronts, he himself planned a swift destruction of the French army via a massive encirclement from the north. At the foundation of such a manoeuvre lay not just Cannae but also the experiences of the wars of 1870/71. The complete failure of the Schlieffen Plan at the beginning of World War I, and especially the devastating effect that this idea had on the conduct of the German high command in the summer of 1914, clearly shows the limits of looking at Classical battles in a completely theoretical way and their apparent direct transferability to modern political and military circumstances.

It was not just within military theory that ancient battles were afforded considerable significance. Because political history was seen as determined by wars, the 'great' battles of European history were frequently examined in the historical and humanistic disciplines. The notion that the outcomes of ancient battles had set the course for later European development was widespread. J.S. Mill even went so far as to make the exaggerated comment that the Battle of Marathon, as an event, was more important for British history than the Battle of Hastings (*Collected Works*, ed. J.M. Robson, Vol. XI, 1978, 273). The idea that the fate not just of the Greek poleis was at risk in the Persian Wars, but also that of the whole of Western culture is echoed here. The Greek victories at Marathon (490 BC), Salamis (480 BC) and Plataea (479 BC) only attained their importance for world history through such interpretations. In 1851 in London, Edward Sheperd Creasy published *The Fifteen Decisive Battles of the World. From Marathon to Waterloo*, aimed at the popular market and which soon became a bestseller. Among the 15 battles that he discusses are six ancient ones. The battles of Alexander are seen as the first successful attempt at a conquest of the East by the civilized West. The Battle of the Teutoburg Forest (AD 9) is seen as decisive for the later European divide into the Roman and Germanic cultural spheres of influence. The successful defence against the Huns at the Battle of the Catalaunian Plains (also known as the Battle of Chalons) (AD 451) is interpreted as the rescue of European culture.

Arguments based on Classical experiences took completely different forms throughout the 20th cent. In *The Decisive Wars of History* (1929) Basil H. Liddell Hart, using examples of battles, explained the theory of the *indirect approach*, a strategy that did not primarily aim at direct confrontation on the battlefield, but rather, in coordination with politics, looked to undermine the leadership of the enemy. The examples he uses from Antiquity are the campaigns of Epaminondas, Philip of Macedon and Alexander the Great, Cassander's successful resistance against Antigonos, the Second Punic War and the Wars of Caesar. Characteristic of his analyses is a strong focus on strategy. He devoted a monograph to Scipio Africanus (1938). John Frederick Charles Fuller, in *A Military History of the Western World* (1954–1957), deals with 30 different battles, six of which date from Antiquity. Bernard Law Montgomery's *A History of Warfare* (1968) starts with the Battle of Kadesh and the campaigns of Belisarius, while Chester W. Nimitz's *Sea Power – A Naval History* (1960) deals with the sea battles of Salamis, the Punic Wars and Actium. Edward Luttwak, in *The Grand Strategy of the Roman Empire* (1976), sees in the broad security considerations of the Romans a model for American politics. The complex siege of Masada (AD 73/74), in particular, made an impression on him. He sees in this action a deliberate demonstration of Roman superiority. Chaim Herzog, the future president of Israel, in a book with Mordechai Gichon called *Battles of the Bible* (1978, rev. ed. 1997) articulated the idea 'that the strategic and tactical lessons of the Bible are still applicable and are as relevant as ever'. 'Ancient Military History' is still taught at the US Army War College, and *The Great Battles of Antiquity* (1994) by Richard A. Gabriel and Donald W. Boose covers warfare from the Battle of Megiddo to the fall of Constantinople (1453).

Politological research into the origins of war has occasionally taken Classical evidence into account. Quincy Wright's *A Study of War* (1942) sees in the ancient Near Eastern, or rather early Greek battles the decisive development of occidental warfare from primitive beginnings. In doing so, military and politological literature draws upon a series of much-used older representations, such as Kromayer/Veith. Further new analyses can be found in W. K. Pritchett's *Studies in Ancient Topography* (1965–1982) and *The Greek State at War* (1974–1991). Other well-known modern researchers include Yvon Garlan (*La Guerre dans l'antiquité*, 1972) and Pierre Ducrey (*Guerre et guerriers dans la Grèce antique*, 1985), who have long separated themselves from the narrow view of a history of battle and are taking into consideration the historical, political and societal contexts. In *Warfare and Agriculture in Classical Greece* (1983) and *The Western Way of War: Infantry Battle in Classical Greece* (1989), Victor Davis Hanson revealed that the laying waste of land, much described in Classical authors, was not as serious as had previously been thought.

V. D. Hanson, Carnage and Culture: Landmark Battles in the Rise of Western Power, 2001; J. E. Lendon, Soldiers and Ghosts: A History of Battle in Classical Antiquity, 2005; J. A. Lynn, Battle: A History of Combat and Culture, 2003

B. Individual Battles and Battlefields
The culture of remembering battles already started in Antiquity. Parallel with the erection of memorials the mythologisation and idealisation of the events of war emerged. Several topoi can be identified, such as the numerical inferiority or the legitimacy of the individual concerns, as well as the memory of those who took part, and especially of those who fell in past battles, the glorification of their deeds and their function as an example. Individual battles always assume metaphorical functions in principal ideological models of explanation.
1. Troy 2. Persian Wars 3. Campaigns of Alexander 4. Punic Wars 5. Numantia 6. Battles of Caesar 7. Battle of Teutoburg Forest 8. Masada 9. Late Antiquity

1. Troy
The Trojan War and the battle memorials associated with it always occupied a leading position → Troy.

2. Persian Wars

Following the broad resonance the Persian Wars had in Greek Antiquity, it was not until the 18th cent. that the battles of Marathon [3], Thermopylae and Salamis reappeared in the general historical awareness. The conflict of the Persian Wars was now linked with the bodies of thought of the → Enlightenment, → Romanticism and → Philhellenism, for example in Jean-Jacques Barthélmy's *Voyage du jeune Anacharsis en Grèce* (1788), François René de Chateaubriand's *L'itinéraire de Paris à Jérusalem* (1811) and Elizabeth Barrett Browning's *The Battle of Marathon: A Poem* (c. 1820). At the centre stood the myth of the struggle for freedom, or even, as in the case of Thermopylae, death for freedom. Numerous paintings addressed these themes, such as the depictions of Leonidas by Alexandre-Evariste Fragonard or Jacques-Louis David (Figs. 1 & 2).

In his *Vorlesungen über die Philosophie der Geschichte* (1833–1836), G. W. F. Hegel assigned to the battles between the Greeks and the Persians a key position in the development of individual freedoms, arguing that oriental despotism and free individualism faced each other from opposing sides. Historiography also saw events in terms of world-historical importance, as articulated by Robert von Pöhlmann or Eduard Meyer.

During the nationalist movements, the Persian Wars took on a new perspective. They became a core myth in the Greek War of Independence. The great sacrifices of the World Wars had the Persian Wars appear in a new light. Self-sacrifice for one's ideals became central (Georg Heym, *Marathon*, 1914). In the period of National Socialism, this approach was continued through the additional integration of the putative virtue and ideals of the Spartans, as can be seen in the writings of Helmut Berve and Franz Miltner. The enthusiasm for all things Spartan during the Third Reich was so great that H. Göring thought he could compare the 'final battle' of Stalingrad to the battle of Thermopylae and misuse it for propaganda purposes: 'When you reach Germany, say that you saw us fighting in Stalingrad, as the law for the protection of our people has ordained' [1. 51f. with comments. 190]. Apostolos Daskalakis still defended Leonidas' sacrifice (1964), although already Karl Julius Beloch in his *Griechische Geschichte* had described the battle of Thermopylae as a destructive defeat to which only later rhetoric could give a false sheen. A memorial to the battle was set up at the pass of Thermopylae in 1955. The barrow at Marathon was restored after 1945. Today the site is an → Archaeological Park, on which were built the facilities for the rowing competitions for the 2004 Summer Olympics.

3. Campaigns of Alexander

The Persian campaigns of Alexander the Great (334–323 BC) were already well-known in Antiquity, and, accordingly, often treated. An impressive pictoral view of the way the Romans saw the battles of Alexander can be gleaned from the Alexander Mosaic in Pompeii (→ Naples, Museo Nazionale Archeologico, Fig.3), although it probably does not represent a specific battle.

The broad reception of Alexander in the Middle Ages emanates from the *Life of Alexander* (3rd cent. AD), ascribed to Callisthenes, and Curtius Rufus' *History of Alexander* in Latin. One of the most influential works in this respect was the epic *Alexandreis* (1178/1182) by Walter of Châtillon which, in the course of the 13th cent., took on a preeminent position as a school book. In 1185, the final version of the *Roman d'Alexandre* by Alexandre de Paris appeared. Around 1150, Pfaffe Lamprecht wrote the oldest Alexander poem (*Alexanderlied*) in the German language. Rudolf von Ems (*Alexander*), 1230/1250) or Ulrich von Eschenbach (*Alexander*), 1271/1282) continued the tradition of the chivalric Alexander epic. Starting with Thomas of Kent's *Roman de Toute Chevalerie* (second half of the 12th cent.), a tradition of Alexander poems also developed in Britain (among others *Kyng Alisaunder*, c. 1300). In these works, the campaigns of Alexander and his battles served as a backdrop against which Alexander was glorified.

In the Renaissance, the works of Arrian and Plutarch were the starting point for the reception of Alexander. A concrete perception of the individual battles became possible from this time on, although medieval traditions continued to have an effect: it was customary to trace back one's genealogy to the Macedonian royal family. The Frankish kings did this, as did the Hapsburg monarchy later on. This resulted in numerous pictorial representations of the Alexander theme as well as the battles. In 1530, Duke Federico Gonzaga decorated the Palazzo del Tè in Mantua with historical motifs for Karl V. We can see Alexander motifs, as well as those of Scipio and Caesar in the Sala del Imperator, as they were also counted among the ancestors of Karl V. Perino del Vaga produced a cycle of frescoes in the Castel Sant' Angelo for Pope Paul III (1545–1547), featuring among others the Battle of the Hydaspes against Porus (326 BC). Wilhelm IV of Bavaria commissioned a cycle of classical battles which includes a painting of the Battle of Issus (333 BC) by Albrecht Altdorfer (1526) (→ War, Fig. 1)

The military successes of Louis II de Bourbon (4th prince de) Condé (Le Grande Condé/The Great Condé) in the 1640s gave the Alexander myth a boost in France. Comparisons were made, for example by Jean Puget de la Serre (*Parallèle d'Alexandre le Grand et de Mons. le Duc d'Anguien*, Paris 1645). After Condé went over to the Fronde, Louis XIV took this as an opportunity to lay claims to Alexander for himself. For this purpose, Charles Le Brun produced a series of Alexander paintings, such as *Le Passage du Granique* (1665), *La Défaite de Porus* or *La Bataille d'Arbèle* (1667–1668). He drew inspiration from the paintings of P. da Cortona, who in 1650 had painted in Rome for Alessandro Sacchetti, then commander of the Pope's forces, the victory of Alexander over Darius. The Battle of Arbela was the subject of a painting by J. Courtois in 1664. After 1670, a distancing from the Alexander mythology took place, which can be understood in connection with the Querelle des Anciens et des Modernes. Nonetheless, the motifs of Alexander retained their popularity. In 1693, Jan Brueghel produced a painting of the battle of Issus, and in 1737, Cornelius Troost one of the Battle of Granicus (334 BC).

In Vienna in 1797, Rhegas Pheraios (Rigas Velestinlis) brought out a pamphlet which, by alluding to the campaigns of Alexander, called on the Greeks to rise up against the Ottoman rule. This drawing of a parallel was the beginning of the Alexander reception in the Greek independence movement. With the advent of the Macedonian Question at the start of the 20th cent., the Alexander myth and associated memories of his campaigns became as relevant then as ever.

In Germany, Alexander and his battles came under greater scrutiny at the start of the 19th cent. as a result of the experience of the Napoleonic Wars. In 1833, Johann Gustav Droysen published the *Geschichte Alexanders des Großen* in which the unifying and civilizing elements of the Alexander campaigns were emphasized. Impressions from the German movement for unification come into play here. Eduard Meyer highlighted the connection between the achievements of Alexander and that of the monarchy. K. J. Beloch dismissed Droysen's analysis, but it retained its influence in the 20th cent. nonetheless. During the period of National Socialism, interpretations of the history of the races gained ground. In turn, William Woodthorpe Tarn described the campaigns of Alexander in terms of a civilizing and unifying mission on Alexander's part (*Alexander the Great*, 1948).

4. PUNIC WARS

The reception of the Punic Wars, for which the deeds of Hannibal and Scipio were central, began in the 14th cent. Petrarch devoted his epic *Africa* to the life of Scipio (1338– *c.* 1350), which describes the hero's deeds from the conquest of Spain to the battle of Zama (202 BC). In 1532, François I. commissioned tapestries with motifs from the Second Punic War. The Battle of Zama was based on an original by Jules Romain (Giulio Romano). Maria, archduchess of Austria, wife of Ludwig II of Bohemia and Hungary, sister of Karl V and governor of the Netherlands, also owned tapestries depicting scenes from Scipio's life (among others the capture of Carthage, the parley between Hannibal and Scipio and the battle of Zama). Emulating Scipio, Karl V. let himself be celebrated as a third 'Africanus' following his victory over the Turks. In 1530, Jörg Breu (the Elder) was commissioned to paint the battle of Zama for a cycle of paintings for Wilhelm IV of Bavaria for which Hans Burgkmair in 1529 painted the battle of Cannae. In general, from the 16th cent. onwards, numerous representations of the Roman general and the Second Punic War were made. Between 1508–1513, Jacopo Ripanda painted a series of frescoes depicting Scipio and Hannibal in the Conservators' Palace in

Rome. In 1515 in the Monastery of St George near Freiburg Ambrosius Holbein created a cycle of paintings about Hannibal and Scipio, which portray the capture of Saguntum and Carthage. In his painting of Napoleon's crossing of the Alps via the Great St. Bernard Pass (1801/02), J. L. David depicts a milestone with Hannibal's name on it in order to emphasize the parallel with Hannibal's alpine crossing (Fig. 3). Jean Desmarets de St. Sorlin's play *Scipion* (1639), Pierre Carlet Mariveaux' *Annibal* (1720) and Christian Dietrich Grabbe's *Hannibal* (1835) all illustrate the popularity of the theme for the stage over the years.

From 18th-cent. travel reports, such as that of Thomas Shaw (1730), we have the first testimonies about the Punic sites in North Africa. However, an archaeological debate did not take place until the 19th cent. In 1807, Chateaubriand travelled to North Africa, visited → CARTHAGE and set out his impressions in his *Itinéraire de Paris à Jérusalem* (1811). Gustave Flaubert travelled to Carthage in 1858 and created a strong legend with his novel *Salammbô* (1862). Nathan Davis searched the whole coastline looking for historical sites of the Punic Wars (*Carthage and Her Remains*, 1861). In 1859, Charles-Ernest Beulé started excavations in Byrsa, which were continued from 1875 by Alfred Louis Delattre.

Scholarly debate about the Punic Wars was heavily influenced in the 19th cent. by Theodor Mommsen's *Römische Geschichte* (1854). Hannibal's crossing of the Alps, the battle of Lake Trasimene or the battle of Cannae have repeatedly stood at the centre of modern research into battlefields.

5. NUMANTIA

The resistance of the Iberian Celts at Numantia (153–133 BC), which ended with Scipio the Younger taking the town and the suicide of all inhabitants, played an important role in the Spanish view of history. Miguel de Cervantes Saavedra's tragedy *Numancia* (1580) or Francisco Mosquera's epic *La Numantina* (1609) are the first notable treatments of the theme. In his *Historia de España* (c. 1830), Alvarez y Marina established a connection with the Napoleonic wars of liberation. La Motte Fouqué as well as August Wilhelm Schlegel translated Cervantes' tragedy at the time of the Napoleonic Wars. Among the numerous illustrations of the last days of Numantia, Alejo Vera y Estaca's *Numantia* (1880) stands out. The erection of a memorial was begun on the hill of Numantia in 1843. In 1879, Eduardo Saavedra created the first sketches of the village, but the excavations, led by Adolf Schulten did not start until 1905 and ran until 1912.

6. BATTLES OF CAESAR

The reception of the battles of Caesar is closely linked to Caesar the individual, due to his reputation as an ideal ruler and general, but also because of his literary works. The first aspect stands in the foreground of the reception in the Middle Ages. The glorious commander, which is how he appears in, for example, *Li Fet des Romains* (1213/14), and which draws on Lucan,

Sallust and Suetonius, served as the forebear for medieval rulers, such as the Hapsburgs, the Tudors and the Burgundian dukes. They happily compared their own military successes with those of their famous 'ancestor'. Four carpets were manufactured for the Burgundian court between 1465 and 1470 that show victorious battles and were based on manuscript-illustrations from *Li Fet des Romains*. Commissioned by the Gonzaga in Mantua, Andrea Mantegna created a cycle of paintings depicting Caesar's triumph 1486–1492. In 1533, for a cycle of pictures for Wilhelm IV, Melchior Feselen took the siege of Alesia as his theme. Melchior Steidl's *Die Überschreitung des Rubicon* (1707–1709), in the Kaisersaal of the Neue Residenz in Bamberg, first and foremost serves to glorify the patron, in this case the archbishop and electoral prince Lothar Franz von Schönborn. On the ceiling of the Palazzo Pitti, Giuseppe Bezzuoli depicted the triumvirate as well as the Battle of Pharsalus (1835/36).

Shakespeare's drama *Julius Caesar* (c. 1599) has to be seen in the context of the mythologizing of Caesar by the Tudors. The declaration of Caesar's ghost that Brutus was to see him again at Philippi (42 BC), which harks back to Plutarch's account (Caes. 69,7), became a well-known quotation at the hands of Shakespeare (IV,3): 'Why, I will see thee at Philippi then'.

Of course, there was also a tradition that was negatively critical of Caesar. Sympathy for the Republic that vanished with Caesar is noticeable in the 15th cent. in the *cassoni* of the Anghiari Master, with scenes from the Battle of Pharsalus and Caesar's triumphal procession. In France, at the time of the religious wars, Caesar was held responsible for the start of the civil wars as can be seen in Robert Garnier's *Porcie* (1568), *Cornélie* (1574) or *Marc-Antoine* (1578).

In the course of the various independence movements within Europe, individual battles attained specific importance; for example in Switzerland the war against the Helvetii, or in France the battles against Vercingetorix.

The localization of the site of Bibracte (58 BC) was the purpose of repeated searches in the course of the 19th cent. J. G. Bulliot (*Fouilles du Mt. Beuvray de 1867–95*, Autun 1899), Xavier Garenne (*Bibracte*, Autun 1867) or Eugène Stoffel (*Histoire des Jules César*, Paris 1887) decided on a spot at Montmort near Toulon-sur-Arroux. The campaign against the Helvetii, especially the outcome of the battle of Bibracte, has been interpreted in very different ways since the second half of the 19th cent. Napoleon III and Th. Mommsen adopted Caesar's reports. Hans Delbrück interpreted the exodus of the Helvetii as a mercenary expedition against Ariovistus. Guglielmo Ferrero questioned Caesar's great success in this battle and wanted to assume at least an undecided outcome.

Throughout the 16th and even more so in the 17th cent., some works championed Vercingetorix [13], though interest in Caesar dominated as before. Nonetheless, Jacques Cassan in 1621 claimed to trace Louis XIII back to Vercingetorix. In 1752, Jacques Auvergnat (J. Ribauld de la Chapelle) wrote an *Histoire de Vercingétorix* (publ. 1834), which accused Vercingetorix of various mistakes. On the other hand, in Pierre. Laureau's *Histoire de France avant Clovis* (Paris 1786) the deeds of the Gauls were glorified.

At the beginning of the 19th cent. the supporters of the French Republic built up the myth of the strong but oppressed Gauls. During the *second empire* of Napoleon III, the republican symbols were reinterpreted as nationalistic icons and as such developed their actual effect for the first time. Napoleon III viewed the Roman conquest of Gaul as an essential and civilizing event for the good of France. To be sure, Vercingetorix was regarded as the first hero who died for his fatherland, but his rebellion against the Roman conquest did have characteristics of a fatal reaction against progress. This interpretation changed after France's defeat in the Franco-Prussian war. The Roman conqueror was compared to the victorious enemy, Germany; Alesia was equated with the defeat of 1870/71 (see Louis-Mathurin Moreau-Christophe, *Les Gaulois nos aieux*, Tours 1880; Camille Jullian, *Vercingétorix*, Paris 1901) and was explained as the result of the Gauls fighting among themselves. Vercingetorix had undertaken a first attempt at unification, albeit in vain, and through his surrender offered himself up for the nation. This scene was often treated pictorially, for example by Louis Royer in 1899 (Fig. 4) or Henri-Paul Motte in 1886. The martyr trait of the Gallic chieftain appears impressively in the sculpture *Aux martyrs de l'indépendance nationale* by Emile Chatrousse, exhibited in 1872. Already in 1865, Napoleon III engaged Aimé Millet to construct a monumental statue of Vercingetorix on the battlefield of Alesia (Fig. 5). In 1902, a memorial was erected on the hill of Gergovia and in 1903, a statue of Vercingetorix on a horse by Frédéric-Auguste Bartholdi was dedicated in Clermont-Ferrand.

In the 20th cent., in the years between the two world wars, France's extreme right made Vercingetorix into a model. In 1942, the Vichy regime hosted a commemoration at Gergovia in order to celebrate the second anniversary of the French Legion, and at which Vercingetorix' sacrifice for France was underscored. The alliance that was formed after the battle of Alesia between the Roman victors and the defeated Gauls as well as the contemporary defence alliance against a threat from the East in union with Germany were seen as historical parallels. In the same period, the French government-in-exile in London saw Vercingetorix as an archetype of resistance against foreign enemies. The myth of the Gauls lost its dramatic political effect in the post-war years. However, in the *Asterix* comic books he celebrates a new triumphal march (→ COMICS).

7. BATTLE OF TEUTOBURG FOREST

The dissemination of Tacitus (primarily through the rediscovery of the *Germania* at the beginning of the 16th cent.) led to a rediscovery of the Germanic past in Germany. Among scholars of the Reformation, the report of the events in the Teutoburg Forest (Tac. Ann. 1,60) met with significant approval as it seemed to exhibit parallels with the battles against the Papacy. Ulrich von Hutten was the first person to describe the Cheruscan chieftain as the liberator of Germany in his *Arminius* (c. 1516/1529). The synonymous labeling of Arminius as Hermann also goes back to its reception during the Reformation. In 1517, Ambrosius Holbein produced an illustration of the *Hermannsschlacht* as the frontispiece for an edition of Velleius Paterculus *Historia Romana*. A woodcut from 1543 by Hans Brosamer for Burkhard Waldis *Reimchronik* shows Arminius with Varus' head in his hand. Daniel Caspar von Lohenstein's novel *Arminius* (1689) continued this patriotic approach.

The subject of Hermann was a much-loved one in the 18th cent.: it can be seen in opera (Johann Adolf Hasse, *Arminius*, 1730) and in literature (Johann Elias Schlegel, *Hermann*, 1743; Justus Möser, *Arminius*, 1748; Friedrich Gottlieb Klopstock, *Hermanns Schlacht*, 1769; *Hermann und die Fürsten*, 1784; *Hermanns Tod*, 1784). Möser's and Klopstock's works stand at the beginning of Germany's myth of self-identification that was to become decisive for the 19th cent. Christoph Otto Freiherr von Schöneich's (Schönaich) epic *Hermann oder das befreyte Deutschland* (1753) moves in a similar direction. The decisive impulse to interpret the slaughter in the Teutoburg Forest as a significant event in the history of freedom and independence in Germany came about only through the Napoleonic Wars. Heinrich von Kleist's play *Die Hermannsschlacht* (1808/09, premiere 1860) or Caspar David Friedrich's painting *Gräber gefallener Freiheitskrieger* (1812/13), in which Arminius' gravestone can be seen gleaming brightly in the Teutoburg Forest, are examples of such interpretations of events under the influence of the Wars of Liberation. Throughout the 19th cent., the battle against Varus remained a central event in German historical awareness. In 1838, Christian Dietrich Grabbe wrote the *Hermannsschlacht*. On the occasion of the opening session of parliament in Frankfurt in 1848 an Arminius memorial coin was issued. The Cheruscan chieftain occupied a prominent position in Ludwig I's Valhalla. Friedrich Gunkel's *Die Hermannsschlacht* (1864) or Wilhelm Lindenschmit the Elder's painting of the same name are striking examples of the vivid visualisation of the motif in this period. In 1875, following the successful war against France and the unification of 1871, a memorial was erected in Grotenburg near Detmold on what was thought to have been the battle site.

In 1871, Theodor Mommsen (*Die Germanische Politik des Augustus*) tried to establish a connection between Arminius' struggle for freedom and German unification, and to attribute the greatest importance to the battle against Varus as a real turning point in Rome's dealings with the Germanic provinces. The acme of this development was reached in 1909 when the battle was commemorated on the occasion of its

1,900th anniversary. That same year, Gottlob Egelhaaf published *Die Schlacht im Teutoburger Wald*, a work that emphasized the nationalistic approach.

If at the start of the war in 1914 the new theatre season opened in Berlin with Kleist's *Hermannsschlacht*, between the acts of which victory announcements were made, the wave of enthusiasm for Arminius was broken after 1918. In the face of the recently suffered defeat, Ernst Kornemann attempted a positive reappraisal of Varus leadership in an article (*P. Quinctilius Varus*, 1922) in order to highlight Arminius accomplishment.

The National Socialist conception of history did not see the Battle of the Teutoburg Forest as a prominent event. Due to of the alliance with Italy it was hardly possible to emphasize antagonism between Germany and Rome. Nonetheless, various works on the theme appeared of which Hans Erich Stier's publications (among others *Die Bedeutung der römischen Angriffskriege für Westfalen*, 1938) was the most important.

In the post-war period, authors such as Hermann Kesting occasionally continued nationalistic interpretations of the Battle of the Teutoburg Forest (*Der Befreier Arminius im Lichte der geschichtlichen Quellen*, 1950), but academic research has distanced itself from this point of view.

8. MASADA

From the beginning of the 20th cent. onwards, the Jewish uprising against Rome in AD 66–73 has been regarded both by the Zionist movement and then by the state of Israel as a crucial milestone in Jewish-Israeli history. Particularly central to this are the siege of Masada in AD 73 and the collective suicide of the Jewish defenders described by Flavius Josephus (bell. iud. 8,8,6).

In Isaac Lamdan's poem *Masada* (1923–24), the Jewish stronghold is seen as the last place of refuge which must never be allowed to fall. This assertion would later become a leitmotif of the Zionist movement and the Jewish state. The heroes' death of the besieged for the freedom and independence of Israel was seen as the calling for that generation. The myth of Masada reached its high point following the site's first excavation by Yigael Yadin in 1963–64. His excavation report *Herod's Fortress and the Zealots' Last Stand* (1967), written for the general public, generated a great deal of interest. The 1,900th anniversary in 1973 resulted in mass rallies at the site. At the same time though, the myth of Masada elicited fierce controversy, and the glorification of the death of the heroes was criticized increasingly (P. Vidal-Naquet, S. Zeitlin).

Apart from Masada, the battles and particularly the siege of Iotapata or Gamala, the latter because of present-day tension due to its position on the Golan Heights, have played an important role. In the same way the destruction of Jerusalem (AD 70) has come to be seen as a core date of Jewish History. The rebellion of the Maccabees as well as the battles around the time of the first temple are also important.

9. LATE ANTIQUITY

As far as the battles of Late Antiquity are concerned, there are two models that play a part in collective memory: first, the model of the battle 'Romans against barbarians'; the second, battles resulting in conversion to Christianity. The defeat of the Romans at Adrianople in AD 378, the fall of Rome in AD 410 and 455, as well as the Battle of the Catalaunian Plains in AD 451 that stopped the advance of the Huns, are examples of the first model. Constantine's victory at the Battle of the Milvian Bridge in AD 312 is an important example of the second type (→ HISTORICAL SUBJECTS, PAINTINGS OF, Fig. 3). The victory of the Franks under Clovis, stylized as the 'novus Constantinus', over the Alemanni became a central event in French history following Gregory of Tours' account which was frequently quoted both in the Middle Ages and the modern era. Gregory is scant with detail on the battle, instead he concentrates on the conversion of the Frankish king in the critical phase of the battle, thanks to which he was able to win. Whether the conversion actually happened during the course of the battle at Zülpich in AD 496, is as questionable as the characterisation of the battle as decisive event between the Franks and the Alemanni. From the 16th cent. onwards, Clovis' conversion during the battle became the basis for the claims of the French Church over the Pope (Gallicanism), as seen in Pierre Pithou (*Traité des libertés de l'église gallicaine*, Paris 1594) or Etienne Pasquier (*Recherches de la France*, vol. 1, Paris 1560). Under Louis XIV the prominent position of the king, chosen alone by God to defend the Church, and justified by Clovis' act, was further emphasized (Jean Desmarets de Saint-Sorlin, *Clovis ou la France chrétienne*, Paris 1654). In Daniel's *Histoire de France* which appeared in 1696, Clovis' conversion in AD 496 was seen as the starting point of the French monarchy, and the name of the Frankish monarch was changed to Ludovicus.

While republican circles developed an increasing interest in the Gallic past in late 18th-cent. France, the monarchists saw in Clovis a symbol for their cause. In his opening speech in 1824, Charles X made an explicit reference to his alleged predecessor. At the same time a new interpretation emerged: no longer the conversion but rather the victory over the Alemanni came to the fore. Accordingly, in the course of the 19th cent., numerous paintings of the battle came into being, such as those by Ary Scheffer 1837 or J. Blanc 1874–1882. Especially following the defeat of 1870/71, the king of the Franks was portrayed as the first victor over the Alemanni (Ernest Lavisse, *Histoire de France illustrée, depuis les origines jusqu'à la révolution*, Paris 1911). In 1896, the Catholic party – via Cardinal B. M. Langénieux – played a significant part in the ceremonies for the 1,400th anniversary of the battle. On this occasion an anthology of writings by Catholic intellectuals, *La France chrétienne dans l'Histoire* (Paris 1896), appeared under the aegis of the Cardinal.

The Clovis myth lost its importance after World War I. Nonetheless, the starting point of French history can still be seen to originate from here as a matter of course. The *Histoire Militaire de la France* (ed. PHILLIPE CONTAMINE) which appeared in 1992–94, starts with Clovis' wars. Numerous publications on the theme were published in connection with the 1,500th anniversary in 1996.

→ Alesia; → Alexander; → Caesar; → Cannae; → Hadrianopolis 3; → Hannibal; → Marathon; → Masada; → Megiddo; → Numantia; → Salamis; → Thermopylae; → Troy; → Tropaion

1 K. CHRIST (ed.), Sparta, Wege der Forsch. 622, 1986 2 PH. CONTAMINE, La Guerre au Moyen Age. Nouvelle Clio 24, 1980 3 M. FLASHAR, Die Sieger von Marathon – Zwischen Mythisierung und Vorbildlichkeit, in: Id., H.-J. GEHRKE, E. HEINRICH (eds.), Retrospektive. Konzepte von Vergangenheit in der griechisch-römischen Antike, 1996, 63–85 4 M. HADAS-LEBEL, Massada, histoire et symbole, 1995 5 W. HAHLWEG, Die Heeresreform der Oranier und die Antike, 1941 6 J. R. HALE, Artists and Warfare in the Renaissance, 1990 7 Id., Renaissance War Studies, History Series 11, 1993 8 M. JÄHNS, Geschichte der Kriegswissenschaft vornehmlich in Deutschland, 3 Vols., 1880–1891 9 CH. RÖCK, Römische Schlachtordnungen im 17. Jahrhundert, in: M. BAUMBACH (ed.), Tradita et inventa. Beiträge zur Rezeption der Antike, 2000, 165–186 10 M. ROUCHE (ed.), Clovis, histoire et Mémoire, 2 vols., 1997 11 CH. TACKE, Denkmal im sozialen Raum. Nationale Symbole in Deutschland und Frankreich im 19. Jahrhundert, 1995 12 M. FANSA (ed.),Varusschlacht und Germanenmythos. Eine Vortragsreihe anläßlich der Sonderausstellung Kalkriese Römer im Osnabrücker Land in Oldenburg, 1993 13 RÉUNION DES MUSÉES NATIONAUX (ed.),Vercingétorix et Alésia, 1994 ADDITIONAL BIBLIOGRAPHY: V. ILARI, Imitatio, restitutio, utopia: la storia militare antica nel pensiero strategico moderno, in: M. SORDI (ed.), Guerra e diritto nel mondo greco e romano, 2002, 269–381; H. VAN WEES, Greek warfare: myths and realities, 2004; R. WIEGELS, WINFRIED WOESLER (eds.), Arminius und die Varusschlacht: Geschichte, Mythos, Literatur, 2003.

LORENZO SGUAITAMATTI

Bavaria

A. FROM MONASTERIES TO HUMANISM
B. EDUCATION AND UNIVERSITIES FROM THE 15TH TO THE 19TH CENTS. C. THE PERIOD OF LUDWIG I
D. THE GEORGE CIRCLE E. UNIVERSITIES AND INSTITUTIONS IN THE 19TH AND 20TH CENTS.

A. FROM MONASTERIES TO HUMANISM

The Carolingian Period in Bavaria is distinguished by an effort to transmit and spread Latin culture. This is born out by the remains of the old → LIBRARIES and scriptoria of the episcopal seats (e.g., St. Emmeram, Freising, Prüfening near Regensburg, Passau, Salzburg) and monasteries where pagan as well as Christian authors are documented: Vergil, Horace, Lucan, Sallust, Ovid, Persius, Statius, Terence, Cicero, and Cato [26. 116–124]. However, because of the Hungarian invasions very little of these libraries has survived. Rebuilding after 955 (victory of Otto the Great) was not without difficulties, but yielded significant achievements until the 11th cent.: Under Gottschalk, Bishop of Freising (994–1005), numerous manuscripts of ancient authors were copied; Bavaria played an important role in the textual tradition of the comedies of Plautus, Hyginus' handbook of mythology, the collection of *sententia* by Publilius Syrus and some of the elegies of Tibullus. Special attention was given to didactic literature, such as Cicero's rhetorical writings and ancient grammars (e.g., Marius Victorinus). In the Middle Ages, the ancient pagan authors were mandatory reading in the monastic schools, although they were only read to facilitate a better understanding of the Christian sacred texts [4]; in general the pagan authors were regarded as dangerous. Thus Othloh of St. Emmeram (c. 1010–1070) reports that as a teacher in Regensburg he fell ill after reading Lucan with too much enthusiasm and now feared divine punishment (PL 146, 347A–353D). His collection of *Proverbia* was intended to replace Avian and Cato in introductory courses (PL 146, 299A–338A), the two authors most used for language instruction in the Middle Ages [8].

Latin literary life in Bavaria started with Arbeo, Bishop of Freising (764–782) [8]; around this time the oldest Latin-German glossary was compiled, called *Abrogans*, after the first entry. The earliest evidence of Latin poetry dates to the late Agilolfingian period (555–788): the rhythmic verses by Liutprand in the Salzburg formularies and the church inscriptions from Tegernsee. In the 11th cent., Latin literature in Bavaria reached its pinnacle; noteworthy are *Ruodlieb*, a chivalrous epic of which about 2300 verses in hexameter have survived, and three religious plays – a literary form popular in Bavaria during the 11th and 13th cents. and in part preserved in the famous manuscript of the *Carmina Burana* (13th cent.), found 1803 in Benediktbeuren (Buranus).

The peak of Bavarian Humanism came with the foundation of Ingolstadt University (1472) [43. 350–353; 4]. Martin Mayr (d. 1481), jurist, alderman and one of Germany's first statesmen with a humanist education, commented in his opening address on the political function of education: '... Since Plato, it has been rightly said that only states whose politicians have a philosophical education can be called happy in every respect' (*...a Platone ... recte dictum est, beatas fore respublicas, quarum gubernatores vel sapientes sunt vel sapientiae studio tenentur*). Education should not aim at preparing for a profession, but at forming the personality: 'This is the only way to improve the situation of humankind' (*una ... superest via, qua meliora et laetiora acquiretis tempora, ut scilicet vobis animos faciatis meliores, quod sine virtute seu litteris fieri nequit*, [49. II 8, 10]). From 1491 to 1492 and 1494 to 1497, Konrad Celtis (1459–1508), an important poet of German Humanism and editor of Tacitus' *Germania* (1500), taught in the faculty of the Liberal Arts at Ingolstadt. His bi-

ographer Ulrich von Hutten called him an 'archhumanist'. With his inaugural lecture he established humanist studies in Germany. He committed himself to reviving ancient poetry, the knowledge of Greek and Roman history and German antiquities. A number of his students, such as Andreas Stiborius (d. 1515), Georg Tannstetter (Collimitius, 1482–1535), Johann Stabius (d. 1522), and Jakob Ziegler (c. 1470–1549), who also wrote commentaries on several ancient scientists, tried to systematically combine the *studia humanitatis* with mathematics and astronomy. Celtis' successor Jacob Locher (Philomusos, c. 1470–1523) became the first German editor of Horace (1498). A vehement controversy erupted between him and the theologian Georg Zingel, a proponent of scholasticism, who fought the pagan poets as 'lascivious and obscene corrupters of morale'. This was the last conservative resistance Humanism faced. Once Johannes Eck (1486–1543) succeeded to Zingel's chair at the university (1519), Humanism flourished, attracting students from all over Europe [4]. When the Reformation overshadowed humanist ideals, drawing almost all life out of the universities, Ingolstadt became an active centre of Catholicism and intellectual opposition to the Reformation. From 1520 to 1521 Johann Reuchlin lectured at Ingolstadt on Aristophanes' comedies and taught Hebrew grammar. A few decades later the Bavarian abbot Wolfgang of Aldersbach said that, in addition to Latin, knowledge of Greek and Hebrew was 'so common that without it nobody could be called a scholar' (cited in [43. 352]). Ingolstadt continued to play a central role, although theological disputes often threatened to take precedence over the interest in Antiquity. Hubert Gyphanius, editor of Lucretius (1566/1595) and Homer (1577), Matthias Rader, commentator of Martial (1602) and Curtius Rufus (1615), were active at Ingolstadt. Humanism gave new impulses to the monasteries as well. The monastic libraries acquired humanist literature. Learned monks and abbots were involved in establishing an *eruditio christiana*, a Christian education (e.g., the Emmeram abbot Leonhard, died 1540, and Wolfgang Haimstöckl, died 1509, provost of the Rohr monastery).

Gradually the interest of the Court in Humanism grew as well. In 1508 Duke Wilhelm employed Johannes Turmair, also called Aventinus (1477–1534), a pupil of Celtis, to tutor Princes Ludwig and Ernst. Aventinus wrote a Latin grammar for them, published 1512 in Munich. Its explanations in German make it the first Latin-German grammar, and for a long time it was the definitive textbook at the university. Aventinus sought to win political support for his humanist ideals: in 1516 he founded a learned society in Ingolstadt, the *Sodalitas litteraria Boiorum*. As the 'father of Bavarian history' (G.W. Leibniz), he initiated a re-evaluation of historical sources: 'We need a new way of looking at sources', he wrote, 'and to understand the new we must refer to the old' [16. 17]. For Aventinus 'sources' were no longer strictly textual (chronicles, official documents, legends and poetry), but also included inscriptions, coins, monuments and archaeological finds. As his teacher Celtis, he viewed Tacitus' *Germania* as an idealised model for the German people. In 1558 the Munich Hofbibliothek (court library) was founded, for which Duke Albrecht V acquired the libraries of the Humanist Johann Albrecht Widmanstetter (d. 1557) and that of the great collector Johann Jakob Fugger (d. 1575). In addition to the library, Albrecht V built the Antiquarium, Germany's first museum, giving rise to Munich's reputation as a cultural city of international rank. The core of the collection also came from the property of J.J. Fugger and was supplemented with acquisitions from Italy. The Bavarian court modelled its activities on those of the Italian nobility and the pope, for whom a collection of antiquities was an expression of *nobilitas* (aristocratic lifestyle). Museum architecture would later return to the principles involved in the design of the building and the arrangement of the collection [29. 310–321].

In 1532 Simon Scheidenreisser (Minervius) became teacher of poetics and city chronicler in Munich; in 1537 he completed the first German Homer translation 'in powerful unaffected Bavarian prose, capturing amazingly well 'Homer's serene unpretentiousness' '(Joseph Nadler). This was an important turning point in the reception of the ancient epic; Scheidenreisser's translation even had a profound effect on the narrative prose of the 17th cent. Willibald Pirckheimer (1470–1530) came from Eichstätt. Along with Erasmus and Reichlin he was one of the most distinguished Humanists, and in the words of Emperor Maximilian 'the most learned doctor to be found in the Empire'. In Landshut, the preeminent publishing town in Bavaria (the first book was printed in 1482), editions of the classics were published along with translations of Sallust, Cicero, Seneca and Lucian by Dietrich of Plieningen (*c.* 1450–1520), one of the principal precursors of the reception of Antiquity in Germany [4].

In the late Middle Ages, Bavaria only reluctantly embarked on the intellectual journey from monastery to university, and from Scholasticism to Humanism; Franconia and Swabia, however, took that route faster and more vigorously [21. 141]. In the early Humanistic period, Franconia did not yet have its own university; talented students had to matriculate at other universities before taking employment as scholars with princes or in cities. This situation allowed Franconian Humanists to put their stamp on the overall intellectual climate in Germany: Johann Müller, also called Regiomontanus (1436–1476), the greatest astronomer of his time, discovered the mathematical writings of Diophantes in Venice; with Johannes Cuspinian (1473–1529) came the critical appreciation of ancient historiographic sources (most important works: *De Caesaribus atque Imperatoribus Romanis*, 1540; *De Consulibus Romanis Commentarii*, 1553); Johannes Cochläus (1479–1552), a vehement opponent of Luther, wrote introductions to the language and culture of Antiquity

and published the cosmography of Pomponius Mela with the famous appendix *Brevis Germaniae descriptio* (1514). Ivo Wittich (d. 1507), editor of the *Epitomai* of Lucius Florus, was Livy's first translator; Georg Dont (d. 1537), editor of Seneca's *De vita beata* (1496), translated Aristotle into Latin; between 1510 and 1516 Veit Werler (born after 1480), edited Plautus, Lucian, Valerius Maximus and Cicero. Joachim Camerarius (1500–1574) came from Franconia as well (Bamberg).

B. EDUCATION AND UNIVERSITIES FROM THE 15TH TO THE 19TH CENTS.

In Bavaria, Franconia and Swabia, esp. in the imperial cities, → LATIN SCHOOLS were established in addition to the old cathedral and → MONASTERY SCHOOLS in the late Middle Ages (after *c.* 1200). They taught Latin, as it was indispensable for singing in the choir, serving as altar boy and for reading prayer books. After *c.* 1500, school regulations revealed the influence of Humanism. In Munich (1489), Freising, Ingolstadt and Nuremberg poets' schools (*Poetenschulen*) were established, in which Greek was also taught. They were typical humanistic educational institutions and, being elitist, they soon found themselves in conflict with scholastic Dominicans as well as poorer Latin schools. In the cities the Humanists themselves operated secular Latin schools. Classical authors were harshly criticised especially by Protestants. In a Bavarian school document from 1548 we read that 'the pagan windbags who deal in pagan fantasies and idolatry' turned the young minds away from God (quoted in [41. 354]). With the abovementioned poets' schools the Humanists created a concept of classical literary education that for the next two centuries would shape instruction at the Gymnasium. The Jesuits finally integrated the Humanistic educational ideal into their system of Catholic instruction. The Jesuit schools, in their Greek and Latin language classes, concentrated on fostering an appreciation for the beauty of language and its practical application.

In Bavaria, as elsewhere in Germany, the majority of schools remained Church schools at first. In the Duchy, and later the Electorate of Bavaria, the Jesuit Gymnasium grew to be the prototype for an institution of higher learning until the middle of the 18th cent. [43. 370–372], while the number of monastic schools also increased from the 17th cent. on. In 1773, when the *Societas Jesu* was dissolved, the responsibility for secondary education (*Lyzealwesen*) in Bavaria was transferred from the Jesuits to the state, and for the first time in its history of 150 years it became a source of constant controversy [46. 33]. Accordingly, the time from 1773 to 1830 is called 'a period of storm and stress in the Bavarian school history' [41. 1]. A tendency towards pedagogical realism is noticeable as early as the 17th cent., with demands to include more 'practical' subjects and modern languages. A vehement dispute erupted between the proponents of the pedagogical ideals of philanthropism and the Enlightenment and those who advocated → NEW HUMANISM. The central figure was a pupil of Christian Wolff, J.A. von Ickstatt (1702–1776), since 1744 Rector of Ingolstadt University, where he attracted a circle of scholars to pursue the ideals of the Enlightenment in Bavaria. He called for vocationally oriented schools and emphasised mathematics and the 'secular disciplines'. Reacting against Jesuit and Latin schools, in his plan for reform (1774) Ickstatt attempted to diminish the importance of Latin grammar in teaching.

Following a suggestion by Johann Georg Lori (1723–1787), a jurist and member of the circle around Ickstatt, the Bayerische Akademie der Wissenschaften (Bavarian Academy of Sciences) was founded in 1759, forming the centre of the movement for school reforms [31]. One of Ickstatt's rivals was Heinrich Braun (1732–1792), whose aim it was to cultivate German language studies – a position more closely associated with Neohumanism. Braun, who in 1765 became Professor of German Language and Rhetoric at the Bayerische Akademie der Wissenschaften, edited Horace and Ovid and Latin grammar handbooks. His policy for schools, a 'milestone of Bavarian school history' [50. 952], introduced Realschulen (secondary schools) as schools for the middle class in Bavaria; the Gymnasium, however, was envisioned as a school for students wishing to enter the university. At the Gymnasium, teaching focused on the old languages. In the introduction of Braun's *Lateinischen Sprachkunst* one finds: *Lektüre! Lektüre der Alten unter der Aufsicht und Erklärung eines geschickten Lehrers, dies ist das einzige Mittel, nicht nur die Sprache der Alten zu erlernen, sondern sich durch ihre Ausdrücke in ihre Denkungsart hineinzudenken, das natürlich Feine ihres Geschmacks zu fühlen, sich ihre Wendungen nicht nur im Lateinischen, sondern durch das Lateinische auch im Deutschen geläufig zu machen* ('The reading! The reading of the ancients with the supervision and help of a skilful teacher, is the only way to learn the language of the ancients, and, through their expressions, to learn to think the way they did, to sense their naturally refined taste, to become conversant with their phrases not only in Latin, but by means of Latin in German as well'). Like Johann Matthias Gesner (1691–1701) before him, he considered the study of language not merely a 'memory business' but an 'occupation for the mind itself'. Even in Braun's curriculum two thirds of the teachers were still Jesuits, and although instruction in the ancient languages, namely Latin, prevailed, the final goal was always 'oratorical proficiency' as demanded by the Jesuits. From 1781 on the prelacy was again responsible for the Mittelschulen (secondary schools). In the new school policies from 1782 the most important issue is translation from Latin into German. At the Lyzeum, Latin was the language used in exams, in instruction and lectures; exercises in rhetoric and poetics were conducted in Latin as well. The Greek language was cultivated on a much more superficial level; its command – as the wellspring of all science and scholarship – was encouraged only in theory.

Philology as an independent subject was introduced only late at Ingolstadt (1788). Even at the university it was limited to the study of language, and was supposed to remedy the deficient command of language resulting from instruction at the Gymnasium. Although Latin no longer was the lecture language, those in logic, metaphysics and physics were still conducted in Latin. *Was im vorigen Jahrhundert (in der Philologie) geleistet wurde, ging nicht über die damals geforderten Bedürfnisse der Schule, welche gering genug waren, hinaus; von eigentlicher Philologie hatte man keinen Begriff* ('The achievements of the previous century (in philology) did not go beyond what was required by the schools at the time, which was very little; philology proper was not really understood'), wrote Leonhard Spengel in 1854 (quoted in [34. 13]). After Ingolstadt University was moved to Landshut in 1800, Anton Drexel, the new Professor of Philology, complained that in Bavaria scholarly study of the ancient languages was a rarity, and that in the instruction attention was given to 'things' rather than grammar. In 1799 Bavaria, too, saw the beginning of the government-supported battle against language schools and against Latin in general. The Kantian Kajetan Weiller (1762–1826), a headmaster in Munich, had been involved in drawing up the curriculum of 1804 and was a proponent of the pedagogy of the Enlightenment, while opposing its encyclopedism. In his opinion, the Latin language was not required for every cultivated person, only for scholars, and even not necessarily for those. It was much better to read the ancient classics in translation. He asked: *Schlägt man mit allem Latein in der Welt eine Armee? Stillt oder hindert man damit einen Aufruhr? Bekehrt oder verscheucht man damit das Laster und seinen Unglauben?* ('Will all the Latin of the world defeat an army? Will it quench or prevent an uprising? Does it reform or drive away vice and its lack of faith?' in: [41. 24]). A new *Lehrplan für alle kurpfalzbayerischen Mittelschulen* (*Curriculum For All Secondary Schools in the Palatine-Bavarian Territory*) by Joseph Wismayr (1767–1858), Studiendirektionsrat in Munich, was published in 1804. In this curriculum, Sachunterricht (social studies and science) outweighed languages, among which Greek apparently fared worst [41. 26; 50. 957]. J.H. Voß, who was offered a new philological seminar in Würzburg by the Bavarian government, rejected the new curriculum and wrote in the *Jenaische Allgemeine Literaturzeitung: Offenbar ist der Wismayrische Studienplan darauf angelegt, die freiere Ausbildung der menschlichen Natur, welche aus den freien Künsten und Wissenschaften der alten Klassiker hervorgeht, mit wohlwollender Miene zurückzuhalten. Seine Zöglinge, wo nicht eigene Kraft sich über die Schranken schwingt, sind noch verdorbener für die alte Humanität als die vormaligen Jesuitenschüler* ('Apparently Wismayr's curriculum intends to curb – with a benevolent smile – the liberal education of human nature that comes from the liberal arts and from studying the ancient classics. Its students, unless their own ener-

gy propels them over boundaries, are even more corrupted for the old Humanitarianism than the former
Jesuit students'...,cf. [41. 25–27]).

In 1805, Friedrich Ast came from Jena, a centre of
Neohumanism, to Landshut University, where he became Professor of Classical Philology, Philosophy and
Aesthetics. In his opening address, *Über den Geist des
Altertums und dessen Bedeutung für unser Zeitalter*
(*On the Spirit of Antiquity and Its Significance for Our
Time*), he revealed himself as a 'philologist with philosophical training and a romantic neohumanist' [34.
54]: 'Just as ... Antiquity is the foundation on which
rests the modern period ... Classical Antiquity is the true
model of our education. Educate yourself the Greek
way'! *Bilde dich griechisch!* was his motto. In the
addendum to his inaugural speech, Ast developed a
plan for establishing the Philology Department at
Landshut. Ast saw the Greeks in an aesthetically normative and quasi-religious way, but not yet from a historical perspective. The ancient world was the model
for any future education; ancient culture was regarded
as the only remedy that would lead to an independent
national culture ([25] with bibliography; [63]). Ast
stood in the older tradition of hermeneutics, yet in his
writings (as in August Friedrich Wolf's) new problems
and issues emerged, especially the need for a philosophical foundation of philology.

Another member of the *Jena Circle*, Friedrich Immanuel Niethammer (1766–1848), was asked by Minister
Montgelas to draw up a new curriculum. In 1804 he
received a position in Würzburg, and by 1808 he held
the position of Studienrat with the *Geheimes Ministe-
rium des Inneren* in Munich. In 1808 he published his
first programmatic essay *Der Streit des Philanthropinismus und des Humanismus in der Theorie des Erzie-
hungsunterrichts unserer Zeit* (*The Dispute Between
Philanthropinism and Humanism in the Educational
Theory of Our Time*) (repr. in [48]). With this essay he
defined the term 'humanism' while attempting to reconcile the differences between humanism and philanthropinism [11; 19]. The main idea was that Humanism
cultivates the intellectual and rational aspects of a person. His essay, therefore, advocates the didactic-philo-
logical reform movement. Not only was his criticism
directed against the utilitarian and eudemonistic pedagogy of the Enlightenment with its encyclopedism, but
also against an idealising concept of Humanism that
does not adequately take into account factual reality
[50. 958–959]. *Die Ideen Niethammers sind ein
Gemeingut der neuen klassisch-deutschen Geistesbe-
wegung; die lebendigere Sprachauffassung geht auf
Herder und Humboldt zurück, die begriffliche Formu-
lierung auf Schelling und Hegel* ('Niethammer's ideas
are part of the new classical German intellectual movement; Herder and Humboldt were responsible for the
more vital concept of language, whereas Schelling and
Hegel created the theoretical framework'), and his
work marked the *Beginn der Verschulung (des Humanismus) im humanistischem Gymnasium und seiner*
*Verwissenschaftlichung in dem großartigen Entwurf
von F.A. Wolf, (Darstellung der) Altertumswissenschaft (1807)* ('the beginning of ('Humanism') as an
educational concept in the humanistic Gymnasium, and
its emerging scholarly dimension as found in the splendid outline of F.A. Wolf, (Darstellung der) *Altertumswissenschaft* (1807)', cf. [11. 322], with bibliography).
According to Niethammer, no field was more suited to
provide material for instruction than Antiquity, *indem
unleugbar wahre Classicität in allen Arten der Darstellung des Wahren, Guten und Schönen in ihrer größten
Vollendung nur bei den classischen Nationen des Alter-
thumes angetroffen wird* ('since' 'undeniably only the
classical nations of Antiquity were able to present in
any manner truth and beauty in the greatest perfection
of true classicism'). In this context the specialised vocational education that was central to instruction at the
Philanthropines) was relegated to secondary status. On
3 November 1808 the so-called Niethammersche Normativ (*Allgemeines Normativ der Einrichtung der
öffentlichen Unterrichtsanstalten in dem Königreiche
Baiern*) was published: In addition to the Progymna-
sium and Gymnasium it also envisioned a Realschule
and a Realinstitut. In Niethammer's concept, the
Lyzeum, although it offered only a fraction of the material covered at the university, was the highest-ranking
educational institution, second only to the university.
Bavarian Lyzeen were typical Catholic products of the
Baroque era, derived from the Council of Trent, to
foster the scholarly education of a new generation of
priests. They were 'early or specialised (semi-) academic
institutions, fulfilling both the mission of the Gymnasium along with scholarly propaedeutics and the *studium generale* of a university' [35. 642–643].

A significant outcome of Niethammer's education
policies were appointments of important personalities:
Hegel was appointed to the Ägydiengymnasium in
Nuremberg. On 7 December 1807 Friedrich Jacobs
began his activities in Munich with the address, *Vom
Zwecke der gelehrten Schulen* (*Of the Purpose of The
Learned Schools*): 'To educate the youth the right way
means to educate them for humaneness – for humanitarianism'. The safest route to this high goal was the
study of Antiquity. Jacobs took the responsibility the
government had imposed on him very seriously: to promote classical literature, especially Greek. He objected
to Wismayr's curriculum: *Mitleid muß es einflößen zu
sehen, daß Leute, die nicht eine Seite im Plato oder
einem anderen alten Philosophen verstehen, über die
Geschichte der Philosophie und die größten Männer
mit einer Keckheit von Hörensagen aburteilen, die sich
kein Kenner erlauben würde* ('One has to feel pity when
one sees people who do not understand one page in
Plato or any other old philosopher pass judgement over
the history of philosophy and the greatest men, based
on hearsay and with a boldness no expert would dare to
assume', cf. [58. 63–65]).

Friedrich Thiersch (1784–1860), a pupil of Gottfried Hermann and Ch.G. Heyne, was transferred from

Göttingen to Munich [20; 36; 40; 61]. In 1811, he was appointed to a chair at the Lyzeum and to head the Philological Institute; through a royal decree of 1812 he received a fixed fund for scholarships and a philological library: Thiersch transformed his private courses into a philological seminar. The ministry gave him permission to publish the *disputationes* of the young members of his seminar. These appeared under the title *Acta Philologorum Monacensium* and contained contributions from Jacobs and Thiersch as well. In the foreword, Thiersch claimed the only route to Classical Studies was the critical knowledge of the Latin and Greek languages. The *Acta* ended in 1828 with the first fascicle of the fourth volume. After 1819 Joseph Kopp (1788–1842) was co-director of the seminar, and after 1823 Leonhard Spengel (1803–1880); on December 14, 1823 the Philological Institute was separated from the Lyzeum and affiliated with the Academy of Sciences. In addition to Munich, the Philological Seminar Erlangen became a training institution for teachers for the Gymnasium. After 1819 J. Ludwig Döderlein (1791–1863), and after 1842 Karl Friedrich Nägelsbach were active in Erlangen [60].

Niethammer's *Normativ* and its proponents from the north encountered vehement opposition from conservative Catholic forces and from the old Bavarian Patriotic Party: Thiersch even suffered an assassination attempt (cf. [20. 438]). Niethammer's new curriculum (1824) put even greater emphasis on the ancient languages, esp. Latin (higher standards in the curriculum). According to Wieland you learned to write well, even in German, 'from Cicero' [50. 962]. Thiersch's school regulation (1829) stipulated that in the Gymnasium other subjects should be 'subordinated in every aspect' to the ancient languages and their literature. This regulation, albeit in a more 'lenient' version of 1830, shaped the Bavarian Gymnasium throughout the 19th cent. (for statistics, see [56]). At Munich University the contingent from Jena, Schelling and Niethammer especially, defended an idealistic concept against the enlightened pragmatism of the ministerial bureaucracy. In 1826 the old Landesuniversität (Bavarian State University) was moved to Munich so that the capital would, in the words of Eduard von Schenk, advisor to Ludwig I on cultural politics, have a 'dominant influence on all of Germany' in intellectual matters. The King was especially influenced by Thiersch's programmatic essay *Über Gelehrte Schulen mit besonderer Rücksicht auf Bayern* (*On Learned Schools With Special Respect to Bavaria*), published by Cotta between 1826 and 1831.

C. The Period of Ludwig I

Like the cultural politics of Ludwig I, Thiersch's neohumanistic programme focussed on art. Ludwig's Italian journey (1804/1805) was a formative experience that awakened his love for ancient art. Ludwig would later remember: *Ich war in Schwetzingen erzogen und keineswegs Kunstfreund, aber die scheußlichen Figuren im Hofgarten von Nymphenburg machten mich der Skulptur abgeneigt, bis ich nach Venedig kam und es mir vor Canovas Hebe wie Schuppen von den Augen fiel* ('I was brought up in Schwetzingen and not an art lover at all; the ghastly statues in the Nymphenburg Hofgarten made me dislike sculpture until I came to Venice where, standing in front of Canova's *Hebe*, the scales fell from my eyes', [29. 23]). In Rome, Ludwig drew up a plan for a collection of antiquities (→ ANTIQUITIES COLLECTIONS); he was influenced by the Palatine painter and poet Friedrich Müller (1749–1825), who belonged to Goethe's circle. Only a few months after his return, Ludwig started acquiring works of art. Until 1810 Müller was his first agent in Rome; other advisors of the crown prince were the sculptor Konrad Eberhardt, the painter Johann Georg von Dillis [33], who later became a gallery director in Munich, and the sculptor and painter Johann Martin von Wagner (1777–1858) of Würzburg. 'In Munich we need what they call *museo* in Rome' – these words of Ludwig signified the birth of the Glyptothek (→ GLYPTOTHEK), a collection which 'should distinguish itself by its quality', as Ludwig wrote to von Wagner (1777–1858) in 1810 [66]. Ludwig only searched for 'the classical', works 'for eternity whose value will only increase with each century'. Ludwig's project combined ideas of Winckelmann and the French Revolution, for the planned exhibition was to serve the artistic education of the people as well [66]. At the same time the crown prince wanted to alleviate a deficiency of German and Bavarian art and support sculpture. 'Glyptothek' is a neologism and refers to an exhibition space for sculptural works of art [29]. The building was intended as a symbol for the rebirth of ancient art, for a new Periclean epoch in Munich. It was 'a bit ridiculous' (*ridikül*), wrote Heinrich Heine in his *Reisebilder*, 'to call the entire city a new Athens' (*Sämtliche Schriften* III 320). The museum was supposed to prove the exemplary character of Antiquity. Nothing could help the project more than ownership of Greek originals. Almost the entire sculpture collection of the Glyptothek was purchased at Ludwig's expense during the time he was crown prince (for a detailed acquisition history, see R. Wünsche in [18]). Max I could not understand what his son liked about these *zerbrochenen schmutzigen Puppen* ('broken dirty dolls', [29. 9]). Once construction started, the strange building became known as the 'crazy house of the crown prince'. In 1811 Ludwig made it known he planned to look in Greece for 'excellent beauty'. He wrote to Carl Haller von Hallerstein (1774–1817), who had been in Greece on a Bavarian scholarship, wanting to hire him as his agent. In the spring of the same year, Haller and the English architect Charles Robert Cokkerell (1788–1863) discovered the famous pediment sculptures of the temple of Aphaia at Aigina; six months later the first fragments of the frieze at Bassai were unearthed.

These discoveries were reported in the European press and made the excavators famous. But the central interest of Haller von Hallerstein and his friends (O.M.

von Stackelberg, P.O. Bröndsted, G. Koes, J. Linckh) was scholarly research. Bröndsted writes: *Wir haben uns vereint zu einer graphischen und historischen Darstellung des Besten von dem, was wir in verschiedenen Teilen von Griechenland gesehen, erfahren und gelernt haben* ('We have come together to produce a visual and historical account of the best of what we have seen, experienced and learned in the various parts of Greece', cited in K. Fräßle in: [3. 22]). Cockerell wanted to expand and improve the *Antiquities of Athens* (4 vols., 1762–1816) [3. 48–49]. Haller wanted to fight 'barbarism', e.g., that of the famous British ambassador Lord Elgin, who had the sculptures of the Parthenon removed and taken to England. Under Haller's influence Ludwig made it his ambition not only to own Greek monuments, but to protect them as well. These two principles can be found in the first *Beschreibung der Glyptothek* (*Description of the Glyptothek*). Future excavation plans were put on hold by Haller's death, but not the museum project, for which Haller had left sketches in his own hand, and which made him the founding father of archaeological classicism in Germany. In 1814 a competition was held for the museum project, demanding that 'the whole and the parts [be] in the purest ancient style' (wording of the announcement of the competition in [29. 98]). Eventually, the architect Leo von Klenze (1784–1864) won the bid [32]. In Klenze's view, the mission of the museum was to teach a historical understanding of all ancient art. He wrote: *Der Grund, welcher uns als der mächtigste für die Wahl einer historischen Ordnung bestimmt, ist die Entfernung unserer Kunstideen von denen der Alten, denen die Idealcharaktere ihrer Götter als religiöser und pantheistischer Grund, der stets lebendig, vor der Seele schwebte. Da diese Aussicht uns aber entrückt, so glauben wir, daß nächst des artistischen Genusses die Verfolgung der historischen Ordnung, und der daraus entspringenden Entwicklung des Ganges der Kunst, uns lebhafter ergreifen muß, als eine unvollkommene Reihe von Idealen, welche unsere religiösen Begriffe verwerfen* ('The most important reason for us in choosing a historical order is how far removed our artistic ideas are from those of the ancients, who constantly had before their soul the ideal characters of their gods as a living religious and pantheistic foundation. Since we are removed from this world view, we think that, in addition to the artistic pleasure, the pursuit of the historical order and the evolution of art that sprang from it should touch us more vigorously than an incomplete series of ideals, which our religious notions condemn', cf. [18. 38]). The museum was opened in 1830; however, it was not until 1862 that the last figure was placed in an alcove. Artists reacted to the building with criticism: the tradition of German architecture appeared to have been betrayed. Ludwig's ambition was to have examples of all architectural styles in Munich, and to transplant 'to one spot', as von Klenze wrote to him, 'an image of pure Hellenism' [64]. The result was a 'mishmash of monuments of all periods' (F.Ch. Gau), a 'building ... completely devoid of style, without any consequence, on which immense sums of money are wasted' (Friedrich Schelling, quoted in [29. 286]). A 'stone catalogue of styles' was created, as Anton Springen put it in 1845. Inspired by Haller's sketches, Klenze built the Walhalla between 1830 and 1842 (Regenstauf on the Danube, 11 km east of Regensburg); Ludwig I had commissioned the reproduction of the → PARTHENON, the Acropolis of Athens, as a hall of fame for notable Germans. Between 1846 and 1862, the Propyläen, modelled on the Propylaia of the Acropolis of Athens, were built at the western side of the Königsplatz in Munich. However, Klenze did not intend merely to copy in Bavaria the Greek originals in their reputedly perfect beauty; instead he attempted a free variation and a transposition of the present ideal. The classicist reference to the Greek models should not be seen simply as an architectural quotation. As an expression of Bildungsarchitektur (educational architecture), its purpose was to showcase the relevance of everything that was associated with Greece.

Klenze's programme, which followed in Haller's footsteps, was articulated in the lecture *Über das Hinwegführen plastischer Kunstwerke aus dem jetzigen Griechenland und die neuesten Unternehmungen dieser Art* (*On Taking Works of Sculptural Art Out of Greece Today and on the Latest Undertakings of That Kind*), delivered on March 31,1821 at the Royal Bavarian Academy of Sciences (Königlich Bayerischen Akademie der Wissenschaften). All 'cultural assets, regardless of which nation they belong to', were part of 'the cultural heritage of all humankind'; the removal of ancient art from Greece, therefore, was not only permitted, it was a responsibility. Klenze planned a German excavation at Olympia, where he hoped to find 'rich treasures of sculpture', the works of Phidias and Miron. C.O. Müller and Friedrich Thiersch took up his plan with great enthusiasm and started raising money. But the end of March 1821 saw the outbreak of the Greek war of independence, in which Bavaria was to play a central role. → PHILHELLENISM is an almost unique example of how an idea was translated into political action [1; 14]. It is inconceivable without German classicism and its worship of Greece. Ludwig I turned the political idea into a reality. Through its practical and intellectual impulses, Bavaria gained a central position in the German Hellenistic movement. Friedrich Thiersch's projects, and especially his publications, supplemented by Emmerich Carl von Dahlberg's expansions and implementation efforts, were largely responsible for the pioneering character of the Bavarian initiatives, both in their practical realisation as well as in their idealistic concept. [59. 255]. From 1814 Thiersch was working with *Hetairie der Philomuse*, an organisation that provided young Greeks with scholarships to come to Germany. Also in that year he founded the *Musenverein* in Vienna, to support Greek culture and the fight for independence. In Munich he founded the *Atheneum*, a study centre for young Greeks. In 1821 he headed the

Münchner Griechenverein; in addition, he corresponded extensively with the patriot and philologist Adaman-
tios Korais and with Johannes Capostria. Thiersch was
the first German scholar to attempt a scholarly treatment of Modern Greek literature and culture; in 1831
and 1832 he promoted the election of the young Otto in
Greece. This made Bavaria the starting point and the
centre of philhellenism. A second wave of philhellenism
rose in Bavaria after Otto was elected King of Greece.
But the Greek revolution of 1843 put an end to the
so-called 'bavarocracy' (*Bavarokratie*). Against this
backdrop, the tradition of studying Middle and Modern Greek was established at Munich University in the
early 19th cent. Among its 19th cent. luminaries was
Karl Krumbacher (1856–1909), pioneer of Byzantine
studies and founder of the Middle and Modern Greek
Seminar, who wrote the *Geschichte der byzantinischen
Literatur* (1891, ²1897) and initiated the *Byzantinische
Zeitschrift* (1892), the first scholarly journal of the discipline.

The classicism of Ludwig's time had literary repercussions as well [22]: the King himself wrote poetry [22;
57] and gave financial support to the main representative of the classical style, August von Platen, who was
very successful in Munich. After his *Romantischer
Oedipus* was published in 1829, he was celebrated as
the 'German Aristophanes' in the journal *Aurora*. The
work, it claimed in a lengthy review, stands 'like a
sculptural work of art of the highest perfection, well-
rounded and complete in all its parts. It affects our aesthetic sensitivity with a serenity as only the most beautiful ancient marbles can' – Winckelmann's interpretation of Greek sculpture is clearly echoed. The article
culminates in a plea for the necessity of a 'developed
form' as opposed to romantic 'error' and 'barbarism'.
To fulfill this requirement, a 'thorough classical education' was required – not to be confused with 'the
pedantic textbook-knowledge of narrow-minded philologists'. Without such an education 'no real salvation'
could be expected for art [22. 68–69]. An epigonic classicism continued to prevail in literary output and literary theory under Max II (especially with Paul Heyse).

D. The George Circle

At the end of the 19th cent., a new understanding of
Antiquity emerged, largely due to the influence of the
poet Stefan George. In the ninth installment of the *Blätter für die Kunst* he celebrated the manifestation of the
divine in the perfect body as 'the Hellenic miracle'; in
the early 20th cent. this powerful model of archaic art
along with the unusual poetry of George had a strong
influence on the generation of archaeologists, historians and religious historians who were members of
George's circle of friends [54]. For instance, in 1935
Horst Rüdiger saw in George's revival of Antiquity a
way for a 'German renewal' [53]. George helped create
a deeper understanding of pre- and post-classical art
[44; 54]. The sentiment for Antiquity in George and his
circle is anything but classicist: it is a new religious ex-

perience. This provided a fresh approach for archaeological research, and for Religious Studies and Classical
Studies in general, i.e. the realisation that great art has a
religious component. 'Art has not always been 'art'' –
the opening sentence of *Vom Sinn der griechischen
Standbilder* (*On The Meaning of Greek Statues*, 1980)
by Ernst Buschor (1942, ²1977), one of the most remarkable personalities of 20th cent. archaeology (cf. K.
Schefold in: [24. 183–203; 54. 94]), had been anticipated in George's poetry. The title of Walter F. Otto's
book *Die Götter Griechenlands* (1929) already marks
it as a 'Gestalt' book in the style of the George Circle:
*Nicht 'die Religion der Griechen', sondern Gestalten
und Mythen, Göttergeschichten, theologia im alten
Sinne also, verspricht dieser Titel, dichterische Schau,
von Hölderlin und von Schillers Wesen aus dem Fabelland inspiriert, nicht Historismus, nicht altphilol.
Emsigkeiten oder gar Ideologiekritik* ('This title does
not promise the 'religion of the Greeks', but rather characters and myths, stories about gods, *theologia* in the
old sense, a poetic vision, inspired by Hölderlin and by
Schiller's *Wesen aus dem Fabelland*, not historicism,
not the zeal of Classical Philology or even Ideologiekritik' [11. 140–141]). It is no coincidence that the
'Bachofen renaissance' of the 1920s had its origins in
Munich, or rather in the circles of the so-called Münchener Kosmiker [55], who wanted to lead a 'pagan'
life, i.e. a natural and archaic life that was not controlled by the intellect. The major figure of this new
paganism, this 'metaphysics of life', was Ludwig Kla-
ges. Rainer Maria Rilke and the young Thomas Mann
gravitated towards the movement, and in 1926 C.H.
Beck published the anthology: *Bachofen. Der Mythus
von Orient und Occident*. It was edited by Manfred
Schröter, with a long introduction by Alfred Baeumler,
the theorist of National Socialism. Baeumler emphasised the significance of the near-eastern 'symbol' as
opposed to the classicistic concept of Greek art.
Baeumler and the Munich 'Kosmiker' viewed Friedrich
Creuzer (1771–1858), the author of *Symbolik und
Mythologie der alten Völker* (Symbolism and Mythology of the Ancient Peoples) (1812, ³1836), as having
paved the way for this anti-classicistic view of ancient
art and mythology.

E. Universities and Institutions in the 19th and 20th Centuries

At Bavarian universities historical research had
always been of great importance [15; 65]: Leopold von
Ranke was a teacher and friend of Max II, and a
number of his pupils were appointed to chairs at Bavarian universities between 1848 and 1864. The *Historische Kommission* at the Academy of Sciences, the
Monumenta Germaniae Historica [27], which counted
the palaeographer Ludwig Traube among its collaborators ([27]; on Traube: [6; 9]), the *Institut für Zeitgeschichte*, the *Osteuropa-Institut*, and the *Südost-Insti-
tut* are all Munich institutions of crucial importance for
the historical disciplines. A pre-eminent champion of

Ancient History in Munich was Robert von Pöhlmann (1852–1914). As an expert in political economy he examined social conditions in the ancient world and destroyed the classicistic and neohumanist myth of an ideal ancient society [12]. In his *Geschichte des antiken Kommunismus und Sozialismus* (2 vols., 1893 and 1901), after the second edition entitled *Geschichte der sozialen Frage und des Sozialismus in der antiken Welt* (*History of the Social Question And of Socialism in The Ancient World*), he consistently applied the economic and social categories of the 19th cent. to his subject, and was criticised for his modernist view of Antiquity. A third, expanded edition appeared in 1925 with an addendum by Friedrich Oertel [24. 316f.].

From 1918 to 1941 Walter F. Otto was Professor of Ancient History in Munich. He had a command of the major languages of the Ancient Orient and a universalist concept of the study of Antiquity. Otto played a unique role in the history of interpretations of Hellenism, which he suggested should include the entire Roman period as well. For Otto, Hellenism was a common Greek culture; with his teacher Ulrich Wilcken he shared the idea that the Hellenistic triumph over political particularism could be instructive for Germans [24. 298f.]. To this was added his hope for an 'all-conquering popular leader', a leader who would bring about the 'revolution', and who has taken concrete shape [24. 304]. Otto was also a major scholarly organizer and published the fundamental *Handbuch der klassischen Altertumswissenschaft* (started by Iwan Müller who taught in Munich and Erlangen).

After Walter Otto, Hermann Bengston (1909–1989) held the Chair for Ancient History in 1942. Bengston also revised the *Handbuch der Altertumswissenschaft* and published seminal overviews of Greek and Roman history; in the winter semester of 1943/1944 Helmut Berve relocated from Leipzig to take up an appointment in Munich. For a long time, Classical Philology in Munich was represented by Wilhelm Christ (1831–1906) [13], editor of the *Geschichte der griechischen Literatur*, which still belongs to the 'enduring core of standard literature in our field' [13. 28], and by Eduard Wölfflin (1831–1908), the founder of the → THESAURUS LINGUAE LATINAE, as it had been envisioned by Friedrich Ritschl. Martin Schanz (1842–1914), a Plato scholar (*Novae commentationes platonicae*, 1871), taught in Würzburg. He was the author of the entry on the history of Latin literature in the above-mentioned *Handbuch* (1890–1914 in various editions, revised by Carl Hosius) [17]. To appreciate the significance of Greek Studies in Munich, we only need to remind ourselves that Eduard Schwartz, 'one of the most imposing figures of Classical Studies ... of all times' (R. Pfeiffer), was professor in Munich [51]. He was succeeded by Rudolf Pfeiffer, who held the chair until the autumn of 1937 [45]. When in March 1946 the heavily damaged university in Munich was reopened, the three professors, Franz Dirlmeier, Richard Harder and Rudolf Till, were removed from office [23]. Albert Rehm (1871–

1949) was appointed as temporary Rector – a position he had already held in 1930, when he overcame radical right-wing student unrest [30; 62]. In his inaugural speech of 1930, *Neuhumanismus einst und jetzt, auf den Spuren von Gesner, Niethammer, Humboldt* (*Neohumanism, Now And Then, In the Footprints of Gesner, Niethammer and Humboldt*), Rehm emphasised the need for a classical education starting with the Gymnasium. Among his great achievements after the war was the salvaging of the *Thesaurus Linguae Latinae* project: an international Thesaurus commission was set up on 7 April 1949. Since he also had credentials as an epigrapher, Rehm expressed interest in an institution for the advancement of epigraphy. His plans were put into practice when the Munich Ancient Historians Alexander Graf Schenk von Stauffenberg, Hermann Bengston and Siegfried Lauffer established the *Kommission für Alte Geschichte und Epigraphik* in 1951 [10]. Since 1959 the *Kommission* has published several volumes in its two occasional series, *Vestigia* and *Staatsverträge des Altertums*, and since 1971 the journal *Chiron*; it also supervises the *Sylloge Nummorum Graecorum Deutschland* (started by H. Gebhardt and K. Kraft).

→ GREECE; → HUMANIST GYMNASIUM; → PHILHELLENISM

1 R. F. ARNOLD, Der deutsche Philhellenismus. Kultur- und literarhistorische Untersuchungen, in: Euphorion, 2. Ergänzungsheft, 1896, 151–161 2 F. BAETHGEN, Die Bayerische Akademie der Wissenschaften, 1909–1959, Tradition und Auftrag, 1959 3 H. BANKEL (ed.), Carl Haller von Hallerstein in Griechenland. 1810–1817, 1986 4 L. BOEHM et al. (eds.), s.v. Das geistige Leben vom 13. bis zum Ende des 18. Jahrhunderts, Handbuch der Bayerischen Geschichte III.1, 1997, 963–1249 5 L. BOEHM, s.v. Das akademische Bildungswesen in seiner organisatorischen Entwicklung (1800–1920), Handbuch der Bayerischen Geschichte IV.2, 1979, 995–1035 6 F. BOLL, Erinnerung an Ludwig Traube, 1907 7 K. BOSL (ed.), Bayerische Biographie, Vols. I–II, 1983–1988 8 F. BRUNHÖLZL, s.v. Die lateinische Literatur, Handbuch der Bayerischen Geschichte I, 1981, 582–606 9 H. BRUNN, E. MONACI et al. (eds.), Ludwig Traube zum Gedächtnis, 1907 10 E. BUCHNER, 25 Jahre Kommission für Alte Geschichte und Epigraphik, in: Chiron 6, 1976, VII–VIII 11 H. CANCIK, Antik. Modern. Beiträge zur römischen und deutschen Kulturgeschichte, 1998 12 K. CHRIST, Robert von Pöhlmann (1852–1914), in: Von Gibbon zu Rostvtzeff. Leben und Werk führender Althistoriker der Neuzeit 1979, 201–247 13 O. CRUSIUS, Wilhelm von Christ. Gedächtnisrede, 1907 14 Der Philhellenismus und die Modernisierung in Griechenland und Deutschland, 1986 15 H. DICKERHOF-FRÖHLICH, Das historische Studium an der Universität München im 19. Jahrhundert, 1979 16 E. DÜNNINGER, E. STAHLEDER, Aventinus zum 450. Todesjahr 1984, 1986 (with bibliography) 17 A. DYROFF, Martin von Schanz, in: BiogJahr 249, 1935, 50–87 18 Ein griechischer Traum. Leo von Klenze. Der Archäologe, Catalogue of the exhibition, 6 December 1985–9 February 1986, Glyptothek München 1986 19 C. VON ELSPERGER, s.v. Friedrich Immanuel von Niethammer, Encyclopädie des gesammten Erziehungs- und Unterrichtswesens V, Gotha 1866, 233–237

20 Id., s.v. Friedrich Thiersch, Encyclopädie des gesammten Erziehungs- und Unterrichtswesens VI, 1867, 432–443
21 R. ENDRES, s.v. Das Schulwesen von c. 1200 bis zum Reformation. Gesamtdarstellung, Handbuch der Geschichte des Bayerischen Bildungswesen, Vol. 1, 1991, 141–188 22 K.-H. FALBACHER, Literarische Kultur in München zur Zeit Ludwigs I. und Maximilians II., 1992 23 Festschrift für Ernst Vogt, (Eikasmos 4) 1993 24 H. FLASHAR (ed.), Altertumswissenschaft in den 20er Jahren. Neue Fragen und Impulse, 1995 25 Id., Die methodisch-hermeneutischen Ansätze von Friedrich August Wolf und Friedrich Ast – Traditionelle und neue Begründungen, in: Philologie und Hermeneutik im 19. Jahrhundert, 1979, 21–31 (Reprint: Eidola 38, 529–539) 26 TH. FRENZ, Das Schulwesen des Mittelalters bis c. 1200. Gesamtdarstellung, Handbuch der Geschichte des Bayerischen Bildungswesen, Vol. 1, 1991, 81–133 27 W. D. FRITZ, Theodor Mommsen, Ludwig Traube und Karl Strecker als Mitarbeiter der Monumenta Germaniae Historica, in: Das Altertum 14, 1968, 235–244 28 Geist und Gestalt. I. Geisteswissenschaften, 1959 29 Glyptothek München: 1830–1980. Jubiläumsausstellung zur Entstehungs- und Baugeschichte, 17. September–23. November 1980 (eds.) K. VIERNEISEL, G. LEINY, K. J. SEMBACH, 1980 30 H. HAFFTER, Albert Rehm, in: Gnomon 22, 1950, 315–318 31 L. HAMMERMAYER, Gründung- und Frühgeschichte der Bayerischen Akademie der Wissenschaften, 1959 32 O. HEDERER, Leo von Klenze. Persönlichkeit und Werk, 1964 33 C. HEILMANN (ed.), Johann Georg von Dillis 1759–1841. Landschaft und Menschenbild 1991 (catalogue) 34 J. HERMANN, Friedrich Ast als Neuhumanist. Ein Beitrag zur Geschichte des Neuhumanismus in Bayern, 1912 35 R. W. KECK, W. WIATER, s.v. Geschichte der Universitäten und Hochschulen. I. Von den Anfängen bis 1900. 2. Von 1900 bis 1990, Handbuch der Geschichte des Bayerischen Bildungswesen, Vol. 4, 1997, 637–717 (with bibliography) 36 H.-M. KIRCHNER, Friedrich Thiersch. Ein liberaler Kulturpolitiker und Philhellene in Bayern, 1996 37 M. KRAUS, J. LATACZ, Zum Geleit, in: U. HÖLSCHER, Das nächste Fremde 1994, I–X 38 M. KRAUS, Vorwort des Herausgebers, in: H. FLASHAR, Eidola, 1989 39 J. LATACZ (ed.), In memoriam Uvo Hölscher (8.3.1914–31.12.1996). Gedenkfeier des Instituts für Klassische Philologie der Universität München am 9. Mai 1997, in collaboration with W. SUERBAUM, 1997 40 H. LOEWE, Friedrich Thiersch. Ein Humanistenleben im Rahmen der Geistesgeschichte seiner Zeit, Vol. 1: Die Zeit des Reifens, 1925 41 Id., Die Entwicklung des Schulkampfs in Bayern bis zum vollständigen Sieg des Neuhumanismus, 1917 42 H. LUTZ, A. SCHMID, s.v. Vom Humanismus zur Gegenreformation, Handbuch der bayerischen Geschichte II, 1988, 861–875 43 K. E. MAIER, s.v. Das Schulwesen von der Zeit der Reformation bis zur Aufklärung. Gesamtdarstellung, Handbuch der Geschichte des Bayerischen Bildungswesen, Vol. 1, 1991, 349–384 44 H. MARWITZ, Stephan George und die Antike, in: WJA 1, 1946, 226–257 45 E. MESCHING, Ein Versuch, Rudolf Pfeiffer 1937 zu helfen? Zur Geschichte der klassischen Philologie in Bayern (1987), in: Nugae zur Philologiegeschichte II, 1989, 93–98 46 R. A. MÜLLER, Akademische Ausbildung zwischen Staat und Kirche. Das bayerische Lyzealwesen 1773–1849, Teil 1 und 2, 1986 47 E. NEUBAUER, Das geistig-kulturelle Leben der Reichsstadt Regensburg (1750–1806), 1979 48 F. I. NIETHAMMER, Philanthropinismus – Humanismus. Texte zur Schulreform (ed.) W. HILLEBRECHT, 1968 49 K. VON PRANTL,

Geschichte der Ludwig-Maximilians-Universität in Ingolstadt, Landshut, München, 2 vols., 1968 50 A. REBLE, s.v. Das Schulwesen, Handbuch der bayerischen Geschichte IV.2, 1979, 950–994 51 A. REHM, Eduard Schwartz wissenschaftliches Lebenswerk, 1942 52 Id., Das Seminar für Klassische Philologie, in: K.A. von Müller (ed.), Die wissenschaftlichen Anstalten der Ludwig-Maximilian-Universität zu München, 1926, 168–173 53 H. RÜDIGER, Georges Begegnung mit der Antike, in: Die Antike 11, 1935, 236–254 – 54 K. SCHEFOLD, Wirkungen Stefan Georges. Auf drei neuen Wegen der klassischen Archäologie, in: Castrum peregrini 173–174, 1986, 72–97 55 G. SCHIAVONI, Bachofen-Renaissance e cultura di destra, in: Nuova Corrente 28, 1981, 597–618 56 L. SCHILLER, s.v. Bayern (D. Die Gelehrtenschulen in Bayern), Encyclopädie des gesammten Erziehungs- und Unterrichtswesens I, 1859, 444–458 57 W. SEIDL, Der Teutschland half, wird Hellas retten! Ludwig I. von Bayern als philhellenischer Dichter, in: E. KONSTANTINOU (ed.), Europäischer Philhellenismus. Die europäische philhellenische Literatur bis zur 1. Hälfte des 19. Jahrhunderts, 1992, 111–118 58 K. SOCHATYZ, Das Neuhumanistische Gymnasium und die rein-menschliche Bildung, 1973 59 L. SPAENLE, Der Philhellenismus in Bayern 1821–1832, 1990 (political aspects) 60 O. STÄHLIN, Das Seminar für klassische Philologie an der Universität Erlangen. Rede gehalten bei der Feier seines 150-jährigen Bestehens am 17. Dezember 1927, 1928 61 H. W. J. THIERSCH, Friedrich Thiersch's Leben, Vol. I: 1784–1830; Vol. II: 1830–1860, Leipzig 1866 62 THESAURUS LINGUAE LATINAE (ed.), Albert Rehm zum Gedächtnis (with index of writings), in: Philologus 98, 1954, 1–13 63 F. VERCELLONE, Lo spirito e il suo altro. L'ermeneutica di Friedrich Ast, in: Identità e dell'antico. L'idea del classico nella cultura tedesca del primo Ottocento 1988, 48–65 64 K. VIERNEISEL, Ludwigs I. Verlangen nach dem Reinen griechischen Stil in: G. GRIMM, TH. NIKOLAOU (eds.), Bayerns Philhellenismus, 1993, 113–145 65 E. WEIS, s.v. Wissenschaftentwicklung im 19. und 20. Jahrhundert, Handbuch der bayerischen Geschichte IV.2, 1979, 1036–1088 66 R. WÜNSCHE, Antiken aus Griechenland – Botschafter der Freiheit, in: R. HEZDENREUTER, J. MURKEN, R. WÜNSCHE (eds.), AA. VV. Die erträumte Nation. Griechenlands Wiedergeburt im 19. Jahrhundert, 1995, 9–46.

SOTERA FORNARO

Beauty see→ BODY, ATTITUDES TOWARDS;→ PROPORTIONS, THEORY OF

Belarus see→ BELORUSSIA

Belgium see → NETHERLANDS AND BELGIUM

Bellum iustum see→ WAR

Belorussia

A. INTRODUCTION B. LITERATURE AND TRANSLATIONS C. LANGUAGE D. THEATRE E. LAW F. ANCIENT STUDIES (PHILOSOPHY AND HISTORY)

A. INTRODUCTION

Belarussian culture evolved under the clear influence of Antiquity as a result of the interaction of two cultural traditions – Byzantine (→ Byzantium) and Western European. By adopting the Greek version of Christianity, Belarussian lands became part of a world-wide historical process. The influence of Classical Antiquity became even stronger after the formation of the Grand Duchy of Lithuania. Orientation towards ancient and Western European cultural traditions became an indispensable part of Belarussian culture from the end of the 15th century onwards. A socio-political doctrine emerged (Jan Zamoysky, *De senatu Romano*, 1563; Andrei Volan, *De principe et proprius eius virtutibus*, 1608; Kazimir Lyshchinski, *De non existentia Dei*, 1686). The role of translated secular literature expanded. Among works transcribed into Old Belarussian in the 15th and 16th cents. were *Alexandria*, *History of Attila*, *History of the destruction of Troy* and *the Legend of the three Royal Soothsayers* by Johann of Hildesheim. Interest developed in novels of chivalry and in stories of wars. The 16th cent. Chronicle *Origo regis* was transcribed from Old Belarussian into Latin. In Catholic, Uniate and Jesuit schools and colleges Greek and Latin were studied alongside the 'seven liberal arts' (→ Artes liberales), Latin also being used as the everyday language. In the Orthodox schools Latin was studied alongside Church Slavonic and Greek. This made it possible for young Belarussian men to study at Latin-speaking universities in Western Europe. The development of printing and the construction of libraries were of particular advantage when it came to education in the Latin language.

B. Literature and Translations

The influence of ancient poetry and poetics is reflected in the Latin-language literature of Belarus and in the Bellum Prutenum (1515) by Jan Vislitsky (1480–1520), as well as in N. Gusovskiy's lyric-epic poem (*c.* 1480 – after 1533) *Carmen de statura feritate ac venatione bisontis* (1523). The first Belarussian printer and educator F. Skaryna (1490 – no later than 1551) was a true connoisseur of classical culture. In his Old Belarussian translation of the Bible he referred to the legacy of the ancients. Exceptional service to the spread of Latin education was rendered by Simeon Polotsky (1629–1680), whose work contains many examples from ancient history, literature and mythology. Ancient subjects, which were used in two anonymous poems of the 19th cent., represent the start of a new era in Belarussian literature (*Eneida navyvorod, Taras na Parnase*). The tradition of using ancient models and subjects was continued by Belarussian writers and poets, e.g. M. Bagdanovich (1891–1917), Janka Kupala (1882–1942), I. Shamiakin (1921), V. Karatkevich (1930–1984) and others. Artistic translation from Classical Languages into Belarussian began with M. Bagdanovich, who translated Virgil and Ovid. Julian Dreyzin (1879–1942) was another who worked on the translation of ancient writers, including *Antigone* by Sophocles (Minsk, 1926) and the 6th book of the *Iliad*. Fragments of translations of Homer by B. Tarashkevich

have been preserved. A translation by L. Barshchevsky of the work *Prometheus in Chains*, ascribed to Aeschylus, appeared in 1993. Neo-Latin literature (N. Gusovsky, *Song of Wisent*) was translated by J. Semeshon (Minsk 1980) and V. I. Schaton (Minsk 1994). The *Prussian War* by Jan Vislitsky was translated in 1997 by Shanna Nekrashevich.

C. Language

At the time of the → Renaissance and even earlier, processes were taking place in the Old Belarussian language which would result in linguistic mixing in both the everyday and literary language. Legal, medical, diplomatic and bureaucratic specialist terms evolved. The effect of the use of Latin in a Belarussian environment was the step by step loss of internationally-held standards for Latin, leading to the development of a Belarussian variant. The influence of Latin and Greek is also evident in foreign and loanwords.

D. Theatre

The culture of Classical Antiquity in Belarus in the 18th cent. was popularized and proliferated in the theatre. The repertoire included both works by ancient authors and plays based on ancient subjects. Some were performed in Old Belarussian and others in Latin. The plays were performed in teaching institutions. The theological school of Schuchin was famous for these, as was the Jesuit College in Novogrudok, where the tragedy *Artaxerxes* and the comedy *Jupiter* were performed. In modern Belarussian theatres, plays by ancient authors such as *Lysistrata* by Aristophanes still run successfully, as do works by modern authors based on ancient subjects, such as *Spartacus* by A. J. Chachaturian, *Penelope* by A. Shurbin, *The Fox and the Grapes* by G. Figeyred and others.

E. Law

The legal system of the Grand Duchy of Lithuania evolved under the influence of → Roman law. This is attested by a statute dating from 1588, one section of which (family and marriage relationships) is based on the principles of Roman law. This statute was translated into Latin in 1619. The tradition was not new; a statute of 1529 had been translated into Latin in 1530, another one dating from 1566 was translated in the same year.

F. Ancient Studies (Philosophy and History)

A remarkable researcher of ancient Greek philosophy was the Belarussian O. A. Makovelsky (1884–1969). His main works are *The Morality of Epictetus* (Kazan 1912) and 'Pre-Socratics' (Kazan 1914-1919). Original works treating ancient Greek philosophy were written by B. B. Viz-Morgules (*Democritus*, Moscow 1979; *Diogor Melosskiy*, Grodno 1996). Interest in the study of ancient history is apparent in works by authors of the 18th and 19th cents. (M. S. Kutorga, 1809–1886:

History of the Republic of Athens, St. Petersburg 1848; *The Persian Wars*, St. Petersburg 1858; *Athenian Politics*, 1896; D. N. Azarevich, 1848–1912: *Patricians and Plebeians in Rome*, 2 vols., St. Petersburg 1875). Scholars in the 20th cent. continued to work on ancient history. The following professors all founded schools of ancient history in White Russia: F. M. Nechay (1905–1990; Monographs: *Rome and the Italic Peoples*, Minsk 1963; *The Founding of the Roman State*, Minsk 1972) and G. M. Livshitz (1909–1986; Monographs: *Class War in Judaea and the Revolt against Rome, Origin of Christianity in the Region of the Dead Sea*, Minsk 1976). The tradition of the Belarussian school of ancient history was continued by: M. S. Korzun (*Sociopolitical Strife in Athens between 444–425 BC*, Minsk 1975); K. A. Revyako (*The Punic Wars*, Minsk 1988). A chair of Classical Philology (Professor, G. Shevchenko) was established at the Belarussian State University in Minsk in 1995.

1 G. I. Baryšev, Teatralnaja kultura Belorussii XVIII veka, Minsk 1992 2 V. J. Doroškevic, Novolatinskaja poesija Belorussii i Litvy, Minsk 1979 3 G. Ševcenko, Latyń belorusskogo srednevekov'ja, in: Echo Latina 1–2, Brno 1997, 25–30 4 Statut Vialikaga kniastwa Litovskaga 1588. Texty. Davednik. Kamentaryi, Minsk 1989 5 S. Tomkowicz, Materialy do historyi stosunków kulturalnych w XVI w. na dworze królewskim polskim, Kraków 1915 6 Iz istorii knigi v Belorussii. Sbornik stat'ej, Minsk 1976

ADDITIONAL BIBLIOGRAPHY: G. SCHEVTSCHENKOV, Phraseology of Antique Origin in Slavic Languages, 2005.
GALINA IVANOVNA SCHEVTSCHENKO

Belvedere Apollo

A. SIGNIFICANCE B. RENAISSANCE C. BAROQUE
D. CLASSICISM E. MODERN ERA

A. SIGNIFICANCE

The Belvedere Apollo (BA) (223 cm, marble, *c.* AD 130–140, Rome, MV) held the greatest fascination for artists and scholars until well into the 19th cent. and has been replicated in numerous works of world art. The Roman copy was probably made after a bronze sculpture by Leochares (*c.* 320/330 BC), which Pausanias describes in the temple of Apollo Patroos in Athens [9. 150]. It has never been possible to verify details about the time and place of the discovery (near Anzio or near Grottaferrata) [4. 44–47]. The two earliest drawings of the BA (Fig.1) are contained in the Codex Escurialensis (library of the Escorial, Madrid), a sketch book dated at 1491 from the studio of Domenico Ghirlandaio [6. 130; 154]. This documents both its state of preservation at the time and its original erection in the garden of S. Pietro in Vincoli (on fol. 53) or else near the titular church of Cardinal Giuliano della Rovere, who was the owner of the statue.

Soon after the start of his pontificate as Julius II (1503–13), he transferred his collection of antiquities to the Belvedere in the Vatican, which Bramante had rede-

signed into a statue gallery. This is first attested by Albertini in his *Opusculum de mirabilibus novae et veteris urbis Romae* (1509/1510) [2. 27]. In situ – erected in a niche flanking the → LAOCOON GROUP – the BA acquired a central role in High Renaissance enthusiasm for antiquities. Due to information from the *Liber Pontificalis* (6th cent.) and Andrea Fulvio's poem *Antiquaria Urbis* (1513) one was led to believe that St. Peter's Basilica had been erected near a temple of Apollo. Raphael's fresco of Parnassus in the *Stanza della Segnatura* (1508, Rome, MV) therefore symbolizes the Belvedere as Apollo's hill of muses of [7. 111; 113]. Also associated with the BA is the metaphor of the return of the Golden Age (*Aetas aurea*), used by Julius II to promulgate a legitimization of his pontificate based on historical mythology [2. 27, 28].

B. RENAISSANCE

Graphic sketches of the BA were already so widespread by 1500 that Dürer was able to base his early studies of proportion on them [13]. The first large sculptural version in Germany, the Apollo Fountain by Peter Flötner, 1531/32 in Nuremberg, came about via this route (Jacopo de' Barbari). In the subsequent period Renaissance graphics tended to reproduce the still mutilated statue as though physically complete, as in the case of Baccio Bandinelli, Marc Anton Raimondi and Agostino Veneziano. The measure of the success of the restoration by Michelangelo's pupil Montorsoli in 1532/33 – he completed the right lower arm and the left hand with the piece of bow (removed again in 1923) – is highlighted by Francesco d'Ollanda and Marten van Heemskerck, et al, in their sketch books [17].

The earliest bronze reduction, closely orientated to the model and partially gilded, by Jacopo Alari Bonacolsi (called Antico) emerged as early as 1497/98 by commission of Cardinal Lodovico Gonzaga (Frankfurt, LH; Fig.2). The silver inlays of the eyes and the perfection of the treatment of the surface are indications of Antico's training as a goldsmith. There was lively production of small bronzes after the BA until well into the 19th cent. Encyclopaedic terms for antiquities were used to label statuettes of this kind in private collections [2. 323–328].

Francis I had more ambitious plans. In order to found a virtual second Rome in Fontainebleau, in 1540 he commissioned Primaticcio to cast the Vatican sculptures. Copies of the BA still acted as courtly displays during the periods of the Baroque and Classicism or were indispensable components of the art academies: Important casts found their way, for instance, in 1549 for Maria of Hungary, to Binche Castle in the Netherlands, in 1650/51 via Velazquez for Philip IV, to Madrid and, *c.* 1760 through the agency of R. Adam, into the vestibule of Syon House in Middlesex ([9. 4, 32, 87–89]; cf. also the cast in the Round Room at Wörlitz).

The first independent monumental sculpture after the ancient model is Baccio Bandinelli's *Orfeo che placa*

Fig. 1: Drawing of the
Belvedere Apollo in the
Codex Escurialensis,
studio of Domenico
Ghirlandaio, 1491

Fig. 2: Jacopo Alari
Bonacolsi, bronze
reduction of the Belvedere
Apollo, 1497/98

Fig. 3: Bertel Thorvaldsen,
Jason with the Golden
Fleece, 1803/1828.
Copenhagen, Thorvaldsen
Museum Library
Photographer:
Ole Woldbye

Fig. 4: Jacopo Sansovino,
bronze figure of Apollo,
1541–1546. Logetta,
Piazza San Marco, Venice

Fig. 5: Peter Paul Rubens,
The Council of the Gods
(detail), 1622–1625.
From the Medici Cylce.
With Permission of Musée
du Louvre, Paris

Fig. 6: Giorgio de Chirico,
Love Song, 1914.
Beeldrecht Amsterdam 2006.
Digital Image © (2005)
The Museum of Modern Art,
NY/Scala, Florence

Cerbero col suo canto (1516/17) in the inner courtyard of the Palazzo Medici-Riccardi in Florence – a humanist-inspired work commissioned by the Medici pope Leo X. [11]. The BA was reinterpreted for the public domain by Jacopo Sansovino (Fig.4). His classically elegant bronze figure at the Logetta on St. Mark's Square in Venice (1541–1546) is endebted to a Raphaelesque, yet androgynous ideal of beauty [3. 76].

C. BAROQUE

The ability of emerging Baroque art to convert the BA in ways that were both naturalistically dynamic and allegorical is shown by Gian Lorenzo Bernini's masterpiece *Apollo e Dafne* (Rome, Villa Borghese) for Cardinal Scipio Borghese (1623/25) [10. 59]. At the same time Rubens was creating his Medici cycle. A BA prevailing over vice is illustrated in the painting *The Power of the Queen* (Paris, LV) for the political and moral glorification of Maria de' Medici (Fig.5). Rubens' concern here was to 'bring alive' the marble model [8].

Engravings of the BA in the drawing textbooks of the *Royal Academy of Art* in France served similar purposes [16]. Charles Le Brun, for instance, in his painting *Le Roi arme sur terre et sur mer* (Galerie des Glaces, 1678–86) in Versailles used the characteristic body motif for the imperious gesture of Louis XIV. Francois Girardon's statue group of *Apollon servit par les Nymphes* (1666–1673) also assimilated the BA, to deify the *Roi Soleil* and to stage a 'sun project' in the parklands of Versailles [5. 200]. The BA was also able to lend respectable stature to clothed state and official portraits (cf. H. Rigaud, Louis XIII, 1701, Paris, LV; J. Reynolds, Commodore Keppel, 1752, London, National Maritime Museum).

D. CLASSICISM

Winckelmann's emphatic description of the BA as the highest 'ideal among all works' in his *Geschichte der Kunst des Alterthums* (History of Ancient Art, Dresden 1764) established classical taste [1. 309, 310]. His hymnic poetic phrasing characterizes the classical concept of physical and spiritual perfection. His words made a lasting impression on both Goethe (Italian Journey, 9.11.1786) and Schiller, who had seen a cast of the BA in the antiquities gallery in Mannheim [15]. An expression of this attitude is *Perseus* in the manner of the BA painted by Winckelmann's friend, A. R. Mengs (St. Petersburg, Hermitage).

The best example of the orientation of the epoch towards late Classical or Hellenistic sculptures is the work of Canova. His *Perseus* (1797–1801, Rome, MV), in its pose alone and in the movement motif, returns to the BA, though differs from it both in iconography and in its sensually soft modelling. The sculpture was bought in 1801 by the papal authorities to replace the BA taken by Napoleon to the Museé Central des Arts in Paris as a victory trophy (1797–1815). The sculpture of *Jason* by Bertel Thorvaldsen (Fig.3, 1803 in plaster, until 1828 in marble, Copenhagen, TM), pro-

duced in competition with Canova, replicated the ancient statue again in a purely formal respect. The BA had thus become related to modern sculpture, which in the eyes of an educated public laid claim to the same artistic rank. After the return of the BA to the Vatican (1816) interest shifted to an archaeological dispute [12. 187].

E. MODERN ERA

The last important position in the history of its reception is held by Giorgio de Chirico. The head of the BA appears in his *Love Song* (1914, New York, Museum of Modern Art) contrasted with symbols of an alien world (Fig.6). The myth of Apollo, which for de Chirico has identificatory significance, clashes in his *Pittura Metafisica* with the disparate reality of modern man [14. 50].

→ Apollo; → Leochares; → Parnassus; → Pausanias
→ ANTIQUITIES COLLECTIONS

SOURCES: 1 J. J. WINCKELMANN, Die Geschichte der Kunst des Alterthums, W. SENFF (ed.), 1964

LITERATURE: 2 H. BECK, P. BOL (eds.), Natur und Antike in der Renaissance, 1985   3 B. BOUCHER, The Sculpture of Jacopo Sansovino, 1991   4 H. BRUMMER, The Statue Court of the Vatican, 1970   5 B. CEYSON, M. F. DELL'ARCO (eds.), Skulptur. Renaissance bis Rokoko, 1996   6 H. EGGER (ed.), Codex Escurialensis. Ein Skizzenbuch aus der Werkstatt Domenico Ghirlandaios, 1906   7 M. FAGIOLO (ed.), Roma e L'Antico – nell'arte e nella cultura del Cinquecento, 1985   8 F. M. HABERDITZEL, Rubens und die Antike, in: Jb. der Kunsthistor. Slgg. des allerhöchsten Kaiserhauses, 1912, 276–297   9 F. HASKELL, N. PENNY, Taste and the Antique. The Lure of Classical Sculpture 1500–1900, 1981   10 H. KAUFMANN, Gian Lorenzo Bernini, 1970   11 K. LANGEDIJK, Baccio Bandinellis Orpheus: A Political Message, in: Mitt. des Dt. Kunsthistor. Instituts in Florenz, Bd. XX, 1976, 33–52   12 F. LICHT, Canova, 1983   13 E. PANOFSKY, Dürers Stellung des Apolls und ihr Verhältnis zu Barbari, in: Jb. Der königlich preußischen Kunst-Slg. 41, 1920, 359–377   14 W. SCHMIED, W. RUBIN, J. CLAIR (eds.), Giorgio de Chirico der Metaphysiker, 1982   15 H. SITTE, Im Mannheimer Antikensaal, in: Jb. der Goetheges. 20, 1934, 150–158   16 G. VALERIUS, Antike Statuen als Modelle des Menschen, 1992   17 M. M. WINNER, Zum Apoll von Belvedere, in: Jb. der Berliner Mus. 10, 1968, 181–199   18 Il Cortile delle Statue – Der Statuenhof des Belvedere im Vatikan, M. WINNER, D. ANDRAE, C. PIETRANGELI (eds.), 1998   FRIEDHELM SCHARF

Fig. 1: The Altes Museum
at the Lustgarten (*c.* 1900).
Bildarchiv Preussischer Kulturbesitz

Fig. 2: The Altes Pergamon Museum
(*c.* 1905)
Bildarchiv Preussischer Kulturbesitz

Fig. 3: Pergamon Museum,
ancient sculpture collection,
room number three (*c.* 1965)
Bildarchiv Preussischer Kulturbesitz

Berlin
I. Staatliche Museen Preussischer
Kulturbesitz, Collection of Antiquities
II. Vorderasiatisches Museum
III. Ägyptisches Museum

I. Staatliche Museen Preussischer
Kulturbesitz, Collection of Antiquities
A. Early History B. The Collections of An-
tiquities after 1830 C. The Collection of
Antiquities after 1901 D. The Collections
of Antiquities since World War Two

A. Early History
The origin of the Berlin Collection of Antiquities
goes back to the 16th cent. It was probably the elector
Joachim II of Brandenburg who laid the foundations of
the holdings of the Curiosity Cabinet in the Schloss in
Berlin, during his reign (1535–1571) and also had antiquities purchased. This first stock was almost completely lost during the Thirty Years' War, but was
replaced after 1640 by new acquisitions (inventories of
ancient coins, 1649, and sculptures, 1672). Building an
independent section for antiquities and medals, separate from the art and natural history rooms, was set in
motion in 1698 by the purchase of the Bellori Collection. It comprised more than 200 antiquities and was
made public by Lorenz Beger, the head of the Curiosity
Cabinet. According to Beger the electoral, from 1701
royal, holdings were also made accessible to an interested public.

The stock of antiquities in the Berlin Schloss suffered
serious setbacks again under the reign of the 'Soldier
King' Friedrich Wilhelm I (1710–1740). Coins of precious metals were melted down; the most important
sculptures were given away to other rulers, mainly to
August the Strong (→ Dresden, Staatliche Kunst-
sammlungen). The situation changed fundamentally
under Friedrich II (reigned 1740–1786). With the intention to endow the park and the buildings of Potsdam-
Sanssouci, but first Schloss Charlottenburg near Berlin,
the king obtained numerous works of art, with ancient
sculptures playing a leading role. The most comprehensive collection, which he purchased soon after the
beginning of his reign, was that of Cardinal Polignac. In
addition to other collections financed by royal moneys
and individual works such as the Praying Boy (Fig. 5),
the collection of his sister Wilhelmine of Bayreuth came
to Sanssouci as an inheritance. The exhibition of antiquities of the time, today extant only in a few parts or
restored, within the Palace buildings at Potsdam-Sanssouci demonstrates that Friedrich II on the one hand
strove to compete with other residences, primarily with
Dresden, and to that end adapted current representational models of Absolutism; on the other hand he endeavoured to present an ideal world derived from the
French Enlightenment. This was realised – a few years
before Winckelmann's writings – in the idealized depiction of a view of Greece, which took shape in the inner

rooms of the pleasure palace of Sanssouci as a social
utopia turned private. In the antiquities set up in the
park and after the Seven Years War in the Neue Palais,
however, the customary absolutist reference frame of
Imperial Rome remained relevant (Fig. 9). Expectations
of civic enlightenment were met by the opening of the
galleries to an interested public. For visitors there were
catalogues of the works of art in list form, compiled by
the gallery inspector Matthias Oesterreich. Furthermore, in accord with contemporary demands for a
museum, in 1770 an original ancient temple was constructed, which made reference equally to English
garden buildings and various conceptions of museums,
especially those of Dresden.

In the post-Friedrich era the Prussian royal acquisition of antiquities declined noticeably. A significant
new phase of acquisition began in the 19th cent. with
the crown prince, later the king Friedrich Wilhelm IV.
But these objects have remained almost without importance to the history of the Berlin Museums, as, in contrast to the majority of objects collected in the 18th
cent., they were not transferred to the capital, but with
few exceptions were integrated into and remained in the
classicistic-romantic ambience of Friedrich Wilhelm
IV's buildings in Potsdam-Sanssouci until today (especially Schloss Charlottenhof and the Roman baths).

B. The Collections of Antiquities after
1830
Attempts to institute an art museum in Berlin go
back to the 18th cent. In 1810 Friedrich Wilhelm III
decided to make available the most distinguished parts
of the royal possessions by contributing them to a
public collection. However, one had to wait for the
return of the holdings which were taken to Paris in
1806, before the plans could assume concrete form. In
1822 Karl Friedrich Schinkel was given a free hand in
siting and constructing an adequate building for them.
The Museum am Lustgarten was dedicated (Fig. 1), and
Eduard Gerhard received a position there in 1833 (from
1855 Director of Ancient Sculptures). Programmatically built opposite the Berlin Schloss on the Spree
Island with a wide entrance hall opening on to the
square in front, the main floor was given over to ancient
as well as more modern sculptures. In the central
rotunda statues of gods were placed, which had previously been located in Potsdam-Sanssouci. The collections of antiquities also included the Antiquarium on the
lower level: a collection of minor art which had been
systematically extended since the 1830s, primarily by
the purchase of Greek vases, in 1885 already numbering 4221 according to Adolf Furtwängler's *Beschreibung*. Moreover, numerous bronzes were added, primarily from the excavations at → Olympia, and the
Hildesheimer Silberfund, which was transferred by royal decree in 1869.

The Museum am Lustgarten, however, proved from
the beginning to be too small. Therefore, in 1855 the
Neues Museum, designed by Friedrich August Stüler,

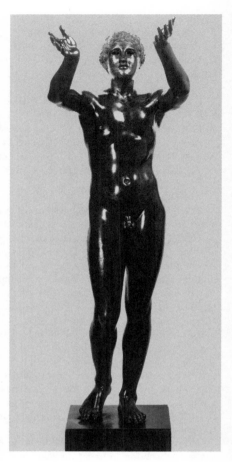

Fig. 4: Pergamon Museum, statue of an enthroned goddess.
Bildarchiv Preussischer Kulturbesitz

Fig. 5: The Altes Museum, statue of the Praying Boy.
Bildarchiv Preussischer Kulturbesitz

Fig. 6: Pergamon Museum,
small frieze from the Pergamum Altar,
Hercules discovering Telephus.
Bildarchiv Preussischer Kulturbesitz

Fig. 7: Pergamon Museum, Pergamum Altar, large east frieze, Zeus panel.
Bildarchiv Preussischer Kulturbesitz

was built at the rear of the Schinkel building, which has subsequently become known as the Alte Museum. The plaster casts, the vases (Fig. 11) and the painted mummy portraits of Fayyum were gradually moved here. In 1911, when Theodor Wiegand took over the directorship of the Department of Antiquities in the Berlin Museums, the plaster casts were transferred to the ownership of the University and set up there in 1921.

C. The Collection of Antiquities after 1901

The history of the antiquities collections in Berlin entered a new phase after the → PERGAMUM ALTAR was discovered in 1873. Together with the collection of sculptures, extended by finds from excavations conducted by the Museum, the frieze panels of the Pergamum Altar (Figs. 6 and 7), which had been brought to Berlin, prompted the planning of a new museum on the 'Museum Island'. The only short-lived first Pergamonmuseum (Fig. 2), built by Fritz Wolff 1897–1899 in late-classicist style, was opened in 1901. The idea of replicating the front of the Pergamum Altar inside the building more or less completely was accomplished only during the construction process. However, the Museum did not receive the support of Kaiser Wilhelm II on account of its less than representational appearance. In fact its planning concept was too small and there were faults in its foundations, so that already in 1908 it was pulled down. The imperial demand to set off the Pergamum Altar in its full height was met in 1907 by the architect Alfred Messel with plans for a new building, which was realised under the direction of Ludwig Hoffmann and dedicated in 1930 at the centennial celebrations of the Berlin Museums. The graecising neoclassical three-wing structure was, however, externally still not complete in all parts. The main entrance, in which a glass hall supports an Attic-style structure instead of the intended pediment, was finished only in 1980.

The opening in the year 1930 was preceded by lively controversy in the press about the costs, in which the discussion was about not only the spending on the building itself, but also the money raised for the purchase of art works. In the case of the acquisitions owed to Theodor Wiegand, for example, there were important archaic sculptures essentially enriching the holdings, such as the *Enthroned Goddess* (Fig. 4) and the *Kore with Pomegranate*, which could be secured for Berlin in 1916 and 1925 respectively. The sculptures were still exhibited in the Alte Museum together with the Antiquarium (terracottas, metal works, gems and glassware) until the outbreak of the Second World War.

The speciality of the (new) Pergamonmuseum was its orientation towards ancient architecture. Building monuments were entirely or partially reconstructed in skylit rooms. In addition to the front of the Pergamum Altar, it was mainly the Market Gate of Miletus (2nd cent. AD, Fig. 8) that fulfilled the requirement to illustrate the proportions and dimensions of ancient archi-

tecture. No less impressive is the reconstruction of the Babylonian Ishtar Gate (6th cent. BC) in the Middle Eastern Department (from 1953 the Vorderasiatische Museum) of the Museum.

D. The Collections of Antiquities since World War Two

During the War the Pergamonmuseum stayed closed. The movable antiquities from all parts of the collection (Alte Museum, Neue Museum, Pergamonmuseum) were evacuated and the fixed installations of the Pergamonmuseum were protected as far as possible. The latter measures, however, proved to be inadequate in the face of British and American bombing raids, so that in 1945 the Market Gate of Miletus (Fig. 8) was seriously damaged. A number of objects, including almost the whole collection of glassware, fell victim to a fire in a Berlin bunker.

The evacuation caused a division of the objects in post-War history. Those that had been moved to western Germany, about half of the Antiquarium including the majority of the vases (Fig. 10) and the *Hildesheimer Silberfund*, were concentrated by the British and American occupation forces, initially in Wiesbaden and Celle, then in 1957/1958 transferred to West Berlin. In 1960 they were given a place there in a garrison built in 1851–1859 by Friedrich August Stüler in front of Schloss Charlottenburg. Set up in 1961 as a Department of Antiquities under the administration of the Stiftung Preußischer Kulturbesitz, for about three decades the later Museum of Antiquities was a counterpart to the Egyptian Department or the Ägyptisches Museum, which was accommodated in a matching building by Stüler opposite the first. The old stock of the Museum of Antiquities was gradually increased by more than 600 new acquisitions and gifts. The initially very plain furnishings of the cabinet-style rooms, modelled on the taste of the 1950s and 1960s, were made more efficient in 1974 with a striking system of showcases and a mixture of artificial and natural light. The visitors especially favoured the treasure room in the basement. The need for space during the last years of the Museum of Antiquities was alleviated by the annexation of rooms in a neighbouring building.

The more extensive stock which in 1945 remained on East German territory was initially moved to the Soviet Union (the Hermitage in Saint Petersburg and the Pushkin Museum in Moscow), and in 1958 for the most part returned to East Berlin, where it was immediately set up in the Pergamonmuseum, preceded by intensive efforts to refurbish the war-damaged architectural rooms. The building, which was made part of the Staatlichen Museen zu Berlin by the government of the → GDR in 1951, was partially reopened in 1954. Until 1965 the refurbishment of further rooms followed. The combination of all genres within one building followed a new concept: whereas Wiegand's arrangement was preserved in the architectural rooms, Carl Blümel, who had been actively responsible for the Pergamonmuseum

Fig. 8: Pergamon Museum, the 'Market Gate of Miletus'

before the war and as its Director since 1947, saw to it that in the sections of the north wing, dedicated to the history of sculpture, the strict lining up of exhibits was abandoned, in favour of forming thematic and chronological ensembles (Fig. 3). The principle of loosening up and concentrating on focuses of content, became even more apparent with the reorganisation of some of the rooms in 1982/1983. While small works of art had also been integrated into the sequence of the sculpture rooms by 1959 and more so in 1982/1983, there was still a predominant classification by genres, with architecture and large sculpture occupying the main floor and minor arts and Roman portraits (Fig. 9), in contrast, concentrated on the upper floor.

The political changes of 1989/1990 led to various considerations of how to consolidate in space and organisation the holdings of the State Museums, divided between the two halves of the city. With regard to the stock of antiquities the decision was soon made to 're-unite' all the works on Museum Island. The Museum of Antiquities in Charlottenburg (West Berlin) was dissolved and from 1995 the building was used for other museum purposes. The present plan of the Museum is of a distinctively restorative character, in that it aimed at directly connecting to the pre-War situation: efforts were made to divide the holdings in the medium term among the Alte Museum, the Neue Museum and the Pergamonmuseum. The tendency to show respect to the old conception can be traced back to the history of the

GDR, as the rotunda of the Alte Museum, which was reconstructed for the 150th anniversary of the Berlin Museums the 1980, had already been completed with ancient statues in imitation of its original following its original design. Since 1998 the main floor of the Alte Museum has housed, until the completion of the renovation, a temporary exhibition of objects of minor arts from Charlottenburg (Fig. 11), augmented by works from the Pergamonmuseum, among which there are also some large-format sculptures. The centre of this presentation is the *Praying Boy* (Fig. 5). The largely chronologically-ordered objects, can be viewed on a walk through the museum with a comprehensive supply of didactic material available.

→ ANTIQUITIES COLLECTIONS; → GREECE

1 Antikenmuseum. Staatliche Museen Preußischer Kulturbesitz (Kunst der Welt in den Berliner Museen), 1980 2 Antikenmuseum. Berlin. Die ausgestellten Werke, 1988 3 Die Antikensammlung. Altes Museum, Pergamonmuseum. Staatliche Museen zu Berlin, ²1988   4 W. AREN-HÖVEL (ed.), Berlin und die Antike. Katalog und Aufsätze, 1979 5 Beschreibung der antiken Skulpturen. Königliche Museen zu Berlin, Berlin 1891 6 C. BLÜMEL, Die archaischen griechischen Skulpturen, 1964   7 Id., Die klassischen griechischen Skulpturen, 1966 8 A. FURTWÄNGLER, Beschreibung der Vasensammlung im Antiquarium, 2 vols, Berlin 1885 9 U. GEHRIG et al., Staatliche Museen Preußischer Kulturbesitz Berlin. Führer durch die Antikenabteilung, 1968 10 G. HERES, M. KUNZE, Antikensammlung I. Griechische und römische Plastik (Staatliche Museen zu Berlin Hauptstadt der DDR, Führer durch die

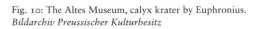

Fig. 10: The Altes Museum, calyx krater by Euphronius.
Bildarchiv Preussischer Kulturbesitz

Fig. 9: The Altes Museum, bust known as 'Caesar'.
Bildarchiv Preussischer Kulturbesitz

Fig. 11: Display of ancient vases in the Neues Museum (currently housed in the Altes Museum).

Ausstellungen), 1984 11 H. HERES et al., Griechische und etruskische Kleinkunst. Römische Porträts (Staatliche Museen zu Berlin Hauptstadt der DDR, Führer durch die Ausstellungen des Pergamonmuseums, Antikensammlung III), 1985 12 V. KÄSTNER, Pergamonmuseum. Griechische und römische Architektur, 1992 13 H. KAUFFMANN, Zweckbau und Monument. Schinkels Museum am Berliner Lustgarten, in: Eine Festgabe für Ernst Hellmut Vitts, 1963, 135–166 14 D. KREIKENBOM, Die Aufstellung antiker Skulpturen in Potsdam-Sanssouci unter Friedrich II., in: Wilhelmine und Friedrich II. und die Antiken, in: Schriften der Winckelmann-Gesellschaft 15, 1998, 43–99 15 M. KUNZE, V. KÄSTNER, Der Altar von Pergamon. Hellenistiche und römische Architektur (Staatliche Museen zu Berlin Hauptstadt der DDR, Führer durch die Ausstellungen des Pergamonmuseums, Antikensammlung II) 16 E. ROHDE, Griechische und römische Kunst in den Staatlichen Museen zu Berlin, 1968 17 A. RUMPF, Katalog der etruskischen Skulpturen, 1928 18 C. THEUERKAUFF, Zur Geschichte der Brandenburgisch-Preußischen Kunstkammer bis gegen 1800, in: Die Brandenburgisch-Preußische Kunstkammer. Eine Auswahl aus den alten Beständen, 1981 19 H. WREDE (ed.), Dem Archäologen Eduard Gerhard 1795–1867 zu seinem 200. Geburtstag (Winckelmann-Institut der Humboldt-Universität zu Berlin, 2), 1997.   DETLEV KREIKENBOM

II. VORDERASIATISCHES MUSEUM
A. INTRODUCTION B. EARLY HISTORY C. HISTORY D. THE STOCK OF THE COLLECTION E. CONCEPT OF THE EXHIBITION

A. INTRODUCTION
The Vorderasiatisches Museum (VAM – Near Eastern Museum) known until 1953 as the Vorderasiatische Abteilung (Near Eastern Section), was founded in 1899 as part of the Royal Museums of Berlin. It is one of the great archaeological museum collections of old Oriental cultures and in Germany is the only one of its kind. Today the VAM is located in the south wing of the Pergamonmuseum, where, together with the reconstructions of the Ishtar Gate and the Procession Road of Babylon (see Fig. 3), it is one of the main attractions.

B. EARLY HISTORY
The development of the Berlin collection of antiquities of the Orient was closely connected with growing German interest in ancient Oriental cultures. Until 1885 the ancient Orientalia were preserved distributed among the Antiquarium, the Collection of Antiquities and the cast collection of the Berlin Museums. Whereas only some stamp seals were moved from the Royal Curiosity Cabinet to the Alte Museum, opened in 1830, the Berlin collections also profited from the large British and French excavations (1842) in Mesopotamia from the beginning. Cylinder and stamp seals were then acquired in well-directed purchases by the Antiquarium. Above all, however, in 1855 and 1858 the acquisition for the Collection of Antiquities of a series of Assyrian reliefs from Nimrud and Nineveh was achieved and they were put on view together in the Assyrian Room of the Alte Museum in 1860. The cast collection also ordered plaster casts of ancient Oriental finds from London and Paris. After the end of the first wave of excavations (c. 1855) interest in ancient Orientalia initially declined even in Berlin. This was changed by the founding of the Reich in 1871, as the Berlin Museums now competed with the collections of the other capitals of Europe. The ancient Oriental collection also profited from this, especially since Assyriology now received general recognition as a scholarly discipline in Germany with the establishment of the first chair at the University of Berlin in the year 1875. In 1885 this initially led to the consolidation of the ancient Orientalia in the Ägyptische Abteilung (Egyptian Section) of the Neue Museum, where in 1889 the first comprehensive exhibition of Near Eastern antiquities was opened. The section director Adolf Erman (1854–1937) endeavoured, together with the general director Richard Schöne (1840–1922), to increase the holdings of the collection. To this end he initiated the first German expedition to Mesopotamia in 1886/1887, which was financed by the cotton dealer Louis Simon. However, this undertaking did not lead to the originally planned excavation in Mesopotamia. Instead, the *Deutsche Orient-Comité*, a private promotional cooperative founded in collaboration with Erman in 1888, organised its first dig in Sendshirli in northern Syria (see Fig. 1). It was the aim of the *Orient-Comité* to sell the finds which reached Germany to the Museums to cover the costs of the excavation. However, this financial concept failed, since the Museums were able to pay off the high costs only in installments and with difficulty, so that the *Orient-Comité* were unable to operate after the first three campaigns. In addition to the expeditions Erman managed to make some spectacular purchases, e.g. a considerable part of the tablets from Amarna and a number of Ur-Artaean and southern Arabian objects. The plan for an excavation in Mesopotamia to augment the collection could only be realised after Germany's entry into 'World Politics' (1897) and its growing economic and political influence in the Ottoman Empire. In 1897/1898 the Museums dispatched a new expedition to identify promising excavation sites. Shortly afterwards, in January 1898, the → DEUTSCHE ORIENT-GESELLSCHAFT (DOG) was founded in collaboration with Erman and Schöne as representatives of the Museums and through the commitment of James Simon (1851–1932). As the first joint project of the Museums and the DOG excavations in → BABYLON were opened in March 1899.

C. HISTORY
Parallel with preparations for excavations, efforts were made to found an independent Vorderasiatische Abteilung (VA) of the Berlin Museums. This finally became possible with the appointment of Friedrich Delitzsch (1850–1922) as professor of Assyriology at the University of Berlin in the spring of 1899, since the post was combined with that of director of the new

Fig. 1: Relief of Barrakib with scribe,
from Sendshirli.
Bildarchiv Preussischer Kulturbesitz

Fig. 2: Bird of Prey, from Tall Halaf.
Bildarchiv Preussischer Kulturbesitz

Fig. 3: Reconstructions of the
Ishtar Gate and Processional
Way of Babylon.
Bildarchiv Preussischer Kulturbesitz

department. This joining of offices was to guarantee close collaboration between academics and museum. At first the collection was moved out of the large exhibition rooms in the Neues Museum to a rebuilt warehouse on Museum Island. The confined spaces were not open to the public. Instead, a large part of the Assyriological research and teaching took place there. The first years of the VA, until the First World War, were shaped by the targeted development of a collection through large-scale digs. To this end the DOG and the Berlin Museums in cooperation organised excavations in Babylon (1899–1917), Assur (1903–1914), Fara and Abu Hatab (1902/1903), Kar Tukulti-Ninurta (1913/1914), Uruk (1912/1913), Hatra as well as in Palestine. A great part of these projects was financed not by the DOG members' dues, but by imperial subsidies and by the Prussian state. The German Reich's good relations with the Ottoman Empire enabled it to secure not only the appropriate excavation permits but also, and primarily, the sharing of finds. Helpful here was the 'sharing agreement' concluded in 1899 between the Berlin Museums and the Ottoman Empire, which stated that the Museums were entitled to half of all the finds from their excavations. However, the latter was properly applied only to the division of the Assur finds in 1914. In addition to the DOG excavations, in this period finds also arrived in the Berlin VA from a another campaign by the *Orient-Comité* in Sendshirli, from the Hittite Boghazköy and from the excavations at Tall Halaf (see Fig. 2). Although a great part of the finds from Assur and Babylon, because of the outbreak of the First World War, did not arrive in Berlin until 1926/1927, a plan had been in existence since 1907 for a large VAM in the south wing of the building, today known as the Pergamonmuseum. Here, from the beginning, the reconstructions of the Ishtar Gate and the Procession Road of Babylon, which were composed of thousands of reliefed brick fragments (Fig. 4), played a central role. Because preparations for construction were beginning, the exhibition sheds had to be emptied, with the result that the VA was accommodated in the basement of the Kaiser Friedrich Museum (now the Bode Museum) from 1911 until the final allocation of rooms in the new museum building in 1927. The economically and politically altered situation during the Weimar Republic permitted excavation projects only to a rather limited extent. At this point the excavation of Uruk should be emphasised. Its first campaign in 1912/1913 was followed from 1928 by further campaigns, financed by the *Notgemeinschaft der deutschen Wissenschaft*. The most important task of the Museum's department, from 1918 under its first principal director Otto Weber (1877–1928), was the assessment of the results and finds of the excavations in the period up to the Second World War.

This work took place in close cooperation with the DOG and was also supported by the *Notgemeinschaft der deutschen Wissenschaft*. Particularly prominent were the preparations for the great exhibition of the VA

Fig. 4: Brick fragments found in Babylon, spread out on long tables in preparation for the reconstructions of the Ishtar Gate and Processional Way.
Bildarchiv Preussischer Kulturbesitz

Fig. 5: Museum view of the reconstructed stone cone mosaic temple façade from Uruk.
Bildarchiv preussischer Kulturbesitz

in the Pergamonmuseum, the arrangement of which was taken over, after the death of Otto Weber in 1928, by Walter Andrae (1875–1956), the former excavator of Assur. The central axis, with the Ishtar Gate and the Procession Road, could be opened in 1930. The other rooms were not finished until 1936, but had to be closed again in 1939 because of the outbreak of the War. Owing to Andrae's opposition to the planned evacuation, the holdings remained almost completely together until 1945. Building damage and theft due to the War threatened the collection in the first post-War years. Furthermore, in 1946 valuable objects were carried off by the Soviet occupation forces. In the following years repair and restoration work had priority, from 1951 led by Gerhard Rudolf Meyer (1908–1977). In May 1953 all 14 rooms of the collection, now renamed the VAM, were finally reopened. In 1958 the objects brought back from the Soviet Union could be reincorporated into the collection. The following years were

Fig. 6: Middle Assyrian tablet of laws

given over principally to further assessment of excavation results, with special concentration on editions of cuneiform texts. Simultaneously, in cooperation with the Akademie der Wissenschaften, the VAM took part in smaller excavation projects and field research in Iraq and Syria. After 1989 collaboration with the DOG resumed, manifested in particular in the Assur Project, i.e., joint assessment of the finds and results from Assur. Furthermore, today the VAM seeks to cooperate with research institutes and museums and to pursue a broader outreach program. As part of the current process of restructuring the museum landscape of Berlin, changes were also imminent at the VAM.

D. The Stock of the Collection

In all, the stock of the collection of the VAM amounts to about 70,000 archaeological objects and 26,500 written historical documents. A large part of the holdings stems from the large excavations in Mesopotamia, northern Syria, Palestine and Anatolia. Furthermore, a series of significant purchases was successfully made. In addition to sculptures and everyday objects, above all the great collection of clay tablets should be mentioned, encompassing about 25,000 tablets. Prominent among these, in addition to tablets from Babylon, Assur (see Fig. 6) and Fara, are those from Amarna and Boghazköy. It is because of the latter that the Museum became a centre of Hittitological research. While a large portion of the objects are from the

period up to the end of the ancient oriental empires, a number of objects are also of more recent date, such as objects from the Parthian period and from Palmyra and southern Arabia.

E. Concept of the Exhibition

The basis of the the VAM exhibition today corresponds to Andrae's concept, with the reconstructions of architectonic contexts corresponding to the idea of a museum of architecture playing a decisive role. Thus the Ishtar Gate and the Procession Road are at the centre of the exhibition. The exhibits in the other rooms are arranged primarily geographically. Whereas the great room, facing the Kupfergraben, is dedicated to finds from Syria and Anatolia, the rooms to the left and right of the central passage are divided between northern and southern Mesopotamia. Within the chronological order of the rooms the architectonic reconstructions, such as a room of an Assyrian palace and a part of the Stifmosaic facade from Uruk (Fig. 5), are also prominent. To explain the (culturally) historical contexts the originals are augmented by plaster copies, such as the replica of the Code of Hammurabi and the large Lamassu Figures. Large wall paintings utilising the oversized height of the rooms illustrate the situation at the place of excavation.

→ Assur; → Babylon; → Hatra; → Hattusa
→ Cast; Cast collections; → Ancient Near Eastern philology and history (Assyriology); → Antiquities collections; → Near Eastern archaeology

1 N. Crüsemann, Vom Zweistromland zum Kupfergraben. Vorgeschichte und Entstehungsjahre (1899–1918) der Vorderasiatische Abteilung der Berliner Museen vor fach- und kulturpolitischen Hintergründen, (unpublished thesis) 1999 2 J. Marzahn, Die Keilschriftsammlung des Vorderasiatische Museums zu Berlin, in: H. Klengel, W. Sundermann, Ägypten-Vorderasien-Turfan. Probleme der Edition und Bearbeitung altorientalischer Handschriften, 1991, 30–50 3 J. Renger, Die Geschichte der Altorientalistik und der Vorderasiatischen Altertumskunde in Berlin von 1875–1945, in: W. Arenhövel (ed.), Berlin und die Antike, Aufsätze, Ergänzungsband zum Katalog der Ausstellung 1979, 151–192 4 Staatliche Museen zu Berlin, Das Vorderasiatische Museum, 1992 5 G. Wilhelm (ed.), Zwischen Tigris und Nil. 100 Jahre Ausgrabungen der → Deutsche Orient-Gesellschaft in Vorderasien und Ägypten, 1998. NICOLA CRÜSEMANN

III. Ägyptisches Museum

A. Definition of Contents B. Legal Form
C. History D. Current Situation

A. Definition of Contents

The official designation 'Ägyptisches Museum und Papyrussammlung, Staatliche Museen zu Berlin – Stiftung Preußischer Kulturbesitz' describes the range of the content and the organisational structure of the largest collection of ancient Egyptian art and culture in the German-speaking countries. The Ägyptisches Museum

Fig. 1: Charlottenburg Egyptian Museum, Column Hall of Sahurê (1994).
Bildarchiv Preussischer Kulturbesitz

Fig. 2: August Stüber, The Egyptian Courtyard in the New Museum (1862).
Bildarchiv Preussischer Kulturbesitz

(ÄM) unites within itself an archaeological collection of classical style and one of the largest collections of papyruses in the world (about 50,000 texts). Whereas the former concentrates on ancient Egypt from the Palaeolithic until the Roman Imperial period, the latter ranges from the early Christian into the Islamic period and has at its disposal, in addition to texts in the ancient Egyptian language from the Old Kingdom until the Graeco-Roman period (written in hieroglyphic, hieratic and demotic scripts), an extremely comprehensive stock of documents in Greek, Latin, Aramaic, Coptic, Pahlavi and Arabic on papyrus, parchment and ceramic and limestone ostraca. In the field of philology the papyrus collection also represents the collection areas of the Collection of Antiquities, the Museum of Late Antiquity and Byzantine Art and of the Museum of Islamic Art and so constitutes a multidisciplinary element of the archaeological museums. The archaeological part of the ÄM comprises with about 40,000 objects the whole material culture of ancient Egypt. The artworks from the Old Kingdom and the Amarna period give the Museum its special character.

B. Legal Form

Formally one of the Royal Museums of Berlin, today the ÄM is one of the 17 institutions of the Staatliche Museen zu Berlin, which are subordinate to the Stiftung Preußischer Kulturbesitz as the legal successor of Prussia. The Foundation (Stiftung Preußischer Kulturbesitz) is financed as a federal authority jointly by federal and state governments.

C. History

The first Aegyptiaca arrived in 1698 with the antiquities of the Bellori Collection from Rome in the Brandenburg Electoral Collections. It may be called a special Egyptian Collection only when in 1822, under Friedrich Wilhelm III of Prussia, the collection of Freiherr Heinrich Menu von Minutoli was acquired for the Antiquarium, which he had assembled on his royally commissioned trip to the Orient. Part of this collection sank on sea transport in the estuary of the Elbe and is still lost today. In 1828 the collection of the Trieste merchant Giuseppe Passalacqua was acquired at the instigation of Alexander von Humboldt. Passalacqua himself became the first principal director of collections and he installed the first independent ÄM in Schloss Monbijou (opposite the Spree Island, today known as 'Museum Island'). The motivation of the Prussian royal house to set up an Egyptian museum by means of the targeted purchase of complete collections lay in the significance of representative collections of art as part of political self-representation and followed the model of other museums: the Louvre in → Paris, the British Museum in → London, the Museo Egizio in Turin, the Rijksmuseum van Oudheden in Leiden, and finally also the Vatican Museums. The 1842–1845 expedition sent by the Prussian king Friedrich Wilhelm IV to Egypt and the Sudan under the leadership of Richard Lepsius may also be considered an act of sovereign representation. With the approval of the viceroy Mohamed Ali, Lepius brought 1500 objects, from small sculptures to whole burial chambers, back to Berlin. During this trip Lepsius formulated his concept for the content of a future Egyptian museum for which the housing conditions had been created by the architect August Stüler with the construction of the Neue Museum on the Museum Island in 1840. The plans of Passalacqua, the director of the collection until 1865, were not taken into consideration by the Director General Olfers or by the king. Lepsius understood the Museum as a monumental representation of the history and religion of Egypt in the medium of large wall paintings following ancient Egyptian models, as they had been documented by his expedition to Egypt and published in *Denkmäler aus Ägypten und Äthiopien* (Monuments from Egypt and Ethiopia). The original objects served as evidential material for this dominant didactic concept, which had already been heavily criticised immediately after the opening of the 'Egyptian Section' (Ägyptische Abtheilung) in the Neue Museum. Subsequently Lepsius considered his interest to be less the Museum than his historical and philological research; his appointment as Director of the Royal Library distanced him further from the work of the Museum. Only under the direction of Adolf Erman (1884–1914) did the Museum undergo a relevant expansion by means of purchases on the art markets of Europe and Egypt. The scholarly standing of the Museum was established world-wide by the project *Wörterbuch der ägyptischen Sprache* (Dictionary of the Egyptian Language), initiated by Erman, which, just like the academic area of → Egyptology, was housed in the Museum. During Adolf Erman's directorship, the great excavation projects of the → Deutsche Orient-Gesellschaft, financed by James Simon, were carried out in Abusir (Pyramids and 5th Dynasty Sanctuary of the Sun) and in Amarna, Akhenaton's and Nefertiti's capital. The objects allotted to James Simon by the division of finds were later transferred as gifts to the ownership of the ÄM. Through the Amarna finds, especially the bust of Queen Nefertiti, the ÄM earned unique status in the sphere of great Egyptian collections, even if the presentation in the rebuilt Greek Court of the overcrowded Neues Museum could in no way do justice to the quality of the collection. The significance of the ÄM for the art history of ancient Egypt was advanced for some time to come by Erman's successor Heinrich Schäfer (Director 1914–1935), whose seminal studies on the art of Egypt were largely based on Berlin material. In 1939 the Museum was closed; while large objects were secured on site against threatening war-damage, the bulk of the holdings were evacuated in and around Berlin. The Neues Museum was partly destroyed by bombing in 1944. In 1945 the evacuated holdings were safeguarded by the Western Allies and the Red Army and taken to Frankfurt am Main (later to Wiesbaden) and Celle or to Moscow and (the then) Leningrad. On their return in the 1950s they were placed in the divided city,

Fig. 3: Charlottenburg Egyptian Museum, Kalabsha temple gate.
Bildarchiv Preussischer Kulturbesitz

Fig. 4: Charlottenburg Egyptian Museum, Rotunda (1998).
Bildarchiv Preussischer Kulturbesitz

partly under the aegis of the *Staatlichen Museen zu Berlin – Hauptstadt der DDR*, on the Museum Island in a temporary exhibition in the Bode Museum. It continued to be updated until 1989 and remained accessible until 1998. The other part became an institution of the *Staatliche Museen zu Berlin – Stiftung Preußischer Kulturbesitz* in Charlottenburg, where since 1967, initially in the eastern part of the Stüler Building, afterwards in the adjoining Royal Stables, a sub-museum existed which, with the bust of Nefertiti, became a magnet for the public. The Temple Gate of Kalabsha (Lower Nubia), presented by the Republic of Egypt to Federal Republic of Germany in 1963 in gratitude for its participation in the rescuing of Nubian antiquities, was given a place in Charlottenburg; together with the columns, reerected in an annex in 1989, from the Sahure pyramid complex, which was to be installed on the Museum Island already around 1910, it conveys, from a museological point of view, a unique impression of ancient Egyptian monumental architecture.

D. Current Situation

Since the reunification of Germany in 1991 the Stiftung Preußischer Kulturbesitz has been the umbrella organisation for the former Eastern and Western institutions of the State Museums. The ÄM will return to the Neues Museum on Museum Island (after 2006) and will become an essential component of a complex, as a *Museum der antiken Welt*, presenting the archaeological collections as a whole with emphasis on the overlapping aspects of disciplines. The Kalabsha Gate and the Sahure Court will become, in the context of the Pergamonmuseum, elements of a museum of architecture, stretching from Egypt through Mesopotamia and Hellenism to the Roman Empire. This integrated concept of archaeological museum will attempt to overcome conventional presentation of strictly separate cultural areas and the particularism of administrative organisations. The tradition of field research in Egypt is being continued in a long-term excavation project in Sudan.

→ Amarna

1 J. Althoff, Das Ägyptische Museum, 1998 2 W. Kaiser (ed.), Ägyptisches Museum Berlin, 1967 3 K.-H. Priese (ed.), Das Ägyptische Museum Berlin, 1991 4 D. Wildung, Ägyptische Kunst in Berlin, ²1999.

DIETRICH WILDUNG

Bible see → Theology and the Christian Church

Bibliotheca Corviniana The Bibliotheca Corviniana (BC), set up in the castle of King Mathias I (Corvinus; 1458–1490) in Buda (today part of Budapest), was in its time, after the Vatican Library, the second largest and most valuable royal Humanist library. The king strove to amass as complete a collection of valuable literature as possible, mainly the classics of antiquity with particular emphasis on Greek authors. A Greek-Latin duality was a characteristic of the library. To give the pre-

cious contents an appropriate form, the king employed the best Italian, mainly Florentine, scribes and illustrators, particularly in the second half of his reign. He also set up a studio in his castle in Buda that produced books of a quality equivalent to those of the Italians in every respect. The number of codices can be estimated at about 2000–2500. In 1526, Sultan Suleiman, who after the battle of Mohács first temporarily captured Buda, took the library as booty, along with other treasures, to Istanbul. Here, with the exception of a few items, its contents disappeared during the following centuries. Sultan Abdul Hamid II gave back what was left at the end of the 19th cent. The fact that only about a tenth of the former material was preserved can be attributed to the fact that under the weak successors of King Mathias foreign humanists, particularly imperial ambassadors, acquired and removed many codices. The authentic codices of the BC known today are scattered over 51 libraries in 43 cities.

→ Library; → Humanism; → Codicology; → Scriptorium; → Hungary

1 Ilona Berkovits, Illuminated Manuscripts from the Library of Matthias Corvinus, Budapest, 1964. 2 Cs. Csapodi, The Corvinian Library. History and Stock, Budapest, 1973 3 Csaba Csapodi, Klara Csapodi-Gardonyi, Bibliotheca Corviniana. The Library of King Matthias Corvinus of Hungary, New York, 1969; 3rd rev. German ed., Budapest,1982; greatly expanded 4th ed. only in Hungarian: Budapest, 1990. 4 Guglielmo Fraknoi, Bibliotheca Corvina, Luigi Zambra (trans.), Budapest, 1927

CSABA CSAPODI

Biography

A. Introduction B. Middle Ages C. Renaissance, Humanism, Reformation D. 17th and 18th Cents. E. 19th and 20th Cents.

A. Introduction

Biography is one of the oldest literary genres and is divided into many different types, among them biographies of heroes, politicians, orators, artists, etc. The various functions and ways in which biographies are presented gave rise to various designations such as individual, collective, parallel, and social or societal biographies, among others. Furthermore, there are several modern biographical genres such as biographical essay, novel, novella, film. Also included under biographics – the term having established itself as a generic concept – are character study, profile, interview, etc. Biography is always a mirror of the currently prevailing notion of individuality. In the case of biography, the history of the genre is marked by the social history of individuation. From Antiquity to Renaissance, the term biography was not used, and it did not become popular until the 17th cent. Before that time, terms such as *vitae, libri de viris illustribus, commentarii de vita* or *rebus gestis, declamationes, epistolae demonstrativae, elegiae,* etc., were common [3. 3]. Up to the Renaissance, biography was strongly influenced by ancient models; the most important and influential ones were Cornelius Nepos' *De viris illustribus* (*c.*36 BC), Suetonius' *De vita Caesarum* (*c.* AD 120), Plutarch's *Bioi parálleloi* (AD 105–115), and Tacitus' *De vita Iulii Agricolae* (98 AD). Furthermore, the tradition of encomia and praise (*enkomion, panegyrikos, laudatio funebris*) was preserved until the 18th cent. (cf. apotheosis, elogium, necrology etc.)

B. MIDDLE AGES

In the Middle Ages, the ancient tradition of the biographies of philosophers, authors, and rulers gave way to the tradition of hagiography. The notion of history as a divinely guided order inspired an interest in the exemplary life stories of saints who turned themselves into God's 'vessels' on earth. The tendency towards hagiography also coloured the vitae of rulers which were still being written as well. Even Einhart's *Vita Karoli Magni* (eds. G. H. PERTZ, G. WAITZ, O. HOLDER-EGGER, ⁶1911) written in *c.* 830 – a work which was unique for the Middle Ages in how closely it was modelled after Suetonius emperors' *vitae* – refers in its prologue to the famous *Vita S. Martini* by Sulpicius Severus from the late 4th cent. (ed. C. HALM, CSEL 1, 1866; ed. J. FONTAINE, 3 vols., 1967–1969). Otherwise, individual emperors' *vitae* – in so far as they were not saints' *vitae* to begin with – managed to maintain a certain independence by their deliberate focus on secular and political aspects along with religious themes (such as the *Histoire de Saint Louis* by Jehan de Joinville written in 1305/06; ed. N. DE WAILLY, 1874). Abbots' *vitae* also tended at times to go beyond the hagiographical framework under the mantle of recording monastic history [1. 272–326]. However, as far as the holders of ecclesiastical or secular offices are concerned (those not revered in a cult-like manner), *vitae* are, on the whole, less common than chronicles or annals, in which only official deeds are selected and related to other thematic contexts.

Beginning with Tertullian, the saints worthy of *vitae* were divided between martyrs and confessors. In the Middle Ages, the martyrs' *vitae*, having grown out of the early Christian *Acta martyrum,* continued to be produced or revised because of martyrdom's significance, although the confessors began to take the lead in number after the persecution of Christians came to an end. In the latter, the focus on the sacrificial death is replaced by recurring and extensive proofs of sainthood spread out between birth and (natural) death. Structurally, these confessors' *vitae* go beyond the model of early Christian, encomiastic biographies [1st vol. 1; 3. 43–59] and refer back to the structural rules established by ancient rhetoric (such as Quint. Inst. 3,7) for the praise of an individual [4. 33–45]. In substance, the various depictions of lives are channeled into highly prominent topics. As a result, the *vitae* appear to be narrative embellishments of a religious catalogue of virtues and make the saints immediately recognisable as such despite historical variations in emphasis. The ten-

dency towards collections of *vitae* is further evidence of the desire to view saints as exemplary representatives of the *Communio sanctorum.* The best known example of this is the *Legenda aurea* (ed. TH. GRAESSE, ³1890, repr. 1965) by Jacobus de Voragine (d. 1298). On the other hand, medieval saints' *vitae* are characterised by a remarkable flexibility at the discursive level. This flexibility is especially apparent in multiple revisions that present the story of a saint's life – no matter how stereotypical it may be – in varying ways specific to the function or audience at hand, thereby exploring the stylistic spectrum between *sermo humilis* and *sermo grandis.* In this sense, saints' *vitae* should not simply be dismissed as naive legends but instead can be regarded – under the premise of an historical understanding of genre – as a specifically medieval manifestation of biography

C. RENAISSANCE, HUMANISM, REFORMATION

Although the Renaissance brought about a new self-awareness for the individual, biography still operated under the principle of → IMITATIO or *aemulatio,* that is, models were found as well as constructed. Biographers continued to write collections of works about famous men and women, often following C. Nepos, Suetonius, and Plutarch. The best known collections are by Vasari, *Le Vite de più eccellenti pittori, scultori e architettori* (1550) and K. van Mander, *Het Schilderboeck* (1604). Furthermore, the first biographies of individuals emerged such as Boccaccio's *Vita di Dante* (1373), Machiavelli's biography of Castruccio Castracani, the tyrant of Lucca (*c.* 1500), W. Roper's *Life of Sir Thomas More* (after 1535, ed. 1626), and C. Cavendish's *Life of Wolsey* (between 1554 and 1557). The translations of Plutarch into French by J. Amyot (1559) and into English by Th. North (1579) made these parallel biographies into the most commonly used sources from Antiquity [2. 129–156]. At first, this resulted in a focus on individual ethics, but the appreciation of political, artistic, scientific, or spiritual activities gradually gained ground as well (cf. R. Agricola's *Vita Petrarchae c.* 1473/74 or the biographical letters and speeches by Erasmus and Melanchthon) [2. 23–96].

D. 17TH AND 18TH CENTS.

Models of ancient biography continued to be used in these centuries and even experienced a new peak: the literary market was dominated by the type of *De viris illustribus* (cf. esp. Brantômes *Vies des Dames illustres* and *Vies des Hommes illustres,* written in 1584–1604, ed. 1665/66) [2. 97–128] as well as by collected biographies of academic professionals, and, above all, by biographical panegyrics (elogium, necrology, dedicational poetry). In France, J. de La Bruyère's translation (1688) of the *Charakteres ethikoi* by Theophrastus (372–287 BC) sparked an interest in anthropological types which also influenced the biographies of actual persons. In the 18th cent., great biographies of individuals were composed in France (cf. Voltaire) and England (cf. S. Knight), the most successful of which was J. Boswell's

Life of Samuel Johnson (1791), because it was the first one to attempt a comprehensive portrait of a life based on intimate personal knowledge and a wealth of documents. Germany saw, above all, the development of a biographical essay (G. Forster, J.G. Herder, Chr.M. Wieland) which would offer new models for the bourgeois public, in particular those from the 16th and 17th cents. Gradually, a new type of biography established itself which placed a life within the broader perspective of cultural history (cf. Goethe's *Winckelmann*, 1805) [7. 9–53].

E. 19TH AND 20TH CENTS.

The 19th cent. became the era of great biographies of individuals that try to offer well-rounded portraits with multiple facets. In addition, the triumph of a new → HISTORIOGRAPHY led to an enhanced appreciation of the genre of biography. A discussion emerged about the position of biography between art and science (cf. J.G.Droysen, *Historik*, 1858; ed. R. HÜBNER, 1937). In 1869, in the introduction to his biography *Geschichte Wallensteins*, Leopold von Ranke refers to Plutarch's distinction between 'history' and 'biography' (in *Alexander*). Biography was therefore still understood to be committed to the ethics of living. Nonetheless, an abundance of historical biographies were composed in Europe as well as in America (cf. R.W. Emerson, *Representative Men*, 1850), which either aimed to glorify (e.g. Th. Carlyle, *The History of Friedrich II of Prussia*, 1858–65) or subjected biography to nationalistic interests (cf. the 'Prussian school' with J.G. Droysen, G.H. Pertz, H. Lehmann, R. Koser, H. v. Treitschke). On the other hand, the 18th cent. tradition of humanistic biographies was continued; examples are the great biographies of individuals by W. Dilthey, Schleiermacher (1870), R. Haym, Herder (1880–85), E. Schmidt, Lessing (1884, 1892). Furthermore, biographers such as C. Justi (Winckelmann, 1866–72) and H. Grimm (Goethe, 1877) produced biographies with a focus on art history and cultural history for the educated classes. The second half of the 19th cent. saw a wealth of biographical essays (O. Gildemeister, H. Grimm, K. Hillebrand, L. Speidel). The genre of biography reached its peak in the era of positivism when biographies combined the interpretation of works with the presentation of a life story ('biographism'). Biographical novels also became very popular with audiences in Europe and continued to develop through the end of the 20th cent. (the *biographie romancée* by A. Maurois, St. Zweig, int.al.).

The early 20th cent. saw the production of a broad spectrum of biographies: → PSYCHOANALYSIS opened up the possibility of a new, 'intimate' type of biography (cf. E. Ludwig, L. Strachey, St. Zweig) first explored by S. Freud in *Eine Kindheitserinnerung des Leonardo da Vinci* (1910). Positivist biography stood in contrast to the new 'mythography' created by Stefan George's circle (cf. E. Bertram, *Nietzsche*, 1918; G. Gundolf, *Goethe*, 1916; E. Kantorowicz, *Kaiser Friedrich der Zweite*, 1927). In the 1920s and 1930s, biography ex-

perienced a boom in the form of biographical novels (*int. al.* H. Broch, A. Döblin, L. Feuchtwanger, H. Mann, Th. Wilde, M. Yourcenar, V. Woolf), biographical essays (e.g. H. and Th. Mann, St. Zweig), and 'historical fiction and poetry', that is, a form of biography that tried to be a form of art and of scholarship at the same time (H. Eulenberg, F. Hegemann, E. Ludwig int. al.). In the late 1920s, a dispute erupted between writers and historians regarding biography (*Historische Zeitschrift* 1928: A. Maurois, Die Biographie als Kunstwerk; E. Ludwig, *Historie und Dichtung*, 1929; S. Kracauer, *Die Biographie als neubürgerliche Kunstform*, 1930 *int. al.*). This conflict between art and scholarship dissipated in the late 1920s as historians recognised that historiography is always a literary construct as well (cf. the debate about narrative in the 1970s and 1980s). Since historical studies have focused increasingly on mental, social, and structural history, the genre of biography has been revitalized, particularly by writers who place the genre on the boundary between art and scholarship, or between subjectivity and objectivity. An example of this, in France, is J.P. Sartre's great study of Flaubert *L'Idiot de la famille* as *roman vrai* (1971/72). In Germany, Dieter Kühn (*Ich Wolkenstein*, 1977), Peter Härtling (*Hölderlin*, 1976), and Wolfgang Hildesheimer (*Mozart*, 1977) represent a new type of biography in which they explore an 'open-ended' kind of writing in analogy to the modern novel while still trying to satisfy demands for verifiable truth. In the 1990s, a new scholarly type of biography was established which followed the same technique and renounced the usual teleological development of life in favour of a complex, discontinuous, and at times narrative representational technique.

→ Biography

1 W. BERSCHIN, Biographie und Epochenstil im lateinischen Mittelalter, 3 vols., 1986–1991   2 Id. (ed.), Biographie zwischen Renaissance und Barock, 1993   3 A. BUCK (ed.), Biographie und Autobiographie in der Renaissance, 1983   4 E. FEISTNER, Historische Typologie der deutschen Heiligenlegende des Mittelalters, 1995   5 D. MADELÉNAL, La biographie, 1984   6 J. ROMEIN, Die Biographie, 1948   7 H. SCHEUER, Biographie, Studien zur Funktion und zum Wandel einer literarischen Gattung vom 18. Jahrhundert bis zur Gegenwart, 1979   8 TH. WOLPERS, Die englische Heiligenlegende des Mittelalters, 1964

ADDITIONAL BIBLIOGRAPHY: H. BÖDEKER (ed.), Biographie schreiben, 2003; T. HÄGG, PH. ROUSSEAU (eds.), Greek Biography and Panegyrik in Late Antiquity, 2000; O. HÄHNER, Historische Biographik. Die Entwicklung einer geschichtswissenschaftlichen Darstellungsform von der Antike bis ins 20. Jahrhundert, 1999; C. KLEIN (ed.), Grundlagen der Biographik. Theorie des biographischen Schreibens, 2002; J. KREMER, Biographie und Kunst als historiographisches Problem, 2004; L. MOOTE, New Bottles and New Wine: The Current State of Early Modernist Biographical Writing, in: French Historical Studies 19 (1996), 911–926; H. SCHEUER, Biographie. Ästhetische Handlungsmodelle und historische Rekonstruktion, in: JOHANN HOLZNER, WOLFGANG WIESMÜLLER (eds.), Ästhetik der Geschichte, 1995, 119–139; H. SONNABEND,

Geschichte der antiken Biographie. Von Isokrates bis zur Historia Augusta, 2002; M. Szöllösi-Janze, Lebens-Geschichte – Wissenschafts-Geschichte. Vom Nutzen der Biographie für die Geschichtswissenschaft und Wissenschaftsgeschichte, in: Berichte zur Wissenschaftsgeschichte 23, 2000, 17–35.   EDITH FEISTNER

Böckh-Hermann Dispute, the
A. SIGNIFICANCE AND ORIGIN OF THE METHOD DISPUTE B. GOTTFRIED HERMANN C. AUGUST BÖCKH

A. SIGNIFICANCE AND ORIGIN OF THE METHOD DISPUTE

The long-lasting dispute between Gottfried Hermann and August Böckh (regarding spelling [5. 15 n.11]) is a part of the general considerations concerning methods [1. 15] in the study of Classical Antiquity that arose in the 19th cent., triggered by the question of how Classical philology viewed itself and its place in scholarship. The opposing positions of Böckh, who was the greater systematist and who continued the work first begun by A. Wolf [2. 80f.] to put Classical philology on a new footing as the scholarship of all Antiquity, and Hermann, the more conservative scholar who insisted on the intrinsic value of Classical philology, were recognised even in the lifetime of the two men as a significant debate over methods; their positions found a place in the history of this field of knowledge under the terms historical-antiquarian philology of objects, or reality-oriented philology (Real- or Sachphilologie), and grammatical-critical text philology (Wortphilologie) [11. 117 n. 44; 5. 102 n. 112]. Although these programmatic abbreviated forms were already current in the 19th cent. to characterise the two camps, and although they do cite key words in the dispute, they must nevertheless be rejected as misleading because an exclusive opposition between an either/or, i.e. 'between object philology or word philology' was never a point of discussion (cf. G. Hermann, Über Herrn Professor Böckhs Behandlung der griechischen Inschriften, Leipzig 1826, 3).

The relationship between Böckh and Hermann, initially based on mutual respect, first began to falter [11. 111] as a result of their differing opinions regarding meter; the actual dispute, however, did not break out until 1825 when Hermann reacted to the first fascicle of the Corpus inscriptionum Graecarum with an unusually sharp review in which he accused the editor Böckh of superficial research and declared him incompetent of accomplishing such a demanding task. This devastating and cutting criticism provoked an full-blown exchange of writings and rejoinders (detailed discussion in [3. 48–62]). The quarrel, which was shared by the two men's respective students [4. 44] as well and continued into the 1830s, escalated (due mainly to Hermann) into such sharp attacks that doubts arose as to whether, as they averred, it was always about professional differences sine ira et studio doubts that were affirmed by the fact that a reconciliation occurred in the 1840s without

a settling of the scholarly controversy itself. The actual points of difference are at times difficult to ascertain, not only because of the personal vehemence but also because of the differing emphasis and elaboration of methodology: Hermann could not and did not want to oppose Böckh's complex theoretical approach (Enzyklopädie und Methodenlehre der philologischen Wissenschaft, 1809–1865; cf. [9. 68]), which had been worked out in many years of teaching. (Hermann's most important treatise on this is De officio interpretis, 1834). He critiqued merely individual points of Böckh's concept of philology but never the systematic structure as a whole.

B. GOTTFRIED HERMANN

Gottfried Hermann (born 28 November 1772 in Leipzig, studied Classical languages in Leipzig and the philosophy of Kant in Jena, professorship in 1803 in Leipzig, died 1 January 1848) viewed the Classical languages as 'the most important thing of all, as the propylaea, so difficult to reach, to all Classical Antiquity' (Über Herrn Professor Böckhs Behandlung der griechischen Inschriften, Foreword, 8), through which alone 'everything else that is characteristic of a people can be felt and understood' (ibid 4). The task of philologists, therefore, consists in the careful study, interpretation and criticism of the texts of Antiquity (interpretatio and emendatio, De officio interpretis, 5), whereas in non-linguistic approaches (e.g. archaeology), the danger lies in looking down and, from a 'bird's eye view', seeing, to be sure, many things which, however, remain blurred, as well as in losing oneself in sonorous but fatuous loquacity (vana ostentatio aut stulta garulitas, De officio interpretis, 102). Correct understanding of a text verifies the timeless human ratio (influence of Kant), which connects the philologist with the concerns expressed in the texts, whereas 'congeniality' is necessary for a translation to be outstanding [11. 116]. Because of his rationalistic and Enlightenment-inspired conviction concerning the ahistoricity of reason, Hermann explained the process of interpretation as a unilineal one.

C. AUGUST BÖCKH

August Böckh (born 24 November 1785 in Karlsruhe, studied Classical languages in Halle, professorships in 1809 in Heidelberg and 1811 in Berlin, died 3 August 1867) turned against the limitation to the formal realm of grammar, narrow exegesis of text and textual criticism. He believed that such 'syllable- and letter-criticism' (Der Staatshaushalt der Athener, Berlin 1817, XIX) could only lead to narrow-minded specialisation. Just how much more broadly he understood the term philology, which at first for him [5. 73f.] included modern philology, and how intensely he incorporated the question about the essence of scholarship in general into his thinking, is shown by his now-famous definition of philology: das Erkennen des vom menschlichen Geist Producierten, d.h. Erkannten ('knowledge of what has been produced by the human spirit, i.e. of what is known', *Encyclopaedia*, 101). This formula – knowledge of what is known –, in which Platonic and Aristotelian views are commingled with those of neo-Humanism and German Idealism, assigns to the philologist not the primary but rather the secondary step toward knowledge: the philologist's task is not for example to accomplish Plato's philosophical work process of understanding, but rather to recognize that which Plato himself understood (*gigónoskei, anagigóskei*). On the other hand, by applying the expression 'things produced' equally to all cultural monuments and historical events, Böckh defined philology as [a part of] historical studies. And by positing ideas as the foundation of each work-*lógoi* that the scholar must discern –, he characterised philology to a large extent as philosophy (Schleiermacher, Schlegel, cf. [5. 32, 41]: *Denn man kann das Erkannte nicht erkennen ohne überhaupt zu erkennen und man kann nicht zu einer Erkenntnis schlechthin gelangen, ohne, was Andere erkannt haben, zu kennen* ('for one cannot recognize that which is known without knowing in general, and one cannot come to knowledge without knowing what others have come to know', *Encyclopaedia*, 17). Through this theoretical definition of philology as *universae antiquitatis cognitio historica et philosopha* (historical and philosophical inquiry into all of Antiquity), the significance of language, though still of utmost importance, is relativised insofar as it is no longer the sole key to understanding Antiquity (*Encyclopaedia*, 54): In this way, language becomes merely one thing among others. Moreover, Böckh believed that philology shared the fate of every true science: because of the infinity of the subject matter, only approximate results can be offered: 'Where infinity stops, science is at an end' (*Encyclopaedia*, 15). The approximative character of philology is augmented through the hermeneutic circle: the accomplishments of single interpretations, whether individual, grammatical, historical or generic [10. 94f.], condition one another mutually, so that neither an understanding of a text without knowledge of the subject nor knowledge of the subject without an understanding of a text can succeed (cf. Hermann's unilineal concept of interpretation). Only the 'divinatory power of the mind' (*Encyclopaedia*, 184) can break through this circle [9. 70f.]; with this notion of genial aesthetics [2. 93f.] Böckh draws close to Hermann's concept of congeniality.

By seeing the legitimation of Classical philology in the fact that 'Greek and Roman culture is the basis of our whole culture' (*Encyclopaedia*, 21), Böckh's argument of foundation goes beyond the argument of the model character, prevalent up to that time, without giving up the pedagogical normative function of the discipline: For 'nowhere does a higher spirit prevail than in Antiquity' (*Encyclopaedia*, 31). The separation embedded here between → HISTORICISM (subject as object of research) and → HUMANISM (subject content as norm) is transcended inasmuch as research is understood as a

philosophical, truth-oriented process toward knowledge [4.50].

The methodological dispute between Hermann and Böckh ('language as the only right way to knowledge'; 'language as one way among others') guided Classical philology in its further development in the 19th cent., without however the sharp confrontation of the two camps being maintained, as some histories of scholarship would have us believe [11.117ff.].

→ NIETZSCHE-WILAMOWITZ CONTROVERSY; → ANCIENT LANGUAGES, TEACHING OF I. GERMANY

1 H. FLASHAR, Zur Einführung, in: Id., K. GRÜNDER, A. HORSTMANN, Philologie und Hermeneutik im 19. Jahrhundert. Zur Geschichte und Methodologie der Geisteswissenschaften, 1979   2 A. HENTSCHKE, U. MUHLACK, Einführung in die Geschichte der Klassischen Philolologie, 1972   3 A. HOFFMANN, AUGUST BÖCKH, Lebensbeschreibung und Auswahl aus seinem wissenschaftlichen Briefwechsel, 1901   4 A. HORSTMANN, August Böckh und die Antike-Rezeption im 19. Jahrhundert, in: L'Antichità nell' Ottocento in Italiae Germania, K. CHRIST, A. MOMIGLIANO (eds.), 1988, 39–75   5 Id., Die Forschung in der Klassischen Philologie des 19. Jahrhunderts, in: Konzeption und Begriff der Forschung in den Wissenschaften des 19. Jahrhunderts, A. DIEMER (ed.), 1968, 27–57   6 Id., s.v. Philologie, Historisches Wörterbuch der Philosophie 7, 561f.   7 O. JAHN, GOTTFRIED HERMANN, Eine Gedächtnisrede, Leipzig 1849   8 C. LEHMANN, Die Auseinandersetzung zwischen Wort- und Sachphilologie in der deutschen klassischen Altertumswissenschaft des 19. Jahrhunderts, 1964   9 F. RODI, 'Erkenntnis des Erkannten' – August Boeckhs Grundformel der hermeneutischen Wissenschaften, in: Philologie und Hermeneutik im 19. Jahrhundert, 68–83   10 I. STROHSCHNEIDER-KOHRS, Textauslegung und hermeneutischer Zirkel zur Innovation des Interpretationsbegriffes von August Boeckh, in: Philologie und Hermeneutik im 19. Jahrhundert, 84–102   11 E. VOGT, Der Methodenstreit zwischen Hermann und Böckh und seine Bedeutung für die Geschichte der Philologie, in: Philologie und Hermeneutik im 19. Jahrhundert, 103–121   12 W. NIPPEL, Philologenstreit und Schulpolitik. Zur Kontroverse zwischen Gottfried Hermann und August Böckh, in: W. KÜTTLER, J. RÜSEN, E. SCHULIN, Geschichtsdiskurs, vol. 3: Die Epoche der Historisierung, 1997, 244ff.   CLAUDIA UNGEFÄHR-KORTUS

Body culture
A. CONCEPT   B. HISTORY

A. CONCEPT
1. DEFINITION   2. REFERENTIAL DISCOURSES

1. DEFINITION
In this context, body culture (BC) describes the reflexive contemplation of the human body and attitudes toward the human body with reference to Greek and Roman Antiquity. Furthermore, this definition is based on a broad concept of culture, comprising not only culture as the collective practice of social groups – life styles, models of interaction, the formation of gender roles, etc. –, founded on and structured by various sets of norms and values, mindsets, and interpretations of

the world [17. 9ff.], but also 'high culture', i.e. works of art (and their reception) which were perceived as such [21. 539ff.]. In the following, BC will therefore be described both in the context of social and individual practice as well as that of historically evolved horizons of meaning.

2. REFERENTIAL DISCOURSES

a) BC correlates with the discourse on a new definition of the nature of humans as individual and socializable beings who relate to the world they live in;

b) BC correlates with the discourse on education;

c) BC correlates with the discourse on the role and social position of men and women;

d) Since the 18th cent., BC has correlated in the aesthetic discourse with the concept of gestalt;

e) Within the political-sociological discourse, BC correlates with the notion of *kalokagathia*.

Beyond the contexts already mentioned, BC has been assigned additional levels of significance that need to be taken into account: bodies as subjects and objects of power (political level); bodies as constituents of the process of civilization and of social interaction (social level); bodies as the media for personal interaction and bearers of meaning (cultural level).

B. HISTORY
1. MIDDLE AGES: 5TH–15TH CENTS. 2. MODERN TIMES: 15TH–18TH CENTS. 2.1 RENAISSANCE/HUMANISM 2.2 ENLIGHTENMENT AND NEO-HUMANISM 2.3 19TH AND 20TH CENTS.

1. MIDDLE AGES: 5TH–15TH CENTS.
In the Early Middle Ages, the human body was initially seen as a token of the transience of human existence, a place of pain and death, a contemptible prison of the soul. The body was tangible evidence of the distance between men and God as a result of Adam's fall from grace [11. 13]. The ideal life was seen as that of the ascetic monk, withdrawn from the world in a community of like-minded people, who in chastity, poverty, and obedience worked physically and spiritually towards the salvation of their souls. The aim was to discipline the body, whose requirements were to be subordinated to spiritual salvation by means of grinding ascetic toil. Even the king, anointed as *rex et sacerdos*, was ideally expected to live like a monk.

The body of a ruler was at the same time also the body of power, as stipulated by the doctrine of the two bodies of a king – one natural and one of salvation, granted by the grace of God, and a part of divine nature. And yet, the king's mortal body was inseparable from his political body. For this reason, the body of a king is not only a symbol of power, it *is* power. After the Investiture Contest and as a consequence of the reception of Roman law in the High and Late Middle Ages, the notion of the sovereign's salvific body belonging to the sphere of the divine shifted to that of the sovereign's salvific body as an aspect of the law and finally one of the state [16].

In the rurally dominated culture of the Early Middle Ages, the ascetic, body-denying ideal of the monk determined the culture of the body. The body at work, at war, or persisting in prayer was a symbol of the divine order of the world on a hierarchical scale of significance (*oratores, bellatores, laboratores*). In the visual arts, bodies were bearers of signs, they pointed to the transcendental world, shrouded and rigid.

The High Middle Ages saw the development of new social spheres like feudal courts and cities. At the municipal institutions of learning, the universities, Greek (espicially Aristotle) and Arab authors were studied alongside the traditional Latin ones; they were re-edited, using the tools of scholasticism, and translated into Christianity [18. 156]. Based on this premise, Anselm of Canterbury (1033–1109) and Peter Abaelard (1079–1142) were among those who introduced reason as a means to perceive God, and combined it with a new evaluation of the individual as an autonomous, thinking subject [12. 191ff., 211ff.].

Gothic art as the art of the new cities liberated itself from the anti-corporeal dogmatism of the early medieval period. Against the backdrop of the spiritual reforms of the High Middle Ages, humans and their bodies received new connotations. In the sculptures of Gothic cathedrals and in paintings, male and female bodies now stood for the perfection of divine creation, which revealed itself in the beauty of nature. The idealized bodies of saints exemplified the harmony of the world and the human position within the cosmos, with humans now seen as self-confident beings enlightened by the grace of God [11. 263ff.]. This reappraisal of the human body occurred as a result of the incipient reception of ancient sculptures. Hildebert of Lavardin (1056–1133) described the reception of ancient sculptures as an opportunity to recognize the ideal nature of man [14. 117ff.]. The representation of the beautiful body thus also gained an educational dimension. The Bamberg Horseman (c. 1235) and the figure of Mary in the Visitation group on the western facade of Reims Cathedral (c.1250) are two examples of high medieval body images that were modelled on the ancient ideal.

Within the framework of courtly culture, the body became the object of a process of civilization and education and thus the bearer of social identity. Referring to the ideal of the just and peacemaking ruler created by Cicero and Augustine (*rex iustus et pacificus*), virtues (such as piety, wisdom, munificence, benevolence) were formulated for rulers, which in the visual culture of the Middle Ages became imprinted upon the body, and were then to be splendidly displayed in ritualized gestures and interactions [9. 385ff.]. Aside from the kings of the Bible, the models for this kind of rulership were the ancient emperors Augustus and Trajan, as well as Alexander the Great. The feudal system, in its ideal of *hövescheit* (courtliness), developed an educational programme for rulers and their courts that was a body-oriented code of conduct and a catalogue of virtues rolled into one [9. 425ff.]. Courtly BC, concretized in courtly love service, created a complex system of behavioural norms, gestures, appearance, communication, and interaction, which could only be achieved through physical training; it demanded of both sexes a newly reflective approach towards their own bodies. It was particularly through the virtues of *mâze* (moderation, avoidance of extremes) and *staete* (constancy, adhering to good), associated with both men and women, that bodies became sensitized to social and interpersonal relationships, while at the same time, as courtly bodies, they remained socially distinct from their environment [9. 416ff.]. Courtly BC resulted in a new definition of masculinity and femininity; this coincided with the tendency of releasing women from their negative typification as daughters of Eve; they were now serenaded as figures of emotional and actual power [9. 451ff.]. The impact of this ideal of courtly life on the everyday reality of feudal gender relations outside of courtly poetry and festivities is difficult to determine.

2. Modern Times: 15th–18th Cents.

2.1 Renaissance/Humanism

Rooted in the urban way of life of the late medieval period and further developing that period's philosophical currents, the authors of European Humanism radicalized the already changing medieval image of man. Within the context of Upper Italian city states and republics, they defined man's mission as a struggle for self-improvement, and the continual improvement of his environment – almost to the extent of man offering to serve as God's assistant on earth [20. 44ff.]. 'We have made you neither of heaven nor of earth, neither mortal nor immortal, so that you may, as the free and extraordinary shaper of yourself, fashion yourself in the form you will prefer' (*Nec te celestem neque terrenum, neque mortalem neque immortalem fecimus, ut tui ipsius quasi arbitrarius honorariusque plastes et fictor, in quam malueris tute formam effingas*, G. Pico della Mirandola, *Oratio de hominis dignitate*, 1486 [text and translation: http://www.brown.edu/Departments/Italian_Studies/pico/text/bori/frame.html]). 'But men, I believe, are not born, rather they are moulded' (*At homines, mihi crede, non nascuntur, sed figuntur*, Erasmus of Rotterdam, *De pueris*, 1529). Breaking with the medieval tradition, Humanists no longer simply re-interpreted Antiquity to fit the Christian world picture. They imitated it constructively as a normative historical model in poetry, philosophy, and as a way of life [7. 2].

The Humanists considered language to be the medium through which humans could achieve education, and which also sets them apart from animals. Language facilitated socialization and allowed man to participate in and shape the world around him. At the heart of the Humanist education were the *studia humanitatis* (Cicero) – scholarly studies –, with the purpose of bringing to full fruition all of man's good aptitudes. The most important element were the ancient authors, who were approached e.g. by means of dialogue, as Francesco Petrarca (1304–1374) did in his letters to Classical authors [7. 1ff.]. Rhetoric as an educational programme combining thought, speech and action dominated the Humanist educational canon. Rhetorical training was to strengthen the autonomy of the individual and aid in his or her socialization. Rhetorical education was more than just a comprehensive linguistic training; as in antiquity, it also aimed to educate the body in the acquisition of a language of gestures which was liberated but moderate, appropriate to the personality of the speaker and the speech situation. Intellectual conversation thus moved away from the scholastic dialogue between teacher and pupil towards a free form of speech based on the models of the Greek agora or the Roman Forum. Like their ancient predecessors, the Humanists were convinced that cultured conversation between individuals or groups required the free movement of the body in space, in the street, or in an urban square [23. 66ff.]. For the Italian Humanists, the relationship between the human body and the republic was as important as that between the body of the king and monarchy in medieval times. Consequently, the Humanist *Specula principum* advocated a programme of physical education for rulers, which made physical and spiritual schooling a prerequisite of just rulership.

The idea of independent self-motivated study as a means of education initially led to the imposition of a new discipline on the body: whether standing, sitting, reading or writing in studious zeal, the body remained motionless, and only differed from that of a medieval copyist in the element of self-determination and the (educational) goal of its actions. Furthermore, the city as the Renaissance stage for social interaction liberated the body from the rigid medieval system of gestures and rituals, which had also served to create recognizable meaning in a world of rare encounters. Both postures -the motionless and the moving body – also point to the controversy and debate amongst Humanist scholars regarding the ideal form of life, i.e. *vita contemplativa* or *vita activa*, the choice of which they left to the individual. Yet, even the *vita contemplativa* was put in relation to the political community, to whose benefit the scholar was to search for truth [7. 5f.].

The Renaissance catalogue of virtues was modelled on Aristotle's *Ethics* and followed the Greek ideal of *kalokagathia*, which combined ethical and aesthetic values. A human being was noble and good if within him the education of the body and that of the mind were combined in visible harmony. Thus beauty became a moral category, insofar as it described a successful process of education [13. 278ff.]. According to Humanist thought, man as a *zoon politikon* (Aristotle) was obliged to socialize. He was no longer to do this merely within a network of rituals, but with an increasing degree of self-organization, while still adhering to the ideals of moderation, usefulness, and virtue, as applicable to the duties of the members of a political commonwealth.

Against this backdrop, Renaissance BC demanded highly sophisticated performances from both male and female bodies on the public stage. Refined table manners, a finely honed rhetoric and a socially adroit demeanour, as well as self-assured role-play and a sense of power grew in importance as urban life became increasingly mobile and complex. Families such as the Borgia and Medici in Italy and the Fugger in Germany are examples of a society that had become mobile. At the same time, however, the family and the state remained the two reference points of the Humanist conception of the world; the individual was not released into a self-regulating society.

In the visual arts, the 'rebirth of man' is celebrated in realistic portraits and in male and female nudes, signaling the return to nature rediscovered in the spirit of ancient models. The human form was measured in both arts and sciences and in its perfect harmonic development elevated to the signum of the new golden age [8. 124ff.]. Examples of this new understanding of the human body are Michelangelo's 'David' in the Florence Uffizi Galleries and Raffael's 'The School of Athens' in the Vatican Museum.

Even though idea of 'new man' still held mainly male connotations, Humanism also brought with it a reappraisal of women. In principle, they were given the same access to Humanist education as men, and female education became a topic of Humanist educational tracts. A woman educated in the arts and sciences was no longer seen as nightmarish, but as part of the new ideal of *humanitas*. However, the male and female spheres remained separate; female education was to be associated with female virtues, with modesty and with care for the family and the house, which were projected as the natural female spheres [8. 18f.].

2.2 ENLIGHTENMENT AND NEO-HUMANISM

In the corporative society of the Ancien Régime, the body was bound by a complex system of rules and restrictions. Human nature, described as selfish and pleasure-seeking in Thomas Hobbes' *Leviathan* (1651), was to be subjected to rules which were to make it possible for humans to live together. A system of gestures and signs in, as well as on, the body was intended to serve as a manifestation – and as a reminder – of the political structure of the community. The codes for dress, marriage, and work of that period reflected this notion. The body thus provided orientation and helped define the individual, whom it also bound firmly to the social order of his birth [24. 86ff.]. As a result of the increasing social mobility of late 17th and 18th cent. society, these codes became less distinct; new social groups evolved that were difficult to integrate into this system of body codes, such as the elite functionaries of the absolutistic state. Against this background, Enlightenment philosophy and pedagogy developed concepts for the relationship between the state and the individual, which encouraged the dissolution of corporative structures or made allowances for them. Immanuel Kant (1724–1804) saw human nature characterized by 'unsocial sociability'. Because every human strives for the best possible development of his natural aptitudes, but is only able to achieve this in confrontation with other humans, inter-

action with others is the only way for an individual to achieve the highest degree of self-development (*Ideen zur allgemeinen Geschichte in weltbürgerlicher Absicht*, 1784). By granting to every human being both reason and the potential for development, Kant shattered the absolutistic notion of an unchangeable order of the world instituted by God (*Beantwortung der Frage: Was ist Aufklärung?*, 1784). Yet, even the philosophers of the Enlightenment remained convinced that humans required governance in order to regulate individual egotism. They entrusted the state with the task of regulating the commonwealth – the maintenance of which would be enshrined in the education of its subjects. Accordingly, Frederick II of Prussia (1712–1786) in his *Lettres sur l'amour de la patrie* (1779) described the Roman Republic as the paradigm of heroic civic virtues, which had established the political community as the highest value in the life of every individual. Regrettably, this 'line of masculine souls, these men of nerve and virtue, seem to have become extinct. Love of glory has been replaced by effeminacy. Idleness has taken the place of watchfulness, and sordid self-love is destroying the love of the fatherland' [8. 338]. Forty years earlier, Charles-Louis de Secondat, Baron de Montesquieu, (1689–1755) had come to a similar conclusion regarding France in his *Considérations sur les causes de la grandeur des Romains et de leur décadence* (1734); he, too, saw in the civic education of the people a main reason for the greatness of the Greek and Roman past [8. 336ff.].

It was not least through the reception of Roman Antiquity that the philosophy of the Enlightenment also posited the equality of all (male) bodies within the state. The body was gradually democratized, while the privilege of the aristocratic body, legitimized by its aristocratic blood, was increasingly questioned [10. 74ff.]. Aristocratic body posture and body language, which had developed into a socially distinctive system of rules governing steps, gestures, and any form of interaction, finally became the butt of ridicule in the French Revolution. The Roman Republic was seen as the role model for a political commonwealth of free men, whose bodies had cast off the constraints of the Ancien Régime. The new freedom of humanity is evident in the expansive gestures on contemporary paintings: Marianne is depicted in a running pose, bearing the flag and leading the crowd.

Through the 'expansion of publicness' [15. 19] in the French Revolution, clothing, too, gained political importance. The Phrygian cap, a short jacket, and long, wide-cut trousers, the attire of the Sansculottes, comprised the uniform of the true Republican [15. 22]. At the same time, mass rallies were staged based on the Roman model, symbolically presenting the people as a single body. In 1794, the Convention asked the painter Jacques Louis David to submit suggestions for a national costume. David drew civic costumes consisting of a 'short, open tunic, held together at the waist with a sash, tight-fitting trousers, short boots or flat-soled shoes, a kind of beret, and a three-quarter length coat' [15. 24f.], an imaginative combination of ancient and Renaissance dress styles. While these designs turned the male body into a representative of the new order and minimized the private sphere as a possible location for counter-revolutionary activity, women and their clothing were carefully excluded from this politicalization to preserve the 'natural order' of the genders. Political displays on the female body were largely restricted to wearing the cockade. In posture and dress, the female body was expected to conform to female 'nature', which was associated with the privacy of home and family and, in contrast to the male sphere of public life, seen as largely ahistorical, i.e. immutable [15. 24f., 29].

On the eve of the French Revolution, Jean-Jacques Rousseau (1712–1778) in his *Discours* described the historical development of human existence from the natural state to civilized society (Gesellschaft) as a secular Fall of Man. Man in his natural state is good; civilized society causes him to develop negative qualities. For that reason it is the task of a future political commonwealth to return to the closest possible approximation of the natural state (*Du Contrat social*, 1762). In Rousseau's educational novel *Emile* (1762), man is led to happiness by his instincts, and the child develops his mental and physical abilities without coercion. Emile gains much from reading ancient authors: 'it is their simplicity of taste, which speaks directly to the heart' [8. 341]. In this instance, the attractiveness of Antiquity lies in its proximity to the natural state.

This connection was taken up above all by the German Neo-Humanists, linking the reception of Greek Antiquity with a reappraisal of nature and a renascence of art, culture, and community. Friedrich Schiller (1759–1805) formulated the basic principles of this new ideal in his essay *Über die ästhetische Erziehung des Menschen* (1795): *Die Griechen beschämen uns nicht bloß durch eine Simplizität, die unserm Zeitalter fremd ist; ... Zugleich voll Form und voll Fülle, zugleich philosophierend und bildend, zugleich zart und energisch sehen wir sie die Jugend der Phantasie mit der Männlichkeit der Vernunft in einer herrlichen Menschheit vereinigen* ('The Greeks not only put us to shame by a simplicity which is alien to our age; ... Combining fullness of form with fullness of content, philosophizing as well as educating, both tender and forceful, we see them unite the youth of fantasy with the manliness of reason in a splendid humanity', [5. 150]). Education, the idea at the centre of Neo-Humanism, implied the active shaping of aptitudes, innate to the individual, into a comprehensively erudite, reflective, and unique personality. Education always involved the 'whole' person; it was to set targets, overcome regional and religious barriers, and advance the political permeation of bourgeois society. After the experience of the French Revolution, the reform of the polity was conceived as starting with the individual whose comprehensive education, comprising reason, emotion, and sensuality, was seen as the precondition for a free con-

stitution of the state. Wilhelm von Humboldt's (1767–1835) anthropological argument of the malleability of men (*Theorie der Bildung des Menschen*, c. 1793, [4. 237]) described this same wholeness: *... in ihm sind mehrere Fähigkeiten, ihm denselben Gegenstand in verschiedenen Gestalten, bald als Begriff des Verstandes, bald als Bild der Einbildungskraft, bald als Anschauung der Sinne vor seine Betrachtung zu führen* ('... [present] in him are various abilities, [enabling him] to present the same subject for his contemplation in different manifestations, be it as a notion of reason, or as an image of fantasy, or as an intuition of the senses'). In order for education to take place, an object needed to be found which could ideally represent the 'oneness and universality' ('Einheit und Allheit', [4. 237]) of the world. For the Neo-Humanists this was Greek Antiquity, in the sense of a cultural peak that embraced all aspects of human life. Through its appropriation and constructive imitation, their own era, too, was to be led to a cultural renewal.

In the aesthetics of the German classicists, the concept of gestalt became the correlative to the 'unity and universality' of Greek Antiquity. Johann Gottfried Herder (1744–1803) developed the concept of gestalt (aesthetic form) in his treatise on Greek sculpture via a theory of empathy ('Einsfühlung'), a feeling of being at one. In a 'curious correlation of sculpture and sense of touch', the sculpted figure and that of the observer become as one, as through tactile exploration the sculpted figure virtually becomes that of the observer: 'my form walks with Apollo', [25. 542]. Thus, the form, through sensual pleasure, opens the way to the experience of a higher level of art. In Friedrich Schiller's view, aesthetic form was predominantly the expression of the formal drive as part of the aesthetic consciousness. In the same way the sensual drive of the aesthetic consciousness was focused on life, the formal drive was tied to the aesthetic form. Schiller understood aesthetic consciousness as a *whole* as referring to the 'living form' (*lebende Gestalt*, [25. 542]): *Solange wir über seine (eines Menschen) Gestalt bloß denken, ist sie leblos, bloße Abstraktion; solange wir sein Leben bloß fühlen, ist es gestaltlos, bloße Impression. Nur indem seine Form in unsrer Empfindung lebt und sein Leben in unserm Verstande sich formt, ist er lebende Gestalt, und dies wird überall der Fall sein, wo wir ihn als schön beurteilen* ('As long as we only think of the aesthetic form (of a human being), it remains lifeless, a mere abstraction; as long as we only feel his life, it remains formless, a mere impression. It is only when his form lives in our feeling, and his life in our understanding, he is the living form, and this will everywhere be the case where we judge him to be beautiful', [25. 542]). In Schiller's eyes, aesthetic 'form' is conceivable as a human being and also as a work of art; both can be the object of a holistic contemplation. The German classicists' concept of gestalt expresses the balance of opposing forces within a successful aesthetic form; it is therefore not only an expression of art's claim to autonomy, but also one of the successful educational processes of the individual. Neo-Humanist and Classical Antiquity thus established an indissoluble link between the production and reception of art and the human body, on the levels of representation and reception within the educational process. Furthermore, Johann Joachim Winckelmann (1717–1768) declared the study of the naked body the very origin of art in ancient Greece: *da zeigt sich die schöne Natur unverhüllt zum großen Unterricht der Künstler. Die Schule der Künstler war in den Gymnasien, wo die jungen Leute ... ganz nackend ihre Leibesübungen trieben ... Diese häufigen Gelegenheiten zur Beobachtung der Natur veranlaßten die griech. Künstler noch weiter zu gehen: sie fingen an, sich gewisse allg. Begriffe von Schönheiten sowohl einzelner Teile als ganzer Verhältnisse der Körper zu bilden, die sich über die Natur selbst erheben sollten; ihr Urbild war eine bloß im Verstande entworfene geistige Natur* ('... beautiful nature revealed itself unveiled for the great instruction of artists. The school of artists was the gymnasium, where young people ... performed their physical exercises entirely in the nude ... The frequent opportunities to observe nature prompted Greek artists to pursue this further: they began to formulate certain general principles of beauty of individual parts as well as entire interrelationships between bodies, which were to rise above nature itself; their archetype was a spiritual nature designed only in the mind', *Gedanken über die Nachahmung der griechischen Werke in der Malerei und Bildhauerkunst*, 1755, [8. 347f.]). Nature and culture are thus combined in the aesthetic form, whose beauty, as in the Renaissance, also contains a moral postulate, as Schiller explained in his *Über Anmut und Würde* (1793) with regard to the beautiful soul: *In einer schönen Seele ist es also, wo Sinnlichkeit und Vernunft, Pflicht und Neigung harmonieren, und Grazie ist ihr Ausdruck in der Erscheinung* ('Thus it is in a beautiful soul that sensuality and reason, duty and inclination harmonize, and physical grace is its outward expression', [5. 75]). Beauty and goodness were joined according to the Greek concept of *kalokagathia*.

While this meant the beautiful body was considered to be the product of a process of education, it also acquired a social connotation as a bourgeois body. In contrast with aristocratic BC, the bourgeois body (male *and* female) was seen as the result of an inner shaping of the human being, as a work of education undertaken by the emerging economic and academic middle classes. In the early 19th-cent. bourgeois catalogue of norms and values, individual achievement and civic freedom became the yardstick for social reform. The 'perfect posture' as a means to avoid extreme gestures and to initiate interaction on an equal footing was no longer an expression of social class, but of character, and was initially seen as equally important for men and women [10. 88ff.; 19. 8off.]. At the same time, male and female bodies were subject to different educational ideals and rules of movement: *Im Kreise der (griechischen) Göttinnen begegnet uns das Ideal der Weiblichkeit zuerst in Dionens Tochter. Der kleine und zarte Gliederbau, welcher jeden schmeichelnden Liebreiz vereint, ... der sehnsuchtsvoll geöffnete Mund, die holde Sittsamkeit ... und die himmlische Anmuth, die, gleich einem Hauche, über ihre ganze Gestalt ausgegossen ist, kündigen ein Geschlecht an, das auf seine Schwäche selbst seine Macht gründet. ... Der eigentliche Geschlechtsausdruck ist in der männlichen Gestalt weniger hervorstechend ... sie (die Natur) verstattet ihr mehr Unabhängigkeit von dem, was nur dem Geschlecht angehört ... Je mehr Kraft und Freiheit auch die Gestalt des Mannes verräth, desto männlicher erklärt ihn selbst das alltägliche Urtheil. ... Daher wird die männliche Schönheit immer in dem Grade erhöht, in welchem die Kraft gestärkt wird, und sinkt immer um so viel herab, als man dem Genuss Uebergewicht über die Thätigkeit verstattet* ('It is within the circle of (Greek) goddesses that we first encounter the ideal of femininity in *Dione's* daughter. Her delicate and lithe build, a combination of all that is graceful, ... her mouth longingly opened, her sweet modesty ... and her divine gracefulness, poured like a breeze over her entire body, announce a gender whose power and strength is founded upon its very weakness. ... The actual expression of gender is less prevalent in the male form ... (nature) grants it greater independence of that which is merely associated with gender ... The more strength and freedom the male form betrays, the greater his maleness in everyday perception. ... For that reason, male beauty is always increased to the same degree that its [the male body's] power is strengthened, and lowered to the same extent, as pleasure is given predominance over occupation', W. von Humboldt, *Über die männliche und weibliche Form*, 1795, [4. 298ff.]). Whereas female gracefulness was associated with nobleness of the heart, male strength was linked to the rational disciplining and shaping of the body. This view of the body has found artistic expression in the *Doppelstandbild der Prinzessinnen Luise und Friederike von Preußen* (double statue of the Princesses Luise and Friederike of Prussia, 1795–1797) by Johann G. Schadow (1764–1850) in the Alte Nationalgallerie Berlin, or in Karl Friedrich Schinkel's (1781–1841) painting *Blick in Griechenlands Blüte* (Glimpse of Greece's Golden Age) (1825), Nationalgallerie Berlin, Gallerie der Romantik.

2.3 19TH AND 20TH CENTS.

In the course of the 19th cent., the middle-class 'perfect posture' led to the cultivation of an increasingly standardized and ever more disciplined body. The growing importance of the middle classes lent exemplary significance to the presentation of the body and its gesticular expressions and it turned into an instrument of social distinction. While Humboldt had still developed his body ideal from the naked body, this became increasingly taboo in the middle class BC of the 19th cent. Moral standards were written into the bourgeois body language [10. 93ff.]. Bourgeois attire in the 19th cent. gradually began to cover the entire body to the extent that, eventually, even the glimpse of a female ankle could be taken as an erotic signal.

Only at the turn of the century in 1900 did the body undergo a reappraisal as part of the critique of civilization and the life reform movement. Naturism, dress and diet reform, Youth Movement, naturopathy and the temperance movement, gymnastics and dance – all of these converged in the emphasis of the natural beauty of the (also naked) body. However, it was not just a simple matter of returning the body to nature, but of re-educating it towards a new naturalness. Like the Neo-Humanists before them, the reformers saw the forerunners of this beauty, which was cultivated through education, in the statues of Greek Antiquity – an era, which was to be detached from scholarly study and, at the same time, to be tied once again to art and daily life as the royal road to education.

The programme was set out in 1894 by Paul Gérardy in his treatise on *Geistige Kunst* (Spiritual Art), published in Stefan George's (1868–1933) *Blätter für die Kunst: Diese worte sollen für diejenigen gelten die einen abscheu empfanden am tage wo das zwanzigste jahr sie aus dem land der fabel in die lebende wirklichkeit versezte. trotz der schulmässigen umhüllung leerer rednerei hatte der schauer vor der geahnten pracht des Altertumes unsre vor bewunderung bleichen stirnen gebeugt, und als wir kühn den göttl. formen zueilen wollten stiessen wir uns an dem leichnam der jahrhunderte* ('These words are addressed to those who loathed the day, when the twentieth year propelled them from the realm of fables into the reality of life. Despite being obscured by the emptiness of schoolmasterly words, the thrill of the splendour of Antiquity, which we could barely sense, bent our foreheads, pale with admiration. But when we boldly rushed towards these divine forms, we stumbled against the corpse of centuries', [3. 111]). Gérardy describes a conflict that has both literary-ideological and inter-generational implications. A new Antiquity, seen through the eyes of youth at the *fin de siècle*, became the symbol of a cultural renewal: *denn die werdende jugend wird darüber lächeln und den vom alter tot zurückgelassenen formen in unerwarteter weise neues und glühendes leben einhauchen* ('because rising youth will smile on this and in unexpected ways breathe new and glowing life into the forms left for dead by the old', [1. 19]). The 'new man' was to be full of beauty and grace; in contrast with the fragmentation and pace of metropolitan life, he was to find a new holistic unity, to discover his 'body-soul' (*Körperseele*). The liberation of the body became part of an ideological framework, combining the new naturalness with a claim to morality, which, originating in an altered perception of the body, could be expanded to include novel concepts of state and society.

The body concept of a new natural femininity was justified through the female body's specific closeness to nature, which led to the assumption not only of a natural biological motherhood but also to that of a 'spiritual motherhood', thus assigning to women a general responsibility for the education of society as a whole. At the same time, the nature of femininity was to be ex-plored and reshaped by naturism and new forms of dance, which were modelled on nature's own rhythms [22].

While the new femininity was largely based on a re-interpretation of 'Deutschtum' ('Germanness', i.e. indigenous culture), it was often imagined in sharp contrast to the male body, which was modelled on ideals drawn from Antiquity, and in rejection of a 'feminized' society (Hans Blüher, *Die Rolle der Erotik in der männlichen Gesellschaft. Eine Theorie der Staatsbildung nach Wesen und Wert*, 1917). The male body was to find its own way back to a unity of body and mind through physical exercise in male communities. Legitimized by the reception of Plato's dialogues, and the Politeia, the male body served to promote a new concept of culture, expressed in terms of all-male fellowships by the Youth Movement, male propagandists of naturism, and also the George Circle. Within the George Circle, the beautiful male body became the vehicle for comprehensive reform plans. Starting from the notion of *kalokagathia* as physical, spiritual and social primacy, beauty as the harmonic union of physical and spiritual education became the aspirational ideal for Stefan George's followers. They also considered it a token of the creative power and the potential for development in those young men who were chosen. Ideals concerning the production of poetic/philosophical works, educational aims, body ideals and ideas of social reform were combined and given full expression within the theorem of the aesthetic form (Gestalt) central to the Circle's ideology. In Heinrich Friedemann's (1888–1915) *Platon. Seine Gestalt* (1914), 'the experience of the opportune moment' (Greek *kairos*) ultimately leads to the perfect poetic or statesmanly work: *Der kairos aber ist die schöpferische stunde, die das chaos zur gestalt zwingt: … und die gestalt ist als fuge von maass und chaos des kairos bleibendes kind* ('*kairos*, though, is the creative moment which forces chaos into aesthetic form: … and the aesthetic form as the juncture of restraint and chaos is the lasting progeny of *kairos*', [2. 40f.]). The authors of the George Circle see the 'living form' of the 'whole human being' as the 'founder of the spiritual empire', whose creative impulse was aimed at the receptive male youth: *An euch, knaben und jünglinge, ergeht unser ruf, soweit in euch noch die reinen feuer des lebens brennen. … Die ewige wahrheit erscheint nur als gestalt und nur im sinnenhaft begrenzten zeigt sie ihre gesetze, eben als gesetze der besonderen leiblichen einheit: darum ist der grösste mensch die tiefste wahrheit, ja der held und herrscher allein ist wahr!* ('We call you, boys and young men, provided that the pure fires of life still burn within you. … Eternal truth only appears in manifest form, and only in the moderation of the senses does it reveal its laws, precisely as laws of a special physical unity: for that reason the greatest of humans is the deepest truth; yes, only the hero and ruler alone is true!', [6. 151]). The George Circle took up the sharp profile given to the gestalt concept by the German Classicists and bent it towards cultural criticism. Freedom as the precondition of education and its firm establishment within society was replaced by the subordination of the individual to the demands of the group. A fellowship-like community concept was developed to counter that of industrial society.

Whereas in the first three decades of the 20th cent. BC was once more defined by the recourse to Antiquity, present-day BC seems to rely solely on set-pieces. The statues of ancient gods and heroes are only playfully reflected in the male body ideal of body builders and their poses, and female BC is opening up to what used to be exclusively male body ideals. The blurring of physical gender contours also opens the way for a playful interaction with previously normative models. However, present day BC is no less subject to a powerful standardization by a society and its ideals, which claims to recognize in a young, slim, and physically fit body an assertive, mobile, creative and flexible personality. In this way, the Greek ideal of *kalokagathia* has indeed found its way into present-day BC, albeit under a different set of norms and values.

SOURCES: 1 Einleitungen und Merksprüche, 3rd series, vol. 4 (1896), in: Blätter für die Kunst. Eine auslese aus den jahren 1892–98, 1899 2 H. FRIEDEMANN, Platon. Seine Gestalt, 1914 3 P. GÉRARDY, Geistige Kunst, in: Blätter für die Kunst. Eine auslese aus den jahren 1892–98, 1899, 111–114 4 W. VON HUMBOLDT, Schriften zur Anthropologie und Geschichte Werke in 5 Bänden, vol.1, 1960 5 F. SCHILLER, Über das Schöne und die Kunst. Schriften zur Ästhetik, 1975 6 F. WOLTERS, Mensch und Gattung, in: F. GUNDOLF, F. WOLTERS (eds.), Jahrbuch für die geistige Bewegung, vol. 3, 1912, 138–154

LITERATURE: 7 A. BUCK, Der italienische Humanismus, in: Handbuch der deutschen Bildungsgeschichte, C. BERG et al. (eds.), vol. 1, 15.–17. Jahrhundert, 1996, 1–56 8 Id., Humanismus. Seine europäische Entwicklung in Dokumenten und Darstellungen, 1987 9 J. BUMKE, Literatur und Gesellschaft im Hochmittelalter, vol. 2, 1986 (Eng.: Courtly Culture: Literature and Society in the High Middle Ages, 1991) 10 U. DÖCKER, Die Ordnung der bürgerlichen Welt. Verhaltensideale und soziale Praktiken im 19. Jahrhundert, 1994 11 G. DUBY, Zeit der Kathedralen. Kunst und Gesellschaft 980–1420, ⁵1987 (Eng.: The Age of the Cathedrals: Art and Society, 980–1420, 1981) 12 K. FLASCH, Das philosophische Denken im Mittelalter. Von Augustin zu Machiavelli, 1988 13 A. HELLER, Der Mensch der Renaissance, 1988 14 K. HELMER, Bildungswelten des Mittelalters. Denken und Gedanken, Vorstellungen und Einstellungen, 1997 15 L. HUNT, Französische Revolution und privates Leben, in: PH. ARIÈS, G. DUBY (eds.), Geschichte des privaten Lebens, vol. 4, Von der Revolution zum Großen Krieg, ed. by M. PERROT, 1992 (Eng.: The Unstable Boundaries of the French Revolution, in: (PH. ARIÈS, G. DUBY (eds.), trans. Arthur Goldhammer) A History of Private Life: From the Fires of Revolution to the Great War, 1990, 13–45) 16 E. KANTOROWICZ, Die zwei Körper des Königs. Eine Studie zur politischen Theologie des Mittelalters (1957), 1990 (Eng.: The King's Two Bodies: A Study in Medieval Political Theology, 1957) 17 W. KASCHUBA, Deutsche Bürgerlichkeit nach 1800. Kultur als symbolische Praxis, in: J. KOCKA (ed.), Bürgertum im 19. Jahrhundert. Deutschland im europäischen Vergleich, vol. 3, 1988, 9–44 18 J. LE GOFF, Das Hochmittelalter, 1965 19 A. LINKE, Bürgertum und Sprachkultur. Zur Mentalitätsgeschichte des 19. Jahrhunderts, 1996 20 K. MEYER-DRAWE, Menschen im Spiegel ihrer Maschinen, 1996 21 TH. NIPPERDEY, Deutsche Geschichte 1800–1866. Bürgerwelt und starker Staat, 1983 22 M. DE RAS, Körper, Eros und weibliche Kultur. Mädchen im Wandervogel und in der Bündischen Jugend 1900–1933, 1988 23 R. SENNETT, Fleisch und Stein. Der Körper und die Stadt in der westlichen Zivilisation, 1995 24 Id., Verfall und Ende des öffentlichen Lebens. Die Tyrannei der Intimität, 1983 25 W. STRUBE, Art. 'Gestalt', in: Historisches Wörterbuch der Philosophie, ed. by J. RITTER, vol. 3, 1974, 540–548

ADDITIONAL BIBLIOGRAPHY: Fragments for a History of the Human Body. Parts 1–3. MICHAEL FEHER (ed.), New York, 1989; RICHARD JENKYNS, The Victorians and Ancient Greece. Cambridge (Mass.), 1980; TH. LAQUEUR, Making Sex. Body and Gender from the Greeks to Freud, 1990.   CAROLA GROPPE

Bohemia see → CZECH REPUBLIC

Bonapartism see → CAESARISM

Bonn, Rheinisches Landesmuseum and Akademisches Kunstmuseum

A. INTRODUCTION B. HISTORY OF THE RHEINISCHES LANDESMUSEUM C. HISTORY AND PRESENTATION OF THE RHEINISCHES LANDESMUSEUM D. HISTORY OF THE AKADEMISCHES KUNSTMUSEUM E. COLLECTION AND PRESENTATION OF THE AKADEMISCHES KUNSTMUSEUM

A. INTRODUCTION

The two Bonn museums that house examples of ancient art developed from common historical circumstances. They did not arise from older court collections, but owe their existence indirectly to the Berlin government, after the Rhineland became annexed to the Prussian state in 1814. The preconditions and bases of the museums' foundation may be considered, on the one hand, as positive effects of Prussia's 'bourgeois' reforms after the Wars of Liberation. On the other hand, they also bear witness to a definite cultural policy, with which the central power tried to promote its ideals within the new province, which was Catholic and by no means well disposed towards Prussia.

B. HISTORY OF THE RHEINISCHES LANDESMUSEUM

In 1820, Chancellor Hardenberg decreed that a collection of regional monuments should be created in Bonn as the *Museum Rheinisch-Westfälischer Alterthümer*. From 1823 to 1874, its holdings were organizationally linked to the University, which was housed in the Bonner Schloss. From 1841 on, the *Verein von Alterthumsfreunden im Rheinlande* (Society of the Friends of Antiquity in the Rhineland), founded as a citizens' initiative and to some extent strongly marked

Fig. 1: Bonn, Rheinisches Landesmuseum,
tomb relief of Marcus Caelius.
Landesverband Rheinland/
Rheinisches Landesmuseum Bonn

Fig. 2: Bonn, Akademisches Kunstmuseum,
view of the exterior with former entrance (*c.* 1990).
Photo: Akademisches Kunstmuseum

Fig. 4: Bonn, Akademisches Kunstmuseum,
portrait of Arsinoe.
Photo: Akademisches Kunstmuseum

Fig. 3: Bonn, Akademisches Kunstmuseum,
calyx krater by the 'Copenhagen Painter'.
Photo: Akademisches Kunstmuseum

by regional patriotism, emerged with its own collection efforts. These collections were combined into the *Rheinisches Provinzialmuseum*, which was subject to provincial authority and moved into its own building in 1893. An extension was added in 1909, and its name was changed to *Rheinisches Landesmuseum* in 1934. The buildings suffered extensive war damage in 1943, while the holdings were, by and large, able to be preserved by being moved to safety. The objects were made accessible to the public once again in 1969.

C. HISTORY AND PRESENTATION OF THE RHEINISCHES LANDESMUSEUM

Antiquity occupies only one segment in the building, albeit an important one. All in all, the time span of the works exhibited in modern-designed rooms extends from the Stone Age to the present. The common denominator of all the objects is their regional connection.

Archeological monuments are not set up primarily as works of art, but as historical evidence. To be sure, aesthetic and stylistic categories also come into play, but on a subordinate level. Although the main room, the skylight hall, is visually dominated by a mosaic set in the floor, some stone sculptures grouped around the centre, and a display of arcades from Aachen, works of other genres, down to simple objects for daily use, likewise find suitable consideration. An outstanding group of monuments with high value as sources for the history of Roman Germania are the gravestones of military personnel, including the well-known relief of Caelius from Xanten (Fig. 1), who fell as a captain in Varus' campaign. A few Altars of the Matronae testify to religious peculiarities and regional cultic traditions. Roman portraiture is represented mainly by a youthful head from Zülpich, from the early Empire, and a bronze head of Emperor Gordian III (reigned AD 238–244).

D. HISTORY OF THE AKADEMISCHES KUNSTMUSEUM

After King Friedrich Wilhelm III had a Prussian university built in Bonn in 1818, it was rapidly decided to establish an archaeological museum at the university as well. Its founder Georg Friedrich Welcker – formerly tutor in the household of Wilhelm von Humboldt at Rome and then the holder of the Chair for Classical Studies – sought to assemble a collection that should awaken 'a sense of appreciation for the essence of the fine arts'. This goal was served less by the collection of originals, initially modest, than by the → CAST COLLECTIONS of ancient sculptures. For several decades, the *Akademisches Kunstmuseum* was developed parallel with the *Museum Rheinisch-Westfälischer (bzw. vaterländischer) Alterthümer* (Museum of Rheinish-Westphalian (or patriotic) Antiquities), which was also affiliated with the university. Close connections had also existed since 1841 between the University and the *Society of Friends of Antiquity*; yet after 1860 this cooperation changed to rivalry and conflict. At the same time, the common administration of both museums at the University broke apart. The official separation was carried out in 1870.

The size of the collection of the Akademisches Kunstmuseum, and especially moisture damage to the casts, increasingly made accommodation in separate quarters a necessity. In 1884 the move, which included the Archeological Seminar, to the former anatomy building (Fig. 2) took place, which, built in 1824 in strictly Classical style, was adapted to its new function and enlarged, on which occasion the question of appropriate lighting by means of a skylight or high sidelight played an important role. The annex, which definitely had more surface-space than the old wing, hosted to the cast collection.

However, as also happened elsewhere, during the second half of the 19th cent., appreciation of the cast collection decreased. Around the turn of the 20th cent., preferences within the Museum shifted entirely in favour of originals, and their numbers were systematically increased. However, since the First World War, new purchases have been drastically curtailed, owing to lack of resources.

E. COLLECTION AND PRESENTATION OF THE AKADEMISCHES KUNSTMUSEUM

The cast collection, begun in 1820, is today among the world's largest. Due to limited space, only a selection of the approximately 900 pieces is presented. Yet even the approximately 250 statues shown in the Annex are exhibited close together.

If initially the cast collection was meant to fulfil a task of aesthetic education, with the emphasis on Classical Greek sculpture, this area of the Museum has evolved to provide an overall view of the history of ancient sculpture, albeit necessarily limited. Its function has been primarily that of an educational collection. This also holds true of the collection of originals. Thus, ceramic production from all phases of Antiquity is documented almost uninterruptedly by characteristic pieces, sometimes only in the form of inconspicuous shards, mostly kept in storage. At the same time, there are outstanding monuments from a wide variety of genres, which deserve interest even outside of university instruction. Let us merely mention a Cycladic idol from the 3rd millennium BC, a portrait of the Ptolemaic queen Arsinoe II (3rd cent. BC, Fig. 4), and an Attic red-figured bell krater by the so-called Copenhagen Painter (c. 470–460 BC, Fig. 3).

Since 1968, the Museum has striven to attract a broader public. Over the last few years, activities have intensified with a view to achieving recognition as an official educational institution, as well as towards integration into Bonn's 'Museum Mile'. This was the goal of an ambitious special exhibition in the early 1990s, carried out with international cooperation. At the same time, proposals were submitted as to how the institution's premises could be better put to use, in order, on the one hand, to reduce the overcrowded profusion of the permanent exhibitions, and, on the other, to set aside space for changing presentations.

1 Antiken aus dem Akademischen Kunstmuseum Bonn, Katalog Rheinisches Landesmuseums Bonn, 1969   2 W. EHRHARDT, Das Akademische Kunstmuseum der Universität Bonn unter der Direktion von F.G. Welcker und O. Jahn, Abhandlungen der Rheinisch-Westfälischen Akademie Düsseldorf, Nr. 68, 1982   3 W. GEOMINY, Das Akademische Kunstmuseum der Universität Bonn unter der Direktion von Reinhard Kekulé, 1989   4 R. KEKULÉ, Das akademische Kunstmuseum zu Bonn, Bonn 1872   5 Rheinisches Landesmuseum Bonn. Führer durch die Sammlungen, 1985   6 Verzeichnis der Abguß-Sammlungen des Akademischen Kunstmuseums der Universität Bonn, DEUTSCHES ARCHÄOLOGISCHES INSTITUT (ed.), 1981   7 F. G. WELCKER, Das akademische Kunstmuseum in Bonn, Bonn 1827, ²1841.   DETLEV KREIKENBOM

Boston, Museum of Fine Arts

A. INSTITUTION   B. HISTORY OF THE COLLECTION
C. MUSEUM ACTIVITIES

A. INSTITUTION

The organization responsible of the Museum of Fine Arts (MFA), which was founded in 1870, is a private foundation (address: MFA, 465 Huntington Avenue, Boston, Massachusetts 02115–5523, USA).

B. HISTORY OF THE COLLECTION

Together with the Metropolitan Museum of Art in New York and others, the MFA is one of the pioneering American museum institutions of the 19th cent.

The Museum was founded on February 4, 1870, and its opening in the building on Copley Square took place on July 4, 1876. In 1909, the rapidly-growing museum moved to its present location, which since then, through extensions built by I.M. Pei, among others, has reached its current dimensions. Europe, with its cultural and, above all, educational ideals, served as model in the museum's conception [1].

The M.F.A.'s collections are indebted to 'genial art'. All areas of world art were collected, among which the collections of ancient, European, and Asian art held a high rank. In sculpture, in addition to originals, plaster casts of representative works were also included initially, since in general 'originals would either remain inaccessible, or else have little value, or else be of doubtful authenticity' [1].

The Department of Antiquities forms a separate department within the MFA: the *Department of Classical Archaeology*, today the *Department of Classical Art*, which was set up in 1885 under the direction of Edward Robinson. It began with, among other objects, a collection of Cypriot sculptures, purchased in 1872 from Luigi Palma di Cesnola, future Director of the Metropolitan Museum in New York. In 1876, for the one hundredth anniversary of the founding of the United States, Charles Perkings made a gift of a group of reliefs which he had evidently brought back from Rome. They included a fragment of the so-called Capaneus from Phidias' shield of Athena Parthenos. Other elements of the collection (1884) came from Assos in Turkey, in the form of objects which the MFA received in return for its participation in excavations at that site. Slightly later, finds from the Greek colony Naucratis in the Nile Delta came to Boston by this route.

Robinson began the selective purchase of originals of objects such as vases, terracottas, and sculptures. True to the Museum's manifesto, its first publication was the catalogue of casts from 1887 [2]. The ancient pieces were presented in 1893 in a vase catalogue with over 600 entries and fragments from Naucratis [3].

The personal interests of a series of benefactors were decisive for the composition of the collection [4]. Among them, E.P. Warren, who actively contributed to broadening the antiquities collection, particularly stands out. Financial donations enabled the selective purchase of Classical art, so that between 1895 and 1904 the collection grew by more than 4000 objects, including more than 1000 Greek coins, as well as sculptures, vases, bronzes, terracottas and gems.

Between 1908 and 1944, the curator L. D. Caskey left his mark on the Antiquities department: it was under his aegis that, for instance, the *Boston Throne* (1908), the Carter collection of ancient glass (1916–1931) and the E.P. Warren collection of ancient gems (1927) were acquired. In 1918, part 3 of the frieze of the temple of Athena Nike on the Acropolis found its way to Boston. Portraits, Etruscan art, and prehistoric Greek art were also acquired in large numbers [4]. This acquisition activity was selectively continued by Caskey's successors. Completed by donations and gifts, the Boston collection impresses today mainly by its breadth, and offers a wide-reaching overview of ancient art, from prehistory to early Byzantium.

C. MUSEUM ACTIVITIES

Among the best-known objects is the *Boston Throne*, which, however, was probably created as a counterpart to the Ludovisi Throne in Rome in the 19th cent. (Fig. 1). There has been a lengthy debate about this relief, which can serve as an excellent example of a fundamental dilemma of antiquities collecting: the difficulty of recognizing → FORGERIES or new creations as such. The acknowledged highlights of the collection include: the post-Geometric statue of Mantiklos from Boeotia, impressive by its 'modern' simplicity (Fig. 2), the fine head of the young Arsinoe II of Egypt (Fig. 3), an example of the important series of ancient portraits, which runs into Late Antiquity. A classic of Greek vase painting is the amphora by the Andokides Painter, which marks the beginning of red-figure vase painting. A large number of outstanding examples of this genre of art and craft, such as the bell krater by the Pan Painter with Artemis and Aktaion (Fig. 4), enable their history to be followed down to the time of Alexander the Great.

In addition to large sculpture and vase painting, the MFA also possesses an impressive collection of minor arts, in which gems, gold jewellery, and small bronzes are represented as much as are coins and medals. Here, too, a broad historical spectrum opens before the visi-

Fig. 1: 'Boston Throne',
in the style of the 5th cent.
BC, 19th cent. Italian

Fig. 2: Statue with votive
inscription to Apollo,
donated by Manticlus,
from Boeotia,
c. 700 – 650 BC

tor, which extends from the Bronze Age to the early Byzantine era.

The MFA. has presented part of its collection in a series of scholarly publications. These include the first catalogue of sculptures [4] by L. C. Caskey; who also published the ceramics, partly in collaboration with Sir John D. Beazley [5]. Already in 1916, G.H. Chase had presented the Arretine sigillata [6], and in 1928 A. Fairbanks had made the Greek and Etruscan vases accessible [7]. A series of further catalogues for individual special disciplines show the progress of work on the Museum's holdings in recent times [8–17]. In addition, the MFA is collaborating on a series of scholarly standard works [18; 19]. It also participated in an excavation on Cyprus, on which occasion it harked back to the archaeological tradition of the 19th cent. [20].
→ Andocides Painter.

1 D. PICKMAN, Museum of Fine Arts, Boston. The First One Hundred Years, Archaeology 23 (2), 1970, 114–119 2 E. ROBINSON, Descriptive Catalogue of Casts from Greek and Roman Sculpture, Boston 1887 3 Id., Catalogue of Greek, Etruscan and Roman Vases, Boston, MA, 1983 4 L. D. CASKEY, Catalogue of Greek and Roman Sculpture, Cambridge, MA, 1925 5 Id., Attic Vase Paintings in the Museum of Fine Arts, Part I, 1931, (with J. D. BEAZLEY) vols. II & III 1954, 1963 6 G. H. CHASE, Catalogue of Arretine Pottery, Boston, 1916 7 A. FAIRBANKS, Catalogue of Greek and Etruscan Vases, 1928 8 A. B. BRETT, Catalogue of Greek Coins, 1955 9 Id., Greek and Roman Portraits 470 BC- AD 500, 1959 10 M. COM-STOCK, C. C. VERMEULE, Greek Coins. 1950 to 1963, 1964 11 A. VON SALDERN, Ancient Glass in the Museum of Fine Arts, 1968 12 M. COMSTOCK, C. C. VERMEULE, Greek, Etruscan, and Roman Bronzes in the Museum of Fine Arts, 1971 13 Greek and Roman Portraits, 470 BC-AD 500, Boston, Museum of Fine Arts, 1972 14 C. C. VERMEULE, Art of Ancient Cyprus. Museum of Fine Arts Boston, 1972 15 M. B. COMSTOCK, C. C. VERMEULE, Sculpture in Stone. The Greek, Roman and Etruscan Collections of the Museum of Fine Arts Boston, 1976 16 C. C. VERMEULE (ed.), Sculpture in stone and bronze in the Museum of Fine Arts, Boston. Additions to the collections of Greek, Etruscan, and Roman art, 1971–1988, 1988 17 J. M. PADGETT, M. B. COMSTOCK, J. J. HERR-MANN et al., Vase-painting in Italy. Red-figure and related works in the Museum of Fine Arts Boston, 1993 18 H. HOFFMANN, Corpus vasorum antiquorum. United States of America, 14. Boston, Museum of Fine Arts, 1. Attic black-figured amphorae, 1973 19 M. TRUE, Corpus vasorum antiquorum. United States of America, 19. Boston, Museum of Fine Arts, 2. Attic black-figured pelike, kraters, dinoi, hydriai, and kylikes, 1978 20 E. T. VER-MEULE, Toumba tou Skourou. The Mound of Darkness. A Bronze Age Town on Morphou Bay in Cyprus. The Harvard Univ. Cyprus Archaeological Expedition and the Museum of Fine Arts, Boston, 1971–1974, 1974.

WOLF RUDOLPH

Botany

A. Introduction   B. Agriculture   C. Medicine and Pharmacy   D. Pure Botany   E. Astrology and Magic

A. Introduction

The term was introduced as early as 1663 by Schorer as *Botanic oder Kräuterwissenschaft* (botany or herbal science), following *botanik-́e* (sc. *epist-́emē*) and Neo-Latin *botanica* (sc. *scientia*) [32] and is encountered in the limited sense of a plant system in 1694 in the title of the *Elemens de Botanique* by Joseph Pitton de Tournefort. Only in the 19th cent. did botany gain the comprehensive meaning of all scientific disciplines involving plants [29]. Before this, botany can only be spoken of in a very limited way.

B. Agriculture

In earliest times, human interest in the surrounding flora was focussed on becoming familiar with and collecting edible plants in order to still their hunger. Trees and bushes bearing fruit and berries, as well as types of grass used to feed animals, were thus the first known. The knowledge was also passed on orally by the various waves of Greek tribes which emigrated from Central Europe. No specialist literature for agricultural botany has been preserved, even from Classical Greece. Traces can be found only in Theophrastus, but hardly any names are connected with them [33. 14–30]. Some older information has been included in the *Geoponica* from the 10th cent. AD and in the works of Latin agricultural authors such as Cato, M. Terentius Varro, Columella and Palladius. In his work *De vegetabilibus libri VII*, Albertus Magnus (about 1200–1280) frequently falls back on Palladius, who was well-known throughout the Middle Ages. Then in the 14th cent. in Germany, Gottfried of Franconia refers to him explicitly in describing old and new grafting techniques for achieving better varieties of fruit and wine. His Pelzbuch continued to have major influence in a (to date unedited) Latin and several German editions. In his *Opus ruralium commodorum*, Petrus de Crescentiis (about 1233 – about 1320) also drew from numerous ancient agricultural works, e.g. that of Palladius, and from his own experience as a country landowner. Other Latin treatises (ed. KIEWISCH) are based more on personal experience than on the reception of ancient texts.

C. Medicine and Pharmacy

The second most important significance for plants was in medicine. However, before Hippocrates who, like Diocles of Carystus later, placed great value on diet, we have no written medical lore. According to W. Jaeger [31. 164, 181–185], the *Rhizotomika* of Diocles was the first, evidently groundbreaking work in pharmacological botany, which presumably was used tacitly by Theophrastus (Hist. pl. Book 9) as well as by Dioscorides, Nicander, and Pliny (cf. [39]). Jaeger took Diocles to be a Peripatetic who lived *c.* 340–260 BC. We do not know whether, as a probable contemporary, he had a closer connection with Aristotle (384–322 BC). From Crateuas, who worked about 100 BC at the court of Mithridates VI, we are aware of only ten fragments from the famous illustrated Greek codex of Dioscorides from 512, prepared for the imperial daughter Julia Anicia, which was donated from the library in Constantinople to the imperial court library in Vienna; they are probably from the scientific ϱιζοθομιχόν and not from the popular herbal with coloured illustrations. In the 1st cent. AD, the Greek physician Pedanius Dioscorides, who used Crateuas as a source, provided many good descriptions along with the discussion of plants as drugs in his pharmacopoeia de *materia medica* (περὶ ὕλης ἰατρικῆς) in five books. As the so-called *Dioscorides Longobardus*, the work is preserved in the vulgar Latin form of the 6th cent. in the Codex Latinus Monacensis 337 in Munich. The second Latin translation in alphabetical order was attributed to Constantinus Africanus (2nd half of the 11th cent.) and revised by Petrus de Abano in the 14th cent. Together with the Greek text first published in Venice [36. 69ff.] in 1499, it then formed the basis for pharmacological instruction (*materia medica*) at medieval universities and was frequently commented in Latin, e.g. by Valerius Cordus in 1561. In its dispute with the botanical information of Dioscorides, botany developed into an independent science from the 16th cent. on. His second work *De simplicibus medicamentis* (περὶ ἁπλῶν φαρμάκων), on the other hand, encompassed only two books and had little effect. Dioscorides was a contemporary of Plinius Secundus (AD 23–79); in the latter's *Naturalis historia* many books are filled with all types of botanical knowledge. Pliny's encyclopaedia was very well-known, particularly after the 12th cent., at first in the form of epitomes, such as the *Defloratio naturalis historiae Plinii* of Robert of Cricklade [first edition: *Roberti Crikeladensis Defloratio Naturalis Historie Plinii Secundi*, BODO NÄF (ed.), 2002], furthermore through numerous publications after 1469 [36. 80], commentaries, and Renaissance works both in support of and in opposition to it. [36. 81–86].

D. Pure Botany

We have only 147 fragments of Aristotle's lost work on plants, which he himself quotes for comparison in some places in the *Historia animalium* and other works. Theophrastus of Eresus (372–285 BC) on the island of Lesbos was a Peripatetic and direct student of Aristotle. He appears to have already possessed botanical knowledge before meeting Aristotle, but it was their daily interaction that enabled him to represent his views systematically in two works. These are a) his botany corresponding to the Aristotelian zoology (*Historia plantarum*) and b) the causes of plants (*De causis plantarum*), which according to Wöhrle [40. 11] corresponds to Aristotle's work *De generatione animalium*. With these two works, Theophrastus became the founder of a scientific botany.

G. Senn [37] arrived at the view – not accepted by scholars – that Botany was compiled from approximately nine individual works of Andronicus about 80 BC, while Wöhrle [40] demonstrates that each book fits well into the plan of the complete work. The organization of a) is [40. 2–3] as follows: Book 1, ch. 1–4: Definition of plant parts and general statements about the most important of them, as well as distinguishing contrasting pairs, such as fruit-bearing and nonfruit-bearing, coniferous and deciduous. At the same time, Theophrastus not only defines many terms precisely, but also creates new terms [37]. Furthermore, the influence of a plant's location on its habitus and characteristics are discussed. Ch. 5–14: The differentiation (διαφοραί) of the parts into trunk or stem, bark, wood, pith, leaves, roots, etc., taking into account the most important types of plants (tree = δένδρον, shrub = θάμος, undershrub = φρύγανον, herb = πόα). 'The tree is considered the ideal case, as the 'model' for the discussion of plants' [40. 149–153]. Book 2, ch. 1–4: The (non sexual) reproduction of various types of plants (the μέγιστα εἴδη). Ch. 5–8: The cultivation and care of 'domestic' (ἥμερα), i.e. fruit-bearing trees (δένδρα). Book 3: The 'wild' (ἄγρια) trees and shrubs. Book 4: The occurrence of trees and other plants in various locations, also discussing plants in lakes, rivers and oceans (cf. [40. 105–108]). In Hist. pl. 4,4,4, Theophrastus describes the Indian banyan (*Ficus bengalensis*) with its mighty aerial roots based on reports from Alexander's expedition [30]. The lifespan of plants, diseases and other negative influences on plants are also discussed [34. 107–120]. Book 5: The various types of wood and their use. Books 6–8: The undershrubs and herbs in detail, including the cereals in Book 8. Book 9: Plant fluids, but also the production of balsam, resin and pitch, as well as the medical-pharmaceutical use of plant parts. b) The work on plant physiology deals with the motive causes of botanical reproduction in six books and is organized as follows [40. 43–46]: Book 1: The types of reproduction, annual sprouting, and fructification. Book 2: The influences of nature, particularly wind, rain and soil conditions, on sprouting and fructification. Books 3–4: The influence of humans on the plants they cultivate. Book 5, ch. 1–7: Uninfluenced, unnatural processes and human efforts for specific results, such as seedless fruit. Ch. 8–18: Plant diseases and plant death. Book 6: The origin of plant fluids and their taste and odour as influenced by location.

In both works, Theophrastus demonstrates thorough botanical knowledge, both theoretical and practical. He knew the agricultural procedures for growing plants [40. 46–51] as well as the various qualities of standard commercial types of wood. Also striking – as with Aristotle in regard to animals – is his excellent geographical knowledge of plants. However, he would not admit the sexuality of plants, i.e. the necessity of pollinating the female style with pollen from the male stamen to produce seeds and fruit. Though he, he had actually been on the track of this process, which paral-

lels animal reproduction based on the artificial pollination of table figs and date palms (Caus. pl. 2,9 and 3,18), he was nonetheless wary of a corresponding generalization [35. 141–194, 166–169]. The work *De plantis* by Nicolaus of Damascus (1st cent. BC) in two short books was long considered to be the lost Aristotelian work. In the Occident, at first, it was of influence only in its incomplete Latin translation (about 1200) from the Arabic by Alfredus Anglicus (de Sareshel) and was translated into Greek from this 100 years later by an unknown Byzantine. Authors of Latin natural history encyclopaedias (13th–15th cent.) occasionally cited it under the name of Aristotle. Following a discussion of the difference in how life is expressed in plants and animals, the author reviews the components of plants, such as wood, pith and bark, parallels the shedding of leaves in winter with the change of coat in some animals, and discusses the differences of plants in their morphological development, their locations, and their reproduction, as in part dependent on humans and meteorological influences. Some types of plants are named as examples.

E. Astrology and Magic

From the Byzantine period there are smaller works extant in which certain plants, such as the mandrake, are interpreted and applied in magical ways [38]. This section includes the translation into Latin of the *Cyranides*, which are cited, for example, around the middle of the 13th cent. by Thomas of Cantimpré in his *Liber de natura rerum*, and the related *Compendium aureum*. → Columella; → Diocles [6] of Carystus; → Pedanius Dioscurides

SOURCES: 1 M. Catonis de agricultura, A. MAZZARINO (ed.), 1962 2 W. D. HOOPER, H. B. ASH, Marcus Porcius Cato, On agriculture, Marcus Terentius Varro, On agriculture, 1934 3 O. SCHÖNBERGER, M. P. CATO, Vom Landbau, Fragmente, lateinisch-deutsch, 1980 4 Pedani Dioscuridis Anazarbei de materia medica, ed. princeps Venedig, Manutius, Juli 1899 (M. WELLMANN (ed.), 3 vol., 1907–1914, repr. 1958) 5 Dioskurides' Arzneimittellehre, J. BERENDES (trans.), 1902, repr. 1970 (see 7) 6 K. HOFMANN, T. M. AURACHER (later H. STADLER), Der Longobardische Dioskorides des Marcellus Virgilius, 1883–1903, in: Romanische Forschung 1, 49–105; 10, 181–247 und 372–446; 11,1–121; 13, 161–243; 14, 602–636 7 DIOSCORIDES, De materia medica, ed. princeps, Colle, Medemblik, Juli 1478 (Eng.: The Greek Herbal of Dioscorides, trans. JOHN GOODYER, AD 1655; edited and first printed, AD 1933, by ROBERT T. GUNTHER. 1959) 8 VALERIUS CORDUS, Annotationes in Pedacii Dioscoridis Anazarbei de medica materia libros V, ed. C. GESNERUS, Straßburg, J. RIBEL, 1561 (see 7) 9 Pedani Dioscuridis ... De simplicibus medicamentis, M. WELLMANN (ed.), Vol. 3, 151–317 (see 7) 10 R. ANKENBRAND, Das Pelzbuch des Gottfried von Franken, Untersuchungen zu den Quellen, zur Überlieferung und zur Nachfolge der mittelalterlichen Gartenliteratur, (Dissertation Heidelberg) 1970 11 G. EIS, Gottfrieds Pelzbuch, 1944, Ndr. 1966 12 Nicolai Damasceni de plantis libri duo Aristoteli vulgo adscripti. Ex Isaaci ben Honayn versione arabica Latine verfit Alfredus, (ed.) E. H. F. MEYER, Leipzig 1841 13 H. J. DROSSA-

ART LULOFS, E. L. J. POORTMAN, NICOLAUS DAMASCE-
NUS, De plantis. Five translations, 1989 (Aristorteles semi-
tico-latinus), 465–561 (Latin edition), 563–648 (Greek
edition) 14 Theophrasti Eresii opera, ed. princeps in: Aristoteles, Opera, vol. 3, Venedig, Manutius, 29. Januar
1497 (Eng.: De causis plantarum, (eds.) B. EINARSON and
G. K. K. LINK Harvard, 1976–1990= Loeb Classical Library, Vols. 471, 474–475) 15 A. HORT, Theophrastus
Enquiry into Plants, 2 vols., 1916 16 K. SPRENGEL, Theophrasts Naturgeschichte der Gewächse, 2 vols., 1822,
repr. 1971 (see 14) 17 Theophrasti c. plant., F. WIMMER
(ed.), 165–319 (see 14) 18 Albertus Magnus de vegetabilibus libri VII, E. MEYER, C. JESSEN (eds.), Berlin 1867
19 Geoponica sive Cassiani Bassi Scholastici de re rustica,
H. BECKH (ed.), Leipzig 1895 20 Lucius Iunius Moderatus Columella, Zwölf Bücher über Landwirtschaft,
Buch eines Unbekannten über Baumzüchtung, lateinisch-
deutsch, W. RICHTER (ed.), 3 vols., 1981–83 (Eng.: On
Agriculture, with a Recension of the Text and an English
Translation, H. B. ASH (ed.), rev. ed. 1968 = Loeb Classical Library, vols. 361, 407–408) 21 S. KIEWISCH, Obst-
bau und Kellerei in lateinischen Fachprosaschriften des
14. und 15. Jahrhunderts, (Dissertation Hamburg) 1995 =
Würzburger medizinhistorische Forschungen, Vol. 57
22 KRATEUAS, Fragmente, M. WELLMANN (ed.), in: Dioscorides, vol. 3, 144–146 23 Palladii Rutilii Tauri Aemi-
liani Opus agriculturae, De veterinaria medicina, De insi-
tione, R. H. RODGERS (ed.), 1975 (Palladius on husbon-
drie. From the Unique MS. of About 1420 AD in Col-
chester Castle, B. LODGE (ed.), 1873–1879) 24 PETRUS
DE CRESCENTIIS, Opus ruralium commodorum, ed. princeps Augsburg, Schüssler, 16. Februar 1471: Ruralia com-
moda. Das Wissen des vollkommenen Landwirts um
1300, Teil 1 (Einleitung mit Buch IIII), W. RICHTER (ed.),
1995 (= Editiones Heidelbergenses 25) 25 C. PLINIUS
SECUNDUS Naturalis historia, ed. princeps Venedig J.
SPIRA, 1469 (ed.) I. IAN, C. MAYHOFF, (eds.) 5 vols., 1892–
1909, repr. 1967 (Pliny the Elder's Natural History, H.
RACKHAM (trans.), 1938–1963= Loeb Classical Library,
vols. 330, 352–352, 370–371, 392–394, 418–419)
26 Textes latins et vieux français relatifs aux Cyranides, L.
DELATTE (ed.), 1942 27 M. WELLMANN, Die Fragmente
der sikelischen Ärzte Akron, Philistion und des Diokles
von Karystos, 1901 (new edition by P. VAN DER EIJK in
preparation) 28 F. WIMMER, Phytologiae Aristotelicae
fragmenta, 1838

LITERATURE: 29 W. BARON, Gedanken über den
ursprünglichen Sinn der Ausdrücke Botanik, Zoologie
und Biologie, in: G. RATH, H. SCHIPPERGES (eds.), Medi-
zingeschichte im Spektrum (= Sudhoffs Archiv, Beiheft 7),
1–10 30 H. BRETZL, Botanische Forschungen des Alex-
anderzuges, 1903 31 W. JAEGER, Diokles von Karystos,
1938 32 F. KLUGE, s.v. Botanik, Etymologisches Wörterbuch der deutschen Sprache, 93ff. 33 E. H. F. MEYER,
Geschichte der Botanik, vol. 1, Königsberg 1854 34 G. B.
ORLOB, Frühe und mittelalterliche Pflanzenpathologie,
in: Pflanzenschutz-Nachrichten Bayer, 26. Jahrgang
1973/Heft 2 (Eng.: Ancient and Medieval Plant Pathology, 1973) 35 O. REGENBOGEN, Eine Forschungsmethode
antiker Naturwissenschaft. (1930), in: KS, F. DIRLMEIER
(ed.), 1961 36 G. SARTON, The Appreciation of Ancient
and Medieval Science during the Renaissance (1450–
1600), 1955 37 R. STRÖMBERG, Theophrastea. Studien
zur botanischen Begriffsbildung, 1937 38 M. H.
THOMSON, Textes grecs inedits relatifs aux plantes, 1955

39 M. WELLMANN, Das älteste Kräuterbuch der Griechen,
in: Festschrift F. Susemihl, Leipzig 1898, 2–23   40 G.
WÖHRLE, Theophrasts Methode in seinen botanischen
Schriften, 1985.   CHRISTIAN HÜNEMÖRDER

Bücher-Meyer Controversy, the
A. INTRODUCTION   B. HISTORICAL AND POLITI-
CAL PRE-CONDITIONS   C. BÜCHER'S THEORY OF
ECONOMIC DEVELOPMENT   D. EDUARD MEYER'S
VIEW OF THE ECONOMY IN ANTIQUITY   E. AGREE-
MENT AND CRITICISM – SUBSEQUENT
CONTRIBUTIONS TO THE DISCUSSION

A. INTRODUCTION
The debate that went on between 1893 and 1902
over the basic features of the economy in Classical Antiquity is referred to in more recent scholarly historical
literature, both in Ancient History as well as the history
of the discipline, as the Bücher-Meyer Controversy
(BMC). The origin of this discussion was the publication in 1893 of a book entitled *Die Entstehung der
Volkswirtschaft* ('Industrial Evolution', 1907) by the
economist Karl Bücher promulgating the view that a
dominance of a home economy was characteristic of
Classical Antiquity. At the third meeting of German
historians in Frankfurt in 1895, historian Eduard
Meyer took a detailed stand vis-à-vis Bücher's thesis in
a lecture entitled *Die wirtschaftliche Entwicklung des
Altertums* ('Economic Development in Antiquity'), in
which he emphasised the modernity of the economic
conditions in those times. The historical significance of
the BMC for scholars lies essentially in the fact that
Meyer's position, despite critical objections by individual historians in the field, was widely accepted and left
its stamp on economic studies of Antiquity well into the
years following World War II; as recently as 1972,
Meyer's work was recognised by Karl Christ as having
the 'status of a definitive synthesis'.

B. HISTORICAL AND POLITICAL PRE-CONDI-
TIONS
Eduard Meyer's exceedingly sharp criticism of
Bücher's theories on the history of economics can be
understood only against the background of the
methods debate among German historians and the education policy after 1890. Shortly before 1895, the
attempt of Karl Lamprecht in his *Deutsche Geschichte*
to realise a new conception of historiographic presentation through the reception of sociological theories of
varying origins and through the inclusion of both the
material and the intellectual culture of a people were
met with rejection by many historians; the prevailing
view at that time was expressed by Georg von Below in
1893 in a critical review in which he accuses Lamprecht
of having neglected the political history while at the
same time he (Below) affirmed the primacy of the history of political events: 'from a work of history we just
want to learn what happened and to be informed about
political events and persons'. Politically important was

the fact that Below called Lamprecht an 'adherent of the materialistic and physiological way of viewing history that is now flourishing', thereby making him appear as an outsider in the rather more conservative fraternity of historians. For Classical Studies at this time the outcome and consequences of the School Conference of 1890 were sobering: the number of (weekly) instruction hours in Greek and Latin had been reduced as well as those in Ancient History within the overall subject of history. That Wilhelm II himself had supported these changes was felt to be especially problematic. In the opinion of the classical historian Robert von Pöhlmann, the challenge in this situation was to emphasise the topicality of Classical Studies and their relevance for the present, on the one hand, and, on the other, to reject any model of a socialist interpretation of Antiquity. Revealing for an evaluation of the BMC is the fact that Pöhlmann dismissed the notion that humanity passes through 'certain stages in accordance with a strict law of history' as the 'historical dogma' of socialist scholarship. Under these conditions, historians of Classical Antiquity could not be interested in approving a theory that postulated economic primitivity in ancient times based on the idea of economic stages.

C. BÜCHER'S THEORY OF ECONOMIC DEVELOPMENT

Bücher's remarks were directed primarily against theoretical assumptions of the historical school of German national economy; he attempted to show that the categories derived from modern economics could not be applied to earlier economic periods, but that national economy is instead a product of historical development. To distinguish the economy of previous epochs, Bücher assumes the economic stages: closed home economy, city economy, and national economy. The postulation of such economic stages is for him an 'indispensable methodological tool'. Characteristic of the closed home economy, in Bücher's view, is the fact that 'the entire economic cycle, from production to consumption, takes place in the closed sphere of the home', so that 'production of goods and consumption of goods' merge. Identification of this economic stage with the economic conditions in Greece, Carthage and Rome was decisive for the ensuing debate. Drawing support from the works of Johann Karl Rodbertus, Bücher was easily able to list an array of arguments for his theory; especially important was reference to the distinct tendency to self-sufficiency on the big Roman estates; the existence of long-distance trade is not denied, but in Bücher's view this trade was limited to 'rare natural products' and handcrafted commodities of high value and was therefore largely insignificant for the economic structure: 'Impetus and direction for every single economy always come from the needs of its members; it must produce whatever it can produce itself to satisfy those needs'.

D. EDUARD MEYER'S VIEW OF THE ECONOMY IN ANTIQUITY

For his lecture in Frankfurt, Meyer chose an economic-historical topic because he believed that in this way the 'significance, which even now in the present contains a correct understanding of the problems which affect ancient history, could emerge clearly', and because he wanted to 'combat as erroneous' the views formulated by Rodbertus and Bücher, which in his opinion were 'an obstacle in the way of a correct understanding not only of Antiquity but also of historical development in the world in general'. Basic to Meyer's view of history was the idea that the Homeric Age in Greece could be conceived as the 'Greek Middle Ages'. Since the beginning of colonisation, then, according to Meyer, maritime trade developed and, as a result, an 'industry working for export'; at the same time, slave labour and a money economy gained in significance. In the Aegean realm, 'distinct trade- and industrial cities existed everywhere', the policies of Athens were 'completely governed by commercial interests', and because of its local textile production, Megara appears as an 'industrial state' in Meyer's writings. As such conclusions show, Meyer saw clear parallels between economic development in antiquity and that of modern times; he even postulates direct correspondences between the two periods: 'In their development, the seventh and sixth centuries in Greek history correspond to the fourteenth and fifteenth cents AD in modern times; the fifth to the sixteenth'. Recapitulating, Meyer says of Hellenistic Greece that 'in every respect this epoch cannot be thought of as modern enough', that to all intents and purposes it can be compared to our 17th and 18th cents. The causes of the collapse of the Roman Empire are to be found, according to Meyer in a general disintegration, in a cultural decline rather than in economic factors, among which, however, the 'growth of big business' and the 'full development of capitalism' are specifically noted; they led to the ruin of the rural population and, in the end, to the destruction of prosperity and culture. With the return in Late Antiquity to a barter economy, however, the 'cycle of development in Antiquity' is again completed. Eduard Meyer argued this complex of topics once again in 1898, in his lecture *Die Sklaverei im Altertum*, in which he repeated his criticism of Bücher's theses. Here, too, he was essentially concerned about the reference to present time: 'And so it is only natural that economic development in Antiquity is granted only a historic interest today; if its conditions were truly fundamentally different from ours in this respect, then it would be self-evident that our times can no longer learn anything from them'.

Meyer's remarks are based largely not on his own research but rather follow most notably the views of Büchsenschütz, who as early as 1869 described extensively the expansion of commerce and industry in the post-Homeric period and specifically pointed out factors that inhibited the development of trade and industry, as for example widespread production for domestic consumption and 'deficiency in the means of transportation'.

E. Agreement and Criticism – Subsequent Contributions to the Discussion

Meyer's modernistic view of Antiquity found concurrence in Julius Beloch, who in his essay *Die Großindustrie im Altertum* (1899) assumed, similar to Meyer, that a number of factories and large firms existed in Athens during the fifth and fourth centuries BC; Italy, according to Beloch, never became 'an actual industrial country'. Bücher's attempt to continue the discussion in his essay *Zur griechischen Wirtschaftsgeschichte* (Festschrift Albert Schäffle, 1901) went largely unnoticed in the field of Ancient History; in a short reply in 1902, Beloch made convincingly clear that data from ancient times pertaining to the custom duties at the port of Piraeus constitute quite sufficient evidence for the volume of exchanged goods in the fifth and fourth centuries BC. Likewise, the considerably expanded version of Bücher's essay (*Beiträge zur Wirtschaftsgeschichte*, 1922) had no further influence on research in the field of Classical Antiquity, despite a number of substantial objections to Meyer's interpretation of the sources.

Nonetheless, other scholars raised critical objections to Meyer's position; here, Ludo Moritz Hartmann must especially be mentioned; in a discussion of the Frankfurt lecture, he emphatically concluded that the view 'that the ancient economy was not essentially different from the modern' contradicts the 'facts that are known'. Hartmann himself was of the belief that no single economic system dominated in Antiquity; rather that 'several types of economy' existed in parallel. Max Weber, finally, who as early as 1896 had expressed the opinion, in clear contradiction to Meyer, that 'little or nothing [could be learned] from the history of Antiquity for the social problems of today', interprets Bücher's remarks in his 1909 article *Agrarverhältnisse im Altertum* as an 'idealised construct of an economic constitution' and at the same time notes the absence of any evidence for the existence of factories in ancient Greece. Summing up, he says that nothing could be 'more dangerous than imagining the conditions of Antiquity as 'modern''. While later authors such as M. Rostovtzeff (1929–30) and W.L. Westermann (1935) in important works took up the theses of Meyer and Beloch and thus influenced our modern image of the economy in ancient times, a reflection of the critical position can be found in the works of Johannes Hasebroek.

After 1970, with growing interest in economic-historical questions, greater attention was once again paid to the BMC. In 1972, Michael Austin devoted a longer section to it in *Économies et sociétés en Grèce ancienne*, and in 1979, Moses Finley, whose concept of ancient economy was strongly influenced by Max Weber and Karl Polanyi, edited the most important contributions of all to the BMC. In the most recent economic-historical research there is no longer any debate about alternative positions like subsistence economy or market production, but rather an attempt to include all the diverse economic forms and their regional and temporal distribution in a differentiated model of the economy in Antiquity.

SOURCES: 1 A. B. Büchsenschütz, Besitz und Erwerb im griechischen Altertum, Halle 1869 2 G. von Below, Rezension von K. Lamprecht, Deutsche Geschichte 1–3, in: HZ 71, 1893, 465–498 3 K. Bücher, Die Entstehung der Volkswirtschaft, 1893 4 R. v. Pöhlmann, Aus Altertum und Gegenwart, München 1895 5 Ed. Meyer, Die wirtschaftliche Entwicklung des Altertums, in: Id., KS 1, 1924, 81–168 6 L. M. Hartmann, Rezension von Ed.Meyer, Die wirtschaftliche Entwicklung des Altertums, in: Zschr. für Sozial- und Wirtschaftsgesch. 4, 1896, 153–157 7 Ed. Meyer, Die Sklaverei im Altertum, in: Id., KS 1, 1924, 171–212 8 J. Beloch, Die Großindustrie im Altertum, in: Zschr. für Social-Wiss. 2, 1899, 18–26 9 K. Bücher, Zur griechischen Wirtschaftsgeschichte, in: Id., Beiträge zur Wirtschaftsgeschichte, 1922, 1–97 10 J. Beloch, Zur griechischen Wirtschaftsgeschichte, in: Zschr. für Social-Wiss. 5, 1902, 95–103; 169–179 11 M. Weber, Gesammelte Aufsätze zur Sozial- und Wirtschaftsgeschichte, 1924 (repr., 1988) 12 J. Hasebroek, Staat und Handel im alten Griechenland, 1928 (repr., 1966) 13 Id., Griech. Wirtschafts- und Gesellschaftsgesch. bis zur Perserzeit, 1931 (repr., 1966) 14 M. I. Rostovtzeff, The Decay of the Ancient World and its Economic Explanations, in: Economic History Review 2, 1929/30, 197–214 15 W. L. Westermann, s.v. Sklaverei, RE Suppl. 6, 894–1068

LITERATURE 16 M. M. Austin, P. Vidal-Naquet, Économies et sociétés en Grèce ancienne, 1972 17 K. Christ, Von Gibbon zu Rostovtzeff, 1972; 18 M. I. Finley (ed.), The Bücher-Meyer Controversy, 1979 19 A. Momigliano, Premesse per una discussione su Eduard Meyer, in: Rivista storica italiana 93, 1981, 384–398 20 M. Mazza, Meyer vs Bücher: Il Dibattito sull'economia antica nella storiografia Tedesca tra otto e novecento, in: Società e storia 29, 1985, 507–546 21 N. Hammerstein (ed.), Deutsche Geschichtswissenschaft. um 1900, 1988 22 W. M. Calder III, A. Demandt (eds.), Eduard Meyer, 1990. HELMUTH SCHNEIDER

Bucolic/Idyll
A. Scope of the Topic B. The Development of Bucolic Poetry during the Renaissance and the Baroque C. Renewal of the Genre of Modern Idyllic Poetry D. Directions of Development in the Idyllic Literature of the 19th and 20th Cents.

A. Scope of the Topic

E.R. Curtius designated Virgil's First Eclogue as a 'Schlüssel zur literarischen Tradition Europas' (key to the literary tradition of Europe) [4]. In order to describe the tradition thus inaugurated we have to begin by justifying why it is identified here with the two concepts, bucolics and idyll. Bucolics (also pastoral poetry) refers to the poetry associated with those poems of Theocritus, authentic or just attributed to him, which evoke a pastoral world. The term idyll, although derived from the designation of the texts of Theocritus as *eidýllia*, must be understood more broadly, namely from the perspective of reception history. Essential is the representation of a limited space, which allows the cultivation of the arts, particularly of poetry and music, and the cultivation of intense human relationships, particularly erotic. Idyllic poetry in this sense can be found already before Theocritus (i.e., in Homer) and developed from the 18th cent. onwards increasingly independent from the pastoral setting. Considering both poetry forms, however, requires the explicit or implicit connection of even the most modern and individualistic idyllic poetry to the ancient models. Decisive for the bucolic-idyllic tradition remains a fundamental structure, which is already present in the ancient models: a tension between the deliberate fictionality of the texts, which shows itself through various signals, and episodes which imitate reality. Since Virgil, the contemporary reality outside the text has often been introduced through allegoric references. Thus in each case an interplay of various textual levels develops, whose unfolding design gains great liberty from the absence of classical normative poetics for this genre which emerged late. However, the ascription of it to the *genus humile*, which has long been established in the various poetics, is important. During the reception history, related ancient motifs from other genres merge with the bucolic elements: the depiction of country life (Virgil's *Georgics*), the praise of simple life (Horace's 2nd *Epode*), the Golden Age (the first book of Ovid's *Metamorphoses*).

B. The Development of Bucolic Poetry during the Renaissance and the Baroque

From the rich variety of the Virgilian bucolics (song, poetry, love, friendship, scenery, myth), ancient bucolics ends in the Carolingian period with references to personal and political states of affairs and problems; and it is with these that it starts again in the 14th cent., albeit without continuity. The absence of a comprehensive Christian transformation of ancient bucolic poetry in medieval literature has complex reasons [5]. The new beginning took its place in the dispute between Latin and Italian as literary languages. In a letter composed as a hexameter eclogue, the grammarian Giovanni di Virgilio asked Dante to leave aside his preference for the *volgare* and celebrate the great contemporary events in Latin and to found with him a community of poets in Bologna, proposals which Dante rejected, also using the form of a Latin eclogue transcribed in the bucolic mode (1319/1320). Boccaccio (1347/1348) adopted this new form of the letter-eclogue and published in 1357 a *Bucolicum carmen* consisting of 16 eclogues. In his work, as in the Petrarch's poetry collection of the same name, the bucolic disguise becomes a medium of political opinion regarding the power struggles in Italy. An evasive move away from political reality led the lyric poet Petrarch to the foundation of an important tradition: bucolic-idyllic solitude poetry. Until well into the 17th cent., the allegorical eclogue remained a favoured form of learned discussion. Particularly influential was

the Carmelite Mantuanus (Baptista Spagnuolo), who has the herdsmen discuss in dialogues a wide range of traditional and current topics in his collection *Adulescentia* (1500). Also in Germany, Latin bucolic poetry of the Reformation (Euricius Cordus, Eobanus Hessus, et al) attests to the close theoretical association of idyll and satire, which would be established by Schiller (*Über naive und sentimentalische Dichtung*, 1795). In a parallel development, eclogues were conceived also in the vernacular, e.g. in French by Pierre Ronsard. A particularly complex example of allegorical bucolic poetry is that of Edmund Spenser's *The Shepheardes Calender* (1579). By dedicating an eclogue to each month in a cycle rich in poetic forms and quotations, Spenser introduced to bucolic poetry the motif of the seasons, central for future idyllic poetry. Added commentaries explicitly point to the existence of current reference levels, which are superimposed to an extent that allows multiple readings of the text. [6. 76–92].

Renaissance bucolics developed vigorously in the forms of the pastoral novel and drama. Most important was the Neapolitan poet and courtier Jacopo Sannazaro [10]. In his prosimetric poem *Arcadia* (1502/04), the first-person narrator Sincero wanders, with unhappy love on his mind, through the charming pastoral country Arcadia, where he shares the life and songs of the shepherds, until the homesick hero is at last brought back to Naples by a nymph. In this poem, clouded by the decline of the Neapolitan kingdom, there are references to the historical situation; at the same time though, the pastoral country acquires a coherent fictional existence, characterized by the beauty of the landscape, by a life of leisure, by concentration on love and singing. The name 'Arcadia', which is reminiscent of Virgil's repeated mention of this region as the home of singing, will become from now on the code name for an artistic and textual world situated at the margins of the empirical. With this meaning it appears in Tasso's *L'Aminta* (1573), a drama close to tragedy, about the turning of an Amazon-like shepherdess to love. Its famous choral song on the Golden Age of free love places Arcadia close to blessed primordial times. Guarini's *Pastor fido* (1590) presents an antithetic answer to Tasso's ideal of erotic liberty. Together with the dramas and operas promoted by court culture, numerous pastoral poems and novels would be created during the following two centuries. In the structure of the latter, bucolic love troubles are entwined with the intrigues of adventure novels and with political allegories. The most important are: Jorge de Montemayor's *Siete libros de la Diana* (1559), Miguel de Cervantes Saavedra's *Galatea* (1585), Lope de Vega's *Arcadia* (1598), Philip Sidney's *Arcadia* (1590/93) and Honoré d'Urfés *Astrée* (1607/27). The *Schäferromane* (pastoral novels) translated into German in the 17th cent. contributed to the connection of German literature to European; compared with the latter, the late independent production of novels in Germany attained only limited importance. In contrast, the newly developing Christian bucolic poetry, not only in the Spanish lyric of Juan de la Cruz which was inspired by the Song of Songs, but also in the intimate Christ poems of his German disciple, Friedrich Spee von Langenfeld, reached a high point. The superimposition of the pastoral world on the empirical took place until the end of the 18th cent., also in a real way: in the court performances of pastoral plays and operas, as well as in the poetic societies. The strong presence of bucolic motifs in the cultural life, however, brought about a trivialization which contributed to the necessity of a renewal of this poetic genre.

C. Renewal of the Genre of Modern Idyllic Poetry

The renewal started in France, in the context of the → Querelle des Anciens et des Modernes. In his *Discours sur l'Eglogue* (1688), Bernard de Fontenelle demanded for the contemporary author the right to adapt his depiction of the pastoral world to the modern taste. However, he still maintained an idealization justified by the placement of the pastoral life in a more perfect, primordial time. The first decades of the 18th cent. are marked by the dispute between those who defended what should remain in principle a fictional Arcadia and the advocates of a stronger presence of elements that imitate reality [11]. The latter came especially from England, where in 1713, in *The Guardian*, an extensive discussion about the orientation of pastoral poetry could be read. Motivating the demand for the introduction of local elements were a new sensibility toward nature and a growing awareness of the real life of the country people. However, their misery becomes noticeable precisely when they are entering Arcadia. The impossibility of such an integration was the main argument of those who insisted on fictionalisation. The revaluing of work in the Protestant countries weakened the old bucolic component of leisure and allowed the influence of the *Georgics* on the idyll to become stronger, as the influential poem *Die Alpen* (1729) by Albrecht von Haller shows. The tangled literary situation was decisively changed by the idyllic poetry of Salomon Gessner (1756; 1772), which, unusually quickly and successfully translated into numerous languages, defined the image of bucolic-idyllic poetry until the end of the century. Gessner participated in the new, specifically German, enthusiasm for Antiquity, which, compared with the traditional scholarly conception of Classical literature, aimed at a more lively understanding of it. His model is Theocritus, who, misunderstood as the original poet of nature, became in the last decades of the 18th cent. the guiding star of the renewed idyllic poetry. Thus the term idyll, which refers back to Theocritus, grammatically constructed as feminine from a plural form, prevailed against competing designations and influenced poetical practice through its misinterpretation as 'small image'. Gessner created variations on the form used by Theocritus in musical prose. Coming from the school of ancient bucolics, he drew up a pastoral world, still indicated as fictional by the use of Greek names,

gods and topography, whose inhabitants show, however, a contemporary sensibility toward nature and morality. With the new type of literary text that he created, the relations between the textual levels changed. Whereas in classical bucolic poetry the references to the extra-textual world were made by single elements imitating reality and by allegorical pointers, the latter now fade away and the potential political content is mainly conveyed implicitly. Thus the social structure of Gessner's idyllic world reveals a communal existence of persons of more or less equal status, among whom friendship and helpfulness dominate and the difference between the sexes plays a minor role. Although modern episodes of labour and family are now integrated [3], there is space left for love, song, conversation and story telling. Thus a world is built that stands in contrast to the luxury of the courts and cities as well as to aggressive heroism.

The implicit process allows readers to interpret the idyllic world either as a stimulus toward social change or just as an enticement to evasion – a vagueness which stimulated scholarly discussions, particularly during the 1970s and 1980s. With his classicistic bucolic paintings, Gessner continued the tradition of pastoral painting (Figs. 1 and 2), which started in Italy, and had under the influence of Sannazaro's *Arcadia* and the *Rural Concert*, earlier attributed to Giorgione but now mostly to Tizian, and Poussin's *Les Bergers d'Arcadie,* created perfect images of the ideal Arcadia. In *Faust II* it is shaped once more into great poetic form. In Goethe's diverse idyllic poetic works the close relation to Antiquity repeatedly emerges. With the hexameter poem *Hermann and Dorothea* (1797), he tries to regenerate – in the reduced form of the idyll – the former epic shaping of the fates of the world. The contrast laid bare here between the quiet, small town life and the fundamental upheaval brought about by the consequences of the French Revolution owes its nature to a model linked to Virgil's first eclogue. Because of his political implications, Virgil is, together with Theocritus and Homer, important for Johann Heinrich Voss, for a long time the most popular German author of idyllic poetry. In his early work, replete with social criticism, Voss, an aggressive promoter of the Enlightenment, utilized the hexameter to emphasize the barbaric character of feudal dominance by means of the bucolic model, as André Chenier did by using ancient scenery (*La Liberté*, 1787). On the other hand, in Voss's descriptions of country and bourgeois life (*Luise*, 1795) the Classical model strengthens the illusion of his contemporary readers that here a new humane culture was already in existence

D. Directions of Development in the Idyllic Literature of the 19th and 20th Cents.

The opening up of settings and occupations, explicitly legitimated around 1800 by Herder and Jean Paul, became decisive for the further development of the idyll. This favoured the variety of a more encompassing form of the idyll, allowing its instrumentalisation for the presentation of more complex themes. Thus the authors could compensate for their dissatisfaction with the limitations of the bucolic-idyllic subject matter, which caused Schiller to argue that instead of leading people back to an 'Arcadia' of simple ways of life, the idyll should lead them forward, into the 'Elysium' of greatest development. From the abundance of examples only a few characteristics can be indicated here which reveal, how much the bucolic models remained in the awareness, despite all modern liberties. Even though rural life was now depicted with realism, emphatically free of illusion, this is precisely what often evokes the background of the earlier bucolic poetical depictions. Variously enhanced by modern attributes, the *locus amoenus* and other characteristics of the idyll reappeared in the peasant world (Balzac, George Sand, Jeremias Gotthelf, George Eliot). Particularly in the argument against modernity, protected spaces are evoked as counterimages: gardens, small towns, cozy corners in big city neighbourhoods (Dickens, Hugo, Zola, Keller, Raabe and others). Their endangerment and destruction is a constant topic of the 19th cent.; however the destruction does not come only from the outside, but also from the tensions born in a small enclosed world. Since Romanticism, growing psychological acumen finds in the layout of such realms a form for the description of narcissistic or morbid states of mind (Tieck, Stifter, Tennyson). In lyric poetry the Petrarchistical idyll of solitude unfolded again, a solitude that became the origin of reflection and art (Leopardi, Mörike, C.F. Meyer, Pascoli). As a modern eclogue poet, Baudelaire observed closely the awaking city in the form of the programmatic poem of his *Tableaux parisiens* (1857 and [complete] 1861), but he also constructed within the lyric a topical idyllic world.

In the 20th cent. the position of bucolic-idyllic poetry is closely connected to historical events and mentality transformations, particularly in Germany. The instrumentalisation of the love of nature and of rural poetry by National Socialist ideology (→ NATIONALSOCIALISM) left behind a distrust of the idyll as an expression of an evasive, if not an entirely conformist attitude. This situation changed, at least in literary studies, during the left wing intellectual movement of the 1960s, when the political potentialities of the bucolic-idyllic counterimages were discovered. The genre, disregarded for some time – not least because of its trivialization during the 19th cent. – benefited from the new ecological impetus. However, more important for its persistence is the almost 'quiet' practice, as it were, of idyllic writing, from Léon-Paul Fargue to Philippe Jacottet, from the miniatures of Robert Walser to Musil's *Bildern*. Peter Handke and Gerhard Meier developed in their idyllic prose a new interplay of textual levels from the tension between enclosed space and comprehensive reflection and fantasy, both related at the same time fictionally and to the extratextual world.

→ Bucolics; → Vergilius
→ ARCADIANISM

1 K. BERNHARDT, Idylle. Theorie, Geschichte, Darstellung in der Malerei 1750–1850, 1977   2 R. BÖSCHENSTEIN-SCHÄFER, Idylle, 1977   3 Id., Arbeit und Muße in der Idyllendichtung des 18. Jahrhunderts., in: G. HOFFMEISTER (ed.), Goethezeit, 1981, 9–30   4 E. R. CURTIUS, Europäische Literatur und lateinisches Mittlelalter, 1948, Ch. 10: Die Ideallandschaft (Eng.: European Literature and the Latin Middle Ages (trans. W. R. TRASK), 1953, Ch. 10: The Ideal Landscape)   5 W. SCHMID, Tityrus Christianus, in: K. GARBER (ed.), Europäische Bukolik und Georgik, 1976, 44–121   6 W. ISER, Das Fiktive und das Imaginäre, 1991   7 K. KRAUTTER, Die Renaissance der Bukolik in der lateinischen Literatur des XIV. Jahrhunderts.: von Dante bis Petrarca, 1983   8 B. LOUGHREY (ed.), The Pastoral Mode, 1984   9 R. POGGIOLI, The Oaten Flute, 1975   10 E. A. SCHMIDT, Arkadien: Abendland und Antike, in: A&A 21, 1975, 36–57   11 H. J. SCHNEIDER (ed.), Deutsche Idyllentheorien im 18. Jahrhundert, 1988   12 H. U. SEEBER, P. G. KLUSSMANN (eds.), Idylle und Modernisierung in der europäischen Literatur des 19. Jahrhunderts, 1986   13 W. WEHLE, Arkadien. Eine Kunstwelt, in: W. D. STEMPEL, K. STIERLE (eds.), Die Pluralität der Welten, 1987.

ADDITIONAL BIBLIOGRAPHY: W. L. GRANT, Neo-Latin Literature and the Pastoral, 1965.   RENATE BÖSCHENSTEIN

Bulgaria
A. GENERAL   B. MIDDLE AGES   C. 15TH–17TH CENTS.   D. 18TH–20TH CENTS.

A. GENERAL
The region corresponding to the territory of the modern Republic of Bulgaria had been on the near periphery of the ancient world since the end of the 8th cent. (colonisation) and had, to various extents, been Hellenised, Romanised and, as a hinterland of → BYZANTIUM in Late Antiquity, exposed to strong Byzantine influence. There is no evidence that at this time ethnic and cultural groups of the former indigenous Thracian inhabitants existed to a significant degree.

B. MIDDLE AGES
In the 6th and 7th cents. AD, when first Bulgars, then larger groups of Slavs, later followed by smaller bands of Turkic peoples, all of whom were to some extent already familiar with Byzantine culture, settled in the territory of modern Bulgaria, they came upon a thinly settled, largely Christianised land with a population in which ancient traditions were also continued. Although these were largely destroyed, driven away or assimilated, a number of elements of the ancient culture continued to exist: the Romance linguistic element persisted among the Wallachians, and Greek among the population of the cities of the Black Sea (chiefly Mesambria, Sozopol and also Philippopolis inland). Various ancient elements of the cult and the tradition which had survived Christianisation are still retained in the folklore. Nevertheless, the migrations of the Bulgars and

Slavs meant a new cultural beginning, so that ancient cultural elements had to be reacquired, in part by way of Byzantium.

The Greek language was officially recognised and used by the Bulgarian Khans: the inscriptions described as 'Proto-Bulgarian' are all in good contemporary Greek; imported with them were terms relating to the state. Greek was widely disseminated among the higher classes of the Slavonic Bulgarian state after Christianisation under Tsar Boris I (from 864). The Latin language was little known and experienced only a short flourishing between 866 and 870, when Roman clerics came to the country. So far three Latin inscriptions have been found, in Pliska and Preslav.

All higher state and Church dignitaries of the First Bulgarian Kingdom had a Hellenic education. Slavonic literature, which began in the 9th cent. actually strengthened the teaching of Greek in the church schools, because it had to be translated out of Greek. After the parallel use of Bulgarian and Greek in the earliest Old Slavonic literature, the spread of bilingualism at the end of the 9th and in the 10th cents. increased. The true creators of Old Slavonic literature, Brothers Constantine (Cyril, 826/7–869) and Methodius, had received a high level of Greek education in the Magnaura School in Constantinople etc., and also under Photios, who in 850 taught philosophy at the same school. Probably in 855 he created a Slavonic writing system, known as Glagolitic, based on Greek minuscules with the addition of letters for specifically Slavonic phonemes. The Cyrillic alphabet however, which had already developed through the use of Greek uncials in state chanceries before the introduction of Slavonic writing, began to displace Glagolitic towards the end of the 9th cent.; replacement was total in the 10th cent. Old Bulgarian inscriptions are recognised by their mixture of Greek and Glagolitic letters. As a highly educated man, who in the course of the early Byzantine pre-Renaissance knew the Ancient Greek authors and the Byzantine programme of education, Cyril allowed this archaising style to influence his Old Bulgarian writings. It then also influenced Old Bulgarian literature and its language and all the Old Slavonic literatures that developed from it. At the end of the 10th cent. and towards the beginning of the 10th, Old Bulgarian literature developed mainly in the literary schools in Preslav and Ohrid. It flourished during the reign of Tsar Symeon (893–927). Most of the works of these schools were translations of Greek ecclesiastical literature, though original Old Bulgarian books were also written. The most important representatives of this new generation of authors were Kliment Ohridski, Chernorizec Hrabar, the bishop Konstantin Preslavski etc. Tsar Symeon himself was a highly educated man who had also studied in Constantinople and actively supported these schools both with commissions and with his own authorial activities. Through him many important early Byzantine works were disseminated in Old Bulgarian translations covering the whole of Sla-

vonic literature, such as e.g. On Poetic Figures by Georgios Cheiroboscos. At his behest Chernorizec Hrabar wrote collections, compilations and translations of similar Byzantine collected works on e.g. problems of rhetoric, philology, and natural history. He wrote, among other things, a history of the alphabet, in which he showed a very good knowledge of ancient literature and philosophy. Konstantin Preslavski was the author of a short history from the creation of the world up to the year 894, which itself had Byzantine models. In 906 the four 'Speeches Against the Arians' by Athanasius of Alexandria were translated and copied. John Exarch was another representative of the Preslav School, a philosopher, dogmatist, priest, translator, author and poet. The upper educated classes in particular applied themselves to his writings. Problems of ancient natural history and philosophy became better known through his translation of the *Theologia* of John of Damascus. He expounded on his knowledge of ancient pagan writings primarily in his *Shestodnev* Hexameron. The most important model for this was Basil the Great. The description of nature, animals and people was extensively influenced by Aristoteles (hist. an.), even if he worked from the summary by the monk Meletios. In it he mentioned a series of ancient authors, such as Thales, Democritus, Parmenides etc., who do not appear in this version but were added by John Exarch, as were the quotations from Plato. This work became the basis for further development of natural history and anthropology in the Slavonic languages.

Byzantine language and culture had even greater influence in the years 1018–1186, after the first Bulgarian kingdom was destroyed by Basileios II and the territory of what is modern Bulgaria fell to Byzantium. Greek was not only the official language, used predominantly by the Church, which in many places suppressed Slavonic, but also widely used by the people, particularly in urban areas. By placing itself at the service of Byzantium the Bulgarian upper class received an obligatory Greek education. There were Greek schools not only in the cities on the Black Sea coast but in all of the larger cities such as Plovdiv, Vidin, Tarnovo etc. More and more people bought Greek books. From the the Byzantine side also came stirring cultural propaganda against 'barbaric Slavdom'. This massive cultural invasion from Byzantium did encounter resistance however, and a countermovement came into being: in the Old Bulgarian Apocryphal Literature of the time, which was largely dependent on the Byzantine, moments of Bulgarian history were depicted with evident propagandist purposes. Ancient and early Byzantine achievements were not mentioned; everything being ascribed to the Bulgars, such as e.g. the founding of Drastár (Durostorum) etc. During the second Bulgarian kingdom (1186–1393) the recognised cultural standing of Greek education also remained high and developed according to the contemporary Byzantine pattern. The Greek schools continued to be popular among the higher social classes, all the more because in contrast to the purely ecclesiastical Bulgarian schools they also taught secular knowledge: basic natural science and particularly the writings of ancient Greek philosophers. In the library of Bachkovo monastery at the time of the second Bulgarian Kingdom there were also collected editions of ancient Greek literature, e.g. with excerpts of the works of Sophocles and Euripides. There are Greek inscriptions on icons, stone inscriptions and even Greek marginalia in Old Bulgarian manuscripts (Tomichov Psalter from the middle of the 14th cent.). Large parts of the population spoke Greek to some extent: the southern parts of the country were Greek-speaking, and in the churches Greek and Bulgarian were taught and spoken. Outstanding authors of this time, such as Teodosiy Tarnovski, Grigoriy Camblak, Kyprian etc, who were educated and influenced by the Tarnovo School in particular, had full command of the Greek language. Noteworthy in these works, too, are efforts to push individual views and tastes. Following on the growing interest of Byzantium in ancient Greek culture and particularly in ancient Greek philosophy, these evidently received wide circulation in Bulgaria. This is shown by the appearance of their type of rationalism in Bulgarian works (*The Theory of Varlaam and Akindin*) and by the Church's polemic against such occupations (e.g. an anathema from the Synod of Borilov: 'Those who occupy themselves with Hellenic erudition and learn it not only for their education but follow its unreasonable thoughts and hold them to be true (...) and sometimes even draw others to them and instruct them in it: may they be cursed!'). The works of Pseudo-Caesarius, Kosmas Indikopleustes and others, which had been translated by the 8th and 9th cents., received wide circulation in both languages. The Bulgarian Tsars set the trend for this tendency in their own way: Ivan Alexander (1331–1371), for example, owned a significant private library, for which he commissioned works and which contained both Bulgarian translations and Greek originals. One of the most informative of these manuscripts is the Tomichov Gospel. At the wish of the Tsar the story of the Trojan War was added to the Vatican's manuscript of the Manassi Chronicle. Stories of heroic history were generally much loved, and this is shown in the Bulgarian translations of the Greek originals. From Antiquity in particular there were modernised Byzantine versions of the Trojan War and the Romance of Alexander. The latter in the Bulgarian versions bears especially strongly nationalistic traits: the king of Macedonia is portrayed as a Bulgar, and Tsar Ivan Alexander is named 'the second Alexander of the ancient period'. Aesop's fables were also circulated as models for new folklore stories (Hitǎr Petǎr).

Though the first Proto-Bulgarian and Slavonic settlements and buildings were primitive and modest, they changed very quickly with the formation of the Bulgarian Slavonic state. Both under the influence of Byzantine architecture and, no less, under that of chanced upon remains of late Antiquity, urban building developed very quickly (see particularly Preslav and Pliska,

where Late Antiquity building materials come from the nearby cities of Marcianopolis and Nicopolis on the Danube). To decorate the new imposing buildings not only were Hellenistic and Roman buildings (capitals, columns etc.) utilised, but these architectonic elements were also mixed with ones both Byzantine and newly created, so that a unique decorative sculpture came into existence. There was a similar development in monumental sculpture, for which the 9th cent. *The Madara Horseman* is particularly representative: judging by its iconography it is very close to the Thracian equestrian hero from the Imperial period. The art of jewellery similarly adopted both contemporary Byzantine and ancient elements on the basis of an early mediaeval nomadic style, widespread in the Eurasian steppes. By about 864 churches had begun to be built, often on top of pagan sanctuaries, wholly following Byzantine tradition and frequently using late ancient foundations for new buildings. The church of Saint George in Sofia for example, a square domed building with murals from the 9th–10th cents., stands on much older foundations. From time to time such ancient ground plans also influenced the architecture of other churches.

C. 15TH–17TH CENTS.

The Turkish conquest of Bulgaria put an end to the independent development of cultural creativity and education. The clerical and political upper class, if not destroyed, emigrated (mostly to Italy), also taking valuable manuscripts out of the country. The Bulgarian Church was placed under the Patriarch of Constantinople. Whereas Slavonic cultural assets were poorly cared for in some monasteries (by making copies etc.), Greek education was preserved to a limited extent, primarily in the Black Sea cities (particularly Sozopol, Nesebar, and the somewhat smaller Varna), whose inhabitants were mostly Greeks. A book of Pindar's Odes together with *scholia* appeared in 1515; in 1557 one of the tragedies of Aeschylus. Books with works by Aristotle, Thucydides, Apollonius Rhodius and others have been found in these cities. Greek was also spoken and taught in some churches and monasteries in Southern Bulgaria, where the mostly Greek clergy was active. Some interesting murals from the end of the 16th and 17th cents., found in monasteries, show that, despite everything, a living knowledge of the ancient heritage remained intact. The refectory of Bachkovo monastery was decorated in 1643 with murals provided with Greek inscriptions. In addition to various ecclesiastical and religious subjects the composition *The Stem of Jesse* and the depiction of 12 ancient Greek philosophers and poets can be seen here, with names indicated, if not always correctly written. Like Christian saints they are each holding a scroll, on which Greek apocryphal and prophetic inscriptions can be read. Similar depictions can also be seen in the Church of the 'Nativity' in Arbanassi.

In the 16th and 17th cents. Catholic influence in Bulgaria grew, initially in the town of Chiprovci. The

Catholics founded several schools, at which Italian Humanists also taught. Through them the mastery of Latin also spread to a modest extent. The connexion with Italy and the opportunity for younger Bulgarians to acquire a classical education by studying at Italian schools and universities were important. Latin works were written at this time by P. Bogdan, P. Parchevich, and F. Stanislavov. P. Bogdan was the Bulgarian Catholics' most significant leader in the 17th cent. He had studied in Rome and had a command of Latin and Italian. In his work he utilised and cited ancient authors. Furthermore, owing to his interest in ancient inscriptions and sites of ruins, he can be described as the first Bulgarian archaeologist and epigraphist.

D. 18TH–20TH CENTS.

The 'Period of Bulgarian Rebirth' began with the 18th cent. Its roots lie primarily in modern Greek cultural rebirth, which was due to the influence both of the church and of the Greek part of the population in the country. The first libraries and → SCHOOLS of a secular character were Greek, and the mastery of this language again became a prerequisite for a better education. These institutions imparted both ancient Byzantine heritage and ideas of Western Enlightenment. Ancient Greek language and literature were among the obligatory subjects. A great number of leading politicians, authors and journalists of this period went through such schools, e.g. I. Dobrovski, G. Rakovski, Seliminski. With the opening up of their country, rather isolated for so long, Bulgarians went abroad; Russia, France and Austria being the most important countries where young people sought education. N. Bonchev, who was one of the most passionate proponents of classical education in Bulgaria at the time, studied in Russia. Bonchev, Parlichev and others at first translated excerpts from Homeric epic into Bulgarian. Neither was the connexion with Italy broken. For example, the metropolitan Ierotej studied medicine in Padua at the beginning of the 18th cent. before teaching at the Bej Academy in Bucharest. His successor, the metropolitan Athanasis, worked on translations of ancient Greek authors and also brought the writer Palaeologis from Constantinople to teach there. The Academy of *Saint Sava* also played no small role in Bucharest at the beginning of the 18th cent. It was there that Partenij Pavlovich, for example, had heard parts of Aristotelean theory and many influential Bulgarian authors and scholars received their education. Enlightenment scholars such as L. Photiadis, Nikola Pikolo and A. Bogoridi taught Ancient Greek poetry and philosophy there. Sofronij Vrachanski, who translated Aesop's fables into Bulgarian and also introduced readers of the time to ancient Greek philosophy, also studied there. His writings, defined by or borrowing from Greek ones, have had a lasting influence on modern Bulgarian literature. It is characteristic of this period of rebirth that all leaders who had enjoyed a good education saw it their primary task, to raise the general level of education in their country by building schools and publishing newspapers and books in order to give classical education the importance that it enjoyed in other countries. From the 1850s to the 1870s the influence of modern Greek culture and language disappeared because of the struggle by the Bulgarians for the permanent restoration of their autonomous Church. 'Greek' acquired a pejorative sense. Modern Bulgarian literature developed only later and relatively slowly in comparison with that of the other Balkan peoples; this was due on the one hand to the rather long lasting Turkish rule and on the other hand to major geographically conditioned isolation. Since its main themes were national liberation and a glorious past and it borrowed heavily from folklore in its form, fitted itself to the level of education of the people and abandoned Greek elements on account of the ecclesiastical campaign mentioned above, ancient elements were only seldom to be found, although many of the great poets and authors of the period of rebirth had received a classical education. Nevertheless, in some of the works of I. Vazov, G. Rakovski, S. Mihailovski, Pencho Slavejkov and others, assonances and associations with ancient literature were apparent. After spiritual (1870) and political (1878) freedom was obtained, the need for classical education grew rapidly. By the early years Humanist gymnasiums had been founded. At first → SCHOOL TEXTBOOKS were translated (mostly from German), but these were also soon replaced by original compositions. In 1888 a college came into being in which ancient Greek and Latin were taught. Teachers were recruited from abroad to satisfy the additional demand. The Czechs I. Brožka, K. Jireček, the brothers K. and H. Škorpil and Dobruski were primarily responsible for laying the foundations for ancient history and archaeology in Bulgaria. Apart from their teaching activities their painstaking research work also made extraordinarily great advances. In 1921 the college mentioned above became the University of Sofia, at which classical philology was taught from the year of its foundation.

The next generation of teachers and professors was made up of Bulgarian scholars. Classical education continued to spread only because of the schools. In 1937 a journal of classical philology *Prometheus* was founded, which also made ancient culture accessible to other classes of people. Its editor-in-chief was A. Balabanov, a professor of Classical philology, author and translator of several Greek tragedies, lyricists and quite a large part of the Homeric epics and for his time, generally one of the most important figures in the cultural life of Bulgaria. Scholars such as A. Milev, D. Dechev, V. Beshevliev and others wrote textbooks of Classical philology. Thorough research into the early history of Bulgaria on the basis of ancient authors was written primarily by G. Kacarov, J. Todorov and others, driven by the ancient archaeology of B. Filov and I. Velkov. In the spheres of Late Antiquity and the Byzantine period I. Dujchev led the way. This high esteem for the ancient heritage led to every educated Bulgarian learning Greek and Latin.

This influenced literature to a certain extent (in form and aesthetics) until the Second World War.

After the 'Socialist Revolution' abolished the humanistic gymnasiums in 1944, schooling was reformed in accordance with the Soviet model. Work on Antiquity was forced into the background as ideologically irrelevant and even harmful. Research on ancient times was confined to Bulgarian history: Thracians, Proto-Bulgarians and Slavs were in the forefront. Ancient history proper was treated as a backdrop. Although the general availability of Classical education and its influence on culture declined greatly, and despite the isolation of the country, i.e. the absence of opportunities for communication, the lack of scholarly literature and the ideological restrictions, the works of individual scholars of this time were path-breaking, mainly those of the philologists, historians and epigraphists V.Beshevliev, B. Gerov, D. Dechev, G. Mihailov, Chr. Danov and V.Velkov. The study of Classical languages was obligatory only for the study of medicine; the Chair of Classical philology was barely occupied and the field continued to exist with only a minimum of student enrolment. Indeed it was only there that the students learnt Classical languages, and for this they received a very broad introduction to the study of ancient times, which included history, epigraphy, historical grammar, history of culture, history of literature etc. Apart from this chair, ancient studies had only the history of the Thracians and Bulgarians as topics. Collections of sources (*Sources for Bulgarian History, Sources for Thrace and the Thracians*) and numerous series (*Thrakia, Studia Thracica, Terra Antiqua Balcanica* etc) came into being. Only at the beginning of the 1970s did humanistic education again slowly gain a more positive assessment, through numerous initiatives by L. Zhivkova, the daughter of the Communist head of state. An Institute for Thracology (1972) and a Classical Gymnasium (1977) were founded in Sofia, and knowledge of a Classical language became obligatory for the study of history. Greek and Latin authors also began to be translated intensively again. In this connexion the State promoted to a great extent from the beginning archaeological research in an attempt to bring to light the material culture of the past and with it primarily the cultural achievements of the Thracians, Proto-Bulgarians and Slavs. By means of systematic excavations the Greek Cities on the Black Sea (Dionysopolis, Odessos, Anchialos, Mesambria, Apollonia etc.) and inland (Kabyle, Philippopolis etc.), Thracian settlements (Seuthopolis, Sveshtari etc.), Roman cities and forts on the Limes (Oescus, Novae, Durostorum, Iatrus etc.) and in the interior (Abritus, Nicopolis ad Istrum), early Byzantine centres (Marcianopolis, Serdica etc.) and the Old Bulgarian settlements and cities (Pliska, Preslav etc.) were researched. Every city, and even most villages, have an archaeological museum or at least a collection. Since the political change in 1989 humanistic education has again received greater significance, as is evidenced by numerous new translations of Greek and Latin

authors, original works on ancient culture and philosophy and a more noticeable inclusion of ancient elements in contemporary Bulgarian art. At the private *New Bulgarian University* founded in 1992 there is a faculty of ancient history and culture.

→ Alexander Romance; → Alexander [4] the Great; → Bulgari

→ Humanist Gymnasium; → University

1 R. Aitzetmüller, Das Hexameron des Exarchen Johannes, 1958; IV, 1966　2 D. Angelov, Obštestvo i obštestvena misăl v srednovekovna Bălgarija, 1979　3 S. S. Averinčev, Drevneslavjanskie literatury i tradicija ellinizma, in: Slavjanskie kul'tury i Balkany, 1978　4 V. Beševliev, Părvobălgarski nadpisi, 1992　5 Fr. Bakšič, Petri Bogdani episcopi Galliponensis et coadiutoris Sophiensis de statu ecclesiae suae relatio accuratissima. Cum notis cuisdam in margine adposuit E. Fermendzin, Acta Bulgariae ecclesiastica ab anno 1565 usque ad annum 1799. Monumenta spectantia historiam slavorum meridionalium, vol. 18, Zagabriae 1887　6 A. Camariano-Ciorau, Les académies princières du Bucarest et de Jassy et leur professeurs, 1974　7 P. Dinekov, Starobălgarskata literatura I, 1950　8 I. Dujčev, Les débuts littéraires de Constantin Philosophe-Cyrille, in: Slavica 41, 1972, 357–67　9 Id., Klassisches Altertum im mittelalterlichen Bulgarien, in: Renaissance und Humanismus in Mittel- und Osteuropa, 1962　10 Id., Drevnoezičeski misliteli i pisateli v starata bălgarska živopis,1978　11 N. Genčev, Bălgarskoto văzraždane, 1988　12 Id., Bălgarskata Kultura XV–XIX v., 1988　13 V. Gjuzelev, Učilšta, skriptorii, biblioteki i znanija v Bălgarija, XIII–XIV v., 1985　14 Istorija na filosofskata misăl, 1970　15 Izsledvanija v pamet na K. Škorpil, 1961　16 C. Jireček, Beiträge zur antiken Geographie und Epigraphik von Bulgaren und Rumelien, in: Monatsbericht der Königlich Preußischen Akademie der Wissenschaft zu Berlin, 1881　17 D. Kosev (ed.), Istorija na Bălgarija, vol. II, 1981　18 C. Kristanov, I. Dujčev, Estestvoznanieto v srednovekovna Bălgarija, 1954　19 N. Mavrodinov, Starobălgarskoto izkustvo, 1959　20 G. Mihailov, Aleksandăr Balabanov, 1989　21 K. Mijatev, Arhitekturata v sredovekovna Bălgarija, 1965　22 K. Ohridski, Prostranni žitija na Kirili Metodij, in: Săbrani cačinenija, vol. 3, 1973　23 K. Škorpil, Pametnici ot stolica Preslav, in: Bălgarija 1000 godini, 1930　24 M. Stojanov, Livres anciens grecs à la bibliotheque nationale de Bulgare, in: Studia in honorem V.Beševliev, 1978, 96–99　25 E. Teodorov, Drevnotrakijsko nasledstvo v bălgarskija folklor, 1972　26 V. N. Zlatarski, Istorija na bălgarskata dăržava, vol. 1–3, 1918–1940.　Iris von Bredow

Burlesque see→ Adaptation

Byzantine Studies

A. From 1453 to the 18th Cent.　B. 19th and Early 20th Cents.　C. The Most Recent Period　D. Art-Historical Research　E. Museums

A. From 1453 to the 18th Cent.

Soon after the Fall of → Constantinople in 1453, the Ottoman advance stimulated interest among the scholars of Central Europe in Byzantine historians as a source of the history of the Turks. Hieronymus Wolf (1516–1580) had published historical works by Niketas Choniates and Nikephoros Gregoras with precisely this aspect in mind; he was also the first to recognise the intrinsic value of the Byzantine world, fixing its conventional range as the period from Constantine the Great to Constantine XI (1453) and also inventing the term 'Byzantine'. This he did regardless of the fact that the so-called Byzantines had always understood and described themselves as Romans (ῥωμαῖοι). Other stimuli for the study of Byzantine culture, in particular theological matters, arose with the Reformation, and the interest developed by both denominations in Orthodoxy as an opponent or a potential comrade-in-arms.

An elective affinity of European Absolutism with the uniquely Byzantine synthesis of Romanness, imperial authority, Christian nation and religion, had a positive effect on the development of Byzantine Studies (BS), especially in France, Germany and Russia. In Paris in 1648 an appeal was made to the international scholarly community to help compile a complete edition, a *Corpus Byzantinae Historiae*, under the patronage of Louis XIV and Jean Baptiste Colbert. The project had already been started three years earlier, significantly with a historical work by a crowned author, John VI Cantacuzenos (1292–1383). In this Paris Corpus there were 42 volumes in total. The image of the Eastern Roman Empire that is still present in the consciousness of many educated people today and which is limited to the sequence of emperorships and to the medieval imperial capital of Constantinople, was first conceptualised by the jurist Du Cange (1610–1688), one of the collaborators on the Paris Corpus. With his two-part work *Historia Constantinopolitana* he created the first history of the emperors and the first compendium on the development and topography of Constantinople [1]. However, this pioneering achievement also aimed at conferring an historical past on Absolutism. Du Cange projected the ideas of his time about the power of the French monarch and his capital city of Paris on → BYZANTIUM, but scarcely acknowledged the cultural achievements of the Eastern Roman Empire as a mediator of ancient culture and as a world of thought whose own power helped shape Eastern and Southeastern Europe.

Moreover, by compiling a Middle Greek lexicon which incorporated extensive colloquial material from predominantly unedited works available in manuscript form at the Paris Bibliothèque Royale, Du Cange supplemented the *Thesaurus linguae graecae* (→ LEXICOGRAPHY I. GREEK) of H. Stephanus [2]. Scholarly collections of Greek manuscripts, which had been built up by ecclesiastical or secular princes (primarily the Vatican, Paris, London, Venice, Milan, Cambridge, Oxford, Saint Petersburg, Leiden), generally enabled the expansion of BS. At the same time diplomatics (Jean Mabillion, 1632–1707 [3]) and → PALAEOGRAPHY (Bernard de Montfaucon, 1655–1741 [4]) came into being, and these were applied to ecclesiastical and legal historical

sources. Disdain for the Eastern Roman Empire proved persistently influential, on the one hand, with the philosophers of the Enlightenment, who arbitrarily equated Byzantine autocracy with despotism and decline, and on the other hand with the interpreters of world history according to schemes of cultural spheres, who either looked to Byzantium for an identity-forming counterpart to a Europe inspired by Charlemagne, or suspected Byzantium behind the Russian colossus. In this context Edward Gibbon and his *History of the Decline and Fall of the Roman Empire* [5] should be mentioned, and also the ingenious publicist Jakob Philipp Fallmerayer, who believed he had recognised a cultural thread originating in Byzantium and uniting the Orthodox peoples against the West [6]. The negative statements of renowned personalities of the → ENLIGHTENMENT, including a remark by Voltaire about Byzantium as a 'stain on humanity', are legion [7]. It is important to note, however, that such a distorted image was able to emerge because the Byzantine imperial archives, which would certainly have conveyed a more realistic view of *homo byzantinus* than that which had been derived from theological literature, had been lost.

B. 19TH AND EARLY 20TH CENTS.

In any case, the untenable view that Byzantium had been a symbol of cultural decline for a millennium found few adherents among early proponents of → HISTORICISM. In 1828 Barthold Georg Niebuhr (1776–1831), Classical philologist, Classical historian and influential functionary in the up-and-coming state of Prussia, published the works of Agathias, initiating the Bonn *Corpus Scriptorum Historiae Byzantinae*, which was to encompass 50 volumes (in part reprints from the Paris Corpus). The historical critical method, the new opportunities for archival research (Athos monasteries, Venice) and the general political climate together led to a resurgence of BS.

The Humanists' turn to Byzantine themes (unavoidable since access to Greek Antiquity was possible only through Byzantium) had led to Byzantine philology in particular becoming an offshoot of Classical philology and taking over its methods. The organisation and institutionalisation of BS as an independent study of the culture and history of the Eastern Roman Empire was eventually accomplished by Karl Krumbacher (1856–1909). Krumbacher wrote the first history of Byzantine literature [8], founded the scholarly journal of the discipline, the *Byzantinische Zeitschrift* (still a most important journal), which, with great foresight, he arranged according to the organisation of BS, and he turned the world's first university institute for BS (*Institut für Mittel- und Neugriechische Philologie*) that was set up for him in Munich into a centre for international research. Another prime concern of his at the time was the establishment of a corpus of medieval Greek documents; this undertaking took on a more diverse character after the World Wars: in addition to various subprojects, work on the Byzantine imperial documents continued in Munich [9], while members of the Assumptionist Order took on the records of the Constantinople patriarchy [10]. Responsibility for an edition of the documents in the archives of the Athos monasteries was handed over to France [11].

Already in the 19th cent., there was a tendency in Russian BS to construe from Byzantine sources evidence for an alleged early Slavic influence on land distribution in Byzantium, i.e. the early formation of states among Eastern Slavs independent of Byzantium and the Normans (Vasiliy G. Vasilevskiy, 1838–1899) – a trend that could also be observed in Soviet times. The conceptual vocabulary of Marxist BS (→ MARXISM) proved to be inadequate in the 20th cent., simply because it was shaped by feudal conditions, but stress on economic and socio-historical aspects did have a productive effect. In France, the turn to agrarian and socio-historical issues was due to the influence of the Annales School; in the United States this turn resulted from the application of quantitive methods.

C. THE MOST RECENT PERIOD

The 20th cent. boom of BS in the United States was in part precipitated by scholars of European descent emigrating to the US or seeking refuge there, either as established scholars or at a younger age (especially P. Charanis, F. Dvornik, H. Grégoire, E. Kitzinger, A.A. Vasiljev, K. Weitzmann [12]). In addition to engaging in basic research, now as natural for American scholars as it is for those of other cultured nations, it was hoped that BS in the United States would provide better insights into supposedly Byzantine-influenced cultures such as that of Russia. In the countries of Eastern and Southeastern Europe, Byzantine sources have occasionally been interpreted in terms of national history to serve a contemporary political agenda. A greater role and responsibility, particularly for the preservation and the accessibility of the archaeological remains of Byzantine culture has fallen to Byzantine scholars in Turkey.

Fortunate circumstances also helped BS prosper in the 20th cent. Notable examples are the activities of Mildred and Robert Woods Bliss in the United States and Herbert Hungers in Vienna. The culturally-minded Blisses established the → DUMBARTON OAKS Centre in Washington, D.C., furnished it with a rich collection and put it under the control of Harvard University. Dumbarton Oaks has become one of the world's leading Byzantine research institutes [13]. The Classical philologist Hunger came to BS by way of cataloguing the Greek manuscripts of the National Library in Vienna. Against the backdrop of the traditional interest of Austrian scholars in Southeastern Europe he built an Institute for Byzantine and Modern Greek Studies at the University of Vienna and a Commission for BS at the Academy of Sciences there, both of which are producing outstanding achievements in the systematic preparation of sources for the discipline's core areas of philology and the history of thought, but also in its ancillary disciplines.

The international character and the openness of BS is exemplified in the fact that the most significant project to date is now called the *Corpus Fontium Historiae Byzantinae*, and a number of centres in the Old and New World are working on it simultaneously. The diverse initiatives, the firm establishment of BS in the canon of academic subjects worldwide (not least through the flourishing of archaeology and art history [14]), the internationalisation of research and the combination of tradition and modern methodology contribute to an ever more thorough understanding of the fundamentals.

→ Byzantium

SOURCES: 1 C. DU FRESNE DOMINO DU CANGE, Historia Byzantina duplici commentario illustrata, 1: Familiae ac stemmata imperatorum Constantinopolitanarum, 2: Descriptio urbis constantinopolitanae, Paris 1680 (repr. 1964) 2 Id., Glossarium ad scriptores mediae et infimae Graecitatis, Lyon 1688 (repr. 1958) 3 J. MABILLON, De re diplomatica libri VI, Paris 1681 4 B. DE MONTFAUCON, Palaeographia Graeca, Paris 1708 5 E. GIBBON, The History of the Decline and Fall of the Roman Empire, London 1776–1788 (passim) 6 H. SEIDLER, Jakob Philipp Fallmerayers geistige Entwicklung, 1947 7 A. A. VASILIEV, History of the Byzantine Empire, I, ⁵1964, 6–13 8 K. KRUMBACHER, Geschichte der byzantinischen Litteratur, München ²1898 9 F. DÖLGER, Regesten der Kaiserurkunden des Oströmischen Reiches, I–V, 1924–1965 (partially revised by P. WIRTH) 10 V. GRUMEL, Les regestes des actes du Patriarcat de Constantinople, I–VII, 1932–1991 11 P. LEMERLE, Archives de l'Athos, 1937ff. 12 K. WEITZMANN, Sailing with Byzantium from Europe to America: The Memoirs of an Art Historian, 1995 13 http://www.doaks.org 14 http://www.gzg.fn.bw.schule.de/lexikon/byzanz/contents.htm

LITERATURE: 15 H.-G. BECK, Kirche und theologische Literatur, ²1970, 7–23 16 G. OSTROGORSKY, Geschichte des byzantinischen Staates, ³1963, 1–18 (Eng.: History of the Byzantine State, 1969; rev. ed., 1999) 17 E. HÖSCH, s.v. Byzanz, in: Sowjetsystem und demokratische Gesellschaft, I, 1966, 972–984 18 La filologia medievale e umanistica greca e latina nel secolo XX (Atti del Congresso Internazionale ... Roma 1989), 1993 19 O. MAZAL, Handbuch der Byzantinistik, 1988, 7–22 20 R.-J. LILIE, Byzanz. Kaiser und Reich, 1994, 258–271 21 P. SCHREINER, Byzanz, ²1994, 98–113 22 F. TINNEFELD, Byzantinistik im deutschen Sprachbereich, in: Das Mittelalter 2, 1997, 178–180

ADDITIONAL BIBLIOGRAPHY: Society for the Promotion of Byzantine Studies (http://www.byzantium.ac.uk/); P. SPECK, S. A. TAKÁCS, Understanding Byzantium: Studies in Byzantine Historical Sources, 2003; J. P. THOMAS, A. C. HERO, Byzantine Monastic Foundation Documents: A Complete Translation of the Surviving Founders' typika and Testaments, 2000.

D. ART-HISTORICAL RESEARCH

Interest in Byzantine art, as in medieval art generally, only emerged – somewhat hesitantly – at the end of the 18th cent.: after all, the art of Byzantium had also fallen under the classicistic verdict, not least determined by Johann Joachim Winckelmann but also following a

Fig. 1: Fragment of a chancel screen (?),
Saint Peter in a Miracle Scene;
Constantinople, last third of the 5th cent.
Bildarchiv Preussischer Kulturbesitz

Fig. 2: Two relief icons: Maria Orans
and the Archangel Michael;
Constantinople, third quarter
of the 13th cent.
Bildarchiv Preussischer Kulturbesitz

Fig. 3: Winged altarpiece (triptych):
Crucifixion of Christ, Apostles,
Constantine and Helena, Church Fathers;
Constantinople, 11th cent.
Bildarchiv Preussischer Kulturbesitz

Fig. 4: Frieze panel, Christ on Horseback
Accompanied by Two Angels; Egypt, 6th/7th cent.
Bildarchiv Preussischer Kulturbesitz

communis opinio, according to which art had been in a state of steady decline since the end of Antiquity. Nevertheless, there is evidence quite early on for an occasional burgeoning of interest in collecting art of the 'Eastern Church'. It clearly differed from the medieval acquisition of relics, although it must be assumed the owners were not aware of the art-historical provenance of the objects (icons, ivory and soapstone reliefs etc.). At least from the end of the 16th cent., a considerable amount of travel literature about the Christian Orient provided ever more detailed reports of the buildings and monuments of Byzantium, some supplemented by celebrated views of the city that were of great topographical value [4].

The conscious perception of 'Greek portraits of saints' began in the 17th cent. The *Acta Sanctorum*, first published by the Bollandists in 1643, contained numerous engravings of icons and miniatures of the Eastern Church to illustrate the saints' lives. The first antiquarian study in German of a Russian *vita* icon of Theodoros Stratilates in the church at Kalbensteinberg (Franconia) was offered by Heinrich Alexander Döderlein in 1724 [3. 251–253; 6]. The Roman cardinal Alessandro Albani had the *Menologion* by Basileios II published in a three-volume edition in 1727, in which some 400 miniatures were reproduced in astonishingly faithful copper engravings (*Menologium Graecorum iussu Basilii imperatoris graece olim editum tres vol.*, Urbini). In 1756, the Arabist and philologist Johann Jakob Reiske, to whom we owe the discovery and first edition of the ceremonial book of the emperor Constantine VII Porphyrogenitus, published a (since lost) Byzantine soapstone relief with important observations on the iconography and hagiographical significance of the saints depicted on it [3. 253–255]. Perhaps the most interesting art-historical treatment of Russian art was attempted by the Göttingen art scholar Johann Dominikus Fiorillo [3. 255–257]. Arguably the most comprehensive catalogue of early Christian and Byzantine art is offered in the monumental work of the French autodidact Jean-Baptiste Seroux d'Agincourt, which appeared – for the most part posthumously – in six volumes between 1811 and 1824 (*Histoire de l'art par les monuments, depuis sa décadence au IVme siècle jusqu à son renouvellement au XVIme*, Paris, 1825). It contained scores of engravings, albeit in rather curious combinations [2]. The term 'Byzantine', from the time of Hieronymus Wolf (1515–1580) used in a strictly historiographical sense, was first applied to the art of Byzantium in the correspondence between Goethe and Sulpiz Boisserée exchanging their views on art in 1810. It eventually replaced other words in use at the time, such as 'graecizing' and 'ancient Greek' etc. [1]. Further initiatives of note towards a serious occupation with Byzantine art can be found in the German Romantic movement (e.g. Friedrich Schlegel). Art historiography, which started in the early 19th cent., (Carl Friedrich von Rumohr, Gustav Friedrich Waagen, Anton Springer, Franz Theodor Kugler and others) gradually over-

came the unfavourable judgment of Byzantine art and thus drew closer to a systematic and comparative review of the art of the Middle Ages.

The actual scholarly treatment of Byzantine art set in between the end of the 19th and the beginning of the 20th cent. in Germany, England (O.M. Dalton), France (Ch. Diehl, J. Ebersolt) and Russia (F.I. Uspenskiy, D.V. Aynalov, N.P. Kondakov), and, for the most part included the Christian monuments of Late Antiquity that until then had been the exclusive domain of denominational → CHRISTIAN ARCHAEOLOGY. The standard work *Altchristliche und byzantinische Kunst*, published by Oskar Wulff between 1914 and 1918 (two volumes, 1914–1918; with a bibliographical critical supplement, 1935), presents an overview of the development of Christian art from the end of the Roman imperial period to the end of the Byzantine empire (1453). It is distinguished by great expertise and may even today be considered a milestone in the exploration of Byzantine art.

By the middle of the 20th cent. Byzantine art history had established itself as an independent branch within the general study of art history, and branched out into several specialised fields (study of architecture, sculpture, monumentalisation, book illustration, ivory carving etc.). This was due not least to a considerable growth in monuments that were systematically recorded, archaeologically recovered or saved through large-scale restoration projects. An international community of scholars is engaged in its study. Nevertheless, a historical survey of the discipline, its intentions and methods is still lacking.

E. MUSEUMS

In the late 1880s Wilhelm von Bode began building a systematic collection of early Christian and Byzantine art in the Berlin museums. The first public exhibition followed in 1904 at the newly opened Kaiser Friedrich Museum (now the Bode Museum), where it formed the 'Sculptures of Christian Epochs section' (now the Sculpture Collection and Museum of Byzantine Art of the → BERLIN State Museums). This marked the first time Byzantine art was recognized as a 'museumworthy' period in art history. Primarily, the museum holds outstanding pieces of rare 5th to 11th cent. figurative stone sculptures from Constantinople, Asia Minor and Greece (Figs. 1 and 2) as well as exceptional examples of architectural sculpture, ivory carvings (Fig. 3) and one of the world's largest collections of Coptic art (Fig.4; [7]).

In other European countries and the United States, Byzantine collections of similar importance were created as separate entities or added to existing museums (Athens: Benaki Museum, Byzantine Museum, Istanbul: Archaeological Museum, → LONDON: British Museum, Paris: → LOUVRE; St. Petersburg: Hermitage Museum, Washington: → DUMBARTON OAKS Collection et al.). Outstanding objects of Byzantine art have been held in many European church treasuries and libraries, some without interruption for nearly 1,000 years.

1 A. Effenberger, Goethe und die 'Russischen Heiligen-bilder'. Anfänge byzantinischer Kunstgeschichte in Deutschland (= Beiträge der Winckelmann-Gesellschaft 18), 1990 2 Id., Goethe und Seroux d'Agincourt. Anfänge byzantinscher Kunstforschung am Vorabend der Französischen Revolution, in: La Grecia antica. Mito e simbolo per l'età della Grande Rivoluzione. Genesi e crisi di un modello nella cultura del Settecento (eds. Ph. Boutry et al.), 1991, 323–332 3 Id., Frühes Ikonenstudium in Deutschland, in: Studien zur byzantinischen Kunstgeschichte. Festschrift für Horst Hallensleben zum 65. Geburtstag (eds. B. Borkopp, B. Schellewald, L. Theis), 1995, 249–258 4 J. Ebersolt, Constantinople byzantine et les voyageurs du Levant, 1918 (repr. 1986) 5 J. D. Fiorillo, Versuch einer Geschichte der bildenden Künste in Rußland, in: Id., Kleine Schriften artistischen Inhalts, vol. 2, Göttingen 1806 6 H. Lohse, Die Ikone des heiligen Theodor Stratilat zu Kalbensteinberg, eine philologisch-historische Untersuchung (= Slavistische Beiträge 98), 1976 7 A. Effenberger, H.-G. Severin (eds.), Das Museum für Spät-Antike und Byzantinische Kunst. Staatliche Museen zu Berlin, 1992

Additional Bibliography: R. Cormack, Byzantine Art, 2000; J. Lowden, Early Christian & Byzantine Art, 1997; H. Maguire, The Icons of Their Bodies: Saints and Their Images in Byzantium, 1996; L. Rodley, Byzantine Art and Architecture: An Introduction, 1994; L. Safran, Heaven on Earth: Art and the Church in Byzantium, 1998.

ARNE EFFENBERGER

Byzantium
I. History   II. Literature   III. Art

I. History
A. Introduction B. Reception of Antiquity
C. Transmission of Ancient Culture

A. Introduction
The term Byzantium (B.) initially denoted the eastern part of the Roman Empire, from the foundation of → Constantinople by the emperor Constantine the Great as a 'second Rome' on the extended territory of the town of Byzantion on the Bosporus in AD 330. After the end of empire in the western part of the Roman Empire in the late 5th cent., it designated the Roman Empire as it continued to exist in the East until 1453.

The rediscovery of Classical Antiquity in the 18th and 19th cents. had as a result that for a long time, scarcely any independent value was attributed to the culture of the Byzantines; instead, they were essentially credited with only the preservation and transmission of ancient tradition. More recent research, however, has given a more positive evaluation of B.'s own contribution, which it sometimes provided also in confrontation with the ancient 'heritage' [13]. However, it is indisputable that it made an essential contribution to the preservation and transmission of this heritage, especially to the West. At any rate, for every Byzantine period the qualification holds that intellectual life as a whole, and consequently also the reception of Antiquity, was sustained only by a small social group. At the least, a basic linguistic and rhetorical education, oriented towards the ancient standard, was always the shared property of a broad subgroup of persons, which primarily included the extensive State and Church bureaucracy.

The first phase of Byzantine history falls within Late Antiquity (4th–6th cents.), a period when urban culture flourished, and was clearly still shaped by the ancient educational canon. Under the pressure of external catastrophes for the Empire in the 7th cent., above all the victorious march of Islamic Arabs into the eastern provinces, and the invasion of the Balkan peninsula by Slavs and Bulgarians of Turkish descent, it experienced a drastic decline, which affected almost every cultural domain. An exception in some cases was theological literature, where ancient philosophy lived on at a high linguistic level in Christian garb (e.g. in the works of Maximus Confessor, John of Damascus). However, an increased recourse to the cultural tradition, which initially followed models of Late Antiquity, had already begun towards the end of the 8th cent. [19].

This current emerged in about 840 as a phase of Byzantine cultural history that extended till the late 10th cent., which has been described as the 'Macedonian Renaissance'. The term Renaissance was correspondingly also used for later Byzantine periods [22]. However, whereas the Western Renaissance of the 15th and 16th cents. can be understood as a new cultural point of departure, in B. the continuity of the connection with ancient culture in the four spheres of language, script, literature and fine arts was never wholly interrupted [18]. In any case, around the middle of the 9th cent. works by authors of Antiquity and Late Antiquity began to be systematically collected and copied; at the same time, the development of the fine arts was influenced by recourse to stylistic forms from Late Antiquity [24].

Following this phase of collection, scholars of a later period (11th–12th cent.) turned to the content of ancient texts more intensely, made a conscious choice in the reception of materials, and varied the forms of confrontation. Thus, for instance, the realities of everyday B. were illustrated by ancient examples, or allusions to Antiquity were used for ironic distancing [13]. The period from about 1250 until the end of the Empire (1453) was indeed characterised by progressive political decline, but also by a renewed, particularly intensive preoccupation with the ancient heritage, whether with the content of texts, with questions of style, or with the textual tradition. Even some works of Classical Latin literature were now made accessible by translation into Greek. This development of intellectual life was in part favoured by the attempt to compete with the high standard of Western learning in the Scholastic period [20].

B. Reception of Antiquity
In what follows, the term reception is used in the sense of a concrete cultural recollection, in the context

of the continuing connection of Byzantine culture with Antiquity, and is considered with regard to the areas of literature, philosophy, law and the sciences, as well as architecture and fine arts.

1. LITERATURE 2. PHILOSOPHY 3. LAW 4. THE SCIENCES 5. CONTINUING INFLUENCE OF ANCIENT ELEMENTS IN ARCHITECTURE AND THE FINE ARTS

1. LITERATURE

Byzantine literature was indebted to the categories of rhetoric established in Antiquity, and therefore always more or less strove for conscious imitation [11] of ancient literature, as it had already been postulated and theoretically grounded in the late Hellenistic and early Imperial periods. In the framework of the ideal of mimesis, particular efforts were made to emulate ancient authors, whether linguistically (Atticism), stylistically, or in merely individual formulations [1]. Byzantine authors quoted from their [i.e., the ancient authors] works (including some particularly beloved standard citations), alluded to individual *loci*, or took over entire passages in more or less altered form. When this happened in historical works, such dependency could lead to falsifying historical reality, though there were also authors who transformed an adopted message so skilfully that the adaptation served to raise the literary level, while the essential points of information remained reliable [12]. Reference was also made to heroes and events of ancient mythology and history, which were often reinterpreted allegorically. Many ancient heroes, such as Hercules, appeared with stereotypical frequency. Some authors, however, also consciously chose allusions to little known personalities and events, like Johannes Tzetzes (12th cent.) in his letters, which he subsequently explained in a poem of 12000 verses [9 vol. 2. 118]. In many authors, especially the historians, the linguistic imitation of Antiquity went so far as to defamiliarise expressions from everyday life, current terms of bureaucratic language or of the calendar, as well as geographical and ethnographical names by means of archaisms [9 vol. 1. 407, 414, 446, 452].

In poetry [9 vol. 2. 87–180], ancient meters were emulated (hexameter, elegiac distichs, iambic trimeters and anacreontics), although this imitation remained quite superficial owing to the loss of distinction in quantity and the transition from tonal accent to stress in Koine Greek. As a result of the linguistic development, the trimeter became the Byzantine dodecasyllable. Many ancient poetic genres were continued in B. in more or less modified form, e.g. mythological, historical and didactic epic, the novel, drama (which were not, however, intended for performance), satires, epigrams and other minor forms. In much Byzantine poetry, ancient verses were cited with such frequency that they approached the form of a *cento* (e.g. in the anonymous Christian poem *Christós páschon*, which is especially indebted to the dramas of Euripides). Again, other authors, particularly the above-mentioned Johannes

Tzetzes, annotated or paraphrased works of Antiquity in verse form.

2. PHILOSOPHY

[9 vol. 1. 3–62] The influence of ancient philosophy in B. has still not been fully researched. However, at least since the Patristic period, it was always present in Byzantine theology, above all in its outstanding representatives Plato (partly through the intermediary of Neoplatonism) and Aristotle, and in many cases a direct confrontation with ancient philosophy in commentaries and essays can be shown as well. Among those who, following Porphyry and Iamblichus, concerned themselves with Plato were first and foremost the Schools of Athens (Proclus, Damascius) and Alexandria (Ammonius, Olympiodorus) in Late Antiquity, Michael Psellus and his circle in Constantinople in the middle Byzantine period, and in the 15th cent. Georgius Gemistus Plethon in Mistras [28], together with his most important pupil Bessarion, who lived in Italy from 1444 as a Roman cardinal and was an outstanding expert on Platonic dialogues. Plethon, too, stayed in Italy on the occasion of the Council of Ferrara-Florence (1438–39). The last Byzantine Platonist, the Athenian Demetrius Chalcocandyles (Chalcondyles), taught in Padua from 1463 and in Florence from 1475. However, the most significant Italian Platonists, such as Marsilio Ficino, tended to be self-taught, and the influence on them of Byzantine philosophers such as Plethon is generally considered insignificant [6].

Porphyry was to become the first mediator of Byzantine Aristotelian studies with his *Eisagoge*. Important Byzantine interpreters of Aristotle in Late Antiquity included Themistius, Simplicius, Johannes Philoponus and the Alexandrians mentioned above; in the 11th and 12th cents. Johannes Italus, Eustratius of Nicaea and Michael of Ephesus, in the 13th cent. Nicephorus Blemmydes and Georgius Pachymeres, in the 14th cent. Theodorus Metochites and Sophonias, in the 15th cent. Georgius Scholarius (later patriarch of Constantinople as Gennadius II), Georgius Trapezuntius from Crete, and Johannes Argyropoulus. The last two worked in their later years as teachers in Italy, Trapezuntius also as a transmitter of Byzantine rhetoric.

3. LAW

Byzantine law was based on Roman law, as it was first established and further developed by professional jurists, and later through dispositions by the Imperial Chancery. Roman law achieved a lasting claim to validity through the codifications by Emperor Theodosius II (5th cent., Imperial laws) and above all Justinian I, who in the 6th cent. collected the laws developed by jurists in the *Digests* in addition to the Imperial Laws, and himself amended numerous laws. This validity was reconfirmed by Leo VI's collection of laws (late 9th cent.) known as the *Basilica*. Many decisions of the *Basilica*, however, no longer corresponded to the altered social circumstances, for which smaller legal collections such as the 8th cent. *Ecloge* and judicial practice were better adapted.

4. THE SCIENCES

The sciences (geography, mathematics, astronomy, zoology, botany, mineralogy, medicine, military science) [9 vol. 2. 221–340] in B. were largely indebted to the knowledge of Antiquity, primarily of the Hellenistic and Imperial periods. For geography and astronomy Claudius Ptolemaeus (2nd cent. AD) had set standards that were not surpassed until early modern times. No pioneering innovations are to be found in B. in the other sciences mentioned, or in engineering; yet in all these areas transmitted material was keenly studied and handed down in treatises. Military science, which was pursued particularly in the 10th cent., the period of the great victories of the Byzantine armies, was as a rule largely indebted to the ancient tradition (e.g. Onosander, 1st cent. AD), yet in the anonymous work *Perí paradromés* (about 965), for instance, we have a handbook of mobile warfare wholly oriented towards Byzantine practice.

5. CONTINUING INFLUENCE OF ANCIENT EL-EMENTS IN ARCHITECTURE AND THE FINE ARTS

The Byzantine architecture of Late Antiquity takes up earlier building forms. It was primarily the profane building type of the longitudinal → BASILICA (market or assembly hall) that proved productive in the area of Christian church building [23. 27–31; 3], but so did the form of a domed central building, used in the Imperial period as a mausoleum and often adopted in the Christian period for the tombs of martyrs (*martyria*) and for baptisteries [23. 31f.]. These initiatives underwent further creative development since the 6th cent., so that in the architecture of later centuries ancient elements can be distinguished from innovative ones only with difficulty.

Antiquity had a clearer influence on sculpture and painting [17]. It should be borne in mind that statues of Greek Antiquity, as well as ancient wall paintings in Constantinople and other places had survived intact for many centuries, thus maintaining a living tradition. In Late Antiquity, artists initially adhered to the ancient models: in sculpture, to traditional realistic shaping, and in → PAINTING to such illusionist techniques as chiaroscuro, architectonic perspective and allusions to landscapes. Human emotions were shown in sculpture and painting by means of gestures and expressions. At first, even ancient myths and heroes remained as artistic subjects. We once again find artistic representations of ancient themes from the middle Byzantine period, which however remained restricted to particular areas. Thus, for instance, in a commentary probably composed in the 6th cent. by a certain Nonnus, explaining mythological allusions in the sermons of Gregory Nazianzen to Christians, corresponding illustrations were added to four manuscripts of the 11th–12th cents. Mythology is also found in later centuries as decoration on household objects, textiles, silverware and ivory boxes, but historical and mythological themes of Antiquity were also represented in wall paintings, as is known from numerous descriptions [8]. The resump-tion of ancient stylistic forms did not remain restricted to the profane; they were also used, primarily in ivory carving and in book illustration, to represent Christian religious themes.

C. TRANSMISSION OF ANCIENT CULTURE

1. THE PRESERVATION OF TEXTS 2. THE TRANSFER OF THE ANCIENT HERITAGE TO THE WEST

1. THE PRESERVATION OF TEXTS

As the successor to the Greek empire of Alexander the Great and his diadochs, the Byzantine Empire was the natural heir to ancient Greek culture. In its territory, ancient Greek texts were essentially preserved, primarily in the great libraries: in → ALEXANDRIA (where, after the destruction of the Museum-Library in 48/47 BC, only the Serapeum Library probably remained; its holdings were affected but not destroyed in 391 AD), → ATHENS, Ephesus, Smyrna, Pergamum and Caesarea/Palestine, and from the 4th cent. also in Antioch and Constantinople. It should be remembered that there were doubtless many smaller, mainly private libraries.

The development from the older customary (cursive) script of the minuscule script, which was used more and more in place of majuscules from about 800, was of great significance for the preservation and transmission of these classical texts in the Byzantine period. Since the minuscule script was more versatile, it permitted faster copying and so increased book production, which from about 900 was also facilitated by the gradual introduction of oriental paper, and later in the 13th cent. still more by the introduction of western paper. With the awakening of intensified antiquarian interest in the period of Leo the mathematician and Photius, the later patriarch of Constantinople, more and more texts from ancient times began to be transcribed into minuscules [7]. Photius himself wrote a collection of reports and excerpts from ancient and late antique works (*Library*), which conveys at least an idea of the content of many texts that no longer exist today [21], and at the same time, he contributed to an improved understanding of ancient texts by compiling a lexicon. In about 900 Arethas of Patras, later metropolitan of Caesarea, commissioned copies of numerous ancient philosophical and other texts, on some of which he commented in his own hand [15. 243–270]. For instance, the earliest manuscripts of Plato's Dialogues include Oxford Bodleian CLARK 39 and Vat. gr. 1 (the first ones certain to have been copied by order of Arethas), and Paris. gr. 1807, which may have been copied before Arethas [15. 247–250]. Copying activity in minuscule script was continued in the following cents., and it is responsible for the preservation of most ancient Greek texts down to our own time.

In contrast, the collections of excerpts with moral aims, instigated by the emperor Constantinus VII in the 10th cent., of which only a fragment is extant, concentrated for the most part on authors more recent than

Late Antiquity [15. 323–332]. Both ancient and late antique epigrams are contained in the Byzantine collection compiled by Constantinus Cephalas in about 900, known today as the *Anthologia Palatina*. Maximus Planudes produced a revised edition of this work in 1299, to which he added numerous epigrams, yet he also omitted a series of epigrams, especially those which seemed to him indecent (*Anthologia Planudea*). In the 12th cent. Johannes Tzetzes, the man of letters with antiquarian interests, wrote commentaries and allegorical interpretations in prose and verse on works by ancient authors (Homer, Hesiod, Aristophanes, Lycophron and others) and produced abridged versions of their works, e.g. of Porphyry's *Eisagoge* [9 vol. 2. 59–63]. The most significant Byzantine commentator on Homer, as well as of Pindar and Aristophanes, however, was Eustathius, a contemporary of Tzetzes and later metropolitan of Thessalonica [9 vol. 2. 63–67]. These two authors also influenced the textual history of the works they dealt with. Finally, it should be remembered at this point that southern Italy, which was still partly in Byzantine hands until the late 11th cent., made an independent contribution to the transmission of ancient literature [7].

In 1204, the conquest and the approximately 60-year occupation of Constantinople by Western Crusaders and the Venetians led to the loss of many more ancient texts. However, in the context of the interest in Antiquity, which increased once again from about 1250, a number of Byzantines carried out valuable philological work on the texts of ancient works. For instance, the learned monk Maximus Planudes worked on the poets Hesiod, Pindar, Sophocles, Euripides, Theocritus, Aratus, and Tryphiodorus; the author of Late Antiquity, Nonnus and the *Anthologia Palatina*, as well as on Plutarch's *Moralia* and Ptolemy's *Geography*. The philological qualifications of his student Manuel Moschopoulus are disputed, yet he did text-critical work on Pindar, Sophocles, Euripides and Theocritus, as well as on Homer and Aristophanes. The most significant philologist of the era (first half of the 14th cent.) was Demetrius Triclinius, who did valuable work on the textual transmission of such poets as Hesiod, Pindar, Aeschylus, Euripides and Aristophanes. The philological achievement of his contemporary Thomas Magister is the least valued [20].

2. The Transfer of the Ancient Heritage to the West

By the middle of the 14th cent., Italian Humanists were already showing an interest in learning Ancient Greek from a Byzantine. The first was the poet Petrarch, in about 1340; his teacher was the Calabrese monk Barlaam, who had lived quite a long time in Constantinople [16]. Towards the end of the 14th cent., the Humanist and statesman Lino Coluccio de'Salutati invited the Byzantine man of letters Manuel Chrysoloras [2] to the 'Studium' (University) of Florence, and a series of Italian Humanists studied Ancient Greek under him from 1397–1400, including Leonardo Bruni

Aretino, later an important translator of Plato's Dialogues into Latin. On the invitation of Giangaleazzo Visconti of Milan, Chrysoloras later taught at Pavia until 1403, before returning to Constantinople. Some of his pupils, like Pier Paolo Vergerio, were themselves later active as teachers of Greek in Italy. From 1414 to 1418 Guarino Veronese transmitted to Italy the knowledge of Greek he had previously acquired in Constantinople. Greek was also taught by Georgius Trapezuntius of Crete at Vicenza from 1420 and at Venice from 1427–1437, and by Andronicus Callistus of Constantinople at Bologna from 1449–1473, and then at Florence for approximately another year.

Contemporary with these linguistic contacts, interest was awakened among the Italian Humanists in the manuscripts of ancient Greek authors, which could be found in abundance in B. [7]. They arrived in large numbers in Italy for the first time when, soon after Chrysoloras's teaching activities in Florence, some Humanists such as Guarino Guarini, Francesco Filelfo and Giovanni Aurispa went from there to Constantinople and began to collect manuscripts systematically. Niccolò Niccoli based his collection on the manuscripts Chrysoloras had brought with him to Italy. Yet Greeks who came to Italy were also active collectors and copyists of Greek manuscripts: for instance, the previously mentioned scholars Georgius Trapezuntius, Bessarion, Johannes Argyropoulus and Andronicus Callistus, as well as in the late 15th cent. Constantinus Lascaris (copyist) and Johannes (Ianus) Lascaris (collector and editor of ancient texts).

The oldest large collection of manuscripts on Italian soil around 1450 was that of the Vatican, thanks to the collecting activity of Pope Nicholas V, who had learned Greek from Filelfo. It was not surpassed until a few years later, by the collection of Bessarion, who since 1455 had engaged Michael Apostoles to buy up Greek manuscripts in Crete. However, he also owed much to the important library of the southern Italian monastery of San Nicola di Casole at Otranto, which had existed since the Middle Ages. He further augmented its holdings with copies, which he commissioned from Johannes Rhosus and others. It was only toward the end of the 15th cent. that Padua and Venice became important trans-shipment centres for Greek manuscripts, when Aldus Manutius began printing ancient Greek texts at Venice in 1494 [5; 27].

In so far as Byzantine art transmitted ancient elements in the manner described above, it also transmitted them to other cultures in the context of overall reception, primarily to the West [4; 14; 25]. The periods of increased absorption of ancient elements, borrowed from B., into Western art, especially in book illustration and ivory carving, were those of Charlemagne and the Ottonians and Salians. This last phenomenon can be explained primarily by the influence and posterity of the presence in the West of Theophano, the influential Byzantine wife of Otto II.

→ Byzantium; → Constantine [1]

1 A. CAMERON, Herodotus und Thucydides in Agathias, in: ByzZ 57, 1964, 33–52 2 G. CAMMELLI, I dotti bizantini e le origini dell'umanesimo, I, Manuele Crisolora, 1941 3 F. W. DEICHMANN, Wandsysteme, in: ByzZ 59, 1966, 334–358 (on the ancient character of early Christian basilicas) 4 O. DEMUS, Byzantine Art and the West, 1970 5 D. GEANAKOPLOS, Greek Scholars in Venice, 1962 6 J. HANKINS, Plato in the Italian Ren., 1990 7 D. HARLFINGER (ed.), Griech. Kodikologie und Textüberlieferung, 1980 (particularly the contributions by A. DAIN, J. IRIGOIN, R. SABBADINI) 8 A. HOHLWEG, Ekphrasis, in: Reallex. zur byz. Kunst, 2, 33–75 9 H. HUNGER, Literatur 10 Id., et al. (eds.), Geschichte der Textüberlieferung der antiken und mitteralterlichen Literatur, 1961, 1 (repr. 1975) 11 Id., On the Imitation (Mimesis) of Antiquity in Byzantine Literature, in: Dumbarton Oaks Papers 23/24, 1969/70, 17–38 12 Id., Thukydides bei Johannes Kantakuzenos, in: Jb. Österr. Byz. 25, 1976, 181–193 13 A. KAZHDAN, L'eredità antica à Bisanzio, in: Studi classici e orientali 38, 1989, 140–153 14 E. KITZINGER, The Art of Byzantium and the Medieval West, 1976 15 P. LEMERLE, Byzantine Humanism. The First Phase, 1986 (translation of the French original of 1972 with an expanded bibliography) 16 P. L. M. LEONE, Barlaam in Occidente, in: Annali Università di Lecce 8–10, 1977–80, 427–446 17 H. MAGUIRE, s.v. Antico, area bizantina, Enciclopedia dell'arte medievale 2, 108–111 18 P. SCHREINER, 'Rennaissance' in Byzantium? in: W. ERZGRÄBER (ed.), Kontinuität und Transformation der Antike im Mittelalter, 1989, 389f. 19 P. SPECK, Ikonoklasmus und die Anfänge der Makedonischen Renaissance, in: Poikíla Byzantiná 4, 1984, 175–209 20 F. TINNEFELD, Neue Formen der Antikerezeption bei den Byzantinern der frühen Palaiologenzeit, in: IJCT 1/3, 1995, 19–28 21 W. TREADGOLD, The Nature of the Bibliotheca of Photius, 1980 22 Id., Renaissances before the Renaissance, 1984 23 W. F. VOLBACH, J. LAFONTAINE-DOSOGNE, Byzantium und der christliche Osten (Propyläen Kunstgeschichte), 1968 24 K. WEITZMANN, The Classical Heritage in Byzantine and Near Eastern Art, 1981 25 Id., Art in the Medieval West and its Contacts with Byzantium, 1982 26 Id., Greek Mythology in Byzantine Art, ²1984 27 N. WILSON, The Book Trade in Venice c. 1400–1515, in: H.-G. BECK et al. (eds.), Venezia: Centro di mediazione tra Oriente e Occidente (secoli XV–XVI), 1977, 381–397 28 C. M. WOODHOUSE, George Gemistos Plethon

ADDITIONAL BIBLIOGRAPHY: G. OSTROGORSKI, Geschichte des byzantinischen Staates, 1940 (=History of the Byzantine State (trans.) Joan Hussey, 1956; J. SIGNES CONDOÑER, Translatio studiorum: la emigración bizantina a Europa Occidental en las décadas finales del Imperio (1353–1453), in: P. Bádenas de la Peña & I. Pérez Martín (Eds.), Constantinopla 1453, Madrid 2003, 187–246; F. TINNEFELD, Abendland und Byzanz: ein Europa?, in: P. Segl (Ed.), Byzanz – das »andere« Europa (= Das Mittelalter 6, 2), Berlin 2001, 19–38   FRANZ TINNEFELD

II. LITERATURE

A. INTRODUCTION AND REMARKS CONCERNING METHODOLOGY B. THE TRANSITION PERIOD AND THE EARLY BYZANTINE PERIOD (4TH–MID 7TH CENTS.) C. THE 'DARK CENTURIES' (MID–7TH CENT. – c. 800) D. ENCYCLOPAEDISM AND THE REAPPROPRIATION OF ANTIQUITY (9TH–10TH CENT.) E. PROTO-RENAISSANCE (11TH–MID–13TH CENTS.) F. THE ERA OF THE PALEOLOGANS. RESIGNED FLOURISHING AND DISSOLUTION (MID–13TH-MID–15TH CENTS.)

A. INTRODUCTION AND REMARKS CONCERNING METHODOLOGY

As is also customary in the corresponding Classical disciplines, the treatment of the history of Byzantine literature includes, the whole of 'literature', including philosophy, law, medicine and other sciences. This corresponds to the concept of the Byzantines themselves, who subsumed everything having to do with culture, science and 'literature' under the term *lógoi*. By 'Byzantine' we understand the cultural area that, on an ideological level, was shaped by a Christian world view, and on a linguistic one was dominated by Greek (although this hegemony was not exclusive). It was essentially identical to the respective borders of the Eastern Roman ('Byzantine') Empire, albeit with temporary displacements, especially in the Near East (Syria, Palestine) and in Sicily/Lower Italy. Here, Byzantine literature in Greek arose even after the conquest of these lands by the Arabs in the 7th or the Normans in the 11th cent. There are no generally-accepted principles of classification of Byzantine literature; the handbooks' division [4; 5; 9] into literary-profane, colloquial and theological literature is increasingly seen as less than satisfactory [10; 11; 13]. It is extremely problematic to delimit a 'profane' area in a society which, like that of B., was so permeated by Christianity in all its manifestations. Above all, many authors escape such a categorisation; with this method they are perceivable as total literary persons, either not at all or only in parts at any one time. Nor are *levels of style* any longer seen as a simple bipartition into 'literary' and 'colloquial language', but in a much more differentiated way, and in the light of their function in the relationship between author and public [18]. A true history of Byzantine literature has yet to be written. Only in recent times has research begun to evaluate Byzantine literature, at least in part, as an aesthetic phenomenon *sui generis* [1; 13a; 15; 15a], instead of starting out from the prejudice that it consisted only of symptoms of decline and more than a thousand years of sterility. The inner boundaries between individual periods of Byzantine literature are to some extent variously defined; however, there is widespread agreement on its beginning in the 4th cent. (the inauguration of the new residence at Constantinople by Constantine I in AD 330, if one wishes to specify a fixed date of political history), and general agreement on its end point (the conquest of Constantinople by the Ottomans in 1453).

In what follows the individual eras of Byzantine literature will be considered only under the special aspect their reception of Antiquity. Some genres, many of their achievements, and the people responsible for them will therefore be left out of the discussion. In any case, the aspect of the reception of Antiquity includes a central peculiarity. An essential trait of Byzantine literature is → MIMESIS [8] in a dual sense: mimesis of a form of language seen as canonical, as it developed out of Atticism in the Second Sophistic as a written language, and mimesis of literary forms, which had been used by the treasured authors of Antiquity and the imperial period, including Biblical and Patristic models. It is due less to Byzantine literature than to the aesthetic categories of their onlookers that play with these linguistic and literary forms was chiefly evaluated negatively (that is, as uncreative or unoriginal) in the 19th and 20th cents.

B. THE TRANSITION PERIOD AND THE EARLY BYZANTINE PERIOD (4TH-MID 7TH CENTS.)

The most important orientation for the whole of Byzantine literature consisted in the fact that despite the new ideological direction of Byzantine society (the adoption of Christianity by Constantine I, Christianity as the state religion under Theodosius I, the struggle against paganism), Greek Antiquity remained the determining cultural force. The emperor Julian (361–363), himself highly educated and productive in various literary genres, tried in vain to exclude Christians by law from the ancient cultural tradition during the short phase of the pagan reaction he led. Rhetoric and philosophy were placed in the service of the new world view. The (*Progymnasmata*) of Aphthonius (end of the 4th cent.), together with the earlier (*Corpus*) of Hermogenes and the two treatises by Menander of Laodiceia on epideictic eloquence, constituted the fundamental rulebooks for Byzantine authors of all periods, which were commented on repeatedly for use in higher education. Throughout the Byzantine millennium, moreover, → ARISTOTELIANISM and → NEOPLATONISM remained the all-determining system of thought. It was crucially important that the great Church Fathers of the 4th cent. (the 'Cappadocians' Gregory of Nazianzus, Gregory of Nyssa, and Basil the Great, as well as John Chrysostom) allowed the whole of ancient literature, including poetry and philosophy (particularly Plato, by way of Neoplatonism), to find its way into their system of thought and their literary production. Ancient epideictic eloquence celebrates new triumphs in the preaching of these Church Fathers. The exclusion of contents of ancient literature that contradicted Christianity remained a constant problem, which authors repeatedly attempted to solve through recourse to formal or Euhemeristic/allegorical interpretation. Justinian I sought to counter direct competition from ancient philosophy administratively by closing the philosophical school at Athens (529), while the Christian-oriented variants in Alexandria succumbed to the Arab conquest (642). However, on the road towards the formation of

Christological dogma, Aristotle had long since found himself within the fold of Christian literature (his logical writings were also ideologically innocuous). By way of Synesius of Cyrene, Nemesius, Gregory of Nyssa and above all Pseudo Dionysius Areopagita (beginning of the 5th cent.), Platonism was an element of Byzantine thought that was always viewed with mistrust, but henceforth indissociable. In all, literary production was also dominated by the ancient tradition, with its international and also interreligious character, although this diminished towards the end of this period. Latin too still played a role as a literary language in the East: the Antiochan Greek Ammianus Marcellinus wrote his historical work, and the Alexandrian Greek Claudian his panegyric poetic work in Latin, while on the other side Romanus, a Syrian from Emesa, made originally Syrian literary forms fruitful for Greek, as creator and completer of the ecclesiastical poetry of the *Kontákion*. Poetic genres inherited from Late Antiquity such as → EPIC and → EPIGRAM were further cultivated: with his *Dionysiaca* the Egyptian Nonnus (first half of the 5th cent.), who was only one of many poets, created the most extensive epic in the Greek language in particularly rigid and artificially constructed hexameters. Tradition was maintained particularly in the epigram, alongside the new accentual verse of the Byzantine dodecameter (developed from the quantitative ancient iambic trimeter) and anacreontics, also used accentually. The pagan Palladas (of Alexandria, 4th cent.) and the Christian Agathias (of Myrina in Asia Minor, 6th cent.) used the same forms, while Agathias, with his collection of new epigrams, placed himself in the tradition of older collections. Efforts, which are only partially preserved, to exploit ancient, particularly epic, forms for Christian subjects (Apollinaris of Laodiceia in the 4th cent., Nonnus with his paraphrase of Saint John's Gospel, the Homerocentra of Eudocia, 5th cent.) met with limited success at best. Another area was successfully developed further: ancient biography was made useful and transformed to promote a new human ideal. In a radical renunciation of ancient values, life in the solitude of the desert was praised. The *Vita Antonii* by Athanasius of Alexandria (mid–4th cent.) was the prototype at the beginning of a new and extremely fruitful genre, the hagiographic Vita. Continuity and recourse to the linguistic and compositional models of Antiquity were at their most striking in → HISTORIOGRAPHY, the crowing discipline of Byzantine literature. In addition to the newly developed genre of the chronicle, with its emphatically Christian view of a linear course of history (the first work of this type to survive complete is the 6th-cent. Chronicle by John Malalas of Antioch) and the equally new genre of ecclesiastical history (from Eusebius of Caesarea in the 4th cent. to the compilation of his predecessors' work by Theodorus Lector in the 6th cent.), the ancient form of contemporary historical writing continued in style and conception, and was to continue uninterrupted until the end of the Byzantine Empire. From the period of time outlined here, we have, besides extensive fragments of other authors, the works of Procopius of Caesarea (mid–6th cent.), of Agathias (second half of the 6th cent.), already mentioned as a lyricist, and of Theophylactus Simocattes (beginning of the 7th cent.). Among the literature of this time that absorbed Antiquity in the wider sense, the great collections on individual subjects must be included: medical material in the compilations by Aetius of Amida and Alexander of Tralles, legal material in the (*Corpus Iuris Civilis*) instigated by Justinian I, literature in the sense of *belles lettres* in the excerpts by John Stobaeus, and in the lexicon by Hesychius. In all, ancient → CULTURE was further transmitted in this era; its forms continued to be used or reshaped, and its contents lived on. In so far as they did not flagrantly contradict Christianity, they were successfully integrated.

C. THE 'DARK CENTURIES' (MID–7TH CENT. – *c.* 800)

As far as literature on the whole is concerned, the validity of this standard term is disputed or at least limited in more recent research. It remains a fact, however, that in the period after the government of Heraclius (610–641) literary and other 'artistic production' decreased. The older explanatory model, according to which this was causally connected with 'Iconoclasm', which split Byzantine society between 730 and 843 and plunged it into a severe crisis, is evidently false [20]. Even from a chronological point of view, the phases simply do not coincide. Moreover, the controversy over the legitimacy of icon worship had an effect which was stimulating rather than debilitating. Thus, John of Damascus outlined a differentiated theology of icons in his speeches on icons, with the help of Aristotelian thought-categories. Instead, it seems plausible that there was a connection with the general breakdown of ancient urban culture which occurred at this time, as well as with the empire's foreign policy troubles, due to the conquest of the south-eastern provinces (Egypt, Syria, Palestine, Mesopotamia) by the Arabs, and the occupation of the Balkan peninsula by Avar and Slavonic tribes. Nevertheless, the break with tradition in Syria-Palestine was not drastic, even under Arab rule [7]. Quite apart from this, literary creativity did not cease by any means; yet its focus shifted quite clearly to the theological sector. Here it was mainly the genres of liturgical verse, with John of Damascus and Andrew of Crete, the 'inventor' of canon-verse, which replaced the earlier *Kontákion*, and of homiletics, that flourished. In the sermons of Sophronius of Jerusalem, Andrew of Crete and Germanus I, patriarch of Constantinople, it became clear that the ancient cultural tradition had not been uprooted, either among the orators or their public. The same holds true for philosophy. By adopting the ideas of Pseudo Dionysius Areopagita, Maximus Homologetes (580–662) anchored the connection of Aristotelian and Platonic approaches even more firmly in Byzantine theology. The break in the strands of tradition that went back to Antiquity is at its clearest in the narrative genres of historiography and hagiography. The chain of archaising contemporary historians was not immediately continued after Theophylactus Simocattes. The Chronicle of Theophanes the Confessor (*c.* 760–817/18), which covered the years 285 to 813, could not by any means be considered an example of literature inspired in any way by mimesis of Antiquity. This is less true for the parallel source, the *Historia Syntomos* of the Patriarch Nicephorus I (written in about 780, it dealt with the years 602–769), yet on a linguistic and stylistic level, it remains, like this author's theological writings directed against the Iconoclasts, within the framework of the inherited rhetorical ideal. The same holds true for a few products of hagiography, in general poorly represented, such as the Life of Theodorus of Sicyon and parts of the Life of Symeon Salus by Leontius of Neapolis in Cyprus. In contrast, the majority of this Life, like most of the same author's Life of John Eleemon, follows other linguistic and stylistic tendencies, much more indebted to everyday spoken language. The 'Dark Centuries' of Byzantine literature were not as dark as was long thought; as a cultural force, however, Antiquity is present in the background, rather than as a direct model of literary production or a subject of philological study.

D. ENCYCLOPAEDISM AND THE REAPPROPRIATION OF ANTIQUITY (9TH–10TH CENT.)

By the end of the 8th cent. there began, timidly at first, a period which then consciously and decisively revived its connection to the late antique tradition prior to the crisis of the 7th cent., and hence to Antiquity itself [12]. It is often designated in modern literature, with somewhat different boundaries, as the 'Macedonian Renaissance'. Yet both components of the term are problematic: the Macedonian Dynasty (so called after the place of origin of Basilius I, founder of the dynasty) ruled from 867 to 1056, and the inflationary use of the term Renaissance is misleading. In the 9th and 10th cents., the looking back to Antiquity did not yet bear any direct connection to the autonomy of the individual or to a radical change of overall world-view [21]. Instead it took place primarily in two areas: the philological and literary study of the texts themselves, as well as a rich neo-classically-oriented literary production in many fields. The edition of ancient texts by the Byzantine philologists of this period was of great importance, not least because almost the whole of ancient Greek literature that has come down to us had to pass through the needle's eye of the so-called *metacharakterismós* (i.e. the transcription from majuscule into minuscule script, which emerged at the beginning of the 9th cent.). Significantly, as in Hellenism, the philologists who did the collecting were often the very ones who were creatively active. The outstanding figures of the first phase, up to the beginning of the 10th cent. were Leo the Mathematician (*c.* 790 to after 869), Photius (Patriarch of Constantinople 858–867 and 877–886) and Arethas (*c.* 850 to after 932, from 902 Archbishop of Caesarea in Cappadocia) [22]. Leo the Mathematician, who taught at the private academy founded by Bardas in Constantinople after 843 [19], collected primarily mathematical and scientific manuscripts, thereby contributing substantially to the preservation of various ancient writings on astronomy, as well as algebra and geometry (Ptolemy, Euclid, Apollonius of Perga, Diophantus). Yet he can also be shown to have studied Porphyry, Plato and Achilles Tatius. Entire editorial projects of the 9th cent. are known through surviving manuscripts, for instance the so-called *Philosophical Collection* from the middle of the century, containing a nucleus of manuscripts of various works by Plato and commentaries on Platonic and Aristotelian works. At the end of the century, Plato and Aristotle can also be found among the surviving manuscripts in the library of Arethas, flanked, apart from Christian authors, by Lucian, Aelius Aristides and Euclid. From Arethas's autograph *scholia,* a comprehensive classical education, including the tragedians and comedians, is clearly apparent. The most impressive figure in this respect as well, as a scholar with a comprehensive humanistic training, is nevertheless Photius. As an author active in many fields (e.g. dogmatics, exegesis, homiletics, epistolography, constitutional law), his importance for the history of reception of Antiquity lies above all in his lexicon of words of Attic authors, with its treasurehouse of numerous invaluable citations from otherwise lost works, and his (*Library*), a literary-historical inventory of 280 codices, recording a total of 386 works of ancient and Byzantine literature. A whole series of ancient historians and other works are known to us only from Photius's reports.

Here and in many other undertakings, does the encyclopaedic spirit of the era become clear. It culminated in the second phase in the figure of the emperor Constantine VII Porphyrogennetus (born 905, ruled 945–959). Long kept from power, Constantine put into operation a gigantic programme of collecting excerpts: the entire historical literature of Antiquity and the early Byzantine period, classified by subject, geoponics, iatrics and hippiatrics as well as other projects not relating to Antiquity. The collection of imperial biographies by the author known as Theophanes Continuatus can also be traced back to Constantine, and he himself, in a return to the genre of ancient imperial vitae, contributed an encomiastic biography of his grandfather, the dynastic founder Basilius I, in Book V. In the genre of historiography, we find the same neo-classical tendencies in the imperial biographies (for the years 813–886) by the anonymous author conventionally named Joseph Genesius, who also wrote at the court of Constantine, as well as in Leo Diaconus (writing at the end of the 10th cent., on the years 959–976), who was wholly indebted to ancient form. Great general encyclopaedias emerged: in the 9th cent. the *Etymologicum Genuinum* [2] and, probably also in Constantine's circle, the Suda. Both contained a wealth of material from ancient litera-

ture. Ancient law was edited for current use through recourse to Justinian's collection of laws in the gigantic (60 volumes) work *Basilica,* begun under Basilius I, and completed under Leo VI, probably in 888 [17]. The same emperor Leo VI emerges as an author of highly rhetorical homilies, in complete conformity with characteristic neoclassical style. Lucianic satire found its rebirth and continuation in the anonymous dialogue Philopatris (10th cent.). Nor did hagiography lag behind. Symeon Metaphrastes (died in about 1000) collected lives of saints, some of which he composed himself, while others he rewrote with a view to raising them to a neo-classicist level of language and style, into a menologion normally organised into 10 volumes, classified according to the Church calendar. The same tendencies are found in the field of poetry: the revival of archaising forms (anacreontics, dodecasyllables taking account of ancient prosody, elegiac distichs) and encyclopaedic collecting. The rules of ancient prosody were observed once again by Theodorus Studites (759–826) in his epigrams, and the most important poet of this entire era, John the Geometer (second half of the 10th cent.) was deeply marked by ancient models. At the beginning of the century, Constantine Cephalas had compiled a large collection of epigrams, which, as was often the case in other fields, united ancient and Byzantine material. His sources were both the great classical anthologies (Meleager of Gadara, Philip of Thessalonica) and the *Cyclus* of Agathias. This collection was reorganised and extended by an anonymous editor (Constantine Rhodius, according to Cameron) a few decades later, and this is the form it which it has come down to us under the modern designation *Anthologia Palatina* [6]. Overall, the revival of ancient linguistic and literary form led to greater productivity. Here we shall omit discussion of new forms that emerged at the same time without recourse to ancient models, e.g. the fifteen-syllable *versus politicus,* which was used in stichic verse for the first time in funerary poems for Leo VI (died 912) [2a], and would later become the main Byzantine and Modern Greek verse form.

E. Proto-Renaissance (11th–mid–13th Cents.)

The term has been chosen to resonate with that of *pre-Renaissance,* coined by Kazhdan [14. 146]. Without it being the case that a genuine Renaissance ensued, there were clear Renaissance-like traits, primarily a wholly new interest in individuality, both that of persons portrayed in literature and of the authors themselves. Interest in ancient literature no longer took the primary form of encyclopaedic collecting, but that of individually creative transformation. This holds for quite different genres: in poetry, the great mystic Symeon the New Theologian stood apart from neoclassical forms in his hymns, with their expression of personal mystical experiences; yet the two other great poets Christopher of Mytilene and John Mauropus combined personal statements with archaising forms

[14a]. Historiography sketched individual psychological portraits of its protagonists; the models here were not so much Thucydides and Herodotus as Polybius, Diodorus, and later authors. Here, too, the great master was the universal scholar and statesman Michael Psellus (1018–1079), who shone in almost every field of literature, but especially in his *Chronographia* (for the years 976–1077) [10b; 15b]. In her *Alexias* (on the reign of her father Alexius I Comnenus, 1081–1118), Anna Comnena combined event-focused history, biography and encomium with strong autobiographical elements, using the Homeric *Iliad* as a constant intertextual frame of reference [7a]. Nicetas Choniates, who dealt with the following period (1118–1206), cultivated at the highest literary and intellectual level a mimesis that is quite pronounced on the level of detail. The anonymous *Christus Paschon* wove verses and verse segments from Euripides, Aeschylus and Lycophron together into a new whole. The likewise anonymous dialogue *Timarion* continued the reception of Lucian with an ironic and parodistic tone, even with regard to Christian dogmas. The *Catomyomachia* by the universal man of letters Theodorus Prodromus parodied classical tragedy. Recourse to Platonic-Neoplatonic thought and to Aristotle led to a clash with the guardians of Orthodox belief: Michael Psellus narrowly avoided an accusation, the teachings of his pupil John Italus were anathematised in 1082. In the chivalrous spirit of the era, the Hellenistic novel inspired the revival of this genre, of which four 12th-cent. works survive [1a]. The novelistic epic by Digenes Acrites linked this tradition once again with elements of folk poetry [10a]. Great commentaries on ancient authors were written by Eustathius of Thessalonica (on Homer, Aristophanes, Dionysius Periegeta, Pindar) and by John Tzetzes (on Homer, Hesiod, Aristophanes, and Lycophron), who also documented their comprehensive classical culture in their rhetorical works. Overall, this era was characterised by the trend towards creative, genre-spanning departures, which made use, in grand style, of stimuli from ancient literature for new purposes.

F. THE ERA OF THE PALEOLOGANS. RESIGNED
FLOURISHING AND DISSOLUTION
(MID–13TH–MID–15TH CENTS.)

The political and economic decline of the Byzantine Empire after the conquest of Constantinople by the so-called Fourth Crusade in 1204 was accompanied by an astonishing cultural zenith, whose basically resigned tone is quite unmistakable. In addition to intensive work on Antiquity, which was more philological than literary, new trends began to be sketched: an opening up to non-Byzantine, particularly Western, literature, and a new interest in popular genres (chivalric novels, satirical animal stories). Even authors of Latin Antiquity were absorbed: out of primarily literary interest, Maximus Planudes (second half of the 13th cent.) translated such authors as Augustine, Ovid, Cicero, Macrobius and Boethius, while Demetrius and Prochorus

Kydones (14th cent.) translated Thomas Aquinas as well as Augustine and Boethius, mainly out of philosophical interest. This was the high period of Byzantine philology. Particularly outstanding as editors and textual critics were above all Planudes (epigram collections, Plutarch, Aratus), Manuel Moschopoulus (Pindar, Aristophanes), Thomas Magister (Pindar, the tragedians, Aristophanes) and especially Demetrius Triclinius (Hesiod, the tragedians and the comic poets). A remarkable series of great polygraphs, active in various literary fields and interested in science and philosophy, extended from the Empire of Nicaea (1204–1261) into the period after 1453, from Nicephorus Blemmydes (various philosophical works) through his pupils, the emperor Theodorus II Lascaris (1254–1258) and Georgius Acropolites (historian and teacher), Georgius Pachymeres (historian, author of philosophical, mathematical, rhetorical, and juridical writings), Nicephorus Gregoras (historian, author of rhetorical and theological treatises, including philosophical controversies in the form of a Platonic dialogue) to Georgius-Gennadius Scholarius (Patriarch of Constantinople 1454–1456, 1463 and 1464–1465) and his circle of intellectuals interested in philosophy and theology. An important place among these polygraphs was occupied by Theodorus Metochites (1270–1332), who in his numerous writings (including commentaries on Aristotle, essays on philosophical, scientific, historical and literary-historical questions, hexametric poems, and an introduction to astronomy) displayed a comprehensive training in Antiquity. He gave clear expression to the apocalyptic mood, accompanied by a feeling of inferiority with regard to Antiquity [3]. However, Antiquity did not cease inspiring authors, both on a literary and a philosophical level, including those who had not, like Bessarion and many others, gone to the West and played a role there in the Italian Renaissance. Georgius-Gemistus Pletho (c. 1360–1452) combined Platonic, Neoplatonic and Zoroastrian ideologies to draft a new religion and political reform based on it. The historians Laonicus Chalcocondyles and Critobulus of Imbrus moved the Ottomans to the centre of their historical representation. As it had been previously, however, mimesis of ancient authors was constitutive of the literary form of their work: Thucydides for Laonicus; Arrian, first and foremost, along with Thucydides, Herodotus, Flavius Josephus and Aelius Aristides for Critobulus. Thus, until and beyond the end, a part of Byzantine literature remained focused on Antiquity.

1 P. AGAPITOS, Narrative Structure in the Byzantine Vernacular Romances. A Textual and Literary Study of Kallimachos, Belthandros and Libistros, 1991 1a P. AGAPITOS, D. R. Reinsch (ed.), Der Roman im Byzanz der Komnenenzeit, 2000 2 K. ALPERS, Eine byzantinische Enzyklopädie des 9. Jahrhunderts. Zu Hintergrund, Entstehung und Geschichte des griechischen Etymologikons in Konstantinopel und im italo-griechischen Bereich, in: G. CAVALLO, G. DE GREGORIO, M. MANIACI (eds.), Scritture, libri e testi nelle aree provinciali di Bisanzio, vol. I, 1991, 235–269 2a TH. ANTONOPOULOU, The Homilies

of the Emperor Leo VI, 1997   3 H.-G. BECK, Theodoros Metochites: Die Krise des byzantinischen Weltbildes im 14. Jahrhundert, 1952   4 Id., Kirche und theologische Literatur im byzantinischen Reich, 1959   5 Id., Geschichte der byzantinischen Volksliteratur, 1971. 6 A. CAMERON, The Greek Anthology from Meleager to Planudes, 1993   7 G. CAVALLO, Qualche riflessioni sulla continuità della cultura greca in Oriente tra i secoli VII e VIII, in: ByzZ 88, 1995, 13–22   7a TH. GOUMA-PETERSON (ed.), Anna Komnene and Her Times, 2000   8 H. HUNGER, On the Imitation (Μίμησις) of Antiquity in Byzantine Literature, in: Dumbarton Oaks Papers 23–24, 1969–1970, 17–38 9 Id., Die hochsprachliche profane Literatur der Byzantiner, vols I–II, 1978   10 Id., s.v. Byzantinische Literatur, LMA 2, 1182–1204   10a E. JEFFREYS, Digenis Akritis. The Grottaferrata and Escorial versions edited and translated, 1998   10b A. KALDELLIS, The Argument of Psellos' Chronographia, 1999   11 A. KAMBYLIS, Abriß der byzantinischen Literatur, in: H.-G. NESSELRATH, Einleitung in die griechische Philologie, 1997, 316–342   12 P. LEMERLE, Le premier humanisme byzantin, 1971 (Byzantine Humanism: The First Phase (trans.) HELEN LINDSAY and ANN MOFFATT, 1986)   13 A. KAZHDAN, s.v. Literatur, ODB 2, 1234–1237   13a A. KAZHDAN, A History of Byzantine Literature (650–850), 1999   14 Id., L'eredità ant. à Bisanzio, in: Studi Classici e Orientali 28, 1988, 139–153   14a M. D. LAUXTERMANN, Byzantine Poetry from Pisides to Geometres, 2003   15 J. LJUBARSKIJ, Why is the Alexiad a Masterpiece of Byzantine Literature, in: J. O. ROSENQVIST, ΛΕΙΜΩΝ. Studies Presented to Lennart Rydén, 1996, 127–141   15a P. ODORICO, P. A. AGAPITOS (eds.), Pour une »nouvelle« histoire de la littérature byzantine, 2002   15b E. PIETSCH, Die Chronographia des Michael Psellos. Kaisergeschichte, Autobiographie und Apologie, 2000   16 G. PODSKALSKY, Theologie und Philosophie in Byzantium, 1977   17 A. SCHMINCK, Studien zu mittelbyzantinischen Rechtsbüchern, 1986   18 I. ŠEVČENKO, Levels of Style in Byzantine Prose, in: Jb. der Österreichischen Byzantinistik 31/1, 1981, 289–312   19 P. SPECK, Die Kaiserliche Universität von Konstantinopel, 1974   20 Id., Ikonoklasmus und die Anfänge der Makedonischen Renaissance, in: ΠΟΙΚΙΛΑ BYZANTINA 4, 1984, 175–210   21 W. TREADGOLD (ed.), Renaissances before the Renaissance, 1984   22 N. WILSON, Scholars of Byzantium, 1983 (²1996).

DIETHER RODERICH REINSCH

III. ART
A. OUTSIDE THE BYZANTINE EMPIRE (726–1453)
B. AFTER THE FALL OF THE BYZANTINE EMPIRE (1453–17TH CENT.)

A. OUTSIDE THE BYZANTINE EMPIRE (726–1453)
1. INTRODUCTION   2. WESTERN MIDDLE AGES (8TH–12TH CENTS.)   3. ITALY (11TH-BEGINNING OF THE 14TH CENT.)   4. BALKAN COUNTRIES   5. KIEVAN RUS' AND RUSSIA   6. THE CRUSADER STATES

1. INTRODUCTION
Two kinds of reception of Byzantine art may be distinguished: one contemporaneous with its state of de-

Fig. 1: Rome, Santa Maria Antiqua in the Roman Forum; fresco in the Theodotus chapel, c. 750

velopment at a given moment, and another, which first began after its end. However, after the end of Iconoclasm (726–843), Byzantine art returned repeatedly to classical models transmitted by the art of Late Antiquity, both with regard to theme (iconography) and especially to form, and it therefore became usual to speak of a 'Macedonian', 'Comnenian' or 'Palaeologan Renaissance'. Decisive for the influence and posterity of Byzantine art, however, was the fact that it was the determining form in the Christianised regions bordering the Mediterranean (and, to a severely limited extent, in the provinces of Syria, Egypt, and Northern Africa, occupied by the Arabs since the 7th and 8th cents.), as well, particularly after the Schism of 1054, as in all the eastern and south-eastern European lands that had joined the Orthodox Church. It could thus wield influence in two respects, insofar as 1) it exported its theologically-based formal canon, and 2) at the same time, it transmitted the ancient heritage, more or less clearly preserved in its complex creation of images, to the recipient lands. Examples include the 'classical' body-clothing scheme, with clearly recognisable echoes of balance, still effective even in expressive or stiffly linear representations of figures; but also such opposing compositional principles as the hieratic manner of presentation (frontality with regard to the viewer; portraits), or narrative description (continuous vs. sequential image sequences; paintings or reliefs of stories), and finally the way of integrating the figure(s) into the surrounding pictorial space (illusionist perspective). In any case, this was certainly a considerable reduction of the ancient tradition, since figurative art in B. had remained essentially limited to the genres of painting (wall and mosaic,

Fig. 3: Ivory relief: Christ crowning
Otto II and Theophano,
c. 982. Paris, Musée Cluny

Fig. 2: Ivory relief, Christ crowning the
emperor Romanus II and Eudocia, *c.* 945.
*Reproduced with the permission
of the Bibliothèque nationale de France*

book illustration, enamelling) and bas-relief (stone relief, ivory carving, shallow casting) and statuary played scarcely any role.

2. WESTERN MIDDLE AGES (8TH–12TH CENTS.)

In the West, the contemporaneous reception of Byzantine artistic forms was never really interrupted. There had been a strong Greek colony In Rome since the 6th cent., while Lower Italy and Sicily, but also Ravenna and Venice, had been under Byzantine rule for a long time, and so remained under the defining influence of Byzantine art. Popes of Greek origin who were sensitive to art and were active as patrons, such as John VII (705–707) and Zacharias (741–752) leant prestige to Byzantine spirituality and art in Rome. Itinerant or, after Iconoclasm, emigrant groups of Byzantine artists, who were active in Rome and Italy, disseminated Byzantine pictorial models and stylistic methods, as is shown by Roman miraculous images of the 7th/8th cents. and the frescos in Santa Maria Antiqua (Fig.1). In addition, Byzantine works of art were brought to the West throughout this period by imperial legations, pilgrims, travellers, and merchants. During the Iconoclastic peri-

od, however, it was to be expected that there were scarcely any exports of Byzantine art worth mentioning, owing to the considerable decrease in artistic productivity. One can nevertheless assume, however scant the surviving Byzantine evidence may be, that something like an artistic unity was preserved in East and West in the 'Dark Ccenturies' (*c.* 600–800).

In contrast, the → CAROLINGIAN RENAISSANCE which began *c.* 780 out of opposition to Byzantium and in accordance with the consciously pursued idea of a 'renovatio' of the Western Roman Empire, unequivocally took up the art of Western (Latin) Late Antiquity, whose transmitted products (primarily ivory works, illuminated manuscripts, architectonic *spolia*) it appropriated and, as it were, transformed [21]. In contrast, Byzantine art began its significant achievements only gradually, in the late 9th cent. There was a strong influx of Byzantine works of art of beginning with the Ottonian period (mid–10th cent.) into the West (Italy, the Saxon Empire), above all courtly art (illuminated manuscripts, ivory carvings, silk fabrics, and gold, silver and enamel works). This led to a peculiar reception, characterised on the one hand by new forms of reuse (e.g. Byzantine ivory icons as cover decoration for Western liturgical manuscripts) and on the other hand by conscious imitation (Figs. 2 and 3). It had consider-

Fig. 4: Interior of San Marco, Venice

able influence on the development of Western art north of the Alps in the 10th and 11th cents. [2. 434–507].

3. ITALY (11TH-BEGINNING OF THE 14TH CENT.)

In Italy the conditions for the reception of Byzantine art were especially favourable. Even during Norman rule (1091–1189) in Lower Italy and particularly in Sicily, the Byzantine canon of forms developed after Iconoclasm remained decisive in mosaic painting [7] (Palermo, Cappella Palatina, 1132–1140, Santa Maria dell'Ammiraglio, 1143, Monreale, cathedral, 1185–1189) [14]. Venice was a special case, as the city, originally a Byzantine duchy, remained in a tense relationship with B., despite its gradual separation from Constantinople. The Church of San Marco, erected between 1063 and 1094 with decoration continuing until the 13th cent. [8], was in many respects a copy of the Justinian Church of the Apostles in Constantinople, completed in the year 550. It is richly furnished with architectonic and figurative *spolia* of Byzantine origin and with mosaic programmes [9], which, although Venice belonged to the Catholic West, were executed wholly in the sense of Orthodox spirituality (Fig. 4).

The arrival of numerous Byzantine works of art in Italy, France and Germany after the conquest and plundering of Constantinople during the Fourth Crusade (1202–1204), together with the influx of Byzantine artists, who migrated to the West during Latin rule (1204–1261), led to a renewed confrontation with Byzantine art [2. 441–449]. The Venetian 'proto-Renaissance' of the 13th cent., evidence of which is often hard to distinguish from genuine Byzantine works, was therefore as much a product of the undiminished continuation of Byzantine influence as the 'maniera greca', which dominated Italian panel painting in the 12th/13th cents., mainly in Tuscany, and decisively shaped the artistic creativity of important painters such as Cimabue, Duccio and Giotto [15]. Here, the term 'maniera greca' describes not so much a simple imitation of current Byzantine figurative types, for instance the Byzantine variations on the enthroned Mother of God, as their appropriation and development, and also, not least, the invention of new kinds of supports (e.g. polyptychs, altarpieces, monumental triumphal crucifixes). From the synthesis of the Byzantine model, whose recognised archetypical authority continued to remain influential,

Fig. 5: Sopocani, Church of the Holy Trinity, Dormition of the Mother of God, *c.* 1265.
Sopocani Monastery, Kosovo

also in the new creations, and an altered relation to the image, which grew out of the desire to have the person portrayed turned towards the observer, Italian panel painting gradually overcame Byzantine standardisation [5].

4. BALKAN COUNTRIES

Greece, including the islands (more or less within the modern borders), together with Asia Minor, formed the core region of the Byzantine state since the 7th and 8th cents., after the loss of the eastern provinces to the Arabs. It thus always remained immediately connected to Byzantine art [1] and thereby also influenced the neighbouring regions of the Balkan peninsula (Macedonia, Bulgaria, Serbia) as far as approximately the lower Danube [4]. From the mid–7th cent., migrating Slavs encountered the culture of the late ancient and early Byzantine population here, and gradually founded their own dominions. The first Bulgarian empire (651–1018) thus emerged out of several ethnic groups (Slavs, proto-Bulgars), whose cultural peculiarities mixed with the influential late ancient and early Byzantine substrate [2. 321–335]. With the acceptance of Orthodox Christianity as a state religion under Boris I (867), the Bulgarian empire fell wholly under the influ-

ence of Byzantine art, but preserved many traditional elements (for instance, the basilical type of church: Pliska, Great Basilica, 870–880). With the relocation of the Imperial residence to Preslav under Tsar Symeon (893–927), Byzantine influence was accentuated (e.g. adoption of the type of the cruciform domed church, albeit simplified), yet completely independent creations did emerge (Preslav Round Church, about 900). With the end of the first Bulgarian empire and the re-establishment of Byzantine rule over → BULGARIA, Macedonia and Serbia (1018–1186), the influence of the art of B. was again reinforced (wall-paintings of Sofia, Saint George Rotunda, *c.* 1000, Bačkovo Monastery, 11th/12th cents.), yet even during the second Bulgarian empire (1186–1396), with its capital at Veliko Tŭrnovo, the characteristics of mediaeval Bulgarian art remained clearly recognisable, particularly in architectural decoration, monumental painting and crafts (Bojana, Church of Saints Nicholas and Panteleimon, 1259; Nessebar, Pantocrator Church, 14th cent.). With the Turkish conquest, the living reception of Byzantine art ended [18] and later merged with the general post-Byzantine development.

Fig. 6: Vladimir Mother of God icon,
11th/12th cent.

In contrast, owing to its geographical position,
Serbia was always an area typified by West-East contact
[17], especially in 13th/14th-cent. architecture and
sculpture, where elements of local forms mix with Romanesque and early Gothic ones (Studenica, Church of
the Holy Mother, after 1190, Dečani, Church of the
Ascension, 1327–1335). After the Byzantine reconquest of further areas of the Balkans (1018) and the
reestablishment of the archbishopric of Ohrid, Macedonia became an important centre of Byzantine culture.
Particularly in monumental wall painting, the decisive
influence first of the Comnenian style (Ohrid, Saint
Sophia's, c. 1050, Nerezi, Saint Panteleimon's, 1164,
Kurbinovo, Saint George's, 1191), and later also of the
Palaeologan style is clearly visible [13]. Under the Serbian Nemanjid dynasty (1168–1371) the Serbian
Orthodox Church obtained its independence. Art,
however, particularly monumental wall paintings in
churches and monasteries, remained indebted to Byzantine art. This was especially true under Latin rule (1204–
1261), when the activity of émigré artists from the capital shifted precisely to the Balkan region (Studenica,
Church of Saint Mary, 1209; Mileševa, Church of the
Ascension, c. 1235; Peć, Church of the Apostles, 1235–
1250). In Sopoćani (Church of the Holy Trinity, c. 1265
etc.) mediaeval Serbian monumental painting reached
its summit, and already anticipated elements of the
early Palaeologan style (Fig. 5). Under King Milutin

(1282–1321), who founded many new churches,
schools of painting arose in Serbia and the part of
Macedonian territory it had annexed that were contemporaneous with the beginning of the Palaeologan style,
some with artists known by name such as Michael
Astrapas and Eutychius (Ohrid, Church of Peribleptos,
1297, Studenica, 'King's Church', 1313/14, Gračanica
Monastery, Church of the Annunciation, 1321, Dečani,
Church of the Ascension, c. 1340). Under the Lazarević
dynasty (1371–1427) parts of Serbia (primarily Macedonia) were lost to the Turks (Battle of Kosovo, 1398).
After the brief interlude of the 'Morava School', henceforth limited to only a small area (e.g. Ravanica:
Church of the Ascension, c. 1375, Kalenić: Church of
the Holy Mother, c. 1410), the mediaeval Serbian artistic era came to an end in 1459 [13].

5. KIEVAN RUS' AND RUSSIA

With the conversion to Orthodox Christianity (988)
of the archduke Vladimir of Kiev (1015) the development of Old Russian art, initially under decisive influence from Byzantium, began [2. 281–319]. In this process, Byzantine builders, immigrant artists and imported materials determined church architecture [10] as
well as the mosaic and monumental painting of the new
capital Kiev (Tithe Church, 989–996), which first flourished under Yaroslav the Wise (1015–1054). The
nucleus of Sophia Cathedral, erected between 1037 and
1043, a five-nave cruciform domed basilica with five
apses, 13 domes and a gallery on three sides (extended
in the 12th cent.), already offers a clearly independent
reception of Byzantine building forms, while the
mosaics and frescos (1043–1046) were executed by immigrant Greek and indigenous artists. Kievan architecture became the model for further centres, such as Cernigov (Church of the Redeemer, 1036) and the far
northern cities of Smolensk, Polock (Sophia Cathedral,
c. 1050), Pskov and Novgorod (Sophia Cathedral,
1042–1052). In the course of the 12th cent., the cruciform domed basilica, built over four columns in brick,
or brick and plaster, and with simple decoration, established itself henceforth as the leading form of Russian
sacral architecture (Cernigov, Church of Paraskeva-
Pjatnica, end of the 12th cent.). Byzantine panel paintings (Fig. 6), illuminated manuscripts, and gold and
silver work reached Rus' and other cities, where they
acted as models and stimulated a highly developed local
artistic creativity. As in mediaeval Serbia, Byzantine
and Western Romanesque influences mixed to form a
synthesis in the architecture and architectural sculpture
of Vladimir-Suzdal', where a further centre of Old Russian art emerged in the 12th cent. (Vladimir, Saint
Demetrius Cathedral, 1193–1197). With the Tatar
invasion (1237–1241) the first phase of reception of
Byzantine art came to an end in almost all Russian principalities, with the exception of the city republics of
Novgorod and Pskov, where the entire Byzantine canon
of themes and forms was preserved in monumental and
panel painting, partly in a clearly local version.
Through the influx of Byzantine painters such as Theo-

phanes the Greek (d. 1410), the late Paleologan style reached Novgorod in the 14th and 15th cents., and here initially influenced monumental painting, while the Novgorod Style developed in panel painting. After the victory over the Tatars at Kulikovo (1380), the rise of Moscow to the position of the decisive political and cultural centre of Russia began. It now took over the Byzantine-Russian heritage, which had been preserved and further developed primarily in Novgorod and Pskov. Immigrant Russian and Byzantine painters founded the Moscow School, at whose beginning were Theophanes the Greek and Andrei Rublev (d. *c.* 1427/30), and which reached its acme in Dionisy, after the fall of B. [4. 285–315].

6. THE CRUSADER STATES

B.-influenced art presents a particular problem in the dominions established by the Crusaders in the Holy Land [11], in Constantinople and in parts of Greece (Antioch, 1098–1268, Latin Kingdom of Jerusalem, 1099–1291, Latin Empire of Constantinople, 1204–1261, Cyprus, 1275–1291). Works created in these regions by indigenous Greek or Syrian and/or Frankish artists (wall paintings, book illustrations, crafts) often cannot be unambiguously categorised owing to this overlapping network of influences; alternatively, precisely because of the various stylistic components, they show themselves to be typical products of the Crusader period [2. 389–401].

B. AFTER THE FALL OF THE BYZANTINE EMPIRE (1453–17TH CENT.)
1. INTRODUCTION 2. GREECE AND THE GREEK ISLANDS 3. OTTOMAN ARCHITECTURE

1. INTRODUCTION

The literary heritage of Antiquity, which had been preserved almost undiminished in B., was transmitted after the end of the Byzantine Empire (1453) to the West, where it inspired a literary reception, including Byzantine historiography (→ BYZANTINE STUDIES). At the same time, the 'national styles' that emerged under Byzantine influence lived on in the art of the post-Byzantine period in the 15th–17th cents., despite Turkish rule, primarily in the Orthodox regions of southeastern Europe (Greece, Serbia, Bulgaria, Romania). Although one can no longer speak of a living reception of the vanished Byzantine art, a 'Koine' ('Maniera Bizantina') established itself on the basis of the respective artistic traditions, which drew its comprehensive strength, binding the various ethnicities together, from the preservation of Orthodox spirituality. It produced complete innovations in wall painting (Athos, Meteora), yet its characteristic field of activity was in (private) icon painting and in crafts, and no longer displayed any echoes of the classical epochs of Byzantine art [20].

2. GREECE AND THE GREEK ISLANDS

The island of Crete, which had been under Venetian sovereignty since 1201, occupied a special position within post-Byzantine painting [6]. There had already been a lively artistic exchange with Constantinople during and after the end of Latin rule. After 1453, many artists emigrated from the capital to Crete, where they transplanted the achievements of the 'Palaeologan Renaissance' in wall and panel painting. In the subsequent period, Heraclion/Candia in particular developed into an important spiritual and artistic centre with strong influence on the post-Byzantine painting of the Greek mainland (Athos, Meteora) and the Greek islands (Patmos), primarily through the export of icons. Its influence reached as far as Sinai and Venice. On the other hand, from the end of the 15th cent. Cretan painting took its impetus from the Italian Renaissance, which led to an eclectic style (Italo-Cretan School, 'Maniera Italiana'). Unusually large numbers of the names of artists have been transmitted and are confirmed archivally. The best known are Andreas and Nicholas Ritzos, Nicholas Tzafouris, Theophanes the Cretan, Michael Damascenus, Georgios Klontzas, Emanuel Tzane and, finally, Domenicos Theotocopoulos (El Greco). During the Turkish-Venetian war (1630–1669), many artists abandoned the island, thus contributing to a wide dissemination of characteristic Cretan features, especially in the Ionian islands (e.g. Zakynthos) and the mainland. This development finally culminated in the so-called Heptanesian School, a tendency strongly marked by Western Baroque influences [19].

3. OTTOMAN ARCHITECTURE

In contrast, a genuinely creative confrontation occurred in the architecture of the Ottoman Empire, namely with the early Byzantine church architecture of the early Justinian period [12]. The model for all great mosques built in Istanbul after 1453 [16] was Hagia Sophia (Fig. 7), whose central main dome, held up by support domes and a system of concealed buttresses, inspired new variations on domed central spaces and solutions to the associated technical and constructional problems. Already in 1462, Mehmet II Fatih had the dilapidated Justinian Church of the Apostles demolished and built in its place the enormous complex of the Fatih Camii. The Beyazıt Camii arose in the years 1500–1506. Under Sinan, the most important Ottoman architect (1490–1588), the Şahzade Camii (1543–1548) and, as probably his greatest achievement, the Süleymaniye Camii (1550–1557, Fig. 8) were built one after the other, almost exactly matching Hagia Sophia in their dimensions.

→ ARMENIA; → BASILICA; → GEORGIA; → Iconoclasm

1 A. CUTLER, J.-M. SPIESER, Das mittelalterliche Byzantium 725–1205, 1996 2 The Glory of Byzantium. Art and Culture of the Middle Byzantine Era AD 843–1261, H. C. EVANS, W. W. WIXOM (eds.), The Metropolitan Museum of Art, 1997 (exhibition catalogue) 3 R. KRAUTHEIMER, Early and Christian Architecture, ⁴1986 (revised by R. K. and SL. ĆURČIĆ) 4 W. F. VOLBACH, J. LAFONTAINE-DOSOGNE, Byzantium und der christliche Osten (Propyläen Kunstgeschichte, vol. 3), 1968 5 H. BELTING, Bild und Kult. Eine Geschichte des Bildes vor dem Zeitalter der Kunst, 1990 6 M. CHATZIDAKIS, Études sur la peinture postbyzantine, 1976 7 O. DEMUS,

The Mosaics of Norman Sicily, 1950 8 Id., The Church of San Marco in Venice: History, Architecture, Sculpture (Dumbarton Oaks Studies 6), 1960 9 Id., The Mosaics of San Marco in Venice, vol. 1: The Eleventh and Twelfth Centuries, 1984 10 H. Faensen, W. Iwanow, Altrussische Baukunst, 1972 (Early Russian Architecture (trans.) M. Whittal, 1975) 11 J. Folda, The Art of the Crusaders in the Holy Land, 1098–1187, 1995 12 G. Goodwin, A History of Ottoman Architecture, 1971 13 R. Haman-Mac Lean, H. Hallensleben, Die Monumentalmalerei in Serbien und Makedonien vom 11. bis zum frühen 14. Jahrhundert, 3 vols, 1963–76 14 E. Kitzinger, The Mosaics of St. Mary's of the Admiral in Palermo (Dumbarton Oaks Studies 27), 1990 15 V. N. Lazarev, Geschichte der byzantinischen Malerei, 1986 16 W. Müller-Wiener, Bild-Lexikon zur Topographie Istanbuls. Byzantion – Konstantinupolis – Istanbul bis zum Beginn des 17. Jahrhunderts, 1977 17 Sv. Radojčic, Geschichte der serbischen Kunst von den Anfang bis zum Ende des Mittelalters, 1969 18 A. Chilingirov, Die Kunst des christlichen Mittelalters, in Bulgarien vom 4. bis 18. Jahrhundert, 1978 19 D. D. Triantaphyllopulos, Die nachbyzantinische Wandmalerei auf Kerkyra und den anderen ionischen Inseln. Untersuchungen zur Konfrontation zwischen ostkirchlicher und abendländischer Kunst (15.–18. Jahrhundert), = Miscellanea Byzantina Monacensia 30A, 1985 20 Thesauroi tou Hagiou Orous, 1997 (exhibition catalogue, Greek) 21 799 – Kunst und Kultur der Karolingerzeit. Karl der Grosse und Papst Leo III. in Paderborn (Exhibition).   ARNE EFFENBERGER

C

Caesarism

A. Introduction   B. Definition   C. Historical Preconditions and Dissemination
D. Looking Ahead

A. Introduction

The concept of Caesarism covers only one part, albeit an important one, of the historical reception of
Caesar in modern times. Its use in the political discourse
of the 19th and early 20th cents. was complemented by
scholarly, artistic and literary interpretations (e.g.
Thornton Wilder, *The Ides of March*, 1948; Bertolt
Brecht, *Die Geschäfte des Herrn Julius Caesar*, 1957,
[17. 119ff.; 13. 247ff.] and its adaptation and use in
films such as *Little Caesar*, 1930; *Cleopatra*, 1963; and
Asterix and the Laurel Wreath, from the *Asterix* series,
1972).

B. Definition

The concept of Caesarism was shaped and became
influential from the second half of the 19th cent.
onwards in reaction to the rule of Napoleon III (President of France 1848, French emperor 1852–1873). It
became in many respects synonymous with Bonapartism as 'the new Caesarism' ('... thus Napoleon gives his
name to a new Caesarism, to which only he who is most
capable and is of the best will is entitled', Heinrich
Heine, Französische Zustände von 1832, Bulletin for
20 August, in: H. Heine, Säkularausgabe 7, 1970, 210,
[20. 741]) and can thus also include the specific structures of governance under Napoleon I, including his
expansionist foreign policy. Caesarism was spread by
the writings of French essayist A. Romieu, *L'ère des
Césars* (1850) [4]. According to Romieu, Caesarism
means, on the one hand, a political dictatorship that is,
as was the case with the Roman emperors, based upon a
union of the military imperium and tribunicial rule of
the people. Thus, to a large extent, it overrides or even
supplants entirely traditional power-structures [22.
1814ff.]. On the other hand, this kind of dictatorial rule
can become an historical necessity on occasions when
the traditional bonds of people and society break down,
social crises arise, and civil war threatens, thus calling
for an outstanding leader as a saviour. This curious
mixture of historical model, contemporary societal processes and new leadership structures guaranteed Caesarism its enigmatic and contentious character. As a
contemporary political term it appears in all the major
European reference dictionaries and → ENCYCLOPE-
DIAS of the second half of the 19th cent. (e.g. *Meyers
Konversations-Lex.*, 4th ed. 1886 and [1; 9]). Caesarism is defined as an 'absolute monarchy with pseudo-
constitutional institutions. The Caesar (emperor) exercises his absolute power as the agent of the people, and
his will enjoys equal status to decisions made by the

people' [6. 1195]. He is the highest representative of the
people and has full responsibility, while the people can
make known its will by means of a plebiscite [23. 525].
Depending upon political orientation, Caesarism can
approach despotism, → TYRANNIS, dictatorship and totalitarian rule. In all these systems, decision by plebiscite and a military basis for rule are constitutive.

C. Historical Preconditions and Dissemi-
nation

The widespread and mostly ideological use of the
concept is based upon historical preconditions in the
19th and early 20th cents that were specific to that period. In Europe, the French Revolution had called into
question once and for all the role and function of the
traditional monarchy and placed the problem of a valid
contemporary representation of nation and people on
the long-term agenda. The nobility, the bourgeoisie and
the gradually developing so-called fourth estate were
undergoing significant changes as a result of the industrial revolution. New political and social organisations
arose (societies, associations, parties) that needed well-
thought out publicity. These far-reaching changes went
hand in hand both with a sharper historical awareness,
which sought to understand the political and social
problems of the age by comparing them with those of
the past, especially those of Greek and Roman antiquity, as well as with a complementary counter-tenden-
cy towards contemporary → HISTORICISM, which focused upon the individuality and uniqueness of historical phenomena. The example of Caesar, his military
successes, his populist politics, his ending of the civil
war and his dictatorial one-man rule seemed both to
illustrate and to legitimise the rule of Napoleon [28.
120ff.; 15. 135ff.] (cf. figs 1 and 2). In general terms, the
Roman Caesardom or imperium represented an important model of reference for Napoleon I in its outward
form as well. In Napoleon, Hippolyte Taine (1828–
1893) saw 'the Diocletian of Ajaccio, the Constantine
of the Concordat, the Justinian of the Civil Code, and
the Theodosius of the Tuileries', by whose efforts modern France had taken its shape as an 'exemplary model
of the classical spirit' [11. 180, 187]. Thereafter, the
Napoleonic or Caesar-based model for rule presented a
challenge in theory as well as in practice. A great
amount of evidence for this was provided by the coup
d'etat of Napoleon III in 1851, which represented the
'birth of Caesarism in France' (Stürmer) (detailed discussion in [19]).

Mommsen's brilliant sketch of Caesar in his *Römische Geschichte* [vol. 3. 461ff.] also owes its fascination
not least of all to its proximity to contemporary Caesarism of the Bonapartist type [30. 3, 636, 649, 651ff.; 14.
151ff.]. In the third edition of his *Römische Geschichte*,
Mommsen attempted to correct and distance himself
from this widespread impression by inserting a passage

Fig. 1: Place Vendôme, Paris

[3. 477f.] that insists upon the uniqueness of the classical instance; 'where Caesarism develops under other circumstances, it is simultaneously a farce and a usurpation' (*Römische Geschichte*, vol. 3, 478). Nevertheless, Mommsen's picture of a powerful and democratic king who founded a Mediterranean monarchy upon the ruins of decayed aristocratic rule (*Römische Geschichte*, vol. 3, 567f.) had a great effect, not only in France, where Napoleon III himself produced a literary tribute to the brilliant general Caesar (*Histoire de Jules César*, I–II, 1865/6), but also, and to an equal extent, in Italy and in the rest of Europe. The tension between political reality in the figure of Napoleon III and the historical model made Caesarism a highly ambiguous concept that lent itself to use in the debate over the proper political order of Europe. For J. G. Droysen (1808–1884) Caesarism was a symptom of a pan-European crisis and an element of transition in state and society (*Zur Charakteristik der europäischen Krise*, 1854). That radical social changes, tensions in the bourgeoisie itself and the rise of a proletariat provided fertile soil for the growth of Caesarism or Bonapartism was noticed in various quarters (K. Marx, W. H. Riehl and others; for details, see [23. 21f.]), and was interpreted in various ways depending upon political standpoint. In the form of French Bonapartism, modern Caesarism was understood in Germany as a warning against the unrestricted sovereignty of the people and the introduction of democracy ('Caesar-style democracy', Karl Hillebrand, 1873 [20. 763]), which, according to a certain

natural logic, would result ultimately in a *Führer*-figure gifted with the instinct for power. In this sense, the 'Caesarism of Caesar' (cf. [16. 275f.]), a fortuitous historical combination of absolute rule and the needs of the people peculiar to its own time, served as a contrast to its modern distortion in the shape of Bonapartism [8; 21. 74f.], whose place in the historical process was seen as a warning sign.

'The main means of advancement for Caesarism is the thought that one would rather be devoured completely by a lion than by ten wolves, or a hundred jackals, or a thousand rats.' This is according to the interpretation by the economist and historian W. Roscher (1817–1894) in his *Politik* (Geschichtliche Naturlehre über Monarchie, Aristokratie und Demokratie, Stuttgart 1892, 492 [24. 279f.]) of the 'natural' movement from a democracy that has fallen into chaos towards an autocracy by plebiscite (with links to classical theories of circulation: [22. 1808f.; 20. 764ff.]). Roscher's pupil R. von Pöhlmann built on this outline when he spoke about the 'Janus-head of Caesarism', which shows an 'extreme monarchic and an extreme democratic, and even ochlocratic face' [3. 284]. A similar genesis occurs in the related political system of tyranny, i.e. in 'the emergence of a proletarian revolution and in the combination of personal ambition with the power of the fist latent in the masses' [3. 282]. The initial systematisation of Caesarism by Roscher and Pöhlmann forms a bridge to a sociological interpretation [20. 764ff.] and makes it possible to assume the Greek tyrants, the

Fig. 2: Napoléon I as Caesar Imperator: etching of
the statue in the Place Vendôme, c. 1810

Roman Caesars, the autocratic rulers of the city states
of Upper Italy, Cromwell, Napoleon I and Napoleon III
all under the collective term Caesarism and to analyse
them using comparable criteria such as populism,
eagerness for achievements abroad, building frenzy,
personality cult, talent for stagecraft and propaganda,
desire to provide for succession, and employment of the
military apparatus [5. 491ff.]. In M. Weber's (1864–
1920) sociology of rule, Caesarism also grows out of
democracy [10. 707], uses mass demagogy, and represents a special form of selection of leaders not only in
state organisations [10. 1094f.] It is based upon accla-
mation and emotional fealty and thus contrasts both
with bureaucratic and traditional forms of rule. Caesarism can, therefore, acquire a quite general dimension
within modern systems of government. It may be
applied to Cavour or Bismarck [10. 1988] just as to the
populist Kaiser Wilhelm II, to Hindenburg's presidency, supported as it was by plebiscite [26. 1958], or
to modern dictatorships, since it represents a precursor
and working parallel for them [19. 73ff.; 26, 233ff.; 12.
161f.]. For Otto Spengler (1880–1936) Caesarism represented a phenomenon associated with decay and
apocalypse in cultures that have degenerated to civilisations and a 'formless' rule by 'great men of great action',
which uses modern military possibilities to establish
personal power without any substantive program [7.
1080ff., esp. 1101ff.]. As the heir of democracy and
parliamentarianism, Caesarism moves towards the
final battle, to the decisive struggle on the world-historical stage that will be fought out between Caesarism
and democracy, between the commanding forces of a

dictatorial plutocracy and the purely political desire for
the order of the Caesars [7. 1144]. 'The rise of Caesarism smashes the dictatorship of finance and its political
weapon, democracy' [7. 1193]. The suggestion of this
dismal apocalyptic vision owes more than a little to the
experience of the First World War and the spiritual and
political breakdown that it occasioned. Spengler's *Decline of the West* ensured for Caesarism, yet again, a
broad resonance, and provided, especially in intellectual circles, for understanding and affirmation of the
rising totalitarian dictatorships.

D. LOOKING AHEAD
The word Caesarism is a product of the classically-
educated 19th cent. and its understanding of Caesar
himself, whose mythically elevated person also seemed
to hold abundant remedies for the societal and political
crises of the age. In the course of the 20th cent.the concept lost its functionality, its analytical usefulness and
its power of self-identification and was largely displaced by dictatorship and the Führer-principle. [22.
1819]. In Italian → FASCISM, Caesar the dictator became once again an important reference figure, who,
together with Princeps Augustus, provided a model for
military virtue and expansionist foreign policy and
helped to form an imperial ideology of Romanità or
Italianità [13. 90ff., 249ff.; 14. 267ff.; 19, 5ff.]. This
political strand in the reception of Caesar ended in
1945, even though leaders arising from the masses, with
a talent for power, continued to exist as a type next to
and indeed inside of parliamentary democracies and
helped to determine the political landscape of the second half of the 20th cent.
→ Augustus; → Caesar; → Ruler
→ RULER, FASCISM

SOURCES: 1 P. GUIRAUD, s.v. Césarisme, Grande Encyclopédie, (ed.) A. BERTHOLET, Vol. 10 (Paris 1892), 13f.
2 K. MARX, Der 18. Brumaire des Louis Bonaparte, in: Id.,
F. ENGELS, Werke Vol. 8, 1960, 111–207 (1rst ed. 1852,
2nd ed. 1869) 3 R. PÖHLMANN, Aus Altertum und Gegenwart Vol. 2, 245–293 (Die Entstehung des Cäsarismus), 2.
ed. 1911 4 A. ROMIEU, L'ère des Césars, 1850 5 W.
ROSCHER, Politik, Geschichtliche Naturlehre der Monarchie, Aristokratie und Demokratie, 1892 (Repr. 1933)
6 H. SACHER (ed.), s.v. Cäsarismus, Staats-Lexikon I.5,
1926, 1195f. 7 O. SPENGLER, Der Untergang des Abendlandes, Umriß einer Morphologie der Weltgeschichte,
1923 (Repr. 1969) 8 H.v. TREITSCHKE, Frankreichs
Staatsleben und der Bonapartismus (1865), in: Historische und politische Aufsätze III.4, Leipzig 1871, 43–113
9 H WAGENER (Ed.), s.v. Cäsarismus, Staats- und Ges.-
Lex. 5 (1861), 122f. 10 M. WEBER, Wirtschaft und Ges
I–II, 4. ed. 1956 11 H. TAINE, Les Origines de la France
Contemporaine 3.1, Paris 1891

LITERATURE: 12 P. BAEHR, Max Weber as a Critic of
Bismarck, in: Archive of European Sociology 29, 1988,
149–164 13 L. CANFORA, Ideologie del classicismo, 1980
14 K. CHRIST, Caesar. Annäherungen an einen Diktator,
1994 15 M. ERBE, Der Caesarmythos im Spiegel der
Herrschaftsideologie Napoleons I. und Napoleons III., in:
R. STUPPERICH (ed.), Lebendige Antike, 1995, 135–142

16 R. Etienne, Jules César, 1997   17 E. Frenzel, Stoffe
der Weltliteratur, 8th ed., 1992   18 F. di Georgi, Science
humane e concetto storico: Il Cesarismo, in: Nuova Rivista Storica 68, 1984, 323–354   19 H. Gollwitzer, Der
Cäsarismus Napoleons III. im Widerhall der öffentlichen
Meinung Deutschlands, in: HZ 173, 1952, 23–75   20 D.
Groh, C., Napoleonismus, Bonapartismus, in:
Geschichtliche Grundbegriffe 1, 1972, 726–771   21 F.
Gundolf, Caesar im 19. Jh., 1926   22 A. Heuss, Der
Cäsarismus und sein antikes Urbild (1980), in: GS III,
1995, 1803–1830   23 G. Jellinek, Allgemeine Staats-
lehre 3. ed. 1914   24 W. Meyer, Demokratie und Cäsa-
rismus, Konservatives Denken in der Schweiz zur Zeit
Napoleons III., 1975   25 A. Momigliano, Per un riesame
della storia dell'idea di Caesarismo (1956), in: Secondo
Contributo, 1960, 273–282   26 F. Neumann (ed.), The
Democratic and the Authoritarian State, 1964   27 A. de
Riencourt, The Coming Caesars, 1958   28 M. Stürmer,
Krise, Konflikt, Entscheidung: Die Suche nach dem neuen
Caesar als europ. Verfassungsproblem (1977), in: Id., Dis-
sonanzen des Fortschritts, 1986, 119–137   29 R. Visser,
Fascist Doctrine and the Cult of Romanità, in: Journ. of
Contemporary History 27, 1992, 5–22   30 L. Wickert,
Theodor Mommsen. Eine Biographie, 3–4, 1969 and
1980.   HANS KLOFT, JENS KÖHLER

Cairo, Egyptian Museum
A. History   B. The Current Exhibition
C. Plans for a New Museum

A. History

A *firman* (decree) concerning the preservation of antiquities was issued in Egypt for the first time in 1835,
after the country's monuments had for very many years
been plundered by native and foreign treasure-hunters
and sent to Europe. At the same time, the scholar Refaa
el Tahtawi was commissioned by the Wali (governor)
Mohamed Ali to set up a museum for Egyptian antiquities under his supervision, which was to be located in
the Ezbakiah Garden in downtown Cairo. Once the
museum was completely filled up with monuments,
around 1850, the state found another, larger building
for these treasures, in the Citadel of Saladin. Five years
later the Khedive (viceroy) Abbas Pasha donated the
Egyptian collection to Archduke Maximilian of
Austria.

The French archaeologist Auguste Mariette, who
had been carrying out excavations in Egypt since 1850,
was appointed in 1858 as the first director of the commission for overseeing Egyptian antiquities. In 1863,
Mariette built a new museum in the former harbour
buildings at Bulaq on the banks of the Nile. This
museum was under constant threat from fires in the
harbour warehouses and workshops. In 1878 it was
even inundated during a particularly high Nile-flood-
ing, so that a large number of smaller items were damaged or lost. When Mariette died in 1881, Gaston Mas-
pero was appointed as his successor.

In 1890 the state found a temporary storage site for
the monuments in a warehouse near the palace of the
Viceroy Ismail Pasha in Giza, until a new museum could
be built.

Fig. 1: Scribe. Limestone, Fifth Dynasty.
Cairo, Egyptian Museum

Fig. 2: Prince Rahotep and his wife Nofret. Limestone,
Fourth Dynasty. Cairo, Egyptian Museum

1896 saw the announcement of a world-wide competition for the construction of the new museum, and
more than 70 designs were submitted. The submission
by the French architect Marcel Dougnon was deemed
the most suitable, and the foundation-stone was cer-
emonially laid as early as 1 April, 1897. The plan of the
museum was based on those of Egyptian temples of the
New Kingdom and the Ptolemaic period, although the
façade and the inner galleries were still in neo-classical
style. While the façade was embellished with statues,
decorative features and inscriptions, the reception hall
was covered with a massive dome. The galleries, with
walls 1.20 metres thick, were connected to make the
exhibits easy to visit. The galleries received natural light
and sufficient ventilation through skylights on the
upper level and large windows at ground level. Concrete was used for the building for the first time in
Egypt, in addition to such traditional building materials

Fig. 3: Triad of Menkaure/Mykerinos (?).
Greywacke, Fourth Dynasty. Cairo, Egyptian Museum

Fig. 4: The dwarf Seneb and his family. Limestone,
Fourth/Fifth Dynasty. Cairo, Egyptian Museum

as marble, quartzite, limestone, iron and brick. At the time of its formal opening by Viceroy Abbas Helmi on 15 November 1902, it already contained nearly 40,000 items. Today, the Egyptian Museum shelters more than 160,000 exhibits, about ten per cent of them well exhibited, while the rest are kept in closed cabinets or storerooms.

B. The Current Exhibition

The ground floor holds large sarcophagi, sculptures and reliefs, set out clockwise in chronological order:

1) The sculptures of King Chephren (4th dynasty), found in 1860 by Mariette in the Valley Temple of the king at Giza. The most impressive is a diorite statue of the king on a throne with the falcon of Horus, the sun and sky god, behind his back, spreading out his wings to protect the king. The modelling of the sculpture reflects the king's strong personality, and symbolises the connection between god and man (or king).

2. Three triads of King Mycerinus (4th dynasty) in greywacke, also found in the Valley Temple of the king's pyramid (Fig. 3). Each triad shows the king between two other figures, one of which is the goddess Hathor while the other symbolises the personification of a region or town, with its emblems above their heads. These sculptures bear witness to the great skill of Old Kingdom sculptors, who were able to model the human body in a most impressive way and polish the hard stone to perfection.

3) The wonderful statues of Prince Rahotep, son of Snofru, and his wife Nofret (4th dynasty). These two statues of painted limestone with inset eyes are so lifelike that Mariette's workers were terrified when they found them (Fig. 2).

4) The wooden statue of the lector-priest Ka-aper (better known as Sheikh el Beled) from the 5th dynasty, which was found in Saqqara in 1860. This sculpture is perhaps the finest example of private sculpture in the round from the Old Kingdom. Here the perfection of the sculptor's art is complete, as he successfully reproduces the physiognomy and individualism of Ka-aper (Fig 1).

5) The limestone statue-group of the chief of all the palace dwarfs, Seneb, his wife Sentites and their two children, from the 4/5th dynasty, which were discovered in Giza in 1926–27 (Fig. 4). This group shows the close family relationship, with the man lovingly embracing his wife and the children completing the image of their father.

6) The grave furniture of Queen Hetep-hetres, wife of Snofru (4th dynasty), found in 1924–25 to the east of the great pyramid of her son Cheops in Giza. These objects were recently placed in a gallery of their own between the Old Kingdom rooms. Among them is a baldaquin of particular historical value (including gilded wooden pillars), and a litter.

7) The statue of Mentuhotep-Nebhepetre, of the 11th dynasty (c. 2061–2010 BC) is of special historical

Fig. 5: Perfume vessel of Tutankhamun.
Gold, silver and semiprecious stones.
Eighteenth Dynasty. Cairo, Egyptian Museum

Fig. 6: Perfume vessel of Tutankhamun
with Nile deities. Alabaster, Eighteenth Dynasty.
Cairo, Egyptian Museum

and artistic significance, since it represents the king who reorganised and reunited the state after many years of discord between the north and the south. From an artistic viewpoint, this statue, which Howard Carter discovered by accident in 1900, beautifully painted and in very good condition, is particularly valuable on account of its still provincial style.

8) The museum possesses several 12th dynasty sculptures of Kings Sesotris III (c. 1878–1842 BC) and Amenemhet III (c. 1842–1798 BC), which no longer show the idealised and fine facial features of the rulers of the Old Kingdom, but bear witness to a new style, characterised by a hard and exaggerated severity in the features.

9) The Egyptian Museum has numerous excellent 18th dynasty statues of Queen Hatshepsut (1490–1470 BC) and Thutmosis III (1490–1439 BC). Here, the artists returned to the idealistic and at the same time realistic forms of statuary. The two rulers are portrayed with beautiful features.

10) From the Amarna period (c. 1365–1349 BC) the museum has several important sculptures of Akhenaton and Nefertiti and their daughters, which give expression to the new artistic tendency and the new concept of kingship. We may note in this context the characteristic and almost realistic, sometimes even exaggeratedly represented physical features of Akhenaton and his daughters.

11) Numerous sculptures of Ramses II (1290–1224 BC) show the king in massive figures with his individual features. Special mention must be made of the gigantic statue of the falcon-headed Hauron: the king is shown as a squatting child, with his back and head protected by the breast and the beak of Hauron (illustrated in [2. no. 203]). The artist sought to translate the abstract name of Ramses (Ra-mes-su) into pictures, by using the sun's disk (for Ra), the child (mes) and an ear of grass (su).

12) The museum's Greek and Latin manuscripts are kept in two rooms on the ground floor.

Grouped finds and thematic collections are to be found on the upper floor: a) the monuments of Hemaka, a high-ranking official from the period of King Udimi (or Den, 1st dynasty, c. 2900 BC), found by the Egyptian Antiquities Commission in 1931 and 1936 in North Saqqara. Various interesting items belong to this find, notably some decorated disks of stone and metal, wooden agricultural tools with copper and flint blades, a wood casket inlaid with other materials, inscribed ebony labels and drawings of animals on limestone fragments. b) The grave-goods of Meketre, chancellor and senior administrator of the 11th dynasty (c. 2000 BC), which were found by the *Metropolitan Museum of Art* (New York) at Thebes in 1919–1920. While half went to New York under a division agreement, the other half remained in Cairo. The find consists of artistically painted wooden models, showing a miniature version of Meketre's earthly environment, in the form of grave-goods intended to help him in the afterlife. These include a woman offering sacrifice, Meketre's garden, his workshops (joinery and weaving mill), boats for transport and fishing, and models of his livestock. c). The very important and sumptuous jewellery of the princesses Chnumit, Sat-Hathor, Sat-Hathor-Junit, Ita, Neferuptah, Mereret, and Wereret, from the 12th dynasty (*c.* 1930–1800 BC), discovered in Dahshur, Lahun and Hawara in 1894, 1914, 1920, 1956 and 1994. d) The treasure of Queen Ahhotep, wife of Seqenenre-Taa, beginning of the 18th dynasty (*c.* 1554–1529 BC) found in West Thebes in 1858. e) The finds from the Theban grave of the whisk-bearer Maiherperi, which represent the personal belongings and coffins of a senior official (period of Hatshepsut and Thutmosis III) in the 18th dynasty (*c.* 1450 BC). f) The grave goods of Juja and Tuja, the parents of Queen Teje, wife of Amenhotep III, 18th dynasty (*c.* 1400 BC), discovered in the Valley of the Kings (Thebes) in 1905. These include sarcophagi, mummies, papyri, furniture, personal belongings, statues, vessels and a chariot. g) The unique and practically complete collection of items from the grave of Tutankhamun, 18th dynasty (*c.* 1349–1339 BC), found in the Valley of the Kings in 1922. This is an impressive representation of the opulence of a king's grave-goods in pharaonic Egypt (Figs 5 and 6), consisting in more than 4000 objects. Among them are numerous statues, furniture for everyday life and for the afterlife, jewellery and personal belongings, sarcophagi, six ceremonial and war chariots, vessels, toys, clothes, weapons and many other items. Of special note are the golden mask and the solid gold inner coffin. h) The grave furniture of the artisan Sennedjem and his family, from the time of Ramses II (1250 BC), found in 1886 in Deir el-Medinah (west of Thebes). Half of this collection remained in Cairo, while the other half is exhibited in the Metropolitan Museum (New York). i) The collection of mummies of kings of the New Kingdom from the royal repository at Deir el-Bahri (1881) and from the grave of Amenhotep II in the Valley of the Kings (1898). As part of a new presentation, eleven royal mummies are already on view in a climate-controlled room (Seqenenra-Taa, Amenhotep I, his wife Queen Meritamun, Thutmosis II, Thutmosis IV, Setos I, Ramses II, Merenptah, Ramses V, Queen Mutnedjemet and Queen Henut-Tawi). A new gallery is to be provided for sixteen further mummies. j) The sarcophagi of the priests of Amun-Ra and Khonsu, 21–22nd dynasty, from Deir el-Bahri (1891). k) Jewellery and other objects from the graves of kings and dignitaries of the 21–22nd dynasty from Tanis (*c.* 1054–970 BC): Psusennes, Sheshonq, Heqa-Cheper-Re, Undjebau-en-Djed, Hornakht and Amunemopet, discovered in 1939. l) The wooden coffins of various epochs discovered in Deir el-Bahri (West Thebes). m) Statues from various periods and materials found in the celebrated 'Karnak repository'. They are preserved or exhibited in various parts of the museum; originally there were more than 700 stone and 16,000 bronze statues. n) Objects associated with everyday life from the prehistoric and dynastic periods.

The museum possesses an extensive specialised library, as well as workshops for restoration and photography. There is a data-base of the collection, protected by an electronic security system.

At the beginning of the 20th cent., there were no more than 500 visitors daily. Now, with 5,000–7,000 daily visitors, and in view of pollution problems, the Egyptian Museum badly needs state-of-the-art climate-controlled rooms and a lighting system compatible with the most modern demands.

C. PLANS FOR A NEW MUSEUM

A new museum for the Egyptian monuments will soon be built in Giza, at the beginning of the desert road to Alexandria. The greater part of the Cairo collection will be accommodated here, including the treasures of Tutankhamun and monuments from various places and repositories in Egypt. The museum will make use of the most recent advances in procedures and technology, and will have an area of around 48,000 square metres. There will also be a large library, a research centre and an auditorium.

→ Amarna; → Echnaton; → Mycerinus; → Sesostris; → Thutmosis; → Tutankhamon

1 H. GRIMM, Kunst der Ptolemäer- und Römerzeit im Ägyptischen Museum, Cairo, 1975 2 M. SALEH, H. SOUROUZIAN, Das Ägyptisches Museum, Cairo, 1987

ADDITIONAL BIBLIOGRAPHY: R. GREGORY, Grand project. The Architectural Review 1 Aug. 2003: 17,19.; Website of new Grand Museum of Egypt: http://www.gem.gov.eg/index/main.htm; B. HANSEN, Grand Museum of Egypt to Complement Giza Pyramids. Civil Engineering. 75.7 (Jul 2005): 14. MOHAMED SALEH

Calendar

A. TRADITIONS B. THE JULIAN CALENDAR AS A SYSTEM OF CALCULATING TIME C. GRAPHIC FORM D. THE CALENDAR AS A MEDIUM

A. TRADITIONS

Of the many calendar systems of Greek and Roman Antiquity only the Jewish and the Julian Calendars survived in use beyond the late classical period. For many other systems, such as the Gaulish calendar, or that of Coligny, or the conventional lunisolar calendar of the Eastern Mediterranean, there are clear breaks in the tradition after the 4th cent. AD. The Julian Calendar, the system adopted by the Roman administration, was taken over by the Christian Church by the 4th cent. as its sole calendar and was thus continued as a broad-based living institution into the Middle Ages. There have been insufficient studies of the spread and parallel usage of the Jewish lunisolar calendar; it must certainly have been used and disseminated on a continuous basis in religious centres in Palestine. Scholarly work on the

Jewish calendar has been concerned with reconstructing it in detail and examining its popular use (e.g. [1;22]). With the spread of Islam around the Mediterranean there appears in the European history of the calendar after the 7th cent. a further, purely lunar calendar (augmented, it is true, by a system that is linked to the tropic year and based on the rising and setting of stars, *anwâ*, and which is also found in written form in almanacs). In addition, the passing-on of classical astronomical or antiquarian learning ensured that the knowledge of alternative (historical) systems was preserved by specialists.

This article concentrates upon the effects of the Julian Calendar. Alongside the technical aspects, which are typically in the foreground of historical analyses, attention is paid also to the graphic form of the calendar and its insertion within sources.

B. THE JULIAN CALENDAR AS A SYSTEM OF CALCULATING TIME
1. THE MIDDLE AGES 2. THE GREGORIAN REFORM 3. ACCEPTANCE AND CRITICISM 4. FURTHER ATTEMPTS AT REFORM

1. THE MIDDLE AGES
With an average year's length of 365.25 days and the automatic insertion of a day every four years, the Julian Calendar represents a fairly precise and easy-to-use system for the calculation of time and seems to have been used without interruption since the time of Augustus. The average excess of 0.0078 days per year did not occasion until the late Middle Ages – from the 13th cent. onward – any significant deviation (bringing forward the start of spring according to the calendar), which then led to various suggestions for reform. The principal problem was the date of Easter, which had been defined by the Council of Nicaea (in accordance with Roman and Alexandrian practices) as the Sunday after the first full moon in spring. Increasingly, this definition could not be brought into line with the dates between which the feast had to occur (i.e. 22 March and 25 April as 'Easter limits'). The intense debates at the Councils of Rome (1412), Constance (1415) and Basle (1434) and finally the reform suggestion of Nicholas of Cusa (Cusanus) all failed, in the face of the increasingly serious problems of the time, to give rise to any organised reform [6. 253]. It was not until the Council of Trent took up the task and after the work of the Calendar Commission (1576) that the reform-decretal was formulated which Pope Gregory XIII promulgated at the end of 1581 (summary of the background to and implementation of the reform in [3]).

2. THE GREGORIAN REFORM
The reform itself consisted of several elements. First, to maintain the traditional dates of spring, the accumulated 'deficit' of the solar year vis-à-vis the calendar year was eliminated by shifting the date from the 4th to the 15th of October 1582. This step in the reform had the most unfortunate long-term consequences, in that it led at once to constant differences in setting the date with all those states that did not implement the reform. Also the corrective efforts of the Orthodox Church to establish a more precise length of the year did not fully carry out this reform.

The second element was the modification of the rules for leap years: There was to be no leap year in those years where the century-years (1700, 1800, 1900) were not completely divisible by four. The threatening spread of divergence because of this rule caused many European states to adopt this reform in 1700. Finally, there was a need for regulation in the reckoning of the date of Easter. In this case, the suggestion made by the physician Aloisi Giglio (A. Lilius) in the form of new epact tables was accepted. The basis for this traditional form of reckoning was the ability to calculate the spring full moon from the progress of the phase of the moon at New Year. From a long-term calculation of the cycle, one could determine for every year-for centuries in advance-figures that, with the help of a few rules, permitted calculation of the date of Easter. Associated with the tables were also a number of 'tricks' that, by means of an actually false moving forward of the date of the full moon (on which the Jewish Feast of the Passover, on the 14th of Nisan, was based), permitted Easter to fall on the 14th of Nisan. It was accomplished without this 'quartodecimal' and hence, as the polemical reproach put it, 'Judaising' Easter dating – which was criticised at Nicaea – being noticeable as such in the tables. An empirical alternative, namely the observation of the moon, could not even be be considered in view of problems associated with observation as well as communication.

3. ACCEPTANCE AND CRITICISM
A glance at the details shows just how open to attack the scheme of reform actually was. In the century of the Reformation, such a calendar reform, in the discussion of which the Protestant states had not been involved, could not simply be adopted across the board. At soon as this reformed calendar was announced, Protestant polemics began to appear, primarily arguing from the point of view of the astronomical calendar (e.g. Michael Eychler, *Was von dem newen Bäpstischen Gregorianischen Calender zu halten sey*, Lemgo 1584; Lucas Osiander, *Bedencken Ob der newe Päpstische Kalender ein Notturfft bey der Christenheit seie/unnd wie trewlich diser Papst Gregorius XIII. die Sachen damit meine ...*, Tübingen 1583; Michael Maestlin, *Ausführlicher und gründlicher Bericht ... Sambt erklärung der newen Reformation/welche jetziger Bapst zum Rom Gregorius XIII. in demselben Kalender hat angestellet / und an vilen Orten eyngeführet/Und was darvon zuhalten seye*, Heidelberg 1583). The result was a considerable delay in its acceptance. Whereas most of the Catholic states of Europe immediately accepted the calendar (Spain, Portugal and, to a large extent, Italy and Poland; 1583 in Catholic Germany; Austria, Bohemia and some of the Swiss cantons only in 1584; Hungary in 1587), many of the Protestant states, which used different date-adjust-

ments, followed only in 1700 (especially Germany, Denmark and the Netherlands), England in 1752, Sweden not until 1753 (after experimenting from 1700 onwards). Attempts at an 'improved calendar' that would replace the (imprecise) cyclical changes by using astronomical-empirical methods – which, in spite of the acceptance of the Gregorian Calendar, still sometimes led to different dates for Easter – were abandoned at the end of the 18th cent. The Eastern Orthodox countries only accepted the reform (and sometimes without adjusting the dates) around 1920 (Albania 1913, Russia 1918, Greece 1923, the Greek-Orthodox Church 1924) [6. 266–77; 7. 26–28]. In 1924, the technically more precise orthodox calendar reform stabilised the synchronisation of leap years until 2700. Beyond Europe, the Gregorian Calendar was adopted in 1606 by the United Maronites in Syria (further attempts at negotiation with the Patriarch in Constantinople broke down). Japan introduced it in 1873. Its use began to take hold in China at the start of the 20th cent., and Turkey introduced it on 1 January 1926.

4. Further Attempts at Reform

Criticism of the Gregorian Calendar, which originated with the Reformation and which was, not least of all, based on the diplomatic ineptitude of its introduction, has continued to the present. In 1702, Quidus Ubaldus listed in his *Remonstratio fundamentalis et succincta errorum quibus tam Novum quam Vetus Calendarium graviter laborat. Nec non Remediorum...* a series of older suggestions for reform, including that fixed times be used for Easter (5 April or the first Sunday thereafter). The strongest motivations for reform, apart from the problem of the dates for Easter, were the unstable relationship between days of the week and dates of the months and the unequal lengths of the quartals (see, for example, the *Journal of Calendar Reform* 1ff., 1931ff.). Problems of adaptation to new reforms proved their greatest obstacles.

The sole critical suggestion that was realized to any appreciable extent is represented by the French Revolutionary Calendar, which was introduced on 24 October 1793 (i.e. 3 Brumaire in year 2 of the Republic) by decree of the National Assembly. In this case, a rational criticism of the calendar – albeit in favour of a technically weaker system, starting as it did from an annual average of 365 days – was combined with the organization in calendar terms of ideological alternatives to Christianity. This included the replacement of Sunday by *Décadi* and of the divine service by the cult of reason and by celebrations of the revolution. The claims of the calendar were manifest not only in its regular thirty-day months but also in the systematized roots and suffixes of the names of the months:

Vendémiaire, Brumaire, Frimaire (autumn)
Nivôse, Pluviôse, Ventôse (winter)
Germinal, Floréal, Prairial (spring)
Messidor, Thermidor, Fructidor (summer).

The structure shows obvious parallels with the German names of the months introduced by Charle-

magne (beginning, however, with January, Einhard, *Vita Caroli Magni* 29):

uuintarmanoth, hornung, lenzinmanoth,
ostarmanoth, uuinnemanoth, brachmanoth,
heuuimanoth, aranmanoth, uuitumanoth
uuindumemanoth, herbistmanoth, heilagmanoth.

These names for the months were widespread in Germany throughout the Middle Ages. The French Revolutionary calendar was modified by the Concordat with the Catholic Church in 1802 and was done away with on 31 December 1805 in spite of ongoing reservations about the Gregorian Calendar.

The French experiment with the calendar made it clear that large-scale interference in private life is linked with the rhythms of the weeks [13]. Experiments in the Soviet Union took this into account in the introduction of continuous five or six day weeks. These provided only for individual rhythms and eliminated a shared day of rest for the whole society. This was intended to increase productivity and at the same time supplant the Christian tradition, which was promulgated on Sundays. Begun in the wake of the massive industrialisation of the 1920s, these experiments were discontinued at the start of the war with Germany. Unlike the much more frequent introduction of new designations for eras (like that of Mussolini in 1922 and also for Nazi Germany), far-reaching calendar reforms had such an effect on the structure of time of individual societies that any possible gain in rationalisation seemed hardly adequate to justify them.

C. Graphic Form

Unlike all other calendar systems of the ancient Mediterranean world, the representational form developed by Rome for its conventionalised months offered (after the Julian reform) an overview of the year in twelve similar columns (→ Calendar). This representation was continued beyond Classical times in the traditional forms of mural painting and monumental inscriptions. The 'Kalendarium marmoreum' in Naples, roughly 5.5 meters across and probably from the middle of the 9th cent., provides evidence for this continuation. In terms of content, it summarises several regional lists of saint's feasts and, in particular, martyrdom dates. In religious texts of the high and late Middle Ages, this calendar-form mostly shows the following columns: the 'golden number' (for calculating Easter); the Sunday letter (A-G: the letter, which changed at the the beginning of the year, thus indicated all the Sundays in the year in a calendar that was in principal 'eternal'); numbered days of the month (this form of date notation arises after the early Middle Ages and is the dominant form by the late Middle Ages); Roman date forms; and saints' days. In breviaries, the pitch for the prayers of the canonical hours (*III., IX tonus*) may also be given. As was already the case in classical times, this representation could be augmented by astronomical information (e.g. zodiac signs) or prognostic information (e.g. weather forecasts) – a practice that came to fruition with the enormous rise of astrology after the Renaissance. In Germany from the beginning of the 15th cent. onward, one encounters large numbers of 'practica' or 'almanacs' in book form (initially as manuscript books). These spread the monthly columns over a double page that gives information in a number of columns about moonrise and sunrise and moonset and sunset as well as information over the movements of the planets. An example of the genre, the *Practica* of Johann Schindel was designed for use over a nine-year (lunar) cycle (1410, 1439; [9. 180]), which remained the norm for book-calendars for a time [23. 365]. Alongside these one also finds broadsheets, for a long time printed as woodcuts, which typically contain only isolated dates and not the whole calendar for the year.

The arrangement of 'one month per page' was not obligatory, and frequently the format is more continuous, with the page-break occuring at a random date. Where the one-page-per-month format was preserved, one often finds in more expensively produced manuscripts a continuation of the classical tradition of representing the months. Mural paintings (e.g. the fasti beneath Santa Maria Maggiore in Rome) or mosaics are older than, or independent of, the written calendars, but the calendar in the Chronograph of 354 is still the oldest known example of the combination in book format. The manuscript tradition of this illustrated calendar (see most recently [18. 249–268], with individual copies from the 6th to the 10 cents. as well as a number of copies from the late 15th to early 17th cents., characterises the interest in the calendar. Breviaries and books of hours continue to carry these representations (alongside monumental forms) through the Middle Ages [4; 23. 364, note 64]. With the start of the 15th cent., the pattern was disseminated across a variety of other secular genres [14. 378] and achieved a great deal of popularity in the 17th cent. [23. 426f.]. A wall calendar combining a picture with the schematic representation of a month is nowadays one of the most popular forms of calendar; admittedly, the pictures often go well beyond the representation of individual months in the narrower sense.

D. The Calendar as a Medium

As a systematic means of conveying information, the calendar, as early as the classical period, went beyond the simple representation of the months. Lists of magistrates (i.e. Roman consuls and also civic officials or officers of societies), which could be expanded into actual chronicles, regularly accompanied Roman fasti [17]. In the Chronograph of 354 there is already a wealth of different materials. The characteristics of individual months (e.g weather and feasts) were treated poetically in single lines of verse, couplets or quatrains – this is also the case in the Chronograph of 354 and in Ausonius (14, 1ff.: *Eclogues*). This tradition continues throughout the Middle Ages [8] and into Renaissance verse (as in Heinrich Ranzovius's *Ranzovianum Calendarium ad elevationem poli 55. Grad....*, Hamburg

1590). As a mnemonic for the feasts and memorial days of the church year, the Cisio Ianus – named after its first words (*Circumcisio...*) and known in various forms (e.g. that of Philipp Melanchthon) – takes on a similar but almost canonical function. Thus, it is absent from very few of the early printed calendars. The understanding of how to replace a stored memory by the intermediary of writing as memory-store gives way here to the function of writing as a mnemonic auxiliary (on such perception problems, see [5]).

In spite of the numerous variations in classical calendars, the medieval calendars show a great uniformity when, as liturgical aids, they accompany texts of various types, including Bible manuscripts (e.g. Gotha membr, II 65, fol.1r–2v). A particularly important impetus for the extension of the calendric scheme was astrology (→ Natural sciences), which was at its height in Europe from the 15th to the 17th cent. After manuscripts that are clearly older (e.g. the Calendarium of 1305[9. 179f.], astrological predictions constitute, as indicated above, an important part of calendar production ([23. 358, note 50]: *c.* 392 incunabula printings after 1462). The calendar published by Johannes Regiomontanus in 1475 (and reprinted) represents for Germany the start of an abundant production. Calendars of this type combine the astronomical material mentioned with a whole range of prophecies and especially with medical advice. This is the case as early as 1483 with an 84–page untitled calendar from Strasbourg (Gotha, Mon.typ. 1483,4deg.,2 = Hain 9734) that offers extensive systematic discussions and pieces of advice particular to specific months. The various items are ordered according to the astrologically determined days for bloodletting (hence the German term 'Lasszettel' (letting-sheet) for such calendars or for single-page compilations of the appropriate dates [11. 15]; also on further calendar forms). Comparable 'practical' texts form part of popular mass-literature into the 19th cent.

As far as the reception of classical material is concerned, a second line of development, which derives from Ovid's *Libri fastorum*, is more important. Ovid's poetic calendar commentary offered historical explanations and mythological stories associated with the Roman *fasti* in a text that jumped from date to date and failed to include all the days of the year. The work was massively popular and there are more than 170 manuscripts, many of them from the Renaissance. In 1516, Johannes Baptista Mantuanus (G. B. Spagnoli) composed his *Fastorum libri XII*, which was not only an expansion but also an *updating* of Ovid. In 1550, the Wittenberg professor of grammar and later Reformation theologian Paul Eber [21] composed a *Calendarium historicum* of 482 pages under the influence of Ovid – a fact that scholarship has not previously noted but which is suggested by the Praefatio (p. 4: *Sic cernimus in fastis Ouidianis*. (See also the concluding elegy with its imitation of Ovid and its final comment *Cumque tuis forsan Naso mea scripta legentur*.) Eber's work was also influenced by the *Fasti triumphales*, which was discovered in Rome in 1548 and from which he, beginning with 1 January, frequently took material. After many editions, Eber's sons, Johannes and Martin, expanded it yet again, translated it and published it in German. This text is considered the beginning of the genre of the historical calendar ([23. 369f.;10.47f.] for an opposing view [3]). That genre, by including not only dates associated with a particular year but also by increasingly including short narratives of an historical or legendary nature, stands in direct connexion to the classical calendar stories of Johann Jakob Christoffel von Grimmelshausen, Johann Peter Hebel and finally – separated from the overarching genre of the 'calendar' – of Oskar Maria Graf and Bertolt Brecht (on the later development, see [15. 10]). The great interest in the genre of the historical calendar that had derived from the reception of Ovid is clear from the steady flow of new editions and imitations, among which the work of Caspar Goltwurm stands in the first place. Goltwurm followed his secular historical calendar in 1570 with an *Ecclesiastical Calendar*, which offered a series of saints' lives on the appropriate days and appeared a century before the work of the Bollandists. As early as 1551, there appeared in Wittenberg the *Cisio Ianus, hoc est, Kalendarium syllabicum* of Lucas Lossius, which was intended for school use and which offered in question-and-answer format explanations of the contemporary and Roman calendars as well as extracts (*historiae*) from Paul Eber's calendar. The heavy reference to classical history that typifies Eber's calendar was quickly lost in the following period (e.g. Michael Beuther of Carlstadt, *Calendarium Historicum* Frankfurt/M. 1557) when early modern and Reformation period dates came to predominate.

→ Eras; → Chronographer of 354; → Fasti; → Ovidius Naso, Publius

1 L. BASNIZKI, Der jüdische Kalender, 1938 (repr. 1989)
2 A. BORST, Computus, 1990 3 G. V. COYNE, M. A. HOSKIN, O. PEDERSEN, Gregorian Reform of the Calendar, 1983 4 H. DORMEIER, Bildersprache zwischen Tradition und Originalität. Das Sujet der Monatsbilder im Mittelalter, in: 'Kurzweil viel ohn' Maß und Ziel', 1994, 102–127 5 M. GIESECKE, Der Buchdruck in der frühen Neuzeit, 1991 6 F. K. GINZEL, Handbuch der mathematischen und technischen Chronologie, vol. 3, 1914 7 H. GROTEFEND, Taschenbuch der Zeitrechnung des deutschen Mittelters und der Neuzeit, ¹³1991 8 J. HENNIG, Kalender und Martyrologium als Literaturformen, in: Id., Literatur und Existenz, 1980, 37–80 9 W. KNAPPICH, Geschichte der Astrologie, ²1988 10 J. KNOPF, Die deutsche Kalendergeschichte, 1983 11 K. MASEL, Kalender und Volksaufklärung in Bayern, 1997 12 K. MATTHÄUS, Zur Geschichte des Nürnberger Kalenderwesens (Archiv für Gesch. des Buchwesens 64/65), 1968 13 M. MEINZER, Der französische Revolutionskalender, 1992 14 M. OHM, Die zwölf Monate, in: Geburt der Zeit, Katalog Kassel, 1999, 378–381 15 L. ROHNER, Kalendergeschichte und Kalender, 1978 16 J. RÜPKE, Kalender und Öffentlichkeit, 1995 17 Id., Geschichtsschreibung in Listenform, in: Philologus 141, 1997, 65–85 18 M. R. SALZMAN, On Roman Time, 1990 19 R. SCHENDA, Die Lesestoffe der Kleinen Leute, 1976 20 T. SCHMIDT, Kalender und Gedächtnis, 2000 21 C. H. SIXT, Dr. Paul Eber, der Schüler, Freund und Amtsgenosse der Reformatoren, 1843 22 A. SPIER, The Comprehensive Hebrew Calendar, 1952 23 H. SÜHRIG, Die Entwicklung der niedersächsischen Kalender im 17. Jahrhundert, 1979 24 H. ZEMANEK, Kalender und Chronologie, ⁵1990

ADDITIONAL BIBLIOGRAPHY: A. K. MICHELS, The Calendar of the Roman Republic, 1967.; J. RÜPKE, Zeit und Fest: Kulturgeschichte des Kalenders, München 2006
JÖRG RÜPKE

Cambridge School see→ RELIGION, HISTORY OF

Cambridge, Fitzwilliam Museum see→ UNITED KINGDOM

Campania
A. INTRODUCTION B. THE MIDDLE AGES C. RENAISSANCE AND HUMANISM D. GEOGRAPHICAL AND TRAVEL LITERATURE E. FICTION

A. INTRODUCTION

The land between the Volturno in the north and the Sorrento peninsula in the south gained in the Roman period a great significance over and above its geographical and political importance. Factors favouring this were: the continuation of Greek culture in the coastal settlement centres (Naples as *Graeca urbs*; Tac. ann. 15,33,2; cf. Strabo 5,4,7), the arrival after the 2nd cent. BC of Roman citizens as visitors either for health reasons (thermal springs) or in search of the good life (made very vivid in Strabo 1. c), and as a result the uninterrupted construction of luxury villas and parks along the coastal strip (Strabo 5,4,8)[3]. Added to this is the wealth-producing fertility of the hinterland ('felix illa Campania'): Pliny, Nat. 3, 60) and not least the beauty of the whole region (Pol. 3, 91). The land as a whole, individual places (Capua, Baiae), or their products (Falernian wine, Lucrine oysters) became indicators for a particular mind-set and life-style, most notably of the *dolce vita* (e.g. Sen. dial. 9,2,13). These indicators outlasted the material decline of the area after the 3rd cent. AD (SHA Tac. 7, 5–7; 19,5; Symm. epist. 2,17,2). They also allowed for the literary transfer of Campania (C.) onto other places and areas, to Nomentum (Martial 6. 43), to the Moselle (Auson. Mos. 345–347; 208–219), to the Auvergne (Sidon. carm. 18), and to Istria (Cassiod. var. 12, 22). The comparative basis for this transfer was not the material comparability of the places, but rather the intellectual status which they embodied. The elegant and fashionable spa of Baiae was used as a trope, as antonomasia for any other spa (Sidon. carm. 23, 13; epist. 5,14,1) or bathing-places (Anth. Latina, ed. D. R. Shackelton Bailey 99; 108; 112;169;202;372;CLE 1910;2039). The land became a code for the site of mythical and historical events, but having become a code, it also determined the poetic, oratorical or historical representation of those events. They attached themselves to the various places as reminiscences, often in a particular literary context. Cumae and Lake Avernus could be seen only through Virgil's (*Aeneid* VI) eyes (Ov. met. 14, 85ff.; Sil. 12, 113ff.; 13, 395ff.; Stat. silv. 4,3,114ff.). On the other hand, the image of Campanian villa culture was formed by various writers: Cicero, Varro, Horace, Seneca, Statius. In each case it was the literary and not the actual landscape in which the literature dealt with Campanian events [15].

B. THE MIDDLE AGES
Cassiodorus, without having seen the places concerned, was the last to praise C. in literature (var. 9,6). After him its fame declined, as did the area itself. The nadir is reached when, in a 9th-cent. version of the *Acta Petri et Pauli*, much-praised Baiae appears as 'a place called Baiae' (12) [5]. The use of the thermal springs for bathing on the Campi Phlegraei did continue through the whole Middle Ages [11; 12]. One poetic result of this is the *De balneis Puteolanis* by Pietro da Eboli, probably dedicated to Frederick II before 1220, consisting of 35 epigrams on the healing effects of the individual baths [7: 19]. The work (20 manuscripts of the 13th–15th cents., ten of them illuminated) is the starting point for a rich individual balneological tradition which continued into the 19th cent. and linked with the fame of the Phlegraei Fields in Antiquity [10; 4]. The poetic work itself is practically orientated, and sparing with classical allusions.

C. RENAISSANCE AND HUMANISM
The idea of a memorable journey, offering more to the spirit than to the eyes, was first formulated by Petrarch in the *Itinerarium ad sepulcrum domini nostri Iesu Christi* of 1358. The west coast of Italy is afforded in that work more space than the Holy Land, with the Bay of Naples as the central point in the report. In his preface, Petrarch justifies the imaginary journey through landscapes of the mind on the basis of the impossibility of himself being able to take part in the journey in the actual sense (7–9).The details in the description go back to a visit to the Campi Phlegraei on 23 November 1343, which he describes in a lively fashion, with relevant quotations, in the *Familiares* (5,4). Echoes of Virgil also play a major part here. For Boccaccio (in Naples 1327–39) it is Roman love poetry which is called to mind by the landscape [11. 398–400]. This becomes the dominant theme for an entire collection of poetry during the high period of Aragonese rule in Naples with Giovanni Pontano's (1426–1503) *Hendecasyllaborum seu Baiarum libri duo* (begun in 1490). In this case Baiae certainly represents a spiritual attitude, somewhat one-sidedly that of love and dalliance. But Virgil is invoked as well. He sang – and bathed – here (1,31; 2,6). In the *Arcadia* (first version begun in 1480) of Pontano's friend Sannazaro (1457–1530) the spiritual Arcadia is juxtaposed with a spiritual C. (Prose XII and XIII).

D. GEOGRAPHICAL AND TRAVEL LITERATURE
Petrach's *Itinerarium* (see above) already established the importance for the geographical and touristic reception of the Campanian landscape of memory. The Campi Phlegraei are the central point of reference, on the one hand as the land of Homer and especially that of Virgil, and on the other as a site of Roman history. To this must be added the rich, leisure loving and educated city of Naples; occasionally, because of Hannibal's winter camp, the once-flourishing Capua; further Capri, rarely visited but rich in reminiscences of Emperor Tiberius; and finally fire-spewing Vesuvius, which, together with the thermal phenomena of the Campi Phlegraei, provides the physical interest in the region. The journey from Rome to Naples was a mental preparation for the visitor rather than for the geographer. Here the traveller was accompanied not only by historical memories, but by those of Horace's *Iter Brundisinum* (sat. 1,5) [16]. The mention of the three aspects by which the land addresses the spirit – poetically, historically and physically – belongs to the topoi of the literature in question. The regions are 'interessant durch die Geschichte, reitzend als Gefilde der Poesie, interessanter noch und reitzender durch die Natur' (interesting for their history, delightful as the fields of poetry, and made still more interesting and delightful through nature) writes Friedrich Leopold Graf zu Stolberg in his *Reise in Deutschland, der Schweiz, Italien und Sicilien in den Jahren 1791–92* (²1822, vol. 2, 367). To be sure, the enthusiasm was nurtured less by a coherent study of the classical texts themselves than by reading various works of historical geography and local guide-books, which appeared in large numbers and presented the ancient sites in a pleasing way. Here, a pioneering effort is represented in the *Italia Illustrata* of Flavio Biondo, produced in 1449–1453 and printed in 1474. It was followed by the *Descrittione di tutta Italia* of Leandro Alberti (1550), and on an entirely new critical level by the *Italia antiqua* of Philipp Clüver (1624). The first guidebook to the transcendent central part of the area, the Campi Phlegraei, appeared in 1570: Ferrante Loffredo's *Le antichità di Pozzuolo et luoghi convicini*. This brief and reliable work was followed by Scipione Mazzella's *Sito, et antichita della citta di Pozzuolo, e del suo amenissimo distretto* (1591), Giuseppe Mormile's *Descirittione dell'amenssimo distretto dell citta di Napoli, et dell'antichita della citta de Pozzuolo* (1617), Giulio Caesare Capaccio's *Il Forastiero* (1630), Pompeo Sarnelli's *Guida de' forestieri* (1685) and many others [6; 15]. Foreign traveler's handbooks and travel-descriptions were influenced by these 'as they influenced each other', so that a tradition of seeing and writing developed which was astonishingly uniform and encouraged the transmission of errors and narrative phantoms [17]. The guidance offered by the *Itinerarium Italiae Nov-Antiquae* of Martin Zeiller (1640), who had never visited Naples, does not differ much from other 'Wahrhafften und curiösen Reiß-Beschreibungen' of the same period.

In spite of the gradual decline, Biondo, who visited the Campi Phlegraei in 1452, was enchanted by the number and the excellent state of preservation of the monuments (fol. L7r), as was Alberti, whose visits were made in the years 1526 and 1536. He saw and described many things which later travellers did not see but described anyway. But even in Petrarch's descriptions there are occasional comments upon the ruinous state of the objects. Set against its one-time glory, these comments gradually build up to form a lament on temporality. Hieronymus Turler, in *De peregrinatio et agro Neapolitano Libri II* (1574, 80) saw the decline as 'evidens argumentum fragilitatis humanae, & quam nihil stabile aut perpetuum sit in vita' (a clear sign of human fragility and that nothing is immutable or permanent in life). The volcanic eruption on 29 September 1538 was fatal: it raised up the almost 140 metre high Monte Nuovo between Lake Avernus and Monte Barbaro, and buried under it the greater part of the sea-inlet which had replaced the Lucrine lake [9]. This struck at the heart of the *regio Baiana*. A large part of its glory was now lost to sight. However, the material loss augmented greatly the spiritual aspects of the landscape. The relationship between object and memory had shifted in favour of the latter. Discussion of C., which had been going on since ancient times, could now increasingly leave reality aside. Richard Lassels (*The Voyage of Italy*, 1670) referred to this as 'Travelers losse' and 'mans comfort' (266). Although most visitors happily went on copying out the classical passages and carried phantom descriptions from book to book, after the turn of the 17th and 18th cent. a minority began to feel cheated by the earthly paradise which C. was supposed to represent. The antiquities of Pozzuoli 'ne sont pas que de vieux bâtimens' (are nothing but old buildings), wrote Charles Bourdin in his *Voyage d'Italie* (1699,224). Perceptive observers like President de Brosse (1709–1777, in Naples in 1739) recognised clearly the underlying situation. Having returned from an expedition into the Campi Phlegraei, he determined 'que tous les grands plaisirs que j'avais goûtés étaient beaucoup plus en idée qu'en réalité' (that all the great delights that I have experienced were more in the idea than in reality); the objects described are, he said 'délicieux par réminiscence et tirent un agrément infini des gens qui n'y sont pas'(delightful through reminiscence and elicit boundless pleasure from the people who are not there: *Lettres d'Italie*, ed. Y. BEZARD, 1931, vol. 1, 457). The catalyst for this perception was the rediscovery of the Vesuvius towns (official excavations in → HERCULANEUM after 1738). For there one could contrast the grandiose realm of memory with the modest, but immediate and visible presence of Antiquity in a Roman country town [18]. Of the antiquities in the Campi Phlegraei, Lady Morgan wrote later that 'there are few sufficiently perfect to interest the general enquirer, by their power of illustrating the internal oeconomy of civil life, like those of Pompeii' (*Italy*, 1821, Vol. 2, 354). In→ POMPEII, on the other hand, Mark

Twain was able to determine in the vestibule of a house the place 'where presumably the hat-stand had been' (*The Innocents Abroad*).

The impression of worn-out ruins making a huge claim to be a spiritual landscape gave rise after the end of the 18th cent. to three different reactions: 1. a blind obedience to tradition: 'jeder Blick regt ein classisches Gefühl auf' (every glance inspires a classical emotion: J. I. v. Gerning, *Reise durch Östreich und Italien*, 1802, vol. 2, 181); 2. rejection: August von Kotzebue broke off his visit on the grounds of the 'Ueberdruß, Steinhaufen anzugaffen, die nichts mehr ähnlich sehen [...] Fabeln und Mährchen anzuhören, die nichts bedeuten' (weariness from staring at piles of stone that do not resemble anything [... and] listening to fables and fairy-tales that mean nothing: *Erinnerung von einer Reise aus Liefland nach Rom und Neapel*, 1805, vol. 1, 357f.); 3. sublimation: William Beckford went against the grain of the tradition of sight and memory in his *Dreams, Waking Thoughts, and Incidents: in a series of Letters, from various parts of Europe* (1783), and placed the spiritual value of the landscape into an overall mood that is hard to grasp; President Dupaty spoke similarly and almost at the same time [14]. These attempts had, however, no successors. What lasted was the feeling of weariness. The landscape, which was no longer able to address the spirit, was condemned for not being picturesque enough. To be sure, C. has survived in a few stereotypical images in recent travel-books and contemporary essays (L. De Crescenzo et al).

E. FICTION

Modern fiction does not distinguish itself in its perceptive mode from geography and travel literature. As far as C. is concerned literature's role is a receptive one. This can be inferred from well-known works such as Wilhelm Heinse's *Ardinghello* (1787), Jean Paul's *Titan*, Hans Christian Andersen's *Improvisatoren*(1835) and many others; it is also easy to see in Mme de. Staël's *Corinne ou l'Italie*(1807), the prose epic *Les Martyrs* of Chateaubriand (1809) or the *Histoire de Juliette* of the Marquis de Sade (1796), since the authors in these case are all following their own travel notes. For guides and travel descriptions, modern literature places itself as a second layer of memory upon the reminiscences about Antiquity. Benedetto di Falco places Pontano and Sannazaro alongside the classical eulogists of the Bay of Naples (*Descrittione dei luoghi antiqui di Napoli e del sua amenissimo distretto*, 1535, passim); for Anna Jameson, Corinne has 'superadded romantic and charming associations quite as delightful, and quite as true' as the *Aeneid* and the *Odyssey* (*The Diary of an Ennuyée*, 1836, 91); Felix Mendelssohn claims to have 'had lunch' with the woman from Goethe's *Wandrer* (Letter of 7 May, 1831, (ed.) P. SUTERMEISTER, 1979, 148)

1 R. J. CLARK, Giles of Viterbo on the Phlegraean Fields: A Vergilian View?, in: Phoenix 49, 1995, 150–162 2 Id., The Avernian Sibyl's Cave: From Military Tunnel to Me-

diaeval Spa, in: CeM 47, 1996, 217–243 3 J. H. D'ARMS, Romans on the Bay of Naples. A Social and Cultural Study of the Villas and Their Owners from 150 B. C. to A. D. 400, 1970 4 R. DI BONITO, R. GIAMMINELLI, Le Terme dei Campi Flegrei. Topografia storica, 1992 5 M. FREDERIKSEN, Una fonte trascurata sul bradisismo puteolano, in: I Campi Flegrei nell'archeologia e nella storia, 1977, 117–129 6 A. HORN-ONCKEN, Ausflug in elysische Gefilde. Das europäische Campanienbild des 16. und 17. Jahrhunderts und die Aufzeichnungen J. F. A. von Uffenbachs (AAWG 111), 1978 7 C. M. KAUFFMANN, The Baths of Pozzuoli. A Study of the Medieval Illustrations of Peter of Eboli's Poem, 1959 8 S. MASTELLONE, L'Umanesimo napoletano e la zona flegrea, in: ASNP 30, 1945–46, 5–36 9 A. PARASCANDOLA, Il Monte Nuovo ed il Lago Lucrino, in: Bollettino della Società dei Naturalisti in Napoli 55, 1944–46, 151–312 10 L. PETRUCCI, Le fonti per la conoscenza della topografia delle terme flegree dal XII al XV secolo, in: ASPN 97, 1979, 99–129 11 E. PONTIERI, Baia nel Medioevo, in: I Campi Flegrei nell'archeologia e nella storia, 1977, 377–411 12 C. RUSSO MAILLER, La tradizione medioevale dei Bagni Flegrei, in: Puteoli 3, 1979, 141–153 13 L. SCHUDT, Italienreisen im 17. und 18. Jahrhundert, 1959 14 E. STÄRK, Die Überwindung der Phlegräischen Felder. Vom träumerischen Umgang mit der Antike am Ausgang des 18. Jahrhunderts, in: A&A 40, 1994, 137–152 15 Id., Kampanien als geistige Landschaft. Interpretationen zum antiken Bild des Golfs von Neapel, 1995 16 Id., Wallfahrten auf der Appischen Straße – Das Iter Brundisinum und der Tourismus, in: H. KRASSER, E. A. SCHMIDT (eds.), Zeitgenosse Horaz, 1996, 371–391 17 Id., Antrum Sibyllae Cumanae und Campi Elysii. Zwei vergilische Lokale in den Phlegräischen Feldern, 1998 18 G. VALLET, Les 'antiquités des Champs' Phlégréens dans les récits des voyageurs du XVIIIe siècle, in: Il destino della Sibilla, a cura di P. AMALFITANO, 1986, 43–57 19 F. K. YEGÜL, The Thermo-Mineral Complex at Baiae and De Balneis Puteolanis, in: The Art Bulletin 78, 1996, 137–161

ADDITIONAL BIBLIOGRAPHY: E. W. LEACH, The Social Life of Painting in Ancient Rome and on the Bay of Naples, 2004.   EKKEHARD STÄRK

Canada see → NORTH-AMERICA

Cannae see→ BATTLEFIELDS

Canon Until the dawn of the modern era, the term was unusual in the sense in which it is now used by literary scholars; namely, to mean 'standard', 'rule', or 'model' (first used by D. Ruhnken in 1768 to mean a literary corpus), although the contrasting sense of the 'inspired' canon of the Bible, or religious law and 'apocryphal' writings, was available to suggest an analogy that could be applied to secular items.

Concentration and extent of transmission are indicators of canonicity. As early as the manuscript tradition of, for example, the Greek tragedians, one notes a selection from the entire *oeuvre* (Euripides: 17 of 75 tragedies attested by Varro). With the earliest canon, transmitted from Alexandria or rather Byzantium, of five (later three) tragedians, nine lyricists or ten rhetors,

the factor of symbolic numbers, as well as a fixation on author figures (not works), can be seen at work. This is perhaps analogous to the apostolic number of twelve 'old masters' of courtly lyric who were venerated by the mastersingers of the 16th cent. and were later replaced by the same number from their own master craftsmen.

Canon marks the conflict and interplay between continuity and innovation, the tension between *imitatio* and *aemulatio* (or translation [11. 104–126]), in which, for the period between Late Antiquity and the late Middle Ages, stress was laid on the exemplarity of the *auctoritates*. A canon is articulated; its propagation determines textual forms [13. 21–39], such as books of *sententiae*, accessus, florilegia, library catalogues, lists of writers and even catalogues of literary works that had been circulating from the time of Jerome, Cassiodorus and Bede but more intensively from the Carolingian Renaissance (e.g. Alcuin) on, as the precursor of a literary historiography (Konrad von Hirsau, Hugo von Trimberg) that was always intended to be commendatory in character. Thus, school reading-lists from the 9th to the 12th cents. included only a few *auctores*, and the teaching of grammar within the framework of the *artes liberales* was based on a selection of Classical Latin writers regarded as linguistic-poetic models (epic writers, satirists, writers of comedy; Cicero, the *Ilias latina*; [5. 253–276]). In moralistic writing the fables of Avianus, and later of Aesop, together with the *Disticha Catonis*, play a special role. After the rise of a genuinely Christian-Latin hymnody and narrative literature, the literature of the times from the 12th and 13th cents. on sets itself off more clearly from the literature of Antiquity. The Classical canon survived through its *interpretatio christiana* (Virgil, Ovid, Lucan, Statius). Dante's enumerations (Inferno, IV passim) are both a commendation of Classical Latin poetry and a transition to the emancipation of vernacular poetry. New features at the dawn of the Renaissance are self-canonisation, evident precisely in Dante [13. 139–152], as well as the poet-crowning ritual, based not on texts but rather on authors (e.g. in Petrarch 1341). Humanism reversed the decanonization of pagan writers, as well as the scant attention paid to Greek literature, which had developed distinct strands of reception by way of Byzantium and Arabic translation. At the same time, a negative canon evolved, based on theological criteria, through works being placed on the Index, through censorship and the Inquisition. This yardstick of religious or confessional orthodoxy was not eliminated until the 'Romantic' period, which granted autonomy to aesthetic discourse. By then printing had facilitated the dissemination of the canon, and simply ensuring the survival of what had been handed down was no longer a primary concern.

The criterion of 'timeless' value lies at the heart of any debate about a canon. In the 16th and 17th cents. the *Querelle des anciens et des modernes* [17] led to a historically relativising point of view that first enabled the paradigm shift of the Romantics. Through their canon of medieval and modern authors (Dante, Cervantes, Shakespeare, Goethe–as supplementary to the literature of Antiquity, which has never been seriously challenged to this day), the Romantics defined themselves as strategically opposed to the Enlightenment. This incursion of medieval and especially modern texts into the domain of Antiquity marks the first questioning of canon in the modern sense. Thus, the genesis of the modern study of literature in the 18th and 19th cents. was accompanied by the opportunity to canonize something new. Goethe's notion and concept of 'world literature', with its diverse connotations and political functions of compensation, served as a frame of reference in contrast to the concept of a European Classical literature.

In pluralistic societies a uniform canon that applies to the whole of humanity is difficult to draw up, even in theory. As the product of literary evaluation and manifold filtering, it gets drawn up, experimented on, organized and revised by the practising members of the literary establishment [2. 3–32] and forms a microcosmic portrait of the cultural memory. On the assumption of a difference between normative and descriptive poetics, canon essentially belongs to the former, but all general statements concerning literary theory are also based on bodies of texts. Thus, a canon in its normative function helps determine the future of literature but also has a role in determining what is conserved. If since European Romanticism the semantic background of canon has afforded at least a metaphorical 'sanctification' [1. 114121] of work and artist, even to the point of a cult of genius, there has been a tendency since the First World War, in reaction to this, to destroy such an aura; but that has not diminished the Classical canon in academic circles (cf. the 2000th anniversaries of Virgil's birth and death [19]). Political democratisation and philosophical questioning of authority, hierarchies and centres were currents eating away at traditional canons, especially in the latter part of the 20th cent. The middle-class canon, cultivated in schools and universities and cementing Western cultural hegemony in particular, has been massively called into question in European and American circles from a feminist or minority perspective, but also by those fundamentally sceptical of norms to the point of deconstruction. Whether models of interpretation can also be termed canonical remains a contentious issue. Against this decanonisation, more and more emphasis is being placed on the support function that the canon – insofar as it is not understood restrictively or repressively – can have for the underprivileged. Moreover, the idea of a canon stands right at the centre of any integrative discipline, such as comparative literature, that is dependent on the preservation of a platform for discussion. On another level a canon has this function for all distinct literatures. The provocative [10. 47–59] counter-movement of H. Bloom [3], for whom canon is based on the eternal conflict of authors, appears, when viewed in a historical and philosophical sense, as an automatic, if only temporary reaction. Against a background of universal

availability, postmodernism, and the digitalization and globalization of an expanding textual tradition, the usual criteria for a canon, namely, exemplarity, innovativeness, singularity, classicity, and literary-historical relevance (in more recent thinking, the greatest possible universal connective) are largely reduced, in the context of a potentially limitless library, to a choice based on economic constraints but, for the individual, to the time available for reading during a lifetime [12. 9f.]. These insights call for the timely re-canonisation of 'classic writers' in general and the liberalization of the canon in particular.

→ Artes liberales; → Carolingian Renaissance; → Querelle des anciens et des modernes; → Censorship

1 J. Assmann, Das kulturelle Gedächtnis: Schrift, Erinnerung und politische Identität in frühen Hochkulturen, ²1997   2 G. Berger, H.-J. Lüsebrink (eds.), Literarische Kanon-Bildung in der Romania, 1987   3 H. Bloom, The Western Canon. The Books and School of the Ages, 1994   4 G. Buck, Literarischer Kanon und Geschichtlichkeit, in: DVjS 57, 1983, 351–365   5 E. R. Curtius, Europäische Literatur und lateinisches Mittelalter, 1948 (Eng.: European Literature and the Latin Middle Ages, trans. Willard R. Trask, 1953)   6 Geschichte der Textüberlieferung der antiken und mittelalterlichen Literatur, vol. I, 1961   7 G. Glauche, Schullektüre im Mittelalter, 1970   8 J. Gorak, The Making of the Modern Canon, 1991   9 J. Guillory, Cultural Capital. The Problems of Literary Canon Formation, 1993   10 R. v. Heydebrand (ed.), Kanon macht Kultur. Theoretische, historische und soziale Aspekte ästhetischer Kanonbildungen, 1998   11 G. Highet, The Classical Tradition, 1949   12 H.-W. Ludwig (ed.), Kriterien der Kanonbildung, 1988   13 M. Moog-Grünewald (ed.), Kanon und Theorie, 1997   14 B. Munk Olsen, L'étude des auteurs classiques latins aux XIe et XIIe siècles, 1982–1989   15 Id., I classici nel canone scolastico altomedievale, 1991   16 L. D. Reynolds, N. G. Wilson, Scribes and Scholars. A Guide to the Transmission of Greek and Latin Lit., 2nd ed., 1974   17 H. G. Rötzer, Traditionalität und Modernität in der europäischen Literatur, 1979   18 H. Rüdiger, Literatur ohne Klassiker? Tradition und Kanonbildung, in: Wort u. Wahrheit 14 (1959)   19 W. Taegert (ed.), Vergil 2000 Jahre Rezeption in Literatur, Musik und Kunst, 1982.   20 J. Werner, Zur Überlieferung der antiken Literatur, in: Symbolae Philologorum Posnaniensium 4 (1979)   21 C. Martindale (ed.), Virgil and his Influence: Bimillennial Studies, 1984

ADDITIONAL BIBLIOGRAPHY: G. Allan, Higher Education in the Making. Pragmatism, Whitehead and the Canon, 2004; B. Allmendinger, Ten Most Wanted. The New Western Literature, 1998; R. Alter, Canon and Creativity. Modern Writing and the Authority of Scripture, 2000; A. K. Ansari, English-Canadian Literary Canon. Emergence and Development, 2003; I. Armstrong, V. Blain (eds.), Women's Poetry in the Enlightenment. The Making of a Canon: 1730–1820, 1999; A. E. Boyd, Writing for Immortality. Women and the Emergence of High Literary Culture in America, 2004; B. Lyon Clark, Kiddie lit. The Cultural Construction of Children's Literature in America, 2003; J. Csicsila, Canons by Consensus. Critical Trends and American Literature

Anthologies, 2004; D. DAMROSCH, What is World Literature?, 2003.; R. DANSON, S. GUPTA (eds.), The Popular and the Canonical, 2005; A. DELBANCO, Required Reading. Why our American Classics Matter Now, 1997; M. DEPEW, D. OBBINK (eds.), Matrices of Genre. Authors, Canons, and Society, 2000; D. DONOGHUE, The American Classics. A Personal Essay, 2005; S. FENDLER, Feminist Contributions to the Literary Canon. Setting Standards of Taste, 1997; M. FINKELBERG, G. G. STROUMSA (eds.), Homer, the Bible and Beyond. Literary and Religious Canons in the Ancient World, 2003; A. FLEISHMAN, The Condition of English. Literary Studies in a Changing Culture, 1998; M. GAMER, Romanticism and the Gothic. Genre, Reception, and Canon Formation, 2000; L. GLASS, Authors Inc. Literary Celebrity in the Modern United States. 1880–1980, 2004; J. GORAK (ed.), Canon vs. Culture. Reflections on the Current Debate, 2001; A. HOLGATE, H. WILSON-FLETCHER (eds.), The Test of Time. What makes a Classic a Classic?, 1999; G. S. JAY, American Literature and the Culture Wars, 1997; D. JOHNSON, The Popular and the Canonical. Debating Twentieth-Century Literature 1940–2000, 2005; F. KERMODE, R. ALTER (eds.), Pleasure and Change. The Aesthetics of Canon, 2004; K. L. KILCUP, (eds.), Soft Canons. American Women Writers and Masculine Tradition, 1999; E. D. KOLBAS, Critical Theory and the Literary Canon, 2001; J. B. KRAMNICK, Making the English Canon. Print-Capitalism and the Cultural Past, 1700–1770, 1998; A. LUNDIN, Constructing the Canon of Children's Literature. Beyond Library Walls and Ivory Towers, 2004; D. L. MADSEN (ed.), Post-Colonial Literatures. Expanding the Canon, 1999; J. MORAN, Star Authors. Literary Celebrity in America, 2000; L. MORRISSEY (ed.), Debating the Canon, 2005; L. N. ODOZOR, Contemporary Nigerian Literature and the Idea of a Canon, 2004; L. S. ROBINSON, In the Canon's Mouth. Dispatches from the Culture Wars, 1997; T. ROSS, The Making of the English Literary Canon. From the Middle Ages to the Late Eighteenth Century, 1998; H. L. SINAIKO, Reclaiming the Canon. Essays on Philosophy, Poetry, and History, 1998; J. SPENCER, Literary Relations. Kinship and the Canon, 1660–1830, 2005; B. M. STABLEFORD, Yesterday's Bestsellers. A Journey through Literary History, 1998; M. SZEGEDY-MASZÁK, Literary Canons. National and International, 2001; id. (ed.), National Heritage, National Canon, 2001; J. THIEME, Postcolonial Con-Texts. Writing back to the Canon, 2001; G. WESTFAHL, G. SLUSSER (eds.), Science Fiction, Canonization, Marginalization, and the Academy, 2002; R. R. WISSE, The Modern Jewish Canon. A Journey through Language and Culture, 2000.   ACHIM HÖLTER

Canonists Experts in Church law, and thus of canon(ical) law, were termed 'canonists', from the Greek *kanón* = 'rule', in particular, religious rule. The term canonist came into use in the 12th cent., to distinguish them from 'civilists', experts in the Roman *Corpus iuris civilis*, who appeared from that time on in Church courts in competition with canonists.

The word '*canon*' was applied in medieval Latin mainly to excerpts from juridical texts of authoritative writings. *Canones* were taken from the Bible, conciliar decisions, the writings of the early Church Fathers, early medieval books of penitence (*libri poenitentiales*),

and from the laws of the Frankish kings (*capitularia*). In addition, papal letters (*litterae decretales*) were also cited. From the late 12th cent. on, these became the most important source of law.

Rules of Church law had actually been collected as early as the 2nd cent., but collections were not officially promulgated until 1210. Of the many collections, the following should be mentioned because they were widely known and influenced others that came later: the Greek *Syntagma Canonum* (2nd half of the 4th cent.), *Statuta Ecclesiae antiqua* (c. 450), *Collectio Dionysiana* (c. 500), *Concordia Canonum Cresconii* (a reordering of the *Dionysiana*), the great Greek *Nomokanones*-collection (c. 629, revised in 883 and 1080), *Collectio Hispana* (c. 633, revised several times), *Collectio vetus Gallica* (c. 600), *Collectio Hibernensis* (c. 700), *Dionysio-Hadriana* (sent by Pope Hadrian I to Charlemagne in 774), *Dacheriana* (1st half of the 9th cent.). Between 847 and 857 four collections were compiled in France, possibly in Reims, with partly falsified and partly fabricated material. They are known today collectively as 'Ps.-Isidorian', as one them had been attributed to Isidor of Seville (d. 636). Later collections copied many of these falsifications and, to some extent, their questionable *modus operandi* as well; for example, the *Collectio Anselmo dedicata* (c. 882, northern Italy) and the *Liber Decretorum* of Burchard, Bishop of Worms (1000–1025). A *Collection in 74 Titles* was compiled about 1075 as a manual for Gregorian reform. It was the basis for the much-used *Collection of Anselm*, Bishop of Lucca (c. 1083) and at least five other collections championing the reform. In contrast, the three collections of Bishop Ivo of Chartres (end of the 11th cent.), the *Tripartita*, *Decretum* and *Panormia*, followed a middle path between reform and old Church law. The *Polycarpus* of Cardinal Gregory of St. Chrysogonus (c. 1109–1113), on the other hand, was sympathetic to the Gregorian reform.

The 'Collection of Gratian' (of whose life we know nothing reliable) had such resounding success that no other collections of *Canones* were created after it. Its first version appeared in the 1120s. The last version was published immediately after the Lateran Council of 1139. Within a short time canonists everywhere used the *Decretum Gratiani* as a reference work.

Later in the 12th cent. collections of authoritative material 'extra Decretum' were compiled. These collections mainly contained new papal decrees. A collection of decrees promulgated by Pope Gregory IX in five books had from 1234 the status of *Liber Extra*. It drew on five earlier collections of decrees which by then had been repealed (*Compilationes antiquae*). In 1298, Pope Boniface VIII published a *Liber sextus decretaliumas*, a supplement. It was enlarged by a collection of decrees by Pope Clement V (d. 1314) (*Clementinae*) and by *Extravagantes* up until the middle of the 14th cent. This body of texts consisting of the *Decretum Gratiani* and the collection of decrees, taken in its entirety, was termed the *Corpus iuris canonici*.

Later conciliar and papal pronouncements were collected only on a private basis (*Bullarium*). In 1917 canon law was codified. The *Codex iuris canonici* of 1917 was replaced by another in 1983.

Documents about the juridical literary activity of the canonistic → GLOSSATORS of the 12th and early 13th cents. were already using the term *canonist*. Up until the early 16th cent. canonistic writings always significantly exceeded 'civilistic' in quantity and were much more widespread. Especially influential from the middle of the 13th cent. were the *summae* and commentaries of Innocent IV (Sinibald Fliscus), Hostiensis (Henry of Segusio), Goffredus of Trano, Raymond of Pennaforte, abbas antiquus (Bernard of Montemirato), *archidiaconus* (Guido of Baysio), William of Montelauduno, Zenzelinus of Cassanhis, Iohannes Monachus, Iohannes Andreae, Anthony of Butrio, Iohannes of Imola, Iohannes of Lignano, Peter of Ancharano, Baldus of Ubaldis, Dominic of Sancto Geminiano, Iohannes Calderinus, Abbot Panormitanus (Nicolaus of Tudeschis), Franciscus Zabarella, and Felinus Sandeus. For procedural law, the short manual by Egidius of Fuscarariis was most widely used. The procedural law encyclopaedia of *Speculator* (Guilielmus Durantis, end of the 13th cent.) was regarded as a standard work until the 17th cent.

Many canonists served as judges (*officiales*) in the court of an archdeacon or bishop (*officialatus*). These courts had, until the early modern era and in many places even longer, unrivalled jurisdiction over suits against clerics and religious legal persons, as well as over marital cases, the execution of wills and, in general, over any case where the Church saw fit to publicly restrain open sinfulness, when it was thought that the relevant secular authority was not taking effective action against it.

Appeals could be made to the pope against a judgment by a bishop's or archbishop's court. Appeals could be made even against out-of-court decisions, e. g. in matters of administrative law (*appellatio extraiudicialis*). Since the pope could personally adjudicate only a few, especially significant cases, most proceedings were assigned to authorized judges (*iudices delegati*), who conducted the appeal hearings on the pope's behalf. Most frequently, trustworthy persons were selected who lived near the two parties. On the other hand, any trials that were important to the Holy See were allocated to a legal scholar, an *auditor*, at the papal court. This was particularly the case with disputes arising from papal intervention in local affairs, especially the allocation of religious stipends and benefices.

As the number of Church stipends and benefices fluctuated, so did the legal proceedings arising from them. The number of *auditores sacri palatii apostolici* gradually increased from the 12th cent. on to over 30 in around 1335 and then dropped to twelve. Every *auditor* was independently responsible for the trials assigned to him and thus was the sole judge. However, because under canon law no one could decide cases without having first obtained expert counsel, the *auditores* consulted with their colleagues and met regularly for that purpose two or three times a week. In the 14th cent. in Avignon they meet in a circular shaped room (*rota*). The room's name was transferred to the *auditores* who met there. The papal court is still known even today as the *Sacra Rota Romana*.

Collections of rulings by the *Rota* started being published towards the end of the 14th cent. They had an extraordinarily broad circulation and were much used and quoted. A large number of other rulings by the *Rota* were printed beginning in the middle of the 16th cent. Juristic theories often gained authority if the *Rota* assented to them.

Today the *Rota* handles marriage annulment cases almost exclusively, because its former fields of activity have in the meantime been allocated to other papal institutions, above all to the *Signatura Apostolica* and the *Sacrae Congregationes*.

Until the early 16th cent. there were many more canonists than 'civilists'. At universities outside Italy, in particular, it was canon law, not Roman law, which was predominantly studied. There were only a few 'civilist' teaching chairs and even these were intended mainly to educate Church jurists, as Roman law was important in the Middle Ages mainly as an element of Church law. The Church actually followed Roman law, except where it had established its own rules under ecclesiastical legislation. *Canones* and *decretales* extended and interpreted Roman law. All canonists, therefore, learned at least the legal fundamentals of the *Corpus iuris civilis*. There was much more canonical than civil-law writing, and more of its works were widely disseminated. Roman law in Europe was spread mainly by canonists and, indeed, not only by the relatively few fully trained canonists but, for the greater part, by the large numbers of half-trained or partly trained canonists.

Until the 16th cent. not only canonists but also civilists survived for the most part on income from Church benefices. Even secular princes or cities relied on having their legal advisers and office-holders being maintained by the Church. Ordination was not necessary for religious offices that did not involve any pastoral duties (*sine cura*), such as cathedral canons (*canonicatus*).

Even today canon law can be studied at many universities in the world. Only a few students, however, become canonists. Since 1500 canon law has gradually lost its earlier importance. The primary cause has been that over time Church courts have had to relinquish more and more jurisdiction to secular courts and public authorities. Secondly, disputes over religious property and stipends gradually became rarer and rarer. Church property was nationalized. Princes of the Church ceased being secular princes as well. And in the Church, as also in secular offices, office-holders were no longer remunerated by Church stipends but by fixed salaries. Today's canonists are almost exclusively concerned with internal religious matters and marriage annulment cases.

Canonists from the 12th to the 18th cents. strongly influenced some legal fields that are now regarded as secular law, in particular, procedural law, disciplinary law, marriage law, law of inheritance, insurance law, cheque and currency law, and law concerning 'unjustified profit-making'.

→ Apostolical Constitutions; → Didache

1 Altera continuatio, vol. 1–9, Rome 1840–1856   2 A. BARBERI et al. (eds.), Prima Bullarii Romani continuatio, vol. 1–19, Rome 1835–1857   3 G. LE BRAS et al. (eds.), Histoire du droit et des institutions de l'église en occident, 1955 –1996, 10 vol.   4 CH. CHENEY, Church and Government in the Middle Ages, vol. 1–2, 1976–1978   5 ST. CHODOROW, W. HOLTZM ANN (eds.), Decretales ineditae saec. 12, 1982   6 Codex iuris canonici, 1917   7 Codex iuris canonici, 1983   8 G. DOLEZALEK, Die handschriftliche Verbreitung von Rechtsprechungssammlungen der Rota, in: Zschr. der Savigny-Stiftung für Rechtsgesch. 89, kanonistische Abteilung, 58, 1972, 1–106   9 Id., Bernardus de Bosqueto, seine Quaestiones motae in Rota (1360–1365) und ihr Anteil in den Decisiones Antiquae, in: Zschr. der Savigny-Stiftung für Rechtsgesch. 93, kanonistische Abteilung 62, 1976, 106–172   10 Id., Quaestiones motae in Rota: Richterliche Beratungsnotizen aus dem 14 Jahrhundert, 99–114, in: Proceedings of the Fifth International Congress of Medieval Canon Law Salamanca 1976 (Monumenta iuris canonici, series C: Subsidia, 5), 1980   11 Id., Litigation at the Rota Romana, particularly around 1700, vol. 1, 339–373 und vol. 2, 457–485, in: Case Law in the Making. The Techniques and Methods of judicial Records and Law Reports, A. WIJFFELS (ed.), 1997   12 Id., Reports of the 'Rota' (14th – 19th centuries), 69–99, in: Judicial Records, Law Reports, and the Growth of Case Law, J. H. BAKER (ed.), 1989   13 CH. DUGGAN, W. HOLTZMANN (eds.), Decretales ineditae saec. 12, 1982   14 G. ERLER (ed.), Dietrich v. Nieheim. Der Liber Cancellariae Apostolicae vom Jahr 1380 und der Stilus Palatii abbreviatus, 1887, (repr. 1977)   15 AE. FRIEDBERG (ed.), Corpus juris canonici, vol. 1–2, 1879–1882, (repr. 1959)   16 Id. (ed.), Quinque compilationes antiquae, Leipzig, 1882, (repr. 1956)   17 CH., M. CHENEY, W. HOLTZMANN, Studies in the Collections of 12th Century Decretals, 1979   18 O. HEGGELBACHER, Geschichte des frühchristlichen Kirchenrechts bis zum Konzil von Nizäa 325, 1974   19 S. KUTTNER, Gratian and the Schools of Law 1140–1234, 1983   20 Id., Studies in the History of Medieval Canon Law, 1990   21 P. LANDAU, Kanones und Dekretalen, 1997   22 FR. MAASSEN, Geschichte der Quellen und Literatur des kanonischen Rechts im Abendlande, vol. 1, Die Rechtssammlungen bis zur Mitte des 9. Jahrhunderts, Graz 1870, reprint 1956   23 Magnum Bullarium Romanum, vol. 1–32, 1727–1762   24 I. D. MANSI (ed.), Amplissima collectio conciliorum, vol. 1–53, Paris 1901–1927, (repr. Graz 1960–61)   25 G. MAY, Kirchenrechtsquellen I, Theologische Realenzyklopädie 19 (1990), 1–44   26 P. MICHAUD-QUENTIN, Sommes de casuistique et manuels de confession au moyen âge (12–16 siècles), 1962   27 X. OCHOA (ed.), Leges Ecclesiae post Codicem iuris canonici editae, 1966 – 1987, 6 vols.   28 E. v. OTTENTHAL (ed.), Regulae Cancellariae Apostolicae. Die päpstlichen Kanzleiregeln von Johannes XXII bis Nicolaus V, Innsbruck 1888, reprint 1968   29 W. PLOECHL, Geschichte des Kir-

chenrechts, vol. 1–6, 1959–1969   30 B. SCHILLING, C. F. F. SINTENIS, Das Corpus iuris canonici ... ins Deutsche übersetzt, Leipzig 1834–1837   31 J. FR. V. SCHULTE, Die Geschichte der Quellen und Literatur des kanonischen Rechts von Gratian bis auf die Gegenwart, vol. 1–3, Stuttgart 1875–1880, (repr. Graz 1956)   32 Supplementum ...: Collectio conciliorum recentiorum ..., Vol. 1–20, 1901–1927   33 J. TARRANT (ed.), Extravagantes Iohannis XXII, 1983   34 W. ULLMANN, The Church and the Law in the Earlier Middle Ages. Selected essays, 1975   35 Id., The Papacy and the Law in the Middle Ages, 1976   36 Id., Jurisprudence in the Middle Ages, 1980   37 Id., Law and Jurisdiction in the Middle Ages, 1988.

GERO DOLEZALEK

Capitoline museums see → ROME

Caricature

A. DEFINITION   B. THE EARLY MODERN PERIOD
C. THE BAROQUE   D. THE 18TH CENT.   E. THE
19TH CENT.   F. THE 20TH CENT.

A. DEFINITION

The concept of caricature, which arose around 1600 in Italy, refers first of all to 'loaded', i.e. exaggerated, humorous portrait drawings [7. 346]. Already in drawings of the Middle Ages, however, techniques of exaggeration, distortion and contrast are found [7. 13–17] which are today seen as characteristics of caricature. The objects of Classical caricature are Classical works of art and the themes of Classical mythology, but also the Classical studies pursued by contemporary artists, amateurs and archaeologists. A consideration of the historical context is needed to establish the precise target at which the sharp weapon of caricature is aimed.

B. THE EARLY MODERN PERIOD

Copies of the coin portraits of Galba (68–69) appear around 1490, in the context of a type of Leonardo's grotesque heads characterised especially by its variati-

Fig. 1: Leonardo da Vinci, *A fragment: Two Grotesque Profiles Confronted.* Drawing, *c.* 1490. *The Royal Collection © 2006 Her Majesty Queen Elizabeth II*

Fig. 2: Niccolò Boldrini, Monkey-Laokoon, after Titian. Woodcut, *c.* 1550.
© *Board of Trustees, National Gallery of Art, Washington*

ons on the theme of antithetical juxtaposition (Fig. 1) [6]. The precursors of these physiognomic experiments are medieval drolleries, whose themes largely go back to classical times [15]. An extreme example comes from Titian in around 1550 with his → LAOCOON GROUP [11] (Fig. 2). The exchange of people for monkeys contrasts the moral and aesthetic force of the Christianised original image with a scene that is ridiculous. Captions and some of the attributes prepare the grotesque heads in Martino Rota's etching (*Pagan Gods*) (before 1583) for the mockery of the Olympians [7. 95].

C. THE BAROQUE

Classical parodies provided material in the 17th cent. for drama and painting [5.113]. In Rembrandt's painting (*The Rape of Ganymede*) (1631) the obvious susceptibility to the force of gravity of the child, who is weeping and urinating in his terror, runs counter to any idealisation [1. vol. 1, 192–95]. Rembrandt thus emotionalises the myth and trivialises its Neoplatonic and indeed astrological connotations [cp. 2. 107f.] The interpretation of Ribera's drawing of a grimacing toga-wearer (*c.* 1625) as a caricature of republican portraits is not sufficiently convincing [16. 215]. The exaggerated orator's pose, which anticipates the caricatures of archaeologists [17] by Pier Leone Ghezzi (1674–1755), speaks more for a contemporary inspiration.

D. THE 18TH CENT.

Since Winckelmann's *Gedanken über die Nachahmung der griechischen Werke in der Malerei und Bildhauerkunst* (*Reflections on the Imitation of Greek Works in Painting and Sculpture*, 1756), caricature has been defined as an aesthetic category in its own right, one used not least in the battle against the baroque and against absolutism. Thus, the concept could henceforth be applied to all genres of pictorial art and to literature [14. 696]. Justified only ironically in the sense of a 'negative ideal', caricatures were seen as subordinate to high art, and banished to the private worlds of neoclassical artists [4.22]. Private drawings by Füßli and Sergel served as a corrective to the official picture of a calm classical world by exposing voluptuous aspects of Homer [4. 184], and distorted classical formulas of pathos for private tales of suffering [4. 102ff.]. On the other hand, Hogarth's etching (*Boys Peeping at Nature*) (Fig. 3), which presents the academic study of nature in the form of boys as putti and satyrs looking at the statue of → DIANA of Ephesus, was intended for the public [8. 142]. The questionability of education along classical lines is already apparent in the comfortable contemporary clothing of the statue. Only the satyr boy is trying to look under the skirts to get the whole truth, but is prevented from doing so. Neither faithful imitation, the putto on the left, nor the imagination, on the right, can truly reveal nature – only satire can do so. In 1731, this sheet was a counterfoil for the cycle (*A Har-*

Fig. 3: William Hogarth, Boys Peeping at Nature. Etching 1730/31, second version. (Caption: 'necesse est Indiciis monstrare recentibus abdita rerum dabiturque Licentia Sumpta pudenter. Hor.').
The Royal Collection © 2006 Her Majesty Queen Elizabeth II

Fig. 4: Joseph Anton Koch, *The Painter as Hercules at the Crossroads*. Water-colour drawing, 1791. *Staatsgalerie Stuttgart/Graphische Sammlung*

Das antike Knie oder das Vorrecht der Wissenschaft.

Wie mit Recht behauptet werden kann, daß Raphael auch ohne Hände geboren, der größte Maler gewesen wäre, so wage
ich kühnlich aufzustellen, daß auch leider ohne Hand dies göttliche Fragment der vollendetste Arm genannt zu werden verdient.
O herrliches Vorrecht der Wissenschaft, wie Goethe sagt: „aus dem Bekannten das Unbekannte zu entwickeln."

Fig. 5: The Ancient Knee,
or The Scholarly Prerogative.
Woodcut after Moritz von
Schwind, in: Fliegende Blätter, no.
285, vol. XIII, 1850/51.
(The caption reads: 'As it can be
rightfully claimed that even if
he had been born without hands,
Raffael would have been the
greatest painter, I dare make the
bold assumption that even with its
hand sadly missing this divine
fragment deserves to be
considered the most perfect arm.
O glorious scholarly prerogative,
as Goethe says: 'to uncover the
unknown from the known.')

Fig. 6: Honoré Daumier, At the World's Fair – Egyptian
Section. Lithography, 1867

lot's Progress), with which Hogarth attempted to depict contemporary everyday life and raise caricature to a higher level [4. 23–25]. This mixture of history and everyday life ushered in a new era of caricature, which now for the first time laid claim to the moral authority of the Classical world. In 1790, literary parody of the world of the Olympians was followed by pictorial burlesque in Chodowiecki's (*Aeneid*) [8. 150]. Koch used the Classical world in two ways in his (*Self-Portrait as Hercules at the Crossroads*) of 1791 (Fig. 4). On the one hand, he turns towards a muse, who is based on a Classical Athena-type, with the caption (*imitatio*). On the other hand, he is chained, in a contorted rococo-pose, to a chimaera, whose body is made up of arabesques, baroque architectural features and the breasts of the Diana of Ephesus. In the repressive feudal conditions of the Stuttgart Academy, Koch took refuge in Winckelmann's image of Greece [12.8]. At the same time, he offers us two opposing artistic distancings from nature and points forward to the 19th century's stylistic battles between Classicism and Romanticism.

E. The 19th Cent.

In the wake of an emerging mass media, and assisted by new reproduction techniques, caricature in the 19th cent. was elevated to a genre of great significance for the modern world. While historical consciousness in postrevolutionary France called into question the use (already present in the *Ancien Régime*) of the Classical world as a model, German and English caricatures used Classical monuments and myths to legitimise the rights of the people. Thus Marx, editor of the *Rheinische Zeitung*, which was banned in 1843, was shown as Prometheus in chains [7. 415]. However, with the entry of the Classical world into modern everyday life, some loss of dignity was inevitable. This is visible in 1848, when the 'deutscher Michel' figure is shown as Laocoon fighting against the serpentine princedoms [9, fig. 1]. In 1827/28, Ramberg's *Iliad-cycle*, based on the → Parthenon-frieze, where the serious and the comic are played off one against the other, made fun of the Classical desire for order and hierarchy [5.121ff; 9. 146ff.]. After the failed 1848 revolution, Classical education became associated in France with the forces of reaction, and in Germany too it became synonymous with discipline and order [9. 138f.]. Hence there emerged a mass of burlesque drawings based on the deeds of the Homeric heroes. Unlike Füßli, despairing in 1778 in the face of the greatness of Classical ruins, [13. 265], Moriz von Schwind turned the Classical fragment in 1848 into an emblem of other-worldly scholarship (Fig. 5). Within a circle of respectful dilettanti, and under the gaze of a more-than-life-sized bust of Socrates, an archaeologist lectures on the perfect body to which this fragment of a knee once belonged. The target was not just the positivist claims and habits of a discipline which justifies itself by over-fastidious reconstructions. Behind that stands the debate about the value of Classical education, which Daumier had already examined in his

(*Histoire ancienne*) in 1842/3 [10]. Daumier's lithograph (*A l'Exposition Universelle – Section égyptienne*) (Fig. 6) of 1867 juxtaposes the transitoriness of his contemporaries, shown in perspective, with the enduring nature and greatness of the monument. By having the ugly, animal-headed Egyptians admired by visitors who are no more beautiful themselves, the educational value and aesthetics of the ancient world are called into question. At the same time, Daumier rejects the legitimising function of Egyptian art, which was used in France as part of the representation of empire. The Farnese Hercules (12. 92], Mercury [9, Fig. 14], the Three Graces [4. Fig. 111] and the Medici Venus were all knocked off their pedestals in the 19th cent., the last-named verbally by Wilhelm Busch [12. 74]. Daumier replaced them with contemporaries.

F. The 20th Cent.

Although criticism of the Classical world has, together with the commitment to the Humanities, diminished in general relevance, caricatures of the Classical world are still current [12], though nowadays they are more inclined to mock the privileges of a Classical education. Meanwhile, → comics have released students from the burden of classes in Classical history and Latin.

→ Grylloi; → Caricature
→ Grotesque

1 C. Brown et al., Rembrandt. The Master & His Workshop, 2 vols., 1991   2 W. Busch, Nachahmung als bürgerliches Kunstprinzip, 1977   3 H. M. Champfleury, Histoire de la Caricature antique, Paris 1865   4 B. Collenberg-Plotnikov, Klassizismus und Karikatur, 1998   5 F. Forster-Hahn, Johann Heinrich Ramberg als Karikaturist und Satiriker, 1963   6 E. Gombrich, Leonardo's Grotesque Heads, in: The Heritage of Apelles, 1976, 57–75   7 H. Guratzsch et al. (eds.), Bild als Waffe, 1984   8 K. Herding, Die Schönheit wandelt auf den Straßen – Lichtenberg zur Bildsatire seiner Zeit, in: Im Zeichen der Aufklärung, 1989, 127–162   9 Id., Inversionen. Antikenkritik in der Karikatur des 19. Jahrhunderts, in: Id., G. Otto (ed.), Karikatur, 1980, 131–171   10 K. Herding, Kritik der Moderne im Gewand der Antike. Daumiers Histoire Ancienne, in: Hephaistos 9, 1988, 111–142   11 H. W. Janson, Apes and Ape Lore in the Middle Ages and the Renaissance, 1952, 355–368   12 M. Kunze (ed.), Antike(n) – Auf die Schippe genommen, 1999   13 G. Lammel, Karikatur der Goethezeit, 1992   14 G. and I. Oesterle, s. v. Karikatur, Historisches Wörterbuch der Philosophie 4, 696–701   15 R. Schilling, s. v. Drolerien, Reallexikon zur deutschen Kunstgeschichte 4, 567–588   16 N. Spinosa, A. di Pérez Sánchez, Jusepe de Ribera (1591–1652), 1992   17 L. M. Tentori, Scoperte Archeologiche del Secolo 18 nella Vigna di San Cesario, in: Rivista di Reale Istituto d'Archeologia e Storia dell'Arte 6, 1937/38, 289–308

Additional Bibliography: E. Lucie-Smith, The Art of Caricature, 1981.; U. Pfarr, Comics as Mythology of the Modern Age. Myths in a Rationalised World. In: Kassandra Nakas, Funny Cuts. Cartoons and Comics in Contemporary Art, 2004, 104–129.   Ulrich Pfarr

Carmen figuratum see→ FIGURED POEM

Carolingian Renaissance
I. POLITICAL II. ART III. OLD HIGH GERMAN BIB-
LICAL POETRY

I. POLITICAL
A. CONCEPT B. THE BEGINNINGS C. POLITICAL
CONTEXT D. WAYS AND MEANS E. INTENTIONS
F. RECEPTION OF THE CLASSICS

A. CONCEPT
The enormous renewal of Latin writing according to
classical models, the extensive copying of classical writings beginning around 780 and extending well into the
9th cent., and not least the intellectual and literary efforts of numerous scholars arising apparently out of nowhere at the court of Charlemagne meant that the term
renaissance, chosen by analogy with the 'Italian Renaissance', seemed appropriate. Nevertheless, the concept
of a renaissance was also seen early on as inappropriate.
As early as 1923 E. Patzelt drew attention to numerous
fundamental traits and premises for the Carolingian
Renaissance (CR) that had also been present in the
Merovingian empire, so that from the perspective of
continuity the concept of a CR was not viable. The
notion of a renaissance was also called into question in
the field of art history. R. Krautheimer demonstrated in
1942 that the decisive models for this 'Carolingian renewal' were not to be found in classical times, but rather in late antiquity and were largely of a religious nature. Already in 1953 J. Fleckenstein provided an overall picture of the 'educational reforms of Charlemagne'
which also fitted in with this view of things. P. Lehmann
argued in 1954 against the rejection of the concept of a
CR, however, and suggested that the notion should be
retained, though one should make allowances for differences from the Italian Renaissance. Then, in 1964,
P. E. Schramm emphasised the religious aspect of the
CR and suggested, taking into account the religious and
literary aspects, using the term *correctio*. If it is possible
to speak of a CR, then, it is not to be seen as a movement
comparable with the Italian Renaissance, but rather,
taking full account of its different nature, as a renewal
(*renovatio*) brought about with the help of classical
knowledge and forms. The great importance afforded
to liturgy and theology from the very beginnings of this
Carolingian renewal makes it questionable to give a
prominent role to the reception of Classical ideas for the
CR. Classical Antiquity was not conceived of as a pure
model which one should strive to reach; rather, its cultural premises were often seen as a standard which
could be bettered and could be placed then in the service
of a Christian (that is, a more worthy) society. W. Ullmann (1969) sees the concept of the CR, therefore, also
as a description of the renewal of Frankish society and
its disposition as a *populus Dei*, to which end the cultural efforts of the Carolingians and thus also their intensive reception of Classical Antiquity were an essential
tool.

B. THE BEGINNINGS
Pippin the Younger had recognised the importance
of the Church and its organisation for monarchic rule
and therefore made great efforts in Church renewal. In
the area of liturgy and missionary activity, initially principally in the hands of the Irish and Anglo-Saxons, he
was above all else concerned to ensure dissemination
and standardisation of the Christian divine service. His
elevation to King of the Franks (751) made this task
easier. But only the strengthening of the monarchy
under Charlemagne led to greater successes, first with
the reform of the liturgy and efforts to provide a unified
monastic rule (continued under Louis the Pious under
the supervision of Benedict of Aniane), and then with
such undertakings as the revision and dissemination of
the *lex Salica* and of other Germanic laws.

C. POLITICAL CONTEXT
Charlemagne himself may be considered the prime
mover in the movement for renewal, and his biographer
Einhard attests (Vita Caroli 25) to a special interest on
his part in education, and to his understanding of an
extremely varied range of other areas of knowledge,
which also manifests itself in questions posed by Charlemagne in letters to different scholars. Because of his
interest in furthering education, both personally and in
his position as a ruler, Charlemagne drew to his court
from the end of the 770s onward emigré scholars from
all those countries of Europe in which the knowledge of
Classical culture had been better maintained than in the
Frankish empire. These included most importantly the
Anglo-Saxon Alcuin of York (soon after 781), who
quickly took over the central task of educational renewal. In addition, there came, for example, the Lombards
Paulus Diaconus and Paulinus, the Irishmen Jonas and
Dungal, and the Visigoth Theodulf (around 780). In
this way a circle of scholars grew up from which the
court school also profited. Its members often belonged
for a time to the court chapel, which became also a
political instrument insofar as it was partly responsible
for Charlemagne's chancery. As a result of their service
at court a good number of scholars received either a
bishopric or the abbacy of a monastery. Thus, for example, Modoin, at Charlemagne's court from 804, was
made Bishop of Autun in 815: Paulinus later became
Patriarch of Aquileia: and in 798 Theodulf became
Bishop of Orleans and Abbot of Fleury.

D. WAYS AND MEANS
The most important means by which the reforming
efforts were carried out was though the capitularies, in
which the most varied matters were determined to be
universally binding. The two composed by Alcuin merit
special emphasis: the *Admonitio generalis* of 789
(MGH Cap. I, Nr. 22, 52–62), which principally dealt
with matters of ecclesiastical politics, and the *Epistola
de litteris colendis* on 784/85 (MGH Cap. O, Nr. 29,
78f.), which had as its main aim the renewal of Frankish
society by means of educational reform. An essential

Fig. 1: Terence manuscript (probably Aachen, *c.* 825). *BAV Vat. Lat. 3868, author's portrait folio 2 recto*

prerequisite for the CR as educational reform was the exchange of books and letters between key figures, such as the leading bishops and abbots. The monasteries and cathedral schools with their libraries and teachers were the real instruments of the education reforms, not least because they could provided the necessary continuity through their older collections of books. To maintain the new educational levels over a longer period of time it was of some importance that the position of bishop or abbot was in many cases filled from the immediate or extended circle of scholars around Charlemagne and his successors. Their efforts in exchanging and copying books was made considerably easier by the replacement of the insular scripts with Roman scripts, above all others, with the Carolingian minuscule, the Carolingian book script.

E. Intentions

The renewal of monarchical rule and the development of the idea of the state are closely bound together with the renewal of the Frankish church, programmatically designated as *populus Dei* in the *Admonitio generalis*. The renewal of learning was intended to contribute to raising the educational level of the ordinary clergy and thus to influence the education and Christian piety of the populace at large. To this end, too, the number of parishes was increased considerably in Frankish territories under the Carolingians. A particular aim was to disseminate the *Bible* in its entirety and in the most reliable form possible. It was the basis not only for the religious attitudes of the Carolingians, but also for their political views. The rule of the Frankish kings benefited from the heavy emphasis in the books of the Old Testament on almost unrestricted monarchic rule. To this end, Alcuin and Theodulf of Orleans in particular undertook to cleanse the text of older copy errors, using their wide-ranging philological, especially gram-

matical, skills. In essence, Carolingian culture was a Latin culture which may be seen as the opposite of the Greek culture of Byzantium. In this, too, lies the seeds of a re-birth, that of Latinity.

F. Reception of the Classics

It was an essential part of the CR to gather together Latin writings on the widest possible range of cultural and civilizing matters, and above all else efforts were made to copy the writings of the Church Fathers, who were themselves indebted to the cultural heritage of pagan writers; and this led, with a slight delay, to the spread of those texts, too, in greater numbers. Those Classical Latin texts now extant essentially go back to 9th-cent. copies, and preference was given in copying to works by Virgil, Horace, Lucan, Juvenal, Terence (Fig. 1), Statius, Sallust, Pliny the Elder, Justinian and Vitruvius. Rather rarer were works by Plautus, Lucretius, Livy, Ovid, Tacitus, Columella and Ammianus. Not least important were the extensive efforts made to renew the seven liberal arts (→ Artes liberales). Beside the philological skills, which were demanded above all for the correction of earlier texts and for proper expression in the writers' own principally theological works, mathematics, geometry, astronomy, chronology and architecture were all given special attention. All these sciences, and linked with them the reception of Classical writings, were needed for the recognition and establishment of the divine order, for example, for the reckoning of Easter. In the circle of scholars at the court, biblical names were taken (Charlemagne himself was David), and beside these, also names from famous Classical writers, such as Homer (Angilbert) and Naso (Modoin). Alcuin himself had the name Flaccus. The poetry written in the circle of scholars gathered around Charlemagne and his successors (especially Lewis the Pious and Charles the Bald) was linked both in choice of vocabulary and in form with Vergil's writings, with a key role played for poetry by Venantius Fortunatus (6th cent.), while the bucolic poets Calpurnius Siculus (1st cent.) and Nemesianus (3rd cent.) also had a certain importance. Beyond the adoption of poetic forms there may, especially in the → PANEGYRIC, possibly be an indication that the Carolingian poets and their poetry looked towards the Augustan court as a model, although it was rather the court of King David that was stressed. (→ RULER)

1 W. BRAUNFELS, P. E. SCHRAMM (eds.), Karl der Große, 4 vols., 1965 2 G. BROWN, The Carolingian Renaissance, in: R. MCKITTERICK (ed.), Carolingian Culture, 1994, 1–51 3 F. BRUNHÖLZL, Renaissance, Karolingische, in: LMA 7, 1995, 718–720 4 P. BUTZER, M. KERNER, W. OBERSCHELP (eds.), Karl der Große und sein Nachwirken, vol. 1, 1997 5 J. J. CONTRENI, The Carolingian Renaissance, in: W. TREADGOLD (ed.), Renaissances before the Renaissance, 1984, 59–74 6 J. FLECKENSTEIN, Die Bildungsreform Karls des Großen, 1953 7 Id., Bildungsreform Karls des Großen, in: LMA 2, 1983, 187–189 8 P. GODMAN, The Poetry of the Carolingian Remaissance, 1985 9 Id., Louis the Pious and his Poets, in: Frühmittelalterliche Studien 19, 1985, 239–289 10 H. W. GOETZ, Vergangenheitswahrnehmung, Vergangenheitsgebrauch und Geschichtssymbolismus in der Geschichtsschreibung der Karolingerzeit, in: Settimane di Studio 46, 1999, 177–225 11 R. KRAUTHEIMER, The Carolingian Revival of Early Christian Architecture, in: Art Bulletin 24, 1942, 1–38 12 P. LEHMANN, Das Problem der karolingischen Renaissance, in: Settimane di Studi di Spoleto 1 (1954), 309–358 13 R. MCKITTERICK (ed.), Carolingian Culture, 1994 14 A. MONTEVERDI, Il problema del Rinascimento Carolino, in: Settimane di Studi di Spoleto 1, 1954, 359–377 15 E. PATZELT, Die karolingische Renaissance, 1923 (repr. 1965) 16 P. RICHÉ, École et enseignement im haut moyen âge, ²1989 17 CH. STIEGEMANN, M. WEMHOFF (eds.), Kunst und Kultur in der Karolingerzeit, 3 vols., 1999 18 P. E. SCHRAMM, Karl der Große, in: HZ 198, 1964, 306–345 19 N. STAUBACH, Rex Christianus, 1993 20 W. M. STEVENS, Karolingische Renovatio in Wissenschaft und Literatur, in: [17. Vol. 3, 662–680] 21 G. W. TROMPF, The Concept of the Carolingian Renaissance, in: Journal of the History of Ideas 34, 1973, 3–26 22 W. ULLMANN, The Carolingian Renaissance and the Idea of Kingship, 1969.

II. ART

In the visual arts of the Carolingian period, too, it is true that Classical Antiquity provided less of a model than Christian Late Antiquity; there was a thoroughly critical attitude towards the temptations of the works of art of Classical Antiquity, caused by their strong aesthetic attraction [6]. The *renovatio* of the Classical world was not an end in itself but was grounded in politics and theology, and an approach to the Classical world that was solely aesthetic and self-sufficient in its subordination to art would demonstrate precisely the difference to the reforms [8]. Any recourse to Classical models in art could only be one of various means of putting regulation into effect, and geometric and numerological patterns were also employed [7; 8]. Even

the reception of the Classical world in manuscript illustration clearly had the principal aim of showing the preeminence of the Scriptures [3].

That the CR is not limited to the time of Charlemagne himself is also made clear by the fact that most Carolingian works of art are the products of the 9th cent., just as the reforms only became effective after their wider dissemination in the empire, especially among the West Franks under Charles the Bald (d. 877). The (Constantinian) basilica as a model is first taken up by Fulrad of St Denis for his new church there (consecration 755); here as in Fulda (consecration 819) the basilica of St Peter in Rome is being used as a model. The most important surviving Carolingian building, Charlemagne's Palace Chapel in Aachen, did not only use the architecture of the church of St Vitale in Ravenna (6th cent.) as a model. From that town came the columns and other spoils that were taken for use in its construction. The adoption of Roman names for individual elements in the construction of the Palace Chapel in Aachen ('Lateran') refers back to Christian Rome. The Palace Great Hall, still preserved in modified form in Aachen, is modelled on the type of hall found in Late Antiquity, such as that in Trier. A further early major building is Theodulf's chapel in Germigny-des-Prés (consecration 806). On the other hand, Angilbert's church in Centula/St Riquier (consecration 799), in which the so-called Carolingian 'Westwerk' appears for the first time, has not survived. The Carolingian forerunner of the Cologne cathedral and also the monastery plan of St Gallen (c. 820) show the type of church with a double choir. The porch in Lorsch (c. 790) imitates triumphal arches such as that of Constantine.

Wall-paintings are rare and survive only in fragmentary form. That great biblical and historical cycles existed is clear from descriptions and especially from captions. Surviving examples come from the second half of the 9th cent. and are found mainly in remote places: Naturns and Mals (Tyrol), Müstair (Graubünden, the most complete example) and Auxerre. The mosaic in the apse of Theodulf's chapel in Germigny-des-Prés depicts the Ark of the Covenant and Seraphim. In Rome the Carolingian mosaics are almost exclusively just copies (triclinium of Leo III, apse mosaic of St Susannah with Leo III and Charlemagne). One fragment from Corvey depicts an unusual motif: Odysseus and Scylla (c. 855).

Many works of representational art in Charlemagne's palace at Aachen were imported from Italy,;for example, the equestrian statue of Theoderich from Ravenna, which is no longer extant (and of which there is a critical evaluation by Walahfrid Strabo: MHG Poet. II, 370–378), the Classical she-bear (2nd cent.) and perhaps the pine-cones (Classical or Carolingian) and the Prosperina sarcophagus (2nd cent.) used for Charlemagne's tomb. The attempt has been made to reconstruct a large Carolingian statuary group on the basis of questionable fragments, to which would belong, apart from the works already mentioned, the plaster statue of

Fig. 1: Aachen Book of Gospels, portraits of the four Evangelists. Illuminated manuscript, *c.* 800.
Aachen, Domschatz, folio 14 verso.
Photo: Ann Münchow, copyright: Domkapitel Aachen

Charlemagne in Müstair, the plaster statues of female saints in Cividale and the sculpture of a cleric in Seligenstadt [2]. In each case the influence of Late Antiquity is clear. A further surviving image of Charlemagne is a bronze statuette, based on equestrian statues from Late Antiquity (*c.* 860) which is preserved in the Louvre. The court workshop reached a very high level around 800 with the Classical-style bronze screens and doors of the Aachen cathedral. The arts of gemstone-cutting (for example, the so-called Lothar crystal in London, from the mid–9th cent., a gem with scenes from the story of Susannah) and ivory carving were practised along post-Classical lines, and in the case of the latter, Classical pieces were often re-used. Alongside manuscript illumination, works in ivory belong to some of the best-preserved works of art of the period. Examples from Charlemagne's court school include the cover of the

Lorsch Gospel Book (London, Victoria and Albert Museum and Alba Julia/Romania), and from a later period the plates with scenes from the labours of Hercules on the so-called Cathedra Petri in Rome (*c.* 870) and the ivories of the so-called Liuthard-group (3rd quarter of the 9 cent.). Coins and semi-precious and precious stones are also used as splendid and ennobling additions in the art of the book, especially in the court manuscripts of Charlemagne (e.g. the Gospel Book in Aachen, Cathedral, Fig. 1), in Tours and in the court school of Charles the Bald.

Numerous objects, for example, three of Charlemagne's tables decorated with gold, are known only by description, and the pediment of a cross in the form of a → TRIUMPHAL ARCH known as Einhard's Arch is known only in a later drawing.

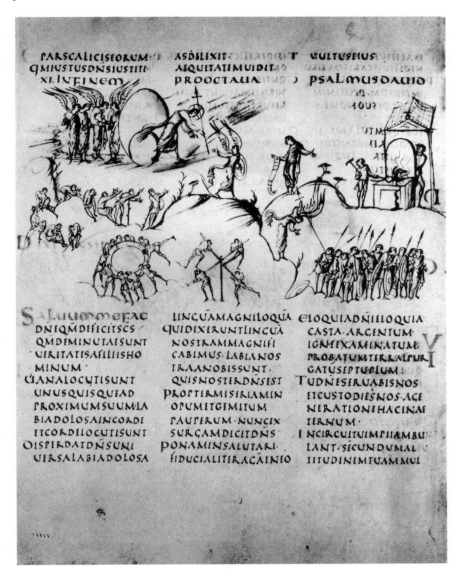

Fig. 2: Utrecht Psalter, illustration of Psalm 11. Illuminated manuscript *c.* 830.
Reproduced with permission of the Universiteitsbibliotheek Utrecht,
Ms. 32, folio 6 verso

The predominance of the book and of the Scriptures is evident from how well they are preserved and shows that the book is a central point in the Carolingian *renovatio*; the use of Classical models in images of the evangelists, for example, serves only to underline this predominance [3; 8]. Charlemagne's court manuscripts have a precursor in the *Gundohinus Gospel Book* (Autun, Bibl. mun. 3, Burgundy, after the middle of the 8th cent.), which in spite of its regionally limited character and its modest quality, permits us to recognise in its series of evangelist portraits a similar Classical model. After the 780s, two groups of manuscripts appeared at roughly the same time under Charlemagne's auspices

which are of the highest decorative quality (gold and silver inks, purple parchment, whole-page miniatures). The court school of Charlemagne, or 'Ada-group' produced with the exception of the *Dagulf Psalter* (Vienna, Österr. Nat. Bibl. 1861) only gospel books, such as the *Godescalc Gospel* (Paris, Bibl. Nat. nouv. acq. lat. 1203), the *Harley Gospel Book* (London, Brit. Library Harl. 2788) and the *Soissons Gospel Book* (Paris, Bibl. Nat. lat. 8850). Sixth cent. codices from Ravenna have been determined as models. A completely different style is that represented by the groups linked with the *Vienna Coronation Gospel Book* (Vienna, Schatzkammer), the work of an Italo-Byzantine artist; the nervous, impres-

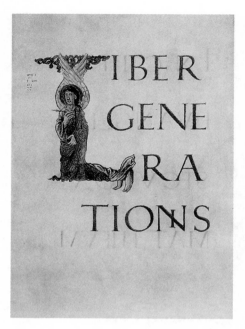

Fig. 3: Drogo Sacramentary, incipit to Matthew.
Illuminated manuscript, *c.* 850. Paris, Bibliothèque
Nationale lat. 9388, folio 17 verso.
*Reproduced with the permission of the Bibliothèque
Nationale de France*

sionistic line and the atmospheric representations of
landscape are related to the wall-paintings in Castelse-
prio and demonstrate great familiarity with Late Classical works of the 4th cent. (e.g., the Quedlinburg Itala-
fragment, Berlin SBPK theol. lat. fol 485).

At the court of Louis the Pious several exact copies of
Late Classical manuscripts were produced; for example, the *Leiden Aratea* (Leiden, Library of the Rijksuniversiteit Voss Lat. Q79). There is a portrait of Louis
as the first Carolingian ruler in the pictorial poems *De
laudibus sanctae crucis* of Hrabanus Maurus. Models
for *carmina figurata* like these are derived from Constantine's court poet Porphyrius; the image of the ruler
with shield, nimbus and staff with a cross also points to
Late Classical models (copy *c.* 840: Vatican, Bibl.
Apost. Vat. Reg. Lat. 124, fol. 4v).

In general, individuals from the court may be identified as having commissioned the non-court manuscripts. Scriptoria were established in centres such as
Tours or Rheims. In Rheims/Hautvilliers under Archbishop Ebo (d. 851) a series of quasi-Classical/illusional
codices were produced, which betray knowledge of the
Vienna Coronation Gospel Book among other works.
The most important are *Ebo's Gospel Book* (Epernay,
Bibl. mun. 1) and the *Utrecht Psalter*) (Utrecht, Library
of the Rijksuniversiteit 484, Fig. 2), which imitate Late
Classical manuscripts in its almost square format and
its text in *rustic capitals*. On the other hand, artists in
the service of Drogo of Metz (d. 855) produced positively Classical solutions for the completely un-Classi-

cal historicised initials, based on Classical materials
(*Sacramentary of Drogo*, Paris Bibl. Nat. lat. 9428,
Gospel Book, Paris Bibl. Nat. lat. 9388)(Fig. 3). In
Tours, under Alcuin's successors Fridugis (d. 834),
Adalhard and Vivian altogether almost 100 illustrated
collections of biblical excerpts were produced, with a
fully developed layout – a hierarchical sequence of Classical letter-types (*square capitals*, *rustic capitals*, *uncials*
and *semi-uncials*) used as differentiating scripts, initials
and title pages. The iconography of the biblical scenes
reproduced derive from Late Classical models. The
Vivian Bible (Paris Bibl. Nat. lat. 1, Fig. 1) dedicated to
Charles the Bald contains one of the frequent images of
Charles, which turn up also in the splendidly decorated
codices that come out of his court school, the location
of which has not been determined. There are examples
in the *Codex Aureus of St Emmeram* (Munich, Bayer.
Staatsbibl. Clm 14000) and in the *Metz Sacramentary
Fragment* (Partis Bibl. Nat. lat. 1141). The high point is
reached with the *Bible of S. Paolo fuori le mura*
(Rheims(?), *c.* 870).

Towards the end of the 9th cent. monastic scriptoria
come to predominate. The so-called Franco-Saxon
school shows a preference for aniconic, non-Classical
ornamentation of insular provenance. The scriptoria at
St Gall and in the Reichenau take us on into the art of
the book in the Ottonian period. (→ Ottonian Renaissance I.)

1 A. ANGENENDT, Das Frühmittelalter. Die abendländi-
sche Christenheit von 400 bis 900, 1990.   2 C. BEUTLER,
Statua. Die Entstehung der nachantiken Statue und der
europäische Individualismus, 1982.   3 B. BRENK, Schrift-
lichkeit und Bildlichkeit in der Hofschule Karls des Großen, in: Testo e immagine nell' alto medioevo, Vol. 2,
1994, 631–691   4 R. MCKITTERICK (ed.), Carolingian
Culture: Emulation and Innovation, 1994   5 F. MÜTHE-
RICH, J. GAEHDE, Karolingische Buchmalerei, 1976   6 L.
NEES, A Tainted Mantle. Hercules and the Classical Tradition at the Carolingian Court, 1991, esp. 3–17   7 B.
REUDENBACH, Das Godescalc-Evangelistar. Ein Buch für
die Reformpolitik Karls des Großen, 1998   8 Id., Recti-
tudo als Projekt: Bildpolitik und Bildungsreform Karls des
Großen, in: U. SCHAEFER (ed.), Artes im Mittelalter, 1999,
283–308   9 C. STIEGEMANN, M. WEMHOFF (eds.), 799.
Karl der Große und Papst Leo III. in Paderborn. Kunst und
Kultur der Karolingerzeit, Ausstellung Paderborn, 2 vols.
and essay volume, 1999 (with a bibliography of earlier
literature)   10 W. TREADGOLD (ed.), Renaissances before
the Renaissance: Cultural Revivals of Late Antiquity and
the Middle Ages, 1984.

III. OLD HIGH GERMAN BIBLICAL POETRY

The reception of Classical Antiquity becomes an
ongoing feature in the German literature of the Carolingian period by way of biblical poetry. The first two
works of this kind are the *Evangelienbuch* of Otfrid of
Weissenburg and the Old Saxon *Heliand*. Neither
belongs to the period of Charlemagne, but rather, in the
case of the *Heliand*, probably to that of Louis the Pious
and in the case of Otfrid to the time of Louis the German. Because of his poetic treatment of the biblical text

Fig. 4: Vivian Bible, dedication page. Illuminated manuscript 845/46.
Paris, Bibliothèque Nationale, lat. 1 folio 423 recto.
Reproduced with the permission of the Bibliothèque Nationale de France

in the tradition of post-Classical biblical poetry, Otfrid may be seen as a vernacular offshoot of the CR. The work of Otfrid of Weissenburg, monk and teacher at the monastery of Weissenburg in Speyergau, now in France in the Departement Bas-Rhin, is datable to the period between 863 and 871 by its dedicatory letter to Archbishop Liutbert of Mainz, Otfrid's metropolitan, and by the dedicatory poems to King Louis the German and Bishop Salomo I of Constance [23]. It is the largest full-scale piece of poetic writing in early German literature. The letter seeking the approbation of Archbishop Liutbert of Mainz provides a poetological accompaniment, and also concerns itself with the problems of German grammar, phonetics and orthography con-

fronting the author. His subject is the life of Jesus. Although there are only four gospels, Otfrid divides the work into five books to correspond to our five senses, because the holy evenness of the Gospels (*quadrata aequalitas sancta*) adorns the unevenness of our five senses (*quinque sensuum inaequalitatem ornat*) and raises our works and thoughts toward heaven (vv. 51–55, references according to [5]). The work is also a gospel harmony, though not one that is based on Tatian's *Diatessaron*, as might have been expected from someone who had been a pupil of Hrabanus Maurus at Fulda, but rather one put together by Otfrid himself. Interpretative sections are frequently interpolated into the narrative chapters with the headings *spiritaliter*, *moraliter* and *mystice*. The title *Liber evangeliorum* thus covers a variety of textual types: beside the gospel narrative there is interpretation, but also prayers, hymnic passages and homiletic addresses to the audience. The fact that a biblical poetry has emerged in the vernacular is a new beginning which cannot simply be understood in the context of a renaissance. That the *Heliand* might be a generation older is of no help here. If Otfrid knew about it, he certainly did not draw attention to its existence to legitimize his own efforts [11; 15]. Carolingian Latin literature had produced no biblical epic, and the large scale epic form was restricted to *gesta*, *vitae* and didactic works. If Otfrid wanted to call upon any models, he needed other paradigms. Referring to such works, Otfrid falls back, in his letter to Liutbert, on the main *desideratum* for his own time; namely, to present the gospel in his mother tongue: 'Together with this request they [his fellow monks and the matron Judith] complained that pagan poets like Virgil, Ovid, Lucan and very many others had told of the deeds of their people in poetic form in their own language .... They went on to praise the achievement of excellent men of our own faith, such as Juvencus, Arator, Prudentius and many others, who placed the words and miracles of Christ in an appropriate poetic form in their language' (vv. 14.–21)[trans. as in 3]. The selection does not always make clear to which works Otfrid was referring and how well he knew them, and in fact they do not reveal any indication of formal models or sources [22]. Otfrid probably knew about them from the literature classes of his teacher Hrabanus [5. 396]. They do not represent a fixed poetological genre of 'biblical epic' [16], and Otfrid could be diffuse in his expression. Nevertheless, they do indeed function in the way he says they do; namely, that the Christian writers put Christ's words and deeds into poetic form. This is certainly true in the case of the Spanish priest Juvencus (mid–4th cent.) in his epic *Evangeliorum libri IIII* and the Roman subdeacon Arator (6th cent.) in his epic-allegorical version of the 'Acts of the Apostles'.

To answer the question of which studies led in the Carolingian period to this kind of vernacular writing, it is necessary to look at the origins and use made of various components. After years of research the sources have essentially been established: the usual biblical commentaries used in the Carolingian period (Bede on Luke, Alcuin on John and Hrabanus on Matthew). Otfrid himself excerpted these commentaries and put them together to make a catena (Wolfenbüttel, Cod. Weißenburg 26) [17], which left its mark on the *Evangelienbuch* , too, even if it does not explain everything [13]. If one assumes that Otfrid had read all the Latin works that he mentions and had had the relevant manuscripts in his hand when he was developing the library at Weißenburg, then the history of the transmission of Juvenus' work emerges as being of particular significance. Only one manuscript exists from the 7th cent. (C, now in Corpus Christi College, Cambridge). Its provenance is unknown, although there are indications

pointing to Spain. There are three manuscripts from the 8th cent. (from the Reichenau, Freising and Canterbury: Huemer in [6. 27]). Finally, five are known from the 9th cent. References in library catalogues also have to be taken into account – St Gall, Reichenau, Murbach (all 9th cent.)[20. vol 1, 81, line 1 and 252, ll. 9, 11 and 14f.], and there are manuscripts of the 10th cent. in Bobbio (Huemer in [6. 13]). It is almost the same with the Arator-tradition: a single manuscript of the 7th cent. (B) is followed by numerous surviving manuscripts and references in catalogues from the 9th cent. onward [20, vol. 1, 81, l. 3; vol. 4.1, 26, l. 61]. This confirms the image of the CR proposed by Lehmann— that Late Classical material flowed into the Carolingian period in a thin stream, which then broadened considerably and was able to serve as a legitimisation for Otfrid's poetry. Glosses in these MSS indicate their frequent use and are found in, for example, MS A (formerly) from the Reichenau, and (Clm 6402), originally from Freising. The layout of the older Juvencus-codices C and R (Huemer in [6.13]) rank with Otfrid in their high scriptorial-aesthetic level. In the impressive Viennese manuscript Codex Vindobonensis 2687 (from Weißenburg), which contains the first pictorial illustrations in German literature, Otfrid's own hand is discernable[17], and he also entered glosses in manuscripts of Priscian and Prudentius that were originally in Weißenburg.

The question of why Otfrid, who was after all concerned principally to establish the gospels in his mother tongue, chose to do so in verse, requires us to investigate further aspects of the reception of the Classical period. Here, too, he is part of a scholarly tradition, although authors have given different reasons, from the desire to surpass Homer and Virgil to the idea (of Sedulius) that people tend to read verse more carefully [16. 39, 67]. The poet of the *Heliand* before Otfrid, and after him, though working from different premises, the early Middle High German partial adaptations of the Bible, such as the *Vienna/Millstatt Genesis* and *Exodus* poems, also chose verse forms. In the case of these last two poems it cannot be ruled out that Otfrid himself was still effective as a model, even if his work as such was no longer read. Some account has to be taken, too, of Otfrid's own assertion that his poetry was also intended as competition for existing worldly poems which it was intended to supplant. This was clearly so successful that we are no longer able to get any real idea of this *laicorum cantus obscenus* at all. Whether or not this means that Otfrid's verse was also designed for singing cannot be proved, even though this was initially assumed. The notion, however, that 'whoever can read the gospel in his own language and thus can keep in his mind the deeds of Christ ... has in his life no room for secular poetry' [9. 143] seems in this case to have had much going for it.

It cannot be deduced from the two verses in the Heidelberg Codex Pal. Lat. 52 [1, 1st vol. Book I, chapter 5, v. 3f., fol. 7v], which have been provided with neumes, that they were indeed sung, since those neumes were added later and might equally be seen as an experiment with script or composition, or the private notes of a singer [9. 58ff.]. In manuscripts of the poems in Latin hexameter, neumes are occasionally found, as for example in the oldest Juvencus manuscript (noted above). In any case, Otfrid can be linked in formal terms less with the *cantus obscenus* than with the poems in hexameters [22. 136–139], with Carolingian rhythmi or with the strophic Ambrosian hymn. Otfrid may also have used as models attempts made in Late Antiquity to turn into hexameters or iambic trimeters even prose works with no poetic aspirations whatsoever, presumably to claim a higher value for them as didactic poems or to attract a more favourably disposed audience [10. 514–522].

Jerome's idea (Ep. 58), which was passed on by Hrabanus, that certain books of the Old Testament were poems in their original language, will not have been applied to the gospels; even less would it have applied to Arator's version of *Acts*. But even if the form can be explained from its context as a non-liturgical *lectio*, Classical rhetoric was nevertheless a factor at the start once again. Regardless of how Otfrid's verse is to be understood and whence it derives, the *series scriptionis* (apparently the line as written down on the parchment), which is not metrically formalised (*metrica subtilitate constricta*)(l. 83f.), has as its salient feature Otfrid's end-rhyme, which he himself refers to as a ('schema omoeoteleuton')(l. 84). But this description is not enough to reconstruct Otfrid's metrical system, which almost resembles doggerel. His theory lags behind his practice. Otfrid must have had other concepts in mind for his verse-form than he documents. There is much to be said for the possibility that the 'Otfridian strophe', which consists of two long-lines rhyming at the end of each half-line, optically clear in the manuscripts, has an affinity with the rhythmic strophe of the Ambrosian hymn [21].

Even if the literary-historical ancestry is not clear from Otfrid's German work itself, the list of Christian and pagan authors mentioned leads straight to the intellectual centre of the CR, namely to the education of the extremely influential Alcuin. He was the teacher of Hrabanus Maurus in Tours, whom Otfrid proudly names as his teacher with great self-deprecation (*a Rhabano venerandae memoriae (...) educata parum mea partvitas est*), lines 135ff.) Alcuin names nearly all of the works by Church Fathers, historians and grammarians, and the Christian and pagan poets, as having been in his home monastery of York. Alcuin's text is a versified library catalogue and a masterpiece of poetical rhetoric, a memoir of the educational origins of one man [8. vv. 1525–1561] and a programme for an epoch. [18. 128f.] Thus it is also perfectly understandable for Hrabanus in his teaching of grammar to list not only the Christian writers, including the two biblical poets Juvencus and Arator, but also the older pagan writers [5.395]. The older texts are not suppressed; rather, their use is justified.

By taking up foreign writers, in Christian adaptation where necessary, Otfrid brought into literary history something new, and it needed legitimisation. He got this, as he had his poetic technique, from the Classical world, especially from the literature and rhetoric of Late Antiquity (as is clear in his acrostic). To a certain extent it has been modified by use in monastic communities and adapted to their needs. (The *veneranda matrona nomine Judith*) (l. 9f.), who has unfortunately not been identified, will hardly have lived within the walls of the monastery of Weißenburg, but she may possibly have lived in its vicinity). Here, then, the preliminary work of Charlemagne and his circle exerts a delayed influence on vernacular literature, although the literary context has to be seen in this cultural surge. Otfrid can almost be described as a Latin poet employing the language of the Franks. He is supported by the proud feeling that he is a member of a new race, the Franks, who are the equals of the Romans and are descended from Alexander the Great. He says as much in Chapter 1, 1, where he justifies his use of the vernacular (*Cur scriptor hunc librum theodisce dictaverit*). Why should the Franks alone refrain from singing God's praises in the Frankish tongue? (v. 33f.)

God's sermon brings with it its own poetic form (v. 41f.). After all, the Franks are just as brave as the Romans and in no way inferior to the Greeks. They have the same intellectual abilities and skill with weapons. Their land is richly endowed and their neighbours are subordinate to them. They are descended from the Macedonians (v. 91). Only a native king may rule over them (v. 93), and they defend him against all others with their horsemanship. Thus the Franks should not be the only ones who have to refrain from singing God's praises in their own language. He has, after all, gathered them amongst His faithful. These are ideas of a beginning that could have been formulated under Charlemagne, although Otfrid's king, Louis, is *orientalium regnorum rex*, and although the actual historical situation (fathers against sons, brothers in conflict) might have been less than ideal.

Almost none of this applies to the other great Bible poem, the *Heliand*. To be sure, it also has a Latin preface, two of them, in fact, that contradict each other to an extent; it, too, is dependent upon a Carolingian King Louis; here, too, the aim is to render the gospel into the *lingua theodisca*, but the foreword evokes a quite specific and very different context. The royal command in Part A to a Saxon who is reckoned among his own people to be a great poet (*vir de gente Saxonum, qui apud suos non ignobilis vates habebatur*) is not given to someone whom one can picture, like Otfrid, in the context of a scriptorium. The *Ludovicus piissimus Augustus* named in the prose preface is probably Louis the Pious (814–840). The task given to a bard in his sleep who had previously been unaware of his gifts (*vates dum adhuc artis huius penitus esset ignarus*, Praefatio B), and also the form, the alliterative long-line, represent a real or fictive biographical context for oral poetry in Old Saxon, without the *Heliand* itself necessarily having to be seen as oral poetry. The pseudo-oral diction allows the poem, which is scarcely less learned than Otfrid's, to hide its erudition in the variation style that is part of the genre [12. 121–126, 148f., 203–207]. The only element in this Old Saxon context that points to a scholarly tradition is the bucolic *versus de poeta et interprete huius codicis*. The rural setting, the motif of a 'bucolic retreat,' the ideal of the modest peasant or herdsmen who, then, by divine inspiration (like the Anglo-Saxon poet Caedmon) becomes the herald of Christ and proclaims redemption to the world are all probably quite unthinkable without the bucolic revival by the Carolingian poets Peter of Pisa, Alcuin and Modoin (Naso) (24. 93–97]. Taken together with the Old Saxon *Heliand*, the *Versus* is in any case somewhat alien and says less about the poet than about a particular concept of what a poet is, a concept completely compatible with the idea of a CR as a renewal of Classical genres. More difficult to answer is the question what the indirect reference to Caedmon in the story of divine inspiration, which derives originally from Bede (Hist. eccl. 5, 24), might mean for the composition of the *Heliand*. Clearly there is no intention here of liturgical use, just the justification of putting sacred events into a language that was until then not at all sacred. The source is the 'Gospel Harmony' of Tatian, which had been translated into German at Fulda.

SOURCES: 1 Otfrids von Weissenburg Evangelienbuch. Text, Einleitung, Grammatik, Metrik, Glossar, 3 vols., J. KELLE (ed.), 1856–1881 (repr. 1963) 2 Otfrids Evangelienbuch, O. ERDMANN (ed.), ⁶1973 by L. WOLFF 3 Otfrid von Weißenburg, Evangelienbuch. Auswahl (Selections), G. VOLLMANN-PROFE (ed., trans. with commentary), 1987 4 Heliand und Genesis, B. TAEGER (ed.), ¹⁰1996 5 Hrabanus Maurus, De clericorum institutione, PL 107, 293–419 6 Juvencus, Evangeliorum libri quattuor, J. HUEMER (ed.), 1891 (CSEL 24) 7 Arator, De actibus apostolorum, A. P. McKINLAY (ed.), 1951 (CSEL 72) 8 Alkuin, Versus de patribus regibus et sanctis euboricensis ecclesiae, in: E. DUEMMLER(ed.), Poetae latini 1, 1891, 169–206

ADDITIONAL SOURCES: OTFRID VON WEISSENBURG, Evangelienbuch, W. KLEIBER, E. HELLGARDT (eds.), vol. 1: Edition nach dem Wiener Codex 2687, W. KLEIBER, R. HEUSER (eds.)2004; vol. 2 Einleitung und Apparat, 2004; The Heliand. The Saxon Gospel, G. RONALD MURPHY (trans. and commentary), 1992; Heliand, Text and Commentary, J. E. CATHEY (ed.),2002

SECONDARY LITERATURE: 9 M. BIELITZ, Die Neumen in Otfrids Evangelienharmonie, 1989 10 L. J. ENGELS, H. HOFMANN, (eds.), Spätantike, 1997 (= Neues Hdb. der Literaturwiss., vol. 4) 11 W. FOERSTE, Otfrids literarisches Verhältnis zum Heliand, in: NdJb. 71/73, 1948/50, 40–67 12 K. GANTERT, Akkomodation und eingeschriebener Kommentar. Untersuchungen zur Übertragungsstrategie des Helianddichters, 1998 13 E. HELLGARDT, Die exegetischen Quellen von Otfrids Evangelienbuch, 1981 14 R. HERZOG, Bibelepik 1, 1975 15 D. KARTSCHOKE, Altdeutsche Bibeldichtung, 1975 16 Id., Bibeldichtung. Studien zur Geschichte der epischen Bibelparaphrase von Juvencus bis Otfrid von Weißenburg, 1975

17 W. KLEIBER, Otfrid von Weißenburg. Untersuchungen zur handschriftlichen Überlieferung und Studien zum Aufbau des Evangelienbuches, 1971 18 P. LEHMANN, Das Problem der karolingischen Renaissance, in: Id., Erforschungen des Mittelalters, vol. 2, 1959, 109–138 19 W. MILDE, Der Bibliotheskatalog des Klosters Murbach aus dem 9. Jahrhundert, 1968 20 Mittelalterliche Bibliothekskatalog Deutschlands und der Schweiz, vol. 1, 1918/1969, vol. 4,1, 1977 21 R. PATZLAFF, Otfrid von Weißenburg und die mittelalterliche versus-Tradition: Untersuchungen zur formgeschichtlichen Stellung der Otfridstrophe, 1975 22 H. RUPP, Otfrid von Weißenburg und die spätantike Bibeldichtung, in: Wirkendes Wort 7, 1956/57, 334–343 23 H. D. SCHLOSSER, Zur Datierung von Otfrids Evangelienbuch, in: Zschr für d Alt 125, 1996, 386–391 24 V. SCHUPP, Studien zu Williram von Ebersberg, 1978.

ADDITIONAL LITERATURE: D. H. GREEN, Zur primären Rezeption von Otfrids Evangelienbuch, in: R. BERGMAN, H. TIEFENBACH, L. VOETZ (eds.), Althochdeutsch, vol. 1, Grammatik, Glossen, Texte, 1987, 737–771; D. H. GREEN, The Carolingian Lord. Semantic Studies on Four Old High German Words: balder, fro, truhtin, hero, 1965; D. A. MCKENZIE, Otfrid von Weissenburg: Narrator or Commentator? A Comparative Study, 1946; G. RONALD MURPHY, The Saxon Savior. The Transformation of the Gospel in the Ninth-Century Heliand, 1989; H. RUPP, The Adoption of Christian Ideas into German, with Reference to the Heliand and Otfrid's Evangelienbuch, in: Parergon 21, 1978, 33–41; J. C. RUSSELL, The Germanization of Early Medieval Christianity, 1994

VOLKER SCHUPP

Carthage
I. ARCHAEOLOGICAL EXCAVATIONS II. HISTORY AND CULTURAL MEMORY

I. ARCHAEOLOGICAL EXCAVATIONS
A. FROM THE BEGINNINGS TO THE SETTLING OF THE 'WHITE FATHERS' IN 1875 B. FROM 1875 TO THE BEGINNING OF THE UNESCO-CAMPAIGN IN 1973 C. PERSPECTIVES ON THE UNESCO-CAMPAIGN 'POUR SAUVER CARTHAGE' AND ARCHAEOLOGICAL INVESTIGATION UNTIL THE END OF THE CENT.

A. FROM THE BEGINNINGS TO THE SETTLING OF THE 'WHITE FATHERS' IN 1875
Legends about the untold riches of the Punic metropolis have always fascinated treasure hunters, starting with Scipio's soldiers, who ransacked and razed the city in 146 BC, and with Pompey's legionnaires, who, two generations later, after the victory against the Numidian king Hiarbas near Utica (83 BC), scoured the nearby desert looking for booty (Plut. Pompeius 12,6). However, the earliest example of a targeted excavation must be considered the undertaking of the emperor Nero, dated in AD 65, who sent a military expedition to Carthage (C.) in order to recover 'Dido's treasure'. He credulously relied on the report of a certain Bassus, apparently a citizen of Punic origin of the *Colonia Iulia*

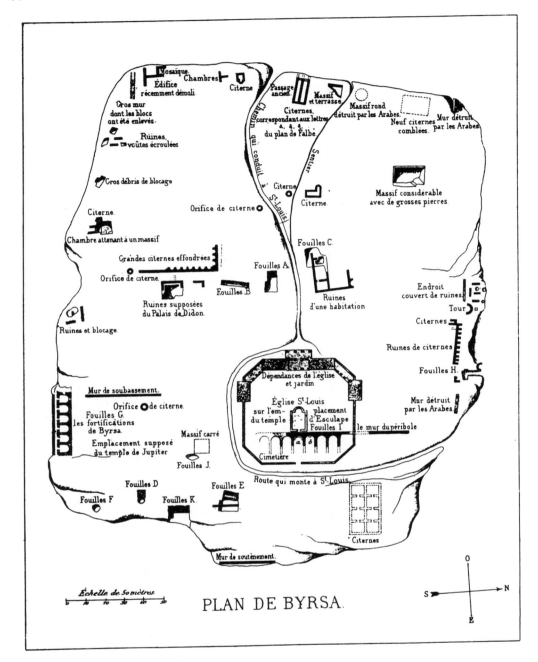

Fig. 1: Plan of the Byrsa Hill by Charles Ernest Beulé (1859)

Concordia Carthago, founded by Caesar and organized by Augustus, who claimed that on his land there was, at great depth, a cavern with heavy slabs and upright pillars of gold nearby (Tac. ann. 16,1–3) Whatever one may think of this report [10.143], it described a plausible situation, one which could have arisen anywhere in the city, which had been leveled to the depth of a meter over a large area for the new foundation. People working at foundations for new houses could have found, for instance, the rubble-filled ruins of a Punic peristyle building.

The splendid edifices from the Roman Imperial period still impressed the Andalusian Arab chronicler and geographer El-Bekri (1094) in the 11th cent., who, among other things, describes the city wall, the amphitheatre and the baths of Antoninus, and also the geographer El-Idrisi (1099–1164), who was active less than half a century later at the court of Roger II, the king of

Sicily. However, the latter already referred to the transformation of the city into a 'quarry': ('the marble is brought to all God's countries and all the outgoing ships are fully loaded') [2. 42; 20]. Stone from C. was used in the mosques of Tunis and Kairouan and also in the cathedrals of Genoa and Pisa; nevertheless, in 1270 there was enough construction material available for the army of the Seventh Crusade led by Louis IX to entrench itself behind walls on the Byrsa hill after the failed attempt to seize Tunis. However, after the king's death in August of the same year and the withdrawal of the crusaders, the Hafsidic prince El Moustancir ordered that everything be razed to the ground, in order to exclude any repetition of such an undertaking. The city was transformed into a desert and the chronicler Ibn Khaldoun (1332–1406) assures his readers that not even the remains of a ruin could be recognized [7. II 77 sq; 23. 8 sq].

Chr. T. Falbe is unanimously recognized as the 'father' of the archaeological investigation of C. As Danish consul at the court of the Bey of Tunis between 1822 and 1830, he made a first, very accurate, archaeological map of C. and its immediate surroundings, including the modern port La Goulette, of Sidi Bou Said and Gamart, which he published with commentaries in 1833 in Paris [13]. Meanwhile the first archaeological remains and collections were sent abroad: for instance, the collection of Punic funerary stelae assembled by the Dutch hydraulic engineer J.L. Humbert between 1825 and 1827 and sent to Leiden (now in the Rijksmuseum van Oudheden) [16], or the Roman and Late Antique mosaics from the villas of the coast and of the periphery of C. sent to London and preserved in the British Museum (→ LONDON, BRITISH MUSEUM). *The Société pour l'exploration de Carthage*, founded in 1837, with the participation of many French aristocrats, intended to support itself by selling antiquities. To these can be added the more than two thousand funerary and votive stelae apparently found in a stone storehouse created during the leveling work of the Early Empire and shipped in 1874/1875 to Paris by the 'Senior Dragoman' of the French Consulate in Tunis, E. de Sainte-Marie (half of the cargo sank with the ship Magenta in the Toulon harbour, where, during dives made a few years ago, some of their remains were apparently recovered).

By 1859, Ch.-E. Beulé, known because of his successful research on the Acropolis of → ATHENS, started the excavations on the Byrsa hilltop (Fig. 1) at the request of the *Institut de France*, of which he was a member. At that time he did not recognize that the great open plaza, now crowned by the former cathedral, had only been created during the early Roman Empire in order to be a central representative forum, and tried to recover from the preserved underlying structures the remains of Dido's Palace and of the fortifications described by Appianus in his account of the capture of the citadel in 146 BC. The limited success of his undertaking explains why archaeological field research has focused more precisely on other objectives: the necropoleis of Punic Carthage.

B. FROM 1875 TO THE BEGINNING OF THE UNESCO-CAMPAIGN IN 1973

The next almost one hundred years of research were significantly shaped by two institutions: First, by the order of the 'White Fathers', which received from Pope Pius IX the custody of the cenotaph of St. Louis. In 1875 the Archbishop of Algers, who later became the Cardinal Lavigérie, appointed Father Alfred-Louis Delattre, who was born in America, 'chaplain' of the sacred place, which had already been marked in 1841 at the behest of King Louis-Philippe of France with a chapel on the Byrsa hill. His mission bore the explicit mandate to research the city's ancient past. Dedicating himself to this gigantic task for over half a century until his death (1932), Delattre concentrated his work, praiseworthy despite a lack of professional training [15. 15], on the necropoleis of the Punic city and on the large cemetery churches to the north of C., the 'Damous el-Karita' (not: *domus caritatis* [10. 207]), with its nine naves, and the basilica of St. Cyprian (excavated in 1915). However, by the criteria of modern monument preservation, the activity of the 'White Fathers' was by no means only beneficial; the monumental buildings erected on and dominating the Byrsa plateau – the St. Louis cathedral (1890), the Musée Lavigérie (now the Musée National de C.) along with the buildings of the monastic order – destroyed more or less completely the centre of the representative forum of the Early and Middle Imperial Periods.

The Bardo Treaty of 1881 made Tunisia a French protectorate. The *Service des Antiquités*, created by the Bey of Tunis, exercising the autonomy still granted him, was the second institution which substantially influenced the archaeological investigation of C. It was placed under the supervision of the Paris Academy and Ministry of Education and so remained dependent on the goals of European research on Antiquity at that time. One of the first directors was the talented field archaeologist Paul Gauckler (born in 1866), who was dismissed in 1906 in 'disgrace' for immoral conduct and killed himself in Rome in 1911 [28]. The sketches and notes preserved in his account notebooks, edited in facsimile by his former collaborator D. Anziani in 1915 [14], are today the only source of information about the hundreds of intact graves he unearthed between 1895 and 1905.

In 1921, a fortuitous find led to the discovery, west of the harbour, of the 'Tophet', a still controversial cemetery for sacrificed first-born or stillborn children and for those who died early [15. 170–197; 3. 330–333]. Investigation of this cemetery was conducted under an unlucky star from the beginning. Besides unconstrained excavations – their leaders competing among themselves, often in bitter hostility – made by untrained explorers and greedy land owners, there were the official excavations of the authorities charged with the protec-

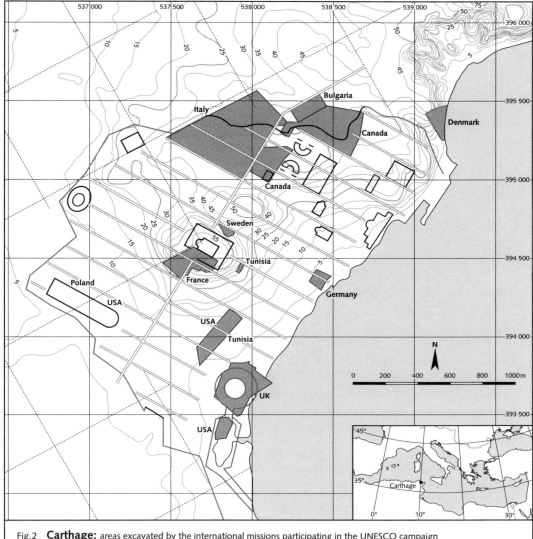

Fig.2 **Carthage:** areas excavated by the international missions participating in the UNESCO campaign 'Pour sauver Carthage', superimposed on the map of the city of the Imperial period

tion of the monuments [29], as well as those undertaken by the University of Michigan and led by F. Kelsey, financed by Count Byron Khun de Prorock, a wealthy US citizen of Hungarian origin, which were however abandoned after few years [17; 19; 22. 248–264]. Most of the excavations' reports remained unpublished and are now lost or can be reconstructed only with great difficulty. This is particularly true of the alleged 'foundation depository' of C. (the so-called 'chapelle Cintas'), discovered in the deepest level during the excavations in the 'Tophet' from 1944–1947 by P. Cintas, an unusually creative, enthusiastic and talented amateur archaeologist, who switched over to the Antiquities Service from the Customs Administration. Only recent careful analysis of the ceramic finds has allowed a suit-

able interpretation of the site as a rich grave, with locally-produced imitations of Greek models of the second half of the 8th cent. BC as burial gifts [4]. In keeping with work on the Phoenician-Punic epochs, are (1) the surveys and larger excavations in the area of the city undertaken by F. Rakob, during which perhaps work on the Apollo temple described by Appian, Lib. 19, p. 127, was commenced [31], and (2) the Hamburg excavation beneath the Decumanus Maximus [27] and, not least, the excavations begun by R.F. Docter (then University of Amsterdam, now University of Ghent) in the area of the city (Flur Bir Messaouda) [8]. Owing to these, there is important new information about the city's topography, especially about the assumed course of the early city wall [9]. Important progress has also

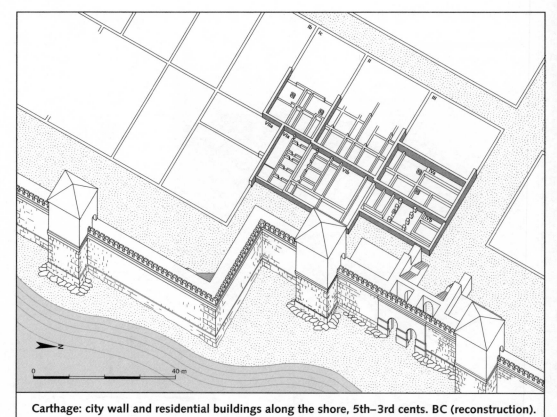

Carthage: city wall and residential buildings along the shore, 5th–3rd cents. BC (reconstruction).

been made through reappraisal and interpretation of the older excavations in the so-called Tophet [1].

C. PERSPECTIVES ON THE UNESCO-CAMPAIGN 'POUR SAUVER CARTHAGE' AND ARCHAEOLOGICAL INVESTIGATION UNTIL THE END OF THE CENT.

After Tunisia's declaration of independence in 1956, archaeological investigation of C. at first lost momentum. The emphasis was now on the investigation of the surrounding area. The report on archaeological research in Tunisia, presented by Mhamed H. Fantar in 1969, at the colloquium of the *Centro di Studio per la Civiltà Fenicia e Punica*, an institution founded by Sabatino Moscati in Rome, still relied mainly on works from the time of the French protectorate [25. 75–89] for data concerning C. At the same time, however, the still extensive ruins, part of a fashionable suburb of prosperous and rapidly growing Tunis, were increasingly threatened by modern construction. In this situation, responsible archaeologists of the country succeeded in persuading UNESCO to include Carthage in the inventory of the World Cultural Heritage. The appeal launched on May 19, 1972 by the General Director R. Maheu to the community of states to take part in the action 'Pour sauver Carthage' [12. 231–234], and the

exemplary hospitality of the Tunisian authorities have led to the involvement of twelve 'missions' from various nations (Fig. 2: Germany, Canada, France, Great Britain, the USA, among others), in which several hundred scholars and students from the widest range of disciplines related to Antiquity were temporarily active in Carthage between 1973 and 1984 [11; 30]. The chronological, thematic and methodological spectrum of the projects was broadly diverse and included interdisciplinary approaches (e.g. local geology, the reconstitution of the ancient coastline, surveys in the hinterland). Individual projects were continued until the 1990s [12].

Among the outstanding results of this absolutely unique international cooperation in archaeology is that today certainty exists about the place where the first city was founded around the middle of the 8th cent. BC, at the bottom of the east slope of the Byrsa hill; that the urban development of the great Punic metropolis and its significance in the Mediterranean context from archaic times to its destruction in 146 BC (Fig. 3) is discernable, at least in outline; and, finally, that, based on well-founded reconstruction, the monumental urban profile of the *splendidissima urbs* during the Roman Empire (Fig. 4) and Late Antiquity can be described with reasonable accuracy. Thus, at the end of the 20th

Fig. 4: Carthage in the
Roman Imperial period.
Reconstruction by
Jean-Claude Golvin.
Musée National de Carthage

cent., the city, deeply lodged in European memory through education and culture as one of the leading forces of Mediterranean history and civilization, has attained an objectively secure position in the consciousness of the present as well, and can present itself for the first time in a contemporary form, sufficiently complete, clear, and comprehensible. It is certainly not by coincidence that the exhibition about the history and the impact of C. [5], organized in 1995 in Paris, under a common French-Tunisian aegis, dedicated considerable space to the dimension of reception history.

→ Carthage; → Kerkouane

1 H. BÉNICHOU-SAFAR, Le tophet de Salammbô à Carthage: essai de reconstitution (2004). Collection de l'École Française de Rome, 342. 2 A. BESCHAOUCH, Karthago, 1994 3 C. BONNET, P. XELLA, La religion, in: [18. 316–333] 4 CHR. BRIESE, Die Chapelle Cintas – das Gründungsdepot Karthagos oder eine Bestattung der Gründergeneration? in: R. ROLLE, K. SCHMIDT, R. F. DOCTER (eds.), Archäologische Studien in Kontaktzonen der antiken Welt. Veröffentlichungen der J. Jungius-Gesellschaft. Nr.87, 1998, 419–452 5 Carthage. L'histoire, sa trace et son écho. [Exhibition Catalogue] Musée du Petit Palais, 1995 6 P. CINTAS, Céramique punique, 1950 7 Id., Manuel d'archéologie punique I, 1970; II, 1976 8 R. F. DOCTER, F. CHELBI, B. M. TELMINI, Carthage Bir Massouda. Preliminary Report on the First Bilateral Excavations of Ghent University and the Institut National du Patrimoine (2002–2003), BABesch 78 (2003) 43–71. 9 R. F. DOCTER, Carthage Bir Massouda: Excavations by the University of Amsterdam (UVA) in 2000 and 2001, CEDAC Carthage 21 (2002) 29–34. 10 W. ELLIGER, Karthago. Stadt der Punier, Römer, Christen, 1990 11 A. ENNABLI, La campagne internationale de sauvegarde de Carthage (1973–1984). Resultats et enseignements, in: Carthage VI. Actes du Congrès international sur Carthage, Québec Trois-Rivières 10–13 octobre 1984, Vol. 3., 1985, 21–35 12 Id., Pour sauver Carthage. Exploration et conservation de la cité punique, romaine et byzantine, 1992 13 C. T. FALBE, Recherches sur l'emplacement de Carthage, suivies de renseignements sur plusieurs inscrip-

tions puniques inédites, de notices historiques, géographiques etc., 1833 **14** P. GAUCKLER, Nécropoles puniques de Carthage, 1915 **15** M. GRAS, P. ROUILLARD, J. TEIXIDOR, L'Univers phénicien, 1989 **16** R. B. HALBERTSMA, Benefit and Honour. The Archaeological Travels of Jean Emile Humbert (1771–1839) in North Africa and Italy in the Service of the Kingdom of The Netherlands. MededRom 50, 1991, 301–316 **17** F. KELSEY, A Preliminary Report on the Excavations at Carthage 1925. AJA Supplement, 1926 **18** V. KRINGS (ed.), La civilisation phénicienne et punique. Manuel de recherche. HbdOr I Bd. 20, 1995 **19** B. KUHN de Prorock, Digging for Lost African Gods, 1926 **20** Z. van Laer, La ville de Carthage dans les sources arabes des XIᵉ-XIIIᵉ siècles, in: E. LIPIŃSKI (ed.), Studia Phoenicia VI. Carthago. Orientalia Lovanensia Analecta 26, 1988, 245–248 **21** S. LANCEL, J. DENEAUVE, Un siècle de fouilles sur la colline de Byrsa. Historique des recherches, in: S. LANCEL (ed.), Byrsa I. Rapports préliminaires des fouilles 1974–1976 (1979), 11–55 **22** S. LANCEL, Carthage, 1992 (Engl.: Carthage. A History, 1995) **23** A. LÉZINE, Les thermes d'Antonin à Carthage, 1969 **24** J. LUND, The Archaeological Activities of Christian Tuxen Falbe in Carthage in 1838, in: Carthage VIII. Actes du Congrès international sur Carthage, 3. Québec Trois-Rivières 10–13 octobre 1984 (1986), 9–24 **25** S. MOSCATI (ed.), Ricerche puniche nel Mediterraneo centrale. Studi Semitici, 36, 1970 **26** H. G. NIEMEYER, Das frühe Karthago und die phönizische Expansion im Mittelmeerraum, 1989 **27** H. G. NIEMEYER et al., Die Grabung unter dem Decumanus Maximus von Karthago. 2. Vorbericht, in: MDAI(R) 102 (1995) 475–502. **28** G.-CH. PICARD, La recherche archéologique en Tunisie des origines à l'indépendance, in: Carthage VI. Actes du Congrès international sur Carthage, Québec Trois-Rivières 10–13 octobre 1984, Vol. 3 (1985), 11–20 **29** L. POINSSOT, R. LANTIER, Un sanctuaire de Tanit à Carthage, RHR 1923, 31–68 **30** F. RAKOB, Die internationalen Ausgrabungen in Karthago, Gymnasium 92, 1985, 489–513 (reprinted in: W. HUSS (ed.), Karthago. Wege der Forschung, Vol. 654, 1992, 46–75). **31** F. RAKOB, Forschungen im Stadtzentrum von Karthago. Zweiter Vorbericht. MDAI(R) 102 (1995) 413–461   HANS GEORG NIEMEYER

II. HISTORY AND CULTURAL MEMORY
A. HISTORY   B. CARTHAGE'S PAST (FROM THE MIDDLE AGES TO THE 19TH CENT.): AWARENESS AND SCHOLARSHIP   C. CARTHAGE IN CULTURAL MEMORY   B. THE HISTORICAL DEVELOPMENT OF CAST COLLECTIONS

A. HISTORY
After its new foundation in 44 BC by Caesar and in a continuous process of integration into the structures of the Roman Empire, C. had developed economically, politically and culturally; especially under the Severi it became one of the important metropolises of the ancient world. It was able to maintain this status well into Late Antiquity – a development in stark contrast to the political and economic crisis which started in the 3rd cent. in the other western provinces. According to panegyrics of Late Antiquity celebrating cities, C. competed for second place after Rome within the Empire (Auson. Urb. 2 and already Hdn. 7,6,1). Together with Alex-

andria, Milan and Antioch, C. was known as one of largest cities of its time (Lib. Or. 15,59; 20,40). While the epoch of the Severi was a time of assimilation into Roman culture, the fate of the city after the 3rd cent. was marked by Christianisation. After Rome, C. had one of the oldest and earliest organized Christian communities of the ancient West. It quickly developed into the centre of North African Christianity. As a late Roman metropolis, C. experienced the conflicts with the schismatic Donatists and hosted important Church gatherings. The activities of the Church Fathers Tertullian, Cyprian and Augustine in the area, influenced by the metropolis C. and its rich intellectual traditions, stimulated numerous movements which would be important for the whole of Christianity. When the Vandals, who had invaded North Africa as early as 429, conquered C. in 439, their goals were economic and political-strategic. Therefore the Roman element (*romanitas*) remained dominant in many areas of life. The conquerors limited themselves to the installation and the provisioning of a ruling class and to the introduction of Arianism. Justinian's intervention in 533 ended the Vandals' rule. In line with the restructuring of the regained territory now known as Carthago Iustiniana, with C. as its capital, there was an attempt to consolidate the new status of the city as an administrative centre and, beginning in the 6th cent., as residence of the exarch, through building measures and bestowal of privileges. However, the intended renaissance of C. was hindered by military conflicts with hostile Berber tribes and by disagreements within the army. A short phase of regeneration was followed by economic decline and the end of *romanitas*. The plans of the exarch Heraklius to make C. the capital of the Empire were doomed to failure. The city's demise was sealed by its conquest by the Arabs: in 698 C. was destroyed. Its successor cities were Kairouan and, especially, Tunis. After the 7th cent. the city's ruins were used for a long time as a marble quarry, for Arab buildings as well as for cathedrals, for instance those in Genoa and Pisa.

B. CARTHAGE'S PAST (FROM THE MIDDLE AGES TO THE 19TH CENT.): AWARENESS AND SCHOLARSHIP
Whereas C.'s past was still celebrated in the Middle Ages by Arab court chroniclers and poets (11th cent., El Bekri; 12th cent., El Idrissi; 13th cent. El Abdery), during the Ottoman domination, under which Tunis became the Arab-Islamic center of North Africa, memory of the region's ancient roots was gradually lost. The conflict between Islam and Christianity, which manifested itself in increasingly acute forms during the 18th cent. contributed to this in no small measure. The scholarly approach to C. initially arose in a Europe influenced by the principles of the humanistic Renaissance. Until the archaeological investigation of C. in the middle of the 19th cent., knowledge of the city was based almost exclusively on Greek and Roman sources, which could offer only little information about the early

Phoenician phase and were strongly influenced by the one-sided perspective of Roman historiography in the numerous accounts of the military conflicts between C. and Greece and Rome. Though C. became an object of detailed historical and philological analysis at an early stage; it did not become a central object of scholarship until the works of A.H.L. Heeren (1760–1842). Relying on Heeren's research, W. Bötticher wrote the first general presentation of Carthaginian history (*Geschichte der Carthager*, 1827). At the beginning of the 19th cent., the first important and decisive contributions to Northwest Semitic epigraphy are linked to the names of W. Gesenius and E. Renan. The accurate integration of new epigraphical and archaeological sources and a marked sensitivity for political realities characterize O. Meltzer's *Geschichte der Karthager*, a work continued and finished, however, by U. Kahrstedt (1879–1913).

C. Carthage in Cultural Memory
1. The Identity of Carthage and the Sources of Later Memory 2. Middle Ages to the Early Modern Period 3. 17th and 18th Cents. 4. 18th Cent. 5. 19th Cent. 6. 20th Cent.

1. The Identity of Carthage and the Sources of Later Memory
Throughout its history, C. has undergone very different historical phases, dominated by very different cultures, without losing its importance. Punic C. has held a particular fascination in cultural memory. Its constitution provoked early interest, e.g., from Aristotle (Pol. 1272 b 24ff.). Later C. became an important subject for historians and also for literary adaptations particularly as a dreaded *aemula imperii*, as Rome's rival in the Mediterranean power struggle. Because of the lack of Carthaginian-Punic literature, which either did not exist or was lost, knowledge of C. is based mainly on Greco-Roman sources. The impact of the name C. on the cultural memory of the West up to the present is essentially due to writings of authors like Polybius, Livius or Silius Italicus as well as to authors like Appian, Plutarch or Valerius Maximus, who used them as models. Therefore it is not surprising that the discovery of C. as an object of cultural reception was tied to renewed interest in and study of the ancient sources – e.g. Virgil in Carolingian times and historians mainly of the Renaissance. Against the background of this literary tradition, in cultural memory C.'s name, in general, evokes an image of power, greatness and prestige, in particular the remembrance of images of the great men and women of C., such as Dido, Sophonisba or Hannibal, who as a figure received great attention in all periods of European literature. Scipio Africanus (the Elder) as well, Hannibal's Roman antagonist, has a secure place in this context. The pre-Roman Punic sources re-entered public consciousness only after the archaeological investigation of C.'s ancient territory. The history of the impact of C. is a rich one. Because of the overabundance of material, the following overview of the reception history can only sketch its main contours.

2. Middle Ages to the Early Modern Period
The political-historical dimension of C. was, for the most part, overlooked in the Middle Ages. However, C. certainly survived as a motif and symbol in the literary tradition of the Middle Ages and of the Early Modern period. This tradition is based on the ubiquity of Virgil's *Aeneid*, which continued to be integrated into Western educational canon as no other literary work of Roman Antiquity. The intellectual reference to C. derives from the 'Carthaginian episode' presented in the fourth book of the *Aeneid*, the encounter of Aeneas with Dido-Elissa, the Carthaginian queen. Already in the reception of Late Antiquity this episode contributed to the *Aeneid*'s increased popularity, and inseparably tied Dido's name to that of C. Thus Silius Italicus coined the adjective *elissaeus* from her other name as a synonym for *punicus*-Carthaginian. During post-Antiquity periods as well, no other book of the *Aeneid* was so often quoted and imitated. Thus the *historia Didonis*, of particular interest for courtly poetry (*Roman de la Rose*, 13th cent.) because of its erotic-tragic component, came into its own in the epics about Aeneas or C., which appeared after the 12th cent. in Romance, Anglo-Saxon and Germanic literatures (*Roman d'Aeneas*, 1160; H. von Veldeke, *Aeneid*, 1170/1190), as a subject independent of the general context of the Aeneas-narrative. The psychological and moralizing evaluation of the main characters, quite typical of these adaptations, was based on the traditions of Late Antiquity (Tert. Apol. 50,5; Aug. Civ.; Hier.) and adopted from them a positive notion of C., derived from a positive evaluation of Dido's actions and thus associated C. with *castitas* (chastity). Influenced by Virgilian allegorism, the concept of C. in the early Renaissance resembled rather a medieval Christian perspective. The Humanists Christoforo Landino and Bernardus Silvestris were very much influenced in their works by the Virgil commentaries of Servius and Fulgentius, which stylized Dido and C. into an epitome of the libido. In Ladino's interpretation, C. symbolizes a secular striving for power and becomes an allegory of the *vita activa*.

3. 17th and 18th Cents.
The strong affinity for the representation of tragic sentiments in literature, music and painting characterized the image of the reception of C. during the Baroque. Thus the history of the Punic Wars was perceived rather in its epic-tragic components and C.'s fate was taken as an allegory of transience. Particularly in France, C.-related themes were adapted in many tragedies, the stories about Dido, Sophonisba and, for the first time, about Hannibal, being among the popular subjects (Montreux, *Sophonisbe*, 1601; Mayret, *Sophonisbe*, 1629; Desmarets, *Scipion*, 1629; P. Corneille, *Sophonisbe*, 1663; Th. Corneille, *La Mort d'Hannibal*, 1669; Marivaux, *Annibal*, 1720 etc.). In

these works, the historical content is greatly reduced to its tragically human aspect so that against this background C. appeared often as an almost arbitrary imitation of an ancient, oriental setting. A similar condensation of the narrative material of Carthaginian themes also took place in painting, which discovered the protagonists of the Carthaginian 'epic' as prototypes for epic heroes, made tragic by their deaths, as G. de Lairesse explained in his treatise on painting (mid–17th cent.). The death of Dido or that of Sophonisba were among the popular themes of Baroque historical painting → HISTORICAL SUBJECTS, PAINTINGS OF (cf. Simon Vouet, *La Mort de Didon*, 1642–43; Mattia Preti, *La Morte di Sofonisba*, around 1660). However, the iconography of handcrafted art objects (enamels of P. Reymond and J. Pénicaud, as early as the middle of the 16th cent.; other representations on fayences and tapestries) was dominated by scenes from the Virgilian Dido narrative. But, the preferred medium for the representation of C.-related narratives during the 17th–18th cents. was theatrical representation through the Baroque opera, with its predilection for exotic elements (Purcell, *Dido and Aeneas*, 1689; Steffani, *Il trionfo del Fato*, 1695; Albinoni, *Didone*, 1726; Metastasio, *Didone abandonnata*, 1724).

4. 18TH CENT.

With the publication of several Renaissance editions of Titus Livius (by Petrarch, Bersuire and Bruni), which often included in their appendices editions of Polybius, historical and political aspects of Carthaginian history were finally given attention. In the Early Modern period Carthaginian history was discovered as a medium for political argumentation, in the tradition of Machiavelli's treatment of Antiquity from the perspective of political philosophy. At first the anti-Carthaginian perspective transmitted by Roman historiography was uncritically adopted. Against this background, the iconography of official art had, since the 16th cent., used representations of episodes of the Scipio narrative (the Battle of Zama, Continentia Scipionis, the triumphal march of Scipio) for the praise of a ruler and as the expression of the legitimation of political rule (e.g. the picture cycle of the tapestries made in the style of Jules Romain, Brussels, 16th cent.). A radical transformation of C.'s image can, however, be noted since the turn of the 18th cent. The more positive connotations of C. and particularly of Hannibal, as its most illustrious exponent, was a consequence of an intense study of the sources. A first echo of this new perspective can be found in Machiavelli's praise of Hannibal's military achievements (Principe, c. 16). The edition of Polybius's universal history, published in Paris in 1728, with a French translation and a military commentary, gave further impulse to the appreciation of Hannibal's strategic abilities. The 18th cent. works of political philosophy and constitutional theory now emphasized in typological comparisons the paradigmatic significance of Carthaginian history for the present. Montesquieu (*Considérations sur les causes de la grandeur des Romains et de leur décadence*, 1734) and Chateaubriand (*Essai sur les révolutions*, 1791) compared the rivalry between France and England with the conflict between Rome and C. and Malborough with Hannibal. These reflections on the philosophy of history are echoed in the painting style of → CLASSICISM, which thematizes the flourishing and decadence of contemporary political regimes, namely the British Empire, by associating it with Carthaginian history (cf. W. Turner, *Dido Building Carthage, or the Rise of the Carthaginian Empire*, 1815; *The Decline of the Carthaginian Empire*, 1817). C. and Hannibal were elevated to positive models, also in the context of the French Revolution. Napoleon's identification with Hannibal is of programmatic importance, since he viewed himself as the latter's successor especially during his Italian campaigns (*Mémorial de Sainte Hélène*). Vicenzo Monti, a supporter of the French Revolution, celebrated Napoleon as 'the second Hannibal' (*Prometeo*, 1797).

This association was taken up also by the painting of the 18th cent. An iconographical transposition of this comparison can be found in David's equestrian portrait, *Bonaparte franchissant les Alpes au Grand Saint Bernard* (1801), where Hannibal, together with Charlemagne, is evoked as a political model for Napoleon,.

5. 19TH CENT.

Within the context of the general fascination of Romanticism with oriental subjects and against the backdrop of a political vision of a 'third C.' (*troisième Carthage*), dominated by France after Tunisia had become a French protectorate, C. clearly entered the consciousness of the French Belle Époque. Thus, Flaubert's novel, *Salammbô*, published in 1862, which describes an episode during the Punic mercenary wars, fully corresponded to the spirit of the times. Innovative was the choice of an episode of ancient history familiar to the contemporary public, but unknown in its details, and the adoption of the perspective of the 'vanquished', quite unusual for the literary genre of the historical novel. Despite Flaubert's efforts to learn about the historical reality by travelling and by studying the sources, the novel remained mostly fictional and its historical setting was pushed into the background under the influence of an orientalising splendour 'Bedouin East' (*orient du Bédouin*). Thus a stylistically rigorous adaptation of 19th cent. aestheticism and the inclusion of allegorically-coded references to the (post)revolutionary present were possible. It is a paradox that this fictional novel has decisively shaped the image of C. in the 19th and 20th cents., although it appeared at a time of beginning scientific objectivisation of knowledge. Thus *Salammbô*'s success has inaugurated a renaissance of C.-related themes in all the arts (plastic arts: sculptures of Th. Rivière and D. Ferrary; opera: E. Reyer *Salammbô*, 1890; S. Casavoel, E. Mucci, *Salammbô*, 1948).

6. 20TH CENT.

At the beginning of the 20th cent., against the background of World War I, especially in connection with the Second Punic War, C. became once again a subject of reflection on politics and on the philosophy of history. The treatise of General von Schlieffen on the battle of Cannae not only stylised Hannibal as an idol of modern warfare, but also C. as symbol for pro-war politicians, victorious despite being smaller in numbers. After the end of the war there was a discussion about the Second Punic War from the perspective of the war guilt question, in which parallels between the situation of Germany and that of C. and between the Versailles treaties and the peace of 201 BC were noted. Views on C. during the 'Third Reich' were also influenced by the previous (political and military) heroisation of Hannibal. It perceived C. above all as shaped by Hellenistic culture and Hannibal as a model of modern warfare.

After the long domination of the ancient Romano-centric perspective, it was in the 19th cent. that the image of C. was for the first time increasingly objectivised and freed from ideological references through the accomplishments of the scholarly disciplines. Only then did it become possible to objectively integrate the peripheral Punic cultures within the context of universal history. Nevertheless the reception of C. during the 20th cent. was characterized rather by a subjective and idealising view of Carthaginian history, particularly of Hannibal (whose best-known supporter was arguably S. Freud), than by a scholarly understanding of the historical background. Starting from Flaubert's novel *Salammbô*, C.-related topics were increasingly popularised after the end of the 19th cent. The predominant media were film (V. Jacet, *Dans les Ruines de C.*, 1910; L. Maggi, *Didone abandonnata*, 1910; L. Maggi, *Delenda Carthago*, 1910; G. Pastrone, *Cabiria*, 1912–1914; G. Sidney, *Jupiter's Darling*, 1955), as well as literary fiction (historical novels: M. Jelusich, *Hannibal*, 1934; M. Dolan, *Hannibal of Carthage*, 1956; G. Haefs, *Hannibal*, 1989; Ross Leckie, *Hannibal*, 1996, *Scipio Africanus: The Man Who Defeated Hannibal*,1998, *Carthage: A Novel*,2001). Together, however, they constitute an image of C. consisting mainly of stereotypical commonplaces.

→ Carthage

1 Carthage. L'histoire, sa trace et son écho, 1995 [Exhibition Catalogue] 2 A. AZIZA, Carthage, le rêve en flammes, 1993 3 A. BESCHAOUCH, La légende de Carthage, 1993 4 F. DECRET, De Carthage à Kairouan, 1982 5 A. ENNABLI, Carthage retrouvée, 1995 6 M. H. FANTAR, Carthage, la cité punique, 1995. ALEXANDRA KOPKA

Cartography Maps – in the broader sense of graphical representations facilitating spatial understanding – were made by the Greeks and the Romans in many forms since early times. The assumption – still detectable in novels and films – that maps played in those cultures a role comparable to their function in our contemporary world is widespread. However, recent research is skeptical about this. It assumes that the maps used by the Greeks and the Romans were only rarely relevant for the organization and recording of the spatial data of the environment. Serious doubts have been raised even about the much-discussed *Map of Agrippa*, questioning if it looked like map at all. Even if the discussion on many aspects is still open, scholars agree that no general concept of 'map' existed in Antiquity, let alone one of 'Cartography' (this word was created only in the 19th cent.). There were no 'all purpose' maps, and certainly not atlases and no mass production.

Because almost all the original maps of Antiquity are lost, it is impossible to establish to what extent the Roman precursors have influenced the representations on the Medieval *mappae mundi* (Hereford, Ebstorf among others [17]), even if a certain influence is probable (cf. [4], especially ch. 1).

In contrast, many geographical writings (mostly in Greek) are preserved. The most detailed and influential of these writings, the *Geography* of Claudius Ptolemaeus, evidently was of interest to the Arab scholars long before Maximus Planudes revived the interest for it in the 13th cent. in Constantinople and commissioned the making of maps for the illustration of the text.

During the late 15th cent. for various reasons an extraordinary enthusiasm for the making and use of maps quickly developed throughout Europe; at the same time the advanced printing technique (using woodcut or copper gravure) allowed a wide dissemination. The upcoming profession of land surveyors revived the techniques presented in the Latin *Corpus Agrimensorum* and copies of this corpus were continuously produced during the Middle Ages. Perhaps it was the addition of illustrations that made those difficult texts surprisingly popular [6; 7; 12]. Ptolemy's *Geography* was first translated into Latin in the early 15th cent. (by Jacopo d'Angelo) and was first printed in 1475. The treatment of the problems of projection and the production of the maps, as well as the comprehensive topographical data, made this work indispensable for cartographers. Until 1600 more than 30 editions with newly drawn maps were published.

During that age of exploration it became also gradually evident that Ptolemy was in many respects either inaccurate or simply ignorant, particularly regarding the existence of a New World on the other side of the Atlantic. Finally Gerhardus Mercator at the end of the 16th cent. gave expression to the spreading opinion that Ptolemy's *Geography* should be regarded as a historical work and not a scientific one, and that it was inappropriate to continue the previous practice of simply supplementing it in the light of new discoveries. Rather, Ptolemy's *Geography* should no longer be trusted and contemporary knowledge should be presented separately in new works. The newly arisen 'Atlas' concept was particularly suited for this; it was named after the figure of Greek mythology who 'sounds the deep in all its depths, whose shoulders lift on high the colossal pillars thrusting earth and sky apart' (Hom. Od. 1,52–54 [Robert Fagles, trans., 1, 63–64]) [5; 1]

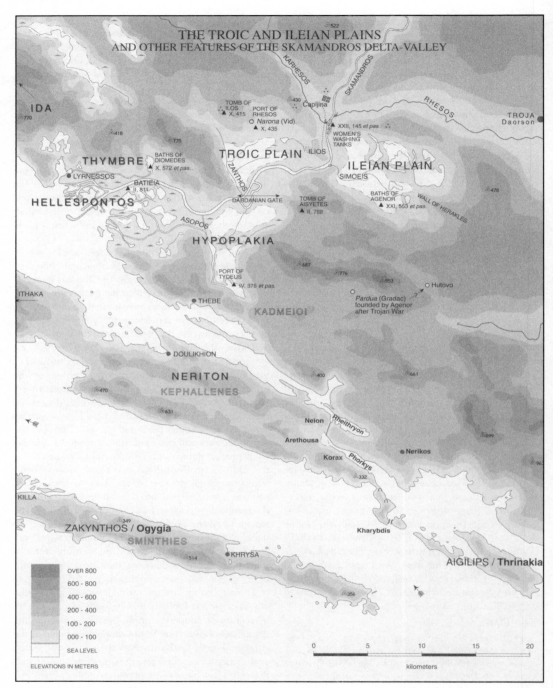

Fig. 1. Features of Homeric geography identified and localized on the central Eastern coast of the Adriatic - from R.S. Price, *Atlas of Homeric Geography*

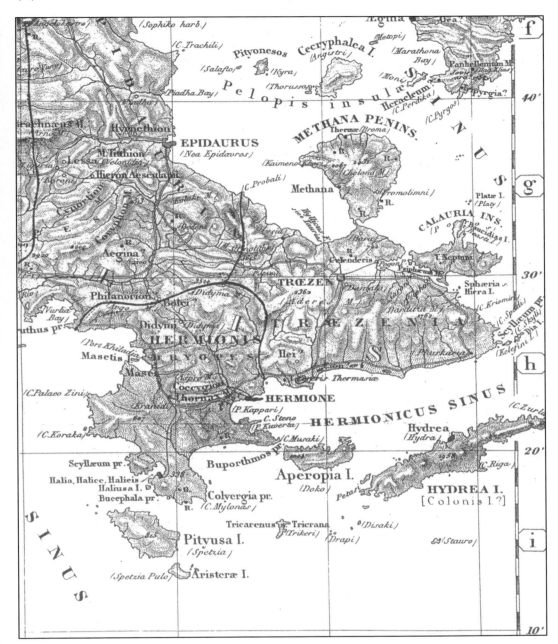

Fig. 2. Section of Map 26 'Peloponnesus', Epidaurus and Hermione region
taken by C. Müller from W. Smith and G. Grove, Atlas of Ancient Geography

From the 16th cent. onwards, the increased importance of Classical Antiquity for European culture and education, as well as the new cartographic consciousness and the development of book printing, have generated a demand for historical maps of the world of the Greeks and Romans. A further incentive was the demand for maps on Biblical themes which, although already present in earlier times, was stimulated in the early 16th cent. both by the Reformation and by the

development of book printing. Bibles and biblical commentaries illustrated with maps were published for the first time in the 1520s. Biblical lands and the Ancient World usually appeared in map collections as a pair, for instance in the late 16th cent., in the *Parergon* to the new and ambitious atlas of Abraham Ortelius, *Theatrum Orbis Terrarum* [2. 4–21, 27–37]. Not the least interesting of the remarkable constituents of the *Parergon* was a map of the wanderings of Odysseus'

('Ulyssis Errores'), an imaginative use of contemporary cartographic knowledge for the interpretation of ancient literature. Such attempts have been repeated ever since (Fig. 1) [13. 143–206].

In 1598 Ortelius published for the first time a facsimile of the *Tabula Peutingeriana*, a map which was incorporated in several subsequent editions of the *Parergon* ('discovered' in 1512, later in the possession of C. Peutinger). Already in 1563 the discovery of the fragments of the *Forma Urbis* in Rome was met with lively interest; it would have a decisive influence on the *Pianta Grande di Roma* of G. B. Nolli (1748, reprinted with an introduction by A. Ceen in 1991) and on the *Le Antichità Romane* of G. B. Piranesi (1756).

An impressive series of atlases of the Ancient World was produced from the 17th to the 19th cents.: those of Philip Kluver (Leiden 1629) and Jean-Baptiste Bouguignon d'Anville (Paris 1738–1740) deserve a special mention. The rendering of the natural landscape profited from the gradual expansion of the discoveries and surveys. Moreover, Cartography became more precise at the end of the 17th cent. because it was now possible to determine the longitude in addition to the geographical latitude. Since the early 19th cent. lithography made the production of maps easier, even if until the beginning of the 20ᵗʰ cent. many authorities did not give up copper gravure as a method of cartographic documentation because of its higher quality [8].

This long tradition of compiling comprehensive atlases of the Ancient World for research and teaching reached its acme toward the end of the 19th cent. with three works: William Smith and George Grove (1872–1874; most maps regarding Antiquity included in this atlas were compiled by Carl Müller, those on the Biblical World by Trelawny Saunders); Wilhelm Sieglin (1893–1909); Heinrich and Richard Kiepert (1894–1914). Only the former work was completed (Fig. 2) [9; 10; 11; 14].

These admirable projects, mostly relying on few people, were outdated both by the emergence of archaeology as a scholarly discipline and by the unprecedented systematic investigation of the Ancient World, followed in its wake by a huge expansion of knowledge. This was reflected in regional cartographic initiatives, such as the *Karten von Attika* (1881–1900), the *Atlas archéologique de l'Algérie* (1911) and the two editions of the unfinished *Atlas archéologique de Tunisie* (1893–1932).

Since World War I the efforts made in mapping the Ancient World did not keep up either with the continuous expansion of relevant information (especially through → AERIAL ARCHAEOLOGICAL IMAGING), or with the huge progress in the compiling and production of maps (through computer technology). The most successful works were limited to regions and relatively large-scaled, such as the *Forma Italiae* and the *Edizione archeologica della Carta d'Italia*. The most recent work of this type makes increasing use of intensive field survey, Global Positioning Systems (GPS), Geographic Information Systems (GIS), and electronic publication [15].

The vision of O. G. S. Crawford of a *Tabula Imperii Romani* with a comprehensive presentation of the Roman Empire in 56 sheets at a scale of 1:1,000,000 on the basis of the *International Map of the World* was brilliant and pursued with considerable success during the 1930s. After World War II, however, the project encountered increasing difficulties, not least because of the principle that each present-day country should be responsible for the mapping of its own territory. This principle was naturally defended by the *Union Académique Internationale*, which has been overseeing the *Tabula Imperii Romani* since 1957. Several valuable pages for Britain, Northern France, Eastern Europe and Northern Italy have been published; since 1991 others for Northern Greece, the Iberian Peninsula, Israel and Poland. The maps of the latter group are, however, even less uniform in their presentation than those of the former, and perspectives for the completion of the work are bleaker than ever.

Important contributions come also from two projects with admittedly different purposes: from the *Tabula Imperii Byzantini* (since 1966) and from the *Tübinger Atlas des Vorderen Orients* (1969–1993). The urgent need for a new initiative on Classical Antiquity finally prompted the *American Philological Association* to assume the patronage over the *Barrington Atlas of the Greek and Roman World*, which was published in 2000 in Princeton. This atlas offers an exhaustive image of the knowledge accumulated over the last hundred years and uses modern cartographic and production methods [16]. Its 180 large maps are complemented by a Map-by-Map Directory (2 vols. and on CD-ROM), which not only offers a comprehensive list of ancient toponyms and sites, but also the appropriate references. The digital production facilitates future revisions and adaptations of the maps. An *Ancient World Mapping Center* was set up at the University of North Carolina at Chapel Hill (USA) in order to coordinate this work and offer assistance to those who, for whatever purpose, are interested in using or compiling maps of the Ancient World.

→ Cartography
→ ATLANTIS

1 J. R. AKERMAN, From Books with Maps to Books as Maps. The Editor in the Creation of an Atlas Idea, in: J. WINEARLS (ed.), Editing Early and Historical Atlases, 1995, 3–48 2 J. BLACK, Maps and History. Constructing Images of the Past, 1997 3 K. BRODERSEN, Terra Cognita, 1995, 12 4 E. EDSON, Mapping Time and Space. How Medieval Mapmakers Viewed their World, 1997 5 A. GRAFTON et al., New Worlds, Ancient Texts. The Power of Tradition and the Shock of Discovery, 1992, Index s. v. Ptolemy 6 F. T. HINRICHS, Die *agri per extremitatem mensura comprehensi*. Diskussion eines Frontintextes und der Geschichte seines Verständnisses, in: O. BEHRENDS, L. CAPOGROSSI COLOGNESI (eds.), Die römische Feldmeßkunst. Interdisziplinäre Beiträge zu ihrer Bedeutung für die Zivilisationsgeschichte Roms, 1992, 348–374 7 R. J. P. KAIN, E. BAIGENT, The Cadastral Map in the Service of the State. A History of Property Mapping, 1992 8 I. KRETSCHMER et al. (eds.), Lexikon

zur Geschichte der Kartographie von den Anfängen bis zum Ersten Weltkrieg, 2 vols., 1986   9 R. TALBERT, Mapping the Classical World. Major Atlases and Map Series 1872–1990, Journal of Roman Archaeology 5, 1992, 5–38   10 Id. Carl Müller (1813–1894), S. Jacobs, and the Making of Classical Maps in Paris for John Murray, Imago Mundi 46, 1994, 128–150   11 Id. Introduction, in: H. (and R.) KIEPERT, Formae Orbis Antiqui, reprint 1996, V–VIII   12 L. TONEATTO, Codices Artis Mensoriae: I Manoscritti degli Antichi Opuscoli Latini d'Agrimensura (V–XIX sec.), 3 vols, 1994–95   13 A. WOLF, H.-H. WOLF, Die wirkliche Reise des Odysseus, 1983   14 L. ZÖGNER (ed.), Antike Welten, Neue Regionen: Heinrich Kiepert, 1999   15 S. E. ALCOCK, J. F. CHERRY (eds.), Side-by-Side Survey: Comparative Regional Studies in the Mediterranean World (2004), especially chapters 13, 16   16 Id., Barrington Atlas of the Greek and Roman World: The Cartographic Fundamentals in Retrospect, Cartographic Perspectives 46, 2003, 4–27 and 72–76   17 S. D. WESTREM, The Hereford Map: A Transcription and Translation of the Legends with Commentary, 2001   18 Ancient World Mapping Center: www.unc.edu/awmc

RICHARD TALBERT

Caryatids see → SUPPORTING FIGURES

Cast; Cast Collections
A. CAST   B. THE HISTORICAL DEVELOPMENT OF CAST COLLECTIONS

A. CAST
1. DEFINITION   2. PRODUCTION AND MATERIALS 3. UTILIZATION

1. DEFINITION
A cast is made by mechanically moulding an already existing plastic work of art or model. Designations such as copy, replicate or reproduction should account for this characteristic on a linguistic level, and always imply a lower valuation; in contrast, one speaks of a replica when the model is reproduced using the same manufacturing method. In everyday language, the notion of a copy somewhat vaguely designates both replicates and replicas. Whereas in the process of manufacturing replicas, changes in relation to the model are inevitable, the cast reproduces the plastic surface structure and three-dimensional extension of the model with a precision other copying procedures cannot attain, and therefore probably do not even attempt to accomplish.

2. PRODUCTION AND MATERIALS
Two procedures are necessary in order to make a cast: first, shaping the mould through casting the model or the original; second, filling the mould with the preferred material. Already in Antiquity, hardening as well as durably plastic materials were used as moulds ([6]: Lucian, Iupp.trag. 33). Hardening forms (of clay, plaster and wax for smaller objects) must be assembled from many parts, which leave a characteristic network of casting burrs on the cast. Plastic moulds (of pitch, bone glue, gelatine, Formalose, latex, or silicone rubber) have the advantage that only a few mould parts are

used, even for complicated divisions of the model. Depending on the material and condition of the model, as well as on the material chosen for the mould, a separating substance must be applied between the model and the mould (shellac, soap solution, potter's clay, wax, talcum; with silicone: soap solution, wallpaper paste, petroleum jelly, paraffin, metal foil) [2; 4; 6; 7; 14; 15]. In 1984 an ancient bronze, the equestrian statue of Marcus Aurelius from Rome, was for the first time moulded or 'contoured', not following the usual, mechanical method, but photogrammetrically, without surface contact [1].

Until modern times, plaster and metal were most often used for cast (zinc was added in the 19th cent. [13], and aluminium from about 1880), as well as waxes [8]. Over the last few decades, one also finds mixtures of white cement, grey concrete and artificial stone, as well as various mixes of polyester resin (with steel, copper, brass, mica, gold bronze powders or with metal chips for metal imitations; with marble chips, glass sand, kaolin, chalk, volcanic ash, graphite, slate flour, cork flour, cotton flocks or crushed bottle glass for stone imitations; wood flour for wood imitations), which aim to achieve better durability and/or a more realistic imitation. Metal casts are produced as before by lost wax casting, but also by electrolytic methods like galvanoplasty [7; 14].

3. UTILIZATION
A distinction is to be made between the use of casts as independent art objects or as substitutes for them (see below, section B.; for Antiquity e.g. Plin. HN 35,4–11; Paus. 1,40,3–4; 9,32,1; Juv. 2,4–5; Plut. Mor. 984; SHA Sev. 22, 3; Tert. de idol. 3, 2; Lucian, Nigr. 2; Arnob. 6, 14ff.), and the use of casts as aids in the production of objects made of metal, terracotta or stucco (e.g. Theophr. de lapid. 64–67; Plin. HN. 33,156ff.; 35,153. 155–157; cf. 35,151), or for the production of stone replicas by means of pointing [9]. Because plaster remains do not survive in the soil, ancient examples are only rarely available. Excavations attest the use of casts in Egypt since the middle of the 3rd millennium BC. The most famous examples come from the workshop of Thutmose at Amarna (c. 1340 BC) [19]. This use of casts probably goes back to early times in the Greek cultural area as well. Casts of sculptures have been found especially at Baiae, Sabratha and Rome (shield from the Via Appia, with the representation of an amazonomachy), plaster moulds for toreutic products or terracottas, especially at Memphis, Kara-Tobe (Crimea) and Begram (Afghanistan). These finds show that ancient artists already possessed a highly developed casting technique [2; 6; 15]. In the written sources, we first hear of impressions and casts from the time of Theophrastus. Ancient technical terms that occur include *apomágma* (Theophr. de lapid. 67), *sphragís*, (Lucian, Iupp. trag. 33,16), *apomáxasthai* (Plut. mor. 984) or, only in later occurrences, *gypsoplástes* (Cassiod. var. 7,55) and *gypsoplasía* (Nilus Ancyranus epist. 4,61).

B. The Historical Development of Cast
Collections

Since the 15th cent., the causes that led to the establishment of cast collections (CC) of ancient sculptures
were often subject to fundamental changes in content,
so that we are justified in speaking of four generations
of CC up to the present.

1. Cast Collections as Tools for Artists and
as Surrogates for Non-Marketable Originals   2. The Revaluation of Cast
Collections since Classicism

1. Cast Collections as Tools for Artists
and as Surrogates for Non-Marketable
Originals

First came the possession of casts, already common
in former times, which served as tools for sculptors and
painters in their work. The explicit use of casts of ancient sculptures is attested for the first time by Francesco Squarcione (1397–1468) in Padua. At that time,
they were introduced merely as models for new art
objects in the style of the Renaissance. Casts of ancient
works of art did not yet possess their own value as ideal
models for art. Although small casts, e.g. of ancient portraits, occasionally appeared in the 'art cabinets' of
scholars or high-ranking personages, such as bishop
Ludovico Gonzaga (1458–1511) at Mantua, the encyclopaedic scholar Konrad Peutinger (1465–1547) at
Augsburg or the legal scholar Marco Mantova Bena-
vides (1489–1582) at Padua, this was no homage rendered to the objects' artistic value, but an allusion to the
owner's culture. Similar phenomena are already attested in antiquity (Juv. 2,4–5), although casts then bore
the stigma of an inferior surrogate: those who could not
afford a first-class self-representation, i.e. a bronze or
marble sculpture, and therefore had recourse to cheaper
reproductions, exposed themselves to ridicule.

The prestige derived from the access to 'first class'
ancient sculptures was the motive force for the emergence of the second generation of CC, beginning with
the 16th cent. [11]. A canonical artistic taste, practiced
especially in Renaissance Italy, whose criteria had in
part been extracted from the study of ancient sources
(especially on Pheidias, Praxiteles, and Polycleitus [10;
18; 19; 21]), determined what 'first class' sculptures
were. How the development of qualitative criteria was
related in individual cases to the codification of canonical pieces or to the available supply of antiquities is not
relevant for the history of CC. The course of events
shows that it was the way the sculptures were displayed,
and not only their quality, that determined their artistic
value and celebrity throughout the centuries. The first
collection of originals to have a profound impact on the
history of CC developed in the Vatican, beginning with
Pope Julius II (1503–1513). At his command, Donato
Bramante (1444–1514) built a courtyard for this collection in the Vatican Palace, the so-called Cortile delle
Statue (the topmost court of the Cortile del Belvedere),

in which Julius displayed the sculptures he had bought
or which had been found on his properties. The most
significant were the → BELVEDERE APOLLO , the Belvedere Laocoon, the so-called Commodus as Hercules,
the so-called Cleopatra, the Venus Felix, and the so-
called Belvedere Antinous (all in the Vatican), as well as
the Tiber (Paris, LV; see [11], Cat. Nos. 8, 52, 25, 24, 4,
79). These statues gained worldwide celebrity at the
time through the work of the Bolognese painter Francesco Primaticcio, who, on the orders of King François I
of France (reigned 1515–1547), moulded them from
1540–1543 and displayed the original-size bronze casts
in the gallery of Fontainebleau. François I's goal was to
possess not just any ancient statues, even if they were
originals, but such as would furnish proof of his first-
class taste. Such highly-rated originals were jealously
guarded by their owners, primarily the Farnese, Medici,
Borghese and Ludovisi families, and were not for sale.
Until the end of the 17th cent., only King Louis XIV
managed to transport two top-ranking originals to
France (the so-called Germanicus and the so-called Cin-
cinnatus), both in the Louvre; see [11], Cat. nos. 42,
23]. The means of choice were thus outstanding casts,
at least of plaster, if not of bronze, in original size. The
fact that the acquisition of casts, or the authorization to
produce moulds were extremely expensive and complicated, even being the subjects of diplomatic negotiation, underlines the importance of casts and CC as court
or princely prestige objects. An ensemble of originals
with a success comparable to that of the Cortile delle
Statue was completed up to 1688, in the so-called Tribuna, an octagonal art cabinet in the → UFFIZI gallery
of Florence; from here, the statues that had the greatest
influence and subsequently were present in every CC,
were the Venus de'Medici, the Florentine Wrestlers, the
Arrotino, the Dancing Satyr and the Venus Victrix (all
at Florence, UF; see [11], Cat. nos. 88, 94, 11, 34, 91).
The Farnese Hercules (now at Naples, MN; see. [11],
Cat. no. 46) was also moulded after its discovery in
1546 or 1556, and we hear of casts in Rome and Alca-
zar in 1666, and of one in Paris in 1669.

Until the middle of the 18th cent., the sculptures of
the Cortile delle Statue and of the Tribuna were present
at European courts in the form of plaster or bronze
casts, or as marble copies, where they were used either
as exhibition pieces or, until the end of the 18th cent., in
the context of specially created royal art academies,
promoted to the status of an arsenal for the forms of
canonized good taste (Copenhagen 1682, Berlin
1695/1696), Augsburg 1757, St. Petersburg 1758,
London 1768, Stockholm and Warsaw between 1780
and 1790, New York and Philadelphia 1805). France
was once again the pioneer in this development. Louis
XIV had already created a French art academy at Rome
in 1666, which was to provide French artists the same
advantageous conditions as those long enjoyed by Italian artists. Until 1684 more than 100 large-sized casts
of the most famous sculptures were collected in
→ ROME, and in the course of time they reached

→ PARIS. French court artists made marble or bronze copies of these models for Versailles, and developed the basis for a state art of the highest possible taste. Around 1713, only Düsseldorf under Prince-elector Johann Wilhelm could boast a comparable CC outside of Italy, thanks to his marriage into the Medici family. At any event, he did not evaluate it according to the French model.

2. THE REVALUATION OF CAST COLLECTIONS SINCE CLASSICISM

Beginning with the 2nd half of the 18th cent., the scholarly study of antiquities on an encyclopaedic basis achieved great success in the context of the courtly usage of ancient sculptures. A pioneer in this regard was J.J. Winckelmann (*Geschichte der Kunst des Altertums*, Dresden 1764), who was in the service of Cardinal Albani from 1758 on. The newly gained knowledge initiated an integrated attitude towards Antiquity (in Germany especially to Greek Antiquity [16]), in which surviving remains were assigned an importance that went far beyond previous reception, which was merely representative. Antiquity became a symbol of greatness and perfection. The structure and the laws of a past life envisaged as ideal, its religion and political order, questions of social and juridical order, as well as literature and art could be studied in the case of Antiquity, and were to be made fruitful for the present in the sense of an ideology supporting the state. This introduced a third generation of CC, with its centre of gravity in Germany, which was intended to be received by the general public as illustrating recently formulated social values. Many of these CC came into being at universities (e.g. Göttingen since 1767, Bonn since 1819, Tübingen since 1830, Kiel since 1840, Erlangen and Zürich since 1855), partly together with the newly established and sumptuously equipped chairs of → CLASSICAL ARCHAEOLOGY (e.g. Leipzig 1840, Halle 1841, Heidelberg 1848, Munich 1869, Strasbourg 1872, Marburg since 1876, Münster since 1883, Frankfurt 1914). Integration within academic studies was to provide popular education at the highest level, and casts became embodiments of a didactic program. In this context, all other genres became important as well (pottery, tools, gem impressions, architectural specimens and models). About half of the approx. 130 CC known until today are in German-speaking countries, a third in other European countries and rest outside Europe. At the same time, the private possession of casts as symbols of culture became once again fashionable. Alongside this orientation, huge CC, continuing the idea of art academies under the sign of the new boom conditions, arose in the 19th cent. as cabinets of models or as documentation centres for ancient styles or outstanding works of art from all Mediterranean cultures, from early periods to the present (e.g. Paris, Musée des Études de l'École Nationale Supérieure des Beaux-Arts, since 1666, and Paris, Trocadéro, Musée des Monuments Français 1882; Berlin, Neues Museum 1856; New York, CC of the Metropolitan Museum since 1883; Dresden, Alber-

tinum 1891; Lyon 1899/1948; Copenhagen, Royal CC 1885). Such CC were sometimes more valued than the collections of originals, and many filled large museum wings all by themselves (cast holdings at the beginning of the 20th cent.: Dresden approximately 5000, New York approx. 2600, Berlin approx. 2270, Munich approx. 1700). With the beginning of the decline of the artistic and humanistic educational ideal (cf. the controversy over the polychromy of ancient sculpture) a discrepancy developed, recurring throughout the history of almost all CC, between the (outmoded) ideological charge of the casts and the financial support currently awarded to them. The spectrum of the events reached the point of throwing casts, which had come to be perceived as didactic patronization, out the window. It was also the ambiguous symbolic value of casts that, during and after World War II, led to the decline or complete demise of some of the greatest CC in Europe (Berlin, Leipzig, Munich; Frankfurt, Kiel, Münster were also destroyed; the collections at Dresden and Strasbourg were evacuated in 1940/45; Lyon's collection was put in storage in 1962; that of the Paris Musée des Études was evacuated in 1970 to Versailles; the one at New York was evacuated in 1938, and since 1987 is partly in Munich).

Since about the 1960s there has been a resurgence of the value of casts and of CC in science, public opinion and art [5]. Especially in the universities, the CC of old have been rebuilt (Berlin; Munich, the Mannheim Antikensaal since 1983; the storage depot at → DRESDEN; Halle and Leipzig (under construction); Strasbourg since 1982, and Lyon (reopened in 1985 on a smaller scale)). Here, as fourth generation CC, they are primarily of use to archaeological research, but they can also be experienced as contemporary witnesses to the flourishing Humanism of the 19th cent.

→ Copies; → Gypsum; → Imagines maiorum

1 G. ACCARDO, M. MICHELI, L'utilizzazione di modelli per lo studio di problemi strutturali e formali. Una metodologia per realizzare copie senza calco, in: Bolletino d'Arte 41, 1987, 111–125 2 G. BARONE, Gessi del Museo di Sabratha, 1994 3 A. H. BORBEIN, Klassische Architektur in Berlin, in: Berlin und die Antike. Aufsätze, Kongress-Berichte Berlin 1979, 99–150 4 F. BURKHALTER, Moulages en plâtre antiques et toreutique alexandrine, in: N. BONACASA, A. DI VITA (eds.), Alessandria e il mondo ellenistico-romano, 1984, 334–347 5 H.-U. CAIN, Gipsabgüsse. Zur Geschichte ihrer Wertschätzung, in: Anzeiger des Germanischen Nationalmuseum 1995, 200–215 6 F. DONATI, Processi di riproduzione artistica: l'uso della pece bruzia e i calchi antichi, in: Klearchos 125–128, 1990, 105–148 7 K. FALTERMEIER, in: CIBA-GEIGY (ed.), Technik der Nachbildung durch Abgiessen (n.d.) 2–16 8 H. I. FLOWER, Ancestor Masks and Aristocratic Power in Roman Culture, 1996 9 C. GASPARRI, s.v. copie e copisti, EAA Suppl. 2, 1994, 267–280 10 N. GRAMACCINI, Mirabilia, 1996 11 F. HASKELL, N. PENNY, Taste and the Antique. The Lure of Classical Sculpture 1500–1900, 1982 12 N. HIMMELMANN, Utopische Vergangenheit. Architektur und moderne Kultur, 1976, 138–157 13 F. KOBLER, Über Zink, in: Anzeiger des Germanischen

Nationalmuseum 1995, 228–237   14 G. KOLLMANN, in: WACKER-CHEMIE GMBH (ed.), Die Kunst zu bewahren, 1997, 11–13 and 168–171   15 CHR. LANDWEHR, Die antike Gipsabgüsse aus Baiae. Griechische Bronzestatuen in Abgüssen römischer Zeit, 1985, 12–25   16 S. L. MAR-CHAND, Down from Olympus. Archaeology and Philhellenism in Germany, 1750–1970, 1996   17 Moulages, copies, facsimiles. Actes des IXèmes journées des restaurateurs en archéologie, Soissons 1993, in: Bull. de liaison. Centre d'études des peintures murales romaines 11, 1994, 5–167   18 A. THIELEMANN, Phidias im Quattrocento, 1992   19 D. WILDUNG, Einblicke. Zerstörungsfreie Untersuchungen an altägyptischen Objekten, in: Jb. Preußischer Kulturbesitz 29, 1992, 148–155   20 H. WREDE, Römische Reliefs griechischer Meister?, in: CHR. BÖRKER, M. DONDERER (eds), Das antike Rom und der Osten, 1990, 219–234   21 F. ZÖLLNER, Policretior manu – zum Polykletbild der frühen Neuzeit, in: Polyklet. Der Bildhauer der griechischen Klassik, exhibition catalogue Frankfurt 1990, 450–472.   INGEBORG KADER

Cathedral School
A. DEFINITION   B. CHRONOLOGY   C. SYSTEM

A. DEFINITION
Schools established in the centres of power and organisation of bishoprics for the primary purpose of training diocesan clerics. Beyond that, they also fulfilled an important educational function for the maintaining of the political structure through the so-called *schola exterior*.

B. CHRONOLOGY
Since the mid–8th cent. the function of the Cathedral School (CS) had been programmatically as well as organisationally established in the interplay between the ancient Roman legacy on the one hand and the → MONASTIC SCHOOL on the other. The schools of the Roman Empire essentially guaranteed the replication of the political system and the upholding of the cultural tradition, while the monastic schools that emerged primarily through the Irish-Frankish and Anglo-Saxon mission in the Merovingian and Frankish Empires were striving for the model of a life centred around the Christian faith.

Schools at bishoprics were already present in Christian Late Antiquity (Augustine) and had been called for at Visigothic Church convocations beginning with the Council of Toledo (527) although they did not yet occupy their later central role in the structure of society. Under Bishop Chrodegang of Metz (d. 766), the demand was made to reform, within the framework of the CS, the way of life even of the diocesan clergy according to the model of (Benedictine) monasticism (*vita communis*). In this way, the need for educated secular priests was to be met who, in view of the established integration of political and religious authority in medieval society, were structurally accorded the representation of ruling legitimation.

Within the context of Charlemagne's efforts to reform the organisation of schools (→ CAROLINGIAN RENAISSANCE) the demand was formulated at the Synod of Aachen in 798 to establish schools in all cathedral chapters, which were to follow the model of the CS of Metz. Coupled with this demand, the desire for reform also aimed at improving the language competence of clerics so that the religiously legitimised ruling structure could be based on a reliable and binding Christian message. The practice of Christianity as a book religion served political interests as well. At the same time, language competence, which was to be acquired using religious material, was essential for the reading, transmission, and composition legal texts. And last but not least, as the leading, i.e. integrative European language, Latin, owing to the interconnection of spiritual and secular education, had to assure communication in the political sphere. All of these purposes were to be served by instruction in written characters, grammar, psalms, singing, the calculation of Church feast days (computus), the cultivation of the liturgy and the development of the scribal staff (scriptorium). This reform practically went hand in hand with the demand for an empire-wide training of clergy which had already been formulated in 789 in the *Admonitio generalis*, Charlemagne's pedagogically trend-setting decree. Along with this generalizing tendency, the capriciousness of individual school directors was to be balanced by means of the ruler's proclamation of binding basic standards in school education (→ COURSE OF INSTRUCTION).

The practice and the program of CS and monastic schools was caught in the tension between withdrawal from and openness towards the world. This conflict manifested itself especially during the reign of Louis the Pious when there was much debate about the contours of a life lived according to Christian faith. Debated were the treatment of non-Christian literature on the one hand and, on the other, the use of (scholarly) reflection as such. This debate was manifested in a curricular view in the devaluation or absolute rejection of scholarly studies in the curriculum, in a personal respect by the admittance–from time to time–of only those students who were destined for religious orders (*scholares canonici*), and finally, in a structural sense, and as a medium-term reaction to the tension, in a separation between an inner school for young canons (*schola interior*) and an outer school (*schola exterior*) where the secular clergy and other adolescents could be educated.

In Germany, England, and France, the CS enjoyed its peak from the 10th to the 12th cent. Among the most important schools were those in Mainz, Münster, Hildesheim, Salzburg, Canterbury, Laon, Chartres, and Reims. In the High Middle Ages, the CS lost importance due to two counter currents within the comprehensive change in the educational realm. On the one hand, the emerging → UNIVERSITIES took over from above the transmission of scholarly studies in the *septem* → *artes liberales* and especially in the fields of law, medicine, and (scholastic) theology. On the other hand, writing schools emerged from below that were led, at first, by freely operating teaching masters who aimed to satisfy the secular desire for education, above all in the trades and in commerce. Thus, the comprehensive monopoly on education held by the CS over the entire diocese, the diocesan town, or over certain parts of both gradually eroded, with the result that schools at cathedral chapters still existed but had lost their central significance for societal organisation.

C. System

The teaching content of school instruction was fundamentally integrated within the interpretive context of Christianity–this also held true for the study of the ancient classical writers, who were to serve either technically for language instruction or in terms of content as an introduction to the teachings of the Bible. The educational foundation were the *septem artes liberales,* which were followed in individual CS by advanced studies of, above all, theological problem analysis (the *quaestio* and *disputatio* of the scholastic method) and of legal problems. The tension between the educational goals of contemplation, detached from the world, on the one hand and secular learning on the other hand accompanied the curricular discussion of CS over the years. This controversy is apparent in the libraries that were equipped with ancient authors. The educational techniques were oriented towards building competency in speaking, reading, and writing. The starting point was oral repetition, with much emphasis placed on correctly accentuated → PRONUNCIATION. Various levels of competency must be differentiated, from rote learning of elementary Church formulas to the sophisticated ability to read and write. The basic learning of writing on wax tablets prepared students for the important function of a scribe. Chanting played a special role–the school director (*magister scholarum*) or an independent choir was in charge of it. The school director, usually a member of the cathedral chapter, was responsible for the structure of the CS as a whole which largely followed the model of monastic schools in its daily routines and in the ideal of communal life for the *scholares canonici.* The reputation of the individual institution was usually marked by the personality of the school director.

→ artes liberales; → Augustinus
→ AUGUSTINISM; → CHURCH; → SCHOLASTICISM;
→ SCHOOL SYSTEM

1 J. EHLERS, s.v. Domschule, LMA 3, 1226–1229 2 M. M. HILDEBRANDT, The External School in Carolingian Society, 1992 3 M. KINTZINGER, S. LORENZ, M. WALTER (ed.), Schule und Schüler im Mittelalter, 1996 4 L. MAITRE, Les écoles épiscopales et monastiques en Occident avant les universités (768–1180), 1924 5 F. A. SPECHT, Geschichte des Unterrichtswesens in Deutschland von den ältesten Zeiten bis zur Mitte des 13. Jahrhundert, Stuttgart 1885
ADDITIONAL BIBLIOGRAPHY: M. COLISH, Medieval Foundations of the Western Intellectual Tradition, 1997.

RALF KOERRENZ

Causa The word *causa* is linked, with considerable changes, in medieval and common law scholarship to the respective applications in Roman legal sources, i.e., *causa stipulationis, causa conditionis* and *iusta causa traditionis.* European common law scholarship has, however, not achieved a uniform concept of *causa.*

The Justinian sources already recognised the *causa stipulationis.* The *stipulatio* had become causal: the declaration of the debtor alone could no longer be the basis of his obligation. The relationship between creditor and debtor had to be accompanied by a reason, e.g. a loan received. In the case of innominate contracts, in the Justinian sources supported by an action of performance if the party in question has unilaterally fulfilled the agreement, this advance payment was called a *causa* and it made the contract actionable. The → CANONISTS were the first to introduce the identification of the *pactum* (contract) with the *stipulatio.* The theory of the *causa* was its most important element. A simple *pactum* which had not been given the form of a *stipulatio* was seen as binding, and as a result the theory of the necessity of a *causa* had been adopted, as it had been developed in Justinian Law for the *stipulatio* (cf. esp. Dig. 44,4,2,3). As a result Baldus extended the concept of *causa* also to every *causa extrinsica* in the sense of Scholastic logic. A preceding obligation of debt as in the case of the *stipulatio* was no longer regarded as necessary. A *causa impulsiva,* i.e. a reasonable motive, was now also sufficient. The proposition *ex pacto nudo actio non oritur* ('no action from a mere promise') obtained a new meaning as a result; it was now related to a *pactum nudum a causa.* This theory was also adopted by the → GLOSSATORS from the end of the 15th cent. The *pactum,* the → CONTRACT, had to make the *causa* recognisable. A simple promise of debt was seen as void. A *causa falsa* or *erronea* made the statement of contract void. The French, Spanish and Italian general law doctrines appeared to have held to these theories until the end of the general law period (18th cent.). They made the presence of a *causa* into an element of a valid contract. In contrast, the authors of the Netherlands and German → USUS MODERNUS (GERMAN) allowed this theory to move the background from the second half of the 17th cent. An abstract statement of obligation was indeed not binding, as its *causa* had to be demonstated and proved. This requirement is, however, no longer dealt with in terms of a *causa.* In the definition of contract the necessity for a *causa* no longer occurs.

The French *Code Civil* (1804) did retain this requirement (Articles 1108 and 1131). There was, however, no demand for the *causa* to be expressly contained in the contract. It can in case of dispute also be proved otherwise (Article 1132). It follows the *Ancien Droit* in that a contract in which a *cause érronée* or *illicite* occurs is declared void (Article 1131). According to the theory of the German Usus modernus neither the Prussian General National Law (1794) nor the Austrian General Civil Law Code (1811) speak of the necessity of a *causa* in a contract. German → PANDECTIST STUDIES at first abided by the traditional general law theory: a *causa* is needed for an effectual obligation. Savigny named as *causa* the promise or performance of *donandi causa, solvendi causa* or *credendi causa*. By the development of the theory of an abstract promise of debt in later pandectics in the second half of the 19th cent. the theory of the necessity of a contract *causa*, e.g. in Windscheid's pandectic textbook, was ultimately abandoned.

General law theory also speaks of *causa* as an entitlement to property transfer in the case of *traditio*. As *causa (titulus)* for the transfer of property, any contractual agreement oriented towards transfer was seen as *iusta et ad transferendum dominium habilis* ('suitable for the transfer of property'), thus especially a contract of purchase or gift. The requirement for a *causa iusta* was understood to mean that the title was not unlawful and the contract was not null. On the question of whether a *causa erronea* or *putativa* was sufficient the general law theory was at variance and encountered the contradiction between Digest 12,1,18 and Digest 41,1,36. The theory of a *iusta causa traditionis* as a *titulus* in property transfer received explicit recognition in the Austrian ABGB (1811). In Savigny's theory of contract, in contrast, the theory of the abstract, real legal transaction was developed out of it. The *iusta causa traditionis* was reduced in this to the motive of the parties to want to transfer the → PROPERTY. The new theory also lies at the basis of the formation of derivative property acquisition in the German BGB (1900) (BGB §§ 929ff.). To this extent, Savigny's theory and the dogma constructed on it in German civil law unified the *causa* of the *traditio* with the *causa* of the *condictio indebit* (performance condition; §§ 812ff. BGB).

→ Causa; → Condictio; → Stipulatio; → Traditio

1 E. BATTISTONI, La causa nei negozi giuridici. Dal diritto intermedio al codice civile italiano, 1932 2 I. BIROCCHI, Causa e categoria generale del contratto. Un problema dogmatico della cultura privatistica dell'età moderna. I. Il Cinquecento, 1997 3 G. CHEVRIER, Essai sur l'histoire de la cause dans les obligations. Droit savant du moyen-âge. Ancien droit français, 1929 4 H. COING, I, p. 304; 402–403; 495; II, p. 394–395; 435–437 5 J. P. DAWSON, Gifts and Promises. Continental and American Law Compared, 1980 6 H. KIEFNER, Der abstrakte obligatorische Vertrag in Praxis und Theorie des 19. Jahrhunderts, in: COING/WILHELM (eds.), Wissenschaft und Kodifikation des Privatrechts im 19. Jahrhundert, 1977, 74ff. 7 TH. MAYER-MALY, Fragmente zur causa, in: Festschrift W.Wilburg, 1975, 243ff. 8 E. M. MEIJERS, Les théories médiévales concernant la cause de la stipulation et la cause de la donation, in: TRG 14, 1936, 379ff. 9 F. RANIERI, Die Lehre der abstrakten Übereignung in der deutschen Zivilrechtswissenschaft des 19. Jahrhunderts, in:COING/WILHELM, as [6], 90ff. 10 A. SÖLLNER, Die causa im Kondiktionen- und Vertragsrecht des Mittelalters bei den Glossatoren, Kommentatoren und Kanonisten, in: ZRG 77, 1960, 212ff., esp. 264f. 11 A. STADLER, Gestaltungsfreiheit und Verkehrsschutz durch Abstraktion, 1995 (fundamental for comparative law) 12 R. ZIMMERMANN, The Law of Obligations, 1990, 549f.; 556f.; 867.

FILIPPO RANIERI

Celtic Languages

A. THE POLITICAL AND GEOGRAPHICAL SITUATION B. LITERARY TRADITION AND WRITTEN RECORDS C. INFLUENCES OF GREEK AND LATIN

A. THE POLITICAL AND GEOGRAPHICAL SITUATION

Of the Celtic languages (CL) only the so-called insular CL have survived to the present day: Irish (or Irish Gaelic), Gaelic (or Scots Gaelic), Welsh (Cymric) and Breton. In the Republic of Ireland Irish [13; 15; 16] has had since 1937 – alongside English – the status of an official language, but it is increasingly giving way to English [17]. In the census of 1981 around 58,000 Irish people claimed to be able to speak and understand Irish, but only around 10,000 use the language as native-speakers [8. 248f.]. Breton (in Brittany, France) [9; 18; 20], Scots Gaelic (in the North-West of Scotland and in the Hebrides, UK) [5; 14] and above all Welsh (principally in West Wales, UK) [11; 12; 22] are still spoken, but have no formal status as official languages. A change in attitudes, not, unfortunately, apparent before the 20th cent., towards minority languages and the need to preserve them has nevertheless led to the fact that in the United Kingdom the relevant CL may be used in teaching. Welsh obtained the right in Wales, as early as 1907 and at first restricted to schools, that 'any of the subjects on the curriculum may (...) be taught in Welsh.' [11. 563]. But it was not until the *Education Reform Bill* of 1988 that Welsh was guaranteed an equal status with English on a large scale (within the Welsh education system, English pupils are obliged to learn Welsh), so that the numbers of Welsh-speakers are growing once more. [11. 571f.] The *Education Act* of 1918 permitted Scots Gaelic 'to be taught in Gaelic-speaking areas', but this was, however, only an entitlement, rather than an obligation [14. 514], which might have led to its official acknowledgement as a national language. The situation of Breton is worse. In 1951 a *Comité d'Études et de Liaison des Intérêts Bretons* was set up which is indeed able, with the financial backing of the French government, to support the preservation and spread of Breton language and culture [9. 612f.], but the Breton language has been unable to establish itself either as a school or as an official language. With the exception of Welsh, the numbers of native speakers of the CL are dwindling rapidly [3; 8]. The insular CL were ousted by English, died out, and have since been revived by language enthusiasts and language preservation groups; these are: Cornish ([4]; formerly in Cornwall, spoken to the end of the 17th cent., closely related to Welsh) and Manx ([2]; on the Isle of Man, died with the last native speaker in 1974, closely related to Irish [19. 61–68]).

B. LITERARY TRADITION AND WRITTEN RECORDS

The literary tradition of the insular CL began at different times and in varying degrees: Irish is well-attested on a continuous basis from the 8th cent. AD to the present (only in the Ogham script from the 5th–8th cents.) [1; 15], first in Gaelic script (originally a Latin semi-uncial), and now principally using modern Roman script. Modern Irish demonstrates a very clearly historical orthography: even with far-reaching changes in pronunciation, the older orthography derived from Old and Middle Irish has largely been retained in modern Irish (Old Irish *lebar*, Middle Irish *lebhar*, pronounced approximately as l'evar, but modern Irish *leabhar* [l'aur] 'book'; Middle Irish *abainn*, roughly [avan'], but modern Irish *abhainn* [' aun'] 'river'. Early loanwords are also affected by these changes in pronunication (*unga* 'ounce' < Latin *uncia*; *dúr* 'hard' < Latin *durus*, see below). Modern loanwords are rendered according to contemporary orthographic rules. Scots Gaelic was taken to Scotland and to the Hebrides by Irish settlers from the 5th/6th cents. onward. Scots Gaelic is therefore a dialect of Irish. A native literature appeared from the 12th cent., but in larger quantities only after the 17th cent. in Roman script. The orthography is, as with Irish, historical, given that the connection with, and orientation towards, Irish remained constant until the early modern period (and therefore in the following, references to Irish will also include Scots Gaelic). Welsh is attested sparsely from the 6th cent., then more extensively as a literary language on a continuous basis from the 11th cent. to the present, written in Roman script. Breton, actually a close relative of Welsh (arising from the emigration of British Celts in the 5th, 6th and 7th cents. in the wake of the Anglo-Saxon invasions) is initially sparsely, then continuously attested from the 12th cent. onwards. The orthography is partly influenced by French (⟨ch⟩ for [š], ⟨j⟩ for [ž], but with native ⟨c'h⟩ for [χ] and ⟨z⟩ for [θ]). In contrast to Irish and Scots Gaelic, Welsh and Breton is written on a largely phonemic basis.

C. Influences of Greek and Latin

Greek and Latin vocabulary items were taken over as borrowings into the CL in various ways and at different times. Typical of words borrowed in the early period (1st–7th cent. AD) is above all the loss of the final syllable (Welsh *dur*, Breton *dir* 'steel' < Lat. (*ferrum*) *durum*; Irish *dúr* 'hard' < Lat. *durus*; Breton *ster*, irish *stair* via British-Latin *stória* < Lat. *história* from Greek ἱστορία 'history'); modern loanwords are largely adopted unchanged. The stress is usually adapted to the Celtic language (Irish and Scots Gaelic have a fixed stress, normally on the first syllable; in Welsh and Breton it is on the penultimate). As a result of the conquest and settlement of Britain by the Romans (1st–5th cents. AD) numerous loanwords were adopted into the CL from a variety of semantic areas [6; 7; 10. 78f.; 12., 71f.; 16. 439f.; 21]: Lat. *Calamus* > Welsh *calaf* 'reed, pipe'; *molina* > Breton *milin*, Irish *muileann* 'mill'; *fructus* > Welsh *ffrwyth*, Breton *frouezh* 'fruit'; Lat. *Piscis* > Welsh *pysg*, Breton *pesk* 'fish' (agriculture and animals); Lat. *Fenestra* > Welsh *ffenestr*, Breton *fenestr*,

prenestr, Irish *seinistir* (with Old Irish substitution of *s* for *f*; the usual Irish word is now *fuinneog* < Engl. *window*) 'window'; Lat. (*ferrum*) *durum* > Welsh *dur*, Breton *dir* 'steel' (architecture, technology); Lat. *cingula* > Welsh *cengl* 'belt'; Lat. *oleum* > Welsh *olew*, Breton *olev*, Irish *ola* 'oil', 'anointing'; Lat. *coquina* (via Vulg. Lat. *cocina*) > Welsh *cegin*, Breton *kegin* 'kitchen', Irish *cuigeann* 'butter-tub' (everyday life, food); Greek γραμματική via Lat. *grammatical* > Welsh and Breton *gramadeg*, Irish *gramadach* 'grammar'; Greek ἱστορία via Lat. *Historia* > Breton *ster*, Irish *stoir*, *stair*, 'history'; Greek. σχολή via Lat. *Schola* > Welsh *ysgol*, Irish *scoil* 'school'; Greek/Lat. *Discipulus* > Welsh *disgybl*, Breton *diskibl*, Irish *deisceabal*, 'pupil' (education); Lat. *imperator* Welsh *ymherawdr* 'ruler'; Lat. *populus* (via British-Lat. *poplus*) > Welsh and Breton *pobl*, Irish *pobal*, 'people'; Lat. *Civitas* > Welsh *ciwed* 'people', Breton *keoded* 'old town,' 'town centre' (military and administration); Lat. *Aprilis* > Welsh *Ebrill*, Breton *Ebril* (later borrowed again from French as *Avril*) 'April'; Lat. *Ianuarius* > Welsh *Ionawr*, *Ionor*, Breton *Genver*, Irish *Eánair* 'January'; Lat. (*dies*) *Solis* > Welsh (*Dydd*) *Sul*, Breton *Sul* 'Sunday' (calendar). In the context of the conversion to Christianity (5th–7th cents. AD) words were borrowed particularly in the religious sphere; Irish took these words over partially from Welsh, and, therefore, evidences linguistic elements of the latter [10. 122f.]: Greek ἄγγελος via Lat. *angelus*, Welsh *engyl* > *angel*, Irish *aingeal* 'angel'; Lat. *Divinus* > Welsh *dewin* 'divine'; Greek ἐπίσκοπος via Lat. *episcopus* (with British-Lat. stress and syncope of the i: *ep(i)scópus*) > Welsh *esgob*, Breton *eskob*, Irish *easpag* (with metathesis of the p and g) 'bishop'; Lat. *benedictio* > Welsh *bendith*, Breton *bennaz*, Irish *beannacht* 'blessing'. In the Middle Ages and in the Early Modern period, Latin vocabulary came into Welsh and Irish by way of English (just like inherited English language) and into Breton by way of French (like inherited French language – for this reason Breton has the largest amount of originally Lat. vocabulary items). Irish *fabhar* 'favour' (Vulg. Lat. *favorem*); *páiste* 'page' (Lat. *pagina*). Welsh *cwc* 'cook', *cwcio* 'to cook' (with Welsh morpheme *-io*) from English (*to*) cook (British-Lat. *cocere*); *actio* 'to act' (Lat. *agere*, *actum*; with Welsh morphem *-io*); *biff-io*, from English 'beef' (from French *boeuf*, Lat. *bos*, *bovis*); but Welsh *ffortun* (pron. [fortyn]) presumably directly from French *fortune*. Breton: *pôd* < French *pot*, 'pot'; *sich*, *sij* [siš], [siž] < French *siège*, 'chair' (derived from Vulg. Lat. *sedicare*). Modern loanwords formed with Greek or Latin elements (principally technical terms in technology, science and the Liberal Arts) have been adopted into Welsh, Irish and Scots Gaelic by way of English, and into Breton by way of French. As a rule they have been adapted to the relevant orthography, and may be provided with native affixes: Irish: English *hydropshere* > Irish *hidrisféar* [hidrəsf'ər]; *hydraulic* > Irish *hiodrálach* [hidraləch] (Irish morpheme *-ach*); *policy*, Irish *polasai* [poləsi], but English *political party* > Irish *páirti polaitíochta* [polit'icht] (Irish morpheme *-iochta*); English *plant*, Irish *planda* (Irish nominal suffix *-a*); *gráimear* 'grammar-book' from English *grammar* [13; 16. 439f.]. Welsh and Breton: Welsh *sinema* < English *cinema*; *hidroleissio* [hidrolisio] < English (*to*) *hydrolyse*; Breton *hiperbol* < French *hyperbol e* 'hyperbole'; *politikel* and *histeriel* (Breton suffix *-el*) < French *politique*, *hystérique*.

→ Celtic languages

1 M. J. BALL, J. FIFE (eds.), The Celtic Languages, 1993 2 G. BRODERICK, Manx, in: [1. 228–285] 3 V. E. DURKACZ, The Decline of the Celtic Languages, 1983 4 K. GEORGE, Cornish, in: [1. 410–468] 5 W. GILLIES, Scottish Gaelic, in: [1. 145–227] 6 H. B. HAARMANN, Der lateinische Lehnwortschatz im Kymrischen, 1970 7 Id., Der lateinische Lehnwortschatz im Bretonischen, 1973 8 R. HINDLEY, The Death of the Irish Language, 1990 9 H. L. HUMPHREYS, The Breton language: its present position and historical background, in: [1. 606–643] 10 K. H. JACKSON, Language and History in Early Britain, 1953 11 R. O. JONES, The Sociolinguistics of Welsh, in: [1. 536–605] 12 H. LEWIS, Die kymrische Sprache ([Datblygiad yr Iaith Gymraeg, 1931], German version by W. Meid), 1989 13 G. MACEOIN, Irish, in: [1. 101–144] 14 K. MACKINNON, Scottish Gaelic Today: Social History and Contemporary Status, in: [1. 491–535] 15 K. McCONE (ed.), Stair na Gaeilge (History of Irish), 1994 16 D. MCMANUS, An Nua-Ghaeilge Chlasaiceach (Classical Modern Irish), in: [15. 335–445] 17 M. Ó MURCHÚ, Aspects of the Social Status in Modern Irish, in: [1. 471–490] 18 I. PRESS, A Grammar of Modern Breton, 1986 19 P. RUSSELL, Celtic languages, 1995 20 J. STEPHENS, Breton, in: [1. 349–409] 21 J. VENDRYES, De hibernicis vocabulis quae a Latina lingua originem duxerunt, 1902 22 T. A. WATKINS, Welsh, in: [1. 289–348]

SABINE ZIEGLER

Celtic-Germanic Archaeology

A. DEFINITION B. MIDDLE AGES C. EARLY MODERN PERIOD (16TH–18TH CENTS.) D. SCIENTIFIC APPROACHES (19TH CENT. – WORLD WAR II) E. INTERNATIONALISATION (TO THE PRESENT)

A. DEFINITION

Celtic/Germanic Archaeology (CGA) is a part of prehistoric archaeology (= prehistory, early prehistory and protohistory). Based on archaeological evidence (finds, monuments), the largely non-written history and culture of the Celts and the Germani are investigated using → ARCHAEOLOGICAL METHODS. Its scholarly and scientific development and reception can be broken down into several stages. In doing so the main criteria are the steps that lead to a recognition of archaeological finds as historical sources and also the general development of adequate methods for an analysis of these sources.

B. MIDDLE AGES

The pre-scientific phase of the Middle Ages was determined, almost without exception, by references in the Bible to the origin and development of humans. Further questions which could have been prompted by the numerous surviving Germanic sagas or from place names or the names of regions (for example the Alemanni, Helvetii, Chatti) never arose. Even burial mounds (Celtic or Germanic barrows or the Celtic rampart surrounding Manching which was identified as a 'pale' as early as 1417) did not bring about attempts to identify these as the remains of ancestors or the like. They were generally described as the work of giants and burial urns were thought to have grown in the ground.

C. EARLY MODERN PERIOD (16TH–18TH CENTS.)

With the rise of Humanism and especially during the → RENAISSANCE a gradual process of separation from theological authority towards a history of humans and the world began. In particular, the rediscovery of the ancient authors who had written about the Celts and the Germans (especially Tacitus and Caesar) encouraged scholars to search for the origins of these peoples in the same texts. Initially these were only individual cases that had no scholarly and even less archaeological basis. Archaeological finds were much noticed, but more as strange and rare objects which were kept in the cabinets of curiosities that became popular among aristocrats and archbishops, rather than as remains of early human life. From the 17th cent. and increasingly from the 18th cent. a change was noticeable in this area too. Scholars such as the Dane O. Worm (1588–1654), the Welshman E. Lhwyd (1660–1708) or the North German A. A. Rhode (1682–1724) conceded that finds may have had a direct connection with the humans of antiquity. Their and their contemporaries' preoccupation with local 'antiquities' was noticeably determined by specific questions about the identity and way of life of the original users. They developed first attempts at dealing methodologically with finds by giving exact descriptions, recording the place where an object was found, writing reports, developing excavation techniques etc.

D. SCIENTIFIC APPROACHES (19TH CENT. – WORLD WAR II)

A rigorous scientific and scholarly approach to CGA was only developed towards the end of the 18th cent. By then geological and anthropological research had finally disproved the still widespread concept of the 'biblical age' of humankind, and archaeological evidence came to be accepted as a valid source of information. A crucial factor on the way towards a scientific approach was the development of reliable dating methods that were able to put finds in their historic context. The development of the Three-Age system in around 1830, which was closely linked to the Danish antiquarian C. Thomsen (1788–1865), became the basis of any classification of time periods. For the first time a system had been developed out of the archaeological evidence, of which the latest period, the Iron Age, provideds a chronological framework for CGA up to the present day. At the same time, and over the course of the romantic period (→ ROMANTICISM) with its emphasis on national traditions, there was a noticeable increase in the preoccupation with archaeological finds. Scholarly associations and societies were established in Germany and abroad. Their main focus was on local (in Germany often 'patriotic') antiquities and the evidence they were believed to provide for the respective ancestors (Celts or Gauls in France and Switzerland, Germanic people in Germany or Scandinavia and England). Their sometimes significant membership numbers, their collections of antiquities and the appearance of many society publications for the first time brought archaeological finds to the attention of wider sectors of society. That the underlying ideology of this development was a national one is imposingly exemplified by the construction of the Hermann monument in the Teutoburg Forest (1830–1875) and the Vercingetorix monuments in France (e.g. in Alesia in 1865). In Germany a further important step was the amalgamation of numerous associations into a 'single society for German history and antiquity' in 1852 and at the same time the creation of a central (research) museum, the *Römisch-Germanisches Zentralmuseum* in Mainz. In France similar developments were promoted by Napoleon III, who in the late 1850s and 1860s had Gallic sites from the time of Caesar (Alesia and others) identified and investigated by having them excavated. Prior to this several extensive excavation projects had been undertaken, partly paid for with public funds, such as e.g. the burial ground at Hallstatt (after 1846) or the site of La Tène, which were of central importance for Celtic archaeology and provided the basis for the distinction between the remains of the Celtic and Germanic and other peoples. In Germany and abroad these developments were reflected in literature (e.g. H. v. Kleist, *Hermannsschlacht*, 1808; W. Raabe, *Keltische Knochen*, 1869; G. Freytag, *Die Ahnen*, 1872; F. T. Vischer, *Auch Einer*, 1879), in paintings (with countless pictures of Germanic people or Gauls) and in music (R. Wagner, *Ring des Nibelungen*, 1876, which had a huge effect on the general perception of the Germanic peoples).

The second half of the 19th cent. saw more advances in methodology. Thus, in 1885 the Swede O. Montelius (1843–1921) proposed a combination of typological and other methods (stratigraphy etc.) for the relative dating of objects. In the 1880s the Iron Age of the Three-Age system was divided into multiple sub-periods by O. Tischler (1893–1891) and others and these were applied to Celtic and Germanic finds. The excavation process was refined methodologically, particularly for features specific to central Europe (ditches, post holes). In Britain this development was primarily linked to A. Lane-Fox Pitt Rivers (1827–1900), in Germany to systematic research into the Roman *limes* and its surrounding area by the Reichslimeskommission, newly established in 1892. In connection with this, the relationship with → ANTIQUARIANISM (HUMANISM UNTIL 1800), which had until then mostly been dismissive of prehistoric archaeology, also improved. This explains why native antiquities rarely appeared in schoolbooks and educational pamphlets compared with classical history until the second half of the 19th cent. Nationalistic representations of history increased during this period, however, and began to draw more and more strongly on these antiquities.

At the beginning of the 20th cent. a further step towards the organisational establishment of CGA was taken. In 1902 the *Römisch-Germanische Kommission* of the → DEUTSCHES ARCHÄOLOGISCHE INSTITUT was founded as a central research facility in particular also for CGA. In many countries efforts were made for the creation of legal protection of archaeological monuments. Prehistoric archaeology was increasingly integrated within the university curriculum, supported by related subjects; e.g. by J. Heierli in Switzerland or G. Kossinna in Berlin, there in the subject of philology. Fundamentally, however, there still was no subject-specific training for prehistorians, particularly as there was also no actual job market for them. All the academics involved with CGA came from other fields (geology, anthropology, literature, ethnology, less from classical fields (see above)). In 1927 the first institute specifically devoted to the subject was set up in Marburg. During the inter-war period the emphasis on the early and desirably extensive settlement areas of various peoples increased in the context of discussions surrounding territorial restructuring in Europe. In his focus on Germanic areas G. Kossinna (1858–1931), and other scholars, among them 'race anthropologists', but also French colleagues who supported an idea of Gaul extending to the Rhine, delivered corresponding results. An extreme case was represented by the Third Reich with the political and ideological take-over of prehistoric archaeology. Germanic archaeology was intensively, but also exclusively, supported by the Third Reich and its leading institutions, the 'Amt Rosenberg' and the 'Ahnenerbe'. Many important and extensive research projects were carried out, especially if they conformed to the objectives of 'Germanentum' and its long history (Neolithic, Bronze Age). Overall, however, the subject as a whole, as well as the majority of academics and their research, were deployed, or rather abused, for an inhuman, chauvinist and fascist ideology with all its consequences. In many aspects of their life the population was inundated (e.g. schoolbooks, novels, advertisements in the shape of the Erdal collectable cards, pins from various organisations and causes, etc.) with images of Germanic people that at times diverged wildly from research results. All cultural life (drama, film, literature) was correspondingly affected. During the war years archaeological research came to a halt in most parts of Europe.

E. INTERNATIONALISATION (TO THE PRESENT)

After the war hardly any archaeological research on the Germanic people was undertaken, and later only in a fairly neutral form ('Cultures of the pre-Roman and Roman Iron Age'). Only in East Germany (GDR) did intensive archaeological research into the Germanic people take place. A two-volume handbook *Die Ger-*

manen – Geschichte und Kultur der germanischen Stämme in Mitteleuropa which appeared in the 1980s was a notable achievement. Research into the Vikings played an important role in Scandinavian countries and also in Britain. Research in West Germany (FRG) tended more towards Celtic archaeology. Two overriding developments left their mark on the second half of the 20th cent. On the one hand, a variety of new methods, particularly in the fields of prospection techniques (aerial photography, geophysics), dating (dendrochronology, radiocarbon dating) and material science (metal analysis), had to be incorporated and their results integrated. On the other hand, there was the desire, from early on, for an intensive opening up and collaboration with international research, such as with common research projects (e.g. the excavations in Manching, on the Heuneburg, in Zavíst near Prague, in Alesia and Bibracte) or with international organisations and various conferences (*oppida*-questions, Celtic art etc.). These activities have led to a huge increase in knowledge and data about Celtic archaeology in Europe. In the last decades, a proper 'Celtomania' developed which was, above all, reflected in the number of large exhibitions (*Die Hallstattkultur – Frühform europäischer Einheit* in Steyr/Austria 1980, *Die Kelten in Mitteleuropa* in Hallein/Austria 1980, *I Celti* in Venice 1991, *Das keltische Jahrtausend* in Rosenheim 1993 and others) that witnessed a huge public response. Frequently these exhibitions have been a vehicle for the propagation of a European ideology. Many television documentaries followed up on the newly awoken public interest. Over the last decades the popular reception of CGA has reached a completely new dimension in terms of coverage, audience, the media, themes, etc. In the entertainment sphere, this includes crime novels (many examples, some even written by archaeologists e.g. G. Daniel, based on precursors ranging from Sir Conan Doyle in 1917 to Nick Carter in the 1970s/80s) and historical novels, in which druidical themes and Viking figures undergo symbioses which frequently lead into the fantasy genre. A whole range of TV series and computer games is of a similar nature. → Comics are a specific area, in which the Asterix characters of course stand out. They have been known worldwide since 1959 and unite all the established elements including megaliths (Obelix), and to this day certainly have had particular influence on the image of the Celts (Gauls). Tourism, leisure activities and general commercialisation has lead to the creation of archaeological theme parks (e.g. Archéodrôme/Isère in France) and corresponding hotels etc. These widely incorporate CGA themes in advertising (the famous Gauloises packet with the Vercingetorix monument was only an early and discreet precursor). By now the attraction of the Celtic world can also be seen in the Internet, where sites on Celtic customs and ways of life, druidic religions etc. are widespread. A return to tradition, the search for one's own roots etc. probably play only a secondary role in this development. Up to now little research has

been undertaken into its driving forces: Is it the search for the mystic and mythic? The exotic? The ancient and unknown? The primordial? Or do other aspects lie behind this? Old traditions and also ideologies have by no means disappeared. Nationalist images of the Germanic people are being perpetuated on national and international levels within a political or mystical framework while the Celtic world is also not only maintained in folkloristic contexts in Brittany and Ireland, but is often ideologically incorporated into their independence movements.

→ Alesia; → Caesar; → Gallia; → Germani, Germania; → Germanic archaeology; → Hallstatt culture; → Heuneburg; → Celts; → Celtic archaeology; → La Tène culture; → Manching; → Tacitus; → Vercingetorix → Druids

1 H. Beck (ed.), Germanenprobleme in heutiger Sicht, 1986 2 R. Bollmus, Das Amt Rosenberg und seine Gegner, 1970 3 B. Cunliffe, The Ancient Celts, 1997 4 G. Daniel, A Short History of Archaeology, 1981 5 M. Dietler, Our Ancestors the Gauls? Archaeology, Ethnic Nationalism, and the Manipulation of Celtic Identity in Modern Europe, in: American Anthropologist 96, 1994, 584–605 6 E. Gran-Aymerich, Naissance de l'archéologie moderne (1798–1945), 1998 7 H. Gummel, Forschungsgeschichte Deutschland, 1938 8 M. H. Kater, Das 'Ahnenerbe' der SS 1935–1945, 1974 9 B. Krüger (ed.), Die Germanen, vol.1, 1988, especially 13–30 10 V. Kruta, Die Kelten, 1978 11 E. Wahle, Geschichte der prähistorischen Forschung, in: Anthropos 45, 1950, 499–538 and 46, 1951, 49–112.

ADDITIONAL BIBLIOGRAPHY: B. Arnold, The Past as Propaganda: Totalitarian archaeology in Nazi Germany, Antiquity 64, 1990, 464–78; J. Collis, The Celts. Origins, Myths, Inventions, 2003; H. Hassmann, Archaeology in the 'Third Reich', in: H. Härke (ed.) Archaeology, Ideology and Society: the German Experience, 2000, 65–139; S. James, The Atlantic Celts. Ancient People or Modern Invention?, 1999; W. Pohl, Die Germanen, 2000; A. Schnapp, French Archaeology: Between National Identity and Cultural Identity, in: M. Díaz-Andreu, T. Champion (eds.) Archaeology and Nationalism in Europe, 1996, 48–67; I. Wiwjorra, German Archaeology and its Relation to Nationalism and Racism, in: M. Díaz-Andreu, T. Champion (eds.) Archaeology and Nationalism in Europe, 1996, 164–187 VOLKER PINGEL

Cemeteries, culture of see → Sepulchral art

Censorship

A. Introduction B. State Censorship in Antiquity C. Ecclesiastical Censorship and Censorship-Like Procedures D. Morally Motivated Censorship E. Institutionalisation of Censorship in Modern Times F. Secular Censorship

A. Introduction

Censorship as 'silencing' and as the practice of 'cultural regulation' [9] refers to the Roman state office of the censor that came into existence in 366 BC. As a judge in matters of morality, the modern-day successor to that office protects the general public from pornography and depictions of violent acts and those in power from subversion and criticism. The examination of public pronouncements for their admissibility, 'so that nothing harmful to religion or the state has been left in them' [36. vol. 5. 1817], is subject to religious, later denominational, political and, in certain cases, military criteria. Censorship monitors discourse and, by means of the processes of differentiation required to do this, also plays a role in establishing the autonomy of art. In the service of authority or tyranny, it is immediately directed against oppositional thinking as well as emancipatory traditions. In a broader sense, social and economic pressures can also be seen as indirect censorship. Self-censorship takes effect as anticipatory reaction; conversely, texts activate the censor as an implicit reader. The institutions of censorship work toward partial or complete elimination of individual texts, or of the entire works of an author; their manifestations range from publication that is conditional or even under permanent control (the main purpose of pre-censorship is approval of publication) all the way to book burning. The ban is in part specifically directed at adolescents; to this end there is expurgation and editing *ad usum delphini* especially of school textbooks. Grammarians (or literary historians, critics, editors) and censors [30. 179] work in a complementary fashion inasmuch as they expunge textual passages that are considered 'false' or 'harmful'. One must distinguish here between suppression of a Greek or Latin original text, a new edition, and a → TRANSLATION. Censorship occurs through the regulation and limitation of textual interpretation and is therefore related to hermeneutics. The interrelation with positive selection, as it is present in the canon, makes censorship appear as its negative; classical reception, however, traditionally occupies a broad intermediary zone between what is explicitly allowed and what is absolutely forbidden and is therefore hardly relevant to the major modern areas of censorship – the press, theatre and film, whether in risqué or even obscene variants.

B. STATE CENSORSHIP IN ANTIQUITY

In 440 BC, Protagoras was punished for godlessness. Plato recommended that Homer be censored (Rep. 387 b) and kept inaccessible especially to youth. Hellenistic rulers could punish critics with death; in Rome, the office of the censor directed its activities against the public forms of literature – the theatre and political poetry. Tacitus had made the attraction of the forbidden a theme [22. 47]. Some writings about magic and astrology were proscribed during the Imperial Period. The Roman emperors – most rigourously Tiberius and Domitian – prosecuted instances of lèse-majesté, in which cases exile brought about censorship as a secondary effect. The anticipatory modes of writing that are so much discussed today are of little consequences for reception, despite the fact that self-censorship [3] oc-

curred, as for example in the case of Ovid. As late as around the time of the beginning of the Common Era, 'book executions' [22. 134] were carried out in Rome against Republican writings. Diocletian had Christian writings burned; after Christianisation, this practice was continued with the contrary objective against 'heresies'. Additionally, the 'decline in copying activities' to the detriment of the 'frequency of transmission of Hebrew, Greek and Latin texts' [15. 1035] is to be taken as a consequence of censorship.

C. ECCLESIASTICAL CENSORSHIP AND CENSORSHIP-LIKE PROCEDURES

In addition to state censorship since Justinian, there was ecclesiastical censorship, beginning in the 5th cent., practised from the Middle Ages on at the universities. In → BYZANTIUM, book burning was replaced by total suppression of manuscripts [22. 137]. After the first Nicene Council, 'heretical' writings were repeatedly banned in both the western and eastern branches of the Church. Reading them, making copies of them, and disseminating copies were all made punishable by law. The manuscripts themselves – whether pagan (magic rituals, lascivious texts), heretical, or Jewish – were to be destroyed, a measure that remained controversial. Arnobius actively opposed the truth-fearing practice of *intercipere scripta et publicatam velle submergere lectionem* ('intercept[ing] writings and suppress[ing] published text[s]', Arnob. 3,7). To be sure, the theological character of literature was so prominent that poetic-fictional literature came within the purview of the censor only in exceptional cases. The censorship of historically remote texts is a completely different matter insofar as all the strategies of authorial contention with the censors, which were often aesthetically productive, no longer apply or are reduced to a secondary involvement on the part of editors and printers who comply with the dictates and get around the prohibitions by means of a foreword, commentary, or publishing tricks–especially vis-à-vis political censorship in the 19th cent. The principal allegations – 'blasphemy', 'treason', 'libel', 'immorality' [2. 19] – can apply only indirectly to the texts of Classical Antiquity. Whereas Jerome rejected the reading of pagan authors, the Interpretatio christina succeeded as a mode of productive censorship (*Ovide moralisé* among many others). The → ALLEGORISM, especially of Ovid and Virgil, was at first a means of preserving their texts and keeping the myths dealt with in them – but also e.g. in Cicero's *De natura deorum* – acceptable. Censorious activity was therefore not directed at the original text, which in the case of Theodulf von Orléans was now regarded as the mere 'packaging' of Christian truth, but rather at the interpretation instead. The more extensively the body of rules governing interpretation was formulated into a highly differentiated exegetical hierarchy, the more potent the performative aspect of censorship became in the form of reinterpretations. Paradoxically, the conveyance of the *sensus litteralis* beneath the allegorical level of meaning was thereby preserved. Ever since John of Salisbury (*Policraticus* 2,26), Gregory the Great has been considered the destroyer of the pagan library on the Palatine. With that destruction serving as an example to be followed, a skull alleged to be that of Livy was defiled in Padua as late as 1413 [5. 52]. In contrast to such extreme cases, censorship in the Middle Ages came about more indirectly: through the choice of the Codices to be copied-the degree of suppression of obscenities at the time of copying by the monks is debatable [28. 104–107]-and through supervisory measures intended to limit access to the manuscripts. It was in this sense, for example, that Aristotle's *Metaphysics* was banned at the University of Paris in 1215 [24. Vol. 1. 17]. Effective censorship could also take the form of cumbersome cataloguing with restricted access. In any event, until modern times, the librarian had, in agreement with the abbot, control over keys to the books: *Noxii libri & vetiti in pluteo clave obsignato custodiantur a Superiore; nec cuiquam, sine ipsius licentia, legi permittantur* ('harmful and forbidden books shall be kept in the cabinet of the Superior under lock and key and be read by nobody without his permission', *Constitutiones Congregationis S. Mauri*, XII).

D. MORALLY MOTIVATED CENSORSHIP

With reference to the texts of Antiquity, one can only talk of post-censorship and, with reference to reprints of those texts, of pre-censorship. Which authors were censored, either completely or in part, was primarily a question of image. Erotic narratives and lyrics ('Priapea') could fall under that type of verdict. To be sure, Plautus and the more popular Terence were suspicious in the eyes of the clergy [23. 31f.], but they were nevertheless handed down, adapted and performed with great intensity. Lucretius was difficult to get through the censor; he was accepted only if the theological refutation of his materialism was also published in the commentary [24. Vol. 2. 159]. Most problematic of all was Ovid's reception [29. 131–139, 146]. Fiscal prosecutors confiscated his works as 'dirty' or 'immoral' [17. 79]. In 1599, some elegies translated by Christopher Marlowe were burned in England [16. 4]. Censors took legal steps against 'suggestive', 'slanderous' publications, as for example in Augsburg in 1777 against the publication of *De amore*, by confiscating the copies [34. 81f.]. In 1497, Ovidian iconography caused the Patriarch of Venice to prohibit or impose conditions on indecent illustrations (coitus of Mars and Venus, seduction of Lotis by Priapus), measures that in the end proved certainly to be unsuccessful so that complaints about *inhonestates tam mulierum quam aliter* ('immorality of women and others') appeared anew [12. 184]. The Index of Paul IV. even suppressed a 1484 Ovid allegorisation [24. Vol. 1. 285]. In 1612, the Spanish Index forbade the vernacular *Ars amatoria*, which moreover had already been removed from Roman libraries during the reign of Augustus [26. 58]. One should not pass over in silence the fact that adaptations of the *Meta-*

morphoses, like the one by Anguillara in 1563, could also have the opposite effect [18. 44]. In 1776, writings by Voltaire and Ovid, which were deemed 'immoral', were burned in Cologne [36. 234]. In particular, translations of Ovid and Anacreon into Italian were placed on the Index at the beginning of the 18th cent. [24. Vol. 2. 158]. As recently as the 1920s and 1930s, importation of Aristophanes' *Lysistrata*, Ovid's *Ars amandi* and Apuleius' *Golden Ass* were forbidden in the US.

E. INSTITUTIONALISATION OF CENSORSHIP IN MODERN TIMES

If even the Inquisition could not exercise total control, the printing of books made censorship more difficult to implement, with the targets being at first primarily Humanist authors. Immoral works of Catullus and Ovid fell victim in 1497–98 in Florence to the *bruciamenti* ('book burnings') of Savonarola [22. 142]. In 1486, a censorship office was founded in Mainz and Frankfurt. Following the Reformation, censorship appeared in strengthened fashion in Catholic regions. Often, mere publication by a Catholic press was positive criterion enough; abstention from censorship was thus a factor favouring places of printing. Universities (e.g. Paris, Louvain), academies, and religious orders possessed local or regional censorship rights. In 1501, a papal bull, the first of its kind, codified the right of bishops to pre-censor. The *Index librorum prohibitorum* was first drawn up in 1559 (published in 1564), but writers of Classical Antiquity hardly figured in it. A revision of the Indices, as exists for the censoring of vernacular writers like Petrarch, Pulci and Boccaccio [6. 18–51, 67–88], is absent. The Tridentinum formalised the process and enacted a prohibition of lewd texts under penalty of punishment, but permitted pagan writings 'because of their elegance and beauty of description', although these books continued to be excluded from use in schools [24. vol. 1. 338]. Until 1596 examination of individual texts when drawing up the Indices was the exception. Not infrequently, the Indices contain positive lists that decree prohibitions only as an exception: for example, the Diocesan Synod of Cologne decreed in 1550: In rhetoricis (*tradi conveniet*) ... *Virgilium, Horatium, Ovidium, praeterquam de arte amandi et Epistolas Heroidum* ('Of the poets, circulation of Virgil, Horace, and Ovid is suitable, with the exception of the latter's *Art of Love* and the *Heroides*') etc. [25. 80]. In some cases, nudity in Renaissance book illustrations became a problem (cf. censoring of pictures in a 1497 Venetian edition of the Metamorphoses: [13. 11–36]). In addition to Ovid, Catullus and Propertius, Virgil was to be decanonised in 16th cent. → SPAIN [13. 117]. The Spanish grammarian Juan L. Vives castigates Roman authors as poisonous seducers to *luxuria* (Ovid), *superbia* (Martial), *impietas* (Lucretius), among other things [13. 116], in his work *De tradendis disciplines* (1531). Similarly, an 'uncritical reading of Cicero' could 'lead to boastfulness and self-praise' [30. 187]. In 1579, the Jesuit Mariana called for the prohibition of courtly epics, among other things (which Cervantes then depicted in the sixth chapter of his *Don Quixote* as a parodistic *auto da fé*), as well as of 'Virgil, Ovid, Martial, Catullus, Tibullus and Propertius' [30. 190]. Censorship was at times realised through explicit counter-recommendations. School regulations in Bavaria in 1569 specify that Marco Gerolamo Vida and Baptista Mantuanus be read instead of Virgil; Prudentius, Falminius and Johannes Pedioneus instead of Horace; Ambrosius Novidius instead of Ovid; and the letters of Jerome rather than those of Cicero and Pliny [24. vol. 1. 470].

F. Secular Censorship

Secular prohibition lists came into use in the 16th cent. as well, as for example through book commissions and council decrees. In France, the censor increasingly controlled the secular → THEATRE after spiritual plays had been almost entirely forbidden. In general, the states reacted to the advent of book publishing with pre-censorship and by making licenses obligatory. Increasingly, intervention occurred only as a result of complaints; legal prosecution replaced prevention. After religious and moral censorship had been replaced by political censorship in the 18th cent., the bourgeoisie, especially, pursued its abolition as a goal between the 17th and 19th cents., and success finally came through the constitutional prohibition of censorship that is in effect in most modern democracies. Globalisation of data networks makes national censorship entirely ineffective, so that the 21st cent. is faced by a permanently ongoing ethical and technical discussion of the basis and limits of censorship on the internet [37].
→ Censorship

1 P. S. Boyer, Purity in Print. Book Censorship in America from the Gilded Age to the Computer Age, ²2002 2 D. Breuer, Geschichte der literarischen Zensur in Deutschland, 1982 3 P. Brockmeier, G. R. Kaiser (eds.), Zensur und Selbstzensur in der Literatur, 1996 4 S. Buchloh, 'Pervers, jugendgefährdend, staatsfeindlich'. Zensur in der Ära Adenauer als Spiegel des gesellschaftlichen Klimas, 2002 5 T. Buddensieg, Gregory the Great. The Destroyer of Pagan Idols, in: JWI 28, 1965, 44-65 6 A. Coseriu, Zensur und Literatur in der italienischen Renaissance des 16. Jahrhunderts, in: A. Noyer-Weidner (ed.), Lit. zwischen immanenter Bedingtheit und äußerem Zwang, 1987, 1-121 7 D. Fellmann, The Censorship of Books, 1957 8 J. Fessler, Das kirchliche Bücherverbot, 1858 9 L. Gil, Censura en el mundo antiguo, 1961 10 P. Godman, Weltliteratur auf dem Index. Die geheimen Gutachten des Vatikan, 2001 11 W. K. Gotwald, Ecclesiastical Censure at the End of the 15th century, 1927 12 B. Guthmüller, Ovidio Metamorphoseos vulgare. Formen und Funktionen der volkssprachlichen Wiedergabe klassischer Dichtung in der italienischen Renaissance, 1981 13 J. Jankovics, S. Katalin Németh (eds.), Freiheitsstufen der Literaturverbreitung, 1998 14 D. Jones (ed.), Censorship. A World Encyclopedia, 4 vols., 2001 15 K. Kanzog, s. v. Zensur, literarische, in: Reallexikon der deutschen Literaturgeschichte, Vol. 4, ²1984, 998-1049 16 A. Lyon Haight, Banned Books, ³1970 17 J. A. McCarthy, W. v.d. Ohe

(eds.), Zensur und Kultur, 1995 18 M. Moog-Grünewald, Metamorphosen der 'Metamorphosen', 1979 19 A. Parkes, Modernism and the Theater of Censorship, 2002 20 J. Plamper, Abolishing Ambiguity. Soviet Censorship Practices in the 1930s, in: The Russian Review. An American Quarterly Devoted to Russia Past & Present 60, 4, 2001, 526-544 21 R. C. Post (ed.), Censorship and Silencing, 1998 22 H. Rafetseder, Bücherverbrennungen, 1988 23 K. v. Reinhardstoettner, Plautus. Spätere Bearbeitungen plautinischer Lustspiele, Leipzig 1886 24 F. H. Reusch, Der Index der verbotenen Bücher, 2 vols., Bonn 1883-1885 25 Id. (ed.), 'Die Indices librorum prohibitorum' des sechzehnten Jahrhunderts, Tübingen 1886 (The following replaces Reusch: J. M. de Bujanda, F. M. Higman, J. K. Farge (eds.), Index des livres interdits, 10 vols., 1984-) 26 H. J. Schütz, Verbotene Bücher. Eine Geschichte der Zensur von Homer bis Henry Miller, 1990 27 R. Seim, J. Spiegel (eds.), 'Ab 18.' Zensiert, diskutiert, unterschlagen - Beispiele aus der Kulturgeschichte der Bundesrepublik Deutschland, 2001 28 W. Speyer, Büchervernichtung und Zensur des Geistes bei Heiden, Juden und Christen, 1981 29 W. Stroh, Ovid im Urteil der Nachwelt, 1969 30 Ch. Strosetzki, Zensor und Grammatiker im Siglo de Oro, in: H.-J. Niederehe (ed.), Schwerpunkt Siglo de Oro, 1986, 177-194 31 V. Wehdeking, Die literarische Auseinandersetzung mit dem Themenkomplex Staatssicherheit, Zensur und Schriftstellerrolle, in: Id., Mentalitätswechsel in der deutschen Literatur zur Einheit (1990-2000), 2000, 43-55 32 S. Weinstock, Die platonische Homerkritik und ihre Nachwirkung, in: Philologus 82, 1927, 121-153 33 H. Wolf (ed.), Inquisition, Index, Zensur. Wissenskulturen der Neuzeit im Widerstreit (= Römische Inquisition und Indexkongregation, Vol. 1), 2001 34 W. Wüst, Censur als Stütze von Staat und Kirche in der Frühmoderne, 1998 35 S. Zala, Geschichte unter der Schere politischer Zensur. Amtliche Aktensammlungen im internationalen Vergleich, 2001 36 J. H. Zedler, Großes vollständiges Universallexikon aller Wissenschaften und Künste, vol. 5, Leipzig 1733 37 Ch. Zelger, Zensur im Internet, 1999 38 P. F. Grendler, The Roman Inquisition and the Venetian Press, 1540-1605, 1977 ACHIM HÖLTER

Ceremony see → Festive processions/Trionfi

Chanson de geste see → Epic

Character Theory see → Psychology

Chemistry see→ Natural sciences

Chicago, Oriental Institute Museum The foundation of the Oriental Institute Museum (OIM) dates back to 1896, when – just five years after the inauguration of the University of Chicago – its *Semitic Language Department*, in which both its then President William Rainey Harper and his brother Robert Francis Harper taught Hebrew and Assyriology, moved to new premises: the Haskell Oriental Museum. The galleries were arranged for the study of the Near East. The collection consisted of plaster casts and bought objects, but was soon to expand considerably as the result of archaeological expeditions. The OIM in its current form is the

Fig. 1: Ivory plaque with depiction of a gryphon from Megiddo.
Courtesy of the Oriental Institute of the University of Chicago

Fig. 2: Poster from the 1930s.
Courtesy of the Oriental Institute of the
University of Chicago

Fig. 3: Sumerian statues from the Diyala region.
Courtesy of the Oriental Institute of the University
of Chicago

Fig. 4: Head of a bull from Persepolis.
Courtesy of the Oriental Institute of the University
of Chicago

brainchild of James Henry Breasted, the first to hold a Chair for Egyptology in the US, whose aim it was at the beginning of the 20th cent. to research the role of the Near East in the development of Occidental civilization. He had in mind a kind of 'laboratory' to investigate the rise of the earliest advanced civilizations as well as civilizatory progress prior to the Classical era: the OIM was founded in 1919 with financial support from John D. Rockefeller Jr. and in 1931 moved into new purpose-built premises.

The institute soon became one of the most important research establishments for the history of the Near East, not least thanks to the appointment of German-Jewish scholars who had been forced to leave Nazi Germany – among them Benno Landsberger, Leo Oppenheim, Hans-Gustav Güterbock and Ernst Herzfeld. The OIM, which started off as a study collection, now houses more than 110,000 registered and c. 200,000 unregistered finds from more than 30 surveys and excavations in Egypt, Mesopotamia, Iran, Anatolia and Palestine. Particular mention should be given to: the *Epigraphic Survey*, based in Luxor; the excavations in the Diyala region (Henri Frankfort), the basis for establishing the chronology of Mesopotamian artefacts; the continuation of excavations at Khorsabad (the Assyrian capital founded by Sargon II) and Nippur; the excavations at Persepolis, Megiddo, in the Amuq region as well as of prehistoric settlements in Syria and Iran. The unregistered finds consist mainly of cramics from the prehistoric project under the direction of Robert and Linda Braidwood and also from the excavations at Khirbet-al-Kerak and Choga Miš (Iran).

The OIM is unique in its focus on the Near East and also in its combination of philological and archaeological research on the one hand with a substantial museum collection on the other. Furthermore, the OIM holds the most complete research library in the field of the Ancient Orient. It offers a number of lectures and classes that are aimed at an interested lay audience. An extension, which complies with modern requirements for the preservation of antiquities, was completed in the summer of 1998 and the collections reopened in 1999.

The Egyptological part of the collection (mainly purchased items) provides a vivid illustration of the daily life of ancient Egyptians. Among other exhibits, a complete collection of agricultural implements and building tools provides an insight into the technology employed in these fields at the time. Among the artistically exceptional pieces are the bust of a life-size statue of a god from the 18th Dynasty and three painted reliefs from the tomb of Mentuemhat, a 25th Dynasty governor of Thebes. Within the Mesopotamian department, the early dynastic period and the Assyrian period are particularly well represented. The trove of statues found in the Diyala region and others from Nippur as well as relief-decorated door plates form the largest collection of Sumerian sculptures in one place. Two exceptional Old Babylonian bronze statuettes of a four-faced pair of deities likewise come from the Diyala region, while a

neo-Sumerian stone head of a ruler, still bearing its original painted decoration, is from from Bismaya. The Assyrian period comes to life in the colossal statues that had once guarded the palace gates and the reliefs from the palace at Khorsabad. In difference to Egypt, preserved epigraphical sources by far outnumber extant sculptural objects in the Mesopotamian tradition: the OIM holds about 8000 clay tablets, ranging form the late 4th millennium to the Seleucid period. Particularly remarkable is a stone tablet listing all the peoples under Achaemenid rule shortly after the uprisings at the time of Xerxes' accession to the throne. The centrepiece of the Iranian department is a monumental bull's head from Persopolis, originally belonging to one of the pair of snorting bulls that once adorned and guarded the entrance to the Hundred-Column Hall. It is worked in the characteristic style of the Achaemenid court and probably once had horns made of gold that are missing now. Iran is also the origin of high-quality painted ceramics from the early period as well as Luristan bronzes from normal excavations.

The Palestine collection comprises among others some bronze statuettes of Canaanite deities and also two parchment fragments from Qumran, one of them with its associated storage vessel. Among the finds from Megiddo, particular mention should be made of the ivory carvings from the 2nd and 1st millennium BC, of great importance in the definition of local styles, and also a proto-Aeolian capital and a horned altar. The Syrian and Anatolian collections mainly originate from the excavations in the Amuq region or respectively at Ališar Höyük, and mainly consist of ceramic finds.

→ EGYPTOLOGY

1 A Guide to the The Oriental Institute Museum. The Univ. of Chicago, 1982   2 The Oriental Institute Museum: Highlights from the Collection (n.d., n.p.) 3 Oriental Institute Communications, 1922ff   4 Oriental Institute Publications, 1924ff.   5 http://www.oi.uchicago.edu/OI/MUS (Website).   CLAUDIA E. SUTER

Children's and Young Adults' Literature
A. INTRODUCTION B. CLASSICAL FABLES AS READING FOR CHILDREN   C. ADAPTATION OF CLASSICAL MYTHS AND EPICS   D. HISTORICAL REPRESENTATIONS   E. PAN AND THE PUER AETERNUS

A. INTRODUCTION
In accordance with recent definitions, children's and young adults' literature (CYAL) embraces the whole spectrum of fiction and non-fiction writing for children and young people. What is involved here are not only texts specifically written for children (CYAL as such) but also texts expressly recommended for reading by children and young people (intentional CYAL). Thus consideration will be also given to writings not originally produced with children as the target audience (such as adaptation of adult literature for children); further, we shall include school texts and readers, which until

the middle of the 19th cent. cannot be precisely distinguished from CYAL.

B. Classical Fables as Reading for Children

From Classical times onward, the 'Fables' of Aesop (*Mythōn Synagōgē*, 6th cent. BC) were read in schools, and thus belonged to the earliest canonical reading material for children. In the 12th cent. Konrad of Hirsau made them compulsory reading in monastery schools. The fables served four purposes: they were used in the teaching of reading; they provided exercises for grammar instruction; they were an introduction to authoritative wisdom and guidance in the conduct of one's life; and they offered a basic introduction to the knowledge of ancient language and culture[5]. The reception of Aesop's Fables received a fresh impetus in those fable-collections, also designed to be read by children, such as the *Fables* (Paris 1668–1694) of Jean de la Fontaine, the *Fabeln und Erzählungen* (Fables and Tales) (Leipzig 1746–1748) of Christian Fürchtegott Gellert and *Basni* (Fables) (St Petersburg 1809) of Ivan Krylov. Illustrated editions of Aesop's 'Fables' and editions designed for children are still widely available.

C. Adaptation of Classical Myths and Epics

Classical themes from world literature have been appearing since the 16th cent. in literary adaptations for children, and pride of place has been given to the Homeric epics and to the tales of the gods. The Humanists encouraged the reading in schools of Classical myths on grounds of educational theory. However, there was constant opposition to this from the theological and moral side. Guilielmus Gnaphaeus' drama *Acolastus. De filio prodigo* (Acolastus, On the Prodigal Son) (Cologne 1530), which combines the Classical Palliata-tradition with a biblical theme became, as a *comoedia sacra*, the model for numerous Jesuit school dramas, which differ from medieval mystery plays and from popular theatre through the integration of Classical themes. The comic epic *Froschmeuseler* (Magdeburg 1595) by Georg Rollenhagen, an adaptation for young people of the (*Batrachomyomachia*), wrongly ascribed to Homer, is distinctive for its encyclopaedic orientation.

In the 17th and early 18th cents. Classical myths were used to emphasise the distinctive nature of Christianity as opposed to the belief in the pagan gods. Thus the *Orbis sensualium pictus* (The Visible World in Pictures) (Nuremberg 1658) of Johann Amos Comenius contains a section on the most important gods of Greece and Rome. The most significant work in the 17th cent. was, however, the novel of education *Suite du quatrième livre de l'Odyssée d'Homère, ou les aventures de Télémaque, fils d'Ulysse* (Continuation of the Fourth Book or Homer's Odyssey-Or The Adventures of Telemachus, Son of Ulysses) (Paris 1699) by François de Salignac de la Mothe Fénelon, written for the heir to the

French throne, in which Christian and Classical ethics were combined. Translated into a number of European languages, Fénelon's novel came to be a central work of older CYAL, and was still being used in French instruction until the beginning of the 20th cent.

The classical view of Antiquity emanating from Joachim Heinrich Winckelmann represents a turning point in CYAL. Classical myths were now interpreted as poetic works which had sprung from a poet's imagination, and were thus no longer liable to theological criticism. From now on, a knowledge of the Classics was regarded as an essential element in the aesthetic education of the young [2]. This new standpoint found an expression in, among others, Friedrich Justin Bertuch's *Bilderbuch für Kinder* (Picturebook for Children) (Weimar 1790) and Friedrich Wilhelm Hempel's *Mythologie für die Jugend oder Götter- und Heldengeschichte zum Gebrauch für Schulen* (Mythology for Young People-Or Stories of Gods and Heroes for the School) (Leipzig 1802). From the middle of the 18th cent., re-tellings of Classical myths and sagas were increasingly circulated as popular reading material for young people. In the German-speaking countries, Gustav Schwab's *Die schönsten Sagen des klassischen Altertums* (The Most beautiful Tales from Classical Antiquity) (Stuttgart 1838–1840) was instrumental in the establishing of the heroic saga as a genre in CYAL. It is to his credit that Schwab gathered the Greek sagas from diverse traditions together into one unit and developed for this a unique narrative style, based on that of the chapbook [4]. Charles Kingsley (*The Heroes, or Greek Fairy Tales for My Children*, London 1856) and Nathaniel Hawthorne (*A Wonder Book for Girls and Boys*, Boston 1852) turned Classical myths into fairy-tales and adapted them to suit the romantic image of childhood. In his work, Hawthorne also paved the way for the development of fantasy literature for children in the US [6]. Under the influence of Romanticism and of early Victorian/Biedermeier values, moral norms reasserted themselves. Nevertheless, the study of Classical myths and epics remained a canonical part of the curriculum in secondary schools until the beginning of the 20th cent.

Modernised adaptations for children and young adults appeared in the 20th cent. too (for example Padraic Colum, *The Adventures of Odysseus and the Tale of Troy*, 1918; Leon Garfield, *The God beneath the Sea*, 1970). Children's literature in the former German Democratic Republic played a special part in this respect. In accordance with the doctrine of 'democratising the cultural inheritance', Classical myths were turned into socio-political, didactic texts (Franz Fühmann, *Das hölzerne Pferd* (The Wooden Horse), 1968; *Prometheus*, 1972), or into cultural-historical presentations for children (Gerhard Holtz-Baumert, *Daidalos und Ikaros* (Daedalus and Icarus), 1984)[8].

Since the middle of the 19th cent. there has been an increasing amount of differentiation in the use of Classical myths and legends in CYAL. One noticeable tendency is that of intertextual allusion to motifs, themes and characters from Classical Antiquity, the knowledge of which is either assumed or indicated: examples are the myth of Persephone in George MacDonald's *The Princess and the Goblin* (London 1872) and Ted Hughes' *Season Songs* (1975), the tales of Hercules in James Krüss' *Mein Urgroßvater, die Helden und ich* (My Great-Grandfather, the Heroes and I) (1967), Aesop's fable of the ant and the grasshopper in Rogelio Sinán's *Chiquilinga o la gloria de ser hormiga* (Chiquilinga – Or the Glory of Being an Ant) (1961), the *Odyssey* in Richard Adams' *Watership Down* (1972), Francisco Espínola's *Saltoncito* (1930), C. S. Lewis' *The Chronicles of Narnia* (1950–1956) and Lisa Tetzner's *Die Kinder aus Nr. 67 – Odyssee einer Jugend* (The Children from No. 67–Odyssey of Youth) (1933–1949). Pamela Travers' fantasy novel *Mary Poppins* (1934) contains a particularly large number of allusions to Classical mythology [1]. Parodies of Classical myths and legends may also be found in CYAL: examples are that of Aristophanes' *Batrachoi* in Yrjö Kokko's *Pessi ja Illusia* (Pessi and Illusia) (1944) or of the battle between Odysseus and the suitors in Kenneth Grahame's *The Wind in the Willows* (1908). Peter Hacks provided a satire on Fénelon's educational novel in his *Prinz Telemach und sein Lehrer Mentor* (Pince Telemach and his Teacher Mentor) (1997).

D. Historical Representations

The transmission of Classical history has had a significance place in school education since the Humanist period. Based at the beginning in the tradition of artes-literature, knowledge of Classical history was also widely spread in the literature of *civilitas, officia* and *virtus*. This group contained books structured according to the standard rhetorical formula of *praecepta-exempla-imitatio*, and were used in the teaching of history and of ethics. The philanthropists stressed the exemplary nature of Classical history: Joachim Heinrich Campe in his *Historisches Bilderbüchlein* (Little Picture-Book of History) (Brunswick 1801) or Karl Christoph Reiche in *Die Geschichte Roms* (The History of Rom) (Leipzig 1778) Alongside the dissemination of basic knowledge and that of the ways of the world, from the middle of the 19th cent. nationalist education took centre stage, in which context the development of one's own country was compared with that of ancient Rome. Beside these historical presentations, from the beginning of the 20th cent. historical novels on Classical themes began to appear. Rudyard Kipling was in the vanguard with *Puck of Pook's Hill* (1906). Rosemary Sutcliffe is regarded as one of the most significant writers of historical novels for children, favouring in her works the political and cultural conflicts of the Roman empire in England (*The Eagle of the Ninth*, 1954). The influence of Classical history upon the present is at the centre of Alan Garner's *Red Shift* (1973). Two special categories are represented by the fantastic journey into Antiquity (Edith Nesbit, *The Story of the Amulet*,

1906) and the detective story for children set in ancient Rome (Henry Winterfeld, *Caius ist ein Dummkopf* (Caius is a Fool), 1953).

E. Pan and the puer aeternus

The aesthetic reflections of Robert Louis Stevenson in *Virginibus Puerisque* (London 1881) and of Kenneth Grahame in *The Golden Age* (London 1895) on the child's quasi-innate ability to commune with nature and its affinity to music led to a perception of the child as a representative of the pastoral god Pan [7]. This connotation is encountered in a number of significant children's books: among others in Luigi Capuana's *Scurpiddu* (Turin 1898), Frances Hodgson Burnett's *The Secret Garden* (1911) and Cecil Bødker's *Silas og den sorte hoppe* (Silas and the Black Filly) (1967). The work of James Matthew Barrie that was first conceived as a play (*Peter Pan, or the Boy Who Would Not Grow Up*, first produced in London 1904) and later turned into prose *Peter and Wendy* (1911) combined the figure of Pan with the motif of the *puer aeternus*, an image of the child that cannot or will not grow up, and in the years which followed it inspired numerous international works of CYAL, e.g. Natalie Babbitt's *Tuck Everlasting* (1975) or Ana María Matute's *El polizón del Ulisses* (The Stowaway on the Ulysses) (1965).
→ Aesop; → Aristophanes; → Homer

1 S. Bergsten, Mary Poppins and Myth, 1978 2 T. Brüggemann, Zur Rezeption antiken Mythologie in der Kinder- und Jugendliteratur der Goethezeit, in: Imprimatur N. F. 12, 1987, 93–115 3 M. Halub, Das literarische Werk Gustav Schwabs, 1993 4 S. Jentgens, Gustav Schwab. Die schönsten Sagen des klassischen Altertums, in: O. Brunken, B. Hurrelmann, K. U. Pech (eds.), Hdb zur KJL 1800–1850, 1997, 721–734 5 B. Kümmerling-Meibauer, Klassiker der Kinder- und Jugendliteratur. Ein internationales Lexikon, 1999 6 L. Laffrado, Hawthorne's Literature for Children, 1992 7 J. Perrot, Pan and *Puer Aeternus*. Aestheticism and the Spirit of the Age, in: Poetics Today 13, 1992, 155–167 8 S. Warnecke, Neu- und Nacherzählungen antiker Mythen, Sagen und Epen für Kinder und Jugendliche in der DDR, in: M. Dahrendorf (ed.), KJL, 1995, 185–191.

Additional Bibliography: B. Kümmerling-Meibauer, Kinderliteratur, Kanonbildung und literarische Wertung, 2003; M. Rutenfranz, Götter, Helden, Menschen. Rezeption und Adaption antiker Mythologie in der deutschen Kinder- und Jugendliteratur, 2004; J. Stephens, R. McCallum, Retelling Stories, Framing Culture. Traditional Story and Metanarratives in Children's Literature, 1998 Bettina Kümmerling-Meibauer

China As an ancient high culture, China possesses not a few of its own 'classical' models in the plastic arts, literature and philosophy. Classical Antiquity of the West, a thousand-years younger, is of restricted interest in China only because of its standing overseas.

There were indeed occasional contacts in Antiquity between the Roman Empire and China; in particular, the Silk Road provided opportunities for commercial and cultural exchange, so that in Xian, e.g., Nestorian Christianity is attested epigraphically. But these contacts remained for the most part isolated and without consequence.

Nestorian Christians actually intrigued against the Franciscan missionary Giovanni di Montecorvino, who proselytized for Catholicism at the court of the Tartar Khan in Beijing between 1294 and 1328. He nevertheless had some missionary success. Over time he bought 40 boys, whom he educated and also instructed in Latin. During the 2nd half of the 14th cent., after the end of Mongol rule, his parish vanished.

The Jesuit Matteo Ricci was a missionary at the Chinese imperial court at the end of the 16th cent. He translated Euclid's teachings on geometry into the national language, and in a collection of maxims (→ APHORISM) and a treatise on virtue even propagated Ancient thought (*inter al.* Epictetus) in Chinese.

Catholic missionary schools and seminaries (Shanghai, Wuhan) arose in the Middle Kingdom during the 19th cent., teaching Latin and even using it as a language of instruction at senior levels (→ ANCIENT LANGUAGES, TEACHING OF). They persisted in a variety of forms until the Cultural Revolution during the 1960s; since the 1980s Catholic seminaries have re-emerged, where limited familiarity with Latin and the philosophy of western Antiquity is provided.

Apart from this ecclesiastical approach, the literary and academic areas offer further potential for contacts. There have been and are several initiatives for the translation of Ancient texts into Chinese. Thus in recent times there have been translations for theatrical productions, e.g. *Antigone, Oedipus, Medea*, which were performed in China (Beijing, Harbin, Shijizhuang) and came to Europe as traveling productions. But other plays too have been translated, along with texts from Plato, parts of Homer, Thucydides and Livy, in addition to texts of Aristotle, Herondas, Aesop, Sallust's monographs, Caesar, Ciceronian writings, Cornelius Nepos and Pliny's letters.

The reading of such texts in the original is restricted to a tiny minority. Since 1985 the *Institute for the History of Ancient Civilisations* (= IHAC), supported by Beijing, is based at the Northeast Normal University in the former capital of the puppet state of Mandschukuo, the modern Changchun in the north-eastern province of Jilin. Here instruction in ancient Greek and Latin, classical history, mythology and philosophy is offered to a few historians of the ancient world from the whole of China. The students are taught in English by non-Chinese scholars; some of them even study for a time in Europe or the USA. A library, well stocked by Chinese standards, offers collections for Hittite, Egyptian, Mesopotamian and Classical studies in the original languages, in translation and as secondary literature. IHAC also publishes the annual *Journal of Ancient Civilisations* (= JAC), and publishes editions, translations and studies. In 1997 Changchun was also host to the 2nd International Conference on Ancient World

History; the first having taken place in 1993 at Nankai University in Tianjin. Upon completing their studies a number of the graduates have become active throughout the country as teachers of ancient world history at universities, or they work as researchers at the Chinese Academy in Beijing. The foundation of similar centers has been undertaken in Tianjin, Wuhan and Shanghai; their future remains uncertain.

During the Japanese invasion prior to the middle of the 20th cent., even public buildings were erected in colonial style, combining heavy cement architecture with Greek embellishments. Thus Changchun is adorned here and there with Corinthian and Doric columns. It is also possible to come occasionally across casts of Greek sculptures; these have their origin in the collection of casts (→ CAST; CAST COLLECTIONS) belonging to Xu Bei Hong, the former President of the Central Academy of the Arts in Beijing, and are used in art classes as models for the creation of figures in the style of Socialist Realism.

The overall situation is poor. A visit by Sir Gilbert Murray, which was supposed to encourage the foundation of a Chinese society for western Classical Antiquity, met with no success. The enthusiasm of Zhuo Zuo Ren (1885–1966) for Greek culture had hardly an echo beyond his own work. It remains clear that, although the world's most populous state deals with the history of the ancient world in its universities, lasting cultural influences have yet to take hold.

→ China; → Nestorius, Nestorianism; → Silk Road

1 F.-H. MUTSCHLER, 'Western Classics' im Reich der Mitte, in: Wissenschaftliche Zeitschrift der TU Dresden, Fakultät Sprach- und Literaturwissenschaft, 44, 1995, 45–52 (seminal, with bibliography) 2 G. BRUGNOLI, C. SANTINI, Latinitas Sinica, in: Bolletino di Studi Latini 20, 1990, 381–386 3 B. KYTZLER, Classics in China, in: Mitteilungsblatt des deutschen Altphilologenverbandes 31, 1988, 30–32 4 JI CI LE (= B. KYTZLER), Chila Luoma Yanjiu zai Zhongguo, in: Dongbei Shida Xuebao 6, 1988, 61f. 5 W. BRASHEAR, Classics in China, in: The Classical Journal 86, 1990, 73–78 6 Y. C. WANG, Chinese Intellectuals and the West, 1966 7 J. G. LUTZ, China and the Christian Colleges 1850–1950, 1971 8 D. W. TREADGOLD, The West in Russia and China. Religious and Secular Thought in Modern Times, vol. 2: Ch. 1592–1949, 1973 9 LIN ZHI CHUN et al., The study of Classics in China and the West, in: Journal of Ancient Civilisations 8, 1993, 1–24 10 LI PING, Klassische Philologie in China, in: Desiderius 1992, 545–547. BERNHARD KYTZLER

Chrêsis (χρῆσις)

A. INTRODUCTION B. PRE-CHRISTIAN ANTIQUITY C. CHURCH FATHERS/PATROLOGY D. OUTLOOK

A. INTRODUCTION

The notion of proper use (*chrêsis dikaía, usus iustus*) or simply words that mean 'use' (often more clearly defined by adverbs or by naming the specific purpose) were used by the Church Fathers (→ PATRISTIC THEOLogy/Patristics) to describe their approach to dealing with ancient culture. In this way, they absorbed a didactic message with a long tradition in pre-Christian thinking. Of all the authentic Patristic terms, this one is particularly suited to encompass their entire outlook. It offers a hermeneutic key to understanding the conflict between Antiquity and Christianity.

B. Pre-Christian Antiquity

The twin realizations that possession is of no avail if it is not used, and that the value of an object depends on the nature of its use are simple truths based on general life experience; however, when reflected by scientists, particularly medical scientists [2. 40ff.], they acquire terminological acuity. The principle of proper use is invoked by the Sophists [5. 16–24; 2. 30f.], particularly in the defence of rhetoric (Pl. Grg. 456B–557B). It represents one axis of Platonic thinking, and in this context appears closely linked to the notion of superior knowledge and its application [2. 31ff.; 5. 60–85]. The Aristotelian *Protrepticus* is also centred around this axis. In his didactic writings, Aristotle uses the concept pair 'to possess' and 'to use' in order to illustrate the relationship between potentiality and actuality, as reflected in his definition of eudaimonia as *enérgeia kaí chrésis aretés teleía* (Aristot. Pol. 7,13,1332 a 9) [2. 34–36; 5. 86–113]. The Stoa teaches that the world was created for the benefit of humans who, thanks to the power of reason, are the only ones able to make use of it (Cic. Nat. D. 2,157; Lactant. Ira 13). The doctrine of proper use was particularly well developed by Epictetus in the later Stoa [2. 36ff.]. In its path through philosophy and science, the notion of *chrésis* thus acquired an intrinsic value beyond the limits of each individual system: associated with it is the demand that action be submitted to a guiding value, and the imperative of having to decide between right and wrong.

C. Church Fathers/Patrology

In that way, *chrésis* became a useful instrument for ecclesiastical thinkers and in itself an example of Christian use [2. 52]. Even in such early works as those of Tertullian, Clemens of Alexandria, and Origenes, it appears with terminological consistency [2. 45–63]. It is supported by the NT (Rom. 1: 26f.; 1 Cor. 7: 31), and further developed through allegorical exegesis (→ Allegorism) of the OT [2. 57f., 59f., 76–79, 89f.] as well as through analogies taken from nature [2. 16f., 102–133; 3. 83–86]. A Christian sees himself as being placed into a world that is created by God and therefore good (Gn. 1: 31; 1 Tim. 4: 4), but also into a world of idolatry and moral perversion, whose elements are to a greater or lesser degree removed from their God-given designation, i.e. abused [2. 44]. The diacritical task of *chrésis* is thus a general one, and into this wider framework belongs the *chrésis* of cultural tradition (Greg. Naz. Or. 43,11), seen exemplified in Paul's speech on the Areopagus (Acts 17:23. 28 [2. 124–129; 3. 79f.]). *Chrésis* is based on the belief that there are truth-bearing seeds

within the pre-Christian spiritual world, but that they only existed in a blend with the wrong and the bad [2. 13–16; 3. 177–186]. Justin Martyr (around AD 150) attempted to explain this fact by using the Stoic tenet of *lógos spermatikós* [4. 35–40]. The elements of truth, goodness and beauty have to be isolated and 'returned' to God as their rightful owner [3. 79f.], defined by Justin as a Christian duty. In the same way that the Israelites during the exodus from Egypt followed God's orders, taking with them gold and silver vessels as well as garments belonging to the Egyptians (Ex. 3: 21f.; 11: 2; 12: 35f.) in order to furnish the inner sanctum of their temple, it is the duty of Christians to use goods that are misused by pagans in order to worship God.

This exegesis clearly shows the terminological sense of *chrésis*, its theocentric orientation, and its universal application. It is first found in Irenaeus, then in Origen [2. 57f.], Gregory of Nyssa [2. 89f.], Augustine (Aug. Doctr. christ. 2,40,60f. [2. 94]) and others. However, *chrésis* is not only seen as a selective measure, but also as a creative and unifying power. Bees were seen as one of nature's examples: they collect useful substances from all kinds of flowers, but produce new vessels (honeycomb) and a new substance (honey) [2. 102–133]. Yet the purpose of *chrésis* is not to expand the revelation, but to protect it, to prepare for it, and to illustrate (i.e. 'adorn') it: in that way, it becomes a general tool in the conversion of an individual as well as of an entire culture [2. 134–140; 3. 93–127]. It is related to, but not identical with, *synkatábasis (condescensio)*, the pedagogical, or missionary, adaptation to customary ways of living and thinking [2. 63f.; 3. 81f.]. The ultimate model for both is God who condescended to adapting his word to the human one [3. 31, 82], and who makes good use of everything, even evil (Aug. Civ. 11,17f.; 18,51; de natura boni 36f.). The notion of *chrésis* was further expanded theologically by Augustine who integrated it into his structure regarding use and enjoyment: the sole object of *frui* is the Trinity, everything else falls under *uti*. The *fruitio Dei* constitutes the highest purpose of human existence; everything else, including science and the arts, is no more than a means to serve this end ([2. 80–91] with bibliography).

D. Outlook

The views of the Church Fathers form a pool of thought which could be drawn upon in the defence of Classical → education from a Christian perspective. With reference to the Augustinian exegesis of the Egyptian treasures, Cassiodorus (6th cent.) was able to save the profane authors for the education of monks (Cassiod. Inst. Var. 1,28,4), and later Hrabanus Maurus (780–856) used the same argument regarding the instruction of clerics (De institutione clericorum 3,26; quoting verbatim). Christian Humanism used the same arguments, even though its ultimate aim was significantly different from the *chrésis* of the Church Fathers [1]. Petrarch referred to the Egyptian gold and silver (*De sui ipsius et multorum ignorantia*, 1366) in his justification of why Cicero's works should be read [2. 89]; Erasmus (*Antibarbari*, 1520) used this famous allegory in his defence of the whole concept of Classical Studies (Amsterdam edition: Opera omnia 1, 1969, 116–118), and, together with the old images, the old terminology also returned (*uti, usus* in *Antibarbari*). But the terminology can be absent, as long the concept itself is understood: John Henry Newman understood and penetrated it, even though he used a different terminology (*Essay on the Development of Christian Doctrine*, 1845, ²1878). Within the Church, *chrêsis* remains a living principle, intrinsically linked above all with the practice and theory of mission. For that reason, it is retained in Church documents into modern and most recent times – including those of the Second Vatican Council –, acquiring some very concise definitions in the process [2. 33, 121ff., 165–176]. The Indologist Paul Hacker [4] rediscovered the value of the *chrêsis* concept and attempted its fruitful application to the problem of inculturation.

→ Artes liberales; → Education/Culture

1 A. Buck, Der Rückgriff des Renaissance-Humanismus auf die Patristik, in: K. Baldinger (ed.), Festschrift W. von Wartburg, vol. I, 1968, 153–175   2 Ch. Gnilka, ΧΡΗΣΙΣ. Die Methode der Kirchenväter im Umgang mit der antiken Kultur I. Der Begriff des rechten Gebrauchs, 1984   3 Id., ΧΡΗΣΙΣ. Die Methode der Kirchenväter im Umgang mit der antiken Kultur II. Kultur und Conversion, 1993   4 P. Hacker, Theological Foundations of Evangelization, 1978 (= Veröffentlichungen des Instituts für Missionswissenschaft der Westfälischen Wilhelms-Universität Münster 15, 1980)   5 R. Nickel, Das Begriffspaar Besitzen und Gebrauchen. Ein Beitrag zur Vorgeschichte der Potenz-Akt-Beziehung in der aristotelischen Ethik, 1970

Additional Bibliography: J. J. Pelikan, Christianity and Classical Culture: The Metamorphosis of Natural Theology in the Christian Encounter with Hellenism, 1993; E. G. Weltin, Athens and Jerusalem: An Interpretative Essay on Christianity and Classical Culture, 1987.

CHRISTIAN GNILKA

Christian Archaeology

A. Definition   B. To the Beginning of the Modern Era   C. 16th to 18th Cents.   D. 19th and Early 20th Cents.   E. To the Present

A. Definition

Christian Archaeology (ChrA) is a recent area of academic research which studies the material remains of early Christianity – originally exclusively – but now also their wider context, from approx. AD 200. Corresponding to historical conditions, the subject now focuses on the entire area of the Roman Empire and on neighbouring Christianised regions. The research period is delineated by events such as the Arab invasions (7th/8th cents.), the Iconoclastic Controversy (8th/9th cents.) or the beginning of the Romanesque period in the West, at the latest. The discipline of ChrA occupies a precarious but fertile mediatory position between subjects such as → Classical archaeology/ → Provincial Roman archaeology early history, art history and Church history, and → Byzantine studies. It shares its aims (to record and protect monuments, to narrate and interpret history, to consolidate cultural awareness), its methods (finding and studying of sources, also by excavation, documentation, analysis of construction methods, iconography, style criticism) and the distinctions into genres (architecture, → painting, sculpture etc.) with its neighbouring historical and cultural disciplines. It also encompasses non-artistic remains, esp. inscriptions and craftwork. In an attempt to distance the subject from long-standing denominational demands to incorporate it into Church history as an complementary science [7] some German academics favour the replacement of 'Christian' with 'Late Ancient' [22; 25]. This would facilitate the necessary inclusion of secular monuments and of paganism and Judaism, without which Christianity cannot be understood.

B. To the Beginning of the Modern Era

ChrA, as a tool for the objective clarification of historical contexts, was unknown in both Antiquity and the Middle Ages, even though there was great interest in tangible religious artifacts, exemplified by Helena's 'finding' of the True Cross in the 4th cent., the great cult of the tombs of the martyrs in the Roman catacombs and the 'discovery' of the grave of St. James in the 9th cent. The constant access to and occasional resetting of memorials, bones or even minute relics meant that there was intensive contact with early Christian antiquities. However, their physical presence and (supposed) ability to bear witness was primarily of interest in the context of their salvatory qualities and their liturgical implementation. Secondary advantages of a dogmatic (e.g. *c.* AD 200 in the Montanist controversy at the grave of St. Philip at Hierapolis and the tropaia of the Apostles in the city of Rome) or political/economic nature could arise. Even in the high Middle Ages there was little concern for accurate representation; exceptions were the descriptions of Old St. Peter's by P. Mallius and of the Lateran church by J. Diaconus in 12th cent. Rome which showed great commitment but sprang from acute competitiveness. The humanists of the 14th cent. (Petrarch) still lacked a rigorous scholarly approach, but the 15th cent. saw the emergence of scholarship that was firmly focused on Antiquity, in particular on the collection of epigraphic evidence and on topographical and building studies (F. Biondo, d. 1436; M. Vegio, d. 1458; A. Fulvio, 16th cent.). This revealed the passion of the → Renaissance for Antiquity which ultimately also paved the way for the development of ChrA.

C. 16th to 18th Cents.

Although the emerging ChrA served theological and apologetic ends, this period saw the gaining of an enduring understanding of the monuments. Initially this was mostly limited to Rome and to Italian researchers.

Fig. 1: Drawing and explanation of an arcosolium in the catacomb of Santi Marcellino e Pietro

In the context of the Counter-Reformation, O. Panvinio's (d. 1568) ambitious publications on Church history created a broad scholarly foundation for early Christianity, making use of material evidence and written sources. C. Baronio (d. 1607), author of the *Annales ecclesiastici*, and others working in the spirit of the Roman Oratorians, also stood for Catholic reaffirmation, but maintained a receptive objectivity towards the archaeological evidence. The inventory of Constantinian Christian monuments in Rome suffered severe losses during this period, with valuable buildings being destroyed or concealed (Old St. Peter's: demolished 1506–1618; Lateran Basilica: converted mid 17th cent.; dome mosaic in the supposed *Templum Bacchi* of S. Costanza: suppressed 1620). The 'reborn' ancient forms that were adapted by early modernity thus conflicted with authentic late ancient ones. On the other hand, we are indebted to men of the Church for the documentation of Old St. Peter's (T. Alfarano, d. 1596; G. Grimaldi, d. 1623) and the correct classification as Christian of the dome mosaic in S. Costanza. In this latter case P. Ugonio (d. probably 1613) sadly could not make himself heard, as his *Theatrum urbis Romae* remained unfinished.

At the same time, the catacombs caused the inventory of monuments to grow substantially and particularly because of inscriptions and images. Their exploration would prove the most fruitful branch of ChrA: in 1578 the discovery of the richly painted Via Anapo catacomb, which was at first erroneously named after

Priscilla, caused a sensation. Soon more sites could be explored in the Roman tuff (Domitilla, SS. Marcellino and Pietro), and they all appeared – if their date was early enough – to reveal the very foundation of Roman Catholic Christianity and of the practice of the cult of the martyrs, which were both needed for defence of dogma. Three collaborating foreign scholars turned their attention to the catacombs: A. Chacón/Ciacconio (d. 1599), the accomplished draughtsman P. van Winghe (d. 1592) [21] who was driven by genuine antiquarian and scholarly enthusiasm and J. L'Heureux/ Macarius (d. 1614), the author of the *Hagioglypta* [3], the first compendium of early Christian iconography. The most thorough explorer of the catacombs and the true founding father of ChrA was A. Bosio (d. 1629). He was of paramount importance, despite his ideological links to the Counter Reformation and the severe losses of his work – only a single volume of *Roma sotterranea* [1] (see Figs.) appeared posthumously. He even documented lost or inaccessible sites. His followers were A. Boldetti (d. 1749) and G. Marangoni (d. 1753), among others. G. Ciampini (d. 1698) worked on standing Christian monuments in and outside of Rome. He created drawings of many early mosaics, thereby safeguarding our knowledge of them. The demand for redrawing the disintegrating ancient images was met most prominently by P.S. Bartoli (d. 1700), who had a tendency towards fantastic elaboration, e.g. of the dome mosaic of S. Costanza (which was only noticed in the 19th cent.). In the Settecento, the monuments became the background for denominational polemics, while innovative approaches remained absent. In France, too, research began to be undertaken [15], such as the publications of the *Daurade* of Toulouse (O. Lamothe) in the 17th cent. and of the grave of Childeric I (J.-J. Chifflet); Spain followed in the late 18th cent. with J. Córnide's study of Segobriga.

D. 19TH AND EARLY 20TH CENTS.

The *Histoire de l'art* of the Frenchman J.B.L.G. Séroux d'Agincourt (d. 1814) appeared posthumously. Its title indicated its aim – the artistic renewal of the 16th cent. – beginning with the *décadence au IVe siècle*. His countryman E. Le Blant (d. 1897) emphasised the internationalization of ChrA also in terms of the range of material studied: his seminal works on epigraphy and on sarcophagal art in Gaul, in particular in Arles, showed him to be a pioneer of modern ChrA in France [15. 340f.]. This diverted much interest away from the Eternal City. R. Garrucci (d. 1885) also promoted a widening of the focus by aiming to prepare the first complete illustrated catalogue of early Christian art in 1873. It retains great archival value. Nonetheless, Rome remained the supreme arena of ChrA. It was here that the German Protestant C.C.J. Bunsen (d. 1860) wrote his thesis on the local Christian basilicas. G.B. De Rossi (d. 1894) [20] undertook his monumental life's work mainly in Rome and rigorously focused it on early Christian antiquities. He was another proponent of the transition of ChrA to a modern and independent discipline and he expressly did not see himself as a theologian. De Rossi began the *Inscriptiones christianae urbis Romae* and in 1863 he founded the *Bullettino di Archeologia cristiana* (whose modern equivalent is the *Rivista di Archeologia cristiana*). It was the subject's first periodical and for decades he was its sole contributor. He devoted his *magnum opus, Roma sotterranea cristiana,* to the Catacombs. He rediscovered the Lucina region in the Callixtine complex and, as expected, found the tombs of a number of early Roman bishops which had been attested in documentary sources. He was supported by the *Pontificia Commissione di Archeologia Sacra,* founded specially in 1852 by Pius IX, who also promoted the activities of the Vatican Museum in this area. In 1879/1881 T. Roller pioneered the photographic publication of the catacomb paintings. German ChrA, too, was now gaining importance: F.X. Kraus (d. 1901) [2] disseminated the findings of De Rossi, whose status as the 'doyen' of the subject in Rome was assumed by J. Wilpert (d. 1944) [20; 23; 27]. The latter accumulated a vast bibliography, above all three multi-volume folio works, which were authoritative, magnificently illustrated and are still indispensable today: on the catacomb paintings of Rome (1903), on the early figurative art of churches of Rome and Italy (1916) and on Christian and antique sarcophagi (1929–36). He came into conflict with his Protestant countrymen, such as F. Piper (d. 1889), less because of the latter's attempt to incorporate the early Christian monuments into a distinct sub-discipline 'monumental theology' [4] but because Piper unabashedly demonstrated that early Christians made use of non-Christian imagery, which was considered scandalous in Catholic circles, and because Piper rightly suspected Christian art in its own right to have developed only in the 3rd cent. AD. In 1889 a dispute broke out between Wilpert [6] and other Protestants (who were to help German ChrA achieve acceptance at universities and to develop a modern academic character) over the concept of independent agency. Spokesman for the latter was V. Schultze (d. 1937) who accused Wilpert and Catholic ChrA of making cases according to the demands of Church and following a 'directive of predetermined results'. On the contrary, he stated, the monuments ought to be seen as pieces of evidence, which *aus ihrer Eigenart und ihrer Zeit verstanden und nach den Regeln historischer Untersuchung behandelt werden wollen. Sie sind nicht ... danach zu befragen, ob sie irgend eine dogmatische oder ethische Anschauung beweisen, sondern was sie ihrem Wesen und Inhalte nach sind* ('are intended to be understood in the context of their individuality and time and examined according to the rules of historical enquiry. Questions ought not ... to be asked as to whether they prove some dogmatic or ethical viewpoint or other, but as to what they are in nature and content') [5. esp 29f.]. Wilpert's work, which was centred on Rome and emphasised early dating, corresponded to his argument for the primacy

of Rome in the 'Orient-or-Rome?' debate, which arose in the years after 1900. New research was producing ever more spectacular antiquities of the Christian Orient, to which the Austrian J. Strzygowski (d. 1941) in particular accorded primacy.

E. To the Present

After 1907 the *Dictionnaire d'archéologie chrétienne et de liturgie,* the great project of F. Cabrol and H. Leclercq, attempted to do justice to this gradual, sweeping expansion into a research area which encompassed the entire Mediterranean and its peripheries. Later research in particular was shaped by the unexpected riches appearing outside of Rome and Italy; the Occident offered a plethora of important monuments, but it was the wider east Mediterranean region that attracted the legitimate main interest of ChrA. The subject was now also becoming technically more and more advanced. The sensational discovery of the synagogue and house church at Dura Europos on the Euphrates, each decorated with paintings from the 2nd quarter of the 3rd cent. AD, upset Rome's claims to have been the cradle of Christian art. Researchers now predominantly came from Germany, France, Britain, Russia, the USA etc. As the subject and its researchers, who were increasingly not members of the clergy, became internationalized, the influence of Catholic authorities diminished. Their displeasure was particularly aroused by the innovative typological approach. Based on the works of A. Riegl (d. 1905) and F. Wickhoff (d. 1909) it was pursued by L. von Sybel (d. 1929) in the early 20th cent.: by studying its typology, early Christian art was easily proven to have been a component of late ancient art. It could thus be seen as the younger sister of rather than being antagonistic to pagan art, as the religious traditionalists would have it. Comparative style criticism made it possible to establish more clearly the late inception of catacomb paintings around AD 200 and of Christian sarcophagal sculpture in the 3rd cent., long after the early Christian period. As far as is known today, no earlier Christian art exists. Correspondingly, excavations underneath St. Peter's in Rome in the 1940s only succeeded in tracing the origins of the building as far back as *c.* AD 200; the tropaion (see above) represented the earliest phase. Nonetheless, the Curia insisted that the true grave of St. Peter had been discovered. However, A. Grabar, F.W. Deichmann and R. Krautheimer, who were more sober in their interpretations, were able to determine events to an increasing degree. Special mention must also be made of T. Klauser. He followed the research of F.J. Dölgers (d. 1940), promoted the *Reallexikon für Antike und Christentum* for decades after its first publication in 1941 and founded the *Jahrbuch für Antike und Christentum* alongside it [12]. The former has now reached approximately 40% of its planned scope, is supplied by international authors and, as the *Sachwörterbuch zur Auseinandersetzung des Christentums mit der antiken Welt* (enclopedia for the analysis of the relationship between Christianity and the ancient world), has a remit extending beyond the narrow field of ChrA, for which it nonetheless represents the most important international reference work. Since 1894, there have been 14 international congresses for ChrA, most recently in Vienna in 1999, which was accompanied by an exhibition on the origins of ChrA in Austria.

→ EPIGRAPHICS; → HUMANISM

SOURCES: 1 A. BOSIO, Roma sotterranea, 1632 (Repr. 1998) 2 F. X. KRAUS, Über Begriff, Umfang, Geschichte der Christlichen Archäologie, Freiburg im Breisgau 1879 3 J. L'HEUREUX (Macarius), Hagioglypta, Paris 1856 4 F. PIPER, Einleitung in die Monumentale Theologie, Gotha 1867 (Repr. 1978) 5 V. SCHULTZE, Die altchristlichen Bildwerke und die wissenschaftliche Forschung, Erlangen 1889 6 J. WILPERT, Principienfragen der Christlichen Archäologie, Freiburg im Breisgau 1889

LITERATURE: 7 C. ANDRESEN, Einführung in die Christliche Archäologie, 1971 8 X. BARRAL I ALTET, Les étapes de la recherche au XIXᵉ siècle et les personnalités, in: Naissance des arts chrétiens, 1991, 348–367 9 G. BOVINI, Gli studi di archeologia cristiana dalle origini alla metà del secolo XIX, 1968 10 C. CECCHELLI, Origini romane dell'Archeologia Cristiana, in: Roma 7, 1929, 105–112 11 J. CHRISTERN, Christliche Archäologie, in: Mitt. des Dt. Archäologen-Verbandes 11/2, 1980, 13f. 12 E. DASSMANN, Entstehung und Entwicklung des RAC und des Franz Joseph Dölger-Instituts in Bonn, in: JbAC 40, 1997, 5–17 13 F. W. DEICHMANN, Einführung in die Christliche Archäologie, 1983, 7–45 (rev. W. Gessel, in: Theologische Rev. 79, 1983, 353–362) 14 J. ENGEMANN, s.v. Christliche Archäologie, LThK 1, 943–945 15 P.-A. FÉVRIER, Naissance d'une archéologie chrétienne, in: Naissance des arts chrétiens (no ed.), 1991, 336–347 16 W. H. C. FREND, The Archaeology of Early Christianity, 1996 17 G. P. KIRSCH, L'Archeologia Cristiana, in: Rivista di Archeologia cristiana 4, 1927, 49–57 18 W. E. KLEINBAUER, Early Christian and Byzantine Architecture. An Annotated Bibliography and Historiography, 1992 19 G. KOCH, Frühchristliche Kunst, 1995, 14–18 20 V. SAXER, Zwei christliche Archäologen in Rom: Das Werk von G.B. de Rossi und J. Wilpert, in: Röm. Quartalschrift 89, 1994, 163–172 21 C. SCHUDDEBOOM, Philips van Winghe (1560–1592) en het ontstaan de christelijke archeologie, 1996 22 H. R. SEELIGER, Christliche Archäologie oder Spät-Ant. Kunstgeschichte?, in: Rivista di Archeologia cristiana 61, 1985, 167–187 23 R. SÖRRIES, Josef Wilpert (1857–1944). Ein Leben im Dienste der Christlichen Archäologie, 1998 24 M. SCHMAUDER, R. WISSKIRCHEN (eds.), Ausstellungs-Katalog: Spiegel einer Wissenschaft. Zur Geschichte der Christlichen Archäologie vom 16. bis 19. Jh. (rev. H. R. SEELIGER, in: Röm. Quartalschrift 87, 1992, 112–115) 25 R. WARLAND, Von der Christlichen Archäologie zur Spät-Antiken Archäologie, in: Zschr. für ant. Christentum 2, 1998, 3–15 26 A. WEILAND, Zum Stand der stadtrömischen Katakombenforschung, in: Röm. Quartalschrift 89, 1994, 173–198 27 J. WILPERT, Erlebnisse und Ergebnisse im Dienste der Christlichen Archäologie, 1930 28 W. WISCHMEYER, Die Entstehung der Christlichen Archäologie im Rom der Gegenreformation, in: ZKG 89, 1978, 136–149

ADDITIONAL BIBLIOGRAPHY: M. GUARDUCCI: La tomba di Pietro: notizie antiche e nuove scoperte, 1959 (Eng.: The Tomb of St. Peter: The New Discoveries in the Sacred Grottoes of the Vatican, 1960); R. R. HOLLOWAY, Constantine and Rome, 2004; P. FREMIOTTI, La Riforma Cattolica del secolo decimosesto e gli studi di Archeologia Cristiana, 1926; Acta XIII Congressus Internationalis Archaeologiae Christianae (Split – Porec 1994), vol. 1, Città del Vaticano – Split 1998; JESÚS ÁLVAREZ GÓMEZ, Arqueología cristiana, 1998, 15–30; NORBERT ZIMMERMANN, Werkstattgruppen römischer Katakombenmalerei, 2002, 13–31; JOSÉ ANTONIO ÍÑIGUEZ HERRERO, Tratado de arqueología cristiana, 2002, 23–70; GIOVANNI LICCARDO, Introduzione allo studio dell'archeologia cristiana, 2004, 11–38, 166–171. ACHIM ARBEITER

Christianity see → THEOLOGY AND THE CHRISTIAN CHURCH

Chronology
I. CLASSICAL ARCHAEOLOGY
II. CRETAN-MYCENAEAN   III. GREEK   IV. LATIN

I. CLASSICAL ARCHAEOLOGY
A. COMPARATIVE CHRONOLOGY   B. ABSOLUTE CHRONOLOGY AND CHRONOLOGICAL NETWORK

A. COMPARATIVE CHRONOLOGY
Before any artefacts can be placed within an historical time scale, it makes sense to determine their relationship to each other (comparative chronology) by means of stratigraphy and by observing how morphological changes in objects take place.

The basic principles of stratigraphy were established by geologists during the first half of the 19th cent. In 1847, J. Boucher de Perthes applied the observations made about the layers of the earth to the archeological remains found in them; the realization that the order of layers corresponded to their chronological sequence was truly seminal. Even before that, L. Ross had already made observations concerning the stratification on the Acropolis in Athens (see below), and in the late 19th cent., G. Fiorelli in Italy, A. Conze and E. Curtius in Greece started to document strata in detail. It was not until the later the 20th cent., however, that stratigraphy became common practice in classical archaeology.

Winckelmann was the first to perceive art as part of a sequence of historical events and thus create typology as a specific tool of classification. Comparisons of style (observations of changes in technique, form or type) are based on his original notion that simpler versions are found at the start of a development process and subsequently become more refined and ever more complex. In the mid–19th cent., Heinrich Brunn provided the foundations for a comparative chronology of sculptures; in his *Geschichte der griechischen Künstler* [History of Greek Artists], he compiled all the information available in ancient literature regarding the creative period, works and style of ancient sculptors, and on that basis, in a profound analysis of form and style, described the development of Greek art. At the end of the 19th cent., this method was further improved by Adolf Furtwängler in his *Meisterwerke der griechischen*

Plastik [Masterpieces of Greek Sculpture]. The formal analysis of style was developed mainly in Germany during the first half of the 20th cent.; however, the 'biologistic' model which this concept implies has remained problematic, because it leaves little room for the appearance of concurrent, but stylistically different works of art. In the field of ceramics, it was the Oxford scholar John D. Beazley who in the first half of the 20th cent. established the basis for a comparative chronology by examining more than 65,000 vases and ceramic figures; he assigned more than 17,000 of them to individual artists or their respective workshops [2].

A new technique, developed first in the computer age and as yet not exploited to its full potential, is that of seriation. This method is based on the premise that objects within a self-contained site (such as a grave) date to about the same period, and, consequently, that graves with similar grave gifts are roughly contemporary. Given a sufficient number of graves, it is possible to establish their probable chronological order and, using the statistical method of correspondence analysis, to provide a graphical representation.

B. Absolute Chronology and Chronological Network

Scientific methods, which have been adopted in recent decades, are, with the possible exception of dendrochronology (see below), of little importance for Classical archaeology. Radiocarbon dating, developed in the USA in 1949, measures the remains of the radioactive isotope C14 which exists in every living organism and begins to decay after its death; its accuracy, however, becomes increasingly unreliable after about 1000 BC. The same applies to the dating method known as thermoluminescence, which, putting it simply, measures the radiation absorbed by clay objects after firing; it has an error margin of up to 10% and is thus mainly used to establish the authenticity of objects.

Linking archaeological findings with historical events allows comparative chronology to be anchored within the absolute timeline. Classical archaeology has the advantage but at times also the disadvantage (see below), that this link is not only based on information on the objects themselves, but is often also provided by literary texts.

1. Geometric and Archaic Period
2. Classical and Hellenistic Period
3. Roman Period and Beyond

1. Geometric and Archaic Period

The period, prior to the onset of official archives and historiography, is problematic and will remain so; even ancient historians and chronographers could not agree on dates in their reconstruction of earlier events from the Classical period onward. However, at the same time this provides a good backdrop for the illustration of the methodological problems involved.

One attempt to find a solid external link for the early period, whose pottery had become known primarily through the excavations in Athens' Kerameikos district after 1870, was based on the imports of Greek geometric pottery to the Middle East, especially in Tell Abu Hawam, Samaria, and Megiddo, where shards were believed to have been found in clearly datable stratigraphies or in destruction layers which form the framework of J. N. Coldstream's valid fundamental chronology [5], cf. [6]. However, the chronology of Palestine has since been revised several times; the destruction layer in Tell Abu Hawam alone has been variously ascribed to Pharaoh Sheshonq I (*c.* 926 BC), the Syrian king Hazael (815 BC) as well as Jehu, king of Israel (*c.* 840 BC); the most recent argument was for that stratum to continue to as late as 750 BC. Similarly, the stratigraphy and chronology of Samaria are the subjects of vigourous debate [11]. For that reason, these sites can no longer be seen to provide firm evidence for dating. The Syrian Hama seems to be a safer option; it was destroyed by the Assyrians in 720 BC and was, according to its excavators, not rebuilt until the Hellenistic period (however, differently in [10]); consequently, the Attic late Geometric ceramic fragments should be dated to the period prior to its destruction. Recent research [23] has emphasized the importance of the three Israeli sites of Ashkelon, Tel Miqne-Ekron, and Tel Batash-Timnah where the destruction layer, which yielded mainly eastern Greek ceramics (Ionic bowls), was linked with the campaign of Nebuchadnezzar II between 605 and 595 BC, as recorded in the Babylonian Chronicle; if this link can be maintained, it would confirm the traditional chronology of the 7th cent. BC.

The 'absolute' chronology of Archaic Corinthian ceramics, providing the basis for the entire chronology of Archaic Greek ceramics, – now generally referred to as orthodox – had been developed in 1931 by H. Payne [18], based on the simple assumption that Thucydides (6,3–5) provides the foundation dates of the Greek colonies in Sicily: the earliest pottery found in a particular settlement shows the style which was in use at that time; the information can then be used to work out an entire system of reference. These dates were further supported by the finds in a late 8th cent. grave in Pithecussae on Ischia, which contained a number of Greek vases, amongst them three proto-Corinthian aryballoi, together with a scarab of Pharaoh Bocchoris (*c.* 720–715 BC). A methodological problem arises from the fact that Thucydides provides no absolute dates, but only a chronological sequence of the colonies in relation to each other, with the starting point for the absolute chronology being the information that Megara Hyblaea was destroyed 245 years later. The fact that not only none of the colonies is completely excavated and researched, but also that historical events or rather their reflection in archaeological findings often remain ambiguous, gives rise to another problem: it is hardly possible to pin down these complex demographic processes to a single year – it is always possible for material to have reached the sites in question prior to colonization, e.g. as the result of trade, and it is not possible to establish the length of time that items had been in circulation before being placed in graves [17. 54–58]. These questions gained particular pertinence in Selinus in 1958, when excavators discovered pottery that was earlier than the previously earliest finds which had been dated to the founding of the colony in 628 BC, a conflict that was resolved in a rather unsatisfactory manner by assuming that for the foundation of just this one colony Thucydides' date was wrong and to switch to the date found in Eusebius (650 BC) [20. 54–56; 9].

Nevertheless, these datings, which are not always convincing in isolation, lend each other sufficient support to allow a sensible interpretation of the finds; in any case, to date no satisfactory alternative has been found (see below). Even the most recent research [13. 98] suggested only one modification, i.e. to move the end of the Athenian late Geometric vases from c. 700 BC to 675 BC – probably a leeway well within the acceptable limits for that period; in any event, one should always be aware of the fact that ultimately all fixed dates in that period are based on the literary tradition (above all, Thucydides) and that there is no 'independent' archaeological chronology [3]. These uncertainties continue into the Archaic period because of the comparatively small number of monuments and the lack of criteria other than style.

L. Ross, from 1834 senior curator in Athens, was the first to properly survey the strata on the Acropolis; he identified the 'Persian rubble'(see below), in which he discovered a red-figured plate with scorch marks, thus proving that the beginnings of red-figured vase painting date back to before the Persian Wars. In 1887, Studnicka positioned the Attic vase paintings within their contemporary history by linking dedications to historical persons (on the problems of this approach, cf. [14. 78–93]). Langlotz [15. 9f.; 14. 28–30] established a link between the oldest extant Panathenanaic prize amphora and the start of the Great Panathenaea in 566/565 BC; he also developed a system to compare styles in different media.To name but a few examples: the *columnae caelatae* of the Artemisium in Ephesus, whose column drums with epigraphic fragments confirm the information transmitted in Herodotus (1,92,1), i.e. that they were a donation by the Lydian king Croesus, which dates them somewhere between his ascent to the throne in 561/560 and his deposition in 547/546; similarly stylized cloaked figures and the slant of the cloak folds can, for example, also be found on vases from Amasis and Execias. The second fixed point, used by Langlotz to create such cross-links – which are still valid today for Attic red-figured pottery, the Caeretan hydriae, and the Clazomenian sarcophagi – is the architectural sculpture of the Siphnian Treasury in Delphi, which can have been built by the rich island at most only a few years before Siphnos was laid waste by the Samians in 525 BC (Hdt. 3,57f.) (for further fixed points for early chronology, cf. [14]).

Accepting the so-called Persian rubble as a chronological fixed point and an epoch boundary, as already Winckelmann did, is based on the assumption that, following its destruction, the Acropolis was fairly quickly cleared and terraced. However, in the middle of the 19th cent., excavations were frequently unsystematic – since the layers were dug up in a treasure-seeking mentality down to bare rock – and insufficiently documented; already for Langlotz [15. 99],' the 'Persian rubble' was already beginning to lose its applicability for dating' (similarly [22. 581–583]). Nowadays, it is generally accepted that the filler layers contain also post-Persian material; it is likely that the work of clearing the site continued into the 440s BC, and additional material was transported in from the surroundings. Clear indications for classification as Persian rubble are scorchmarks and, to a lesser extent, mechanical damage [16].

The uncertainties tainting the chronology of Classical archaeology, particularly with regard to the early period, the frequently very positivistic approach in associating material with actual dates, together with the implicit assumption (as noted already by Langlotz himself [15. 6f.]) that within the different media a uniform and concurrent development of styles took place, motivated, above all, E. D. Francis and M. Vickers in the 1980s to move the entire chronology forward by about 60 years [7]. They argue, for example, that Herodotus made an error regarding the building date of the Siphnian Treasury; they took (1,4) as the more reliable source Vitruvius, who dated the origin of the Caryatids (as personifications of the fate awaiting Persian sympathizers) to after 479 BC; furthermore, they claim that at that time Siphnos was still a wealthy island. By a different argument the evidence of destruction found in the 'Persian rubble' did not necessarily have to be the result of the Persian invasion; the *korai* were evidence of 'post-war affluence' in Athens and were only destroyed in the 'cultural revolution' of 462/461 BC. These two examples suffice to reveal the methodological weaknesses of this chronology which, not surprisingly, never succeeded in gaining acceptance: in the first example, the evidence of an author still comparatively close in time to the events is dismissed in favour of a much later and much less reliable one; in the second example, an entirely convincing assumption is replaced with the postulation of an event for which there is no supporting evidence anywhere.

Tölle-Kastenbein [22] attempted a not very convincing compromise with her suggestion that the arithmetic average between controversial dates be taken (as e.g. in respect of Leagros' age, celebrated on vases as a young man at the time that he held the office of *strategos* in 465/464, as recorded in Hdt. 9,75).

2. CLASSICAL AND HELLENISTIC PERIOD

For the chronology of the 5th and 4th cent. BC, several well dated monuments provide a firm framework; the situation regarding Attic marble sculptures is particularly favourable, because the names of the eponymous archons, in an almost completely preserved list, also appear on the building and accounting documents, recording and dating the building activity on the Athenian acropolis (Parthenon: metopes 448–442 BC, frieze 442–438 BC, gables 438–432 BC; Propylaea: 437–432 BC; Erechtheion: korai 421–413 BC, frieze 409–407 BC; Nike balustrade 408 BC; for the research history, see → ATHENS). The document reliefs, too, contain the names of the archons.

One fixed point is the sanctuary of Zeus in → OLYMPIA, systematically excavated since 1875, because both Thucydides (1,108) and Pausanias (1,29,9) report that the Spartans had a gilded shield fitted to the gable of the temple of Zeus after their victory at Tanagra in 457 BC, paid for out of the tithe of their war booty; as is clear from Pausanias (5,10,4), the lavish architectural sculpture must have been completed by that time. The excavations in Kerameikos (since 1870) and in the agora have provided a number of additional fixed points (grave stele of Dexileos 394 BC; state grave of the Lacedaemonians 403 BC). As far as the razing of cities is concerned (e.g. Olynthus 348 BC; Gela 405 BC), it is now clear that they did not always entail such a radical end as previously assumed, and that life frequently continued, albeit on a much more modest level; for that reason, they cannot be used unreservedly as chronological fixed points.

In the Hellenistic period, in spite of numerous fixed historical dates (founding of Alexandria 331 BC; Demetrius of Phaleron's sumptuary law concerning tombs in Athens 317 BC; inscriptions of the ruling Ptolemies on the hydrias of Hădra between 271 and 209 BC; destruction of Corinth 146 BC and many others), considerable problems still arise when one attempts to establish a relative chronology of events, and even more in attempting to locate these more firmly with the aid of written records. The eclecticism of Hellenistic sculpture, the references and adaptations of earlier styles on the one hand, combined simultaneously with daring innovations on the other, soon illustrate clearly the limits of any analysis of style (whose 'reliability' is ironically postulated in [1], where otherwise the variously differing interpretations and chronological placements are treated very polemically). An additional problem is posed by the sometimes contradictory or ambiguous information about Hellenistic artists and art works in Pliny, in whose view in any case art as such 'ended' in this period (Plin. HN 34,52). Ultimately, the ongoing debates about the Sperlonga group [12. 66–71] the *Laocoon*, the latter ever since the days of Lessing and Winckelmann, show how little conclusive those statements are that can be made about the chronology of the Hellenistic period, apart from the fact that here, too, the decisive role played by correct interpretation of written sources in defining criteria outside of style and form is retained.

3. ROMAN PERIOD AND BEYOND

Historical reliefs (triumphal arches), inscriptions, imperial portraits and coins provide important cornerstones for the chronology of the Roman period; as early as the 14th cent. Italian scholars had realized their importance as well as their ability to be linked to liter-

ary accounts, and had already suggested some quite accurate datings for well-known monuments. However, the framework for Roman chronology, allowing finer distinctions of subperiods such as 'Augustan', 'Flavian' etc., was not created until the mid–19th cent. with the compilation of the *Corpus Inscriptionum Latinarum* (CIL) and the chronology of Roman pottery as a result of large-scale excavations of locations datable by historical events; of particular importance here are the Augustan and Tiberian border fortifications in Germania that had been occupied during the main export period of Italian *terra sigillata* (some of them even during the early period of workshops in southern Gaul). Among the fundamental works are those of S. Loeschcke in Haltern and E. Ritterling in Hofheim [21]. H. Dressel recognized as early as 1891 [4] the usefulness of stamped bricks, which were very common in the early Imperial period, and which since the Trajanic period also bore the names of consuls as well as that of the emperor; however, problems can at times arise from the fact that bricks may be stored for lengthy periods or reused, as e.g. in Rome's Aurelian wall.

Considerable amounts of wood have been preserved from the Roman provinces, whose value as a chronological source has, however, only recently been exploited: one example for the potential of this material is the Roman bridge near Trier, for which it was established by dendrochronology that the trees used in its construction had been cut in AD 119 [8].

The strongest critic of the fundamental assumptions behind the traditional method of chronology has been Snodgrass [20. 36–66]; it is a justifiable objection that, because daily life continued unaffected, historical events thought to have been important by ancient authors are often not reflected in the archaeological material. Catastrophes such as the one that destroyed → POMPEII and → HERCULANEUM in AD 79, leaving a truly complete body of evidence, are rare (with regard to other methodological problems, cf. above). However, the conclusion that there are few points of contact between history and archaeology, acting in different levels of reality, is equally exaggerated and has been disproved by the great number of historical monuments or else monuments built in response to historical events.

'New Archaeology' considers chronology as a whole to have little relevance in a broad social-science approach, and furthermore faults traditional chronology for representing a concept of time which is far too modern (and in Antiquity too alien), while neglecting those social contexts and practices that constituted time, and thus calls into question the alleged neutrality of typological schemes. Nevertheless, even the proponents of 'New Archaeology' use traditional chronology as a frame of reference, and so it continues to provide a reliable framework, albeit one to be used with due caution.

→ EPIGRAPHY, GREEK; → Pottery; → Triumphal Arches → Inscriptions; → Pottery, production of; → Colonization IV. The 'Great' Greek Colonization; → Corinthian vases; → Panathenaic prize amphorae; → Relief; → Triumphal arches

1 B. ANDREAE, Fixpunkte hellenistischer Chronologie, in: H.-U. CAIN, H. GABELMANN, D. SALZMANN (eds.), Festschrift für N. Himmelmann, 1989, 237–244   2 W. R. BIERS, Arts, Artefacts and Chronology in Classical Archaeology, 1992   3 H. BOWDEN, The Chronology of Greek Painted Pottery: Some Observations, in: Hephaistos 10, 1991, 49–59   4 CIL XV,1 fasc. 1   5 J. N. COLDSTREAM, Greek Geometric Pottery, 1968 (esp. 302ff.)   6 R. M. COOK, A Note on the Absolute Chronology of the Eighth and Seventh Centuries BC, in: The Annual of the British School at Athens 64, 1969, 13–15   7 Id., The Francis-Vickers Chronology, in: JHS 109, 1989, 164–170   8 H. CÜPPERS, Vorrömische und römische Brücken über die Mosel, in: Germania 45, 1967, 60–69   9 J. DUCAT, L'archaisme à la recherche de points de repère chronologiques, in: BCH 86, 1962, 165–182   10 E. D. FRANCIS, M. VICKERS, Greek Geometric Pottery at Hama and Its Implications for Near Eastern Chronology, in: Levant 17, 1985, 131–138   11 L. HANNESTAD, Absolute Chronology: Greece and the Near East c. 100–500 BC, in: [19. 39–49]   12 N. HIMMELMANN, Sperlonga. Die homerischen Gruppen und ihre Bildquellen, 1995   13 P. JAMES et al., Centuries of Darkness. A Challenge to the Conventional Chronology of Old World Archaeology, 1991   14 J. KLEINE, Untersuchungen zur Chronologie der attischen Kunst von Peisistratos bis Themistokles, 1973   15 E. LANGLOTZ, Zur Zeitbestimmung der strengrotfigurigen Vasenmalerei und der gleichzeitigen Plastik, 1920   16 A. LINDENLAUF, Der Perserschutt der Athener Akropolis, in: W. HOEPFNER (ed.), Kult und Kultbauten auf der Akropolis, 1997, 46–115   17 I. MORRIS, The Absolute Chronology of the Greek Colonies in Sicily, in: [19. 51–59]   18 H. PAYNE, Necrocorinthia, 1931   19 K. RANDSBORG (ed.), Absolute Chronology. Archaeological Europe 2500–500 BC (Acta Archaeologica 67) 1996   20 A. M. SNODGRASS, An Archaeology of Greece, 1987   21 M. TODD, Dating the Roman Empire: The Contribution of Archaeology, in: B. ORME (ed.), Problems and Case Studies in Archaeological Dating, 1982, 35–56   22 R. TÖLLE-KASTENBEIN, Bemerkungen zur absoluten Chronologie spätarchaischer und frühklassischer Denkmäler Athens, in: AA 1983, 573–584   23 J. C. WALDBAUM, J. MAGNESS, The Chronology of Early Greek Pottery: New Evidence from Seventh-Century BC Destruction Levels in Israel, in: AJA 101, 1997, 23–40.   BALBINA BÄBLER

II. CRETAN-MYCENAEAN
A. HISTORY OF RESEARCH   B. COMPARATIVE CHRONOLOGY   C. ABSOLUTE CHRONOLOGY

A. HISTORY OF RESEARCH
As early as 1906, only a few years after the discovery of the palace of → KNOSSOS (March 1900), which had opened the world of Bronze Age high culture to research, A. J. Evans [9], the leader of the excavation team, produced the outline of a chronological structure, dividing Minoan development into three main periods, based on the changing styles of pottery: an Early, Middle and Late Minoan period (abbreviated as EM, MM, and LM). Evans further divided each of these main periods into three phases, designated by the Roman numerals I–III, some of which he in the course of his later work further specified with letters (e.g. LM I A and LM I B). The fundamental and frequently voiced criticism that Evans, proceeding from 19th cent. notions of evolution, had designed a system mainly modelled on biological sequences such as growth, bloom, and decay, can be negated by Evans' differentiation of structures and his own evaluations of the periods (for instance, MM III and LM I as the peak periods of Minoan culture – i.e. periods beyond simple numerical symmetry). The objections that ceramic or generally artistic styles create by their very nature no clear-cut epoch boundaries but rather gradual transitions, are, of course, basically correct, but apply in equal measure to all chronological schemes in archaeology (thus also to the division of Greek art into Geometric, Archaic, Classical and Hellenistic periods with their respective subdivisions). In practical archaeological work, Evans' system with its additional differentiations has proven its worth as a useful classification tool.

As an alternative, N. Platon [21] suggested in the 1950s the classification of Minoan culture into a Pre-, Old, New and Post- Palace Period (with finer subdivisions), a system of nomenclature that corresponds strongly to the building lines of the palaces and historical periods and is thus of value in the classification of the main stages of development, but by the same token is only of limited use in the dating of actual finds.

Following Evans' model, A. J. B. Wace and C. W. Blegen [24] divided the cultural development of Bronze Age mainland Greece into an Early, Middle, and Late Helladic (or Mycenaean) period (EH, MH, LH, each with subdivisions). The classification of the Late Helladic period was further refined by A. Furumark [10–12]. Finally, an analogous structure has gradually been developed for the region of the Cyclades [3] (Early, Middle and Late Cycladic).

B. COMPARATIVE CHRONOLOGY
The comparative sequence of the Minoan, mainland Greek and Cycladic levels of civilization seems to be established now on the basis of stratigraphic observations as well as the sequence of complete grave inventories; furthermore, the correlation of the regional stages to each other has largely been clarified by means of the numerous ceramic importing relationships between the regions [28].

Individual Periods:

Crete [4; 23; 25–27]: EM I is characterized by fine burnished pottery, grey monochrome ware, or with red and brown painted decorations on a light-coloured background, EM II (A-B) initially by sophisticated painted ware, later by the mottled ('Vassiliki') pottery, EM III by white painting on a dark background. MM I (A-B) is typified by Barbotine and early Kamares style painted pottery; the Minoan palaces were built in the course of MM I. MM II (A-B) comprises the peak of the mostly abstract, curvilinear classical Kamares pottery; MM III (A-B) is the period in which the old palaces were destroyed and the building of the newer palaces began, also the late phase of Kamares ware with a preference for plant motifs, together with a white gloss (*firnis*) on a dark coated ground. During LM I A, gloss painting (*Firnismalerei*) became prevalent (spiral ornaments, plant motifs, *rippled ware*); LM I B is a period of more refined, palatial gloss painted pottery with motifs of plants or sea life (floral style, marine style, alternating style); at the end of this period, the Minoan palaces – with the exception of Knossos and numerous settlements fell victim to an island-wide sweep of destruction. LM II sees the appearance of the palatial style as well as the Ephyraean style, influenced by mainland models. LM III A – C are characterized by later developments of gloss painting in various levels of formal development, with a tendency toward ornamental patterns of decoration; the exchange in arts and crafts with the mainland increased; the destruction of the palace of Knossos is likely either to have taken place in LM III A, or during the transition of LM III A 1 to 2, or early in III A 2 (sometimes it is dated even later to LM III B). This was followed by a short sub-Minoan period, marking the transition to the proto-Geometric development of the 1st millennium BC.

Mainland Greece [7; 10–12; 18–20]: The Early Helladic period is one of predominantly monochrome styles; EH II: *urfirnis* pottery, with the sauce boat (beaked bowl) as the leading form, in EH III painted ware, the first evidence of pottery wheels. The subsequent Middle Helladic period (MH) is characterized by matt-painted pottery, Minyan ware, and novel monochrome styles. With the beginnings of the Mycenaean culture, we see the appearance of Minoan style gloss painting – the early LH phases still exhibit a strong Minoan influence (LH I and II A, parallel with LM I A and B). The shaft graves of Mycenae, illustrating the onset of the advanced Mycenaean civilization, belong to the end of the Middle Helladic period and LH I. During LH II B (parallel with LM II), independent concepts in arts and crafts come to the fore; consequently, changes in vessel shapes and decorative styles–with increasing tendency toward abstraction–permitted further and more refined subdivisions (LH III A 1 – 2 and B 1– 2). LH III A is the period of the development of the great Mycenaean palace and fortress centres, which were destroyed at the end of LH III B. LH III C – together with several subdivisions – is characterized by well-developed regional styles. The sub-Mycenaean period marks the transition to the proto-Geometric one.

The division of the Cycladic Bronze Age development [3] is still under discussion, particularly with respect to the nomenclature and definition of the individual stages and also their correlation with the Minoan and Helladic sequence (e.g. at the end of the Early Cycladic period). Because of an insufficient number of grave finds and very sparse settlement material, thus making it likely that the sequence of styles remains incomplete, little is known about the Early Cycladic period; however, it is clearly characterized as an independ-

ent local culture (EC I: Pelos – Kampos level, II: Syros level, III: beginnings of matt-painted pottery). During the Middle and beginning Late Cycladic periods, various types of matt-painted pottery dominated (alongside monochrome and white-painted ones), with various degrees of local characteristics and Minoan influence. In the course of the Late Cycladic period, the islands became integrated into the Mycenaean cultural sphere.

C. ABSOLUTE CHRONOLOGY

In order to establish absolute dates [1; 2; 6; 15; 16; 28], archaeologists initially used the traditional method of studying the links of the Aegean region with historically dated Near Eastern or Egyptian civilizations, and investigating the potential information yielded by objects from these regions which had been found in graves and within stratigraphical contexts within the Aegean as well as Aegean exports into the eastern Mediterranean. In so doing, one needs to take into account that the historical chronology of the Near East itself is subject to considerable variation, and that even the sequence of dynasties and pharaohs in Egypt is still – though to a lesser extent – subject to fluctuation. The difficulty in estimating the lifespan of imported goods presents a fundamental problem; the lifespan of pottery is likely to be quite limited, but for scarabs, seals, and other valuable items, it could be considerably longer. For some decades now, new scientific dating methods have been available, especially the radiocarbon or C14 method, the results of which, however, show a high uncertainty factor; and, more recently, dendrochronology and other tools [16; 22]. A central problem in most recent discussion has been the establishment of the absolute chronology of the volcanic eruption that destroyed the late Bronze Age settlement of Akrotiri on the island of → THERA during the advanced LM I A. Currently, there are two schools of archaeological thought, one of which largely relies on the archaeological findings themselves, while the other pays far greater heed to the scientific data. There are wide variations in dating especially regarding the early periods of the Late Bronze Age.

Even though the existence of trade links with the east has been verifiably established, there are no precisely datable import and export records which can help to define the various levels of the Early Minoan, Early Helladic, and Early Cycladic cultures; for that reason, C14 dating is of particular relevance in this context [15]. It is likely that the Early Bronze Age comprised the entire 3rd millennium BC, possibly even extending back into the 4th millennium. Exact dates seem problematic.

For the Middle Minoan period, ceramic exports from Crete to Egypt (Qubbet el Hawa, Kahun, Abydos, Tell Dab'a) are available, as are Egyptian scarabs in Cretan contexts. They permit the establishment of a correlation between MM I and the early 12th dynasty (20th cent. BC), between MM II with the established 12th (19th cent.) as well as with the 13th dynasty (18th and first half of the 17th cent.). MM III (A) can possibly be dated by an alabaster lid with the cartouche of the Hyksos pharaoh Khyan (after the mid–17th cent. BC) in Knossos (MM I: *c.* 2000–1900 BC, MM II: 1900–1700, MM III: 1700–1600/1550).

Considerable uncertainties remain regarding the beginnings of the Late Minoan and Late Helladic periods, because most of the Aegean ceramic imports to Egypt have been found in contexts that are not clearly stratifiable. A LH II B jug in the tomb of Maket in Kahun seems to be contemporary with the rule of Thutmosis III (*c.* 1479–1425). Traditionally, the beginning of the Aegean Late Bronze Age is set at around 1600/1550 BC (LM I A/LH I: *c.* 1600/1550–1500, LM I B: 1500–1450, LH II A: 1500–1460, LM II: 1450–1400, LH II B: 1460–1400). Ph.P. Betancourt, S. Manning et. al. [5; 16] have recently attempted to date the final catastrophe of Akrotiri (in LM I A) with the aid of C14 data, which tend to be higher, and other scientific data, by linking a climatic event of 1628 BC, which is evident in northern hemisphere dendrochronological graphs, to the volcanic eruption of Thera [8; 13]and similarly to traces of volcanic ash in the Greenlandic ice pack (1645 *c.* 20) – accordingly LM I A: 1675–1600/1580, LM I B: 1600/1580–1500/1490, LM II: 1500/1490–1440/25, LM III A 1: 1440/25–1390/70. However, the assumption that the volcanic eruption caused global climatic changes is speculative, and the correspondence of the Greenlandic ashes with those of the Thera eruption has been disputed by scientists. Recent archaeological finds argue against such a connection: in Tell Dab'a, the ancient Avaris in the Nile delta, pottery of the Late Cypriot period (contemporary with LM I A/LH I) is found only in the context of the early New Empire (XVIII dynasty, roughly mid–16th cent. BC), the same as findings of Theraean pumice [2]. Images of luxurious metal vessels, gifts from Minoan emissaries (*keftiu*), found in the graves of 15th cent. Egyptian dignitaries, clearly indicate in their typology that the transition from LM I B to LM II (or respectively LH II A to LH II B) cannot have happened earlier than the latter years of the rule of Thutmose III (mid–15th cent.) [17].

The different systems continue to interlock throughout the LM III/LH III period. LM III A 1 is fixed in time by the scarabs of Amenophis III (early 14th cent. BC), LH III A 2 by Mycenaean pottery in Amarna, the residence of Amenophis IV -Akhnaton (1351–1334); LH III B can be assumed to be largely concurrent with the rule of Ramses II (1279–1213), though starting somewhat earlier. However, the exact absolute chronological definition of LM/LH III C as well as of the subsequent Subminoan/Submycenaean period requires further investigation – LM/LH III A: *c.* 1400–1340/30, LM/LH III B: 1340/30–1200, LM/LH III C: 1200–1100, Subminoan/Submycenaean: 1100–1050/1000.
→ Amenophis [3].→ Amenophis [4]; → Ramesses [2] R. II.; → Thutmosis [3] Th. III.;

1 P. Åström (ed.), High, Middle or Low? Acts of an International Colloquium on Absolute Chronology held at the University of Gothenburg 1987, vol. 1–3, 1987–1989 2 M. S. Balmouth, R. H. Tykot (eds.), Sardinian and Aegean chronology, 1998 (contributions by Ph.P. Betancourt, S. W. Manning, M. H. Wiener, M. Bietak, P. Warren) 3 R. L. Barber, The Cyclades in the Bronze Age, 1987 4 Ph. P. Betancourt, The History of Minoan Pottery, 1985 5 Id., Dating the Aegean Late Bronze Age with Radiocarbon, Archaeometry 29, 1987, 45–49 6 M. Bietak (ed.), The Synchronisation of Civilisations in the Eastern Mediterranean in the Second Millennium B. C., 2000 7 O. T. P. K. Dickinson, The Origins of Mycenaean Civilisation, 1977 8 T. H. Druitt et al., Santorini volcano. Geological Society Memoir 19, 1999 9 A. J. Evans, Essai de classification des époques de la civilisation minoenne, revised ed. 1906 10 A. Furumark, Mycenaean pottery. Analysis and classification, 1941, ²1972 11 Id., The Chronology of Mycenaean Pottery, 1941, ²1972 12 Id., Mycenaean Pottery. Plates, 1992 13 D. A. Hardy, A. C. Renfrew (eds.), Thera and the Aegean World III, 1990 14 V. Karageorghis (ed.), The White Slip Ware of Late Bronze Age Cyprus, 2001 15 S. W. Manning, The absolute chronology of the Aegean Early Bronze Age, 1995 16 Id., A Test of Time: The Volcano of Thera and the Chronology of the Aegean and East Mediterranean in the mid-Second Millennium B. C., 1999 17 H. Matthäus, Representations of Keftiu in Egyptian Tombs and the Absolute Chronology of the Aegean Late Bronze Age, in: BICS 40, 1995, 177–186 18 P. A. Mountjoy, Mycenaean Decorated Pottery, 1986 19 Id., Mycenaean Pottery, 1993 20 Id., Regional Mycenaean Decorated Pottery, 1999 21 N. Platon, La chronologie minoenne, in: Chr. Zervos, L'art de la Crète néolithique et minoenne, 1956, 509–512 22 M. Schoch, Die minoische Chronologie, 1996 23 V. Stürmer, MM III. Stud. zum Stilwandel der minoischen Keramik, 1992 24 A. J. B. Wace, C. W. Blegen, The Pre-Mycenaean Pottery of the Mainland, ABSA 22, 1916–1918, 175–189 25 G. Walberg, Kamares. A Study of the Character of Palatial Middle Minoan Pottery, 1976 26 Id., Provincial Middle Minoan Pottery, 1983 27 Id., Middle Minoan III – A Time of Transition, 1992 28 P. Warren, V. Hankey, Aegean Bronze Age Chronology, 1989 (seminal).

HARTMUT MATTHÄUS

III. Greek

A. Development of Chronology B. Methodology and Problems of Dating

A. Development of Chronology

The German term 'Zeitrechnung' [lit. 'calculation of time'] came into common use at the beginning of the 18th cent. as the translation of the Latin term *chronologia*, which in turn had been defined in its academic sense first by Joseph Justus Scaliger (1540–1609) [3. 86ff.]. Scaliger used this term to institute a new academic discipline in his *Opus de emendatione temporum* (1583) and *Thesaurus temporum* (1606); in these works, he meticulously reconstructed a firm framework of dates from events recorded by ancient historians – the more ancient, the better. In addition, his *Thesaurus* also contained the first edition of the Chronicle of Eusebius and Jerome and their successors. Eusebius' accounts were partially corrected by Scaliger with the aid of further sources through combination and text-critical emendation. In that way, Scaliger laid the foundations for any further study of the chronology of ancient history and literature [2. 92ff.]. He converted the reckoning of the Olympiads in the ancient sources into what he referred to as 'Julian years'. The continuous numbering of years began with 4713 BC and was in competition with the 'anno domini' reckoning of years as suggested by Dionysius Exiguus in 525, but was adopted in historiography only much later (Venerable Bede). Scaliger's motivation was to disentangle chronology from any kind of religiously motivated reckoning. His chronology has to be seen within the context of a wider 16th cent. interest in questions of calendar reform and time reckoning (cf. the Gregorian reform of the calendar in 1582). Basically, Scaliger's chronography is an uncritical continuation of ancient chronographical methods and also adopts mythical references such as the dating of the Trojan War. In the 17th/18th cent., it was further completed by improved chronologies and histories of literature (esp. DIONYSIUS PETAVIUS, *Opus de doctrina temporum*, 1672; HENRY DODWELL, *De veteribus Graecorum Romanorumque cyclis*, 1701), and first editions of ancient chronographical works (*Chronicon Alexandrinum*, ed. MATTHAEUS RADER 1615; *Historicae poeticae scriptores*, ed. THOMAS GALE 1675), as well as by the discovery of fragments of the *Marmor Parium* 1627 (ed. JOHN SELDEN 1628), and also an edition of the lists of eponymous archons (*Fasti Attici*, ed. EDUARDO CORSINI 1744–56). In the 18th cent., the ancient reckoning on the basis of Olympiads and the Julian dates used by Scaliger were replaced by references to 'after' and (following August von Schlözer) especially 'before the birth of Christ'. It was only from the latter half of the 18th cent. onward, in the course of the → ENLIGHTENMENT and → ROMANTICISM, that chronography distanced itself from slavishly copying ancient methodology. Following J. J. Winckelmann's *Geschichte der Kunst des Alterthums* (1764), in the study of literature, too, there was an attempt to establish independent datings with the aid of a historical-critical method, as e.g. J. G. Herder (*Von der Griechischen Litteratur*, 1766), the brothers August Wilhelm and Friedrich Schlegel, and the philologist August Boeckh (1785–1867) [4. 311–28]. However, they were not the first; an early similar attempt had been made by Jacob Perizonius (Voorbroek; 1651–1715). Particularly Homer, the progenitor of all poetry, and the Bible were increasingly understood in terms of their historicity as well; however, both Richard Bentley and Friedrich August Wolf still assumed that Homer's 'songs' dated back to prehistoric times. In the 18th cent., ancient texts were also examined in relation to each other, in order to – e.g. in the case of the Gospels – establish a relative chronology on the basis of intratextual criteria (G. E. Lessing, F. Schleiermacher). Eduard Woelfflin developed a statistical approach to language which could be used for dating purposes. In the course of the 19th cent., a period char-

acterized by → HISTORISM and Positivism, the knowledge of Antiquity grew immensely, through increased activity in collecting in both archaeology and epigraphy, the deciphering of cuneiform script (Old Persian 1802–1837 by Grotefend and Rawlinson; Babylonian-Assyrian gradually from c. 1850 onwards by Talbot et. al.) and Egyptian hieroglyphs (from 1821 by Champollion), and finally through the start of a massive increase in papyrus finds. The thus accessible Egyptian and Oriental sources (lists of kings, chronicles) made it possible to examine and review ancient chronologies independently and critically (e.g. those of Manetho and Berossos). Only on that basis could the full range of dating methods now be applied, not only those based on what were in some instances speculative intratextual criteria. In Ancient History, it was B. Niebuhr (1776–1831) who first used the newly acquired tools. In the study of ancient Greek, Boeckh's pupils led the way, particularly Karl Otto Müller with his *History of the Literature of Ancient Greece* (1840) and Adolf Kirchhoff, whose studies covered the Greek alphabet, epigraphy, and the chronologies of Homer and Herodotus. In the course of the 19th cent., the sheer quantity of available ancient chronographical material increased considerably, e.g. after the discovery of the *didaskalia* inscriptions for Greek plays, as well as ancient biographies and Aristotle's *Athēnaíōn politeía*, the latter containing, among other things, an outline of Athenian history. Despite the continuing discovery of new source material (esp. papyri), there was no further methodological advance in the 20th cent., even though in individual cases, dating could be improved on the basis of new findings (e.g. the literary novel), while is still the subject of lively debate (early Greek literature).

B. METHODOLOGY AND PROBLEMS OF DATING
1. EARLY GREEK LITERATURE   2. CLASSICAL LITERATURE   3. HELLENISTIC LITERATURE   4. LITERATURE OF THE IMPERIAL AGE   5. CHRISTIAN LITERATURE

1. EARLY GREEK LITERATURE
Epic: Already in Antiquity, Homer and Hesiod were seen as the most ancient Greek poets (e.g. Hdt. 2,53), with Aristotle (metaph. 983b28) placing both of them far earlier than any conceivable dating. Today, their exact dating is still controversial because of the lack of unambiguous text-external evidence such as a reference to contemporary historical events. Attempts have been made to establish a comparative chronology of the two epic poets in relationship to each other. In antiquity, Homer and Hesiod were frequently mentioned together and were seen as contemporaries, as e.g. shown in the poem about the competition between Homer and Hesiod (*certamen Homeri et Hesiodi*). Nowadays, it is generally assumed that Homer predated Hesiod; but see [38]. Absolute dating of Hesiod is based on the reference to the funeral games of Amphidamas, an aristocrat from Chalcis, in the *Erga* (654). The only other refer-

ence to this person is by Plutarch (b. before AD 50, d. after 120) (mor. 153f–154a), who dated Amphidamas' death to the period of the Lelantine War, dated by archaeologists to around 700 BC [26; 34]. The *terminus ante quem* for Homer is often taken to be the late-Geometric Cup of Nestor, found in Ischia and dated by some archaeologists and epigraphists to the 8th, but by others to the 6th cent. BC; the inscription on the cup is thought to presuppose the action of the *Iliad* (11,632–637). The *terminus post quem* is the introduction of the alphabetic script in Greece, which has not been dated with certainty but is generally set at around 800 BC, because the complexity of Homer's epics in their transmitted form implies that they were most likely written down. Archaeologists also use the images of scenes from the Iliad, appearing on Geometric vases after about 625 BC, in the dating process [11; 10; 38]. With regard to the details, even today the results of different academic disciplines still vary widely: the majority assumes that Homer's epics date back to the 8th cent., e.g. [18; 22; 23; 31], a minority [5; 10; 38] argues for a more recent date in the 7th cent. According to Bukert, the *Iliad* reference to the 'hundred-gated Thebes' in Egypt can only refer to the city's heyday under Ethiopian rule between 715 and 663 BC [5]. Another general assumption for Homer is that the *Iliad* predates the *Odyssey*. This is based on the postulate of a more archaic conception of the world in the *Iliad* with its aristocratic hero ethos as opposed to the more gentrified and humane traits of the *Odyssey* with its notion of property and possession combined with a wider geographical horizon. The attempt has also been made to further underpin the *Iliad*'s priority with alleged quotations from it in the *Odyssey*, e.g. [37].

Lyric poetry: The dating of early Greek lyric poets and pre-Socratic philosophers is difficult and uncertain, even though or maybe because their extant works contain nonfictional biographical references such as wars (Archilochus, Tyrataeus), political unrest with banishment (Sappho, Alcaeus), contemporary non-Greek personalities (Croesus) or solar eclipses; for instance, the solar eclipse of 648 secures the dating in the case of Archilochus who mentions it and probably experienced it firsthand. Chronologically fixed points provided by epigraphical documents, such as lists of archons or Olympic champions, are not known for this period. Almost all of the early Greek authors are mentioned by Herodotus, who had extracted his biographical information from the poems themselves. These can be synchronized with the aid of his – partly fictitious – list of kings and non-Greek personalities from the 6th cent. on. In turn, a number of later ancient Greek authors depended on early Greek literature [33] for their biographical information. A second – ancient tradition, differing significantly from Herodotus, began with Aristotle and was continued in the *Marmor Parium*, Eusebius' chronicle and the Suda lexicon. This tradition assumes the dates for early Greek personalities to be one or two generations earlier than Herodotus. Most

scholars and handbooks follow the latter tradition, even though the later Herodotean dating is directly or indirectly more likely on the basis of references in Isocrates' or Plato's works.

The dating of the Athenian lyric poet and politician Solon is instructive; according to Aristotle (pol. 5,2; 13,1), he served as archon in 594/3 and afterwards went travelling for 10 years. According to Herodotus (1,29–33), he supposedly met the Lydian king Croesus on his travels. However, again according to Herodotus and confirmed by the Neo-Babylonian Nabonidus Chronicle, Croesus' rule was significantly later (*c.* 560–547). Herodotus' later dating is made more plausible by references in Plato (Charm. 157 e 6; Tim. 20 e 2f.), according to which Solon was still personally known to the grandfather and great-grandfather of Critias, born around 460 BC (similarly in Isoc. Or. 12,148f.) [30]. Moreover, no other author before Aristotle mentions that Solon served an archonship. Thus the information in the handbooks that Solon was born *c.* 640 BC and served as archon in 594/3 remains speculative. The year of his birth, in turn, is calculated backwards from reaching the *akmé* in life, which, according to Greek understanding, was at about 40 years of age. Similar problems are encountered with respect to the → Pre-Socratic Thales, who on the one hand – according to Herodotus (1,74) – supposedly predicted a solar eclipse, first identified by Pliny the Elder (HN 2,12,53) as that of 585 BC. On the other hand, Herodotus claims that 50 years later, Thales was still serving as an adviser to Croesus. It is still unresolved how Thales was able to calculate and predict this solar eclipse based on the astronomical knowledge available at that time. It is thus more probable that this prediction of a spectacular and historical eclipse of the sun was retrospectively attributed to the most famous of the Seven Sages. At any rate, it cannot be taken as a source for secure biographical data for Thales.

On the whole, after Aristotle, [9] quite a number of early Greek personalities were – against the older tradition – only secondarily dated to the early 6th cent. (582 'Proclamation of the Seven Sages' according to Demetrius of Phalerum: Diog. Laert. 1,22) in order to achieve a synchronism, especially of the 'Seven Sages'. The meeting of the Seven Sages in Delphi is a humorous fiction by Plato (Prot. 343a1–c5); qualified in [28]. However, as there are quite a number of poets who are dated in relation to Pittacus, Solon and others, it follows that these were also dated earlier, secondarily, than according to the older Herodotean tradition. So far, this theory has not gained much ground within historical research on Antiquity, quite likely also for practical reasons: so as to avoid having to work without the familiar framework of dates supplied by the later sources.

2. Classical Literature

Chronologies do not become clearer until the Classical period, when data transmitted after the Persian Wars can be taken as firm. The reference to the battle of

Salamis (480 BC) with the first mention of an archon (Calliades) in Herodotus (8,51) is the first exactly definable date in Greek literature and thus also the chronological 'anchor', by which all further dates from 500 onward are defined. There is a wide range of options available outside of literature, as the comparison with historical events and, for plays, for instance, detailed information regarding the actual performance of a particular drama. Furthermore, from the 5th cent. onward, lists of archons were kept and archived in Athens, which enable exact chronological matches even for later ones. From the last quarter of the 5th cent., lists of Olympic champions were introduced for literary use, which served to synchronize local historical events and thus could be used in the Panhellenic region. In literature, reckoning by Olympiads continued even after the Olympic Games had been banned by emperor Theodosius in AD 393.

The exact dates of the births and deaths of important Classical authors such as the tragedians or Socrates and Plato, are recorded in the Hellenistic *Marmor Parium*. A special record for the 5th cent. Attic drama is the Didascalia which originally listedall information relevant to the performance of a particular play, such as date of performance, victory in a competition, author, title, *choregos*, etc. Aristotle used these records, archived by the authorities in charge, as the basis for his (lost) works *didaskalíai* and *níkai Dionysiakaí astikaí kaí Lēnaikaí* ('Victories at the municipal Dionysia and Lenaea') [27]. In turn, these form the foundation for research on the Peripatetic school (e.g. Aristotle's pupil Dicaerchus), the fragmentary extant Didascalia inscriptions from the 2nd half of the 4th cent. (e.g. IG 2², 2318–2325 and [7]), the *Marmor Parium*, the *hypothéseis* and *scholia* information, and also the Suda lexicon.

The exact chronology of the classical prose works was of no interest to ancient philologists; for that reason, there are no detailed references. The comparative dates of origin for the works of Plato [6; 35], Xenophon or Isocrates was not established until the end of the 18th cent. (1792 W. G. Tennemann for Plato), using intratextual tools, i.e. style, language statistics, criteria regarding developmental history, some aspects of which are still controversial (e.g. Xenophon). For some works such as Thucydides *historíai*, but also Xenophons *Hellēniká*, autobiographical data included in the text provide some information regarding their respective dates of origin: thus Thucydides served as *strategos* at the time of the lost battle of Amphipolis in 422 (5,26,5; cf. Xenophon, *Hellēniká* 6,4,37 – written after 358/7). Herodotus' work must already have been known in 424 BC because of Aristophanes' parody of it in the *Acharnians* (523ff.). For Attic orators such as Lysias, Isocrates, Demosthenes et al, biography and chronology of works can be gleaned from the speeches themselves, which were often written on the occasion of specific historical events. The speeches have also been used as source material for the ancient biographies of orators, e.g. by Dionysius of Halicarnassus and Plutarch.

3. HELLENISTIC LITERATURE

The Hellenistic period saw a blossoming of general and also specifically literary-historical interest in chronography. Apart from the extensive compilations by the Alexandrian philologists, this is also evident in chronographers such as Eratosthenes, the founding father of ancient critical chronography (3rd cent.), with his works on *olympioníkai* (reconstruction of the lists of Olympic champions) and *chronographíai*, an overview of Greek history since the fall of Troy, using the lists of Olympic champions as well as those of Spartan kings. Even earlier, Timaeus of Tauromenium (3rd/4th cent.) had been instrumental in establishing the historiography based on the reckoning of Olympiads. Eratosthenes was followed by Apollodorus (*c.* 180–110) with his *chroniká*. The famous, if somewhat incomplete inscription, discovered in Paros in 1627 – the Marmor Parium of 264/3 (FGrH 239) – contains, in the form of a universal chronicle, besides historical-political facts also a great number of references to cultural-historical events [16]. The chronicle has its beginning in mythical times with Cecrops (1581/0) and ends in 264/3.

Paradoxically, exact biographical data for the great Hellenistic poets and an absolute or comparative chronology of their works is only insufficiently documented, as the chronographical research of the Hellenistic period was directed toward the literature of the Archaic and Classical periods.

Information about the Attic writer of comedies, Menander, is sparse and not very reliable, originating from much later sources such as the compendium of the Suda lexicon and the anonymous *perí kōmōdías* (CGF 1,9) [19]. The inscription IG 14,1184 states – in contradictory fashion – that Menander was born under the archonship of Sosigenes (342/1) and died aged 52 under the archonship of Philip (293/2). According to Strabo 14,638, both Menander and Epicurus, whose birth date is confirmed as 342/1, belonged to the same *ephebe* (*synépheboi*) and so were the same age, thus confirming Menander's birth date. Other dates remain uncertain: According to the anonymous *perí kōmōdías*, Menander began to write comedies under the archonship of Philocles (322/1); according to Eusebius' Chronicle, his first work was supposed to have been *Orgé*; the *Marmor Parium* records his first victory for the year 316/5. By contrast, according to the *hypóthesis* of the papyri with the first complete play *Dýskolos*, only discovered in 1959, this play was the one with which Menander supposedly achieved his first victory under the archonship of Demogenes in 317/6.

Some of Theocritus' poems were written to commemorate actual events and can thus be dated: *Eidyllion* 17 to Ptolemy II was written between 274 and 270 BC. Similarly, Callimachus' *Lock of Berenice* can be dated to 246/5 on the basis of historical and astronomical allusions. Apart from that, only the later Suda lexicon provides other chronographical data for both authors (with the exception of Gell. 17,21,41 on Callimachus). The MSS of the *Argonautiká*, however, also contain vitae for Apollonius Rhodius that are both contradictory in themselves and speculative in nature; they might have originated with Theon (1st cent. BC). Further information comes from P Oxy. 1241 (2nd cent. AD). Arat's *Phainómena* (c. 276) are taken as the *terminus post quem* for the *Argonautiká*, because it makes use of them. Furthermore, based on theoretical observations concerning their poetry, Callimachus and Apollonius Rhodius are viewed as contemporaries.

4. LITERATURE OF THE IMPERIAL AGE

At least comparatively exact life dates can generally be established for the well-known authors of the imperial age from autobiographical references within their works, though here, too, the chronology of the works themselves presents a problem. This is true, for example, for the orators Dion Chrysostomus and Aelius Aristides, whose orations, which were held on specific occasions, permit chronological fixing.

Scattered throughout his entire body of work, are Plutarch's numerous references to himself and his family, while the information about him in the Suda lexicon is rather sparse. Plutarch's life first became the subject of research as early as 1624, in the edition by Rualdus. Based on Plutarch's statement that as a young man (*néos*) he had listened to Ammonius during Nero's stay in Greece in 66/67 (de E 385b), his date of birth can be determined as sometime between AD 45 and 50. Based on Eusebius, who in his *Chronicle* for the year 2135 after Abraham (= AD 119) refers to Plutarch as a very old man, the latter's date of death must have been later than 119. Because the pseudo-Lucian treatise *Macrobii* does not list his name among the 'long-living' (*makróbioi*), he did not reach the age of 80, i.e. he must have died between c. 120 and 129. Based on this statement of Eusebius, in which it is also mentioned that Plutarch was acquainted with the philosophers Sextus Empiricus and Oenomaus, Jerome, the later editor and translator of the *Chronicle* into Armenian, wrongly assumed that the *akmé* of these three men would have been around 119, i.e. Plutarch was only about 40 years old at that time. It is not possible to determine the chronology of his works, as they rarely contain any hint regarding their date of origin; in his biography of Sulla (cap. 21), Plutarch mentions, for example, that the battle of Orchomenus (AD 85) was fought about 20 years previously; more information in [41. 708ff.]. Research has concentrated, in particular, on the relative chronology of the biographies: On the one hand, there are references by Plutarch himself, describing Demosthenes-Cicero as the fifth biographical pair, Pericles-Fabius Maximus as the 10th, Dion-Brutus as the 12th, whereas Theseus-Romulus was one of the last ones written (Demosthenes 3,1; Pericles 2,5; Dion 2,7; Theseus: introduction); on the other, the biographies contain 48 self-quotations, some of them reciprocal, suggesting that several of them may have been written concurrently. The situation regarding Lucian is similar, as he mentions in his works contemporary events and persons.

The chronology of the Greek novel is particularly complex, originally dated by Rohde to Late Antiquity [29]. Within the genre of the novel, he dated Xenophon of Ephesus and Chariton as 5th cent., later than the others, because of their unadorned style, which he interpreted as rhetorical mannerism. New papyrus finds have completely overthrown this chronology: according to them, Chariton's work may have originated around the time of Christ's birth. 1st cent. AD papyri of the Ninos novel have been found (P Berol. 6926; PSI 1305); as a result of the finds, Achilles Tatius is now dated to the 2nd cent. (P Oxy. 3836) [21]. A further criterion for a comparative chronology of the novels is their increasing narrative complexity; in consequence, the works of Chariton and Xenophon are seen as early examples of their genre, whereas the bucolic Longus and the sometimes self-deprecating Achilles Tatius are dated to the Second Sophistic movement (2nd cent. AD). Heliodorus' novel is generally seen, in terms of its narrative, as the most sophisticated and thus the last love story, even though its actual dating, based on alleged historical allusions or else religious tendencies, varies between the 3rd and the 4th cent. [14].

5. CHRISTIAN LITERATURE

For the chronography of Greek Christian literature, distinctions have to be made between a) the books of the New Testament, b) the other early Christian literature up to Eusebius (mainly apologetics), and c) the remaining Patristic works.

a) The academic chronography of the writings of the New Testament, already beginning with G. E. Lessing as early as the end of the 18th cent., is very complex, because, with the exception of the authentic epistles of Paul, the authors, contrary to the early Christian tradition of naming authors, remain unknown or anonymous. A comparative chronology of the gospels can be established by uncovering their mutual and reciprocal use: Mark is the first and is used by both Matthew and Luke, the latter in turn is used by John. Furthermore, theologically Mark appears early because of his expectation of the *parousia* in the immediate future, whereas John with its comparatively well developed Christology may have been written much later. A guiding question for the absolute chronology is on the one hand, whether the writers of the gospels had already been aware of and influenced by the destruction of the Temple in AD 70: this is assumed for Matthew (22,7) and Luke (21,20–24), but remains controversial for Mark (13: Jesus' 'apocalyptic speech'). Furthermore, the author of Luke seems to have written about Jesus' martyrdom already under the influence of the persecution and the much stricter religious laws introduced by the emperor Domitian (from 92 onward). Matthew must have been written prior to 110, because Ignatius is familiar with this gospel. For John, there are meanwhile a number of papyri which confirm in their script a *terminus ante quem* of c. 100 (P 52, 66, 75). The *Acts of the Apostles* by Luke continues where Luke's gospel leaves off and probably originated soon after [32; 36; 39]. Paul's letters with their wealth of internal references to the stops on his travels make it possible to draw up a comparative chronology, beginning with 1 *Thessalonians*. The absolute chronology of Paul's work is determined by reference to Gallio's period of office as administrator of Corinth in 51/2; it is a matter of controversy whether his letters were written in the years before or after (majority view) [15; 39].

b) The remaining early Christian literature (e.g. apologetics, Clemens of Alexandria, Origen) can either be dated by references within the works themselves, or with the aid of dates provided by Eusebius of Caesarea, the first Christian chronographer and church historian, who wrote in the 3rd/4th cent. All of this information is contained in the *Chronicle* with its synoptic tables of universal historical events from Abraham to AD 303 (also the *terminus post quem* for this book), and also the *History of the Church* (10 bks.); cf. [25; 39]. The *History of the Church* also serves as a source from which to glean information about the life of Eusebius himself (e.g. 3,28,3 and 7,28,3: birth prior to 265); he was still alive during the rule of Constantine the Great, to whom he dedicated a panegyric (*laus Constantini*).

c) Regarding the chronography of most other patristic authors such as Gregory of Nazianzus, Basil the Great, Gregory of Nyssa, Athanasius, John Chrysostom etc., similar criteria apply as to pagan Imperial Age literature: intratextual references, often autobiographical in character, have to be combined with external historical dates. Generally, the exact chronology of the works themselves is not clearly known, especially with respect to particularly comprehensive bodies of work such as that of John Chrysostom.

→ Archontes; → Chronicles; → Didaskaliai; → Eusebius [7] Eusebius of Caesarea; → Herodotus [1]; → Homerus [1]; → Marmor Parium; → Novel; → Suda → EPOCHS, CONCEPTS OF; → HOMERIC QUESTION; → PHILOLOGY

1 K. J. BELOCH, Griechische Geschichte, vol. 1,2, ²1913 2 J. BERNAYS, Joseph Justus Scaliger, Berlin 1855 3 A. BORST, Computus, 1990 4 E. BRATUSCHECK (ed.), Enzyklopädie und Methodologie der philologischen Wissenschaft von August Boeckh, Leipzig 1877 5 W. BURKERT, Das hunderttorige Theben, in: WS 89, 1976, 5–21 6 L. BRANDWOOD, The Chronology of Plato's Dialogues, 1990 7 E. CAPPS, Greek Inscriptions, in: Hesperia 12, 1943, 1–11 8 S. DÖPP, W. GEERLINGS (eds.), Lexikon der antiken christlichen Literatur, 1998 9 D. FEHLING, Die sieben Weisen und die frühgriechische Chronologie, 1985 10 Id., Die ursprüngliche Geschichte vom Fall Trojas, 1991 11 K. FITTSCHEN, Untersuchungen zum Beginn der Sagendarstellungen bei den Griechen, 1969 12 A. v. HARNACK, Geschichte der altchristlichen Literatur, ²1958 13 R. HELM, s. v. Lukianos, in: RE 13,2, 1725–1777 14 N. HOLZBERG, Der antike Roman, 1986 15 H. HÜBNER, s. v. Paulus, in: TRE 26, 133–153 16 F. JACOBY, Apollodors Chronik, 1902 17 Id., Das Mamor Parium, 1904 (repr. 1980) 18 R. JANKO, Homer, Hesiod and the Hymns, 1982 19 A. KÖRTE, s. v. Menandros, in: RE 15,1, 707ff. 20 Id., s. v. Menandros, in: RE Suppl. 12, 854ff. 21 R. KUSSL, Papyrusfragen griechischer Romane, 1991

22 J. LATACZ, Homer, ²1989 23 A. LESKY, s. v. Homeros, in: RE Suppl. 11, 687–846 24 F. MILLAR, A Study of Cassius Dio, 1964, 5–72 25 A. MOSSHAMMER, The Chronicle of Eusebius and Greek Chronographic Tradition, 1979 26 V. PARKER, Untersuchungen zum Lelantinischen Krieg, 1997 27 REISCH, s. v. Didaskalíai, in: RE V,1, 394–403 28 W. RÖSLER, Die Sieben Weisen, in: A. ASSMANN (ed.), Weisheit. Archiv der literarischen Kommunikation, vol. 3, 1991, 357–365 29 E. ROHDE, Der griechische Roman und seine Vorläufer, ⁴1914 30 E. RUSCHENBUSCH,πάτριος πολιτεία, in: Historia 7, 1958, 398–424 31 W. SCHADEWALDT, Homer und sein Jahrhundert., in: Id., Von Homers Welt und Werk, ³1959, 87–129 32 W. SCHMITHALS, s. v. Evangelien, in: TRE 10, 570–626 33 H. STRASBURGER, Herodots Zeitrechnung, in: W. MARG (ed.), Herodot, 1965, 688–736 34 K. TAUSEND, Der Lelantinische Krieg – Ein Mythos?, in: Klio 69, 1987, 499–514 35 H. THESLEFF, Studies in Platonic Chronology, 1982 36 H. THYEN, s. v. Johannesevangelium, in: TRE 17, 200–225 37 K. USENER, Beobachtungen zum Verhältnis der Odyssee zur Ilias, 1992 38 M. L. WEST, The Date of the Iliad, in: MH 52, 1995, 203–219 39 A. WIKENHAUSER, J. SCHMID, Einleitung in das Neue Testament, ⁶1973 40 F. WINKELMANN, Eusebios von Kaisareia, 1991 41 K. ZIEGLER, s. v. Plutarchos, in: RE 21, 639ff. (Life), 708ff. (Chronology), 899ff. (Biographies).
PETER KUHLMANN

IV. LATIN

A. BASIC PRINCIPLES B. METHODS C. MEDIEVAL TRANSMISSION OF DATES D. CRITICAL-PHILOLOGICAL ACHIEVEMENTS OF THE RENAISSANCE HUMANISTS E. CHRONOLOGICAL PROBLEMS IN MODERN RESEARCH

A. BASIC PRINCIPLES

1. TEXTUAL REFERENCES WHICH EXPAND OUR SOURCE MATERIAL BEYOND THE WORK IN QUESTION 2. CHRONOLOGICAL RESEARCH BY ROMAN LITERARY HISTORIANS 3. JEROME'S LITERARY-HISTORICAL WORKS

1. TEXTUAL REFERENCES WHICH EXPAND OUR SOURCE MATERIAL BEYOND THE WORK IN QUESTION

Didaskalia: A main source for the ancient Roman drama is the *Didaskalia*, public records providing us with information not only about the author and title of a play, but also with the details of the relevant festival and the names of the consuls in the year of its premiere. For Plautus' comedies, only two of these festival records are extant (in the *Codex Ambrosianus*), enabling us to date *Stichus* and *Pseudolus*. By contrast, all six of Terence's comedies are datable with the aid of the *Didaskalia*, preserved as manuscripts, and references in the Donatus commentary [30].

Inscriptions: Among contemporary documents, inscriptions can provide clues for the reconstruction of dates. The minutes of the Centenary of 17 BC on an inscription found in 1890 [1] thus provide us with the information that on the third and final day (3 June) a choir performed Horace's *Carmen saeculare* in a solemn conclusion of the celebrations.

Autobiographical documents are among the most important sources for research on the biography and chronology of works. Besides the author's actual work as the often only source of information for his life and date of origin of his works, secondary sources, i.e. documents by contemporary or later authors, can also provide clues as to the date (e.g. Plin. Ep. 3,5 on Pliny the Elder's life and the chronology of his works).

2. CHRONOLOGICAL RESEARCH BY ROMAN LITERARY HISTORIANS

The fundamental framework of our chronology of Latin literature is based on literary-historical research by Roman scholars. The beginnings of Roman literature did not become the subject of antiquarian research in Rome until about one century after the first performance of a play by the dramatist Livius(85 BC). In his *Didascalica*, a work on the history of literature, written at least partially in verse, the tragedian L. Accius (170 – c. 85 BC) also addresses questions of dating. His erroneous dating of the Roman dramatists (Livius Andronicus, Naevius, Pacuvius) can be only indirectly deduced from Varro's critical discussion in his *De poetis*, of which only fragments are extant [12]. Varro's achievement is the establishment of a chronology of dramatic performances in Rome with their starting date of 240 BC, and – closely linked to this date – the appreciation of Livius Andronicus as the forefather of Roman poetry. Varro, to whose literary-historical research we also owe the datings of Naevius, Ennius, and Plautus' ἀκμή, arrived at his dates by evaluating the information provided by the poets themselves in their works, but also on the basis of official documents (particularly Didascalian records and senatorial decrees).

For the older Roman poets, subsequent annalists and biographers could take recourse to these few exact dates, first among them Suetonius in his *De poetis*, a work that is still partially reconstructable. For his collection of biographies of Roman authors (*De viris illustribus*) up to the end of the 1st cent., Suetonius, who (at least until AD 122) enjoyed access to the original sources deposited in the imperial archives, could, in addition, resort to his own research.

Several streams of literary-historical tradition flow into the synchronistic chapter of the *Noctes Atticae* (17,21), in which Gellius provides a Greco-Roman chronology of literature from the foundation of Rome to the end of the Second Punic War, interlinked with that period's political history [25].

3. JEROME'S LITERARY-HISTORICAL WORKS

In its transmission of the biographical dates of Latin authors, Jerome's universal chronicle plays a particularly important role because of the addenda which Jerome included in his adaptation of Eusebius' (largely lost) two-part chronicle; there are even some dates for which it is the main source. In around 380, Jerome translated the *Canones*, the so-called second part of the chronicle of Eusebius of Caesarea (d. 339),which covered the period up to AD 325/326, extended its coverage to 378, and supplemented Eusebius' data tables with mainly literary-historical dates transmitted from Latin,which he excerpted mainly from Suetonius. Following Eusebius' example, Jerome also presented his work in tabular form: between the synoptically arranged annual tables of the various eras since Abraham's birth (dated to 2016 BC), set in parallel columns, he inserted the chronologically important column of short political and literary notes on individual the years [2]. While Jerome wanted his accounts to refer to a specific year, he often found that his Suetonian original did not provide him with an exact chronological point [18] so that his assignment of news to specific years sometimes results in obviously wrong dates. For that reason, critical philologists from the Renaissance (Petrarch, J. J. Scaliger) to the present time [18. 95] urge greater caution with Jerome's dates, whose long unquestioned authority has gradually been shattered in the course of modern research to the point where they now bear the reproof of 'notorious unreliability' [33. 31].

Jerome provides a firm basis for the chronology of Latin and Greek Christian authors in his little treatise *De viris illustribus*. In 392 or 393, he compiled a catalogue of church writers in chronological order; for Jerome and his successors, particularly Gennadius of Marseille (late 5th cent.), Isidore of Seville (d. 636), and Ildefons of Toledo (d. 667), see [9. 98–130].

B. METHODS

1. METHODS FOR DETERMINING THE LIFE DATES OF AN AUTHOR

1.1 ᾿Ακμή AND SYNCHRONISMS – GENUINE METHODS OF ANTIQUITY

Following the example of scholarly philological achievements in the Hellenistic period, Roman scholars, too, in the absence of other information tried to determine the life dates of an author on the basis of his time of prime (ἀκμή). Jerome, however, did not, in his chronicle, adopt these flexible datings, typified by vague expressions such as *floruit, insignis/clarus habetur*, etc. rather, he fixed them to a specific date.

Synchronisms, linking the death of a poet to the maturing of a young and rising talent to follow him, were also established in the Roman tradition, following the model of the famous synchronism of these ancient literary historians, who linked the three great Attic tragedians in different ways to the battle of Salamis. There are several references, particularly in the oldest of the ancient biographies of Virgil, to the fact that Virgil assumed his *toga virilis* on the very same day that the poet Lucretius died.

1.2 RECONSTRUCTION OF AN AUTHOR'S DATE OF DEATH

In the absence of an author's life dates, it is common practice to assume that the end of his literary production is his date of death. However, that the absence of literary output cannot necessarily be equated with the death of the author, is illustrated by the example of determining the year of death of the rhetor M. Cornelius Fronto: as his datable letters cease in about 166, and as Fronto claims in a letter on the death of his grandson (165) to feel close to death himself (*De nepote amisso* 2,8 = p. 238 Van den Hout), the obvious conclusion was to assume that his death occurred around this time. The reference to Commodus coins (first minted in 176) in a letter to M. Aurelius (p. 159,12 Van den Hout), however, endorses a later date of death; [28. 486]; furthermore, the published correspondence is not completely extant [29].

1.3 Autobiographical Statements

The spectrum of autobiographical statements includes the entire range from references scattered throughout an author's work to specific autobiographical poems (Ov. Tr. 4,10). Whereas – quite rightly – the historicity of an autobiographical statement is regarded ever more sceptically [31; 20], important dates in an author's life, references to historical events, dedications and the poems addressed to contemporaries can still be of use in the reconstruction of a biography.

2. Methods for Determining the Date when a Work was Written or Published

Allusions to datable events or people generally permit the date of origin to be determined; this date,is, of course, different from the date of publication. Greater difficulties arise in the chronological placement of anonymously transmitted works or work whose author may be named, but is not known outside of this work. A method to determine the approximate date of origin of a text, increasingly used in modern research and continuously being refined, is an analysis of the text based on criteria of language and style. Starting with ancient philologists and particularly with the Italian humanists, questions regarding dating and authorship, arising in conjunction with a debate on literary genuineness, have been dealt with on the basis of stylistic arguments. Thus Coluccio Salutati (1331–1406) used mainly stylistic arguments alongside anachronisms in his proof that Seneca could not have written the *Octavia* transmitted under his name [37]. More recently, in a study important primarily for its methodology, Bertil Axelson succeeded in narrowing down the date of origin of an anonymously transmitted work – using lexical and stylistic evidence and particularly an analysis of the clausula technique – and thus ruled out the previously claimed authorship of Firmucus Maternus [7]. Regarding the methodology for finding clues for a comparative chronology of Seneca's plays, see [41]; for determining the order of Plautus' works, see [40]. However, stylistic studies and observations about an author's development with respect to his verse technique rarely result in more than probabilities. A prime example of how arguments over questions of comparative chronology can be reversed could be the *Carmina Priapea*, an anonymously transmitted anthology of 80 epigrams: apart from a clarification of its authorship, the date of origin of the *Corpus Priapeorum* remains controversial. Proposed

dates range from the Augustan, early Imperial, or Neronian periods to the time immediately following Martial [17; 39].

C. Medieval Transmission of Dates

The formal structures established by Jerome for the transmission of noteworthy information on the life and work of famous authors, i.e. his universal chronicle, enriched with literary-historical data and the chronologically ordered catalogue of church writers, became the foundation and model for the medieval transmission of the ancient authors (regarding the genesis of medieval literary history: [14. 53–57; 6. 58–61]). If there was any interest in a literary-historical account of pagan Roman authors at all, little attention was paid to questions of chronology; often, a rough dating of the author's prime period was deemed sufficient, but sometimes there are not even references to the period in which an author had lived (still fundamental P. Lehmann [24; 9. 137–202]). This aspect of neglecting the chronological context has been illustrated in an exemplary fashion by P. L. Schmidt for the Cicero biography of Johannes Vallensis (John of Wales), an English Franciscan of the late 13th cent.[32].

In his *Speculum historiale*, the main part of the *Speculum maius*, the most comprehensive late-medieval encyclopaedia, Vincent of Beauvais (d. 1264) also included the Classical Latin authors within the context of world history. The rough chronological order of the authors provided Vincent, a Dominican monk, only with the framework in which to insert his florilegium of popular-philosophical and ethical maxims [34]. The lack of interest in an exact chronology and the total absence of critical assessment of transmitted data are a characteristic feature, common to the literary-historical passages in nearly all of the medieval world chronicles. A more intensive study of the literary historicity of pagan Antiquity, influenced by Johannes Vallensis, is evident in the *De vita et moribus philosophorum* by the English scholastic Walter Burley (Burleigh, b. about 1274/75, d. after 1344), including not only philosophers, but also general authors (however, according to [23], Walter is not the author of this work, for which the date of origin is before 1326). The Late Middle Ages saw the compilation of a number of compendium-style anthologies that also recorded the life dates and main works of famous ancient authors. The *Liber de viris illustribus*, written by the Dominican Giovanni Colonna [10. 533–563] between 1332 and 1338, and Guglielmo da Pastrengo's catalogue of authors from around 1350 deserve particular mention.

D. Critical-philological Achievements of the Renaissance Humanists

As they did in matters of the transmission of texts and the authenticity of ancient and Christian literature, so also in questions of chronology, Humanist philologists developed an independent critical approach to the tradition; they looked through the copious compiled materials for contradictions and made improvements with firm confidence in their own critical abilities. After the long period of mainly uncritical acceptance of the dates defined by Roman literary historians, which stretched from Gellius, via Jerome to the medieval chroniclers, the Renaissance Humanists hearkened back to the critical methods of Varro or Suetonius, because the situation regarding the available sources for determining an exact chronology remained basically unchanged.

Francesco Petrarca (1304–1374) used Eusebius' *Chronicon* in Jerome's Latin translation as the starting point for his treatment of the problems in chronology of Latin literature. With the aid of Petrarch's sharp-witted comments in the margins of his copy of the Chronicle, Billanovich could illustrate how Petrarch used his own immediate knowledge of the sources to recognize contradictory statements about the life dates of various authors [8]. For example, Petrarch annotated Jerome's entry on the death of M. Terentius Varro *prope nonagenarius moritur* (164a H.) with a higher age: *imo prope centenarius*; his likely source for this different age reference was Val. Max. 8,7,3 [8. 44]. Petrarch's doubts regarding the credibility of transmitted data is best characterized in a critical remark in his historiographical work *De viris illustribus* 2,12 [3].

Sicco Polenton(e), an Italian Humanist (1375/6–1447), who completed his 18 book *magnum opus* about the Latin authors from Livius Andronicus to Petrarch – often referred to as the first history of Latin literature – between 1433 and 1437, frequently focused on the biographical data of Roman writers. The technique for establishing an author's place within the chronological order – in complete contrast to that used in the compendium-style anthologies and medieval chronicles – is based on a critical assessment of the sources in combination with independent conclusions. An instructive example for Sicco's independent judgement can be found in this treatment of Virgil's biography: D. R. Stuart has demonstrated how (and why) Sicco Polenton – with explicit criticism of Servius and Donatus – wanted a timeline to prevail that was different from that traditionally employed for Virgil's biography [38. 8f.].

The beginnings of aesthetic literary criticism are found in the literary-historical *De poetis Latinis libri V* (first published in Florence 1508) by Petrus Crinitus (Pietro Crinito, Ricci or Riccio, 1465–c. 1505), in which he introduces Latin poets from Livius Andronicus to Sidonius Apollinaris in more or less chronologically ordered short chapters. His view of the tradition was not uncritical, and occasionally he also directed his attention to biographical details (cf. his expositions regarding the life dates of Lucretius in bk 2, ch. 19).

Whereas the Humanist Petrarch had used Eusebius' chronicle as a chronological aid in his reading of Latin authors, the emphasis shifted during the later Renaissance: with his reconstruction of Eusebius' chronicle, Joseph Justus Scaliger (1540–1609) made a seminal contribution to the establishment of modern chronology as a subdiscipline of the study of classical antiquity, with the systematic provision of the specialist's knowledge required for historical-critical source-based research; he was preceded by Carlo Sigonio (1523/4–1584), who had attempted a reconstruction of Roman chronology on the basis of the fragments of the *Fasti Capitolinii*, discovered on the Forum Romanum in 1546 [36; 27]. Scaliger takes Eusebius' work in Jerome's translation as the starting point for his attempted reconstruction and co-ordination of Biblical and ancient systems of time reckoning. Almost as a by-product of his antiquarian research, Scaliger also revised Jerome's chronological errors, as is illustrated in exemplary fashion in his criticism of the dating of Catullus. Scaliger recognized that the date of death could not have been correct and supported his findings in his *Thesaurus temporum* (Leiden 1606, Amsterdam ²1658) with allusions to historical events in Catullus poems that took place after the date that Jerome had set for the poet's death [16. 621f.; 18. 37–39].

E. CHRONOLOGICAL PROBLEMS IN MODERN RESEARCH

Chronological tables with dates regarding Latin literature, as so frequently found in literary histories [5; 15], are the result of a lengthy process, in the course of which not only reliable, but also uncertain dates have been elicited and transmitted; as a result, questions relating to the biography of an author, the date of a work's origin of, and the chronology of different works are still the subject of academic debate. Within M. von Albrecht's frequently republished history of Roman literature, the section 'Life and Dates' takes up a considerable share of the similarly structured chapters for each author.

Special studies of problems of dating for Roman authors, a mainstay of especially the second half of 19th cent. research [35; 13], are still being written; an entire monograph is still dedicated to even such a well researched field as Cicero's chronology [26].

To provide just a few examples of controversial problems with dating: one of the most discussed topics within the research on Lucilius is the determination of the satirist's age, especially his date of birth [11. 71–74; 19]. Also, the date of origin of Lucretius' didactic poem has been the topic of a recent study [21]. A much debated complex of problems concerns the date of origin of Claudian's mythological epic *De raptu Proserpinae* [22. 12–14]. In view of the uncertainties, the following postulates with respect to chronological problems in Latin literature remain as valid as ever: transmitted dates have to be critically assessed; they have to be analysed for contradictions and, if necessary, corrected; missing dates have to be approximately reconstructed from a combination of various records and sources (*Terminus ante/post quem*), sometimes with a certain range of possibility. The closer the insight into the genesis of the chronological representation of Latin literature, the more one's scepticism grows vis-à-vis too great a confidence in the reliability of the elicited and transmitted dates. In many cases, it would be quite justifiable to indicate dates with a question mark, thereby highlighting fragmentary transmission and other contradictions.

→ Chronicles; → Hieronymus II (Roman); → Suetonius [2] S. Tranquillus, C.; → Varro [2] V. Terentius, M. (Reatinus);

→ LITERARY CRITICISM

SOURCES: 1 CIL 6, 32323 (= ILS 5050) 2 R. HELM (ed.), Eusebius, Werke, Vol. 7., GCS 47, ²1956 3 PETRARCA, De viris illustribus, G. MARTELLOTTI (ed.), 1964 4 B. L. ULLMAN (ed.), Sicconis Polentoni Scriptorum illustrium Latinae linguae libri XVIII, 1928

LITERATURE: 5 ALBRECHT, 1457ff. 6 K. ARNOLD, De viris illustribus. Aus den Anfängen der humanistischen Literaturgeschichtsschreibung..., in: Humanistica Lovaniensia 42, 1993, 52–70 7 B. AXELSON, Ein drittes Werk des Firmicus Maternus? Zur Kritik der philologischen Identifizierungsmethode, 1937 8 G. BILLANOVICH, Un nuovo esempio delle scoperte e delle letture del Petrarca, L''Eusebio- Girolamo Pseudo Prospero', 1954 (notes in Petrarch's copy published on pp. 26–56) 9 R. BLUM, Die Literaturverzeichnung im Altertum und Mittelalter, 1983 10 W. BRAXTON Ross Jr., Giovanni Colonna, Historian at Avignon, Speculum 45, 1970 11 J. CHRISTES, Lucilius senex – vetus historia – Epilog zu XXVI–XXX, in: Philologus 142, 1998, 71–79 12 H. DAHLMANN, Studien zu Varro De poetis, 1963 (= AAWM 10, 1962, 557–676) 13 J. DÜRR, Das Leben Juvenals, Gymnasium-Programm, Ulm 1888 14 M. FUHRMANN, Die Geschichte der Literaturgeschichtsschreibung von den Anfängen bis zum 19. Jahrhundert., in: B. CERQUIGLINI, H. U. GUMBRECHT (eds.), Der Diskurs der Literatur- und Sprachhistorie, 1983, 49–72 15 F. GRAF (ed.), Einleitung in die lateinische Philologie, 1997 (as supplement: Synopse der römischen Literatur) 16 A. GRAFTON, Joseph Scaliger. A Study in the History of Classical Scholarship, II Historical Chronology, 1993 17 F. GREWING, Martial, Book VI, 1997, 459–464 18 R. HELM, Hieronymus' Zusätze in Eusebius' Chronik und ihr Wert für die Literaturgeschichte (= Philologus, Supplemental Vol. 21,2), 1929 19 G. HERBERT-BROWN, Jerome's Dates for Gaius Lucilius, satyrarum scriptor, in: CQ 49, 1999, 535–543 20 N. HOLZBERG, Ovid. Dichter und Werk, 1997, 31–37 21 G. O. HUTCHINSON, The Date of De rerum natura, in: CQ 51, 2001, 150–162 22 T. KELLNER, Die Göttergestalten in Claudians De raptu Proserpinae, 1997 23 M. LAARMANN, Art. Walter Burley, LMA VIII, 1999, 1994f. 24 P. LEHMANN, Literaturgeschichte im Mittelalter, in: Erforschung des Mittelalters, Band. 1, 1941 (originally 1912), 82–113 25 O. LEUZE, Das synchronistische Kapitel des Gellius (Noct. Att. XVII 21), in: RhM 66, 1911, 237–274 26 NINO MARINONE, Cronologia ciceroniana, 1997 27 W. McCUAIG, The Fasti Capitolini and the Study of Roman Chronology in the Sixteenth Century, in: Athenaeum 79, 1991, 141–159 28 TH. MOMMSEN, Die Chronologie der Briefe Frontos, in: Hermes 8, 1874, 198–216 (= Schriften IV, 469–86) 29 K. SALLMANN, M. CORNELIUS Fronto, in: HLL 4, 1997, 283f. 30 SCHANZ/ HOSIUS, Vol. 1, 104–107 31 E. A. SCHMIDT, Catull, 1985, 11–15, 53f. 32 P. L. SCHMIDT, Das Compendiloquium des Johannes Vallensis – die erste mittelalterliche

Geschichte der antiken Literatur?, in: D. H. GREEN, L. P. JOHNSON, D. WUTTKE (eds.), From Wolfram and Petrarch to Goethe and Grass. Studies in honour of Leonard Forster, 1982, 109–123 (= Traditio Latinitatis, 2000, 247–258) 33 Id., C. SUETONIUS Tranquillus (Literarhistorische Schriften), in: HLL 4, 1997, 27–44 34 S. SCHULER, Excerptoris morem gerere. Zur Kompilation und Rezeption klassisch-lateinischer Dichter im Speculum historiale des Vinzenz von Beauvais, in: FMS 29, 1995, 312–348 35 L. SCHWABE, Quaestionum Catullianarum liber I: De vita Catulli, de personis Catullianis, de temporibus carminum Catullianorum, Gießen 1862 36 C. SIGONIUS, Regum, consulum, dictatorum ac censorum Romanorum Fasti, Modena 1550 37 W. SPEYER, Italienische Humanisten als Kritiker der Echtheit antiker und christlicher Literatur (= AAWM 3), 1993, 16f. 38 D. R. STUART, Biographical Criticism of Vergil since the Renaissance, in: Studies in Philology 19, 1922, 1–30 39 H. TRÄNKLE, Entstehungszeit und Verfasserschaft des Corpus Priapeorum, in: ZPE 124, 1999, 145–156 40 E. WOYTEK, Sprach- und Kontextbeobachtung im Dienste der Prioritätsbestimmung bei Plautus, in: WS 114, 2001, 119–142 41 O. ZWIERLEIN, Prolegomena zu einer kritischen Ausgabe der Tragödien Senecas, 1983, 233–248.   THOMAS A. SCHMITZ

Church see → THEOLOGY AND THE CHRISTIAN CHURCH

Church history see → PATRISTIC THEOLOGY/PATRISTICS

Ciceronianism
A. THE TERM AND ITS MEANING [8] B. HISTORY [7; 9]

A. THE TERM AND ITS MEANING [8]
The term Ciceronianism was coined in the 19th cent. as a term for a Renaissance tendency to use the linguistic form and substance of Cicero's (106–43 BC) writings. The suffix -ism was added to Ciceronianus ('a supporter of Cicero'). The term now means 'something fashioned, in linguistic form and in philosophical content, in imitation of Cicero'. It is also an expression for a classicistic pattern of behaviour. The originator of the term is unknown; it gained currency through the Storia del Ciceronianismo of R. Sabbadini (1886). While the term Ciceronianism is free of any connotation implying a value judgement, the noun Ciceronianus, from which it was derived and which was itself commonly used in the Renaissance, could have either the negative sense of a narrow and pedantic imitation, or be positive in the sense of a free and creative imitation. It was more frequently used in this positive sense.

Ciceronianism in the Renaissance had an antecedent in Antiquity that is relevant to the substance of the term. Quintilian, the Roman teacher of rhetoric in the early Imperial period (c. 35–c. 100), argued in his Institutio oratoria (Rhetorical Training) for the classicity of Cicero's works by virtue of their linguistic form and the material to which they gave expression. From Cicero's work he gleaned the ideal of the perfectus orator, the accomplished orator, who was both an orator and philosopher in one. Thus, the highest form of education is a marriage of *eloquentia* ('eloquence') and *sapientia* ('wisdom'), as Cicero had called for. This ideal of Cicero did not fail to have an effect on the Christian concept of education. Thus the Church Father Jerome (*c.* 345–419) was to hear God's reproach in a dream (Epist. 22,30): 'Ciceronianus es, non Christianus' ('You are a Ciceronian, not a Christian'). In his work *De doctrina christiana* ('On Christian Teaching') Augustine (354–430), in particular, articulated Cicero's significance for the Christian tradition. He not only related Cicero's teaching on eloquence to Christian preaching but also acknowledged in Cicero's philosophy a relevant pagan precursor of Christian 'wisdom'. While Ciceronian 'wisdom' retained its appeal in the Middle Ages, Ciceronian language held no privileged position in medieval Latin. Medieval Latin became the repository of the entire Latin linguistic tradition. No distinction was drawn between ancient Christian and ancient profane authors. Moreover, semasiological and lexical innovations were common. Scholastic Latin, in particular, is characterised by such innovations. The sentence structure was simple and frequently reinforced in prose by rhyme. In syntax and morphology colloquial language regularly prevailed. Occasional attempts to correct this trend by recourse to Classical forms had no lasting effect (Servatus Lupus, 9th cent.; Gerbert of Aurillac/Silvester II, *c.* 940–1003; Bernhard of Chartres, *c.* 1100 – *c.* 1160; Peter of Blois, died *c.* 1200) [6].

Change arrived with the all-encompassing Classicism of the Renaissance. The Ciceronian ideal of education, as envisaged by Quintilian, established itself on a wide front. Ciceronianism in the early modern period was never an educational ideal of purely linguistic form but received its special quality in the theory of the period through an educational process combining linguistic form with philosophical content, even if, in practice, the linguistic formal aspect frequently managed to emancipate itself. In principle, the Ciceronianism of the early modern period is nothing but the dominant form of the *studia humanitatis*. Typical of its theoretical claim are titles of works such as *Oratio de studiis philosophiae et eloquentiae coniungendis* (Oration on the Necessity of Joining Philosophy and Eloquence; P. de la Ramée/ Ramus, 1546) and *De philosophiae et eloquentiae coniunctione* (On Combining Philosophy and Eloquence; M.A. Muret, 1557). It was in this same sense that Landino (1424–1504) programmatically formulated Ciceronianism in the preface to Cicero's *Tusculanae disputationes* [5]: *Perfectissima eloquentia existimanda est, quae a sapientiae studio non sit seiuncta, sed et bene vivendi et bene loquendi simul rationem habeat* ('Perfect eloquence has to be considered as that which is not distinct from the pursuit of wisdom but takes into consideration at the same time both living well and speaking well'). Thus, Cicero's 'wisdom', especially from *De officiis* ('On Duty'), *Tusculanae disputationes* ('Tusculan Disputations') and *De finibus*

bonorum et malorum ('On the Ends of Good and Evil') was acquired either as a (usually disguised) alternative to Christian education or as its extension and amplification in the Augustinian sense of an intellectual relationship between pagan Ciceronian philosophy and Christianity. With eloquence, emphasis was put on the imitation of vocabulary, figurative expression and tropes (*ornatus*), elaborate sentence construction (*compositio*) in complex sentences (periods), sentence rhythm (*numerus, numerositas*), propriety of diction (*latinitas*), 'clarity' (*perspicuitas*), the 'aptness' (*aptum*) of content, context and 'elegance' (*elegantia*). In the process, the focus was generally on Cicero's linguistic form, which was removed from the style of ancient Asianism (rich in figurative expression, tropes and rhythms) that Cicero had indeed cultivated in his early works but later modified in favour of the less artificial Atticist writing style. As a consequence of Renaissance interest in Cicero's linguistic style, medieval Latin came to be thought of as a barbaric form of Latin to be renounced both in theory and in practice. Medieval Latin has still not recovered today from this denunciation by Ciceronians, especially in the anti-barbaric literature (L. Valla, 1407–1457, *Elegantiarum linguae Latinae libri VI*, (Six Books of Refinements of the Latin Language),1440, ed. princeps 1471; Hadrian/Adriano Castello, *c.* 1458 until after 1517, *De sermone Latino et modis latine loquendi*, On Latin Speech and Ways of Speaking Latin, 1505). Its reputation does not correspond to its actual quality. Because it gave language a philosophically justified foundation, Ciceronianism became in the early modern period an international stylistic ideal that seemed best suited to the various needs of such different forms of linguistic discourse as poetry, courtly patterns of speech, teaching in schools and fields of knowledge like poetics, philosophy, theology and rhetoric.

B. History [7; 9]

Ciceronianism has its origins in Italy in the first half of the 15th cent. After becoming fashionable there in the second half of the century, it developed into an international stylistic ideal, especially in France, Germany and England. Ciceronianism, however, was not a homogeneous phenomenon. There were vigorous struggles concerning various points that concealed in their polemic what Ciceronians shared in common. The cause of conflict was the degree of Ciceronian imitation. Those in the radical camp of (orthodox, strict purist, fundamental) Ciceronianism were mocked as *simii Ciceronis* ('apes/mimics of Cicero') (according to A. Poliziano) by their adversaries. There was also a moderate (free, liberal) Ciceronianism, frequently termed anti-Ciceronianism. Radical Ciceronianism was interested only in Cicero's language (P. Cortesi, 1465–1510 [2]; P. Bembo, 1470–1547 [1]; G. Budé/Budaeus, 1467/68–1540; E. Dolet, 1509–1546 [3]). It was therefore focused on the systematic collection of Ciceronian vocabulary. Such collections had developed into such a mania by around 1500 that Erasmus of Rotterdam, in his *Ciceronianus* (1528) made fun of an invented author, a radical Ciceronian [4. 17f.]. The most important foundation for recording Ciceronian language was laid by M. Nizolio in his *Observationes in Ciceronem* (1535), later published under the titles *Thesaurus Ciceronianus* and *Lexicon Ciceronianum*. C. Estienne published a *Thesaurus M. Tullii Ciceronis* in Paris in 1556. Because of its rigorous concentration on Cicero, orthodox Ciceronianism was often latently anti-Christian. Moderate Ciceronianism was more open. Thus, for example, A. Poliziano (1454–1494), in a dispute with P. Cortesi [2], advocated imitating authors from the early Imperial period especially Seneca and Tacitus, because they first created the opportunity for individual style. Petrarch's bee image (fam. 1,8; drawing on Seneca ep. 84,3f.; 16,7: bees produce something new and unique, honey, from the nectar of many different flowers) refers in this way to productive → IMITATIO. German Humanists, in particular, argued with determination and effectively for a free Ciceronianism, because they held the view that the modern Christian world could not be comprehended just using the linguistic and intellectual categories of Cicero. Opinion shapers were Erasmus of Rotterdam (c. 1469–1546) in his satirical dialogue *Ciceronianus: Sive de optimo dicendi genere* (*Ciceronianus: or On the Best Form of Speaking*) [4]. This dialogue is structured in individual sections in keeping with the treatise *Lexiphanes* of the Greek satirist Lucian of Samosata (c. 120–c. 180). Taking aim at the rigid Greek Atticism that gave recognition only to the linguistic elements of Classical Attic literature in the pre-Christian 5th and 4th cents., Erasmus argued thus: Radical Ciceronianism offends against a fundamental principle of style, that of the *aptum*, because strict Ciceronian style, including its vocabulary, is suited only to old Ciceronian-pagan material, not to Christian, and thus modern thought. In a world that has become Christian there is no room for strict Ciceronianism; and thus restricting oneself to using Ciceronian vocabulary is particularly nonsensical.

The reformist pedagogue Philipp Melanchthon (1497–1560) used a similar line of argument in his *Elementa Rhetorices* (1532): close imitation of Cicero is impossible, for 'alia forma nunc est imperii, religio alia est quam Ciceronis temporibus. Quare propter rerum novitatem interdum verbis novis uti convenit' ('There is now another form of empire, another form of religion than in Cicero's time. It is therefore permitted, because of the newness of the situation, to use new words occasionally'. *Elementa Rhetorices libri duo*, 1532, fol. EGr). When however P. de la Ramée (Ramus) with his *Ciceronianus* (1577) became involved in the dispute over the correct form of Ciceronianism, in the same vein as Erasmus, Ciceronianism had passed its zenith. Mannerism, with its highly artificial stylization of heaping up figurative expressions and tropes (in the manner of ancient Asianism) and Tacitism, with the reception of forms of speech from Tacitus, had replaced the *Querel-les ciceroniennes*. → TACITISM, in particular, developed, in the manner of an ancient history of style, into a determined anti-Ciceronianism. It was called Lipsianism after its passionate supporter, J. Lipsius (1547–1606). The relevance of this Tacitism was based on the relationship between the absolutism of the Roman Imperial period and that of the early modern period. Tacitism, however, was short-lived, because Latin was everywhere being pushed aside by national languages. Ciceronianism retained a strong footing in schools and universities but, as a result, developed into an exclusively formalistic language phenomenon. It underwent a late flowering once again, with a strong anti-Tacitus and anti-Seneca emphasis, in schools and universities in the second half of the 19th cent. when it, together with the language of Caesar, became the linguistic norm, that even into the present has had no small impact on the way that Latin language and style are taught to university students, as demonstrated by the indestructible H. Menge and his *Repetitorium der lateinischen Syntax und Stilistik* (Repository of Latin Syntax and Stylistics) ([10]1914, [11]1953).

→ Cicero

→ ANCIENT LANGUAGES, TEACHING OF; → RHETORIC

SOURCES 1 P. BEMBO,Letter: De imitatione (1513) to G. Pico della Mirandola (Text: Le Epistole De imitatione di G. Pico della Mirandola e di P. Bembo (ed.) G. Santangelo, 1954, 46. Partial translation: A. Buck, Humanismus: seine europäische Entwicklung in Dokumenten und Darstellungen, 1987, 206f.; Eng.: Scott, Controversies over the Imitation of Cicero in the Renaissance: With Translations of Letters between Pietro Bembo and Gianfrancesco Pico, On Imitation; and a translation of Desiderius Erasmus, the Ciceronian (Ciceronianus) 1991, 1910) 2 P. CORTESI, Brief über die literarische Nachahmung (n. d.) des A. Poliziano an P. Cortesi, Text and German translation: E. Garin, Geschichte und Dokumente der abendländischen Pädagogik, Vol. 2: Humanismus, Quellenauswahl für die deutsche. Ausgabe von E. Keßler, 1966, 246–248 (German translation: Die Kultur des Humanismus. Reden, Briefe, Traktate, Gespräche von Petrarca bis Kepler (ed.) N. Mout, 1998, 42f.) 3 E. DOLET: Dialogus de imitatione Ciceroniana, Lyon 1535 4 ERASMUS VON ROTTERDAM, Ausgewählte Schriften,Vol. 7 (ed.) W. Welzig, translation by Th. Payr, 1972, 1–355 (C. R. THOMPSON (ed.), Literary and Educational Writings. vol. 6, in: The Collected Works of Erasmus, 1974) 5 C. LANDINO, Scritti critici e teorici, R. CARDINI (ed.), vol. 1, 1974, 5–15

LITERATURE: 6 E. NORDEN, Die antike Kunstprosa, vol. 2, [2]1909, 699–719 7 TH. PAYR, German introduction to: Erasmus von Rotterdam, vol. 7, W. WELZIG, ed., German translation by TH. PAYR, 1972, XXXV–XLII 8 F. TATEO, 'Ciceronianismus,' in: Historisches Wörterbuch der Rhetorik 2, 1994, 225–229 9 Id., B. TEUBER, R. E. SCHADE, 'Ciceronianismus,' in: Historisches Wörterbuch der Rhetorik 2, 1994, 230–247

ADDITIONAL BIBLIOGRAPHY: C. MOUCHEL, Cicéron et Sénèque dans la rhétorique de la Renaissance, 1990; D. MARSH, The quattrocento Dialogue: Classical Tradition and Humanist Innovation, 1980. MANFRED LANDFESTER

Circus see→ STADIUM

Citizen
A. ANTIQUITY   B. MIDDLE AGES
C. ARISTOTELIAN AND ROMAN TRADITION
D. CITIZENS AND CITIES IN THE HOLY ROMAN EM-
PIRE   E. 19TH AND 20TH CENT.

A. ANTIQUITY
In Greek as well as in Roman Antiquity, the concept of citizenship (Greek *polítes*, Lat. *civis*) had a dual dimension: on the one hand, as citizen of a town or city, and on the other, as a citizen of the state, because a city state comprised both town and country (regarding the *civis Romanus*: Dig. 1,5,17; Dig. 50,1,1; Cod. Iust. 10,40,7). This is where the modern understanding of citizenship, predominantly in political and legal terms, but also in social, cultural, and economic ones, as well) has its roots and has led to various definitions, in terms of content, associated with the development of cities, states and their respective constitutions. In the Greek understanding of the term, 'citizen, defined in simple terms, is someone who can participate in judging and in governing.' (Aristot. Pol. 1275 a 23). For the Romans as well, it was participation in the government of a city that turned a mere resident into a citizen. This close association with political participation can be seen as a constant element in the development of the concept of citizenship. In Rome, the legal status of the *civis* was defined in accordance with the *ius civile*. Hence, the main elements of citizenship, apart from the obligations to pay taxes and to perform military service, were the *ius suffragii* (right to vote in the citizens' assembly), the *ius provocationis* (right to appeal to the citizens' assembly against capital punishment), and also the *ius honorarium* (eligibility for publice offices) and legal protection [12]. Only the *pater familias* enjoyed the full legal capacity of a *civis Romanus*. Citizenship was acquired by birth, award, adoption (Cod. Iust. 10,40,7; Dig. 50,1,1), and sometimes by treaty. In line with the expansion of Roman power and the subjugation of foreign peoples in the 3rd cent. BC, the *ius gentium* as the law governing aliens was developed alongside Rome's *ius civile*. The necessary legal assimilation of the *peregrini* (foreigners) to the legal status of the Roman citizen added a further dimension to citizenship: the rights enjoyed by the citizens of the city of Rome became extended to the Roman state; then, in the imperial age they further expanded into the *imperium Romanum*. With the *constitutio Antoniniana*, all free inhabitants of the empire, with the exception of the *dediticii* (those who had surrendered unconditionally to Rome), became Roman citizens, and Roman law thus became the standard law of the Roman empire [19. 91]. Isidore's general definition of citizenship (Etymologiae 9,4,2) was: *cives vocati, quod in unum coeuntes vivant* ... ('they are called citizens because they live coming together into one'). The equal legal status for all citizens of the state has been a steadily developing tendency, extending into modern times, towards a state without class distinctions. The Christian religion was incompatible with the Roman concept of citizenship; however, the term *civis* was adopted by the Church Fathers in their notion of the citizen of earth, as opposed to the *civis caeli*. It was also used to describe the members of Augustine's *Civitas dei* [10. 544].

B. MIDDLE AGES
In the Early Middle Ages, the concept *civis Romanus* of Late Antiquity only appears in reference to freedmen [7. 98]. *Civis* refers to any fellow town dweller – *communiter vivens*, translated into German as *geburo*. Cumulative or alternative words found in the High Middle Ages are *burger, civis*, and *burgensis*, depending on chancery style and regional origin. In the 13th cent., *burgensis*, compared with *civis*, had a 'psychologically induced added linguistic value' [17. 120], but at the same time indicating a different legal implication. The adoption of *civis* into the language of official documents highlights the change towards its becoming a legal concept associated with the acceptance of the Roman *ius civile* as 'civil law', which came later [7. 35, 100]. The legal concept of the citizen is understood in reference to a medieval town, which in turn was legally defined by its immunity, affirmations of protection by the overlord, privileges, *coniuratio* and incorporation. Legally essential elements in the concept *citizen*, which varied with region and time, were freehold property, the payment of a fee, and the swearing of an oath of loyalty 'as an oath of initiation added to the oath sworn by all citizens, from which it took its legal validity' [3. 117; 5]. From this followed the clearly defined legal status of the citizen of a town or city, involving compulsory military service, tax liability, right of inheritance and freedom of movement. Citizenship was characterized, in particular, by judicial legal protection, the free and equal legal status for all citizens and, most of all, by the citizen's participation and share in the political rights of the town or city. Although the level of political participation was not the same in all medieval cities, it still showed a direct correspondence to Aristotle's definition of a citizen (Pol. 1275 a 23). Elements of the rights of medieval citizens, conveyed through the corporate structure, should not, however, be seen as the result of the reception of ancient concepts of citizenship; rather, they are merely evidence of partial structural identity and functional equivalents. From the late 14th cent. on, however, the translation of Aristotle's *Politics* by William of Moerbeke (late 13th cent.) enabled the *scientia politica* to apply or adapt Aristotelian political theories regarding *civis* and *civitas* to the medieval city.

C. ARISTOTELIAN AND ROMAN TRADITION
The city or town was the preferred subject in the medieval interpretation of Aristotelian politics. Although both the Greek *polítes* and the *civis Romanus* were landowners, whereas the citizens of medieval

towns were predominantly merchants and craftsmen [16. 676], these differences were either not taken into account or reinterpreted [13. 122]. The class distinctions, as well as the political and legal demarcation between citizens and subjects (*cives et subditi*), contradicted the Aristotelian notion of citizens in the polity as a community of free men equal to each other. In accordance with the various Aristotelian constitutions and criteria, the political tracts of the 14th and 15th cents. were, for example, able to bar craftsmen and tradesmen from access to political participation in the government of the city, to restrict the definition of citizenship exclusively to the nobility, or to consider only the *principes* as *cives*. Conversely, they might expand the definition of citizenry to include craftsmen and merchants, whom Aristotle had excluded from his definition of citizenship; or they might equate day labourers and wage workers with Aristotle's category of slaves [9. 15]. Ultimately, the classification according to the criteria of class was only possible contrary to or outside Aristotelian concepts [14. 48f.]. However, Aristotle's narrow requirement for citizenship, that each citizen should be capable of governing, though commented upon, was not taken up as a political demand. Nevertheless, Johann von Soest did attempt to transcend Aristotle and to link the *animal politicum* to the concept of *civis*, interpreting *vivere civiliter* to include ethical and Christian postulates within the definition of a city of free citizens [15. 15ff., 63]. Also, Aristotle's *Politics*, which was used throughout the period as a reference in studies on politics [13. 125ff.], permitted one to apply a broader definition of citizen to cities, as well as to the empire as a whole with its gradual differentiation of classes (*species civium*) and, at the same time, retain Aristotle's criterion of participation in government (*civis simpliciter, civis secundum quid, civis subjectus*) [14. 53]. For this, Althusius referred directly to the 'Romana libertas, consistens in juri civitatis Romanae' (Roman liberty consisting in the right of Roman citizenship) [4. 202], by carefully listing and explaining the private and political status rights of the *plenus civis Romanus* (full Roman citizen; *Politica*, 3. ed., Herbornae Nassoviorum 1614, cap. 5 n. 4, reprint 1932, 40). The result was a division of Aristotle's political concept of citizen into those enjoying political rights and those in a state of submission. The opposites *civis – subditus*, *civitas – respublica* and participation – submission (manorial and seignorial rule) [13. 106] characterized this division. Bodin used this relationship between submission and sovereignty in his definition of the citizen as a subject (*civis urbanus* or *bourgeois*), in direct contradiction to Aristotle's definition of citizen (Bodin, *Six livres de la République*, Paris 1583, Bk.I, chap. 6, 77) [16. 678].

D. CITIZENS AND CITIES IN THE HOLY ROMAN EMPIRE

The subsidiary validity of the *ius commune* in the 'Holy Roman Empire' (→ SACRUM IMPERII ROMANUM)

gave immediate efficacy to the language of legal codification within the empire. Bartolus' formula *civitas superiorem non recognoscens* (a city recognizes no overlord), expanded by him to the statement *civitas sibi princeps* (a city is its own ruler), could also be used to reach decisions in the question of imperial immediacy or intermediacy [15. 150, 175]. The Aristotelians adhered to the criterion of participation, thus recognizing as *cives imperii* (imperial citizens) only the representatives of the estates present at the imperial diets, including the *civitates imperiales liberae* (free imperial cities) [2. 100–101]. Pufendorf countered the resulting expansion of the subject class within the empire with the historical argument that Aristotle's criterion of participation applied only to the citizens of the Attic *polis* [16. 681]. On the other had, the estates of the empire were also defined as subjects, and yet referred to as *civis*. The right to political participation thus receded: *Civis est persona sui juris* (a citizen is an independent person. J. J. MÜLLER, *Institutiones politicae*, Jena, ²1705, 150) [4. 202]. *Civitas* represented a neutral legal validity for the citizens: ... *nomen civitatis accipitur pro coetu et multitudine civium iisdem legibus et moribus viventium* (the word citizenry stands for an assembly and large number of citizens living under the same laws and customs. PH. KNIPSCHILD, *De juribus et privilegiis civitatum imperialium*, Argentorati, ³1740,Bk. I, chap. 1, n. 21), with reference to Cicero (*Somnium Scipionis* and rep. 1,25,39). The Aristotelian postulate of political participation as part of the definition of citizenship was not thereby excluded and could be reactivated.

E. 19TH AND 20TH CENT.

The modern debate concerning the definition of citizenship still has as its basic prerequisite the Aristotelian postulate of political participation, which was given new dynamism by the French Revolution. Kant reflected on the importance of this event for the definition of citizenship from an emancipatory point of view: *welcher das Stimmrecht in dieser Gesetzgebung hat, heißt ein Bürger (citoyen, das ist Staatsbürger, nicht Stadtbürger, bourgeois). Die dazu erforderliche Qualität ist ... die einzige: daß er sein eigener Herr (sui juris) sei, mithin irgendein Eigentum habe ... folglich, daß er niemanden als dem gemeinen Wesen ... diene,in: Über den Gemeinspruch: Das mag in der Theorie richtig sein, taugt aber nicht für die Praxis* ('...whoever has the right to vote in this making of laws is called a citizen (*citoyen*, i.e. citizen of the state, not *bourgeois*, i.e. citizen of a city). This only requires a single quality: that he be his only master (*sui juris*), i.e. own some property .... and, consequently, that he serve none other but the commonwealth', in: *Werke* VI, 378f. ed. CASSIRER). Hegel, too, who defined human rights as the rights of the citizen, used the ancient examples from the Attic *polis* and the declining years of the Roman Republic as illustrations for his thoughts on the political *citoyen* (as opposed to the *bourgeois*, who only follows his own private interests) within 'civil society' [16. 707]. In the

19th cent., the historical explanation of the notion of citizenship and adding to its meaning became a preoccupation. Bluntschli saw the 'bourgeoisie' as the *Verbindungsglied aus dem Mittelalter zur neuen Zeit. Das heutige Staatsbürgerthum wurzelt vorzüglich in dem Begriffe der mittelalterlichen Stadtbürgerschaft* ('link from the Middle Ages to modern times. The modern concept of a citizen of the state is excellently rooted in that of the citizenry of the medieval city', [1. 302]). The freedom of the medieval city, alongside a liberal defence against the state, reappears mainly in the form of self-determination and municipal self-government, i.e. as political participation in the public life of the city or state. This is entirely in line with Aristotle's definition of citizenship. *Der demokratische Zug der neuen Zeit fand daher auch vornehmlich in den Städten den eifrigsten Anhang* ('The democratic tendency of the new era thus found its most ardent support predominantly in the cities', [1. 306]). The attempt to harmonize civil and political freedom, which had failed in the 19th cent., also implied, for the political movements of the 19th and 20th cents., the activation of ancient elements of citizenship, i.e. the certainty of the law in the sense of Roman law and Aristotelian political participation in government and legislation. [18. 93, 105]. Property and economic independence became the main criteria for the liberal citizen of the state, expressed by Max Weber as the contrast between the medieval *homo oeconomicus* and the *homo politicus* of Antiquity [20. 1022].

→ Aristoteles [6]; → Citizenship; → Civitas; → Constitutio Antoniniana; → Pater familias; → Polis

1 J. C. BLUNTSCHLI, Bürgerstand, in: BLUNTSCHLI/BRATER, Deutsches Staatswörterbuch, II, Stuttgart/Leipzig 1857, 300–307 2 W. BRAUNEDER, Civitas et Cives Sancti Romani Imperii, in: G. LINGELBACH et al. (eds.), Deutsches Recht zwischen Sachsenspiegel und Aufklärung, Festschrift für Rolf Lieberwirth, 1991, 95–117 3 G. DILCHER, Bürgerrecht und Stadtverfassung im europäischen Mittelalter, 1996 4 H. DREITZEL, Grundrechtskonzeptionen in der protestantischen Rechts- und Staatslehre im Zeitalter der Glaubenskämpfe, in: G. BIRTSCH (ed.), Grund- und Freiheitsrechte von der ständischen zur spätbürgerlichen Gesellschaft, 1987, 180–214 5 W. EBEL, Der Bürgereid als Geltungsgrund und Gestaltungsprinzip des deutschen mittelalterlichen Stadtrechts, 1958 6 J. F. GARDNER, Being a Roman Citizen, 1993 7 G. KÖBLER, Civis und Ius Civile im deutschen Frühmittelalter, 1965 8 R. KOSELLECK, K. SCHREINER (eds.), Bürgerschaft. Rezeption der Begrifflichkeit im hohen Mittelalter bis in das 19. Jahrhundert, 1994 9 Id., Einleitung: Von der alteuropäischen zur neuzeitlichen Bürgerschaft, in:Id., Bürgerschaft, 11–39 10 K. KROESCHELL, Bürger, in: Handwörterbuch zur Deutschen Rechtsgeschichte I, 1971, 543–553 11 E. LEVY, Libertas und Civitas, in: ZRG 78, 1961, 143–172 12 H. VOLKMANN, Bürgerrecht, LAW 1, 515f. 13 A. LÖTHER, Bürger-, Stadt- und Verfassungsbegriff in frühneuzeitlichen Kommentaren der Aristotelischen Politik, in: R. KOSELLECK, K. SCHREINER, Bürgerschaft, 90–128 14 U. MEIER, Burgerlich vereynung, Herrschende, beherrschte und mittlere Bürger in Politiktheorie, chronikalischer Überlieferung und städtischen Quellen des Spät-Mittelalters, in: R. KOSELLECK, K. SCHREINER, Bürger-

schaft, 43–89 15 Id., Mensch und Bürger. Die Stadt im Denken spätmittelalterlicher Theologen, Philosophen und Juristen, 1994 16 M. RIEDEL, B., Staatsbürger, Bürgertum, in: Geschichtliche Grundbegriffe, vol. 1, 1972, 672–725 17 R. SCHMIDT-WIEGAND, Burgensis/Bürger in: J. FLECKENSTEIN, K. STACKMANN (eds.), Über Bürger, Stadt und städtische Literatur im Spätmittelalter, 1980, 106–126 18 K. SCHREINER, Jura et libertates, in: H.-J. PUHLE (ed.), Bürger in der Gesellschaft der Neuzeit, 1991, 59–106 19 F. SCHULZ, Prinzipien des römischen Rechts, 1954 20 M. WEBER, Die nichtlegitime Herrschaft. Typologie der Städte, in: Wirtschaft und Gesellschaft, vol. II, 1964 21 P.-L. WEINACHT, Staatsbürger. Zur Geschichte und Kritik eines politischen Begriffs, in: Der Staat 8, 1969, 41–63 22 F. WIEACKER, Recht und Gesellschaft in der Spätantike, 1964. HEINZ MOHNHAUPT

Civilists

A. INTRODUCTION B. HISTORY C. SIGNIFICANCE D. WORKS E. INFLUENCE

A. INTRODUCTION

Roman law, to be precise, the *ius commune* (translated as *civil law*), which was prevalent on the European mainland and based on Roman canonical sources, played an important role alongside *common law* in England's legal system. It was practised by lawyers known as civilists, was taught at universities, and formed the basis of academic work. Owing to its connection with the Tudors and Stuarts, it was of particular importance in the 16th and 17th cents. for a number of important courts outside the royal courts of Westminster.

B. HISTORY

The earliest beginnings were in the 12th cent., at the time when people first began to study Roman and canon law at the English universities of Oxford and Cambridge. From then onwards for almost 600 years, until Blackstone became Professor of English Law in 1758, Roman law and, until the Reformation, canon law as well, were the only kinds of law taught at universities. The real history of civilists began around 1500. In about 1511 a group of jurists who were studying *civil law* and had obtained university degrees joined together to form a professional association, modeled on the *Inns of Court* of *common law*, with its headquarters near St. Paul's Church. The original core was formed by the *Advocates* or *Doctors of Law* of the ecclesiastical court of the *Court of Arches*. However, jurists educated in Roman *civil law*, who made up the staff of the *Admiralty Court*, also belonged to it almost from the start. After the Reformation *canon lawyers* disappeared as a class of their own. The courts of the Anglican Church still continued to apply traditional canon law, but all offices at the ecclesiastical courts were now accessible solely to civilists. In addition, in founding or reorganizing some courts important to him, Heny VIII needed the support of the civilists. The founding of *Regius Chairs* for *civil law* in Oxford and Cambridge in 1540 was of great significance. This measure served to create a replacement for the study of canon law but was also part of the Humanist agenda of fostering the study of ancient cultures. The first important holder of the chair at Oxford was Alberico Gentili (1552–1608), who subscribed to the *mos Italicus*. The first incumbent of the chair at Cambridge was Thomas Smith, who was greatly influenced by Humanism.

In 1568 the association of civilists moved into an imposing building called, like the association itself, *Doctors' Commons*. Shortly after the move, the *Court of Admiralty* and a few smaller ecclesiastical courts began to hold their meetings at *Doctors' Commons*. However, in contrast to the *Inns of Court,* the association of civilists never participated in educating new generations. This remained the task of the universities. There was initially a certain dependency on *Trinity Hall* in Cambridge. It was not until 1768 that the association was recognized as fully independent by *Royal Charter* as the *College of Doctors of Law exercent in the Ecclesiastical and Admiralty Courts*.

The civilists regarded themselves as a juristic elite equal in rank to the *Serjeants at law*. While it is true that in his time as *Chief Justice* Sir Edward Coke (1552–1634) had already tried to compete with them, it was not until 1857, during the course of 19th cent. legal reforms, that the secular courts became responsible for marital questions and matters relating to wills. In 1859 the civilists also lost their monopoly in matters for which the *Admiralty Courts* had been responsible. The last twenty six members of *Doctors' Commons* therefore decided in 1858, after a long period of decline, to disband the association. The building was sold and the library with its excellent collection of international legal literature dispersed.

C. SIGNIFICANCE

Civil law was applied by a large number of courts with far-reaching jurisdictions. The most significant of these courts were the Consistorial Court, responsible for matters relating to marriage and wills, and the *Court of Admiralty*, which passed judgment on matters of maritime law and international commerce. Until 1857 all wills drawn up in the archdiocese of London had been kept at *Doctors' Commons*. The general European law of *lex mercatoria* was adopted in England by a decision of the Admiralty. Arrangements unknown in *common law,* such as stocks and shares, insurances, bills of lading, etc. were dealt with here. The courts designated collectively as *Conciliar Courts* also included the *Privy Council, Star Chamber, Court of Requests, Court of High Commission, High Court of Chivalry, High Court of Delegates, Council of the North* and the *Council of Wales*. There were also the courts martial and the courts of the vice-chancellors of the two English universities of Oxford and Cambridge. The civilists were faithful servants of the king in public administration and diplomatic service, but they were excluded from major politics. Sometimes both types of

jurists served at the courts side by side, though many jurists had both qualifications. There were rarely more than twenty to twenty-five civilists in *Doctors' Commons* at the same time. Compared with the number of jurists practising *common law*, which was always about 400, this was not a very large number. Therefore, though they were in competition with the *Common Lawyers*, they were never really any threat to them.

D. WORKS

The list of civilists, who were important due primarily to their scholarly achievements, contains in a first group or, as Coquilette says, *generation* the following names: Christopher St. German (1457–1539), Thomas Smith (1513–1571), Alberico Gentili (1552–1608), William Fulbecke (1560–1603) and John Cowell (1554–1611). Smith, Gentili and Cowell were *Regius Professors*.

St. German was, to be sure, a *common lawyer*, who, however, with his discussion on the common features and differences between *civil law* and *common law* – the principal theme of this first generation – is regarded as the intellectual progenitor of the *civilists*. Fulbecke studied under Gentili at Oxford and became the most important of the civilists. Cowell emphasized more the similarities between the two legal systems and thus tried to introduce a course in *common law* at his university. The differences between *civil law* and *common law* played a particularly major role in the area of commercial law, where Thomas Ridley (1549–1629) represented *civil law* and Charles Molloy (1607–1690) *common law*.

Prominent among later generations of civilists were Arthur Duck (1580–1648), Richard Zouche (1590–1662), Thomas Wood (1661–1722), William Strahan and John Ayliffe (1676–1732). In his book *De usu et authoritate iuris civilis Romanorum in dominiis principum Christianorum*, written in 1653, Duck continued to follow Cowell's line. He was concerned with ' the common ideas of law and equity, shared by all European nations', though it was generally held that their roots lay in Roman law. Zouche, like Duck a pupil of Gentili's successor Budden, defended the jurisdiction of the *Admiralty* and the principles of the *ius inter gentes*. With Wood the influence of the modern law of nature in the style of Jean Domat began to assert itself and reached its pinnacle in Strahan's translation of Domat in 1722.

E. INFLUENCE

Civil law was also important for the development of English law in general. Particularly noteworthy is the contribution the civilists made in their writings on the formation of general juristic principles and methods of legal thinking as well as on the representation of law in scholarly systems. 'Method' means that the judge does not follow the *precedents* drafted in the *abridgements*, but subsumes the cases under abstract rules, suitable for representation in systematic jurisprudence and for teaching at universities. The idea that as *ius gentium* there must be generally accepted basic principles of justice was disseminated by the civilists and made useable by *common law*. The civilists were the founders of comparative law and international private law and, for this reason, of great significance for the development of commercial law and procedural law.

Among the *common lawyers* who were open to the influence of civilists, one of the most prominent was Francis Bacon. He was followed in the attempt to treat law as a rational science by Thomas Hobbes, John Seldon, Matthew Hales, John Holt, Lord Mansfield as well as Jeremy Bentham.

→ Great Britain; → Roman Law

1 C. T. Allmand, The Civil Lawyers, in: Profession, Vocation and Culture in Later Medieval England, C. H. Clough (ed.), 1982, 155–180   2 D. R. Coquillette, The Civilian Writers of Doctors' Commons (= Comparative Studies in Continental and Anglo-American Legal History, vol. 3), 1988; H. Coing, Das Schrifttum der englischen Civilians und die kontinentale Rechtsliteratur in der Zeit zwischen 1550 und 1800, in: Ius commune – Veröffentlichungen des Max-Planck-Instituts für europäische Rechtsgeschichte, vol. V, 1975, 1–55   3 N. Horn, Römisches Recht als gemeineuropäisches Recht bei Arthur Duck, in: Studien zur europäischen Rechtsgeschichte, W. Wilhelm (ed.), 1972, 170–180   4 B. Levack, The Civil Lawyers in England, 1603–1641, 1973   5 Id., The English Civil Lawyers 1500–1750, in: Lawyers in Early Modern Europe and America, W. Prest (ed.), 1981, 108–128   6 G. Squibb, Doctors' Commons, 1977   7 P. Stein, Continental Influences on English Legal Thought, 1600–1900, in: La formazione storica del diritto moderno in Europa, 1977, III 1105–1125   8 Id., Römisches Recht und Europa, 1997, 145–147.   KLAUS LUIG

Classical Archaeology
I. General   II. New Finds   III. Contextual Archaeology

I. General
A. Terminology   B. From the Beginnings until the Middle of the 18th Cent.   C. The Founder of Classical Archaeology: J. J. Winckelmann, his Contemporaries and Successors   D. The 19th Cent. and the Age of the Great Excavations   E. 20th Cent. F. Perspectives

A. Terminology
A peculiarity of the discipline is the absence of a generally accepted concept of Classical Archeology (CA), which in a good third of German-speaking universities is simply called Archaeology, either by way of obvious simplification or by way of conscious extension of the subject-matter, thereby sacrificing the aspect and claim of the 'Classical'. One of its most prominent research bodies, the → Deutsches Archäologisches Institut [20; 55; 89], was founded in Rome in 1829 as the *Istituto di corrispondenza archeologica*, the terms 'Ar-

chaeology' and CA being taken as synonymous as a matter of course. In a similar vein, F. A. Wolf in 1807 [112] understood 'the Archaeology of ancient art and technology' in the context of a discipline that did not hesitate to confine the very term Antiquity to the two peoples (i.e. the Greeks and Romans).

In any case, there is agreement to the present day that CA as a scholarly discipline is concerned with the material remains of Greek and Roman culture [101. 9–12], and more precisely: with that aspect of the ancient world 'that has material substance and is formed or structured by the human hand, and whose meaning finds expression in that form and structure' [82. 8]. 'It embraces the entire lived cultural context insofar as this is of a material nature and thus visibly perceptible' [3. 198]. The extent to which the attribute 'Classical' is used in these contexts as a term describing value or merely as a conventional means for describing a particular past culture, and the degree to which, out of a highly diverse legacy, only Classical art, i.e. the plastic arts of the Greeks and Romans, is declared as its real theme or its main task [7. 17; 91. 4], or whether its attention is directed towards the entire cultural complexity [3. 199], depends upon the individual research perspective or the generation or disciplinary tradition to which the author belongs: 'Each period has its own view of history (or archaeology)' [10. 796].

The investigation of its own history has therefore long been perceived as a legitimate and necessary task for CA. Its goals and methods are, in fact, to a large extent determined by its development as a discipline. In common with all humanistic disciplines dedicated to the understanding of history, CA has always directed its attention, not only to its object of research, but also to the insights, modes of thinking and interpretative methods that have been arrived at in the past – at the very least it has not entirely ignored them. Unlike the case of the natural sciences, the results obtained by past generations of researchers by no means always represent absolutely measurable and thus exactly determined values that can be seen either as still valid or obsolete and accordingly susceptible (or not) of being incorporated into research utilizing a new approach. Rather, these results of past research are themselves conditioned by a particular historical situation as regards intellectual and scholarly understanding, and are comprehensible only after appropriate assessment. Critical reconstruction of the continuous discourse of the last 500 years on monuments, their significance and their place in the larger picture lends new relevance and validity to the results of past research. On the other hand – e.g. in the field of chronology or in our knowledge of monuments – there are always new discoveries that in terms of topicality and reliability are the match of those produced by the natural sciences, and simply render older insights obsolete. As soon, however, as the endeavours of researchers go beyond the search for this kind of fact they are subject to historical qualification.

B. From the Beginnings until the Middle of the 18th Cent.

In almost all attempts to present an account of CA, and usually before any other aspect has been taken up, it has been regarded as essential to provide a survey of the discipline's historical development. There is today an abundant literature covering both the development of the study of ancient monuments from its first beginnings in Antiquity and in the Middle Ages (esp. in Rome itself) via the enthusiasm of the Renaissance for ancient objects to the scholarship of the 17th and 18th cents. and the history of the early journeys and emergence of the first European museums [19; 60; 63; 65; 92; 95; 115].

Whether the desire for 'archaeological' knowledge is directed towards the consolidation of one's cultural identity or towards establishing aesthetic paradigms for the plastic arts, the beginnings of archaeology may be discerned in Antiquity itself: Over a period of years the last king of Babylon, Nabonid (556–539 BC), successfully carried out excavations to discover documents from the time of the founder of the Akkadian empire [27]. Cimon had similar intentions in undertaking the supposedly successful rediscovery of the grave of Theseus on Scyros, reported by Plutarch (Cimon, ch. 8). The admiration of the Roman aristocracy for the plastic arts of classical Greece and the already extensive writings on art history in the context of Hellenistic scholarship are well-exploited themes of CA itself, and an essential precondition for our understanding of all 'post-Classical' art [54; 68].

The beginnings of CA may be discerned as early as the Middle Ages, e.g. in the 12th-cent. *Mirabilia urbis Romae* by the canon Benedict of St. Peter's, the oldest topographically organised treatment of that city's buildings and works of art. In subsequent centuries, too, Rome was always at the centre of the antiquarian and soon also scholarly interest that was stirring from the time of the Renaissance and of which Cola di Rienzo (1314–54) and Flavio Biondo (1392–1463) are usually regarded as the earliest representatives. Individual travellers such as the merchant Cyriacus of Ancona (1391–1455) acquired direct experience in Greece and the Aegean as well.

On 27th August 1515 Pope Leo X appointed the most noted artist of his time as prefect of all Roman antiquities: Raffaello Santi [31. 482]. In 1506 the → Laocoon group had been found in the *Domus Aurea*; it was immediately recognised by Giuliano da Sangallo and Michelangelo as the work mentioned by Pliny the Elder (HN XXXVI 37–38), and soon transferred by Pope Julius II to the Cortile del Belvedere in the Vatican, which had been converted into a museum. In 1511 in Venice Fra Giocondo was able to publish an emended edition of Vitruvius. In 1540 the French king François I sent the painter Primaticcio to Rome to buy antiquities and castings. At the same period Philip II of Spain charged his court painter Velázquez with drawing the statues in the Belvedere in Rome. Even these few selected names demonstrate how during the decades before and after the *sacco di Roma* of 1527 (the plundering of Rome by the troops of Charles V) artists of genius and inspired humanists, learned antiquarians and cultured spiritual and secular rulers, continually in competition and at the same time in closest association one with the other, were able to promote the objective of a revival of the ancient world. But this was scarcely an appropriate foundation for CA inH the sense of a historical discipline. And the part of Antiquity that formed the object of this interest, essentially sculpture and monumental architecture determined by the taste of the late Hellenistic and Roman Imperial periods, together with coins and gemstones, was a merely one section of the whole.

The separation between the plastic arts and scholarly research does not begin to emerge clearly until the Baroque Age. 'The first seething passion for rediscovered Antiquity is past' [88. 46]. Its place is taken by the endeavour to attain a systematic approach and a profound, encyclopaedic knowledge of the monuments. The beginnings of this process may be discerned around the middle of the 16th cent., for example in a Coburg codex containing drawings of antiquities arranged according to mythological criteria [33]. In the 17th cent. the word 'archaeology' emerges as a name for this branch of scholarship. Following ancient terminology, it is first used in *Miscellanea eruditae antiquitatis* by the physician and humanist Jacques Spon, published in 1685 [22]. *L'antiquité expliquée et représentée en figures* ('Antiquity explained and illustrated') by Bernard de Montfaucon (1655–1741), in ten volumes with some 40,000 illustrations on 1,200 plates (!), appeared in 1719, almost at the end of the period, and remained a standard work for many generations. At the same time, interest remained basically of an antiquarian and encyclopaedic nature. There was still no well-founded historical or stylistic differentiation within genres and in the appreciation of works of art.

This remains true of 18th cent. enthusiasm for art, which developed into a European passion for travel and collecting, concentrated on Italy and on Antiquity. This enthusiasm finds a particular focus in the British aristocratic phenomenon of the 'Grand Tour' [114], a cultural journey to Italy, often lasting several years and setting the seal on an individual's higher education, and giving rise in England to the emergence of impressive privately owned museums of sculpture (e.g. Holkham Hall 1734 [108]); at the same time the continental European version of the Grand Tour to Italy ('Kavalierstour') is accorded high status value, with the antiquities collections in Rome in particular achieving new levels of importance [63].

In this climate of general enthusiasm for Antiquity a specifically British philhellenism develops, which in 1732 culminates in the foundation of the → Society of Dilettanti. It was with the support of this society that in 1762 the first volume of the monumental *The Antiquities of Athens* by the architect Nicholas Revett and the painter James Stuart appeared (the second volume did not follow until 1787!), resulting from a three-year tour (1751–53) and to some extent not superseded to this day. Likewise in 1751 the Society commissioned Robert Wood's journey to the most important ruin sites of Syria (*The Ruins of Palmyra*, 1753; *The Ruins of Balbec otherwise Heliopolis*, 1757). In 1766 began the expedition of Richard Chandler, Nicholas Revett and William Pars to western Asia Minor, the results being published as early as 1769 in the large-format illustrated *Ionian Antiquities*.

C. THE FOUNDER OF CLASSICAL ARCHAEOLOGY: J. J. WINCKELMANN, HIS CONTEMPORARIES AND SUCCESSORS

The → CLASSICISM of the later 18th cent. is responsible for the emergence of CA as the study of Greek and Roman art. Its beginnings in Germany are marked by the figures of Lessing and above all Winckelmann, whose literary work was of decisive importance. Johann Joachim Winckelmann, born the son of a shoemaker on December 9, 1717 in Stendal and murdered on 8th June 1768 in Trieste, was able-even in his youth-to acquire a wide knowledge of ancient written sources by means of broad-based patronage and the extraordinary energy of the social climber. After his initial theological studies at Halle and a lengthy period as a private tutor, he entered the service of Count Bünau in Nöthnitz near Dresden in 1748 as a librarian. In the nearby capital he came to know, and apparently despise, contemporary art and artists. Having adopted the Roman Catholic faith in 1754, he went to Rome in 1755, and there in 1763 as 'Antiquario della camera apostolica' became the supervisor of antiquities in and around Rome [56; 62].

Even before his departure for Rome, in 1755 he published his *Gedanken über die Nachahmung der griechischen Werke in der Malerei und Bildhauerkunst* (*Reflections Concerning the Imitation of the Grecian Artists in Painting and Sculpture*), a work which largely if not exclusively aimed at the renewal of contemporary art and raised ancient Greek art to the status of an absolute standard. This work and the year of its appearance have justifiably been singled out as being epoch-making in German intellectual history; it shaped one of the central traditions of German CA, which since the beginning of the 19th cent. has considered Winckelmann its founder. [16].

Annual Winckelmann celebrations, initiated in 1840 by Otto Jahn in Kiel and since observed on his birthday in a scarcely interrupted tradition in almost all the more important centres of CA in Germany are a living token of the affection that has been and continues to be felt for its founding hero. It is significant that Christian Petersen, director of the library and teacher at the 'Gymnasium' in Hamburg, a city that was at that time entirely oriented towards overseas commerce, and where a university was not established until 1919, was able with his *Erinnerung an J. J. Winckelmanns Einfluß auf Literatur, Wissenschaft und Kunst* (Memoir of J. J. Winckelmann's influence on literature, science and art), given in public in 1842, only two years after Kiel, to introduce the same tradition over a period of some decades.

Winckelmann's original 'approach' is made clear by two quotations from his first book: after a long passage on the *Laocoon group* in the Belvedere at the Vatican he writes: *das wahre Gegenteil ist der gemeinste Geschmack der heutigen, sonderlich angehenden Künstler* ('Its true opposite is the most vulgar taste and strange antics of today's artists, especially the younger ones'). Some paragraphs previously one reads: *das allgemeine und vorzügliche Kennzeichen der griechischen Meisterstücke ist endlich eine edle Einfalt und stille Größe ... so zeigt der Ausdruck in den Figuren der Griechen bei allen Leidenschaften eine große und gesetzte Seele* ('The overall and excellent characteristic of the Greek masterpieces is in the final analysis their noble simplicity and quiet greatness... thus Greek figures, for all their passion, show in their expression a great and sober soul'). These words have time and again been seen as characteristic of Winckelmann's and German Classicism's image of the Greeks, and continue to exert their influence on German CA to this day. The juxtaposition of the terms 'simplicity' and 'greatness' may be rediscovered in only slightly altered form in Winckelmann's masterpiece, his *Geschichte der Kunst des Altertums* (*History of the Art of Antiquity*), whose first edition, completed in 1761, appeared in 1764. He says there: *durch die Einheit und Einfalt wird alle Schönheit erhaben ...: denn was in sich groß ist, wird, mit Einfalt ausgeführt, erhaben* ('Through unity and simplicity all beauty becomes sublime ... for what is great in itself, if executed with simplicity, becomes sublime'). And, although Winckelmann by his choice of title had now set himself the task of writing the 'history' of the art of Antiquity, he wanted this to be understood under that higher purpose programmatically expressed in the title of his first work: *meine Absicht ist, einen Versuch eines Lehrgebäudes zu liefern ... Das Wesen der Kunst ist ... der vornehmste Endzweck* ('My intention is to attempt the creation of a didactic edifice ... The essence of art is ... its most important goal').

In his study, *Das Griechenbild J. J. Winckelmanns* (J. J. Winckelmann's image of the Greeks) Fritz Blättner was able to show that the Greek world which arose out of Winckelmann's encounter with it was its observer's creation, one that enriched the study of Antiquity to an astonishing degree, but which was intended to be and in fact was more than that: 'A life-signifying image, i.e. religion' [10]. Egon Friedell (1878–1938), as perceptive as he was sardonic, wrote: 'He also had invented something: Greek man', significantly in the chapter [30 vol. II. 376] entitled 'Die Erfindung der Antike' ('The Invention of Antiquity') of his *Kulturgeschichte der Neuzeit* ('A Cultural History of the Modern Age').

In Winckelmann were fruitfully combined the two diverging tendencies embodied in the preoccupation with Antiquity: on the one hand the scholarly approach, on the other aesthetic-dogmatic interest. 'He was, as R. Pfeiffer put it, the creator of a neohellenism' [58. 19].

Quite apart from the classicistic impulse, which not least can be traced back to Winckelmann's views, a monument-orientated CA must ask itself: In front of which ancient monuments did Winkelmann [stand and] gain the knowledge upon which such a readily adopted 'doctrine' was based. When he wrote his treatise on the imitation of Greek works, which was seminal for him and for all his later writings, he did indeed possess a comprehensive knowledge of ancient writers, but of ancient monuments the ones he knew were for the most part the representations of Roman statues on old and contemporary engravings. So far as direct observation went, the Dresden collection of statues acquired by the Electors of Saxony between 1723 and 1736 was available to him only to a very restricted extent, however, since it was at that time housed in garden pavilions in a far from satisfying manner [51].

It was only during his years in Rome that Winckelmann was able to develop that knowledge of monuments that found expression in the Geschichte der Kunst des Altertums. But even these artefacts, with very few exceptions, originated from the Roman Imperial period, and were representatives of Roman Classicism; some of them were copies of Greek originals, some of them original Roman creations indebted only in a general sense to Greek classical art of the 5th and 4th cents. BC. The significance of the few precious Greek originals that had been found on Roman soil or had reached there by way of Venice during the 16th and 17th cents. was as yet unknown to Winckelmann: to him they were Etruscan works. Thus the only knowledge Winckelmann had of Greek Antiquity, which in his work became 'Classical', was through the distorting mirror of Roman Classicism. Moreover he often saw the statues in the form in which they had been completed according to the taste of the time. Archaeology is nevertheless beholden to Winckelmann for two important insights: first the realisation that those very antiquities he became acquainted with in Rome must be interpreted on the basis of Greek mythology; an axiom that often still applies today, even in those cases where we no longer view the statues as copies of Greek originals, as Winckelmann did, but as original Roman works [37]. More significant is the fact that Winckelmann introduced the concept of development, and thus of a sequence of separate stylistic periods, into the study of ancient art and art in general. In his Geschichte der Kunst he distinguished the 'archaic style', the 'high style', the 'elegant style', the 'imitative style' and finally the 'decline of art'. The element of all this that still applies is the introduction of the concept of development itself, which in the course of two cents., especially since the turn of the 20th cent., has inevitably undergone many transformations, until today it has become a quite different concept, no longer coloured by a classicistic entelechy.

CA as a research and teaching discipline has Classical Philology as its second root. Winckelmann's influence was as vital as anyone's, but he had neither been an academic teacher nor had pupils in the narrower sense. But the archaeologists who from the beginning of the 19th cent. filled the chairs that were gradually being established by universities for the new discipline, and who developed archaeology into the great edifice we see before us today, all began as students of classical philologists. In their scholarly practice, therefore, they were philologists as well as archaeologists. Christian Gottlob Heyne (1729–1812), from 1763 Professor of Eloquence at Göttingen, belonged among the first academics to comprehensively deal with ancient monuments in their lectures (Archäologie der Kunst des Altertums, insbesondere der Griechen und Römer (Archaeology of the Art of Antiquity, especially that of the Greeks and Romans, published as a book in 1767). His pupils included the translator of Homer Johann Heinrich Voß, the classical philologist Friedrich August Wolf, the brothers August Wilhelm and Friedrich Schlegel, the archaeologists Georg Zoega and Karl August Böttiger as well as Wilhelm von Humboldt. Beginning with Zoega (1759–1809), an unbroken tradition may be traced to many of today's academic teachers, e.g. via Friedrich Gottlob Welcker (1784–1868), whom Zoega had introduced to archaeology in Rome, via Heinrich Brunn (1822–1894), Adolf Furtwängler (1853–1907), Ludwig Curtius (1874–1954) and Ernst Buschor (1886–1961).

D. THE 19TH CENT. AND THE AGE OF THE GREAT EXCAVATIONS
Meanwhile, however, the stage of splitting up and differentiating Altertumswissenschaft (study of Antiquity), which for F. A. Wolf in his often-quoted Darstellung der Alterthumswissenschaft nach Begriff, Umfang, Zweck und Werth (Account of the study of Antiquity in terms of its concept, purpose and value) of 1807 was still a unified whole, had long been embarked upon. Wolf had concluded his account with a 24–point comprehensive 'survey of the elements of the study of Antiquity' [112], four of those points applying to archaeological matters in the narrower sense: 'XVIII. Introduction to archaeology and its techniques, or an account of the surviving monuments and artworks of the ancients; XIX. Archaeological theory of art, or the fundamentals of ancient drawing and sculpture; XX. A general history of ancient art; XXI. Introduction to the knowledge and history of ancient architecture' (ibid.). With this, a history of Greek and Roman Antiquity, completely along the lines developed by Winckelmann, was conceived, and in the same vein K. O. Müller stated as late as 1835, in the second edition of his Handbuch der Archäologie der Kunst (Handbook of the archaeology of art) that he 'wanted to exclude everything that does not directly further our knowledge of the ancient plastic arts' (preface to the second edition, [78]).

It is true that even prior to this time the stock of monuments had altered appreciably in origin and character. Apart from the Roman statues before which

Winckelmann had conceived his ideas, for the first time more Greek originals from the 5th cent. had become available to research: thus the frieze from Phigalia-Bassae, bought by the British Museum in 1812, the Parthenon sculptures acquired by the same museum in 1816 from the collection of Lord Elgin, and the Late Archaic figures from the gable of the Temple of Alphaia at Aegina, which came to the Munich Glyptothek in 1828. Works from the 6th cent. BC soon followed: in 1822 and 1823 the first of the Archaic metope reliefs were excavated at Selinunt. In 1853, with the High Archaic *kouros* found near Corinth in 1848 and then still called the *Apollo of Tenea*, the first work of some significance from the time *c.* 560 BC came to the Munich Glyptothek.

But even these new finds corresponded entirely with conceptions of Archaic monuments that had been formed during the decades after Winckelmann's *Geschichte der Kunst des Altertums*. Even the painted Greek vases that came to light in the ancient necropoleis, first in Lower Italy (esp. Nola) then in ever greater numbers in Etruria, fitted this picture: for K. O. Müller they attested to the 'artistic soul of the Greek nation, which manifests itself even in these simple artifacts' [78. 456], and were considered to be illustrations of Greek mythology and Greek life; vessels without figurative designs and less interesting pieces continued to be largely ignored. And in 1850 at the eleventh conference of philologists and academics in Berlin Eduard Gerhard, who in 1833 had been appointed as an 'archaeologist' to the royal museums in Berlin and since 1844 had also held a full professorship at the Berlin University, still described archaeology as *denjenigen Zweig der klassischen Philologie welcher, im Gegensatz litterarischer Quellen und Gegenstände, auf den monumentalen Werken und Spuren antiker Technik beruht* ('that branch of classical philology that depends not on literary sources and texts but on monumental works and the remains of ancient technology') [90. 55]. Nevertheless, in an argument developed on the same occasion he expressed the opinion that it was the 'task of archaeology … to record not only a selection of artistic monuments but the entirety of the monumental stock, … of the overall experience of life in Antiquity' (*ibid.*). In fact during these years developments had already begun that would decisively alter the general conception of archaeology, the first thing that must be emphasised was the huge increase in the stock of monuments in the course of the great excavations, which were carried out on a new scale, initially in the Near East and Egypt, and whose goal, as in the previous century in the case of the excavations in Rome and the cities near the Vesuvius, was to acquire new artistic works. For example A. H. Layard the excavator of Nineveh declared: 'I determined … to economize as far as it was in my power – that the nation might possess as extensive and complete a collection of Assyrian antiquities as … it was possible to collect' ([67. Vol. I. 327]; cf. [72. 17]).

Thus, as early as 1711 looting excavations in the theatre at Herculaneum had brought to light the two famous clothed female statues known as the Herculaneum Matron and the Herculaneum Maiden, both initially going to Vienna into the ownership of Prince Eugene of Savoy, and after his death in 1736 into the collection of the Electors of Saxony in Dresden. In 1748 excavations had been carried out at Pompeii at the instigation of the Viceroy of Naples, Don Carlos III of Bourbon [34], and during the years from 1806 to 1832 the centre of the city and a few large private houses were almost entirely revealed. The immense public reaction to this first opportunity for the lay world to gain an insight into daily life in Antiquity is reflected in one of the first historical novels, Edward Bulwer-Lytton's *The Last Days of Pompeii*, (1834). To ensure the proper instruction of the interested public, the organisationally gifted Eduard Gerhard had in 1833 founded the *Archäologisches Intelligenzblatt der Hallischen Literatur-Zeitung (Archaeological Gazette of the Halle Literary Journal* – until 1838), and functioned as its publisher [15. 27].

At the same time there was an extraordinary increase in (looting) excavations of the necropoleis of southern Etruria (esp. Vulci), whose finds, above all– again– painted Greek vases, quickly arrived on the flourishing art market and formed the basis of substantial collections in many large museums outside Italy. Especially active in this field was Luciano Bonaparte, Napoleon's youngest brother, whom Pope Pius VII had made Prince of Canino. In order to provide a degree of scientific observation of and accompaniment to the explosive increase in excavational activity, the *Istituto di Corrispondenza Archeologica* had been founded in 1829 as an international body among the circle of academics, cultured diplomats and artistically knowledgeable laypeople in Rome, at the instigation of Eduard Gerhard (1795–1867), a pupil of the Berlin philologist and epigraphist August Boeckh (1785–1867).

Finally, especially in the 19th cent., the increasingly apparent interest of cultured lay-people both in indigenous prehistoric monuments and in those of the Roman past had a not inconsiderable influence on the development of CA in Germany. The merging of the two strains occurred to a large extent after the model of the *Society of Antiquaries* (founded in 1751), which had already been successful in England in the 18th cent. While the *Archäologische Gesellschaft*, brought into being in Berlin in 1841 (again by Eduard Gerhard), proclaimed by its very name and by its annual publication of the *Berliner Winckelmannsprogramme* its attachment to ancient Italy and Greece, for the *Verein von Altertumsfreunden im Rheinlande*, founded in the same year, the legacy of the Romans in Germany was further in the forefront of interest [29. 92], as was the case with other associations of this kind, e.g. the *Nassauische Gesellschaft für Alterthumskunde und Geschichtsforschung*, founded in 1821. The primarily historical-antiquarian interests of this cultured milieu extended back beyond Winckelmann; as early as 1723 the Weißenburg headmaster J. A. Döderlein had written a monograph describing the Upper Germanic *limes*.

CA was slow in recognising, let alone accepting, that its attention should also be directed towards the archaeology of the provinces of the Roman Empire. In 1892 the *Reichs-Limeskommission* was founded at the instigation of Theodor Mommsen as the successor institution of the *Commission zur Erforschung des limes imperii Romani*, which had been founded in 1852 at the same time as the *Römisch-Germanisches Centralmuseum*. The leading institution of CA, the *Archäologisches Institut des Deutschen Reiches*, at first remained unaffected, although the development meant de facto the creation of a major research project of the German empire. After the *Istituto di corrispondenza archeologica*, founded in Rome in 1829, had been taken over by the Prussian state in 1859 and in 1874 recast as an imperial commission complemented by a branch in Athens, it had lost its status as an international organisation. The founding of the *Römisch-Germanische Kommission* in 1902 in Frankfurt am Main [61] as a semi-autonomous branch of the → DEUTSCHES ARCHÄOLOGISCHES INSTITUT represented a significant step within the new development towards integration, although it was controversial at first and later also did not meet with universal approval. The prehistoric research expertise embodied in the new commission which was familiar from early on with giving painstaking attention to the slightest peculiarities of the excavated site, so as to detect perishable wood and earth structures from discoloration of the earth and organic remains and which had developed the technique of stratigraphic arrangement of historical sediments, provided an important methodological basis for CA, involved as it was in 'practical' excavations in Mediterranean countries.

In 1871 Heinrich Schliemann, a loner who had acquired great wealth as a businessman [35; 72], had launched the age of the great excavations in the Mediterranean by his admittedly not always systematic uncovering of the city mound of Troy, which he followed, already in 1876, with the excavation of Mycenae. Already, however, it was clear that the purpose of these excavations was no longer merely the accumulation of finds. His concern was rather 'to light up the darkness that covered the prehistory of the Greek world' [64. 91]. In a similar spirit, the purpose of the 'official' CA excavations begun in 1873 on Samothrace and in 1875 at Olympia was above all the furtherance of scholarly knowledge, as has been the case for all systematic excavations since. From this time at the latest we may speak of a certain evolution and 'scientification' of archaeology, which may in principle be ranked as a technical, methodological 'aid' to a whole series of historically orientated disciplines. One hundred years after Schliemann, within the context of → ARCHAEOLOGICAL METHODS, a dedicated publication, the *Journal of Field Archaeology* (Vol. 1ff., 1974ff.), was finally created for

this area of endeavour, and comprehensive systematic descriptions are available [30; 80]. From these beginnings, fruitful initiatives for interdisciplinary collaboration with the natural sciences (archaeo-botany, -metallurgy, -zoology etc.) have been developed and successfully tried.

But the first great excavations of the 1870s initially did nothing to alter the fundamental priorities in CA, and the discipline only gradually began to realise that they had decisively changed the composition of the stock of monuments and had broadened the research spectrum into ancient cultures. Even after this time, on many excavations all undecorated vessels continued to be discarded without being recorded. But those researchers with an open mind had to admit that previously neglected prosaic craft products and the trappings of simple everyday life had now taken their place alongside the statues, architecture and paintings, those marks of high Greek and Roman artistic achievement: undecorated kitchenware, nails, brackets and tools, farm buildings and gutters and much more– objects that did not fit comfortably into the conceptual framework of Classicism. At the same time, on those occasions when the location and chronological juxtaposition of finds revealed an abundance of different cultural contexts on one and the same site, or where there were plant remains and the bones of animals and humans to analyse and interpret, those very excavations brought the essential involvement with neighbouring disciplines into clear focus.

The change brought about by this development is demonstrated by the definitions of archaeology, which, depending on the period from which they originate, bear witness to the discipline's altered image of itself. For Eduard Gerhard (1795–1867) in his *Grundzüge der Archäologie* (1833), it was this: 'that half of the general discipline of Classical Antiquity that is based on the knowledge of monuments'. A generation later, influenced by the beginning of art-historical studies, Alexander Conze (1831–1914) in his inaugural lecture in Vienna declared: 'At the intersection of Classical Philology and Art History, there and precisely there lies the field of Classical Archaeology'. For his posthumously published manual of 1880 C. B. Stark (1824–1879) described archaeology as the 'scholarly study of the art of Antiquity'; but Adolf Furtwängler (1853–1907) gave the authoritarian formulation: 'Archaeology is nothing other than the history of ancient art, and therefore a component of the overall history of art' [82. 27].

E. 20TH CENT.

1. DEVELOPMENTS UP TO 1945   2. THE FINAL DECADES OF THE 20TH CENT.

1. DEVELOPMENTS UP TO 1945

Only a little later, however, H. Bulle (1867–1945) in his introduction to the first fascicle of the new *Handbuch der Archäologie* in 1913 understood it 'not merely as Art History, but as the study of monuments in the broadest sense'. It is therefore not without reason that he omitted the word 'Classical' from the title of his handbook. 'The isolation of 'Classical' Archaeology', he wrote, 'is on the wane'. The English archaeologist A. Evans had already stated the position even more clearly in a letter to E. Freeman in 1883: 'To restrict a Chair in Archaeology to the classical period appears to me to be as sensible as the creation of a Chair in 'Insular Geography' or 'Mesozoic Geology'' [82. 27–28].

F. Schlegel had been the first in 1797 to link the exclusive attribute 'Klassisch' to the concept of 'Altertum' (Ancient History), thus displacing the use of the terms 'Antike' (Antiquity) and 'Die Antiken' (Ancient peoples), which in the early classicistic period had had the same exemplary content as was now understood under 'Klassische Altertum' (Classical History). Throughout the 19th cent., this combination of words was the preferred means of celebrating the exemplary in ancient art and literature, thus expressly – and quite in the spirit of Wolff – restricting the attribute to the culture of the Greeks and Romans. The discipline of archaeology as an accompaniment to 'Classical' Philology and the study of the history of 'Classical' Antiquity did not receive the specifying adjective 'Classical' and achieve autonomous stature as CA until later; until then it was regarded as sufficient to classify it as the archaeology of art in the 'context of the study of Classical History'.

The return to a new idealisation of the Classical art of Greece was not slow to follow, not least provoked by the cataclysm of the First World War in Europe, which had for the time being brought excavations and the constant process of 'monuments accumulation' to a halt. Of the currents of thought designed to serve inner contemplation, which was felt to be of urgent importance, the so-called Third Humanism [52; 88], arising within the framework of Classical Philology, exerted a substantial influence on CA. For many in the discipline it represented a challenge to collaborate intensively in *Die Antike* [101. 377], the journal founded by W. Jaeger in 1925 and aimed at a cultured public whose enthusiasm for the normative content of Classicism was regarded as ripe to be rekindled. It was no accident that in the same year *Gnomon. Kritische Zeitschrift für die gesamte Altertumswissenschaft* was brought into being for the actual specialists, preserving the traditional name created by F. A. Wolf.

At the centre of this 'Classical' Antiquity in the realm of Greek art now stood Phidias and the Parthenon; a new inclusion was Archaic art and the art of the 'Severe Style', for the assessment of which the illustrated volume on the sculptures of the Temple of Zeus at Olympia, published in 1924 by E. Buschor and R. Hamann, provided a basis that was as much in step with the artistic taste of the time as it was with scholarly standards. Newly included in the narrower field of 'Classicism' was also the classicistic art of the early Imperial period [45. 4f.]. This positive evaluation of Roman art, which up to then had been judged to be of low artistic stand-

ard, had been encouraged by the belated impact of two works that had been published around the turn of the century, and which were of fundamental importance for the new vision: the introduction to the edition of the Wiener Genesis manuscript by F. Wickhoff (1853–1909); and in particular the investigation of the Late Roman Art 'industry' by the Viennese art historian A. Riegl (1858–1905). The same is true of the *Kunstgeschichtliche Grundbegriffe (Fundamentals of Art History)* by H. Wölfflin (1864–1945), first edition published in 1915. His observation *daß sich, mit engerer oder weiterer Wellenlänge, gewisse gleichlautende Entwicklungen schon mehrfach im Abendland abgespielt habe n* ('that, in shorter or longer 'waves', certain similar developments have taken place more than once in the history of Western art') [110. 268], which he presented as an undisputed fact for Art History in general, was transferred to CA and led to a 'relativistic' conception of development here as well. It helped create the 'splendid edifice of order' [36. 17] of an historical course of art and crafts, into which even the stock of anonymous monuments was fitted– in the better researched areas often precise to the decade [81. 229–232].

Riegl's text, which was also theoretically demanding, was reprinted in convenient format in 1927, and was extensively praised in *Gnomon* by G. Kaschnitz von Weinberg as a 'turning point in the historical study of the fine arts'. It is in this review that one finds the first explicit mention of what was sometimes termed 'Formgeschichte' (history of form), sometimes 'Strukturforschung' (structural analysis), and nowadays correctly as 'archäologischer Strukturalismus' (archaeological Structuralism) [4]. It was *i.a.* Riegl's concept of a superindividual 'Kunstwollen' (artistic volition), and observations by Wickhoff, such as that concerning a 'continuierende Erzählweise' (continuous narrative method) characteristic of Roman art, that suggested the identification of an *Italic structure*. The principle of internal formal organisation, as G. Kaschnitz von Weinberg defined structure, was determined by the sum of the creative powers of an epoch or historical period, and had to be capable of being recognised even from the individual work. This concept could be understood as a function of *Ethnos* (race), landscape and period, and in the framework of such factors could be related to smaller as well as larger entities. Thus for example, a 'Near-Eastern' structure was described, whose heterogeneity was due to 'the complex and constantly changing ethnic base' [57. 89]; or an 'Aegean' structure, which addressed the common formal features of a geographical space (the Aegean in its broadest sense), of an enormous temporal span (the Neolithic and Bronze Age), and finally of a more or less uniform ethnic substrate (an ancient Mediterranean population) [75].

Such a theoretical construct – which also had its parallels in the prehistoric field – was inevitably attractive to the ideologues of the National Socialist regime of 1933–1945. A sober [e.g. 53. 47–56], comprehensive treatment of the complexities and also dangers that resulted for the discipline and its institutions is still lacking [5. 23]. On the other hand, it is clearly evident that the paradigms of structural archaeology, to which CA owes significant achievements, are used successfully to this day (cf. e.g. [12. 532]). This is shown with particular clarity in the presentation of *Strukturalistische Artefakt- und Kunstanalyse* (The structural analysis of artefacts and art) by M. Bachmann [4], which is consistently argued on a sound philosophical basis. Finally, Stefan George (1868–1933), to whose circle of friends many archaeologists from the generation born around and after the turn of the century felt themselves drawn [74; 94], exerted a certain influence even beyond his death, and this even though the relationship of George himself to Antiquity and to ancient art was more of a generally idealizing kind. The predominant position of works of art nevertheless remained unaffected in research and teaching. Even though the visible legacy of the past gave the discipline wide scope for research, for E. Buschor (1886–1961), a pupil of Furtwängler, 'the fine arts [remain] at the centre of attention as the most precious legacy from the past' [16. 3], and for A. Rumpf (1890–1966), who had emerged from the philology/Ancient Studies-oriented school of F. Studniczkas (1860–1929) 'that art which is rightfully termed Classical [could maintain] its old sovereignty' [91. 4].

In the same spirit, there was no change in the general rejection of H. Schliemann and of the new opportunities he had opened up for an archaeology devoted to the past cultures of the Mediterranean in general. Although Schliemann's significance for a development in this sense and as the founder of the sub-discipline of 'Mycenaean Archaeology' was acknowledged and appreciated by a few [83], it was not given proper prominence and critical attention until the occasion of the 100th anniversary of his death in 1990. As recently as 1953, A. Rumpf saw the discipline as in growing danger of being diverted from its real purpose. 'For almost two generations it has squandered its finest efforts on prehistory' [91. 94]; and this situation of 'rejection or, at best, disregard, in particular by CA' has remained substantially the case in Germany [101. 250]: any critical survey of the situation at the end of the 20th cent. could not but conclude that Minoan and Mycenaean archaeology, while enjoying impressive progress internationally, must in Germany be counted among those branches of research that have substantially withered away [46; 83].

2. THE FINAL DECADES OF THE 20TH CENT.

Characteristic of the situation of CA after 1945 and into the 1960s was the return to positivist, innocuous approaches to research (intrinsic interpretation, style- and iconography-based investigation, editions of monuments). In the first volume of the newly rebegun *Handbuch der Archäologie*, this time under the direction of U. Hausmann, which appeared in 1969 under the title *Allgemeine Grundlagen der Archäologie*, the articles, authored for the 1939 edition by E. Buschor

and B. Schweitzer respectively, *Begriff und Methode der Archäologie* (written in 1932) and *Problem der Form in der Kunst des Altertums* (written in 1931), were reprinted unaltered. The evident theoretical deficit was perceived to be serious, and it was noted more clearly than before that in contemporary practice: *die Fragestellungen, die hinter den sichtbaren Fortschritten stehen, im allgemeinen ziemlich gleichartig und monoton sind. Wie vordergründig diese Fortschritte in geistiger Hinsicht sind, zeigt sich sogleich, wenn über die Bestimmung und Klassifizierung hinaus die Frage nach der Bedeutung gestellt und das Problem des Verstehens aufgeworfen werden* ('the questions behind visible progress are in general rather alike and monotonous. How superficial this progress is from an intellectual point of view immediately becomes evident when, over and above considerations of identification and classification, we pose the question of meaning, and are confronted with the problem of understanding') [38. 189].

On the other hand, the endeavour to approach the assessment of ancient monuments from a wider basis was already unmistakable. As an appropriate area for iconological investigation, i.e. investigation based on meaning, intention and message [18] as practiced by the sociological approach championed in Italy, especially by R. Bianchi Bandinelli and his school, the political art of the Roman Empire seemed especially suitable. The ground for this emergence of Roman art, a subject long unloved by CA, into the focus of research had also been prepared by the activities of G. Rodenwaldt (1886–1945) [13]. The broad range of public architecture characterised by a political purpose inevitably presented a prime target for such research. In this spirit, 'the consideration of all forms of social intercourse, insofar as they manifest themselves in figurative form' was formulated as object of research [119].

A concentration on particular categories of monument suggested itself, e.g. on portraits of politicians or rulers [32; 117; 118], on the decorative imagery on state monuments and official buildings as a medium for political messages [25; 41; 42], and on individual social groups and their characteristic visual testimonies [113; 114]. At the same time the question of the function of the sculptures and paintings employed to decorate buildings and public spaces and of their character as 'message-bearers' in the ancient social context was posed anew [73; 106; 114; 122], and this approach was also projected onto the epochs of Greek art [39; 40; 96], or, conversely, an examination was made of the role of Greek mythological images in the Roman context [105]. By this means, and on the basis of questions developed in the 1970s, insights have been gained into the psychological history of bourgeois culture in the early Roman Imperial period [116; 117].

In assessing the complex relationship between the psychological and formal tendencies of an epoch [11; 69], the definition of the language of artistic forms in Roman art as a semantic system was of particular importance [43], and in this context the observation that in Roman art 'different models from different epochs of Greek art had been taken up for different thematic categories' could be linked to the axiom of 'stylistic genre' dating from the beginning of the century. In the context of this 'semanticisation of styles' it emerged that, by the Augustan period at the latest, a certain canon of modes of representation and image types had developed, i.e. a more or less fixed imagery, and that, although the semantic system did not exclude a change of style, it underwent no further alterations during the first and second cent. AD. The systematised, static imagery for the transmission of messages and for communication in general in the Roman empire, and the manifest tendency towards the norm in art were thus established as characteristic of Roman imperial culture, and in doing so, the familiar problem of the 'contemporaneity of the uncontemporaneous' [70] was solved as well.

CA increasingly sees itself faced by the task of regarding all formed, visually perceptible cultural utterances, not only artistic works, as reference points for forms of everyday experience in Antiquity. The concept of the artwork as a component of a larger overall stock of material legacies from Antiquity is a necessary prerequisite for the fulfillment of the wish 'to obtain an insight into the anthropological dimension shared by art and lived culture'. This approach allows the ancient world to be seen no longer as 'a model or as an obligatory or inescapable tradition', but as 'an experiential and experimental space for different but not altogether foreign possibilities of cultural existence' [47. 11].

The endeavour to obtain a more holistic insight also lies behind the many approaches to the investigation of the city in Antiquity. If at first the problem was seen as one purely of urban planning and design, and the indicated task of a technical nature, the sociological and cultural dimensions of the project were now quickly recognised. In fact, the city in its multitudinous manifestations and functional forms, representing as it does the centre of social and political life in Antiquity, offers an extensive context for the incorporation of the results of archaeological research into a broader anthropological inquiry [21; 48; 49; 50; 93; 107; 111].

In view of this development, the criticisms that have demanded a debate on theory and method since the 1968 movement must be seen in a relative light [1; 5]. The shortcomings of CA in the German-speaking world are obvious, and the discipline is increasingly aware of them. It must also be said, however, that up to now they have not been sufficiently resolved by those who raise them so vehemently.

The attempt by the so-called *Hamburg School* to understand the world of monuments as components of a 'system of signs', and to define it anew by using criteria from communication and interaction theory [24; 97; 99;], remained a more or less isolated phenomenon within CA. It remains to be hoped that theoretical discussion in advance of and in the context of the Mainz special research area 'Kulturelle und sprachliche Kon-

takte: Zentren und Peripherien im historischen Raum Nordostafrika/Westasien' (Cultural and linguistic contacts: centres and peripheries in historical North-East Africa and Western Asia), established in the late 1990s, will lead to the development of new approaches in this sense, approaches that may, beyond the boundaries of linguistics and philology, also prove fruitful for CA [2; 3; 86].

Discussion at present is for the most part restricted to lectures, colloquia and newspaper articles, and therefore difficult to summarise. One fundamental dilemma has recently been given explicit mention: 'Reconstructing historical conditions of life means not only asking more comprehensive questions, but at the same time conducting more detailed research in more detail. Praxis often founders on this contradiction' [44]. It is furthermore only too easy to overlook the fact that the well advanced discussion in the USA and elsewhere in Europe is in most cases coming from a fundamentally different structure of cultural and Antiquity studies, and bears the mark of an archaeological establishment that has an entirely different conception of itself. For these reasons, only the pre- and early-history branch has taken up the engaged polemic that took place pro and contra *New Archaeology* in the 1970s and 1980s [5. 38–84]. One reason why this polemic was not taken up by CA in Germany is that the discipline's immense, heterogeneous and complex array of source material, combined with a written tradition of like nature, appears at first sight at least to militate against the use of models and systems deriving from cultural theory. Warnings that architectural evidence may be pushed aside in favour of theoretical constructs are therefore numerous, and are not leveled exclusively 'from the other side'. The clear message is that the discipline must keep its eyes open to 'the full power of the archaeological record' [102. 174].

F. Perspectives

Of the abundance of tasks indicated here to be confronted by CA, three of a more general nature can be identified. First there is the obligation to keep interdisciplinary discourse alive in the context of ancient studies, and where necessary give it new life. Efforts to find ways towards re-integration are becoming clearly evident. The *Mommsen-Gesellschaft* as an association of German researchers in the field of Greek and Roman Antiquity had been founded as early as 1949 not only in order to give expression to the discipline's unity in a land that was then divided, but also, regardless of the inevitable specialisation into sub-disciplines, to highlight their common object of research. Special areas of research and graduate programs fostered in the field of ancient studies by the *Deutsche Forschungsgemeinschaft* were also set up with the aim of creating a new basis for this endeavour. These intentions are made manifest in the first reports on work in progress, for instance in the graduate program 'Vergangenheitsbezug antiker Gegenwarten' at Freiburg University [26. 9–16].

Secondly, in view of the interdisciplinary dimension of one's own approach to research, which is focused on the transmission of material objects, there is the challenge to incorporate the outcomes of specialist research into an overall science of the past. As a first step, this requires a greater acceptance of the close cultural involvement of Classical Antiquity of the Greeks and Romans with the ancient Near East, with the entire Mediterranean area and with the so-called marginal cultures of Europe, from the Iberians and Celts to the nomadic cultures of Eastern Europe and the Eurasian Steppes. The setting up of the Eurasian department within the *Deutsches Archäologisches Institut* in 1996 is an initiative in the spirit of this challenge. Furthermore, it is important to determine the position of CA in the widest context of general and comparative archaeology – thus the name ('Allgemeine und vergleichende Archäologie') of a commission of the *Deutsches Archäologisches Institut* founded in 1979 [79] – as a research area of human culture of the past. And in this regard in particular, German CA will not be able to avoid engaging with theoretical constructs originating from abroad, such as the thought-provoking structural models provided by, among others, the *Annales* school of historians in France [8; 59].

Finally, in the course of the last generation CA has been confronted by a particular responsibility with which the discipline is only gradually coming to terms, especially since it concerns the apparently secondary area of 'communication' with the so-called interested public and associated didactic activities, on top of the task of caring for state-protected ancient monuments and the display of objects in museums. There are in this area omissions for which CA has to make up. For it may almost be regarded as certain that less than ever before since the end of Antiquity will future generations in their upbringing be characterised by a classical and humanistic, indeed by even as much as a historical education. In this future, CA as a discipline concerned with the visible and the tangible will more than ever bear the responsibility for ensuring that the heritage of the ancient Mediterranean world can be experienced and thus remain alive, not only in its works of arts but also in its manifold evidence of the general culture of everyday life, by means of 'first-hand experience' and in the form of 'exhibitions of the living past'.

→ Cast; cast collection; → Antiquities collections; → Archaeological methods; → Museum; → Style, Style analysis, Stylistic analysis

1 S. Altekamp et al. (eds.), Posthumanistische Klassische Archäologische Historizität und Wissenschaftlichkeit von Interessen und Methoden. Akten des Kolloquiums Berlin (18.–21.2. 1999), 2000   2 J. Assmann, Die Macht der Bilder. Rahmenbedingungen ikonischen Handelns im Alten Ägypten, in: VisRel VII, Genre in Visual Representation, 1990, 1–20   3 Id., Probleme der Erfassung von Zeichenkonzeptionen im Abendland, in: R. Posner et al. (eds.), Semiotik. Ein Handbuch zu den zeichentheoretischen Grundlagen von Natur und Kultur 1, 1997, 710–729   4 M. Bachmann, Die strukturalistische Artefakt- und Kunstanalyse. Exposition der Grundlagen anhand der vorderorientalischen, ägyptischen und griechischen Kunst, OBO 148, 1996   5 R. Bernbeck, Theorien in der Archäologie 1997   6 R. Bianchi-Bandinelli, Römische Kunst, zwei Generationen nach Wickhoff, in: Klio 38, 1960, 267–283   7 Id., Klassische Archäologie. Eine kritische Einführung, 1978   8 J. Bintliff (ed.), The Annales School and Archaeology, 1991   9 F. Blättner, Das Griechenbild J. J. Winckelmanns, A&A 1, 1944, 121–132   10 J. Boardman, Review of A. M. Snodgrass, An Archaeology of Greece. The Present State and Future Scope of a Discipline, in: Antiquity 62, 1988, 795–797   11 A. H. Borbein, Die griechische Statue des 4. Jahrhunderts vor Christus, in: JDAI 88, 1973, 43–212   12 Id., Review of W. Fuchs, J. Floren, Die griechische Plastik I: J. Floren, Die geometrsiche und archaische Plastik. HdArch, 1987, in: Gnomon 63, 1991, 529–538   13 Id., Gerhart Rodenwaldts Bild der römischen Kunst, in: Römische Geschichte und Zeitgeschichte in der deutschen und italiänischen Altertumswissenschaft, 2, 1991, 175–200   14 id., Die Klassik-Diskussion in der Klassischen Archäologie, in: H. Flashar (ed.), Altertumswissenschaft in den 20er Jahren. Neue Fragen und Impulse, 1995, 205–245   15 Id., Eduard Gerhard als Organisator, in: H. Wrede (ed.), Winckelmann-Institut der Humboldt-Universität zu Berlin 2, 1997, 25–30   16 S. G. Bruer, Die Wirkung Winckelmanns in der deutschen Klassischen Archäologie des 19. Jahrhunderts, 1994   17 E. Buschor, Handbuch der Archäologie I (1939), 3   18 F. Coarelli, Classe dirigente romana e arti figurative, in: Dialoghi di Archeologia 4–5, 1970–71, 241–265   19 G. Daltrop, Antikensammlungen und Mäzenatentum um 1600 in Rom, in: Antikenrezeption im Hochbarock, 1989, 37–58   20 Deutsches Archäologisches Institut (ed.), Das Deutsche Archäologische Institut. Geschichte und Dokumente, vols. 1–10, 1979–1986   21 W. Eck, H. Galsterer (eds.), Die Stadt in Oberitalien und in den nordwestlichen Provinzen des römischen Reiches, Kolloquium Köln, 1991   22 R. Étienne, J.-C. Mossière (eds.), Jacob Spon. Un humaniste Lyonnais du XVIIIe siècle, 1993   23 J. Evans, Time and Chance: The Story of A. Evans and his Forebears, 1934, 261f.   24 B. Fehr, Bewegungsweisen und Verhaltensideale, 1979   25 K. Fittschen, Das Bildprogramm des Traiansbogens von Benevent, in: AA 1972, 742–788   26 M. Flashar, H. J. Gehrke, E. Heinrich (eds.), Retrospektive. Konzepte von Vergangenheit in der griechisch-römische Antike 1. Bericht über die Arbeit des Graduiertenkollegs 'Vergangenheitsbezug antiker Gegenwarten' der Universität Freiburg, 1996   27 G. Frame, Nabonidus and the History of the Eulma-Temple of Akkadia. Mesopotamia 28, 1993, 21–50   28 E. Friedell, Kulturgeschichte der Neuzeit, vol. I–III, 1931   29 R. Fuchs, Zur Geschichte der Sammlungen des Rheinischen Landesmuseums Bonn, in: Rheinisches Landesmuseum Bonn. 150 Jahre Sammlungen 1820–1970 (= Führer des Rheinischen Landesmuseums Bonn Nr. 38), 1971, 1–158   30 E. Gersbach, J. Hahn, Ausgrabung heute. Methoden und Techniken der Feldgrabung, 1989   31 L. Giuliani, Bildnis und Botschaft. Hermeneutische Untersuchungen zur Bildniskunst der römischen Republik, 1986   32 G. Grimm, Von der Liebe Raffaels zur Antike, in: Antike Welt 29, 1998, 481–496   33 R. Harprath, H. Wrede (eds.), Antikenzeichnung und Antikenstudium in Renaissance und Frühbarock, 1989   34 R. Herbig, Don Carlos von Bourbon als Ausgräber von Herculaneum und Pompeji, in: MDAI(Madrid) 1, 1960, 11–19   35 J. Herrmann (ed.),

Heinrich Schliemann. Grundlagen und Ergebnisse moderner Archäologie 100 Jahre nach Schliemanns Tod, 1992 **36** N. HIMMELMANN-WILDSCHÜTZ, Der Entwicklungsbegriff der modernen Archäologie, in: Marburger Winckelmann-Programm 1960, 13–40 **37** Id., Winckelmanns Hermeneutik, 1971 **38** Id., Utopische Vergangenheit. Archäologie und moderne Kultur, 1976 **39** T. HÖLSCHER, Ideal und Wirklichkeit in den Bildnissen Alexanders des Großen, 1971 **40** Id., Die Nike der Messenier und Naupaktier in Olympia, in: JDAI 89, 1974, 70–111 **41** Id., Die Geschichtsauffassung in der römischen Repräsentationskunst, in: JDAI 95, 1980, 265–321 **42** Id., Staatsdenkmal und Publikum vom Untergang der Republik bis zur Festigung des Kaisertums in Rom, 1984 **43** Id., Römische Bildsprache als semantisches System, 1987 **44** Id., Fremdgewordener Kanon. Klassische Archäologie in unklassischer Umgebung, in: Frankfurter Allgemeine Zeitung, 23.11.1988 **45** Id., Die unheimliche Klassik der Griechen. Thyssen-Vorträge: Auseinandersetzungen mit der Antike, H. FLASHAR (ed.), 1995 **46** Id., Klassische Archäologie am Ende des 20. Jahrhunderts: Tendenzen, Defizite, Illusionen, in: E.-R. SCHWINGE (ed.), Die Wissenschaft vom Altertum am Ende des 2. Jahrtausends nach Christus, 1995, 197–228 **47** Id., R. LAUTER (eds.), Formen der Kunst und Formen des Lebens. Ästhetische Betrachtungen als Dialog. Von der Antike bis zur Gegenwart und wieder zurück, 1995 **48** W. HOEPFNER, L. SCHWANDNER (eds.), Demokratie und Architektur. Der hippodamische Städtebau und die Entstehung der Demokratie. Konstanzer Symposion vom 17. bis 19. Juli 1987. Wohnen in der klassischen Polis, 2, 1989 **49** Id., Haus und Stadt im klassischen Griechenland, ²1994 **50** W. HOEPFNER, G. ZIMMER (eds.), Die griechische Polis. Architektur und Politik, 1993 **51** J. IRMSCHER, K. ZIMMERMANN, H. PROTZMANN, Die Dresdner Antiken und Winckelmann. Schriften der Winckelmann-Gesellschaft 4, 1977 **52** W. JAEGER (ed.), Das Problem des Klassischen und die Antike. Acht Vorträge Naumburg 1930, 1933 (²1961) **53** U. JANTZEN, Einhundert Jahre Athener Institut 1874–1974. Das Deutsche Archäologische Institut. Geschichte und Dokumente, 10, 1986 **54** H. JUCKER, Vom Verhältnis der Römer zur bildenden Kunst der Griechen, 1950 **55** K. JUNKER, Das Archäologische Institut des Deutschen Reiches zwischen Forschung und Politik 1929–1945, 1997 **56** C. JUSTI, Winckelmann und sein Jahrhundert, ³1923 **57** G. KASCHNITZ VON WEINBERG, Kleine Schriften zur Struktur. Ausgewählte Schriften I, H. v. HEINTZE (ed.), 1965 **58** H. KLOFT, Antikenrezeption und Klassizismus, Jahrbuch der Wittheit zu Bremen 1993/94, 17–23 **59** A. B. KNAPP (Hrsg.), Archaeology, Annales, and Ethnohistory, 1992 **60** F. KOEPP, Geschichte der Archäologie, in: W. OTTO (ed.), HdArch I, 1939, 11–66 **61** W. KRÄMER et al., Festschrift zum 75-jährigen Bestehen der Römisch-Germanischen Kommission, BRGK 58, 1977, Beiheft 1979 **62** M. KUNZE (ed.), Johann Joachim Winckelmann. Neue Forschung. Schriften der Winckelmann-Gesellschaft 11, 1990 **63** Id. (ed.), Römisches Antikenmuseum im 18. Jahrhundert, 1998 **64** H. KYRIELEIS, Schliemann in Griechenland. JRGZ 25, 1978, 74–91 **65** H. LADENDORF, Antikenstudium und Antikenkopie. Vorarbeiten zu einer Darstellung ihrer Bedeutung für die mittelalterlichen und neueren Zeit, ²1958 **66** E. LANGLOTZ, Klassische Antike in heutiger Sicht. Vortrag im Freien Deutschen Hochstift, 1956 **67** A. H. LAYARD, Niniveh and its Remains, London 1849 **68** Foundation Hardt pour l'étude de l'antiquité classique (ed.), Le clas-

sicisme à Rome aux 1ers siècles avant et après J. C. Entretiens sur l'antiquité classique Vandoeuvres – Genève 21–26 août 1978. Entretiens 25, 1979 **69** A. LEIBUNDGUT, Künstlerische Form und konservative Tendenzen nach Perikles. Ein Stilpluralismus im 5. Jahrhundert vor Christus? Trierer Winckelmannprogramme 10, 1989 **70** A. LEIBUNDGUT-MAYE, Gleichzeitigkeit des Ungleichzeitigen. Die Stilebenen in der trajanischen Kunst und ihre Botschaft, in: Johannes Gutenberg-Universität Mainz, Antrittsvorlesungen vol. 5, 1989, 15–29 **71** R. LULLIES, W. SCHIERING (eds.), Archäologenbildnisse, 1988 **72** F. G. MAIER, Von Winckelmann zu Schliemann – Archäologie als Eroberungswissenschaft des 19. Jahrhunderts, 1992 **73** H. MANDERSCHEID, Die Skulpturenausstattung der kaiserzeitlichen Thermenanlagen, 1981 **74** H. MARWITZ, Stefan George und die Antike, WJA 1, 1946, 226–257 **75** F. MATZ, Strukturforschung und Archäologie, Studium generale 17, 1964, 203–219 **76** A. MICHAELIS, Ein Jahrhundert kunstarchäologischer Entdeckungen, 1908 **77** C. MOATTI, Rom. Wiederentdeckung einer antiken Stadt, 1995 **78** K. O. MÜLLER, Handbuch der Archäologie der Kunst, ³1848 **79** H. MÜLLER-KARPE, Die Gründung der Kommission für Allgemeine und Vergleichende Archäologie, in: Beiträge zur allgemeinen und vergleichenden Archäologie 2, 1980, 1–22 **80** W. MÜLLER-WIENER, Archäologische Ausgrabungsmethodik, in: Enzyklopädie der geisteswissenschaftlichen Arbeitsmethoden, fasc. 10, Methoden der Geschichtswissenschaft und der Archäologie, 1974, 253–287 **81** H. G. NIEMEYER, Methodik der Archäologie, Id., 217–252 **82** Id., Einführung in die Archäologie, ³1983 **83** Id., Heinrich Schliemann, die Klassische Archäologie und die Entdeckung der Vorgeschichte Griechenlands, in: Das Altertum 43 (Heft 2), 1997, 85–91 **84** H. OEHLER, Foto+Skulptur. Römische Antike in englischen Schlössern. Ausstellungskatalog Cologne, 1980 **85** E. PÖHLMANN, W. GAUER (eds.), Griechische Klassik, Erlanger Beiträge zur Sprache, Literatur und Kunst 75, 1994 **86** R. POSNER, Kultur als Zeichensystem. Zur semiotischen Explikation kulturwissenschaftlicher Grundbegriffe, in: A. ASSMANN, D. HARTH (eds.), Kultur als Lebenswelt und Monument, 1991, 37–71 **87** W. REHM, J. J. Winckelmann, Briefe, vols. I–IV, 1952–1957 **88** K. REINHARDT, Die klassische Philologie und das Klassische, in: Von Werken und Formen, 1948, 419–457 (with literature on the Third Humanism) **89** G. RODENWALDT, Archäologisches Institut des Deutschen Reiches 1829–1929, 1929 **90** D. RÖSSLER, Eduard Gerhards 'Monumentale Philologie', in: H. WREDE (ed.), Winckelmann-Institut der Humboldt-Universität zu Berlin 2, 1997, 55–61 **91** A. RUMPF, Archäologie I. Einleitung. Historischer Überblick, 1953 **92** B. SAUER, Geschichte der Archäologie, in: B. BULLE (ed.), Handbuch der Archäologie, vol. I, 1913, 80–141. In the context of the Handbuch der klassischen Altertumswissenschaft, vol. VI, (ed.) W. OTTO **93** H.-J. SCHALLES, H. v. HESBERG, P. ZANKER (eds.), Die römische Stadt im 2. Jahrhundert nach Christus. Der Funktionswandel des öffentlichen Raumes. Kolloquium Xanten 1990, 1992 **94** K. SCHEFOLD, Wirkung Stefan Georges, Castrum Peregrini 35, 1986 (fasc. 173/74), 72–97 **95** W. SCHIERING, Zur Geschichte der Archäologie, in U. HAUSMANN (ed.), Allgemeine Grundlagen der Archäologie, HdArch VI, 1, 1969, 11–161 **96** L. A. SCHNEIDER, Zur sozialen Bedeutung der archaischen Korenstatuen, 1975 **97** Id., B. FEHR, K.-H. MEYER, Zeichen-Kommunikation-Interaktion. Zur Bedeutung von Zeichen-, Kommunikations- und Interaktionstheorie für die Klassische Archäologie, Hephaistos 1, 1979, 7–41   98 Id., Die Domäne als Weltbild. Wirkungsstrukturen der spätantiken Bildersprache, 1983   99 Id., P. ZAZOFF, Konstruktion und Rekonstruktion. Zur Lesung thrakischer und skythischer Bilder. JDAI 109, 1994, 143–216   100 A. SHERRATT, What can Archaeologists learn from Annalists? in: A. B. KNAPP (ed.), Archaeology, Annales, and Ethnohistory, 1992, 135–142   101 H. SICHTERMANN, Kulturgeschichte der Klassischen Archäologie, 1996   102 D. B. SMALL, Monuments, Laws and Analysis: Combining Archaeology and Text in Ancient Athens, in: D. B. SMALL (ed.), Methods in the Mediterranean. Historical and Archaeological Views on Texts and Archaeology, Mnemosyne 135, 1995, Suppl., 143–174   103 C. B. STARK, Handbuch der Archäologie der Kunst I, Systematik und Geschichte der Archäologie der Kunst, 1880, 80–400   104 V. M. STROCKA, Das Bildprogramm des Epigrammzimmers in Pompeji, MDAI(R) 102, 1995, 269–290   105 E. THOMAS, Griechisches Mythenbild und augusteische 'Propaganda', in: E. G. SCHMIDT (ed.), Griechenland und Rom. Vergleichende Untersuchungen zu Entwicklungstendenzen und -Höhepunkten der antiken Geschichte, Kunst und Literatur, 1996, 252–263   106 M. TORELLI, Typology and Structure of Roman Historical Reliefs, 1982   107 W. TRILLMICH, P. ZANKER (eds.), Stadtbild und Ideologie. Die Monumentalisierung hispanischer Städte zwischen Republik und Kaiserzeit. colloquium Madrid 1987, 1990   108 G. B. WAYWELL, Hand-guide to the Classical Sculptures of Holkham Hall, Houghton Hall, Chatsworth, Castle Howard, Duncombe Park and Newby Hall. Classical Sculpture in English Country Houses. 11th International Congress of Classical Archaeology London, 1978   109 A. WILTON, I. BIGNAMINI (eds.), Grand Tour. The Lure of Italy in the Eighteenth Century. Exhibition Catalog London, 1996/97   110 H. WÖLFFLIN, Kunstgeschichtliche Grundbegriffe. Das Problem der Stilentwicklung in der neueren Kunst, 1915   18 1991 (Eng.: Principles of Art History: The Problem of the Development of Style in Later Art, 4 1932)   111 M. WÖRRLE, P. ZANKER (eds.), Stadtbild und Bürgerbild im Hellenismus, Kolloquium München 1993, 1995   112 F. A. WOLF, Darstellung der Alterthumswissenschaft nach Begriff, Umfang, Zweck und Werth, Berlin 1807 (reprint Acta Humaniora, 1986, with an epilogue by J. Irmscher)   113 H. WREDE, Das Mausoleum der Claudia Semne und die bürgerliche Plastik der Kaiserzeit, MDAI(R) 78, 1971, 125–166   114 Id., Die spätantike Hermengalerie von Welschbillig, 1972   115 Id., Die Entstehung der Archäologie und das Einsetzen der neuzeitlichen Geschichtsbetrachtung, in: W. KÜTTLER, J. RÜSEN, E. SCHULIN (eds.), Geschichtsdiskurs vol. 2, 1994, 95–119   116 P. ZANKER, Grabreliefs römischer Freigelassener, JDAI 90, 1975, 267–315   117 Id., Die Bildnisse des Augustus. Herrscherbild und Politik im kaiserlichen Rom, 1978   118 Id., Provinzielle Kaiserporträts. Zur Rezeption der Selbstdarstellung des Kaisers, 1983   119 Id., Augustus und die Macht der Bilder, 2 1990   120 Id., Pompeji. Stadtbild und Wohngeschmack, 1995   121 Id., Mythenbilder im Haus, in: Acts of the 15th Internat. Congress of Classical Archaeology Amsterdam 1998, 1999   122 G. ZIMMER, Locus datus decreto decurionum. Zur Statuenaufstellung zweier Forumsanlagen im römischen Afrika, 1989.

ADDITIONAL BIBLIOGRAPHY: J. BERGEMANN, Orientierung Archäologie, 2000; A. H. BORBEIN, T. HÖLSCHER, P. ZANKER (ed.), Klassische Archäologie, 2000; P. BOURBIN, Qu'est ce que l'archéologie, 1982; T. HÖLSCHER, Klassische Archäologie: Grundwissen, 2002; F. LANG, Klassische Archäologie, 2002; U. SINN, Einführung in die Klassische Archäologie, 2000   HANS GEORG NIEMEYER

II. NEW FINDS
A. INTRODUCTION   B. 19TH CENT.   C. 20TH CENT.

A. INTRODUCTION

CA, in common with all branches of archaeology, is almost specifically oriented towards the accumulation of new material and new finds, and this not only in recent times. At the same time, the quantity of new finds has long become a problem for the discipline. In the following we will accordingly ask what it is that new finds contribute to the state of the discipline, and whether it would not do better to exploit known sources anew and more thoroughly. How does the discipline of CA cope with new finds? What is the situation regarding the reception of new finds within this discipline and beyond? What are the real reasons for the concentration on new finds? Are those researchers right who argue that it is only on the basis of new material from documented new findings that problems and solutions can be formulated? Does not the quest for new finds suggest the old conception of the magnificent discovery, long influential in archaeology but now long invalid? Are not the *findings* much more important than the *finds*? So what is the reason for beginning a new excavation or continuing an existing one? As a more modern history of archaeology, taking into account the discipline in its entirety and not just individual institutions or aspects, has not yet been written, only fragments of the whole picture can be discussed here.

B. 19TH CENT.

The question of the effects and consequences of new finds has its own tradition. In this connection, the early reception of the great discoveries of the 18th cent., e.g. at → HERCULANEUM [1], → POMPEII [25; 17], Paestum [30] and → ATHENS [37], is not being further pursued because, whatever contemporary consequences these excavations and publications had, they fall prior to the establishment of CA as a specialist discipline in the first half of the 19th cent. It is illuminating to see how two publications at the turn of the 19th to 20th cent., differing from one another not only in scope but also in approach, regarded the previous century in retrospect.

Reinhard Kekule von Stradonitz [2], in his rector's address at Berlin in 1901 [23] makes sculpture his sole theme entirely on the premise: 'The change in our conception of Greek art has been for the most part and above all provoked by the discovery of evidence of that art that were not previously available to us' [23.4]. Kekule sees four high points in the discoveries of the → PARTHENON sculptures, the Temple of Aphaia on → AEGINA, the Temple of Zeus at → OLYMPIA and the

Great Altar of → PERGAMUM, but in summing up he gives as the most significant achievement of the 19th cent. 'the heightened understanding and better appreciation of archaic and Hellenistic art' [23. 27]. For the time being the Olympia sculptures are consigned to a position between the Aeginetan Marbles and the Parthenon sculptures [23. 19]; the time was not yet ripe for the special qualities of the 'Severe Style' to be appreciated in their own right. The fact that the Aeginetan Marbles, after being regarded as unusual for decades throughout the 19th cent., had only become more comprehensible after 1885 with the new Archaic finds from the Athenian acropolis, remains as a reservation regarding his Kekule's retrospective. But above all: he speaks only of finds and artworks; the actual excavations and assessments are ignored, even though the excavations at Olympia had advanced the use of stratigraphy as a method for the first time in CA [26. 121–129], and although as director of the Berlin Museum Kekule had previously initiated and promoted excavations in Asia Minor and on Samos. His speech once again attempts to view new finds in an idealistic light. New finds are sought and understood as individual artworks out of the epistemological interest of the archaeology of art. The desire for the 'discovery of new evidence' manifests itself as a non-specific interest in an influx of 'high' art.

Five years later, Adolf Michaelis' [13] book [26] paints a different picture. He counts archaeology among the 'conquering sciences of the 19th cent'. [26. 1]; 'the archaeology of the spade' [26. VII] has remained a byword within the discipline. At that time Michaelis stood (as did Kekule, in fact) at the centre of the process of transforming the subject from its origins in philology and art history into a complex, methodologically-rich and -aware historical discipline, more specifically into an excavation-based science, and this is the topic covered in the chapters of his book: 'Excavation strives everywhere for the whole picture without neglecting the individual detail. It strives to establish the original nature of the overall site as well as its individual components, to pursue gradual transformations over the course of epochs, to assign a fixed place to every detail in this process, and thus to make the excavation at the same time a reconstruction of the entire lost complex' [26. 152].

The alteration in attitudes to new finds had begun early in the 19th cent., as can be seen from the *Denkschrift über Notwendigkeit und Zweck der Hyperboreisch-Römischen Gesellschaft* from the 1820s [33. 5–20, esp. 18ff.] dealing with the foundation of the *Istituto di Corrispondenza Archeologica*, from the early history of that institution, and the treatment of new finds in its regular colloquiums [28. 9–12]. But the real revolution in epistemological interest towards a science of excavation does not occur until the second half of the century.

After the middle of the 19th cent., the insight that Charles Darwin's theory of evolution included human beings [10] led to the conclusion that *Homo sapiens* had

a long history behind him, a longer one than had once been envisaged by the old calculations of the creation of the world. This cleared the way for renewed and less inhibited appraisal of human artifacts from earlier times. At the same time, however, during these years national interests in archaeology begin to become evident and to have consequences ('archaeology as a conquering science'). The *Istituto di Corrispondenza Archeologica* becomes an institution of the Prussian state (1859); the → École Française d'Athènes is founded in Greece (1846). The other national research institutions in the motherlands of Greek and Roman culture follow at intervals corresponding to political development, i.e. after the foundation of the Second Reich in the case of Germany. With the foundation of the national research institutions the association between politics and the archaeological discipline was everywhere intensified. Research projects were planned with national prestige in mind, and this is the spirit in which excavations began at many locations within the Mediterranean world. This area, which belongs in the more extensive chapter on 'Archaeology and society', must become one of the central chapters of a future history of archaeology. In the present context it is significant that in this manner the fund of archaeological monuments, excavations and findings grew to an extraordinary extent in a very short time, and that researchers were granted many opportunities to develop and refine their new excavational techniques. Archaeology definitively became 'the science of the spade'. Delos and Delphi, Olympia and Pergamum, → MYCENAE and → KNOSSOS: these are bywords that immediately and distinctly call to mind the pioneering spirit of those decades. One could and should extend the list to include the great archaeological sites of Egypt and Mesopotamia. Without the technical and mechanical aids available today, in the 2nd half of the 19th cent. huge problems of archaeological fieldwork were tackled (and overcome!), and projects were now increasingly carried out in the sense of a systematic science of excavation. The fact that at the same time field archaeology as a search for treasure persisted for a long time is one of the dark chapters of CA and its sister disciplines.

But it was not archaeologists in the Mediterranean region and the Orient who were at the forefront of progress towards a systematic science of excavation, but people like the Dane J. K. Worsaae with his excavations in Jutland or Pitt Rivers with his in England [24. 36–39]. Giuseppe Fiorelli at Pompeii [15; 16], Alexander Conze at Samothrace [9], Ernst Curtius and Wilhelm Dörpfeld at Olympia [10], Heinrich Schliemann at → TROY and → MYCENAE (first [34; 35]) and Flinders Petrie in Egypt [29; 30] followed after an interval. But from then on, there was no turning back. Archaeology became a discipline with its own particular structure and of its own type.

From its first beginnings the progress of excavational methodology has not ceased. Technological developments and discoveries in the natural sciences have exerted a continuous influence on archaeological methods. At the same time, of course, the improvement in excavational methods has had its price. Necessarily, the progress of the excavation is slowed in a way that brings it into permanent conflict of many kinds with the patron, who is soon no longer willing to accept the increasing costs; with the public, which soon sees itself, once again, being cheated of its right to be informed; and with the site itself, where the risks of damage, either accidental or wilful but in either case undocumented, increase. And finally the 'big excavation' has to accept the accusation that the large amount of money concentrated on it contributes indirectly to the demise of many small sites, which are then neglected. Nonetheless, in recent times modern archaeological exploratory techniques have been able to partially remedy this situation (e.g. [19]).

The aim of excavational methods in CA is unambiguously, or, once again, historical (see below), but its procedures have affinities with those of the natural sciences, and make their contribution to the further development of technical and scientific methods and equipment. Categories of finds also are no longer he main purpose of the excavation and its publication; it is no longer a matter of finds of classes of material (which of course continue to assert their right), but of ensembles of finds provide insight into the social reality of those who bequeathed these finds. The *New Archaeology* of the 1960s summarised this in its dictum 'archaeology is anthropology or nothing' [14. 9]. Excavations provide at first facts, pieces of evidence, that are measurable and must be measured and documented. This gives rise to the hope that the archaeological sciences are no longer reliant on the humanities-orientated, hermeneutic method, and research has on occasion expressed this aspiration with pride. *New Archaeology* saw archaeology overall as a natural science, and from that derived its entitlement to arrive at generalisations having the character of laws, which in turn gave rise not only to the interest in quantification and similar lines of inquiry but also to conflict with the idea that history is unrepeatable and unique [14; 4. 35ff.]. Moreover, if they are not submitted to a subsequent hermeneutic line of inquiry, findings and finds give up only the first half of the information they contain; an early expression of this is contained in the contradictions of the very systematic excavator Flinders Petrie, which are as entertaining as they are programmatic: 'the only rule that may be called general is, that digging must be systematic' is followed, two sentences later, by: 'the main acquirement always needed is plenty of imagination. Imagination is the fire of discoverment' [30. 156]. It is to the archaeological fieldwork of those times that we owe the decisive paradigm shift represented by the redirection of leading interests onto the path of historical inquiry. History and archaeology came closer to one another, but archaeology changed more than did Ancient History. Henceforth it became the unambiguous goal of all → ARCHAEOLOGICAL methods and procedures to reconstruct

the past and to learn to understand the people of Antiquity as socially active individuals or groups. Of course this paradigm shift was not an abrupt event, and not everywhere was it readily accepted. The increase in quite new, hitherto unknown categories of monuments opened up historical epochs that on the basis of the sources available hitherto were scarcely accessible, but the new situation was to some extent only partially and tardily discerned. Triumph and defeat of the new archaeological methods were never far apart.

The excavation of the Acropolis of Athens stands as a momentous defeat [7]. Once the young Greek state had cleared the citadel of its inhabitants and Schinkel's idea of establishing the royal residence there had fallen through, the ruler handed it over to the archaeologists. The fact that scientific methods of excavation did not yet play any role in the initial operations prior to the middle of the century can be explained by the state of science at the time. The great exploratory campaign initiated by Greek and German archaeologists in common in 1882, and assuming its full scope from 1885 on, in the first place satisfied, on the one hand, the fateful decision that the purpose would be to restore the Acropolis of the 5th cent. BC, the citadel of the time of Pericles. The outcome was that everything else was consigned to oblivion, and virtually nothing was documented. On the other hand, work was carried out in full understanding of stratigraphy and its significance. As the layers of millennia on the Acropolis could by no manner of means remain undisturbed, the archaeologists were soon at a loss. In this unexpected situation they did not come to the conclusion that they should wait a while, but abandoned the entire hard-won methodical apparatus, and simply tipped all the 'soil' down from the Acropolis. The stratigraphy of the Acropolis was thus lost for ever. Instead, they concentrated on finds, and in this way the various Archaic-period sculptures that had so splendidly adorned the Acropolis prior to the destruction of 480 BC came to light. Now monuments became visible from a time known only from fragments of Archaic poetry -and even of that, considerably less was known than today. The Archaic sculpture of the votive statues and the decoration of the Archaic structures were so new and strange that the generation of archaeologists scarcely knew how to appreciate them.

The excavation of Olympia stands out, in contrast, as a success story, even if on the basis of simpler premises [10; 20. 203–207]. Once the Alpheius had completely buried the remains of the half-destroyed sanctuary and traces of the last Early Byzantine settlement under its alluvial sands during the Early and Late Byzantine Period, the site remained as good as untouched for centuries. Although the early attempt to pursue stratigraphical methods disregarded the site's final settlement phase, below it were found many undisturbed layers. Today therefore, the only reliable starting point for the archaeology of early Greek religion is, so far as the sanctuary is concerned, Olympia; it cannot be → DEL-

PHI, which was begun without any regard for stratigraphy. Here at Olympia researchers first encountered the passion of pious Greeks from Homer's time for sacrifices and offerings, in the form of thousands of both small and large bronze objects. At Olympia, for the first time, researchers and the public in general had the opportunity to gain an insight not only into the religious experiences but also into the religious compulsions of the early visitors to the sanctuary. Of the sculptures of the Temple of Zeus little had been removed by the unsystematic excavations of earlier expeditions; for the most part, however, at the beginning of the German excavations from 1875 the fragments were found, apart from single pieces which were farther removed, in the vicinity of the structure. For this reason, the distribution of the fragments on both pediments was for the most part clear from the beginning, and the archaeologists were already able to produce a reconstruction that, while requiring adjustment in its details later on, provided an appropriate encounter with that characteristic post-Archaic but pre-Classical formal world, later given the name 'Severe Style' [8]. Although the then generation of archaeologists recognised the strangeness and absolute novelty of this art [5], they could not go beyond acknowledging that strangeness. Only the subsequent generation could really enter fully into its world and recognise it as a distinct stage of Greek cultural history [8]. It is characteristic that Praxiteles' Hermes, found at the same time, was immediately admitted into the salons of bourgeois houses as a → SOUVENIR in the form of miniature copies of details in marble and clay – that same Hermes to which Aristide Maillol reacted with distaste a generation later in 1909 ('sculpté comme dans du savon de Marseille') [5. 59f., 69]. It took considerably longer for the sculptures of the Temple of Zeus to fall prey to the souvenir industry. The period of their discovery was, as it were, not yet ready for them.

C. 20TH Cent.

In saying that the progress towards scientific excavation was irreversible, we include the experience of the modern day. In view of the young age of the area as a consciously methodological, historical discipline, the position as regards source material for archaeological work can only be bad. Either the old stock of objects has not been sufficiently appraised and publicised, or sufficient source material to answer the questions that preoccupy the researcher is simply lacking. Thus everyone is continually faced with the decision to secure sufficiently meaningful sources for himself within his area of expertise. The decision may be for a targeted excavation, with the idea that it will provide the material looked for. This brings with it the implication and the 'risk' that the excavator then assumes responsibility for material that was neither looked for nor expected. When investigation of the inhabited quarter was begun in post-war Pergamum it was a question of finding the quarters of the Hellenistic and early Roman 'bourgeoisie' that related to the palaces of the upper city, and of

finding out how they interacted. In reality, what was found was Early Byzantine Pergamum, and nowhere in the Eastern Mediterranean can more be learned about the cultural context of Early Byzantine urban life than at Pergamum [31]. Old finds cease to be perceived as the outcome of an excavation, so that a recent dissertation on houses in Pompeii can maintain in its introduction that its ideas are based 'not on excavations, but solely on visible findings above ground', but at the same time ingenuously offers the consideration that 'experience shows that targeted follow-up excavations for the testing of hypotheses seldom produce the desired outcome; indeed they always carry with them the risk of increasing the quantity of unsolved problems' [12. 16f.]. Nowadays, it is not only 'spade-based archaeology' that offers itself as an appropriate means of acquiring source material: fascinating new methods of exploration continue to prove their worth (e.g. [18]), just as new techniques refine the possibilities for interpreting long-familiar monuments (cf. e.g. Fig. 1).

Meanwhile, an entire discipline has grown up around the growth caused by new excavations and new finds. Wherever possible, every university carries out 'its' excavation or collaborates in an expedition led by others. And yet at the same time the growth in new finds and new findings becomes a separate entity and distances itself from us. The immense push for modernisation in Mediterranean lands during the last 50 years altered the settlement of the Classical countries more than for whole centuries previously, so that new finds of less crucial significance than those supplied by big excavations (*big digs* to our American colleagues), now became everyday occurrences on a massive scale. Local archaeological services incessantly document chance findings and store the finds. In all Mediterranean countries within the former *Imperium Romanum* there are national periodicals – usually several in individual countries – that do nothing but publicise new excavations and finds. When the NSA began to be suffocated by its duty to publish, BA for a time took on the job of presenting new excavations and results of excavations. When this journal was no longer up to the task it was joined by the BOLL. DI ARCH. (1, 1990ff.). In addition, in Northern Italy the superintendents of the individual regions publish periodicals devoted to finds (*pars pro compluribus: Soprintendenza Archeologica della Lombardia. Notiziario* 1981ff.; *Notizie Archeologiche Bergomensi* 1, 1993ff.). In Greece, apart from *Praktika*, the bulletins of the Archaeological Society in Athens, and its abridged version in the annual working report *To ergon*, there are the weighty state volumes or double volumes of the annual chronicle of the bulletin *AD*. This in turn is supplemented by regional reports such as the fast-swelling annual reports from Macedonia *To archeologikó érgo sti Makedonía ke Thráki* 1, 1987ff. In Turkey, too, several new periodicals providing reports on excavations and new finds are available alongside the old ones, etc. etc.

Fig. 1: Delphi, detail from the North Frieze of the Siphnian Treasury: Athena and Achilles (?) fighting with the Giants. The inclusion of new photographical methods (ultraviolet and sidelight photography, etc.) has since the mid-1960s produced a wealth of observations and documentations equalling that of new finds. The decoding of the colourful decoration of Greek archaic sculpture has begun and will alter its appreciation considerably.

It is no longer possible for the individual researcher even merely to register the abundance of material that annually accumulates in these volumes. Scholarship frequently is carried on without notice being taken of the multitude of new findings and when, in the midst of this stream of material, something occasionally shows up that is spectacular and of importance for cultural history in general, it meets with resentful scepticism. Or the very novelty and strangeness of significant individual works prevents them from fitting into existing categories, leaving researchers bewildered or reacting with incomprehension. Figs. 2–5 from the realm of Greek sculpture illustrate some examples whose reception researchers found and still find characteristically difficult. Occasionally, however, new finds provide access to areas of ancient art that were believed to be lost to us for ever, such as Greek painting (cf. Figs. 6a-b). Attempts have been and still are being made by particular journals to collate and summarise information on new excavations and finds for particular regions within the Mediterranean area. For decades Mechthild Mellink reported in the AJA on *Archaeology in Asia Minor*. After her death attempts were for a while made to maintain the tradition, but now it appears to have lapsed. The → Deutsches Archäologisches Institut in Rome has for many decades provided information on research in Italy and North Africa in the form of summaries of find-reports in the AA. But a mood of resignation has for the time being put an end to these reports. There remain for the time being the journal of the BCH and the summaries of the Archaeological Reports. The duty to document new finds and findings is unarguable. And it is to be expected that media developed in the new information technologies will be used both alongside

and in place of printed publications. But the resignation caused by the flood of material is unmistakable.

And yet that attitude of expectation with respect to new finds, that orientation towards the new, whatever it may be, persists. But the fact that many old questions are still awaiting an answer, that old answers either must be reassessed or evidently no longer apply, that other old answers and insights may indeed remain apt and appropriate even for today's generation, and in the light of positive reassessment could cause us to alter our positions: all this is rendered foggy and indistinct by the focusing of our attention on new finds. Lecturers in the course of their work may experience this when, on the one hand, they realise with some agitation how little of what they thought two decades ago may still apply to a particular theme, but on the other hand first-year students, caught up in this tense and excited voyage of discovery, pour out their hearts and complain that they had expected to learn more about new ceramics etc., and now are faced with going over old ground. This is not only the familiar case of the pedagogical failure of a lecturer who has not managed sufficiently to communicate his academic enthusiasm, but also the general truth that it is the new that counts. Mountains of academic knowledge and source material threaten to bar access to the 'reality' of Antiquity, and this has often been the case throughout the history of ancient studies, most recently and very clearly in the late 19th cent.

In conclusion: archaeological research is today caught in a double paradox. Its thirst for knowledge is characterised by the urge for new finds: it seeks them, and indeed must seek them. At the same time it is no longer capable of receiving and reviewing the continuous and voluminous flood of new data, contexts and

Fig. 2: Portrait herm of Themistocles. Copy after a lost
original, *c.* 470 BC. Ostia, Museo.
When the sculpture was found in 1940, the actual
'portrait value' and the realism of the work were
felt to be so novel that scholars were at first reluctant
to learn and accept the fact that Greek portraiture
in the narrow sense already set in during the Severe Style.
Deutsches Archäologisches Institut

Fig. 3: Statue of a young man, found in 1979
at the site of a Punic settlement on the island of Mozia
off the west coast of Sicily.
Mozia, Museo Whitaker.
For twenty years, the iconographic uniqueness,
the apparent contrast between the Severe Style head
and the 'much later' elements of the body, as well
as the surprising realism of various details have left
scholars if not perplexed then at least at odds
with each other. A commonly accepted identification
and explanation of the statue has yet to be reached.

Fig. 4: Bronze portrait, recovered in 1969 from
the sea off Porticello (Calabria).
Reggio Calabria, Museo Nazionale.
Other finds from the same site have helped date
the shipwreck to the late fifth/early fourth cent. BC.
Because of its expressive physiognomy the sculpture
was initially published as a Hellenistic work of art.
This despite the fact that the excavation findings told
a different story. It simply would not fit in with the
then-known history of Greek portraiture.
*Su concessione n. 1 del 10/01/2006 del Minsterio per I Beni
e le Attività Culturali – Museo Nazionale Archeologico
di Reggio Calabria*

Fig. 5: Statue of a hero, recovered from the sea off Riace
(Calabria). Reggio Calabria, Museo Nazionale.
With the discovery of the two statues in 1972, the stock
of original classical bronze sculptures was doubled
in one fell swoop. The almost tangible physical presence,
the exactness of single shapes, the unexpected realism
within a larger concept of ideality – all this surpassed that
which had been known from Imperial copies of classic
sculptures. This revised image of classical sculpture has not
yet been universally accepted: the 1984 publication of the
Riace statues (L.V. Borelli, P. Pelagatti (eds.), Due Bronzi
di Riace I–II, with ingenious measuring and drawing
methods) failed to set the standard for new sculpture
publications.
Hirmer Photoarchiv, München

Fig. 6a: Royal Hunt, fresco over the entrance to Tomb II in the Great Tumulus of Vergina (Macedonia).
Reconstruction after M. Andronicos, Vergina. The Royal Tombs, 1984, 102f.
Deutsches Archäologisches Institut

Fig. 6b: Drawing of the hunting scene, with additional material, according to Lorenz Baumer. The excavation of the royal
tombs of Vergina began in 1977, but their publication will not be completed for quite some time. Because of the authority
of the excavator, the attribution of the main tomb to Philip II has long remained undisputed. New interpretations have
raised doubts, and later occupants (Kassander, Philip III) have been suggested. In any case, the depictions full of passion
are the first original examples of great painting from the late fourth cent. BC – they show an affinity to the masters
whose names we only know from ancient art criticism. In the long-running controversy over the beginning of ancient
landscape painting, the new find at Vergina finally tipped the scales in favour of an early onset in early Hellenism.
Deutsches Archäologisches Institut

finds in such a way as to combine the splinters of individual observations and chance outcomes into history, adequately and in an appropriate timeframe. At the same time, however, semi twilight has fallen over the old familiar monuments and rendered them unimportant to us. The discipline no longer has the courage to take the old familiar, so-called masterworks quite seriously as regards anything they might have to say to the modern generation. The sociological approach reveals particular aspects of ancient societies; but, to take just one example, the graves in the post-Classical necropoleis of Athens and Apulia when examined along sociological lines (e.g. [3; 18]) give only a partial account of the society surrounding those graves. Hermeneutic interpretation of tomb reliefs and Apulian vase-paintings reveals realities that are not accessible to a contextual examination of the grave complex (e.g. [22; 36]).

How, in conclusion, can we find a way to overcome the paradoxes outlined above? There is of course no simple solution, but our search should probably begin by addressing the current debate between *New Archaeology* and post-modern archaeology, which prefers to be called post-processual archaeology, and by making our position clear. The post-modern assault of a

Michael Shanks [37], who, in his call for a 'prehistory of classical Greece', makes himself the advocate of a pluralism of historical truths, merits our involvement and our outright opposition [27]. If pluralism of methods were directly parallel to a pluralism of truths that were all of equal worth, then an accumulation of data and finds would at best broaden our reconstruction of history, but it would no longer be capable of altering our picture of ancient society. A plea should be made for the old ways once again to be taken seriously, namely for examining when a truth is capable of being verified or falsified. In this way, the significance for our lives of that which is new and old among our views and finds will, as it were, become completely visible.

→ ATHENS; → NATIONAL RESEARCH INSTITUTES

1 Antichità di Ercolano, 9 vols., Naples 1757–1792 2 G. BAADER, Reinhard Kekule, in: NDB 11, 1971, 424–426 3 J. BERGEMANN, Demos und Thanatos. Untersuchungen zum Wertesystem der Polis im Spiegel der attischen Grabreliefs des 4. Jahrhunderts vor Christus und zur Funktion der gleichzeitigen Grabbauten, 1997 4 R. BERNBECK, Theorien in der Archäologie, 1997 5 C. BLÜMEL, Hermes eines Praxiteles, 1948 6 H. BRUNN, Die Skulpturen von Olympia, in: SBAW 1877, I 1, 128 (repr. in: Id., Kleine Schriften 2, 1905, 201–217 und abridged [19. 203–210])

7 J. A. Bundgaard, The Excavation of the Athenian Acropolis 1882–1890, 1974   8 E. Buschor, R. Hamann, Die Skulpturen des Zeustempels von Olympia, 1924 (Text, E. Buschor; reprinted [19. 221–235])   9 A. Conze et al. (eds.), Archäologische Untersuchungen auf Samothrake, 2 vols. Wien 1875–1880   10 E. Curtius et al. (eds.), Ausgrabungen zu Olympia, 5 vols., Berlin 1876–1881   11 Ch. Darwin, On the Origin of Species by Means of Natural Selection, or the Preservation of Favoured Races in the Struggle for Life, London 1859   12 J. A. Dickmann, domus frequentata. Anspruchsvolles Wohnen im pompejanischen Stadthaus, 1999   13 H. Döhl, Adolf Michaelis, in: NDB 17, 1994, 429f.   14 St. L. Dyson, A Classical Archaeologist's Response to the New Archaeology, in: BASO 242, 1981, 7–14   15 G. Fiorelli, Appunti autobiografici (ed. and introduction St. De Caro), 1994   16 G. Fiorelli, Giornale degli scavi di Pompei 1, 1850ff.   17 L. Garcia y Garcia, Nova Bibliotheca Pompeiana 1–2, 1998   18 D. Gräpler, Tonfiguren im Grab. Fundkontexte hellenistischer Terrakotten aus der Nekropole von Tarent, 1997   19 M. Heinzelmann, Arbeitsbericht zu einer zweiten geophysikalischen Prospektionskampagne in Ostia Antica, in: MDAI(R) 105, 1998, 425–429   20 H. V. Herrmann, Olympia. Heiligtum und Wettkampfstätte, 1972   21 Id. (ed.), Die Olympia-Skulpturen, 1987   22 N. Himmelmann, Attische Grabreliefs, 1999   23 R. Kekule von Stradonitz, Die Vorstellungen griechischer Kunst und ihre Wandlung im 19 Jahrhundert. Rede bei Antritt des Rectorats, 1901   24 F. G. Maier, Neue Wege in die alte Welt. Methoden der modernen Archäologie, 1977   25 F. Mazois, Les ruines de Pompéi, 4 vols. Paris 1812–1838   26 A. Michaelis, Die archäologischen Entdeckungen des 19. Jahrhunderts, 1906 (Second edition: Ein Jahrhundert kunstarchäologischen Entdeckungen, ²1908 cited here)   27 N. Müller-Scheessel, 'Archaeology is nothing if it is not critique'. Zum Archäologieverständnis von Michael Shanks und Christopher Tilley, in: M. K. H. Eggert, U. Veit (eds.), Theorie in der Archäologie: Zur englischsprachigen Diskussion, 1998, 243–271   28 R. Neudecker, M. G. Granino Cecere, Antike Skulpturen und Inschriften im Institutum Archeologicum Germanicum, 1997   29 W. M. Flinders Petrie, Seventy Years in Archaeology, 1931   30 Id., Ten Years Digging in Egypt 1892 (²1893 cited here)   31 J. Raspi Serra (ed.), Paestum – idea e immagine. Antologia di testi critici e di immagini di Paestum 1750–1836, 1990   32 K. Rheidt, Die byzantinische Wohnstadt. Altertümer von Pergamon 15.2, 1991   33 A. Rieche (ed.), Die Satzungen des Deutschen Archäologischen Instituts 1828 bis 1972, 1979   34 H. Schliemann, Ithaka, der Peloponnes und Troja, 1869   35 Schliemann und Troja. Ausstellungskatalog (exhibition catalogue) Munich, Prähistorosche Staatssammlung, 1992   36 M. Schmidt, Aufbruch oder Verharren in der Unterwelt? Nochmals zu den apulischen Vasenbildern mit Darstellungen des Hades, in: AK 43, 2000   37 M. Shanks, Classical Archaeology of Greece: Experiences of the Discipline, 1996   38 J. Stuart, N. Revett, Antiquities of Athens, 3 vols., London ²1762–1794.

DIETRICH WILLERS

III. Contextual Archaeology
A. Terminology   B. From Art in Context to Contextual Archaeology   C. Pompeii as a Case in Point   D. Problems of Contextual Archaeology

A. Terminology

The term Contextual Archaeology (ContA) is used to describe an archaeology in which the context of material remains is taken as a basis for the investigation of the ancient living world [*Lebenswelt*] [50], the purpose being to formulate a cultural history of Antiquity [58; 54]. Cont. A. takes account of linguistic and literary material, but places emphasis on the autonomy of visual sources (for the figurative context: [38; 83]). Cont. A. is founded on a synchro-spatial conception of context with regard the three findings categories of grave, sanctuary and settlement [25. 264–268], without, however, orienting its interpretations strictly on these types of context. This conception of ContA differs from the 'Contextual Archaeology' propagated by Hodder [35. 118–146], since Hodder does not restrict himself only to defining context in spatial terms, embracing everything from the tiniest perceptible archaeological entity to archaeological culture [36. 85], but also includes research constructs such as typological or stylistic groups and categories and system relationships (critique: [8]). It is assumed that conclusions as to the living world can be reached on the basis of archaeological contexts, over and above the information provided by literary sources, the contextual approach being in Whitley's words 'the *sine qua non* of any attempt to write cultural history from archaeological evidence' [78. 52]. This is based on the consideration that archaeological contexts – quite apart from post-depositional aspects – cannot be regarded as reflecting the circumstances, not even the material circumstances, of Antiquity, but rather should be seen as evidence of a chronologically and spatially fixed selection which is determined by specific human actions and conceptions [69. 356–358; 38.151].

B. From Art in Context to Contextual Archaeology

Although the context of findings has been an aspect of modern archaeology since the beginning of scientific excavations oriented toward the determination of the wider interconnections within ancient locations in the late 19th cent, archaeology has, until far into the 20th cent., de facto been characterised by the incorporation of decontextualised finds and images or motifs into typological, stylistic or iconographic groups and categories, which were then interpreted on the basis of actualistic borrowings from the literary tradition. Accordingly, both in Panofsky's concept of art history as well in the art-historical archaeology of Bianchi Bandinelli between the wars, archaeology was conceived of virtually as reconstruction of the contexts of ancient artworks, and thus, at the same time, as mere preliminary work for iconological or formal interpretation [59. 19–28; 15. 362].

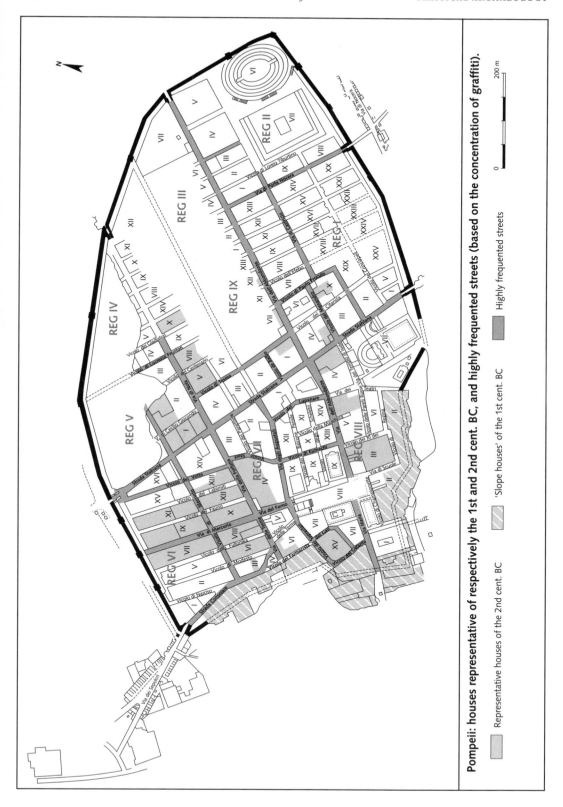

Pompeii: houses representative of respectively the 1st and 2nd cent. BC, and highly frequented streets (based on the concentration of graffiti).

Representative houses of the 2nd cent. BC

'Slope houses' of the 1st cent. BC

Representative houses of the 1st cent. BC

Highly frequented streets

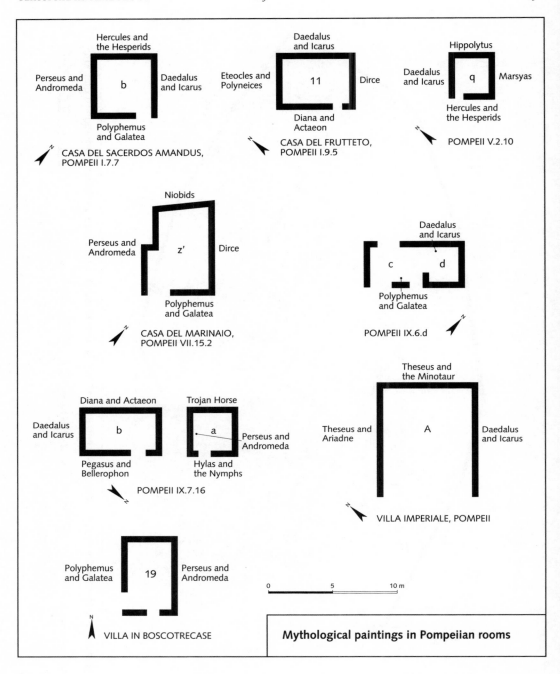

CASA DEL SACERDOS AMANDUS, POMPEII I.7.7

Hercules and the Hesperids — Perseus and Andromeda — Daedalus and Icarus — Polyphemus and Galatea — b

CASA DEL FRUTTETO, POMPEII I.9.5

Daedalus and Icarus — Eteocles and Polyneices — Dirce — Diana and Actaeon — 11

POMPEII V.2.10

Hippolytus — Daedalus and Icarus — Marsyas — Hercules and the Hesperids — q

CASA DEL MARINAIO, POMPEII VII.15.2

Niobids — Perseus and Andromeda — Dirce — Polyphemus and Galatea — z'

POMPEII IX.6.d

Daedalus and Icarus — Polyphemus and Galatea — c — d

POMPEII IX.7.16

Diana and Actaeon — Trojan Horse — Daedalus and Icarus — Perseus and Andromeda — Pegasus and Bellerophon — Hylas and the Nymphs — b — a

VILLA IMPERIALE, POMPEII

Theseus and the Minotaur — Theseus and Ariadne — Daedalus and Icarus — A

VILLA IN BOSCOTRECASE

Polyphemus and Galatea — Perseus and Andromeda — 19

0   5   10 m

Mythological paintings in Pompeiian rooms

Since the 1960s, however, context has been regarded as the key to overcoming the – in the final analysis politically motivated [44; 9. 100–102] – conflict between iconology and the hermeneutics of form. With the concepts of genre and decorum [29] or function, genre and medium [10] suggested by Gombrich and Belting, access to a view of monuments in the context of human actions and the way to a reception-oriented research has also been opened through the emphasis on context for the interpretation of works of art. To this extent, context provides us with a reflective method by which to lay bare the preconceptions implicitly overlaid onto sources by the researcher (interpretatively speaking: 'the contextual conditions of knowledge' [36. 68]). In CA too since the 1960s a sociological approach has been used to reconstruct the contexts of ancient artworks and monuments: in German archaeology primarily in relation to prestigious monuments (survey: [14]); in Italian Marxist-oriented archaeology [7. 181–184] directed also towards the lower classes, initially in

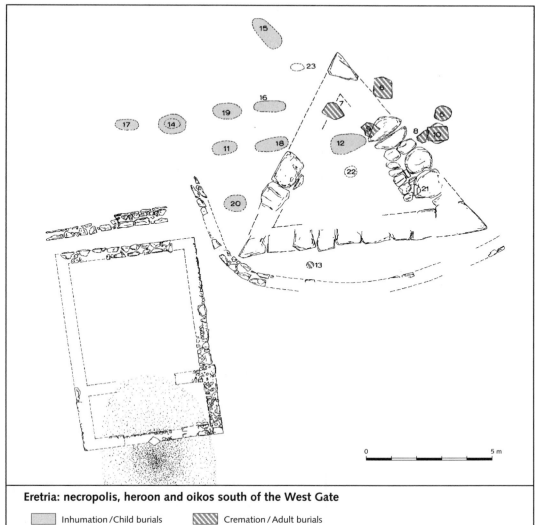

Eretria: necropolis, heroon and oikos south of the West Gate

Inhumation / Child burials   Cremation / Adult burials

relation to artworks and monuments, but then also extending to the 'cultura materiale' [16; 19]. The share of archaeological contributions in modern historical surveys is a sign of this socio-historical orientation (cf. in Italian research: *Storia di Roma* [51]; but internationally, also with contributions on reception history: *I Greci* [67]).

In contrast to art history, in which the context of monuments almost always represents a reconstruction-thus, borrowing on the one hand from Derrida, critical remarks regarding context as the basis of interpretation [6. 176–180], and on the other hand the demand for an interdisciplinary, contextual art history [40] archaeology has the context of material remains as its fundamental base. Even if the acquisition of archaeological contexts is subject to the conditions of archaeological research, ContA is capable of providing insights into the way culture and images were experienced in Anti-

quity, into figurative worlds and thus into conceptions and representations of space, religion [18] and politics. A precondition of ContA turns out to be a post-structuralistic, cultural-anthropological approach based on action theory (semiotically speaking, emphasising the pragmatic or signifier level [63] or the materiality of communication [33]), taken up into CA as a direct loan from cultural-anthropological studies via New Archaeology [68. 132–143; 69] and Post-Processual Archaeology [21; 68], via the ethnological orientation of French Antiquity studies ([47. 376–381; 75] cf. [61]), or within the framework of the increasing anthropologisation of humanities disciplines (New Cultural History).

C. POMPEII AS A CASE IN POINT

Even if, in recent years, → POMPEII (excavation history: [57. 16–19]) has long since lost its aura of a vir-

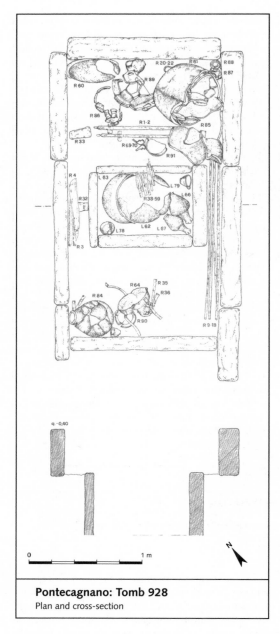

Pontecagnano: Tomb 928

Plan and cross-section

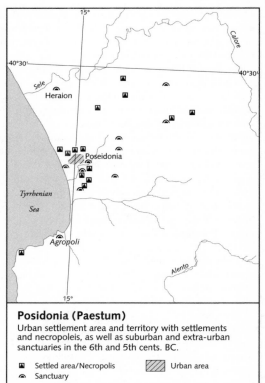

Posidonia (Paestum)

Urban settlement area and territory with settlements and necropoleis, as well as suburban and extra-urban sanctuaries in the 6th and 5th cents. BC.

▣ Settled area/Necropolis   ▨ Urban area

◠ Sanctuary

phasis on the domestic area [23] with its revaluation of the terms *privatus* and *domesticus* [27; 43] and the reassessment of the relationship between the private and the public space [79], there is still work to be done on central state monuments of Rome such as Trajan's Column [67] and the Imperial forums [82], if only with regard to the history of reception (cf.: [26; 80]).

Typical of the most recent research on Pompeii is the emphasis on the interaction between socially engaged activities and material culture, and thus among researchers a mutually interactive reassessment of material and literary sources. This entails analysis of the house as a living space and a display place for the *familia* [28; 76] on the basis of the association between rooms, room-sequences and furnishings, as well as the way the house integrates with the urban space. Another element is the interpretation of houses, streets and public facilities in the context of the urban structure, not only on the basis of form but also by reconstructing the way they were used. Thus streets are differentiated not only by reference to their course and width and their relationship to gates and public buildings, but also on the basis of graffiti (Fig. 1) and the entrances to houses [42], traces of wear and tear and street barriers, and the location of shops and taverns [42; 77]. The analysis of houses is no longer oriented towards a classification of house- and room-types on the basis of function, but towards the context of the architectural design and decoration. From this investigation, which also embra-

tually frozen social environment with objects *in situ*, only waiting to be excavated [3] as a result of the extension of the sociological approach orientated towards middle-class self-display to cover the investigation of urban life (cf. [24. 7; 81. 7–32]), it has become an experimental field for ContA in the framework of its modern investigation of the house and the town (overview: [49]; article [4]). In this respect, however, even for the Roman period, esp. the High and Late Imperial period, other sites must not be ignored. ContA in respect of the figurative environment and architecture is possible in the realm of mosaics in the absence of standing walls ([55. 19–47]: overview). And, notwithstanding the em-

ces the historical development of the structures concerned, has emerged a picture of the highly flexible use of space in buildings that are not at all of a type, but designed to answer particular needs [23; 24; 56], in which display houses and public buildings are associated with smaller private and commercial rooms in the same *insula*, i.e. the same building complex [60]. As regards mythical imagery, interest is moving away from reconstruction of the originals, the iconography of individual myths, from figurative programs derived from the combination of decontextualised myths within the framework of a generalised conception of Roman value systems, to concentrate on the analysis of mythical images in their architectural context, and thus the re-interpretation of their content on the basis of references, including formal references, arising from combinations or juxtapositions of images within the same space [13; 14] (Fig. 2).

The Casa del Fauno (Regio VI, Insula 12), always a central object of research, typifies the scope of ContA, both on the basis of the Alexander Mosaic and the size of the house, filling an entire *insula* as it does, and also on account of the so-called First Pompeian style of its decor, with its prestigious facade of tuffa blocks. In contrast to earlier methods, which examined the Alexander Mosaic as an autonomous object, a reflection of Greek painting, the decoration of the house in the context of the typology of Pompeian wall paintings, the architecture as an example of the development of the typical Pompeian house during the Hellenistic period, the emphasis now is on analysing the house as a structure with variously decorated rooms within the context of social life during the early Imperial period. It is only this approach that reveals the significance of a house that was begun in the 2nd cent. BC and fundamentally extended and luxuriously refitted around the turn of the same century in the context of a town belonging to the 3rd quarter of the 1st cent. AD [24; 30; 81, 40–49; 84; 85].

D. PROBLEMS OF CONTEXTUAL ARCHAEOLOGY

The new investigation of Pompeii during the 1990s was preceded by earlier action-theoretical structuralist approaches in other areas of archaeology. But problems of acceptance arise here, first because conservation and/or documentation of the material records seldom allows of anything beyond the level of microanalysis, and second because of a lack of contemporary literary material with contextual relevance. Favourable to interpretation are small, manageable contexts of findings such as the heroon over the necropolis at the western gate of Eretria (Fig. 3), where the cult building's association with the small necropolis results from the stratigraphy and from topographical proximity [11], or an individual grave such as Pontecagnano, grave 928 (Fig. 4), where the relationship between the topographical complexity of the tomb structure and the distribution of the various burial objects can be easily seen [1]. Larger necropoleis on the other hand require statistical

analysis, whose outcome, for example with regard to population structure, can then no longer be represented in an analogous manner. This applies to the modern excavations of the necropoleis of Pithekoussai [65] and Osteria dell'Osa [17] as well as to the archaic Kerameikos of → ATHENS, whose interpretation by Morris [52] became the subject of intense controversy for this very reason (cf. [53; 41. 9–19]), with the result that more recent work proceeds from smaller units such as a burial mound [39; 41].

Similar problems arise in the investigation of the extra-urban sanctuary (cf. [5; 45]), because here the conception developed from archaeological sources, in this case the geographical disposition of the sanctuaries and/or the finds and findings associated with them, cannot be set against a literary tradition. Like many topics in archaeology, that of the extra-urban sanctuary goes back to the beginning of the 20th cent. when, by virtue of the increasing number of excavations, names known from literary tradition, such as those of the great sanctuaries of *Magna Graecia*, acquired entirely new connotations by their association with finds and also from their topographical location. In one particular case a number of nude female statuettes from the sanctuary of Persephone, lying close outside the city walls of Locri Epizephirii, led to the thesis of an 'indigenous' background to the sanctuary, and thus of its functioning as a site of interaction between new Greek settlers and the local population under a religious shelter. This interpretation of a Greek sanctuary outside the protected settlement area, held particularly by Italian historians, as indicating an indigenous origin led to the firm anchoring of the extra-urban sanctuary in Italian archaeological discourse since the 1920s. Vital to the development of the concept of the extra-urban sanctuary, however, was a 1967 article by Vallet, [74] differentiating the sanctuaries of Greater Greece into urban, suburban and extra-urban, most clearly represented (today) by the city and *chora* of Posidonia (Fig. 5). However, Vallet conceived the extra-urban sanctuary not as a site of interaction, but as a sign of territorialisation associated with the foundation of Greek settlements. Fundamental to this interpretation is the structural conception of the Greek *polis* conveyed in particular by the historian Lepore (cf. [46]), adjusted to the 'colonisation situation' of *Magna Graecia* insofar as the relationship between city and country was conceived as analogous to that between Greeks and natives. This conception, which uses the distribution of material culture to explain historical events, and in reconstructing the way in which the Greek settlers adapted to their environment also reconstructs their living culture, has widely asserted itself among Italian researchers. Various aspects already touched upon by Vallet have been further developed subsequently: the territorial aspect in the direction of 'santuari di frontiera' [20; 34; 70], the aspect of commerce by association with the concept of the *emporion* ([71; 72] cf. [46]), the liminal aspect in the direction of rites of initiation [32]. In this context the finds themselves were brought back to the fore. The iconography of the metopes of the *Heraion* at the mouth of the Sele and that of the great extra-urban sanctuary of Posidonia are associated with the function of the sanctuary as a site either of interaction [62] or of territorialisation [73]. But it was not until De Polignac transferred the concept to the Greek motherland that this discourse was extended beyond the confines of Italian archaeology ([22], cf. [37]), and, as in the case of Morris's work, by its claim to provide a contribution to the question of the emergence of the polis became quite controversial (on the discussion cf. the congresses: [2; 39; 48]). The application of the archaeological concept is rejected by the historical side, since an interpretation of the extra-urban sanctuary is not explicitly attested by literary sources, and because of the high degree of generalisation this is regarded as unhistorical [48]. On the other hand, this provides the very basis for a transfer of the concept to the cities of Etruria and Latium [72], and thus for a comparative archaeology.

→ ARCHAEOLOGICAL METHODS; → CULTURAL ANTHROPOLOGY; → RECONSTRUCTION/CONSTRUCTION; → STRUCTURALISM

1 B. D'AGOSTINO, Tombe 'principesche' dell'orientalizzante antico da Pontecagnano, in: Mon. Ant. ined. 49, Ser. Misc. 2, 1977, 1–110 2 S. ALCOCK, R. OSBORNE (eds.), Placing the Gods. Sanctuaries and Sacred Space in Ancient Greece, 1994 3 P. ALLISON, Artefact assemblages. Not 'the Pompeii premise', in: E. HERRING, R. WHITEHOUSE, J. WILKINS (eds.), Papers of the Fourth Conference of Italian Archaeology 3, 1992, 49–56 4 Id., Lables for Ladles. Interpreting the Material Culture of Roman Households, in: Id. (ed.), The Archaeology of Household Activities, 1999, 57–77 5 D. ASHERI, A propos des sanctuaires extraurbains en Sicile et Grand-Grèce. Théories et témoignages, in: Mélanges P. Lévêque, vol. 1., Religion, 1988, 1–15 6 M. BAL, N. BRYSON, Semiotics and Art History, in: Art Bulletin 73, 1991, 174–208 7 M. BARBANERA, L'archeologia degli Italiani. Storia, metodi e orientamenti dell'archeologia classica in Italia. Con un contributo di Nicola Terrenato (175–192), 1998 8 J. C. BARRETT, Contextual Archaeology, in: Antiquity 61, 1987, 468–473 9 M. BAUMGARTNER, Einführung in das Studium der Kunstgeschichte, 1998 10 H. BELTING, Das Werk im Kontext, in: Id., H. DILLY, W. KEMP, W. SAUERLÄNDER, M. WARNKE (eds.), Kunstgeschichte. Eine Einführung, 1985, 186–202 11 C. BÉRARD, L'Héroon à la porte de l'ouest, (= Eretria 3) 1970 12 B. BERGMANN, The Roman House as Memory Theater. The House of the Tragic Poet in Pompeii, in: ArtBulletin 76, 1994, 225–256 13 Id., Rhythms of Recognition. Mythological Encounters in Roman Landscape Painting, in: F. de Angelis, S. MUTH (eds.), Im Spiegel des Mythos. Bilderwelt und Lebenswelt, Symposium 19.–20. Februar 1998 (= Palilia 6), 1999, 81–107 14 M. BERGMANN, Repräsentation, in: A. H. BORBEIN, T. HÖLSCHER, P. ZANKER (eds.), Klassische Archäologie, Eine Einführung, 2000, 166–188 15 R. BIANCHI Bandinelli, Archeologia e critica d'arte, in: La Nuova Italia 1, 1930, 360–364 16 Id., Arte plebea, in: Dialoghi di Archeologia 1, 1967, 7–19 17 A. M. BIETTI SESTIERI, The Iron Age Community of Osteria dell'Osa. A Study of Sociopolitical Development in Central Tyrrhenian Italy, 1992 18 H. CANCIK, H. MOHR, s. v. Religionsästhetik, in: Handbuch religionswissenschaftlicher Grundbegriffe 1, 1988, 121–156 19 A. CARANDINI, A. RICCI, Settefinestre. Una villa schiavistica nell'Etruria romana, 1985 20 Confini e frontiera nella grecità d'Occidente, Atti del 37. convegno di studi sulla Magna Grecia, Taranto 1997, 1999 21 M. CUOZZO, Prospettive teoriche e metodologiche nell'interpretazione delle necropoli. La Post-Processual Archaeology, in: Annali di Archelogia e storia antica dell'Instituto Orientale di Napoli 3, 1996, 1–37 22 F. DE POLIGNAC, La naissance de la cité grecque. Culte, espace et société, 1984, ²1995 23 J.-A. DICKMANN, Der Fall Pompeji. Wohnen in einer antiken Kleinstadt, in: W. HOEPFNER (ed.), Geschichte des Wohnens vol. 1, 5000 v. Chr.–500 n. Chr., Vorgeschichte, Frühgeschichte, Antike, 1999, 611–678 24 Id., *domus frequentata*. Anspruchsvolles Wohnen im pompejanischen Stadthaus, 1999 25 H. J. EGGERS, Einführung in die Vorgeschichte, 1959 26 J. R. ELSNER, Art and the Roman Viewer, 1995 27 E. GAZDA (ed.), Roman Art in a Private Sphere. New Perspectives on the Architecture and Decor of the Domus, Villa, and Insula, 1991 28 M. GEORGE, Repopulating the Roman House, in: B. RAWSON, P. WEAVER (eds.), The Roman Family in Italy. Status, Sentiment, Space, 1997, 299–319 29 E. H. GOMBRICH, Symbolic Images, Studies in the Art of the Renaissance, 1972, 1–25 30 M. GRAHAME, Public and Private in the Roman House. The Spatial Order of the Casa del Fauno, in: [43. 137–164] 31 Id., Material Culture and Roman identity, in: R. LAURENCE, J. BERRY (eds.), Cultural Identity in the Roman Empire, 1998, 156–178 32 G. GRECO, Santuari extraurbani tra periferia cittadina e periferia indigena, in: La colonisation grecque en Méditerranée occidentale, Actes de la rencontre scientifique en hommage à Georges Vallet, 1999, 231–247 33 H. U. GUMBRECHT, K. L. PFEIFFER (eds.), Materialität der Kommunikation, 1988 34 P. G. GUZZO, Schema per la categoria interpretativa del santuario di frontiera, in: Scienze di Antichità 1, 1987, 373–379 35 I. HODDER, Reading the Past. Current Approaches to Interpretation in Archaeology, 1986 36 Id., The Archaeological Process. An Introduction, 1999 37 T. HÖLSCHER, Öffentliche Räume in frühen griechischen Städten, Schriften Heidelberg 7, 1998 38 Id., Bildwerke. Darstellungen, Funktionen, Botschaften, in: Klassische Archäologie (see [14.]), 147–165 39 S. HOUBY-NIELSEN, The Archaeology of Ideology in the Kerameikos. New Interpretations of the 'Opferrinnen', in: R. HÄGG (ed.), The Role of Religion in the Early Greek Polis. Proceedings of the Third International Seminar on Ancient Greek Cult, 1996, 41–54 40 W. KEMP, Kontexte. Für eine Kunstgeschichte der Komplexität, in: Texte zur Kunst 1, 1991.2, 89–101 41 E. KISTLER, Die Opferrinne-Zeremonie. Bankettideologie am Grab, Orientalisierung und Formierung einer Adelsgesellschaft in Athen, 1998 42 R. LAURENCE, Roman Pompeii. Space and Society, 1994 43 Id., A. WALLACE-HADRILL (eds.), Domestic Space in the Roman World, JRA Suppl. 22, 1997 44 I. LAVIN, Ikonographie als geisteswissenschaftliche Disziplin, in: A. BEYER (ed.), Die Lesbarkeit der Kunst. Zur Geistes-Gegenwart der Ikonologie, 1992, 11–22 45 R. LEONE, Luoghi di culto extraurbani d'età arcaica in Magna Grecia, 1998 46 E. LEPORE, Colonie greche dell'Occidente antico, 1989 47 F. LISSARRAGUE, A. SCHNAPP, Tradition und Erneuerung in der Klassischen Archäologie in Frankreich, in: Klassische Archäologie (see [14]), 365–382 48 I. MALKIN, Territorial Domination and the Greek Sanctuary, in: P. HELLSTRÖM, B. ALROTH (eds.), Religion and Power in the An-

cient Greek World, Proceedings of the Uppsala Symposium 1993, 1996, 75–81 49 G. P. R. Metreaux, Ancient Housing. Oikos and Domus in Greece and Rome, in: JSAH 58, 1999, 392–404 50 A. Möller, 'Die Gegenwart töten', in: H.-J. Gehrke, A. Möller (eds.), Vergangenheit und Lebenswelt. Soziale Kommunikation, Traditionsbildung und historisches Bewußtsein, 1996, 1–8 51 A. Momigliano, A. Schiavone (eds.), Storia di Roma I, II 1–3, III 1/2, IV, 1988–1993 52 I. Morris, Burial and Ancient Society. The Rise of the Greek City-State, 1987 53 Id., Burial and Ancient Society after Ten Years, in: S. Marchegay, M.-T. Le Dinahet, J.-F. Salles (eds.), Nécropoles et pouvoir. Idéologies, pratiques et interprétations, 1998, 21–36 54 Id., Archaeology as Cultural History. Words and Things in Iron Age Greece, 2000 55 S. Muth, Erleben von Raum – Leben im Raum. Zur Funktion mythischer Mosaikbilder in der römisch-kaiserzeitlichen Wohnarchitektur, 1998 56 S. C. Nappo, Urban transformation at Pompeii in the late 3rd and early 2nd century B. C., in: [43. 92–120] 57 Id., Pompeji. Die versunkene Stadt, 1999 (Italian 1998) 58 O. G. Oexle, Geschichte als historische Kulturwissenschaft, in: W. Hardtwig, H.-U. Wehler (eds.), Kulturgeschichte heute, 1996, 14–40 59 E. Panofsky, The History of Art as a Humanistic Discipline (1940), in: Id., Meaning in the Visual Arts: Papers in and on Art History, 1955 60 F. Pirson, Mietwohnungen in Pompeji und Herkulaneum. Untersuchungen zur Architektur, zum Wohnen und zur Sozial- und Wirtschaftsgeschichte der Vesuvstädte, 1999 61 K. Pomian, Entre l'invisible et le visible: La collection, in: Id., Collectionneurs, amateurs et curieux. Paris, Venise XVIᵉ-XVIIIᵉ siècle, 1987, 15–58 62 A. Pontrandolfo, Poseidonia e le comunità miste del golfo di Salerno, in: M. Cipriani, F. Longo (eds.), I Greci in Occidente. Poseidonia e i Lucani, Paestum, Museo Archeologico Nazionale, 1996, 37–39 63 R. Posner, Semiotik diesseits und jenseits des Strukturalismus. Zum Verhältnis von Moderne und Postmoderne, Strukturalismus und Poststrukturalismus, in: Zeitschrift für Semiotik 15, 1993, 211–233 64 L. Richardson, Pompeii, An Architectural History, 1988 65 D. Ridgway, The First Western Greeks, 1992 66 S. Settis, La colonne Trajane: l'Empereur et son public, RA 1991, 186–98 67 Id. (ed.), I Greci. Storia, cultura, arte, società 1–2.3, 1996–98 68 M. Shanks, Classical Archaeology of Greece. Experiences of the Discipline, 1996 69 A. Snodgrass, Archäologie in den angelsächsischen Ländern. Im Westen was Neues?, in: Klassische Archäologie (see [14.]), 347–364 70 M. Torelli, Greci e indigeni in Magna Grecia. Ideologia religiosa e rapporti di classe, in: StudStorici 18.4, 1977, 45–61 71 Id., Il santuario greco di Gravisca, in: PdP 32, 1977, 398–458 72 Id., Riflessione a margine dell'emporion di Gravisca, in: T. Hackens (ed.), Navies and Commerce of the Greeks, the Carthaginians and the Etruscans in the Tyrrhenian Sea, PACT (Rev. du groupe européen d'études pour les techniques physiques, chimiques, biologiques et mathématiques appliquées à l'archéologie) 20, 1988 (1993), 181–188 73 Id., Per un'archeologia dell'Oinotría, in: S. Bianco et al. (eds.), I Greci in Occidente. Greci, Enotri e Lucani nella Basilicata meridionale, Policoro, Museo Nazionale della Siritide, 1996, 123–131 74 G. Vallet, La cité et son territoire dans les colonies grecques d'occident, in: La città e il suo territorio, Atti del 7. convegno di studi sulla Magna Grecia, Taranto 1967, 1970, 67–142 75 J.-P. Vernant, Entre Mythe et Politique, 1996 76 A. Wallace-Hadrill, Houses and Society in Pompeii and Herculaneum, 1994 77 Id., Public Honour and Private Shame. The Urban Texture of Pompeii, in: T. J. Cornell, K. Lomas (eds.), Urban Society in Roman Italy, 1995, 39–62 78 J. Whitley, Protoattic Pottery. A Contextual Approach, in: I. Morris (ed.), Classical Greece. Ancient Histories and Modern Approaches, 1994, 51–70 79 A. Zaccaria Ruggio, Spazio privato e spazio pubblico nella città romana, 1995 80 P. Zanker, Nouvelles orientations de la recherche en iconographie. Commanditaires et spectateurs, in: RA 1994, 281–293 81 Id., Pompeji. Stadtbild und Wohngeschmack, 1995 82 Id., In search of the Roman viewer, in: D. Buitron-Oliver (ed.), The Interpretation of Architectural Sculpture in Greece and Rome, 1997, 179–191 83 Id., Bildräume und Betrachter im kaiserzeitlichen Rom, in: Klassische Archäologie (see [14.]), 205–226 84 F. Zevi, La casa del Fauno, in: M. Borriello, A. d'Ambrosio, S. De Caro, P. G. Guzzo (eds.), Pompei, Abitare sotto il Vesuvio, Ferrara, Palazzo dei Diamanti, 29 settembre 1996–19 gennaio 1997, 1996, 37–57 85 Id., Die Casa del Fauno in Pompeji und das Alexandermosaik, in: RM 105, 1998, 21–65.

BEAT SCHWEIZER

Classical period see → Epochs, concept of

Classicism

I. Art II. Literature (Great Britain) III. Literature (German and Romance)

I. Art

The epochal terms 'classic' and 'classicism' are the result of the development of historical thinking. Sulzer recognizes the adjective 'classical' (or 'classic'), as intended to convey a striving towards perfection [10. 541ff.], but it is not until Hegel characterizes the sequence of epochs as 'symbolic, classical, Romantic' in his aesthetics that the term becomes a term for an epoch. In 1839 Jeitteles therefore speaks of the 'classical period' [6. 150], and this is quite correct as long as one realizes that 'the term classicism was born out of the debate over the term Romantic' [3. 102]. Thus, in Franz Reber's *Geschichte der Neueren Deutschen Kunst* (1876), 'classicism' appears for the first time as a term denoting an epoch. The careers of the terms 'classicism' and 'historicism' ran parallel in time.

Classicism as an epochal term, though it is more accurate to speak of neo-classicism, as in English and Italian linguistic usage to distinguish it from all the other classicisms, is an international style and its birth place was Rome. The necessary pre-condition for it was the emergence of historical archaeological research, which surpassed mere antiquarian studies in that, among other things, it systemized the procedures of research, as they had already been carried out in palaeography, epigraphy and verification of sources or genealogy. At the same time, these new methods of approach resulted in art being displayed in museums, in new methods of inventory and ordering and in the founding of academic research institutes, which undertook to correct history in grand style. For instance, the 'Accademia Etrusca' was founded in Cortona in 1727 and the 'Accademia delle Romane Antichità' in Rome in 1740. The Egyptian section of the Capitoline Museum in Rome was set up in 1748. The London 'Society of Dilettanti', founded in 1732 as a 'dining club' for gentlemen who had travelled in Italy and had dedicated themselves to Italian opera, was increasingly transformed into a club to promote contemporary art and, more particularly, archaeological research. The society financed publications, excavations and systematic fact-finding trips up to the time of James Stuart's and Nicholas Revett's *The Antiquities of Athens*, the first volume of which appeared in 1762. As far as Greek Antiquity was concerned, it had its forerunner in David LeRoy's *Les Ruines des plus beaux monuments de la Grèce* in 1758 and, for the Far East, in Robert Wood's *Ruins of Palmyra* of 1753 and his *Ruins of Balbec* of 1757.

The impulse for this European mania had emanated from the discoveries and subsequent excavations at Herculaneum in 1738 and Pompeii in 1748. The knowledge and publication especially of the Pompeian wall paintings created quite a stir. The first four volumes dedicated to painting alone appeared under the title *Le Antichità di Ercolano esposte* between 1757 and 1765 and, in spite of their luxurious presentation and correspondingly high price, were disseminated throughout the whole of Europe in more than two thousand copies. This publication in particular triggered a pan-European style of decoration, initially in the form of the English Adam style. One major influence on Robert Adam as an architect and archaeologist was Charles Louis Clérisseau, who was at the French Academy in Rome from 1749 to 1753 and travelled with Adam to Dalmatia to record the palace of Diocletian in Spalato (published 1764). Another influence was Giovanni Battista Piranesi and his survey and graphic recording of ancient Roman civilisations. After his return to England in 1758, Adam's delicate arabesque decorative style, which superseded the baroque and also the neo-palladian conceptions of architecture, became hugely popular in England. In France the neo-classical Pompeian fashion for interior decor reached its peak in the design style of Napoleon's chief architects Charles Percier and Pierre-François-Léonard Fontaine. In Germany Weimar classicism or the Munich classicism of Klenze, for instance, reflected this neo-classicism, while Schinkel's Prussian classicism was just one aspect of his historicism, which was equally matched by a marked Gothicism.

Historical paintings (→ HISTORICAL SUBJECT, PAINTINGS OF) were likewise given archaeological impetus by the publications on the excavations of the cities of Vesuvius. Decisive for this was the publication of the vase pictures, particularly in two editions of the → VASE PAINTINGS of the English ambassador to Naples, Sir William Hamilton (published between 1767 and 1776). Johann Heinrich Wilhelm Tischbein was responsible for the second series in a purely outline rendering. The outline engraved rendering of the vase pictures encouraged neo-classical concentration on the Roman style of

Fig. 1: Tommaso Piroli after John Flaxman, *Night Shielding Sleep from the Ire of Zeus*. Engraving. Illustration for Alexander Pope's translation of Homer's *Iliad*, Book 14, 294, 1805, plate 23. London, British Museum

relief. In this area English programmatic painting in Rome led the way. In 1759 Gavin Hamilton began his cycle of histories on Homer's *Iliad*, which, though still having vestiges of baroque, also reflects Antiquity and Poussin. Hamilton's central role as initiator of the new classicism should in no way be underestimated because, in addition, he acted as one of the chief excavators and as an art agent. He sent antiques to England by the shipload, as well as classical Renaissance and Baroque pictures, whose canonical exemplarity he established, for instance, in his work of reproduction *Schola italica* of 1773. French programmatic painting in neo-classical style began in Rome just slightly later with Vien's *Gods of love*, exhibited at the Salon in 1761. These paintings follow very closely Pompeian wall painting, but for all their cult of line and relief still cannot suppress a distinct tone of rococo eroticism. David, in Vien's studio beginning in 1765, was in Rome himself, first from 1775 to 1781, and he then returned there specifically for his *Horatio's Oath*. This incunabulus of French classicistic revolutionary art was exhibited in 1785 in Rome and Paris with great international success. German art hit the scene, also in 1761, with Meng's *Parnassus* in the Villa Albani.

The ideas of Winckelmann were clearly influential in this milieu. He spent some time in Rome from 1755 onwards, first residing as librarian of the Albani in the villa of the same name. Later he was responsible for the pope's antiques. His debut article of 1755 was pub-

Fig. 2: Asmus
Jakob Carstens,
*Ajax and
Tecmessa.*
Drawing, 1789.
*Stiftung
Weimarer
Klassik und
Kunst-
sammlungen
Museen*

Fig. 3: Jacques-
Louis David,
*The Lictors
returning to
Brutus the
Bodies of his
Sons.* Oil on
canvas, Salon
of 1789.
*With
permission of
Musée du
Louvre, Paris*

lished there and, more importantly, his *History of the Art of Antiquity* appeared there in 1764. The initial phase of neo-classicism was primarily characterized by antiquarian archaeology. The second phase, clearly limited to the 1790s, because of the influence of the vase style was careful to suppress volume and perspective in favour of superficial ornamental linearity and abstraction. On the other hand, neo-classicism then gained a dimension, which, using Schiller's term from the mid–1790s, might be called 'sentimental'. For Schiller, aware of an irrevocable break with the past, the sentimental is the only conceivable way under modern conditions to partake of Classical Antiquity, which he thought of as naive. Thus the sentimental is, on the one hand, a form of reflection on what is past and therefore historical and, on the other hand, because of the overwhelming involvement of the observer triggered by the excessively strong sentiment of the depiction, it is the only possibility of attaining natural and therefore naive self-awareness. This was supposed to give art a utopian dimension and enable an unalienated experience of nature to come to light [9. 149–183]. This conception, which, after the political failure of the Revolution, encumbers art with making freedom a reality, has in various versions left its mark on an entire generation of neo-classicists. Again it was begun in Rome, virtually simultaneously by, above all, the Italian Canova, the Frenchman David, the Englishman Flaxman, the German Carstens and, though far away from Rome, but possibly through the influence of Flaxman, to some extent also by the Spaniard Goya. Emulating Tischbein's vase work from 1791 onwards, Flaxman's outline engraved illustrations for Homer's *Iliad* and *Odyssey* of 1793 were of the greatest influence in Europe as a whole and were followed by illustrations of Aeschylus and Sophocles (Fig. 1). With typical classical reservation Goethe's Weimar prize competitions, for instance, (1799–1805) refer constantly to this model, but early Romantic art became equally familiar with this idiom through August Wilhelm Schlegel's review of Flaxman's publications. This style is sentimental insofar as, in its extreme form of stylisation, the abstract three-dimensional structuring directly steers the effect and meaning of what is observed in the way it is received, and the ancient (or old Italian) stylistic level written into this form gives cause for reflection on past idiom. An ideal is evoked in an embellished form, which one remembers with longing but, faced with the experiences of the present, longs for in vain. The conception of programmatic painting is also sentimental. In the centre of the pictures – in an extreme form in Asmus Jakob Carstens, who exhibited his decisive sketches in Rome in 1795 (Fig. 2), but also in David in *Brutus*, for instance, from 1789 (Fig. 3) – stands not a dominating, active hero, but rather a broken hero, incapable of action, who ponders that he can no longer reconcile his official role with his personal feelings. Images emerge of a breakdown in communication, the cohesion of which is guaranteed solely by the abstract artistic form. Form and content no longer coincide. This separates the neo-classical art of the second stage from all Classical art and the terminology used to characterize it.

Also to be attributed rather more to this second stage is the trend in architecture for which the term *revolutionary architecture* has been adopted, although all the important sketches – and most of this architecture has remained in the form of sketches – were created before the French Revolution and owe their moral claims exclusively to the Enlightenment. This art is Classical in the sense of the characteristics mentioned insofar as it is decidedly anti-baroque, proclaiming the cause of reduction and clarity. Yet it goes way beyond traditional Classical or classicistic structures insofar as it suspends the Classical (and also baroque) idea of unity and completeness and no longer fosters a living integration of the parts, but instead, ensures its deliberate destruction. In its extreme preference for pure stereometry, it casts off its antiquating skin. The order of columns, proportional relationships, ornamental frameworks and organization become dispensable, and the parts become independent. However much it is possible to speak of a search for the basic elements of architecture, they no longer fit into an overall order. What would have been called its extreme dual-value stylization in neo-classicistic painting and drawing, is, in architecture, the reduction to stereometric elements which, on the one hand, expose an original language of architecture but, on the other, also aim to illustrate the purpose and the function of the building (*architecture parlante*) directly. In both cases, reflection and sensual presence are intended to be one. This ultimately surpasses all Classical form and is the main characteristic of historically founded neo-classicistic art.

1 W. Busch, Das sentimentalische Bild. Die Krise der Kunst im 18. Jahrhundert und die Geburt der Moderne, 1993   2 E. Battisti, E. Langlotz, Classicism, Encyclopedia of World Art 3, 1960, 674–698   3 G. Hajós, Klassizismus und Historismus – Epochen oder Gesinnungen?, in: Österreichische Zeitschrift für Kunst und Denkmalpflege 32, 1978, 102   4 H. Honour, Neo-Classicism, 1968   5 D. Irwin, English Neoclassical Art: Studies in Inspiration and Taste, 1966   6 I. Jeitteles, Ästhetisches Lexikon, vol. 1, 150   7 Ausstellungskatalog. The Age of Neo-Classicism, The Royal Academy und The Victoria & Albert Museum, London 1972   8 M. Praz, Gusto neoclassico, 1940 (²1959; Engl.: On Neoclassicism, 1969)   9 J. G. Sulzer, Allgemeine Theorie der Schönen Künste, ²1798, 1,514ff.   10 P. Szondi, Poetik und Geschichtsphilosophie, I, Studienausgabe der Vorlesungen, 2, 1974   11 D. Friedberg (ed.), The Problem of Classicism: Ideology and Power, in: Art Journal, 47, 1988, 7–41   12 R. Zeitler, Klassizismus und Utopia, 1954

ADDITIONAL BIBLIOGRAPHY: B. Arciszewska & E. McKellar, Articulating British Classicism: New Approaches to Eighteenth Century Architecture, 2004; Catalogue Exhibition: Vases & Volcanoes. Sir William Hamilton and his Collection, I. Jenkins, K. Sloan (eds.), The British Museum London 1996; Catalogue Exhibition: Grand Tour. The Lure of Italy in the Eighteenth Century, A. Wilton, I. Bignamini (eds.), The Tate Gallery London 1996; B. Collenberg-Plotnikov, Klassizismus und Karikatur: Eine Konstellation der Kunst am Beginn der Moderne, 1998; T. J. McCormick, Charles-Louis Clérisseau and the Genesis of Neo-Classicism, 1990; H. Tausch, Entfernung der Antike. Carl Ludwig Fernow im Kontext der Kunsttheorie um 1800, 2000.

WERNER BUSCH

II. Literature (Great Britain)
A. Introduction B. Previous History, Renaissance C. Classicism

A. Introduction
1. Division into Periods, Terms, and General Observations 2. Contexts of Education and Learning

1. Division into Periods, Terms, and General Observations

The division into periods employed here follows the usage widespread in the study of English language and literature described by a recent annotated anthology as follows: 'In representations of English literary history the 18th cent. is very often combined with the (preceding) Restoration period into one epoch, which is then often given a joint label like (neo)-classicism or Augustan Age' [46. 9]. The Restoration, i.e. the return to the English royal throne of the Stuart monarch from exile on the continent in 1660 after the Civil Wars and the Commonwealth signified a decisive turning point in the cultural and literary life of the country. From then on continental, and especially French, ideas played a more controlling role and, partly in association with this, models from Antiquity were a determining factor. This was not altered by the important changes taking place in the subsequent period in politics, namely, the *Glorious Revolution* of 1688 and the assumption of power by the House of Hannover when George I came to the throne in 1714. The period ended at the end of the 18th cent. with the Romantic movement, when different attitudes towards the legacy of Antiquity gained acceptance. The influence of Antiquity was particularly strong shortly before and after the beginning of the 18th cent., as confirmed by a new study: '... the British century from 1688 must rank as outstanding in the degree to which its cultural and political elite appropriated and assimilated classical, and particularly Roman, habits of mind' [14. 165]. Or this strong influence can be viewed as concentrated within an even shorter period of time: 'In Britain, the appropriation of Roman models was at its strongest in the first half-century following the Glorious Revolution' [14. 166].

In his in-depth discussion of the term *classicism* R. Wellek stresses the late establishment of the expression: 'The English classicists or neo-classicists did not, of course, call themselves by that name; they spoke, at most, of the imitation of the ancients, of the observance of the rules, or similarly' [57. 1049]. Terms such as *classicism* or *classicality* or *pseudo-classicality* had been tried out in the 19th cent., but it was not until the beginning of the 20th cent. that the linguistic usage *classicism* (German: 'Klassizismus') with the adjectival form *classical* gained acceptance. J. W. Johnson quotes in this connection Sir Edmund Gosse, the man of letters who set the tone around the turn of the century: 'The school of writers who cultivated this order ... have commonly been described as the classical, because their early lead-ers claimed to emulate and restore the grace and precision of the poets of antiquity, to write in English as Horace and Ovid were supposed to have written in Latin, – that is to say, with a polished and eclectic elegance' [35. 13]. The term *neo-classicism*, actually attested earlier (1863, cf. [57. 1050]), was not established until later, in the 1920s, especially in the USA [35. 15], to distinguish the classicism of the late 17th and 18th cents. from other periods characterized by classicism, such as the Renaissance, for instance. While it is usually used as synonymous with *classicism* [35. 46], it is also sometimes rejected as tautological [18. 5]. The term 'classics', customary in German and other European literature, has no validity in English literature, as T. S. Eliot notes in his highly regarded study *What is a Classic?*: 'We have no classic age, and no classic poet, in English' [57. 1066].

Even more controversial is another widely-used term: *Augustan Age*, which sought to produce a parallel between the period of the outgoing 17th and early 18th cents. in England and the rule of the Emperor Augustus in ancient Rome, the *aetas aurea* of Virgil, Horace and Ovid. This comparison was already being employed by contemporaries. The 'first application of the word Augustan to English culture' [28. 236] is found as early as 1690. Above all, it was always popular to praise each new ruler as a new Augustus, though according to J. Sambrook in time Tacitus's view of him as a cruel tyrant began to be more widely accepted: 'By the beginning of the eighteenth century an idea of Augustan Rome had maintained a strong presence in English cultural life for over a century: Jonson praised James I, Waller praised Cromwell, and Dryden praised Charles II, under the name of Augustus; but after 1688 the hostile, Tacitean attitude to Augustus is more evident in England' [48. 169]. Doubt about the positive significance of the Augustan model has been expressed in our age with particular intensity by the influential American critic H. D. Weinbrot. For him a cosmeticized understanding of what Augustus meant to the 18th cent. leads to 'an erroneous *vision* of the past' [55. 7]. In a later monograph he reinforces these reservations further and thinks in general: 'Many of the best eighteenth-century authors ... were deeply ambivalent or negative towards classical achievement' [56. 20]. However, on the other hand, he does himself admit: 'There was indeed much deserved and continuing respect for classical literature and values' [56. 74]. It is certainly correct that the appropriation of Antiquity, in particular among leading writers, did not take place in a simple adoption, but in a lively debate; but one should not be blind to the great importance of ancient models in this epoch. H. Erskine-Hill (as also confirmed by [31. 29f.]) gives an essentially more balanced picture by rightly claiming: '... the eighteenth century and the very end of the seventeenth stand out through their reiterated attempts to claim or to deny an English Augustan Age'; and: 'the positive sense of the word *Augustan* was used all through the century from ... 1690 to ... 1802'. While he definitely acknowledges the increasingly strong pre-dominance of the Tacitean point of view in the histori-cal domain, he points out 'the emergence of a largely literary sense of *Augustan*' [28. 265]. This is where the emphasis should lie.

The name 'Augustan Age' for the literature and cul-ture of the epoch also expresses a decisive placing of the main emphasis, as a critic pertinently remarks: '... the Neo-Classical emphasis after 1700 came to be put more strongly on Roman culture than Greek so that eight-eenth century England was led to call itself Augustan rather than *Periclean* or *Alexandrian*' [35. 91]. The classicism of this period is characterized by an unequi-vocal priority of the Roman model: 'One says *classical*, but in fact Greek literature had never much effect upon the age. The eighteenth was a Latin century' [52. 210; 14. 4]. Decisive for the primacy of Latin was possibly not only a mental affinity of contemporaries with an-cient Rome, but also the educational presuppositions of the time.

2. Contexts of Education and Learning

Teaching at the *grammar schools* of the time, which had hardly changed since the 16th cent., was unilater-ally determined by the ancient languages. A telling illus-tration of this: 'The school education of the eighteenth century was based entirely on the classics. ... Other lan-guages and other subjects were scarcely taught at all' [23. 10]. Latin was given distinct precedence not just in the order of languages. Greek was learned after Latin and through Latin. The customary Greek grammars were written in Latin and Greek dictionaries gave Latin, rather than English explanations of words [23. 15]. Therefore it must be assumed that most pupils on leav-ing these schools knew Latin considerably better than Greek and had far better access to Latin writings (which is also confirmed by contemporary biographies). The philosopher J. Locke considers Latin absolutely neces-sary for every gentleman, but Greek only for scholars *Some Thoughts Concerning Education* (1693). In a famous letter to his son, Lord Chesterfield recommends Classical education to him as 'a most useful and neces-sary ornament' and advises him, in particular to learn Greek, whereas a command of Latin almost goes with-out saying: 'there is no credit in knowing Latin for everybody knows it' [23. 11]. This comment needs to be seen in far more relative terms, however, as J. W. John-son convincingly explains: 'Lord Chesterfield's *every-body* meant *everybody who was anybody* or the *elite*' [36. 4]. Almost all women and members of the lower classes were excluded from these languages. This is defi-nitely an important reason why translations of ancient authors were so successful at this time. At the same time this was also the era of R. Bentley, as the poet and phi-lologist Housman later said, 'our great age of scholar-ship', and, in fact, a particular concentration on Greek was to be observed [23. 1]. For the literary world, on the other hand, a different orientation applied: 'A gentle-man should know his Horace and perhaps his Virgil. Authors assumed this knowledge in their readers. An educated man was a man who knew Latin' [52. 201].

B. Previous History, Renaissance

The epoch which preceded the age of classicism in England is often called the 'Renaissance'. (The term 'ba-roque', which German students of English language and literature tried to introduce, did not catch on in English study of literature.) Also at this time, when edu-cational qualifications similar to those at the time of classicism prevailed, the ancient authors were held in high regard. His poet-colleague Ben Jonson acknowl-edges of Shakespeare (1564–1616) in a dedicatory poem in the first complete folio edition (1623): 'thou hadst small Latine, and lesse Greeke'; yet he proves not only in his so-called Roman dramas – *Titus Androni-cus, Julius Caesar, Antony and Cleopatra* and *Corio-lanus,* but also, for example, by his emulation of Seneca in his histories and tragedies that he was very familiar with ancient writings, materials and ideas [17. 305ff.]. Ben Jonson (1572–1637) himself, who was considered superior to Shakespeare by many educated contempo-raries and who occupied the position of *poet laureate*, had an even closer relationship with Antiquity. In his literary notebook *Timber, or Discoveries* he wrote: '*Nothing* can conduce more to letters, than to examine the writings of the Ancients'; at the same time, though, he also warned: 'not to rest in their sole Authority, or take all upon trust from them' [51. 40]. He used Clas-sical themes, especially in the satirical comedy *Poetaster* (1601), which deals, among other things, with the exile of the poet Ovid and in which the author takes to the stage himself in the figure of Horace, and in the trag-edies *Sejanus, His Fall* (1603) and *Catiline, His Con-spiracy* (1611). In his comedies which were very suc-cessful and had a lasting influence on the further devel-opment of the genre in England, he was clearly influ-enced by Plautus, from whom he repeatedly adopted comic figures and situations. He valued Horace particu-larly highly; he often made reference to him and trans-lated the *Ars poetica*. This brought him the honorary title of *English Horace* [28. 231]. J. Dryden later ac-cused Jonson of learned plagiarism of all the ancient authors: 'you track him everywhere in their snow' [39. 24]; yet one certainly has to admit that C. H. Herford and P. Simpson, the publishers of the large Jonson edi-tion, were right: 'We have to do, in Jonson, almost always with reinterpretation or adaptation of classical tradition, not with either blank acceptance or out-and-out revolt' [33 I. 123; 45. 19].

John Milton (1608–74) was of outstanding impor-tance in the adoption of Antiquity in the English Re-naissance. Although Milton was first and foremost a Christian and the great poets of Antiquity were of ne-cessity pagans, he did not see them, as H. D. Weinbrot suggests with a quotation as 'Vain wisdom all, and false Philosophie!' [56. 48]. Instead, in his major work *Para-dise Lost* (1667), which was to become a national epic, he was concerned with a close and living link between Christian and ancient tradition. The epics of Virgil and Homer, and also Greek drama, were obviously the chief models for this work and also for the sequel *Paradise*

Regained (1671), determining the structure, content and style of the depiction (cf. e.g. [32. 248f.]). The most important sources for Milton's mythology are Homer, Hesiod, Virgil and Ovid [42. xlii]. Milton was, even according to the ideas of the time, a universal scholar. In his writings he makes reference to about 1500 authors [24. 51]. Even so, to him there was no doubt that Latin had to represent the basis of education, and in his article *Of Education* (1644) he was concerned only about the correct pronunciation, i.e. that closest to the Italian: 'For we Englishmen, being far northerly, do not open our mouths in the cold air wide enough' [8. 633]. He himself wrote internationally acclaimed pamphlets in Latin and a fairly large number of Latin poems, including seven consecutively numbered elegies, the most famous being the *Epitaphium Damonis* (1640). Dr. Johnson, himself an excellent Latinist, praised him highly for this later: 'In Latin his skill was such as places him in the first rank of writers and criticks' [5 I. 107]; on the other hand, he also said critically: 'The Latin pieces are lusciously elegant; but the delight which they afford is rather by the exquisite imitation of the ancient writers, by the purity of the diction, and the harmony of the numbers, than by any power of invention, or vigour of sentiment' [5 I. 111]. The English compositions are by contrast incomparably more significant. In particular after Milton's status had been enhanced, thanks to J. Addison in the early 18th cent., his diction informed by Latinisms was for a long time the epitome of high poetic style in English. Overall, the following assessment is without doubt apposite: 'Milton ... owed much to the Classics, but always ended by turning his borrowings into something quite contemporary as well as quite his own' [54. 63]. Especially with his great epic poems, Milton's effect was still felt until well into the epoch of classicism and at this time he earned his greatest recognition as a poet.

C. CLASSICISM

1. THEORY: ANCIENTS AND MODERNS, THE BATTLE OF THE BOOKS 2. POETRY AND TRANSLATION 3. DRAMA 4. PROSE

1. THEORY: ANCIENTS AND MODERNS, THE BATTLE OF THE BOOKS

The → QUERELLE DES ANCIENS ET DES MODERNES, the battle between traditionalists and modernists already being hotly contested in France, also experienced an acute stage in England towards the end of the 17th cent. as *The Battle of the Books*. It started when the statesman Sir William Temple published a short paper in 1690 entitled *An Essay upon the Ancient and Modern Learning*, decidedly partisan for the ancients or, from a negative point of view, according to G. Highet 'a ridiculously exaggerated assertion of the primacy of the classics' [34. 282]. In it he praised the *Epistles of Phalaris*, among other reasons because of their great age: 'I think the Epistles of Phalaris to have more grace, more spirit, more force of wit and genius than any others I

have ever seen' [34. 283]). This led in 1695 to a new edition of the Greek text by C. Boyle in Oxford. Previously W. Wotton in *Reflections upon Ancient and Modern Learning* (1694) had taken the opposite view, arguing for a middle position, according to R. Pfeiffer, 'that the ancients were superior in eloquence and poetry, the moderns in science' [44. 151]. According to R. F. Jones this must have been an attitude which had a wide consensus at the time: 'The influence of Ben Jonson and the French critics succeeded in establishing the ancients as literary arbiters, so that Aristotle, who had suffered badly at the hands of the scientists, maintained his prestige in criticism' [37. 282]. Bentley, who was a friend of Wotton and was annoyed about critical comments in the introduction to Boyle's publication on the way he performed his office of librarian, added an appendix to a new edition of the *Reflections* in 1697, *A Dissertation upon the Epistles of Phalaris*, in which he exposed the letters as a crass forgery. Two years later Bentley extended his comments, originally comprising 98 pages, to an impressive volume of more than 600 pages, which shocked some of his contemporaries with its aggressive polemics [44. 151]. J. Swift was one of those who felt himself called upon to intervene in the controversy on behalf of his patron Temple. Against Bentley and for the cause of the *Ancients*, he published in 1704 two of his earliest satires, *A Tale of a Tub* and, in particular, *The Battle of the Books*. In the latter the battle is depicted in a prose parody of an ancient epic. Swift's support for the 'Ancients' is shown to striking advantage, not least in the fable about the spider and the bee recited by the ancient 'warrior' Aesop. The arrogant, poisonous spider stands for the 'Moderns'; it is, as the bee admits, more or less independent, but its radius is limited and it can produce only 'Dirt and Poison'. By contrast the industrious bee, as the representative of the *Ancients*, has, so to speak, an unlimited field of action at its disposal 'by infinite Labor, and search, ... ranging thro' every Corner of Nature', and with its labour it achieves what is most beautiful and most useful, 'furnishing Mankind with the two Noblest of Things, which are Sweetness and Light' [12 I. 149ff.]. Apart from his support in the English stage of the *Querelle*, largely for personal reasons, most striking is the paradoxical fact, already recognized in an early dissertation, 'that it is in fact those who know Antiquity best (Wotton and Bentley) who appear as moderns and those who are less familiar with Antiquity (Temple and Boyle) as representatives of the ancients' [25. 139]. In any case, the battle shows the conspicuous significance accorded this question by contemporaries.

2. POETRY AND TRANSLATION

The leading figures in poetry, which in classicism enjoyed not only high status but also great popularity among the reading public, were J. Dryden (1631–1700) and after him A. Pope (1688–1744). Hence the period was also frequently called *The Age of Dryden and Pope*. For both, the authors of Antiquity had an eminent status, and one critic rightly maintains: 'With them

[Dryden and Pope], antiquity was more than roots, it was the continuing basis of their careers, and they remained the spokesmen of its values all their lives' [30. 270]. With them and other poets of the time the appropriation of ancient models took place at various levels: from translation to imitation to a general orientation based on ancient models and the adoption of individual elements. Ancient authors were highly regarded, but many interested readers, especially women readers, were not able to read the original texts without problems because of the limitations of their education. Thus classicism in England was, among other things, a great age of translations. There had previously been English versions of ancient authors, but at the end of the 17th cent. a particular peak period for verse translations emerged. In one descripton it was stated: 'The art of translation was steadily improving as the classics in English dress were read by more and more people. Roscommon's, Creech's, and Oldham's translations of Horace, Lucretius, Ovid, and others were triumphantly peaked by Dryden's *Sylvae* in 1685' [36. 21]. Both for Dryden and for Pope translation of ancient epics, regarded as the highest literary genre, brought a high level of recognition – and income. Dryden, who by 1693 had already translated Persius and Juvenal, in 1697 published his *Works of Virgil* in *heroic couplets* (i.e. iambic pentameter rhymed in pairs). Pope followed this example by publishing Homer's epics, the *Iliad* (1715–1720) and the *Odyssey* (1725–1726), translated in the same metre. The income he earned from this made Pope the first poet in the history of English literature to become prosperous and independent from aristocratic patrons by his literary works in spite of Bentley's negative verdict: 'a very pretty poem ..., but he must not call it Homer' [44. 157]. In his independent writings Dryden, who also produced a comprehensive oeuvre as a critic and author of dramas, clearly followed Latin models, especially in his satires. One study concludes: 'Dryden ... did not take much from his English precursors, but went direct to the Latin models, above all to Juvenal, who suited him better than Horace. ... Dryden has got the invective force of Juvenal, his inexhaustible variety and resource, his moral superiority, real or assumed, to the men he assails' [52. 203]. It appears to be characteristic of Dryden's close affinity to Antiquity when Dr. Johnson later in the 18th cent. in his life of Dryden illustrates the successful work of the poet by a comparison with Augustus: 'What was said of Rome, adorned by Augustus, may be applied by an easy metaphor to English poetry embellished by Dryden, lateritiam invenit, marmoream reliquit, he found it brick, and he left it marble' [5 I. 332].

A. Pope, who as a poet took on and further developed the legacy of Dryden and who in English literature was possibly closest to achieving the qualities of a classicist [26. 16f.], kept even closer to ancient models than his predecessor, In his entire oeuvre he observed the motto, the orthodox opinion of the age passed on to him early on by his poet friend Garth: 'The best of the modern poets in all languages are those that have the nearest copied the ancients' [52. 205]. The maxim *correctness*, which was recommended to Pope by his poetic mentor Walsh as a leading orientation [15. 154], follows the same direction, and Pope wrote to him accordingly in a letter (dated 22.10.1706), 'the true style of sound is evident everywhere in Homer and Virgil, and nowhere else' [15. 39].

Pope's poetic output clearly follows the *rota Vergilii*, which prescribed for the poet the sequence – pastoral poetry, didactic poetry, epic – as the norm. In his foreword to his *Pastorals* (1709) Pope makes the claim that they represented a concentration of that which the Classical *exempla* contained by way of truly generic elements: 'Of the following Eclogues I shall only say, that these four comprehend all the subjects which the Critics upon Theocritus and Virgil will allow to be fit for pastoral' [16. 50]. The most important model is without doubt Virgil and it is possible to obtain the impression that 'Pope out-Virgils Virgil' or 'their [the Pastorals'] originality ... consists mainly in Pope's cunning selection of themes from the old eclogues', which, however, overlooks Pope's own contribution [16. 57]. Pope's literary friends and patrons felt urged to make a comparison between the promising young poet and the Roman master, and one of them, Granville, in a letter expressed his great anticipation: 'If he goes on as he has begun, in the pastoral way, as Virgil first try'd his Strength, we may hope to see English Poetry vie with the Roman' [16. 49].

Just as Virgil concluded his *Georgics* with the opening line of the *Bucolics*, Pope ended his landscape poem *Windsor Forest* (1713) with a varied reprise of the beginning of the *Pastorals*, the motif of the πρῶτος εὑρετής: 'First in these Fields I sung the Sylvan Strains'. This unmistakably marks 'the poet's georgic phase' [19. 48]. Even though *Windsor Forest* (1713) is not a didactic poem in the strict sense, it is above all the mythologization of the home landscape and the depiction of the *Pax Britannica* as analogous to the *Pax Augustana* that clearly suggest the Roman model.

An Essay on Criticism (1711), on the other hand, is a didactic poem pure and simple. The fact that in this case, however, Horace, not Virgil, constitutes the model was already pointed out by J. Addison in a contemporary review: 'The Observations follow one another like those in Horace's Art of Poetry, without that methodical Regularity which would have been requisite in a Prose Author' [2. no. 253]. However, in this case Virgil or 'young Maro' (l. 130) is presented as an example of the harmony of the traditional rules with nature; for, when he examines the work of his Greek predecessor, he comes, according to Pope, to the surprising conclusion that 'Nature and Homer were, he found, the same' (Z. 135). Pope therefore concludes from this the central maxim: 'Learn hence for Ancient Rules a just Esteem;/To copy Nature is to copy Them' (l. 139f.).

In accordance with Classical concepts, for Pope and his contemporaries the epic was the very highest form of poetry, and Pope very early on nurtured the plan of writing his own epic about the Roman Brutus. However, it never happened, since this age evidently did not provide the philosophical presuppositions for a serious epic. Pope therefore switched to neighbouring fields and, besides the Homer translations, wrote a satirical verse epic, *The Rape of the Lock* (expanded version 1714), in which he parodies the generic elements of the Classical epic in order to draw an ironic picture of contemporary court society. Instead of the epic hero, the beautiful Belinda has the central role. Neither courage in battle nor *pietas* are decisive in the world of the genteel salons, but rather external splendour and beautiful appearance. The frame of reference of the ancient epic manifests itself throughout. After the traditional opening with the naming of themes and the calling upon the muse, in the five cantos we find ironically brought into play, among other things, the arming of oneself with weapons (morning toilette of the beauties), battle descriptions (card game or cutting off the locks), the journey to the underworld (the cave of *Spleen*) and especially the epic 'machinery' (here consisting of sylphs and gnomes). The later poem *Dunciad* (1727) is similar. Here, too, can be seen 'Pope's total immersion in the great epic poems of the past' [21. 242].

In Pope's later output Horace becomes his chief model. Of this N. Callan says: 'As it affects almost all his mature poetry this relationship is by far the most important' [21. 242]. Like Horace in his satire and epistles, Pope examines contemporary people and circumstances in an urbane, colloquial style. *The Imitations of Horace* (1733–1738) are particularly close to the Roman poet. Pope, who published his writings side by side with the Classical models and thus invites his readers to make a direct comparison, responded with extreme flexibility to the Latin original, partly by translating it freely, but partly by transposing it wholesale into similar circumstances in his own present time[50. 23ff.; 47. 61ff.].

In this epoch Horace was generally the most highly regarded ancient author, as is shown, for example, by the fact that it was of his works that the most translations appeared. From 1660 to 1800 there were in all 37 different versions (22 of Homer, 21 of Virgil and 19 of Ovid) [14. 182]. Even such a radical innovator as J. Swift (1667–1745) liked to follow this model, as, for instance, in his poem *To the Earl of Oxford, Late Lord Treasurer. Sent to him when he was in the Tower, before his Tryal* (1716), with the subtitle *Out of Horace*, by rendering as the opening lines from Horace *Dulce et decorum est pro patria mori* with 'How blest is he, who for his Country dies' [11. I, 210]. Swift's contemporary biographer J. Orrery reported that the Dean was particularly proud of his Latin poems *Ad Amicum Eruditum Thomam Sheridan* and *Carberiae Rupes*: 'he assumed to himself more vanity upon these two Latin poems, than upon many of his best English performances' [11. 316; 14. 32]. It also fits in well with this kind of attitude when Swift later in his *Gulliver's Travels*

allows the world traveler on the island of Glubbdubdrib to summon the senate of Rome together with a modern parliament from the underworld and addresses the latter as 'a gathering of heroes and demigods' but the former as 'a mob of pedlars, pickpockets, highway robbers and loudmouths'.

In the generation of poets after Pope and Swift, Samuel Johnson (1709–1784), usually known as Dr. Johnson, continued the classicistic tradition. His knowledge of Latin was excellent and he is regarded as 'one of the great modern masters of the Latin Tongue' [13. 286]. As a student in Oxford he had already translated Pope's *Messiah*, which in turn derives from Virgil's *Fourth Eclogue*, into Latin hexameters [6. 29ff.]. Similar to Milton before him Johnson spoke fluent Latin and kept a Latin diary. It was said of him that: 'Johnson loved Horace – at school, where he translated *Integer vitae* and *Nec semper imbres*, at Oxford, ... and all his life' [13. 299]. But he achieved his greatest poetic success in emulation of another Latin author. *London* (1738), with which he achieved his breakthrough as a poet, is a free adaptation of *the Third Satire* of Juvenal,and *The Vanity of Human Wishes* (1749), his longest poem, regarded by many as his best, is based on Juvenal's *Tenth Satire*. His contemporary biographer J. Boswell has passed on Johnson's comment that 'modern writers are the moons of literature; they shine with reflected light, with light borrowed from the ancients. Greece appears to me to be the fountain of knowledge; Rome of Elegance' [13. 285]. This attitude was to change fundamentally for the Romantic poets at the beginning of the 19th cent. For them, as is shown, for example, in the *Ode on a Grecian Urn* by John Keats (1795–1821), only ancient Greece counts, whose mythology and art, they believed, should be experienced in a living encounter.

3. DRAMA

Classical influence reached the English drama of the era mainly by way of French theories and examples. They set the tone after the Restoration, though of course often with the emphasis on British originality. This is clearly demonstrated in the most important document on the theory of drama of the epoch, Dryden's *Essay on Dramatic Poesy* (1668). In the Ciceronian dialogue of the four friends, Crites, Eugenius, Lisideius and Neander, besides the popular question of the superiority of the *Ancients* or *Moderns*, also discussed is the concept of mimesis and, in particular, the subject of the three unities.

Dryden himself, who was also very successful as an author of dramas, in his tragedy *All for Love, or, The World Well Lost* (1678), usually considered his best play, conspicuously observes neo-classical decorum and the three unities. In his adaptation of the subject matter of *Antony and Cleopatra*, by contrast with Shakespeare, whom he claims as his model on the title page 'Written in Imitation of Shakespeare's Stile', Dryden concentrates on the closing stage of the action with the tragic climax and presents main figures who are far more noble in their deadly conflict between love and honour.

Addison's tragedy Cato (1713), the most discussed play of the period [14. 24], also deals with Roman subject matter. As Pope impresses on the audience in his prologue, the author here intends a connection between ancient Rome and modern England: 'He bids your breast with ancient ardour rise,/And calls forth Roman drops from British eyes'. Cato Uticensis as a champion of republican freedom fascinated contemporaries not only in England, and it is well known that George Washington quoted from no other literary work as frequently as from this, and that he promoted a performance of the play for his troops [58. 77]. Besides Cato, one of the main figures of Roman history popularly represented as *exempla virtutis* in the theatre of the period was the republican Brutus. Nathaniel Lee wrote about him in his play which was suppressed by censorship (1680); William Hunt's *The Fall of Tarquin: or The Distress'd Lovers* (1713) is an apolitical version of the subject; William Duncombe emulates Voltaire with *Junius Brutus* (1735); finally, late in the 18th cent. Richard Cumberland in *The Sybil* emphasized supernatural elements of the story surrounding Brutus. Other popular Roman themes in tragedies are the self-sacrifice of Regulus, the persecution of Christians and the struggle for freedom [58. 79ff.]. In the comedies of the period, on the other hand, which were usually clearly preferred to tragedies by both critics and public, ancient models had only a very indirect effect.

4. PROSE

The most important literary innovations in the era of classicism took place in the domain of prose. So Matthew Arnold is probably justified later in the 19th cent. in calling the age of Dryden and Pope 'an age of prose and reason' [15. 252]. In particular, a new independent canon now gradually became established. By far the most significant change occurred in narrative literature. The novel took on the functional role of the epic as the leading literary genre and the fundamental values of contemporary society, as held to be expressed in Virgil's *Aeneid*, were now increasingly articulated in literature in the long form of narrative prose. It is amazing but, in view of the widespread esteem for Antiquity in this period perhaps not completely surprising, that even with these substantial radical changes and innovations, which were inevitably bound ultimately to reduce the significance of Classical norms and models, the heritage of Antiquity in many instances still played an important role.

In the first two decades of the 18th cent. a new type of periodical emerged, 'in German usually called moral weeklies, even though most of them neither appeared weekly nor were they moral in today's sense' [41. 34]. They consisted mainly of essays, some in the form of letters, dealing with various kinds of subjects of contemporary life and the world in an urbane, conversational, wittily relaxed style. In the world of literature the moral weeklies not least took on the function of extending and educating the contemporary reading audience, which was very limited by today's standards. As a continuation of *The Tatler* (1709–11), *The Spectator* (1711–14), which was run partly by Richard Steele, but principally by Joseph Addison (1672–1719), was the central example of this. As is also evident from his dramatic output, Addison was decisively influenced by Classical education, and it is rightly said of him: 'Addison must be counted among those English writers who have a prevailingly classical or rather Latin Background. There is not much of exaggeration ... in calling him a classical don who took to writing English essays.' In the same passage it is said of Addison's prose style that it was 'perhaps the most Attic in the language' [52. 215].

Addison's Classical background is already recognizable in the objectives he sets. When he announces, 'I shall spare no Pains to make their [my readers'] Instruction agreeable, and their Diversion useful' [2. no. 10], the Horatian *prodesse et delectare* is undoubtedly in evidence behind it. And it is no coincidence that Addison illustrates his mission with a clear reference to an ancient analogy: I't was said of Socrates, that he brought Philosophy down from Heaven, to inhabit among Men; and I shall be ambitious to have it said of me, that I have brought Philosophy out of Closets and Libraries, Schools and Colleges, to dwell in Clubs and Assemblies, at Tea-Tables and in Coffee-Houses' [2. no. 10].

Addison continually speaks in his essays about subjects and themes from Antiquity and often quotes with expertise passages from Latin (more rarely Greek) texts in the original. He principally wanted to produce links to Antiquity. For instance, he formulated the thesis that there is a close essential affinity between the nature of English and Latin authors: 'if we look into the Writings of the old Italians, such as Cicero and Virgil, we shall find that the English Writers, in their way of thinking and expressing themselves, resemble those Authors much more than the modern Italians pretend to do' [2. no. 5]. Calling on Longinus, he sees *imitatio* as a positive process: 'one great Genius often catches the Flame from another, and writes in his Spirit without copying servilely after him' and justifies it by the relationship of Virgil to Homer [2. no. 339]. For Addison the ancient authors set the binding standards, for example, in regard to *imagination*: 'the most perfect in their several kinds ... are perhaps Homer, Virgil, and Ovid' [2. no. 417]. Even in the increased appreciation of native authors he propagated, especially with regard to Milton and British folk ballads, ancient authors were drawn on for comparison and to vouch for his views [43. 419].

Almost naively Addison assumes that his own enthusiasm for ancient languages and their culture is shared by his reading public and he speaks, for example, of 'the natural Love to Latin which is so prevalent in our common People'. In this context he recounts the anecdote of the country parson who enhances his sermons with Latin quotations from the Church Fathers and attracts more and more listeners, while his colleague in office in the neighbouring church increasingly has to preach to empty pews; when the latter realizes the problem he decides to offer his parish Latin as well and, since he does not know the Church Fathers, quotes mnemonic rhymes from Lily, the grammar book widely used in the schools, and is successful [2. no. 221].

Particularly interesting in this connection are the Latin (and sometimes Greek) *maxims* that introduce every copy of the *Spectator*. In contrast to the practice followed by Dr. Johnson later in his periodical *The Rambler* (1750–1752), they remain untranslated. As Addison believes with self-irony, they are supposed to guarantee that there is at least *one* good line in every copy and form for the reader 'a Hint that awakens in his Memory some beautiful Passage of a Classic Author' [2. no. 221]. The frequency with which an author occurs can perhaps be seen as a barometer of the appreciation of that author in Addison and his age. Horace, who is chosen in 215 from a total of 635 copies, takes the lead by a long way. He is followed by Virgil (123) and Ovid (56). After the Augustan poets comes Juvenal (48). Not until fifth place is there a prose author, Cicero (37), who, nonetheless, still occurs more frequently than all the Greek authors combined (28). Terence (22), Persius (19), Martial (19) and Lucretius (9) follow. Seneca (5), Sallust (2) and Tacitus (1) are surprisingly sparsely represented,as are the love poets Tibullus (2), Catullus (1) and Propertius (1).

The moral weeklies are also important as a preparation for the novel, since in emulation of Theophrastus, in English continued by Joseph Hall (1574–1656) and John Earle (c. 1601–1655), they present fictional characters in short contexts of action [52. 215].

The development of the modern novel in the early 18th cent., the most significant radical change of this period, initially progressed without much reference to ancient literature. Daniel Defoe (1660–1731), whom people like to call 'the father of the English novel,' as a dissenter received a non-humanist education, which provided him with mercantile knowledge and modern foreign languages, but not with a familiarity with Antiquity. The same applies naturally to the 'mothers of the novel,' who have recently entered the field through feminist literary history. Also Samuel Richardson (1689–1761), who became an influential pioneer of the new genre with his epistolary novels with their detailed depictions of the psyche, had to forgo a Classical education (and an ecclesiastical career) owing to his father's financial situation and was able instead to prepare himself for his future literary activity by practical experiences with texts as a printer.

In contrast, Henry Fielding (1707–1754), as the son of an aristocratic family, received a humanist education, first by private tutors, then at the prestigious *public school* Eton and finally at the University of Leyden, where he studied Classical literature and law. Because of his education Fielding had a good overview of the wider literary landscape and rightly saw that the

modern novel as a genre had taken on the function of the ancient epic. In his foreword Fielding actually calls his novel *Joseph Andrews* (1742), 'a comic epic-poem in prose' [3. 25]. Incidentally, one of its protagonists, the clergyman Abraham Adams, is a character of thorough classical erudition. Above all, Fielding's magnificent major work *Tom Jones* (1749) makes many references to ancient epics and other literature of ancient Rome and Greece. Even the motto on the original title page points the well-informed reader in this direction: *Mores hominum multorum vidit* (he saw the customs of many men). This is an unmistakable reference to the beginning of the *Odyssey*. Like a modern Odysseus, on his journey the eponymous hero gets to know the various regions of the world and contemporary society. By dividing his novel into 18 books, Fielding wishes to occupy the centre ground between Homer's 24 and Virgil's 12 books. Over and again the author reminds his readers of the analogy to Classical epics by parodying his ancient models, as expressed, for example, in the heading of chap. IV, 8: 'A Battle sung by the Muse in the Homerican Stile, and which none but the classical Reader can taste'. Here a village fight is depicted as an epic battle and the Classically educated reader finds, among other things, invocations to the muses, epic similes, necrology and Fortuna as a force deciding battle. Even in the apology by the narrator, 'All things are not in the power of all' [4. IV, 8], it is possible to recognize Virgil's *Non omnia possumus omnes*. Like Homer or Virgil, whom Fielding addresses as 'masters of all the learning of their times' [4. XIV, 1], he shows himself to be a *poeta doctus*. In this sense we encounter quite a few Latin and Greek quotations, which are admittedly usually translated, to simplify orientation for the 'mere English reader' [3. 25]. In one of his forewords Fielding calls invoking the muses by a modern author 'absurd' [4. VIII,1], and he also heeds the advice of Horace to writers to use supernatural agents only extremely rarely; but he does not keep to this and,besides the muses, also calls for the help of the allegorical power Learning: 'Open thy Mæonian and thy Mantuan coffers, with whatever else includes thy philosophic, thy poetic, and thy historical treasures, whether with Greek or Roman characters thou hast chosen to inscribe the ponderous chests' [4. XIII, 1]. At the end the narrator complains that the modern author, unlike the ancient one, no longer has any mythology at his disposal [cf. XVII,1]; but he still manages to save his protagonist even without a *deus ex machina*. In the final analysis, the heritage of the ancients helps Fielding emancipate himself from it. A similar picture, though less striking, is offered by the novelists Tobias Smollett (1721–1771), Laurence Sterne (1713–1768) and Oliver Goldsmith (1730–1774), all of whom had a good Classical education.

The influence of Antiquity had a stronger and more direct effect on the historiography of the period than in the field of the novel. Cicero's concept of history as a *magistra vitae* and the assumption that, above all, ancient history represented an inexhaustible treasure trove for political experience and that in this area there were examples of civic virtue worth emulating, was generally widespread. At the same time, however, the analogy between Roman and British history was not always seen as positive, and the reservation applied: 'English historians, social critics, and moralists used the analogy to raise apprehensions and self-doubts. As Cato served for an example and warning to the individual, Rome became the model and threat to England' [35. 105].

Even the philosopher and historian David Hume (1711–1776), whose *History of Great Britain*(1754–1757) and *History of England* (1759–1763) was regarded as the first great national history and for a long time as the standard work *par excellence*, was in essential ways molded by his encounter with ancient authors. Instead of studying law, he says of himself, he spent his time devouring Cicero and Virgil; and he writes in a letter about the formation of his personality according to Classical models: 'Having read many Books of Morality, such as Cicero, Seneca & Plutarch, & being smitten with their beautiful Representations of Virtue & Philosophy, I undertook the Improvement of my Temper & Will, along with my Reason & Understanding' [14. 59].

Hume saw history through the eyes of a philosopher. He was convinced that basic constants of human nature are revealed in historical events and processes. Looking into the past could provide valuable patterns of enlightenment for the present. As he was particularly interested in questions of the constitution, in other words, of the political system, Hume began his work of national history with the time of the rule of James I, when for the first time parliament successfully made a claim to the monarch for its own rights. The second volume, which went as far as the Glorious Revolution of 1688, brought Hume wide recognition, so he continued the project. In two stages he worked his way back and first wrote two volumes each on the Tudor age and then on the entire period from the invasion of Julius Caesar to Henry VII's accession to the throne. Hume strove for balance and impartiality and stressed the progress of civilization since the Middle Ages. Even though he did not verify his sources, he had an excellent command of the subject matter and received great applause, above all, for his mastery of style. With Hume, as with his contemporaries, historiography belonged to the area of belles-lettres. For his successor Gibbon, Hume was the 'Tacitus of Scotland' [48. 96].

Probably the best known work of historiography in the English language, *The History of the Decline and Fall of the Roman Empire* (1776–1788) in six volumes, by Edward Gibbon (1737–1794), is not without reason dedicated to an object from Antiquity. Like Hume before him Gibbon consciously schooled his (later much praised) style on ancient models. He mentions Nepos as an early model: 'The lives of Cornelius Nepos, the friend of Atticus and Cicero, are composed in the style of the purest age: his simplicity is elegant, his brevity

copious; he exhibits a series of men and manners; and with such illustrations, as every pedant is not indeed qualified to give, this Classic biographer may initiate a young Student in the history of Greece and Rome' [14. 60]. Later Gibbon read 'all the Epistles, all the Orations, and the most important treatises of Rhetoric and Philosophy' by Cicero and concluded from them the telling recommendation: 'Cicero in Latin and Xenophon in Greek are indeed the two ancients whom I would first propose to a liberal scholar, not only for the merit of their style and sentiments but for the admirable lessons which may be applied almost to every situation of public and private life' [14. 60f.].

The inspiration Gibbon himself gives for the monumental work is famous: 'It was at Rome, on the 15th of October 1764, as I sat musing admidst the ruins of the Capitol, while the barefooted friars were singing vespers in the temple of Jupiter, that the idea of writing the decline and fall of the city first started to my mind' [48. 96]. Gibbon deals with the history of the Roman Empire from the death of Marcus Aurelius (AD 180) to the fall of the Byzantine Empire (1453) in three large sections, which he outlines in the foreword: from the Age of Trajan and the Antonines to the fall of the Western Empire in the assaults by the Huns and the Goths; from the reign of Justinian in the East to the establishment of a second or Germanic empire in the West under Charlemagne; and finally from the revival of the Western Empire to the conquest of Constantinople by the Turks. Gibbon's sympathies were with Diocletian, the hardworking parvenu who restored order and stability to a shattered kingdom, more than with his successor Constantine, whose calculating use of tactics, especially when dealing with religion, he found despicable.

Gibbon depicts the development of the Roman Empire as a continuous decline. He emphasizes the paradoxical fact that, though Rome reached the pinnacle of its civilization under the enlightened despotism of the Antonine emperors, the seeds of ruin had at the same time already been sown when the well-balanced, free constitution of the republic had been given up and 'uniform government ... introduced a slow and secret poison into the vitals of the empire'. Also, in Christianity 'with its doctrines of patience and pusillanimity' [48. 79] Gibbon saw a decisive cause for the decline. In chap. 15 and 16 of the first book, strongly attacked particularly by Anglican clerics, Gibbon critically examines the rise of Christianity, the growing religious fanaticism, the superstition and the treatment of Christians by the Roman Empire up to the time of Constantine. Gibbon shared this negative assessment of the role of the Church with contemporary intellectuals whom he had met in France and Switzerland.

While he was still working on the great work, in 1765 Gibbon founded the *Roman Club*, so as to gather round him a group of like-minded people. Like the previous *Society of Roman Knights* (founded in 1722) or the → SOCIETY OF DILETTANTI (founded in 1732), which later shifted its main interest from Rome to

Greece, this society was actively concerned with fostering ancient cultural assets [14. 61].

Very committed in this sense also was Anthony Ashley Cooper, third Earl of Shaftesbury (1671–1713), the most influential philosopher of his time. He could already converse fluently in Greek and Latin at the age of eleven and an early biographer points out his lifelong intensive involvement with Antiquity. 'Shaftesbury's principal study was of the writings of antiquity, from which he formed to himself the plan of his philosophy'. Further he says: 'Among these writings those which he most admired, and carried always with him, were the moral works of Xenophon, Horace, the Commentaries and Enchiridion of Epictetus as published by Arrian, and Marcus Antoninus' [14. 57].

In contrast to John Locke (1632–1704), the founder of English empiricism, whom he personally regarded highly, Shaftesbury placed the main emphasis in his philosophical thinking on ethics. He was an admirer of what he regarded as the Greek ideal of balance and harmony, and in his view Locke's doctrines of moral and state philosophy would have decidedly gained from a greater consideration of Greek philosophy. For Shaftesbury Aristotle's view of man as ξῷον πολιτικόν was fundamental. In his unsystematic main work, ('the most ingenious way of becoming foolish is by a system'), *Characteristics of Men, Manners, Opinions, Times* (1711, revised 1714), particularly in the treatise contained in it *Enquiry concerning Virtue*(1699), he supports the conviction that man possesses an inherent distinction between right and wrong, between the beauty or ugliness of his actions and feelings. He calls this capability *moral sense*. Even though Shaftesbury's high esteem for Greek Antiquity in an age, when Rome was usually the centre of attention, was somewhat unusual, his body of thought is nevertheless reflected in many novels and in aesthetic and philosophical writings of the 18th cent. [cf. 41. 38].

SOURCES: 1 J. ADDISON, Miscellaneous Works, A. C. GUTHKELCH (ed.), 2 vols., 1914 2 J. ADDISON, R. STEELE et al., Spectator, G. SMITH (ed.), 4 vols., 1907, revised 1945 3 H. FIELDING, Joseph Andrews, R. F. BRISSENDEN (ed.), 1977 4 Id., Tom Jones, R. P. C. MUTTER (ed.), 1966 5 S. JOHNSON, Lives of the English Poets, 2 vols., 1906 (repr. 1952) 6 Id., Poems, E. L. McADAM , JR. (ed.), 1964 7 B. JONSON, Works, C. H. HERFORD, P. UND E. SIMPSON (eds.), 11 vols., 1925–1952 8 J. MILTON, Complete Poems and Major Prose, M. Y. HUGHES (ed.), 1957 9 A. POPE, Poems, J. BUTT (ed.), 1963 10 W. SHAKE-SPEARE, The Riverside Shakespeare, G. BLAKEMORE EVANS (ed.), 1974 11 J. SWIFT, Poems, H. WILLIAMS (ed.), 3 vols., 1958 12 J. SWIFT, Prose Works, H. DAVIS (ed.), 14 vols., 1939–1968

LITERATURE: 13 M. N. AUSTIN, Classical Learning of Samuel Johnson, in: Studies in the Eighteenth Century, R. F. BRISSENDEN (ed.), 1968 14 P. AYRES, Classical Culture and the Idea of Rome in 18th Century England, 1997 15 F. W. BATESON, N. A. JOUKOVSKY (eds.), Alexander Pope. A Critical Anthology, 1971 16 R. BORGMEIER, The Dying Shepherd. Die Tradition der englischen Ekloge von Pope bis Wordsworth, 1976 17 Id., Die englische Litera-

tur, in: Einfluß Senecas auf das europäische Drama, E. LEFÈVRE (ed.), 1978, 276–323 18 B. H. BRONSON, Facets of the Enlightenment, 1968 19 R. A. BROWER, Alexander Pope. Poetry of Allusion, 1959 20 H. BROWN, Classical Tradition in English Literature: A Bibliography, in: Harvard Studies and Notes in Philology and Literature 18 (1935), 7–46 21 N. CALLAN, Pope and the Classics, in: P. DIXON (ed.), Alexander Pope, 1975, 230–249 22 M. L. CLARKE, Classical Education in Britain. 1500–1900, 1959 23 Id., Greek Studies in England. 1700–1830, 1986 24 D. DANIELSON, Cambridge Companion to Milton, 1989 25 O. DIEDE, Streit der Alten und Modernen in der englischen Literaturgeschichte des 16. und 17. Jahrhunderts, 1912 26 T. S. ELIOT, What is a Classic?, 1974 (1945) 27 H. ERSKINE-HILL, Augustans on Augustanism, 1655–1759, in: Renaissance & Modern Studies 2 (1967), 55–83 28 Id., Augustan Idea in English Literature, 1983 29 D. M. FOERSTER, Homer in English Criticism, 1947 30 W. FROST, Dryden and the Classics: With a Look at his *Aeneis*, in: E. MINER (ed.), John Dryden, 267–296 31 J. FUCHS, Reading Pope's Imitations of Horace, 1989 32 J. H. HANFORD, Milton Handbook, ⁴1961 33 C. H. HERFORD, P. SIMPSON (eds.), Ben Jonson. The Man and His Work, 2 vols., 1925 34 G. HIGHET, Classical Tradition. Greek and Roman Influences on Western Literature, 1949 35 J. W. JOHNSON, Formation of English Neo-Classical Thought, 1967 36 Id., 'Classics and John Bull,' in: H. T. SWEDENBERG (ed.), England in the Restoration and Early 18th Century, 1972, 1–26 37 R. F. JONES, Ancients and Moderns. A Study of the Background of the Battle of the Books, 1936 38 C. KALLENDORF, Latin Influences on English Literature from the Middle Ages to the 18th Century, Annotated Bibliography of Scholarship, 1945–1979, 1982 39 L. C. KNIGHTS, Tradition and Ben Jonson, in: J. A. BARISH (ed.), Ben Jonson, 1963, 24–39 40 H. LEVIN, Contexts of the Classical, in: Contexts of Criticism, 1957, 38–54 41 V. NÜNNING, A. NÜNNING, Englische Literatur des 18. Jahrhunderts, 1998 42 C. G. OSGOOD, Classical Mythology of Milton's Poems, 1964 (1900) 43 H. PAPAJEWSKI, Die Bedeutung der Ars Poetica für den englischen Neoklassizismus, in: Anglia 79 (1961), 405–439 44 R. PFEIFFER, History of Classical Scholarship. From 1300 to 1850, 1976 45 K. A. PREUSCHEN, Ben Jonson als humanistischer Dramatiker, 1989 46 D. ROLLE (ed.), 18. Jahrhundert I (Die englische Literatur in Text und Darstellung), 1982 47 N. RUDD, Classical Tradition in Operation, 1994 48 J. SAMBROOK, The 18th Century. The Intellectual and Cultural Context of Literature, 1700–1789, 1986 49 B. N. SCHILLING (ed.), Essential Articles: For the Study of English Augustan Backgrounds, 1961 50 F. STACK, Pope and Horace: Studies in Imitation, 1985 51 C. J. SUMMERS, T.-L. PEBWORTH, Ben Jonson, 1979 52 J. A. K. THOMSON, Classical Background of English Literature, 1948 53 Id., Classical Influences of English Poetry, 1951 54 E. M. W. TILLYARD, Milton and the Classics, in: Essay by Divers Hands 26 (1953), 59–72 55 H. D. WEINBROT, Augustus Caesar in Augustan England, 1978 56 Id., Britannia's Issue. The Rise of British Literature from Dryden to Ossian, 1993 57 R. WELLEK, Term and Concept of Classicism, in: Proceedings of the International Comparative Literatures Association, 1966, 1049–1067 58 C. WINTON, The Roman Play in the 18th Century, in: Studies in the Literary Imagination 10 (1977), 77–90

ADDITIONAL BIBLIOGRAPHY: B. BALDWIN, Samuel Johnson and the Classics, in: Hellas: A Journal of Poetry and the Humanities (Fall 1991), 2 (2): 227–38; J. BUXTON, The Grecian Taste: Literature in the Age of Neo-Classicism, 1740–1820, 1978; V. COLTMAN, Classicism in the English Library: Reading Classical Culture in the Late Eighteenth and Early Nineteenth Centuries, in: Journal of the History of Collections 11 (1999), 35–50; R. HOBERMAN, Gendering Classicism: The Ancient World in Twentieth-Century Women's Historical Fiction, 1997; A. A. M. KINNEGING, Aristocracy and History: Classicism in Political Thought, 1997.   RAIMUND BORGMEIER

III. LITERATURE (GERMAN AND ROMANCE)
see → CLASSICISM AFTER CLASSICAL ANTIQUITY

Classicism after Classical Antiquity

A. TERMINOLOGY PROBLEMS AND GENERAL
B. CLASSICISM AS A STRATEGY FOR LITERARY MODERNISATION IN 17TH CENT. FRANCE
C. CLASSICISM AS A WAY OF DEFINING THE FUNCTION OF LITERATURE ON THE BASIS OF A PHILOSOPHY OF HISTORY IN GERMANY TOWARD THE END OF THE 18TH CENT.

A. TERMINOLOGY PROBLEMS AND GENERAL

The use of the term *classicism* as a name for peak periods in literature, accordingly also in music and, sometimes, art history, is a late neologism. It did not appear widely in German literary history until the end of the 19th cent. and then after the First World War (unlike in the study of German language and literature abroad, where it is still little used today) quickly gained acceptance. It is commonly referred to more precisely as 'German' or 'Weimar' classicism, to characterize aspects of literary development regarded as formative around the turn of the 18th to the 19th cent. In the wake of the term's wide acceptance, it was also applied, besides in the history of music ('Viennese' classicism), to other national literatures, in particular, to French literature, whose classicism in the 17th cent. has commonly been called 'French classicism' in the study of Romance languages and literature in Germany since the 1920s. Influenced by problems of legitimizing national literature, it is an appropriation of the French term *classicisme* into German terminology. The term *classicism* is, in fact, already found in isolated instances in Germany as a derivation from the adjective and noun *classique*, taken mainly from 18th cent. French discussions (and along with its alternative noun form 'classicity'), in works of literary criticism and theory since the end of the 18th cent. Also in the 19th cent. the term is found in some treatises on literary history, though initially only as a term of literary evaluation. Because its use, so natural today at least from a German point of view, as the name for an epoch, is the result of a late separate development, it is necessary, especially because the literary periods known as classicism in Germany and France are portrayed as having a connection to the ancient literatures of Greece and Rome, to include a discussion of the

historical semantic field from which the term *classicism* developed and in which it received its specific meaning (cf. on general history of terminology [18. 253ff.; 37]; on the specific problems of the German and French tradition of the terms 'classicism' or *classicisme* as the name for an epoch [14; 23; 29; 27; 32. 1–44] and various contributions in [15]).

The starting point for this semantic field is the Latin *classicus*. Aside from its military usage, it has a predominantly social meaning in Latin writings and is applied only in very isolated instances to questions of literary evaluation. A much-quoted appropriate reference is found in the phrase *classicus adsiduusque aliquis scriptor, non proletarius* (a certain wealthy, upper-class writer, one not from the lowest class) in Aulus Gellius (19,8,15), where the social hierarchy in the double attribute *classicus adsiduusque* is obviously used as a model for a literary hierarchy. From the Renaissance on especially, a meaning of the semantic field developed which assumes the initially undisputed value of ancient literature but, at the same time, can be explained by its importance for teaching. For example, *classique* employed to describe exemplary ancient authors, especially those used for reading in schools- 'auteurs qu'on lit dans les classes' ('authors one reads at school'),– is still a definition in Furetière's *Dictionnaire universel* of 1690. At the same time, however, this usage does make clear that evaluating contemporary literature itself as 'classical' was inconceivable in 17th cent. France. Not until after the → QUERELLE DES ANCIENS ET DES MODERNES did it also become possible to use the semantic field *classique*/'classical', without reference to Antiquity, to mean exemplary 'in a literary sense' or 'perfect', and therefore to apply the idea of perfection to authors of the respective national literatures. In this sense, *classique* is first found in France as early as 1548 in Th. Sebillet's *Art poétique françois* ('bons et classiques poètes français', 'excellent and classical French poets'), but the term did not become common for describing and evaluating authors of the recent past or, much less, the present until the 18th cent. By 'bons auteurs du siècle de Louis XIV et de celui-ci' ('excellent authors of the age of Louis XIV and the present') the entry *classique* in the *Encyclopédie* (1754), for instance, defines a meaning of the term corresponding to similar tendencies in Voltaire's *Le Siècle de Louis XIV* (1752/53). In Germany a debate took place sometime between 1795 and 1797 about whether classical works and authors existed in the present. In this debate, it is significant that Goethe, in opposition to representatives of the Enlightenment and Romanticism, still denied the possibility of this, referring to the lack of a national state and the cultural prerequisites [6th vol. 40. 196–203]. In spite of his warning 'to use the expressions *classical author* and *classical work* extremely rarely' [6th vol. 40. 198], from about the turn of the century on, terms such as 'classical writer' or 'German classicist' became increasingly common in Germany. The terms appeared in collections of writings and treatises as a qualification for authors regarded as outstanding in terms of national literature as well as for their works (references in [14. 350f.]). This occurred, as it had in France, long before such evaluations became the basis for distinguishing epochs.

The idea that there are peak epochs in national literature which are clearly distinguishable is, in all European countries, a product of the constructs of literary history flourishing in the 19th cent., though, historically, the beginning of the process can be traced to the end of the 17th cent., with the elevation of the 'Siècle de Louis XIV' serving as model and impetus. As a name for this period considered the peak period of French 17th cent. literature, the neologism *classicisme* (not commonly used to signifiy an epoch until later) was formed in the 1820s in France. It was initially intended to denote primarily the antithesis to the literature of Romanticism and was directed against the positive evaluation of Romanticism in the dichotomy, championed primarily by the Schlegel brothers, of 'classical/romantic', which Mme de Staël had disseminated in France. Initially, the particular significance of the relationship of this peak period in national literature to Antiquity played no more a major role in this terminological development than in the epochal construct opening up parallel to, and in competition with France in Germany. Alongside a devaluation of Romanticism, nationalistic motives were paramount in both countries. This can be seen both in the epochal term the 'Age of Frederick the Great,' common in the second half of the century and modeled on the French example (cf. e.g. [33. 436ff.]), and in the term 'classicism' itself, which was substituted for it later. As to its acceptance into German, 'Trübner's German Dictionary' still notes in 1943, not without a quiet national pathos, that 'happily for our language, twisted neologisms' from the French 'have fallen out of use'. The epochal terms *classicisme* and 'classicism' itself, like the entire semantic field, thus initially denoted competing peak periods in national literature. These posited peaks have a relationship to Antiquity principally insofar as the exemplary nature of ancient literature, which originally constituted the meaning of the semantic field, is applied to periods in modern national literature. Both French and German classicisms, in the sense of peak periods, only took on a relationship to ancient literature as an essential component of their validity in subsequent, more carefully articulated justifications of the term as used to delineate an epoch, especially when employed to signify similarities in genesis and value.

However, efforts of this kind to differentiate national literatures can have been influenced by the fact that the confrontation with the French model was already part of those processes during which, towards the end of the 18 th cent., a literary construct, later described as classicism, was formed in Germany. From the time of Lessing's *Hamburgischer Dramaturgie* (1767–1769) at the latest, the question of the appropriation and further development of ancient texts already played a part in

this development. And a new interpretation of basic Aristotelian terms, directed by Lessing against the tragedy of French classicism, took the position that French classicism, which had been considered until then exemplary (for instance in Gottsched's attempts at reform), was reinterpreted as a false orientation created by a superficial appropriation of Antiquity. For instance, Friedrich Schlegel, in his *Gespräch über die Poesie* (1800) stated that *es sei aus dem mißverstandenen Alt. und dem mittelmäßigen Talent … in Frankreich ein umfassendes und zusammenhängendes System von falscher Poesie, welches auf einer gleich falschen Theorie der Dichtkunst ruhte entstanden* ('in France, from misunderstood Antiquity and mediocre talent … a comprehensive and cohesive system of false poetry has evolved which was based on an equally false theory of the art of poetry', [12th Vol. 2. 302]). In a comparison of the two epochs credited as classicism, evaluative contrasts such as that between superficiality and depth or between external order and existential reflection are played out over and over again, principally from the point of view of the study of German language and literature. Part of the point of all this is to prove the superiority of German classicism because of the particular way it (as opposed to French classicism) understood and employed ancient literature(cf. [22, Vol. 1. 23ff., 146ff.; 24. 11ff.; 28. 18ff.]). Such evaluations resulted in a perspective which, because of the suppositions of the term *classicism,* had a unifying effect on the conception of national literature. Both French and German classicism appeared as self-contained epochs. How each of the two national literatures appropriated and reinterpreted the ancient models then raises questions about the validity of viewing these constructs as really existing coherent epochs. This kind of examination, contrasting the German and the French cases, appears justified in that their ancient points of reference clearly differ from one another (Roman Republic and literature of the Augustan age in French classicism; Homeric epic and Greek *polis* in German classicism). The two periods are nevertheless basically comparable in regard to their self-legitimization, which is derived from their both following ancient texts and using them to construct and develop their national literatures as these evolved in modern times.

Although a recent summarizing portrayal complains that the term German classicism has attained 'an apparently irrefutable validity' in spite of the 'most astute objections' to retaining it, [23. 1] (cf. on this also [31]), we shall not pursue further these general problems about its use to signify an epoch. In any case, it can be assumed that it finds justification principally, if at all, in the fact that it denotes a special relationship between attempts to legitimize new interpretations of ancient points of reference and literary modernisation. Even if one takes a skeptical attitude towards towards attempts to grasp epochal coherences in the term *classicism*, the periods described as classicism in both the German and the French cases had tendencies at least towards a kind of poetological reflection and style of writing which the authors considered justified because of their relationsip to ancient literature. This stands both in contrast to periods in the other national literatures canonized as peak periods (such as the Spanish *siglo de oro* or the English *Elizabethan Age*) and in comparison with other periods in French and German literature (such as the Enlightenment or Romanticism), in which appropriation of ancient texts does not play a major role. On the other hand, compared with other periods of classical orientation in literature, such as the Renaissance or even the neo-classicism of the 18th cent. in Spain, Italy and England, it would be possible to distinguish both French and German classicism from these by calling them 'intensive' classicisms because they considered Antiquity to be not only a model or source of inspiration, but also to be the object of an aesthetic construct (particularly in the case of France) and historical-philosophical construct (particularly in the case of Germany) in which both the legitimacy of literature and the relationship between ancient and modern times are re-conceived (cf. on these questions from very varying perspectives the contributions in [15; 21; 36]). Beyond the traditional paradigms of evaluation, both classicisms are comparable primarily in that they see their conception of Antiquity as a means of legitimizing literary modernisation.

B. CLASSICISM AS A STRATEGY FOR LITERARY MODERNISATION IN 17TH CENT. FRANCE

It only seems to be a paradox that it is possible to mark the disintegration of the Humanist tradition at the end of the 16th cent. as the starting point of French classicism. The exemplary character, rediscovered in the Humanist optimism of the Renaissance and still unreservedly applicable, which was attributed then to Antiquity, seemed increasingly no longer tenable both in terms of the mentality then current (against the background of the religious wars in the latter third of the 16th cent.) and in terms of literature (in the wake of the development of the tendencies of literary Baroque). Also, because of the social and ideological momentum towards modernization after the religious peace of 1594/1598, Humanism became increasingly less important. Literary development at the beginning of the 17th cent. is clearly influenced by a desire for modernity, which initially, against the background of Baroque styles of writing, clearly turned away from the poetological and rhetorical traditions of Antiquity. A fundamental problem of this literary modernisation, though, is that it consists mainly in denying that there are any perspectives capable of forming a consensus for modernisation, or any general assumptions or principles according to which it could be devised (cf. Ch. 4 in [32]). This constituted a fundamental problem of legitimization all the more as authors increasingly found themselves confronted with demands as to their role, a result of the literary policies of an absolute monarchy which aimed at political integration and regulation of litera-

ture. From about 1630 Richelieu intensified these efforts. They found expression in the founding of the *Académie française* (1635) and also in poetological attempts at standardization which he initiated and were later continued, for example, by the gratification policies pursued by Colbert (from 1663). In the conflict between such attempts at political functionalization and authors pushing for autonomy, adopting and reinterpreting ancient points of reference opened up possibilities of legitimizing and affirming literature's autonomous value, even though these points of reference had been established in opposition to the humanist appropriation of Antiquity. A constellation therefore developed out of the contradictions and internal dynamics of which basic problems of French classicism could be more meaningfully outlined, specifically with respect to its relationship to Antiquity, than by enumerating epochal boundaries and dominants which were controversial and problematic anyway. Without pursuing further debates on this matter or depicting in greater detail the literary field in which classical orientation, albeit as only one of several competing factors, is a partial determinant, from about 1630 and 1680 its significance can be calculated primarily in the context of a process of modernisation which contributed to the creation of a relatively autonomous field of literature (cf. on this [32; 35]).

Even though the appropriation of Antiquity by the Humanists gave French classicism a broad inventory of models, it is nevertheless indicative of the way it dealt with this tradition that, from this range, it is primarily literary, philosophical and political elements from the final period of the Roman republic and the beginnings of the empire that were taken up, most particularly, elements from the Age of Augustus, which was reinterpreted to address the problems of the present. This selection does indeed follow tendencies of Renaissance classicism, for instance, in the doctrine of poetry, long regarded as formative in France. Julius Scaliger's *Poetices libri septem* (printed in Lyons in 1561), in spite of its neo-Aristotelian orientation, not only declares that the epic is the highest form of poetry, but also sees Virgil as the unequalled master of the genre, while harshly denigrating Homer, and, in a broadly argued comparison, elevates Latin literature far above Greek literature because of the quality of its rhetorical style. This evaluation remained dominant in France throughout the 17th cent. (It still held sway without reservation in Nicolas Boileau's *Art poétique*, the most famous poetological text of French classicism, and even later in Charles Perrault's *Parallèle des Anciens et des Modernes*, the most comprehensive anti-classical treatise in the context of the *Querelle des Anciens et des Modernes*.) It leads away, however, from a Humanist scholarly discussion of the value of ancient tradition as a norm and towards a reinterpretation of it in terms of aesthetic criticism. Reflected in the way the epochs regarded themselves and their claims of literature's importance, the Augustan Golden Age in particular becomes an idealized projection of literary relationships in the conflict between literature's claim to autonomy and attempts at its political regulation.

Informative clues to this are found in various treatises written in the 1630s by Guez de Balzac on politics and culture in the Augustan age. Balzac was not only a leading representative of attempts to modernize literature but, after he had fallen from grace after various overtures to Richelieu, also the most important advocate of classicism in the first half of the 17th cent. In his treatises he depicts an image of Rome in which warlike *virtus* retreats behind the *urbanitas* of social circles in which communication not inhibited by a power structure constitutes the idealized ancient culture (cf. on this [1. 92f.]). He justified this interpretation by changing the Humanist perspective on Roman history, which was orientated towards the Republic, to the Empire: 'for the Republic may permit me to admit that the Age of Augustus ... was the golden age of art, science and, in general, of all good discoveries. During this period of government everything was smoothed out and refined, everyone was erudite and inventive at this court, from Augustus down to his servants' [1. 94]. In the light of a universal cultural prosperity, the Age of Augustus was stylized into a Utopian place of equality of mind, where education overcomes social barriers and, over and above this, as in the peripeteia of *Cinna*, a tragedy by Pierre Corneille (1643) depicting an attempt to revolt against Augustus, humanity becomes the basis of rule. With the famous 'let us be friends, Cinna' (V, 3, V. 1701), with which he seals his reconciliation with the conspirators who had acted against him, Augustus retains his claim to power as *Imperator* by accepting his detractors as equals in the private sphere. Balzac highlighted precisely this element of Utopian idealization of Roman life in the light of the present when he writes to Corneille about his drama: 'You show us Rome just as it can exist in Paris and did not destroy it by changing it. (...) Where Rome was made of bricks, you are rebuilding it in marble' [2nd Vol. 1. 675f.].

This Utopian modelling of the Augustan Age – and this is the decisive achievement of French classicism – allows one to imagine a relatively autonomous place for literature. In declaring the private sphere to be the really important centre of the Age of Augustus – one worthy of entering tradition, the literary discourses, reduced to this, attain an autonomous dignity which reflects back even into the public domain. As in Balzac's above-quoted reversal of perspectives, the intellectual rank of Augustus's court constitutes its real importance. Such interpretations enable one to think of literary discourses as having an independent dignity, even though they are excluded from the political realm. This was an essential prerequisite for their autonomy, which began about mid-century.

This development was also promoted ultimately by French literature's much discussed turning to a poetics of rules in the tradition of neo-Aristotelism which, rooted in the Italian Renaissance, spread across Europe.

Discussed at length in France from the end of the 1620s, this prescriptive poetics is hardly of practical significance except in the theatre, in spite of its patronage by Richelieu. Even though the mighty cardinal probably had the idea that a poetics of rules provided a way of controlling the literary *inventio*, it nevertheless, at the same time, paved the way for autonomous discussions about texts by legitimizing discourse on literature that sticks to judging it according to the logic of poetics (in fact, a poetic of rules) (cf. on this, in general, [32, 196ff.]). This functional ambivalence became very obvious in the *Querelle du Cid* (1637), a fierce literary battle over Corneille's successful play, which the *Académie française*, at Richelieu's instigation, was supposed to bring to an end with their verdict. On the one hand, the intervention of this politically sponsored institution did bring the literary debate to a conclusion; on the other hand, however, the Academy in its *Sentimens de l'Académie françoise sur la tragicomédie du Cid* had to admit that an evaluation based on rules did not allow an unequivocal judgement of a literary work and that, in spite of its infringements of the rules, the *Cid* was worthy of 'an appreciable standing in French literature' [5. 417]. Balzac expressed the ambivalence of this judgement sarcastically in the quote 'maior ille est qui iudicum abstulit quam qui meruit' [5. 457], thereby introducing the authority of public taste as a modern criterion of literary value, which disempowers the claim that rules have to validity.

The recourse to authentication by Antiquity and its ambivalent function served the modern tendency towards the autonomy of literature. According to the conviction of contemporaries, this poetics of rules was considered the poetics of ancient literatures. *De facto*, it is rather an invention of neo-Aristotelianism and, in French discussions, seems to be primarily indebted to Cartesian principles. It contributed, in any case, to the formulation of a theory of literature as autonomous without functioning as an evaluative standard for the literary production of those very authors who were among the most important in French classicism. Examples are the already mentioned Corneille and also Molière, in whose *Malade imaginaire* a ludicrous doctor dogmatically clinging to the ancient orthodox tradition is told: 'The ancients, old chap, are the ancients and we are living in the present' (Act II, Scene 6). La Fontaine, too, adopted an extremely relaxed, sometimes positively ironic and playful way of dealing with the rules. Where they are more or less observed as, for instance, in some of Molière's comedies and, in particular, in Racine's tragedies, this is done principally not out of respect for the (pseudo-)ancient dogma, but because the dramatic conflicts characteristic of these works are internal and require structures of action that can fit in with the requirements of the famous three unities. In any case, it cannot be substantiated from the works themselves that they were the basis for a so-called *doctrine classique*, ascribed to French classicism as a form of standardization of works following the rules of poetry (fundamental for this [16]). The fact that Boileau's *Art poétique*, to which a standardizing function is usually attributed, was not written until the last phase of classicism in the 17th cent. is not the only reason why it scarcely counts as evidence of this (1674); Boileau's poetics also turns the exemplary character of Antiquity itself towards aestheticism. The expected hyperbolic praise of Virgil does indeed appear there at a poetologically central point in the section on epic; but Boileau emphasizes the aesthetic qualities of evoking ancient mythology primarily in order to turn it against the religious-monarchistic products of his contemporaries (*L'Art poétique*, 3rd verse, in particular V. 173ff. [3]). A judgement based on the value of ancient texts enables ideologically heteronomous texts to break the boundaries of literary orthodoxy, yet allows its autonomy to be stabilized at the same time.

As these few examples show, the reinterpretation of ancient literature directed towards the present in French classicism contributed to creating legitimacy for a freedom for literature beyond political and ideological restrictions. It offered reasons why discourse about literature should be relatively autonomous. Undoubtedly such a discourse is anything but narrowly focused. Nor can boundaries created by using ancient texts functioning as norms be thought of as a prerequisite for a flourishing of literature that is inherently consistent. What the classical orientation of literature in France in the 17th cent. does, however, is to allow room to manoeuvre – room which can be used and was used in a multitude of ways, and can be scrutinized by literary discourses of very different orientations and scope.

C. Classicism as a Way of Defining the Function of Literature on the Basis of a Philosophy of History in Germany toward the End of the 18th Cent.

The autonomy devised in French classicism and consolidated in the literary development of the 18th cent. moved in German classicism into the centre of a literary orientation that sought to justify its legitimacy and function from a historical-philosophical reconstruction of the relationship between Antiquity and the present. Though, as already mentioned, this happened at a critical distance from the French model, at least the social location of literature there, exerted an undeniable power of fascination. Even though both Goethe and Schiller rejected the application of the French model to German circumstances, not least because of the consequences of the Revolution, it is nevertheless at least implicitly present in their efforts to promote the development of a national literature around the turn of the century with a classicistic programme, since that seemed to offer the possibility of stability and hierarchical order (cf. on this in general [25; 30]). Not least the attempt to produce unity, achievable in literature if not in politics, in the short period of mutual programmatic and practical efforts by Goethe and Schiller around the turn of the century in Germany contributed to the increased interest in

Antiquity that can be regarded as an essential component of German classicism in a Germany which was fragmented equally in terms of literature and politics between the late Enlightenment and early Romanticism.

The need for legitimization that Antiquity had to satisfy is indicated by the titles of periodicals such as the *Hori* or the *Propylaeae* and also by the joint collection of distichs, the *Xeniae*, with which the two men from 'Weimar' tried to strengthen their position in the disparate literary field under the patronage of Martial, as explicitly set forth by Goethe in a letter to Schiller (23.12.1795). Besides a series of invectives against literary competitors, one also finds there reflections designed to locate and legitimize the orientation of literature aspired to against the political situation, including, in particular, the famous 85th *Xenia Das deutsche Reich*: 'Deutschland? aber wo liegt es? Ich weiß das Land nicht zu finden./Wo das gelehrte beginnt, hört das politische auf' (the German Empire: Germany? but where is it? I do not know where to find this country./Where learning begins, politics stops). From this perspective, in which the intellectual nation appears to be in decay in relation to the nation as a political entity, the following *Xenia* (*German National Character*) devises an autonomous humanistic project: 'Zur Nation euch zu bilden, ihr hoffet es, Deutsche, vergebens./ Bildet, ihr könnt es, dafür freier zu Menschen euch aus' (Germans, you are hoping in vain to make yourselves into a nation./Rather, you can do this: make yourselves more freely into human beings). Such reflections indicate the perspective of radical autonomy with which Goethe and Schiller sought to justify their position in literature by seeing themselves beyond history and society. They turn away from an 'interest limited to the present'. Against this they posit 'a general and greater concern, namely, in that which is purely human and elevated above all influence of ages' (the announcement in the *Hori*, 8th Vol. 22, 107). This journalistic project expressly implores the eponymous goddesses, handed down by, among others, Hesiod, to be 'Garantinnen einer welterhaltende[n] Ordnung, aus der alles Gute fließt' (guarantors of a world-sustaining order from which all goodness flows). With this mythological reference they hoped to propagate a new order based on aesthetics and philosophy. 'Die politisch geteilte Welt unter der Fahne der Wahrheit und der Schönheit wieder vereinigen' (To reunite the politically divided world under the banner of truth and beauty (ibid.): this claim posits the idea of an autonomous artistic beauty, attested to by Antiquity and opposed to the confusion of history, that will propagate a literary discourse structured by a classicistic orientation dominated by the men of 'Weimar' (on the literary political aspect of the 'Weimar' constellation cf. [17; 19]).

The literary movement of the turn of the century certainly did not exhaust itself in such tussles for literary turf and in the attempts by Goethe and Schiller to build a hierarchy, even though the later epochal structure was quite exclusively tailored to the two Weimar classicists and is sometimes even limited to the decade which began their collaboration with writings like those previously quoted. Yet the reduction of this period to its 'leading figures' should not be underestimated any less than in the case of France. Intentions of literary strategy were hardly the least of the factors contributing to the intensity of this classicistic orientation and giving it that appearance of duration and coherence which made possible its epochal codification as classicism. At any rate, it was possible for Goethe and Schiller to position themselves programmatically in this way with a symbolic capital schooled in Antiquity only because they were able to fall back on an increased interest in (principally Greek) Antiquity which had begun to emerge from the middle of the century. Its point of departure is Winckelmann's 1755 work *Gedancken über die Nachahmung der griechischen Wercke in der Malerey und der Bildhauerkunst* ('Reflections concerning the Imitation of the Grecian Artists in Painting and Sculpture', 1766). This treatise, considered exemplary until well into the 19th cent., adopts an ambivalent position regarding intellectual history. On the one hand, it followed an Enlightenment perspective of progress: 'der gute Geschmack, welcher sich mehr und mehr durch die Welt ausbreitet, hat sich angefangen zuerst unter dem griechischen Himmel zu bilden' (good taste, which is spreading more and more throughout the world, first started to form under Greek skies) [13. 29]; and it tried to explain the superior rank accorded to Greek art by climatic and living conditions, thereby historicizing it. On the other hand, it tried to depict it as inimitable and unsurpassable (in the famous words: 'eine edle Einfalt, und eine stille Größe' (a noble simplicity and a quiet greatness) [13. 43], for instance). Decisive for Winckelmann's acceptance was that he created for Greek art a philosophy of art and of history by introducing 'the concepts of wholeness and perfection into the nature of Antiquity' as a point of reference intended to reform in the artist 'the concepts of the split in our nature' [13. 38]. This was comparable to the starting point of French classicism and went beyond a scholarly, Humanist ('antiquarian') position.

This points to a way of thinking that became defining for German classicism: the conception of Greek art as an idealized point of reference, from which the problems of the present can be pondered. Towards the end of the century, in Schiller's programmatic writing *Über naive und sentimentalische Dichtung*, (1795) and Schlegel's *Über das Studium der griechischen Poesie* (1795/1797), following Winckelmann's interpretation, the authors depict Antiquity as an idealized place of unity, where the artistically beautiful, according to Schlegel, can be thought of as 'original nature' [12th Vol. 1. 276], as perfect and harmonious. Both the point of departure and the point of reference for this construct are an awareness of the present in which such unity and perfection in modernity, though an admired ideal, appears at the same time impossible. Schlegel cha-

racterizes the predicament of the artistically beautiful in the present, the impossibility of its harmony, with the idea of the 'interesting', which is supposed to portray a 'lack of general validity', the 'rule of the mannered, characteristic and individual' as the hallmark of 'the entire aesthetic education of modern people' [12th vol. 1. 252]. Schiller does this with the term 'sentimental', which means an orientation in poetry in which a unity with nature that has been lost is configured as an unattainable ideal [8th Vol. 20/1. 437ff.]. Whereas Winckelmann still had a tendency to consider ancient art as a standard which, even if not attainable, should still be aimed at. Schlegel and, in part, also Schiller emphasize the possibility of self-reflection and of finding oneself in the present by means of the idealizing construct of ancient art. Schlegel is not concerned with a Schillerian 'naive' repetition of ancient idealism, but rather with a historical and philosophical process of modern self-reflection on art. In this march forward, at least at times, he considers Goethe to embody the synthesis, as a person who has sich zu einer 'Höhe der Kunst heraufgearbeitet' habe, 'welche zum erstenmal die ganze Poesie der Alten und Modernen umfaßt, und den Keim ewigen Fortschreitens enthält' (worked his way up to a level of art which, for the first time, embraces the entire poetry of the ancients and moderns and contains the seed of perpetual progress) [12th vol. 2. 347].

In this development, which constituted German classicism, the aspects of projection and construct in the image of Antiquity are very much more obvious and deliberate than in French classicism. Lessing and Herder had already raised objections on the basis of historical criticism to the unifying reduction of Winckelmann's image of Antiquity. Lessing not only insisted on the difference between fine art and literature but also raised questions about the religious functionality of Greek art and literature [10th Vol. 6. 414ff.]. Herder, principally out of a skepticism schooled on the → *Querelle des Anciens et des Modernes* towards the idea that repetition of Antiquity is possible at all, interpreted the representatives of modern German literature through analogies with Greek Antiquity [9. 285–356]. The classicism of the turn of the century, on the other hand, gains coherence from the fact that the nature of the construct of Greek Antiquity is deliberately represented as fictitious. This is evident in Goethe's turning away from the open forms and the contradictory content of the works of the *Sturm und Drang* and his overstating a Utopian humanitarian perspective inscribed in ancient mythology in his *Iphigenie auf Tauris* (1779–1787) (cf. on this [17. 177ff.; 20]. The transitions to this classicism gain contours clearly seen in Schiller's famous poem *Die Götter Griechenlands* (1788), where the mythological figures of idealistic beauty appear from the very beginning as 'Beautiful Beings from the Land of Fable' [8th vol. 2/1. 336]. In the *Athenäums-Fragmente* (1797/98) F. Schlegel therefore firmly insisted that Winckelmann, 'who read all the ancients as though they were one author', by this very reduction revealed 'the absolute dissimilarity between the ancient and the modern', Shortly afterwards he noted: 'Everyone found in the ancients what he needed or wished for; especially himself' [12th vol. 2. 188f.]. Goethe, finally, with the collected volume *Winckelmann and his Century* (1805) attempted to draw up a kind of balance-sheet of the new adoption of Antiquity. In his introductory essay, he characterizes Winckelmann's view of Antiquity with the words of Wilhelm von Humboldt as 'being dragged violently into a past seen by us somehow, maybe even by necessary delusion, as noble and exalted'. And in Humboldt's letter, which he quotes, Goethe concluded: 'Only from a distance, only separated from everything in common, only as past, must Antiquity appear to us' [6th vol. 46. 38f.].

The idealizing distance, into which Greek Antiquity is thus moved in German classicism for reasons of literary politics and in view of the question raised by philosophers of history as to how one should locate literature in the present, should not conceal the fact that – otherwise completely analogous to the French development – a construct of Antiquity in the 19th cent. contoured in such a way also had an eminently formative effect on educational policy that was carried out largely through measures associated with the above mentioned Wilhelm von Humboldt. Even Goethe, at least temporarily, intended to make orientational and educational capital out of the idealized and exaggerated deference to Antiquity. He did this, for instance, by establishing prize competitions for fine artists around the turn of the century in the short-lived *Propylaeae*. Here, as the model for the prize works, he proposed all the scenes from Homer's epics, because there a world had been created 'to which every genuine modern artist so much likes to take himself back, where all his archetypes and his highest goals exist' [6th vol. 48. 4]. By relinquishing the historical and philosophical differences, Antiquity attained a normative function among the educated classes and in the educational system, which was to retain its vitality beyond the 19th cent. as a fiercely defended world opposed to the disorientating and fragmentizing tendencies of social modernisation (cf. on this [26]). Comparable tendencies were already at work in the didactic novel *Les aventures de Télémaque* (1699), in which, at the end of French classicism, Fénelon collected an assorted mixture of elements from Homeric and Virgilian epics for moral instruction against the immense variety of present-day experiences. The ambivalence of the two classicisms codified as classicism in France and Germany, their contradictory functionalization as an instrument of aesthetic modernization and, at the same time, as a construct of an aesthetically moral standard is further evidence of the things they have in common structurally.

→ BAROQUE; → HUMANISM; → RENAISSANCE

SOURCES: 1 J.-L. GUEZ DE BALZAC, Oeuvres diverses, (ed.) R. ZUBER, 1995   2 Id., Oeuvres, 2 vols., Paris 1665 (repr. 1971)   3 N. BOILEAU, Oeuvres complètes, F. ESCAL (ed.) 1966   4 P. CORNEILLE, Oeuvres complètes, G.

COUTON (ed.), 3 vols., 1980–1988   5 A. GASTÉ (ed.), La Querelle du Cid, Paris 1898 (repr. 1970)   6 Goethes Werke. Weimarer Ausgabe, Weimar 1887ff. (repr. 1987)   7 MOLIÈRE, Oeuvres complètes, G. COUTON (ed.), 2 vols., 1971–72   8 Schillers Werke. Nationalausgabe, 1943ff.   9 J. G. HERDER, Sämtliche Werke, B. SUPHAN (ed.), Berlin 1892 (reprint 1967)   10 G. E. LESSINGS sämtliche Schriften, K. LACHMANN (ed.), Berlin 1953ff.   11 CH. PERRAULT, Parallèle des Anciens et des Modernes, 3 vols., Paris 1688ff. (repr. 1964, H.-R. JAUSS, ed.)   12 F. SCHLEGEL, Sämtliche Werke. Kritische Ausgabe E. BEHLER et al. (eds.), 1958ff.   13 J. J. WINCKELMANN, Kleinere Schriften, Vorreden, Entwürfe, W. REHM (ed.),1968

LITERATURE: 14 E. BECKER, Klassiker in der deutschen Literaturgeschichtsschreibung zwischen 1780 und 1860, in: J. HERMAND, M. WINDFUHR (eds.), Zur Literatur der Restaurationsepoche 1815–1845, 1970, 349–370   15 R. BOCKHOLDT (ed.), Über das Klassische, 1987   16 R. BRAY, La Formation de la doctrine classique, 1927   17 CHRISTIAN BÜRGER, Der Ursprung der bürgerlichen Institution Kunst. Untersuchung zum klassischen Goethe, 1977   18 E. R. CURTIUS, Europäische Literatur und lateinisches Mittelalter, 6 1967   19 H.-D. DAHNKE, B. LEISTNER (eds.), Debatten und Kontroversen. Literarische Auseinandersetzungen in Deutschland am Ende des 18. Jahrhunderts, 2 vols., 1989   20 E. FISCHER-LICHTE, Probleme der Rezeption klassischer Werke am Beispiel von Goethes *Iphigenie*, in: K. O. CONRADY (ed.), Deutsche Literatur zur Zeit der Klassik, 1977, 114–140   21 G. FORESTIER, J.-P. NÉRAUDEAU (eds.), Un classicisme ou des classicismes?, 1995   22 H. A. KORFF, Geist der Goethezeit, 4 vols., 4 1957   23 K. R. MANDELKOW, Deutsche Literatur zwischen. Klassik und Romantik aus rezeptionsgeschichtlicher Sicht, in: Id. (ed.), Europäische Romantik I, 1982 (Neues Handbuch der Literatur-Wissenschaft, Vol. 14), 1–26   24 F. NEUBERT, Die französische Klassik und Europa, 1941   25 G. OESTERLE, Kulturelle Identität und Klassizismus, in: B. GIESEN (ed.), Nationale und kulturelle Identität, 1991, 304–349   26 L. O'BOYLE, Klassische Bildung und soziale Struktur in Deutschland zwischen 1800 und 1848, in: HZ 207, 1968, 584–608   27 H. PEYRE, Qu'est-ce que le Classicisme?, 2 1964   28 W. REHM, Griechentum und Goethezeit, 4 1969   29 H. SCHLAFFER, Rezension von W. VOSSKAMP (ed.), Klassik im Vergleich, 1993, in: Poetica 25, 1993, 441–446   30 H. STENZEL, Geschichte auf Distanz oder sublimiert? Vergleichende Überlegungen zur deutschen und französischen Klassik, in: Romanistische Zeitschrift für Literatur-Geschichte 17, 1993, 56–73   31 Id., Ein obskures Objekt literaturwissenschaftlicher Begierde, Romanistische Zeitschrift für Literaturgeschichte 18, 1994, 402–414   32 Id., Die französische Klassik. Literarische Modernisierung und absolutistischer Staat, 1995   33 W. SCHERER, Geschichte der deutschen Literatur, 1893   34 P. SZONDI, Poetik und Geschichtsphilosophie, S. METZ, H. H. HILDEBRANDT (eds.),1974   35 A. VIALA, La naissance de l'écrivain, 1985   36 W. VOSSKAMP (ed.), Klassik im Vergleich, 1993   37 R. WELLEK, The Term and Concept of Classicism in Literary History, in: Id., Discriminations. Further Concepts of Criticism, 1970, 55–90   HARTMUT STENZEL

Clothing see → FASHION

Cnidian Aphrodite

Cnidian Aphrodite The Cnidian Aphrodite (CA) was sculpted by Praxiteles about 340 BC for the temple of Aphrodite Euploia in Cnidus. She was said to be the first and also the most perfect sculpture of a completely naked goddess and woman. According to Pliny the Elder, it was the world's most famous marble sculpture, turning Cnidus into an important tourist destination (HN 36,20). The fame of this larger than life late-Classical statue is also reflected in numerous references and epigrams [3], as well as by the fact that it is the most copied of Greek sculptures: the number of large-scale copies exceeds 50 [2], in addition to countless smaller statuettes. A speculative concession to a particular visitor interest is evident in the unusual – secondary – placement of the cult image, which could apparently be viewed from the rear as well as from the front (in a circular temple?). The bizarre amorous attack of a man beguiled by the beauty and 'liveliness' of the statue also took place *a tergo*, as reported by Pliny, the pseudo-Lucian *Erotes*, Philostratus, Valerius Maximus, and others. This legend of the love for a statue is one in a long line of fables about splendid sensual illusions of men and animals in the face of lifelike works of art, both painted and sculpted (cf. Zeuxis' depiction of grapes), and thus part of the standard ancient repertoire of popular praise for the arts. Notwithstanding, though, the story caused a rare scandal, which outlived its marble archetype in both oral and written transmission and which remains unforgotten to this day. This provided the material for a unique reception, an affective history that cannot be described by means of material results, but that requires a sifting of the collective psychological profile of Christian Antiquity and the Middle Ages, as it were.

The statue itself was lost, its assumed temple (a tholos) excavated in about 1970. It was only in the 18th cent. that the iconography of the CA, which became the prototype for Hellenistic Aphrodite statues, could be identified with the aid of Cnidian coins (by Jonathan Richardson senior and junior, Amsterdam 1728) (Fig. 1). The *Venus Colonna* (Rome, Vatican Museums), from the Hadrianic-Antoninian period, is considered the most reliable, albeit in parts wrongly completed copy (Fig. 2). The different paths of verbal as well as artistic and material transmission, already separate in the ancient period, finally completely detached in the early Christian period. Because of its popularity and its odium of offending the sense of modesty, already the early apologist Church Fathers used the Cnidian assault

Fig. 2: Venus Colonna. Roman copy after Praxiteles, Aphrodite of Cnidos.
Courtesy of the Vatican Museums

Fig. 1: Cnidian coin from the time of Caracalla, contour drawing

as a main argument against pagan idols (and works of art): 'such was the ability of art to deceive that it became the downfall of wanton men', so Clemens Alexandrinus on the CA [5. 97]. Statues were now seen as idols, the dwellings of demons. They had become contagious through their very artistic quality and charm, turning people to become idolatrous, and thus hurling them into sin and perdition (Arnobius, Athenagoras, Tatian) [5. 96–106]. The titillating mimesis legend (→ MIME-SIS, MYTHS ABOUT) mutated into a pathological case of demonic love for a statue. The sexual character of pagan image worship, based on the Cnidian legend, was extended to all Venus statues, as well as to anthropomorphous sculptures in general in Late Antiquity and the Early Middle Ages. This is evident in numerous reports of sexually motivated destructions of idols and exorcisms in the early Christian period, as well as the late-medieval illustrations of the demonological chapters of Augustine's *Civitas Dei*.

In the High Middle Ages, when pagan statues had long been removed from view, the legend of the demonic powers of Venus statues renewed and transformed itself: the story was told that a young man had placed his wedding ring (for safekeeping) on the finger of a statue that happened to be close by, and thus made a binding promise of marriage. It was Venus who then claimed her right to the wedding night ('mecum concumbe!'), and who actively prevented the young couple from consummating their marriage. It took a gruesome exorcism to solve this problem eventually and to regain the ring (William of Malmesbury, *Gesta regum Anglorum, c.* 1125, ed. R. M. THOMSON & M. WINTERBOTTOM (1998) II, 205). In the Middle High German version of the *Kaiserchronik* (*c.* 1150, MGH Dt CC I., 13103–13392) the statue even initiated the action, which, in psychological terms, is interpreted as projection.

This motive, originally inspired by the CA, but mutated from image to imagination, shows both the yearning for images of beauty and sexuality, and the fear of them. However, the devilish passion for the pagan goddess soon was transformed into the true love of the Virgin Mary. In one of his Marian miracles (*c.* 1200), Gautier de Coincy replaced the fatal image with a graceful statue of the Madonna – with a similar result: the man enters into a lifelong celibate union with the heavenly bride. In another story from the same period, the Madonna herself intervenes: 'the devils are given images, so why not I?' [5. 149f.; 153ff.]. During the Gothic period, meanwhile, 'beautiful' statues were once again the order of the day (albeit no nude ones) and had to be reconciled – retrospectively – with the old iconoclastic dogmas.

The motive of the miraculous ring betrothal continued its passage and spread, until finally – even though much later – it became 'a distinctive topic of world literature' [4], with the most important titles being: J. Cazotte, *Le Diable amoureux* (1772), J. W. Goethe, *Die Braut von Korinth* (1798), Cl. Brentano,

Fig. 3: Venus Belvedere, bronze copy (without hydria). Musée de Fontainebleau

Godwi (1802), *Romanzen vom Rosenkranz* (1803–1818), J.A. Apel, *Der Brautring* (1812), A. v. Arnim, *Päpstin Jutta* (1813), W. v. Eichendorff, *Die zauberische Venus* (1816), J. v. Eichendorff, *Das Marmorbild* (1819), E.T.A. Hoffmann, *Die Geschichte vom verlorenen Spiegelbilde* (1815), W. Alexis, *Venus in Rom* (1828), P. Merimée, *La Vénus d'Ille* (1837), H. Heine, *Florentinische Nächte* (1836), G. d'Annunzio, *La Pisanelle ou la mort parfumée* (1913).

The experience of ancient and medieval love for a statue does not (in contrast with the Pygmalion legend) seem to have developed its own visual imagery; perhaps it is reflected in Dürer's engraving *Traum des Doktors* (*c.* 1498), showing Venus wearing a ring [5. 195]. However without being explicit, a number of Renaissance

Fig. 4: Venus Colonna with apron (old photograph).
Courtesy of the Vatican Museums

paintings of Venus (e.g. by Cranach the Elder) seem, by means of their lifelike and beautiful depictions, almost to toy with the knowing awareness of the connoisseurs so that the latter are warned not to fall in love with the paintings. Moreover, the story, almost like a whispered secret, keeps reappearing in the letters of connoisseurs and learned treatises on art.

The CA did not enjoy an artistic reception because of ignorance about its physical existence, However, from

an early stage, two famous versions were on display in the Papal Belvedere palace: first the *Venus felix* (1509), followed by the *Venus Belvedere* (from 1534 onward), of which Francis I of France, with a sure eye for its qualities, had a bronze copy made by Primaticcio (Fig. 3; drawn by Fr. da Hollanda and H. Goltzius; engraved in Charles Perrier's collection of the most famous ancient statues, Rome 1638).

The identification of the CA by the Richardsons, which Winckelmann did not accept due to his preference for more pleasing statues like the *Venus de' Medici*, led, in the prudish 19th cent. (under Pope Gregory XVI), to the covering of the *Venus Colonna* with a metal apron, because of the danger it represented for the general public, as documented in literary sources. This addition required an alteration to the statue's right hand (Fig. 4). To be sure, this cover was removed in 1932 (the hand is still wrong), the statue cannot be viewed from the rear or by the general public: it stands in the Gabinetto delle Maschere in the Belvedere wing.

The artistic preoccupation with the CA in more recent times is quite limited, in complete contrast to the → VENUS OF MILO, who represents a much more fashionable type of woman. Attention should be drawn here to Renoir's early attempt, by means of his painting, to enliven evocatively the marble statue and to remove it from the purely masculine observation (*Baigneuse au griffon*); also Salvadore Dalí's *Apparition of the Aphrodite of Cnidus* (1981. Figueras, Fundación Gala-Salvador Dalí), a more general homage to classical beauty and the Mediterranean. Also into this category fall Paul Klee's treatments of the CA during and after his journey to Rome in 1901, though this has not attracted any further research. A number of more recent poems about the statue can be found in G. Kranz (*Das Bildgedicht*, 1–3, 1981–1987, vol. 3, 159f.).

1 FR. V. BEZOLD, Das Fortleben der antiken Götter im mittelalterlichen Humanismus, 1922   2 CHR. BLINKEN-BERG, Knidia. Beiträge zur Kenntnis der praxitelischen Aphrodite, 1933   3 A. CORSO, Prassitele. Fonti epigrafiche e letterarie, I–III, 1988–1991   4 E. FRENZEL, Stoffe der Weltliteratur, ⁶1983   5 B. HINZ, Aphrodite. Geschichte einer abendländischen Passion, 1998   6 CHR. MITCHELL HAVELOCK, The Aphrodite of Knidos and Her Successors, 1995   7 W. PABST, Venus und die mißverstandene Dido, 1955.   BERTHOLD HINZ

Cnidus Owing to its prominent position on the maritime route that connects the Aegean to the Levant, the urban site of Cnidus (C.) at the tip of the Cnidian peninsula (Tekir Cape, formerly Cape Krio) had become accessible for archaeological research at an early stage. Thus, first steps were taken in the wake of naval expeditions that opened up the Aegean coast of Asia Minor in the first half of the 19th cent. The important European naval powers of the time, especially England and France, played an important part in this process. Travelers, in particular the Englishman William Leake in 1812 under the auspices of the → SOCIETY OF DILETTAN-

TI [23], visited C. and gave an initial description of the site, usually without accompanying excavations. This also holds true for the investigation undertaken in the urban area and the necropolis by Charles Texier [25] in the 1830s, commissioned by the French government. These early surveys are of no small importance as they document features that are no longer or only partially preserved.

On the other hand, C.'s exposed location also endangered its ancient monuments. Thus, in the 1830s, Muhammad Ali, Pasha of Egypt, had several shiploads of marble removed from C. for the construction of his palace. Later, the theft of stones for the construction of the Dolmbahçe Palace in Istanbul added to the damage. In 1856, C. saw the beginning of the period of archaeological excavations, undertaken by Charles Newton [20] and commissioned by the British government. Newton, who possessed considerable material and personnel resources, carried out excavation and salvage work over a 17–month period. As previously in Halicarnassus and Didyma, Newton's expedition was also oriented towards the acquisition of museum pieces. With this goal in mind, Newton undertook excavations in the urban area and the necropoleis, whose finds – primarily sculptures and inscriptions – were taken away by ship. Like most undertakings of the time, the excavations were not documented in detail. The plans and sketches that documented the results often combined exact measurements with interpretative completion of the features. Nevertheless, research is indebted to Newton for a detailed plan of the city with a description of the major features and the salvaging of many monuments, most of which are now in the British Museum in London.

Newton's investigations were followed by a lengthy phase of inactivity, determined among other factors by the First World War. Armin von Gerkan [14], who planned a systematic excavation of C. in the 1920s, was not able to realize his project. American excavations began in 1967 under the direction of Iris Love [15–19], especially in the area of the temple courtyard, where, among other things, the temple and altar of Apollo Carneius and a Hellenistic rotunda were uncovered. To this were added numerous trial-trenches in the urban area and excavations in the necropolis. Excavations were suspended after 1973, and an excavation report remains to be published. Renewed investigations have been carried out at C. since the 1980s by the Selçuk Üniversitesi in Konya, under the direction of Ramzan Özgan, and with the participation of foreign scholars.

A. von Gerkan [13. 92] had already pointed out that no finds from the High Classical and Archaic periods (8th/7th – 5th cents. BC) could be confirmed at the urban site of C., which lead him to the conclusion that the city on the cape was displaced in Late Classical – Hellenistic times from an as yet unknown location to the tip of the peninsula. The investigation of the Cnidian peninsula, carried out from 1949 onwards by George Bean and John Cook [2] confirmed this theory.

Some 30 kilometers east of the Cape, in the district of Burgaz near the village of Datça, Bean and Cook identified an extensive urban site with a fortified acropolis and several harbor facilities; its high antiquity could be determined by the archaic pottery found there and in the necropoleis. Inscriptions showed that this city also bore the name of C. Since 1993, the urban site at Burgaz has been the object of archaeological investigations, carried out by the Ortadoğu Teknik Üniversitesi of Ankara, under the direction of Numan Tuna [27]. The excavations have brought confirmation to the theory of the displacement of the urban settlement site. Evidence for a settlement found up until now dates from the 8th–5th cents. BC In contrast, traces of housing construction from the Hellenistic period are lacking. A new inscription bearing the Cnidians' decree of friendship in favor of Epameinondas of Thebes (c. 364 BC) [8] is another piece of evidence. The urban site near Burgaz can therefore be called Old C., and the city on the Cape New C. So far, the precise date at which the city's displacement took place is being debated, as is the historical context in which this measure was taken. There are many indications that strategic and politico-economic factors were prominent in the process [5].

From the beginning of the archeological investigation of C., an important concern for research has been the search for the sanctuary of the League of the Doric Hexapolis, the so-called Triopion. According to historical evidence, this shrine, which had presumably existed since the Doric occupation, was dedicated to Apollo, and was located in the vicinity of the town of C. All attempts on the part of previous research to locate the shrine had failed due to the erroneous assumption that the urban site at the tip of the peninsula was already located there in the Archaic period. The localization of Old C. at Burgaz/Datça resulted in a new starting position. A plausible location for this sanctuary had to be identified not at the Cape, but near Old C. The terraced site at Emecik [4; 6], approximately 15 kilometers east of New C., proved to be a place that featured all requisite preconditions. Older epigraphic evidence proves that a temple to Apollo was situated there. The lower terrace wall dates from the Archaic period (7th/6th cents. BC) on the basis of its architectural style and a graffito, and may be considered as evidence for the high antiquity of the site. Architectural finds clearly show the existence of various inner structures. An inscription discovered in 1998 confirms Apollo as the divinity of this temple and points to some oracular activity. Excavations have been underway in the Temple of Apollo at Emecik since 1998, carried out under the direction of Numan Tuna, with the participation of foreign archaeologists.

→ HALICARNASSUS; → LONDON, BRITISH MUSEUM;

1 H. BANKEL, K. Der hellenistische Rundbau, in: AA 1997, 51–71 2 G. BEAN, J. COOK, The Cnidia, in: ABSA 47, 1952, 171–212 3 Id., The Carian Coast, in: ABSA 47, 1952, 85–87 4 D. BERGES, N. TUNA, Ein archäologisches Heiligtum bei Alt-Knidos, in: AA, 1990, 19–35 5 Id., Alt-Knidos und Neu-Knidos, in: MDAI(Ist) 44,

1994, 5–16   6 Id., Knidos und das Heiligtum der dorischen Hexapolis, in: Nürnberger Beiträge zur Archäologie 12, 1995/96, 103–120   7 W. BLÜMEL, Die Inschriften von Knidos I, 1992   8 Id., in: EA 24, 1994, 157–158   8a A. BRESSON, Guide à l'époque classique, in: REA 101, 1999, 83–114   9 CHR. BRUNS-ÖZGAN, Fries eines hellenistischen Altares in Knidos, in: JDAI 110, 1995, 239–276   10 H. CAHN, KNIDOS. Die Münzen des 6. und des 5. Jahrhundert vor Christus, 1970   11 J. COOK, Cnidian Peraea and Spartan coins, in: JHS 81, 1961, 56–72   12 N. DEMAND, Did Knidos Really Move, in: Classical Antiquity 8, 1989, 224–237   13 A. v. GERKAN, Griechische Städteanlagen, 1924, 117   14 Id., Ausgrabung einer antiken Stadt, in: Von antiker Architektur und Topographie 1959, 88–93   15 I. LOVE, TürkAD 16, 2, 1967, 133–160   16 Id., in: AJA 74, 1970, 149–155   17 Id., in: AJA 76, 1972, 393–405   18 Id., in: AJA 77, 1973, 413–424   19 Id., A Brief Summary of Excavations at Knidos 1967–1973, in: Proceedings of the 10th International Congress of Classical Archaeology, 1973, 1111–1133   20 CH. NEWTON, A History of Discoveries at Halikarnassos, Cnidus and Branchidae 2, London 1865, 346 and 366–526   21 J. NORDBØ, The Coinage of Cnidus after 394 B. C., in: Proceedings of the 10th International Congress of Numismatics 1986, 51–56   22 R. ÖZGAN, Ein neues archäeologisches Sitzbild aus Knidos, in: Festschrift N. Himmelmann 1989, 47–51   23 Society of Dilettanti, Antiquities of Ionia, London 1840, 18–35   24 N. STAMPOLIDES, Der Nymphenaltar in Knidos und der Bildhauer Theon aus Antiochia, in: AA 1984, 113–127   25 CH. TEXIER, Description de l'Asie Mineure faite par ordre du gouvernement français de 1833 à 1837, 3, Paris 1849, 171–176   26 N. TUNA, J.-Y. EMPEREUR, Rapport préliminaire de la prospection archéologique turco-française des ateliers d'amphores de Reşadiye-Kiliseyanı sur la péninsule de Datça, in: Anatolia antiqua 1987, 47–52   27 N. TUNA, in: 19. Kazı Sonuçları Toplantısı 2, 1998, 445–464.

DIETRICH BERGES

Codicology

A. CONCEPT   B. OBJECTS OF STUDY
C. CONGRESSES, JOURNALS, AND OTHER
PUBLICATIONS   D. INTERDISCIPLINARITY

A. CONCEPT

Alphonse Dain [8; 76] lays claim to both the invention of the term *codicologie* as well as to its introduction into the French language; in 1959, it was entered in the *Grand Larousse encyclopédique* and very quickly gained international acceptance. In a definition that not all scholars agree upon, codicology refers to the study of the late-antique and medieval book, i.e. the *codex*. At present, a distinction is made between a narrow and a wider definition of the term. In the narrower sense, codicology is only concerned with the external properties of individual codices, which it treats-in a practice analogous to that of archaeology-as individual artifacts of the material culture. Thus, it examines the material that the book is written on, the method of its preparation, its layout and its cover. In the wider sense, however, and in the only sense Dain himself understood the term that he had invented, codicology also comprises everything that concerns the history of an individual codex or a group of codices, irrespective of whether the information on this is found in the codex itself or elsewhere. To that end, it evaluates possible notes added to the codex by the copyist(s) regarding the patron and the location where the book was copied. Additionally, it is concerned with entries by later owners, other marginal notes, and older signatures. And outside of the codex, it looks for the historical traces that a codex may have left, e.g. within the correspondence of scholars, in old library inventory lists [26; 32], and in edited texts. Palaeography in the stricter sense, i.e. as the science concerned with the development of scripts, is not the subject of codicology. Of course, codicology existed even before the new name had been invented. Thus older palaeographical handbooks appearing after the establishment of palaeography as a separate science at the turn of the 17th to the 18th cent., dealt with questions now considered part of codicology. The German term 'Handschriftenkunde' comprises both codicology (in the narrower and in the wider sense) as well as the palaeography of Latin script and book illumination [22; 25].

B. OBJECTS OF STUDY

Codicology in the narrower sense examines: 1. the qualities of the book block; 2. the writing materials themselves; 3. the layout (*mise en page*) of the pages; 4. the cover; and 5. the inks and pigments. Re 1: Apart from the determination of format and thickness, the main focus is on the order and nature of the individual quires (quaternions, quinions etc., the number of quires and irregularities). Modern manuscript catalogues use fixed systems of notation. Re 2: The main writing materials are parchment and paper. (Papyrus is the domain of papyrology). As concerns parchment, apart from observations regarding the animal species and the quality of the parchment, the most important ascertainment is the distribution of skin sides and flesh sides of the processed animal skin in the formation of the quires (compliance with the *lex Gregory* [12]). In recent decades, parchment research has experienced an upswing [9; 30; 2]. Paper plays a very important part in determining the origin and dating of a book; Codicology distinguishes among Oriental-Arabian (*Bombazine*), 'Western' Arabian-Spanish [7; 16], and European (Western) paper. Because of the presence of watermarks (*filigranes*) since the 13th cent., European paper is an excellent tool in the dating of codices. Under consideration of all pertinent variables such as twin watermarks, order on the sheet, countermarks, and laid- and chain-lines, and with an exact reproduction of the watermark in the medium of a drawing or photograph, it is possible under ideal conditions to achieve a dating accuracy to within about about five years [14]. Comprehensive repertories are available for comparative analyses [e.g. 27; 21; 4; 28; 29; 15]. Re 3: When considering the aesthetic aspect of the layout, there is a close co-operation between codicology and palaeography. Thus, in the identification of

Fig. 1: Binding of a Latin
manuscript of the 12th century.
Berlin, Deutsche Staatsbibliothek,
cod. lat. 4° 651

copyists and scriptoria, codicology supplements the insights already gained through palaeography [24; 23]. For parchment manuscripts, it is important to determine the ruling pattern. Here, a distinction is made between the type of ruling used (i.e. the placement of the line guides for the script on the recto pages) and the ruling system (i.e. which side on which folia of a quire the line guides are marked). Recent specialized studies provide an overview of the various systems that were used [19; 31]. Such studies also consider the tools and instruments employed in the ruling [13; 10]. Re 4: The study of book covers is a separate discipline and is organized according to regions and periods. Most codicological handbooks discuss the discipline in detail and provide extensive bibliographies [25; 211–242, 298–300]. Recent studies focus more on the techniques of covering books (Fig. 1) than on their decoration. Attempts have also been made to use dendrochrono-

logy for the dating of wooden book covers [17]. Re 5: It has only been very recently that scientific methods have made possible an exact analysis of the composition of the ink, rather than just a superficial classification according to its colour [34; 33]. The same applies to pigments used in the illumination of books.

C. CONGRESSES, JOURNALS, AND OTHER PUBLICATIONS

From the mid-20th cent. on, codicology experienced a significant upswing, particularly in France, Belgium and Italy, but also in other European countries. Special codicological publications and journals have been established. The most important are: *Scriptorium. Revue internationale des études relatives aux manuscrits*, published by the *Centre d'étude des manuscrits in Bruxelles*, founded in 1946 by C. Gaspar, F. Lyna, and F. Masai and published from 1959 onward with the *Bul-*

letin codicologique and a Supplément codicologique under the title of Tables de Scriptorium II for the years 1946–1976; Scrittura e civiltà, edited by the Istituto di Paleografia dell'Università di Roma, has been published in Turin since 1977; and Codicologica. Towards a science of handwritten books; Vers une science du manuscrit; Bausteine zur Handschriftenkunde. Rédacteur: A. Gruys, Rédacteur adjoint: J. P. Gumbert, Leiden 1976ff. Cod. manuscripti. Zeitschrift für Handschriftenkunde, established in 1975 by O. Mazal, Vienna. The Comité international de paléographie latine as well as the Comité international de paléographie grecque et byzantine hold regular international congresses in which codicology plays an important role. Special congresses in France and Italy have been dedicated exclusively to codicology, for example: Les techniques de laboratoire dans l'étude des manuscrits, Paris 13–15 September 1972, Paris 1974. C. Questa, R. Raffaelli (eds.), Atti del convegno internazionale 'Il libro e il testo', Urbino 20–23 settembre 1982, Urbino 1984. M. Maniaci, P. F. Munafò (eds.), Ancient and Medieval Book Materials and Techniques (Erice, 18–25 September 1992), 2 vols. (Studi e Testi, 357–358), Città del Vaticano 1993 (in each case, with several essays on parchment, paper, spectrophotometrical differences between inks and pigments and on book covers, including those of Islamic and Hebrew codices).

D. INTERDISCIPLINARITY

In recent years, codicology has worked towards better co-operation with various sciences and also has become open to quantitative approaches [3]. Furthermore, the codicology of Latin and Greek no longer operates in isolation from that of other scripts like Hebrew [1], Coptic, Syrian and Arabian. Despite its independence as an academic discipline, codicology-in order to satisfy its wider definition-entails close co-operation with other disciplines, particularly palaeography and textual philology, art history, political history, liturgical studies, and the history of music [5; 270].

→ Book; → Codex

→ PALAEOGRAPHY

1 M. BEIT-ARIÉ, The Making of the Medieval Hebrew Book: Studies in Paleography and Codicology, 1993 2 F. M. BISCHOFF, M. MANIACI, Pergamentgröße – Handschriftenformate – Lagenkonstruktion. Anmerkungen zur Methodik und zu den Ergebnissen der jüngeren kodikologischen Forschung, in: Scrittura e civiltà 19, 1995, 277–319 3 C. BOZZOLO, E. ORNATO, Pour une histoire du livre manuscrit du Moyen Âge. Trois essais de codicologie quantitative, 1980 4 C. M. BRIQUET, Les filigranes. Dictionnaire historique des marques du papier, 4 vols., 1907, ²1968 5 P. CANART, Nouvelles recherches et nouveaux instruments de travail dans le domaine de la codicologie, in: Scrittura e civiltà 3, 1979, 267–307 6 Id., Paleografia e codicologia greca. Una rassegna bibliografica, 1991 7 Id., S. DI ZIO, L. POLISTENA, D. SCIALANGA, Une enquête sur le papier de type 'arabe occidental' ou 'espagnol non filigrané', in: Studi e Testi 357, 1993, 313–392 8 A. DAIN, Les manuscrits, ³1975 9 A. DEROLEZ, Codicologie des manuscrits en écriture humanistique sur parchemin, 2 vols., 1984 10 M. DUKAN, De la difficulté à reconnaître des instruments de réglure: planche à régler (mastara) et cadre-padron, in: Scriptorium 40, 1986, 41–54 11 Id., La réglure des manuscrits hébreux au moyen âge, 1988 12 G. R. GREGORY, Les cahiers des manuscrits grecs, in: Comptes rendus des séances de l'Académie des Inscriptions et Belles-Lettres, 1885, 261–268. 13 J. P. GUMBERT, Ruling by Rake and Board. Notes on Some Late Medieval Ruling Techniques, in: P. GANZ (ed.), The Role of the Book in Medieval Culture, I (Bibliologia, 3), 1986, 41–54 14 D. HARLFINGER, Zur Datierung von Handschriften mit Hilfe von Wasserzeichen, in: Id., Griechische Kodikologie und Textüberlieferung, 1980, 144–169 15 D. UND J. HARLFINGER, Wasserzeichen aus griechischen Handschriften, 2 vols., 1974–1980 16 J. IRIGOIN, Les papiers non filigranés. État présent des recherches et perspectives d'avenir, in: Studi e Testi 357, 1993, 265–312 17 C. LAVIER, Apport de la dendrochronologie à l'étude d'ais de manuscrits: l'exemple de la Bibliothèque Municipale d'Autun (Saône-et-Loire), in: Scriptorium 52, 1998, 380–388 18 J. LEMAIRE, Introduction à la codicologie, 1989 19 J. LEROY, Les types de réglure des manuscrits grecs, 1976 20 Id., Quelques systèmes de réglure des manuscrits grecs, in: K. TREU (ed.), Studia Codicologica (Texte und Untersuchungen zur Geschichte der altchristlichen Literatur, 124), 1977 21 N. P. LICHAČEV, Paleografičeskoe značenie bumažnych vodjanych znakov, 3 vols., St. Petersburg 1899 22 K. LÖFFLER, W. MILDE, Einführung in die Handschriftenkunde, 1997 23 M. MANIACI, E. ORNATO, Intorno al testo. Il ruolo dei margini nell'impaginazione dei manoscritti greci e latini, in: Nuovi annali della Scuola speciale per archivisti e bibliotecari 9, 1995, 175–194 24 H.-J. MARTIN, J. VEZIN (ed.), Mise en page et mise en texte du livre manuscrit, 1990 25 O. MAZAL, Lehrbuch der Handschriftenkunde, 1986 26 W. MILDE, Über Anordnung und Verzeichnung von Büchern in mittelalterlichen Bibliothekskatalogen, in: Scriptorium 50, 1996, 269–278 27 Monumenta charta papyraceae, 15 vols. 28 V. A. MOŠIN, S. M. TRALJIĆ, Filigranes des XIIIe et XIVe siècles, 2 vols., 1957 29 G. PICCARD, Die Wasserzeichenkartei Piccard im Hauptstaatsarchiv Stuttgart, Findbuch I–XVII, 1961–1997 30 P. RÜCK (ed.), Pergament. Geschichte, Struktur, Restaurierung, Herstellung, 1991 31 J.-H. SAUTEL, Répertoire de réglures dans les manuscrits grecs sur le parchemin (Bibliologia, 13), 1995 32 R. SHARPE, Accession, Classification, Location: Shelfmarks in Medieval Libraries, in: Scriptorium 50, 1996, 279–287 33 V. TROST, Gold- und Silbertinten. Technologische Untersuchungen zur abendländischen Chrysographie und Argyrographie von der Spätantike bis zum hohen Mittelalter, 1991 34 M. ZERDOUN BAT-YEHOUDA, Les encres noires au Moyen Âge (jusqu'à 1600), 1983.

DIETHER RODERICH REINSCH

Codification

A. Introduction B. Antiquity C. The
Middle Ages and the Early Modern Period
D. The Replacement of *ius commune* by En-
lightenment Codification E. The Codifica-
tion Controversy F. The Second Wave of
Codification in the 19th and 20th Cents.
G. Decodification and Recodification

A. Introduction

The idea of carrying out a legal reform through summarizing, revising and finally entering in a codex or
corpus those elements of traditional law that are still to
be valid at a certain point in time can be traced to Antiquity. The various efforts to carry out this type of legal
reform, and the proposals for its realization, will be
referred to here as 'codification' in the broadest sense of
the word. In this context, various Latin-derived terms
have been used, such as *compilatio/compilation, con-
solidatio, reconcinnatio, incorporation*, etc. In contrast, the concept of 'codification' in the modern, technical sense originated from the Humanists' criticism of
the prevailing *ius commune* (common law), and the Enlightenment doctrine of legislation. This concept of
codification in the sense of a materially comprehensive,
systematic, abstract and rational regulation of an entire
area of the law in a statute book (codex) was first defined by Jeremy Bentham. He spoke of *codification* in
an 1815 letter to Czar Alexander I of Russia, contrasting it sharply with *ordinary legislation* 'taking for its
subjects matters of detail' [4.518]. These concepts were
worked out by Bentham in great detail, especially in the
works he published under the title *Papers relative to
codification* (1817) and *Codification proposal to all
Nations professing Liberal Opinions* (1822). As a creator of neologisms, Bentham also uses the term *panno-
mion* in this context, to denote the 'complete body of
law' [4.506], a particularly striking example of his recourse to ancient terminology.

With the validity of this type of codification, the
direct applicability of Common Law came to an end.
Since one of the goals of modern codification was the
unification and fixation of law for a specific territory,
its coming into force replaced the universal validity of
ius commune by separate national systems of law and
jurisprudence.

B. Antiquity

The word codex originally meant 'tree trunk', 'split
wood' or 'log'. It then came to denote a writing tablet
made of wood or some other material. Finally it signified a book, especially a statute book or collection of
laws, consisting of several such tablets, or later also
parchment. Important collections of laws used the
codex-form (*Cod. Gregorianus, Cod. Hermogianus*,
late 3rd cent. AD). There was also a change from the
original scrolls to the codex-format in the composition
of biblical manuscripts. Thus, 'codex' came to be used
currently to mean 'book', 'statute book', as well as collections of source texts. Systematically arranged collections of legal texts intended for the safeguarding and
revision of laws became important for late antique legal
practice and jurisprudence (*Codex Theodosianus*, 438)
and above all Justinian's great legislative work *Corpus
iuris civilis* (529 – 535), which was not denoted as such
until the 12th–13th cent. It consisted of *Digests*, the
Codex Iustinianus, Institutions and *Novellae*. As the
beginning of Justinian's legislative project, the *Codex
Iustinianus* aimed at combining the still-valid constitutions from the *Codex Gregorianus*, the *Codex Her-
mogenianus* and the *Codex Theodosianus* with later
imperial laws [33.53ff.]. The revision of laws, the resolution of contradictions and systematic re-arrangement
are important aspects, which aim particularly at the
practical application of law. They are a constant feature
in similar enterprises undertaken in later epochs. The
Institutiones ('Instructions', 533), in their prototype of
a textbook endowed with official force, constitute a
model that was to recur frequently in the history of
codification (so, for instance, in the first draughts of the
civil law code of Prussia and Austria). The *Digests* (or
Pandects, derived from Greek πανδέκται, 'all-embracing'), 533, are a compendium of extracts from classical
legal writings, offering models for the solution of cases
[34.271]. Novels (*novellae constitutiones*) are imperial
laws, mostly in Greek, published after the conclusion of
the legislative project. They were transmitted in various
anthologies. Down to the 19th cent., the term *corpus
iuris* was often used in the sense of a collection of laws
or sources, as comprehensive as possible, applied to a
circumscribed area of law (e.g. the *Corpus iuris Con-
foederationis Germanicae* for the Public Law of the
German Confederation). Justinian's legislative work
displays several characteristics that also correspond to
the modern concept of codification, such as systematisation, exclusive validity and comprehensive regulation. It has been and sometimes continues to be designated in legal-historical literature as a 'codification',
more often by 'Romanists' than by 'Germanists'. In any
case, the use of the concept 'codification' for the mere
collecting and writing down with regard to archaic
laws, or in general for major public or private record of
laws, appears questionable, since it is a modern projection [11.xxx; 24,2].

C. The Middle Ages and the Early Modern Period

Both at the level of the Holy Roman Empire and at
that of its individual territories, as well as in numerous
other parts of Europe, the Middle Ages and the Early
Modern Period also witnessed attempts to clarify, safe-
guard and record both state and church legislation on a
major scale. Examples of state legislation include, for
instance, medieval law books, early modern reforms of
municipal and state law and at the imperial level the
Constitutio Criminalis Carolina (1532); examples of
Church legislation worth mentioning are the *Decretum
Gratiani* and *the Corpus iuris canonici*. None of these

undertakings, however, can be classified under the modern concept of codification in intention, claim to validity, structure or extent.

D. THE REPLACEMENT OF *ius commune* BY ENLIGHTENMENT CODIFICATION

On several occasions in the 16th cent., representatives of Humanistic jurisprudence appealed to the Emperor (as the 'second Justinian') for a new redaction of Roman law. The demands for reform by French Humanists went further: they sought to overcome the universal validity of Roman law by creating a national system of legal sources. The criticism directed against current Roman law since F. Hotman's *Antitribonian* was two-pronged: it attacked its lack of systematicity, its overly-varied casuistry and its lack of comprehensibility. It also attacked legal practice: there are recurring complaints about fragmentation, legal uncertainty, disputes, and doubtful questions of law. This was the starting point for concrete demands for legal reform, mainly through the collection and rearrangement of existing laws, their consolidation through new legislation, as well as the clarification of disputed points (compilation). Insofar as legislative power is considered a constitutive element of the concept of sovereignty, the quest for comprehensive, centralising and generalising legislation also come to the forefront. The 17th and 18th cents. saw legislative efforts in many European countries, which, although widely different in objectives, content and scope, form the transition from the compilatory to systematic legislation. Examples of such legislation in France include the *Grandes Ordonnances* of Louis XIV (*Ordonnance civile touchant la réformation de la justice*, 1667; *Ordonnance criminelle*, 1670; *Ordonnance du commerce*, 1673, *Ordonnance de la marine*, 1681). Each of these aimed at the complete and systematic regulation of a specific legal domain, which was to be exclusively valid throughout the realm. The civil ordonnances of the 18th cent., edited by the Chancellor d'Aguesseau (*Ordonnance sur les donations*, 1731; *Ordonnance concernant les testaments*, 1735; *Ordonnance concernant les substitutions*, 1747) must also be seen, in many respects, as precursors of codification. G.W. Leibniz suggested the creation of a *Corpus iuris reconcinnatum* for the Holy Roman Empire in 1672. In a few territories, there were attempts at legal reform that went beyond isolated attempts at improvement, and aimed at 'codification' in the sense of a codex: Hesse-Darmstadt (F. C. v. Moser, 1762ff., proposal for a *Cod. Ludovicianus*), Hesse-Kassel (F. B. Rieß, 1805, charged with a *Cod. electoralis Hassiacus Wilhelminus*); Baden (J. M. Saltzer, 1754, Reform of State Law; J. G. Schlosser, 1787, charged with *restoring the Justinian Laws to their principles* and *drawing up the Roman Code according to the draughted plan*); Hannover (F. E. Pufendorf, draught of a Hanoverian State Law, 1772); Mecklenburg (E. A. Rudloff, E. J. F. Mantzel, 1758–1775, partial draughts of a new state and feudal law); Kursachsen (Chr. G. Gutschmid,

1762ff., project for creating a *Cod. iuris civilis et criminalis*). New viewpoints came to be added to the objectives of creating a *ius certum* by revising and systematizing traditional legal material, such as 'natural equity', the demand for conciseness and clarity, or the 'well-proven adaptation' to the respective state constitution. All these bespeak the ideas of the legislative doctrines of the Enlightenment and natural law, especially the teachings of Montesquieu. These attempts at codification were unsuccessful in the short term, but were in some cases taken up again, under different auspices, from the beginning of the 19th cent., henceforth as codification in the modern sense. Kreittmayr's Bavarian codes are often considered to mark the transition from compilation to modern codification. It is true that the three parts of Maximilian's legal reform: *Cod. Juris Bavarici Criminalis*, 1751; *Cod. Juris Bavarici Judiciarii*, 1753; *Cod. Maximilianeus Bavaricus Civilis*, 1756, correspond to some of the technical requirements of the theory of legislation (legal unification and certainty, systematization), but they fail to match its content, i.e. fundamental reform in the sense of the Enlightenment. The breakthrough of the codification idea took place in the second half of the century, when the formal postulates (the comprehensive, complete and systematic regulation of a large legal domain, clear, comprehensible language, etc.) were combined with political ones (legal uniformity as a part of state unity) and the substantive demands of the more recent natural law (guarantee of civil rights such as liberty and property). This idea was then realized through the structuring ambitions of an enlightened absolutist monarch (Prussia, the Hapsburg monarchy) or the new power that emerged from revolution (France). Whereas the legislative work dragged on for half a century in Austria and Prussia, its implementation in revolutionary France took a mere decade – albeit through recourse to preliminary work. The 'General regional Law of the Prussian States' (*Das Allgemeine Landrecht für die Preußischen Staaten*, 1794) was conceived as an overall codification, embracing administrative, penal and procedural law, in addition to all norms valid for all the citizens of a region in their legal relations with one another. In contrast, the *Code civil* (1804) and the *Allgemeines Bürgerliches Gesetzbuch* (German Civil Code (1811) standardized only 'civil' law in the strict sense, leaving other subjects, such as criminal law, procedural law and commercial law, to separate codification.

As far as systematization is concerned, the first modern codifications followed a modified Roman model: both the German Civil Code and the *Code civil* were based on the Institutions system: (*personae, res, actiones*). Later developments towards the modern system of civil law also utilize elements of ancient law as their point of departure. The five-part system of pandects designed by Georg Arnold Heise for his Göttingen lectures has served as a source for the arrangement of a large number of civil statute books and draughts, such as the Civil Code of Saxony of 1863/1865, and the Civil Code for the German Reich.

Both the *Allgemeines Landrecht* (Prussian Civil Code, ALR) and the German Civil Code (ABGB) reflect the corporative order still in existence at the time. Thus, the ABGB formulates the fundamental individual liberty and equality of citizens, but formally brackets traditional class differences from the code by numerous references to the 'political laws', while leaving them materially untouched. The *cinq codes* of the Napoleonic era (*Code civil* 1804, *Code de procédure civile* 1806, *Code de commerce* 1807, *Code d'instruction criminelle* 1808, *Code pénal* 1810), together with the restructuring of the administrative and legal systems, formed the basis for a bourgeois liberal constitutional state. They were defended throughout Europe in the 19th cent. as the basic 'institutions' of such a state, or else were postulated as models for state and legal reforms in pre-constitutional environments.

E. The Codification Controversy

The idea of envisaging national legal unification through one or more codifications as a means, or at least under the auspices of national unification, was at the basis of the demand formulated shortly after the Wars of Liberation by the Heidelberg professor of civil law A. F. J. Thibaut *On the necessity of a general civil law for Germany* (1814) (where, however, 'civil law' as the law of 'civil relations' was also to embrace penal and procedural law). F.C. von Savigny countered him in his famous treatise *On the Vocation of Our Age for Legislation and Jurisprudence* (1814), rejecting all codification, partly though sharp criticism of the extant codes ALR, ABGB and the *Code civil*, as undue interference by the legislator with the 'organic' growth of law and contrary to 'the spirit of the people'. His scientific program, which spelled the beginnings of the → HISTORISCHE RECHTSSCHULE and of → PANDECTIST STUDIES, called for recourse to Roman legal sources, and their further development through jurisprudence, which was to permeate them systematically, instead of a renewal of law through the intervention of lawgiver. This program was highly influential in the first half of the 19th cent. in Germany, hindering the movement towards national codification for a long time.

F. The Second Wave of Codification in the 19th and 20th Cents.

Although pandectics became the dominant school of German legal thought on a national level, regional efforts to promote codification continued. This was mainly due to the influence exerted by the adherents of liberal political theory, and corresponded to the demands made by deputies in the newly formed corporative assemblies. Several German federal states created, or at least attempted to create, legal codes for such major legal domains as civil law, criminal law, procedural law, as well as commercial law. Demands for national codification were brought forward mainly by liberal Germanists (Assemblies of Germanists 1846, 1847; Paulskirche constitution of the Reich). Not until the unification of the Reich, in 1873, did central authority for all of civil law, and consequently the creation of the Civil Code for the German Reich (1896/1900), become a reality.

Parallel developments can also be observed, for instance, in the pre-unification Italian states and the Swiss cantons, where codification measures for individual states and cantons were accompanied by discussions about the national unification of law, which increased in intensity especially in the second half of the century. Legal-political and above all federal arguments played a role in this process, alongside jurisprudential considerations. In Germany as in Switzerland, the codification of commercial and economic law was the driving force behind the unification of civil law, even though the two countries opted for different models ('*code unique*' vs. separate statute books). The Swiss ZGB (Civil code) (1907/1912), which attempts *to grasp and further develop tradition by means of the system and concepts of common law* [8.920] is considered a particularly successful product of the 'second wave of codification'.

In the 19th and early 20th cents., this wave swept across nearly all states of continental Europe and resulted in the codification of the most important legal domains, with the *Code civil* (and, albeit to a lesser degree, the '*cinq codes*' of France) becoming the preferred model in Romance countries. Spain's *Código civil* (1888/89), Portugal's *Código civil* (1867) and Italy's *Codice civile* (1865) were influenced to varying degrees by the French model. Penal and procedural codes were adopted in large numbers in the course of the century. The creation of these separate legal systems on a national level in the 19th cent. was characterised by the close connection of the idea of codification with that of a national state [13.II, 15].

G. Decodification and Recodification

The adoption of a code was often followed, through diversification of individual domains of law, and through the emergence of particular legal areas, as occurred for instance in private law through new labour or social regulations, by a phase in which codification was diluted, a phenomenon which has been termed 'decodification' since the Italian scholar Irti. In recent years, however, discussion of codification has resumed with increased intensity, whereby the status of the code in the system of legal sources has been to some extent questioned. This may occur against the backdrop of a recodification, as we might call the formal restructuring through *codification à droit constant*, which is currently ongoing in France (*Commission supérieure de codification*, since 1989), or as a new effort at codification, like that of the Czech Republic [11.30; 39. 95ff.]. Most recently, the possibilities and limitations of a codified private law for the European Community have been debated [39.106; 17], whereby to some extent a reconnection with common Roman legal tradition is sought.

1 A. J. ARNAUD, Les origines doctrinales du Code civil français, 1969 2 R. BAUER, H. SCHLOSSER (ed.), Freiherr von Kreittmayr. Ein Leben für Recht, Staat und Politik, 1991 3 J. BENTHAM, A General View of a complete Code of Laws (1802), in: Works, J. BOWRING (ed.), vol. 3, 1962, 155–210 4 Id., Papers relative to Codification, in: Works, J. BOWRING (ed.), vol. 4, 1962, 451ff. 5 Id., On the Anti-codification, alias the Historical School of Jurisprudence (1830), in: Denkschriften und Briefe zur Charakteristik der Welt und Literatur 4, Berlin 1840, 247–253 6 R. BONINI, Crisi del diritto romano, consolidazioni e codificazioni nel Settecento europeo, 1985 7 W. BRAUNEDER, Das ABGB für die gesamten Deutschen Erbländer der österreichischen Monarchie von 1811, in: Gutenberg-Jb. 62, 1987, 205–254 8 P. CARONI, Kodifikation, in: HRG 2, 907–922 9 Id., Privatrecht, – eine sozialhistorische Einführung, 1988, 53–99 10 Id., Grundanliegen bürgerlicher Privatrechtskodifikation, in: Gesetz und Gesetzgebung im Europa der Frühen Neuzeit, 1998, 249–273 11 Id., (De)Kodifikation: Wenn historische Begriffe ins Schleudern geraten, in: P. CARONI, H. V. MÁLY (eds.), Kodifikation und Dekodifikation des Privatrechts in der heutigen Rechtsentwicklung, 1998, 31–47 12 H. COING (ed.), Handbuch der Quellen und Literatur der neueren europäischen Privatrechtsgeschichte III/1–5, 1977–1988 13 Id., Europäisches Privatrecht, I–II, 1985–1989 14 B. DÖLEMEYER, Kodifikation-Pläne in deutschen Territorien des 18. Jahrhunderts, in: Gesetz und Gesetzgebung im Europa der Frühen Neuzeit, 1998, 201–223 15 ST. GAGNÉR, Studien zur Ideengeschichte der Gesetzgebung, 1960 16 J.-L. HALÉPRIN, Le Code civil, 1996 17 A. S. HARTKAMP, M. W. HESSELINK (eds.), Towards a European Civil Code, 1994 18 H. HOFMEISTER (ed.), Kodifikation als Mittel der Politik, 1986 19 H. HÜBNER, Kodifikation und Entscheidungsfreiheit des Richters in der Geschichte des Privatrechts, 1980 20 N. IRTI, L'età della decodificazione, 1989³ 21 Id., Codice civile e società politica, 1995 22 J. VAN KAN, F. Hotman en de codificatiepolitiek van zijn Tijd, in: TRG 3, 1922 23 Id., Les efforts de codification en France, 1929 24 W. OGRIS, Kodifikation, in: Ergänzbares Lex. des Rechts 1/780, 1991 25 PH. RÉMY, La recodification civile, in: Droits 26, 1997, 3–18 26 K. SCHMIDT, Die Zukunft der Kodifikationsidee, 1985 27 P. STEIN, Römisches Recht und Europa, 1996 28 M. SUEL, Les premières codifications à droit constant, in: Droits 26, 1997, 19–32 29 G. TARELLO, Le ideologie della codificazione nel secolo 18, 1971 30 J. VANDERLINDEN, Le concept de code en Europe occidentale du 13e au 19e siècle, 1967 31 Id., Code et codification dans la pensée de J. Bentham, in: TRG 32, 1964, 45–78 32 Id., À propos de code et de constitution, in: Liber amicorum John Gilissen, 1983, 427–440 33 W. E. VOSS, Rechtssammlungen, in: Der Neue Pauly 3, 53–55 34 P. WEIMAR, Corpus iuris civilis, in: Lex. des MA 3, 270–277 35 F. WIEACKER, Das Sozialmodell der klassischen Privatrechtsgesetzbücher und die Entwicklung der modernen Geschichte, 1953 36 Id., Aufstieg, Blüte und Krisis der Kodifikationsidee, in: FS G. Boehmer, 1954, 34–50 37 Id., Privatrechtsgeschichte der Neuzeit, ²1967, 249–347 38 W. WILHELM, Gesetzgebung und Kodifikation in Frankreich im 17. und 18. Jahrhundert, in: Ius Commune 1, 1967, 241–270 39 R. ZIMMERMANN, Codification: History and Present Significance of an Idea, in: European Review of Private Law 3, 1995, 95–120

ADDITIONAL BIBLIOGRAPHY: B. DÖLEMEYER, Wohin Napoleons Gesetzbuch kommt, da entsteht eine neue Zeit, eine neue Welt, ein neuer Staat, (epilogue and bibliography to: Napoleons Gesetzbuch/ Code Napoléon) [Faksimile-Nachdruck der Original-Ausgabe von 1808, 2001, 1056–1107]; C. R. NÚÑEZ, El Código napoleonico y su recepción en América latina, Lima 1997; Le Code civil. 1804–2004. Un passé – un présent – un avenir, Paris 2004; R. ZIMMERMANN, The Transition from Civil Law to Civil Code in Germany: Dawn of a New Era?, in: Id. (Ed.), Roman Law, Contemporary Law, European Law, 2001, 53–105.   BARBARA DÖLEMEYER

Coin Collections

A. DEFINITION B. THE MOST IMPORTANT COIN COLLECTIONS C. COIN COLLECTIONS AND CLASSICAL STUDIES

A. DEFINITION

Coin collections (CC), also known as coin cabinets, go back to the Renaissance and the penchant of the time for Classical Antiquity and its monuments, among which coins are certainly counted. The first famous coin collector was Petrarch (1304–1374). Most of the now state-owned CC came into being during the period of Absolutism, as part of royal art collections [19. 436]. It is in these collections that ancient coins (i.e. from the Celts, Greeks, Romans and Byzantines) constitute one of the main emphases. Coin cabinets are frequently to be also found in city and state museums, as well as universities.

B. THE MOST IMPORTANT COIN COLLECTIONS

1. WESTERN AND CENTRAL EUROPE
1.1. FRANCE

Until about the middle of the 19th cent., the *Cabinet des médailles de la Bibliothèque nationale* in Paris was the most important and largest CC in Europe. It goes back to the royal collections of jewellery, coins, gems and other valuables that were kept in the various palaces. Under the reign of Charles IX (1560–1574), the collections were moved to the Louvre, where they were merged together, with a *garde particulier des médailles et antiques du roi*, a 'special guard for the king's medals and antiquities' in charge of protecting them. Under the reign of Louis XIV (1661–1715), who significantly enlarged the coin collection, the coin room was transferred from the Louvre to the Royal Library in 1667. During the 18th, 19th and 20th cents. as well, its holdings were constantly expanded through purchases, discoveries of coins and donations. Since 1917, the collection has been located in its present rooms in the Rue de Richelieu. The collection of coins amounts to over 500,000 pieces, of which the ones from Antiquity are the largest part [16]. These have been and continue to be made public, e.g. B. E. BABELON, *Catalogue des monnaies grecques de la Bibliothèque nationale*: I. *Les rois de Syrie, d'Arménie et de Commagène*, 1890, II. *Les Perses Achéménides, les satrapes et les dynastes tri-*

butaires de leur empire, Cypre et Phénicie, 1893; Id., *Inventaire sommaire de la Collection Waddington*), 1898; SNG France, 1983ff.; J.-B. Giard, *Catalogue des monnaies de l'empire romain* I, 1976; II, 1988.

1.2. GREAT BRITAIN

The *Department of Coins and Medals* of the British Museum in London first started-with the founding of the Museum in 1753-as a division of the *Department of Manuscripts*. In 1803, the collection was transferred to the *Department of Antiquities*, in 1863, the independent *Department of Coins and Medals* was created, which then in 1893 moved to museum's west wing still used today. The department saw a big revival as a result of the endowments of the royal collection made by George VI in 1823, and of the collection of the Bank of England in 1877. Because of the colonial past of the United Kingdom, Oriental coinage provides a major focus with its 71,000 pieces, but the outstanding and most important collection is represented by the ancient coins: 85,000 Greek and 84,000 Roman and Byzantine pieces. Taylor Combe published in 1814 the inventory of Greek coins under the title *Veterum Populorum et regum numi qui in Museo Britannico adservantur*; Payne Knight followed him in 1830 with *Nummi Veteres Civitatum Regum Gentium et Provinciarum, Londini in Museo Richardi Payne Knight asservati, ab ipso, ordine geographico, descripti*. Between 1873 and 1927, 29 volumes were published with the inventory of Greek coins (BMC, Gr). In 1910, three volumes were dedicated to the coins of the Roman Republic (*Coins of the Roman Republic in the British Museum*, BMCRR), six other ones from 1923 to 1962 dealt with the imperial period *Coins of the Roman Empire in the British Museum* (BMCRE) [4]. The Universities of Oxford [10] and Cambridge [17] also have large collections of ancient coins.

1.3. THE NETHERLANDS

The beginnings of CC in Leiden date back to the first half of the 18th cent. under the reign of Prince Wilhelm IV. The first inventory of the year 1759 recorded 170 ancient gold coins, 463 silver and 2,741 bronze Greek coins, 731 Roman Republican silver coins, as well as 3,740 gold and 8,404 bronze coins from the imperial period. At present, the collection of ancient coins amounts to about 60,000 pieces [18].

1.4. BELGIUM

The *Musée d'armes anciennes, d'armures, d'objets d'art et de numismatique* was founded in 1835. Three years later, the numismatic division was attached to the newly founded *Bibliothèque Royale*. Ancient coins make up a substantial part of the 210,000 objects contained in the collection [9].

1.5. GERMANY

The largest CC in Germany are the *Münzkabinett* in Berlin and the *Staatliche Münzsammlung* in Munich. The first surviving inventory of the Berlin coin cabinet dates back to 1649, with a collection of 5,000 coins. When the Königliche Museum was founded in 1830, the coin cabinet became integrated into the so-called Antiquarium and was opened to the public; in 1868, it received the status of an independent museum, and in 1904, it moved to the present site at the Kaiser-Friedrich-Museum, now Bodemuseum. Since 1992, the cabinet has been part of the Staatliche Museen zu Berlin – Preußischer Kulturbesitz. Its collection amounts to about 500,000 objects, including 104,000 Greek and 45,000 Roman and Byzantine coins [8]. One part of the ancient coins has been published in A. V. SALLET et al., *Beschreibung der antiken Münzen*, 1888–1894. The beginnings of the Staatliche Münzsammlung München go back to the second half of the 16th cent. when Duke Albrecht V (1550–1579) founded the Kunstkammer. By the end of the century, its collection already amounted to 7,000 coins, mainly from Classical Antiquity. After the Wittelsbach Palatinate and Bavaria were united in 1777 under the Elector Carl Theodor, the distinguished Kurpfalz CC of Mannheim was also moved to Munich. As a result of the secularisation at the beginning of the 19th cent., important pieces and consignments from monasteries found their way into the CC, where especially the division 'Roman Antiquity' made important acquisitions. In 1807, the 'Königliche Münzcabinet' was integrated into the *Akademie der Wissenschaften*; now it is an autonomous collection. In the 19th cent., the private collections Cousinéry, Astuto, Avellino and Longo were acquired for the area of Greek Antiquity. The Antiquity division of the collection was especially patronised by King Ludwig I (1825–1848), who was a passionate devotee of Classical Antiquity. It contains about 100,000 coins (Celtic, Greek, Roman, Byzantine), partly published in the SNG and in exhibition catalogues [20; 5; 7; 14; 15].

1.6. AUSTRIA   2. NORTHERN EUROPE
2.1. DENMARK   2.2. SWEDEN   3. SOUTHERN
EUROPE   3.1. SPAIN   3.2. ITALY   3.3. GREECE
4. EASTERN EUROPE, THE AMERICAS

1.6. AUSTRIA

The Vienna coin cabinet originated in the CC of the Hapsburgs. Ferdinand I (1521–1564) was fond of ancient coins, and there are two inventory lists of the collection stemming from his time (after 1547). The 18th cent. was of crucial importance for the development of the cabinet: Karl VI (1711–1740) created a unified coin cabinet, by having all pieces that were to be found in various places recorded and assembled. Under the reign of Maria Theresia, since 1774, Joseph Hilarius Eckhel was director of the antiquities division. With his major work *Doctrina numorum veterum* (8 volumes, Vienna 1792–1798), he founded the scientific field of numismatics. The Vienna cabinet contains about 500,000 objects, a considerable part of which consists of ancient coins [6].

2. NORTHERN EUROPE
2.1. DENMARK

The Copenhagen coin cabinet evolved from the royal art collection of Frederik III (1648–1670). The first Roman coins arrived in 1654 in the collection; from the

18th cent. on, the stock of ancient coins has been constantly enlarged. After the end of the absolute monarchy in 1848, the Danish state took over the then royal collection. At present, the collection contains over 400,000 objects, with a large share of Greek coins, which were published from 1939 until 1977 in 43 fascicles of the SNG [12].

2.2. SWEDEN

The Stockholm coin cabinet, whose early beginnings date back to the late 16th cent., ranks among the oldest CC in Europe. Queen Kristina (1632–1654) possessed the first major collection of ancient coins, which had been partly seized in Munich (1632) and Prague (1648) during the Thirty Years' War. Approximately half of the total 400,000 coins stems from Swedish hoards, a large part of the ancient coins are donations, such as the one from King Gustaf VI Adolf (1950–1973). Four volumes (1974–1995) have been published so far as part of the SNG [21].

3. SOUTHERN EUROPE

3.1. SPAIN

The history of the Madrid coin cabinet goes back to 1712, when Felipe V founded the Biblioteca Real, where the coins of the royal palace were integrated. The collection is now part of the Museo Arqueológico Nacional. It has an important collection of Roman Republican bronze coins and denarii, coming for the most part from findings. The most significant and most complete is the series of Roman Imperial coins with its 65,000 pieces [2]. A volume of SNG was published in 1994.

3.2. ITALY

Two CC are kept since 1918 in the Castello Sforzesco in Milan, the national collection of the Gabinetto Numismatico di Brera and the Civiche Raccolte Numismatiche of the city of Milan. The cabinet of Palazzo di Brera – housed there since 1817 – was founded in 1808 as Reale Gabinetto di Medaglie e Monete; the Milan collection came into being in 1832, with the donation of the Castiglioni collection. Both collections count over 140,000 coins, of which about 11,000 are Greek. Roman and Byzantine coins make up the largest part, with over 65,000 pieces [1]. Eleven volumes of SNG have been published since 1988 from the Civiche Raccolte Numismatiche and nine volumes since 1990 *Sylloge Nummorum Romanorum*. The collection of the Museo Nazionale Romano in Rome is more substantial than Milan's collections, though its specialty are Italian coins of the Middle Ages and the Early Modern period. There are numerous CC to be found in many places in Italy.

3.3. GREECE

The largest Greek CC is the Numismatic Museum of Athens, founded in 1829 as part of the National Museum in Aegina. It started with the Jossimades collection with its 20,000 Greek, Roman and Byzantine coins and medals from the Middle Ages and the Early Modern period. From 1889 until 1922, the well-known numismatist Ioannis Svoronos worked at the cabinet. In

this period, the collection was transferred to the Academy, and later on to the National Museum. The collection has more than 500,000 coins, mainly Greek, Roman and Byzantine ones, although their numbers are constantly on the rise due to findings and excavations [13].

4. EASTERN EUROPE, THE AMERICAS

The most important East European CC with ancient coins are the cabinets in St. Petersburg, Moscow and Sophia, made again more easily accessible to research after the change of the political situation. The most important CC in the Americas is the American Numismatic Society (ANS) in New York, with a total of almost 800,000 coins, of which about 120,000 are Greek and 95,000 Roman/Byzantine. Coins of the Hellenistic rulers form a particular focus. ANS has published seven SNG volumes since 1961 [11].

C. COIN COLLECTIONS AND CLASSICAL STUDIES

Besides written evidence and archaeological monuments, ancient coins are an important source of information for scholarly research. Already known material is constantly supplemented and extended by findings and excavations. It is the responsibility of CC and the respective researchers, to classify them and make them accessible to experts by publications or other means – photos, plaster casts, presentation during visits. With modern means of communication and the vast possibilities of travelling at their disposal, scholars can easily find access to CC. It is for that reason that, especially in the last century, coins became an important source of information for the study of Classical Antiquity.

1 E. A. ARSLAN, Il Gabinetto numismatico dei civici Musei di Milano, in: Commission Internationale de Numismatique. Compte rendu 22, 1975, 39–47   2 C. ALFARO ASINS, El Departamento de Numismática y Medallística del Museo Arqueológico Nacional de Madrid, in: Commission Internationale de Numismatique. Compte rendu 39, 1992, 39–47   3 F. DE CALLATAŸ, Les principales collections publiques de monnaies grecques, in: Commission Internationale de Numismatique. Compte rendu 41, 1994, 66–78 (provides an overview on all coin collections with Greek coins.)   4 R. A. G. CARSON, The Department of Coins and Medals, BM, in: Commission Internationale de Numismatique. Compte rendu 21, 1974, 35–45   5 J. GARBSCH, B. OVERBECK, Spätantike zwischen Heidentum und Christentum, 1990 (Exhibition catalogue)   6 H. JUNGWIRTH, Die Sammlung von Medaillen, Münzen und Geldzeichen des Kunsthistorischen Museums in Wien, in: Commission Internationale de Numismatique. Compte rendu 37, 1990, 47–54   7 D. KLOSE, G. STUMPF, Sport – Spiele – Sieg. Münzen und Gemmen der Antike, 1996   8 B. KLUGE, Das Münzkabinett der Staatlichen Museen zu Berlin – Preußischer Kulturbesitz, in: Numismatisches Nachrichtenblatt 46, 1997, 401   9 J. LIPPENS, Bruxelles: Le Cabinet des Médailles de la Bibliothèque Royale, in: Commission Internationale de Numismatique. Compte rendu 37, 1990, 39–41   10 D. M. METCALF, The Heberden Coin Room, Ashmolean Museum, Oxford, in: Commission Internationale de Numismatique. Compte rendu 25, 1978, 40–44   11 W. E. METCALF, The American Nu-

mismatic Society, 1958–1996, in: Commission Internationale de Numismatique. Compte rendu 42, 1995, 49–55 12 O. MØRKHOLM, The Royal Collection of Coins and Medals, Copenhagen 1780/81 – 1980/81, in: Commission Internationale de Numismatique. Compte rendu 27, 1980, 31–42 13 M. OECONOMIDES-CARAMESSINI, Musée Numismatique d'Athènes, in: Commission Internationale de Numismatique. Compte rendu 29, 1982, 28–30 14 B. OVERBECK, Rom und die Germanen. Das Zeugnis der Münzen, 1985 (exhibition catalogue) 15 Id., D. KLOSE, Antike im Münzbild. Lehrausstellung zum Einsatz im Unterricht, 1986 16 M. PASTOUREAU, Paris: Le Cabinet des Médailles de la Bibliothèque Nationale, in: Commission Internationale de Numismatique. Compte rendu 23, 1976, 56–61 17 J. G. POLLARD, The Department of Coins and Medals, Fitzwilliam Museum, Cambridge, in: Commission Internationale de Numismatique. Compte rendu 26, 1979, 41–51 18 M. SCHARLOO, A History of Rijksmuseum – Het Koninklijk Penningkabinet, in: Commission Internationale de Numismatique. Compte rendu 44, 1997, 64–74 19 F. v. SCHRÖTTER (ed.), Wörterbuch der Münzkunde, ²1970, s. v. Münzsammeln und M., 435–437 20 G. STUMPF, Zur Geschichte der Münchner Münzsammlung, in: Numismatisches Nachrichtenblatt 47, 1998, 361 21 U. WESTERMARK, Stockholm: Royal Coin Cabinet. National Museum of Monetary History, in: Commission Internationale de Numismatique. Compte rendu 23, 1976, 50–56.   GERD STUMPF

Coins, Coin minting

A. ANTIQUITY   B. MIDDLE AGES AND MODERN AGE

A. ANTIQUITY

The coin, to this day a common type of legal tender, was invented in Lydia in Asia Minor during the second half of the 7th cent. BC and soon spread across all areas then inhabited by Greeks. [1] Because of the political structure and the number of cities and rulers issuing coinage, the Greek minting system was not uniform. Every city or ruler had its own coin face. Likewise the standards of coinage, i.e the systems of weight the minting was based on, varied to some extent. Not until the reign of Alexander the Great (336 – 323 BC) did one currency, that of Macedon, become standard legal tender in an area of any considerable size.

The Roman Empire had a standardized currency. In all mints the coins were struck according to a single standard and were legal tender throughout the imperial territory. The gold solidus, introduced by the Emperor Constantine in AD 312. was the mainstay of the Byzantine currency system up to the middle of the 14th cent. Because of its high degree of fineness the Byzantine gold currency became the international base currency of the Middle Ages. [8]

B. MIDDLE AGES AND MODERN AGE

In the age of the Germanic migrations the coinage of the kingdoms of the Vandals, the Ostrogoths, the Visigoths, the Suevi, the Langobards and the Merovingians was modelled on the Byzantine system. Alongside these

Fig. 1: Louis the Pious, gold solidus, 814–840, obverse. Legend D(ominus) N(oster) HLVDOVICVS IMP(erator) AVG(ustus), diameter 20 mm, weight 4.38 g, mint undetermined.
Munich, Staatliche Münzsammlung

coinages, however, Roman silver denarii, dating back to the first and second cents. AD were still in circulation. Such coins were found in the tomb of the Merovingian king Childerich (d. 482) and in some Viking sites of the 9th to the 11th cents. Until the late Middle Ages the Latin term *denarius* as used in official documents denotes the most common coin of the period, the Pfennig (penny). Likewise the French term *denier* and the abbreviation θ for Pfennig, still used until the 20th cent., are derived from this.[4]. The Carolingian coinage standards were based on the Roman pound: From 755 under the reign of Pippin 264 denarii were struck from one pound of silver; from around 781 on under Charlemagne, the figure was lowered to 240.

Coins did not just function as legal tender. Through their iconography and the message of their legends they also served as media for news and propaganda. In Imperial Rome coins spread the news of the accession of a new emperor to the far corners of the Empire, while reverses reflected the ruler's achievements or programme during his reign as evidenced by legends such as 'Abundantia', 'Aequitas', 'Concordia', 'Felicitas', 'Pax'.

Unlike Roman coins Carolingian ones do not display the ruler's image, but show a cross on the obverse and a temple on the reverse. It was only after 804 that the Emperor Charlemagne had denarii struck which placed him in the tradition of the Roman emperors. The obverse depicts the draped bust of the Emperor wearing the diadem. The encircling legend says: KAROLVS IMP(erator) AVG(ustus); The iconography and the (encircling) legend are closely modelled on their ancient example. Just as ancient coins frequently refer to religion by depicting pagan deities the reverse of Charlemagne's coins displays a temple encircled by the legend + XPICTIANA RELIGIO (Christiana Religio). The coins clearly demonstrate Charlemagne's claim as a

Fig. 2: Frederick II, augustalis, after 1231. Diameter 19 mm, weight 5.27 g. mint of Brindisi. *Munich, Staatliche Münzsammlung*

Christian ruler to be the successor of the Roman emperors. Louis the Pious (814 – 640) had similar portrait coins minted [3] (Fig. 1). However, in the late Carolingian period no such use is made of the the ruler's portrait.

Not until Otto I. (936 – 973) was the ruler's portrait again found on coins, not, however, based on prototypes from Antiquity. Portrait coins that were struck in the Lower Lorrainian mints of Maastricht, Liege, Huy and Namur in the 10th and 11th cents. were again based on models from Late Antiquity, but their artistic quality falls short of their models.

In 1231 the Hohenstaufen Emperor Frederick II laid the foundations for the minting of gold coins in late-medieval Europe. He had the so-called gold augustales, – 'nummi aurei qui augustales vocantur' [5; 7; 10. 49] – minted in Messina and Brindisi. These coins are counted among the most famous gold coins of all time and are regarded as being among the most beautiful of all medieval coins both because of their artistic and technical perfection and because of the non-contemporary style of the Emperor's portrait (Fig. 2). The obverse portrays in profile the Emperor in his laurel wreath facing right. The (encircling) legend says CESAR AVG(ustus) – IMP(erator) ROM(anus). The reverse displays a highly naturalistic eagle, the symbol of the Hohenstaufen dynasty, the (encircling) legend +FRIDE-RICUS names the emperor depicted on the obverse. The augustalis was the copy of a coin issued by the Roman emperor Augustus (27 BC to 14 AD). With this coinage Frederick suggests that the Augustan Age, characterized by the *Pax Augusta*, and with it the age of Christ has returned.

Coinages of the later Middle Ages and the Modern Age continued the classical tradition only insofar as they used Latin legends. Thus on coins the ruler of the Holy Roman Empire is called *Imperator Romanus Semper Augustus* 'Roman Emperor and constant ex-

pander of the realm'. The 'history coins' of King Ludwig I of Bavaria (1825 – 1848), however, represent a conscious return to the tradition of ancient coinage. Their reverses were dedicated to important events or contemporaries. Like the coins of Antiquity they did not simply serve as legal tender, they were also a medium for the sovereign to address his subjects. [9]

1 M. R. ALFÖLDI, Antike Numismatik, 1978, 71–74 2 P. BERGHAUS, Antike Herrscherbildnisse auf niederlothringischen Münzen des 10./11. Jahrhunderts, in: Scripta archaeologica Groningana 6, 1975, 83–90 3 Id., Das Münzwesen, in: Karl der Große – Werk und Wirkung, 1965, 149–156 4 Id., s. v. Denar, Lexikon des Mittelalters 3, 1986, 694 5 W. JESSE, Quellenbuch zur Münz- und Geldgeschichte des Mittelalters, 1924, Nr. 204 (aus der Chronik des Ryccardus de S. Germano) 6 E. KANTOROWITZ, Kaiser Friedrich II., ⁶1985, 205 7 H. KOWALSKI, Die Augustalen Kaiser Friedrichs II., in: SNR 55, 1976, 77–150 8 C. MORRISSON, s. v. Münze, Münzwesen, Lexikon des Mittelalters 6, 1993, 921f. 9 B. OVERBECK, Geschichtstaler König Ludwigs I. von Bayern – Zitate nach römischen Münzen, in: JNG 39, 1989, 27–35 10 F. v. SCHRÖTTER (ed.), Wörterbuch der Münzkunde, ²1970.

GERD STUMPF

College
A. DEFINITION B. HISTORY C. COLLEGES TODAY

A. DEFINITION
The term College indicates institutions of the British and (US)American educational system belonging either to high school, or to university education. The original meaning of college refers to the community of scholars and their masters (*collegium*) in the Middle Ages, or *fellows* and *students* sharing their studies and everyday life together. The concept of college is neither clearly defined nor protected by statutes. In Great Britain and

the USA, 'college' may stand for general and vocational educational institutions, as well as for university institutes of teaching and research. Universities may consist of several colleges (cf. Oxford, Cambridge), and special university institutes may be so called, but institutes of higher education or universities specialised in technology may also bear that name. Even adult education programs in the USA may be called colleges. They all share the idea of community and intensive open contact between teachers and students, who form a temporary community of studies and life.

B. History

The birth and development of colleges are closely connected with the history of universities in western Europe. Their origin is to be found in the monastically-organised college houses of the Middle Ages, where mainly destitute theology students lived together with and received lessons from their unmarried professors/teachers. As interest in the cultivation of the mind and the demand for lawyers, solicitors and physicians rose during the period of Scholasticism, independent teaching and living communities were formed alongside the colleges. These independent corporations made up of scholars and their pupils constituted the basis for the establishment of universities (Bologna 1119, Oxford 1163, Paris, Salerno, Padova 1200, Cambridge 1249), since they were approved by church and state, and were granted the privileges of academic teaching, examination, graduation and self-administration (cf. *universitas magistrorum et scolarium*, the law college made up of teachers and pupils, as a designation for the new educational establishment known as a 'university'). Colleges lost their importance between the 13th and the 16th cents. as a result of the rise of universities, and became business-like organised boarding schools. However, they regained their status as scholarly institutions in the 16th cent., since academic work took place more and more in their halls and buildings. Thus, in many places in the 16th/17th cents., colleges constituted a university within a university, or were themselves established as universities (cf. the colleges of the Orders throughout Europe). In the 19th cent., the university prevailed over the educational institutions of college, academy and lyceum.

With its concept of a community of study, the college, which was customary in Europe from the Middle Ages to the → Enlightenment, has survived down to the present only in Great Britain. The basic concept of the British college, to live and study in a community of fellows (bachelors, masters and doctors with teaching and administration authority) and students, goes back to William of Wykeham, the founder of New College in Oxford (1386). During the colonial period, colleges were established in New England for the education of the sons of wealthy families (cf. for example the College of William and Mary at Williamsburg, Harvard College, Yale College) on the British model, as educational institutions with a shared community life. Ever since,

community life beyond one's specific subject of study has been considered an essential element of physical, moral and social education.

The foundation of new autonomous colleges on campus over the course of centuries has had as a result, for example, that the tradition-rich Oxford University now consists of about 40 colleges, which are coordinated only by the University administration, led by the Chancellor. In the mid–19th cent., an organisational reform began in the US, giving American schools and universities an independent profile, though without drawing a clear conceptual distinction between colleges and universities or vocational institutes.

C. Colleges Today

Among colleges in Great Britain, the first to be mentioned are the traditional, private secondary boarding schools as Eton, Harrow, Rugby or Winchester, where entrance is reserved primarily for the wealthy, aristocratic classes. The traditionally-oriented universities of Oxford and Cambridge are also elitist, with their standard of demands and admissions. They are made up of various autonomous colleges, which accrued to them in the course of their history. The British Sixth-Form colleges are to be distinguished from them. About one third of all British pupils with a GCSE (General Certificate of Secondary Education) apply for them, in order to reach the A-Level after two years' study, as a qualification for university admission.

American colleges of post-secondary education are extremely variegated. There are over 1500 such institutions, all of which grant the Bachelor degree as B.A. (*Baccalaureus Artium*) or B.S. (*Baccalaureus Scientiarium*) after a basic four-year course of study. Some also confer the Master's degree (*Magister Artium*) or the Ph.D. (*Philosophiae Doctor*). The majority of these are humanities-oriented (liberal arts colleges), which offer an all-round education, and may be part of a university (university colleges) or independent. They are the core of the American higher educational system, and serve as basis for the university's graduate courses in (graduate schools), as well as for specialised courses in 'professional schools' or 'vocational-technical colleges'. Land-grant colleges and universities are also well represented. For the first two years of study, there are also Junior Colleges, a special kind of school with a curriculum of a general education, which can belong either to a high school or to a university from an organisational viewpoint. Also connected to universities are evening colleges for adult education. Finally, adult education institutions with general and vocational offerings are (still) called community colleges in America.

The education of theologians at British traditional colleges was responsible for the central position occupied by the (*litterae humaniores*) and ancient languages until the turn of the 19th/20th cent. This changed dramatically with the development of mathematical and scientific subjects of study after the First World War. Since Latin and Greek have lost their importance, only

perhaps 2% of all pupils study these languages as optional courses in Sixth-Form colleges. A similar development took place in the American school system. Until
about 1914, Latin was predominant in the high schools,
but with the reforms at the beginning of the 1960s, it
definitively lost this position.

→ Ancient languages, teaching of; → Great Britain; → United States of America; → University

> 1 O. A. Singletary (ed.), American Universities and Col-
> leges, 1968 2 Ch. E. Mallet, A History of the University
> of Oxford, 1968 3 R. Ollard, An English Education. A
> Perspective of Eton, 1982.   Werner Wiater

Cologne
I. Post-Antiquity Era II. History of the
Excavations III. Römisch-Germanisches
Museum

I. Post-Antiquity Era
A. History B. Topography C. Reception of
Antiquity

A. History
Roman rule in Cologne (C.) ended in the middle of
the 5th cent. In any case, in 459 C. was in the hands of
the Franks. Written sources prove that the transition
took place without a great deal of destruction
(Amm.15,8; 16,2–3; Salv.gub.6,39; Epistolae 1,5–6).
Archaeological evidence, for example, indicates continuous use of the burial ground of St. Severin by the
Franks and the Romance people as well as traces of
occupation in Kastell Deutz (see below). C. was the
capital city of a Rhine – Frankish kingdom which
encompassed parts of the earlier provinces of *Germania
secunda*, *Belgica prima* and perhaps the northern part
of *Germania prima* including Koblenz and Mainz as
well as areas to the east of the river Rhine (Greg.Tur.
Franc.2,37ff.). After Clovis took power at the start of
the 6th cent., the city formed part of the Merovingian
empire. Kings' sojourns as well as those of the Carolingian seneschals on various occasions are attested. Coins
continued to be minted, the Frankish nobility took up
residence in the town (Salvian, Epistolae 1,5–6), in other words, after the fall of the Roman Empire there was
neither anarchy nor a time when C. was without a government.

Since Late Antiquity C. has been a bishopric. The
boundaries of the civitas in Late Antiquity are still preserved in the bishop's diocese. The presence of Maternus, the first bishop of C., is documented at the synods
of Rome (313) and Arles (314). The names of Euphrates
(342/343) and St. Severin (397) are also recorded. Yet
the gaps in the lists of bishops until the time of Caren-
tinus (565) and Ebergisil are certainly not an indication
of an actual vacancy, rather they are probably due to
the loss of the early C. archives. It can, however, be
assumed that there was a partial return to paganism in
the 5th cent. Gregory of Tours records that around 520
St. Gallus destroyed a heathen temple in C. (Greg.
Tur.vit. patr. 6,2).

The written sources as well as the recently excavated
archaeological finds leave no doubt that C. in the early
Middle Ages continued to exist as an urban centre of
political, cultural and economic activity. At first the ancient buildings were to a large extent maintained even if
they were put to different uses. The main part of settlement lay in the areas to the east of the Hohe Straße
where the economically active and wealthier section of
the population lived. The western part of the town was
by no means uninhabited but there was a clear difference in social status between the west and the east. In
any case, the Roman street system was retained in the
main thoroughfares of the town (Hohe Straße, Breite
Straße). There is no evidence for appropriate use of the
Roman supply and waste disposal system in the Middle
Ages. Two events were of central significance for the
transformation from the mainly Roman city to the medieval one: a powerful earthquake around 770/780
which did such lasting damage to several large buildings
that they had to be abandoned, demolished to be precise
(see below), and the destruction and plundering by the
Normans in 881.

B. Topography
The wall dating from the time of the colonial Roman
times partly fulfilled its function up until the last expansion of the city in 1180. Even after that long stretches of
it were preserved, especially on the north and east sides.
The middle Roman Rhinegate, the Marspforte, was demolished in 1545, the Northgate in 1826 and the last
remains were moved in 1897. Numerous parts of the
wall and towers are still visible today [13; 30] (Fig. 1).

The governor's palace, the Praetorium, is mentioned
as the *Regia* in 4th and 5th cent. sources (Amm. 15,8;
Greg.Tur. vit. patr. 6,2). In Christian times a palace
chapel, dedicated to Laurentius, its patron saint, was
probably part of it. According to the archaeological and
building evidence, the palace survived in its late-classical form [24. Phase IV,2] until a severe earthquake
around 780 [12] (Fig. 2). Afterwards the buildings were
demolished, the area was leveled and divided again into
plots. Charlemagne adopted elements of its design for
the Imperial palace in Aachen [28]. Only in a small area
by the Rhine wall, did space remain to build the new
royal administration centre, the forerunner of the later
city hall.

According to more recent scholarship the southern
parts of the building complex, which were interpreted
by Precht [24] as the *Regia*, were not part of the Praetorium [12]. Their use during the 1st–3rd cents. is still
not sufficiently understood. The 4th cent. building has
been very cautiously identified as a synagogue from
Late Antiquity (references to the Jewish community in
C. under Constantine in 321 and 331, Cod. Theodosianus 16,8,3,4).That building of Late Antiquity was in
use into the second half of the 8th cent. and then fell
victim to the same earthquake as the Praetorium. Today
the semi – circular forecourt lies open as a site of historic
evidence on the city hall square.

Fig. 1: The Roman Tower in Cologne from the northwest. Water colour, *c.* 1810. Cologne Municipal Museum. *Rheinisches Bildarchiv Köln*

Fig. 2: S. Schütte, The Praetorium in Late Antiquity (4th cent. AD). Reconstruction of the eastern façade; preserved sections of the wall are shaded.

How long and in what form the vast forum area continued to exist has been resolved just as little as the identity of the forum which, in later sources of 887, was called Forum Iulii. According to archaeological evidence the forum was damaged by an earthquake in the 4th cent. After that, parts of the basement of the semi-circular exedra [large recess with a row of seats] were filled in, but the upper storey continued to be used. It is possible that at the time of the earthquake at the end of

the 8th cent. the forum once again suffered damage and then was completely done away with in the 10th cent.

In C.'s local folklore there was no tradition at all about the Ara Ubiorum. Only from the 16th cent. on did scholarly research occupy itself again with the Ara, however without precise indications as to location, function and significance.

A Christian church [19] was established in the Roman Capitoline temple, by making use of the middle

cella wall. Its foundation probably goes back to Plek-
trudis, the wife of Pippin of Heristal. Parts of the Temenos wall of the temple are still preserved today. The
entire Temenos area is clearly distinguishable on the
plats of the original official real estate registry in
1836/1837.

The C. location of the ancient temple of Mars had
only survived through the names 'Marspforte' for the
Roman Rhine gate and 'Obermarspforten' for the street
running toward it. The temple itself was demolished at
the latest in Merovingian times and possibly even earlier in Late Antiquity.

On various occasions ancient residential buildings
were converted for the purpose of Christian worship as
in the case of St. Kolumba's church. Also the building
which preceded the parish church of St. Alban stood
directly over Roman remains.

According to the most recent research it cannot be
proved that the complex under the cathedral was used
for religious purposes in Late Antiquity [25]. Only the
Baptisterium, Phase III, is definitely part of a building
for Christian worship. The remains of a Merovingian
cathedral can definitely be shown to have existed in the
last third of the 6th cent. through the ambo [elevated
rostrum in the centre of the nave] and the solea [a raised
level often connecting the sanctuary to the ambo]. As a
result of this research, the medieval tradition in C.
claiming that the oldest cathedral was situated near St.
Peter/St. Cäcilien has to be reconsidered, especially as
the interpretation of the Roman remains on the monastery grounds as thermal baths is under close investigation.

As early as the 2nd cent. there was no longer an
island in the Rhine in front of the city [27]. The excavations at the Heumarkt [2;3;11] showed uninterrupted occupation and trading activity from Antiquity
down to modern times. The south wing of the ancient
horrea [warehouse] was converted into a Christian
church dedicated to St. Martin, which was probably the
church of the market settlement. Today the Roman stonework is still preserved in the north wall of the nave far
up into the vertical masonry [16; 31]. A further large
Roman building over 120 metres long and about 8
metres wide, whose purpose remains unknown, was excavated at the Heumarkt. It stood as a ruin until it was
demolished in the Carolingian era [3; 11].

The Constantinian Kastell Deutz was still occupied
after the withdrawal of the border units in the first decades of the 5th cent. After that, traces of Frankish occupation were found to have existed. The Kastell remained a state property, probably with an early church,
and provided the name for the Deutz district. The
demolition of the Roman inner buildings and replacement by a completely new internal structure took place
in the Carolingian era. In 1002/1003 archbishop Heri-
bert founded a Benedictine abbey here. The Kastell
walls which had so far remained completely intact were
only demolished in 1242 on the demands of the citizens
of C. [4; 9]. However, the exact date of the destruction,

Fig. 3: S. Schütte, St Gereon. Reconstructive section through
the Late Antique central-plan building, view from the north.

or rather, the collapse of the Constantinian bridge over
the Rhine is unknown (the bridge is mentioned by
Eumenius, Paneg.7,13,1–5). By the 8th cent. at least,
though probably as early as the 6th, the bridge was no
longer usable, but remains of it were still visible into the
18th cent. [9].

As in other Gallic civitates in Late Antiquity and the
Merovingian era, churches were built from early Christian (catacomb) buildings established on the Roman
burial grounds. They became the nuclei of important
convents and monasteries. Pride of place goes to St.
Gereon (*ad sanctos aureos*) (Fig. 3), which was built in
the middle or in the first half of the 4th cent. C. local
tradition claims that it was founded by St. Helena, but
archaeological evidence points to the post- Constantinian era. The church dedicated to St. Gereon, or, to be
precise, to the legendary martyrs of the Theban legion,
played a particular role in the Frankish kingdom of
Austrasia (Gregory of Tours, *Liber in Gloria Martyrum*; *Liber Historiae francorum*). By the middle of the
6th cent. the Late Classical central building had been
altered once and an atrium, surrounded by columns,
was situated in the front no later than the second building phase. At the end of the 8th cent., Charlemagne
took over the structural design and perhaps also spolia
to create the imperial chapel in Aachen. In the decagon
of the present church [10; 26], the ancient central structure still forms part of the vertical stonework, to a
height of 16.5 metres. Also the churches of St. Severin
and St. Ursula go back catacomb chapels of the 4th
cent. According to the famous inscription of Clematius
in memory of the virgin martyrs around 400, St. Ursula
was completely restored and enlarged. This church
gained significance as the centre of the so-called Ager
Ursulanus, the Roman burial ground from which relics
of the Holy Virgins were gathered continuously and
which secured a prominent position for C. as a Holy
City in the Middle Ages [17]. Roman buildings have
also been shown or assumed by archaeologists as the
forerunners of other churches.

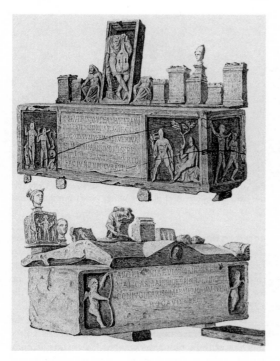

Fig. 4: J.P. Weyer, West façade of the first 'hall of antiquities' of the Wallrafianum, sarcophagus of C. Vitalis (top) and sarcophagus of Apollonia Victorina Bessula (below). Water colour, between 1838 and 1842, in: Kölner Alterthümer, vol. XXX, 12. Cologne Municipal Museum. *Rheinisches Bildarchiv Köln*

C. RECEPTION OF ANTIQUITY

Knowledge about the city's Roman roots was never lost. Moreover, the scholars of the High Middle Ages possessed an excellent knowledge of the Classical writers as well as of the preserved monuments and artefacts. At the beginning of the 12th cent. Rupert of Deutz wrote a report about the controversy of whether the Kastell Divitia [Deutz] had been built in the time of Caesar or Constantine, and he supports his view with the building inscription (CIL XIII 8502) [8;9] which was found and pieced together again during his period as abbot. Abbot Rudolf of St. Pantaleon handed down to us a precise report from the year 1121 of Norbert of Xanten's excavations in St. Gereon, which presupposed a knowledge of high-ranking burials inside the central building [10]. In 1333 Petrarch spent several days being shown around the city so that he could view the Roman remains (Epistolae, lib. I,V).

In addition to that, there is a strand of legendary traditions, which make it difficult to separate the genuine core from the later poetic additions. The most important concern is the elevation of C. to a Holy City (*Sancta Colonia*) by recourse to its Christian-Classical past with its saints' lives such as the *Passio Gereonis* (around 1000) and the *Passio Ursulae* (around 970), which, however, reflect earlier concepts of martyrdom

in Late Antiquity. Another network of themes served to legitimize the city's constitution and independence: The legend of the hero Marsilius is part of this and the tradition that the Emperor Trajan had 15 families uprooted from Rome and moved to C., from whom notable 15th cent. patrician families in C. are descended. The governing committee of the two mayors is traced back directly to the Roman consular constitution. Important knowledge about C. in Roman times is lacking in the historiography of the late Middle Ages. For example the city's name is derived from Marcus Agrippa. Caesar and Tacitus served as primary sources of information while Suetonius was not mentioned at all.

This changed completely with the beginning of Humanism in the 16th cent. In 1571 Arnold Mercator presented illustrations Roman stone monuments around the edges of the first bird's-eye-view map of C. and pointed out places on the map in which Roman remains were still clearly visible. In the labeling he gave a short outline of the city's history in which he correctly placed the founding of the colonial settlement during the time of Claudius and quoted as his sources Caesar, Suetonius, Tacitus and Ammianus Marcellinus.

The most important expert in C.'s topography is Stephan Broelmann (1551–1622). His work surpasses all others in thoroughness of research, knowledge of sources and critical judgement. As law professor and the city's legal adviser, he devoted his life to researching C.'s Roman history although his main work *Civilium rerum memoria dignarum civitatis Ubiorum et Coloniae Claudiae Augustae Agrippinensis commentarii* was never printed (MS in C.'s historical archives). He published only a series of views under the title *Epideigma sive specimen historiae...*, which show imaginative views of Roman C. After that he drew up outstandingly accurate maps, e.g. on the course of the Eifel aqueduct to C. and especially one marking the location of the remains of the Roman bridge over the Rhine, which he himself had calculated by means of triangulation. The accuracy of the location of the Roman Rhine island which had definitely not been in existence since the middle of the 2nd cent. is astonishing [27].

The works of Aegidius Gelenius (1595–1656) became more widely known than Broelmann. Unfortunately he often approached his sources uncritically and without quoting their origin. He placed legends and factual documents side by side giving them equal value (main work: *De admiranda sacra et civili magnitudine Coloniae Claudiae Agrippinensis Augustae Ubiorum Urbis*, C. 1645).

As early as the 16th cent. the study of C.'s ancient past had resulted in significant private collections such as those of the mayors, Arnold von Siegen (1484–1579) and Konstantin Liskirchen (d. 1580), the scholars Stephan Broelmann and Georg Cassander and that of the city councillor Johann Helmann, whose collection is the source for most of the monuments depicted on the Mercator map. However Count Hermann of Manderscheid-Blankenheim (1534–1604) who had acquired parts of the previously mentioned collections, possessed by far the most extensive collection of Rhenish finds [7].

The collections of the Enlightenment at first grew out of educational and didactic interests. This is true of the Jesuit collection which was taken by the French administration to France at the end of the 18th cent., as well as the only large collection remaining in C., that of Franz Ferdinand Wallraf (1748–1824), professor of botany, natural history and aesthetics at University of C. [20]. His collection of ancient works included several thousand coins and over 1,000 small Roman antiquities as well as larger stone monuments (Fig. 4). In 1818 it passed into the possession of the city of C. and formed the basis of the Antiquity section of the later Wallraf-Richartz Museum, that is, the present Römisch-Germanisches Museum (RGM).

SOURCES: 1 C. HEGEL, (ed.), Die Chroniken der deutschen Städte XII–XIV (Cöln I–III), 1875–1877

LITERATURE: 2 N. ATEN, D. BENTE, F. KEMPKEN, E. LOTTER, M. MERSE, Ausgrabungen auf dem Heumarkt in Köln. Erster Bericht zu den Untersuchungen, in: Kölner Jb. 30, 1997,345–404 3 N. ATEN et.al., Die Ausgrabungen auf dem Heumarkt in Köln. 2. Bericht zu den Untersuchungen, in: Kölner Jb. 31,1998, 481–596 4 M CARROLL-SPILLEKE, Das römische Militärlager Divitia in Köln-Deutz, in: Kölner Jb. 26, 1993, 321–444 5 O. DOPPELFELD, W. WEYRES, Die Ausgrabungen im Dom zu Köln, 1980 6 E. EWIG, Rheinische Geschichte, 1,2, 1980 7 O. H. FÖRSTER, Kölner Kunstsammler, 1931 8 M. GECHTER, Das Kastell Deutz im Mittelalter, in: Kölner Jb. 22, 1989, 373–416 9 Id., Zur Überlieferung der Bauinschriften des Kastells Divitia (Deutz), in: Kölner Jb. 24,1991, 377–380 10 Id., Frühe Quellen zur Baugeschichte von St. Gereon in Köln, in: Kölner Jb. 23,1990,531–562 11 Id. and S. SCHÜTTE, Der Heumarkt in Köln, in: Geschichte in Köln 38, 1995,129–139 12 Id. and S. SCHÜTTE, Ursprung und Voraussetzung des mittelalterlichen Rathauses und seiner Umgebung, in: W. GEIS, U. KRINGS (eds.), Köln. Das gotische Rathaus und seine historische Umgebung, 2000, 69–195 13 H. G. HORN, Die Römer in Nordrhein-Westfalen, 1987 14 H. KEUSSEN Topographie der Stadt Köln im Mittelalter, 2 Vols. 1910 15 J. KLINKENBERG, Das römische Köln, 1906 16 C. KOSCH, Neue Überlegungen zu den Ostteilen von Groß St. Martin, in: Colonia Romanica 12, 1997, 35–100 17 W. LEVISON, Das Werden der Ursulalegende, in: Bonner Jb. 132, 1928, 1–164 18 W. LUNG, Zur Topographie der frühmittelalterlichen Altstadt, in: Kölner Jb. 2, 1956, 54–70 19 S. NEU, St. Maria im Kapitol, Die Ausgrabungen, in: H. KIER, U. KRINGS (eds.), Köln. Die romanischen Kirchen, 1984, 331–344 20 P. NOELKE, Im Banne der Medusa – Die Antikensammlung Ferdinand Franz Wallrafs und ihre Rezeption, in: Kölner Jb. 26,1993, 133–216 21 B. PÄFFGEN, S. RISTOW, Die Römerstadt Köln zur Merowingerzeit, in: Die Franken, Exhibition Catalogue 1996, Vol.1, 145–159 22 B. PÄFFGEN, Die Ausgrabungen in St. Severin zu Köln, 3 Vols.1992 23 H. VON PETRIKOVITS, Rheinische Geschichte, 1,1, 1978 24 G. PRECHT, Baugeschichtliche Untersuchung zum römischen Praetorium in Köln, 1973 25 S. RISTOW, Das Baptisterium im Osten des Kölner Domes, in: Kölner Domblatt 58, 1993, 291–312 26 S. SCHÜTTE, ... träumen zwei Kapitel von besseren Zeiten

... Baugeschichtliche Anmerkungen zur frühen Geschichte von St. Gereon in Köln, in: Colonia Romanica XIV, 1999 53–66 27 Id. and M. GECHTER, Stephan Broelmann und die Folgen, in: Kölner Mus.-Bulletin 1, 1999, 4–26 28 Id., Überlegungen zu den architektonischen Vorbildern der Pfalzen Ingelheim und Aachen, in: Krönungen, Exhibition catalogue Aachen 2000,203–211 29 H. STEUER, Die Franken in Köln, 1980 30 U. SÜSSENBACH, Die Stadtmauer des römischen Köln, 1981 31 E. WEGNER, Die ehemalige Benediktinerabtei Groß St. Martin in Köln, in: Kölner Jb. 25, 1992, 143–349. MARIANNE GECHTER

II. HISTORY OF THE EXCAVATIONS
A. INTRODUCTION B. MIDDLE AGES C. RENAISSANCE D. 18TH AND 19TH CENTS. E. END OF THE 19TH CENT. TO 1914 F. 20TH CENT.

A. INTRODUCTION

Since the middle of the first cent. AD C., the *Colonia Claudia Ara Agrippinensium*, *CCAA*, was the capital city of Germania Inferior, that is *Germania Secunda*, after it had been founded around the time of Christ's birth as *Oppidum Ubiorum*. C.'s status as the provincial capital, the future headquarters of the Frankish kings of the East kingdom (Austrasia) and the headquarters of the seneschals until the Carolingian era established the self-assurance of the episcopal city in the high and late Middle Ages. It remained the most densely populated and economically strongest metropolis of the German-speaking lands into the 17th cent. In the 12th cent. C. still outshone Paris and London in some areas. Around 1200 the city was encircled by a wall approximately nine kilometres long, which exactly enclosed the area which had been used in Antiquity. Without its ancient past the extraordinary status of the city in the Middle Ages would have been unthinkable. C. is the only German city with a continuous history of urban settlement where large areas were not abandoned or left deserted. Today the ancient routes of the streets still shape the ground plan of C. The knowledge of the city's early past was never lost, with the result that the study of Antiquity never actually stopped. The awareness of being a Roman city was especially pronounced in the Renaissance. Even today this consciousness is reflected in the city's historical awareness, in which the tangible presence of its antiquities has always played a specific role.

B. MIDDLE AGES

Even before the year 1000 sporadic excavations were made of alleged saints' graves. Around 1100 a brisk, religiously inspired series of excavations began in C. The burial ground near St. Ursula, the so-called *ager ursulanus*, together with Niederich, the fortification of the urban expansion in the north around 1106, became a rich source of finds in the form of the bodies of the so-called 11,000 virgins. A first, almost modern sounding excavation report exists of the ancient central building of St. Gereon, in which Norbert of Xanten discovered and excavated sarcophagi from Late Antiquity or

Fig. 1: The so-called Marsilstein in Cologne (ancient wall remains with sarcophagus); page from the album amicorum of Olivier de la Court, 1595. The illustration also shows the Renaissance inscription of the Cologne Council. Cologne Municipal Museum, Collection of Prints and Drawings. *Rheinisches Bildarchiv Köln*

the Merovingian era. The raising of holy bodies was the main motivation of the excavating clerics even if a duly 'archaeological' method of working can already be detected. On the other hand, a clear historic interest in the city's past had been established as well. In the middle of the 13th cent. Roman mosaics were mentioned by Albertus Magnus at the time of the new construction of the cathedral [11]. The comments of Francesco Petrarca refer to the visible remains which he saw at the time of his visit in 1333 and for the first time testify to the interest in the ancient topography of C. He was able to classify what he saw as he drew direct comparisons to Italy.

C. RENAISSANCE

With the awakening historical interest found in C. in the last third of the 15th cent. the study of the ancient history of the *CCAA* and the *Oppidum Ubiorum* intensified rapidly, though the knowledge of their existence had never been missing and was being directed increasingly toward written sources as well as material evidence. Since the end of the 15th cent. there had been an increase in attention paid to '*rudera*', that is to say, the remains of the Roman bridge (Koehlhoffsche Chronik, 1491), for example, and of Kastell Deutz and other structures such as the ancient city wall. The first excavated inscriptions were published, e.g. by Willibald Pirckheimer and Mariangelus Accursius around 1530. At the same time, in educated circles to which people like the cartographer Arnold Mercator belonged, one started assembling collections of antiquities, which also presupposed digging specifically on the burial grounds to obtain ancient inscriptions, glasses, ceramics and coins (Fig. 1). In the 16th cent. significant collections of C. antiquities were in the hands of the counts of Neuenahr and the families Rinck, Broich, Liskirchen and von Siegen. Johann Helmann can be verified as the author of a first study – before 1574 – of finds and topography based on observations of terrain and archeological finds of ancient C[11].

At the end of the 16th cent. archaeological field research in the modern sense commenced with the law professor and C.'s adviser on legal matters, Stephan Broelmann (1551–1622). Broelmann was the first to combine written sources with on site observations and with the aid of navigational instruments used the most modern methods of the time, such as triangulation. Broelmann wrote an extensive work on the city's history, which remained unpublished and from which only one example was printed in 1608 (*Epideigma sive specimen historiae...*) [2]. Only after that were sources, which are lost today, put at his disposal, allowing him to clarify the topography of ancient C. so effectively that the basic framework developed by him was not surpassed until the second half of the 20th cent., because his knowledge had in the meantime been lost. Also his research on the Roman aqueduct leading to C. was surpassed only shortly before 1900 and his statements on the river island only after 1994 (Fig. 2). For its time Broelmann's work represents a highly respected pioneering achievement [17].

As early as 1620 he knew the exact location of the ancient city wall, the Kastell Deutz, the Constantinian bridge across the Rhine, the Praetorium, the Marspforte and the temple of Mars, the Kapitol, the river island, some necropoleis, the C. aqueduct and further items, even if not all were unearthed. It is true that the works of the brothers Aegidius and Johannes Gelenius in 1645 [3] and of Peter Alexander Bossart in 1687 also used material gained through excavations, significantly adding to Stephan Broelmann's stated views on topography, though they did not fundamentally surpass them [11].

D. 18TH AND 19TH CENTS.

The economically bad and, in C., intellectually stagnant periods during the second half of the 18thcent. until the city came under French rule after 1794, are shaped on the one hand by an historical interest in the city and on the other hand purely by the enthusiasm for collecting antiquities. Especially worthy of note are the

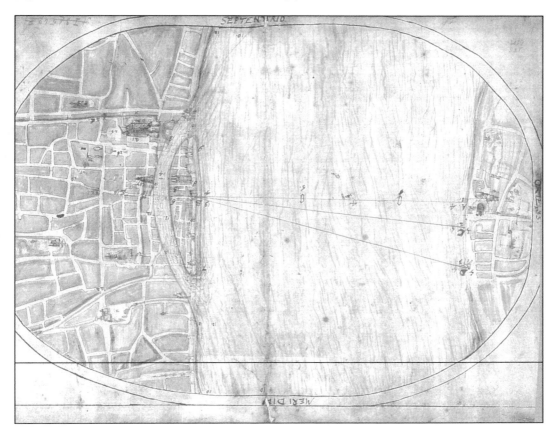

Fig. 2: Map (pen-and-ink drawing): Reconstruction of Cologne's ancient topography.
Stephan Broelmann, pre-1621. Kölnisches Stadtmuseum, graphic collection. The triangulation lines surveying the
Constantinian Rhine bridge between the Roman town and Castellum Divitia (on the right), the Roman city walls and
the exact reconstruction of the island are clearly visible. The numbers precisely indicated the position of ancient
buildings, such as the praetorium. The 17th-cent. town map is superimposed.

Aldenbrück collection and those of von Hartzheim, the
curate Blasius Alfter and the collections and research of
Franz Karl Joseph von Hillesheim and Baron Hüpsch.

Merely the observations by A. Aldenbrück of the
ancient Rhine bridge at low water level in 1765 inspired
a renewal of interest in topography by, among others,
J.M. de Laporterie, whose work before 1824 remained
unfinished [11.15].

With the dissolution of large amounts of church
property during the secularisation, there began not only
an intensified phase of historical investigation but also
an awakened interest in the archaeology of the city,
even if it was more apparent elsewhere. Thus the Landesmuseum was founded in → Bonn around 1820 only
at Dorow's instigation while in C. no such interest apparently existed. In C., in addition to the purely accu-
mulative activities of numerous private collectors, the
prominent collector and museum founder Ferdinand
Franz Wallraf (1818) [21] and particularly Ludwig
Ennen (1861 and 1863ff.) [5], as well as Chr. von
Stramberg (1863) discussed the historical as well as the

topographical and antiquarian problems of the Roman
city. The city's history was then substantially spurred
on by the work of Franz Ritter (1851) and particularly
by the terrain observations of Professor Heinrich Düntzer (1813–1901). Since the middle of the 19th cent.,
C.'s economic flowering through the intensification of
inner city development has brought to light vast
amounts of finds and evidence, which on the one hand
were reflected in large collections [11] (e.g. Mertens-
Schaaffhausen, Merlo, Disch, Herstatt, Wolff, von
Rath, Merkens and Niessen amongst others), and yet
on the other hand only in very few cases led to exact
observations or even documentary accounts, a situation
which was strongly regretted in Bonn as early as 1860.
The level of knowledge in Bonn and even in Xanten
outstripped by far the interest of the citizens of C. in
archaeology. C. also later lost the mass of finds that
were in private collections. In 1843 the famous Roman
burial chamber in Weiden was discovered which was
acquired and restored by the Prussian state and not the
city of C. Locally the C. of Antiquity was for the first

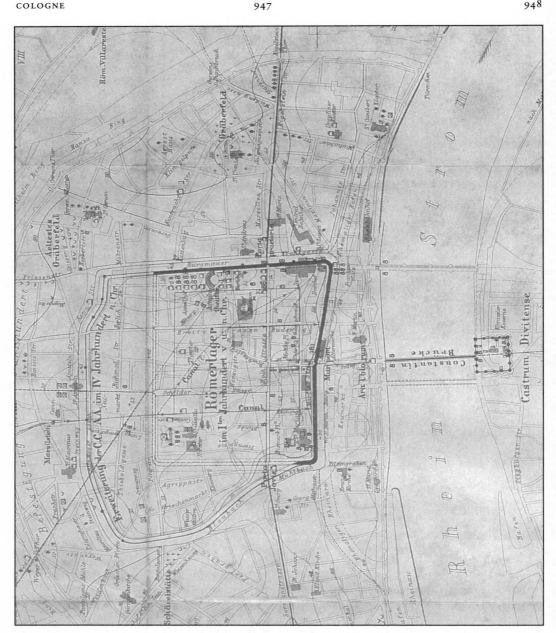

Fig. 3: Reconstructed topography of ancient Cologne after Carl Veith, 1885 (detail from the foldout map);
ancient fortifications, streets, single finds and burial grounds are marked.
Rheinisches Bildarchiv Köln

time represented in a museum in the Roman section of
the Wallraf Richartz Museum, which was opened in
1861 in C. and whose earliest catalogue was compiled
by Düntzer.

E. END OF THE 19TH CENT. TO 1914

The *Classis Germanica* on the Alteburg (excavated
in 1870/1872 and 1899, until 1905 by Lehner from the
Provinzial Museum in Bonn); numerous mosaics and
ancient remains of buildings not yet identified. Kastell

Deutz had been successfully excavated further between
1879 and 1882. Some commercial enterprises were
identified and some parts of the suburbs as well as several terracotta pottery works, e.g. the workshop of *Ser-
vandus* at the *Forum Hordiarium* and installations of
the water supply and waste water disposal (collecting
basin). Questions remained open about the theatre and
circus (see below), the *Ara Ubiorum* and the location of
the *Oppidum Ubiorum*. Nevertheless it can be said that
by the beginning of the 20th cent. the essential features

Fig. 4: Excavation work in the burial ground on
Luxemburger Straße. Photography, *c.* 1900.
Cologne Municipal Museum. *Rheinisches Bildarchiv Köln*

of the city's Roman history, its topography, installations (structures etc.) and inscriptions were already well-
known [11].

F. 20TH CENT.

As almost all the files relating to archaeological finds
were burnt during World War II, the information about
excavations before 1929 is based on a map of the findings which L.S. Haake drew up in 1930, based on
Schultze and Steuernagel's map and on the few publications.

On the basis of the 1914 Prussian law on excavations, the Roman department of the Wallraf Richartz
Museum (occasionally the city conservation curator)
dug to the left of the Rhine while the Museum für Ur-
und Frühgeschichte, which only existed until 1945, to
the right of the Rhine. The latter museum had only been
opened in 1907 under Carl Rademacher, who was the
director until 1931 and was replaced by Werner Buttler
who successfully carried out the excavations of the
Neolithic village (finds of band ceramics) in Cologne-
Lindenthal. After a three year vacancy he was replaced
by Werner von Stokar. The RGM took over the old
Museum für Ur- und Frühgeschichte after 1946 [15]. At
the beginning of the 20th cent. the Roman section of the
Wallraf Richartz Museum was under the direction of
Josef Poppelreuther and between 1922 and 1959 Fritz

Fremersdorff was in charge of the excavations in C.
With the founding of the RGM in 1946 and Fritz Fremersdorff as its first director, this museum, now with
increased personnel, dug in the entire city area. As early
as 1939 Otto Doppelfeld was appointed as Fremersdorff's assistant in C. In 1959 he became his successor
as director of the RGM and due to his enormous
achievements [15] he is the most significant figure in
C.'s post-war archaeology. In 1972 he was replaced by
Hugo Borger who later became director-general of the
C. museums and who, in turn, was followed as museum
director by H. Hellenkemper in 1990. After the new law
for the protection of monuments came into effect in
North Rhine – Westphalia in 1981 the care of in-ground
monuments has been managed successively relying on
the work of the RGM or, at times under the historic
museums and from 1990–1995 under the leadership of
the director general Hiltrud Kier and Sven Schütte [10]
as the independent office for the archaeological care of
in-ground monuments in the city of C. After that period
the RGM took over complete responsibility again.

Besides the maintenance of the official in-ground
monuments there were always large private collections,
a tradition which, following the introduction of the
1914 Prussian law on excavations, was supported with
the approval of the 'official archaeology' from excavation sites in C. Even after the introduction of the 1981

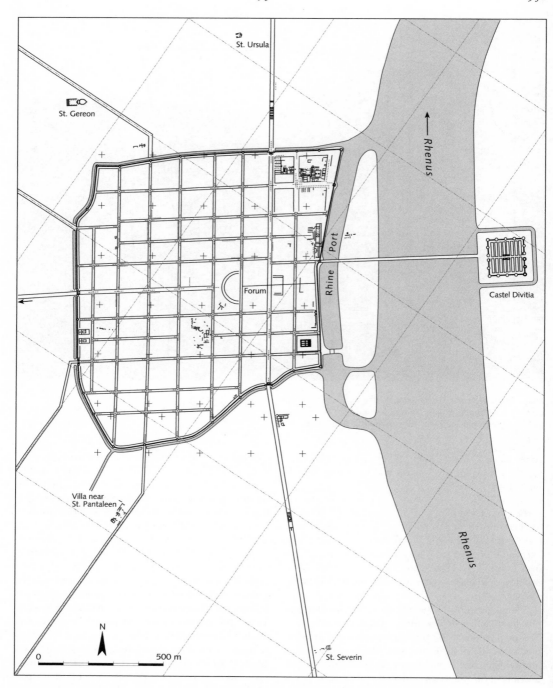

Fig. 5: Map of ancient Cologne after G. Precht, 1973; it incorporates the centuriation grid according to Klinkenberg, identified building remains, mosaics as well as street porticos.
Rheinisches Bildarchiv Köln

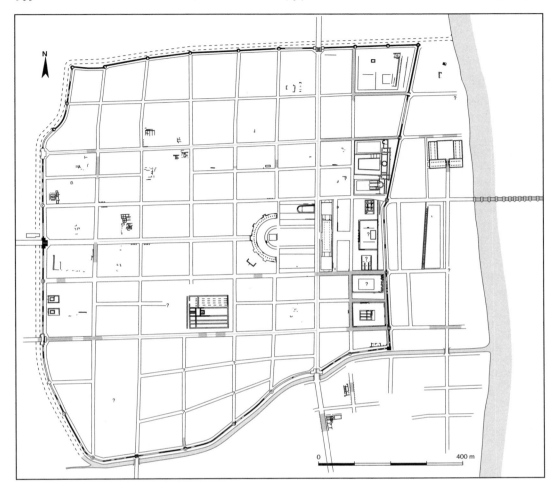

Fig. 6: The topography of Late Antique Cologne after Schütte, 2000, depicting known wall remains and the now revised topography, according to which bridge and island did not exist simultaneously. It also includes the recent findings on the Forum and Haymarket.
Rheinisches Bildarchiv Köln

Protection of Monuments Act in North Rhine – Westphalia 'approved' grave robbers were a constant accompaniment to C.'s archaeology. In the 21st cent. the illegal trade in antiquities in C. still represents a serious problem. In the 20th cent. important finds in the museum collections were acquired from private collections, e.g. the 'privately' excavated, enormous *Poblicius* monument in the RGM, also the well known ancient glass shoes [8] and entire collections such as those of Niessen, Jovi and Lückger, which had been created entirely alongside the official excavation activities. Again and again at the end of the 20th cent. such purchases were still leading to fierce disputes.

In 1974 H. Borger complained that Klinkenberg's fundamental work of 1906 concerning C.'s ancient topography had 'not been updated after almost 80 years' [15]. This description was indeed generally correct and applicable to the furthest corners of the city until

around 1990 (Fig. 5), although the great excavation projects of the Fremersdorff and Doppelfeld era, in particular, contributed essential additions, especially in the 1950's. As early as 1924–1926 under Fremersdorf extended excavations took place under and around St. Severin, which were directed towards the classical and Middle -Ages necropoleis [12]. They were continued well into the 1950's. The excavations at Kastell Deutz (begun 1879–1882) were continued from 1927–1938 and the excavations at the fort of *Classis Germanica* on the Alteburg from 1927 –1928. Nevertheless there were still occasional complaints in the 1930s about the lack of interest in C.'s Roman past and inadequate research methodology.

World War II signified the most serious turning point in C.'s excavation history. Before the war vital finds were already coming to light through the building of bunkers and protective measures, then, during the war, in 1941 for example, the famous Dionysos mosaic and parts of an enormous Peristyle house were unearthed during the construction of the so-called cathedral bunker. While over 90% of the city was destroyed, nevertheless many and diverse observations could be made during the rebuilding, which, in its magnitude and structural progress, brought with it then and now, both many positive results as well as the destruction of much archaeological material. As early as the 19th cent. Roman remains had been unearthed in the cathedral area. Immediately after the war a large excavation began in and around the cathedral which enabled Fremersdorff and later Doppelfeld in a short time to survey the earlier structures in the cathedral area from the ancient to Ottonian times [4]. A few metres to the south the big excavation on the Praetorium took place, 1953–1956, the results of which were presented in 1972 by Gundolf Precht following Doppelfeld's earlier report of 1956; a new updated report of its findings is still awaited today [7]. Immediately afterwards parts of the Jewish quarter, the synagogue and the ceremonial bath, were unearthed and partly presented and made known in 1959. Here, too, an updated report proved to be necessary [7]. There were excavations in almost all the destroyed Romanesque churches, and discoveries were made about their origins in Late Antiquity, for the most part, and the early Middle-Ages and they were partially presented (the most important excavations: St.Alban 1956, 1972, 1994; St. Andreas 1953, 1954, 1958; St Aposteln 1943,1956; St. Cäcilien 1930, 1948–1955, 1976; St. Georg 1927–1931, 1956/1957; St. Gereon 1949, 1950, 1979; St. Kolumba 1924, 1974/1976; St. Kunibert 1978–1981, 1994; St. Maria im Kapitol 1910, 1957–1961, 1964, 1975, 1977; St. Maria Lyskirchen 1968, 1972, 1988; Groß St. Martin 1965/1966, 1973; St. Pantaleon 1955–1962; St. Peter 1953, 1956, 1999; St. Severin 1925–1943, 1953–55; St. Ursula 1942/1943, 1960, 1967). These are part of the great achievements of C.'s archaeology [9]. In this context the 1949 excavations of Armin von Gerkan in St. Gereon and the work of Peter La Baume (since 1953) on Roman and early Christian C. are especially noteworthy. In St. Pantaleon (Mühlberg) part of a ancient suburb was unearthed under the church; the origins (Capitoline Temple) of St. Maria im Kapitol and the forerunner structure of St. Georg with the 'Benefizarierstation' [road station manned by *beneficiarii*, former Roman legionnaires in charge of collecting tolls] were identified, all dating from Antiquity. In addition, a large number of private properties were examined where, among others, the successful discovery of the round porticus in the central forum was made after 1970. Two temples of a Gallic-Roman design were uncovered in the west of the city and more temple podiums were identified (R.Thomas). Glass kilns, potteries and workshops were unearthed not only in the suburbs. Large excavations also took place in the necropoleis of Antquity. The results and on-site finds were presented and made accessible in preliminary reports and larger publications [13; 14; 15; 16].

The enormous achievements of post-war archaeology are partly overshadowed by the counterbalancing losses and the lack of publications. The last annual report on the maintenance of in-ground monuments appeared in 1971 for the year 1960 [13]. Another (single) annual report (Archäologie in Köln [10]) did not appear until 1992. The mass of finds and evidence of the last four decades of the 20th cent. remains to a great extent unassessed or unpublished. This applies to long term research projects, such as the cathedral excavation and the giant excavation in the cathedral area 1969–1972 [8]. In comparison, however, important results were occasionally presented, such as the so-called Ubiermonument (corner tower of the Oppidum, around 0/4 AD) by J.Bracker (1966/1967), or the discovery of the atrium of St. Gereon by Günther Binding and research by Johannes Deckers (1979).

Starting in 1974 the most important ancient finds have been exhibited in their own museum building at the cathedral (RGM). But the display, which remained almost unchanged up to the beginning of the 21st cent., was subject to some strong criticism in the years after the opening. Yet today the RGM is one of the greatest museums of archaeology in Germany [15].

In 1980, due to the conference of the German antiquity societies in C., the possibility arose of a cursory gathering of finds and evidence [16] which in its initial stages had earlier been attempted by Doppelfeld and La Baume.

While Fremersdorff and Doppelfeld still pleaded for a continuous development from Antiquity to the Middle Ages, the following generation under Borger rejected this vehemently (Steuer, Hellenkemper) [7]. Meanwhile, vital new knowledge had been acquired about private dwellings, the production of glass and pottery, numismatics, burial sites and particularly about early Christian C. and early medieval burial sites. Also, in contrast to the beginning of the century, fundamental discoveries had been made about the area surrounding the Roman city with its villas and trading districts. Admittedly after Doppelfeld's era, over 900 excavations took place between 1971 and 1990 though only very few were presented. Furthermore, they have often been inadequately excavated. Among these were the important excavations in the so-called *Horrea* (warehouse) in the Rhine suburbs near Groß St. Martin and further large projects such as the excavation of the foundations of the new Wallraf Richartz Museum from which Stefan Neu was at least able to make the rescued architectural sculpture known (1989). Moreover, finds from older building complexes were presented, as for example the graves of St. Severin (Bernd Päffgen 1992 [12]) or wall paintings (Renate Thomas [20]). The construction of the subway in the 1970s, which dug enormous passages through the inner city, remained completely unrecorded, as well as the entire Rhine bank tunnel situated near the edge of the old city. At that time the entire ancient waterfront of the city was destroyed without being recorded, as extensive building projects were often not overseen by archaeologists.

In the first half of the 1990s preliminary excavations on the location and structure of the *Oppidum Ubiorum* were started by the department for the maintenance of archaeological in-ground monuments (M.Carroll/S. Schütte) [3], which led to an overall location of ditches and fortifications. More recent investigation (Leuschner 1995 [7]) dated the structure of the wood and earth fortification, which at that time could be shown to have existed at the time of the Battle of Varus around AD 9. Scientific investigations were carried out into the geological substrata and the location of the island [17], as well as the topography of ancient C. [7] (Fig. 6). The historical disappearance of the harbour island (1st cent AD) and the Constantinian bridge over the Rhine (4th cent. AD) were issues which were thoroughly resolved [7.17]. For the first time the internationally accepted procedure of digging in natural layers was consistently applied to all excavations, which led to a greatly increased output of finds and to a phenomenal increase in knowledge. Now for the first time the layers above the above era were methodically examined. Investigations of the city's origins revealed the lack of finds and evidence before the birth of Christ. Research and excavations pointed clearly to the city's continuing existence after the era of Antiquity. S.Seiler was the first person to succeed in establishing the structural evidence for the Temple of Mars [19].

After 1996 a change was introduced once again. The largest long-distance trading market in Central Europe, the Heumarkt, could be explored with a test excavation (until 1995) but was to be unearthed by private firms. However on that occasion around half the layers, particularly the ancient ones, were then removed over a large area by a mechanical digger (1997–1999)[1]. Probably the most significant discovery here was a row of over 40 stone-built rooms of over 120 metres in length dating from the 4th cent. AD.

As before, important questions concerning C. archaeology remain unresolved, such as the question of the location of the *Ara Ubiorum*, the circus and the theatre [22]. Research in recent years has posed many new questions about the settlement of the city area and its further development following the era of Antiquity. In view of the current state of research, a thorough revision of the first thousand years of C.'s history is therefore still to appear.

1 N. ATEN, G. FRASHERI, F. KEMPKEN, M. MERSE, B. SCHMIDT, P. GROOTES, K.-H. KNÖRZER, B. PÄFFGERN, G. QUARG, Die Ausgrabungen auf dem Heumarkt in Köln. Zweiter Ber. zu den Untersuchungen von Mai 1997 bis April 1998, in: Kölner Jb. Für Vor- und Frühgesch. 31, 481–596   2 S. BROELMANN, Civilium rerum memoria dignarum civitatis Ubiorum et Coloniae Claudiae Augustae Agrippinensis commentarii. (Cologne, unpublished manuscript 1608/1622, Historisches Archiv der Stadt Köln)   3 M. CARROLL, Neue vorkoloniezeitliche Siedlungsspuren in Köln, in: Arch. Informationen 18/2, 1995, 143–152   4 O. DOPPELFELD, W. WEYERS, Die Ausgrabungen im Dom zu Köln, (= Research in CologneC Vol.1), 1980   5 L. ENNEN, Geschichte der Stadt Köln, 5 vols, Cologne and Neuss 1863–1880   6 A. GELENIUS, De admiranda sacra, et civili magnitudine Coloniae Claudiae Agrippinensis Augustae Urbis libri IV, Cologne 1645   7 M. GECHTER, S. SCHÜTTE, Ursprung und Voraussetzungen des Kölner Rathauses. Stadtspuren, vol.26, 2000   8 H. G. HORN, Die Römer in Nordrhein-Westfalen, 1987   9 H. KIER, U. KRINGS (eds.), Köln: Die Romanischen Kirchen. Stadtspuren, vol. 1, 1984   10 H. KIER, S. SCHÜTTE (eds.), Archäologie in Köln, vol. 1, 1992   11 J. KLINKENBERG, Das Römische Köln. Die Kunstdenkmäler der Stadt Köln. Section II, 1906 (=P. CLEMEN (ed.), Die Kunstdenkmäler der Rheinprovinzen, vol. 6)   12 B. PÄFFGEN, Die Ausgrabungen in St. Severin zu Köln, 3 vols., 1992 (=Kölner Forschungen, vol 5)   13 RGM der Stadt Köln (ed.), Kölner Jahrbuch für Vor- und Frühgeschichte (subsequently: Kölner Jahrbuch)   14 RGM der Stadt Köln (ed.), Kölner Forschungen (7 vols. to 1993)   15 RGM der Stadt Köln (ed.), Römer Illustrierte, vol. 1, 1974   16 Römisch-Germanisches Zentralmuseum. MAINZ (ed), Führer zu Vor- und Frühgeschichtlichen Denkmälern, vols.37 and 38, 1980   17 S. SCHÜTTE, STEFAN BROELMANN und die Folgen. Karten Kölns, der konstantinischen Rheinbrücke und der römischen Wasserleitung nach Köln aus 380 Jahren, in: Kölner Mus.-Bulletin. Ber. und Forsch. aus den Mus. der Stadt Köln. 1, 1999, 4–26   18 R. SCHULTZE, C. STEUERNAGEL, Colonia Agrippensis. Festschrift der XLIII. Versammlung deutscher Philologen und Schulmänner gewidmet vom Verein von Altertumsfreunden im Rheinlande, Bonn 1895   19 S. SEILER, Die Ausgrabungen im Kölner Stadtteil St. Alban, in: H. KIER, S. SCHÜTTE (eds.), Archäologie in Köln, vol. 1, 1992, 46–55   20 R. THOMAS, Römische Wandmalerei in Köln (= Kölner Forschungen vol. 6), 1993   21 F. F. WALLRAFF, Beiträge zur Geschichte der Stadt Köln und ihrer Umgebungen, Köln 1818, in: L. Ennen, Ausgewählte Schriften von F. F. Wallraf, Köln 1861, 1–59   22 G. WOLFF, Das Römische Köln, Guide, ⁵2000 (rev. ed.).   SVEN SCHÜTTE

III. RÖMISCH-GERMANISCHES MUSEUM

A. HISTORY   B. RÖMISCH-GERMANISCHES MUSEUM

A. HISTORY

C. awoke early to an awareness of its own ancient past. Private collections of local monuments had existed since the 16th cent. That the idea to found a museum evolved from this tradition in the 19th cent. is due to Ferdinand Franz Wallraf (1748–1824) snce after his death his rich collection of Roman and medieval artefacts became the property of the city which then felt itself obliged to erect an appropriate building for the collection. Also, middle class patronage came to the assistance of the building project with a large donation from Johann Heinrich Richartz from C. The opening of the Wallraf Richartz Museum took place in 1861. In addition, private collections were still being built up; the most significant of them, for which we have to thank C.A. Niessen, likewise came into the museum's possession in the 20th cent.

The antiquities of the Wallraf Richartz Museum, whose core collection was made up of stone monuments from Roman imperial times, were set up in the basement and on the ground floor. The works contrasted with the historically medieval architecture which, as a visible point of reference, assigned the antiquities a preparatory role in local history. Because of its outstanding artistic significance, the museum's post-Antiquity collection was granted greater attention by far.

B. RÖMISCH-GERMANISCHES MUSEUM

The RGM's nominal hour of birth in 1946 coincided with the moment when the Dionysos mosaic, which was discovered in 1941 next to the cathedral, was made accessible to the public. From now on, the museum was organizationally independent, and in continuation of existing practice both excavation work as well as a systematic purchasing policy stood the collection in good stead and guaranteed steady expansion.

The invitation to tender bids for a separate building for the RGM took place in 1962, at a time when the Dionysos mosaic was still covered over by a bunker, and a number of objects had found a provisional home in the Alte Wache. The building, which was completed in 1974, triggered divided reactions among experts, but nevertheless it enjoyed wide popularity with visitors right from the beginning. Built immediately adjacent to the cathedral, its structure developed from cubes and its exterior divided into quadratic surfaces forms a vigorous contrast to the filigreed shapes of the church building, especially of the choir. On its completion the museum was nevertheless praised from the point of view of town planning as being in harmony with the city's architecture.

The building corresponded to contemporary maxims of 20th cent. architectural style in the 1970s. It imparts 'lightness' and 'openness' to the outside through the recessed basement above which the upper part, which is built diagonally to the base, appears to hover despite its weighty mass. There was also no façade design since the primary function of the walls is to act as a 'skin' for the interior, not to reflect an image of the latter. The available floor areas, which are spread out on several levels without enclosed units of space ('anonymous succession of space'), permitted a seemingly free arrangement of the exhibits, which are for the most part assembled on plinths ('stages'). Particular emphasis was laid on the fact that the exhibition must not be subsumed to the 'spatial characteristics of a room'. The visitor is offered a maximum of individual experiences of the monuments, whether he moves intellectually on different levels past the monument of Poblicius, or whether he thinks he is able to grasp compacted complexes at a glance.

Those responsible for the exhibition did not dispute that it was a matter of 'staging', and even regarded it as an advantage. In a very similar manner to the presentation of the exhibits, publications, through their selection of topics and treatment of subject matter, sought to remove the distance between them and the reader.

1 H. BORGER et al., Colonia antiqua, 1977 2 F. FREMERS-DORF, Die Neuaufstellung der Römischen Abteilung des Wallraf-Richartz-Museums zu Köln, in: Westdeutsche Monatshefte 1, 1925, 43–59; 3 Katalog des Museums Wallraf-Richartz in Köln. Verzeichniss der Gemäldesammlung. Verzeichniss der römischen Alterthümer Cologne 1862 4 Kölner Römer-Illustrierte 1, 1974 5 H. KIER, F. G. ZEHNDER (eds.), Lust und Verlust. Kölner Sammler zwischen Trikolore und Preußenadler (exhibition catalogue), 1995 6 A. KRUG, Antike Gemmen im RGM Köln, 1981 7 I. LINFERT-REICH, Römisches Alltagsleben in Köln, ¹1975, ³1977 8 P. NOELKE, Im Banne der Medusa. Die Antikensammlung. Ferdinand Franz Wallrafs, in: Kölner Jb. 26, 1993, 133–216 9 Id., Statuen haben auch ihr Schicksal. Zwei neuerworbene Togasta-tuen im RGM zu Köln, in: Kölner Mus.-Bulletin 4, 1998, 42–63 10 G. PRECHT, Das Grabmal des L. Poblicius. Rekonstruktion und Aufbau, 1975.   DETLEV KREIKENBOM

Column/Monumental Column

A. INTERPRETATIO CHRISTIANA OF ILLUSTRATED
COLUMNS   B. PERSONALISED COLUMNS
C. SPOLIA COLUMNS IN BUILDING

A. INTERPRETATIO CHRISTIANA OF ILLUS-TRATED COLUMNS

Whether in architectural contexts or isolated as monumental columns, scarcely any building element in post-classical times is linked so closely with reference to Antiquity as the column. This is true both positively, in the sense of a conscious *renovatio* of Classical or Christian Antiquity, and negatively, in connexion with idols as the embodiment of vanquished paganism.

Columns with standing 'idols', mostly nude, became almost a topos in the art of the later Middle Ages and the Renaissance. In many representations (e.g. the Flight to Egypt) the overcrowded illustrated column makes the collapse of paganism particularly graphic. In Piero della Francesca's panel painting of the Scourging of Christ in Urbino the illustrated column and its idol are identical with the Scourging Column of the Passion of Christ (Fig. 1), in order to demonstrate the cause and the purpose of the Passion. From 1223, the stump of a column was venerated in Santa Prassede in Rome as a relic of the Scourging Column that was supposed to have been imported from Jerusalem by way of Constantinople. Since the 14th cent. the same provenance had also been ascribed to the column known as the Colonna Santa, which was venerated in Saint Peter's in Rome and was considered to be the column on which Christ had leaned during the Sermon in the Temple. This was a column wreathed in vine-tendrils, one of a series of six, which Constantine had acquired as → SPOLIA from Greece to decorate the grave of Saint Peter, and which Pope Gregory III (731–741) then doubled to twelve. Their form and their marble were already admired in the early Middle Ages, yet of course the formation of its legend began only later: from the 12th cent. on, when the first copies were made in the circle of Roman *marble-masons*, they were believed to

Fig. 1: Piero della Francesca, *The Flagellation*. Panel painting, *c.* 1450. Urbino,
Galleria Nazionale delle Marche.
Copyright by Zeitschrift für Kunstgeschichte (Aachen/Basel)

have come from the Temple of Apollo at Troy. 200
years later, they were considered as spolia from the
Temple of Solomon in Jerusalem and so became a connecting link between the Old Testament, antiquity, the
triumph of the early church, and the present. Beginning
at Rome towards the end of the 15th cent., this column
then began to be widely accepted in art and architectural treatises, although the latter occurred almost exclusively in Italy [9]. Bernini's presentation in the newly
built Saint Peter's was outstanding, and provided new
impetus for further reception: here, he transformed the
ancient columns used to frame the reliquary tabernacle
into transept pillars, and formally linked old and new
with the bronze columns of the Baldachin over the tomb
of Saint Peter. These, however, are recognisable simultaneously as innovations and as copies of Constantine's
spiral columns.

Another way of symbolising the triumph over paganism by means of columns consisted in seizing upon
illustrated columns. The rather bizarre phenomenon of
quasi-animated illustrated columns in the form of column saints remained limited to the early Byzantine
East. In the West, bn contrast, statues of revered saints
were already placed on columns at the beginnings of the
resurgent grand sculpture of the High Middle Ages.
Bishop Stephen of Clermont-Ferrand, who in the
middle of the 10th cent. had had one of the earliest
attested statues of Mary made, had placed it on a
marble column behind the altar for reverence and admiration [1]. It remains unclear whether this should be

understood as a conscious Christianisation of ancient
monumental columns. It is clear, however, that this is
the case for the Column of Bernward (*c.* 1020, Hildesheim Cathedral), where Trajan's Emperor Column is
transformed into a column of Christ, and then in the
Counter-Reformation, when ancient triumphal and votive monuments were taken up by means of columns of
Mary [4]. Also under the banner of the Counter-Reformation was the raising of gilded bronze statues of the
Princes of the Apostles on the Roman honorific
columns of Trajan and Marcus Aurelius: they had belonged among the *mirabilia* since the High Middle
Ages, and now, by Papal order in 1587/88, they were to
convert the ancient triumphal symbolism manifest in
the columns into a Christian one (→ TRAJAN'S COL-
UMN).

Alongside this Christian tradition of victory and
memorial columns, there had already been a secular one
since the High Middle Ages [5]. In 1072 the Norman
duke Robert Guiscard had marble columns brought to
his Apulian homeland 'in signum victoriae suae' from
the conquered Arab residential city of Palermo (MGH
SS 19,407), but their location remains unknown. This
was not the case for the porphyry columns, which just
50 years later, according to Giovanni Villani, the city of
Florence received from neighbouring Pisa later as
thanks for services rendered and in memory of the victory over the Saracens. They still stand in front of the
Florentine Baptisterium today (and so may allude to the
columns *Jachin* and *Boaz*, which stood in front of the

Fig. 2: Chartres, Cathedral. Portal figures of the western façade, central and right portal, *c.* 1145.
Photograph H.R. Meier

Temple of Solomon). Like the illustrated pillars in front of Saint Mark's in Venice, this is a case of spolia, as is revealed not least by their foreign material. In contrast, the corresponding monuments of modern times are usually new constructions, which, from a formal viewpoint, return to the corresponding ancient columns. This was the case for Sir Christopher Wren's *Monument* commemorating the Fire of London in 1666, as it was for the column glorifying Napoleon in Place Vendôme at Paris, and the Victory Column with its crowning statue of Victoria placed in front of the Reichstag Building in Berlin in 1873, which was augmented and removed to its present site in the Tiergarten in 1938 as a part of National Socialist plans for monumental reconstruction of the capital of the Reich.

B. Personalised Columns

Although the above examples of Christian interpretation of single ancient columns first began in the late Middle Ages, the allegorical interpretation of columns as human forms goes far back into Antiquity, and through the Biblical exegesis of the Church Fathers it experienced an early Christian flourishing, which was to become particularly important for mediaeval architectural allegory. The naming of the above-mentioned Mary Columns as 'Columnae Novae Legis' and 'Columnae Fidei' is significant in this regard, and it had an influence on later emblematics, where the column became a sign of strength of belief and trust in God, as well as in the attributes of the virtue *Fortitudo* [4]. The identification of columns with the Apostles (later also

Fig. 3: Magdeburg, cathedral choir, first half of the 13th cent.

the Prophets), which support the *Ecclesia*, became more important for architectural exegesis. Exemplary was the interpretation of the columns in the new choir of the Abbey-Church of Saint Denis by Abbot Suger in the middle of the 12th cent.: *Medium quippe duodecim columpne duodenarium apostolorum exponentes numerum, secundario uero totidem alarum columpne prophetarum numerum significantes* ... ('However, the middle of the building was suddenly raised up by twelve columns representing the twelve apostles, and secondly by the same number of columns in the aisles signifying the number of prophets', *De Consecratione*, 58). In view of such interpretations, it was a small step to further personalise columns and to enclose relics in them or in their capitals, as is attested e.g. for Saint Michael's in Hildesheim, the Cathedral of Magdeburg, but also for far less significant churches such as Saint Angelo's in Spata in Viterbo. Finally, one of the motives for the column figure developed in the Île-de-France in the 12th cent., where the portal columns were given human form (Fig. 2), might have been to illustrate the identification of column and person.

C. Spolia Columns in Building

Probably the most immediate connexion with Antiquity was realised in mediaeval architecture by use of ancient spolia columns, already alluded to several times above. Scholars dispute whether this phenomenon was connected, already in late ancient architecture, with an idea of *renovatio* [6]. The situation is different for the Carolingian period: Charlemagne's programmatic intentions are apparent from the fact that his new imperial palace in Aachen was fitted out with columns from Rome and Ravenna. In view of the enormous logistical cost, it is evident that what was important for Charlemagne was the origin of the columns, and not just their ancient provenance or material, as it was later for Bishop Gerard of Cambrai, who in the 11th cent. had 'lapides columnares' dug up near his city in order to expedite the building of his new cathedral. The vitality of the topos of Rome and the efforts undertaken for its realisation also become clear from the report of Abbot Desiderius of Monte Cassino, who went to Rome in 1086/87 in connexion with his new abbey church, 'where he got in touch with his best friends and paid a lot of money to acquire numerous columns (...) of various colours and have them transported by ship down the Tiber to Campania' (MGH SS VII, S. 717). Accounts of similar efforts are often transmitted: for instance, Emperor Otto the Great also ennobled his new cathedral building in Magdeburg with a set of ancient columns. In the rebuilding of the cathedral in the 13th cent., these spolia, which now also reminded people of their predecessors, were used in the choir in a manner that did not correspond to the canon of Gothic architecture, and so made the columns stand out in a particularly striking way (Fig. 3), a procedure that can also be observed at approximately the same time in Saint Lorenzo's in Naples. A decline in the use of spolia

columns can generally be observed In late mediaeval architecture, but even in the Renaissance ancient columns were reused in Rome, which rejoiced in spolia. Here, too, however, reference to antiquity subsequently took the form of adherence to classical → COLUMNIATION, rather than that of the reuse of ancient materials, so that anticlassical polemics at that time (e.g. the young Goethe, *Von Deutscher Baukunst, D. M. Ervini a Steinbach*, 1773) turned against column architecture in general. Columns were attributed scant significance in the architecture of the → MODERN AGE (cf., in contrast, the skyscraper project in the form of a gigantic Doric column by Adolf Loos for the *Chicago Tribune* in 1922), whereas in the Post-Modern period they were once again introduced emblematically (e.g. in Charles Moore's *Piazza d'Italia* in New Orleans), but were sometimes also ironically broken (cf. the baldachins with spolia columns in the house by the same architect in Orinda).

→ Column; → Monumental Column; → Spolia; → Stylite

SOURCES: 1 R. RIGODON, Vision de Robert, abbé de Mozat, au sujet de la basilique de la Mère de Dieu, in: Bulletin historique et scientifique de l'Auvergne 70, 1950, 55

LITERATURE: 2 G. BANDMANN, Mittelalterliche Architektur als Bedeutungsträger, 1951 3 W. HAFTMANN, Das italienische Säulenmonument, 1939 4 S. JOHN, s. v. 'Säule', in: Marienlexikon vol. 5, 1993, 620–626 5 H. R. MEIER, Vom Siegeszeichen zum Lüftungsschacht, in: Id., M. WOHLLEBEN (ed.), Bauten und Orte als Träger von Erinnerung, 2000, 87–98 6 J. POESCHKE (ed.) Antike Spolien in der Architektur des Mittelalters und der Renaissance, 1996 7 B. REUDENBACH, Säule und Apostel, in: FMS 14, 1980, 310–351 8 J. RYKWERT, The Dancing Column, 1996 9 H.-W. SCHMIDT, Die gewundene Säule in der Architekturtheorie von 1500 bis 1800, 1978

ADDITIONAL BIBLIOGRAPHY: ONIANS, JOHN Bearers of Meaning: The Classical Orders in Antiquity, the Middle Ages, and the Renaissance, 1988.   HANS-RUDOLF MEIER

Columniation

A. DEFINITION, CHARACTERISATION   B. HISTORY

A. DEFINITION, CHARACTERISATION

The term *columniation* is used to denote a fundamental element of form in ancient and classical modern architecture, comprising the supporting element of the column and the supported element of the horizontal entablature. Unlike other support and articulation systems, columniation is governed by fixed formal and proportional rules: a column of human proportion (→ PROPORTIONS, THEORY OF) consists of a base, a shaft and a capital, and an entablature of an architrave, a frieze and a cornice. Whereas freestanding columns in ancient temples have an architectural function, the half-columns or pilasters which mask the walls of many modern buildings reproduce only a semblance of the basic tectonic principles of bearing and loading. The description of Doric, Ionic and Corinthian temples by

Fig. 1: Filippo Brunelleschi,
nave of San Lorenzo, Florence.
Begun 1419

Vitruvius, the theoretician of ancient architecture, influenced the naming of individual elements and the classification into various kinds of columniation, corresponding to the structure of the details. In Antiquity, however, neither the general concept of columniation current in modern times nor the canonical system of the 'Five Orders' was known [17]. Across countries, styles and periods, the theory of columniation has formed a kernel of architectural theory since the → RENAISSANCE, with which building architecture has always stood in tense interrelation.

B. HISTORY
1. MIDDLE AGES   2. ITALIAN RENAISSANCE: THE CANON OF THE FIVE ORDERS   3. THE RENAISSANCE OUTSIDE ITALY   4. BAROQUE
5. CLASSICISM   6. 20TH CENT.

1. MIDDLE AGES
Understanding of ancient columniation appears to have been mostly lost in the Middle Ages. It is true that from early Christian times columns were imitated more and more, even to the point of using ancient → SPOLIA, as for instance in the 12th and 13th cent. basilicas in Rome. However, with a few exceptions (e.g. Florence, Baptisterium, 11th cent.) the tectonic relationship with the entablature was not maintained, and columns were integrated into mediaeval articulation and arch systems (Pisa, cathedral, 1063–1121).

2. ITALIAN RENAISSANCE: THE CANON OF THE FIVE ORDERS
Thanks to the interest of the Italian Humanists and architects in ancient building and Vitruvius's treatise, columniation was rediscovered in the 15th cent. The Florentine Filippo Brunelleschi was the first architect of post-Antiquity to recognise the tectonic principle of columniation, and he took the epoch-making step of transferring it from ancient temples to contemporary buildings such as churches and palaces (Florence, Saint Lorenzo's, begun in 1419, Fig. 1) [9]. An exact differentiation of the various kinds of Vitruvian columniation still played no role in the 15th cent., other than for the erudite Florentine Humanist and architect Leon Battista Alberti, who accomplished an accurate description of columniation in his architectural treatise (1452). It was not until the beginning of the 16th cent. that Donato Bramante used four distinguishable classical orders for his Roman buildings (Tempietto of Saint Pietro in Montorio, 1502, reconstruction of Saint Peter's, from 1506).

Following detailed study of Antiquity, the next generation of architects, including Raphael, Baldassare Peruzzi and Antonio da Sangallo the Elder, then developed the canonical system of Five Orders, which was published and thus made known throughout Europe by Serlio in 1537 (Fig. 2). The fundamental idea of this canon, which extended the three Vitruvian orders to include the Tuscan and Composite orders, was a specific arrangement for each member of each order on the hierarchical principle that the orders, in the sequence Tuscan, Doric, Ionic, Corinthian and Composite with proportions of from 1:6 to 1:10 (column diameter) were increasingly more slender and richer. In this way the ancient heritage was converted into a new, rationally comprehensible system which could be translated into any architectonic context, isolated from the paradigm of temples, i.e. which could be used both in the fashioning of walls and in connexion with arch and vault constructions (Antonio da Sangallo the Younger, Rome, Palazzo Farnese, from 1513; Andrea Palladio, Vicenza, Basilica, from 1549). For multi-storey buildings, a vertical alignment of columniation in the canonical sequence was preferred (Superposition). The essential meanings of columniation formulated by Vitruvius in the context of his 'decorum'- rules for a design commensurate with the social, political and religious func-

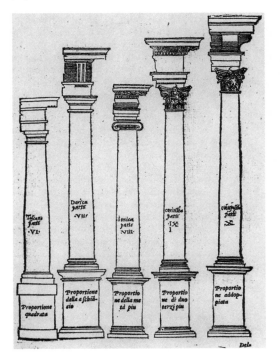

Fig. 2: Sebstiano Serlio, *The Five Orders.*
Regole generali di architettura, IV, Venice 1537

tion of the building – were given a Christian reinterpretation. The Doric order, for example, was appropriate for Christ and male saints, the Ionic for female saints, and the Corinthian for the Virgin Mary.

The subsequent Italian theoreticians Vignola (1562), Andrea Palladio (1570) and Vincenzo Scamozzi (1615) confirmed the canon of columniation, and dedicated themselves primarily to the question of proportionality. The easily applied modular system developed by Vignola for calculating the correct ratios in practical building was particularly successful. In his villa projects, Palladio demonstrated the theoretically justified transference of ancient temple fronts to houses (Vicenza, Villa Rotonda, *c.* 1567) [17].

In contrast, Michelangelo and Giulio Romano broke the rules of the Renaissance in some buildings by their unconventional relationship with columniation, and their invention of new individual elements (Florence, Biblioteca Laurenziana, 1524–1526; Mantua, Palazzo Tè, 1524–1534). In the Conservator's Palace on the Capitol in Rome in 1546, Michelangelo for the first time replaced organization by storeys with a truly Colossal arrangement, unifying all storeys, a solution that paved the way to Baroque architecture.

3. The Renaissance outside Italy
Following Serlio's isolated publication on column theory, numerous 'column books' appeared outside Italy, especially in Germany and the Low Countries. Like the buildings themselves, however, and except from a few works which still maintained strong Italian

influence (Jean Bullant, 1546; Hans Blum, 1550), these departed from the Classical models for want of direct familiarity with Antiquity and the Italian Renaissance, and adapted columniation to the contemporary northern European stylistic sensibility by combining it with phantastical ornamentation (Vredemann de Vries, 1565; Dietterlin, 1598; Heidelberg, Schloß, Ottheinrichsbau, 1556–1560) [8]. Philibert Delorme, the most significant French Renaissance theoretician, added a sixth, French national order to the canon [13].

In England, unlike in other northern European countries, architectural theory and practice from the end of the 16th until into the 18th cent. was influenced predominantly by Palladio (Inigo Jones, London, Banqueting House, 1619–1622; Colen Campbell, *Vitruvius Britannicus*, 1725).

4. Baroque
Although the column theory canonised in the Renaissance theoretically retained its validity in the Baroque, and even supplied the basic vocabulary for building practice, architects first in Italy and later also in Central Europe cultivated a freer relationship with traditional columniation, to the point of carrying out innovative transformations. By means of rhythmic grouping, graduation and rotation, combined with strong entablature mouldings, columniation was introduced as never before, to accentuate building components and portions of façades and spaces, as well as to develop lively sculpted wall reliefs (Gianlorenzo Bernini, Rome, Palazzo -Odescalchi, 1664; Pietro da Cortona, Rome, Saint Luca and Saint Martina's, 1635–1650; Balthasar Neumann, Wallfahrtskirche Vierzehnheiligen, 1743–1772). The preferred variety of rich Corinthian or Composite orders was occasionally distinguished by phantastical capital variants with symbolic motifs. With his unusual capital inventions and pierced or upturned entablatures, Francesco Borromini even questioned the Vitruvian canon (Rome, Oratorio e Casa di San Filippo Neri, 1637–1650).

From a theoretical viewpoint, only Guarino Guarini reacted to this changed relationship with columniation: at the same time, he was also the first to recognise the Gothic order, while for the Solomonic order introduced by Villalpando's reconstruction of the Temple in Jerusalem (1596), he adopted the torsion of the legendary spiral columns of Saint Peter's in Rome. From the late 17th cent. on, theoreticians of every country applied themselves more and more to inventing national orders [13].

In France, theorists of Classical architecture defended the traditional theory of columns against the influences of the Italian High-Baroque, and later against Rococo as well, and discussed the acceptable degree of freedom for new inventions and the 'correct' concept of proportion (cf. the dispute between François Blondel the Younger and Claude Perrault concerning the coupled columns of the eastern façade of the Louvre, 1667) [7]. Not all authors went as far as Fréart de Chambray (1650), who dogmatically demanded a return to the three Greek orders of Doric, Ionic and Corinthian. From the second half of the 17th cent., a strict concept of 'decorum', allowing complete columniation only for high public or sacred types of building, often led to façade arrangements with reduced columniation or even without any, particularly in private *palais* in France [15].

5. CLASSICISM

During the 18th cent., traditional column theory was increasingly brought into question. Led by Marc-Antoine Laugier and his famous essay on primitive 'cabanes' (1753), theoreticians of aesthetic effect denied columniation its sense-giving significance as a motif of wall elements and accepted it only as a truly constructional component of architecture. The famous parody of columniation by William Hogarth compared it to wigs: *The Five Orders of Periwigs*, engraving, 1761. In addition, European architects were enlightened both by the rediscovery of the temples of → PAESTUM and Sicily in about 1750, and by the publication of James Stuart and Nicholas Revett's survey of the ancient buildings of Athens (1762; → SOCIETY OF DILETTANTI). It discussed the characteristics of Greek architecture and its Doric order, which was distinguished by lack of a base, fluted shaft and stouter proportions. In a return to ancient Greek architecture (→ GREEK REVIVAL), many buildings appeared in England, France and Germany from the late 18th cent. with Doric porticos, often in front of the unstructured body of the building (Karl Friedrich Schinkel, Berlin, Neue Wache, 1816).

6. 20TH CENT.

The new building materials that had appeared since the mid–19th cent. – concrete, steel and glass, together with the conscious renunciation of historical style in all stylistic trends, characteristic of the turn of the century, whether in Jugendstil or in the influential rationalistic Bauhaus concept of architecture, all but completely banished columniation from architecture (J. M. Olbrich, Vienna, Sezessionsgebäude, 1897–98; W. Gropius, Bauhaus in Dessau, 1919–1926). The buildings of Peter Behrens are among the few exceptions (Saint Petersburg, German embassy, 1911–12). Their columniation (columns without base or capital, entablature without moulding), inspired by Antiquity but simultaneously completely abstract, adopted Fascist and National Socialist architecture in monumentalized form (Albert Speer, Berlin, new Reichs-Chancery, 1938–39, destroyed; Marcello Piacentini & al., Rome, buildings for the World Exposition EUR, 1936–1942; → FASCISM, → MODERN AGE, → NATIONAL SOCIALISM II. ART AND ARCHITECTURE).

In the so-called Post-Modern architecture of the late 20th cent., columniation again finds application, but mostly in the form of arbitrary and abstract theatrical settings (James Stirling & al., Stuttgart, Staatsgalerie, 1977–1984).

→ Angle triglyph problem; → Epistylion;→ Column
→ ARCHITECTURAL THEORY/VITRUVIANISM

1 J. ACKERMAN, The Tuscan/Rustic Order: A Study in the Metaphorical Language of Architecture, in: Journal of Society of Architectural Historians 42, 1983, 15–34 2 J. CROOK, The Greek Revival, 1972 3 F. DEICHMANN, Säule und Ordnung in frühchristlicher Architektur, in: MDAI(R) 55, 1940, 114–130 4 C. DENKER Nesselrath, Die Säulenordnung bei Bramante, 1990 5 E. FORSSMAN, Säule und Ornament, 1956 6 Id., Dorisch, Ionisch, Korinthisch: Studien über den Gebrauch der Säulenordnung in der Architektur des 16.–18. Jahrhunderts, 1961 7 G. GERMANN, Einführung in die Geschichte der Architekturtheorie, 1987 8 H. GÜNTHER (ed.), Deutsche Architekturtheorie zwischen Gotik und Renaissance, 1988 9 H. GÜNTHER, C. THOENES, Gli ordini arcitettonici: rinascita o invenzione?, in: Roma e l'Antico nell' arte e nella cultura del Cinquecento, 1985, 261–310 10 J. GUILLAUME (ed.), L'emploi des ordres dans l'architecture de la Renaissance, 1992 11 H.-W. KRUFT, Geschichte der Architekturtheorie, 1985 (with detailed bibliography) 12 J. ONIANS, Bearers of Meaning: The Classical Orders in Antiquity, the Middle Ages and the Renaissance, 1988 13 J. M. PEROUSE de Montclos, Le Sixième Ordre de l'Architecture, ou la Pratique des Ordres suivant les Nations, in: Journal of the Society of Architectural Historians 36, 1977, 223–240 14 U. SCHÜTTE, Ordnung und Verzierung. Untersuchung zur deutschsprachigen Architekturtheorie des 18. Jahrhunderts, 1986 15 Id., 'Als wenn eine ganze Ordnung da stünde...'. Anmerkungen zum System der Säulenordnung und seiner Auflösung im späten 18. Jahrhundert, in: Zschr. für Kunstgesch. 44, 1981, 15–37 16 J. SUMMERSON, The Classical Language of Architecture, 1980 17 C. THOENES, Vignolas 'regola delli cinque ordini', in: Röm. Jb. für Kunstgesch. 20, 1983, 345–376 18 M. WILSON JONES, E. DWYER, S. L. SANABRIA, M. LYTELTON, N. COLDSTREAM, s. v. Orders, architectural, in: J. TURNER (ed.), The Dictionary of Art, vol. 23, 1996, 477–494.   ANNA ELISABETH WERDEHAUSEN

Comedy

A. METHODOLOGY B. TAXONOMY C. HISTORY

A. METHODOLOGY

Modern European comedy arose from the adaptation and transformation of ancient comedy, to which was added -sporadically – the influence of autochthonous forms and institutions of 'carnivalesque' play. In its further development it took continual recourse to the forms and concepts of ancient comedy. In addition to straightforward adaptations, indirect influence was exerted where specific forms and types of comedy that were derived from ancient models – such as the commedia dell'arte – became highly influential in their own right and were thus able to transmit their ancient heritage. Roman comedy was already an example of indirect reception, but the mediating link – the comedies of Menander – was missing: the rediscovered comedy *Dyscolus* was not published until the mid–20th cent. (1959); fragments of other plays by Menander have since been added. As a rule, when establishing the history of reception for any text, the occurrence of analogous phenomena does not necessarily prove that a process of reception has taken place. Specific forms of comedy (e.g. metatheatre, the neutralization of established hierarchies, play-within-a-play structures), specific plot patterns (e.g. the provocation of derision), specific character types (e.g. the Foolish Old Man, the Clever Slave or Servant) or specific character constellations (e.g. young lovers in conflict with the older generation) are found both in ancient and in modern comedies. A reception of ancient patterns need therefore not be present, since these forms and models refer to conditions or needs that are either anthropologically or socially constant, or else are essential components of comedy itself. One can speak of a reception of ancient comedy with greater certainty when not merely a single element but an entire set of elements or an elaborate subject matter rather than a single motif is appropriated

B. Taxonomy

According to the nature and extent of the fields in which reference is made to ancient comedy, various types of reception can be distinguished. There is integrative reception when a set of elements of ancient comedy is adapted in a specific arrangement, or a material formed in Antiquity is continued, or contemporary plot, character or language patterns are combined using constitutive moments of ancient comedy. Such constitutive moments are: first of all, the orgiastic aspect which annihilates the principle of distinction. It is rooted in the 'komos', the festive-ecstatic procession of a wandering crowd in the service of Dionysus, god of intoxication. Considered to be the origin of comedy, the 'komos' is provided by the latter with the structural support inherent in its institutional, dramaturgical and overall poetic organization. The rejection of the universal – of the concept – also belongs to comedy. Its principle is singularisation, whether it refers to people or things, to the point of rejecting every kind of 'firmness and control'. On the level of plot, singularisation corresponds to the episodic principle, the centring in the isolated case, which can be formed into a 'plot' only through recourse to an order situated beyond this comicality (for instance, a narrative order or the established combination and succession of speech forms in Old Attic comedy). With regard to plot, another constitutive moment is that of self-reflexivity (manifesting itself in play-within-a-play structures): each conflict is solved by confronting its originator with himself, i.e. the comic plot observes itself. From a pragmatic point of view, another constitutive element of comedy since Antiquity has been not only the act of elevating the oppressed, the release of a claim to pleasure that is usually channelled into a system of order, but also the act of degradation: the aggression of derision, which is, to be sure, not 'fatal'. The beaten body, which appears in some kind of modification in every comedy, rises again and is immortal. The act of reversal – integral to derisive, contrastive comedy – has always invited didactic functionalisation (within a social or individual pedagogical frame).

There is selective reception when isolated elements are adopted, for instance the principle of transgression, embodied in the parabasis (in Old Attic comedy, the illusion of the performance was broken when the chorus stepped forward to address the actual audience). This is the origin of such comedy techniques as improvisation (which went on to determine the structure of the commedia dell'arte) and extemporization (attempts were made, especially in the 19th cent., to reign in the latter as an anarchic moment of comedy). The event character of theatrical action is accentuated by the parabasis: the physical presence of the players in the here and now (as opposed to the world presented in the play), and with it comedy's characteristic resistance against the hegemony of the text in the theatre. A further element subject to isolated reception is the plot based on a (fantastic) invention, particularly in the tradition of Aristophanes. The comedial moments of the fantastic, of wit and surprise derive from this principle of invention. Masks and masques have a paradoxical dimension. Masks create distance, representing the principle of distinction; at the same time something that is surging up against it is held back, which in turn links masks to the principle of metamorphosis. Yet another element of ancient comedy that is susceptible to isolated reception, this time on the level of plot, is the ending that hints at marriage – essentially an affirmation of the body breaking out of its fixed boundaries, ready to enter into contact or a union with other bodies. One last element of ancient comedy that is susceptible to isolated reception is its diversity of media: song and dance, both constitutive moments of the 'komos', are added to the dramatic presentation.

There is derivative reception when moments of ancient comedy are adapted by way of forms that are themselves standing in the tradition of ancient comedy, but have become independent of their origin and have acquired their own history of influence. The most conspicuous example of such a process of reception is the transmission of ancient comedy through the commedia dell'arte. Also worth mentioning is the 'farce with songs' of the Vienna Volkstheater, which led to the development of the operetta and the musical – a testament to the continued influence of the 'cantica', the quite significant portions of sung passages in Plautine comedy. A further example is given by the figurations of the Melancholic and the Fool, facilitating figures in the comedial world of Shakespeare, in which the principles of invention and transgression of ancient comedy continue to be influential (in the figure of the Fool – along with his biblical tradition) as well as in the borderline figure who must always be included (the Melancholic), but who is in opposition to the comedial world.

C. History

1. Late Antiquity 2. Middle Ages 3. 14th –
16th Cents.: Development of Modern Comedy in Italy 4. 15th – 17th Cent. Germany
5. 16th and 17th Cent. France 6. 16th and
17th Cent. England 7. Reception after the
18th Cent.

1. Late Antiquity

Plautus and Terence received commentaries. The
Terence commentary by the grammarian Aelius Donatus (4th cent. AD) also contains notes on the stage performance of the plays. Both authors, as mediators of an
'elegant' Latin, were used as school authors.

2. Middle Ages

Terence remained a literary model. Terence manuscripts of the Carolingian period were in part furnished
with illustrations of scenes (probably copied from versions of Late Antiquity). In the 10th cent., the canoness
Hroswitha of Gandersheim (935–973) wrote six comedies – Latin reading dramas (dramatisations of legends
or stories of martyrs) – as a Christian substitute for the
plays of Terence: a unique appropriation of ancient
drama in the Middle Ages, when drama was known
only in the guise of ecclesiastical miracle or mystery
plays. In the 12th cent., Vitalis of Blois adapted plays by
Plautus (including *Amphitruo* in the Latin comedy
Geta).

3. 14th – 16th Cents.: Development of
Modern Comedy in Italy

Roman comedies (especially those of Terence) were
read in schools, both as linguistic models and for the
ethics expressed in them (the ideal of '*humanitas*').
With orientation on the plays and performances of individual pieces of Plautus and Terence, as well as a
number of Seneca's (in the field of tragedy), the rebirth
of drama and the reestablishment of the institution of
theatre took place. The predominance of Terence in
comedy declined after Nicholas of Cusa discovered in
1429 twelve more plays by Plautus, in addition to the
eight that were known throughout the Middle Ages.

In the Quattrocento, new Latin comedies were written in the tradition of the Roman comedy, which had
been continued by readings and performances of individual plays by Plautus and Terence in Rome, Venice
and Ferrara. This was the 'commedia umanistica' type.
Among the dramatists were Pier Paolo Vergerio, Ugo-
lino Pisani, Pietro Aretino and Aeneas Silvius Piccolomini (Pope Pius II). In the Renaissance, Plautus was especially popular. There were numerous translations of
both Plautus and Terence into Italian, increasingly with
intermezzi inserted into them, and these then took on a
life of their own. In Ferrara and Mantua in the Cinquecento a 'commedia erudita', now written in Italian,
developed out of the commedia umanistica and the
intermezzi. Its main representatives were Publio Filippo
Mantovano, Ariosto, Bernardo Dovizi da Bibbiena,
Benedetto Varchi, Angelo Beolco, and Machiavelli. His
comedy *La Clizia* (1525) has Plautus' *Casina* as a mod-

el; Machiavelli's comedy *La Mandragola* (c. 1518) can
be viewed as the first Italian Renaissance comedy independent of ancient models.

The most significant element connecting ancient
(Latin) comedy, Italian Renaissance comedy and European baroque and bourgeois comedy was the commedia dell'arte. As improvisational theatre it was based
not on fully formulated texts but on patterns of plot; it
emphasised the physicality of acting (acrobatics as an
element of artistic performance), accentuating the presence in the here and now, which is of course a manifestation the Dionysian carnivalistic aspect of comedy and
of the moment of parabasis. In the *lazzi* there is a return
to the Aristophanic moment of invention, and in the
witty dialogue, the concetti, the verbal wit of Aristophanes and Plautus. The first evidence of a commedia
dell'arte being performed dates to 1545 [25. 10]. Its
disappearance from the stage around 1750 coincided
with the historical situation when the bourgeoisie started to dominate the theatre. The theatrical troupes of
the commedia dell'arte shaped and conveyed the understanding and experience of 'comedy' throughout
Europe. The origins or, rather, the sources of the commedia dell'arte cannot be clearly established (without
doubt the commedia erudita, but also Roman comedy,
e.g. in the re-shaping of character types such as transformation of the *miles gloriosus* into the 'Capitano', the
senex type into Pantalone and Graziano, the slave character into Harlequin; possibly elements of the Roman
improvisational comedy, the Atellana, were involved as
well). Each theory of origin depends on what is being
defined as an essential component of the commedia
dell'arte. The commedia dell'arte is closer to Plautus
than to Terence, to his theatricality and musicality, his
verbal wit and his enthusiasm for farce. In accentuating
sensuality, which is to say physical presence, it is close
to parabasis and, in general, to the Dionysian element
of Aristophanic comedy. For all this, however, contemporary phenomena can also be identified: carnival customs, subjects of the commedia erudita, the jokes, the
lazzi, the physical acrobatics, and the element of improvisation without artifice could also have been introduced by contemporary quacks, jesters and other per-
formers at the annual fairs.

Aristophanes' posthumous fame was based on reading; this was the case with Hellenistic philologists and
during the Byzantine period. The plays that were favoured before the 18th cent. were *Plutos*, being easy to read
and pedagogically useful, *The Clouds*, because of
Socrates' appearance in it and *The Frogs*, because the
three great tragedians appear in it. In 15th cent. Italy,
Aristophanes was translated into Latin. The first printed edition of his plays (nine of the eleven surviving,
omitting *Lysistrata* and *The Thesmophoriazousai*) was
published by Aldus Manutius in Venice in 1498.

4. 15th – 17th Cent. Germany

Latin and Greek comedies were read in the schools.
Terence was often translated. As in Italy, a Latin Humanist comedy emerged from ancient models, which in

turn developed into an independent German comedy, for instance Jakob Wimpheling's *Stylpho* (1480) and Johannes Reuchlin's *Henno* (1497), both modelled on Terence. Melanchthon wrote prologues to four comedies by Terence and one by Plautus. The study of Aristophanes began in Germany with an edition of *Plutos* (Hagenau 1517). Erasmus of Rotterdam placed Aristophanes first among the Greek poets to be read by students, even above Homer and Euripides (but only because Menander was thought to be lost). Reuchlin gave a lecture in 1520 on Aristophanes' *Plutos* and Melanchthon edited it in 1528 together with *The Clouds*. One important mediator of ancient comedy, who also gave impulses to German comedy, was Nikodemus Frischlin (1547–1590). A Greek edition of Aristophanes prepared by him appeared in 1586. It contained *Plutos, The Clouds, The Frogs, The Acharnians, The Knights*, with Latin translations attempting a precise rendition of the metre. In the foreword there is a notable definition of the chorus as being located *inter actum et actum*. Thus the plays were divided into acts, with choral songs marking the ends of the acts. Frischlin defended Aristophanes against the criticism of Plutarch. His own comedies (*Frau Wendelgard* 1579; *Phasma* 1580 and *Julius Redivivus* 1582, both in Latin) absorb traits of Aristophanic comedy in their sharp caricaturisation and their method of associating characters with idiomatic language. The plays were successful, as they combined learned Humanist drama with popular theatre. Hans Sachs, who was primarily influenced by the traditional carnival play, also adapted ancient tragedies and generally drew considerable material inspiration from ancient authors. The great distance from the originals (owing to the use of translations or only indirectly) also gave rise to criticism from his contemporaries (e.g. Jonas Bitner).

With the plays of Andreas Gryphius German-language comedy won its independence. The learned Gryphius was acquainted with the ancient comedy authors. His own comedies, however, were more strongly rooted in the commedia dell'arte. His early comedy *Horribilicribrifax* (written between 1647 and 1650) demonstrates a successful appropriation of the two comedy traditions within the intellectual horizon of his own time. The character of the Capitano/*miles gloriosus* became the figure of reflexion in Baroque representation.

5. 16TH AND 17TH CENT. FRANCE

French comedy arose through the adoption of both ancient and Italian comedy (Ariosto, Bibiena, Firenzuola). Plays by Terence and Plautus were often translated in the 16th cent., as were comedies by Aristophanes. In the 1549 publication outlining the programme of the → PLÉIADE, du Bellay called for an adaptation of ancient works which would transpose them into French. The most eminent author of the period, Pierre de Larivey (1550–1612), confessed himself to be a conscious imitator of Greek, Latin and modern Italian comedy; both Molière and Regnard drew inspiration from him. In the early 17th cent., in addition to the Italian influence, the more complex Spanish comedy began have an effect on French comedy, especially on Corneille. Jean Rotrou (1609–1650) adapted plays by Plautus (*Menaechmi, Captivi, Amphitruo*). With Boileau's *L'Art Poétique* (1674) the (theory of the) adaptation of Antiquity reached a new level, which is comprehensively and forcefully reflected in the → QUERELLE des anciens and the modernes. Antiquity was understood as a realisation of the contemporary artistic ideal, of '*grace*' within the boundaries of '*moralité*' and '*bon sens*'. Correspondingly every kind of 'base' humour was rejected, Aristophanes and Plautus were deprecated, Menander virtually and Terence in fact raised to the status of model authors, an assessment which in theory as well as in practice remained in effect until the 18th cent. Surprisingly, though, Racine, a contemporary of Boileau and, like him, a partisan of the '*anciens*', took a play by Aristophanes (*The Wasps*) as a model for his only comedy (*Les Plaideurs*, 1668). Racine's adaptation, however, was only loosely based on the original work. Rather, it sought to prove that even Aristophanes' comedies could be adapted without contravening the requirements of '*moralité*' and '*bon sens*'. Racine explicitly emphasised this point in his foreword, which can be seen as a distancing of himself from Molière's comedies, which remained open to the boundary-dissolving Dionysian moment of ancient comedy and thus to farce as well. Molière gave to comedy the process of anchoring humour discursively. This also determined the nature of its relationship with ancient comedy. To be sure, the humour in Molière's plays is located in the immediately eye-catching constellations of derision, or in the readiness to open up to laughter, liberating that which is suppressed (humour of shared laughter). The principal field of humour, however, lies in the discursive structure of his plays: in each case the excluding force (whether it be the extreme demands of the singled-out individual or those of sociability) is always shown as referring back to that which it excludes. In this balance, the comedy succeeds in achieving, in a representative way, the ideal of the social realisation of ethical demands. His reception of Plautus and Terence is objectively demonstrable; most widely known is his adaptation of *Amphitruo*, other striking references are exhibited by *L'Avare* to Plautus' *Aulularia* and Ariosto's *I Suppositi, Les Fourberies de Scapin* to Terence's *Phormio*, and *L'École des Maris* to Terence's *Adelphoe*. In Molière's plays, a stronger presence than that of Roman comedy, however, is that of the commedia dell'arte (character types, plot patterns and concept of what is comical). The closeness was also spatial. Molière's company occasionally alternated with the Comédie-Italienne playing the same theatre. In addition to and after Molière and the Comédie-Italienne no comparable productive reception of ancient comedy took place in France; rather Molière's comedies and the commedia dell'arte were the reference points for the creation of comedies. Aristophanes was of limited appeal; the only significant opposition was presented by Anne le Fèvre (Dacier), who not only published editions of Plautus and Terence, but also defended Aristophanes emphatically by translating and commenting on *The Clouds* and *Plutos*. In Brumoy's *Théâtre des Grecs* (first edition 1730, continually expanded and new editions) there are translations with commentaries of all the plays of Aristophanes, which became instrumental in spreading awareness of the author. Lessing, Wieland and Goethe became acquainted with Aristophanes through this edition. A greater effect (on Gottsched and Lessing, among others) was achieved by Jean François Regnard's adaptations of Plautus. The sentimental and moving comedy (*Lustspiel*) of the late 17th and early 18th cents. could not have been further removed from ancient comedy. An echo of the inherent playfulness of ancient comedy and the principle of parabasis may be found, at best, in Marivaux' celebration of play-acting, the world of appearances through which his heroes must go.

6. 16TH AND 17TH CENT. ENGLAND

English comedy grew into a genre of its own in the course of the 16th cent., drawing on indigenous traditions of comic play (mediaeval mystery plays, 14th and 15th cent. allegorical morality plays and interludes, which emphasised the farcical and developed '*vice*' – tempter and mischievous buffoon in one – as an autonomous comic character) and on both direct and indirect adaptations of Roman comedies. Roman comedies were read and performed in schools and universities. The first English comedy, *Ralph Roister Doister* by Nicholas Udall (1552), was based on Plautus' *Miles Gloriosus* and, in part, on Terence's *Eunuchus*. Plautus was an important point of reference for creation of comedies in the subsequent decades (e.g. Lyly). In Shakespeare's comedies there are many motifs which are known from ancient comedy (e.g. gender swapping, duplication of love affairs, lost children). The figure of the Fool also goes back, although not exclusively, to the Servant in Italian comedy and the Slave in Roman comedy. Even though he may no longer control the play in Shakespeare, his position has become structurally more comprehensive: for him, everything is play; he negates the principle of distinction by multiplying those distinctions. In this way he becomes a quintessential component of the comedic world, like his complementary counterpart the Melancholic, who interprets everything as play and pretence and insists on the absolute difference between it and the 'truth'. Over and above material reminiscences (especially of Roman comedy), characteristic features of ancient comedy that are more markedly developed in Aristophanes than in Plautus and Terence (including the dissolving of boundaries, parabasis, singularisation, self-reflexivity) appear in Shakespeare, made comprehensively productive. As original creations and types in their own right, these comedies preserve the fundamental achievements of ancient comedy and pass them on. This can already be observed in the *Comedy of Errors*, an early adaptation of the *Menaechmi*; later the figure of Falstaff, for in-

stance, demonstrates how typical characters of the Roman comedy (the *miles gloriosus*, the Parasite, the Foolish Old Man) can be amalgamated into one completely independent complex character with an enigmatic comic quality of its own – one that is always capable of turning into its opposite. Comedy thus reveals an inner paradox, which was most closely captured by Aristophanes in the *Birds*.

Ben Jonson wrote with an excellent knowledge of ancient literature, including Latin and Aristophanic comedies. In part, the subject matter of his early comedies was closely modelled on ancient comedies (especially those of Plautus); Plautus' character types are brought together in *Every Man in his Humour* (1598). As in Shakespeare, the adaptation of ancient comedy goes far beyond mere reference to subject matter. The characteristic features of ancient comedy are preserved and newly formed in independent creations: the *vis comica* of Aristophanes, his combination of accurately observed, satirical realism with fantastical elements, as well as verbal parody. Latin comedy's figure of reversal became newly productive: as a figure, for instance, in the continuously recurring central character of the deceived deceiver (*Volpone or the Foxe*, 1606, *The Alchemist*, 1610), situational in the adaptation of the Saturnalia at the annual fair, which became the paradigm for a comical view of the world (*Bartholomew Fayre*, 1614). One consequence of Ben Jonson's theory of '*humours*', however, (a person can be improved through the satirical exposure of his inflexible character and/or moral rigidity as *humores*) was a distancing from ancient comedy and resulted in the promotion of a pure comedy of derision, which only the Enlightenment would later recognise.

7. RECEPTION AFTER THE 18TH CENT.

During the 17th cent., European comedy became differentiated into several independent varieties, which then developed their own shere of influence. Accordingly, the path of transmission for ancient comedy became increasingly indirect. In the following, only examples will be cited that marked a new turn in the reception of ancient comedy.

The moral and pedagogical functionalisation of comedy in the Enlightenment is far removed from the boundary-dissolving Dionysian element of ancient comedy (especially in Aristophanes and Plautus). The theatre reforms (Gottsched's and Goldoni's) tried to suppress this boundary dissolving and latently nonsensical element of comedy. In his early occupation with Plautus (translations of two plays and a treatise on the author) Lessing still argued wholly in this spirit. In the *Hamburgische Dramaturgie* he would then, like Möser and Krüger, censure Gottsched's banishment of Harlequin from the stage. With the self-criticism of the Enlightenment in the Storm and Stress period (and in Romanticism) ancient comedy once again came to the fore. In this connection, J.M.R. Lenz must be mentioned, above all, as a translator of plays by Plautus and author of his theory of comedy. With ancient comedy Lenz verified his idea that comedy could affect the 'whole' nation, both the educated and the general populace (self-review of the *New Menoza*). Lenz further recalled the common origin of tragedy and comedy in the Dionysus cult, maintaining, however, that comedy – since it does not separate the laughter from the tears – was closer to this 'ur-drama' than tragedy. The return to the origins of drama now became the aim of comedy writing; the comedies of Aristophanes and Plautus became an ideal in retrospect, also because the comical/satirical genre was interpreted as genuinely republican. In the same spirit, and from a revolutionary perspective, Beaumarchais transformed the dramaturgical function of the slave in Roman comedy into a master-servant dialectic. Lenz was already displaying signs of the rekindled interest in Greek comedy, which in the following decades was a unique feature of the German reception of ancient comedy. Goethe, in his post-Italian years, professed a predilection for Terence. By turning to farce (e.g. in *Das Jahrmarktsfest zu Plundersweilern*) in his Strasbourg, Frankfurt and early Weimar years, however, Goethe had regained for comedy the boundary-dissolving Dionysian moment. The Aristophanic moment of boundary transgression appears radicalised in a world of light-hearted, inconsequential play, of moral indifference, of cheerfully conducted nonsense, of the fragmentary and the chaotic. Later revisions by Goethe attempting to impose order on the carefree, turbulent plays could only fail. In general Goethe's outlets for the Dionysian moment of ancient comedy are always counterbalanced by organisational principles. Programmatically this is demonstrated in his work *Das römische Carneval*, which 'contains' the anarchic boundary-dissolving nature of the carnival in a tightly structured narrative.

A new level in the reception of Aristophanic comedy was achieved during Early Romanticism. The individual subjects or forms of ancient comedy were not of primary interest. Instead, constitutive moments of Greek comedy were envisioned anew in the authors' own conceptions of literature. Friedrich Schlegel's *Vom ästhetischen Wert der griechischen Komödie* (1794) was pioneering in this regard. Schlegel returned comedy to its Dionysian origins: celebration of the god Dionysus as 'a strange and hidden god', as god both of immortal joy, of wondrous abundance and of eternal liberation. Greek comedy became a model for literature: for all its faults, it was an unsurpassable example of beautiful mirth, sublime freedom and comic power. This 'comic power' was expected to fulfil the specific task of art to unite the physical and spiritual aspects of human existence. Accordingly, the formal principles of Romantic literature were developed from those of Greek comedy: the principle of parabasis in the sense of boundary transgression in the central element of irony (as 'permanent parekbasis'); dissolving of boundaries also as elevation of the oppresse, as realization of freedom; further, the turning to the large audience which also included crude jokes and satire, to which F. Schle-

gel would later lay claim for Romantic literature as 'impudence'. Friedrich Schlegel's emphatic embracing of Greek comedy was epoch-making for German literature. Tieck has creatively adopted the moment of parabasis in his comedies which intensifies the play and its disillusionment. This new reception was accompanied by rigorous philological research (F.A. Wolf, G. Welcker) and translation activity (complete translations of Aristophanes by Voß, 1821ff., Droysen, 1835ff., Seeger, 1845ff.).

In Kleist's reworking of *Amphitryon* (1807), which expressly drew on Molière but through him and other adaptations (J.D. Falk) hearkened back to Plautus, Latin comedy received its most significant realisation for the 'Kunstperiode', and remains alive in the theatre today. The question of identity appears to be coming to a more dramatic head in Kleist's comedy than in any of his predecessors', in that it is not only transposed to the level of the powerful but also centred on the female character; this has from the earliest beginnings of comedy (e.g. in Euripides, not preserved) been conducive to the introduction of tragic accentuations. However, not Plautus, but Aristophanes was the point of departure for the adaptation of ancient comedy in the German 'Kunstperiode'. Hegel celebrated Aristophanes, but he reduced the presence of the boundary-dissolving Dionysian element of Greek comedy in Romantic poetry. In Hegel's aesthetic, Aristophanes does not stand for the breaking-down and crossing of boundaries, but rather for the humoristic subject, serene and aloof, celebrating itself through comedy. Having thus been associated with a more mature, mellowed brand of humour, Aristophanes' literary reception in the 19th cent. was of a largely epigonic character (Rückert, Platen, Bauernfeld, Glassbrenner). Only in Nestroy, in his wit, his unleashing of anarchic pleasure, his extemporisations (which can be seen as a return of the parabasis) and the inclusion of music in his farces with songs, do we find a potency approaching that of Aristophanic comedy.

A new intensification in the continuing 'work on myth' (Blumenberg) of Amphitryon was achieved by Giraudoux in his comedy *Amphitryon 38* (1929) which, with the number mentioned in the title itself, presupposes a public awareness of the productive continuation of this myth – and of Latin comedy, which preserved it for posterity. At its centre we now find the perfect couple of Amphitryon and Alcmene, through which people liberate themselves from the capriciousness of the gods. The area in which this is mainly achieved is a subtle play on language arising from a particular 'dialogicity': a reversal of words by means of the 'answering you', which brings everything hidden out into the light of day. What F. Schlegel had undertaken for the concept of Romantic poetry, a kind of mediatisation of the characteristics of ancient comedy, is continued here-for the literature of the classical Modern-on the conceptual level of language. It roughly coincides with Bakhtin's works on the 'dialogic word' examining what Bakhtin would later refer to as the 'carnivalesque principle'.

Victorian England maintained its distance from ancient comedy. Robert Browning showed a most knowledgeable appreciation of Aristophanes, albeit with the tenor of a preference for Euripides, in his verse epic *Aristophanes' Apology including a Transcript from Euripides; being the Last Adventure of Balaustion* (1875). George Bernard Shaw's comedies were rightfully associated with Aristophanes because of their satirical edge, their ridicule and their variety of techniques of parody. Nevertheless, the founding of this *vis comica* in an appellative rational optimism also marked an unbridgeable distance. In the quotational universe of Joyce's *Ulysses* (1922) there is no lack of Aristophanic comedy. Noteworthy are the aesthetic methods developed from it: an embracing of that which is hateful/disgusting (quotation from *The Ecclesiazusae*) and the technique of the interior monologue (quotation from *The Clouds*). T.S. Eliot took the opposite approach in the drama fragment *Sweeney Agonistes. Fragments of an Aristophanic Melodrama* (1926/27): contemporary figures and problems are cast in the mould of Aristophanic comedy.

The poetic mediatisation of the characteristics of Aristophanic comedy continued after 1945, with Friedrich Dürrenmatt (*Theaterprobleme*) and Elias Canetti (*Die Fackel im Ohr*) assuming particularly striking and influential positions. They each, in their own *Poetik des Einfalls* (poetics of invention), refer to Aristophanes.

With the necessary caution when discussing the development of types, two fundamentally different but surprisingly enduring types of reception can be established for Aristophanic and Latin comedy since the 18th cent.: one referring serially to the appropriating world, the other surpassing it and pointing to the original figure or problem constellation in an ever new manner. The adaptation of Aristophanic comedy hinges upon the introduction of poetic elements or a specific subject-matter, a motif or an idea into the appropriating constellation, where it acts as a catalyst generating, tracing the outlines of or reinforcing certain poetic techniques (the case of poetic mediatisation). Or it will make apparent current conditions or problem complexes (e.g. the longing for peace or the escapist tendencies of an age, a society, a school of thought). Each appropriation is directed towards the appropriating world; thus the adaptations sit serially side by side. The more closely the original constellation is being transferred, the greater the analytical power of the appropriation. This is why Peter Hacks's adaptation of *Peace* in Benno Besson's production of 1962 became one of the greatest theatrical successes in the history of the → GDR, whereas Hacks' s adaptation of *The Birds* (1975) and Karl Kraus's earlier adaptation *Wolkenkuckucksheim* (1923) failed. In accordance with the above-mentioned 'rule', the frequent reworkings of *Lysistrata* either display an analytical political power (Fritz Kortner: *Die Sendung der Lysistrata*, 1961) or are merely programmatic (Rolf Hochhuth: *Lysistrata und die Nato*, 1973, Walter Jens: *Die Friedensfrau*, 1986). The mechanism

of appropriation for Latin comedy is one by which each new adaptation seeks to delineate the pre-existing character types (self-tormentor/misanthrope, braggart, miser, etc.) or the once-established problem constellation (Amphitryon and the problem of identity, the Menaechmi and the encryption of the world) more acutely, thus surpassing earlier ones. The thrust of the appropriation is directed towards the original, pre-existing characters and conditions. Every new adaptation, with its new set of conditions and circumstances, is an opportunity to formulate those questions even more precisely or more pointedly, to set up an even more complex experimental arrangement, and to add perspectives and views of problems that previous attempts failed to take into account. Amphitryon is the best-known example of this, the self-tormentor comedy is another (examples: Menander *Dyscolus*, Terence *Heautontimorumenos*, Shakespeare *Timon of Athens*, Molière *Le Misanthrope*, Nestroy *Der Zerrissene*, Hofmannsthal *Der Schwierige*).

The extremely productive, rich and varied history of influence of ancient comedy, its founding of modern European comedy and its continuing effect on it, as well as its enduring presence in the basic orientations of poetic theory and practice in general, unrivalled by other genres, is itself a realisation of the comical, its union of boundary setting (as derision) and boundary-dissolving (as liberating laughter) in the comic pleasure as the pleasure of a body opening itself up to others instead of closing in on itself.

→ Dionysus; → Comedy

→ GERMANY; → FRANCE; → GREEK COMEDY; → ITALY;
→ LATIN COMEDY; → UNITED KINGDOM

1 N. ALTENHOFER (ed.), Komödie und Gesellschaft. Komödientheorien des 19. Jahrhunderts, 1973   2 G. ATTINGER, L'esprit de la commedia dell'arte dans le théâtre français, 1950   3 R. BAADER (ed.), Molière, 1980   4 M. BACHTIN, Die Ästhetik des Wortes, R. GRÜBEL (ed.), 1979   5 Id., Literatur und Karneval. Zur Romantheorie und Lachkultur, 1990   6 K.-H. BAREISS, Comoedia. Die Entwicklung der Komödiendiskussion von Aristoteles bis Ben Jonson, 1982   7 R. BAUER, Die Komödientheorie von J.M.R. Lenz, die älteren Plautuskommentare und das Problem der 'dritten' Gattung, in: S. A. CORNGOLD et al. (eds.), Aspekte der Goethezeit, 1977   8 Id., 'Plautinisches' bei Jakob Michael Reinhold Lenz, in: H. MAINUSCH (ed.), Europäische Komödie, 1990   9 H.-D. BLUME, Plautus und Shakespeare, in: A&A 15, 1969   10 F. S. BOAS, Shakespeare and his Predecessors, 1896   11 R. W. BOND, Early Plays from the Italian, 1911   12 C. H. CONLEY, The First English Translators of the Classics, 1927   13 K. O. CONRADY, Zu den deutschen Plautusübertragungen. Ein Überblick von Albrecht von Eyb bis zu J.M.R. Lenz, in: Euphorion 48, 1954   14 H. FLASHAR, Inszenierung der Antike. Das griechische Drama auf der Bühne der Neuzeit, 1991   15 P. FRIEDLÄNDER, Aristophanes in Deutschland. Studien zur antiken Literatur und Kunst, 1969   16 B. GREINER, Die Komödie. Eine theatralische Sendung. Grundlagen und Interpretationen, 1992   17 R. L. GRISMER, The Influence of Plautus in Spain before Lope de Vega, 1944   18 M. T. HERRICK, Italian Comedy in the Renaissance, 1960   19 W. HINCK, Das deutsche Lustspiel des 17. und

18. Jahrhunderts und die italienische Komödie. Commedia dell'arte und Théâtre italien, 1965 20 K. Hölz, Die gespaltene Ordnung in Molières Komödien oder vom problematischen Grund des Lachens, in: Romanistische Zeitschrift für Literaturgeschichte 4, 1980, 386–412 21 H. R. Jauss, Poetik und Problematik von Identität und Rolle in der Geschichte des Amphitryon, in: O. Marquard, H. Stierle (eds.), Identität, 1979 22 W. Krömer, Die italienische Commedia dell'arte, 1976 23 E. Lefèvre, Römische und europäische Komödie, in: Id. (ed.), Die römische Komödie: Plautus und Terenz, 1973 24 L. E. Lord, Aristophanes, his Plays and his Influence, 1925 25 V. Pandolfi (ed.), La commedia dell'arte. Storia e testo, 1957–1961 26 W. Preisendanz, R. Warning (eds.), Das Komische, 1976 27 U. Profitlich (ed.), Komödientheorie. Texte und Kommentare. Vom Barock bis zur Gegenwart, 1998 28 D. Radcliff-Umstead, The Birth of Modern Comedy in Renaissance Italy, 1969 29 K. v. Reinhardstoettner, Plautus. Spätere Bearbeitung plautinischer Lustspiele, 1886 (repr. 1980) 30 L. Salingar, Shakespeare and the Traditions of Comedy, 1974 31 I. A. Schwartz, The commedia dell'arte and its Influence on French Comedy, 1933 32 A. Stäuble, La commedia umanistica del Quattrocento, 1968 33 W. Süss, Aristophanes und die Nachwelt, 1911 34 J. M. Walton, Living Greek Theatre, 1987 35 O. Weinreich, Zur Geschichte und zum Nachleben der griechischen Komödie, in: Aristophanes, Sämtliche Komödien, übertragen von L. Seeger, 1970

Additional Bibliography: R. Miola, Shakespeare and Classical Comedy: The Influence of Plautus and Terence, 1994.
BERNHARD GREINER

Comets see → Natural sciences

Comics
I. Genre   II. Motivational Aids in Teaching   III. In the Media

I. Genre
A. Definition   B. General

A. Definition
Comics are a special kind of picture story, originating in the United States at the end of the 19th cent. They can be described as a form of story in which text and pictures are organised in a narrative sequence, and arranged, for the most part, chronologically. Comics developed from the political and satirical caricatures of the 18th and 19th cents.[1]. Long dismissed as trivial and juvenile literature, comics acquired a refined image and were accepted as a mass medium with specific art-historical and socio-cultural characteristics through the adoption of some of their elements in avant-garde art (painting: Roy Lichtenstein, Andy Warhol, Picasso; cinema: Jean-Luc Godard, Quentin Tarantino) and as a result of their commercial success since the 1970s. The combination of pictures and text (seldom with the same illustrator and author) has developed autonomous story techniques with their own narrative structure ('picture-within-picture' or 'cut-up' technique, speech balloons, onomatopoeia), which go beyond mere loans from literature, painting and cinema. Today, and particularly in France and the United States, comics are recognised as a form of everyday art. Artists such as Carl Barks, Hal Foster and Frank Miller have demonstrably exercised very great influence on the language and perception of modern society [2]. Comics transmit everyday myths [3]. Comic characters such as *Superman* and *Donald Duck* long ago won themselves a permanent place in the cultural thinking of many peoples. High circulation and massive dissemination have contributed to the development of a multifaceted mass medium, which in its thematic and stylistic breadth (underground comics, political comics, adult comics, funnies, superhero comics etc.) can hardly be overlooked. To a significant extent comics have contributed to an objective popular art form relating to the regulated civil society [4]. Finally they play an important role as a medium of communication in modern educational techniques. By mediating and practicing teaching material picture stories have proved themselves as a support for making accessible the content of texts, as an aid to understanding grammatical, structural and historical phenomena and not least as a stimulus for motivation and learning [5; 6].

B. General
Antiquity plays only a subordinate role in comics. Few comics have it as a setting or make use of themes and characters from Antiquity (e.g. Plautus: Ghost Stories, Mostellaria, 1971 and [7]), as historical settings and identifiable characters are often no longer available to be called to the consciousness of a traditionally young reader class that is seldom educated in the humanities. Hence the content is often standardised; traditional clichés recur and are amplified, and the ancient background is reduced to the minimum that can be expected of the reader. The best known comic series is Asterix, which was conceived in 1959 by author René Goscinny and illustrator Albert Uderzo and which, after more than 30 comic books, is considered the most successful comic of all [8]. It describes the adventures of the Gaulish hero Asterix (French *Astérix*), who, together with his gargantuan friend Obelix (French *Obélix*) and with the aid of a magic potion brewed by the druid Getafix (French *Panoramix*), defies Roman conquest in around 50 BC. In addition to the artistic, linguistic and symbolic techniques the charm of the stories lies in the satirical depiction of the national characteristics of the French and other nations and in the clever play with ancient cultural tradition. Besides Astérix, the Alix l'Intrépide series created by Jacques Martin in 1948 (about the Gaulish adopted son of a Roman patrician) and the twelve part series *Jugurtha* which appeared between 1967 and 1970 ([9] cf. also [10]) by Hermann Huppen and Jean-Luc Vernal (based on the *Bellum Iugurthinum* by Sallust) found international recognition owing to their graphic appeal and historical foundations. During the Franco-Algerian conflict *Jugurtha* even called for

Fig. 1a: The narrative techniques of a comic strip and an ancient pictorial frieze.

block of text (describing the situation)

sequence (consisting of multiple frames) → temporal sequence

hiatus (leap in time)

frame (single picture)

balloon with pointer

habitus (frame bordering), regulates the levels of narrated time

I thank you, gentlemen! Let me come to the point right away:

Everyone in the auditory is listening intently as Superman begins to speak

Supermanne iffe wanna boxe, lettine come to Italia! I punchimme KO!

Superrman speaks in congrress! Zis cannot be trrrue!

The incredible message travels around the world. The dictators tremble in their bomb-proof bunkers.

, By my ancestors! The miserable worm!

Gentlemen! It's my pleasure to give the floor to a very important person. A true American will speak to you: Superman!

prompt political activity [11] (since 1976 continued by the artist F. Drappier; cf. also [12]).

1 A. C. KNIGGE, Comics, 1996, 7–10   2 B. FRANZMANN, H.-J. KAGELMANN, R. ZITZLSPERGER, Comics zwischen Lese- und Bildkultur, 1991   3 P. HERMAN, Epopée et Mythes du Western dans la Bande Dessinée, 1982   4 G. METKEN, Comics, 1970, 177   5 M. FUHRMANN, Asterix der Gallier und die 'römische Welt', in: Alte Sprachen in der Krise?, 1976, 105–127   6 T. VISSER, Bilder(geschichten) und Grammatik, in: AU 36, 1994, 8–26   7 Caesaris commentarii belli Gallici: bellum Helveticum pinxit Faber, composuit Rubricastellanus, 1988   8 A. STOLL, Asterix. Das Trivialepos Frankreichs, 1975   9 R. LEHNER, Jugurtha, in: Comixene 36, March 1981, 17   10 B. DE CHOISY, Uderzo-storix, 1991   11 A. C. KNIGGE, in: Jugurtha. Kampf um Numidien, 1983, 91–93   12 TH. GROENSTEEN, Hermann, 1982, 13ff.;

ADDITIONAL BIBLIOGRAPHY: F. G. GENTRY, Asterix and Obelix: The Genesis of the Vernacular Heroic Tradition, in: U. MÜLLER, M. SPRINGETH (eds.) Paare und Paarungen. Festschrift für Werner Wunderlich, 2004, 373–386   KLAUS GEUS

II. MOTIVATIONAL AIDS IN TEACHING
A. INTRODUCTION   B. SPECTRUM OF AVAILABLE COMICS

A. INTRODUCTION

In the case of 'Latin comics' we are confronted with a special case of the reception of Antiquity in the comic literary form. The question of the kind of reception, which can take on such differing forms as e.g. Antiquity as a colourful backdrop for the plot or as a productive coming to terms with features of the present [19. 22], does retain its significance, but takes second place to the aspect of the language and the didactic consideration of the provision of language with this resource. Since the beginning of the 1970s, an adaptation by H. Oberst of a comedy by Plautus (1971) [5] and the first translation of a volume of *Asterix* (1973) [1], the availability of comics in Latin and (in a few cases) also Ancient Greek has continually grown [18. 293–295; 13]. Kipf cites 40 comics that have been translated into Ancient Greek (2) or Latin (38) [15. 6f.; 29. 37–38]. Comics receive particular interest if they appear to promise an increase in motivation [12; 14. 61]. At first sight they combine a multitude of advantages: they deal with child-oriented themes, they use a combination of words and pictures which suits the reading behaviour of children [12. 54ff.], they correspond to the demand for vividness [20. 3] and they present an up-to-date form of presentation close to the materials used in teaching modern foreign languages [20. 5].

The publication of Latin comics coincided on the one hand with a detailed discussion of 'comics' as a literary form in the context of research into popular literature [8. 228ff.], and on the other hand the beginning of Latin didactics taking up the (re)formation of the canon of reading matter in the middle of the 1970s. M. Fuhrmann argued for the 'minor genres', to make

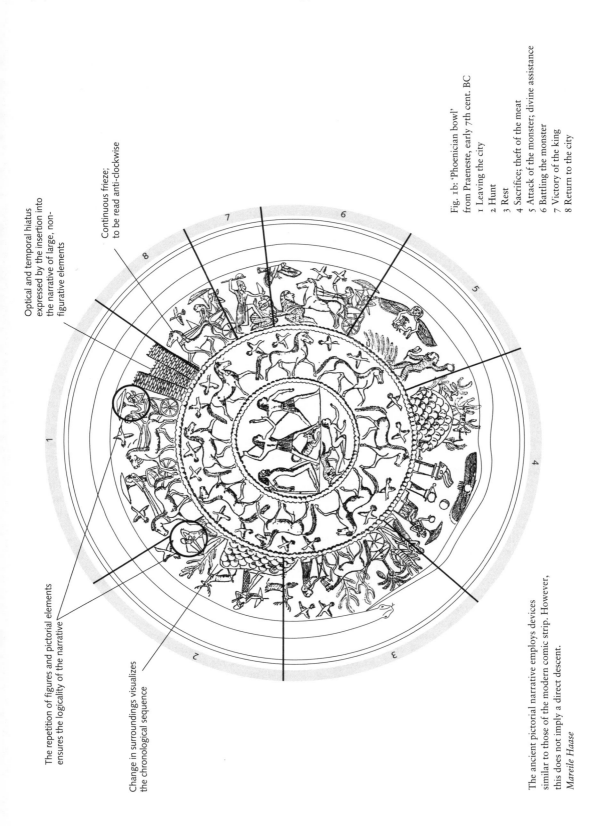

Optical and temporal hiatus expressed by the insertion into the narrative of large, non-figurative elements

Continuous frieze; to be read anti-clockwise

The repetition of figures and pictorial elements ensures the logicality of the narrative

Change in surroundings visualizes the chronological sequence

Fig. 1b: 'Phoenician bowl' from Praeneste, early 7th cent. BC
1 Leaving the city
2 Hunt
3 Rest
4 Sacrifice; theft of the meat
5 Attack of the monster; divine assistance
6 Battling the monster
7 Victory of the king
8 Return to the city

The ancient pictorial narrative employs devices similar to those of the modern comic strip. However, this does not imply a direct descent.
Mareile Haase

teaching stronger and more appropriate to the age and needs of pupils and achieve a gain in motivation at the cost of more trivial subject matter [11]. As a result, neo-Latin translations, primarily of traditional picture stories (Max and Moritz, Straw Peter), particularly also the translations of the *Asterix* comics and the comedy comics of Oberst entered the didactic field of vision [9]. Whereas M. Fuhrmann identified the particular form of reception of Antiquity in the German edition of the *Asterix* series as potential for teaching Latin and principally saw in it a means of stimulating pupils to come to terms with Antiquity in a positive way [12], means were subsequently sought to exploit this potential for the provision of language as well. To this end the qualities of Latin comics as early reading matter were sounded out [10; 17]. In addition there were repeated attempts [4; 6] to expand teaching materials with the help of comics. From the 1980s activity-oriented initiatives were presented in the professional periodicals (*Altsprachlicher Unterricht, Anregung*), explaining the advantages of a creative version of reading matter (of all levels of difficulty) in the form of comics by pupils [18; 13].

B. Spectrum of Available Comics

Comics are traditionally divided into funnies and adventure comics [8. 326]. There are further subcategories (humour, action and adventure, real life, fantasy and serious [19. 22]) as well as a multitude of mixed forms, which resist any unambiguous classification [8. 289ff.]. Latin comics also occur in astonishingly large numbers. Examples can be found of funnies (*Disney lingua Latina*, 1984ff.), semi-funnies (*D. Browne, Haegar terribilis, miles sine timore vitiisque*, translated into Latin by K. ULRICHS, 1986), adventure (*Hergé lingua Latina: De Titini et Miluli facinoribus* = Tim und Struppi, in Latinam convertit C. EICHENSEER, 1987ff.). This traditional classification however gives only limited information about the special properties of the texts and their pros and cons for the teaching of ancient languages. For the group of comics which explicitly deals with Antiquity, the perceptions of the lessons of history are more helpful. These can also develop, supplementing language teaching, information for the transmission of the study of the material environment and the facets of the modern reception of Antiquity.

For 'historical comics', a description transcending the distinctions typical of the genre, Pandel (relying on Eco's typology of historical novels) differentiates five kinds [19. 22]: source comics (witnesses of their time), comic romances ('history as a backdrop': circumstances do not determine the action), comic novels (foreground and background narration are interwoven), comic epochs (actions and thoughts of the fictional characters serve as the best understanding of the story), comic histories ('illustrated history books'). The qualities which have been developed for working with comics in teaching history are also available in this case for teaching Latin: 'they deepen sensual and emotional experience

and thus make a contribution to the aesthetics of historical consciousness and to the rhetoric of historical narratives' [19. 23]. Since the demands of history teaching necessitate primarily a classification by typology of the content of texts and in addition Latin teaching must reflect the dimension of conveying language, it seems to be sensible to divide the available comics into two groups: 1. translations of 'relevant' comics, 2. comics which are consciously produced to convey Latin language and literature.

1. TRANSLATIONS OF 'TOPICAL' COMICS
2. COMICS CONCEIVED FOR TRANSMITTING LATIN LANGUAGE AND LITERATURE

1. TRANSLATIONS OF 'TOPICAL' COMICS

Besides translations of 'historical' comics [1; 2; 3], there is also a series of Latin comics exhibiting no historical relation to Antiquity. Here the choice has fallen in many cases on titles which are considered to be 'classics' of their literary form [16. 342ff.]. Their popularity is supposed to allow them to relate to pupils and thus motivate them. Of course, in such cases one is confronted with the problems specific to neo-Latin texts; when the majority of translators tend towards the normative Latin of Caesar and Cicero [20.5; 2. 49], for vivid dialogue they have to resort to spoken forms (e.g. interjections), which are known primarily from Roman comedies [20. 5]. To this can be added the problem of modern vocabulary and onomatopoeia typical of the genre. Only few translations are handled with such care that the 'bang words' are Latinised (as e.g. by Rothenburg and Eichenseer). However, even conscientious translations are seldom wholly Ciceronian, and a check of vocabulary indexes similarly shows great differences. In the case of an entire work as reading matter, teaching is made more difficult in that the benefits of the literary form (dynamism, suspense, humour) for motivating the pupils are available to them only if they read fluently. A further possibility is to use excerpts to make the teaching of grammar more relaxed ([17. 36]: 'Quarry for innumerable grammatical problems').

2. COMICS CONCEIVED FOR TRANSMITTING LATIN LANGUAGE AND LITERATURE

a) GRAMMAR LESSONS

There are examples of conscious attempts to tailor the medium of comics to teaching languages. Such publications place their emphasis on grammar [6] or methods of translation [4], to which end they offer vocabulary exercises and helpful worksheets for grammar. The pictorial portion condenses a comprehensive verbal context, so that the attention of the pupils can be drawn to the sentences conveying the grammatical point. Added to this is the idea of a potential for motivation immanent in the genre of comics. Of course the problem of this genre consists in achieving the goal of a successful balance of words and pictures, since one cannot fall back on comics which have already demonstrated their popularity.

HE SAYS ARTIFIS PAID HIM TO THROW HIS CARGO IN THE NILE AND THERE'S STILL STONE IN THE QUARRY, LOTS OF STONE, AND HE'LL BE HAPPY TO GO AND GET IT AND PLEASE DON'T HIT QUITE SO HARD AND SWEARS BY ISIS, OSIRIS AND SERAPIS NEVER TO DO IT AGAIN.

Fig. 2a: The use of ancient sources in a modern comic strip: panel from 'Asterix and Cleopatra' Albert Uderzo, the graphic artist of the Astérix series, has copied some of the peculiarities of transcription practice: supplementary passages in square brackets, an unusually-styled hieroglyph and the bold bars indicating (in the now outdated view of the editor) the beginning of a new sentence. It is therefore highly likely that Uderzo based his drawings on the edition of the Book of the Dead by E.A. Wallis Budge. Portions of the Egyptian text have been omitted.

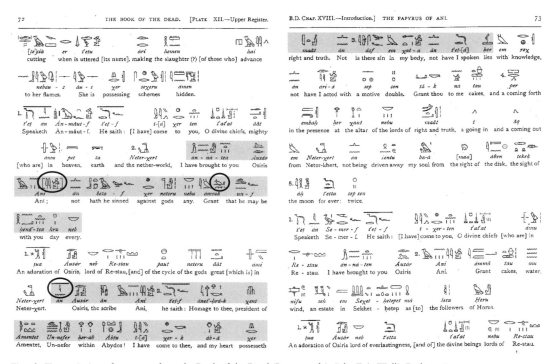

Fig. 2b: Transcription of a passage from the Book of the Dead (Payprus of Ani) by E.A. Wallis Budge, 1895 (relevant passages are highlighted, circles indicate idiosyncrasies also found in the example from Astérix)

b) Illustrated Classics

Comics belonging to this group place their emphasis on awakening interest in and providing access to original ancient texts. They follow in the tradition of the Illustrated Classics editions [9. 48]. The fundamental difficulty of successful adaptation lies in achieving an interpretative combination of words and pictures appropriate to the character of the original. For a comic version selection of the passages and, in some circumstances, textual reworkings are necessary, which seldom receive general approval. Whereas comedy comics of Plautus and Terence have been criticised for polishing and shortening the text [9], those of Von Rothenburg take a different path. He adapts non-dialogue texts to the comic form of presentation. In the case of the 'Caesar Comics' (*Caesaris Bellum Helveticum picturis narratum*, pinxit Faber [= W. SCHMID], composuit Rubricastellanus [= K. H. VON ROTHENBURG], 1987) he intervenes in the text, changing e.g. indirect speech to direct. In the *P. Ovidii Nasonis Metamorphoses selectae*, composuit Rubricastellanus, pinxit M. FREI (1996), he keeps the text closer to the original form in the captions, while composing a simplified dialogue for the speech balloons. In editions of

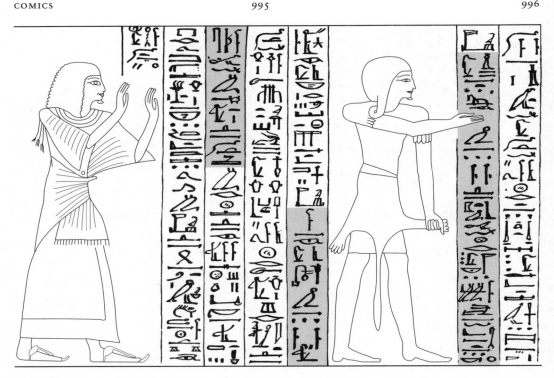

Fig. 2c: Book of the Dead (pBM 10470; *c.* 1250 BC) The priest Anmutef introduces the deceased ('Osiris') scribe Ani to the gods; Ani offers a greeting. The translation of the passage reads: 'I have brought unto you the Osiris Ani. He hath not committed any act which is an abomination before all the gods. Grant ye that he may live with you every day. [The Osiris the scribe Ani adoreth Osiris, Lord of Rasta, and the Great Company of the Gods who live in Khert-Neter.] He saith: Homage to thee, Khenti Amenti, Un-Nefer, who dwellest in Abtu. I come to thee. My heart holdeth Truth. There is no sin in my body. I have not told a lie wittingly...'
Mareile Haase

this kind the intention is to minimise 'reader shock' [20. 2] and access to the text is made easier by conveying information in pictures.

→ ANCIENT LANGUAGES, TEACHING OF

SOURCES   1 R. GOSCINNY, A. UDERZO, Pericula quaedam Asterigis. Composuit Goscinny, pinxit Uderzo, in Latinum convertit Rubricastellanus (= K. H. VON ROTHENBURG), 1973ff.   2 J. MARTIN, Alix. Spartaci filius, in Latinam. convertit C. AZIZA, M. DUBROCARD, 1983   3 J. MARTIN, Alix. Ho Athenaios Pais, ins Griechische übertragen von einer Schulklasse unter der Leitung von R. Ringele, 1994   4 W. MISSFELDT, Comics zur Analyse lateinischer Sätze, 1976   5 H. OBERST, Plautus in Comics Die Gespenstergeschichte (Mostellaria) mit dem lateinischen Text, 1971   6 J. RICHTER-REICHHELM, Casus in Comics, 1982   7 Terenz, Die Brüder, K. BARTELS (ed.), in Comics gezeichnet von H. OBERST, 1975

LITERATURE: 8 B. DOLLE-WEINKAUFF, Comics: Geschichte einer populären Literaturform in Deutschland seit 1945, 1990   9 U. FRINGS, Comics im Lateinunterricht?, in: Gymnasium 85, 1978, 47–54   10 Id., H. KEULEN, R. NICKEL, Lexikon zum Lateinunterricht, 1981   11 M. FUHRMANN, Caesar oder Erasmus?, in: Gymnasium 81, 1974, 394–407   12 Id., Asterix der Gallier und die 'römische Welt'. Betrachtungen über einen geheimen Miterzieher im Lateinunterricht, in: Id., Alte Sprachen in der Krise? Analysen und Programme, 1976, 105–127   13 D.

GERSTMANN, Bibliographie: Lateinunterricht. Didaktik, Methodik, Realien, Sachbegriffe, Eigennamen, Grammatik, 1997   14 D. GRÜNEWALD, Comics. Kitsch oder Kunst?, 1982   15 S. KIPF, Mediensammlung zum Altsprachlichen Unterricht 1995 (Mitteilungsblatt des Deutschen Altphilologenverbandes, Sonderheft 1995) 16 A. C. KNIGGE, Comics: Vom Massenblatt ins multimediale Abenteuer, 1996   17 E. LÜTHJE, Asterix als Motivationshelfer im lateinischen Grammatikunterricht, in: AU 22/5, 1979, 34–47   18 A. MÜLLER, M. SCHAUER, Bibliographie für den Lateinunterricht. Clavis Didactica Latina, 1994   19 H.-J. PANDEL, Comics-Literatur und Geschichte, in: Geschichte lernen 37, 1994, 18–26 20 K.-H. GRAF VON ROTHENBURG, Comics im Lateinunterricht, in: Lateinisch und Griechisch in Berlin 33/1, 1989, 2–10.   BIRGIT M.HAA. EICKHOFF

III. IN THE MEDIA
A. INTRODUCTION   B. ASTERIX   C. HERACLES/ HERCULES

A. INTRODUCTION

A mark of modern marketing strategies is propagation in the media. A product which is successful in one medium is exploited in others, in both literary and non-literary sectors. In the transference medium-specific changes and/or (re)interpretations of the original text are made ([5] = example of a case study). At the same time a certain recognisability factor is necessary in order to be able to fully exploit its popularity in secondary/tertiary etc. use. From the beginning of the literary form topics and characters have been taken over from comics and converted to other kinds of text and other media [2. 249; 4. 316ff.], and this process also affects comics based on Antiquity. As a result, the theme of Antiquity moulded by the end product has an after-effect in other forms of publication.

B. ASTERIX

As in the case of the Asterix series, the literary form of comics can be the result of this process. These had their beginning in episodes published in the periodical *Pilote* and since 1961 have been collected in comic book form [2. 213ff.; 1. 16ff.]. Over time, there has been a development of the characteristics of the series, recurring characters, plot patterns, style of drawing etc. [2. 215–217]. The first shift of medium to animated film ensued in 1967 [1. 22ff.]. Since then six animated films have been produced. Despite the closeness of these two genres [4. 316ff.] modifications resulted from the conditions of aesthetic production. Obvious changes arise e.g. in the creative use of music and sound effects, but also in the use of movement and voices for characterisation. Comic-specific means of expression however get lost. An example is the inclusion of script as a graphical element – particularly virtuoso in the Asterix volumes – primarily for the representation of foreign languages (Egyptian, Gothic etc.). The cinema version can consist of a newly conceived story or a compilation from different books. At the stage of tertiary versions there are film booklets, in which a paraphrase of the cinema version is illustrated with stills from the film (e.g. *Asterix et la Surprise de César*, 1986). Such publications are accompanied by versions in the non-literary sector: motifs from the Asterix series appear on textiles, stationery, toys, in role-playing games, computer games etc. In 1989 even an Asterix theme park was opened [1. 23]. The first non-animated film was *Astérix et Obélix contre César* (1999) directed by Claude Zidi, in which the action is built up from motifs from various comic books. The international popularity of Asterix was expressed in a French-German-Italian coproduction, reflected also in the international cast list. A leitmotiv of the series, the victory of the weak against the apparently overwhelming opponent, is projected directly onto its *raison d'être*: 'Dans la lutte héroïque que mène le village du cinéma français assiégé par les centurions hollywoodiens, enfin vinrent Astérix et Obélix. Dieu, quel tapage!' (Pierre Georges, in: Le Monde, 3 February 1999). The prestige value of this production was also clear from the amount invested in this film: its budget of about 42.81 million euros was the highest for a French language film in a long time (Le Monde, 3 February 1999). Since then a second film, *Astérix & Obélix: Mission Cléopâtre*, has appeared and yet a third one,

Astérix aux jeux olympiques, is said to be in production and scheduled for a 2007 release.

C. HERACLES/HERCULES

In the two following examples the literary form of comics is a stage in the realisation of an end product based on Antiquity. 1. Disney's *Hercules*: in 1997 the Disney film *Hercules* appeared and became the starting point for further exploitation in the media. In this case elements of the legend of Hercules were reshaped into a family viewing format as mere colourful show. In addition the ancient myth was broadened with features from the modern 'myth' of Superman (foundling, heroic deeds, external appearance with cape and symbol) and expanded with media-critical initiatives (satire on the merchandising). The plot of the film was posed as a guiding question: how do you become a hero? The merchandising was of the kind typical of Disney [4. 59]. The plot became the basis of a novel (e.g. LISA ANN MARSOLI, *Disney's Hercules*, 1998), the official comics of the film (E. SKOLNICK et al., *Disney's Hercules: Official Comic Movie Adaptation*, 1997), and computer games. The soundtrack of the film, the score, toys etc. appeared and were incorporated into the Disney theme parks. For the new animated television series (USA 1998) an aspect of the film, the childhood and education of Hercules, was singled out. He visits the 'Academy of Prometheus'. New characters developed for the series (Icarus, Cassandra, Adonis) were brought together with those already familiar from the film (Hades as villain with his accomplices, and Philoctet as educator).

2. *Hercules's Legendary Journeys*: The myths of Hercules were also taken up in a series of five two-hour television films (*Hercules and the Amazon Women*, 1994, *Hercules and the Circle of Fire*, 1994, *Hercules and the Lost Kingdom*), 1994, *Hercules in the Maze of the Minotaur* 1994, *Hercules in the Underworld*, 1994) [6. 36ff.], which can be seen as belonging to the tradition of 'sandal and toga films'. In the following years the concept turned into a weekly one-hour series (*Hercules: The Legendary Journeys*, 1995). At their centre stands the demigod Hercules, who with his friends wanders through a fictional ancient Greece, helps people in need and often fights mythical monsters. Out of this series meanwhile two further series (*spin-offs*) appeared (*Xena, Warrior Princess*, 1996, *Young Hercules*, 1998) and an animated film (*Hercules and Xena – The Animated Movie: The Battle for Mount Olympus*, 1998). These series are accompanied by novel and comic publications, which do not merely retell the televised series, but also contain independent stories. They are similarly based on ancient myths and stories, but in them the ironic tone, which together with the escapist adventure stories is an element of the series, is reinforced. In the product palette of the merchandising again there are computer games, role-playing games, soundtracks, action figures etc. [6. 261f.].

The World-Wide Web is also used on one hand for advertising on official pages and on the other as an opportunity for private exchanges of opinion [6. 259]. The specific form of the theme of Antiquity for this group of products is illustrated by a co-producer's (R.J. Stewart) position on this question: 'R.J. Stewart, who since childhood has read many myths, stresses their value, as long as they are regarded simply as a starting point and not as fetters condemning authors to repeat these old stories verbatim: ... knowledge of these myths is important but *never*, in any generation, have they, as far as is known, been slavishly repeated'. And this attitude, Stewart claims, also corresponds to that of the ancient Greeks themselves: 'Because there was this chap called Euripides, who wrote plays and was much closer to the sources of these myths than we are. In his play *Helena* he has Helen go not to Troy but to Egypt. What for? He must have been aware that in most myths he had heard she went to Troy. I bet somebody said to him: 'Euripides, we've got such a great setting with a pyramid!' So Euripides acted pragmatically and it worked out. And that is how it has always been'. [7. 48]

→ Heracles; → Hercules

1 P. BILLARD, Asterix & Obelix gegen Cäsar. Das Buch zum Film, 1999   2 B. DOLLE-WEINKAUFF, Comics: Geschichte einer populären Literaturform in Deutschland seit 1945, 1990   3 J. HANIMANN, Seifen- statt Sprechblasen, in: FAZ, 5 February 1999   4 A. C. KNIGGE, Comics Vom Massenblatt ins multimediale Abenteuer, 1996   5 R. STROBEL, Die 'Peanuts' – Verbreitung und ästhetische Formen. Ein Comics-Bestseller im Medienverbund, 1987   6 J. VAN HISE, Hercules & Xena. The Unofficial Companion, 1998   7 R. WEISBROT, Xena. Warrior Princess. Der offizielle Führer zur Serie, 1998   8 'Anticomix' Antike in Comics T. LOCHMANN (ed.), (exhibition catalogue) 1999.   BIRGIT EICKHOFF

Commentary
I. GENERAL   II. LATIN LITERATURE   III. BYZANTINE LITERATURE

I. GENERAL
Commentary, the continuous explication of a text, was a widespread phenomenon even in Antiquity. The earliest fully extant ancient commentary on a Latin work was that of the grammarian Servius on Virgil (early 5th cent. AD). Its impact extended into the Middle Ages and the Renaissance. The influence of the history of genres is apparent in the linguistic and factual analysis of words and phrases and in the citing of sources and parallel passages, and also in the way an introduction addressed questions of authorship, title, structure, purpose, etc., becoming a model for the medieval *accessus ad auctores*. Important commentaries from the early Middle Ages are, among others, those of Remigius of Auxerre (after 841–908), whose *Commentum in Martianum Capellam* has been preserved in over 70 MSS (*Remigii Autissidorensis Commentum in Martianum Capellam*, Libri I–II, ed. C. E. Lutz, 1962). From the 12th cent. on commentary was used in the most varied fields of knowledge, particularly in phi-

losophy, and became 'the most important form of scholarly literature' [8. 215]. Likewise, there are signs in Servius, more distinct in the Virgil commentary of Fulgentius (end 5th cent. AD), of an emphasis on allegorical interpretation, which was to become especially significant in the Middle Ages and reached its most systematic development in the allegorical commentary of Bernardus Silvestris (d. after 1159) on the sixth book of the *Aeneid* and in his allegorical commentaries on Ovid's *Metamorphoses*. Analysis of ancient works was especially pursued in schools and universities, where commentary might take the form of continuous exegetical paraphrase. The language used was Latin, the universal language and language of scholars, but vernacular commentaries on the *volgarizzamenti* of ancient authors and on Dante's *Commedia* appeared in Italy quite early on [2].

In no period was commentary as popular, with so many forms, as in the period of Humanism and the → RENAISSANCE; the very many terms applied to it, not always displaying any clear distinction between them, give eloquent testimony to its vitality (*commentarius, interpretatio, enarratio, expositio, explicatio, adnotationes, glossae, scholia* etc.). Raphael Regius 'commentary, published many times over in the 15th and 16th cents. on Ovid's *Metamorphoses* (*Ovidii Metamorphosis cum luculentissimis Raphaelis Regii enarrationibus*, Venice 1493) might well be seen as the very epitome of a typical Humanistic commentary [1. 119–139]. Regius, who was professor of Latin, Greek, and rhetoric at the universities of Padua and Venice and who, in addition to his commentary on Ovid's *Metamorphoses*, had commented on the *Rhetorica ad Herennium* and Quintilian, saw his main task to be the production of a flawless text as much as to elucidate its particular linguistic and contextual difficulties. He chose to explain the Latin poem in terms of 'ut reddita sibi esse Metamorphosis ipsa videatur' (so that the *Metamorphosis* itself might seem to have been given back to itself; dedicatory preface), i. e. the work should reappear in its original form and content. Regius highlights the linguistic-stylistic artistic devices used by the poet and explains the structure of the narrative. The annotations of a factual nature range from relevant mythological explanations through the philosophical, historical and geographic to the astrological and scientific. According to Regius, Ovid's *Metamorphoses* offers an entire encyclopaedia of ancient knowledge that the commentary intends to make accessible. Such an encyclopaedic claim is peculiar to the humanistic commentary. In the extreme it can result in works like the *Cornu Copiae* of Niccolò Perotti, in which the planned commentary on Martial is expanded into a comprehensive, linguistic-encyclopaedic dictionary (first edition, 1489) [6]. Regius acknowledges that the *Metamorphoses* offers not only factual knowledge but can also have other important educational functions. By virtue of its stylistic qualities it is especially suited to guide the reader in correct speech and writing and, by virtue of the *virtutum vitiorumque exempla* (models of virtues and vices) contained in the poem, it offers a model for proper conduct. Regius avoids the allegorical method altogether; his interpretations engage in little speculation and aim instead at passing on practical wisdom.

Another distinctive feature of many Humanistic commentaries, striking us today as rather strange, is only barely discernible in Regius' somewhat reserved commentary: the close link between one's own experiential existence and the text being analysed, between the Humanist's real and personal point of reference and the ancient authors that he is commenting upon. In *De ratione dicendi* (1532) Juan Luis Vives draws a distinction between the *commentarius simplex* (notes in the style of the *Commentarii* of Caesar) and the *commentarius in aliud* (elucidation of an author) and within the latter distinguishes the short commentary (*brevis, contractus*), which analyses a text in a focused way, from the long commentary (*diffusus*), in which the commentator attempts to contribute something of his own (*De ratione dicendi* 3,11). Regius' commentary can be regarded as an example of the first type; regarding the second, Vives was thinking primarily of commentaries on philosophical, medical and legal works: but it can even include commentaries on literary works. Thus, in the *Commentarii in Asinum aureum Lucii Apuleii* (Venice, 1500), his best-known and most ambitious commentary [7], Filippo Beroaldo combines lexical and contextual elucidation with rather lengthy digressions, only loosely connected to the actual textual analysis, on such themes as magic, mythology, religious history and geography, where he engages in lively dialogue with the ancient author. Moreover, he examines the text against the background of his own experience, juxtaposing modern and ancient *exempla*, and making observations on the social reality of his own time. In two especially lengthy and elaborately framed *excursus,* he describes the villa of a patrician friend of his from Bologna and, on the occasion of his own marriage, delivers an enthusiastic oration on marriage. 'Beroaldo's interpretations, therefore, display a lively interaction between the reception and actualization of the text' [7. 172]. Beroaldo shares Regius' scepticism towards allegorical interpretation. He strives to avoid allegory in favour of philosophical-historical methods, so as not to seem to be a *philosophaster* rather than a *commentator* (edition of 1501, f. O6v).

After the Renaissance, vernacular commentaries on major national authors, with an orientation similar to that of the Humanistic commentary on ancient authors, became increasingly important.

1 A. BUCK, O. HERDING (eds.), Der Kommentar in der Renaissance, 1975   2 A. BUCK (ed.), Die italienische Literatur im Zeitalter Dantes und am Übergang vom Mittelalter zur Renaissance, GRLMA X,1–2) 1987–1989   3 Catalogus Translationum et Commentariorum: Mediaeval and Renaissance Latin Translations and Commentaries (eds.), V. BROWN, F. E. CRANZ, P. O. KRISTELLER, Vols. I – VII, 1960–1992   4 J. CÉARD, 'Les transformations du genre du commentaire', in: L'Automne de la Renaissance, 1981, 101–115   5 Id., 'Les mots et les choses: le commentaire à la Renaissance', in: L'Europe de la Renaissance. Cultures et civilisations, 1988, 25–36   6 M. FURNO, Le Cornu Copiae de Niccolò Perotti, 1995   7 K. KRAUTTER, Philologische Methode und humanistische Existenz. Filippo Beroaldo und sein Kommentar zum Goldenen Esel des Apuleius, 1971   8 P. O. KRISTELLER, 'Der Gelehrte und sein Publikum im späten Mittelalter und in der Renaissance,' in: Medium Aevum vivum, Festschrift für W. Bulst, 1960   9 G. MATHIEU-CASTELLANI, M. PLAISANCE, eds., Les commentaires et la naissance de la critique littéraire, 1990   10 S. PRETE, 'Die Leistungen der Humanisten auf dem Gebiete der lateinischen Philologie,' in: Philologus 109 (1965), 259–269.

R. STILLERS, Humanistische Deutung: Studien zu Kommentar und Literaturtheorie in der italienischen Renaissance, Düsseldorf 1988   BODO GUTHMÜLLER

II. LATIN LITERATURE
A. BEGINNINGS   B. THE CLASSICAL PERIOD
C. FROM LATE ANTIQUITY to the RENAISSANCE

A. BEGINNINGS

As a technical term, *commentarius (liber)* or *commentarium* encompasses a broad spectrum of meaning from 'treatise' or 'monograph' to the modern 'explication of a literary text' [2]. This range of meaning makes it difficult to date precisely the origins of commentary in the latter sense, but they are surely more or less contemporaneous with the beginning of school education (initially in Greece) in Rome [6; 9]. Of the Roman *grammatici* of the 2nd cent. BC Suetonius (gramm. 2,2) reports that they carried out their work 'carmina parum adhuc diuulgata ... legendo commentandoque' (by reading and commenting on poems very recently published). Although its content remains unknown to us, Suetonius writes of an 'opusculum ... Annalium Enni elenchorum' of M. Pompilius Andronicus (early years of the 1st cent. BC), which might well have been one of the earliest published commentaries in the modern sense. Suetonius (gramm. 8,1) also tells of Lucius Crassicius Pansa of Tarentum, who seems to have published a commentary of this kind in the 3rd decade of the 1st cent. BC: 'commentario Zmyrnae (i. e. of Cinna) edito'.

B. THE CLASSICAL PERIOD

The first four or five centuries of the Empire produced an enormous variety of commentaries on an extensive body of literary works, but only a small percentage of these has survived [28]. The extent of this loss can be judged from a famous passage in Jerome's *Apologia contra Rufinum* 1,16 (CCL 79. 15. 26): 'Puto quod puer legeris Aspri in Vergilium ac Sallustium commentarios, Vulcatii in orationes Ciceronis, Victorini in dialogos eius, et in Terentii comoedias praeceptoris mei Donati, aeque in Vergilium, et aliorum in alios, Plautum uidelicet, Lucretium, Flaccum, Persium atque Lucanum' ('I think that you might read when young the commentaries of Asper on Virgil and Sallust, those of Vulcatius on the orations of Cicero, those of Victorinus on his [Cicero's] dialogues, and those of my teacher Donatus on the comedies of Terence, as well as on Virgil, and those of others on other authors, such as Plautus, Lucretius, Flaccus, Persius, and Lucan'). From that list, only Aelius Donatus' commentary on Terence is still extant, and even it is not entirely in the original version. From the extant commentaries on Cicero and Virgil, however, we can form a rough impression of what has been lost.

Of all these commentaries, the earliest extant is the (fragmentary and possibly condensed) work of Q. Pedianus Asconius from AD 54–57, which treats the five orations of Cicero In Pisonem, Pro Scauro, Pro Milone, Pro Cornelio and In toga candida [3]. This detailed study places an Argumentum ('list of contents') at the beginning of each oration, followed by a commentary that quotes the relevant point in the text as a lemma. As expected, the contents emphasize the historical, including a great deal of prosopographic details, as well as information on juridical matters and issues of constitutional law. Similar in nature are the commentaries of Marius Victorinus (4th cent.) on De inventione [11. 153–304], Grillius (5th cent.), likewise on De inventione [11. 596–606], Macrobius (5th cent.), Commentarii in somnium Scipionis, Boethius (5th to 6th cent.) In topica Ciceronis [27; 23], as well as the Scholia in Ciceronis orationes Bobiensia, an anonymous work that exists in a palimpsest of the 5th cent., its author probably having used Asconius as one of his sources [12].

Because of his predominance in the school curriculum, commentaries on Virgil were the most frequent. His near contemporary, C. Iulius Hyginus, librarian of the emperor Augustus, wrote a work entitled either Commentaria in Vergilium or Libri de Vergilio, of which the only surviving fragments treat the Eclogues and the Aeneid. Carvilius Pictor wrote a polemic against the Aeneid under the title Aeneomastix, to which Asconius responded with his Liber in obtrectatores Vergilii. Only three works have survived from the extremely extensive literary output of the Empire. The earliest is the Interpretationes Vergilianae of Tiberius Claudius Donatus (c. AD 350), a detailed (principally moralistic and rhetorical) analysis devoted exclusively to the Aeneid, written for his son and distinguished by its outraged rejection of traditional commentators (Proem, 1,5, ed. Georgii: 'cum aduerterem nihil magistros discipulis conferre quod sapiat. since I notice that teachers are offering students nothing sensible')[26]. All that this work borrows from traditional forms of commentary is the use of lemmata to indicate the points under discussion in the text. Apart from that, the style is rather long-winded; the author is especially concerned with the 'correct' interpretation of Virgilian words, rather than, for example, linguistic details useful for classroom teaching. Next are the peculiar Scholia Veronensia from the 5th cent., a fragmentary text of Virgil's Eclogues, Georgics and Aeneid with numerous marginal comments of unknown authorship but clearly indebted to the lost scholiastic tradition [1]. As with Servius, this work makes us only too aware of how many scholarly commentaries have disappeared. We learn here of Virgil commentaries from the pens of Asper (18 quotations), Cornutus (5), Haterianus (5), Longus (8), Probus (3), Scaurus (3) and Sulpicius (1). Last of the three to be mentioned are the wide-ranging Commentarii of M. Servius Honoratus. It would not be inappropriate to mention also the Saturnalia of Macrobius (early 5th cent.). They contain a lot of material from Virgil commentaries, although in dialogue form, and even have the then famous Servius appear as a participant in the conversations. A good portion of the highly influential (but since lost) work of Aelius Donatus (c. AD 350) can be reconstructed from these dialogues.

By far the best example of a perfectly constructed commentary is that of Servius on Virgil. As is apparent from internal cross-references, it was drawn up in the sequence Aeneid, Eclogues, and Georgics [29; 13; 20]. It contains a detailed introduction to each of Virgil's works, including one on the Aeneid, which is the most intact, with numerous (not always reliable) details of the poet's life and references to the background of each individual work; for example, observations on Homer, Theocritus and Hesiod as the respective models for the Aeneid, the Eclogues and the Georgics. The commentary takes the reader through each of Virgil's texts line by line, sometimes even word by word, with frequent references to what has already been explained through comments such as, ut supra diximus (as we said above). Servius constantly brings up questions that he was familiar with through his lengthy experience as a schoolteacher. Thus, he attempts to illustrate his observations by alluding to both Greek and Latin sources. Among the very many key areas in which he was interested are: grammar and the Latin language, textual criticism, metrics, literature, history, mythology, philosophy, religion and geography. In all these areas he makes frequent references to earlier grammatici, a profession to which he himself belonged. Often, however, he writes of them in a condescending and dismissive tone and with special acerbity when he comes to speak of his great predecessor Aelius Donatus. He is, nonetheless, fair in many of his judgements; when he is not himself sure which interpretation is to be preferred, he leaves the choice among various explications open, just as if he had taken to heart the exhortation of Jerome in the Apologia contra Rufinum 1,16 (CCL 79,14,15): 'Commentarii quid operis habent? Alterius dicta edisserunt, quae obscure scripta sunt plano sermone manifestant, multorum sententias replicant, et dicunt: Hunc locum quidam sic edisserunt, alii sic interpretantur'. (What is the task of commentaries? They explain the words of someone else; they make clear in plain speech words that have been written darkly; they repeat the opinions of many and state: some persons explain the passage this way, others interpret it that way).

Servius' work is preserved in many hundreds of MSS, from the early 8th cent. up to the late 15th cent., including the earliest: Marburg, Hessisches Staatsarchiv, Fragment 319; Pfarrarchiv Spangenberg (Depositum) HR no. 1, a collection of excerpts with occasional Anglo-Saxon glosses, written in southwest England and clearly intended for school-use. Some of the texts have been transmitted in their presumed original form, i.e. as a unified work. A magnificent specimen is to be found in Leiden, Bibliotheek der Rijksuniversiteit B. P. L. 52 [15]. Other texts are simply marginal commentaries on Virgil's text. Two impressive examples of this are the 9th cent. MS collection from Bern, Bürgerbibliothek 363 [10] and the two-volume Holkham Hall 311 from the late 15th cent. that not only contains the Virgil text in its entirety but reproduces in the margin the complete text of Servius and that of Tiberius Claudius Donatus on the *Aeneid* as well. At the other end of the spectrum we find hundreds of texts containing marginal glosses or interlinear notes derived from Servius, either as literal excerpts from his commentaries or as a modified borrowings. In fact, only very rarely do we come across MSS of Virgil that contain no form of annotation. Thus, for example, we find a great number of Virgil texts with the interlinear annotation of *bella* over *arma*, the first word of the *Aeneid*.

C. From Late Antiquity to the Renaissance

The history of the following 1000 years is one of both continuity and innovation. Where extant, the earlier commentaries (e.g. Servius on Virgil, Grillius and Victorinus on Cicero, Lactantius Placidus on the *Thebais* of Statius) were copied and remained in use; new commentaries that drew on older ones also appeared, and, finally, to meet a demand, entirely independent commentaries came into being [24; 21; 14].

Immediately after completion of his work, no commentary had been prepared on Martianus Capella. Yet at least from the 9th cent. on, the needs of pedagogues began to be addressed and two commentaries appeared, one of which was ascribed (wrongly, it seems) to Dunchad and the other to Iohannes Scottus Eriugena [18; 19].

Cicero constantly aroused the interest of commentators, especially his rhetorical and philosophical writings. A fascinating example is an early 9th cent. copy of his *De inventione* (codex Parisinus, Bibliothèque Nationale, latinus 7774), the lacunal text of which was partly supplemented in the manuscript of the prominent scholar Servatus Lupus of Ferrières; moreover, the text is filled with interlinear and marginal notes in this same MS of Lupus. During the extremely productive 12th cent., the famous Thierry of Chartres, in addition to his study on Boethius, composed commentaries on *De inventione* and on the pseudo-Ciceronian *Ad Herennium*. This once again underlines the continuing relevance of these works for teaching in schools [5; 7]. Cicero's orations also continually attracted scholarly interest. The following commentaries, each dealing with a selection of his orations, are extant: pseudo-Asconius (of unknown date, on the *orations against Verres*); the *Scholia Gronoviana* (contained in an early 9th cent. MS written in Tours), the *Scholia Cluniacensia* (MS from the 9th cent.); the *Scholia Ambrosiana ac Vaticana* (10th cent. MS). The Renaissance displayed a constant interest in such explications, which became all the more necessary as knowledge spread about the MSS that had been discovered by French and Italian Humanists [25].

As one might expect, Virgil was more often the subject of commentaries than other classical authors. In the early Middle Ages, a series of commentaries followed the Servius model, in particular, that of Iunius Philargyrius on the *Eclogues* (in two different versions, both of which give evidence of the influence of Christianity and of Irish glosses) and the *Scholia Bernensia* [8]. In the Laon MS, Bibliothèque Municipale 468, copied by Martin Hiberniensis [4], we obtain good insight into the way that Virgil was treated in schools. In addition to many similar works, the 12th cent. produced the extensive commentary that is linked to Anselm of Laon, even though it is apparently not by him. Modeled in form and, to a very large extent, in detail as well on the commentary of Servius, it brought to the fore much new material from other sources. In addition, it provided a very clear picture of teaching in the schools of that period. Of course, Christian elements were liberally grafted onto the Servius text, and the emphasis that Servius placed on Greek models is considerably weakened in 'Anselm'. In the 13th cent., the English Dominican Nicholas Trevet composed a commentary on the *Eclogues* 22; 17], while in the 14th cent. Ciones (or Zono) de Magnali(s) of Florence [16] produced a commentary on the *Eclogues*, the *Georgics* and the *Aeneid*. In the same century, Benvenuto da Imola commented on the *Eclogues* and the *Georgics*. In the 15th cent., Italy plays the major role and, in particular, the works of Pomponio Leto, Cristoforo Landino, Domizio Calderini und Antonio Mancinelli stand out. Landino's commentary was printed in Florence as early as 1487/88, and Mancinelli's commentary (along with those of Servius, Donatus and Landino) appeared in book form in a Venetian edition of 1491–92.

It should also be acknowledged that even the translation of a literary work into another language represents a form of commentary. It could even be claimed that in the 10th cent., with his Anglo-Saxon translations of authors like Augustine and Boethius, King Alfred started a genre that expanded considerably in the 14th and 15th cents. Translations of Valerius Maximus, for example, appeared in Sicilian and Tuscan dialects, and in German, French and Catalan.

1 C. Baschera, Gli Scolii Veronesi a Virgilio. Introduzione, edizione critica e indici, 1999   2 F. Bömer, Der Commentarius, in: Hermes 81, 1953, 210–250   3 A. C. Clark, Q. Asconii Pediani Orationum Ciceronis quinque enarratio, 1907   4 J. J. Contreni, Codex Laudensis 468. A Ninth-Century Guide to Vergil, Sedulius, and the Liber-

al Arts, 1984 5 M. DICKEY, Some Commentaries on the De inventione and Ad Herennium in the Eleventh and Early Twelfth Centuries, in: Mediaeval and Renaissance Studies 6, 1968, 1–41 6 R. A. KASTER, C. Suetonius Tranquillus De Grammaticis et Rhetoribus, 1995 7 K. FREDBORG, The Latin Rhetorical Commentaries by Thierry of Chartres, 1971 8 G. FUNAIOLI, Esegesi Virgiliana Antica, 1930 9 Id., Grammaticae Romanae Fragmenta, 1907 (repr. 1964) 10 H. HAGEN, Augustinus, Beda, Horatius, Servius, alii. Codex Bernensis 363 phototypice editus, Leiden 1897 11 C. HALM, Rhetores Latini Minores, Leipzig 1863 12 P. HILDEBRANDT, Scholia in Ciceronis Orationes Bobiensia, 1907 13 R. A. KASTER, Guardians of Language. The Grammarian and Society in Late Antiquity, 1988 14 P. O. KRISTELLER (et al.), Catalogus Translationum et Commentariorum: Mediaeval and Renaissance Latin Translations and Commentaries (7 vols.), 1960–1992 15 G. I. LIEFTINCK, Servii Grammatici in Vergilii Carmina Commentarii. Codex Leidensis B. P. L. 52, 1960 16 M. L. LORD, A Commentary on Aeneid 6, Ciones de Magnali, not Nicholas Trevet, in: Medievalia et Humanistica 15, 1987, 147–160 17 Id., Virgil's Eclogues, Nicholas Trevet, and the Harmony of the Spheres, in: Mediaeval Studies 54, 1991, 186–273 18 C. E. LUTZ, Iohannis Scotti Annotationes in Marcianum, 1939 19 Id., Dunchad Glossae in Martianum, 1944 20 P. K. MARSHALL, Servius and Commentary on Virgil, 1997 21 B. MUNK OLSEN, L'étude des auteurs classiques latins aux XIe et XIIe siècles (3 vols.), 1982–1985 22 A. A. NASCIMENTO, J. MANUEL Díaz de Bustamante, Nicolas Trivet Anglico. Comentario a las Bucolicas de Vergilio, 1984 23 J. C. ORELLI, J. G. BAITER, Ciceronis Opera, vol. 5, Zürich 1834 24 L. D. REYNOLDS, Texts and Transmission. A Survey of the Classics, 1983 25 R. SABBADINI, Le Scoperte dei Codici Latini e Greci nei Secoli XIV e XV, 1905–1914 26 M. SQUILLANTE SACCONE, Le Interpretationes Vergilianae di Tiberio Claudio Donato, 1985 27 T. STANGL, Ciceronis Orationum Scholiastae, 1912 28 W. H. D. SURINGAR, Historia Critica Scholiastarum Latinorum (2 vols.), Leiden 1834 29 G. THILO, H. HAGEN, Servii Grammatici qui feruntur in Vergilii Carmina Commentarii (3 vols.), Leipzig 1881–1987.

III. BYZANTINE LITERATURE

Byzantine literature is a regular reflection of and on Antiquity, and commenting on texts from Classical Antiquity belongs to its most important activities, a practice that often derived from oral exposition in school. Thus, the term 'commentary' can be understood broadly to include also: scholia, paraphrases, allegory, epimerisms (grammatical and linguistic commentaries on profane authors; those on Homer were particularly extensive, but also those on biblical and religious texts) and schedographia (from the 11th cent. on: short exercise texts in prose, sometimes opening with verses).

This short and almost index-like overview, which is necessarily limited to profane authors, begins with the ancient and Late-Antiquity commentaries on Aristotle and Plato that extend from Aspasius and Alexander of Aphrodisias (2nd–3rd cents. AD) to Stephanus and David (7th cent. AD); likewise belonging to Late Antiquity is the commentary by Hierocles of Alexandria (d. 431/2) on the pseudo-Pythagorean Carmen aureum.

The commentaries not only allow a glimpse into the thinking of the Neoplatonic and Aristotelian schools but, because the Greek commentaries or their Arabic versions were translated into Latin in the 12th and 13th cents., they made a significant contribution to Aristotelian transmission. It was thus that the Latin Middle Ages came to know Aristotle, which opened the way for European philosophy of the Renaissance and the early modern period. The grammarian Georgius Choiroboskos, active at the turn of the 8th cent. into the 9th, commented on, among other things, the Κανόνες περί κλίσεως ('rules for declension and conjugation') of Theodosius of Alexandria and the Encheiridion ('a manual on metre') of Hephaestion. In exemplary fashion his work displays that process of rendering and elucidating ancient grammatical texts (e.g. Dionysius Thrax and Apollonius Dyskolos) that characterizes the whole Byzantine millennium. Photius (c. 810–893), Patriarch of Constantinople, in addition to the chapters on categories in a section (Ch. 77; 137–147) of the Amphilochia (a treatise in question and answer format on theological and philosophical themes), which, however, should not be considered real commentaries, composed scholia on the Eisagoge of Porphyrius and on the categories of Aristotle. The middle of the 9th cent. or a little later marked the production of the so-called philosophical collection of a homogeneous group of at least 12 MSS containing predominantly Platonic commentators (Proclus, Damascius and Olympiodorus). Arethas, Archbishop of Caesarea (c. 850–944), wrote commentaries on classical and religious texts as well as on texts from the Old and New Testaments (John's Revelations). The scholia on Aristotle's Organon in cod. Urbinas graecus 35 (about 900) are probably his own work, whereas it is still questionable whether the corpus of scholia on Platonic texts in the cod. Vindobonensis phil. graecus 314 (dated to 925) is to be ascribed to him. Between the 10th and 11th cents., the orator Johannes Sikeliotes commented on the rhetors Hermogenes and Aelius Aristides. The orator Johannes Doxopatres (not to be confused with his predecessor) belonged to the first half of the 11th cent. and composed homilies (lectures) on the Progymnasmata of the rhetor Aphthonios and a commentary on Hermogenes. Toward the end of the Macedonian dynasty (867–1056), the impressive commentary on the collection of laws of the Basilica was prepared (probably completed in 888), for which the material of the Antecessores of the 6th cent. was also used. Michael Psellus (1018–1078) composed a commentary on Aristotle's Physics, which, although conventional in its presentation, displays a deliberate independence of judgement. He also wrote a paraphrase of Aristotle's De interpretatione and a prose paraphrase of the Iliad. For political and religious reasons the works of Johannes Italos (1023–c. 1085) were accorded no great success; nevertheless, a palimpsest-Codex (Marcianus graecus 265) has, in its upper writing, preserved, among other things, his commentary on Books. II–IV of Aristotle's Topics that draws on the commentaries of Alexander of Aphrodisias.

Within the philosophical circle around the princess Anna Comnene, the figures of Eustratios of Nicaea (*c.* 1050– shortly after 1117) and Michael of Ephesus (11th.–12th cent.) feature prominently. To the former we are indebted for commentaries on Book. I of Aristotle's *Posterior Analytics* (quite in the style of Johannes Italos) and on Books. I and VI of the *Nicomachean Ethics* (with a strong Platonizing tendency against Aristotelian criticism). Michael, on the other hand, shows a broader interest in Aristotelian philosophy. In addition to his commentary on the *Organon*, he also commented in a clear and sober manner on the *Metaphysics* (Books. 6–14), the *Nicomachean Ethics* (Books. 5, 9 and 10), the biological and zoological writings and, as the only Byzantine to do so, the *Politics* and the treatise *De coloribus*. His commentaries on the *Topics* and the *Rhetoric*, however, have been lost. A little later, Gregorius Pardos (*c.* 1070–1156), Metropolitan of Corinth, exerted great influence. Apart from commenting on the liturgical *Canons* of Cosmas of Jerusalem and Johannes of Damascus, he commented on the treatise Περί μεθόδου δεινότητος ('On the Acquisition of Skill in Rhetoric') of Hermogenes. Among the prolific output of Theodorus Prodromos (*c.* 1100–shortly before 1158) there is a commentary of a logical-pedagogical nature on the second book of the *Posterior Analytics*. The most significant figures of the Comnene period (1081–1185) are Johannes Tzetzes (d. after 1180) and Eustathius of Thessalonica (d. 1192/4). The former composed a great number of commentaries on ancient authors, especially poets: Hesiod, Pindar, the tragedians, Aristophanes (the so-called Byzantine triad: *Clouds, Frogs, Plutus*), Lycophron (also attributed to his brother Isaac), the *Halieutika* of Oppianus, and Nicander. He also dedicated fifteen-syllable verses to the *Corpus Hermogenianum* (only partly published) and 1700 twelve-syllable paraphrasing poems to the *Eisagoge* of Porphyrius. Finally, he composed an allegoresis of the *Iliad* and the *Odyssey* in 9741 lines. Eustathius' encyclopaedic knowledge is displayed in his extensive Homeric commentaries that have survived as autographs. He is also the author of an explanatory paraphrase and commentary on a geographical didactic poem by Dionysius Periegetes and a commentary on Pindar, of which only the proem has survived. Also belonging to the Comnene period are the two canonists Alexius Aristenos and Theodorus Balsamon, authors of a popular commentary on the *Nomocanon XIV titulorum*.

After the cultural and political hiatus of the Latin domination of 1204–1261, a period in which, nonetheless, there appeared Michael Senacherim's hitherto only partly published commentary on Homer and probably also Leon Margentinos' commentary on the *Organon*, the period of the palaeologists (1259–1453) witnessed a surprising cultural revival. MSS of classical authors were again copied in remarkable quantities. Four towering figures belong to the first phase of this era: 1. Manuel/Maximos Planudes (1255–1305), a translator of Latin authors into Greek and philologist, but also an

editor and commentator on ancient texts. His rich work includes editions of Aesop and the first two books of Diophantus' *Arithmetic*, both with commentaries. He also authored scholia on Hesiod (*Erga*), Sophocles, Euripides, Aristophanes, Thucydides and Euclid, and epimerisms on the first book of Philostratus' *Eikones*. 2. Regarding Manuel Moschopulos (*c.*1265 – *c.* 1316) we can reconstruct, though with some difficulty, the scholia of a predominantly paraphrasing and grammatical nature on Hesiod, Pindar (*Olympic Epinicia*), Sophocles and Euripides (in each case the 'Byzantine triad'), Theocritus (the first eight poems), Aristophanes (*Plutus*), as well as 'Technologies' (grammatical introductions) to the *Iliad* and to Philostratus. 3. Thomas Magistros (d. shortly after 1346), composer of an influential Atticist lexicon, was an editor of and commentator on the tragedians, Aristophanes (three comedies), Pindar (paraphrasing scholia predominantly grammatical and stylistic in nature) and the letters of Synesius. 4. His pupil Demetrius Triklinios (*c.*1280–*c.* 1340) was undoubtedly the most important philologist and textual critic of his time. Deserving special mention of his prolific output are the editions and commentaries (with numerous excerpts from the *scholia vetera*) on Hesiod, Pindar (especially scholia on metre), Aeschylus (five tragedies), Sophocles (particularly the first four tragedies), Euripides (autograph), Aristophanes (the triad, an autograph), Theocritus and Aratus, for which he also used material from Planudes.

Alongside these scholars, other figures gained prominence, such as the historian Georgius Pachymeres (1242–*c.* 1310), who composed an exegetical paraphrase of almost the whole Aristotelian corpus (extant in two autographs), the monk Sophonias (d. before 1351), composer of at least one paraphrase of the Aristotelian writings *De anima* and *Sophistici Elenchi*. Also active was the *Chartophylax* and *Megas sakellarios* (Director of Archives and Financial Administrator) Johannes Pediasimos (*c.* 1240–1310/1314), whose allegorical paraphrase of the *Iliad* 1–4, scholia on the *Prior Analytics* and part of the *Posterior Analytics* (his main source being Johannes Philoponos), on Hesiod (*Theogony* and *Aspis*), Theocritus (*Syrinx*) and Cleomedes have survived. The politician Theodorus Metochites (1270–1332) wrote paraphrasing commentaries on a large part of Aristotle's writings (excluding the *Organon* and the *Metaphysics*). Georgius Lakapenos (13th–14th cents.) wrote a school commentary on Epictetus. Finally, one should mention the numerological interpretation of a Johannes Protospatharios (13th–14th cents.), whom we cannot identify more precisely, on the *Works and Days* (*Hemerai*) of Hesiod, and the allegories on the *Theogony* of Diakonos Johannes Galenos, whose transmission history links him closely to Protospatharios. To the 14th cent. belongs the great polyhistor Nicephorus Gregoras (*c.* 1293–*c.* 1359/1361), who was, among other things, the author of a commentary on Synesius' treatise Περί Ενυπνίων ('On Dreams') and also had attributed (dubiously) to him elementary scholia on Ptolemy's *Geography*. Additional works and authors of the 14th cent. are: an anonymous paraphrase on the *Nicomachean Ethics* that had been erroneously assigned to Emperor Johannes VI Kantakuzenos, and the commentaries on Aristotle's works on logic by the 'Antipalamiter' (i.e. opponent of the Byzantine theologian Gregorius Palamas) Isaac Argyros (*c.* 1300– *c.* 1375) and later by the monk Joseph Philagres/Philagrius written on Crete between 1392 and 1395. Falling within the 15th cent. is the Metropolitan of Selymbria Johannes Chortasmenos (*c.* 1370–1436/7), a MSS-collector and writer to whom we are indebted for paraphrases of Aristotle's works on logic and explications of Aphthonius' *Progymnasmata*. Also in the 15th cent., the Patriarch of Constantinople Georgius Gennadeios Scholarios (1400/1405–*c.* 1472) composed very many clear and succinct commentaries on Aristotle and Porphyry, in which he used ancient, Arabic and Medieval Latin sources (e.g. Thomas Aquinas).

Byzantine exegetical activity did not cease with fall of Constantinople (1453) but rather received a new impulse from the encounter with Italian Humanists and the new style and method of Western commentary.

1 J. ASSMANN, B. GLADIGOW (eds.), Text und Kommentar, 1995 2 A. BUCK, O. HERDING (eds.), Der Kommentar in der Renaissance, 1975 3 F. E. CRANZ et al. (eds.), Catalogus translationum et commentariorum, 1960ff. 4 HANS-CHRISTIAN GÜNTHER, The Manuscripts and the Transmission of the Palaeologan Scholia on the Euripidean Triad, 1995 5 H. HUNGER, Die hochsprachliche profane Literatur der Byzantiner, 1–2, 1978 6 R. SORABJI (ed.), Aristotle Transformed. The Ancient Commentators and Their Influence, 1990 7 N. G. WILSON, Scholars of Byzantium, ²1996. PAOLO ELEUTERI

Communism see → SOCIALISM

Consolation Literature
A. CHARACTERISTICS OF THE RECEPTION
B. GENRES C. ERAS AND MAIN WORKS

A. CHARACTERISTICS OF THE RECEPTION
Owing to its immediate relevance to practical life, consolation literature (CL) was guaranteed an unbroken continuity in the Middle Ages and in modern times, also-and precisely-in its forms that have their origin in Antiquity. However, in the course of the time the corpus has shown an increasing differentiation both with regard to form and content. In addition, the genres of CL were adopted to a varied degree. Moreover, with Christianity ancient secular CL was faced with theological CL, which, apart from a corresponding tradition of treatises and letters, is attested in the broad stream of sermon literature and also shows a continuous history. A further new Christian form of CL was developed in the High Middle Ages by the German mystics (cf. Meister Eckhart's *Buch der göttlichen Tröstung* [7. 308ff.] and Heinrich Seuse's letter of consolation to Elsbeth Stagel (Großes Briefbuch, no. 12) [1. 1050]). Since the late Middle Ages there has been an extremely fruitful tendency of creatively developing further traditional forms and topoi of CL in other textual genres.

B. GENRES
The development of the genres of CL was virtually exhausted in Antiquity. The narrower thematic focus of CL is the *consolatio mortis*, which is a funeral oration, a letter of consolation or a poem of consolation addressed to a particular, usually prominent person on the occasion of a death. With regard to the subject matter the philosophical *consolatio* is more flexible and productive. It systematically deals with the nature and the overcoming of grief. Here, too, the occasion can be an individual misfortune, often of the author himself (usually imprisonment or exile). A philosophical *consolatio* often makes use of the dialogue. The formative model of mediaeval and modern CL, however, was not an ancient text but the *Consolatio Philosophiae* by Boethius. The second main genre of philosophical *consolatio* is the letter (with Cicero and Seneca as the most important models); the contribution of CL to the development of the literary letter must be highly rated. Finally, for poetic CL (primarily the *epicedium*) the → ELEGY and the epigram (→ EPIGRAMMATIC POETRY) are the most important genres. Here, the ancient models are primarily the pseudo-Ovidian *Consolatio ad Liviam* and Statius's *Silvae*.

For the letter of consolation a continuous history of reception is available. Letters of consolation in the narrower sense dominated primarily in the Middle Ages. The survival of ancient poetical CL was most closely connected with the phases of reception of the ancient canon of lyrical forms. Throughout all eras and genres a theme of consolation that in fact originated in Antiquity remained present [2. 90ff.].

With regard to the exordial topos itself, i.e. the occasion of grief, CL proposes to deal with an individual case which, at the same time, it stylizes as an exemplary case. This apparent discrepancy culminates, on one hand, in the intimate tone of CL and, on the other hand, in a virtually exemplary rhetorical and topical organization of the genre. The dialectical step from the individual to the examplary, which is to be understood as a fundamental literary strategy and which is responsible for the process of identification, was carried out in an exemplary way in CL. Thus, CL represents a literary phenomenon whose poetological effect has not yet been sufficiently acknowledged. This effect is probably also the reason why significant works of European literary history had their thematic starting point in the *consolatio*.

C. Eras and Main Works
1. Middle Ages 2. Renaissance, Humanism and Baroque 3. Enlightenment, 19th and 20th Cents.

1. Middle Ages

The liminal text of CL between Antiquity and the Middle Ages is the *Consolatio Philosophiae* by Boethius (written in 534 shortly before his execution). By systematically bringing together ancient consolatory subject matter and topics it arrives at a comprehensive ethics of life and a concise metaphysics that were totally obliged to the secular philosophy of Late Antiquity (primarily neo-Platonism) but could also unproblematically be understood in a Christian way. Thus, consolatory writings could also advance to become a concise textbook of ancient philosophy. The complementation of discursive prose with *carmina*, known as a prosimetrum, provided a powerful formal solution. Allegorization, interpretation of myths and dialogue (between the author and philosophy personified) were based on ancient models, but also foreshadowed central hermeneutic and rhetorical methods of the Middle Ages. All this explains the success of the text, which substantially contributed to the continuation of ancient philosophical CL and which resulted in a comprehensive tradition of translations, applications and commentaries [4]. Following Boethius numerous other Latin letters of consolation originated from the 11th cent. [1. 1048f.].

In addition, from the early Middle Ages on there was a broad tradition of Latin (from the 12th cent. also vernacular, initially French) letters and poems of consolation, which referred to ancient (Cicero, Seneca, Statius) and patristic (Ambrose, Jerome, Augustine) models [6].

In the High Middle Ages a specific form of CL developed in the context of courtly love discourse, based on Ovid's *Ars Amatoria* and *Remedia amoris*. Mediaeval examples are the correspondence between Abelard and Heloise (c. 1135?) and the treatise *De Amore* by Andreas Capellanus (c. 1185). Occasions, means and topoi of this *consolatio amoris* permeated novel, lyrics and love didaxis. In a song by the German minnesinger Heinrich von Morungen (Des Minnesangs Frühling XXII; late 12th cent.), for example, a mistress appears to the lovelorn singer in the manner of Boethian philosophy in order to console him.

2. Renaissance, Humanism and Baroque

The transition to modern times is marked by a series of texts that transcend the narrower context of CL and foreshadow their manifold possibilities of development. Thus, a mixture of courtly *consolatio amoris* and philosophical *consolatio mortis* formed the thematic nucleus of Dante's *Vita Nova* (c. 1290). The *consolatio* because of Beatrice becomes a *consolatio* by Beatrice in the *Commedia* (1307–1321), in which consolation as such represents one of the main themes. Petrarch's comprehensive allegorical dialogue work *De remediis utriusque fortune* (1366, comprising 122 dialogues between *Ratio* and *Gaudium* and 132 dialogues between

Ratio and *Dolor*) is a consolatory work in the narrower sense [5]. His *Canzoniere* (c. 1327–1374) mediated the topic of courtly *consolatio amoris* to the love lyrics of the Baroque.

In German literature the *Der Ackermann und der Tod* ('The Ploughman of Bohemia') by Johannes von Tepl (c. 1401) presents an unusual witness of early humanistic CL. Here, the *consolatio mortis* was not given in the form of a consolatory dialogue but rather in the form of an *altercatio*, i.e. a dispute between the poet, grieving for his wife, and death. Admittedly the text was also influenced by the genuine late mediaeval theme of death as it was tangible in the *Ars moriendi* and in the dance of death. In addition to the contributions of Erasmus [3. 371], humanistic CL reached a height in the systematic *Dyalogue of Comfort agaynst Tribulacion [etc.]* (with fictional speakers), which Thomas More completed in the Tower in 1534, shortly before his execution (in 1535) (this already reveals the close connection with Boethius). Besides traditional consolatory passages, which justify More's stand against royal power in the sense of a philosophical, but in contrast to Boethius an explicitly Christian ethics of life, the work deals also with questions of the theory of the state, among other things.

The topic of consolation permeated Baroque lyrics in particular. In German literature, due to the experience of the Thirty Years War, it is often linked with the (Christian) topos of vanity and refers not only to the individual occasion of grief but also to the fate of the country. Andreas Gryphius's sonnet *Tränen des Vaterlandes* (1636) and, above all, Martin Opitz's *Trost-Gedichte in Widerwertigkeit des Krieges*, a poetic consolatory work in 4 vols. (1621) are worth mentioning. Opitz also wrote several neo-Latin *epicedia*, including *O clara divae stella* on the occasion of the death of Sophie Elisabeth von Anhalt-Dessau (1622).

3. Enlightenment, 19th and 20th Cents.

It was the professed practical goal of ancient philosophical CL to compensate grief as an emotion by rational reflection. Thus, *consolatio* was also a central theme of Enlightenment literature and philosophy; examples are Denis Diderot and Immanuel Kant, among others [8. 1526]. Voltaire's *Candide* (1759) can be understood as a pointedly secular discussion of consolatory Christian moral philosophy and metaphysics. A parodic catalogue of CL and the topic of consolation can be found in *Tristram Shandy* by L. Sterne (Bk. 5, ch. 3, 1759–1767).

An interesting development of poetic CL was provided by the elegy and elegaic poetry of German idealism. With Friedrich Schiller's *Nänie* (1800) and *Die Götter Griechenlands* (with the loss of Antiquity itself as a consolatory theme, 1788/1800) they opened to CL a historical-philosophical perspective, which started from a *consolatio mortis* also in Novalis's *Hymnen an die Nacht* (written in 1797 under the impression of the death of his mistress Sophie von Kühn).

The crisis of traditional rhetoric during the 18th cent. resulted also in a crisis of traditional CL, as attested e.g. in Goethe's *Werther*. The process leads to a fundamental scepticism with regard to a systematically arguing CL in A. Schopenhauer and F. Nietzsche, who, however, acknowledges (in a witty remark) an Epicurean attitude (Menschliches, Allzumenschliches II.2, 7) [8. 1526]. Apart from survivals in trivial forms, owing to historical experiences and aesthetic and philosophical development, the 20th cent. marked the end of conventional consolatory genres and topoi, although to a limited extent exile literature and Holocaust literature could be viewed as new forms and grief remained both a central theme of philosophy and literature (particularly epistolary literature) and a concern of psychotherapy and pastoral theology.

→ Ambrosius; → Augustinus, Aurelius (Augustine); → Boethius; → Cicero; → Dialogue; → Hieronymus; → Letter; → Neoplatonism; → Ovidius Naso, Publius; → Seneca

1 G. BERNT, L. GNÄDINGER, R. GLEISSNER, W. SCHMIDTKE, s. v. Trostbuch, LMA 8, 1048–1051 2 E. R. CURTIUS, Europäische Literatur und lateinisches Mittelalter, ¹⁰1984 (Eng.: European literature and the Latin Middle Ages, W. R. TRASK (trans), ⁷1990) 3 A. GRÖZINGER, s. v. Consolatio, Historisches Wörterbuch der Rhetorik 2, 367–373 4 M. HOENEN, L. NAUTA (ed.), Boethius in the Middle Ages, Latin and Vernacular Traditions of the Consolatio Philosophiae, 1997 5 G. W. MCCLURE, Sorrow and Consolation in Italian Humanism, 1991 6 P. VON MOOS, Consolatio, Studien zur mittelalterlichen Trostliteratur über den Tod und zum Problem der christlichen Trauer, 4 vols., 1971/72 7 K. RUH, Geschichte der abendländischen Mystik, vol. 3, 1996 8 F.-B. STAMMKÖTTER, s. v. Trost, HWdPh 10, 1524–1527. MANFRED KERN

Constantine, Donation of The 'Donation of Constantin' (DC) is the current term for a document forged between the middle of the 8th and the 9th cents., probably in Rome. Its forger gives the impression that it is a copy of an original from the time of Constantine the Great, in which the Emperor transfers imperial sovereignity over the western half of the Empire and primacy over all dioceses (*super omnes in universo orbe terrarum ecclesias Dei*) to Pope Silvester I and his successors. This document, better known as the *Constitutum Constantini*, consists of two parts: 1. the *Confessio*, in which the Emperor describes his being cured of leprosy by the baptism which he received from Silvester, and which ends with recognition of the faith, and 2. the *Donatio* proper, in which discussion is of the transfer of the insignia of temporal and spiritual power to the Pope and the conferring of senatorial rank on Roman clergy.

The oldest known version of the DC is contained in the collection of pseudo-Isidorian *decretals* originating in the middle of the 9th cent., but there are indications that there must have been still older texts. The essential parts of the *Donatio* were included as *palea* in the *Decretum Gratiani*. In this form the document determined discussion among theologians and jurists of the Middle Ages.

From the time of the Investiture Contest popes also based their claim to supremacy over the emperor on the DC. The criticism triggered by this was directed not at the authenticity of the text, but at its content. It was raised both by theologians and by jurists. In the theological view, appeal to the DC was not unproblematic, as, according to it, the pope owed his spiritual and temporal power to the gift from the emperor and not divine intervention. From the time of Leo IX the Church reacted to this protest by interpreting the DC as the emperor's restoring authority originally bestowed on the pope by Christ, saying that by way of the *translatio imperii* the pope had in return then transferred temporal power back to the emperor. Further protests were connected with the objection that bestowing the insignia of temporal power on popes had induced them to neglect their Petrine office (Bernhard von Clairvaux). Such objections were also raised by heretics and early reforming movements (Waldensians, Hussites, Wyclif). Some jurists (Baldus and others.) called into doubt the legal validity of the DC In their opinion it was above all the title *Augustus* that would have prevented Constantine from giving away a part of the Empire. In the end jurists remitted the DC, but rather into the sphere of faith than that of the law. Nicholas of Cusa had already shown that the DC had to be a forgery (*De concordantia catholica*, 1433). This evidence received greater attention however only through Lorenzo Valla's *De falso credita et ementita Constantini donatione* (1440, first published anonymously in 1506). Valla's criticism rested on an historical and philological analysis of the text. In it he was concerned with uncovering the truth as a contribution to Church reform, not with a polemic against the pope. Only when republished by Ulrich v. Hutten (1518 and 1519) did Valla's writings achieve wide circulation. In Luther's view it corroborated his fundamental criticism of the papacy.

SOURCES 1 H. FUHRMANN, Constitutum Constantini, MGH, Fontes iuris Germanici antiqui X, 1968 (introduction and text)

LITERATURE 2 D. MAFFEI, La Donazione di Constantino nei giuristi medievali, 1964 3 H. FUHRMANN, Konstantinische Schenkung und abendländisches Kaisertum, in: Dissertation Abstracts 22, 1966, 63–178 4 Id., Pseudoisidor und das Constitutum Constantini, in: In Iure Veritas: Studies in Canon Law in Memory of Schafer Williams, STEVEN B. BOWMAN, BLANCHE E. CODY (eds.), 1991, 80–84 5 J. PETERSMANN, Die kanonistische Überlieferung des Constitutum Constantini bis zum Dekret Gratians, in: Dissertation Abstracts 30, 1974, 356–446 6 W. SETZ, Lorenzo Vallas Schrift gegen die Konstantinische Schenkung, 1975 7 E.-D. HEHL, 798 – ein erstes Zitat aus der Konstantinischen Schenkung, in: Dissertation Abstracts 47, 1991, 1–17. CHRISTOPH BERGFELD

Constantinople
A. Introduction B. Constantinople in Political Propaganda C. The Popular Reception of Constantinople D. Constantinople through the Eyes of Strangers E. Constantinople as a Cultural Model F. History of Research

A. Introduction
Constantinople's (C.) development as a city reached its zenith in the time of Justinian I (AD 527–565), though building activity continued until about 600. The deep political crisis which began in the Byzantine Empire after that had incisive results for C.: because of the Persian occupation of Egypt, grain deliveries ended in 618 and the aqueducts were destroyed in 626 during the siege by the Avars. The number of inhabitants, which was at a maximum of about 250,000–300,000 in the early 6th cent., had diminished considerably as a result of the plague in 542 to about 50,000–70,000, and for a long time the people were forced to feed themselves from fields and gardens in the city or its immediate vicinity. From 674 to 678 and in 717/18 C. suffered sieges by the Arabs and in 860 by the Russians. After the middle of the 8th cent. the city began to recover slowly, but the population never again attained its former levels. Many great buildings of the early period had collapsed. To be sure, the aqueducts had been partially rebuilt, but the great hot springs had not been made functional again. The cityscape was increasingly characterised by a multitude of small churches and monasteries, often built on the sites of older demolished buildings. With the political stabilisation of the Empire from the late 9th cent., foreigners arrived in the city in greater numbers. From the 10th to the 12th cents. the Imperial bodyguard was provided predominantly by Russians, Vikings and Englishmen. In 1082 Venice established a trade settlement in C. and other Italian cities followed suit. The growing dominance of the Italians in trade together with the religious schism between Catholics and Orthodox Christians led to a deterioration in relations with the indigenous population and in 1183 this was given vent in a harsh pogrom. In 1203 and 1204, occupied by the Venetians and the army of the Fourth Crusade, C. was devastated by several conflagrations. C. swiftly declined as the capital of a 'Latin' empire, and art treasures and relics were to a large extent removed to Western Europe. After reconquest by the Byzantines in 1261 there was short-lived prosperity, followed by C.'s final decline, while the Genoese city of Pera (Galata) on the other side of the estuary flourished. C. ended up merely a walled agglomeration of villages interspersed with gardens, fields and wooded areas. For instance, after 1360 the city was cut off on the land side by the Ottoman Turks and became reachable only by water. In 1453 the Turks eventually captured C. and made it the capital of the Ottoman Empire, though a large minority of Greeks continued to live in the city.

B. Constantinople in Political Propaganda
From the late 4th cent., but particularly after the loss of the competing metropolises of Antioch and Alexandria in the 7th cent., C. was the undisputed political centre of the Byzantine Empire. The propagating of C. as a second, then a new Rome played a significant political role in the 4th and 5th cents. That designation is contained in the titles of the Patriarch of C. to this day [4. 43–47, 454–461]. A result of the analogy with Rome is the early Byzantine division of the city into 14 regions. In contrast, C. was not described as a city of seven hills until the late 7th cent. in apocalyptic texts. In eulogies, C. was glorified as an imperial city, the eye of the world, or a city under divine protection [6]. In traditional Modern Greek usage C. has become simply the Polis, 'the City'. The *Megale Idea* ('grand idea') of recreating the Byzantine Empire with C. as its capital played a role in the foreign policy of modern Greece until the collapse of the Ottoman Empire and the subsequent war against the Turkish Republic between 1919 and 1923.

A conscious connection with Byzantine tradition in the political sphere underlay initiatives attempted by the Ottoman conqueror Mehmet II Fatih (1451–1481), but these conflicted with the state religion of Islam and ceased to be pursued after his death.

C. The Popular Reception of Constantinople
The main source for the popular view of C. in the Middle Ages is a collection of short texts, edited into their final form in about 990 and known as the *Patria Konstantinoupoleos* [1; 13], on the monuments of C., having the character of something between a local history and a guide for travellers. They also include the *Parastaseis syntomoi chronikai* from the early 9th cent. [2] and the legendary story, the core of which can probably be traced back as far as the 6th cent. [16], of the building of Hagia Sophia.

The need for historical legitimation of the political role as capital led to a prolonged period of legend creation in Greek and Roman times. The idea arose of a trio of founders: Byzas, the legendary founder of the city in the 7th cent. BC, Emperor Septimius Severus, who had Byzantium demolished and presumably rebuilt after a civil war in 196, and Constantine the Great [5. 61–97]. The propagation of C. as a New Rome was reflected in various popular traditions, e.g., the settling of C. with members of the Roman urban aristocracy was ascribed to Constantine. The idea that with the founding of the city the Trojans' claim to rule returned to the place of its origin led, on the one hand, to the legend of a failed first founding by Constantine at Troy and a secret removal of the Palladium from Rome to C., on the other.

In addition to political legitimation there was religious legitimation, which was effected e.g. by discovering and moving important relics to C. The words 'Solomon, I have conquered you', spoken, according to leg-

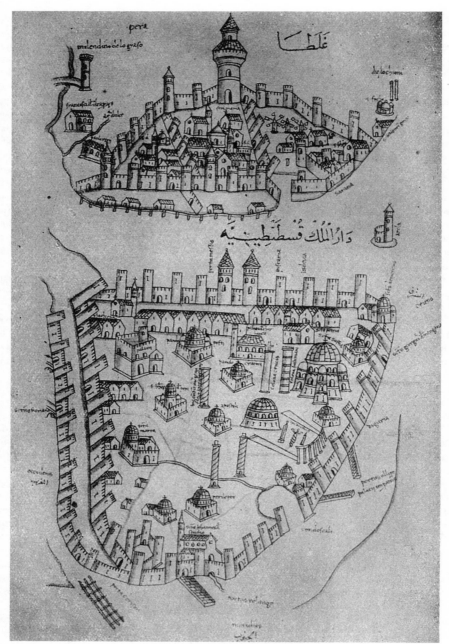

Fig. 1: The earliest bird's eye view of Constantinople from the south, in the traveloque
of Christoforo Buondelmonti. Codex Par. lat. 2383. Istituto di Studi Bizantini e Neoellenici
a cura di Silvio Guieppe Meracti, Rome

end, by the emperor Justinian on first entering Hagia
Sophia, may have an historical basis in that the church
of St. Polyeuktos in C., which had, in fact, been built
shortly before and according to the dimensions of the
Temple in Jerusalem, was to be surpassed [5. 303–309].
In legend however, they became the basis of a far-reaching ideological comparison of the Temple with Hagia

Sophia. From an Islamic point of view, particularly that
of the Ottoman Turks after 1453, Justinian could be
wholly displaced by the figure of Solomon [17. 99–153].

The legend of the construction of Hagia Sophia cites
various regions of the Empire and ancient temples as
sources of the building materials, although precisely
this church was one of the last not to be built predomi-

nantly with → SPOLIA. The reason for this is that in the numerous ruins of the early Byzantine period there was almost unlimited building material available and so beginning in the 7th cent. this material was used as spolia in almost all buildings, until eventually other methods of building were no longer conceivable. The churches of the martyrs Menas and Mokios were presented in a later legend as rebuilt ancient temples, probably at one time because of the use of spolia, or at another because of the idea of substitution of cults. The archaeological record shows that old building components were often used in inconspicuous places in the foundations etc., and only seldom consciously as architectonic citations. An exception is porphyry, which is reserved for imperial use and which sources often call 'Roman stone' owing to its ideological function and because for the most part it arrived in C. by way of Rome.

The subjects of the many ancient statues which had come from all over the Empire to C. as spolia were later reinterpreted in popular literature as characters from local history, mostly emperors. An example is the Tetrarch group from the entrance to the Capitol in C., today in Saint Mark's in Venice, which since at least the 9th cent. had been considered a representation of the fraternal love of the sons of Constantine the Great and so had been generally described as Philadelphion. On the other hand, early Byzantine statues of emperors were later interpreted as Biblical characters, e.g. a statue of Theodosius I in Tauros Square was taken to represent Joshua owing to the fact that its hand was raised towards the southeast, another in the Basilica to represent Solomon looking enviously at Hagia Sophia. Belief in the magical power of statues spread. To some sculptures was ascribed the ability to keep the city free of the animals portrayed, e.g. storks, mosquitoes, and snakes. Talismans of this kind were initially considered to be works of the magus Apollonius of Tyana; in the late Byzantine period they were also ascribed to the emperor Leo VI 'the Wise' (886–912). The use of sympathetic magic, which was supposed to harm or kill the person connected by magic with the statue, resulted in the destruction of a whole series of ancient artworks [12. 55–64]. Owing to the decline in the knowledge of other languages, Latin inscriptions could no longer be read and were often interpreted as prophecies or spells, understood only by the initiated.

D. Constantinople through the Eyes of Strangers

Despite the loss of prosperity compared with the early Byzantine period, the wealth of the city, the splendid court ceremonial, and the Hippodrome games played a central role in descriptions of the city, from the anonymous 7th cent. Chinese account [13] to the historians of the 1204 conquest, Geoffrey de Villehardouin and Robert de Clari [15. 540–552]. Ostentatious displays of wealth in receiving foreign delegations were employed as an instrument of policy in C., as can be

seen e.g. from the account of the German ambassador Liudprand von Cremona (in C. 949 and 968). The account of Hārūn ibn-Yahyā in 911 laid the foundation for an Arabian tradition of stories about C., in which the talismans mentioned above and later also Islamic prophecies concerning C. as a future Islamic city, played a particular role. Representative writers are Al-Harawi (end of the 12th cent.), Ibn Baṭṭūṭa (in C. c. 1332) and Al-Wardī (15th cent.) [15; 17. 85–93, 99–111]. From the late 11th cent. the role of C. increasingly gained prominence in the sagas of Vikings and the accounts of Englishmen and Crusaders as a store of relics. Regular pilgrimages to C. for predominantly religious reasons were undertaken only later however, chiefly by Russians. Antony of Novgorod visited the city in 1200, shortly after numerous relics had been carried off to the West by the Crusaders, and the other Russian pilgrims came to C. in the 14th and 15th cents. [11].

As a result of the East-West confrontation at the time of the Crusades, the depiction in Western sources of the city of C., just as of the whole Byzantine Empire, became increasingly negative from the 12th cent. on. The accounts of travellers in the late period, such as Ruy Gonzalez de Clavijo (1403), Cristoforo Buondelmonti (1422), Hans Schiltberger (1427), Bertrandon de la Brocquière (1433) and Pero Tafur (1438), were unanimous in their descriptions of the city's decline, of the inhabitants' alleged immorality, as well their hatred for Western Europeans [15. 664–669]. Cristoforo Buondelmonti's writings [7] hold a special importance owing to the appended bird's eye view of the city from the south (Fig. 1). Significantly for historical topography, it is the oldest source of illustrations of C., although here too most of the buildings are rendered in a strongly stylised way. The illustration appears in manuscripts in numerous versions with various degrees of detail, occasionally even taking the first Ottoman buildings into consideration. Buondelmonti's view moulded the image of C. in Western Europe until the early 16th cent., being displaced around 1480 by a new view, disseminated after about 1530 and known today under the name of the printer Andreas Vavassore. There were more realistic views of the city after the middle of the 16th cent., by which time the cityscape was dominated by the great Ottoman mosques.

E. Constantinople as a Cultural Model

Byzantine art exercised a great influence on the peoples of the Balkans, where Orthodox missionaries had worked, on Russia, and also on the Western Mediterranean. Especially since the 11th cent., significant buildings of C. were imitated architectonically; e.g. the complex of Hagia Sophia and the nearby palace gate influenced the chapel in Kiev and other Russian centres of government, and the five-domed cruciform Church of the Holy Apostles was a model for Saint Mark's in Venice. Hagia Sophia itself has had no imitators in Christian architecture and has had an influence only on Ottoman mosque architecture.

F. History of Research

Scholarly research on Byzantine C. began with Pierre Gilles (Petrus Gyllius), who went to Istanbul with a French legation and resided there from 1547 till 1550. In his *Topographia Constantinopoleos* [8], which appeared posthumously in 1561, Gilles related his direct observation of the contemporary state to the analysis in written sources. A great number of travel diaries appeared in the 17th and 18th cents., few of which aimed to delve into the history of the Byzantine period. One which did so is the Ch. Du Cange's *Constantinopolis Christiana* of 1682 [3], which was based exclusively on the study of sources and became the standard work for a long time. Only with the increasing openness of Turkey in the 19th cent., particularly after the restoration of Hagia Sophia by the Swiss architects Gaspare and Giuseppe Fossati 1847–1849, was the groundwork laid for broader scholarly work on Byzantine C., carried out at first primarily by members of the Greek minority such as the patriarch Constantios I (1770–1859) and by Western Europeans living in the city.

1 A. BERGER, Untersuchungen zu den Patria Konstantinupoleos, 1988 2 A. CAMERON, J. HERRIN (eds.), Constantinople in the Eighth Century, 1984 3 CH. DU CANGE, Constantinopolis christiana, in: Historia byzantina, Paris 1682 4 G. DAGRON, Naissance d'une capitale, 1974 5 Id., Constantinople imaginaire, 1984 6 E. FENSTER, Laudes Constantinopolitanae, 1968 7 G. GEROLA, Le vedute di Costantinopoli di Cristoforo Buondelmonti, in: Studi bizantini e neoellenici 3, 1930, 247–279 8 P. GYLLIUS, De topographia Constantinopoleos, Lyon 1561 (Eng.: P. GILLES, The Antiquities of Constantinople, ²1988 9 R. JANIN, Constantinople byzantine, ²1964 10 Id., La Géographie ecclésiastique de l'empire byzantin, ²1969 11 G. P. MAJESKA, Russian Travelers to Constantinople in the Fourteenth and Fifteenth Centuries, 1984 12 C. MANGO, Antique Statuary and the Byzantine Beholder, in: Dumbarton Oaks Papers 17, 1963, 53–75 13 P. SCHREINER, Eine chinesische Beschreibung Konstantinopels aus dem 7. Jahrhundert, in: Istanbuler Mitteilungen 39, 1989, 493–505 14 Scriptores originum Constantinopolitanarum, (ed.) TH. PREGER, 1901–1907 15 J. P. A. VAN DER VIN, Travellers to Greece and Constantinople, 1980 16 E. VITTI, Die Erzählung vom Bau der Hagia Sophia, 1986 17 S. YERASIMOS, Légendes d'empire. La fondation de Constantinople et de Sainte-Sophie dans les traditions turques, 1990

ADDITIONAL BIBLIOGRAPHY: N. IORGA, Byzantium after Byzantium (Introduction by Virgil Cândea; trans. LAURA TREPTOW), 2000; C. A. MANGO, Studies on Constantinople, 1993; P. MANSEL, Constantinople: City of the World's Desire, 1453–1924, 1996. ALBRECHT BERGER

Constitution

A. ISSUE COMPLEX AND DEFINITION
B. ANTIQUITY C. TYPOLOGY OF FORMS OF STATE IN THE MIDDLE AGES D. EARLY MODERN ERA
E. THE CONSTITUTION OF THE OLD REICH
F. SCHLOSSER'S TRANSLATION OF THE ARISTOTELIAN G. 19TH CENT. H. THE 'POLITICAL' IN THE CONSTITUTION OF THE 20TH CENT.

A. ISSUE COMPLEX AND DEFINITION

By the 18th cent., the concept of a constitution took on greater and greater breadth of definition, parallel to the formation of the modern state and the expansion of the 'political realm' in general [27. 1–59]. Today, its unstable plethora of definitions still influences the much discussed contemporary work on a 'Constitution for Europe'. State and constitution are largely complementary concepts today, mutually dependent on each other, so that a constitution can be referred to as the 'exact counterpart of the state' [41. 187]. This close link between 'constitution' and 'state' was already expressed by Aristotle in form of what can be understood as a timeless characterization: 'Whoever intends to investigate what the essence and the characteristics of various constitutions are, must first ask about the state, namely what it might be like. One is actually not in agreement about this... The constitution... is a kind of arrangement amongst those who populate the state' (pol. 1274 b 35). Today, one needs to differentiate between a juristic and an extra-juristic concept of constitution. The juristic concept of constitution is aimed at the normative order of established law, which is formed by legal rules, institutions and structures which in turn define the polity as state and society as well as their political environment. These criteria are also followed by modern constitutional history [58. 2f.]. By contrast, the extra-juristic concept of constitution connects up with either a supralegal order of a legitimate rulership or aligns itself with the actual power constellation in a society. In the pre-constitutional state, the two types of constitution overlap each other. If there is a question of which factors of a normative and extra-normative kind constitute the polity as a state and define its political order, then the criteria which allow an identification of constitution in Antiquity should be given as a starting point in order to be able to trace the path these criteria followed into the present day. This is not possible without definitions based in the present; for neither the Greek *politeía* nor the Roman *constitutio* nor the German term 'Verfassung' – in its original meaning of status, order, as well as documentation and codification – are congruent terms. Fundamental elements of the constitution of a state were first determined in Art. XVI of the Declaration of Human and Civil Rights dated 26.8.1789 according to which a society does not have a constitution at all unless a guarantee of these rights is assured and the separation of powers has been determined. G. Jellinek for example defines constitution as the 'quintessence of those legal statements describing the highest organs of the state, laying down the way in which they are to be created, their mutual relationship with each other and their area of validity, determining furthermore the basic position of the individual in relation to the powers of the state' [21. 491]. Relevant modern literature extends the catalogue of constitutional elements even further: limitation and shaping of rulership by the law (separation of powers, rule of law); responsibility of a government; individual rights and their protection, territorial structure; legal form of political order [33. 26f.]. An attempt has been made to firmly establish the current concept of constitution involving up to 16 structural characteristics – consisting of eight formal and eight material elements [54. 148–202]. When reviewed retrospectively in comparison with the situation in Antiquity, this highly differentiated modern catalogue essentially finds its equivalent only in the following characteristics: in the idea of order, in the form of the polity as a state and participation in decision-making as well as, conditionally, in the concept of liberty pertaining to the democratic form of government. These points form the test case for power of ancient tradition and its share in the formation of the modern constitution as well as its conceptuality. Thus, one can only use partial identities and functional equivalents as a starting point.

B. ANTIQUITY
1. GREEK *politeía*   2. ROMAN 'CONSTITUTION'
AND 'RES PUBLICA'   3. MIXED CONSTITUTION

1. GREEK *politeía*

Central concepts in 6. cent. Greek thinking about state and constitution are the *eunomía* ('good order') and the *isonomía* which, translatable as 'equality of rights', suggests a political dimension [24. 196ff.; 8. 55ff., 459f.]. The latter is directed at an arrangement of increased political participation on the part of citizens in the governing of the *polis* which made possible the conceptual establishment of 'democracy' as the rule of the people. In the classical 'three-constitutions-system' with its three negative deviations, democracy forms only one of a total of six constitutional variants which are structured according to the possible rulers: monarch, aristocracy, people – i.e. only one rules, some rule, all rule – and according to the way they exercise power. However, the variation of rulers also indicates social categories relating to aristocrats and the people, that is between the rich and the poor. Aristotle differentiates the following types of constitution: '... we have differentiated three true forms of constitution, i.e. royalty, aristocracy and polity, and three deviations, i.e. tyranny from royalty, oligarchy from aristocracy and democracy from polity' (pol. 1289 a 26). The negative deviations – the 'transgressiones' in Thomas of Aquinus' translation – are measured against the ethical-political yardstick of general benefit: 'tyranny is an autocratic rule for the benefit of the ruler, oligarchy a rulership for the benefit of the rich and democracy one for the benefit of

the poor. But none takes the common benefit to all into account' (pol. 1279 b 6). For the modern concept of constitution, *politeía* became the decisive reference. This term simultaneously means 'citizenry', i.e. involvement in court and in government (pol. 1275 a 23), and 'constitution' [24. 211]: 'Constitution ... is a type of arrangement amongst those who populate the state' (pol. 1274 b 38). Plato (rep. 8,1 544 b-e) and Aristotle use *politeía* for the various types of constitutional pattern. In that sense, the *politeía* as 'constitution' rather represents individual forms of government or state and not so much a comprehensive constitutional system. This can be observed right up to the 18th cent. Aristotle also defines *politeía* as a principle of order: 'For constitution is the order of the state – πολιτεία μὲν γάρ ἔστι τάξις ταῖς πόλεσιν – with respect to the question as to how the government is structured, which authority decides on matters of constitution and what forms the objective of each individual community' (pol. 1289 a 15). As the 'common purpose' of types of state and 'any constitution', the restrictions imposed on power are discernible (pol. 1308 b 10). At the same time, these restrictions indicate the degree of freedom in the democratic form of government (pol. 1310 a 25–35; 1317 a 39–b 16). The structure of the leading magistracies – and not the entire arrangement of social and governmental structures – shapes the Aristotelian concept of *politeía* [2. 303]. Therefore, the usual translation of *politeía* as 'constitution' goes too far [37. 4; 27. 8].

2. ROMAN 'CONSTITUTION' AND 'RES PUBLICA'

Cicero's doctrine on forms of government are based on Greek philosophy of state. The central Roman concept of 'constitution' is the *mos maiorum* ('traditional conduct') in the sense of a historically 'developed constitution' [25. 56–63] that comprises the responsibilities of the organs of state, administrative conduct and the structure of public offices [25. 119]. Its normative legal meaning for the political order has its foundation in customary law. Clear definitions of constitution are missing in Roman legal language. The word 'constitution' did not exist in Rome [16. 36] even though there were partial equivalents such as '... rem publicam constituere' [16. 317ff.], whereby *res publica* represented an abstraction of common public interest. In Cicero's understanding, *constitutio* approximates the usual sense of constitution since the 18th cent.: 'Haec constitutio primum habet aequabilitatem quandam magnam, ... deinde firmitudinem ...' ('In the first instance, such a constitution offers a certain high degree of regularity... and secondly a secure constancy', rep. 1,45,69). Authority, regularity, freedom-preserving responsibility and constancy form elements of this understanding of constitution [27. 12] which, however, apparently found no emulators in this combination [29. 11]. When assessing Rome's governmental conditions, Cicero also speaks of the *status rei publicae* ('status of the polity') and *status civitatis* ('status of the state, the citizenry'), terms which can be translated as constitution to the extent [16. 19] that the meaning of the actually existing status is discernible in it [51. 62–66], a meaning which has shaped the German term *Verfassung* up to modern times [27. 13]. Under the generic term 'status rei publicae' – comparable to *politeía* in the sense of constitution – Cicero also subsumes the forms of state – 'forma rei publicae' – democracy, aristocracy and monarchy [51. 11f.]. Cicero's ideal state, however, is one composed of several forms of state, dealt with under the heading 'de optimo civitatis statu...' ('concerning the state's best status', rep. 1,46,70).

3. MIXED CONSTITUTION

The forms of state representing a constitution and a codification were rarely realised in pure form. For the creation of an optimal constitution, a combination of the various forms of state was, already in Antiquity, a much-discussed question regarding governmental structures, also in relation to the balancing of social stratification. The objective and effect of this mixture could thus have as its goal the integration of the citizenry, stabilisation and the balancing of power [29. 42ff.]. For Aristotle, the ideal mixture ('míxis', pol. 1294 a 35–b 35) is achieved when everyone is interested in the continuation of this constitution [57. 24], i.e. in the sense of a virtuous life. Plato's mixture of democracy and monarchy (leg. 3 693 d) is aimed at a mixture of freedom and rulership [57. 40]. Polybius (6,11,12–13) and Cicero ('e tribus esset modice temperatum', 'mixed moderately out of the three forms of state', rep. 2,39,65) assign groups of the population to certain organs of the constitution in order to thus achieve a common interest in the continuation of the constitution [57. 42f.]. Aristotle, but also Polybius and Cicero, develop the system of the mixed constitution on the basis of historical examples. Up to the 19th cent., these served as a basis for the discussion regarding the best constitution under the changed political aims and conditions obtaining at the time [29. 160ff.; 57. 46ff.].

C. TYPOLOGY OF FORMS OF STATE IN THE MIDDLE AGES

With the reception of Aristotle's works in the Latin West in the 12th cent., the theory of forms of government as a systematic way of assessing statehood was also taken up. For Aristotle, the best constitution ('ἀρίστη πολιτεία') finds its counterpart in Thomas Aquinus' 'optima politia', 'bene commixta ex regno, inquantum unus praest' ('in the best constitution which is formed appropriately within a monarchy led by one person' [53. 503]. The 'ordo dominantium in civitate' (*commentarium* 393 in: [52. 139]) is regarded as equivalent to the Aristotelian 'polity'. This corresponds to the Aristotelian principle 'politia quidem est civitatis ordo' ('the polity forms the structure of the state', pol. 1289 a 12) which Thomas rephrases in his commentary as 'politia est ordo principatuum in civitate' ('the politia – constitution – forms the underlying structure of government in the state', *commentarium* 536 in: [52. 190]). This refers to the priority of the *politia* as a constitutional principle of order over against the laws which have to

adapt to the constitution: '...' 'leges omnes ... ferri debent secundum quod competit politiae per se, et non e converso ...' ('all laws must intrinsically conform to the constitution and not the other way around') (*commentarium* 536 in: [52. 190]). In this, a ranking becomes evident which clearly comes close to the predominance of a constitution in the modern sense as a principle of order guiding all other norms. As a criterion for the negative deviations from the three-constitution-system, Thomas employs an ethical principle, namely whether the 'bonum commune' ('common good') or the 'utilitas propria' ('the self-interest') is pursued by the rulers of the day (*commentarium* 393 in: [52. 139]). This also corresponded to the criterion used by Bartolus in order to be able to differentiate the Aristotelian 'tres bonos et tres malos modos regendi' ('three good and three bad ways of governing') [4. II. 95, 153]. Just like Aristotle (and later the scholastics (Timpler) of the 16/17th cent. [14. 382ff.]), Bartolus, who refers to Aegidius Romanus, considers the monarchy to be the 'regendi modus optimus' (the best form of government) [4. II. 95, 153] of the six forms of government. In contrast to Aristotle, Bartolus even creates a seventh group of state forms, which he deduces from his actual Roman experience: 'Est et septimus modus regiminis, qui nunc est in civitate Romana, pessimus. Ibi enim sunt multi tyranni per diversas regiones ... Quod regimen Aristoteles non posuit ...: est enim res monstruosa ... Certe monstrum esset. Appellatur ergo hoc regimen monstruosum' ('There is also a seventh form of government which can now be found in the Roman state, – and this is the worst of all. Namely that there are many tyrants in various regions. Such a form of rulership has not been mentioned by Aristotle ...: For this is a monstrous matter indeed... It is certain that it would be an ambiguous creation in terms of constitutional law. Therefore, such a government is also referred to as a deformed one') [4. I. 65–75, 152]. Thus, Aristotelian theory of forms of state was not suitable for defining all occurring types of state on the basis of their distribution of power; consequently, they fell through the cracks and formed an ambiguous creation as 'res monstruosa'. Bartolus' phrasing is seen again in 1667 in Pufendorf's famous evaluation of the old German imperial constitution. In regarding the question 'quis sit meloir modus regendi' ('Which is the better kind of government?'), Bartolus decides on the basis of the state's size. For a small state, the 'regimen ad populum' ('government by the people') is regarded as appropriate, for a larger state the 'regi per paucos' ('government by the few') and for a 'populus maximus' the 'regi per unum' ('for a very large state the government by one person') [4. II. 295–400, 162–166]. The constitutional question was thus also a question of the optimal governability of the state's territory and its population, which was decisive in the consideration of the appropriate form of state.

D. Early Modern Era

1. Idea of Order　2. Change in the Forms of State　3. Appropriateness of the Forms of State

1. Idea of Order

In the 16/17th cents., the idea of order is tied to the theories of forms of government and, in particular, to the monarchical form of state. This form is regarded as the 'status politicus primus et perfectus' ('premier and perfect political constitution') in order to govern a large number of people securely and purposefully in terms of the objectives of the state, in a firm unified order [22. 7, 29–39]. The *ordo civitatis* ('the order of the state') becomes meaningful only in the definition of *respublica* ('polity'), *majestas* ('sovereignty'), *civitas* ('state') and the distribution of power between ruler and subjects [7. 29, 35] and has no independent content. The theory of the rights of the *subditi* ('subjects') and *imperantes* ('governing ones/rulers'), Besold, with reference to the Aristotelian *politica*, calls the 'doctrina de civitatis constitutione' ('theory of the constitution of the state') [7. 34], whereby the Latin term 'constitution' emerges as a term encompassing constitutional characteristics in the sense of an order of forms of state. Precise definitions of this sort receive primary focus in the *politica* literature which operates fully in the tradition of Aristotle [48. 80–90; 104–124]. Althusius, in that sense, juxtaposes 'ordo et constitutio civitatis' ('order and 'constitution' of the state') by which all actions of citizens are steered and guided [1. 16, 5]. In the idea of a society based on law (*ius symbioticum*), Althusius expressly ties together the Aristotelian constitutional elements αὐτάρκεια ('independence'), εὐνομία ('good regulation') and εὐταξία ('good order') into a governmental principle of order. Comparing the thinking in Antiquity, Arnisaeus associates the idea of order with the concept of a state, but without regarding them as equivalent: 'Quam Graeci πολιτείαν, Latini vocant Rempublicam. Eam plerique confundunt cum civitate ...'. ('What the Greeks called governmental order, the Romans refer to as the [state] polity. This is associated with the state by most') [3. 39]. For Anisaeus, the decisive and essential characteristic of the *respublica* does not lie in its *materia* ('content'), but in its *forma*. Here, too, the Aristotelian concept of order of τάξις (pol. 1289 a 15) serves as a starting point: 'Respublica est definienda per ordinem' ('the [state] polity is to be determined by its structure, pol. 1275 a 38, 1278 b 9 [3. 43]'). For the legal meaning of the form of state, however, it becomes important that the 'forma Reipublicae' can also be defined by certain laws and be restricted for the public good [3. 42; 27. 35]. Thus, for the class of rulers the *Wahlkapitulationen* [election pacts] in the Old Reich are counted as the necessary rules and structures of which so many 'useful teachings ... can be read in Aristotle, Plato, Xenophon, Isocrate, Cicero, Plutarch' [59. I]. C. Ziegler counts the *Wahlkapitulationen* amongst the power-restricting 'leges fundamentales' [59. 1–6]. While they have had a part in shaping the European concept of constitution, they do not occur as a term in the ancient tradition [27. 62–66; 26. 121ff.]. In accordance with their power-restricting function, however, they build a bridge from the *lex fundamentalis* as a positive legal norm to the political theory of Antiquity.

2. Change in the Forms of State

The Aristotelian three or six-constitution-system does not represent a static quantity. Forms of state can change into different forms or completely disintegrate (pol. 1301 a 25, 1302 b 33, 1304 b 18). This was associated with changes in legislation which in turn redefined the codification of political power structures. Accordingly, the theoretical possibilities and actual experiences of *mutationes* ('changes'), *conversiones* ('revolutions') and the *status mixtus* ('mixed constitutions') were examined using the benchmarks inherent in the writings of Aristotle, Livy, Cicero and Polybius, while also referring to the example of the ancient Roman state [15. §VIf.]. As a result of the change from monarchy to aristocracy and democracy, the increased freedom of the people, observed after forcing back the *optimates* ('aristocrats') and during the phase 'post reges sub consulatu' ('after the kings' rule under the consulate') [15. §XIV–XX], is highlighted. The Aristotelian democratic state was characterised by the principles of majority and freedom (pol. 1310 a 30) which, however, in the 17th cent., were still a long way away from the emancipatory movement of the Age of Enlightenment, but into which they proceeded [40. 10f.; 9. 468, 299].

3. Appropriateness of the Forms of State

The multitude of the possible forms of state evokes the question about the best constitution (Aristot. pol. 1288 b 22–35, 1323 a 14). The Aristotelian standard for this is happiness (pol. 1328 a 37–b 1). This is not an absolute quantity, but 'dependent on appropriate, material foundations' (pol. 1325 b 36–40), amongst which Aristotle counts population size and geographical extent of the state, but also climatic conditions (pol. 1327 b 20f.). Besold in 1641 placed this Aristotelian constitutional question under the heading 'de Republicae forma, ad populi naturam aliasque circumstantias adaptanda' ('on the form of state and its adaptation to the nature of the people and other circumstances') [6. 195f.]. Montesquieu regarded such Aristotelian conditions of influence as the basis for appropriate legislation and the constitution of states in the sense of individual forms of state or government [28. B. III–VIII, XIV–XIX]. In the 18th cent., the size of the country was often considered the measure for the most appropriate form of government for the state: 'History teaches us this much, namely that small states have very often chosen a democratic or an aristocratic form of state, or a combination of both, and that this resulted in a most steady condition. The Greek states confirm my experience, and also Rome [55. 30].' The reason for this choice of constitution can be found in the technical governability of states covering a large area, 'where the collection of votes and ... opinions' in case of 'a democratic or an aristocratic form of government must pose difficulties'. Therefore, in line with Aristotle and Montesquieu, the monarchy [55. 35f.; 13. 72] is regarded as the 'best' one for large states and a 'despotic government' as 'the most natural one' for China [50. 288f.; 39. III. 29. n. 29]; for the small 'Respublica Helvetiorum', the 'respublica mixta ex Optimatum et populi imperio' ('polity with a mixed aristocratic and democratic rulership') is considered to be an example of model character [44. 194f.]. In the 18th cent., the 'wise organisation of the constitution' was not only a question of governmental technique, but the Aristotelian search for the 'best constitution' became a question with legal and ethical dimensions: 'Which form of government actually is a just one?' [5. 338]. In relation to its 'form', J. A. Bergk in 1796 refers to democracy as 'the most just arrangement' of a state [5. 343]. Disagreement in finding an answer to this question in the aftermath of the French → REVOLUTION [5. 350] extended the controversy over constitutions into the constitutionalism of the 19th cent.

E. THE CONSTITUTION OF THE OLD REICH

The constitution of the Old Reich was constantly gauged against the yardstick of the Aristotelian theories of forms of government, after J. Bodin had reignited the debate with the new criterion of sovereignty and had judged the Reich to be a pure aristocracy [48. 172ff.; 11. 242]. Thus, the evaluations [48. 214ff.] swung between the aristocracy of estates (Hippolithus a Lapide), monarchy (D. Reinkingk), mixed constitutions (J. Limnaeus) and federal organisation (Besold, Leibniz). The Aristotelian theories of forms of government, examined in light of the example of the Old Reich, showed inadequacies in relation to actual and empirical assessment. Arnisaeus does not refrain from taking a critical stance with regard to Aristotle's authority (1615): 'Ex sententia Aristotelis incertum fieri numerum rerumpublicarum' ('from Aristotle's theories a fluctuating number of forms of state can be postulated') [12. 264]. Weissenborn declares in 1782: 'We now have a form of government in Europe which by itself makes Aristotle's division an imperfect one; I mean the one in Germany' [55. 25]. The *aporia* of the Aristotelian theories when applied to the Reich, is confirmed by Pufendorf's famous article published in 1667 under the title *De statu Imperii Germanici*, which takes the condition of the imperial constitution as its starting point and rates the Reich as an 'irregulare corpus', that is a 'systema irregulare' ('an inappropriate body of state', i.e. 'an inappropriate arrangement'). That the form of state of the Reich, stood outside all the rules, meant that it had an ambiguous position – 'monstro simile', which had the Reich hover between monarchy and federation ('aliquid inter haec duo fluctuans', Cap. VI, §9). An assignment 'ad simplices rerumpublicarum formas' ('to the simple basic forms of states, Cap. VI, §1') of the Aristotelian system of forms of state was not possible [34.

181, 199]. This made it difficult to determine the state's rationale in its dependence on the form of state [27. 66–70]. A radical conclusion was drawn by Hegel between 1798 and 1802, who equates form of state with constitution: 'There is no dispute any more about the concept under which the German constitution could be placed. What can no longer be understood, does not exist' [20. 11]. This was a negation of the Aristotelian canon of forms as a decisive authority. Hegel measures Germany by the criterion of the state as a power and says 'that its constitution probably was the worst one, its condition that of anarchy' [20. 62]. Beyond the Classical system of forms of state, Aristotle's question about the best constitution was answered in the negative.

F. SCHLOSSER'S TRANSLATION OF THE ARISTOTELIAN
Politeia

Schlosser's translation is, just like Hegel's article (cf. E. above), a reaction to the French Revolution, but pointing in the opposite direction. This updating serves as a pedagogic *ethicizing* of politics, which Schlosser sees as having been lost due to the French Revolution and to irrational passion in the discussion 'between the aristocrats and democrats, ... monarchomats' [39. I. p. III]. Schlosser expressly calls Aristotle's *politeia* his 'theory of state constitutions' which he wants to employ against the 'boasting of our aristocrats ... and the trickery of our demagogues in the ongoing dispute about the best constitution of a state' [39. I. p. V]. For Schlosser, the Aristotelian *politeia* is cause and standard for historical reflection about revolutionary modernity and its dispute 'over forms of state, revolutions, citizenship and the duties of rulers' [39. I. p. III], which he evaluates under the concept of 'constitution'. He is conscious of the difference between the ancient and modern state in the face of changing forms of state in France and leads to a new concept of 'citizen', for the 'state' was not realised, as Aristotle says, in a large number of citizens (pol. 1274 b 41), but rather, conversely, the concept of the citizen as a relational concept 'must be explained from the starting point of the concept of the state' [39. I.218; 36. 300f.]. To endow the constitution with laws, 'to maintain law and order' as well as 'to educate the virtuous citizen' are topoi which accompany the 'reading of Aristotle's Politics' [39. I. p. XVII, XXXVII f.]. 'The new politics could never move so far away from the old one that it could be allowed to lose sight of Aristotelian morality, i.e. worthiness' [39. I. p. XXXIX f.].

G. 19TH CENT.
1. FORMAL AND MATERIAL CONSTITUTION
2. VARIANTS OF THE THEORIES OF FORMS OF GOVERNMENT

1. FORMAL AND MATERIAL CONSTITUTION

The more the legal elements of individual and civic freedom in the aftermath of the French Revolution were put into concrete terms in order to form a material concept of constitution involving a state founded on the rule of law with guaranties regarding the separation of powers and judicial protections, the more the theories of forms of government became a question of a formal constitution.

However, the Aristotelian typology remained important to the extent that the question was raised as to which of the Aristotelian forms of state and their traditional theories would best be able to serve in implementing material legal principles. Particularly in relation to a mixed constitution, questions regarding the shaping of society and of political participation were discussed against the background of the structure of the estates and the claims of equality. The ancient model of the mixed constitution was able to be employed here as a means and goal of easing matters amongst those suffering social and political inequality [47. 141–156]. The discussion reflected conservative, liberal and socialist positions [57. 106–196].

2. Variants of the Theories of Forms of Government

Variants in the theories of forms of government indicate a changed political consciousness of society and state between conservatism and liberalism. C. L. v. Haller reduces the Aristotelian system of three to the two categories of 'principalities (individual rulers) or republics (a number of rulers, polities) ... A third version cannot be conceived of at all' [18. I. 494]. The Aristotelian division is rejected as 'hair-splitting', 'unsatisfactory' and 'inaccurate'. Aristocracy and democracy are considered to be only 'apparent subdivisions of the republics' [18. I. 496]. Thus, democracy was excluded as a form of constitution in its own right: '... all authority of princes and republics rest not on assigned, but only on their own personal ... rights' [18. IV. 563]. Thus, problems of derivation and legitimisation could not arise at all: '... with the principalities and the republics, the whole of political science, indeed we may say the theory of all societal arrangements, is complete' [18. VI. 560]. Against this, C. T. Welcker placed his modified Aristotelian system of the 'three constitutional manifestations': 1. 'Despotism' (monarchy), 2. 'theocracy' (aristocracy) and 3. 'state founded on the rule of law' [56. 50f.]. He considered the Aristotelian 'division to be correct in principle and important up to the present day', but in 1843 he emphasised at the same time that the 'whole legal relationship of the threefold constitution has and will become a totally different one' [56. 68, 51]. By emphasising the legal categories, Aristotle, in Welcker's opinion, 'had he stayed on this path, ultimately [would have] had to arrive ... at the state founded on the rule of law' [56. 69]. Thus, Aristotle was seen as the precursor of the liberal conception of a state and was used as a support when arguing for the state founded 'on the rule of law in order to securely grasp the true justice and need of our time'. Thus, legal approach and liberty can be united in history [56. 73]. This freedom meant – alongside the harmonious order

of the state and morality – freedom in terms of private law as well as political liberty. In 'General Theories of State', the Aristotelian theories of forms of government – inconsistently also referred to as constitution – continue, but with a discernible reference to discussions about monarchic or republican predisposition within the German empire. The Aristotelian 'numeric relationship' is retained as a criterion for differentiating the individual forms of state, 'the arithmetic boundary ... is also recognised as a juristic boundary'; however, the political categorisation of the forms of state is assessed by the 'greatest actual predominance' within the state [35. 188f.]. For the monarchic state favoured by him, H. Rehm (1899) develops four 'organisational principles', all of which incorporate Aristotelian elements: 1. structure of rulership, 2. unity of the state's power through the monarchy, 3. participation of the subjects ('principle of the constitutional state'), 4. social mixture of the peoples representatives [35. 205]. Rehm emphasises the 'logical' derivation of these principles even though, historically, the beginnings of 'the idea of a constitutional state can already be found in the Greek theories and practice of state' [35. 206]. Up to the 20th cent., the Aristotelian theories of forms of government offer the basis for argumentation and legitimisation for questions regarding political and constitutional order. As recently as 1909, J. Hatschek declared in a survey of the current forms of state: '... despite all modifications, Aristotle is still dominant to the present day' [19. 5f.].

H. The 'Political' in the Constitution of the 20th Cent.

With the establishment of parliamentary democracy in Germany in 1919, the ancient theories of forms of government lost their relevance as a source of concrete constitutional models. The Aristotelian *Politics* was regarded as 'the treasure trove of practical politics, being re-exploited time and again' [42. 49] in order to determine the political in the constitution. The experience of diversified statehood under the Weimar constitution of the Reich determined the course of the discussion. From Carl Schmitt's point of view, the theories of forms of government created the potential political space in which the decisions between rulers and ruled are made. In this sense, 'Aristotle's theory of state retains its classical importance' [43. 216]. In 1928, C. Schmitt viewed the civic state as being comprised of two components: 1. the protection of civic liberty, i.e. keeping the state at bay and 2. the 'political component from which the form of state proper (monarchy, aristocracy or democracy, or a *status mixtus*) can be determined' [43. 41]. In the mixture combining the principles of citizenship and the rule of law with formative 'political principles', he saw the 'modern constitution' containing the opportunity to effect 'political unity' [43. 216, 21]. In 1923, R. Smend used as his starting point the 'inapplicability of the ancient theories of forms of government', whose three categories he reformulated as 'integration types' or 'integration factors' [45. 25, 22; 46. 68]. In order to integrate the state into a 'unity, ... a whole', the static form of state of ancient states was replaced by the 'dynamic-dialectic' integration factor. From this point of view, constitution could not be a 'mechanistically objectified technical apparatus' [46. 85]. If the ancient theory of state forms was able 'to be a theory of the pure forms of constitution', Smend reshaped these, in the sense of a mixed constitution, into types of integration processes of 'the state in modern constitutional life' [45. 25]. To that extent, the force of tradition inherent in the ancient models has also had an effect on the structure of the 'political' up to the present day: 1. In the *new constitutionalism*, the participation of citizens in the decision-making processes of state and society forms an essential element with a link to the Aristotelian concept of citizenship [33. 27]; 2. in much-discussed problems regarding a just arrangement of social order as well as solidarity in society, one sees, at the same time, 'a chance for Aristotelian thought to play a role in the political spirit' of our times [38. 99].

→ CITIZEN

1 J. ALTHUSIUS, Politica methodice digesta, atque exemplis sacris et profanis illustrata, ³1932 (¹1614)   2 ARISTOTELES, Politik, trans. and with introduction by O. GIGON (Bibliothek der Alten Welt), ²1973   3 H. ARNISAEUS, De Republica seu relectiones politicae libri duo ..., Frankfurt 1615   4 BARTOLUS, Tractatus de regimine civitatis, in: D. QUAGLIONI, Politica e diritto nel trecento italiano, 1983, 149–170   5 J. A. BERGK, Die Konstitution der demokratischen Republik (1796), in: Z. BATSCHA, J. GARBER (eds.), Von der ständischen zur bürgerlichen Gesellschaft, 1981   6 C. BESOLD, Synopsis politicae doctrinae, Amsterdam ⁵1643   7 Id., Discursus politici, V: De Reipublicae formarum inter sese comparatione; et quaenam earum, praestantior existat?, Straßburg 1641   8 J. BLEICKEN, Die athenische Demokratie, ²1994   9 W. BURGDORF, Reichskonstitution und Nation. Verfassungsreformprojekte für das Heilige Römische Reich Deutscher Nation im politischen Schrifttum von 1648–1806, 1998   10 CICERO, De re publica (= Werke: 16th vol.), 1988   11 H. DENZER, Bodins Staatsformenlehre, in: Id. (ed.), Jean Bodin, 1973, 233–244   12 H. DREITZEL, Protestantischer Aristotelismus und absoluter Staat. Die Politica des Henning Arnisaeus (c. 1576–1636), 1970   13 J. A. EBERHARD, Über Staatsverfassung und ihre Verbesserung, 1973   14 J. S. FREEDMAN, European Academic Philosophy in the Late Sixteenth and Early Seventeenth Centuries. The Life, Significance and Philosophy of Clemens Timpler (1563–1624), Vols. I–II, 1988   15 M. J. C. FUGMANN, Disputatio politica de mutationibus reipublicae romanae, Wittenberg 1674   16 H. GRZIWOTZ, Das Verfassungsverständnis der römischen Republik. Ein methodischer Versuch, 1985   17 Id., Der moderne Verfassungsbegriff und die Römische Verfassung in der deutschen Forschung des 19. und 20. Jahrhunderts, 1986   18 C. L. v. HALLER, Restauration als Staatswissenschaft, vols. I–VI, Winterthur ²1820–1825   19 J. HATSCHECK, Allgemeines Staatsrecht auf rechtsvergleichender Grundlage, 1909   20 G. W. HEGEL, Über die Reichsverfassung, H. MAIER (ed.), 2002   21 G. JELLINEK, Allgemeine Staatslehre, ²1905   22 B. KECKERMANN, Systema disciplinae politicae ... seosorsim accessit synopsis disciplinae oeconomicae, Hannover 1608   23 W. MAGER, Respublica und Bürger. Überlegungen zur Begründung frühneuzeitlicher Verfassungsordnungen, in: Res publica. Bürgerschaft in Stadt und Staat, (= Der Staat/Beiheft 8), 1988, 67–84   24 C. MEIER, Der Wandel der politisch-sozialen Begriffswelt im 5. Jahrhundert vor Christus, in: R. KOSSELECK (ed.), Historische Semantik und Begriffsgeschichte, 1978, 193–227   25 Id., Res publica amissa. Eine Studie zur Verfassung und Geschichte der späten römischen Republik, ²1980   26 H. MOHNHAUPT, Von den leges fundamentals zur modernen Verfassung in Europa. Zum begriffsgeschichtlichen Befund (16–18. Jahrhundert), in: Ius Commune 25, 1988, 121–158   27 Id., D. GRIMM, Verfassung. Zur Geschichte des Begriffs von der Antike bis zur Gegenwart. Zwei Studien (= Schriften zur Verfassungsgeschichte 47), ²2002   28 C.d.S. MONTESQUIEU, De l'Esprit des lois, Genf 1748   29 W. NIPPEL, Mischverfassungstheorie und Verfassungsrealität in Antike und früher Neuzeit, 1980   30 PLATON, Gesetze (= Werke: vol. 8), K. SCHÖPSDAU (ed.), 1977   31 PLATON, Der Staat (= Werke: vol. 4), D. KURZ (ed.), 1971   32 POLYBIUS, The Histories, 1979   33 U. K. PREUSS, Der Begriff der Verfassung und ihre Beziehung zur Politik, in: Id. (ed.), Zum Begriff der Verfassung, 1994, 7–33   34 s. v. Pufendorf, Die Verfassung des Deutschen Reiches, H. DENZER (ed.), 1994   35 H. REHM, Allgemeine Staatslehre, Freiburg i. B. 1899   36 N. RIEDEL, Aristotelestradition am Ausgang des 18. Jahrhunderts, in: Alteuropa und die moderne Geschichte, 1963   37 H. RYFFEL, ΜΕΤΑΒΟΛΗ ΠΟΛΙΤΕΙΩΝ. Der Wandel der Staatsverfassungen (Diss.), 1949   38 J. SCHÄFERS, Ordnungspolitische Aspekte im Wandel der sozialen Frage, in: N. ACHTERBERG et al. (eds.), Recht und Staat im sozialen Wandel. Festschrift für H. U. Scupin, 1983, 85–99   39 J. G. SCHLOSSER, Aristoteles Politik und Fragment der Oeconomik, 1.–3. Abtheilung, Lübek und Leipzig 1798   40 J. SCHLUMBOHM, Freiheitsbegriff und Emanzipationsprozeß, 1973   41 R. SCHMIDT, Die Vorgeschichte der geschriebenen Verfassungen, in: Zwei öffentlich-rechtliche Abhandlungen als Festgabe für Otto Mayer, 1916   42 Id., Allgemeine Staatslehre, vol. I, 1901   43 C. SCHMITT, Verfassungslehre, 1928   44 J. SIMLER, De Republica Helvetiorum, Jiguri 1734   45 R. SMEND, Politische Gewalt im Verfassungsstaat und das Problem der Staatsform, in: Festgabe der Berliner Juristischen Fakultät für Wilhelm Kahl, 1923, 3–25   46 Id., Verfassung und Verfassungsrecht, 1928   47 D. STERNBERGER, Drei Wurzeln der Politik, 1978   48 M. STOLLEIS, Geschichte des öffentlichen Rechts in Deutschland, I: 1600–1800, 1988   49 G. STOURZH, Vom aristotelischen zum liberalen Verfassungsbegriff. Staatsformenlehre und Fundamentalgesetze in England und Nordamerika im 17. und 18. Jahrhundert, in: Id., Wege zur Grundrechtsdemokratie, 1989, 1–35   50 J. THOR Straten, Systematische Abhandlung von den Regierungsformen, Flensburg 1760, 288f.   51 W. SUERBAUM, Vom antiken zum frühmittelalterlichen Staatsbegriff, ³1977   52 THOMAS VON AQUIN, In libros politicorum Aristotelis expositio, P. M. SPIAZZI (ed.), 1951   53 Id., Summa theologica, in: Opera omnia, vol. 2, R. BUSA (ed.), 1980   54 P. UNRUH, Der Verfassungsbegriff des Grundgesetzes, 2002   55 J. WEISSENBORN, Über Staatsverfassung und Gesetzgebung, Berlin 1782   56 C. T. WELCKER, Staatsverfassung, in: K. v. ROTTECK, K. WELCKER (eds.), Staats-Lexikon, vol. 15, Altona 1843, 21–82   57 V. WEMBER, Verfassungsmischung und Verfassungsmitte. Moderne Formen gemischter Verfassung in der politischen Theorie des beginnenden Zeitalters der Gleichheit, 1977   58 D. WILLOWEIT, Deutsche Verfas-

sungsgeschichte, ³1997   59 C. Ziegler, Wahl-Capitulationes, Frankfurt a.M. 1711.

Additional Bibliography: D. Grimm, Die Zukunft der Verfassung, 1991; K. Beckmann et al. (eds.), Eine Verfassung für Europa, ²2005   Heinz Mohnhaupt

Constitution, Types of
A. Introduction B. Late Antiquity and the Middle Ages C. Modern Era up to the French Revolution D. 19th and 20th Cents.

A. Introduction
The idea behind types of constitution (also types of state, government, rule, etc.), as it was developed in Antiquity by Aristotle, Polybius and Cicero, largely maintained its validity in the Middle Ages and in the early modern era. Until well into the 18th cent., all attempts to understand and systematically order existing constitutions were made by referring to that system. No textbook on constitutional law, no political treatise is conceivable without considering this chapter of → political theory to a greater or lesser extent. However, in the 16th and 17th cents., the internal and external circumstances of states brought about the beginnings of differentiations and modifications in the old constitutional theories. This process intensified during the 18th cent. and led to their complete abandonment in the 20th cent.

B. Late Antiquity and the Middle Ages
Augustine still refers extensively to the constitutional system in Cicero's De re publica (Aug. Civ. 2,21). Thereafter, however, Aristotle's and Cicero's works were no longer known, and these constitutional theories were not taken up again until the reception of Aristotle in the 13th cent. The Greek terms were translated into Latin [23. 178–182] by Wilhelm von Moerbeke and, in the 2nd half of the 14th cent., for the first time into a vernacular language by Nicolaus of Oresme, namely into French [58. 127–150]. With Albertus Magnus, the terms for the three good constitution types (monarchia or regnum, aristocratia and politia) and those for the three bad ones (tyrannis, oligarchia or timocratia and democratia) became established [3. 237–240]. Thomas Aquinas refers to the six-constitutions-theory (Summa Theologiae 1–2,95,4) and considers the monarchy the best type of constitution. Although he allowed that peace and stability were most likely guaranteed by a constitution composed of the three good forms (1–2,105,1), there was clearly an unreserved preference for the monarchy on his part [75. 123–125]. Here, he concurred with most of the subsequent authors of the Middle Ages, e.g. Aegidius Romanus [2. 453–458], Dante (Monarchia 1,12,9–13), William of Ockham [22. 794–796], Marsilius of Padua (Defensor pacis 1,8) and Aeneas Silvio Piccolomini [33. 66]. The constitutional model is most often mentioned but briefly, and then passed over in an uncritical fashion.

C. Modern Era up to the French Revolution
In the modern era, the system of the six constitutions remained largely in force. Some authors, it is true, introduced important modifications; however, these were only partially incorporated into general political theory. While Niccolò Machiavelli knew Polybius' writings about the mixed constitutional type and adopted them in part verbatim [47. 95–98], his actual interest focussed on the stability of governments and the maintenance of power. And these latter ones differ depending on whether they are republics or principalities, i.e. inherited or newly acquired principalities (Il Principe 1,1–2; 1532) [47. 5]. A more significant modification was effected towards the end of the 16th cent. by Jean Bodin. To start with, Bodin rejected the differentiation between good and bad types of constitution as well as the concept of a mixed constitution. The only criterion for the differentiation of constitutional types can be found in the number of those who possess sovereignty within the state: a single person (monarchy), several (aristocracy) or all (democracy or 'estat populaire'). In addition, Bodin differentiated between the form and the government of a state: a monarchy, for example, can be run democratically ('populairement') if the king distributes offices to others without taking their aristocratic origins into consideration; or it can be run aristocratically if the offices are distributed only to aristocrats. Finally, Bodin also differentiated monarchies in terms of whether they are run 'royale ou legitime', or whether they are run 'seigneuriale'. In the first instance, the king rules according to firm laws and his subjects have to observe only those; in the latter, the king rules over his subjects as persons and over their possessions, i.e. he rules like a pater familias over his servants. A monarchy would be tyrannical if it did not observe even → natural law and treated its subjects like slaves [9. 252, 272f.]. For the other two types of constitution, however, this differentiation was not made consistently [84; 90].

Bodin's separation of political and sovereign monarchy goes back as far as Aristotle via Thomas Aquinas: Aristotle clearly differentiated monarchs from the pater familias, political rulership from that over a household (Aristot. Pol. 1,5,1254 b 3f.). However, in the early modern era, absolutist thinkers in particular claimed that the king was entitled to rule benevolently over his subjects like a pater familias, i.e. without the participation of parliament and the estates [31. 23f.; 19. 84–86, 93f.].

In the numerous text books and treatises on politics that appeared in the 16th and 17th cents., the old constitutional typology for constitutions was, as a rule, passed on intact or with only minor modifications; it stands out, for example, in the writings of Erasmus of Rotterdam [14. 162f.], Justus Lipsius [43. 58], Francesco Suarez [74. 184], Bartholomäus Keckermann [36. 534–595], Christoph Besold [8. 83–125] and Johannes Althusius, who does not accept Bodin's differentiation of the form and the government of a state and instead supports a different 'temperata et mixta Reipublicae speciem' [4. 948]. The German Reich is often referred to as a mixed constitutional form (e.g. [42. Additiones 95f.; 87]), but occasionally also as an aristocracy [10. 21]. Venice is likewise put forward as an example of a mixed constitutional type [59. 440f.; 11. 276, 298]. Later, Samuel Pufendorf caused a sensation with the idea that he no longer attributed a mixed constitutional form to the Reich, but that he conceived of it as an association of sovereign states which, it is true, are led by a king, but are an 'irregulare aliquid corpus' [62. cap. 6. §9]. Some authors, who otherwise retained the conventional model of a constitution and who elaborate on it [7. 164–267], had to deal with Bodin extensively, however, even if they, in contrast to him, defended the aristocratic monarchy ('monarchie seigneuriale') [6. 550–560; 85]. In the 16th cent., the term *democratia* moved up a level, just as it did occasionally with Polybius, to refer to the good form of rule of or for all. The bad one is then called *ochlocratia* [41. fol. 1r]. Among the three good types of constitution, monarchy is generally clearly favoured, even if the mixed type, for example, was considered to be best. The 'pinnacle' of the state should be occupied by just one person [86].

A turning point in the history of constitutional theory was reached when Thomas Hobbes began to judge a type of constitution solely by that which would most likely guarantee peace and security; this purpose of the state is best served by the 'monarchy' that is most unrestricted. 'Bad' types of constitutions are only insulting names to the 'good' ones [28. 145f.; 29. 185–187]. With John Locke, the question of the separation of powers came to be involved: legislative power is organised such that it is placed either in the hands of one person (monarchy), of several (oligarchy) or or of all (democracy) [44. 287f.]. Thus, in 18th cent. England, the earlier model of a constitution gradually lost its importance and, instead, the problem of the 'implementation' of government moved into the foreground. It is typical, for example, that Adam Ferguson examines the two kinds of constitution in a republic and a monarchy to test how they can guarantee equality and independence of citizens while at the same time safeguarding the common good [17. 351]. David Hume observed with regard to contemporary states that both in a monarchy as well as in a republic, liberty and the arbitrary exercise of power can occur. Therefore, he places less importance on the constitutional framework than on the laws and the type of public administration prevailing within it. However, absolute monarchy and democracy without representation do not guarantee the liberty and stability necessary in a state [30. 95f., 98]. For emphasis, Hume and his contemporaries liked to cite Alexander Pope: 'For forms of government, let fools contest/ What'er best administer'd is best' [60. 74].

In 18th cent. France, the traditional typology of constitutions was reformulated, above all by Montesquieu and Rousseau. Charles-Louis de Montesquieu reduced the former six constitutional forms to three or four: a republican one which devolves into democracy (where sovereignty lies in the hands of the 'peuple en corps') and aristocracy (sovereignty in the hands of a part of the people), monarchy (government in the hands of a single person, based on firm laws) and despotism (government of a single person, without laws) [55. 239]. Thus, Montesquieu combines quantitative aspects with qualitative ones. But this outer form ('nature') of a constitution must first be put into practice in accord with its own 'principles' and filled with life: in democracy by political virtue, i.e. love for one's country and for equality, in aristocracy by restraint, in monarchy by honour, i.e. the striving for awards, and in despotism by 'fear' [55. 250–259, 274f.]. Jean-Jacques Rousseau made further readjustments. He called any form of constitution (democracy, aristocracy, monarchy) a 'république' or 'républicain', if it is bound by laws as 'actes de la volonté générale' [66. 379f.]. Democracy, however, where sovereignty is vested in the people, is only suitable for small, easily managed states; an election-based aristocracy, where only the wisest govern, would really be the best; but that requires restraint on the part of the rich and contentedness on that of the poor. A monarchy is suitable for large states, but it suffers from the fact that the personal qualities of the king do not necessarily guarantee good government [66. 404–413]. Thus, Rousseau does not recommend a particular constitution per se, but only one which is appropriate for the size of the country and the wealth of its inhabitants [66. 415]. The highest rule for a 'gouvernement légitime ou populaire' must be its orientation towards the common will [65. 247].

Other reformers, who sought to limit or overcome absolutism, looked back to the mixed constitutional form of Antiquity as a model and recommended for France a mixture of monarchy and democracy [5. 164] or of aristocracy and democracy whereby one is guided either by ancient Rome [45. 287f.] or by the newly established United States of America [46. 379]. The founding fathers of the USA itself, however, usually understood their type of state, without reference to an ancient constitutional model, as a republic or a representative democracy, even though they occasionally borrowed from earlier authors such as Montesquieu (→ UNITED STATES) [24. 97, 114f., 244f.].

In Germany, until the middle of the 18th cent., the old constitutional theories were often maintained, e.g. by Christian Wolff [80. 90–292; 79. 175–179], Johann Gottlieb Heineccius [27. 405–407], Georg Achenwall and Johann Stephan Pütter [1. 785–829]. But there, too, they lost in importance more and more so that Friedrich Carl von Moser, for example, was able to claim that the various forms of government do not 'provide the correct yardstick for assessing the liberty or servitude of a people' [56. 179f.]. And Moses Mendelssohn responded to the question regarding the best type of constitution: 'For each people, at any level of culture, ... a different form of government may be the best one.'

The important matters are the 'customs and good morals' of the citizens [50. 268]. To this, Honoré-Gabriel de Mirabeau replied that a 'république bien constituée' was preferable to any monarchy and certainly to any arbitrary rule (despotism or anarchy) [52. 54f.].

During the French → REVOLUTION, the terms 'republic' and 'democracy' were used with an emphatically positive connotation, particularly in opposition to 'aristocracy' and 'despotism'. These latter ones, as a German observer detected, turned into 'accusations'; by using these terms, a person became 'suspicious' [71. 45f.]. However, a broad discussion about a particular type of constitution did not occur during the revolution. Only before abolishment of the monarchy was there a debate about it. Jean-Joseph Mounier, the president of the National Assembly, supported a constitutional monarchy, not least because it would protect against 'popular despotism' [57. 91–96]. And Louis-Sébastien Mercier pleaded for a democracy tempered by monarchy, i.e. he fully excludes aristocracy because it was, in his view, responsible for all previous ills [51. 84]. Mirabeau, on the other hand, saw the main difference among the types of constitution in the distribution of powers; besides, monarchies are also 'en un certain sens ... républiques'. Only despotism and anarchy are bad [53. 157].

Probably the decisive break with the old European constitutional typology was introduced by Immanuel Kant who consequently also took account of the changes brought by the French Revolution. First, Kant makes a distinction between the type of constitutions or 'form(s) of rule', namely 'autocracy' (here, this term stands for 'monarchy'), 'aristocracy and democracy', and the form of government ('forma regiminis'); the latter decides how the will of the people is determined and how the state will exercise its power. This can occur either in a 'republican or despotic' manner, i.e. by the determination of laws involving the separate powers or as the 'high-handed implementation of laws by the state, which the state itself created'. Then, only the 'private will' of the ruler has validity as law. In 'republicanism', on the other hand, laws are determined by representatives who, when doing so, are not simply pursuing their own personal interests. Because, in autocracy, the number of rulers is low, it is most likely republican for Kant; (non-representative) democracy, on the other hand, is 'necessarily despotism' because, here, 'everyone wants to be master'. Thus, Pope's dictum can be correct if it means the form of government (it is then a tautology, of course); it is 'utterly wrong' if it is merely related to the form of state. For there may be individual 'examples' of well-run states; but they still prove 'nothing about the type of government' [34. 352f.]. States must be based on the separation of powers and representation: 'Every true republic is, and can be nothing else but, a representative system of the people'. The names of the old types of constitutions are 'mere letters', and 'they may remain such', if the 'type of government' is organised according to 'the only legitimate constitution, namely that of a republic' [35. 341f.; 81. 350–360; 82; 83].

D. 19TH AND 20TH CENTS.

Although some authors continued to consider the constitutions of Antiquity to be valid [13. 3], Kant's transformation of constitutional theory was taken up and developed further by others, e.g. by Wilhelm Traugott Krug [38], Johann Benjamin Erhard [15] and Friedrich Schlegel [67]. Johann Gottlieb Fichte drew even more far-reaching conclusions: When the purpose of the state, liberty and equality of all citizens, has been achieved, it is actually irrelevant whether the government is held 'in the hands of all or ... several or ... in that of a single person' [18. 315f.]. And Friedrich Daniel Ernst Schleiermacher stated that the 'great new constitutions' could no longer be subsumed under the old constitutional forms. For Schleiermacher, the contemporary form of state essentially had to consist of the combined action of the two (the only independent) powers, namely the legislative and the executive [68. 246–286]. For Georg Wilhelm Friedrich Hegel, too, the 'old division of constitutions' had lost its justification; the question about the best constitution had become 'idle'; 'of such forms, one can only speak in historic terms', even though modifications implemented at the time were valuable [26. 254, 276, 282]. 'The principle of our times' for any constitution that wants to be called such is liberty-the abolishment within the state of the opposition of people and government. As a result, the earlier differentiations of constitutional types into democracy, aristocracy and monarchy had become 'abstract' [25. 142f.]. For Hegel's pupil Eduard Gans, the ancient constitutional model was also of historical interest only [21. 172].

Therefore, the numerous constitutional typologies designed in the 19th cent., usually had to employ new concepts in order to be able to appropriately understand political reality. For Karl Theodor Welcker, for example, the old designations only played a subordinate role; more important was the historical development of constitutions: from initial despotism via theocracy to the state of the present time, founded on the rule of law, as the 'state of reason' [77. 12–26, 100f.; 78. 382, 385]. Robert von Mohl recognised a similar historical development; however, it followed a course from the 'patriarchal states' of the 'family and tribal way of life' via 'the patrimonial states', the theocracies of Classical Antiquity and despotic regimes to the state of modern times founded on the rule of law [54. 4f.]. The four constitutions set out by Pierre-Joseph Proudhon, the monarchy (i.e. patriarchy), panarchy (communism), democracy and anarchy (individuals governing themselves), are also conceived of as a process of historical development: For they can be reduced to two principles, the rule of authority and the rule of liberty, and they are engaged in a constant struggle against each other. Only in a society based on the principle of federation will they be reconciled [61. 30–70].

In the meantime, classical constitutional theory was still restated by a few liberal scholars of constitutional law, albeit with modifications, e.g. by Friedrich Christoph Dahlmann [12. 48], Carl von Rotteck [64. 208] and Wilhelm Roscher [63. 8]. It served as a model even for authors like Julius Fröbel, who did not favour a monarchy as was frequently the case, but who described democracy as the highest form 'in the realm of morality' [20. 63–70]. However, it could no longer be applied where one's starting point was the fundamental difference between society and state: Lorenz von Stein recognised in aristocracy and democracy no longer only forms of state and constitution, but rather two great principles which, at the level of society, struggle against each other: the principle of preservation and order on the one hand, and that of development and progress on the other. These are 'the two great principles according to which the whole of humanity ... moves forward' [73. 76, 86]. Their reconciliation is only effected by the state: the kingdom of social reform or, in case that fails, the republic that represents the sovereignty of the people [72. 11, 134]. Thus, for Stein, the earlier state or constitutional forms become principles of social dynamics, with the state being destined to effect their reconciliation [88]. Karl Marx went one step further still: Since he did not approve of the separation of state and society, democracy was no longer a form of constitution for him, but 'the essence of all that is constitutional' in states, the 'solved riddle of all constitutions' [48. 231]. Beyond that, all debates about constitutional types are outdated: 'All struggles within a state, the contest between democracy, aristocracy and monarchy ... (are) nothing but the illusory frameworks ..., within which the true struggles of the various classes are carried out among each other' [49. 33].

While the old constitutional model is occasionally still taken as a starting point in the 20th cent., it must be modified or differentiated more and more if one wishes to be able to properly understand the state and constitutional reality. Georg Jellinek wanted to transcend the 'old model' by recognising only two basic types of constitution, monarchy and republic, which are then divided into many subforms. But with the forms of the state and constitution being identical, he saw an element from the time of Antiquity that continued to be active [32. 661, 665]. For Max Weber, however, the three pure types of legitimate rule take the place of the forms of constitution: the rational (legal), traditional and charismatic ones [76. 124]. Rudolf Smend considers the old theory of constitutional forms to be 'inapplicable'. Instead, he sees in the new parliamentarism a 'form of state in itself' since it forms an 'integration factor' for societal opposites [70. 85f.]. While for Carl Schmitt the 'constitution of the modern bourgeois state' founded on the rule of law 'is always one with a mixed constitution', further development of monarchy and democracy into a written constitution means that none of the two constitutional types has been realised in pure form, rather it will always appear 'restrained by the principles

of a state' founded on the rule of law [69. 200–202]. Even Hans Kelsen's work, which takes the Classical division as its starting point and extensively examines the individual types of constitutions of a monarchy, republic, autocracy and democracy [37. 320f., 370f.], is rather a witness to the fact that the old theory of constitutional types can no longer lay claim to any validity.

It is true that, in the period after World War II some authors still used the former theory of constitutional types as the basis of their work [40. 100]; the numerous differentiations and specifications which then became necessary, e.g. with Erich Küchenhoff [39], demonstrated, however, that the various 'systems of rule' (as expressed by Theodor Eschenburg) could no longer be forced into the traditional templates [16. 275].

→ Constitution

→ RULER; → TYRANNIS; → CONSTITUTION; → INTERNATIONAL LAW

SOURCES: 1 G. ACHENWALL, J. ST. PÜTTER, Elementa iuris naturae, Göttingen ²1753 2 AEGIDIUS ROMANUS (EGIDIO COLONNA), De regimine principum, H. SAMARITANUS (ed.), 1607 (repr. 1967) 3 ALBERTUS MAGNUS, Commentarii in octo libros politicorum Aristotelis III, 5, Opera omnia, A. BORGNET (ed.), vol. 8, Paris 1891 4 J. ALTHUSIUS, Politica methodice digesta, ³1614 (repr.1961) 5 R.-L. D'ARGENSON, Considérations sur le gouvernement ancien et présent de la France (1764) 6 H. ARNISAEUS, De republica, Frankfurt a.M. 1615 7 Id., Doctrina politica, Amsterdam ²1651 8 CH. BESOLD, Synopsis politicae doctrinae (1637), L. BOEHM (ed.), 2000 9 J. BODIN, Les six livres de la république, 1583 (repr. 1961) 10 B. PH. VON CHEMNITZ, Dissertatio de ratione status, Freistad 1647 11 G. CONTARINI, De magistratibus et republica Venetorum (1543), in: Id., Opera, 1571 (repr. 1968) 12 FR. CHR. DAHLMANN, Die Politik (1835), M. RIEDEL (ed.), 1968 13 J. A. EBERHARD, Über die Freyheit des Bürgers und die Principien der Regierungsformen, in: Id., Vermischte Schriften, vol. 1, Halle 1784 14 D. ERASMUS VON ROTTERDAM, Institutio principis christiani (1515), in: Id., Opera omnia, vol. IV/1, 1974 15 J. B. ERHARD, Über freiwillige Knechtschaft und Alleinherrschaft, Berlin 1821 16 TH. ESCHENBURG, Staat und Geschichte in Deutschland, 1963 17 A. FERGUSON, An Essay on the History of Civil Society, (1767). 18 J. G. FICHTE, Die Grundzüge des gegenwärtigen Zeitalters (1804), Gesamtausgabe, BAYERISCHE AKADEMIE DER WISSENSCHAFT, (eds.), vol. I/8 1991 19 R. FILMER, Patriarcha (1635), P. LASLETT (ed.),1949 20 J. FRÖBEL, System der socialen Politik, vol. 2, Mannheim ²1850 21 E. GANS, Deutsches Staatsrecht (1834), in: Id., Philosophische Schriften H. SCHRÖDER (ed.), 1971 22 M. GOLDAST (ed.), Monarchia S. Romani imperii, 1611–1614 (repr. 1967) 23 GUILELMI DE MOERBEKA, Aristotelis Politicorum libri octo cum vetusta translatione, F. SUSEMIHL (ed.), Leipzig 1872 24 A. HAMILTON, J. MADISON, J. JAY, The Federalist Papers, in: American Social and Political Thought: A Reader, A. HESS (ed.), 2003 25 G. W. F. HEGEL, Vorlesungen über die Philosophie der Weltgeschichte, vol. 1: Die Vernunft in der Geschichte, J. HOFFMEISTER (ed.), 1955 26 Id., Grundlinien der Philosophie des Rechts (1821), Sämtliche Werke, Jubiläumsausgabe, H. GLOCKNER (ed.), vol. 7, ⁴1967 27 J. G. HEINECCIUS, Elementa juris naturae et gentium, Editio nova & castigatior (1746) 28 TH. HOBBES, De cive (1642), G. GAWLICK (ed.), 1959

29 Id., Leviathan (1651), I. Fetscher (ed.), 1966　30 D. Hume, Essays (1753/54), Philosophical Works, Th. H. Green, Th. H. Grose (eds.), 1882–1886, (repr.) 1964, vol. 3　31 James I., Basilikon doron (1599), in: Id., Political works, Ch. McIlwain (ed.), 1965　32 G. Jellinek, Allgemeine Staatslehre, 1900, ³1921　33 G. Kallen, A. S. Piccolomini als Publizist, 1939　34 I. Kant, Zum ewigen Frieden (1795), Gesammelte Schriften, Akademische Ausgabe, vol. 8, 1912　35 Id., Die Metaphysik der Sitten (1797), Gesammelte Schriften, Akademische Ausgabe, vol. 6, 1907　36 B. Keckermann, Systema disciplinae politicae, Hannover 1616　37 H. Kelsen, Allgemeine Staatslehre, 1925　38 W. T. Krug, Über Staats-Verfassung und Staatsverwaltung, Königsberg 1806　39 A. Küchenhoff, Möglichkeiten und Grenzen begrifflicher Klarheit in der Staatsformenlehre, 2 vols., 1967　40 R. Laun, Allgemeine Staatslehre im Grundriß, ⁹1964　41 H. Lauterbeck, Regentenbuch, Leipzig 1559　42 J. Limnaeus, Juris publici imperii Romano-Germanici libri IX, Straßburg 1629–1634, ⁴1699, vol. 1　43 J. Lipsius, Politicorum sive civilis doctrinae libri sex, 1589 (last edition [Antwerp] 1615)　44 J. Locke, Two Treatises of Government (1690); in: Id. Two Treatises of Government and A Letter Concerning Toleration, I. Shapiro (ed.), 2003　45 G.-B. de Mably, De la législation ou principes des lois (1776), Œuvres complètes 1794/95, (repr. 1977), vol. 9　46 Id., Observations sur le gouvernement et les lois des états unis d'Amérique (1784), Œuvres complètes, 1794/95, (repr. 1977),vol. 8　47 N. Machiavelli, Opere, M. Bonfantini (ed.), 1963　48 K. Marx, Kritik des Hegelschen Staatsrechts (1843), Marx Engels Werke, vol. 1, 1972　49 Id., F. Engels, Die deutsche Ideologie (1845/4), Marx Engels Werke, vol. 3, 1973　50 M. Mendelssohn, Jerusalem oder über religiöse. Macht und Judentum (1783), Gesammelte Schriften, Jubiläumsausgabe, vol. 8, 1983　51 L.-S. Mercier, De J.-J. Rousseau, considéré comme l'un des premiers auteurs de la révolution, Paris 1791, vol. 2　52 H.-G. de Mirabeau, Sur Moses Mendelssohn, sur la réforme politique des Juifs, 1787, (repr. 1968)　53 Id., Sur l'élection et l'institution des juges (National Assembly speech on 5.5.1790), Œuvres, vol. 2, Paris 1834　54 R. v. Mohl, Die Polizei-Wissenschaft nach den Grundsätzen des Rechtsstaates, vol. 1, Tübingen ³1866　55 Ch.-L. de Montesquieu, De l'esprit des loix (1748), Œuvres completes, R. Caillois (ed.), 1949–1951, vol. 2　56 F. C. v. Moser, Beherzigungen, Frankfurt a.M. ³1763　57 J.-J. Mounier, Considérations sur les gouvernements (1789)　58 Maistre Nicole Oresme, Le livre de Politiques d'Aristote, A. D. Menut (ed.), 1970　59 P. Paruta, Della perfettione della vita politica, new edition, Venedig 1586　60 A. Pope, An Essay on Man (1744)　61 P.-J. Proudhon, Du principe fédératif, Paris 1863　62 S. Pufendorf, Dissertatio de republica irregulari, Lund 1668　63 W. Roscher, Politik, Stuttgart ²1893　64 C. v. Rotteck, Lehrbuch des Vernunftrechts und der Staatswissenschaft, Stuttgart ²1840　65 J.-J. Rousseau, Discours sur l'économie politique (1755), Œuvres completes, B. Gagnebin, M. Raymond (eds.), 1959–1995, vol. 3　66 Id., Du contrat social (1762), in: Œuvres complètes, B. Gagnebin, M. Raymond (eds.), 1959–1995, vol. 3　67 Fr. Schlegel, Versuch über den Begriff des Republikanismus (1796), Kritische Friedrich-Schlegel-Ausgabe, E. Behler (ed.), vol. 7, 1966　68 Fr. D. E. Schleiermacher, Ueber die Begriffe der verschiedenen Staatsformen (1814), Sämmtliche Werke, Part 3, vol. 2, Berlin 1838　69 C. Schmitt, Verfassungslehre,

1928, ³1957　70 R. Smend, Die politische Gewalt im Verfassungsstaat und das Problem der Staatsform (1923), in: Id., Staatsrechtliche Abhandlungen, ²1968, 58–88　71 J. v. Sonnenfels, Handbuch der inneren Staatsverwaltung, vol. 1, Vienna 1798　72 L. v. Stein, Geschichte der sozialen Bewegung in Frankreich von 1789 bis auf unsere Tage (1850), G. Salomon (ed.), 1921, vol. 3　73 Id., Demokratie und Aristokratie (1854), in: Id., Schriften zum Sozialismus, E. Pankoke (ed.), 1974　74 F. Suarez, Tractatus de legibus et legislatore Deo, in: Id., Opera omnia, vol. 5, Paris 1856　75 Thomas Aquinus, De rege, Opera omnia, editio Leonina, vol. 42, 1979　76 M. Weber, Wirtschaft und Gesellschaft, ²1925　77 K. Th. Welcker, Die letzten Gründe von Recht, Staat und Strafe, 1813, (repr. 1964)　78 Id., see Staatsverfassungen, in: Das Staats-Lexikon, C. Rotteck, C. Welcker (eds.), Altona ²1845–1848, vol. 12, 363–387　79 Ch. Wolff, Vernünfftige Gedancken von dem gesellschafftlichen Leben der Menschen (⁴1736), Gesammelte Werke, Part I, vol. 5, 1975　80 Id., Jus naturae (1738), Gesammelte Werke, Part II, vol. 24, 1968

Literature: 81 G. Bien, Revolution, Bürgerbegriff und Freiheit. Über die Transformation der alteuropäische Verfassungstheorie, in: Philosophisches Jahrbuch 79, 1972, 1–18　82 Id., Die Grundlegung der politischen Philosophie bei Aristoteles, 1973　83 Id., see Herrschaftsformen, in: Historisches Wörterbuch der Philosophie, vol. 3, 1974, Sp. 1096–1099　84 H. Denzer, Bodins Staatsformenlehre, in: Id. (ed.), Jean Bodin. Verhandlungen der internationalen Bodin Tagung in München, 1973, 233–244　85 H. Dreitzel, Protestantischer Aristotelismus und absoluter Staat, 1970　86 Id., Monarchiebegriffe in der Fürstengesellschaft, 1991　87 R. Hoke, Die Reichsstaatslehre des Johannes Limnaeus, 1968　88 G. Maluschke, Lorenz von Steins Staatsformenlehre, in: R. Schnur (ed.), Staat und Gesellschaft, 1978, 223–243　89 W. Nippel, Mischverfassungstheorie und Verfassungsrealität in Antike und früher Neuzeit, 1980　90 H. Quaritsch, Staat und Souveränität, 1970.　　　　Ulrich Dierse

Contract

A. The Historical Background　B. The Status of Contracts in Continental Codifications　C. Development and Status of Contract Law in English Common Law

A. The Historical Background

Modern continental contract law has its historical basis in the tradition of Roman Common Law. The Roman sources–even at the time of the Justinian Codification–do not recognise a general theory of contract, but only specific types of contract. The Roman consensual contract, for example, the purchase (*emptio venditio*) or the work contract (*locatio operis*), are at the beginning of a development which led to our modern concept of contract as a consensual joining of intentions of two or more parties. Roman contract law underwent substantial changes in Common Law. First, the superseding of the Roman system of individual contract types should be mentioned. Mediaeval legal theory, primarily that of → canonists, took the first steps towards a general concept of contract [21]. By the end of the 16th cent., under the influence of the practice and not least of all because of the theological and juridical theories of late scholasticism, the doctrine of common law succeeded in developing and formulating one all-inclusive category of contract. [3; 4].

As early as the 16th cent., the authors of Common Law no longer thought a special form of law was necessary for promise of obligation to have occurred. Under the influence, first, of mediaeval canon lawyers and, later, of the theories of → NATURAL LAW (17th–18th cents.), it was accepted that every agreement, however informal, could be the basis of binding legal claims [20]. The Roman proposition *ex pacto actio non oritur* was thus abandoned. As a consequence, the modern idea of a general contract of obligation was born [7; 14]. 'Une convention ou un pacte (car ce sont termes synonymes)', wrote the French jurist Robert Joseph Pothier in the middle of the 18th cent. [15], 'est le consentement de deux ou de plusieurs personnes, pour former entre elles quelque engagement, ou pour résoudre un précédent, ou pour le modifier'. This Common Law definition of contract [9] can still be read, almost verbatim, in the older codifications from the end of the 18th cent., especially in Article 1101 of the French *Code Civil* (1804) and in §861 of the Austrian ABGB (*Allgemeines Bürgerliches Gesetzbuch*, 1811). The similarity in formulation of the two regulations points to an obvious common historical background of the French and Austrian law codes. All modern → CODIFICATION in continental Europe make provision for a definition of contract as a joint intention. The German BGB (*Bürgerliches Gesetzbuch*, 1900), without an express, rigid definition (BGB §154 paragraph 1), assumes it to be logical. A comparative reading of the respective regulations also shows that legislative techniques in modern codifications have distanced themselves considerably in language and style from the first historical models (see Article 1 of the Swiss OR (*Öffentliches Recht*, 1912), Article 1321 and 1325 of the Italian *Codice Civile* (1942), Article 232 of the Portuguese *Código Civil* (1966), and Article 213 paragraph 1 and Article 217 paragraph 1 in Book Six of the *Nieuw Nederlands Burgerlijk Wetboek* (1992).

B. THE STATUS OF CONTRACTS IN CONTINENTAL CODIFICATIONS

The construction of continental codifications and particularly the systematic organisation of the legal concept of contract in their overall structure provides an instructive insight into the development of modern legislation [16. 35ff.]. The historically oldest codifications, the French *Code Civil* and the Austrian ABGB, present → PROPERTY and not contract as the systematic orientation point of the law code. It is indicative that the Third Book of the French *Code Civil* is dedicated to the 'différentes manières dont on acquiert la propriété'. Only in the Third Chapter are there provisions for contract and for → DEBT LAW. Here the structure of the French *Code Civil* follows the model of the Justinian

Institutiones. It is not the contract, but the property and its acquisition, therefore, that lie at the basis of the systematic plan of the *Code*. The Austrian ABGB shows a similar orientation in its systematic construction. After 'personal law' in the first part, there are regulations in the second part for 'laws of property', and here, only in a subdivision, are 'laws of personal property' treated. Contracts and contractual relationships of obligation are not mentioned or legally regulated until the 17th main section, which is definitely not the systematic centre of the law code. Numerous codifications of civil law in 19th-cent. Europe, for example, those of the Italian states before unification and of the Italian kingdom (1865), the first Dutch *Wetboek* (1838) and the first Portugese *Código Civil* (1868), all remain true to the system of the model of the French *Code Civil*. The same is true for the core of the Spanish *Código Civil* (1889). However, the Spanish codification, despite the obvious French influence, shows a remarkable innovation in its structure when compared to its model. It has an independent Fourth Book dedicated to contract law and contractual obligations.

The German BGB of 1900 represents in structure and system a complete innovation in comparison with its above-described historical predecessors. The systematics of the German codification is governed by its logical structure and especially by the First Book, in which a 'General Part' is provided for the whole law code. The structuring of the subject matter thus follows logical and conceptual criteria rather than a division of the material according to content. Primacy of place in the code is given to the theory of legal transactions and to the theory of declarations of intent in legal transactions. Contracts are first mentioned after the introduction of general provisions for declaration of intent and, to that extent, also for contractual declaration in Part Two of Section Three of the 'General Part' (BGB §§116–144).

At first, to be sure, the organisation of the German BGB did not at all represent a model for European codifications in the first half of the 20th cent. [16. 35ff.]. The theory of legal transactions and the strictly logical construction mentioned above was seen by many as too abstract and not in touch with reality. Significantly, neither the Swiss legislators revising the law of obligations in 1912 nor the Austrians amending the ABGB in the years 1914–1916 provided specific regulations for legal transactions. The contract is at the centre of the regulations of the Swiss law of obligations. The Austrian legislators left the historical structure of the ABGB intact as far as possible. The German BGB functioned as a model only with regard to the numerous detailed regulations which were introduced at the time into contract law, both in Switzerland and in Austria. The Italian legislators of 1942 were also not prepared to adopt a 'General Part' in their new law code. The legal regulation of the principle of legal transactions, which incidentally was accepted into Italian law at the time, was deliberately avoided. A Fourth Book of the new law code was dedicated to debt law. In this area the legal concept of contract takes a central position.

Only in the most recent European codifications of civil law does the systematic plan of the BGB seem, in part at least, to have been a model [16. 35ff.]. The Portuguese legislators of 1966, when rewriting the old civil law code of 1868, provided a First Book with a 'General Part'. The theory of legal transactions (*negócio jurídico*) received explicit legal regulation. To this extent the Portuguese *Código Civil* distinguishes, as does the German model, between provisions for statements of intent in legal transactions and regulations for contracts. This does not occur until the second chapter of the 'Second Book'. The most recent Dutch civil law code of 1992 also has a 'General Part'. This is, however, not provided until the 'Third Book', and only for property law. In it particular provisions are devoted to legal acts and legal transactions. Systematically separated from this, contracts are not given detailed regulation until the 'Sixth Book'.

C. Development and Status of Contract Law in English Common Law

The current legal concept of *contract* in English Law developed in a different historical context from those discussed above. As is well known, England did not experience reception of Roman General Law either in the Middle Ages or in modern times. *Common Law* developed its rules out of the practice of law in the Royal Courts in Westminster. This is also the case for contract law. In the beginning there were various procedural *forms of action*. The process began with an application by the plaintiff for the grant by the Royal Chancery of a *writ*, i.e. a royal summons of the defendant before the Royal Court. The process was intensely formalised: 'to every case there corresponds a particular form of process, to every *writ* an 'action'' [18. 12]. The starting point for the development of contract law is the complaint of the offence of *trespass*; initially this was a matter of unlawful injury to body or property, which had to have taken place violently, *vi et armis,* in breach of the King's Peace. In the course of granting writs on the case *in consimili casu*, this form of complaint was extended by the end of the 12th cent.,beyond what was originally a very narrowly defined set of facts. Reparation was also granted for damage done by somebody to another's property which they had promised to handle in a particular way. For example, in a case from the year 1372 a blacksmith had undertaken to shoe a horse and in doing so had wounded it. Out of the constellation of cases cited, the English courts developed in the following decades an *action of assumpsit*. This is based not on contractual obligation in the sense of continental law, but rather only on an obligation for compensation in the case of nonfeasance or misfeasance of the promised action. From the procedural perspective of the time, the contractual agreement is to that extent not the basis for a claim for action, but it is only the prerequisite for the possible claims for reparations that might arise out of a broken promise. The contract itself therefore appears at this point in the historical development of *Common Law* rather as a guarantee of an obligation in prospect.

Another possibility for procedurally enforcing a claim that would be contractual in the modern sense was offered by older *Common Law*. This was the so-called *action of debt*. It consisted of an unconditional claim for payment of a precisely defined numerical sum of money. Such a claim regularly had its basis in written evidence or a legal document. Originally such a claim could not be based on a simple consensual contract. According to its nature the complaint of *debt* appears as 'a claim for money which rightfully belongs to the creditor and which the debtor unlawfully withholds' [18. 233]. Out of these two different procedural figures the English courts developed, during the 16th cent., the idea of an agreed upon and procedurally enforceable obligation of contract. The ultimate modification was introduced in the multifaceted decision by the Exchequer Chamber in the famous 'Slade's case' (1602). As a result of this decision the following principles were anchored in English Law by the beginning of the 17th cent. The creditor of a *debt* could bring a case of his own free choice in the form either of an *action of debt* or of an *action of assumpsit*. The creditor could therefore in the form of an action *of assumpsit* also bring a case for a numerical amount and was to that extent no longer limited as before to the reparation for damage in fact suffered as a result of a broken promise. At the beginning of the 17th cent. English law achieved to that extent the final transformation of the *action of assumpsit* from a criminal to a contractual action. The *action of assumpsit* provided a procedural enforcement for fundamentally every informal promise [16. 12–13].

It is worth mentioning that, from the 16th cent. on, English court practice developed a number of criteria for deciding to what extent such a promise could be seen as defensible. After that time, English contract law spoke of the necessity for *consideration*. Thus, by the time of a judgment in 1577, *consideration* was required in the form of a return promise. According to the interpretation of English jurists, this must be presented at the same time. Hence an action already completed by the other party and made part of the agreement is not valid as a *consideration* for this promise. *Past consideration*, therefore, is not sufficient to obtain damages in the case of breach of promise. This awkward legal thinking reflecting the rigid forms of the 16th and 17th cents. still exerts some influence on modern English contract law. An attempt to weaken the constitutive effect of *consideration* into mere evidence and allow the intentions of the parties alone to be a sufficient basis for a binding contract can be traced back to the Scottish jurist and judge Lord Mansfield (1705–1793), one of the most famous jurists in the history of *Common Law*. Under the influence of the theories of the Enlightenment and of continental trade law, he rejected the theory of *consideration* as a superfluous, rationally unjustifiable subtlety: every agreement should in itself be legally binding; the joint intention should suffice and the *consideration* should serve only as an index of the earnestness of the intentions of the parties [16. 25–27]. However, this concept, which would have meant a complete eventual rapprochement to the continental common law theory of contract, did not prevail. It was rejected by the House of Lords a few years later.

By the end of the 18th cent. English law had made its way from individual cases understood in terms of the law of actions to a concept of contract understood in terms of material law. William Blackstone (1723–1780) defined contracts in his *Commentaries on the Law of England* [5] with a formulation which, disregarding the formalism of *consideration*, is not far from the contemporary definition by Pothier cited above: 'Contract is an agreement upon sufficient consideration to do or not to do a particular thing'. This development was advanced and supported by theoretical jurisprudence which had newly come into existence in England in the 19th cent. Its representatives, active in the universities, were greatly influenced by continental law, primarily by German → PANDECTIST STUDIES. It is therefore understandable that the Romanist categories flowed into the textbooks of the time, which then constructed their definition of contract entirely on the continental conception of civil law. This view can still be observed in modern English textbooks on contract law.

→ Consensus; → Contractus; → Emptio venditio; → Obligatio; → Pactum; → Stipulatio

1 J. Bärmann, Pacta sunt servanda. Considérations sur l'histoire du contrat consensuel, in: Revue internationale du droit comparé 1961, 18ff. 2 J. Barton (ed.), Towards a General Law of Contract, 1990 3 I. Birocchi, Saggi sulla formazione storica della categoria generale del contratto, 1988 4 Id., Causa e categoria generale del contratto. Un problema dogmatico nella cultura privatistica dell'età moderna, 1997 5 W. Blackstone, Commentaries on the Law of England, London 1765–1769, Vol. II, chap. 30, 442 6 H. Charmatz, Zur Geschichte und Konstruktion der Vertragtypen im Schuldrecht, mit besonderer Berücksichtigung der gemischten Verträge, 1937 7 Coing, Vol. I, 432ff. 8 R. Feenstra, M. Ahsmann, Contract. Aspecten van de begrippen contract en contractsvrijheid in historisch perspectief, 1988 9 J.-L. Gazzaniga, Domat et Pothier. Le contrat à la fin de l'ancien régime, in: Droits. Revue française de théorie juridique 12, 1990, 37ff. 10 J. Gordley, The Philosophical Origins of Modern Contract Doctrine, 1991 11 R. H. Helmholz, Assumpsit and Fidei Laesio, in: Law Quarterly Review 91 (1975), 405–432 12 M. Hohlweck, Nebenabreden. Pacta im römischen und im modernen Recht, 1996 13 M. Lupoi, Lo statuto della promessa: diritto altomedievale europeo e diritto inglese, in: L. Vacca (ed.), Causa e contratto nella prospettiva storico-comparatistica, 1997, 235ff. 14 K.-P. Nanz, Die Entstehung des allgemeinen Vertragsbegriffs im 16. bis 18. Jahrhundert, 1985 15 R. J. Pothier, Traité des obligations, n. 3, in: Id., Oeuvres complètes, Paris 1835, 411–412 16 F. Ranieri, Europäisches Obligationenrecht, ²2003, chaps. 1–3 (comprehensive bibliography of the history of law and comparative law) 17 T. Repgen, Vertragstreue und Erfüllungszwang in der mittelalterlichen Rechtswissenschaft, 1994 18 M. Rheinstein, Die Struktur des vertraglichen Schuldverhältnisses im anglo-amerikanischen Recht, 1932 19 A. W. B. Simpson, A History of the Common Law of Contract. The Rise of the Action of Assumpsit, 1975 20 A.

Somma, Autonomia privata e struttura del consenso contrattuale. Aspetti storico-comparativi di una vicenda concettuale, 2000 (comprehensive bibliography of the history of law and comparative law) 21 R. Volante, Il sistema contrattuale del diritto comune classico. Struttura dei patti e individuazione del tipo. Glossatori e Ultramontani (= Per la storia del pensiero giuridico moderno 60), 2001 22 P. Wery, L'exécution forcée en nature des obligations contractuelles non pécuniaires, 1993, 29–81 23 F. Wieacker, Die vertragliche Obligation bei den Klassikern des Vernunftsrechts, in: Festschrift für Hans Welzel, 1974, 7–22 24 R. Zimmermann, The Law of Obligations. Roman Foundations of the Civilian Tradition, 1990, 537–582 25 Id., Konturen eines Europäischen Vertragsrechts, in: Juristen-Zeitung, 1995, 477ff. FILIPPO RANIERI

Copenhagen
A. PREFATORY REMARKS B. THE NY CARLSBERG GLYPTOTEKET C. DANSK NATIONAL MUSEET, THE DANISH NATIONAL MUSEUM D. THORVALDSEN MUSEET, THORVALDSEN MUSEUM

A. PREFATORY REMARKS
The city of (C.) possesses three museums with collections of antiquities, which are situated at only a few minutes' distance from one another. The *Ny Carlsberg Glyptoteket* is the public bequest of a single collector, whose foundation created an institution of national importance. The antiquities collection of the National Museum was built around a royal collection, which became national property. Finally, the Thorvaldsen Museum is a one-artist museum, a very early example in this category, comparable to the *Rodin Museum* at Paris.

B. THE NY CARLSBERG GLYPTOTEKET
The *Ny Carlsberg Glyptoteket* (NCG) is a government-approved art museum. The categories of the collection include Ancient art; Egypt; Near East; Etruria; and French and Danish painting of the 19th and 20th cents. The address is: Dantes Plads 7, DK 1556 Kopenhagen.

The NCG is a foundation of the brewer Carl Jacobsen (1842–1914) and his wife Ottilia. This generous gift is today one of the most important art museums in the Scandinavian region. From the viewpoint of museum history, it counts among the most important foundations by industrial sponsorship, whose activities in the second half of the 19th cent., particularly in the United States, made museums like those of → BOSTON, Museum of Fine Arts, → NEW YORK, Metropolitan Museum or → PHILADELPHIA possible. Jacobsen himself was one of the most important private collectors of the 19th cent. His interests leaned toward the art of the Mediterranean as well as to contemporary art (Rodin and the Impressionists).

The NCG was constructed around the brewer's private property in 1882. In connection with two further donations in 1888 and 1899 (antiquities), Jacobsen

Fig. 1: Portrait (Hadrian).
Ny Carlsberg Glyptoteket

Fig. 3: Volute krater.
Ny Carlsberg Glyptoteket

Fig. 2: Bronze of a negro boy.
Ny Carlsberg Glyptoteket

committed C. and the Danish government to support the construction of a new museum. Shortly afterwards, work was begun in the vicinity of the harbor, near the Tivoli Park. In 1902, Jacobsen ensured the financial base of the museum through the *Ny Carlsberg Foundation* (named after the Carlsberg Brewery). Since 1953, the NCG has acted as an independent foundation under the supervision of the Carlsberg Fund, C., and the Danish government. Alongside the National Museum (see below), it plays an outstanding role in Denmark's museum life.

Today's NCG was built in three phases. The first three-winged part (1897) of the present-day building was designed by Vilhelm Dahlerup, who provided it with an exterior facade made up of seven arcs in Venetian Renaissance style and a central Roman portal in the form of a 'triumphal arch'. Jacobsen's gift to the Danish citizens manages without a grandiose 'temple façade' and fits in harmoniously with its surroundings in its proportions. Dahlerup also added the famed Wintergarden (1906) with its high glass dome over the main entrance, which gave the museum its characteristic silhouette. Thus, Jacobsen's idea of a building, influenced by L. von Klenze's Glyptothek in Munich, was realized with the addition of a modern glass dome. At the same time as the Wintergarden, and according to designs by

Fig. 4:
Etruscan urn.
Ny Carlsberg
Glyptoteket

H. Kampmann, the part of the building meant for the Antiquities collection, came into being-grouped around two interior courtyards. After this the outer dimensions of the Glyptothek have remained unchanged since 1906. The way in which the art works were exhibited was of particular importance for the founder, who had chosen the name 'Glyptothek' in order to emphasize its difference from a museum committed to scientific classification. It was to be a place 'where marble sculptures stand and look at you' [16]. In order to provide an ambience corresponding to this approach, great care was taken in the decorating of the rooms. Today, the museum itself has become a monument through its exhibition-oriented Jugendstil decorations [13; 17; 42].

The third and most recent part, built according to plans by H. Larsen, opened in 1996. Embedded in the southeast court of Kampmann's building, it is invisible from outside and thereby endorses the preliminary planning from the beginning of the century. The elegant new galleries for French painting and sculpture utilize available conditions and constitute a convincing example of modern Danish architecture.

The ancient art of the NCG provides an overview of the high cultures of the eastern Mediterranean: Greece, Italy, and the Imperium Romanum from c. 3000 BC to the end of the Roman Empire. Because of the founder's affinity, the sculptural art is represented by numerous high-quality examples in all areas, especially since Jacobsen was advised in his choices by W. Helbig [29].

A distinctive feature of the NCG is that the Museum presents its rich collection of materials in a relatively

manageable space as a broad overview, at the same time pointing out the relations between different cultures and cultural stages within the Eastern Mediterranean region. The decoration of the interior, already conceived at the beginning of the century, contributes to this. In larger museums, like those of London, New York or Paris, such a 'view at a glance' is considerably more difficult, because of the distance between departments.

The Greek and Roman portraits, including a bust of Hadrian (Fig. 1), represent a high point of the collection. There are also funerary reliefs, both Greek and Roman, as well as wall-paintings, small bronzes and a rich Etruscan collection. Attention may be drawn here to the bronze statue of an African boy (Fig. 2) and the Apulian volute-crater (Fig. 3), as well as an Etruscan urn (Fig. 4).

The NCG maintains its own annual journal, *Meddelelser fra Ny Carlsberg Glyptoteket*. Articles in Danish usually have an English summary. Since its foundation, it has been the Glyptothek's goal to make its holdings available quickly and regularly through publications, so that a considerable bibliography has been amassed. Between 1991 and 1998, the entire collection was newly listed in a series of 35 catalogues in Danish and English. In this way, the museum has made its holdings available to the public, and at the same time utilized its own documentary work in a way that allows both scholars and the public to participate in it. In addition to the three volumes on the Near East and Egypt, a series of separate publications deal with the antiquities collection of the Ny Carlsberg Glyptoteket [8; 11; 12; 15; 19; 20; 21; 22; 23; 26; 27; 28; 30; 31; 32; 41]. They each give a complete list of the older catalogues, some of which have become standard [33; 34; 35; 36; 37], and which have been completed, but not fully replaced by the new series.

C. DANSK NATIONAL MUSEET, THE DANISH NATIONAL MUSEUM

The address of the Danish National Museum (DNM) is: National Museet, Frederiksholms Kanal 12, 1220 Copenhagen K, Denmark. Internet: http://www.natmus.dk.

Practically within view of the NCG stands the DNM, an important institution in the history of European museums [14]. It was founded in the time of nationalistic movements on the initiative of C. Nyerup [1807], originally with the goal of registering Danish antiquities in a museum-style manner. This museum had a lasting influence through the activities of J. Vedel-Simson and C. J. Thomsen, who developed the theory of the three ages of prehistory. When the DNM opened in 1819, it had broken with the principle of the 'jumbled curiosity cabinet' and introduced the principle of chronological arrangement its exhibitions. Thus the groundwork was laid for a continuous narrative that would serve the purpose of guiding visitors. Thomsen quite consciously conceived this museum for all segments of the population, as is documented by one of the most important museum guides of the first half of the 19th cent. [24].

The DNM maintains three main collections, dedicated to Danish history and prehistory, ethnography and Antiquity. In addition, it also has special collections. Important sub-departments include Danish prehistory, Danish urban and peasant culture, and ethnographic collections of Greenland and America, as well as Asia.

The antiquities collection includes cultural artefacts of the Eastern Mediterranean from the beginnings to Byzantine times, and is quantitatively the largest in Denmark [25]. In addition to Classical areas, Egypt and the Near East are also well represented [6]. Antiquities had already been consolidated in the capital from various collections, among others a fragment of a metope from the Parthenon, acquired in 1687 [6. 47]. In 1848, the Antiquities department was established with the collection of the late King Christian VIII (1786–1848) as its basis; it thereby extended the already important Department of Danish Antiquities in the direction of the Mediterranean. The King had been an enthusiastic friend of Antiquity, and, as Crown Prince, had organized excavations in Campania, Nola and Cumae [1; 40. 116]. Since then, the DNM has also carried out active research, both in Classical countries and in the Near East [7; 9]. Thus, at the beginning of the century, for instance, finds came to C. from Danish excavations in then-Turkish Rhodes [2; 3].

The vase collection forms the core area, with examples from all epochs, such as a red-figured cup with Poseidon [25]. The many examples of ancient minor arts with terracottas and bronzes, represented by a Mercury from France [25], as well as jewelry and glass, display the collection in its new surroundings on the second floor of the princely palace in a concentrated, clearly laid-out form.

The results of the research of the DNM and its staff are regularly presented [4; 5; 38; 39]; reports are published in the *Nationalmuseets arbejdsmark Nationalmuseet*.

D. THORVALDSEN MUSEET, THORVALDSEN MUSEUM

The address of the Thorvaldsen Museum (TM) is: Porthusg 2, 1213 Copenhagen K, Denmark. Internet: http://www.thorvaldsensmuseum.dk.

The Thorvaldsen Museum is a monument to the life and work of the sculptor, painter and collector Bertel Thorvaldsen (1770–1844). In Germany, he is known mainly for his restoration of the Munich Aeginetan sculptures (1816). The Museum was already begun during the sculptor's lifetime, in 1837, as the home for the foundation of his œvre, and was officially opened in 1848, scarcely four years after the artist's death. At this time, it was also decided to house the founder's grave in the open inner court, which lends a distinctive air to this edifice. As the home of one of its greatest national artist's œvre, the TM plays an important role in Denmark. In addition, it was significantly involved in the development of the Danish museums [10].

The three-storey Museum building is situated next to the royal palace and in the immediate vicinity of the DNM. It was planned by M. G. Bindesbøll and begun in 1839. The classicistic exterior decorations, partly with scenes from Thorvaldsen's life, are a later addition, and a sign of the veneration that this 'national' artist experienced, as well as an example of contemporary Danish classicism.

The collection is distributed over three floors [18]. It contains a large collection of paintings, as well as plaster casts of ancient sculptures in Thorvaldsen's possession, sketchbooks and antiquities. The latter are particularly numerous in the minor arts; in addition to Egyptian objects, there are Greek and Roman bronzes, glass, vases, gems, as well as coins and ancient sculptures.

The periodical *Meddelelser fra Thorvaldsen-Museet* appears irregularly.

1 Antik-Cabinettet 1851. Udgivet I hundreeddaaret af Natinalmuseet, 1951   2 CH. BLINKENBERG, K. F. KINCH, Lindos Fouilles et recherche 1902–1914, vol. I, 1932 3 Id., E. DYGGVE (ed.), Lindos Fouilles et recherche 1902–1914, 1952   4 N. BREITENSTEIN, Catalogue of Terracottas, Cypriote, Greek, Etrusco-Italian and Roman, Danish National Museum, Department of Oriental and Classical Antiquities, 1941   5 Id., W. SCHWABACHER, Sylloge nummorum Graecorum. The Royal Collection of Coins and Medals, Danish National Mus., 1942 (1987)   6 M.-L.

Buhl, A Hundred Masterpieces from the Ancient Near East in the National Museum of Denmark and the History of its Ancient Near Eastern Collections, 1974 7 Id., S. Holm-Nielsen Shiloh, The Danish Excavations at Tall Sail-un, Palestine, in 1926, 1929, 1932 and 1963. The Pre-Hellenistic Remains, 1969 = Serie: Publications of the National Museum. Archaeological-Historical Series 8 J. Christiansen, Greece in the Geometric Period, 1992 9 S. Dietz, The Argolid at the Transition to the Mycenaean Age. Stud. in the Chronology and Cultural Development in the Shaft Grave Period, Kopenhagen, National Museum of Denmark, Department of Near Eastern and Classical Antiquities, Aarhus 1991 10 J. Erichsen et al., Danske museer gennem 1648–1848 (Danish Museums), Exhibition Thorvaldsen Museum, 1974 11 T. Fischer-Hansen et al., Campania, South Italy and Sicily, 1992 12 M. Fjeldhagen, Graeco-Roman Terracottas from Egypt, 1995 13 K. Glamann, Beer and Marble, 1995 14 K. Hudson, Museums of Influence, chap. 2: Antiquarians and Archaeologists, esp. S. 29–31 15 F. O. Hvidberg-Hansen, The Palmyrene Inscriptions, 1998 16 C. Jacobsen, cited after the brochure (The Dahlerup Building), 1996 17 Id., Ny Carlsberg Glyptoteks Tilblivse, 1906 18 B. Jœrnøs, T. Melander, A. S. Urne (eds.), Thorvaldsen Mus. Catalogue, edited on the basis of the Catalogues in English (1961) and Danish (1975). Revised version, 1995 19 F. Johansen, Greek Portraits, 1992 20 Id. et al., Greece in the Archaic Period, 1994 21 Id., Roman Portraits I, 1994 22 Id., Roman Portraits II, 1995 23 Id., Roman Portraits III, 1995 24 Ledetraad til Nordisk Oldkyndighed, Kopenhagen 1836, 'Handbook to Archaeology'. ed. by the Royal Society for Nordic Archaeology, Copenhagen 1837 25 J. Lund, B. Bundgaard Rasmussen, Natinalmuseets vejledninger. Antiksamlingen. Graekere, estruskere, romere, 1994 26 M. Moltesen et al., Greece in the Classical Period, 1995 27 Id, C. Weber-Lehmann, Copies of Etruscan Tomb Paintings, 1991 28 Id., M. Nielsen et al., Etruria and Central Italy, 199 29 Id., W. Helbig, brygger Jacobsens agent i Rom 1887–1914, 1987 30 A. M. Nielsen, J. Stubbe Øster-gaard et al., Hellenism, The Eastern Mediterranean in the Hellenistic Period, 1997 31 Id., The Cypriote Collection, 1992; 32 G. Ploug, The Palmyrene Sculptures, 1995 33 F. Poulsen, Catalogue of Ancient Sculpture in the Ny Carlsberg Glyptotek, 1951 34 V. Poulsen, Les portraits grecs = Publications de la Glyptothèque Ny Carlsberg, No. 5, 1954 35 Id., Catalogue des terres cuites grecques et romaines = Publications de la Glyptothèque Ny Carlsberg, No 2, 1949 36 Id., Les portraits Romains. vol. 1. Republique et dynastie Julienne, 1962 37 Id., Les portraits Romains. vol. 2. De Vespasien à la Basse-antiquité, 1974 = Ny Carlsberg glyptotek. Publications, nos. 7–8 38 O. E. Ravn, A Catalogue of Oriental Cylinder Seals and Seal Impressions in the Danish National Mus., 1960 39 H. S. Roberts, Corpus speculorum Etruscorum. Denmark. vol. 1, Fascicule 1, Odense, 1981 40 W. Schiering, Zur Geschichte der Archäologie, in U. Hausmann (ed.), Allgemeine. Grundlagen der Archäologie, HdArch, 1969 41 J. Stubbe Østergaard et al., Imperial Rome, 1996 42 D. Zanker, Die Bauten von J. C. und C. Jacobsen, 1982.   WOLF RUDOLPH

Copy see → Cast; Cast collections

Corpus Medicorum This research project was begun in 1901 at the suggestion of the Danish scholar Johan Ludvig Heiberg and with the assistance of the Saxon and Danish Academies of Science and the Puschmann Foundation was established in the Berlin Academy of Sciences. Its self-defined task was the editing of all extant ancient medical authors, initially under the directorship of Hermann Diels. Diels' catalogue of manuscripts by Greek physicians (1906), together with a supplement (1907), remains to this day the standard reference for Greek manuscripts on medical topics. The first Greek text edited within the framework of the Corpus medicorum was Max Wellmann's *Philumenus*, published in 1908; the first Latin text was that of Cornelius Celsus edited by Friedrich Marx published in 1915. The Galenic texts not contained in Kühn's edition appeared as supplements after 1934; a *Supplementum orientale* containing translations of Galenic texts into Oriental languages was begun in 1963. Since 1964, the Corpus medicorum also includes German, English, French, or Italian translations of the Greek and Latin texts.
→ Medicine   VIVIAN NUTTON

Cosmology see → Natural Sciences

Course of Instruction
A. The Concept B. History C. The Current Situation

A. The Concept
In general, the phrase *course[s] of instruction* (CI) designates a plan in educational administration in which the goals of formation and education, as well as the learning contents for a type of school are combined though year-long courses into various subjects and transdisciplinary focal points. CI thus provide official information on what subjects should be taught and learned in a socio-historical situation, as well as when and for what purpose. They express what parts of its store of knowledge a society considers worthy of transmission and necessary to transmit. They enable us to recognize which kinds of knowledge and skills, behaviors, attitudes and norms should be taught in the school through instruction and contact. They define which skills should be developed and which knowledge gained before certificates of scholastic completion may be granted. At the same time, CI are used by educational administrations to evaluate teachers' instructional work.

CI provide outlines for the formation of a school, in which the three determining factors of public instruction are coordinated: childhood, with its demand for the recognition of special forms of life and of learning; knowledge, with its need for organization and method, which must become academic knowledge; and society, with its demands regarding the younger generation's behavior. Childhood, knowledge and society stand in a dynamic relationship to one another, which is pre-structured by the course of instruction and must be didactically put into practice by → TEACHERS in the classroom. According to E. Weniger in his theory of CI, modern CI are the result of a confrontation between powers in society, which attempt to incorporate their own interests in school training into students' educa-tion by influencing the goals and contents of school instruction. The modern state has been able to prevail and ensure its particular function in this struggle for influence on CI: 'It is the moving force of CI and the regulating factor ... as long as there have been CI in the modern sense' [6. 33]. In this special role, the state 'as both a partisan interested party and neutral solicitor ... must bring about social consensus on educational ideals and guarantee its didactic implementation in a course of instruction' [3. 119]. Weniger was counting on discus-sions on pedagogy to bring the state to a disinterested position from which it would support pedagogical inte-rests against the claims of other social groups. He there-by assumed a 'relative independence of pedagogical thought' [1. 129], which, in fact, does not exist with regard to political influences. Such an assumption, in its naiveté, actually facilitates the state's exercise of he-gemony.

B. HISTORY

At the earliest, one can speak of a CI-in the sense defined above-at the time of the educational reforms of the 18th cent. However, the the whole question of a CI, rudiments of a theory of CI and preliminary forms of CI can be traced back to Greek Antiquity. Here, (in the 7th and 6th cents. BC, 'as the ancient Greek aristocracy lost its exclusive privileges' [5. 570], a new form of educa-tion arose for the up-and-coming classes based on the cultural model of *kalokagathía* (beauty and good-ness),alongside the ancient educational model of *arête* (virtue). In the 5th cent. BC, the Sophists, as represen-tatives of an enlightened way of thinking, broadened existing educational practice above all by transmitting rhetorical contents. They supplemented traditional learning by adding a 'philological and practical group of subjects' [2. 24]. Their offerings included studies in grammar, rhetoric, dialectics, in arithmetic, music, ge-ometry, and astronomy, but ought not to be designated as a CI. Plato, in his *Politeía*, was the first to formulate a CI, insofar as he established what should be taught and learned, when, with what goal in view, how much, and to what extent subjects should be connected with and distinguished from one another, in order for young men to be trained as citizens of a state and prepared to exer-cise political functions. Aristotle advocated teaching linguistic and mathematico-musical arts in a manner corresponding to age [2. 43]. The question of CI be-came important soon thereafter in the schools of the Hellenistic period, where Homer's poetry constituted the focal point of studies. Reading and writing were obviously necessary as basic knowledge. The following

order was then developed on this basis: elementary edu-cation (reading, writing), liberal arts (grammar, rheto-ric, dialectic, arithmetic, music, geometry, astronomy) and philosophy. This was the form advocated by Cicero, but for Rome he added instruction in Greek as a foreign language for the cultured class. The canon of the seven subjects of study was specified by Quintilian in his *Institutio oratoria* and attuned to the intellectual abilities of adolescents. From then on, the study of the *septem artes liberales* (→ ARTES LIBERALES) formed the indispensable basic education prior to entering the higher schools of the Roman Empire.

This course of study remained the principal form of higher education until the end of the Middle Ages. In the → RENAISSANCE, a new interest in classical (espe-cially Ciceronian) Latin and Greek arose. In the context of the Reformation, this resulted in the founding of new schools with new regulations, including those govern-ing course material. → LATIN SCHOOLS thus arose in the 16th and 17th cents. and, in Catholic regions, Jesuit *Gymnasia* with their own teaching methods (→ JESUIT SCHOOLS). A fundamentally new orientation was of-fered in the writings of Ratke and Comenius in the 17th cent. Comenius rejected the traditional doctrine of the *septem artes* and broadened instruction by addding the vernacular and general sciences. This arranging of study was supposed to correspond to the natural learn-ing process. In the 18th cent., new reformist tendencies were added, which were unthinkable without the intro-duction of rules of study and instructional plans. The concept CI, at any rate, first came into use around 1800 [2. 319] and replaced the concept *curriculum*. Since them, a CI has been understood as 'the plan according to which one learns, structures and organizes learning', as Dolch maintains with reference to Campe [2. 319].

In the 19th cent., the expansion of educational insti-tutions into a three-tiered school system led to the de-velopment of the most varied CI exhibiting a well-founded arrangement of languages, mathematics, natu-ral and social sciences, art and sports, as well as reli-gion. The educational goal behind a CI becomes clear from the amount of time devoted to the individual dis-ciplines. To this extent, CI are also the expression of a political program, since they are used to limit or to de-velop a given kind of schooling. The arrangement of pedagogical material is always determined from the vie-wpoint of a theory of education. In 1880, Ziller struc-tured the contents of elementary school instruction ac-cording to a so-called theory of the stages of culture and tried to optimize its arrangement through the principle of concentration. The various political systems of the 19th and 20th cents. used CI to impart the knowledge that seemed important to them and the way of thinkng connected with that knowledge. Limits on schooling sometimes greatly affected the drafting of a CI.

In the 1960s, a new orientation was brought about by vehement criticism of CI and the way they are estab-lished. This led to experiments with CI geared to learn-ing goals: the so-called curricular CI. In the meantime, the insight has once again become widely accepted that a CI cannot be a conglomeration of possible goals but rather is a means to describe the goals and contents of a type of school and to express what an educational policy hopes to achieve through public education.

Classical languages were traditionally dominant in the CI of higher schools. In the CI of 1816 for the Prussian Gymnasium, Latin and Greek accounted for almost 40 per cent of all instruction. Not until the time of the Second Empire was this predominance rolled back in favor of modern languages. This trend continued under the Weimar Republic. Although humanistic classical-language education briefly regained importance again after 1945, its decline could not be halted. Only Latin was able to hold its ground at a low level, yet it currently suffers from the fact that it need not be continued after Grade 11.

C. The Current Situation

After a period in which learning-goal oriented CI with explicit guidelines were the rule, forms that give teachers greater liberty in their didactic decisions have again become dominant. The broadest form of CI are the relatively open 'framework plans'. This is consistent with the discussion currently underway with regard to the autonomy of various institutions. Modern CI contain a concise theory of types of schools and then distinguish between questions specific to one or to several academic disciplines. They are partially structured in such a way that the basic layered form of organization, already emphasized by Weniger, comes clearly to light: 1) educational and pedagogical goals by type of school; 2) problems within a discipline and problems across disciplines; 3) framework plan, and 4) vocational CI. In this process, the concentration of similar contents and learning objectives as a means of cross-disciplinary co-operation comes to the fore. Thus, CI prove to be a stimulus for the formation of both school and instruction. Even today the fundamental problem facing the formulation of a CI remains: upon what motivation do the choices made rest and how are these choices justified. Arguments are widely used that allude to so-called key problems, or to questions of great political and social significance. It remains obvious, however, that the exemplary nature of a CI and the 'fruitfulness' [4] of what it transmits is of the greatest importance for the development of such human capacities as thinking, and aesthetic as well as moral sensibilities.
→ Ancient languages, teaching of; → Humanist gymnasium

Sources: 1 H. Blankertz, Theorien und Modelle der Didaktik, ⁹1975 2 J. Dolch, Lehrplan des Abendlandes, ³1971 3 S. Hopmann, Lehrplan-Arbeit als Verwaltungshandeln, 1988 4 L. Koch, Logik des Lernens, 1991 5 G. Wehle, Lehrplan, Pädagogisches Lexikon, 1961, 570–573 6 E. Weniger, Didaktik als Bildungslehre, Vol. 1, ⁹1971

Literature: 7 U. Lindgren, Artes liberales, HWdR Vol.1, 1992, 1080–1109. HANS JÜRGEN APEL

Cretan-Mycenaean Archaeology
A. Introduction B. The exploration of Mycenaean Greece C. Research on Minoan Crete D. Situation, Problems, Task

A. Introduction

The sequence Cretan to Mycenaean is appropriate, since it has become clear that the Minoan culture, named after the mythical King Minos, is older than the culture that had one of its most important centres at → Mycenae and is therefore called Mycenaean. Since both cultures extended well beyond Crete and Mycenae, the archaeology undertaken in this area is now also called Aegean archaeology, after the Aegean Sea. In the history of archaeology, the discoveries of Mycenaean archaeology predate the Minoan ones. It therefore makes sense to begin an overview of Cretan-Minoan Archaeology (CMA) with Mycenaean archaeology, that is, with Heinrich Schliemann's excavations at Mycenae (Fig. 1).

B. The exploration of Mycenaean Greece

When Schliemann set out on his first trip to Greece in 1868, all that was known of Mycenae and Tiryns were the 'cyclopean' walls and gates, and in Mycenae the monumental lion relief above the main gate and the 'Treasury of Atreus'. Only with his excavations at Mycenae, and particularly when the shaft graves were opened in 1876 and their finds became known, did the most precious treasures of a then still unknown culture suddenly come to light. Schliemann's excavations at Mycenae were initially followed by investigations of

Fig. 1: Heinrich Schliemann, portrait by Sydney Hodges, London 1877
Berliner Museum für Vor- und Frühgeschichte.
Photograph J.P. Anders. Hirmer Photoarchiv, München

Fig. 2: One of the two gold cups from a
Mycenaean tholos tomb at Vaphio in Lakonia.
Hirmer Fotoarchiv, München

Fig. 3: So-called Warrior Vase. Found by Schliemann
in the remains of a house behind the 'Lion's Gate' of
Mycenae. Mycenean, c. 1200 BC

Fig. 4: Reconstruction of the megaron in the Palace of Nestor, 13th cent. BC.
With Permission of the Ministry of Culture, Hellenic Republic

Mycenaean graves in Attica (among others by Gerhard
Lolling at Menidi, 1879). In 1880, Schliemann directed
his hopes towards → Orchomenus in Boeotia, to which
he became attracted by the myth of Minyas and by a
tholos tomb in the style of the 'Treasury of Atreus' at
Mycenae, but he was disappointed by its other results.
Four years later, he began excavations at Tiryns, which
he largely left in charge of Wilhelm Dörpfeld, an architect and buildings researcher, who since 1882 had been

his closest collaborator at Troy. Christos Tsountas was
the first Greek archaeologist to achieve prominence in
the Mycenaean area. He succeeded Schliemann at
Mycenae (from 1880 to 1902) and in 1888 made the
spectacular discovery of the so-called Vaphio Cup, fashioned by Minoan artisans, in a tholos tomb south of
→ SPARTA (Fig. 2). Mycenaean material was also found
early on in the Copais basin (Gla) in Boeotia and in
Thessaly, as well as elsewhere on the Greek east coast,
on some Aegean islands, and even in Italy.

Regarding the analysis of Mycenaean finds, Adolf Furtwängler and Georg Loeschcke distinguished themselves in 1879 with their publication of the ceramic material known up to that point (cf. Fig. 3) in *Mykenische Thongefässe* and in 1886 with *Mykenische Vasen*. New standards were only set in 1941 with Arne Furumark's reference work *The Mycenaean Pottery*, which was based on a far broader assemblage and most recently with Penelope Mountjoy's treatment of *Regional Mycenaean Decorated Pottery*, published in 1999. Meanwhile, the ever more recognizable particularities and developments of pottery in this and in other works led to ever more detailed classifications of Mycenaean (= Late Helladic) chronology.

After Schliemann's discovery of the shaft graves inside the citadel of Mycenae (1876), Greek and soon also British excavations yielded valuable information about the former appearance and historical development of citadel and city. Prominent among these was the discovery of a second shaft grave circle (called B). A German project has continued working on the citadel and in the lower city of Tiryns from 1905 – with interruptions – until recent times. The results, concerning Mycenaean as well as more recent topics, have appeared in the Tiryns publication. Schliemann's third excavation in the Mycenaean area, in Boeotian Orchomenos, was taken up again after the turn of the century under the mandate of the Bayerische Akademie der Wissenschaften. The results were likewise presented in a separate publication and were completed in 1983, after long interruptions, with the most recent volume edited by P. Mountjoy (*Orchomenos V, Mycenaean Pottery*). In 1908, Dörpfeld found three Mycenaean tholos-tombs near Kakovatos (Triphylia) and tried to link this site to Nestor's Pylos. However, the Mycenaean palace that can plausibly be connected with the Homeric Nestor was discovered only in 1939 by Englianos, near modern Pylos. After the war, the excavations were directed by the American archaeologist Carl W. Blegen, who brought to the task a wealth of experience gained from his excavations in Greece (Korakou and Zygouries in the area of Corinth, Prosymna in the Argolid) and above all from his campaigns at Troy (1932–1938). Not only did this unexpectedly well-preserved unfortified site provide a great deal of information about the historical development, the fresco-decorated construction and the functions of the Mycenaean palace (including the megaron: Fig. 4), but it also significantly extended our understanding of Mycenaean archaeology, not least through the discovery of a complete and instructive archive of Linear-B clay tablets [7]. The valuable Mycenaean finds from graves found during the excavations of the Athenian Agora and in particular also the excavations on the island of Ceos (at Ay. Irini), carried out and published under the auspices of the University of Cincinnati by John L. Caskey, an experienced excavator of prehistoric sites, are among the important contributions of American archaeology to Greek and in particular to Mycenaean prehistory. On Ceos, interest-

ing frescoes and a sanctuary with peculiarly large female clay figurines from the Mycenaean period have added to the history of a fortified settlement from the Early to the Late Bronze Age.

As was noted above, British archaeologists have rendered outstanding services to the continuing investigation of Mycenae (citadel, lower town, graves). Aside from their early involvement on Crete and Melos and from prehistoric excavations in Greece, British archaeologists have also more recently made fundamental contributions to an increasing understanding of the Greek Bronze Age, with settlement excavations that have yielded important results (J. N. Coldstream at Castri on Cythera, M. Popham at Lefkandi on Euboea and A. C. Renfrew at Phylakopi on Melos). Scandinavian archaeology has also played a significant role in research into the prehistory and Mycenaean period of Greece. In addition to pre-Mycenaean settlements like Asea in Arcadia or Malthi in Messene, the Swedish excavations at Asine (Argolid), carried out from 1922 to 1930 by O. Frödin and A. W. Persson, proved fruitful for the Mycenaean period too. Better known however, because of their rich finds, were the graves from Dendra, near the hilltop-town (acropolis) of Midea in the Argolid; they were later published by Persson. Midea has recently been investigated by a joint Swedish-Greek excavation. Scandinavian excavations on the acropolis of Berbati and investigations of nearby tholos and chamber-tombs (between Mycenae and Dendra) have also increased our knowledge of Mycenaean culture. With the excavation of Mycenaen graves on Rhodes (Ialysos) and Cos, Italy contributed to an increasing knowledge of Mycenaean local pottery styles and thereby also to the understanding of Aegean trade relations. Like the continuing German excavations of the Cretan-Mycenaean settlement near Miletus, Doro Levi's excavations at Iasos on the west coast of Asia Minor have also yielded important finds and features that were informative of the historical position of these outposts of the Cretan-Mycenaean spheres of power and trade. We are indebted to French archaeology for the discovery of special ceramic grave goods from furnished graves in the Mycenaean necropoleis at Argos, while previous excavations in → DELPHI that yielded smaller Mycenaean finds (idols, etc.) had already led to a greater understanding of the shrine's early cultic history.

The importance of Greek contributions to research into the Mycenaean period already became apparent in the example of Mycenae. There, George Mylonas earned merit in Mycenaean archaeology by uncovering the shaft grave circle B and with his work inside the citadel (cult centre), but also by uncovering Mycenaean graves in → ELEUSIS. In the same context, Spiridon Iakovidis deserves to be specially mentioned among many ephors of the Greek Archaeological Service, by carrying out the excavation of the necropoleisis of Perati in Attica in the 1960s and by difficult investigations into the history of the Mycenaean acropolis of

→ ATHENS. Later he took on the exemplary publication of the excavations undertaken by J. Thespriadis in 1955–1961 on the walled Mycenaean acropolis of Gla in the Boeotian Copais basin which had already been the object of archaeological reconnaissance in 1893 (F. Noack and A. de Ridder). In the 1960s and 1970s, Belgian archaeologists published studies of a Mycenaean tholos-tomb in the Attic town of Thorikos, known for its silver mines, as well as the finds from this period.

C. RESEARCH ON MINOAN CRETE

The results and experience gained in Greece in the last quarter of the 19th cent. formed the foundation for a new branch of the discipline, 'Mycenaean' archaeology, on which research on Minoan Crete, which began at about 1900, could build further. In the beginning, however, scholars on the largest Aegean island were not sure about whether this culture was an indigenous and even older one than that of the Greek mainland. Early on, Arthur Evans (Fig. 5), the excavator of the Palace of → KNOSSOS, understandably believed the culture he had discovered to be Mycenaean. Only in his second campaign of excavations did he use the term 'Minoan', which had occasionally already been used in research. In 1886, the German archaeologist Ernst Fabricius wrote after a visit to the excavations of Kalokairinos in Knossos: 'one ... can however suppose with great probability that the ruins found there belong to the same period as the palace of Tiryns'. The chronological relationship between Mycenaean and Minoan archaeology was reversed, as soon as finds from Crete were revealed to be older. Since 1894, Italian and British researchers had been investigating the Kamares cave on the southern flank of Mt. Ida, used by Minoan Cretans as a cult site; its ceramic finds were published two years later. These Kamares vases were then found in large numbers during the excavations in the nearby palace of Phaistos, begun in 1900 by Federico Halbherr, and soon also in the palace of Knossos. They had to have been older not only than the palace at Tiryns but also than the finds from Schliemann's shaft graves that dated from the 16th cent. BC. Soon there was even older evidence from Crete, found by the Greek archaeologist Stephanos Xanthoudidis in the early vaulted tombs (of families and clans) on the plain of Mesara below Phaistos. With his excavations at Knossos and their unexpectedly great success, Evans, like Schliemann with his excavations at Mycenae, provided the impulse for a great deal of further archaeological activity, most of which on Crete now focused on the newly discovered Minoan culture. Andreas Rumpf, a traditionalist representative of German → Classical archaeology, considered this rapid development to have had almost disastrous effects on the field – even in 1953. In his Göschen volume on archaeology, he wrote, after having passed a very one-sided judgement on Schliemann, who was recognized as the 'father of Mycenaean archaeology' by British scholars such as Ventris and Chadwick (p. 94): 'When then the finds and research of Arthur Evans in Crete were added to this at the turn of the century, archaeology was in danger of increasingly deviating from its proper goal. For almost two generations it wasted many of its best minds on prehistory'. We shall return to this statement below.

In the Minoan-Cretan area as in the Mycenaean one, the history of research was determined by the results of excavations. Italian, British, French, American, Greek, Swedish and Canadian archaeologists have been continuing their involvement in excavations of Crete's Minoan past. The relatively late beginnings of scientific work on Crete were mainly due to the political situation before 1900. Before the turn of the 20th cent. outside of excavations of sites from the Graeco-Doric period, only smaller undertakings, such as the investigation of the Kamares cave, were devoted to what was then called Minoan culture. The initiatives of the British scholar Evans at Knossos, which focused on large-scale excavations, and the 'Missione Archeologica Italiana a Creta' at Knossos and Ayia Triada, which initially aimed to cover the whole of ancient Crete and whose work on the early Minoan period was supervised by F. Halbherr, L. Pernier and R. Paribeni, were central for the generation of a broader interest in this first European great civilisation.

After the palaces of Knossos and Phaistos and the palace-like villa of Ayia Triada near Phaistos, the palace and residential areas of the town of Mallia began to be uncovered by the Frenchman Fernand Chapouthier from 1921, while the palace and residential district in Kato Zakros in eastern Crete were investigated by the Greek archaeologist Nikolaos Platon from 1960 onwards. All palace excavations showed the palace to have been at the centre of a town. The palaces themselves have in common a lack of defensive walls and a large rectangular central court, while Knossos, Phaistos and Mallia also share a northwards orientation, a western court and the location of storage areas [6]. Peculiarities in the construction, layout and decoration of rooms with private, public and cultic functions were relatively similar in the palaces, the so-called villas and the larger town houses. The chronology, which was first established with stratigraphic information about pottery for the history of the Knossos palace, with Early, Middle and Late Minoan as its main phases, proved to be a useful foundation for the whole Minoan culture. With the ongoing research and interpretation of the Minoan palaces, interest in their immediate environment also grew. Thus, in Knossos the 'Unexplored Mansion', which had been neglected by Evans but was excavated by Mervyn Popham from 1967 on, was added to the villa-style sites from the palace period that had already been uncovered near the palace. In Phaistos Doro Levi excavated an entire sector of the town at the foot of the palace hill (Chalara) and in Mallia Jean-Claude Poursat added the 'Quartier Mu', which was of great interest to the early history of the site, to the already known town quarters and public buildings.

Smaller and larger Minoan towns and harbour settlements, without a palace but with the familiar standard features (central and west court, etc.), had in some
cases been known for some time (Ayia Triada, Gournia,
Pseira, Vasiliki, Palaikastron, Amnisos), but gradually
they attracted more and more interest because of new
and re-excavations (Myrtos-Pyrgos, Kommos, Chania:
Fig. 6). Research into the so-called villas (Nirou Chani,
Tylissos, Vathypetron etc.), which are common across
the island, and their administrative, political and economic functions (perhaps as institutions subordinate to
the palace centres?) also continues. Outside of towns
and settlements, typologically classified graves have
also often been focused upon with questions regarding
their historical and social significance being asked [13].
Minoan peak sanctuaries (Iuktas, Vrissinas etc.) have
convincingly been attributed special religious status,
particularly for the palace-towns.

D. Situation, Problems, Task

For several reasons, CMA is distinct from Mycenaean archaeology. One main reason is that it is easier
to get a good grasp of this relatively small island with its
easily comprehensible geographical structures. The cultural history of Minoan Crete was determined on the
exterior by it being an island and the manifold consequences thereof, and on the interior by mountain ranges, which restricted human habitat, by caves and mountain peaks, which were the focus of cults, by valleys,
which determined pathways, by few fertile plains for
agriculture and by some individual coastal sites, naturally protected and favoured as harbours. While familiarity with these natural conditions helped to locate the
cultural remains, the Minoans themselves also facilitated the rapid progress in the archaeological investigation of their past, by spreading their culture across the
whole island, by their uniform customs (dress, festivals,
cults, burial), their high technical standards, their organizational talent, by prudently storing their goods,
their hierarchical administration with the use of writing
and seals, and not least by their rapidly unified, cleverly
devised construction methods (palace, villa, house).

Many of the tasks which will occupy research for a
long time to come are of a historical nature. They begin
with the origins of palace structures before the Old Palace period, that is, before 2000 BC, and they will continue to be concerned with the use and administration
of the old palaces, their destruction by earthquakes (c.
1700 BC), and the transformations with the construction and fitting-out of the new palaces. The absence of
defensive walls (in the palace period) will have to be
discussed, together with the question of whether the
widespread destructions of Minoan palaces, villas and
towns at the end of the first Late Minoan phase (c. 1450
BC) can be attributed to warfare or to earthquakes and
whether possible violent destructions were caused from
within or from without (Mycenae). In this context the
historical relations between Crete and the Mycenaean
mainland will become more and more important, due

to increasing archaeological knowledge. In the shaft
grave period of the 16th cent. BC a clear dependency of
the Mycenaean world on Crete, at least culturally and
artistically, will probably persist. However, it has also
become more and more certain that Crete, which suffered new destructions in the early 14th cent. was in
Mycenaean hands from then on until the final catastrophe of the palace of Knossos c. 1200 BC For this time
period further archaeological evidence must be collected and the evidentiary value of the Linear B clay tablets
[7] also has to be clarified definitively.

Through recent excavations on the Aegean islands
(Thera, Melos, Samothrace) and on the west coast of
Asia Minor (Iasos, Miletus) the role played by Cretan-
Mycenaean culture in the entire Aegean area has once
again become a focal point of research. Trade with the
West (Lipari, Southern Italy) and the relations to the
South-East (Egypt, the Near East) are constantly being
brought up to date by new finds and excavation results.

The fact that on the one hand many scholars, often
holding or associated with subject-specific professorships in Britain, America, Sweden, France or Belgium,
have occupied themselves primarily and as international leaders in the field with CMA is opposed – particularly in Germany – by Classical archaeology's claim that
this area ought to be included into the discipline as a
sub-field. In 1953, in the remark quoted above,
Andreas Rumpf expressed the view that 'it wasted
many of its best minds on prehistory'. He must have
been thinking of archaeologists like A. Furtwängler, G.
Loeschcke, G. Rodenwaldt, Kurt Müller, A. Fricken-
haus, E. Kunze and F. Matz, all of whom contributed
with outstanding accomplishments both to the proper
goal of the discipline (Rumpf) and to particular tasks of
CMA. Whoever is interested in Aegean archaeology
today has to decide which of these two possibilities he
or she prefers. Obviously, those who commit themselves to the early Aegean with all their efforts stand a
better chance in the field's international arena than a
classical archaeologist who understands CMA. as a
part of the whole of Greek and Roman archaeology.
Finally, it should also be noted that knowledge of the
written tradition (Linear B) will sooner or later become
part of the comprehensive mastery of CMA. understood as a discipline in its own right [7].

1 S. Alexiou, Minoische Kultur, 1976   2 H.-G. Buch-
holz, V. Karageorghis, Altägäis und Altkypros, 1971
3 O. Dickinson, The Aegean Bronze Age, 1994   4 D.
Fimmen, Die kretisch-mykenische Kultur, ²1924   5 A.
Furumark, The Mycenaean Pottery: Analysis and Classification, 1941   6 J. W. Graham, The Palaces of Crete,
²1972   7 S. Hiller, O. Panagel, Die frühgriechischen
Texte aus mykenischer Zeit, ²1968   8 S. Hood, The
Minoans, 1971   9 Id, The Arts in Prehistoric Greece, 1978
10 S. A. Immerwahr, Aegean Painting in the Bronze Age,
1990   11 F. Matz, Kreta, Mykene, Troja, ⁵1965   12 J.
D. S. Pendlebury, The Archaeology of Crete, 1939   13 I.
Pini, Beiträge zur minoischen Gräberkunde, 1968
14 J. C. Poursat, Les ivoires mycéniens, 1977   15 F.
Schachermeyer, Die minoische Kultur des Alten Kreta,
²1980   16 J. Schäfer, Die Archäologie der altägäischen

Hochkulturen, 1998   17 W. Schiering, Minoische Töpferkunst, 1998   18 E. Vermeule, Greece in the Bronze Age, 1964

Additional Bibliography: P. P. Betancourt, The History of Minoan Pottery, Princeton 1985; P. P. Betancourt et al. (Ed.), MELETEMATA I–III, Studies in Aegean Archaeology, Festschrift M. H. Wiener, 1999; E. B. French, Mycenae: Agamemnon's Capital: The Site in its Setting, 2002; E. Hallager, The Master Impression, SIMA LXIX, 1985; Labyrinth Revisited: Rethinking 'Minoan' Archaeology. Yannis Hamilakis (ed.), 2002; F. J. Lesley, The Discovery of the Greek Bronze Age, 1996; F. Matz, J. Pini (eds.), Corpus der minoischen und mykenischen Siegel (CMS) I–V, 1964–2004; Rethinking Mycenaean Palaces: New Interpretations of an Old Idea. Michael L. Galaty, William A. Parkinson (eds.), 1999.   Wolfgang Schiering

Croatia
A. Middle Ages   B. Renaissance
C. 17th–18th Cents.   D. 19th and 20th Cents.

A. Middle Ages

Before the Gothic invasion, the provinces of Dalmatia and Pannonia were numbered among the more advanced parts of the Roman Empire. Evidence from this period includes numerous ancient monuments in the area now known as Croatia (C.). As a result of the split-up of the later Roman Empire, Southern Europe was divided into two linguistic domains: one Greek and one Latin; however, in the Adriatic towns that belonged to Byzantium, Greek was used parallel with Latin until the 12th cent. The Slavs in the western part of Southern Europe adopted Latin as a literary language (c. 8th–9th cents.) shortly after their settling there (6th–7th cents.). The influence of the Benedictines was of central importance for this process. The oldest preserved Latin document of a Slavic ruler is by Prince Trpimir (852). In the second half of the 9th cent., Old Church Slavonic, disseminated by the students of Methodius, pitted itself against Latin. In the course of the educational reforms of the Carolingian Renaissance, and the centralizing reforms of the Roman popes, Latin was established as the most important literary language from the 9th to the 11th cent. Most writings from the Middle Ages have a judicial or administrative character. A strong orientation towards Roman law can be detected in numerous statutes from Dalmatian towns.

B. Renaissance

The Humanistic movement developed in Croatian territories on the basis of the political situation in several cultural centers: first in the coastal towns Zadar, Šibenik, Trogir, Split, Dubrovnik, Hvar, Korčula, etc. (J. Benja, P. Cipiko, M. Resti), and later in the North (Zagreb, Varaždin), as well as at the Croatian-Hungarian court. Many Croatian humanists studied or taught at European universities. Humanistic treatises are not unified either in thematic or stylistic respects, but reflect the main tendencies and groupings of this period, and include poetry and prose, scientific, philosophical, and theological writings.

Croatian literature of the Renaissance evolved only in the last quarter of the 15th cent., with literature in Latin being three to four decades older than vernacular literature. Under the influence of ancient literature, many epics, elegies, epigrams, eclogues, odes and hymns made their appearance. The influence of Virgil is important for religious epics like *Davidas* by M. Marulić (1450–1524), *De raptu Cerberi* and *De vita et gestis Christi* by J. Bunić (1469–1534) or *Solemais* by I. Barbula (born 1472). Of the collections of poetry published at this time, in which many of the motifs of ancient mythology are used as themes, *Elegiarum et carminum libri III* by J. Šižgorić (c. 1420–1509), *De laudibus Gnesae puellae* by K. Pucić (Carolus Puteus, 1461–1522), *Carmina* by L. Paskalić (1500–1551) and *Otia* by A. Vrančić (1504–1573) deserve mention. The greater part of this primarily philosophical and religious reflective poetry has not been published until recently, including the works of important poets like I. Česmički (Janus Pannonius, 1434–1472), I. Crijević (Aelius Lampridius Cerva, 1463–1520), D. Benešić (1477–1539) and M. Marulić. Ancient models are also to be found in the only Croatian pastoral novel of this period, *Planine* by P. Zoranić (1508–1569), in the poetry of D. Ranjina (1536–1607) and M. Vetranović (c. 1482–1576), as well as in the writings of the most important Croatian comic poet, M. Držić (c. 1508–1567).

Historians list in detail the history of their own towns, as well as providing information on 'Dalmatian' or 'Illyrian' history, which was seen as a continuous line from Antiquity to the present, as in *De situ Illyriae et civitate Sibenici* by J. Šižgorić, *Cronicon Dalmatiae et Saloniae* by Martin of Šibenik, *Historia vel de laudibus Dalmatiae* by I. Barbula, *De Sclavinis seu Sarmatis in Dalmatia* by F. Vrančić (1551–1617), *Monumenta vetera Illyrici Dalmatiae* by S. Kožičić Benja (d. 1532), and *De origine successibusque Slavorum* by V. Priboević (Vicentius Priboevus).

Most of the philosophical works belong methodologically to late Scholasticism. Freed from Medieval Latinity, Franjo Petrišević (Franciscus Patricius, 1592–1597) wrote as the most independent philosopher of this time, as did a series of less original authors who above all sought stylistic models in Antiquity. The most important Dubrovnik philosopher, the Peripatetic N. Gušetić (1549–1610), wrote under the influence of contemporary Neoplatonism.

In the Renaissance one also finds sophisticated scholarly works from various disciplines. They include Latin grammars (e.g. Šimun of Trogir, known under the sobriquet Aretophylus, first half of the 16th cent.); commentaries on Greek and Latin authors (I. Barbula); encyclopaedic works and dictionaries (P. Skalić, 1534–1575; I. Crijević; M. Marulić; F. Vrančić and others). A. Vrančić collected ancient epitaphs in the course of his travels. Ivan Vitez of Sredna (1400–1472), who belonged to the so-called Corvinus circle, translated Demosthenes; I. Česmički did the same for Demosthenes and Plotinus, as did N. Petrović-Petreius (*c.* 1500–1568) for Greek medical authors, and so on. Vernacular translations were also undertaken: D. Ranjina (1536–1607) translated Tibullus, Catullus and Martial; P. Hektorović (1487–1572) and H. Lucić (1485–1553) translated Ovid.

Under the influence of Antiquity, interest in natural sciences was also reawakened in this period. F. Grisognono of Zadar commented on Euclid in his *Speculum astronomicum* (1509); M. Getaldić of Dubrovnik (1568–1626) wrote a series of treatises on ancient geometry (*Apollonius redivivus*) and physics (*Promotus Archimedes*); while in the mid–16th cent., Donatus a Mutiis from Dobrovnik wrote a commentary on Galen.

C. 17TH–18TH CENTS.

The Reformation, which had already been rejected in Croatian lands at the beginning of the 17th cent., was of less importance for the development of Croatian culture in the late 16th and 17th cents. than the cultural, political and religious movement of the Counter-Reformation. Characteristic of this period was a gradual renunciation of the dominance of the Latin language; however, Latin continued to be the language of the clergy, diplomacy and science until the second half of the 19th cent.

One finds numerous reminiscences of ancient mythology in the poets of the 17th and 18th cents., some of whom wrote both in the vernacular and in Latin, I. Đurdjević (1675–1737), one of the most important poets of this era, left behind verse in both languages, scientific, historical and literary historical works (*Antiquitates Illyricae*), as well as a treatise called *Bellum Troianum*, in which he raised doubts about Homer's authorship of the *Ilias* and the *Odyssey*, so that he can be considered a forerunner of the long-standing polemics on the so-called → HOMERIC QUESTION. J. Palmotić (1606–1657) integrated episodes from Ovid and Virgil in his writings. The most important Baroque author, I. Gundulić (1589–1638), also started out from ancient models in his early plays. J. Bajamonti (1744–1800), a representative of the Enlightenment, wrote, in addition to Latin verse, the treatise *Il morlaccismo d'Omero*, in which he compared South Slavic folk poetry with the works of Homer.

Of the later generation of poets active in Dubrovnik, some of whom still wrote Latin verse in the first half of the 19th cent., those who deserve mention, among others, are Đ. Hidža (1752–1833), the translator of Virgil, Horace, Tibullus and Ovid into the vernacular. Among the works of Đ. Ferić (1739–1820) there are numerous epigrams and fables. R. Kunić (1719–1794) translated the *Iliad* (*Homeri Ilias Latinis versibus expressa*, 1776), while his student B. Zamanja (Bernardus Zamagna, 1735–1820) translated Hesiod, bucolic poetry, and the *Odyssey* into Latin.

From the 17th cent. on, Latinity also continued to gain strength in North Croatia. Here, the work of the historian B. Krčelić (1715–1778) was important, and M. P. Katančić (1750–1825) was also influential as a poet (*Poemata lyrica*, *Fructus auctumnales*), philologist, literary theorist (*De poesi Illyrica libellus ad leges aesteticae exactus*) and historian.

In the course of the Counter-Reformation a series of linguistic works was composed by Jesuits, who were preparing themselves for missionary work in the Slavic Balkans and had their own seminary at Rome (*Academia linguae illyricae*). Linguistic studies were also continued in the 18th cent., but for different reasons. The Dubrovnik Academy (*Academia otiosorum*), which sought to reinforce the importance of the vernacular, had the idea for a great Latin-Italian-Croatian dictionary, which was finally brought to its conclusion by the Italian Ardelio Della Bella (1655–1737) (*Dizionario italiano-latino-illirico*, 1728). Several dictionaries from this period, which also set out from Latin foundations, still exist only in manuscript. The *Lexicon Latino-Italico-Illyricum* by J. Stulli (1772–1828), a Franciscan from Dubrovnik, was published at the beginning of the 19th cent.

One can also find numerous works on the monuments of ancient culture in the 18th cent. I. J. Pavlović-Lučić (1775–1818) wrote *Marmora Macarensia* and *Marmora Traguriensia*. Archaeological interests are also evident in the works of A. Blašković (1727–1796), J. Salecić (d. 1747), J. V. Ćolić (d. 1764), P. A. Bogetić (d. 1784) and M. P. Katančić. The eminent Dubrovnik scholar A. Banduri (1671–1743) translated still unknown Byzantine authors (*Imperium Orientale*) and composed a series of archaeological and numismatic treatises.

The central figure in the field of the natural sciences was R. Bošković (1711–1787), who produced an important contribution to the modern understanding of the structure of matter with his classic work *Theoria philosophiae naturalis* (1758).   MIRO MAŠEK

D. THE 19TH AND 20TH CENTS.

The long-lived use of Latin in C. had a strong political motivation. As a reaction to attempts to introduce Hungarian, Latin was used in the Croatian parliament until 1847. In the first half of the 19th cent. numerous works were written in Latin, yet in the course of the 19th cent. Latin was replaced entirely by Croatian in all areas of culture.

In the 19th and 20th cents., ancient culture continued to be an important source of inspiration for art and literature. Ivan Meštrović (1883–1962), one of the most important Croatian sculptors, created many ancient figures, that is to say works on ancient models (*Laokoon*, *Psyche*, etc.). Ancient metre inspired many poets of the 19th and 20th cents., such as P. Preradović (1818–1872), S. S. Kranjčević (1865–1908) and V. Nazor (1876–1949). One finds themes and motifs from ancient literature in drama, for instance in *Leda*, a play by M. Krleža (1893–1981), or in prose, as in the novel *Kiklop* by R. Marinković (b. 1913). The important translations of Homer and Virgil by T. Maretić (1854–1938) should also be mentioned here.

In the modern era, Antiquity has increasingly become a subject in its own right. Apart from the Classical philologist A. Musić (1856–1938) – a student of Brugmann and Leskien – and his student N. Majnarić (1885–1966), M. Kuzmić (1868–1945), D. Körbler (1873–1927), I. Kasumović (1872–1945), V. Gortan (b. 1907) and V. Vratović also deserve mention.

From the first half of the 19th cent. on, numerous archaeological excavations have been undertaken in C. (for instance at Solin, since 1821). The *Archaeological Museum* at Split was founded in 1821. In the course of the 19th and 20th cents., additional museums and archaeological departments were opened in various Croatian cities (Zagreb, Pula, Dubrovnik, etc.). A Chair in Archaeology was established at the University of Zagreb in 1896.

→ HUMANISM; → RENAISSANCE

1 A. ANGYAL, Südosteuropäische Spät-Renaissance, in: Rennaissance und Humanismus in Mittel- und Osteuropa. Eine Sammlung von Materialien besorgt von J. Irmscher, 1962, 287–291   2 A. BARAC, Jugoslavenska književnost, 1954 (Engl. History of Yugoslavian literature, 1973)   3 M. D. BIRNBAUM, Croatian and Hungarian Latinity in the Sixteenth Century, 1993   4 Enciklopedija Jugoslavije, 1–8, 1955–1971   5 I. FRANGEŠ, Povijest hrvatske književnosti, 1987 (Ger. Geschichte der kroatischen Literatur, 1995)   6 M. FRANIČEVIĆ, Povijest hrvatske renesansne književnosti, 1983   7 I. N. GOLENIŠČEV-KUTUZOV, Il Rinascimento italiano e le letterature slave dei secoli XV e XVI, vols. 1 and 2, 1973   8 V. GORTAN, V. VRATOVIĆ, Hrvatski latinisti, I–II, Pet stoljeća hrvatske književnosti, vols. 2 and 3, 1969   9 S. JOSIFOVIĆ, Jugoslawien, Griechiche und römische Philologie, in: La Filologia Greca e Latina nel secolo XX, 1989, 651–661   10 A. KADIĆ, Croatian Rennaissance, in: Slavic Review, 21, 1961, 65–88   11 V. VRATOVIĆ, Hrvatski latinizam i rimska književnost, 1989.   MIRO MAŠEK

Crown

A. INTRODUCTION B. MIDDLE AGES C. MODERN TIMES D. CUSTOMS

A. INTRODUCTION

The crown (Latin *corona*, Greek *stémma*) is first and foremost a wreath made of various materials (leaves, twigs, fruits, grass, and later metal)and worn on the head, in order to single out its bearer from among the common people. In Antiquity objects such as sacrificial gifts and ships were also provided with a crown. Decisive for and common to the multiform crown is the magic-religious symbolism of the circle, which served in Biblical times as a head adornment and symbol of rank for kings and priests (OT, 2 Samuel 1,10; 2 Kg 11,12; Ps 89,40; Ps 132,18; Ex 29,6; Ex 39,30). Thus, from the beginning the crown was a symbol for a Chosen One, who, however, did not need necessarily to be a ruler.

The variety of types of crowns in Roman Antiquity attests to this, by means of which distinctions of every kind were made visible on the individual person. In addition to the crown with its multiple uses, there was the diadem, a woolen band,trimmed in precious stones, and knotted at the neck. It served as a sign of the sovereign majesty of the ancient Persians. Since the late Roman Empire, the aureole has represented the sovereign and was supposed to indicate his similarity to God. Crown symbolism denoting the possession of sovereignty seems to have come into focus in the Byzantine Empire. It was primarily adapted from the diadem, insofar as it was fashioned as a metal circle with a jewel at the forehead, usually cruciform, and pendilia. Combining the diadem with the emperor's ceremonial helmet led to the *kamelaukion*, an imperial head ornament for ceremonial purposes. The arched crown, which developed out of this helmet, was reserved for the *basileus*. Princes could keep and wear crowns if they recognized his sovereignty.   LÜCK, HEINER

B. MIDDLE AGES

The cross-shaped enclosed crown originated during the Early Middle Ages as a further development of the diadem, which was still open at the back. Rulers possessed various crowns since the Early Middle Ages, so that a single authentic form cannot be identified. With the imperial coronation of Charlemagne (AD 800) and its subsequent elaboration into the doctrine of the *translatio imperii* (migration of imperial rule from East to West)(→ SACRUM IMPERIUM), the Frankish crown, just one of many crowns in Europe, received special significance as the Imperial crown of the Holy Roman Empire. Its Western-Christian symbolism as the sign of Christ's representative as world ruler and his sacral functions as the Chosen One is characteristic for the entire Middle Ages. The Imperial crown in the Vienna *Schatzkammer*, which dates from the early 11th cent., expresses clearly this meaning in its four enameled plates alluding to Kings Solomon, David and Ezechias with Christ as Pantokrator. Here too, however, the exclusivity of a quite definite crown must not be assumed [9. 50–53]. Like the Imperial crown with Charlemagne, declared a saint in 1165, other crowns have also been associated with saints (crown of St. Stephen of Hungary; crown of St. Wenceslaus of Bohemia). In addition to its function as a symbol, the crown is also an object of practical use 'in the ruler's daily life' [9. 59], since it is worn on specific special occasions. Its presence and having it at one's disposal has constitutive significance for certain legal acts, for instance, in choosing the German king. Alongside the crown as a symbol of sovereignty, which also are found in the form of special women's crowns, votive and funereal crowns also existed in the Middle Ages. With the advent of heraldry after the Crusades, the crown in various forms became a frequent component of coats of arms. Particularly since the 16th cent., it expresses the bearer's rank in the hierarchy of nobility (royal crown, ducal crown, prince's crown and earl's crown). The same holds true, *ceteris paribus*, for representations of crowns on seals and coins.

C. Modern times

Since the later Middle Ages, the concept of 'kingship separated from the person of the ruler' [8. 3] was added to the crown's meaning as a sign of sovereignty. In the constitutional age, *crown* stands as a synonym for national property, separated from the person of its rightful bearer [8. 3–5]. From portraits on coins, the concept of 'crown' was promoted to a monetary denomination, as it still is today in the Czech Republic, in Scandinavian countries and in Estonia. Even in its material form, the crown became part of the specially deposited and guarded state treasury. Today, the crown has official functions only in the few remaining monarchies, where it is worn on occasions determined by the constitution and protocol.

D. Customs

At all times the crown has had a diverse functionality in customs recalling materials and forms from Roman Antiquity. Virginity (bridal crown) and poetic gifts (poet's crown), among other things, were ascribed to its bearers, male and female. Marking the victor of a contest with a crown or a wreath, hanging up a crown (*Richtkrone*) made of leafy twigs upon the erection of a building and the exhibition of a sheaf of grain after a successful harvest (harvest crown) are customs continuing to this day. We are clearly dealing here with a general symbol of joy.
→ Decorations, military; → Basileus; → Diadema; → Wreath, Garland

1 K. Baus, Der Kranz der Antike und des Christentums, 1940   2 H. Biehn, Die Krone Europas und ihre Schicksale, 1957   3 C. Brühl, 'Krone und Krönungsbrauch im frühen und hohen Mittelalter,' HZ 234, 1984, 1–31   4 W. Deér, Die Heilige Krone Ungarns, 1966   5 V. H. Elben, 'Krone', Lexikon des Mittelalters 5, 1544–1547   6 A. Erler, 'Dichterkrönungen', HWB zur deutschen Rechtsgeschichte 1, 728–729   7 H. Fillitz, 'Krone', HWB zur deutschen Rechtsgeschichte 2, 1212–1217   8 F. Hartung, Die Krone als Symbol der monarchischen Herrschaft im ausgehenden Mittelalter, 1941   9 J. Petersohn, 'Über monarchische Insignien und ihre Funktion im mittelalterischen Reich', in: HZ 266, 1998, 47–96   10 P. E. Schramm, Herrschaftszeichen und Staatssymbolik, I–III, 1954–1956   11 M. Schulze-Dörrlamm, Die Kaiser-Krone Konrads II. (1024–1039), ²1992   12 K. Schwarzenberg, Die Sankt Wenzels-Krone, 1960

Additional Bibliography: M. Blech, Studien zum Kranz bei den Griechen, 1982; M. Kramp (ed.), Krönungen. Könige in Aachen – Geschichte und Mythos, 2 vols., 2000; J. Ott, Krone und Krönung. Die Verheißung und Verleihung von Kronen in der Kunst von der Spätantike bis um 1200 und die geistige Auslegung der Krone, 1998; M. Steinicke & St. Weinfurter (eds.), Investitur- und Krönungsrituale. Herrschaftseinsetzungen im kulturellen Vergleich, 2005.   HEINER LÜCK

Cult image see → Cult image

Cultural anthropology
A. Use of the Term   B. History of the Term and the Discipline   C. Anthropology and the Study of Antiquity   D. Central Concepts and Research Topics   E. Current Methodological Problems

A. Use of the Term
1. Differences in Terms   2. Disciplines and National Academic Traditions

1. Differences in Terms
The noun 'cultural anthropology' (CA) and even more so the adjective related to it, cultural anthropological, is one of the terms that, of the current descriptions for academic disciplines, is most dependent on context. What is to be understood in each case by the term depends on the respective context of the academic traditions, disciplines and methods, which vary from nation to nation, within which it is used; its meaning can therefore diverge considerably.

2. Disciplines and National Academic Traditions
Particularly in the USA and in Germany, the term CA had different connotations [146; 105]. In the USA where the term CA first became widespread in the 1920s., it refers to a culturally relativistic and antiracist faction of the school of ethnology that goes back to F. Boas [117; 142. 42–52] and that so strongly dominated almost the entire century within this discipline that CA was even able to be used, to the displeasure of representatives of other specialised factions [129; 131], from the 1930s as a synonym for ethnology [92; 120; 42]. In Germany the term was introduced in 1942 by E. Rothacker as a philosophical one [55], but in contrast to his English-speaking counterparts, with ontological and apologetic, even racist implications [71]. In this region, the term developed after the Second World War so that it was initially particularly influential in the disciplines of philosophy, ethnology and sociology [105. 268–275; 138]. With its links back to American CA and to cultural philosophical traditions primarily developed by German-Jewish scholars (e.g. [15]), the term has now become the symbol of the turning-point in German cultural studies that has taken place since the 1990s [27; 72]. On the other hand, the use of the term CA as a synonym for ethnology, also established in Germany, corresponds to the attempt to make ethnology into a leading discipline within this academic and political process of transformation [168; 169; 156]. In France the expression *anthropologie culturelle* has not yet established itself, either in a subject-specific manner or institutionally [9], but the anthropological analysis of culture has long been firmly rooted there in social history, social science, ethnology and religious history [139]. In contrast, in England, the preference still dominant there for the term *social anthropology* signals an

academic tradition that is not only applicable to ethnology but also to the other humanities and that tends to be behaviourist in its orientation [129; 172].

B. History of the Term and the Discipline
1. Culture and Anthropology 2. Positions, People, Methods 3. Cultural Anthropology Today: Cultural Criticism, its Transdisciplinary Nature, Post-Colonialism

1. Culture and Anthropology

The composition of the term CA is indicative of its dual linguistic origin – its Latin and Greek roots. However, the term anthropology is a coined word developed at the beginning of the 16th cent. by Italian and German humanists who intended to use it in theological criticism [75], and the term culture did not achieve an ideal quality, through its attribution to education (Pufendorf) and the concept of the people (Herder) until the 17th and 18th cents. [78]. The close link between anthropology and psychology as well as with the physiological-biological theory of human nature that has existed since the oldest uses of the term has remained present in later CA right through to the current state of the discipline, while anthropology as a study of human beings in the pragmatic, cultural and technical sense of cosmopolitan knowledge of the world and wise understanding of how to live (Kant [36]) has, in the meantime, lost any academic legitimation it formerly had. In Germany as well as in other countries, anthropology traditionally maintains, aside from ethnology, the closest academic and organizational ties with medicine and psychology. The neo-Kantian 'abstinence' with respect to psychology and ethnology has however resulted in the academic strategic concept of cultural studies and the humanities developed in Germany in the late 19th and early 20th cents. as counter-models to the natural sciences, as well as simultaneous cultural philosophical designs (e.g. G. Simmel [57]; E. Cassirer [14]), which barely incorporate cultural anthropological dimensions. Likewise, cultural history, which in Germany had been out in the cold from the academic political point of view until long after the Second World War, has brought about a change of direction towards historical anthropology that has come late in comparison with other countries [159]. The great socio-cultural enterprise involving the reconstruction of civilizing processes [23] that was published by Norbert Elias in German during emigration in the late 1930s did not find resonance until the German student movement of the 1960s and 1970s.

2. Positions, People, Methods

Depending on the disciplinary perspective, the beginning of a cultural theoretical anthropology can be found during Antiquity [135; 145; 121; 98] while in the early modern period [118] it was localized in the Scottish and in the French Enlightenment [162; 143]. Notwithstanding the various historiographical accentuations, scholars are in agreement that the contact with foreign cultures, facilitated by travel, stimulated anthropological cultural research [170], particularly during the period of Greek Classicism (Herodotus) as well as during the two 'Ages of Discovery' in modern times. To be sure, this initially occurred without a conceptual apparatus already available regarding to the general terms culture and anthropology. The decisive prerequisite for the development of modern CA was not in place until the 19th cent. when historical philosophical models of progress were amalgamated with colonialist coercive pressures of legitimation and the biological theory of evolution. In this sense E. B. Tylor can be regarded as the most important theoretical forerunner of CA [128; 142. 17–28; 127; 124. 80–98]. Tylor, an 'armchair anthropologist' who drew his material from reports by missionaries, travellers and colonial officers of the British empire, took as his starting-point the concept of a uniform human culture that developed from 'primitive' beginnings to its high point, western civilization, albeit with surviving remnants of the former remaining influential in the latter for the time being [60]; consistently, he never uses the plural Cultures [171. 203]. However, F. Boas must be considered to be the founding father of CA; he came from a German Jewish family and after being educated in Germany and going on research trips to the furthermost northern regions of the American continent, he built up a school of thought that made its mark on US American anthropology, changing it in an anti-evolutionary manner [130. 125–151]. Although he inconsistently adheres to the term 'Primitive' [6], he propagates a cultural relativism [116] based on a uniform and racially independent human nature, while at the same time giving up the use of a standard of uniform progression of culture that runs in a legitimate manner and is reconstructed through comparison. Herder's concept of culture is freed here from its Germanic and ethnocentric implications [173]. After Boas and his students, CA has been the science of specifically different, historically particular human cultures whose self-dynamism tends to be reconstructed primarily in practical field research [113. 250–318]. This also applies to the second major founder of CA, B. Malinowski who came from Poland [129. 1–34, 197–199; 125; 142. 128–139]. His concept of 'field research' as participatory observation was until recently unchallenged in its description of normative practice experience within ethnology [31. 73–101]. Malinowski was not of the Boas School but rather owed a debt to the tradition of British social anthropology; he also adapted for his theory elements of the psychoanalysis of S. Freud [26] who for his part followed older English and French social anthropology in his cultural theoretical thinking. Malinowski's functionally oriented cultural theory is based on a romanticizing form of utopism [43; 44; 45] which is also reflected in its privileging of the terms 'Native' and 'Savage' over that of 'Primitive' [172. 233–297, 460–465]. This is equally characteristic of the French founder of structural anthropology [96], C.

Lévi-Strauss [31. 25–48; 157. 243–295] who likewise referred to Freud as well as to Marx, R. Wagner, the school of E. Durkheim [22] and M. Mauss but primarily to the Russian Formalists as well as to the structural linguistics of the Prague School and whose thinking was also moulded during emigration by American social research. After the Second World War his influence brought about the transformation of English ethnology into Neo-Structuralism [129. 135–175, 203f.] and gave the French anthropologists of Antiquity in the circle centred around J.-P. Vernant [63; 64], M. Detienne [17] and P. Vidal-Naquet [67] important impetus for thought that was taken up in other countries as well. In Lévi-Strauss the programmatics of a reconciliation between culture and nature is dominant and because of him is able to find its model in the mechanisms of the 'savage mind' (pensée sauvage) – that are independent of the respective human being and culturally non-specific – and in the mythologies that orchestrate it [39; 40; 41]. Since the 1970s the liberation of CA from its 'age of heroes' has been initiated in the USA by its most recent representative, C. Geertz [29; 30; 31]. He linked concepts and methods from the Boas and Malinowski Schools with the cultural and humanistic theorems of W. Dilthey and M. Weber under the term 'interpretative anthropology', with a cultural hermeneutics that shifts the accent from 'participatory observation' to 'detailed description' [29. 3–30], hence from experience to linguistic forms of representation. Geertz' cultural hermeneutics. which shares with the philosophical hermeneutics of H. G. Gadamer [28] the demonstratively absent reflection on method, has in the meantime led to the process of dissolution with respect to cultural anthropological subjects and methods that is being carried out by many of his students [16; 160], aided by the nihilistic rejection of traditional criteria of reality and truth derived from Post-Structuralism and Deconstructionism [8].

3. Cultural Anthropology Today: Cultural Criticism, its Transdisciplinary Nature, Post-Colonialism

In the final decades of the 20th cent., the process of replacing and supplementing paradigms that had also became influential in all the humanities accelerated tremendously within CA as well. Among the extremely dizzying academic circular movements there were in particular the linguistic, the interpretive and the performative turn. At the turn of the 3rd millennium these tendencies, although still by no means reflected upon in a sufficiently critical manner, appear to be sinking into the shadowy existence of outdated fashions; new trends, among these a pictorial turn that tends where possible to be suited to the global media age, are already becoming apparent. The fact that – in spite of such repeatedly renewed attempts at conceptualization – the intellectual crisis is being felt particularly painfully within anthropology itself [76; 111] and in the handling of eminent anthropological categories and culture may not be surprising, because the unavoidably antagoni-

sticrelationship between universalism and particularism as well as the indissoluble tension between identity and foreignness characterize the history of the theory of CA from its beginnings to the present [102]. Viewing anthropology as experimental cultural criticism that draws its life from exchange among the humanities [47] may not offer a final solution to these problems, but probably promises at least the possibility of handling them in a reflective, and not compulsive manner. Corresponding to this is a transformation process in these disciplines which analyses in an academic historical manner the subject boundaries established since the 19th cent. and which is adjusted to the social, political, economic and cultural needs at that time, questioning them in practical research and deducing from new constellations of aspects or subjects new research perspectives and conditions for the discipline. In this way, the retrospective fact that innovations within CA mostly started with those researchers who were trained in other disciplines like the study of Antiquity, philosophy, physics, medicine, psychology, sociology, law and economics, history, religion, art and literature also becomes prospectively more significant. The institutional and academic sociological tool kit for critical handling of the construct of culture and society [4] as well as the culturally specific contextual dependency of the academic habitus [10] has been available for a long time. Of course a science like CA is affected to a particularly strong degree by radical changes in world politics like those triggered by Post-colonialism. This circumstance has shifted anti-colonial criticism to the centre of current debates. Anthropologists and scholars of literature like T. Asad [1] and E.W. Said (1935–2003) [56] who came from former colonial regions and were trained in the academic institutions of the imperial powers, particularly in the USA, launched in the 1970s a general assault on the colonialist implications of 'western' theories that has not yet waned. That this approach tends [77] to base its argumentation on cultural concepts that have been made absolute and that are milieu-theoretical or geographical and to lose sight of the critical implications of traditional anthropological cultural theories certainly cannot be overlooked [90; 153]. The 'battle of cultures' [34] that is also conjured up from an opposing perspective makes it clear that the cultural anthropological need for clarification at the beginning of the 3rd millennium remains in no small way politically motivated and will not be dismissed for a long time to come.

C. Anthropology and the Study of Antiquity

1. Overview 2. Anthropology in Antiquity 3. Key Figures in Modern Anthropological Studies of Antiquity 4. The Study of Ancient Culture

1. Overview

Since the beginning of the 20th cent. the link between anthropology and the study of Antiquity has been represented either affirmatively or critically and in terms of historiography, particularly in English-language publications. To be sure, the first three publications bear the same title (*Anthropology and the Classics*) but fundamental differences are apparent. While the oldest of these, edited by R. R. Marett, concerns a programmatic Oxford series of lectures by Classical archaeologists, philologists and historians [48], the two which follow the World War II document not only subject-specific divergences from the viewpoints of an ethnologist (Kluckhohn [37]) and a scholar of ancient history (Finley [24]) but also the reasons which prevent a productive convergence of the two areas. This applies analogously to one of the most recent attempts in this direction, one that tends to be rather casual (Redfield [52]). Further, recent academic historical publications pursue a perspective either limited to ancient Greek social and economic history [123], to the relationship between social anthropology and ancient history [148; 149], to narrative [83] or to religious anthropological aspects of Antiquity [157; 73]. While the publications mentioned deal with special themes of CA, they do so at most from the fringe.

2. ANTHROPOLOGY IN ANTIQUITY

Every attempt to attribute an ancient origin to anthropology makes particular reference to the epoch-making work of Herodotus [147]. Actually Herodotus used methodological procedures and heuristic concepts that are reencountered not just among the travelers of the modern period of the 'Age of Discovery' and the forerunners of modern anthropology like Montaigne and G. Forster but also among the ethnographers of the 19th and 20th cents. [114; 149]. Herodotus, in his depiction of Greeks and other peoples, appears to take as his starting-point a uniform view both of human beings and of the concept of diverse cultures which have developed as part of an historical process.

3. KEY FIGURES IN MODERN ANTHROPOLOGICAL STUDIES OF ANTIQUITY

The history of modern anthropological study of Antiquity was characterized up to the mid 20th cent. by impasses and resistance within the guild of scholars of Antiquity. This affected all the countries included in this process, i.e. Germany, England and France, although this resistance occurred in different ways. Among the elements these had in common was the emphasis on anthropological interest in religion related to Antiquity and here the stress was particularly on the relationship between ritual and myth [157. 307–328]. Among the key figures, listed according to the chronology of their most influential and controversial publications and not according to the dates when they lived, are J. G. Frazer (1890 [25; 69]), E. Rohde (1890/1894 [54; 88]), J. E. Harrison (1903 [33; 157. 123–192]), H. Usener (1904 [61; 141]), K. Meuli (1946 [50; 107]), E. R. Dodds (1951 [20; 87]), J.-P. Vernant (mainly since 1965 [63; 18]), L. Gernet (1968 [32; 123. 76–94, 283–288]) and W. Burkert (above all since 1972 [12; 110]). With the exception of Frazer, a scholar trained as a lawyer and classical philologist who is claimed by ethnologists as one of their own, all the aforementioned were career scholars of Antiquity holding positions in institutions of learning. As the methodological focus for the outlines of their anthropological studies, they all shared comparatism which was used to compare the ancient, primarily Greek material with documents from other cultural traditions. There are certainly conspicuous differences between them in that, leaving aside the universal comparatist Frazer, Rohde, Harrison, Dodds and Gernet draw 'primarily' upon comparative material from primitive societies, (in Usener's work it is more common for ethnological sources to serve as evidence as well, -as already evident with Frazer, with reference to W. Mannhardt [46; 124. 120–142]. In the work of Meuli and Burkert palaeolithic and ethological models predominate, whereas in Vernant comparatist access to the sources is the least marked. An additional difference is related to the respective attitudes of these researchers to Christianity. The radical agnosticism of the English and the pointedly secular stance of the French researchers contrast with the anthropologically oriented scholars of Antiquity from Germany and Switzerland who have a greater affinity with Christianity even if it is expressed in a different way in each case. Parallel with this are the differences with respect to social science access to the subjects which is much more clearly defined among the French and English anthropologists than among the Germans. The fact that Rohde, Harrison and Dodds in particular were decisively inspired by Nietzsche noticeably diminished the status of the first two scholars within the study of Antiquity during their lifetimes. K. Kerényi, who came from Hungary, adopted an unique position; his work was versatile in the humanities, phenomenological in religious history and existentialist in the orientation of his anthropological views [136]. He was one of the first to endeavour to push for the recognition in Germany of the English anthropological school inaugurated by Frazer and Harrison ('Cambridge Ritualists') and he attempted also to exploit to the fullest, for the analysis of Greek myths and cults, C. G. Jung's depth psychology theory of archetypes and the faction of cultural morphology prominent in German ethnology [174]. In a more distantly-related sense, Usener's student A. Warburg (e.g. [68]) should be regarded as one of the scholars who were inspired, anthropologically and with respect to the humanities, by Antiquity, particularly by its reception in art [103]. In comparison with the recourse of scholars of Antiquity to anthropology, the recourse of anthropologists to Antiquity is significantly less widespread. Apart from the use, for instance, of the merely analogizing model of the Argonaut in Malinowski [43], Lévi-Strauss in particular utilizes ancient models very much as a *leitmotif* [157. 268–295]. Other instances of ethnologists having recourse to Antiquity tend on the other hand to remain peripheral [163]. Joint projects by ethnologists and scholars of Antiquity have to date been rare [70; 84].

4. The Study of Ancient Culture

At the beginning of the 3rd millennium it is no exaggeration to assert that the study of Antiquity on an international scale is developing increasingly into an explicitly anthropologically-oriented science of ancient culture. In German-speaking Europe this is shown most clearly in ancient history, religious history and archaeology, though less in Greek and Roman philology [164], which may be connected to its institutional dependence on the training of teachers of ancient languages. Culture and anthropology, as key concepts, can no longer be imagined without current research in the study of Antiquity, already apparent from the growing frequency of these terms in essay and book titles (e.g. [167]).

D. Central Concepts and Research Topics

1. Foreignness and Otherness 2. Ritual and Myth 3. Exchange of Gifts and Reciprocity 4. Initiation, rites de passage, Performance 5. Sex and Kinship 6. Cultural Transfer and Mobility 7. Further Aspects

1. Foreignness and Otherness

Foreignness has for several decades been popular as a cultural anthropological category in the humanities as well as in studies of Antiquity, linking up with an ethnology that can be defined as the 'study of the culturally foreign' [126]. The specifically Greek view of the foreigner and this view's effect on later Western definitions has attracted new attention [133; 95]. The position, formerly considered provocative, of understanding even ancient Greek culture not, for instance, as something naturally familiar within the context of the European tradition but as something foreign – which was already propagated in the early 19th cent. by K. O. Müller [86] [158] – is having a productive influence in studies of Antiquity today, not least following the conceptualization devised by J.-P. Vernant of foreignness in the sense of otherness that is illustrated particularly emblematically through the masked nature of the Gorgon Medusa and the figure of Dionysos [65; 66]. Classical Studies today generally tends to regard itself as the study of that which is closest from the point of view of cultural foreignness [104. 177].

2. Ritual and Myth

These two categories of religious history that are derived linguistically and conceptually from the ancient Roman and Greek tradition have been at the centre of cultural anthropological endeavours right from the outset, both within and without studies of Antiquity. From the end of the 18th cent. onwards, the concept of myth had already been ennobled by C. G. Heyne with the aid of ethnological materials so that it became a basic category of religious history [108. 284–294]. Following W. Robertson Smith [53], the school of the 'Cambridge Ritualists' [85] was the first to appreciate extensively the significance of rituals. While debate was initially dominated by the original question as to whether one

arose from the other, today's research tends rather to be dedicated to the specific cultural function of myths and cults – compared with other traditions – in ancient Greece and Rome and so it increasingly incorporates anthropological theories [81; 154; 176; 157; 110]. The structuralist classifications developed by G. Dumézil [21] using Indo-European material have had a stimulating effect, particularly on the analysis of Roman religion [108].

3. Exchange of Gifts and Reciprocity

The category of the gift that was exemplified by Malinowski through the exchange ritual of the 'Argonauts' of the Western Pacific and that shortly afterwards – primarily following research by German political economists – was shaped by M. Mauss [101], the nephew and student of E. Durkheim and precursor of Lévi-Strauss, into a central concept of social anthropology [49], has developed so that it also has had an eminent heuristic influence in studies of Antiquity up to the present time, not least thanks to the further development of this category and its replacement by the concept of reciprocity that was developed to its fullest by the social economist from Hungary, K. Polanyi [51; 123. 31–75, 276–283]. The utopian and nostalgic criticism of modernity that is expressed in these definitions of the terms [179] is typical of the history of other basic terms in CA as well. Recent [100] research, taking a different view, shows how problematical, as well as fruitful, critical treatment of the concept of the gift can be–especially for an understanding of the Greek view of the stranger and the guest or of friendship [115; 155; 140] or for the Roman games [177]–as well as for the concept of reciprocity, for instance, when analysing literary depictions [165].

4. Initiation, rites de passage, Performance

Rites of passage and their dramatic theatrical quality had already proved fascinating to J. Harrison. As central cross-cultural practices, initiation inside and outside ethnology is a particularly suitable [181] topic for cultural comparison and in the meantime has also become a favourite topic for literary scholars. The key term *rites de passage* was coined before the First World War by the multinational ethnologist A. Van Gennep [62] and was further developed after the World War II by the English ethnologist V. Turner using the term *performance* [58; 59]. Beginning with the research by H. Jeanmaire [35] and A. Brelich [11] on ancient Greek rites of puberty that links up particularly with Van Gennep, a research field that had continued to be productive was dedicated to this topic and is being pursued primarily by the Vernant school in France and to the same extent in other countries [82; 67; 144; 150]. Recently *performance* has also succeeded in becoming a favourite topic for Classical philology [97; 106].

5. Sex and Kinship

One of the fundamental areas of interest in anthropology since the 19th cent. has been comparative cultural research into the rules governing kinship. The investigations conducted by L. H. Morgan on rules of kinship and descent among the North American Indians have not only proved stimulating for ethnology [130. 42–75; 142. 29–41] and particularly for structural anthropology, making these rules into a central field of investigation, but have also influenced Marxist theory of statehood (F. Engels). The cultural dependency acknowledged in the process – and not the natural necessity – of family structures and sexual norms has become a significant reflexive driving force in theoretical and practical feminist endeavours. Historical constructs like the one propagated by J. J. Bachofen of an historical sequence of matriarchy and patriarchy were dismissed over time as frivolous [178; 79] and made way for investigation – pursued in great detail – of the cultural construct of relationships between the generations and the 'genders' and even of the term *sex/gender* itself. The very organization of heterosexuality and homosexuality in Antiquity, being independent of reproduction, offers a rewarding field of work here [180; 112], especially as Greek pederasty can be linked with the initiation model [80] as well as primarily with the symposium, an institution typical of Greek culture, within which even the important social function of the *hetaera* is established [94]. Antiquity is also suited to a great extent to the study of culture-specific forms of misogyny with its far-ranging effects [134].

6. CULTURAL TRANSFER AND MOBILITY

Recently the different forms of a cross-border, mutual cultural exchange have more and more become the focus of attention in the disciplines involved in the study of Antiquity, as a specific characteristic of ancient societies, their economies and religions, and this has given additional encouragement to the transfer of knowledge between these and with other specialized fields. Diagrammatic models of 'cultural areas' or even of 'cultural circles', as have been developed within German cultural morphology and in Anglo-Saxon ethnology since the turn of the 20th cent., have in the meantime been disqualified because of their ideological as well as heuristically misleading implications [175]. Research into acculturation and cultural transfer, cultural mobility [91] and forms of cultural mixing are, on the other hand, at present a particularly flourishing field of work in studies of Antiquity as well as in ethnology and other disciplines. After turning away from a fixation on Athens that had admittedly survived for so long because of tradition, mobility was able to be recognized as a decisive characteristic of ancient Greek culture [152; 122]. The consequences arising from this for the investigation into ancient travel have however remained to a large extent merely a suggestion for further work [161]. The debate over post-colonialism and the discourse concerning affirmative ethnicity that goes hand in hand with it because of *political correctness* has also reached the *Classics*. The applicability of a modern concept like that of colonisation to Greek history can however be questioned [137]. An identificatory origin model like the one presented by M. Bernal [5] shows – contrary to

his intention and despite being glossed over by academic historians – that ideological wishful notions and methodological impasses, such as were hatched by supporters of an ideal image of all things Greek in the 19th cent., cannot retain legitimacy even if they come back with a vengeance under different circumstances [132].

7. FURTHER ASPECTS

While many cultural anthropological topics with which even earlier generations of scholars of Antiquity had been occupied, for instance the concepts of taboo, totem and vegetation spirits, have probably finally been shelved (for the concept of origin or the theory of the cultural group this has not occured), other fields that have for a long time been ignored in CA, like magic, madness and ecstasy, death and burial, festivals and other collective customs in particular, continue to be on the agenda in studies of Antiquity. Last but not least, the treatment of ancient imagery under anthropological circumstances should be emphasized, using an especially stimulating example which came out of the Vernant school [3].

E. CURRENT METHODOLOGICAL PROBLEMS
1. COMPARATIVISM 2. ETHNOLOGY 3. SEMIOTICS 4. HERMENEUTICS 5. HISTORICAL ANTHROPOLOGY

1. COMPARATIVISM

Comparison is perhaps one of the most time-honoured cultural anthropological methods, and debate about the pros and cons of comparison has led to clear factional demarcations in the history of ethnology. Comparative religion has been a preferred battle ground [166] here. Within the context of the analysis of myths and customs, comparison with those of indigenous North Americans by representatives of the Enlightenment like J.-F. Lafitau [38] already led in the early 18th cent. to the discomforting insight that the Greeks and the 'savages' tended to resemble each other more than they differed in this regard. At present it appears, in view of the forceful pleas by many scholars of Antiquity in favour of comparison and explanation and against understanding, as if more and more hardened fronts will be built up [99; 19]. The value of these fronts' insights, as with any drive towards an either-or approach, is doubtful.

2. ETHNOLOGY

Undeterred by trends in the 'classics' which run in other directions, the old master of behavioural research in religious anthropology, W. Burkert, presented a new theoretical plan in this regard [13]. However scholars appear, with only a few exceptions, unwilling to follow his lead [74].

3. SEMIOTICS

At present the recourse to semiotics appears more capable of making connections – the decoding of cultural realities as anthropological and epoch-specific signifying systems [151], e.g. with reference to the Russian literary scholar M. Bakhtin [2]. Religious practices of

Antiquity [109], as well as sacred landscapes [89] and testimonials of imagery [119] seem to provide semiotically analysable 'texts'.

4. HERMENEUTICS

The cultural hermeneutics of C. Geertz, especially his contentious essay on 'Balinese cockfighting' [29. 412–453], has in the meantime also inspired Classical philologists, at least by association [93]. The question arises however as to whether it would not be best first to formulate a material hermeneutics [7; 8] suitable for its cultural meaning when interpreting and seeking to understand the ancient Greek tradition as well as literary texts. This may perhaps also be applicable to a material and critical method of interpretation in CA which is now only recognizable in outline form.

5. HISTORICAL ANTHROPOLOGY

A glance at current debates in the Humanities makes resolution easier because the old antitheses of anthropology versus history, and CA versus historical anthropology appear to be no longer sustainable. Without history, including the history of science, without an historical, critical, analytical consciousness, the Humanities would certainly be condemned to being ephemeral exercises. Without anthropological reflection, however, studies of Antiquity too would probably barely do justice to their role of contributing to the multi-dimensional understanding of a temporally and geographically limited and particular but nonetheless surprisingly universal field of human culture which continues to have influence.

SOURCES: 1 T. ASAD (ed.), Anthropology and the Colonial Encounter, 1973 2 M. BAKHTIN, The Dialogic Imagination. Four Essays, 1981 3 C. BÉRARD et al., La cité des images. Religion et société en Grèce ancienne, 1984 4 P. L. BERGER, T. LUCKMANN, The Social Construction of Reality, 1966 5 M. BERNAL, Black Athena. The Afroasiatic Roots of Classical Civilization, 2 vols., 1987/1991 6 F. BOAS, The Mind of Primitive Man, 1911 7 J. BOLLACK, La Grèce de personne. Les mots sous le mythe, 1997 8 Id., Sens contre sens. Comment lit-on?, 2000 9 P. BONTE, M. IZARD (eds.), Dictionnaire de l'ethnologie et de l'anthropologie, 1991 10 P. BOURDIEU, Homo Academicus, 1984 11 A. BRELICH, Paides e parthenoi, 1969 12 W. BURKERT, Homo necans. Interpretationen altgriechischer Opferriten und Mythen, 1972 (Eng.: Homo necans: The Anthropology of Ancient Greek Sacrificial Ritual and Myth, 1983) 13 Id., Creation of the Sacred. Tracks of Biology in Early Religions, 1996 14 E. CASSIRER, Philosophie der symbolischen Formen, 2 vols., 1923/1925 (Eng.: The Philosophy of Symbolic Forms, 1953–1996) 15 Id., Zur Logik der Kulturwissenschaften, 1942 16 J. CLIFFORD, G. E. MARCUS (eds.), Writing Culture. The Poetics and Politics of Ethnography, 1986 17 M. DETIENNE, Les jardins d'Adonis. La mythologie des aromates en Grèce, 1972 (Eng.: The Gardens of Adonis: Spices in Greek Mythology, 1976) 18 Id. et al. (eds.), Poikilia. Études offertes à Jean-Pierre Vernant, 1987 19 Id., Comparer l'incomparable, 2000 20 E. R. DODDS, The Greeks and the Irrational, 1951 21 G. DUMÉZIL, La religion romaine archaïque, 1966 (Eng.: Archaic Roman Religion, 1970) 22 E. DURKHEIM, Les formes élémentaires de la vie religieuse, 1912 23 N. ELIAS, Über den Prozeß der Zivilisation.

Soziogenetische und psychogenetische Untersuchungen, 2 vols., 1939 (Eng.: The Civilizing Process: Sociogenetic and Psychogenetic Investigations, rev. ed. 2000) 24 M. I. FINLEY, Anthropology and the Classics, in: Id., The Use and Abuse of History, 1986, 102–119 25 J. G. FRAZER, The Golden Bough, 2 vols. ¹1890 26 S. FREUD, Totem und Tabu. Einige Übereinstimmungen im Seelenleben der Wilden und der Neurotiker, 1912/1913 (Eng.: Totem and Taboo: Some Points of Agreement between the Mental Lives of Savages and Neurotics, 1950) 27 W. FRÜHWALD et al., Geisteswissenschaften heute. Eine Denkschrift, 1991 28 H.-G. GADAMER, Wahrheit und Methode. Grundzüge einer philosophischen Hermeneutik, 1960 (Eng.: Truth and Method, 2nd rev. ed. 1995) 29 C. GEERTZ, The Interpretation of Cultures, 1973 30 Id., Local Knowledge. Further Essays on Interpretive Anthropology, 1983 31 Id., Works and Lives. The Anthropologist as Author, 1988 32 L. GERNET, Anthropologie de la Grèce antique, 1968 (Eng.: The Anthropology of Ancient Greece,1981) 33 J. E. HARRISON, Prolegomena to the Study of Greek Religion, 1903 34 S. HUNTINGTON, The Clash of Civilizations?, in: Foreign Affairs 72/3, 1993, 22–49 35 H. JEANMAIRE, Couroi et Courètes. Essai sur l'éducation spartiate et sur les rites d'adolescence dans l'antiquité hellénique, 1939 36 I. KANT, Anthropologie in pragmatischer Hinsicht, 1798 (Eng.: Anthropology from a Pragmatic Point of View, 1978; 1996) 37 C. KLUCKHOHN, Anthropology and the Classics, 1961 38 J.-F. LAFITAU, Mœurs des sauvages amériquains comparées aux mœurs des premiers temps, 2 vols., 1724 (Eng.: Customs of the American Indians Compared with the Customs of Primitive Times, 1974–1977) 39 C. LÉVI-STRAUSS, Anthropologie structurale, 1958 (Eng.: Structural Anthropology, 1963–1976) 40 Id., La pensée sauvage, 1962 (Eng.: The Savage Mind, 1966) 41 Id., Mythologiques, 4 vols., 1964–1971 42 D. LEVINSON, M. EMBER (eds.), Encyclopedia of Cultural Anthropology, 4 vols., 1996 43 B. MALINOWSKI, Argonauts of the Western Pacific. An Account of Native Enterprise and Adventure in the Archipelagos of Melanesian New Guinea, 1922 44 Id., Sex and Repression in Savage Society, 1927 45 Id., A Scientific Theory of Culture and Other Essays, 1944 46 W. MANNHARDT, Wald- und Feldkulte, 2 vols., 1875/1876 47 G. E. MARCUS, M. M. J. FISCHER, Anthropology as Cultural Critique. An Experimental Moment in the Human Sciences, 1986 48 R. R. MARETT (ed.), Anthropology and the Classics, 1908 49 M. MAUSS, Essai sur le don, 1923/1924 50 K. MEULI, Griechische Opferbräuche, in: Phyllobolia. Festschrift Peter Von der Mühll, 1946, 185–288 51 K. POLANYI, The Great Transformation, 1944 52 J. REDFIELD, Classics and Anthropology, in: Arion 3. Ser. 1/2, 1991, 5–23 53 W. ROBERTSON SMITH, The Religion of the Semites. The Fundamental Institutions, 1889 54 E. ROHDE, Psyche. Seelencult und Unsterblichkeitsglaube der Griechen, 2 vols., 1890/1894 (Eng.: Psyche: The Cult of Souls and Belief in Immortality among the Greeks, 1950) 55 E. ROTHACKER, Probleme der Kulturanthropologie, 1942, ²1948 56 E. W. SAID, Orientalism, 1978, ²1994 57 G. SIMMEL, Philosophische Kultur, 1911 58 V. TURNER, The Ritual Process. Structure and Anti-Structure, 1969 59 Id., From Ritual to Theatre. The Human Seriousness of Play, 1982 60 E. B. TYLOR, Primitive Culture. Researches into the Development of Mythology, Philosophy, Religion, Art, and Custom, 2 vols., 1871 61 H. USENER, Heiligie Handlung, in: ARW 7, 1904, 281–339 62 A. VAN GENNEP, Les rites de passage, 1909 (Eng.:

The Rites of Passage, 1960) 63 J.-P. VERNANT, Mythe et pensée chez les Grecs, 1965 (Eng.: Myth and Thought among the Greeks, 1983) 64 Id., Raisons du mythe, in: Id., Mythe et société en Grèce ancienne, 1974, 195–250 (Eng.: Myth and Society in Ancient Greece, 1980) 65 Id., L'individu, la mort, l'amour. Soi-même et l'autre en Grèce ancienne, 1989 66 Id., Figures, idoles, masques, 1990 67 P. VIDAL-NAQUET, Le chasseur noir. Formes de pensée et formes de société dans le monde grec, 1981 (Eng.: The Black Hunter: Forms of Thought and Forms of Society in the Greek World, 1986) 68 A. WARBURG, Das Schlangenritual, 1923/1988

LITERATURE: 69 R. ACKERMAN, J. G. Frazer. His Life and Work, 1987 70 J.-M. ADAM et al., Le discours anthropologique, 1990 71 T. W. ADORNO, Kultur, 1951, in: Id., Gesammelte Schriften, vol. 20.1, 1986, 135–139 72 D. BACHMANN-MEDICK, Einleitung, in: Id. (ed.), Kultur als Text. Die anthropologische Wende in der Literaturwissenschaft, 1996, 7–64 73 G. BAUDY, Antike Religion in anthropologischer Deutung. Wandlungen des altertumskundlichen Kult- und Mythosverständnisses im 20. Jahrhundert, in: Schwinge 1995, 229–258 74 Id., Religion als szenische Ergänzung. Paläoanthropologische Grundlagen religiöser Erfahrung, in: F. STOLZ (ed.), Homo naturaliter religiosus. Gehört Religion notwendig zum Mensch-Sein?, 1997, 65–90 75 U. BENZENHÖFER, M. ROTZOLL, Zur Anthropologia (1533) von Galeazzo Capella. Die früheste bislang bekannte Verwendung des Begriffs Anthropologie, in: Medizinhistorisches Journal 26, 1991, 315–320 76 E. BERG, M. FUCHS (eds.), Kultur, soziale Praxis, Text. Die Krise der ethnographischen Repräsentation, 1993 77 H. BHABHA, The Location of Culture, 1994 78 G. BOLLENBECK, Bildung und Kultur. Glanz und Elend eines deutschen Deutungsmusters 1994, ²1996 79 P. BORGEAUD et al., La mythologie du matriarcat. L'atelier de Johann Jakob Bachofen, 1999 80 J. N. BREMMER, Adolescents, Symposion, and Pederasty, in: O. MURRAY (ed.), Sympotica. A symposium on the Symposion, 1990, 135–148 81 Id., N. M. HORSFALL (ed.), Roman Myth and Mythography, 1987 82 C. CALAME, Les chœurs de jeunes filles en Grèce archaïque, 2 vols., 1977 83 Id., Du figuratif au thématique. Aspects narratifs et interprétatifs de la description en anthropologie de la Grèce ancienne, in: Adam 1990, 111–132 84 Id., M. KILANI (ed.), La fabrication de l'humain dans les cultures et en anthropologie, 1999 85 W. M. CALDER III (ed.), The Cambridge Ritualists Reconsidered, 1991 86 Id., R. SCHLESIER (eds.), Zwischen Rationalismus und Romantik. Karl Otfried Müller und die antike Kultur, 1998 87 G. CAMBIANO, Eric Dodds entre psychanalyse et parapsychologie, in: RHR 208, 1991, 3–26 88 H. CANCIK, Erwin Rohde – ein Philologe der Bismarckzeit, in: W. DOERR (ed.), Semper Apertus. 600 Jahre Ruprecht-Karls-Univ. Heidelberg 1386–1986, vol. 2, 1985, 436–505 89 Id., Rome as Sacred Landscape. Varro and the End of Republican Religion in Rome, in: Visible Religion 4–5: Approaches to Iconology, 1985–1986, 250–265 90 J. CLIFFORD, On Orientalism, 1980, in: Id., The Predicament of Culture. Twentieth-Century Ethnography, Literature, and Art, 1988, 255–276 91 Id., Traveling Cultures, 1992, in: Id., Routes. Travel and Translation in the Late Twentieth Century, 1997, 17–46 92 J. A. CLIFTON (ed.), Introduction to Cultural Anthropology, 1968 93 E. CSAPO, Deep Ambivalence: Notes on the Greek Cockfight, in: Phoenix 47, 1993, 1–28, 115–124 94 J. N.

DAVIDSON, Courtisans and Fishcakes. The Consuming Passions of Classical Athens, 1997 95 A. DIHLE, Die Griechen und die Fremden, 1994 96 F. DOSSE, Histoire du structuralisme, 2 vols., 1991/1992 (Eng.: History of Structuralism, 1998) 97 C. DOUGHERTY, L. KURKE (eds.), Cultural Poetics in Archaic Greece. Cult, Performance, Politics, 1993 98 P. A. ERICKSON, A History of Anthropological Theory, 1998 99 E. FLAIG, Verstehen und Vergleichen. Ein Plädoyer, in: O. G. OEXLE, J. RÜSEN (eds.), Historismus in den Kulturwissenschaften. Geschichtskonzepte, historische Einschätzungen, Grundlagenprobleme, 1996, 263–287 100 Id., Geschichte ist kein Text. Reflexive Anthropologie am Beispiel der symbolischen Gaben im römischen Reich, in: H. W. BLANKE et al. (eds.), Dimensionen der Historik. Geschichtstheorie, Wissenschaftsgeschichte und Geschichtskultur heute, Festschrift J. Rüsen, 1998, 345–360 101 M. FOURNIER, Marcel Mauss, 1994 102 M. FUCHS, Universalität der Kultur. Reflexion, Interaktion und das Identitätsdenken – eine ethnologische Perspektive, in: M. BROCKER, H. NAU (ed.), Ethnozentrismus. Möglichkeiten und Grenzen des interkulturellen Dialogs, 1997, 141–152 103 R. GALITZ, B. REIMERS (eds.), Aby M. Warburg. Ekstatische Nymphe ... trauernder Flußgott. Portrait eines Gelehrten, 1995 104 H.-J. GEHRKE, Zwischen Altertumswissenschaft und Geschichte. Zur Standortbestimmung der Alten Geschichte am Ende des 20. Jahrhunderts, in: Schwinge 1995, 160–196 105 R. GIRTLER, Kultur. Entwicklungslinien, Paradigmata, Methoden, 1979 106 S. GOLDHILL, R. OSBORNE (eds.), Performance Culture and Athenian Democracy, 1999 107 F. GRAF (ed.), Klassische Antike und neue Wege der Kulturwissenschaften. Symposium Karl Meuli, 1992 108 Id. (ed.), Mythos in mythenloser Gesellschaft. Das Paradigma Roms, 1993 109 Id., Zeichenkonzeptionen in der Religion der griechischen und römischen Antike, in: R. Posner et al. (eds.), Semiotik/Semiotics. Ein Handbuch zu den zeichentheoretischen Grundlagen von Natur und Kultur / A Handbook on the Sign-Theoretic Foundations of Nature and Culture, 1997, 939–958 110 Id. (ed.), Ansichten griechischer Rituale. Geburtstags-Symposium für Walter Burkert, 1998 111 A. GRIMSHAW, K. HART, Anthropology and the Crisis of the Intellectuals, 1996 112 D. M. HALPERIN, J. J. WINKLER, F. I. ZEITLIN (eds.), Before Sexuality. The Construction of Erotic Experience in the Ancient Greek World, 1990 113 M. HARRIS, The Rise of Anthropological Theory. A History of Theories of Culture, 1968 114 F. HARTOG, Le miroir d'Hérodote. Essai sur la représentation de l'autre, 1980 (Eng.: The Mirror of Herodotus: An Essay on the Representation of the Other, 1988) 115 G. HERMAN, Ritualised Friendship and the Greek City, 1987 116 M. J. HERSKOVITS, Cultural Relativism. Perspectives in Cultural Pluralism, 1972 117 Id., Franz Boas. The Science of Man in the Making, 1973 118 M. T. HODGEN, Early Anthropology in the Sixteenth and Seventeenth Centuries, 1964 119 T. HÖLSCHER, Römische Bildersprache als semantisches System, 1987 (Eng.: The Language of Images in Roman Art, 2004) 120 J. J. HONIGMANN (ed.), Handbook of Social and Cultural Anthropology, 1973 121 Id., The Development of Anthropological Ideas, 1976 122 P. HORDEN, N. PURCELL, The Corrupting Sea. A Study of Mediterranean History, 2000 123 S. C. HUMPHREYS, Anthropology and the Greeks, 1978 124 H. G. KIPPENBERG, Die Entdeckung der Religionsgeschichte. Religionswissenschaft und Moderne, 1997 125 K.-H. KOHL, Bronislaw Kaspar Malinowski (1884–1942), in: Marschall 1990, 227–247, 348–352 126 Id., Ethnologie – die Wissenschaft vom kulturell Fremden. Eine Einführung, 1993 127 Id., Edward Burnett Tylor (1832–1917), in: A. Michaels (ed.), Klassiker der Religionswissenschaft, 1997, 41–59, 364–366 128 A. KROEBER, C. KLUCK-HOHN, Culture. A Critical Review of Concepts and Definitions, 1952 129 A. KUPER, Anthropology and Anthropologists. The Modern British School, 1973 130 Id., The Invention of Primitive Society. Transformations of an Illusion, 1988 131 Id., Culture. The Anthropologists' Account, 1999 132 M. R. LEFKOWITZ, G. MACLEAN Rogers (eds.), Black Athena Revisited, 1996 133 R. LONIS (ed.), L'étranger dans le monde grec, 2 vols., 1988/1992 134 N. LORAUX, Les expériences de Tirésias. Le féminin et l'homme grec, 1989 135 A. O. LOVEJOY, G. BOAS, Primitivism and Related Ideas in Antiquity, 1935, ²1965 136 A. MAGRIS, Carlo Kerényi e la ricerca fenomenologica della religione, 1975 137 I. MALKIN, The Returns of Odysseus. Colonization and Ethnicity, 1998 138 W. MARSCHALL (ed.), Klassiker der Kulturanthropolgie, 1990 139 M.-C. MAUREL, J.-C. RUANO-BORBALAN (eds.), L'anthropologie aujourd'hui = Sciences Humaines, Hors-série 23, Décembre 1998/Janvier 1999 140 L. G. MITCHELL, Greeks Bearing Gifts. The Public Use of Private Relationships in the Greek World, 435–323 BC, 1997 141 A. MOMIGLIANO (ed.), Aspetti di Hermann Usener, filologo della religione, 1982 142 J. D. MOORE, Visions of Culture. An Introduction to Anthropological Theories and Theorists, 1997 143 S. MORAVIA, La scienza dell'uomo nel settecento, 1970 144 A. MOREAU (ed.), L'initiation. Les rites d'adolescence et les mystères, 2 Bde., 1992 145 W. E. MÜHLMANN, Geschichte der Anthropologie, 1948, ³1984 146 Id., E. W. MÜLLER (ed.), Kultur, 1966 147 K. E. MÜLLER, Geschichte der antiken Ethnologie, 1972/1980 148 W. NIPPEL, Sozialanthropologie und Alte Geschichte, in: C. MEIER, J. RÜSEN (eds.), Historische Methode = Beiträge zur Historik 5, 1988, 300–318 149 Id., Griechen, Barbaren und Wilde. Alte Geschichte und Sozialanthropologie, 1990 150 M. W. PADILLA (ed.), Rites of Passage in Ancient Greece. Literature, Religion, Society, 1999 151 R. POSNER, What is Culture? Toward a Semiotic Explication of Anthropological Concepts, in: W. A. KOCH (ed.), The Nature of Culture, 1989, 240–295 152 N. PURCELL, Mobility and the Polis, in: O. MURRAY, S. PRICE (eds.), The Greek City From Homer to Alexander, 1990, 29–58 153 M. SAHLINS, How Natives Think. About Captain Cook, For Example, 1995 154 J. SCHEID, Romulus et ses frères, 1990 155 E. SCHEID-TISSINIER, Les usages du don chez Homère. Vocabulaire et pratiques, 1994 156 W. SCHIFFHAUER, Die Angst vor der Differenz. Zu neuen Strömungen in der Kulturanthropologie, in: Zeitschrift für Volkskunde 92, 1996, 20–31 157 R. SCHLESIER, Kulte, Mythen und Gelehrte. Anthropologie der Antike seit 1800, 1994 158 Id., Mythos, in: C. WULF (ed.) Vom Menschen. Handbuch Historischer Anthropologie, 1997, 1079–1086 159 Id., Anthropologie und Kulturwissenschaft in Deutschland vor dem Ersten Weltkrieg, in: C. KÖNIG, E. LÄMMERT (eds.), Konkurrenten in der Fakultät. Kultur, Wissen und Universität um 1900, 1999, 219–231 160 Id., Kultur-Interpretation. Gebrauch und Mißbrauch der Hermeneutik heute, in: I. KORNECK et al. (eds.), The Contemporary Study of Culture, 1999, 157–166 161 Id., Menschen und Götter unterwegs. Ritual und Reise in der griechischen Antike, in: T. HÖLSCHER (ed.), Gegenwelten: Zu den Kulturen Griechenlands und Roms in der Antike, 2000 162 H. SCHNEI-DER, Schottische Aufklärung und antike Geschichte, in: P. KNEISSL, V. LOSEMANN (eds.), Alte Geschichte und Wissenschaftsgeschichte Festschrift Karl Christ, 1988, 431–464 163 G. SCHREMPP, Magical Arrows. The Maori, the Greeks, and the Folklore of the Universe, 1992 164 E.-R. SCHWINGE (ed.), Die Wissenschaften vom Altertum am Ende des 2. Jahrhunderts nach Christus, 1995 165 R. SEAFORD, Reciprocity and Ritual. Homer and Tragedy in the Developing City-State, 1994 166 E. J. SHARPE, Comparative Religion. A History, 1975, ²1986 167 C. SOURVINOU-INWOOD, Reading Greek Culture. Texts and Images, Rituals and Myths, 1991 168 J. STAGL, Kultur und Gesellschaft. Eine wissenschaftssoziologische Darstellung der Ethnologie und Kulturanthropologie, 1974, ²1981 169 Id., Introduction, in: F. R. VIVELO, Handbuch der Kulturanthropologie. Eine grundlegende Einführung, 1981, 13–24 170 Id., A History of Curiosity. The Theory of Travel 1550–1800, 1995 171 G. W. STOCKING JR., Race, Culture, and Evolution. Essays in the History of Anthropology, 1968, ²1982 172 Id., After Tylor. British Social Anthropology 1888–1951, 1995 173 Id. (ed.), Volksgeist as Method and Ethic. Essays on Boasian Ethnography and the German Anthropological Tradition = History of Anthropology 8, 1996 174 H. STRAUBE, Leo Frobenius (1873–1938), in: Marschall 1990, 151–170, 338–340 175 B. STRECK, Kultur als Mysterium. Zum Trauma der deutschen Völkerkunde, in: H. BERKING, R. FABER (eds.), Kultursoziologie – Symptom des Zeitgeistes?, 1989, 89–115 176 H. S. VERSNEL, Transition and Reversal in Myth and Ritual = Inconsistencies in Greek and Roman Religion II, 1993 177 P. VEYNE, Le pain et le cirque. Sociologie politique d'un pluralisme politique, 1976 178 B. WAGNER-HASEL (ed.), Matriarchatstheorien der Altertumswissenschaft, 1992 179 Id., Wissenschaftsmythen und Antike. Zur Funktion von Gegenbildern der Moderne am Beispiel der Gabentauschdebatte, in: A. VÖLKER-RASOR, W. SCHMALE (eds.), Mythen-Mächte – Mythen als Argument, 1998, 33–64 180 J. J. WINKLER, The Constraints of Desire. The Anthropology of Sex and Gender in Ancient Greece, 1990 181 F. W. YOUNG, Initiation Ceremonies. A Cross-Cultural Study of Status Dramatization, 1965.

RENATE SCHLESIER

Cynicism
A. THE MIDDLE AGES B. MODERN TIMES

A. THE MIDDLE AGES

The reception of Cynicism in the Middle Ages and in modern times is, with few exceptions, simply the reception of Diogenes. The most important source for the knowledge of Diogenes in the Middle Ages was the brief description given of Diogenes' lifestyle by the Church Father Jerome in his work *Adversus Jovinianum* (2, 14). Jerome summarizes what makes Diogenes into a model for him in the statement that Diogenes was 'more powerful than King Alexander and a victor over human nature' (*potentior rege Alexandro et naturae victor humanae*). On the one hand, the allusion here is to Diogenes' extreme freedom from needs and, on the other, to the well-known anecdote according to which Alexander the Great once came to Diogenes when the latter was sunning himself in the opening of his barrel and asked him whether he had a wish; whereupon Diogenes im-

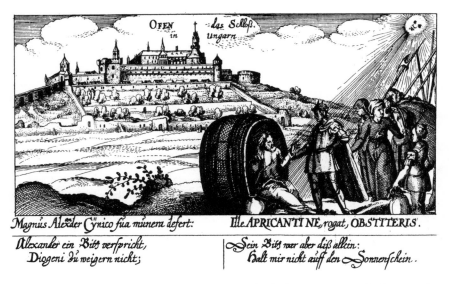

Fig. 1: Diogenes and Alexander, in the background the castle of Ofen (German name for the Hungarian city of Buda), in Daniel Meisner, Thesaurus philopoliticus, Frankfurt 1625–1631, Book I

mediately expressed the wish that Alexander should step out his light a bit (Fig. 1). Anecdotes and apophthegms of Diogenes were also known in the Middle Ages from the works of such pagan authors as Cicero, Seneca and Valerius Maximus. The Diogenes found in these sources is often alluded to in moral-philosophical or, in any case, moralizing texts of the Middle Ages, either in concise form or in imaginative elaboration (extensive collection of texts in: 6. 177–279). The following two frequently used sources came long afterwards. The collection of sayings entitled (*Bocados de Oro*) (Golden Morsels), translated from Arabic to Spanish in the mid-13th cent. and thence into Latin, French and English, contains numerous sayings of Diogenes (Chap. 10). At the beginning of the 14th cent. the earliest biography of Diogenes appeared in the *Liber de vita et moribus philosophorum*, composed after the model of *Diogenes* Laertius' history of philosophy and attributed by tradition to Walter Burley. This work also contains biographies of Antisthenes and Crates (chap. 50, 33, and 19).

B. MODERN TIMES

At the dawn of modern times, Greek sources were added to the Latin sources, which until then had been the only ones available. This considerably broadened the basis of information. From 1472 to 1533, a large selection of letters of the Cynics (later acknowledged as not authentic) and Diogenes Laertius' history of philosophy were printed for the first time, first in Latin translation and then in the original. However, even more influential than these ancient texts was Erasmus' *Apophthegmata*, which quickly spread all over Europe after its first printing (1533). The third volume contained a plethora of sayings by Diogenes, which Eras-

mus had taken mainly from Diogenes Laertius' history of philosophy. In particular, these sayings provided the basis for Hans Sachs who, in a total of eight texts between 1523 and 1563, presented Diogenes to his contemporaries as a teacher of virtue concerned for the well-being of his fellow citizens [6. 300–337]. Also based on these sayings was the anonymous volume that appeared in 1550 in Zurich under the title *Diogenes. Ein Lustige unnd Kurtzwylige History von aller Leer unnd Läben Diogenis Cynici des Heydnischen Philosophi* (Diogenes. A Pleasant and Entertaining History of All the Teachings and Life of the Pagan Philosopher Diogenes the Cynic) [6. 101–165]. The author explains in a preface why the story of Diogenes' life is worthy of being recounted: 'For although Diogenes spoke and did much that was vulgar, coarse, and improper, on the other hand, he also taught and did much from which one can learn a great deal of good'. Saint Jerome had already shown in his work *Adversus Jovinianum* how Diogenes' life story should be read: 'hold onto what is good, let go of what is evil' [6. 103f.].

In Diogenes' person, seriousness and playfulness, wisdom and folly, serenity and provocation were united indissolubly. He was therefore seen as an ancient twin brother of Till Eulenspiegel and, more generally, as an archetype of the wise fool. In one anecdote Diogenes once lit a lantern in broad daylight and said: 'I am searching for a man' (Diog. Laert. 6, 41). This was considered typical of him. In his work *Diogenes Lanthorne* (1607), the Englishman Samuel Rowlands had this Diogenes give sermons on morality on the streets of Athens. They were, of course, really directed at the Londoners of his time (Fig. 2).

In the 17th and 18th cents. as well, Diogenes with his lantern was transferred into one's own time and setting,

DIOGINES
LANTHORNE.

Athens I feeke for honeſt men;
But I ſhal finde thẽ God knows when.

Ile ſearch the Citie, where if I can ſee
One honeſt man; he ſhal goe with me.

Fig. 2: Samuel Rowlands, frontispiece
of *Diogines Lanthorne*, 1607

Die bösen Buben von Korinth
Sind platt gewalzt, wie Kuchen sind.

Fig. 3: Wilhelm Busch, *Diogenes
und die bösen Buben von Korinth*
(Diogenes and the Bad Boys of Corinth).
*Reproduced with the permission of the
Bibliothèque Nationale de France*

both in written works and in pictorial representations.
A new meaning was often associated with the scene.
Diogenes' search lost its original character of being, in
principle, futile and therefore paradoxical, as presented
in the ancient anecdote. Transplanted into modern
times, Diogenes could make productive discoveries. A
particularly interesting feature of this tradition was
Diogenes' transformation into the figurehead of bourgeois resistance to absolutism in 17th and 18th-cent.
France [3]. In an etching from the final phase of this

development, probably originating in 1793, Diogenes,
holding his lantern in his left hand, greets with his right
hand the revolutionary hero Marat, who is stepping out
of his basement window. In the background, Diogenes'
barrel is seen. The inscription reads: 'Diogenes, wearing
a red bonnet (i.e. the bonnet of the Jacobins), leaves his
barrel to give his hand to Marat, who emerges from a
cellar through a window'.

Christoph Martin Wieland had a distinctive sympathy for Diogenes and the Cynics. Three of his novels
were based on materials from them. According to an
ancient tradition, Plato had called Diogenes a 'mad
Socrates' (Σωκράτης μαινόμενος) (Ael. var. 14,33. Diog.
Laert. 6,54), and Wieland chose this saying as the title
of the first of these novels: ΣΩΚΡΑΤΗΣ ΜΑΙΝΟΜΕΝΟΣ
oder die Dialogen des Diogenes von Sinope
(ΣΩΚΡΑΤΗΣ ΜΑΙΝΟΜΕΝΟΣ or the Dialogues of Diogenes of Sinope) (1770; later title: *Nachlaß des Diogenes von Sinope* (The Heritage of Diogenes of Sinope).
This was later followed by the novels *Geheime
Geschichte des Philosophen Peregrinus Proteus* (The
Secret History of the Philosopher Peregrinus Proteus)
(1791), and *Krates und Hipparchia* (1805). Diogenes
played a peculiar role in Goethe's thought. Probably at
the beginning of the Weimar period (1775/76), he composed the short poem 'So wälz' ich ohne Unterlaß, wie
Sankt Diogenes, mein Faß [...])'. (So, like Saint Diogenes, I roll my keg without repose [...]). This verse alludes to the following anecdote (Lucian. hist. conscr. 3):
When the Corinthians first heard that Philip of Macedon was advancing towards the city with his army, they
sought, with a great deal of zeal, to fortify their city in
every conceivable way. Diogenes saw this and immediately began to roll his barrel up and down the hill. When
one of his friends asked him why, he replied: 'I am roll-
ing my barrel in order not to seem idle in the midst of so
many busy people'. From the time of this poem on,
Goethe used the formula that he 'rolls his barrel like
Diogenes' again and again to designate a mode of activity that concentrates itself on itself and cares not at all
for the surrounding hustle and bustle. Goethe, by the
way, also liked to compare himself with Diogenes on
other occasions, especially in his later years. In the draft
of one of Goethe's letters from 1815, we read: 'I would
very much like to let myself be ruled and taxed, as long
as the sun can shine through the opening of my barrel'.

Wilhelm Busch made Diogenes and his barrel the
subject of the story *Diogenes and the Naughty Lads of
Corinth*. In it he recounts in words and pictures how
two youngsters annoy Diogenes by making his barrel
roll. As is to be expected in Busch, the punishment follows quickly after their evil deed. The barrel rolls over
them, and all that is left of them are two stains on the
ground in their shape (Fig. 3).

In Nietzsche, the motif of Diogenes with his lantern
is restored to its original pessimistic meaning. In his
story *The Madman* in *The Gay Science* (Book 3, 125),
the 'mad Socrates' who sought man with a lantern,
turns into the 'madman' who announces to others the

message of the death of God and thereby enlightens them with the news that they themselves have murdered God. Yet it turns out that he has come too soon with his message, and he encounters only misunderstandings and surprises with it. The man who comes too soon, or the untimely one whose message no one will hear, is, of course, Nietzsche himself. He is the new Diogenes, his message the new 'Cynicism' and he proclaims the 'transvaluation of all values', understood as the victory of nature over morality.

In contemporary German, one distinguishes between Cynicism (German *Kynismus*) and cynicalness (German *Zynismus*). The former means the way of life of the ancient Cynics, and the latter expresses an attitude manifesting itself in 'scornfully trenchant, even offensive mockery, which holds nothing sacred' [1]. This distinction, which exists in other linguistic areas but as an orthographical distinction is only possible in German, puts an end, so to speak, to a development that can be traced back to the 18th cent. Already at that time, the concept 'Cynicism' (German 'Cynismus'), usually spelled in this way until the beginning of the 20th cent., showed a tendency to free itself from its connection to its ancient substrate and become independent. This was the beginning of a process, in the course of which what we now call cynicalness finally developed as an offshoot of Cynicism [7].

→ Cynicism; → Diogenes

1 K. DOERING, Antisthenes, Diogenes und die Kyniker, Nachwirkungen,GGPh² 2/1, 1998, 315–321   2 J. FELLE-SCHES,Zynismus, in: Europäische Enzyklopädie zu Philosophie und Wissenschaft, vol. 4, 1990, 1008   3 K. HER-DING,Diogenes als Bürgerheld, in: Boreas 5, 1982, 232–254 (= Id., Im Zeichen der Aufklärung, 1989, 163–181. 219–231)   4 Id., Diogenes als Narr,in: P. K. KLEIN (ed.), Zeitenspiegelung, 1998, 151–180   5 Id., Alexander besucht Diogenes, in: S. ANSELM, C. NEUBAUR (eds.), Talismane. K. Heinrich zum 70. Geburtstag, 1998, 363–424   6 N. LARGIER, Diogenes der Kyniker. Exempel, Erzählung, Geschichte in Mittalter und Früher Neuzeit, 1997   7 H. NIEHUES-PRÖBSTING, Der Kynismus des Diogenes und der Begriff des Zynismus, 1979, ²1988   8 Id., Die Kynismus-Rezeption der Moderne. Diogenes in der Aufklärung, in: M.-O. GOULET-CAZÉ, R. GOULET (eds.), Le cynisme ancien et ses prolongements, 1993, 519–555   9 ST. SCHMITT, Diogenes. Studien zu seiner Ikonographie in der niederländischen Emblematik und Malerei des 16. und 17. Jahrhunderts, 1993   10 P. SLOTERDIJK, Critique of Cynical Reason, (MICHAEL ELDRED (trans.), 1987)

KLAUS DÖRING

Cyprus
I. GENERAL: ANTIQUITY AND MIDDLE AGES
II. EDUCATION AND RESEARCH

I. GENERAL: ANTIQUITY AND MIDDLE AGES
Because of its strategic position, the island of Cyprus (C.) has always been a place where the claims of the various powers of the eastern Mediterranean for supremacy clashed. From the 12th cent. BC on the Greeks

increasingly left their mark; added to this in Antiquity were Phoenicians, Assyrians, Egyptians, Persians and Romans; in the Middle Ages Franks and Venetians; and in the modern period Turks and Britons, all of whom, to varying degrees, left traces of their presence in the culture of the island and largely determined its historical fate. The emergence and the spread of a national consciousness among the Greek population in the 19th cent. which partly also took on nationalistic forms (as in the idea of C. as a geographically and historically purely Greek creation without a break in continuity), gave rise to demands for union with the Greek national state (*enosis*). This ideology, which was also closely related to the reception of Antiquity, was mainly disseminated by the Orthodox Church. Initially the movement was directed against liberation from the Ottoman Empire and after 1878 it gradually developed into an uprising against British colonial rule, but its final consequence was the outbreak of ethnic conflicts that were impossible to subdue even with the proclamation of an independent republic in 1960. They culminated in a coup initiated by the Greek military dictatorship (1967–1974) which resulted in the intervention by Turkey (1974). *De facto* this led to the splitting of the island into two parts. The resulting resettlements and the destruction and looting of antiquities have caused the almost complete disappearance (with the exception of a few communities) of Greek culture and language in the occupied northern part of the island. In the south, the only Republic of C. that is recognized by international law, Greek culture was consolidated completely as being the exclusive basis of national identity.

For the modern Greek population the continuing existence of the Greek language from the Mycenaean era right through to the present and the profession of the Orthodox faith are the decisive factors in their sense of Greek identity. The location of the island and its distance from the Greek mainland meant that C. occupied a marginal position that, depending on the respective ruling powers, led to the long duration of the various acculturation processes. The connection with the Aegean world from the 3rd millennium onwards profoundly shaped the Greek element of C. on a linguistic and cultural level (e.g. the continued existence of the Cypriot syllabary until the 3rd/2nd cent. BC or the archaic political structure with semi-autonomous local rulers that continued right through to the Ptolemaic period). Several inscriptions attest to the existence of non-Greek idioms until the Hellenistic period and reflect an enduring ethnic diversity, although the Greek language component always predominated. During the Hellenistic and Ottoman periods Greek remained the main language of the island. The disappearance of a system of autonomous kingdoms opened the way for the city state. With its annexation by Rome (in 58 BC), Cyprus became a senatorial province; it retained this status until the reign of Diocletian. In late Antiquity, C. was a province of the eastern imperial prefecture and with Justinian it fell under the jurisdiction and power of the *quaestor exercitus* (536). Justinian declared the autocephaly of the Cypriot church, justified by the existence of a local hierarchy of the early Church (325) and the tradition of the mission of the apostle Barnabas. Since then autocephaly has been regarded as a guarantee of independence and as the major mark of Greek identity on the island. In Byzantine times, C. had the status of a colony and was considered a solely agrarian area. Despite the subjugation to Rome dictated in the *Bulla Cypria*, Latin rule (1191–1489) was incapable of eliminating the Graeco-Byzantine sense of identity of the Orthodox Church of C., which regained its autocephaly with the Ottoman conquest of 1571. The Byzantine elite and some of its local supporters moved to Constantinople after the conquest by Richard the Lionheart (1191). This exodus increased after the Fourth Crusade (1204), then to Nicaea, as is attested by Patriarch Gregorios of C., who was one of the most important figures in the tradition of the Classical texts during the Palaeologan renaissance.

→ Cyprus

1 C. N. CONSTANTINIDES, R. BROWNING, Dated Greek Manuscripts from Cyprus to the Year 1570, 1993 2 B. ENGLEZAKIS, Studies on the History of the Church of Cyprus 4th–20th Centuries, 1995 3 A. GAZIOĞLU, The Turks in Cyprus, 1990 4 J. HACKETT, A History of the Orthodox Church of Cyprus, 1901 (repr. 1972) 5 G. HILL, A History of Cyprus, Cambridge, 4 vols., 1940–1952 6 C. P. KYRRIS, Greek Cypriot Identity, Byzantium and the Latins 1192–1489, ByzF 19, 1993, 229–248 7 T. B. MITFORD, Roman Cyprus, in: ANRW II, 1980, 1285–1384 8 I. PÉREZ MARTÍN, El patriarca Gregorio de Chipre y la transmisión de los textos clásicos en Bizancio, 1996.   P. BÁDENAS DE LA PEÑA

II. EDUCATION AND RESEARCH

Under Turkish rule the Orthodox Church had sole responsibility for the education of the Greeks. The influence of the Latin Church on C. gradually decreased; nonetheless, the sharp decline in the population of the island (mid 17th cent.) and the social and political unrest that reached its peak in the 2nd half of the 18th cent. did not allow for the development of any significant cultural life before the beginning of the 19th cent. The establishment of the first Greek high school (1812) in the capital of Nicosia, on the initiative of Archbishop Kyprianos (1810–1821) who had studied in Wallachia, signaled a fresh start. Since the Greek struggle for freedom and the foundation of the Greek national state (and in spite of repeated disappointments as a result of Greek diplomacy with respect to the question of the political future of the island), C. has been receiving much ideological stimulus from Greece that has been definitive for the national consciousness of the Cypriots. In the 19th cent. the educational ideals on C. remained largely oriented towards the humanities and classics, as in Greece, and contrary to the more practically oriented tendencies of the British. The desire for union with Greece (*enosis*) that arose in connection

with Greek irredentism after the arrival of the British (1878) increasingly became an explicit goal of the Church and of conservative and sometimes also of liberal and socialist politicians. This turned the education system into an area in which the opposing interests of the British and the Cypriots clashed.

The *Chronological History of the Island of C.* (1788), written and published in Venice by the Archimandrite Kyprianos, was the first synthetic historical monograph written in Greek during the period of Turkish rule and is one of the central works of the Greek Enlightenment. Until A. Sakellarios' *Kypriaka* (or *The Geography, History and Language of the Island of C. from the Beginnings to the Present*, Athens 1891; the first two of a total of three volumes had already been published in 1854/55) no account of Cypriot Antiquity existed that equalled the history of the Lusignan period by L. de Mas Latrie. In the spirit of his contemporary, Paparigopoulos, Sakellarios attempted to discuss all periods of Cypriot history uniformly, while at the same time aiming to capture the 'national essence' of the Greek population of the island. In this way he contributed to the emergence of a Cypriot ethnology in whose further development the two journals *Kypriaka Chronika* (1923–1937) and *Kypriakai Spoudai* (1937–1968) later played an important part.

While interest in the island even before it was surrendered to the British had led to the drawing up of maps of a quality which went far beyond that of contemporary Mediterranean cartography, the first archaeological research did not even meet the standards of 19th-cent. archaeology. For Luigi Palma di Cesnola, the American ambassador on C. (1865–1876), the discovery and sale of antiquities were a means of personal enrichment; today most of his collection is housed in the Metropolitan Museum of Art in New York. The work of the amateur archaeologist Max Ohnefalsch-Richter (1878–1890) and the British excavations of the 19th cent. also aimed to discover artefacts rather than research the past. The finds in the Metropolitan Museum and in the Cyprus Archaeological Museum, which was founded in 1883, were catalogued on the initiative of John Myres (in 1899 and 1914). The first organized mission that laid the foundations for further systematic research was the Swedish Cyprus Expedition led by E. Gjerstad (1927–1931). It aimed to document systematically the history of the island from the Late Stone Age to the Imperial period. J. Stewart developed a typology of Cypriot ceramics of the early Bronze Age. This paved the way for further research into Cypriot ceramics and sculpture, which, in the 2nd half of the 20th cent., promoted an understanding of the historical and cultural development of the island in prehistory and early history. Systematic archaeological research on the island was supported particularly by the foundation of the Department of Antiquities (1935) which contributed to the rapid development and internationalization of Cypriot archaeology by inviting numerous foreign missions. Its directors included A. H. S. Megaw (1935–1960), P.

Dikaios (1960–1963; previously curator of the Archaeological Museum) and V. Karageorghis (1963–1989), who distinguished himself by his active excavation work and numerous publications and also by his organizational work and regular publication of the *Report of the Department of Antiquities, Cyprus*. The A. G. Leventis Foundation, which generously supports research and restoration work, the Pieridis Foundation and the Pieridis Museum in Larnaca, and the Numismatic Museum of the cultural foundation of the Bank of Cyprus (founded in 1995) are among the private institutions that have been great benefactors of Cypriot archaeological research.

→ Cyprus

1 P. Aström, A Century of International Cyprological Research, 2000   2 V. Karageorghis, Cypriote Archaeology Today. Achievements and Perspectives, 1998   3 V. Karageorghis (ed.), Archaeology in Cyprus 1960–1985, 1985   4 P. Kitromilides, Tradition, Enlightenment and Revolution, Diss. Harvard 1978   5 Archimandrite Kyprianos, Ἱστορία χρονολογικὴ τῆς νήσου Κύπρου, 1971 (repr.)   6 G. Loukas, Φιλολογικαὶ ἐπισκέψεις τῶν ἐν τῷ βίῳ τῶν νεωτέρων Κυπρίων μνημείων τῶν Ἀρχαίων, Athens 1874   7 Th. Papadopoullos (ed.), Ἱστορία τῆς Κύπρου, 1995ff.   8 P. Persianis, Πτυχὲς τῆς ἐκπαίδευσης τῆς Κύπρου κατὰ τὸ τέλος τοῦ 19ου καὶ τὶς ἀρχὲς τοῦ 20 αἰ., 1994   9 A. Sakellarios, Κυπριακά, ἤτοι γεωγραφία, ἱστορία καὶ γλῶσσα τῆς νήσου Κύπρου ἀπὸ τῶν ἀρχαιοτάτων χρόνων μέχρι σήμερον, 1991 (repr.)   10 A. und J. Stylianou, The History of the Cartography of Cyprus, 1980.   ANTONIS TSAKMAKIS

Czech Republic
I. Antiquity in the Medieval Culture of Bohemian countries   II. Antiquity and Humanist Culture in Bohemian Lands   III. Reception of Antiquity in the Latin Literature of Bohemian Lands in the 17th and 18th Cents. (1620–1770)   IV. Ancient Traditions in 19th and 20th Cents. Czech Culture   V. History of the Study of Antiquity

I. Antiquity in the Medieval Culture of Bohemian countries
In the Middle Ages, knowledge of Antiquity found its way to the countries of the Bohemian Kingdom only indirectly and through intermediaries. The spread of this knowledge was largely due, on the one hand, to Bohemians educated in foreign countries who, after completing their studies, brought home ancient literary works or books dealing with the problems of Antiquity and, on the other hand, to those who spent time in foreign countries as members of ecclesiastic or secular missions. Antiquity was reflected more or less passively in the Bohemian environment and, of course, as it was perceived at the time. From his studies in Liège, Cosmas, dean of Prague's cathedral chapter (*c.* 1045–1125), brought with him numerous quotations from ancient authors as well as information from Roman his-

toriographers, which he used in his groundbreaking work of Bohemian historiography, *Chronica Boemorum*. In the rhetorical school on the Vyšehrad of Prague, Master Jindřich Kvas (d. *c.* 1306, also known as Henricus de Isernia or Henricus Italicus), who was educated in Naples, introduced future chancellery officials to a series of ancient verses and names gathered together in the dictamina collections entitled *Formule epistolarum* and *Formule privilegiorum*. New literary works, often clearly influenced by Antiquity, were also brought to Czechia by personages who spent time in foreign countries, esp. at the Papal court. The needs of pastors and educators, as well as those of administrative officials were decisive in the selection of what was to become important.

It was not until the late 13th cent. that a wide range of ancient influences appeared in the Kingdom of Bohemia. They gained intensity under Emperor Charles IV., at the time when the Charles University, founded in 1348, placed higher demands on pastoral, monastery and municipal preparatory schools. In these schools, Aesopian fables were read in their ancient and medieval versions. The *Ezop*, a work in Old Czech verse based on the so-called 'Romulus' (350–500) and the 'Anonymous Neveleti' (second half of the 12th cent.), was composed in the first half of the 14th cent. The *Disticha Catonis* were translated in verse in the mid–14th cent., then transposed into prose in the early 15th cent. Knowledge of Latin improved gradually, while Greek was known only in fragments, transmitted through → Patristics. During the period of the House of Luxemburg (1310–1437), ancient as well as contemporary Latin MSS of ancient authors, together with ancient and more recent commentaries thereon, were brought into the country. The latter served as the basis for new national commentaries, including, for instance, commentaries on Horace's *Epistulae*, prior to 1378; on Seneca's *Declamationes*, between 1376 and 1380; on Prudentius' *Psychomachia*, near the end of the 14th cent.; and on Boethius' *Consolatio philosophiae* in 1417.

In the second half of the 14th cent. and the early 15th cent, Bohemia witnessed an interaction between the so-called → Renaissance of the 12th cent. and emerging Italian → Humanism. Several Central European revisions of works with ancient themes emerged. Eight clerics from Prague compiled a selection of several chapters from the exempla collections entitled *Gesta Romanorum* and *Historia septem sapientum* and retold everything in simple Latin for preachers. This was the origin of the *Gesta Romanorum mystice moralizata*, which were still being translated into Czech and German in the 14th cent. Further minor revisions gave rise to the *Gesta Romanorum mystice designata*, known today from 44 MSS and three German translations. Many ancient themes and their echoes can be traced in the exempla collections: for instance, in the *Tripartitus moralium* of Conrad of Halberstadt (b. after 1354), newly revised in Prague, or the→ Historie

VARIE MORALIZATE, written in Dog Latin in *c.* 1400. The Bohemian King Přemysl Ottokar II (1253–1278 was regarded as a new incarnation of Alexander the Great in the Old Czech *Alexandreis*, written in verse *c.* 1300 and modelled after the *Alexandreis* of Walter of Châtillon. Charles IV (1346–1378) and his son Wenzel IV (1378–1419) also claimed Alexander the Great as their model. In the last years of Charles' reign, the *Privilegium Alexandri Magni Slavis datum* was created as a dictamen. At the end of the 14th cent., version I³ of the *Historia de preliis* was translated into Czech; version I² was adapted by the scribe Macek in the monastery of Postoloprty *c.* 1400. In the second half of the 14th cent., the Trojan War in the tradition of Guido of Columna, dating from the year 1287, was skilfully adapted into Czech as *Kronika trojánská* and translated verbatim in the early 15th cent. Its first incunabulum, mistakenly dated to the year 1468 due to a typesetter's error, was regarded as the oldest Czech incunabulum.

When Petrarch declined to dedicate his work *De viris illustribus* to Charles IV, the pseudo-Burley's *Liber de vita et moribus philosophorum* was procured from Northern Italy and translated into Czech in 1509 and in 1591. Still in the 14th cent., a simplified Latin version arose in Bohemia for pastoral purposes, enriched by additional ancient quotations from various sources. This work has been preserved until today in 55 MSS; in all, this version was translated into Czech three times, together with the *Breviloquium de virtutibus antiquorum principum* by John of Wales (b. *c.* 1303) (end of the 14th cent., beginning and later 15th cent.).

SOURCES: 1 B. BRETHOLZ (ed.), Cosmae Pragensis Chronica Boemorum, 1923 (repr. 1980)   2 H. OESTERLEY (ed.), Gesta Romanorum, Berlin 1872 (repr. 1980)   3 W. DICK (ed.) Die Gesta Romanorum, Erlangen, Leipzig 1890   4 H. KNUST (ed.), Gualteri Burlaei Liber de vita et moribus philosophorum, Tübingen 1886 (repr. 1964, 1967)

LITERATURE: 5 Antika a česká kultura, Praha 1978   6 J. BAŽANT, The Classical Tradition in Czech Medieval Art, G. TURNER, T. CARLISLE (trans.), 2003   7 K. BOLDAN, Sbírka exempel Historiæ variæ moralisatæ v rukopisu Státní knihovny ČSR Praha VIII H 6, in: Miscellanea Oddělení rukopisů a vzácných tisků 5, 1988, 69–88   8 E. RAUNER, Konrads von Halberstadt O. P. tripartitus moralium, in: Studien zum Nachleben antiken Literatur im späten Mittelalter, 1989   9 A. VIDMANOVÁ, La formation de la seconde rédaction des Vite philosophorum et sa relation à l'œuvre originale, in: Medioevo 16, 1990, 253–272   10 Id., K Privilegiu Alexandra Velikého Slovanům, in: J. PÁNEK, M. POLÍVKA, N. REJCHRTOVÁ (eds.), Husitství, reformace, renesance, Praha 1994, 105–115.

ANEŽKA VIDMANOVÁ

II. ANTIQUITY AND HUMANIST CULTURE IN BOHEMIAN LANDS

The influence of → HUMANISM, which asserted itself in Bohemian lands beginning in the second half of the 15th cent., sparked a lively interest in a deeper knowledge of Antiquity. The Bohemian Humanists of this era, usually members of noble or bourgeois families who were devoted to the Catholic Church, undertook educational journeys to Italy and formed personal connections with the Italian Humanists. They were influenced particularly strongly by Enea Silvio Piccolomini and Philip Beroaldus. Upon returning to their homeland, they often devoted themselves to diplomatic or Church service and spread their inclination for Antiquity throughout the learned circles. They often founded extensive libraries, richly supplied with the works of ancient authors. Among the graduates of Italian universities were the important writer Johannes Rabensteinius, a friend of Enea Silvio and Bohemia's greatest Humanist Bohuslaus Hassensteinius of Lobkowicz, as well as his friend Augustinus Olomucensis, who rendered outstanding services to the spread of Humanism in Moravia. Both of them were in contact with Conrad Celtes.

The University of Prague long remained closed to this new intellectual movement. Wenesclaus Pisecenus, dean in the year 1508, strove for a rapprochement to the ideas of Humanism. However, he encountered a tenacious, hard-core resistance from the Scholastics, upon which he resigned from office and travelled to Italy as the companion of his student Sigismundus Gelenius, who was to become a famous philologist. The new type of education found its way only gradually into the universities, where the mid–16th cent. saw a parallel influence of Humanist and Reformation ideas. The primary goal of Bohemian students was now to enter German universities, especially Wittenberg. The Humanist Reformers, above all Melancthon and Erasmus, exerted a decisive influence on them. Back in the homeland, they were usually influential as head teachers of preparatory schools, as university professors or as Protestant pastors.

In the cities, they founded Humanist circles and libraries. Among patrons of Humanist literature, John the Older of Hodieow rendered particularly valuable services. He gathered Latin poets around him, whose works he published in collections entitled *Farragines* in 1561/62. Among his protégés were Sebastianus Aerichalcus, Petrus Codicillus, David Crinitus, Simon Ennius, Thomas Mitis, Thaddaeus Nemicus, Simon Proxenus and others. Foreign Humanists were also active in Rudolfine Prague (1576–1612), outstanding among them the Englishwoman Westonia.

The period following the Battle of White Mountain in 1620 was unfavourable for the further development of Humanism in Bohemia. The famous poet Johannes Campanus, last rector of the University of Prague, fought in vain for the university's survival. He died in the year 1622, shortly after the university was closed. Many Humanists, among them Wenceslaus Clemens and Iohannes Sictor, left their homeland and were active abroad, especially in England and the Netherlands.

In their works, among which poetry was predominant in later times, Bohemian Humanists cultivated ancient literary genres and imitated ancient authors and their metric conventions. Cicero, Seneca, Quintilian, Lucretius, Catullus, Tibullus, Propertius, Virgil, Horace, Ovid, Persius, Martial, Juvenal, Ausonius, Claudian and Sidonius Apollinaris were among their most important models. Following ancient rhetorical prescriptions, they wrote dialogues, diatribes, occasional poetry, topographies and propemptica. Minor forms, such as anagrams and epigrams, were particularly popular. They embellished their works with the ancient mythological apparatus, even when dealing with Christian themes. They used Latin primarily, Greek only rarely. However, Greek titles were favoured for Latin poems.

Wenceslaus Pisecenus had already stressed the importance of Greek. When knowledge of Greek later became important for the Biblical studies of Protestant-oriented Humanists, Matthaeus Collinus in particular became one of its patrons. The curriculum set up by Petrus Codicillus in 1586 for municipal Latin schools assigned an important role to Greek. Only a few Bohemian Humanists achieved the Humanistic ideal of a *vir trium linguarum*. One of them was Matthaeus Aurogallus, who associated with Hassensteinius in his youth and with Melancthon's approval was named professor of Hebrew at Wittenberg in 1521. Nicolaus Albertus a Kamenek did not obtain a professorship for this field at the University of Prague until 1611.

Knowledge of ancient languages made it possible for the Humanists to maintain a lively regional and international correspondence. Their letters, modelled after Cicero, were intended not only for their addressees but for the entire educated world. Epistolographic handbooks arose, whose authors included Augustinus Olomucensis and Rodericus Dubravius. Literary societies, whose founders included Conrad Celtes, offered another possibility for establishing connections. The invention of book printing aided the Humanists' publishing activities. Among the most productive publishers were Thomas Mitis, Georgius Melantrich and Daniel Adam.

The Humanists' scientific achievements were also notable and they counted historians, jurists, natural scientists and physicians among their number. Prominent historiographers included Johannes Dubravius, Martin Cuthenus and Procopius Lupacius, among others. Paulus Koldin and Viktorin of Všehrd were important jurists, while Thaddaeus Nemicus became famous as an astronomer and as the personal physician of Maximilian II. Through their activities, the Humanists contributed to the integration of the Bohemian countries into the European cultural community.

1 A. TRUHLÁŘ, K. HRDINA, J. HEJNIC, J. MARTÍNEK, Rukověť humanistického básnictví – Enchiridion renatae poesis, 1–5, Praha 1966–1982 2 Antika a česká kultura, Praha 1978 3 I. HLOBIL, E. PETRŮ, Human. a raná renesance na Moravě, Praha 1992 4 Id., Humanism and the Early Renaissance in Moravia, Olomouc 1999 5 P. WÖRSTER, Humanismus in Olmütz, 1994.   DANA MARTÍNKOVÁ

III. RECEPTION OF ANTIQUITY IN THE LATIN LITERATURE OF BOHEMIAN LANDS IN THE 17TH AND 18TH CENTS. (1620–1770)

In the aftermath of the defeat of the Bohemian estates at the hands of the Habsburgs in the battle on the Battle of White Mountain (1620), the Bohemian countries underwent a fundamental transformation, which was simultaneously political, religious and cultural. The loss of political influence by the urban estates, the forced emigration of the non-Catholic nobility and the urban educated classes, who had been the main supporters and guarantors of culture in Bohemia prior to the Battle of White Mountain, together with the influx of foreigners into the Kingdom of Bohemia, all yielded an increased penetration of foreign (primarily German and Romanic) influence into the Bohemian cultural realm.

Among those forced to leave their homeland because of their confession were the thinker and educational reformer Johann Amos Comenius, bishop of the Bohemian Brethren and Paulus Stransky, professor at the University of Prague and historiographer. Following the Battle of White Mountain, the Catholic educated priesthood replaced the Protestant intelligentsia. Through their educational institutions, modern, supra-international religious orders propagated a Latin Humanism of Romanic character throughout the lands under the Bohemian crown. Latin served as the means of communication in the Bohemian grammar schools, which were dominated entirely by Jesuits and Piarists during the period of the recatholicization of Bohemian lands and at Prague's Jesuit Carl-Ferdinand University. 17th and 18th cent. Latin was a mixture of the humanist transmission of the language, the style of ancient authors and medieval and modern Church Latin. The 'classical' Latin language of many humanists from the Baroque period was permeated by words and syntactical elements occurring in late and medieval Latin, many Latinized words derived from Greek, *hapax legomena* and instances of archaism and neologism.

The school curriculum that had been drawn up for all Jesuit grammar schools (the so-called *Ratio studiorum* from 1599 (→ JESUIT SCHOOLS) was effective in Bohemian territory as well. The educational system of the Jesuits and Piarists was based on time-tested ancient models, but also on the Church Fathers and perhaps on Latin humanist authors as well. The principles of Jesuit pedagogy can be characterised as Catholic-Humanistic. An important role in Jesuit education was assigned to the *imitatio bonorum*, or the imitation of literary authorities (*auctoritas scriptorum*). It was therefore primarily Cicero's works 'praelectiones Ciceronianae' that were read in the Jesuit grammar schools. In addition to historical works by Caesar, Sallust, Curtius Rufus and Livy, pupils learned selected and 'purified' poems by Ovid, Catullus, Tibullus, Propertius, Virgil and Horace; for rhetoric Cicero was once again used, along with Aristotle and Quintilian. Along with the obligatory Jesuit textbooks (Lat. grammar by Emmanuel Alvarus, the rhetoric of Cyprianus Soarius), teachers also used their own handbooks: the Jesuit Bohuslaus Balbinus, for instance, wrote the schoolbook *Verisimilia humaniorum disciplinarum* based on ancient and humanist poetics and rhetoric, which was also published at Leipzig by Christian Weise.

At the University of Prague, the subjects taught included philology, theology, philosophy, law, medicine, mathematics, logic, physics and astronomy. Rodericus Arriaga, one of the most prominent personalities from the peak of Jesuit scholasticism, surpassed all other theologians and philosophers of the 17th cent. Johannes Marcus Marci gained a European reputation in medicine and in the natural sciences. In the 18th cent., Josephus Stepling became pre-eminent in physics, astronomyand mathematics. Alongside the Jesuit University of Prague and the Jesuit college at Saint Clemens in the historical centre of Prague (the so-called Clementinum), several centres of Latin culture existed in Bohemia and Moravia at this time: the monastery of the Discalced (shoeless) Augustinians in the new town of Prague (Zderaz), the Premonstratensian monastery in Prague-Strahov, the Benedictine monastery at Raigern (Rajhrad)and the Cistercian monastery in Plass. The works of Mauritius Vogt, a member of the Cistercian order, reveal his encyclopaedic knowledge as a geographer, cartographer, geologist, monastery historiographer, music theorist and composer.

The literature of the Baroque period was predominantly religious-propagandistic and educational, resulting in a limitation of topics and genres. Baroque Latin literature (as is true for that written in Czech or German) followed the laws of rhetoric and was often written in accordance with an elaborate concept (e.g., the hagiographical texts by the priest Godefridus Ignatius Bilowsky, or the sermons by the Jesuit Caspar Knittel). The literary genres popular in Antiquity and in Renaissance Humanism were also cultivated in the period of 17th and 18th-cent. Humanism: for instance, the dialogue (Balbinus), the epigram (the Jesuits Balbinus and Sebastianus Labe, the Discalced Augustinian Aegidius a. S. Joanne Baptista), occasional poetry and *carmina figurata*. The stagings of Jesuit dramas, usually performed at great Catholic festivals, were important cultural events in the life of the community. The topics of Latin Jesuit theatre were varied: ancient history or mythology, Biblical stories, lives of saints (e.g. Johann of Nepomuk), contemporary events. Its function was educational, anti-Reformand propagandistic *not excluding anti-Lutheran or anti-Semitic tendencies, among others*. The dramas of some Bohemian Jesuit playwrights were printed (Carolus Kolczawa, Bernardus Pannagl). Poets often worked with a mythological apparatus that imitated Antiquity. In landscape descriptions, for instance, stylised landscapes were represented under the influence of bucolic poetry (Virgil's *Eclogues*, Ovid's *Metamorphoses*, etc.) and in the spirit of contemporary poetics. Poems were composed in classical metres (hexameters, elegiac distichs, iambic trimeters, etc.), but

also in forms of Christian poetry (hymns, litanies). Verse was often inserted into prose works (poetic topographical descriptions in the hagiographic works of Balbinus and in the topographical and geological works of the Cistercian Mauritius Vogt, spiritual lyrics in the sermons of the Jesuit Joannes Kraus). Among the most popular prose genres were sermons, laudatio (esp. university discourses), *elogia* and letters. Historiography and hagiography, often with strongly patriotic tendencies, experienced a great upswing. Of Bohemian historiographers writing in Latin (Thomas Pessina a Czechorod, Georgius Crugerius, Joannes Florianus Hammerschmidt, among others), Bohuslaus Balbinus was influenced most strongly by ancient historians and humanistic Latin authors (Livy, Tacitus and Justus Lipsius among others).

1 I. ČORNEJOVÁ, Tovaryšstvo Ježíšovo. Jezuité v Čechách (The Society of Jesus. Jesuits in Bohemia), Praha 1995 2 Id. (ed.), Dějiny Univerzity Karlovy (History of the Charles University), vol. II: 1620–1802, Praha 1996 3 Z. KALISTA, České baroko (The Bohemian Baroque), Praha 1941 4 Id., Česká barokní gotika a její žďárské ohnisko (The Bohemian Baroque Gothic and its focal point in the Saar), Brno 1970 5 A. KRATOCHVIL, Das böhmische Barock, 1989 6 J. KUČERA, J. RAK, Bohuslav Balbín a jeho místo v české kultuře (Bohuslav Balbín and his place in Czech culture), Praha 1983 7 Z. POKORNÁ, M. SVATOŠ (ed.), Bohuslav Balbín und die Kultur seiner Zeit in Böhmen, 1993 8 M. SOUČKOVÁ, Baroque in Bohemia, 1980 9 S. SOUSEDÍK, Filosofie v českých zemích mezi středověkem a osvícenstvím (Philosophy in Bohemian lands between the Middle Ages and the Renaissance), Praha 1997 10 J. TŘÍŠKA, Studie a prameny k rétorice a k universitní literatuře (Studies and sources for rhetoric and University literature), Praha 1972.   MARTIN SVATOŠ

IV. ANCIENT TRADITIONS IN 19TH AND 20TH CENTS. CZECH CULTURE
A. THE PERIOD OF 'NATIONAL REBIRTH' (1770–1850) B. SECOND HALF OF THE 19TH CENT. TO 1918 C. THE SO-CALLED 'FIRST REPUBLIC' (1918–1938) D. 1938–1989

A. THE PERIOD OF 'NATIONAL REBIRTH' (1770–1850)
Czech culture used Antiquity as an instrument to fulfil its interior needs. In literature, ancient stylisation confirmed the poet's status as an 'elect', in contact with supra-personal and essentially sacred values. The philological character of this culture was bolstered by translations from foreign languages, as a kind of appropriation of the original. Translations of ancient literature became high points of the translator's art. Anacreontic and bucolic poetry flourished; *metra horatiana* (like the ideal of a life *procul negotiis* and of *aurea mediocritas*) characterised the beginnings of lyric poetry; lyric and epic poetry alike were saturated with ancient themes; and the dispute over the character of Czech verse found its expression in the controversy between the representatives of accentuated and quantitative prosody (→ VERSIFICATION).

Milota Zdirad Polák (1788–1856) wrote the first modern Czech travel description. His journey to Italy (1820) yielded many remarkable insights into cultural history *a report on his visit to → POMPEII, an interest in architecture, ancient art and epigraphy, and a wealth of reminiscences of ancient literature, esp. Virgil.*

B. SECOND HALF OF THE 19TH CENT. TO 1918

Architecture, fine arts, aesthetics and physical education: the neo-Renaissance style was chosen for monumental public buildings as well as for representative personal estates. These buildings, reminiscent of the peak of the French or Italian Renaissance (Palladio), could not dispense with tectonic and ornamental elements and motifs of ancient origin.

Josef Zítek (1832–1909), the originator of the National Theatre project and the Rudolfinum in Prague, as well as of the Mühlbrunn colonnade in Karlsbad and the Weimar Galley, together with his collaborator Joseph Schulz (1840–1917) who independently designed the buildings of the National Museum and the Museum for Applied Art, enriched their knowledge of Greek and Roman architecture through studies in Italy. The use of ancient elements became such an expressive component of municipal buildings that one may speak of an inflation of the 'ancient style'. The representative character of the buildings of that period was reflected in their decorative sculptures and paintings. Bohuslav Schnirch (1845–1901) created statues and reliefs inspired by ancient mythology (Apollo and the Muses on the balustrade above the entrance loggia of the National Theatre, the three-horse chariot of Nike on its pylons). Vojtěch Hynais (1854–1925) designed the curtain of the National Theatre (representing the construction of the National Theatre with a winged genius hovering overhead), the lunettes in the Vienna Burgtheater and the painting entitled *The Judgment of Paris.* Joseph Václav Myslbek (1848–1922) also participated in the decoration of the National Theatre with his statues 'Drama', 'Opera' and 'Music' and strove for a synthesis of → CLASSICISM and (→ ROMANTICISM) in a new monumentalism. Here, the concept of Antiquity as a decoratively presented condition of utopian paradise was transformed into a fateful tragedy, which characterises the statues created for the parapet of the Viennese Parliament. *Constancy in attitude* refers to the canon of Greek sculpture, while *Devotion* continues the realistic and psychological expressiveness of Roman art.

Miroslav Tyrš (1832–1884), one of the most important theorists of this tendency and professor of art history at the Prague Technikum towards the end of his life, was one of the cofounders of the sporting association Sokol (1862). He promoted the application of the ancient ideal of kalokagathia in sports (studies: *The Olympic Festival*, 1869; *Laocoon, 1872.* He did not consider the neo-humanist dream of the harmony of mankind and perfected humanity (→ NEW-HUMANISM) as utopian, but saw in it a component of a functioning

society, whose goal was the preparation of each citizen for a free and joyful life (→ SPORTS); (→ PHYSICAL EDUCATION). Tyrš' system of gymnastics (derived from the exercises of the Greek army as described by Xenophon and Arrian), together with his scheme for public exercises at tournaments (slety) became a part of national rituals that were maintained until World War II.

Literature: Ancient tradition dominated the creative work of the writers affiliated with the journal *Lumír* and permeated all contemporary genres. This perspective spanned all of Antiquity, from Homeric Greece and Roman Antiquity to the period of Hellenism and the late Roman empire. Even peripheral spheres, such as Egypt, Judaea and Etruria, played a role. The relatively uniform perception of ancient subjects during the Renaissance period was now replaced by a great stylistic variety and Antiquity was treated in literary works in ways that were deeply solemn, melodramatic and tragic, as well as playful and comical and even burlesque and parodic.

Jaroslav Vrchlický (1853–1912), the most important representative of the *Lumír* group, created an image of humanity and its development in his cycle *Fragments of Epopoeia.* He combines an optimistic evolutionism with the ideal of active human beings living in harmony with a nature inhabited by ancient gods (in the epic *Hilarion*, 1882, in which an early Christian ascetic realises that the meaning of life lies in earthly existence) with scepticism towards the modern era. The ideal form of humanity of ancient Rome is here postponed to an unforeseeable future (*The Legacy of Tantalus*, 1888; *Bar Kochba*, 1897, a work about a small nation's battle for freedom). The authors entire corpus of reflective lyrical poetry is imbued with mythological motifs, with contradictory heroes such as Hercules, Odysseus, Prometheus, Sisyphus and Icarus, or the joyful figures of Erotes, Satyrs, Centaurs and Sileni, as well as Venus and Pomona and, above all, Pan, the erotic god of forests and pastures, who is considered as the 'soul of the world' and who teaches mankind to love life. Over 300 of his poems contain ancient material. Half of his dramas are oriented towards Antiquity: the tragedies *The Death of Odysseus* (1883), *Julian the Apostate* (1885) and *Eponina* (1896) and the comedies *In Diogenes' 'Barrel'* (1883), *Catullus Revenge* (1887), *The Ears of Midas* (1890) and *In Dionysus' Ear* (1900). Whereas here the author concentrated on rather unpretentious intrigues or commentaries on conversations, in the trilogy *Hippodamia* (*Pelops Courtship*, 1890; *Tantalus' Reconciliation*, 1891, *Hippodamias Death*; 1891 he sought to utilise the knowledge of ancient tragedies for structure, dialogue and monologue construction and in the first part, inspired by fragments of the plays of Sophocles and Euripides, even for the construction of the chorus. In its underscoring of fate and in the addition of music by Zdeněk Fibich, the trilogy comes close to Richard Wagner and represents the high point in contemporary efforts at creating a representative work of national drama. Although Vrchlický's connection to ancient tradition was indirect in many ways and conveyed through the modern works of French and Italian poets, he inspired an interest in Antiquity not only in an entire series of his epigones but in future generations as well).

Julius Zeyer (1841–1901) avoided Classical themes, with the exception of the five-part poem *Helena* (1881), written in hexameters and the fantastic story *The Opal Bowl* (1882), in which Socrates appears. His 'Renewed Images' (stories and novellas that paraphrase ancient sources) are primarily inspired by Greek myth (*Quinces*, 1890, on the love between Acontius and Cydippe according to Aristaenetus; *Stratonice*, 1892, after themes from Plutarch; *Evadna*, 1897, after Phlegon of Trallis) or by Roman myth (*Vertumnus and Pomona*, 1893, after Ovid). These prose texts, filled with effective expressions, metamorphoses and recognitions, are not mere copies of alien material. The author never sticks to his sources word-for-word, but enriches his main theme with leitmotifs, using them in a way reminiscent of the methods of the so-called mythological novel of the 20th cent. (see the novel *Jan Maria Plojhar*, 1891, transposed into the present; crucial here is the main theme of a mythical landscape, or a landscape with a historical memory, with episodes that foreshadow the main content).

With his cycle *The Conscience of the Times*, Josef Svatopluk Machar (1864–1942) aimed at representing the destiny of humanity from earliest times to the present, following the models of Victor Hugo and Vrchlický. In the first two books of the cycle (*By the Light of the Hellenic Sun*, 1906 and *Poison from Judaea*, 1906), he created an idealised picture of Antiquity as a world that proclaims earthly happiness and is oriented towards to the natural governance of reason, but is destroyed by Christian religion that suppresses natural spontaneity and hurls mankind into a cruel asceticism. His view of history, whose culmination he sees in Antiquity, is revealed in episodes from his private life, which alternate with vivid narratives recounted in monologues, dialogues, notes and letters, portraits of common people and great personalities. An atmosphere reminiscent of Antiquity is also evoked by free verse, various ancient metres (for instance, an imitation of the Sapphic stanza), rhetoric and a certain archaic flavour of syntactic structure. Above all, he is fascinated by Imperial Rome and the strong individual, who is capable of preserving his integrity. This point of view, partly influenced by Friedrich Nietzsche, also pervades the author's journalism (*Antiquity and Christianity*, 1919) as well as his travel descriptions (*Rome*, 1907; *Under the Italian Sun*, 1918), which constitute a passionate polemics against the church's interpretation of history.

The poet Jiří Karásek ze Lvovic (1871–1951), together with the writers surrounding the journal *Moderne Revue*, pronounced himself against Machar's idealised and didactic conception of Antiquity, because he found the opposition between Antiquity and Christianity artificially exaggerated. Against Machar's cool rationalism, he postulated the necessity to recreate Antiquity with more feeling. In the collection *Sodom* (1895), confiscated by the censors, which was shocking in its unveiling of taboo topics, Antiquity is provocatively represented as a world filled with passion and sensuality, which stands in contrast to the tedious banality of modern life, with its grey everyday reality. In the collection *Endymion* (1909), however, the supposedly Bacchanalian excesses are displaced by sadness caused by the loneliness and futility of love and human destiny. Its symbols are Pygmalion, Echo, Hyacinthus and Sappho.

Theatre: A series of dramas emerged in which individualism, scepticism and the doubts and hopes of the turn of the century were recast into the dream of a new titanism. Thus, Otakar Theer's tragedy *Phaethon* (1916) combines the longing of Helios' son with Promethean obstinacy.

C. THE SO-CALLED 'FIRST REPUBLIC' (1918–1938)

Theatre: The democratic climate favoured the emergence of satire, which found its place on the one hand in excellent stagings of Aristophanes' comedies (*Thesmophoriazusae*, 1926; *Peace*, 1933; *Birds, 1934* and on the other hand in the plays of the *Osvobozené divadlo* ('Liberated Theatre'). Jan Werich (1905–1980) and Jiří Voskovec (1905–1981), authors and protagonists of the 'Liberated Theatre', used events disguised in ancient dress in their plays *Caesar* (1932) and *The Donkey and the Shadow* (1933), while in the play *Heaven on Earth* (1936), they combined Renaissance comedy with the theme of Amphitryon. Their plays, filled with parody of the ancient world and renowned for their puns, aimed at a sharp criticism of individuals, society, literature and politics. Here, with reference to Aristophanic comedy, a special type of revue was created, similar to a parabasis, with lightly sketched characters, flexible plot and fantastical milieu, in which dialogue alternated with songs and slapstick scenes on the proscenium).

The scientist, translator and poet Otakar Fischer (1883–1938) wrote the dramatic poem *Hercules*, a drama of modern individualism influenced by *Faust* and Nietzsche and the tragedy *Slaves*, with Spartacus as protagonist (1925; → SLAVERY).

Architecture and fine arts: The Slovenian architect Josip Plečnik (1872–1957) enriched his monumental renovations of the Prague castle not only with Greek and Roman architectonic elements, but with Cretan and Mycenaean motifs as well. Ancient motifs can be found in the works by the painters Alois Wachsman (*Oedipus washing*, 1934; *Phaethon*, 1941; *The Judgement of Paris*, 1942), Josef Šima (*Return of Theseus*, 1933; *Orpheus' Despair*, 1942) and Emil Filla (*Hercules and the Lion*, 1938).

Music: Operas with ancient themes were created by Bohuslav Martinů (*The Soldier and the Dancer*, 1926–27, modelled after the Plautine *Pseudolus*) and Iša Krejčí (*Antigone*, 1933/34).

D. 1938–1989

The development of Czech culture was violently interrupted several times: through the occupation of Czechoslovakia in 1938, the Communist take-over in 1948 and the invasion of Warsaw Pact member states in 1968, with the result that Antiquity served a replacement function in the second half of the 20th cent. The literature of Antiquity offered the values lacking in contemporary art, so that under its cover problems were concealed that could not have been openly expressed, esp. during the period of the Protectorate and the 'normalisation'. An important function was served both by the publication of translations (the *Ancient Library* by the publishing house Melantrich during the Protectorate, the homonymous series by Svoboda Press, where a total of 67 vols. have appeared since 1969 and the five-volume selection of ancient prose by the publishing house Odeon), as well as popularising literature (*Encyclopaedia of Antiquity*, 1973; *Dictionary of Ancient Culture*, 1974; *Gods and Heroes of Ancient Legends* by Vojtěch Zamarovský, 1965, 1982, 1996).

Theatre: The performance of ancient plays reached an even broader cultural community. They were often used to introduce taboo topics and to clearly articulate ethical questions that troubled society. This task was fulfilled both by the 21 stagings of Sophocles' *Antigone* and by the variations on Sophoclean themes written by Milan Uhde (*The Whore from the City of Thebes*, 1964), Přemysl Rut (*Polygoné*, 1989) and Roman Sikora (*Sweeping away Antigone*, 1998) as well as by performances of Sophocles' *Oedipus Tyrannus*, or Euripides' *Iphigenia at Aulis* and *Troades*.

Important Classical-style performances are still engraved in the public memory, as are the innovative versions with superb scenic collages (*Oedipus – Antigone* at the 'Theatre behind the Gate', 1971; as well as Euripides' plays about the Trojan War in the 'Labyrinth Theatre', 1994). Yet the same is true of the minimalist representations with a strongly reduced set of characters (*Medea* at the 'Studio Forum', 1981).

Literature: Despite its success in the theatre, the traces left by Antiquity in modern literary production were neither lasting nor numerous. There is no literary movement that claims to follow Antiquity programmatically. The use of mythological or historical reminiscences is conditioned exclusively by the particular subject chosen by the author. A few authors have projected their fear of the development of the modern world, rushing towards a global catastrophe, onto Antiquity. This holds true for Vitězslav Nezval and his play *The Sun over Atlantis will set again today* (1956), for the lyrical-epic poems by František Hrubín (*The Metamorphosis*, 1958), Tomás Vondrovic (*Até*, 1975) and Vladimír Janovic (*The House of a Tragic Poet*, 1984). Quite unique is the reference to the ancient system of values in Jiří Kolář's *Epictetus of Vršovice* and in his peculiar poetics, which paraphrases the 53 chapters of the handbook by the Stoic Epictetus. The playful bilingual poetry collection of nonsense poems composed by Eugen Brikcius and Pavel Šrut, entitled *Cadus Rotundus* (A Round Barrel, 1993), belongs to the literature of curiosities.

Jarmila Loukotková contributed to the development of the historical → NOVEL with her tendentiously oriented trilogy about the Roman Slave revolts in (*Spartacus*, 1950; *The Struggle does not end with Death*, 1957; *For Whom the Blood*, 1968). The somewhat romantic novel (*There is no Roman People*, 1949, new version in 1969), set in Emperor Nero's time, whose hero is the poet Petronius and the novel about the life of the Roman dramatist Terence (*Laughing under the Mask*, 1977), were popular with readers. The historical fresco by Joseph Toman *After us, the Flood* (1963) presents finely-chased psychological portraits of the emperor Tiberius and the philosopher Seneca against a background of an eventful plot. The fictitious biography *Socrates* (1975) portrays the philosopher as the embodiment of human wisdom and as a forerunner of modern ideas about social equality.

Music: Important symphonic and vocal compositions were created by Vladimír Sommer (*Antigone*, 1957), Petr Eben (*Apologia Sokratus*, 1967) and by Joseph Berg and Alois Piňos, in modern musical versions of ancient material.

Fine arts: Jan Bauch arranged a series of ancient themes in the context of experiences in Greek and Italian landscapes (*Acropolis*, 1962; *Odysseus' Return*, 1968). The relation to ancient themes was less frequent in the sculptures by Olbram Zoubek (*Iphigenia* cycle, 1984–1986).

1 J. Jiránek, Zdeněk Fibich, 1963 2 O. Jiráni, Antická dramata J. Vrchlického, in: Sborník Společnosti Jaroslava Vrchlického 1921/3, 20–47; 1924/5, 22–40 3 K. Krejčí, Klasicistické tendence v literatuře českého obrození, 1958 4 Id., Umělecký model antiky v českém kulturním vývoji od obrození do současnosti, in: Antika a česká kultura, 1978, 309–327 5 Id., Doba národního obrození, in: Antika a česká kultura, 1978, 328–346 6 J. Ludví-kovský, Antické myšlenky v Tyršové sokolském a národ-ním programu, in: Tyršův sborník 16, 1923 7 A. Matěj-ček, V. V. Štech, Národ sobě. Národní divadlo a jeho umělecké poklady, 1940 8 E. Stehlíková, Tři setkání českÃ© dramatické tvorby s Plautem, in: Acta Universitatis Carolinae 1966, Philosophica et historica 5, 95–115 9 Id., Classical Themes in Czech Drama, in: Listy filologické 91, 1968, 49–54 10 Id., Jeopardized Civilization as Seen in the Mirror of Classical Myths, in: Acta Universitatis Carolinae 1970, Philosophica et historica 1, 73–78 11 Id., Proměna metamorfóz, in: Listy filologické 93, 1970, 59–63 12 Id., Na přelomu staletí, in: Antika a česká kultura, Praha 1978, 360–371 13 Id., Meziválečné období, in: Antika a česká kultura, Praha 1978, 372–382 14 Id., La neve a Firenze ossia Tradizione antica nell'opera di Julius Zeyer, in: Listy filologické 120, 1997, 332–341 15 Id., The Encounter of Theatre and Sculpture, in: Siew Dionizosa, 1997, 163–169 16 F. Stiebitz, Pojetí antiky u české dekadence, in: Práce II. sjezdu klasických filologů, 1931, 283–296 17 Id., Macharova antika, in: Naše věda 15, 1934, 209–214 18 K. Svoboda, Antika a česká vzděl-anost od obrození do první války světové, 1957 19 V. Štěpánek, Májové období, in: Antika a česká kultura,

1978, 346–350 20 Id., Lumírovské období, in: Antika a
česká kultura, 1978, 350–360 21 Z. K. Vysoký, Fische-
rův Herakles a řecká tragédie, in: Listy filologické 72,
1949, 69–79 22 A. Závodský, Tschechische Dramen auf
antiken Motive, in: Antiquitas Greco-Romana ac tempora
nostra, 1968, 313–332

ADDITIONAL BIBLIOGRAPHY: J. Bažant, Friedrich
Nietzsche in the National Theatre in Prague, in: Eirene
XXXVII, 2001, 40–61; D. Čadková, The New Oresteia
of Arnošt Dvořák and the Problem of Oresteian Adaptation, in: Eirene XXXIX, 2003, 7–16; E. Stehlíková,
Antigone and its Czech Audience, in: SKENIKA, Festschrift zum 65. Geburtstag von H.-D.Blume. Darmstadt
2000, 404–408; Id., Central European Medea, in: Medea
in Performance 1500–2000. Legenda, European Humanities Research Centre, University of Oxford 2000, 180–
190; Id., Productions of Greek and Roman Drama on the
Czech Stage, in: Eirene XXXVII, 2001, 71–160; Id.,
Czech Attempts at the Oresteia, in Eirene XXXIX, 2003,
30–48; Id., The encounter between Greek Tragedy and
two Czech Playwrights in the Sixties (J. Topol, M. Kun-
dera), in: Eirene XXXIX, 2003, 229–233

EVA STEHLÍKOVÁ

V. History of the Study of Antiquity
A. Classical Philology and Ancient History
B. Classical Archaeology

A. Classical Philology and Ancient History
1. 1780–1848: The Period of Enlightenment
2. 1848–1882: From the Year of Revolution
to the Czech University 3. 1882–1918: To
the End of World War I. 4. 1918–1948: Democratic Czechoslovakia 5. 1948–1989: The
Era of the Socialist Republic 6. Since 1989:
Return to Democracy

1. 1780–1848: The Period of Enlighten-
ment
Interest in Antiquity grew towards the end of the
18th cent., when the Czech language reawakened after
its repression during the Counterreformation. The first
translations (Pavel Josef Šafařík: Aristophanes' Clouds
in dynamic rhythm) and studies stem from Slovakian
students (at the time, Slovakian was identical to Czech),
who were active in the Jena Societas Latina. An important role was played by the newspapers, calendars,
almanachs and translations of poetry that made the
Czech public familiar with Antiquity. Joseph
Dobrovský used Greek for the study of Old Church
Slavonic. Professors at the University of Prague were
enthusiastic about new methods of interpretation (German: Karl Heinrich Seibt, August Gottlieb Meißner,
Czech: Jan Nejedlý). Nejedlý pointed to the possibility
of comparing Greek and Czech rhythm (1801). His
translation of the Iliad in dynamic rhythm followed
Dobrovskýs views.

The encounter with → New-Humanism inspired
new translations. The historian František Palacký discovered his love of Antiquity at the Preßburg Lyceum: it

manifested itself in his personal encounters with Friedrich Ritschl, Friedrich Wilhelm Thiersch and Johann
Gustav Droysen. His partial translation of Plato's Phaedrus (1828) was significant. However, the new generation (e.g. Josef Jungmann) preferred quantitative
rhythm in translation (e.g. of Moschus poem 3, in
1804).

2. 1848–1882: From the Year of Revolu-
tion to the Czech University
1854 saw the reform of Austrian grammar schools,
whereby Latin was replaced as the language of instruction by the national tongue. This marked the origin of
the German and Czech grammar schools. Since grammar school teachers were required to graduate from the
philosophical faculty, a chair for classical philology was
established at the University of Prague. This development led to a demand for new educational materials,
outstanding among which were a Homeric and a non-
Homeric dictionary by František Lepař (the student of
Georg Curtius).

Freedom of educational resulted in an increase in
nationalistic activities and tendencies. These became
more prevalent following April 1848, when instruction
in both national languages was authorised at the University. Somewhat later (1868), Czech students founded the Assocation of Czech Philologists (Jednota českých filologů), which is still active today as the Association of Classical Philologists (Jednota klasických
filologů). A broader influence was exerted by popularising works and translations; however, the translation
of Aristophanes' Frogs in dynamic rhythm represents
only an isolated case (Václav Bolemír Nebeský, 1870).

Scholarly activity is linked with the name Jan Kví-
čalas (1834–1908). L. Lange obtained a stipend for him
in Bonn, where he studied under Friedrich Ritschl
(1856–57). His first publication Contributions to the
Criticism and Exegesis of Euripides' Tauric Iphigenia
(Vienna 1858) already attracted attention. The Viennese Academy soon named him a corresponding
member (1867). In his Studies on Virgil (Prague 1878),
he focused particularly on alliteration and published
the collation of the Prague Virgil MSS. His works can be
found primarily in the Acts of the Viennese Academy. In
1862, he founded the Library of Greek and Roman
Classics (Bibliothéka klasikův; while in 1873, he became the editor of the first Czech specialist journal,
Listy filologické (Philological Pages), still published
today. He received his habilitation in 1859 and was
appointed dean in 1878. As a member of the Imperial
Parliament at Vienna (1880, he was intensely active for
the benefit of the Czech educational system. His motion
for the establishment of an independent Czech philosophical faculty within the framework of the University
was rejected by the German faction; this led to the independence of the Czech university at Prague, where
Kvíčala moved, together with Joseph Král (who habilitated in 1880).

3. 1882–1918: To the End of World War I.

Robert Novák (1853–1915) confined himself to grammatical and exegetical studies; his many emendations were based primarily on his erudition and wealth of inspiration. He published the monographs *Velleius Paterculus* (1892), *Livius* (1894) and *Ammianus* (1896). Joseph Král (1853–1917) created a wide-ranging oeuvre, in which he studied previously neglected areas (for instance, theatre) and took archaeological results into consideration. He devoted himself esp. to Plato (evaluation of the Viennese MS of the *Protagoras*), metrics and the study of rhythm. In an extensive work, he meticulously analysed all the examples of Greek poetry he had compiled, taking the twofold Greek accent – one musical, the other expiratory – as his starting-point. His work written in Czech (since its author wished to support Czech scholarship) met with only a lukewarm response, as did the posthumous excerpt, already obsolete, from his original work on Greek and Roman rhythmics and metrics (vol. 1–4, 1906–1915) *Contribution to Greek Metrics* (German version 1925). In his studies of Czech prosody, he acknowledged only the dynamic rhythm as the principle of translation. His translations (*Antigone, Electra*) were successfully performed at the Prague National Theatre. As a strict critic and defender of scientific truth, Král became involved in bitter disputes with Kvíčala and other scholars, whereupon Kvíčala founded the new journal *České museum filologické* (1895–1905).

In addition to philology, attention was also devoted to ancient history. Despite his many works on the Near East and Greece – in particular, his *History of the Medes and the Persians down to the Macedonian Conquest* (German version: vol. I, 1906; vol. II, 1910; vol. I–II 1968²) – Justin Václav Prášek (1833–1924) did not receive his habilitation. In 1899, František Groh (1863–1940) was habilitated for Greek epigraphy. His works written in Czech: *Topography of Ancient Athens* (1909, 1913) and *Greek Theatre* (1909, ²1933) were important in their time. Emanuel Peroutka (1860–1912) dealt primarily with the oldest period of Greece. His book *The Constitution of Greek States* (1916), based primarily on inscriptions, was published posthumously by Karel Svoboda. This period (1890) also saw the foundation of the Bohemian Emperor Franz Joseph Academy of Arts and Science (later the Czech Academy of Arts and Science or Czechoslovakian Academy of Science, since 1993 the Academy of Science of the Czech Republic). The philologists and medievalists who belonged to this academy initially supported primarily the cataloguing and edition of Latin written monuments from Bohemian lands and took charge of the edition of translations of ancient authors.

4. 1918–1948: Democratic Czechoslovakia

As early as 1919, two new universities were founded: the Masaryk University in Brno and the Komenský (Comenius) University in Bratislava. A university was also opened in Prague for Russian and Ukrainian immigrants. Contacts between Czech and German universities, however, were limited to individuals. Antonín Salač's efforts (late 1930s) to publish a common journal *Eunomia* met with only a limited response, especially after the German universities raised objections against the participation of its Jewish members (A. Stein, Victor Ehrenberg). (Only) two issues of *Eunomia* were published, thanks to the efforts of Salač and Theodor Hopfner. All Czech institutions of higher education in the so-called Protectorate of Bohemia and Moravia were closed in November of 1939 and almost all Czech professors were forced to emigrate from independent Slovakia. In 1941, Vladimír Groh, the professor of ancient history at Brno, was court-marshalled and shot. The German and Ukrainian universities were closed after the end of the war, because of their pro-Nazi activities.

Among scholars active at the Charles University were Otakar Jiráni (1879–1934, Roman literature), Karel Wenig (1878–1964, Greek literature), Bohumil Ryba (1900–1980, Middle Ages) and Karel Svoboda (1888–1960), a universal mind who dedicated himself in particular to ancient aesthetics (*L'esthétique d'Aristote*, 1927; *L'esthétique de saint Augustin et ses sources*, 1933, Spanish version Madrid 1958, Czech 1996) and later to the history of Czech study of Antiquity as well. His book entitled *Antiquity and Czech Culture from Renaissance to World War I* (Czech 1957) was considered suitable only for offset printing due to its descriptive character, so that it has remained almost unknown. His translations (Augustine, Pre-Socratics) are highly esteemed. In the field of ancient history, Joseph Dobiáš (1888–1972) dealt with the problems of the eastern Roman provinces and the Danubian countries. The classical archaeologist Antonín Salač (1885–1960) is known primarily as an expert on epigraphy (*Fouilles de Delphes* III, with G. Daux, 1932; *Some archaeological Monuments from East Bulgaria*, with K. Škorpil, 1928, in Czech; editor of the *SEG*).

At Masaryk University, F. Novotný (1881–1961) focused on problems of prose eurythmia, on Plato's work and on Latin grammar, esp. semantics: *The Eurhythmia of Greek and Latin Prose* (vol. I 1918; vol. II 1921), in Czech; *État actuel des études sur le rythme de la prose latine*, in: Eos, Suppl. 5, 1929; *Platonis Epistulae commentariis illustratae*, 1930; *Platonis Epinomis commentariis illustrata*, 1960; *On Plato* I–III, 1948, Czech version *O Platonovi*. In this colossal work, he endeavoured to present an overall portrait of Plato based on the philosopher's own statements. Marxist critics objected to the publication of part IV (Posterity); it did not appear until 1970 and in England in 1977 (*Posthumous Life of Plato*). This volume deals with Plato's impact and the reception of his teachings from Antiquity to the 20th cent. Novotný's translation of Plato's complete works, for which he even created a Czech Platonic terminology, is precise as well as elegant. Important instructional texts are his *Historical Grammar of the Latin Language* (1946–1955) as well as his significant contribution to the *Latin-Czech Dictionary* ([18]1980). Ferdinand Stiebitz (1894–1961) habilitated in ancient literature after a year's study in Berlin. His interests were focused on questions of inheritance, new papyrus finds of Greek lyrical poetry and problems of the New Testament. As a translator of ancient poetry, he loosened Král's rigorous rules for translation. His work included lively translations (*Oresteia, Antigone, Oedipus the King, Medea*, a carefully updated Aristophanes, esp. *Acharnaeans, Knights, Birds* and *Frogs*; reconstruction of the *Prometheus*), adaptations for radio (*Mercator, Menaechmi*, as well as Ovid's *Metamorphoses*, a selection of Greek lyric poetry, a selection from Demosthenes under the characteristic title *The Greeks' Last Battle for Freedom*) (1940), *The Golden Ass* by Apuleius and several biographies by Plutarch. His textbooks on Greek ([2]1967) and Roman literature ([3]1966) are highly esteemed.

Antonín Kolář (1884–1963) was active at Komenský University until 1942. His most important contributions included, among others, his monographs on metrics: *Logaoedics* (1933), *De dactyloepitritis* (1935) and *De re metrica poetarum Graecorum et Romanorum* (1947). His translations of Diogenes Laertius and of Cicero's *De natura deorum* are important. Jaroslav Ludvíkovský (1895–1984) was forced to leave the university in 1939 and became professor at Brno. Following his important monograph on the Greek adventure novel (in Czech: *Řecký román dobrodružný*, 1925), in which he pointed to trends and elements that are attributed to the lower classes of the population in modern literature, he dedicated several works to the ancient tradition of Bohemia and Slovakia. Among his translations, that of Epicurus is particularly worth mentioning. The first Slovakian philologist to come to the university (in the late 1930s) was Miloslav Okál (1913–1996), who in 1943 published a work on Seneca and the apostle Paul which was rather bold for the circumstances of its time.

The curriculum at the Palacký University in Olomouc, founded after the war, was organised by Antonín Kolář. The following scholars were appointed as lecturers: L. Varcl (religion, papyrology), Julie Nováková (Roman literature), Karel Janáček (grammar) and O. Pelikán (classical archeology).

5. 1948–1989: THE ERA OF THE SOCIALIST REPUBLIC

As a result of the political changes (1948), Latin was henceforth taught only as an optional subject at grammar schools, leading to a decline of the classical languages. More important chairs were established in University faculties, led by appointed heads who were also responsible for the ideological aspect of instruction. The first heads were professors Antonín Salač (Prague), Václav Machek (Brno), Karel Janáček (Olomouc) and Miloslav Okál (Bratislava).

In the newly founded academy, a cabinet for Greek, Roman and Latin studies was established (led by Antonín Salač; the scientific assistant was Růžena Dostá-lová) and charged with supervision of academic work. It was responsible for cataloguing and publishing national written monuments in Latin and organised working conferences. Salač and George Thomson (Birmingham) instigated the founding of an international organisation of researchers on Antiquity from socialist countries, under the name 'Eirene'. It organised conferences in various socialist countries that were also attended by important researchers from western countries. The cabinet published the journals *Listy filologické* and *Eirene* and developed an intensive cooperation with the Akademie der Wissenschaften in Berlin, largely thanks to Salač and Johannes Irmscher. Scholars from the ČSSR (Jan Burian, Karel Janáček, Václav Marek, Jan Pečírka, Ladislav Vidman and others) contributed to such publications as the *CIL*, *PIR* and *Bibliotheca Teubneriana*. The universities themselves also published scientific journals and monographs. While instruction in Classical languages declined, the art and science of translation continued unabated: suffice it to mention the series *Ancient Library* (*Antická knihovna*, more then 60 vols. so far).

6. SINCE 1989: RETURN TO DEMOCRACY

Despite many efforts, the status of instruction at grammar schools has changed little. In institutions of higher learning, Classical philology continues to be taught at Prague, Brno and Olomouc; only Latin is taught at the new university in České Budějovice. In isolated cases, habilitation or professorships were made possible to those to whom they had previously been denied for political reasons. Although the division into the Czech Republic and Slovakia has led to an independent development in both countries, contacts continue to exist unimpeded. International relations are developing on a larger scale; several libraries have been enriched by valuable publications and many authors have made use of the opportunity to publish in the West. In addition, several reference works have been translated into Czech. The cabinet of the Academy has partially limited Classical studies in favour of late Latin.

1 A. BARTONĚK, History and Bibliography of Classical Scholarship in Czecho-Slovakia, 1900–1987, in: The Classical Bulletin, 68, 1992, 39–62   2 I. LISOVÝ, Stručná česká bibliografie antiky, in: Menerva 2, 1999, 116–119 (A bibliographical index of Czech publications, as well as of individual representatives of Czech Classical Studies) 3 D. ŠKOVIERA, De septuaginta annis studiorum antiquitatis in Universitate Comeniana Bratislavensi, in: Auriga 1994–1995, 13–19 (in Slovenian)   4 MARTIN SVATOŠ, Česká klasická filologie na pražské univerzitě 1848–1917 (působení Jana Kvíčaly a Josefa Krále), 1995 (Bohemian classical philology at the University of Prague: the influence of Jan Kvíčala and Josef Král)   5 K. SVOBODA (ed.), Bibliografie českých a slovenských prací o antice za léta 1901–1950, 1961   5 Id. (ed.), Bibliografie českých prací o antice za léta 1775–1900, 1947   6 L. VIDMAN (ed.), Bibliografie řeckých a latinských studií v Československu za léta 1951–1960, 1966 (Bibliographies for later periods, appearing annually or bianually, are noted in the works by A. Bartoněk und I. Lisový)

ADDITIONAL BIBLIOGRAPHY: M. SVATOŠ, Česká klasická filologie na pražské univerzitě 1848–1917 (působení Jana Kvíčaly a Josefa Krále), 1995; J. HAVRÁNEK (ed.), Dějiny univerzity Karlovy (History of the Charles University) 3, 1802–1918, 1997; ID. (ed.), Dějiny univerzity Karlovy (History of the Charles University) 4, 1918–1990, 1998
RADISLAV HOŠEK

B. CLASSICAL ARCHAEOLOGY

Several plaster collections emerged at the turn of the 18th and 19th cent., the largest of which was established by the Society of Patriotic Friends of Art. The first special courses on ancient art were taught by Franz Lothar Ehemannt at the University of Prague from 1775, then by Jan Erazim Vocel (from 1850/51). The largest collection of antiquities in Bohemia in the 19th cent. was put together by Baron Franziskus Koller (1767–1826) in his Obříství castle near Mělník. His widow, however, sold it to the Prussian king.

A chair for Classical Archaeology was established in Prague in 1872. The first person appointed to it was Otto Benndorf, who remained until 1879. The establishment of the plaster collection in the years 1872/73 was one of his achievements, along with a successful teaching career. His successor, Eugen Petersen, stayed in Prague for only a short time. After the university was divided in 1882 (at which time the collections and libraries remained with the German branch at that time), Miroslav Tyrš (1884), who had habilitated with a study of the Laocoon, taught at the Czech branch, while W. Klein (1850–1922) taught at the German branch from 1885 to 1922. He reconstructed many ancient groups and statues in the Prague plaster museum, with the help of the sculptor Joseph Václav Myslbek. Tyrš' successor at the Czech branch was Hynek Vysoký (1860–1937), who initially habilitated in classical philology. His main works were devoted to antiquities. J. Camillo Praschniker worked as Klein's successor for a few years (1923–1930), followed by Alois Gotsmich until 1945.

After the end of World War I, Vojtěch Birnbaum (1877–1934) came from Vienna to Prague, where he devoted himself to early Christian architecture. Václav Dobruský, the three Škorpil brothers and their cousin Konstantin Jireček made their names as archaeologists in the Black Sea area. Dobruský (1858–1916) founded and directed the Bulgarian National Museum in Sofia from 1893. He retired in 1910, then taught in Prague

for a few more years. Konstantin Jireček, who lived in Bulgaria from 1879 to 1884, concerned himself especially with the topography and epigraphy of that country. Of the brothers Škorpil, Karel (1859–1944) and Hermenegild (1858–1923) were diligent excavators and founders of museums, especially Karel Škorpil, the founder of the Museum of Varna. Václav (Vjačeslav) Škorpil (1835–1918) was founder and, from 1901, director of the Museum of Kerč. The German-Bohemian Anton Gnirs (1873–1933) led Roman excavations in Istria and investigated the Roman camps in southern Moravia and in → SLOVAKIA.

Joseph Ćadík (1891–1979) succeeded Vysoký in 1934. He wrote outstanding works on Greek and Roman glass, jewellery and vases. He barely escaped death on two occasions: first, when he was condemned to death for his activity in the resistance in late 1944, then for the second time in 1950, because of an 'espionage affair'. His assistant and later lecturer and professor Růžena Vacková (1901–1982) had a similar fate. Her most important works are devoted to art historical interpretations of the theatre stage and the general history of style (the last book could be published only after 1989).

Following the detention of the two professors in 1951, the Prague Institute was led until 1958 by Antonín Salač, an important epigraphist also known for his excavations at Cyme, Samothrace and Bulgaria. His assistant was Jiří Frel, an outstanding authority on Greek art, later appointed as professor. He has been working abroad since 1969. In 1985 Jan Bouzek was appointed as lecturer and in 1992 as professor; he led excavations in Beirut, Pistiros in Bulgaria, Mušov and South Moravia, among other places.

In 1945, a seminar of Classical archaeology was founded at Masaryk University in Brno as well, in which Gabriel Hejzlar (1894–1972), Oldřich Pelikán (1913–1987), R. M. Pernička, J. Hrubý and Jan Beneš (1934–1977) were active. The seminar undertook small-scale excavations in South Moravia; Beneš contributed studies on the deployment of Auxilia in Dacia and Moesia. The seminar is currently led by Marie Pardyová. The seminars of Classical archaeology at Olomouc and Bratislava existed for only a short time.

1 J. BOUZEK, Die Geschichte der klassischen Archäologie in den Böhmischen Ländern, in: Eirene 33, 1996, 64–80 (with bibliography). JAN BOUZEK

D

Dance

A. Subject Area/Overview B. Beginning of the 20th Cent.: On the Beauty of the 'Natural Body' C. Mid–20th Cent.: Mythology as a Mirror of Psychic Depths D. End of the 20th Cent./Beginning of the 21st Cent.: Endless Renaissances

A. Subject Area/Overview

The reception of Greek Antiquity in dance reached its acme at the beginning of the 20th cent. in Europe and the USA The first studies of movement, undertaken as early as the end of the 19th cent., drew on the classical Greek body image. In 1885, the American G. Stebbins published her theory of movement [25] which was based on the system of motion pedagogy (aesthetic calisthenics) developed by F. Delsarte. Delsarte linked the idea of a dynamic body image with the static pose of ancient sculptures. These guidelines for posing according to ancient models shaped the work of the dance pioneer I. Duncan, among others. In 1895, M. Emmanuel published his chronophotographic analysis of Greek dance in France [10]. In his comparison of corporeal depictions in Greek vase paintings and poses from the technical movement system of ballet, Emmanuel attempted to decode ancient dance. For each of the above, interest in ancient art went hand in hand with the search for naturalness, individuality and authenticity of human physical expression.

The term → Décadence which emerged around 1900, with reference to dance was clearly defined and alluded exclusively to classical ballet, as opposed to its use in literature or the fine arts. 'Decadent' ballet was often a target for the dance reformers of the time because they regarded the classical vocabulary of movement as unnatural and body-disfiguring. Besides the paintings of the Italian → Renaissance and the artworks of the Pre-Raphaelites that referred to them, collections of antiquities became the major source of inspiration for the representatives of new dance concepts (such as I. Duncan, A. Sacharoff, W. Nijinsky). They understood the representation of Antiquity as a depiction of natural beauty and naturalness, in the sense of a bodily image that had not yet been distorted by processes of civilization and the endeavours of modernity toward mechanization. Seen as the instinctive nature of humanity in the sense of F. Nietzsche [23], nature led to an accentuation of the archaic and Dionysian side of Antiquity. In this way, within classical ballet the adaptation of the Apollo-myth by G. Balanchine (*Apollo Musagète/Apollo*, premiere *Ballets Russes*, Paris) in 1928 became the key work of Neoclassicism in dance. In the second half of the 1940s, the reception of Antiquity was accorded central status in the work of the American choreographer M. Graham. At the end of the 20th cent. and at the beginning of the 21st cent., occasional choreographic works appeared which regarded ancient Greek depictions as a source of inspiration (e.g. those of B. Li) or were themselves citations of the dance-historical 'quotations' of Antiquity (e.g. those by M. Morris).

B. Beginning of the 20th Cent.: On the Beauty of the 'Natural Body'

In 1903, I. Duncan's essay *The Dance of the Future* [8] appeared in which she sought to outline her vision of the new dance. In it she made it clear that she did not seek to return to the dance of the Greeks but to elevate dance once more to a religious art, as it had been in Greek Antiquity. She studied the ancient collections in the British Museum in London and in the Louvre in Paris, as well as the painters of the Renaissance. She read Winckelmann and staged dance evenings, framed by lectures on the revival of dance on the basis of the ancient art. She danced in museums and at the ancient sites themselves. The topos of the artistic understanding of the educated classes accorded to dance the rank of an independent art with equal rights and, hand in hand with the dance reforms, sought new performance locations beyond the stage and backstage area which had been shaped by the theatre of illusions of the 19th cent. [4. 83]. Duncan's efforts to create a new body image were aimed at liberating the body and at dance as the experience of nature. Barefoot and without the corset that was still usual in ballet at that time, she danced dressed in a *peplos* and in this way freed the female body from everything that was constricting and disfiguring (Fig. 1). In numerous lectures and essays she referred to ancient Greek dance as the model for her art of dance. With her recourse to the ancient body as the ideal, she celebrated a natural body that is itself a cultural body [24. 53].

In classical ballet also, the depictions of Antiquity became the source of innovation in dance. In 1907, M. Fokine choreographed *Eunice* for the Ballets Russes. The model was an episode from H. Sienkiewicz's *Quo Vadis?* (1896). The movements (in a similar manner to Duncan's ballets) were based on ancient vase paintings. The dancers were dressed in Greek chitons. Performing barefoot was considered unseemly, so the dancers wore stockings painted with naked feet, and sandals on top. Fokine opened up the classical vocabulary of movement and combined it with unusual bodily images though, in contrast to Duncan, without breaking with the aesthetics of ballet. In 1912 he choreographed *Daphnis and Chloé* (Fig. 2), which still today stands in the shadow of W. Nijinsky' *Afternoon of a Faun*, performed in the same year by the *Ballets Russes*. Nijinsky drew inspiration not only from the bas-reliefs and paintings of Antiquity but also adopted the two-dimensionality of the depiction and applied this to the dancing figures which moved exclusively in horizontal, pose-like

Fig. 1: Isadora Duncan dancing
in the Theatre of Dionysus, Athens.
Photograph Raymond Duncan 1903

Fig. 2: Michel Fokine as Daphnis in
Daphnis and Chloé, c. 1912

motions in profile to the audience. Nijinky's enthusiasm for Antiquity was coupled with an analysis of the avant-garde art of the 20th cent. (Fauvism, Cubism and primitive art) [4. 79].

In Munich it was A. Sacharoff who saw in the body image of Antiquity new opportunities for expression in dance. In close collaboration with the *Münchener Künstlervereinigung* and in a creative exchange with Kandinsky, Münter, Jawlensky and von Werefkin, he choreographed in 1910, among others, his solo *Dionysian Worship*. By lining up poses, he brought to the stage what he had seen in the painting collections of Italy when he was a art student. Like I. Duncan before him, he did not directly cite Antiquity but its interpretations in the artworks of the Italian Renaissance (among others, works by Luca della Robbia) [4. 76].

C. MID–20TH CENT.: MYTHOLOGY AS A MIRROR OF PSYCHIC DEPTHS

In the 1940s there was great interest in the USA in ancient mythologies: the representatives of various fields of art had discovered C.G. Jung and his psychoanalytical studies as a source of inspiration (→ PSYCHOANALYSIS). In dance, the choreographies of M. Graham took as their focal point Greek mythology and its dramas, especially in the second half of the 1940s into the 1960s. As protagonists for her pieces, Graham repeatedly chose female figures from ancient subjects: e.g. her Medea interpretation *Cave of the Heart* (1946), her Ariadne interpretation in *Errand into the Maze* (1947), the Jocasta in *Night Journey* (1947) – a journey

into the past influenced by the theories of S. Freud, *Clytemnestra* (1958) or *Phaedra* (1962; Fig. 3). In contrast to Duncan at the beginning of the century, Graham went back to ancient material in order to illuminate Greek mythology from the perspective of the female figures who became human archetypes in her pieces. The emotional crisis of the respective female protagonist became the symbol of the potential of human beings to rise and fall. It was not so much the mythological plot but the psychological profile of the female protagonists that Graham wanted to have understood as representative of the collective feelings and desires of women [24. 90–91] and that stood at the centre of all her adaptations of ancient works. The language of movement in these pieces shows that Graham's own technique was pervaded by influences from ancient, Oriental and Asian theatre (such as the Nŏ and Kabuki Theatre). Echoes of Antiquity can be discerned above all in the two-dimensional movement performances and in poses reminiscent of ancient vase paintings. But in contrast with, for example, Nijinsky's *Faun*, the movements in Graham's pieces are never purely abstract and decorative but always the expression of an 'interior landscape' [18. 73], a synonym for the state of mind of the protagonist.

In Germany, M. Wigman, at the end of her creative career as a choreographer, turned for a short time to ancient themes: in 1947 she choreographed and staged Ch.W. Gluck's *Orpheus and Euridice* (1762) in Leipzig; among her *Choral Studies II* of 1953 was a piece entitled *Maenadic Rhythm*.

Fig. 3: Martha Graham and Bertram Ross in *Night Journey*. *Photograph Martha Swope, c. 1947*

D. END OF THE 20TH CENT./BEGINNING OF THE 21ST CENT.: ENDLESS RENAISSANCES

Ancient representations of dance, the image of beauty of the Greeks, but above all the depth of human drama in the traditional myths also remained a favourite source of inspiration in the further course of the 20th cent. and also continue as such at the beginning of the 21st cent. Their reception is not limited to classical ballet but is likewise to be found in the pieces of contemporary avant-garde choreographers. Frequently the pieces are themselves renderings of musical adaptations of ancient myths. Example: *Orpheus* by H. W. Henze, choreographed by W. Forsythe in Stuttgart (1979), R. Berghaus in Vienna (1986) and H. Spoerli in Basle (1988). As was already the case in Henze's production which followed the libretto by E. Bond, the myth of Apollo, Orpheus and Eurydice is transposed here to a undefined present time. Also still popular with choreographers is Gluck's *Orpheus and Euridice*. The opera probably saw one of its most famous dance performances in 1975 when it was staged by P. Bausch and her Wuppertal Dance Theatre. Other choreographers who repeatedly tackled Greek myths were M. Béjart (1958 *Orphée in Paris*; 1963 *Promethée* in Brussels; 1984 *Dionysos* in Paris – dedicated to Nietzsche, Wagner and ancient gods); J. Neumeier (1972, 1973 *Daphnis and Chloé* in Frankfurt/M., Hamburg; 1990 *Medea* in Stuttgart; 1995 *Odyssey*, co-production Hamburg and

Athens); J. Schlömer (1995 *Neuschnee in Troja*, his interpretation of the *Odyssey* in Weimar; 1995 *Oresteia* in Ulm; 1997 Ch.W. Gluck's *Orpheus and Euridice* in Basle) or M. Morris (e.g. 1983 *The Death of Socrates* in New York; 1988 *Orpheus and Eurydice* in Seattle; 1989 *Dido and Aeneas* in Brussels). In 1989, a representative of dance theatre again took up an ancient theme: J. Kresnik staged *Oedipus* with his dance theatre in Heidelberg. He placed the myth in the centre of a trilogy at whose start stands *Macbeth* and that ends with the figure of *Lear*. Sophocles' *Oedipus* was interpreted as part of the common theatre canon on the rise and fall of a hero.

In 1998, I. Ivo developed his dance theatre piece *Medea* for the Weimar National Theatre. The interpretation was based on H. Müller's play *Medeamaterial*, published in 1974. This is also a case of a 're-renaissance' of Antiquity.

An up-to-date example of such a 'reception of reception': *The Dream of the Minotaur*, choreographed by B. Li for the Comic Opera in Berlin in 2002 as a full-length ballet. Again, as in I. Duncan's case, above all the vase paintings and ancient sculpture, with their representations of the body, became the source of choreographic inspiration. Central was the idea of ancient art as the depiction of a classical and timeless aesthetic of the body that celebrates naturalness.

Common to all the above-named choreographic approaches is the attempt to apply ancient history to contemporary human and social problems. Dance in the 21st cent. cannot fall back upon ancient representations without also referring at the same time to its own developmental history and its relationship with the body depictions of Antiquity.

→ BODY, ATTITUDES TOWARDS; → NEO-HUMANISM

1 J. ACOCELLA, Mark Morris, 1993   2 C. W. BEAUMONT, Michel Fokine and his Ballet, 1945, 27–29   3 G. BRAND-STETTER, Die Inszenierung der Fläche, in: C. JESCHKE, U. BERGER, B. ZEIDLER, Spiegelungen, 1997, 147–163   4 Id., Tanz-Lektüren, 1995, 58–117, 182–206   5 M. BREMSER (ed.), International Dictionary of Ballet, 1993   6 A. DALY, Done into Dance, 1995   7 D. DUNCAN, C. PRATL, C. SPLATT, Life into Art, 1993   8 I. DUNCAN, The Dance of the Future, 1903   9 Id, My Life, 1927   10 M. EMMANUEL, La Danse Grèque antique d'après les monuments figurés, Paris 1895 (Eng.: The Antique Greek Dance, after Sculptured and Painted Figures (trans. H. J. BEAULEY, 1916)   11 M. FOKINE, Gegen den Strom, 1974, 112–118   12 Id., Über die Entstehung von 'Daphnis und Chloé', in: Programmheft Sächsische Staatsoper Dresden. Drei Ballette von John Neumeier. 12. Oct. 1996   13 R. Garis, Following Balanchine, 1995   14 R. GINNER, The Ancient Greek Dance and its Revival Today, in: The Dancing Times, June 1926, 245–249; July 1926, 355–359; August 1926, 450–453; September 1926, 541–545   15 M. GRAHAM, Blood Memory, 1991   16 E. JAQUES-DALCROZE, Le Rhythme, la Musique et l'Education, 1920 (Eng,: Rhythm, Music and Education, (trans.) H. F. RUBINSTEIN, 1921)   17 D. JOWITT, Time and the Dancing Image, 1988, 199–233   18 N. KAYE, Modern Dance and the Modernist Work, in: Id., Postmodernism and Performance, 1994, 71–89   19 E. KENDALL, Where She Danced: The Birth of American Art-

Dance, 1979   20 H. KOEGLER, Balanchine und das moderne Ballett, 1964   21 H. LINDLAR, Igor Strawinsky: Lebenswege/Bühnenwerke, 1994   22 J.-M. NECTOUX, Nachmittag eines Fauns, 1989   23 F. NIETZSCHE, Sämtliche Werke, 1980   24 J. SCHULZE, Dancing Bodies, Dancing Gender, 1999   25 G. STEBBINS, Delsarte System of Expression, 1885   26 E. STODELLE, Deep Song: The Dance Story of Martha Graham, 1984   27 W. WILLASCHEK, Musik ist tönende Bewegung, in: Anlage zum Programmheft Hamburger Staatsoper Daphnis und Chloé, 20.12.1985, 3–6

ADDITIONAL BIBLIOGRAPHY: L. B. LAWLER, The Dance of the Ancient Greek Theatre, 1964; S. LONSDALE, Dance and Ritual Play in Greek Religion, 1993; F. G. NAEREBOUT, Attractive Performances: Ancient Greek Dance. Three Preliminary Studies, 1997.   JANINE SCHULZE

Décadence 'Décadence', especially in literary criticism and theory, is a concept derived from the comparison of the decline of Imperial and late Ancient Rome with the stylistic characteristics of Rome's literary paradigms. Associated in Ch. Montesquieu's *Considérations sur les causes de la grandeur des Romains et de leur décadence* (1734) exclusively with the decline of the city of Rome and extended in 1750 by J.-J. Rousseau to that city's literature, which was for him both cause and symptom of the decline, 'décadence' becomes in D. Nisard's *Études de mœurs et de critique sur les poètes latins de la décadence* (1834) a pejorative term of the academic, conservative critiques of French romanticism (V. Hugo, A. de Vigny, Th. Gautier). However, since the publication of Ch. Baudelaire's *Notes nouvelles sur Edgar Poe* (1857), 'décadence' has become the central term and a positive concept for the self-understanding of the literary avant-garde and for modernity in general (St. Mallarmé, Th. Gautier, P. Bourget, Fr. Nietzsche, and A. Symons; → FIN DE SIÈCLE).

As early as Nisard, stylistic and technical characteristics become – alongside a content dominated by topics related to decay – defining components of decadence. Later, those characteristics remain definitive for Baudelaire and his followers. Such characteristics include linguistic artistry in syntax and semantics, an excess of description, a tendency towards nuance and detail for the sake of detail, unrestrained word and image choice, and the formative principle of decomposition.

In spite of the numerous stylistic implications that have grown out of the historical development of the concept, the present definition of 'décadence' has become more restricted so as to differentiate it from the concepts aestheticism, symbolism, impressionism and *Art Nouveau* (i.e. *Jugendstil*). Defining elements are: the isolated, artificial worlds of the crystalline (*paradis artificiels*), so distant from and hostile to nature; all that is precious and refined as well as the large cities with their excessive stimuli; literary protagonists marked by biological and genetic depravity involving a susceptibility to stimuli that is at once nervous, exaggerated and pathological; an addiction to reflection and the resulting inability to realize one's wishes. Its cult of beauty

and aesthetic aristocratism is often linked with moral corruption and a longing for death. Dominant types are the *femme fatale, fragile* and *enfant*, the prostitute (coquette and courtesan), the androgyne, the homoerotic figure, the dilettante and the dandy.

Noteworthy examples of decadent literature can be found in drama (M. Maeterlinck, O. Wilde) as well as in lyric (P. Verlaine), but prose is dominant, e.g. H. Bang's *Hoffnungslose Geschlechter* (1880), J.-K. Huysman's *À Rebours* (1884), G. d'Annunzio's *La città morta* (1898), *Il piacere* (1899) and *Il fuoco* (1900) and Th. Mann's *Buddenbrooks* (1901).

1 A. E. CARTER, The Idea of Decadence in French Literature 1830–1900, 1958   2 E. KOPPEN, Dekadenter Wagnerismus. Studien zur europäischen Literatur des Fin de siècle, 1973   3 G. WUNBERG, Historismus, Lexemautonomie und Fin de siècle. Zum Décadence-Begriff in der Literatur der Jahrhundertende, in: Arcadia 30, 1995, 31–61.   KLAUS MÜLLER-RICHTER

Debt law The rules, principles and legal figures of Roman debt law had moulded the continental European *ius commune* since the rebirth of legal instruction in the law schools of the → GLOSSATORS. It was precisely the Justinian sources of the Roman Law of Obligations that stood in the centre of the practical reception of → ROMAN LAW. They have shaped jurisprudence and legal practice throughout continental Europe since the late Middle Ages and so represent the central core of the legal tradition of the *ius commune*. The individual institutions and legal figures of Roman debt law, such as the *mora debitoris* with its increased liability for debtors in arrears, the corresponding legal figure of *mora creditoris*, the problem of *impossibilitas obligationis*, the aedilician legal instrument in purchase law, the Aquilian tort liability and the other legal figures of the Roman Law of Obligations as they appear in the Justinian legal sources, were, therefore, adopted and found a specific application in General Law. The same is true for the systematic organisation of individual problems and legal institutions. The rules and legal figures of Roman debt law still shape significant parts of contract law today. Inspection of the corresponding legal regulations in Continental → CODIFICATION shows how Roman principles have significantly influenced the legal institutions of modern debt and contract law and modern rules of → CONTRACT law even in technical details. This is particularly clear mainly in the German BGB (Civil Code) of 1900. It was debt law in the second book of the BGB that was the foremost of all European codifications to be still modelled on Roman debt law, because in it the framework of → PANDECTIST STUDIES, which were pursued until the year 1900, was essentially codified. Whether this will remain so in the future is certainly more then questionable. A reform of modern German debt law (2001) introduced legal categories, e.g. that of general breach of duty, which are foreign to the Roman tradition and originated in international contract law, built on the Anglo-American model. The same is true e.g. for the final deletion of aedilician legal instruments in purchase law.

Some central institutions of Roman debt law also underwent profound changes both in the context of mediaeval and modern scholarly and practical adoption into the European *ius commune*. The superseding of the Roman system of individual types of contract should be first mentioned here. In mediaeval jurisprudence, mainly that of the → CANONISTS, the first initiatives had been developed towards achieving a general category of contract. Under the influence of practice, but also not least of theological and juristical theories of late scholasticism, the study of general law succeeded at the end of the 16th cent. in developing and creating a general theory of contracts. This finds its final adoption in the codifications of natural law at the end of the 18th cent. The Law of → TORT underwent a similar development. The characteristic figures of liability, which are contained in the Roman legal sources, were superseded during the 16th and 17th cents. both in practice and in scholarly elaborations. The penal character of criminal liability had already come to an end in the practice of 16th cent. general law. Under the influence of the theories of rational → NATURAL LAW scholars of general law formed out of the *lex Aquilia* the idea of a general criminal case. The development concluded in the codification of a general criminal clause in Article 1382 of the French *Code Civil* (1804) and in §1295 of the Austrian ABGB (1811) [2. 140–146].

The system of contractual liability in Roman law also underwent several significant changes in the modern European codifications. A particular break with the traditions of Roman and general law is especially represented by the possibility of cancellation of a contract in the case of default or delay in synallagmatic contracts. In modern civil law, in the case of a delay in fulfillment of a contract on the part of a contractual partner, a dissolution of the contract regularly comes under consideration. The traditions of Roman and general law did not recognise the principle of dissolution of a contract in such a case. A first stage in this development was the auxiliary construction of a resolutory condition in the case of severe breach of duty insinuated by the other party. In the 19th cent. only a fiction of this kind made the compatibility of contract cancellation with the proposition *pacta sunt servanda* appear possible. The *condition résolutoire* of Article 1184 of the French *Code Civil* corresponds to this state of legislation. French law recognises, as does Italian (Article 1453 *Codice Civile* of 1942), dissolution of a contract for this case by means of a court decision (*action résolutoire, azione di risoluzione*). At this point, under the influence of trade law, the German BGB (1900) introduced contract cancellation after setting a period of grace, which is brought about by unilateral declaration of withdrawal (§326 BGB aF and §323 BGB nF). Austrian law (§918 ABGB in the amended version of 1916) and the Swiss Law of Obligations of 1912 (Article 107) have also adopted this solution [2. 82–84].

The system of Roman debt law recognises, not only in classical law but also in the Justinian sources, a rigorous and strict distinction between an *in rem* and debt law → LEGAL CLAIM. This central concept in Roman law is increasingly losing ground in the study of general law. This includes, for example, the development in practice and the adoption in theory of the legal figure of *ius ad rem*. The debt law → LEGAL CLAIM, for example in a sales contract, is seen and handled in the theory of an → USUS MODERNUS (German) with a certain *in rem* character. Such a development, signifying a factual partial superseding of the autonomy of Roman debt law by the *in rem* legal claims, had a characteristic realisation primarily in the French *Ancien Droit* and in the practice of general law in 17th and 18th cent. Italy. In property transfer in 18th cent. French notarial practice, the property transfer of the *traditio* as a precondition for the acquisition of property was reduced to a pure formality in documentary practice. As *constitum possessorium* the necessity to materially transfer the → POSSESSION to the acquirer had already disappeared in the French *Ancien Droit*. This development was ultimately concluded in the French *Code Civil*, in which, according to Article 1138, the conclusion of the purchase contract renders the buyer already the owner of the object of the purchase. With the so-called 'Consensual Principle' of French law and the other Continental law codes following it, e.g. Italian, the boundary between debt law obligation and *in rem* acquisitional conditions is ultimately removed. In these law codes this led to incisive repercussions on the structure of certain legal problems in debt law, such as the question of risk bearing in purchase law or the concretisation of obligations to supply a certain species of goods. In contrast, radically different, yet committed to the principles of Roman law, is the structure of the German BGB, in which the separation and abstraction principle in property transfer leads to a strict division between debt and property law (§929 BGB).

→ Contractus; → Creditor; → Culpa; → Debitor; → Delictum; → Lex Aquilia; → Mora; → Obligatio; → Pactum; → Traditio

1 COING, vol. I, 393–517, vol. II, 430–523   2 F. RANIERI, Europäisches Obligationenrecht, 1999   3 R. ZIMMERMANN, The Law of Obligations. Roman Foundations of the Civilian Tradition, 1990.   FILIPPO RANIERI

Decipherment
I. Ancient Orient and Egypt II. Other Languages

I. Ancient Orient and Egypt
A. Introduction B. Semitic Alphabetic Scripts C. Non-alphabetic Cuneiforms D. Egyptian Scripts E. Other Writing Systems

A. Introduction

In the narrower sense of the word, decipherment is the successful attempt to comprehend the systematics of a text which is based on an unknown script to such an extent that it becomes possible to reconstruct indisputably not only the phonology but also the semantic content of the texts written in this script. The basis of every decipherment is a statistical evaluation of the available inscriptive material, the first goal of which must be to ascertain the total number of different characters used from which one can determine whether the script is logographic, syllabic, alphabetical, or of a 'mixed' type. Which strategy promises the greatest success in the course of the subsequent deciphering process depends on this. Thus, for instance, an analysis of the distribution of characters plays a greater role in the decipherment of relatively simple scripts representing a language of a known type (e.g. the Ugaritic alphabetic characters), while the differentiation of writing variants is of significance especially for the decipherment of complex mixed writing systems (as for example Assyrian-Babylonian cuneiform writing). In a more advanced phase, decipherment deals with the grammar and lexicon of the script's language, whereby it is of course helpful if this language is related to one that is already known. Using the concept in a broader sense, decipherment can also be understood to include interpretation of an unknown language in a known script (e.g. Etruscan; Italic alphabetic script). Many decipherments have been assisted by the discovery of bilingual or even trilingual texts. Through the decipherment of ancient Near Eastern and Egyptian scripts, often owing to the work of brilliant non-experts, much long-buried, ancient history has been uncovered, which, especially in the 19th and at the beginning of the 20th cents. [1. 139–159] (→ Babylon), led to considerable ideological upheavals and controversies.

B. Semitic Alphabetic Scripts

The first successfully completed attempt to decipher an unknown script goes back to the Abbé J.-J. Barthélemy, who succeeded in 1754 in decoding several Palmyrenic inscriptions that had been copied by English travellers. The basis for this were the Greek parallel versions that accompanied these inscriptions. With their help, Barthélemy determined first of all the position of proper names in the Palmyrenic text, so that he could then identify the phonetic values of the unknown script through a comparison with the Greek rendering of the names. Enabled in this way to read the rest of the words in the text as well, he immediately detected the Syrian character of the Palmyrenic language. Further, he recognised the affinity between the Palmyrenic script and the Hebrew and Syrian alphabets, which had never fallen into oblivion. In 1764, Barthélemy deciphered the Phoenician script as well, and in 1768 the Aramaic [5]. Decipherment of the Himyaritic script, undertaken between 1837 and 1841, prerequisite for rediscovering the culture of ancient southern Arabia, was done by W. Gesenius and E. Rödiger; their work was much aided by representations of the script in Islamic-Arabian manuscripts [1. 149]. Still controversial today is the interpretation of the so-called proto-Sinaitic script by A. H. Gardiner, whose attempt at decipherment published in 1916 is based on the idea that the script's apparently alphabetic inventory of signs was derived, in accordance with the principle of acrophony, from Egyptian hieroglyphs [1. 29; 12. 3–50]. In contrast, there are no doubts surrounding the decipherment of the cuneiform alphabetic script of Ugarit, carried out between 1929 and 1933. The decipherers, C. Virolleaud, H. Bauer, E. Dhorme and J. Friedrich, proceeded from the working hypothesis that the language of the Ugaritic texts was western Semitic. Since bilingual texts were not available, a complex investigation of the distribution of signs was required in order to mark first of all prepositions and affixes and, finally, to determine all the phonetic values [1. 153].

C. Non-alphabetic Cuneiforms

Although Babylonian cuneiform writing was still in use at least into the first cent. AD (the last tablet that can be dated stems from AD 74–75), no scholarly discourse arose in Antiquity – in contrast to the discourse over Egyptian hieroglyphs – over the different ancient oriental cuneiforms. (The lost treatise, περὶ τῶν ἐν Βαβυλῶνι ἱερῶν γραμμάτων, DK 2,207, probably wrongly attributed to Democritus, is more likely to have concerned itself with the religious literature of the Babylonians than with their writing.) Thus the existence of cuneiform was almost completely forgotten. Not until European travellers in the Orient in the 17th and 18th cents. (P. della Valle, P. Chardin, E. Kämpfer, C. de Bruin) published copies of cuneiform monuments did this situation change.

Of decisive impetus to decipherment were the copies of Persepolitan cuneiform inscriptions published by C. Niebuhr between 1774 and 1778. Niebuhr himself recognised that these inscriptions had been composed in three different varieties of cuneiform writing and drew up an initial list of signs, comprising 42 items, from the variety that was apparently the simplest. This list became the first focus of attempts at decipherment. By 1800, Niebuhr, O.G. Tychsen and F. Münter were able to determine the direction of the script, identify a word separator and date the script to the time of ancient Persia. The decisive breakthrough was achieved in 1802 by F. Grotefend, a gymnasial teacher in Göttingen who, already as a child, had been fascinated by picture puzzles, rebuses, etc. Proceeding from the working hypothesis that the inscriptions he was examining began with a royal genealogy structurally similar to the genealogies of the Middle Persian royal inscription of Naqsch-i-Rustam as deciphered by S. de Sacy, and convinced that these genealogies surely contained the names of the Achaemenid rulers, known from classical sources (esp. Herodotus), Grotefend was able to read correctly approximately one-third of the Old Persian signs and to interpret correctly the genealogical portions of the inscriptions. By 1846 R.C. Rask, E. Burnouf, C. Lassen and E. Hincks had succeeded in essentially completing the decipherment of Ancient Persian cuneiform writing [3; 6. 101–143; 7. 102–146]. There is no agreement about the extent to which H.C. Rawlinson, working in Iraq, was able to repeat the decipherment of Ancient Persian independently of the work of the forenamed scholars. Above all, Rawlinson rendered outstanding service in the study of cuneiform writing through his 1846 edition of the Old Persian version of the voluminous trilingual text of the Behistun Inscription, which he himself copied.

The Behistun Inscription, made accessible through the work of Rawlinson, served as the basis for the decipherment of the Elamite script by E. Norris (previously also examined by N.L. Westergaard), the second cuneiform variety of the Old Persian trilingual texts. In an essay that appeared in 1852, Norris identified about 90 proper names, known from the Old Persian version, in the Elamite version of the Behistun Text. This enabled him to determine many of the Elamite syllabic values [6. 146–150; 7. 147–166]. Decipherment of the third type of script in the Old Persian texts, the complex Babylonian cuneiform script, proved to be a very difficult undertaking. If proper names had offered a key for successful interpretation in the cases of the two other types of writing, they proved to be more of an obstacle here because of the frequently pronounced logographic nature of the writing. Decipherment of Babylonian cuneiform was furthered by the excavations begun in the 1840s in Assyria and made possible by the efforts of several scholars, among whom E. Hincks, an Irish country clergyman, is especially notable. Through recourse to writing variants in otherwise homonymic texts (including texts written in the Urartian language) and by means of skilful utilisation of the Achaemenid trilingual texts, Hincks recognised between 1846 and 1852 a number of decisive points: 1) The Babylonian script of the Achaemenid and southern Mesopotamian inscriptions is structurally identical with the script found on Assyrian monuments. 2) The script is of a logosyllabic character. 3) The individual signs can have varying syllabic or logographic values, depending on the context (so-called polyphony). 4) The language reproduced through the script is Semitic. Besides Hincks, Rawlinson and J. Oppert also rendered important contributions to decipherment, the latter through the use of Assyrian syllabaries and vocabularies. Decipherment of Babylonian-Assyrian cuneiform writing was completed in the year 1857 when Hincks, Rawlinson, Oppert and W.H. Fox Talbot, independent of one another, transcribed and translated an Assyrian royal inscription with largely consonant results [7. 167–220; 11. 177–227, 293–305, 333–337]. It soon became apparent that the cuneiform variety used for Babylonian and Assyrian had been used also for the reproduction of other languages unknown until that time. An intense dispute broke out in the second half of the 19th cent. between those who opposed a Semitic language connection and those who favored it when dealing with the question of the correct interpretation of the probably oldest of these languages, Sumerian (first made accessible by Hincks, Oppert and P. Haupt, no grammars before the 20th cent.) [4]. Whether the earliest cuneiform documents are in fact Sumerian has yet to be firmly established [8. 17f.]. The rediscovery in 1906 of the Hittite capital Hattusa with its extensive archives led to the decipherment of several other languages that were written in Babylonian cuneiform script, the most important of which, even before Hurrian, is Hittite. The Indo-European character of this language was recognised by B. Hronzny in 1915; in his etymological considerations he could rely on the logograms whose meanings were known in the writing [6. 203–215]. Still unresolved is the question of how the idiom of the cuneiform texts from Ebla dating from the 3rd cent., discovered between 1974 and 1976 and made accessible mainly by G. Pettinato, fits into the sphere of Semitic languages [10].

D. EGYPTIAN SCRIPTS

The Old Egyptian hieroglyphic script (together with the hieratic and the demotic script forms derived from it) remained in use into Late Antiquity and was the object of numerous Greek and Latin treatises. However, the often (neo-) platonically oriented ancient writers were almost solely interested in the 'symbolic' use of script signs that arose at a later period in Egypt, in the link between concrete image and abstract thought, while the phonetic aspects of Egyptian script were hardly considered (beginnings in the writings of Clement of Alexandria). Thus a very distorted and one-sided – but not totally false – picture of the Old Egyptian script system was conveyed, above all, by Chairemon and Horapollo (*Hieroglyphica*), but also by Ammianus Marcellinus, Diodorus, Plotinus, Plutarch, and Porphyry, among others ([9. 38–56; 13. 89–100] with citations). When the authors just named were rediscovered in the 15th and 16th cents. by the Humanists (and their writings began to be fruitful for the 'semiotic discourse' of the early modern period), Old Egyptian culture was long lost, and because of the lack of inscriptive material a critical revision of the ancient descriptions could not yet be accomplished [9. 57–87]. The Jesuit, A. Kircher, whose attempts in the 17th cent. to interpret Egyptian original inscriptions were unsuccessful, nevertheless proposed the correct thesis that this hieroglyphically written language had to be an early form of Coptic, the

Egyptian ecclesiastical language written with Greek letters and some special signs, which he had made grammatically and lexically accessible [6. 49–52; 9. 89–102].

In the 17th and 18th cents., R. Cudworth and especially W. Warburton developed impressive speculative 'grammatologies' on the basis of the information then available about the scripts of ancient Egypt [2. 80–90, 102–115]. Some progress in the understanding of hieroglyphic script was also made by C. Niebuhr, who postulated the existence of phonograms in 1762, and J.-J. Barthélemy, who discovered in the same year that the ring-shaped so-called cartouches contained the names of rulers [6. 52f.; 9. 107–111].

But it was not until the discovery of the *Rosetta Stone*, a hieroglyphic-demotic-Greek trilingual text which came to light in 1799 as soldiers of Napoleon's expeditionary forces were digging trenches in the Nile Delta, that a decisive breakthrough became possible. After the Swede D. Åkerblad, proceeding on the basis of the Greek names, had identified several words in the demotic text in 1802 and, through recourse to Coptic, had ascertained the phonetic shape of the third person singular masculine suffix, and after the English universal scholar Th. Young had also appropriately determined – even if not, for the most part, correctly read – a number of words in the hieroglyphic version in 1818, it was the French Orientalist J.F. Champollion, ardently interested in Egypt from childhood on, who succeeded between 1822 (*Lettre à M. Dacier*) and 1824 in essentially deciphering the Egyptian script, thanks to his knowledge of Coptic and new inscription material. As in the case of Persian cuneiform, his starting point was knowledge of several royal names known from classical sources, from which the sound of both phonograms and semograms could be inferred. Decipherment of Egyptian script was completed by the work of R. Lepsius (discovery of the multiple consonant signs, 1837) and E. Hincks (discovery of the absence of vowels in the script, 1846) [1. 148f.; 6. 53–90; 9. 124–145]. The Meroitic script used in Sudan starting in the 3rd cent. BC, found in monumental script and in a simple variant and in principle an alphabetic script, was deciphered between 1909 and 1911 by F.L. Griffith relying mainly on Nubian place names and titles cited in Egyptian and Greek sources. Because of the absence of bilingual texts, understanding of the language(s) reproduced by the script is to date still inadequate [1. 152; 6. 94–97].

E. Other Writing Systems

As early as 1880, A.H. Sayce conjectured that the pictography affixed to monuments in northern Syria and Asia Minor, known today as hieroglyphic Luwian, was the product of the Hittite civilisation; at the same time, he established the meaning of several determinatives and logograms. But it was not until after Hittite became known that I.Gelb succeeded, between 1931 and 1942, in demonstrating the Hittite-Luwian character of the language reproduced by this script. Further progress in decipherment, using widely varying

methods, was made in the 1930s by J.P. Meriggi and E. Forrer. Discovery of the hieroglyphic Luwian-Phoenician bilingual text of Karatepe by H.Th. Bossert in 1947 not only essentially confirmed previous decipherment, but also made further improvements possible [6. 184–250]. Still considered essentially undeciphered, however, are the 'pseudohieroglyphics' of Byblos, most recently dealt with by G.E. Mendenhall, and the Indus Valley script, examined most thoroughly by A. Parpola [1. 29f., 165–171].

→ Achaimenidai; → Alphabet; → Bilingual inscriptions; → Behistun; → Etruscan; → Hieroglyphs; → Horapollo; → Italy, alphabetical scripts;→ Cuneiform script; → Trilinguals

SOURCE: 1 P. T. DANIELS, W. BRIGHT (eds.), The World's Writing Systems, 1996 (esp. 144)

LITERATURE: 2 J. ASSMANN, Moses the Egyptian, 1997 3 R. BORGER et al., Die Welt des Alten Orients, 1975 4 J. S. COOPER, Posing the Sumerian Question, in: Aula Orientalis 9, 1991, 47–66 5 P. T. DANIELS, Shewing of Hard Sentences and Dissolving of Doubts: The First Decipherment, in: Journal of the American Oriental Society 108, 1988, 419–436 6 E. DOBLHOFER, Die Entzifferung alter Schriften und Sprachen, 1993 7 C. FOSSEY, Manuel d'Assyriologie I, 1904 8 M. W. GREEN, H. J. NISSEN, Zeichenliste der archaischen Texte aus Uruk, 1987 9 E. IVERSEN, The Myth of Egypt and its Hieroglyphs in European Tradition, 1961 10 M. KREBERNIK, The Linguistic Classification of Eblaite, in: J. S. COOPER, G. M. SCHWARTZ (eds.), The Study of the Ancient Near East in the Twenty-First Century, 1996, 233–249 11 M. T. LARSEN, The Conquest of Assyria, 1996 12 B. SASS, The Genesis of the Alphabet, 1988 13 E. WINTER, s.v. Hieroglyphen, RAC XV, 83–103. ECKART FRAHM

II. Other Languages
A. Cypriot B. Linear B C. Iberian
D. Non-deciphered

A. Cypriot

Decipherment of Cypriot syllabic script [1. 48–51] succeeded with the help of the Phoenician-Cypriot bilingual inscription of Idalion [1. 246–48, No. 220]. On November 7, 1871, the British assyriologist George Smith (1840–76) argued for the syllabic character of the script, read a Greek word (Gen. *pa-si-le-wo-se*/*basilē-wos*/of the 'King' Phoenician *mlk*) and postulated that the language was actually Greek. Smith's postulate was confirmed in 1872 by the British Egyptologist Samuel Birch, and in 1873 the German numismatist Johannes Brandis further improved the syllabary. A more thorough exploration was then carried out by philologists, especially Moriz W.C. Schmidt (1874) and, working parallel with him, Wilhelm Deecke and Justus Siegismund as well as the dialectologist Heinrich Ludolf Ahrens (1876), who essentially completed the decipherment. With the syllabary, the so-called Eteo-Cypriot inscriptions can also be read; their language is incomprehensible, however [1. 51, 61].

B. Linear B

Especially impressive is the decipherment of the Linear B script. Thanks to *work notes* that the decipherer, the British architect Michael Ventris (1922–56), regularly sent to friends in the run-up to the breakthrough, the process is documented in detail [1], and an excellent retelling of the story is available (e.g. [3]). The inscriptions, found in Cnossus starting in 1900, were recognised immediately as inventory lists and the like, having for the most part a simple syntactical structure; the script was understood to be a mixture of syllable signs (comparable to the Cypriot signs) and logograms. Publication of the corpus was delayed for decades, however. An exemplary edition of the material found in Pylos since 1939, with a reliable list of signs, did not appear until 1951, the work of the American Emmett L. Bennett Jr. That was one prerequisite for decipherment,.

The second, more important prerequisite was the outstanding preparatory work of the American Alice Kober (d. 1950), who in working with the Cnossian material during the 1940s, compiled lists of 'words' which had the 'same' stem but different 'endings' and determined which forms were functionally the same, aided by the formulaic character that became apparent from the lists – for example (Case I) 26–67–37–57, 3–28–37–57, 69–53–41–57, 70–52–41–57; (Case II) 26–67–37–36, 3–28–37–36, 69–53–41–36, 70–52–41–36; (Case III) 26–67–5, 3–28–5, 69–53–12, 70–52–12. From this she was able to discern that the pair of signs 37 and 5, as well as 41 and 12, each have the same consonant but a different vowel, and further that 37 and 41 as well as 5 and 12 each have the same vowel, and, finally, 57 and 36 also each have the same consonant but a different vowel. This enabled her to construct the beginning of a *grid* with columns of vowels and rows of consonants. Ventris took over at this point in 1950. He brought the grid closer to completion by developing additional such grammatical 'paradigms'. According to *work note 20* of June 1, 1952, the *grid* was sufficiently far along to allow phonetic experiments. For this purpose Ventris also drew on the few Cypriot signs that have plausible correspondences in Linear B (especially *ta, ti, to, pa, lo, na, se*), a strategy which was suggested all the more inasmuch as the counterparts to the Cypriot *ti* and *to* were located in the same row in his 'grid'. His experiment yielded the five vowel qualities (*u* indirectly) and at least several consonant qualities. This subsequently triggered a chain reaction, leading immediately to the identification of several place names, among them the above-mentioned *ru-ki-to* (/Luktos/), *pa-i-to* (/Phaistos/), *tu-ri-so* (/Tulissos/) and *ko-no-so* (/Knōsos/) (Case III), as well as in view of the related ethnic terms ending in *-ti-jo* and/or *-si-jo* (/-tios, -sios/) (Case II) and *-ti-ja* and/or *-si-ja* (/-tiā, -siā/) (Case I), and of several words to the identification of the language as Greek (which was undoubtedly the greatest surprise of all). There is now (almost) no longer any need to argue that Ventris' decipherment is correct. His achievement is impressive above all by virtue of its rigourous methodology and almost error-free development.

C. Iberian

Various scripts were used on the Iberian Peninsula in Antiquity [4. I 132–49], for Iberian in particular the quite uniform Northeast Iberian script, running from left to right (also used for Celto-Iberian), and the more complex South Iberian script running from right to left. The two are undoubtedly related to one another and to the Tartessian (or Southwest Iberian) script that is especially close to the South Iberian. Decipherment was achieved in 1922 by Manuel Gómez-Moreno [4. I 105–10] with a purely analytical approach and without the 'help' of any linguistic affinity (as for example with Basque, as postulated by W. von Humboldt but remaining unconfirmed to this day); definitely helpful, however, was the Iberian inscription of Alcoy, written in the Greek alphabet and found in 1921 [4. II No. G.1.1].

All three scripts show the same mixed system: for the five vowels and the consonantal long sounds (especially /l/, /n/, /r/, /s/,/ś/) there are phoneme signs, but for the occlusives there are five syllable signs each (without differentiation of the two manners of articulation that can be deduced from Greek texts). Thanks to a Tartessian alphabetary with 27 signs, twice inscribed on a stone [5], the origin of these scripts can now be assessed. (The following applies only conditionally to the northeast, with its in part strongly deviating letter forms and therefore possible deviation in the sequence of signs): 1. The foundation of the script is an alphabetary with its normal sequence (numbers 1–13) to which an unusually large number of additional signs were appended (numbers 14–27); the basic sequence was approximately: *a-b(a?)-k(a)-t(u)-i-k(e)-l-m-n-s-p(e)?-ś-t(a)*. 2. A Greek alphabet either formed the basis or at least played a role in early stages of development, because the first additional letter (number 14) after the basic series is the vav [or vau] with the phonetic value /u/ (making clear that the Greek alphabet was undoubtedly the model responsible for the phonemic sound values as well, especially the vowels). 3. The forms of the letters are in part closer to the Phoenician letters (esp. *iota* and *tau*), in part closer to the Greek (esp. *gamma, lambda, san*), a fact that allows no conclusions concerning genealogy, however. 4. Three blocks of letters are eliminated from the basic sequence through reduction reform(s) (*epsilon* to *theta, omikron* (?), *qoppa* to *sigma*); later, however, supplementary letters were again added for some of the sounds involved (/e/,/o/,/r/). 5. To a large extent, *m* is manifestly a 'dead' letter (and for this reason written with uncertainty in the two alphabetaries; on *m* in the northeast see [4. I 153f.]). Thus the alphabetary may be of importance for further decipherment work because knowledge of a possible *ratio* in the succession of additional letters can help to determine a plausible phonetic value for the ones that are uncertain. For this, however, further research by specialists will be necessary.

D. Non-deciphered

Still awaiting decipherment are most notably the scripts (and languages) of the Phaistos Disk, the Cypro-Minoan script, and of Linear A.

→ Alphabet II. The Greek alphabet; → Discus of Phaestus; → Eteo-Cyprian; → Hispania, Iberia; → Italy, alphabetical scripts; → Cypriot Script; → Cypro-Minoan Scripts; → Linear A; → Linear B

SOURCES: 1 O. Masson, Les inscriptions chypriotes syllabiques, 1961, ²1983   2 M. Ventris, Work Notes on Minoan Language Research and Other Unedited Papers (= Incunabula Graeca 90), A. Sacconi (ed.), 1988   3 J. Chadwick, The Decipherment of Linear B, ²1970   4 J. Untermann, Monumenta Linguarum Hispanicarum, III.1 und 2, 1990   5 J. A. Correa, El signario de Espanca (Castro Verde) y la escritura tartesia, in: J. Untermann, F. Villar (eds.), Lengua y cultura en la Hispania prerromana, 1993, 521–62 (with photographs).

LITERATURE: 6 D. Kahn, The Codebreakers, 1968   7 P. Horster, Kryptologie, 1985   8 Y. Duhoux, Th. G. Palaima, J. Bennet (eds.), Problems in Decipherment, 1989   9 E. Doblhofer, Die Entzifferung alter Schriften und Sprachen, 1993.   RUDOLF WACHTER

Decorations see → Medals

Deification see → Apotheosis; → Deification

Delos (Δῆλος)

A. Introduction   B. Excavations 1873–1894
C. Excavations from 1902 to the 1920s
D. Organisation of the Excavation   E. Dissemination of the Results   F. Research on Delos after the 1920s

A. Introduction

There has never been any doubt about the location of Delos (D.), abandoned in the 7th cent. but never forgotten, in the middle of the Cyclades, or that the ancient sanctuary of Apollo was located on it. After the island was shown on maps, beginning in the middle of the 12th cent., and repeatedly described by various visitors in the wake of Cyriacus of Ancona, who sojourned on D. in 1445, the first excavations were carried out at the beginning of the 19th cent., but with disappointing results. The government of Count Capodistrias prohibited them in 1830 in order to put an end to looting. Between 1851 and 1864, the → École française d'Athènes commissioned several of its members to undertake exploratory travel on the island. Although their reports were not very promising for further investigations, the École began excavating in 1873.

B. Excavations 1873–1894

For the most part, A. Lebègue uncovered the peak of Cynthus and explored the grotto on its west flank, which he erroneously regarded as the original Apollo sanctuary. After his departure, P. Stamatakis, commissioned by the Greek government to oversee the exca-

vations, began work in Sarapieion C. In 1877 Th. Homolle undertook excavation of the actual Apollo sanctuary. His hopes were not in vain. Within the period of a few years he was able to bring to the light of day not only remarkable religious architecture from archaic, classical and Hellenistic times but also an extraordinary complex of sculptures and inscriptions. He dealt with a portion of this complex in two works. The first (1885) treated the archaic statues of women and revealed much that was new at the time, since the korai of the Acropolis in Athens were not discovered until a year later; the second (1887) treated the inscriptions composed by the administrators of the sanctuary, making precise knowledge of the administration of a sanctuary available for the first time. At the same time other members of the École francaise were excavating in various parts of the city. Thus the Terrace of the Foreign Gods was uncovered in 1881, the Theatre in 1882, the theatre district in 1883, the Gymnasium in 1886, and the harbour district in 1894. After E. Ardaillon and H. Convert completed an archaeological map of the entire island on a scale of 1:2000, activities were halted in 1894 because the École francaise had decided to concentrate its entire efforts on the sanctuary at → Delphi.

C. Excavations from 1902 to the 1920s

In 1902 excavations were resumed. A large portion of the equipment used for exploration of the sanctuary at Delphi could be used again for this purpose. Moreover, an annual gift of 50,000 francs from the American Joseph Florimond Duc de Loubat (1831–1927) was made available starting in 1903. This patron had distinguished himself prior to that time primarily through endowments for the promotion of research of the American continent and through generous gifts for the benefit of the Vatican; in 1893, he received his title ('duc') from Pope Leo XIII as an honorary title with the motto 'orphano tu eris adiutor' ('you shall be the father of orphans'). Thus although he had no particular interest in D. (which he in fact never visited), he decided on the advice of G. Perrot, Permanent Secretary of the Académie, to finance the excavations; the only condition he imposed was an exact and detailed list of the annual expenses. In addition to this support for the on site work, a Fonds d'épigraphie grecque was set up in 1920 to support the institute, with its income revenues earmarked for the publication of a Choix d'inscriptions grecques de Délos (F. Durrbach 1921) and the Corpus des inscriptions de Délos.

These new technical and financial means made possible systematic excavations, which started with a 'cleaning' of the sanctuary that consisted in dumping the earth that had been cleared away during previous excavations into the sea. Excavation of the sanctuary, the theatre district and the Terrace of the Foreign Gods continued, and by the time of World War I, the Dodecatheon, the Granite Monument, the Terrace of Lions, the Hypostyle Hall, the Minoan Fountain, the first Heraeum, the Lake Palaestra, the Granite Palaestra, the

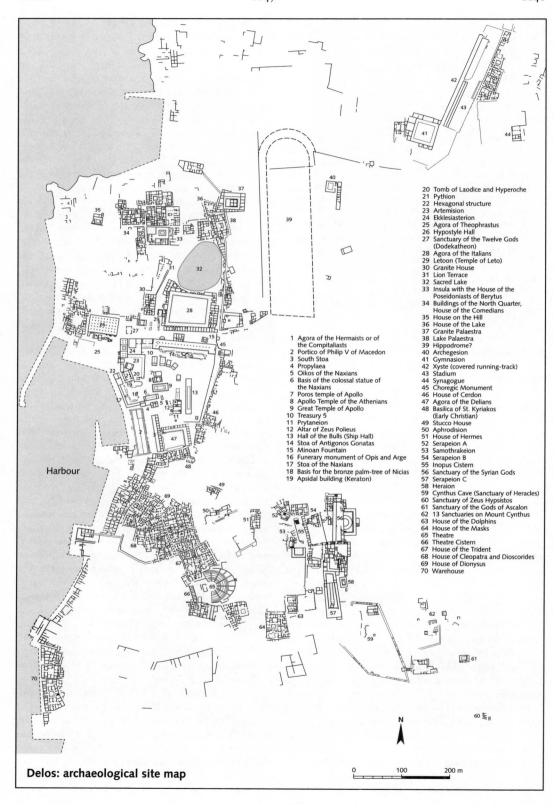

Harbour

1 Agora of the Hermaists or of
   the Compitaliasts
2 Portico of Philip V of Macedon
3 South Stoa
4 Propylaea
5 Oikos of the Naxians
6 Basis of the colossal statue of
   the Naxians
7 Poros temple of Apollo
8 Apollo Temple of the Athenians
9 Great Temple of Apollo
10 Treasury 5
11 Prytaneion
12 Altar of Zeus Polieus
13 Hall of the Bulls (Ship Hall)
14 Stoa of Antigonos Gonatas
15 Minoan Fountain
16 Funerary monument of Opis and Arge
17 Stoa of the Naxians
18 Basis for the bronze palm-tree of Nicias
19 Apsidal building (Keraton)

20 Tomb of Laodice and Hyperoche
21 Pythion
22 Hexagonal structure
23 Artemision
24 Ekklesiasterion
25 Agora of Theophrastus
26 Hypostyle Hall
27 Sanctuary of the Twelve Gods
   (Dodekatheon)
28 Agora of the Italians
29 Letoon (Temple of Leto)
30 Granite House
31 Lion Terrace
32 Sacred Lake
33 Insula with the House of the
   Poseidoniasts of Berytus
34 Buildings of the North Quarter,
   House of the Comedians
35 House on the Hill
36 House of the Lake
37 Granite Palaestra
38 Lake Palaestra
39 Hippodrome?
40 Archegesion
41 Gymnasion
42 Xyste (covered running-track)
43 Stadium
44 Synagogue
45 Choregic Monument
46 House of Cerdon
47 Agora of the Delians
48 Basilica of St. Kyriakos
   (Early Christian)
49 Stucco House
50 Aphrodision
51 House of Hermes
52 Serapeion A
53 Samothrakeion
54 Serapeion B
55 Inopus Cistern
56 Sanctuary of the Syrian Gods
57 Serapeion C
58 Heraion
59 Cynthus Cave (Sanctuary of Heracles)
60 Sanctuary of Zeus Hypsistos
61 Sanctuary of the Gods of Ascalon
62 13 Sanctuaries on Mount Cynthus
63 House of the Dolphins
64 House of the Masks
65 Theatre
66 Theatre Cistern
67 House of the Trident
68 House of Cleopatra and Dioscorides
69 House of Dionysus
70 Warehouse

N

Delos: archaeological site map

0   100   200 m

Fig. 2: The Duc de Loubat

Fig. 3: The statue of Diadumenus, held by two workers, on its discovery in 1894

Fig. 4: Archaeologists of the École française d'Athènes in the hypostyle hall at the beginning of the 20th century

Stadion with surrounding houses, and the Synagogue were all uncovered. During this time, M. Holleaux, director of the École francaise from 1904 to 1912, brought various specialists in geography, geology and hydrography to the island who produced a new map and studied the physical geography of the island. World War I, in the course of which four of the archaeologists from the École francaise active on D. lost their lives, caused a considerable reduction in excavation work. Nonetheless, exploration of the Cynthus was resumed and continued until 1922; the area between the Lake Palaestra and the sanctuary was already laid open.

D. Organisation of the Excavation

Between March 1873, when A. Lebègue alone, with a grant from the Ministry of Education of 1,000 francs, led a small group of workers assembled with the help of the mayor of Mykonos, and the time during which the gift of the Duc de Loubat made possible the simultaneous work of about ten specialists for six months at four or five different sites with more than 200 workers, the equipment, work methods and technical procedures developed substantially.

At the beginning, the work was guided by a single archaeologist; exploratory trenches were laid out to locate the walls and follow them. The excavation leader was in charge of several dozen workers from Mykonos who worked six days a week except on holidays. Living conditions were hard. Evenings one had to seek refuge on Rheneia or sleep on the boat. Starting in 1879, there was one person in charge of a register of the excavated archaeological remains. Initially, this person was an engineer from the Office of Civil Engineering, the brother of Th. Homolle, and, from 1880 on, an architect, P. Nénot who had been awarded the Grand Prix de Rome. Nénot drew a map of the entire sanctuary and studied all of its monuments, to which he devoted the reports of his third and fourth years. After 1902, archaeologists-members or former members of the École francaise worked in groups of several people on the island, making possible concentration on the excavation and study of a particular monument, area or type of material. Two important persons took on the organisation of the excavations. H. Convert, director of the Office of Civil Engineering and in charge of river navigation for the département Seine, was delegated to the École francaise to assume technical leadership of the excavations, as he had done earlier at Delphi. He shared this task with the surveyor J. Replat, who also drew up topographical and architectural registers, studied several buildings, either alone or in collaboration with others, and undertook excavations himself. These two men directed the excavations when, in June 1906, a workers' strike erupted at the instigation of a physician from Mykonos named Andronikos. The demands of the strikers, which were taken up by the Greek national press, involved the disparity between the modest wages and the long working days and hard living conditions. At that time narrow-gauge tracks had been laid at the excavation site, with

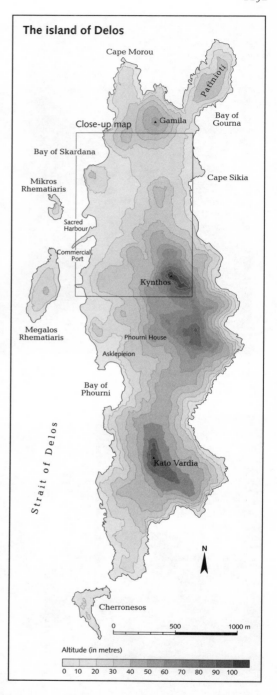

The island of Delos

Cape Morou
Pathnioti
Bay of Gourna
Gamila
Close-up map
Bay of Skardana
Cape Sikia
Mikros Rhematiaris
Sacred Harbour
Commercial Port
Kynthos
Megalos Rhematiaris
Phourni House
Asklepieion
Bay of Phourni
Strait of Delos
Kato Vardia

N

Cherronesos

0   500   1000 m

Altitude (in metres)

0 10 20 30 40 50 60 70 80 90 100

horses and mules pulling the cars; with the help of these light railways, the waste resulting from the excavating (much of which was used for the construction of the present-day landing stage) could be carried away. The work was no longer just with exploratory trenches; now large parts of the town, and especially many of the sanctuaries and public buildings, were being completely uncovered. Living and working conditions were improving. Several houses were built on the island as well

Fig. 5: The museum of Delos in 1909

Fig. 6: The restoration of the peristyle
of the House of Dionysus

Fig. 7: The excavation of the lower Inopus basin

as, beginning in 1904 and in accordance with plans by H. Convert, a museum financed by Greece. After completion of the museum it became possible to keep the moveable discovered objects, until then stored on Mykonos, on D. itself.

Although D. received hardly any visitors at the time of the first excavations, the archaeologists had to give some thought to the safekeeping of the objects at the site of discovery and the protection of the unearthed monuments. More than dealers in antiques and tourists, they – justifiably – feared appropriation of the most beautiful objects by the National Museum in Athens and damage to the walls, stucco work and mosaics by shepherds and their sheep. In order to limit the risk of damage, a wall was built in 1903 separating cultivated land and archaeological zones on the island. The following year, the director of the École francaise submitted a request to the general overseer (*ephor*) of Greek antiquities, M. Stavropoulos, to double the number of personnel (until then only two) charged with guarding the island. The technical means employed in 1902 also allowed restorations as well as the placing of erratic stones in the vicinity of the buildings to which they belonged.

E. Dissemination of the Results

A. Lebègue devoted a complete monograph to the results of his research. As a rule, his successors reported their discoveries annually in the *Bulletin de Correspondance hellénique* as well as in the *Comptes rendus de l'Académie des inscriptions et belles-lettres*. From these first reports, as well as from the notebooks kept during the excavations, one can conclude that there was a preferential interest in sculptures and inscriptions. For the definitive publication of the monuments and the movable discovered objects, the series of books *Exploration archéologique de Délos* was created, its first two volumes appearing in 1909. The inscriptions that were first published by the Berlin Academy in *Inscriptiones graecae* were republished after World War I in the French *Corpus des inscriptions de Délos*. But a broad public also became acquainted with the discoveries, sometimes in a surprising manner: at the 1889 World Exhibition there was a stand devoted to D., and the Hellenist Th. Reinach commissioned E. Pontremoli, who in 1890 had won the Grand Prix de Rome for architecture, to replicate a Delian house complete with antique objects, which, as the Villa Kerylos, embellishes a promontory near Beaulieu-sur-mer (near Nice in southern France).

F. Research on Delos after the 1920s

Excavations were still carried out on D. even after the 1920s, although the means and the perspectives of the research changed. From this time on and down to the present the research has concentrated more on individual buildings than on entire complexes. The Archegesion, the Furni House, the House of Hermes, several houses of the northern quarter, a farmhouse in the surrounding countryside, and burial places on Rheneia were all unearthed. Increasingly, additional

excavations were carried out at the sites of monuments that had already been unearthed for some time in order to be able to complete the publication. This yielded some spectacular results, as for example in 1946 when probing in the Artemision led to the discovery of a pit filled with votive objects. Although more than half of the site has yet to be excavated, work today focuses on the study and classification of the monuments, found objects and inscriptions which, even though some of them were excavated more than 100 years ago, have not yet been completely examined. The work that has already been done is considerable: 36 volumes of *Exploration archéologique de Délos* and nine volumes of inscription have appeared; further, there are some 20 monographs and hundreds of articles that deal specifically with Delian topics. Of those monuments already discovered, a substantial number have not yet been researched; however, this apparent shortcoming can be explained by the scope of the task. It stems not so much from the way research interests have developed in the course of time as from the abundance of discoveries that have been made on D.; apart from the history of foreign settlements on D., all the main topics of present-day research are a continuation of Th. Homolle's and M. Holleaux' programs.

The work on D. pertains not only to the study of the material gained from earlier excavations. Because of the slow but inevitable deterioration of the monuments and the increase in tourism at the archaeological site, which since 1990 has been included in UNESCO's *World Cultural Heritage Sites*, efforts to preserve, restore and organise the exhibition of the monuments have come to the forefront. In the 1950s, N. Kontoléon undertook extensive reconstruction in the theatre district. In recent times several information signboards have been erected at the ruins, and the number of rooms at the museum accessible to the public has been considerably increased. Most of the statues that were previously on display in the open are now in the museum, and removal of the ancient lion statues from the shore of the lake to the museum is also being considered. On the archaeological sites themselves, originals are being replaced by copies. Nonetheless, walls are collapsing with each passing winter, mural paintings are becoming detached from their surfaces, mosaics are disintegrating. Restoration teams are trying to find a remedy, but the means available are inadequate.

→ Athens V. National Archaeological Museum

1 A. Plassart, Un siècle de fouilles à Délos, BCH Suppl. I, 1973, 5–16 2 Ph. Bruneau, M. Brunet, Al. Farnoux, J.-Ch. Moretti (eds.), Délos. Ile sacrée et ville cosmopolite, 1996

Additional Bibliography: V. J. Bruno, Hellenistic Painting Techniques: The Evidence of the Delos Fragments, 1985; R. Hamilton, Treasure Map: A Guide to the Delian Inventories, 2000.

MICHÈLE MORETTI, JEAN-CHARLES BRUNET

Delphi

A. INTRODUCTION B. RESEARCH HISTORY
C. IMPORTANT AREAS OF RESEARCH D. PRESEN-
TATION E. THE EFFECT OF THE EXCAVATIONS ON
THE OUTSIDE WORLD

A. INTRODUCTION

The fame of the Delphi Oracle in Antiquity and the high expectations of the monuments based on sources such as the travel descriptions of Pausanias [5. 200] made the site a desirable location for excavations and led to conflicts about excavation management and excavation methods [5. 194–8]. The discoveries triggered long discussions in academic research both because of their unusualness and as possible fixed points in the chronology. But they were also met with great interest by the broad public. In most recent times, the significance of the site has been duly recognised: in 1972, Delphi (D.) was declared an 'Archaeological Zone' and the area around it a nature preserve; in 1988, D. was added to the UNESCO list of *World Cultural Heritage Sites* [2. 236].

B. RESEARCH HISTORY

The fame of ancient D. aroused the interest of travellers early (Cyriacus of Ancona visited the site in 1436). But the sparse remains of the sanctuary (Castalian Spring, Stadion), directly next to the modern settlement, attracted visitors only in small numbers [5]. Excavations were not carried out until the 19th cent., after the founding of the modern Greek state. These excavations initially consisted of a few smaller projects undertaken by the Greek government (1837 excavation in the Marmaria), by the Berlin Akademie der Wissenschaften (1840 study of a portion of the Polygonal Wall, substructure of the Apollo Temple), and by the → ECOLE Française d'Athènes (EFA) (1860–62 the Polygonal Wall, Temple; 1880 Hall of the Athenians); H. Pomtow undertook an excavation on his own initiative (1887 entrance to the sanctuary) [5]. Extensive excavation of the Apollo sanctuary and of the Athena sanctuary as well as its surroundings (settlement, necropoleis), was possible only after relocation of the modern town of Kastri (renamed 'D.' in 1858) and was carried out between 1892 and 1903 during the 'Grande Fouille' of the EFA under the leadership of its director Th. Homolle. The excavators were at first mainly interested in the archaic and classical sanctuary; they hoped to recover the monuments and art works described by Pausanias and therefore excavated only around the monuments, not under them [2. 235]. After the assessment and restoration of these finds, new explorations were initiated under the directorship of Ch. Picard (1919–1925) [5. 224]. Systematic excavation of the geometrical and Mycenaean levels was expected to reveal the origins of the sanctuary as being in the Bronze Age (1920–22 campaigns under the direction of R. Demangel in the Marmaria; 1934–37 under the direction of L. Lerat in the northeast; between 1936 and 1949 under the direction of P. Amandry and J. Bousquet at other points in the Apollo sanctuary). Accordingly, the Mycenaean clay idols found in the Marmaria led to a dispute whether one should assume there was a Mycenaean precursor to the Athena sanctuary [5. 225]. Not until most recent times were the Mycenaean objects dissociated from this question and considered in the regional context [4]. Other research was concerned with the wider surroundings: between 1936 and 1938, in Kirrha (today Itea), the harbour of D. was studied (H. van Effenterre/J. Roger). After the war the focus was no longer on extensive excavations but rather on probes for the better exploration of individual monuments (e.g. 1956–57 the architecture of the Siphnian Treasure House, since 1985 complete excavation of the Gymnasion) or parts of the sanctuary (e.g. 1991 Monument of the Rhodians was dismantled and parts of the old sanctuary wall under it were exposed; in the 1960s excavation of the necropoleis was continued by the Greek Office of Monuments). The study of topographical questions and of the development of the sanctuary (e.g. by P. de la Coste-Messelière) made new research necessary. Whereas in the beginning the 'more recent' walls were often removed, both in order to make the classical sanctuary better visible and to find reused older stones [5. 265], the emphasis was now on a more thorough study of the Roman period [6. 201; 1. 722ff.] and, since the 1980s, of the early Christian period as well (esp. settlement) [5. 259]. Further, exploration of the surroundings was once again taken up in the 1970s under P. Amandry (the Korykian Grotto, the St. Elias Quarries) [5. 258].

C. IMPORTANT AREAS OF RESEARCH
1. ARCHITECTURE 2. EPIGRAPHY 3. SCULPTURE

1. ARCHITECTURE

When excavations began, a considerable amount of architectural parts was found to have been reused in other ancient buildings (e.g. [5.265]) or built into present-day houses (e.g. [3. 19]). It was therefore the task of the first generation of researchers to assign individual blocks to their respective buildings (sometimes erroneously in the beginning, e.g. blocks from the Treasury of the Cnideans were used in the reconstruction of the Treasury of the Siphnians [3. 51]). As early as the beginning of the 20th cent., inscriptions on the stones were being used as an aid in reconstruction (e.g. by E. Bourguet and A. Martinaud [3. 52], for the Treasury of the Siphnians), and, more recently, a number of buildings have been newly assessed (in part with the collaboration of the Danish architect E. Hansen). The presence in one place of different archaic and classical styles made possible the identification of a group of stone workshops (*Bauhütten*), G. Gruben, 1972), for example.

2. EPIGRAPHY

Of all the scientific works pertaining to D., publications on epigraphy are more numerous than those in any other discipline. In the course of time, a great

Fig. 1: View of Kastri at the beginning of the 'Grande Fouille'

number of inscriptions (esp. contracts, settlement of construction accounts, documents of release) were chiselled into the walls of many of the monuments; after those in Athens, they constitute one of the most important native sources for establishing Greek chronology. One of the very first excavations (K.O. Müller on commission from the Berlin Akademie der Wissenschaften) concentrated on inscriptions. Following the awarding of excavation rights to the EFA, the Parisians and the Berlin Akademie der Wissenschaften agreed to combine the German and French research in a joint publication of inscriptions. However, intense disputes between H. Pomtow (representative of the Berlin Akademie der Wissenschaften) and the EFA [5. 199] ended in the former giving up his rights in 1904 to EFA (his successor: E. Bourguet) [2. 234]. The finds that were made before 1892 are now included in H. COLLITZ (Dialektinschriften. II); those found during the *Grande Fouille* or later were published (after preliminary publication in the BCH [Bulletin de Correspondance Hellénique]) since 1908 in topographical order in Part 3 of the *Fouilles de Delphes*. A systematic presentation according to genres has been available since 1977 in the *Corpus des inscriptions de Delphes* [5. 266ff.].

3. SCULPTURE

By virtue of numerous inscriptions and mentions in the literature of Antiquity, the plastic arts and sculptures of D. yield an array of chronological fixed points, even if the validity of many of the statements made by

writers of Antiquity is being debated by researchers (as in the case of the architectural sculpture of the Treasury of the Athenians). Of special significance is the *Charioteer*, which was celebrated as the first well-preserved, large bronze sculpture found in an excavation; it was accorded an importance equal to that of the Hermes recovered from the German excavation (regarded as the competition) in Olympia [5. 200]. The fragmentary condition of much of the architectural sculpture required at first extensive assembly work to piece together the parts (e.g. as in the case of the sculpture fragments of the Treasury of the Athenians, done by P. de la Coste-Messelière), which was followed, after fairly quick publication by the excavators, by studies of the iconographic and historical problems connected with the works [5. 273].

D. PRESENTATION

To meet the lively interest of the public and of scholars, the excavators endeavoured to make the discoveries accessible as soon as possible. In addition to photographs [5. 197] – a running photographic documentation of the excavation was still new at that time [3.33] – plaster casts (displayed in Paris since 1894) were also widely used for the purpose [3. 46]. As early as 1899, D. was organised as a regular archaeological excavation site; this entailed not only the work of clearing away debris but also the complete or partial erection of important buildings (among others: 1903–06 the

Fig. 2: Western façade of the Siphnian Treasury
(plaster reconstruction, 1905)

Treasury of the Athenians, 1938 the Tholos, 1939–41
the Apollo Temple, 1975–76 and 1983–84 monuments
north of the first segment of the 'Sacred Way'), sometimes with the use of numerous newly produced parts
(e.g. original pieces make up about two thirds of the
Treasury of the Athenians [3. 58]). Arranged by Th.
Homolle, the archaeological finds in need of protection
were to a large extent exhibited in a museum, the first
building of which – financed in part by the Greek state
and in part from the bequest of A. Syngros – was dedicated in 1903. Extensive plaster reconstructions were
produced to meet the public's interest in visual representations, but they were bound to be often inexact (e.g.
the west façade of the Siphnian Treasury, in the reconstruction of which parts of the Cnidean Treasury were
initially used, while other parts where supplemented
with new pieces [3. 46]). Water damage, lack of space,
and new concepts in exhibition led to the construction
of a new museum in 1935–38, set up by the Office of
Historical Monuments (present-day exhibition mainly
by I. Konstantinou and V. Petrakos [7]; the new exhibition of 1938 curated by de la Coste-Messelière was
dismantled because of the outbreak of war and the
evacuation of many works); the extensive inauthentic
additions were subsequently removed and, to the extent
possible, a chronological arrangement became the goal
[5.254].

E. The Effect of the Excavations on the
Outside World
The spectacular archaeological finds of the *Grande
Fouille* resulted in a noticeable increase in the number

Fig. 3: Reconstruction work on the Athenian Treasury

of visitors [5. 200]. Some architects were stimulated anew to use Classical architectural forms (K. Gottlieb, St. Luke's Church in Århus [3. 59]); the hymn to Apollo (engraved on the Athenian Treasury) was recited in numerous countries at various events [5. 196]. The prestige that the excavations brought to the participating countries [5. 141] – to the French as excavators, to the Greeks as inhabitants – can be seen in exemplary fashion in the treatment of individual monuments: a cast model of the west façade of the Siphnian Treasury was shown by the French at the World's Fair in Paris in 1900 [3. 46], and the Athenians financed the reconstruction of the Athenian Treasury, making specific reference to the historical link [5. 201] (cf. also the restoration of the great Altar of Chios by the city of Chios [5. 278]).

→ Delphi

1 P. AMANDRY, Chronique Delphique (1971–1980), in: BCH 105, 1981, 673–769 2 M. MAASS, Das antike Delphi, 1993, 232–236 3 Id. (ed.), Delphi. Orakel am Nabel der Welt, 1996 4 S. MÜLLER, Delphes et sa région à l'époque mycénienne, in: BCH 116/2, 1992, 445ff. 5 O. PICARD (ed.), La redécouverte de Delphes, 1992 6 J. POUILLOUX, Delphes et les Romains, in: ΣΤΗΛΗ 1980, 201–207 7 P. THEMELIS, Kurze Geschichte des Museums, in: Hellenika Jahrbuch 1979, 142f. 8 Centcinquantenaire, BCH 120, 1996

ADDITIONAL BIBLIOGRAPHY: C. MORGAN, Athletes and Oracles: The Transformation of Olympia and Delphi in the Eighth Century BC, 1990; E. C. PARTIDA, The Treasuries at Delphi: An Architectural Study, 2000

HEIDE FRIELINGHAUS